HUMAN RESOURCE MANAGEMENT

A Contemporary Approach

THIRD EDITION

Edited by

Ian Beardwell

and

Len Holden

De Monfort University, Leicester

FINANCIAL TIMES
Prentice Hall

An imprint of **Pearson Education**

Harlow, England · London · New York · Reading, Massachusetts · San Francisco · Toronto · Don Mills, Ontario · Sydney
Tokyo · Singapore · Hong Kong · Seoul · Taipei · Cape Town · Madrid · Mexico City · Amsterdam · Munich · Paris · Milan

Pearson Education Limited

Edinburgh Gate
Harlow
Essex CM20 2JE
United Kingdom

and Associated Companies throughout the world

Visit us on the World Wide Web at:
www.pearsoneduc.com

First published in Great Britain in 1994
Second edition published in 1997
Third edition published in 2001

© Longman Group Limited 1994
© Financial Times Professional Limited 1997
© Pearson Education Limited 2001

ISBN 0 273 64316 9

British Library Cataloguing in Publication Data
A CIP catalogue record for this book can be obtained from the British Library.

10 9 8 7 6 5 4 3 2 1
05 04 03 02 01

Typeset by 30 set in 10pt New Baskerville.
Printed and bound by Rotolito Lombarda, Italy

Contents

Contents

Preface

The first edition of this book emerged at a time when the nature of Human Resource Management was establishing itself amongst practitioners and academics. It was a time of definitions and comparisons, between Personnel Management and HRM, between 'traditional' and 'new', between prescription and practice. The second edition was published when the debate had broadened and policy makers were becoming interested in whether HRM had anything to offer in terms of outcomes; it was a time of 'best fit' and HRM as set of strategic tools. The third edition appears when a number of new and flourishing debates are opening up as to whether or not HRM can be part of the equation in improving organisational performance. Is there a distinctive role, either through the identification of 'bundles' of practice, or the use of particular combinations of policies, that will demonstrate superior levels of outcomes? And are there differences in the way in which sectors within the economy use their human resources to better effect?

Against this background the academic debate has continued unabated. What has changed are the simple dichotomies of the past. There is now active interchange between US and UK analyses, using both large data-set analysis as well as case studies, which are testing HRM further. In the UK the publication of the First Findings from WERS 4 in 1998, and the panel survey analysis in 2000 for the first time provide researchers with a valuable source of research data on many aspects of HRM policy and practice on a systematic and extensive basis. All of this represents an enriching of the research base of HRM out of which critical analysis may flow.

We hope that this book encompasses these issues in a comprehensive and comprehensible manner. The aim, quite simply, is to provide in an accessible form an analysis of some of these major developments combined with some explanation of the processes at work in the field of HRM. This is by no means an easy feat to accomplish, but we believe we have been successful in creating a book which is unique in providing a usable text at both the undergraduate and postgraduate levels. The authors have taken the opportunity to redesign and reshape this edition. There are new contributions on quality management, a rewriting of the training sections in the light of national policy, and rewritten chapters on international HRM, as well as a complete revision of all the chapters in the light of research and policy developments.

Once again this has been a collaborative effort on the part of colleagues within the Department of HRM at De Montfort University. There is no single prescription offered, but a conscious recognition that systematic analysis is required to present the competing arguments in as even handed a manner as possible. We would once again like to thank our fellow contributors for all their hard work. Since the last edition the range of our departmental teaching and research has continued to expand and this book always has to be fitted in with many other commitments. We would also like to thank our spouses, partners and families for putting up with it all over again! As ever, we remain responsible for the final product.

July 2000   Ian Beardwell and Len Holden

Plan of book

PART 1 – HUMAN RESOURCE MANAGMENT AND ITS ORGANISATIONAL CONTEXT	
Chapter 1 An introduction to human resource management	**Chapter 2** Human resource management in context

PART 2 – RESOURCING THE ORGANISATION			
Chapter 3 Human resource management and the labour market	**Chapter 4** Human resource planning: control to seduction?	**Chapter 5** Job design: signs, symbols and re-signations	**Chapter 6** Recruitment and selection

PART 3 – DEVELOPING THE HUMAN RESOURCE		
Chapter 7 Learning and development	**Chapter 8** Human resource development: the organisation and the national framework	**Chapter 9** Management development

PART 4 – THE EMPLOYMENT RELATIONSHIP		
Chapter 10 The employment relationship and contractural regulation	**Chapter 11** Establishing the terms and conditions of employment	**Chapter 12** Reward and performance management
Chapter 13 Employee involvement and empowerment		**Chapter 14** Human resources managment in the public sector

PART 5 – INTERNATIONAL HUMAN RESOURCE MANAGEMENT		
Chapter 15 International human resource management	**Chapter 16** Human resource management and Europe	**Chapter 17** Human resource management in Asia

How to use this book

This text is designed to meet the needs of a range of students who are studying HRM either as a core or option subject on undergraduate degrees in Business and Social Science, MBAs, specialised Masters programmes, or for the CIPD Professional Qualification Scheme. The outlines which follow are intended to indicate how the material in this book can be used to cover the requirements of these varying programmes; the one exception to this scheme is an outline for undergraduates, becuase of the multiplicity of courses at this level which individual tutors will have devised. Nevertheless it is hoped that these suggested 'routes' through the book will be helpful guidelines for tutors who have repsonsiblity for some or all of these courses.

MBA Route
Introduction: Chapters 1 and 2
Core: Chapters 4, 6, 10, 11, 15
Options: Chapters 3, 4, 5, 10, 12, 13, 14, 15, 16

MA/MSc Route
Introduction: Chapter 1 and 2
Core: Chapters: 3, 4, 6, 8, 10, 11, 13, 14, 15
Options: Chapters 3, 4, 5, 7, 12, 14, 15, 16, 17

CIPD Professional Qualification Scheme (PQS)
Introduction: Chapters 1 and 2
People Management and Development: Chapters 3, 4, 6, 7, 8, 11, 12
People Resourcing: Chapters 1, 2, 3, 4, 5, 6, 12
Employee Relations: Chapters 1, 2, 3, 10, 11, 13, 14
Learning and Development: Chapters 7, 8, 9
Employee Reward: Chapters 5, 12
Advanced Practitioner Standards: Chapters 1, 15, 16, 17

The developing range of CIPD specialist modules may be supported by the use of the relevant chapter or part, thus Management Development and Vocational Education and Training can be supported by the whole of Part 3.

Contributors

Editors

Ian Beardwell, BSc, MSc, PhD, is Professor of Industrial Relations, Head of Department of Human Resource Management at Leicester Business School and is currently Vice-President, Membership and Education of the CIPD. Experienced in industrial relations and manpower policy with the CBI, CIR and NEDO, he has researched and published in the areas of low pay, union recognition, public sector labour relations and the management of industrial relations. He has given formal evidence to both the Megaw Committee of Inquiry into Civil Service Pay (1981) and the Review Body for Nursing Pay (1987). His most recent work includes an ESRC supported study of non-union firms in the UK, and contemporary developments in 'new' industrial relations.

Len Holden, BSC(Econ), MPhil, PhD, Cert of Ed, MIPD, is Principal Lecturer in Human Resource Management at Leicester Business School, De Montfort University. He has lived and worked in Eastern Europe and written on the changes which have taken place there since 1989, particularly in Bulgaria. He has researched, lectured and written extensively on Western Europe, notably on Swedish human resource management, and has co-authored a book comparing British and Swedish management styles. He is also co-editor of a book on European human resource management, and was a founding researcher of the Price Waterhouse Cranfield Project on Strategic Human Resource Management in Europe. His current interests are in comparative employee involvement in Britain and Sweden, and a comparative analysis of middle management functions and HRM in other European countries.

Contributors

Ian Clark is Principal Lecturer in Industrial Relations in the Department of HRM at De Montfort University. His teaching and research interests focus on critical interpretations of HRM and the political economy of industrial relations, in particular the location of industrial relations analysis within macro-economic management and performance. Prior to his current appointment, he was ESRC Research Fellow at De Montfort University, working on the Competitiveness of British Industry Project. Ian is currently researching two projects: patterns of corporate governance and HRM, and the role of the state in industrial relations, particularly during the immediate post-war years.

Tim Claydon, BSocSci, MSc(Econ), PhD, is Principal Lecturer in Industrial Relations at Leicester Business School, De Montfort University. He teaches Industrial Relations and Labour Market Studies to undergraduate and postgraduate students, as well as supervising research degrees. He has written on trade union history, union derecognition, and trade unions and training. He has also undertaken consultancy work in the public sector. Currently he is developing research into 'new' industrial relations in the workplace.

Audrey Collin is Professor of Career Studies, De Montfort University, where she teaches Organisation Theory and Behaviour mainly on postgraduate, post-experience courses. Her early career was in personnel management and she is now a MIPM. She was awarded a PhD for her study of mid-career change; career and lifespan studies, mentoring and older workers are the fields in which she has researched and published. Her 1992 book (co-edited with Richard A. Young), *Interpreting Career: Hermeneutical Studies of Lives in Context*, reflects her commitment to interpretive research approaches.

Trevor Colling is Senior Research Fellow in the Department of Human Resource Management, De Montfort University. He has written and published widely on various aspects of public sector industrial relations, particularly the implications of privatisation and contracting-out. His current research interests include the management of labour in business services companies and the influence of systems of labour market regulation on gender inequality in the workplace.

Mike Doyle is Lecturer in the Department of Human Resource Management at Leicester Business School. He joined the Business School after some 20 years in a line management role, managing in both public and private sector organisations. He holds a Masters degree in Human Resource Management and teaches on post-graduate, post-experience management programmes in the area of management development, organisational development and change management. His current research interests include an exploration into empowerment in the workplace and how to develop managers during a time of radical organisational change.

Linda Glover is a Senior Lecturer in Human Resource Management. She teaches on a wide range of undergraduate and postgraduate programmes. She is involved in a number of ongoing research projects. Linda has managed industry funded research projects that have been investigating employee responses to Quality Management and HRM. She has collaborated with Noel Siu of Hong Kong Baptist University on a project examining the human resource issues associated with management of quality in the Peoples Republic of China. She has also written on the human resource problems associated with managing the subsidiaries of multinational companies.

Susan Marlow is Principal Lecturer in Human Resource Management at De Montfort University, teaching on a range of undergraduate and professional courses. Susan has research interests in labour relations in small firms and the role of female entrepreneurs in modern society. Currently she is co-director of two funded studies in these areas which have resulted in a number of refereed publications and papers at international conferences.

Damian O'Doherty graduated from the University of Newcastle-upon-Tyne where he read for an Honours degree in Economics. In 1991 he completed an MA in Industrial Relations at the University of Warwick. He is now a Lecturer at Manchester School of Management (UMIST) and was previously teaching in the Department of Human Resource Management at De Montfort University, Leicester, lecturing on a range of undergraduate degree programmes in Human Resource Management and Industrial Relations. Damian is a doctoral candidate in the School of Management at UMIST where he is studying the processes of construction and deconstruction in the ordering of the organisation in employment relations.

Ian Roberts is Senior Lecturer in Human Resource Management and Organisational Behaviour at De Montfort University. He has a BSc in Management Science and an MA in Industrial Relations which were both awarded by the University of Warwick. He is now involved in setting up an international research project on middle management and the HRM function.

Julie Storey is Principal Lecturer in Human Resource Management at De Montfort University. She joined the University after 10 years' experience in the retail sector. She currently contributes to a range of professional and postgraduate courses, teaching employee resourcing and interpersonal skills. She is also Course Director of the MA in Personnel and Development and an MIPD. Her research interests include HRM in non-union firms and personnel careers.

Mary Wright is Principal Lecturer in Human Resource Management at De Montfort University, lecturing on a variety of undergraduate and professional courses, with specific responsibilities for the part-time IPD programme at the University. She is an active member of the local IPD branch committee. Her current research activity is in international executive search and selection.

PART

1

HUMAN RESOURCE MANAGEMENT AND ITS ORGANISATIONAL CONTEXT

Introduction to Part 1

Human resource management has become a pervasive and influential approach to the management of employment in a wide range of market economies. The original US prescriptions of the early 1980s have become popularised and absorbed in a wide variety of economic settings: there are very few major economies where the nature of human resource management, to include its sources, operation and philosophy, is not actively discussed. As a result the analysis and evaluation of HRM have become major themes in academic, policy and practitioner literatures.

Two related themes run through the first part of the book; both are concerned with the nature of HRM. The first chapter looks at the antecedents of HRM in the USA and its translation to other economies, with particular emphasis on Britain – where the HRM debate has been among the most active and has involved practitioner and academic alike. There are many unresolved questions in HRM: What sort of example is it? Can it be transposed from one economy to another? Does it have qualities that make it truly international? Is it a major contribution to strategic management? The type of questions raised by HRM indicates the extent to which it has disturbed many formerly accepted concepts in the employment relationship. For some it has become a model for action and application; for others it is no more than a map that indicates how the management of employees might be worked out in more specific ways than HRM can adequately deal with.

The second chapter looks at the organisational context in which human resource management has emerged and in which it operates. This is important in understanding some of the assumptions and philosophical stances that lie behind it. The purpose of the discussion is to create a critical awareness of the broader context in which HRM operates, not simply as a set of operational matters that describe the functional role of personnel management, but as part of a complex and sophisticated process that helps us to understand the nature of organisational life.

1 An introduction to human resource management: strategy, style or outcome

Ian Beardwell

OBJECTIVES

- To outline the development of HRM as an area of practice and analysis in terms of:
  - strategy
  - style
  - outcomes.
- To debate the nature of the HRM phenomenon and the different perspectives from which it is viewed:
  - as a restatement of existing personnel practice
  - as a new managerial discipline
  - as a resource-based model
  - as a strategic and international function.
- To review and evaluate the main models of HRM, and to assess likely developments.

INTRODUCTION

The third edition of this book provides an opportunity to reflect on the extent of the debate about human resource management, the changing nature of the employment relationship, and the consequences for how organisations and individuals are managed. It is very nearly ten years since the idea for a comprehensive treatment of HRM was conceived by the authors, and a great deal of the prevailing analysis and data that was available at that time was derived from such sources as the 1984 WIRS 2, the 1988 Company Level Survey and MacInnes' *Thatcherism at Work* (MacInnes, 1987). The story was broadly one of change, but not so much that a radical reshaping of the employment relationship had occurred. Rather, the effects of deflation and recession in the early and late 1980s had wrought greater damage to the infrastructure of employment than any legally enforced reform, while the move to privatisation, and a stronger role for market-based models of economic activity, had shifted the primary scope of industrial relations away from job regulation and collective bargaining towards coping with outsourcing and downsizing.

Despite all these shifts, however, a large part of the analysis and discussion that constitutes the HRM debate today had yet to reveal itself. Some initial studies of non-unionism were only just beginning to see the light of day (McLoughlin and Gourlay, 1992), while the role of HRM in transforming and adding value to organisational performance (Pfeffer, 1994, 1998), the relationship between HRM 'bundles' and business performance (McDuffie, 1995; Huselid, 1995), the role of the psychological contract in gaining employee assent (Guest and Conway, 1997), and wider changes in the infrastructure of the employment relationship (Culley *et al.*, 1998, 1999) would come later in the decade. The situation is now one of a rich and complex diversity of analyses, in which UK-based research and analysis is playing as significant a contribution as that of the USA – even if some of the policy and research initiatives still derive, prima facie, from an American agenda.

What is striking about the HRM debate of the last decade is that two common themes have persisted, and yet neither has turned out to be the determining feature of the way the employment relationship is managed. The first theme is that of HRM's replacement of the older traditions of personnel management and industrial relations. The approach of what might be termed the 'Desperately Seeking HRM' school of analysis seeks to explore the incidence, volume and influence of HRM-based approaches and practices, and to assess whether they are supplanting the historical patterns of UK employee management (Sisson, 1993). The second theme is concerned to examine the specific impact of focused types of HRM – such as high commitment management – in order to assess their superiority over both more generalised HRM interventions and traditional methods. While there are obvious limitations in seeking to assess the total impact of HRM, whether by large-scale survey material or by case analysis, there are similar limitations to measuring discrete choices of 'tools' with the aim of achieving 'best practice', as Purcell (1999) has noted. Thus we have entered the new millennium without a universal model of HRM on the one hand, but, on the other, with a range of HRM activities that are under sustained examination in order to assess their efficacy in achieving superior organisational performance. What is clear is that the HRM agenda still continues to develop and provide opportunities for analysis and prescription. For some commentators HRM seems to have hit its high water mark and is now on the ebb (Bach and Sisson, 2000), while for others (such as Guest, 1997) there is fragmentary but clear evidence that 'HRM works', but we need to put flesh on the bones to consolidate that assertion.

A framework for HRM analysis: strategy, style and outcome

How can we attempt to construct a framework to encompass these divergent views about the relative strength and vitality of HRM? As the subtitle of this chapter suggests, there are at least three approaches to looking at the phenomenon that might help to explain different groups of arguments, based on whether the analysis focuses on the role of strategy, style or outcomes in the conduct of HRM.

HRM as strategy

The strategic emphasis has by far the longest pedigree in the HRM debate; indeed, it is probably the strategic aspirations of the US models that were the defining feature of HRM as it emerged in the 1980s. As we shall see later in the chapter, strategy has been seen as one of the touchstones of HRM's viability. The extent to which HRM has come to play a role in the direction and planning of organisations has been a persistent theme not simply in the academic literature but in practitioner activity too. For example the HRM Initiative currently under way in the UK National Health Service, in the spring of 2000, stresses the key role that HR practitioners will play at both national and regional levels in achieving nationally determined and nationally assessed goals for health care delivery. A key part of this initiative will be the integration of HRM with the strategic goals of the NHS.

Within strategic approaches two further strands might be noted. The first remains centred around macro-strategic issues and the general location of HRM within organisational structures overall – perhaps best summed up by the debate over whether HRM has a seat on the Board. The second strand has been more concerned with the formal inputs that HRM can provide – such as better recruitment and selection procedures or better alignment of reward systems with activity – as a way of providing linkages that are demonstrable and robust. In the NHS, for example, a major factor in stimulating these closer linkages is the realisation that variability of treatment rates between different hospitals may be as much to do with the management of the clinical personnel as with their access to medical technology. Thus the health service provides an excellent example of the strategic positioning of HRM, and the linkage of its inputs. This brings together their respective relationships in the debate over the role of HRM in the health service overall.

A contemporary explanation for HRM's strategic positioning has emerged in the use of the term *business focus*. This has become a popular and widely used phrase to describe a wide range of organisational activity into which HRM is expected to link. However, it has an ambiguity and a potential for use across not only strategy, but also style and outcomes. If it has a meaning, it is probably best viewed as a general description of the territory that HRM now inhabits, rather than the technically defined and narrower role of personnel management of a quarter of a century ago.

HRM as style

The second approach, based around styles of HRM, has also had an active life, and one that has attracted much discussion within the UK. Some of the antecedents to this can be traced back through the analysis of personnel as a function and personnel managers as actors within organisational settings. Thus Watson's (1977) analysis of the professional role of personnel managers and Legge's (1978) analysis of their political location within organisational roles can be seen as important precursors of this approach, while Tyson and Fell (1986) further refined the styles of personnel managers within their tasks. Other antecedents can be traced back to the industrial relations tradition, with the 'unitarist-pluralist' analysis of Fox (1966) and the 'traditionalist/ sophisticated paternalist/sophisticated modern/standard modern' formulation of Purcell and Sisson (1983). The idea that style of personnel management or industrial relations can materially affect the operation of the function is deeply rooted in UK analysis, and suggests too that it has proved difficult to change over time, except through profound disturbance or acute threat. In these contexts the reason why UK management has not demonstrated a greater interest in, or success with, strategic approaches to HRM (in contrast to the US) is largely attachment to a style that is the product of history and institutions over time.

The analysis of HRM in terms of style has also revolved around whether it can be regarded as hard or soft (Legge, 1995) in its intent. *Hard HRM* is sometimes defined in terms of the particular policies that stress a cost-minimisation strategy with an emphasis on leanness in production, the use of labour as a resource, and what Legge calls a 'utilitarian instrumentalism' in the employment relationship; at other times hard HRM is defined in terms of the tightness of fit between organisational goals and strategic objectives on the one hand and HRM policies on the other. *Soft HRM*, by contrast, is sometimes viewed as 'developmental humanism' (Legge, 1995) in which the individual is integrated into a work process that values trust, commitment and communication. What is probably more at issue than either of these two characterisations is the question of whether they are equally routes to work intensification and greater demands on the employment relationship by the organisation at the expense of the employee. As Legge points out, it is quite feasible that hard HRM variants can contain elements of soft practice, while the criticism that can be made of soft variants is that they can be held to deliver hard outcomes in terms of the tightness of the fit with business strategy that is sought. Indeed, just as with the broad definition and usage of the term 'business focus', noted earlier, so with the meaning and use of the term 'fit'. Each of the three descriptions of HRM discussed here – strategy, style and outcome – is concerned with fit and the extent to which each achieves it, with the result that 'fit' has itself become an infinitely flexible term, and one that becomes increasingly difficult to apply to HRM as a single concept.

A more recent approach to the question of style can be found in the work of Ulrich (1998). The tradition that sought to present practitioner roles in terms of the organisational location of their work provides a good background to Ulrich's model of the HRM profession and its contribution to the business. For Ulrich, there are four possible styles or routes that HRM can take. The first is in what he terms *work organisation,* which involves the practitioner servicing the needs of the organisation in as efficient a manner as possible, but no more than that. In this mode, the style of HRM is as a support function 'doing the job right' but with little opportunity to add value or contribute to organisational performance. It might be that there will be minimal HRM mistakes made, but conducting HRM in this manner will not provide any particular competitive advantage for any one organisation. The second style is to become the *employee champion*. In this mode the HR practitioner takes on the role of 'voice' for employees, seeking to reduce the frictional differences between the organisation and its staff and ensuring that senior management are aware of the concerns of employees. While this might be a different role from the maintenance function of work organisation, it still places the practitioner in a servicing role and does not necessarily create a role with added value; the emphasis is still on reducing dysfunctions. In the third mode, that of *agent for change*, the practitioner becomes the protagonist in active change management that has the capacity for added value, while in the fourth mode of *business partner* the practitioner becomes a fully contributing member of the management team, who is able to participate in the corporate planning process and bring the expertise of HRM into the equation with the responsibility to demonstrate how HRM can add value and give competitive advantage. For Ulrich the danger for HRM lies in its inability to move on from work organisation and seize the developmental opportunity of becoming the business partner. The attractions of this approach to style for practitioners are obvious, with its message of hope and a promise of a substantial role at the heart of organisational structures, and Ulrich's work has become particularly popular in the professional associations for HR managers in both the USA and the UK.

HRM as outcomes

Over the second half of the 1990s, a further turn in the HRM debate saw a move away from attempts to define what its 'input' characteristics might be in favour of examining what consequences flowed from applying HRM in fairly tightly defined circumstances. Whereas both strategic and style approaches to HRM analysis had been concerned with its architecture, an 'output' based model concerned itself with examining those organisations that not only constructed their HRM in particular configurations but also found that resultant outcomes could give them a competitive advantage. The impetus for this approach was predominantly American, in particular the work of Arthur (1992, 1994), McDuffie (1995) and Huselid (1995), although UK work has also developed in this area, West and Patterson (1997) in particular.

The unifying theme of these studies is that particular combinations of HRM practices, especially where they are refined and modified, can give quantifiable improvements in organisational performance. Arthur's work studied 54 mini-mills (new technology steel mills using smaller workforces and new working practices) and demonstrated that firms using a 'commitment' model of HRM saw higher productivity, lower labour turnover, and lower rates of rejected production. In other words, it took the HRM style element a stage further in order to establish whether there was an output effect that could benefit the firm. McDuffie's work examined 70 plants in the world car industry, and the use of HR techniques that were regarded as innovative. His analysis argued that it is when practices are used together, rather than simply in isolation or only for the specific effect of some more than others, that superior performance can be achieved. An important part of this analysis is the extent to which employees gave 'extra' in the form of discretionary effort that would otherwise have not been forthcoming without the effect of the chosen practices. Three factors were noted in particular: *buffers* (the extent to which plants adopted flexibility), *work system* (the work arrangements that complemented flexibility), and *HRM policies* (the HRM practices that complemented flexibility). The marked effect on performance was in the combined impact of all three factors working together. This approach moves the impact of HRM from being concerned with strategic choice or style *per se* to following the output consequences of constructing what have come to be known as 'bundles' of HR practice.

Huselid's study examined the relationships between the HR system (the groups of practices rather than individual practices), outcome measures (such as financial performance as well as HR data on turnover and absence), and the fit between HR and competitive strategy in 986 US-owned firms employing more than 100 employees. Huselid's results indicated a lowering of labour turnover, higher sales performance, improved profitability and higher share valuations for those firms that performed well on his indices. In the UK the study by West and Patterson (1997) indicated that HR practices could account for 19% of the variation between firms in changes in profitability and 18% of the variation in changes in productivity. Once again, the complementarity of HR practices was held to be significant.

As a result of these types of analysis a great deal of attention is now being paid to what constitutes a 'bundle' of HR practices that will afford firms superior performance. But this is no easy matter to settle conclusively. What is obvious about each of these studies is that they were examining patterns of HR strategies, choices, applications and refinements after their introduction. We have little information about how all these factors came to be in place in some firms and not in others. For practitioners there is no easy or readily available checklist that can be applied. For each firm contemplating an output model of HRM there has to be a difficult internal process of selecting and testing the bundle that will work in their own circumstances. The mere application of a group of practices, without some assessment of their interconnectedness, is unlikely to have discernible beneficial outcomes.

Thus the debate over HRM, whether it is pursued by analysts, academics or practitioners, continues to expand and develop. So far from reaching the high water mark and ebbing, HRM as a phenomenon continues to thrive. Indeed, the fusion of HRM with business focus, noted above, has ensured that many major organisational changes now intimately involve HRM as part of the equation: thus, in the spring of 2000, the very different circumstances surrounding major reorganisations in the European car industry, banking and retail sectors have all involved important HRM elements as major decisions are taken on plant, branch and store closures.

These changes provide the background against which human resource management has emerged as the predominant contemporary influence on managing employment relationships. It is now commonplace to describe HRM as a managerially derived and driven set of precepts with both line and personnel managers actively involved in its operation. What is new and distinctive about the debate, and perhaps explains its capacity to renew itself after each wave of analysis has been assessed and absorbed, is the shift from the broad question of whether HRM exists at all to more focused analyses – for example, whether particular combinations of HRM policies produce better results in output or services so that competitive advantage might accrue to those organisations that adopt them. Thus HRM continues to provide agendas and prescriptions for debate amongst both practitioners and analysts that are contentious and compelling, and have no settled orthodoxy.

Why should this be so? Part of the answer lies in the perspective brought to bear upon HRM: there is a diversity in the HRM debate, derived from the manner in which particular participants view the essential elements of HRM and what they believe it is representing, that colours the discussion. For the purposes of this analysis four broad perspectives are set out here:

- that HRM is no more than a renaming of basic personnel functions, which does little that is different from the traditional practice of personnel management;
- that HRM represents a fusion of personnel management and industrial relations that is managerially focused and derives from a managerial agenda;
- that HRM represents a resource-based conception of the employment relationship, some elements of which incorporate a developmental role for the individual employee and some elements of cost minimisation;
- that HRM can be viewed as part of the strategic managerial function in the development of business policy, in which it plays both a determining and a contributory role.

HRM as a restatement of existing personnel practice

It is possible to view this first standpoint as a basic but natural reaction to a new and somewhat threatening reformulation of traditional functions. There is, perhaps, an understandable scepticism that HRM can, or ever could, live up to the wider claims of its ability to transform the employment relationship so totally that some of the inherent problems of managing a volatile set of employee issues can be resolved more satisfactorily than by approaches that have grown out of the historical development of personnel management. Throughout the last decade this view has remained as a strong reaction to what is seen as the renaming pretensions of HRM. In large part such a reaction can be explained in terms of the gulf that appears to exist between personnel management 'on the ground' and the rather more theoretical and 'strategic' nature of a great deal of the discussion surrounding human resource management.

For many practitioners the notion that their roles and functions can be seen in anything other than a highly pragmatic light is no more than wishful thinking: there is an important, if straightforward, task of recruiting, selecting, rewarding, managing and developing employees that must be carried out as 'efficiently' as possible. In this sense, HRM might be viewed as no more than another trend in the long line of management prescriptions that have each enjoyed a vogue and then lost favour, while the pragmatic nature of established personnel management has ensured that the operational tasks have been accomplished.

HRM as a new managerial discipline

The second perspective contains more diversity and complexity, and incorporates such issues as the philosophies of personnel and industrial relations, the professional desire to present the management of employees as a holistic discipline (akin to the inclusive approaches of accounting and marketing, for example), and the belief that an integrated management approach can be provided by HRM. This would not only unite the differing perspectives of PM and IR but also create a new and broader discipline as a result of the fusion of these traditional elements. An important outcome of this approach is to view some of these traditional components as now irrelevant or outdated and as dealing with problems that typify past, as opposed to current, practice: this is perhaps most noticeable in the renaming of functional activities so that industrial relations becomes 'employee relations', and training becomes 'employee development'. This retitling is not designed solely to update an image, although that is important in itself, but is more specifically aimed at expressing the nature of the employment relationship in what are seen as changed circumstances. Thus industrial relations is seen as expressing a relationship based upon a manual, manufacturing (and, often by implication, male) unionised workforce – rather than the supposedly wider concept of 'employee relations', which involves a total workforce that includes white-collar and technical staff, of whom many will be female and some or all non-union.

A further significant shift in thinking connected with this second approach is that of the desire by management to extend control over aspects of the collective relationship that were once customarily regarded as jointly agreed between employees (usually via their unions) and management. Treating employees as a primary responsibility of management, as opposed to the jointly negotiated responsibility of both unions and management, suggests an approach that is concerned to stress the primacy of the managerial agenda in the employment relationship, and marks a shift away from one of the fundamental assumptions of the approach (after the Second World War) to managing collective workforces. This shift was underlined in the 1993 employment legislation, which removed from ACAS the duty, originally given to it on its inception in 1974, to promote collective bargaining. In reality, this duty was a reflection of a deeply rooted presumption stretching back throughout most of the twentieth century and, in the UK at least, largely shared by employers, unions and the state, that collective bargaining represented a 'politically' acceptable compromise between management and labour.

More recently, the UK professional body for practitioners, the Institute of Personnel and Development, has sought to establish an agenda that is concerned to show this integration into a business-led managerial discipline. The name of the institute should not be taken as indicative of where HRM lies within its professional portfolio: that is the product of institutional factors that shaped the IPD when it was created by the 1994 merger of its two constituent bodies, the Institute of Personnel Management and the Institute of Training and Development. Instead, it is more instructive to look at the consequences of the adoption of a more integrated approach. The annual autumn conference is now the largest management conference held in Europe, and it attracts the most well-known 'guru' speakers; its annual HRD spring conference is as influential, and presents as extensive a range of speakers within the training and development domain, while setting the programme in a business context. With membership now comfortably over 100 000 the IPD has successfully been granted a Royal Charter from July 2000, in recognition of its role as a major professional management association. Within this framework HRM is one factor in transforming personnel management into a powerful managerial role in its own right. To that extent it is part of a 'transformation' within the profession, which sees a move away from technical specificity towards a more rounded and sophisticated contribution to wider organisational objectives. The extent to which such transformations can be achieved is also connected to the third HRM perspective, which is discussed next.

HRM as a resource based-model

A further perspective has been brought to bear on HRM from those approaches that stress the role of the individual in organisations, rather than the collective employment models outlined so far. Personnel management, to a large degree at least, has always been concerned with the interface between the organisation and the individual, and with the necessity of achieving a trade-off between the requirements of the organisation and the needs of individual employees. Traditional personnel management policies that have been developed to cope with this trade-off have often taken a piecemeal approach to certain aspects of this issue: historically, the early twentieth-century personnel function stressed the 'welfare' role that could be afforded employees so that basic working conditions (both physically and contractually) could be established.

Subsequently, other styles of personnel management sought to introduce, administer or rectify particular aspects of jobs and roles that individuals carried out. This tradition fostered a belief in equitable selection and reward systems, efficient procedures for discipline, dismissal and redundancy, and clear and operable rules for administering large numbers of employees to avoid arbitrary judgements over individual cases. The prevailing rationale behind all these activities could be seen as a desire to manage the difficulties of the organisation/individual relationship in as technically neutral a manner as possible. This emphasis has fostered a culture within personnel management that is characterised as *cost minimisation*, more recently identified with some forms of hard HRM, with the individual as the cost that has to be controlled and contained. In these circumstances employees become one of the aggregate commodities within the organisation that have to be managed within the organisation's resources, in the same way that, for example, the finance available to the organisation has to be managed within a framework and according to accounting conventions. The logical extent of this model is reached in manpower planning with precise numerical assessments of internal and external demand for and supply of labour.

Any alternative to this formalised approach, which treats the individual as a resource rather than an expense and views expenditure on training as an investment rather than a cost, associated with some aspects of soft HRM, poses a profound threat to the conventional wisdom of personnel management.

The conception of personnel as having an enabling capacity for employees has a long tradition, not least in the United States, where organisational analysis has often provided prescriptions concerning the role of supervisors, work groups and work organisation. The advent of Japanese management systems has, however, highlighted the impact of this approach on the employment relationship. Whether sustainable or not in the West, the Japanese large-firm emphasis on developing individual employees along particular job paths while undertaking to provide continuous employment throughout the normal working life of the individual has at least provided a model in which the employer seeks to maximise employment opportunities. This approach goes further, however: it regards all employees as potentially able to benefit from further training and development, from which the organisation itself then benefits. So, far from viewing the employee as a cost, which has to be borne by the employer, this philosophy sees the employee as an actual and potential return on investment, which ultimately strengthens the company. The responsibility of the employer for investment and employment has, at least in the post-war period to date, encouraged large corporate Japanese employers to develop products and markets that have used the invested skills of their workforces.

There has been strong interest in what is termed 'resource-based' HRM, in which human resources are viewed as the basis of competitive advantage. This means that advantage is not only derived from the formal reorganisation and reshaping of work, but is also powerfully derived from within the workforce in terms of the training and expertise available to the organisation, the adaptability of employees which permits the organisation strategic flexibility, and the commitment of employees to the organisation's business plans and goals.

HRM as a strategic and international function

The advent of human resource management has also brought forward the issue of the linkages between the employment relationship and wider organisational strategies and corporate policies. Historically, the management of industrial relations and personnel has been concerned either to cope with the 'downstream' consequences of earlier strategic decisions or to 'firefight' short-term problems that threaten the long-run success of a particular strategy. In these instances the role has been at best reactive and supportive to other managerial functions, at worst a hindrance until particular operational problems were overcome.

In the private sector the well-known case of British Leyland in the 1970s demonstrated a situation where considerable amounts of managerial effort (up to 60% of operational managers' time by some estimates) were devoted to 'fixing' shopfloor problems. In order to re-establish managerial control the company effectively turned the reshaping of industrial relations into its strategy so that it could refashion its product range and market position. In the public sector throughout the 1980s a series of major disputes affected the operations of schools, hospitals and local authorities (among many such examples); in each of these cases changes to the nature of the employment relationship were the root causes of the dislocation. The Leyland case and the public sector experiences are extreme examples, but each demonstrates the impact that the employment relationship can have on total operations.

Human resource management lays claim to a fundamentally different relationship between the organisation's employment function and its strategic role. The assumption behind HRM is that it is essentially a strategically driven activity, which is not only a major contributor to that process but also a determining part of it. From this standpoint the contribution that the management of the employment relationship makes to the overall managerial process is as vital and formative as that of finance or marketing, for example. Indeed, the notion that HRM is central to such managerial decision-making indicates the extent to which its proponents feel that it has come out of the shadows to claim a rightful place alongside other core management roles. In this respect one of the traditional stances of the personnel practitioner – that of the 'liberal' conception of personnel management as standing between employer and employee, moderating and smoothing the interchange between them – is viewed as untenable: HRM is about shaping and delivering corporate strategies with commitment and results.

A further element in this construction of HRM points to its international potentialities. The employment relationship is materially affected – perhaps even defined – by the national and cultural contexts in which it operates. Thus variations in national labour markets have given rise to a wide range of employment structures, policies and relationships within the broad definition of market economies. To the extent that employers operate within national labour markets, these characteristics do not impinge on neighbouring nationalities; but to the extent that employers operate across national boundaries, these different characteristics may become factors that an employer would wish to change or override. Thus international companies that seek to deploy homogeneous employment policies, regardless of national labour markets, have often been cited as seeking and developing broadly based personnel systems that neutralise national differences and stress, by contrast, organisational cultures that are drawn from the strategic goals of the firm. Among the many examples of firms that have been identified as adopting this approach perhaps the best known and most commonly cited is IBM. An important consequence of this approach is that many of the internal policies of such firms have been used to construct approaches to human resource management that are held to be the role models for other organisations to emulate. From this line of argument one arrives at the proposition that HRM is capable of providing a managerial approach to the employment relationship that is 'culturally neutral', is derived and sustained from within the prescriptions of the organisation, and is capable of being translated across national and organisational boundaries. Indeed one might argue that, in these conditions, HRM is best defined as the product of multinational companies' personnel policies, which have the capacity to be translated to other firms regardless of culture. Needless to say, this neutralisation of the strong prescriptive elements of HRM is a highly debatable position, and there are few who would agree that HRM can be so simply defined in terms of its assumptions and values.

SOME ASSUMPTIONS ABOUT HUMAN RESOURCE MANAGEMENT

Figure 1.1 sets out the four perspectives on HRM discussed above, and locates key aspects of the HRM focus within its framework. Such a schematic presentation not only demonstrates the breadth of these operational assumptions, but also underlines their ambiguity. Within many organisations the circumstances in which human resource management is pursued will be critically determined by the state of the labour market at any particular time: it is thus perfectly understandable for an organisation to be moving towards a strategic dimension of HRM in its own terms, but to find it necessary to revert or regroup to a modified version of its original policy. A case in point here might be that of British Airways, which deployed both the developmental

Four perspectives on human resource management

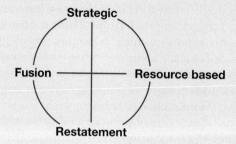

Strategic

Employment policy derived from business objectives; HRM major contributor to business policy; translation of HRM policy across cultures

Fusion

PM and IR no longer seen as operationally distinct; managerially derived agenda; replacement of collectivism with stronger role for individualism

Restatement

PM and IR as prevailing model; HRM style outcomes sought within a pluralist framework

Resource based

Individualistically derived; stress on input provided by organisation on behalf of employee

and strategic/international models of HRM throughout the 1980s in order to support its 'Customer Care' business plan, but found itself increasingly relying on the restatement and fusion models as it sought to reorganise its Gatwick operations (including Dan-Air) in the 1990s. This gave rise to industrial relations difficulties, with strong residual problems over wage levels for cabin staff leading to strike threats in 1996, which were realised in 1997. At a cost of some £125 million BA sustained strike action by cabin crews, worldwide, over pay and conditions. One outcome of the dispute was that BA hired new staff on contracts that were 20% cheaper than those for existing staff, thus further emphasising the cost-minimisation model of hard HRM and linking it with the fusion model.

If further evidence were needed of the shifts in HRM that can occur when businesses come under pressure, then BMW's handling of the Rover group sale and Barclays' branch closure programme, both in the spring of 2000, provide ample evidence that approaches to HRM are prone to severe buffeting, whatever the original intent of the business. In BMW's case it sought to fuse a European style of communication and involvement with the Japanese style already existing within Rover as a result of the latter's Honda collaboration over the previous decade; in Barclays' case it saw the need to maintain its role as a 'big bank in a big world' by cutting 10% of its branch network in one operation. Competitive product and service market pressures can quickly overwhelm the best of HRM intentions.

Although these four interpretations of HRM each contain strong distinguishing characteristics they are by no means mutually exclusive: indeed, it would be surprising if that were so. In this sense they constitute not a model of HRM but a set of perspectives on HRM that organisations bring to bear on the employment relationship. A more useful approach to interpreting these perspectives might be to recognise that many organisations may display at least one of these principal perspectives but will also rely on several characteristics drawn from at least one and probably more of the other three constructs. In this sense HRM, as a set of issues as well as a set of practices, contains ambivalence and contradiction quite as much as clarity and affirmation. In many organisations the tension that arises from this outcome is part of the internal process of the management of uncertainty. With the privatisation of British Rail and the multiplicity of operating companies, there has been a distinct move away from the business-led strategies of the former BR operating divisions to a more traditional pattern of collective agreements involving negotiations between the unions and the individual owners of the new companies. The advent of the Eurostar service to Paris and Brussels has provided another example in this sector. A further discussion of some of these aspects of HRM can be found in Guest (1989a).

THE SEARCH FOR THE DEFINING CHARACTERISTICS OF HRM

An important part of the debate, both in the USA and in the UK, has been the search for the defining characteristics that will describe, analyse and explain the HRM phenomenon. To a considerable extent this quest has proved largely unresolved because of the wide range of prescriptions and expectations placed upon the term, and the relative lack of available evidence to determine systematically whether or not HRM has taken root as a sustainable model of employee management. This difficulty is further compounded if one considers a series of critical questions about human resource management:

- Is HRM a practitioner-driven process that has attracted a wider audience and prompted subsequent analytical attention?
- Is HRM an academically derived description of the employment relationship, to which practitioners have subsequently become drawn?
- Is HRM essentially a prescriptive model of how such a relationship 'ought' to be?
- Is it a 'leading edge' approach as to how such a relationship actually 'is' within certain types of organisation?

Each of these questions leads the search for the innate qualities of HRM along different routes and towards different conclusions. If the first approach is adopted, then evidence is required that would identify the location, incidence and adoption of defined HRM practices and suggest factors that caused organisations to develop those approaches. The second approach would have to locate the HRM debate in the academic discussion of the employment relationship and demonstrate why this particular variant of analysis emerged. The third approach would have to explain why, among so many other prescriptions concerning management, the HRM prescription emerged and quite what the distinctive elements were that permitted its prescriptive influence to gain acceptance. The final approach would have to provide satisfactory evidence that, where HRM had developed within certain organisational contexts, the evidence of the particular setting could be applied to the generality of the employment relationship.

However, when these questions have all been taken into account there still remains the residual problem that none of them can conclusively define the nature of HRM in its own terms to the exclusion of each of the others. What are seen as practitioner-derived examples of HRM can be matched by similar policies in non-HRM espousing organisations; what are seen as academically derived models of HRM are each open to large areas of contention and disagreement between analysts; what are seen as prescriptive models of 'what ought to be' might well be just that and no more; and what could be held up as 'leading edge' examples could be wholly determined by the particular circumstances of organisations that are either incapable of translation into other contexts, or may indeed be unsustainable within the original organisations as circumstances change. Storey (1992: 30) outlines this competing set of considerations within the debate very clearly.

These considerations have not prevented the active debate about the nature of HRM to proceed with increasing velocity and breadth. A significant division can be noted between those analyses that seek to stress the innovative element of HRM, which is claimed to address the fundamental question of managing employees in new ways and with new perspectives, and those that stress its derivative elements, which are claimed to be no more than a reworking of the traditional themes of personnel management. Thus Walton (1985: 77–84), in attempting definitions of HRM, stresses mutuality between employers and employees:

> Mutual goals, mutual influence, mutual respect, mutual rewards, mutual responsibility. The theory is that policies of mutuality will elicit commitment which in turn will yield both better economic performance and greater human development.

Beer and Spector (1985) emphasised a new set of assumptions in shaping their meaning of HRM:

- proactive system-wide interventions, with emphasis on 'fit', linking HRM with strategic planning and cultural change;
- people as social capital capable of development;
- the potential for developing coincidence of interest between stakeholders;
- the search for power equalisation for trust and collaboration;
- open channels of communication to build trust and commitment;
- goal orientation;
- participation and informed choice.

Conversely, some writers, most notably Legge (1989) and Fowler (1987), have commented that personnel management was beginning to emerge as a more strategic function in the late 1970s and early 1980s before the concept was subsumed under the title of HRM, and that in this sense there is little new in HRM practice.

However, allowing for problems of definitions and demarcation lines between various conceptions of human resource management, there is little doubt that HRM became a fashionable concept and a controversial subject in the 1980s, with its boundaries very much overlapping the traditional areas of personnel management, industrial relations, organisational behaviour and strategic and operational management. Its emergence created a controversy, which extends through most of the issues that touch on the employment relationship. Many proponents of HRM argue that it addresses the centrality of employees in the organisation, and that their motivation and commitment to the organisational goals need to be nurtured. While this is by no means a new concept, the HRM perspective would claim at least to present a different perspective on this issue, namely that a range of organisational objectives have been arranged in a strategic way to enhance the performance of employees in achieving these goals. Before examining these arguments in more detail, a brief account of the origins and recent historical development of HRM would be appropriate in order to understand why it emerged when and as it did.

THE ORIGINS OF HUMAN RESOURCE MANAGEMENT

As we saw earlier in this chapter, HRM can be seen as part of the wider and longer debate about the nature of management in general and the management of employees in particular. This means that tracing the definitive origins of HRM is as elusive an exercise as arriving at its defining characteristics. Certainly there are antecedents in organisational theory, and particularly that of the human relations school, but the nature of HRM has involved important elements of strategic management and business policy, coupled with operations management, which make a simple 'family tree' explanation of HRM's derivation highly improbable.

What can be said is that HRM appears to have its origins in the United States in the 1950s, although it did not gain wide recognition until the beginning of the 1980s, and in the UK until the mid to late 1980s. There are a number of reasons for its emergence since then, among the most important of which are the major pressures experienced in product markets during the recession of 1980–82, combined with a growing recognition in the USA that trade union influence in collective employment was reaching fewer employees. By the 1980s the US economy was being challenged by overseas competitors, most particularly Japan. Discussion tended to focus on two issues: 'the productivity of the American worker', particularly compared with the Japanese worker, 'and the declining rate of innovation in American industries' (Devanna et al., 1984: 33). From this sprang a desire to create a work situation free from conflict, in which both employers and employees worked in unity towards the same goal – the success of the organisation (Fombrun, 1984: 17).

In the UK in the 1980s the business climate also became conducive to changes in the employment relationship. As in the USA, this was partly driven by economic pressure in the form of increased product market competition, the recession in the early part of the decade, and the introduction of new technology. However, a very significant factor in the UK, generally absent from the USA, was the desire of the government to reform and reshape the conventional model of industrial relations, which provided a rationale for the development of more employer-oriented employment policies on the part of management (Beardwell, 1992, 1996). The restructuring of the economy saw a rapid decline in the old industries and a relative rise in the service sector and in new industries based on 'high-tech' products and services, many of which were comparatively free from the established patterns of what was sometimes termed the 'old' industrial relations. These changes were overseen by a muscular entrepreneurialism promoted by the Thatcher Conservative government in the form of privatisation and anti-union legislation 'which encouraged firms to introduce new labour practices and to re-order their collective bargaining arrangements' (Hendry and Pettigrew, 1990: 19).

The influence of the US 'excellence' literature (e.g. Peters and Waterman, 1982; Kanter, 1984) also associated the success of 'leading edge' companies with the motivation of employees by involved management styles that also responded to market changes. As a consequence, the concepts of employee commitment and 'empowerment' became another strand in the ongoing debate about management practice and HRM.

A review of these issues suggests that any discussion of HRM has to come to terms with at least three fundamental problems:

- that HRM is derived from a range of antecedents, the ultimate mix of which is wholly dependent upon the stance of the analyst, and which may be drawn from an eclectic range of sources;
- that HRM is itself a contributory factor in the analysis of the employment relationship, and sets part of the context in which that debate takes place;
- that it is difficult to distinguish where the significance of HRM lies – whether it is in its supposed transformation of styles of employee management in a specific sense, or whether in a broader sense it is in its capacity to sponsor a wholly redefined relationship between management and employees that overcomes the traditional issues of control and consent at work.

This ambivalence over the definition, components and scope of HRM can be seen when examining some of the main UK and US analyses. An early model of HRM, developed by Fombrun *et al.* (1984), introduced the concept of strategic human resource management by which HRM policies are inextricably linked to the 'formulation and implementation of strategic corporate and/or business objectives' (Devanna *et al.*, 1984: 34). The model is illustrated in Figure 1.2.

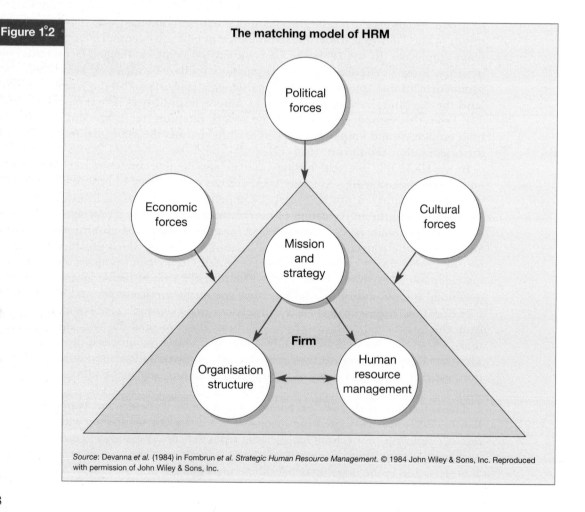

Figure 1.2   **The matching model of HRM**

Source: Devanna *et al.* (1984) in Fombrun *et al. Strategic Human Resource Management.* © 1984 John Wiley & Sons, Inc. Reproduced with permission of John Wiley & Sons, Inc.

The matching model emphasises the necessity of 'tight fit' between HR strategy and business strategy. This in turn has led to a plethora of interpretations by practitioners of how these two strategies are linked. Some offer synergies between human resource planning (manpower planning) and business strategies, with the driving force rooted in the 'product market logic' (Evans and Lorange, 1989). Whatever the process, the result is very much an emphasis on the *unitarist* view of HRM: unitarism assumes that conflict or at least differing views cannot exist within the organisation because the actors – management and employees – are working to the same goal of the organisation's success. What makes the model particularly attractive for many personnel practitioners is the fact that HRM assumes a more important position in the formulation of organisational policies.

The personnel department has often been perceived as an administrative support function with a lowly status. Personnel was now to become very much part of the human resource management of the organisation, and HRM was conceived to be more than personnel and to have peripheries wider than the normal personnel function. In order for HRM to be strategic it had to encompass all the human resource areas of the organisation and be practised by all employees. In addition, decentralisation and devolvement of responsibility are also seen as very much part of the HRM strategy as it facilitates communication, involvement and commitment of middle management and other employees deeper within the organisation. The effectiveness of organisations thus rested on how the strategy and the structure of the organisation interrelated, a concept rooted in the view of the organisation developed by Chandler (1962) and evolved in the matching model.

A more flexible model, illustrated in Figure 1.3, was developed by Beer *et al.* (1984) at Harvard University. 'The map of HRM territory', as the authors titled their model, recognised that there were a variety of 'stakeholders' in the corporation, which included shareholders, various groups of employees, the government and the community. At once the model recognises the legitimate interests of various groups, and that the creation of HRM strategies would have to recognise these interests and fuse them as much as possible into the human resource strategy and ultimately the business strategy.

This recognition of stakeholders' interests raises a number of important questions for policy-makers in the organisation:

> How much responsibility, authority and power should the organisation voluntarily delegate and to whom? If required by government legislation to bargain with the unions or consult with workers' councils, how should management enter into these institutional arrangements? Will they seek to minimize the power and influence of these legislated mechanisms? Or will they share influence and work to create greater congruence of interests between management and the employee groups represented through these mechanisms?   (Beer *et al.*, 1984: 8)

The acknowledgment of these various interest groups has made the model much more amenable to 'export' as the recognition of different legal employment structures, managerial styles and cultural differences can be more easily accommodated within it. This *neopluralist* model has also been recognised as being useful in the study of comparative HRM (Poole, 1990: 3–5). It is not surprising therefore that the Harvard model has found greater favour among academics and commentators in the UK, which has relatively strong union structures and different labour traditions from those in the United States. Nevertheless, some academics have still criticised the model as being too unitarist while accepting its basic premise (Hendry and Pettigrew, 1990).

The first two main approaches to HRM that emerged in the UK are based on the Harvard model, which is made up of both prescriptive and analytical elements. Among

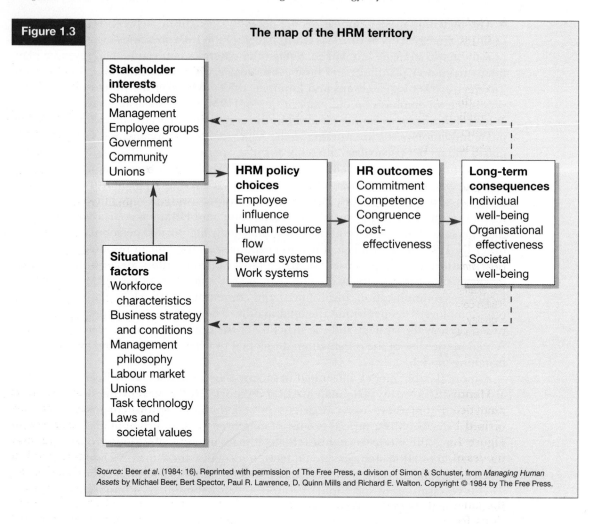

Figure 1.3   **The map of the HRM territory**

Stakeholder interests
Shareholders
Management
Employee groups
Government
Community
Unions

HRM policy choices
Employee influence
Human resource flow
Reward systems
Work systems

HR outcomes
Commitment
Competence
Congruence
Cost-effectiveness

Long-term consequences
Individual well-being
Organisational effectiveness
Societal well-being

Situational factors
Workforce characteristics
Business strategy and conditions
Management philosophy
Labour market
Unions
Task technology
Laws and societal values

Source: Beer *et al*. (1984: 16). Reprinted with permission of The Free Press, a divison of Simon & Schuster, from *Managing Human Assets* by Michael Beer, Bert Spector, Paul R. Lawrence, D. Quinn Mills and Richard E. Walton. Copyright © 1984 by The Free Press.

the most perceptive analysts of HRM, Guest has tended to concentrate on the prescriptive components, while Pettigrew and Hendry rest on the analytical aspect (Boxall, 1992). Although using the Harvard model as a basis, both Guest and Pettigrew and Hendry have some criticisms of the model, and derive from it only that which they consider useful (Guest, 1987, 1989a, 1989b, 1990; Hendry and Pettigrew, 1986, 1990).

As we have seen, there are difficulties of definition and model building in HRM, and this has led British interpreters to take alternative elements in building their own models. Guest is conscious that if a model is to be useful to researchers it must be useful 'in the field' of research, and this means that elements of HRM have to be pinned down for comparative measurement. He has therefore developed a set of propositions that he believes are amenable to testing. He also asserts that the combination of these propositions, which include strategic integration, high commitment, high quality and flexibility, creates more effective organisations (Guest, 1987).

● *Strategic integration* is defined as 'the ability of organisations to integrate HRM issues into their strategic plans, to ensure that the various aspects of HRM cohere and for line managers to incorporate an HRM perspective into their decision making'.

- *High commitment* is defined as being 'concerned with both behavioural commitment to pursue agreed goals and attitudinal commitment reflected in a strong identification with the enterprise'.
- *High quality* 'refers to all aspects of managerial behaviour, including management of employees and investment in high-quality employees, which in turn will bear directly on the quality of the goods and services provided'.
- Finally, *flexibility* is seen as being 'primarily concerned with what is sometimes called functional flexibility but also with an adaptable organisational structure with the capacity to manage innovation' (Guest, 1989b: 42).

The combination of these propositions leads to a linkage between HRM aims, policies and outcomes as shown in Table 1.1. Whether there is enough evidence to assess the relevance and efficacy of these HRM relationships will be examined later.

Table 1.1 A human resource management framework

HRM aims	HRM policies	HRM outcomes
For example: • high commitment • quality • flexible working	For example: • selection based on specific criteria using sophisticated tests	For example: • low labour turnover • allegiance to company

Source: Storey (1989: 11).

Hendry and Pettigrew (1990) have adapted the Harvard model by drawing on its analytical aspects. They see HRM 'as a perspective on employment systems, characterised by their closer alignment with business strategy'. This model, illustrated in Figure 1.4, attempts a theoretically integrative framework encompassing all styles and modes of HRM and making allowances for the economic, technical, and socio-political influences in society on the organisational strategy. 'It also enables one to describe the "preconditions" governing a firm's employment system, along with the consequences of the latter' (Hendry and Pettigrew, 1990: 25). It thus explores 'more fully the implications for employee relations of a variety of approaches to strategic management' (Boxall, 1992).

Storey has recently undertaken a study of a number of UK organisations in a series of case studies, and as a result has modified still further the approaches of previous writers on HRM (Storey, 1992). Storey had previously identified two types of HRM – 'hard' and 'soft' (Storey, 1989) – the one rooted in the manpower planning approach and the other in the human relations school. He begins his approach by defining four elements that distinguish HRM:

1 It is 'human capability and commitment which, in the final analysis, distinguishes successful organisations from the rest'.
2 Because HRM is of strategic importance, it needs to be considered by top management in the formulation of the corporate plan.
3 'HRM is, therefore, seen to have long-term implications and to be integral to the core performance of the business or public sector organisation. In other words it must be the intimate concern of line managers.'
4 The key levers (the deployment of human resources, evaluation of performance and the rewarding of it, etc.) 'are to be used to seek not merely compliance but commitment'.

Figure 1.4

Model of strategic change and human resource management

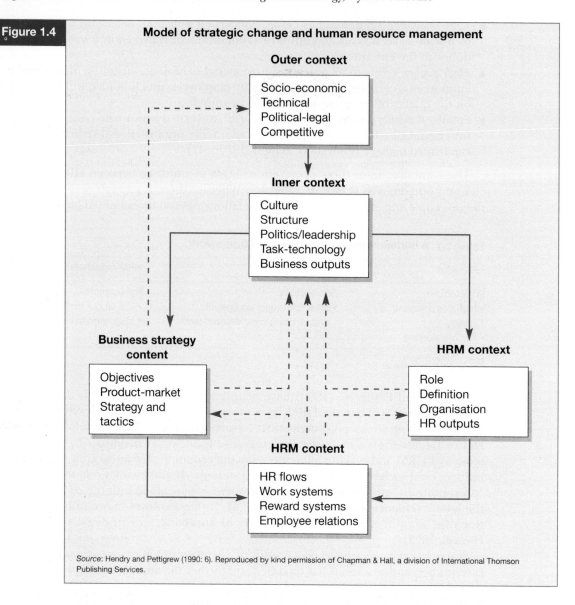

Source: Hendry and Pettigrew (1990: 6). Reproduced by kind permission of Chapman & Hall, a division of International Thomson Publishing Services.

Storey (1992) approaches an analysis of HRM by creating an 'ideal type', the purpose of which 'is to simplify by highlighting the essential features in an exaggerated way' (p.34). This he does by making a classificatory matrix of 27 points of difference between personnel and IR practices and HRM practices (see Table 1.2). The elements are categorised in a four-part basic outline:

- beliefs and assumptions;
- strategic concepts;
- line management;
- key levers.

This 'ideal type' of HRM model is not essentially an aim in itself but more a tool in enabling sets of approaches to be pinpointed in organisations for research and analytical purposes.

Table 1.2 Twenty-seven points of difference

Dimension	Personnel and IR	HRM
Beliefs and assumptions		
1 Contract	Careful delineation of written contracts	Aim to go 'beyond contract'
2 Rules	Importance of devising clear rules/mutuality	'Can-do' outlook; impatience with 'rule'
3 Guide to management action	Procedures	'Business need'
4 Behaviour referent	Norms/custom and practice	Values/mission
5 Managerial task *vis-à-vis* labour	Monitoring	Nurturing
6 Nature of relations	Pluralist	Unitarist
7 Conflict	Institutionalised	De-emphasised
Strategic aspects		
8 Key relations	Labour management	Customer
9 Initiatives	Piecemeal	Integrated
10 Corporate plan	Marginal to	Central to
11 Speed of decision	Slow	Fast
Line management		
12 Management role	Transactional	Transformational leadership
13 Key managers	Personnel/IR specialists	General/business/line managers
14 Communication	Indirect	Direct
15 Standardisation	High (e.g. 'parity' an issue)	Low (e.g. 'parity' not seen as relevant)
16 Prized management skills	Negotiation	Facilitation
Key levers		
17 Selection	Separate, marginal task	Integrated, key task
18 Pay	Job evaluation (fixed grades)	Performance-related
19 Conditions	Separately negotiated	Harmonisation
20 Labour management	Collective bargaining contracts	Towards individual contracts
21 Thrust of relations with stewards	Regularised through facilities and training	Marginalised (with exception of some bargaining for change models)
22 Job categories and grades	Many	Few
23 Communication	Restricted flow	Increased flow
24 Job design	Division of labour	Teamwork
25 Conflict handling	Reach temporary truces	Manage climate and culture
26 Training and development	Controlled access to courses	Learning companies
27 Foci of attention for interventions	Personnel procedures	Wide-ranging cultural, structural and personnel strategies

Source: Storey (1992: 38). Reproduced by kind permission of Blackwell Publishers.

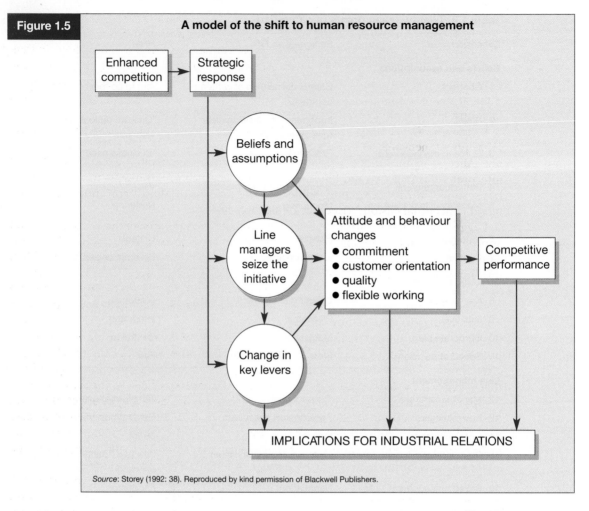

Figure 1.5   A model of the shift to human resource management

Source: Storey (1992: 38). Reproduced by kind permission of Blackwell Publishers.

Storey's theoretical model is thus based on conceptions of how organisations have been transformed from predominantly personnel/IR practices to HRM practices. As it is based on the ideal type there are no organisations that conform to this picture in reality. It is in essence a tool for enabling comparative analysis. He illustrates this by proposing 'a model of the shift to human resource management', shown in Figure 1.5.

HUMAN RESOURCE MANAGEMENT: THE STATE OF THE DEBATE

The question of whether human resource management has the capacity to transform or replace deeply rooted models of personnel management and industrial relations, or could become a fully worked-through theory of management, is one that cannot be answered in a simple manner. Human resource management has many cogent critics and many sceptical supporters. Initial criticism which claimed that it was 'old wine in new bottles', the restatement perspective outlined earlier in this chapter, still has strong adherents (Keenoy and Anthony, 1992). Others see it as a version of 'the emperor's new clothes' (Legge, 1989) or a 'wolf in sheep's clothing' (Armstrong, 1987; Fowler, 1987; Keenoy, 1990a).

Tom Keenoy is one of the most eloquent and persuasive of critics, and his examination of HRM has exposed many of the a priori assumptions and non sequiturs that abound in the reasoning of its supporters. He claims that HRM is more rhetoric than reality and has been 'talked up' by its advocates. It has little support in terms of evidence, and has been a convenient dustbin of rationalisation to support ideological shifts in the employment relationship brought about by market pressures. It is also full of contradictions, not only in its meanings but also in its practice.

In examining the meanings of HRM Keenoy notes that a 'remarkable feature of the HRM phenomenon is the brilliant ambiguity of the term itself'. He later continues: 'On the "Alice principle" that a term means whatever one chooses it to mean, each of these interpretations may be valid but, in Britain, the absence of any intellectual touchstones has resulted in the term being subject to the process of almost continuous and contested conceptual elision.' (Keenoy, 1990b: 363–384).

Legge (1989) has shown that a close examination of the normative models of HRM and personnel management reveals little difference between the two, and that HRM contains a number of internal contradictions. Legge points out that there is a problem with integration in the sense that HRM policies have to integrate with business policy. She asks: 'Is it possible to have a corporation-wide mutually reinforcing set of HRM policies, if the organisation operates in highly diverse product markets, and, if not, does it matter, in terms of organisational effectiveness?' (p.30). She also asks: 'If the business strategy should dictate the choice of HRM policies, will some strategies dictate policies that . . . fail to emphasise commitment, flexibility and quality?' (p.30). Legge also comments on the probable incompatibility of creating an organisational culture that attempts to pursue both individualistic and teamwork policies at the same time.

Other critics have indicated that many organisations are driven by stronger objectives than HRM. Armstrong (1989) has pointed to the financial orientations of most companies, which are incompatible with those prescriptions described as imperative in the practice of HRM. Furthermore, the belief that human resource management can transcend national cultures has attracted considerable critical comment (Pieper, 1990).

The 1990s saw a growing sophistication in the nature of the debate involving HRM. The nature of the debate at the conclusion of that decade was much more extensive than that which ushered it in. One signal factor was the reconstruction and expansion of the most important research 'engine' in the UK, the Workplace Employee Relations Survey of 1998 (Culley *et al.* 1998), which has specifically addressed HRM-based issues of techniques and performance. Part of this development has been promoted by the realisation that traditional sources of competitive advantage, such as technological supremacy, patents and capital, are much less important than they were, in a world in which many countries can display equal advantage in at least some of these critical aspects (Pfeffer, 1994, 1998). Thus the extent to which an organisation can mobilise its internal human resources may hold the key to achievable advantage in the future (Prahalad and Hamel, 1990).

Wood (1995) has examined high-commitment management in terms of what he calls the 'four pillars of HRM' and their ability to deliver significant HRM performance; Guest and Hoque (1996) have examined the concept of 'fit' in the specific circumstances of HRM techniques in greenfield sites and the 'bundles' of practice that might affect performance; Purcell (1996, 1999) has critically examined the notion of 'bundles' but has provided a thoughtful analysis of resource-based HRM in the context of corporate strategy (1995); while Boxall has sought to relate resource-based analysis to the strategic HRM debate (1996).

A further element in the contemporary discussion is the question of whether HRM is now affording line management more control of the personnel function than personnel specialists themselves have. If one of the attributes of HRM is its devolution to the line, then perhaps a logical consequence is the relative loss of influence and control by the erstwhile keepers of the corporate personnel conscience. Does this matter? In the words of Fernie *et al.* (1994), is HRM all 'Big Hat, No Cattle'? The extent to which HRM activity has shifted to the line, and the associated question of whether personnel managers are any more strategic in their role than in the past, is difficult to determine conclusively. The Second Company Level Industrial Relations Survey (Marginson *et al.*, 1993) found no evidence to support general strategic involvement, and some evidence that, without a personnel director on the board, involvement in the formulation of human resource policy was weakened – findings largely supported by Purcell and Ahlstrand's (1994) study of multidivisional organisations. Perhaps the clearest evidence to suggest that personnel management was losing out to the line is provided by Storey's (1992) study of 'mainstream' companies and the introduction of HRM, although a study of 28 organisations by Kelly and Gennard (1994) presented a different picture based on interviews with personnel directors.

In an important sense, therefore, one answer to Storey's (1995) rhetorical question 'HRM: still marching on or marching out?' is that the debate is still progressing, with very little sign that it will abate in the short term. And a reaction to Bach and Sisson's (2000) view that the flood tide of HRM is waning is to note that the tide appears still to be flooding strongly, with new aspects appearing on the agenda or existing issues further strengthening their position. What are the agenda items that are taking us into the new decade? Perhaps three particular aspects can serve from the strategy, style and outcome debate explored at the outset.

From the strategic perspective, an important new area of analysis is concerned with the role played by diffusion: thus Ferner (1997) has argued that country of origin effects within multinational corporations (MNCs) will tend to emphasise HRM practices that have roots in national business cultures and lead to divergent MNC HRM strategies. At the same time, the very processes of operating in different cultural contexts impact on the dominant business culture and moderate the 'export' effect. What we do not yet know is the extent to which these two processes work together or against each other to achieve strategic results.

An approach to the style perspective might be seen in the role of the psychological contract and employee motivation. Guest and Conway (1997) point to evidence that suggests that employees report positive responses to issues such as fairness, trust and delivery on promises. The Fourth WERS survey of 1998 noted that 68% of workplaces with over 500 employees report participation in problem-solving groups. There is a large agenda item that is concerned with examining and assessing the scope and significance of managerial styles in terms of involvement, commitment and delivery on the part of the employer, and the resultant response from employees to give assent and commitment to management systems that stress these aspects of the employment relationship. What is unclear is how these factors hold over time, and whether component elements within this agenda will remain significant or important and thus weaken or strengthen the concept.

The third area for further work lies in the area of outcomes. At the present time there is much work exploring the nature of HRM 'bundles', and one might expect more as the data from WERS 98 are analysed further. Perhaps one strand of this debate is worth emphasis – high-commitment management and the emphasis on work management systems that achieve specific outcomes (Wood and De Menezes 1998). This approach seems to have found good evidence that a particular managerial style, allied to a particular combination of practices, will lead to beneficial business outcomes. Again, whether this is sustainable over time remains a key question. Nevertheless it represents a significant addition to the literature and practice of HRM.

If these three approaches to research, analysis and practice in HRM are indicative of its breadth and strength at the beginning of the new millennium, is there a way in which one can summarise these initiatives? Given that emphasis has been placed in the past on strategy, fit and integration, perhaps one final element ought to be noted as a key ingredient – that of *mix*. Whatever the strategic intent, managerial style, outcomes sought or tight-loose 'fit' adopted by organisations, it will be in the mix of these components that we will find not only some answers to questions but also the further development of HRM as a significant approach to managing employees.

SUMMARY

● Human resource management presents significant issues for the analysis and operation of employment relationships. The management of employees is one of the key elements in the coordination and general management of work organisations. Considerable controversy exists as to the origins, characteristics and philosophy of HRM, and its capacity to influence the nature of that relationship. The debate surrounding HRM can be characterised by these four predominant approaches:

- HRM as a contemporary 'restatement' of industrial relations and personnel management policies;
- HRM as a 'fusion' of industrial relations and personnel management to create a 'new' management discipline and function;
- HRM as a 'resource-based' approach, stressing the potential of the individual employee in terms of an investment rather than a cost;
- HRM as a 'strategic/international' phenomenon, making a determining contribution to corporate strategy and capable of being translated across cultures.

● The origins of HRM may be traced back to the 1950s in the United States. By the early 1980s a number of US analysts were writing about HRM and devising models and explanations for its emergence. Among the most significant of these commentators are Devanna (the matching model), Beer (the Harvard model), and Walton. In the UK significant commentary on HRM has been provided by Guest, Pettigrew and Hendry, Storey, and Poole. More recently Huselid, McDuffie and Arthur have extended the analysis to HRM 'bundles'.

● For Guest the test of HRM is its applicability 'in the field' and its capacity to satisfy some key propositions such as 'strategic integration', 'high commitment', 'high quality' and 'flexibility'. Pettigrew and Hendry stress the analytical elements of the Harvard model, and argue that HRM is characterised by its close alignment with business strategy. Storey defines the 'schools' of HRM – 'hard' (rooted in the manpower planning tradition) and 'soft' (rooted in the human relations approach to organisational analysis), and has developed a model that sets out four areas for analysis: beliefs and assumptions; strategic aspects; line management; key levers as major determinants of HRM practice. Poole has suggested that the Harvard model of HRM is useful in the study of comparative HRM.

● Particularly critical perspectives on HRM in the UK have been provided by Legge, Armstrong and Keenoy. Legge argues that the underlying values of personnel management and HRM differ little, and that organisational constraints may well make a truly integrated HRM approach highly impractical, while Armstrong has noted that financial orientations may well clash with HRM prescriptions. Keenoy sees HRM as being constructed around the highly ambiguous nature of the term, which can come to mean anything to anyone.

● Whatever the perspective taken on HRM, two important points cannot be overlooked: first, it has raised questions about the nature of the employment relationship that have stimulated one of the most intense and active debates to have occurred in the subject over the past 40 years; and second, the management of employment relations and the question of employee commitment to the employment relationship remain at the heart of the debate.

Activity

VP – Human Resources

Headquartered in the US, our client is a Fortune 500 company with sales offices in 59 countries and a turnover exceeding $9 billion. This is an electronics distribution business, which markets, inventories and adds value to the products of the most prestigious manufacturers worldwide.

The European operation, employing over 2000 people with sales of $2 billion, has grown dramatically through recent and extensive acquisitions. The challenge facing the new Vice President of Human Resources is to lead the integration of this newly amalgamated group of companies into a single dynamic entity with high productivity, commitment and morale. He or she must also organise a new Pan European HR team and move it quickly to best practice.

Electronics distribution is an extremely fast-moving and complex business. While previous experience in this industry is not essential, you will definitely need a breadth of European HR experience in a fast-moving and tough business environment, and have high levels of mental agility, flexibility and perseverance.

You will probably have a degree, speak more than one European language, and have excellent interpersonal skills, although ability to deliver is what really counts.

Director of Human Resources

We are one of Britain's leading broadband communications companies, providing residential cable, business communication and network services. Our aim is to create an integrated communications and media group delivering a range of voice, video and interactive services across multiple platforms underpinned by branded digital media content.

We are restructuring our organisational capabilities following rapid year-on-year growth, and are now seeking an exceptional and dynamic individual to join its human resources team. Reporting to the Corporate Human Resources Director the successful applicant will:

● operate as a key member of the senior executive team for the Business, Network and Commercial Services groups, supporting 2500 employees nationwide;
● develop and deliver a human resources strategy that meets current and future business needs;
● manage a diverse brief including resourcing and retention, change management, organisational design, succession planning and performance management.

Candidates will currently be operating at senior human resources management level in a fast-paced consumer goods or service environment, and may now be seeking their first directorship. Qualified to graduate level, with a highly commercial approach and the ability to contribute to strategic decision-making, candidates must be customer focused and results driven, with a strong operational edge. Outstanding drive and leadership skills will be vital in ensuring rapid and professional organisational transition.

This is a high-profile role with one of the UK's most dynamic and fast-growing companies, providing exceptional career development opportunities. The remuneration package will be commensurate with the profile of the role, including an excellent range of benefits.

Examine these two advertisements, which are seeking senior strategic-level HRM positions. Consider the following two points:

1 Assess whether there are any significant differences in either the strategy, style or outcome of the HRM processes described in these advertisements. What factors would you consider to be significant in the organisational profile of each company?

2 In reviewing the person requirements for these two posts, which kinds of personnel experience and development would you consider suitable for this level of appointment?

REFERENCES AND FURTHER READING

Those texts marked with an asterisk are recommended for further reading.

Armstrong, M. (1987) 'Human resource management: a case of the emperor's new clothes?', *Personnel Management*, Vol. 19, No. 8, pp. 30–35.

Armstrong, P. (1989) 'Limits and possibilities for HRM in an age of management accountancy', in Storey, J. (ed.) *New Perspectives on Human Resource Management*. London: Routledge, pp. 154–166.

Arthur, J.B. (1992) 'The link between business strategy and industrial relations systems in American steel mini-mills', *Industrial and Labour Relations Review*, Vol. 45, No. 3, pp. 488–506.

Arthur, J.B. (1994) 'Effects of human resource systems on manufacturing performance and turnover', *Academy of Management Journal*, Vol. 37, No. 3. pp 670–687.

Bach, S. and Sisson, K. (eds) (2000) *Personnel Management*. Oxford: Blackwell.

Beardwell, I.J. (1992) 'The new industrial relations : a review of the debate', *Human Resource Management Journal*, Vol. 2, No. 2, pp. 1–8.

Beardwell, I.J. (1996) 'How do we know how it really is?', in Beardwell, I.J. (ed) *Contemporary Industrial Relations*. Oxford: Oxford University Press, pp. 1–10.

Beer, M. and Spector, B. (1985) 'Corporate wide transformations in human resource management', in Walton, R.E. and Lawrence, E.R. (eds) *Human Resource Management Trends and Challenges*. Boston, Mass.: Harvard Business School Press.

*Beer, M., Spector, B., Lawrence P.R., Quinn Mills, D. and Walton, R.E. (1984) *Managing Human Assets*. New York: Free Press.

Boxall, P.F. (1992) 'Strategic human resource management: beginnings of a new theoretical sophistication?', *Human Resource Management Journal*, Vol. 2, No. 3, pp. 60–79.

*Boxall, P. (1996) 'The strategic HRM debate and the resource-based view of the firm', *Human Resource Management Journal*, Vol. 6, No. 3, pp. 59–75.

Chandler, A. (1962) *Strategy and Structure*. Cambridge, Mass.: Harvard University Press.

Culley, M., O'Reilly, A., Millward, N., Woodland, S., Dix, G., Bryson, A. (1998) *The 1998 Workplace Employee Relations Survey: First Findings*. London: ESRC/ACAS/PSI/DTI.

Culley, M., Woodland, S., O'Reilly, A. and Dix, G. (1999) *Britain at Work: As depicted by the 1998 Workplace Employee Relations Survey*. London: Routledge.

*Devanna, M.A., Fombrun, C.J. and Tichy, N.M. (1984) 'A framework for a strategic human resource management', in Fombrun, C.J., Tichy, M.M. and Devanna, M.A. (eds) *Strategic Human Resource Management*. New York: John Wiley.

Evans, P.A.L. and Lorange, P. (1989) 'Two logics behind human resource management', in Evans, P., Doz, Y. and Laurent, A. (eds) *Human Resource Management in International Firms*. Basingstoke: Macmillan.

Ferner, A. (1997) 'Country of origin effects and HRM in multi-national companies', *Human Resource Management Journal*, Vol. 7, No. 1, pp. 19–37.

Fernie, S., Metcalf, D. and Woodland, S. (1994) *Does HRM Boost Employee Management Relations?* LSE CEP Working Paper No. 546. London: London School of Economics.

Fombrun, C.J. (1984) 'The external context of human resource management', in Fombrun, C.J., Tichy, N.M. and Devanna, M.A. (eds) *Strategic Human Resource Management*. New York: John Wiley, p. 41.

*Fombrun, C.J., Tichy, N.M. and Devanna, M.A. (1984) *Strategic Human Resource Management*. New York: John Wiley.

Fox, A. (1966) *Industrial sociology and industrial relations*, Royal Commission on Trade Unions and Employers' Associations, Research Paper No. 3. London: HMSO.

Fowler, A. (1987) 'When the chief executive discovers HRM', *Personnel Management*, Vol. 19, No. 3.

Guest, D. (1987) 'Human resource management and industrial relations', *Journal of Management Studies*, Vol. 24, No. 5, pp. 503–521.

*Guest, D. (1989a) 'Personnel and human resource management: can you tell the difference?', *Personnel Management*, January, pp. 48–51.

Guest, D. (1989b) 'Human resource management: its implications for industrial relations and trade unions', in Storey, J. (ed.) *New Perspectives on Human Resource Management*. London: Routledge, pp. 41–55.

*Guest, D. (1990) 'Human resource management and the American dream', *Journal of Management Studies*, Vol. 27, No. 4, pp. 377–397.

Guest, D. (1997) 'Human resource management and performance: a review and research agenda', *International Journal of Human Resource Management*, Vol. 8, No. 3, pp. 263–276.

Guest, D. and Conway, N. (1997) *Employee Motivation and the Psychological Contract*, Issues in Personnel Management 21. London: IPD.

*Guest, D. and Hoque, K. (1996) 'Human resource management and the new industrial relations', in Beardwell, I. (ed.) *Contemporary Industrial Relations*. Oxford: Oxford University Press, pp. 11–36.

Hendry, C. and Pettigrew, A. (1986) 'The practice of strategic human resource management', *Personnel Review*, Vol. 15, No. 5, pp. 3–8.

Hendry, C. and Pettigrew, A. (1990) 'Human resource management: an agenda for the 1990s', *International Journal of Human Resource Management*, Vol. 1, No. 1, pp. 17–43.

*Huselid, M. (1995) 'The impact of HRM practices on turnover, productivity and corporate financial performance', *Academy of Management Journal*, Vol. 38, No. 3, pp. 635–672.

Kanter, R. (1984) *The Change Masters*. London: Allen & Unwin.

Keenoy, T. (1990a) 'HRM: a case of the wolf in sheep's clothing?', *Personnel Review*, Vol. 19, No. 2, pp. 3–9.

*Keenoy, T. (1990b) 'Human resource management: rhetoric, reality and contradiction', *International Journal of Human Resource Management*, Vol. 1, No. 3, December, pp. 363–384.

Keenoy, T. and Anthony P. (1992) 'Human resource management: metaphor, meaning and morality', in Blyton, P. and Turnbull, P. (eds) *Reassessing Human Resource Management*. London: Sage, pp. 233–255.

Kelly, J. and Gennard, J. (1994) 'HRM: the views of personnel directors', *Human Resource Management Journal*, Vol. 5, No. 1, pp. 15–30.

Legge, K. (1978) *Power, Innovation and Problem Solving in Personnel Management*. London: McGraw-Hill.

*Legge, K. (1989) 'Human resource management: a critical analysis', in Storey, J. (ed.) *New Perspectives on Human Resource Management*. London: Routledge, pp. 19–40.

*Legge, K. (1995) HRM: *Rhetorics and Realities*. Basingstoke: Macmillan Business.

MacInnes, J. (1987) *Thatcherism at Work*. Milton Keynes: Open University Press.

Marginson, P., Armstrong, P., Edwards, P., Purcell, J. and Hubbard, N. (1993) *The Control of Industrial Relations in Large Companies*, Warwick Papers in Industrial Relations No. 45. IRRV School of Industrial and Business Studies, University of Warwick.

McDuffie, J.P. (1995) Human resource bundles and manufacturing performance', *Industrial and Labour Relations Review*, Vol. 48, No. 2, pp 197–221.

McLoughlin, I. and Gourlay, S. (1994) *Enterprise without Unions*. Milton Keynes: Open University Press.

Peters, T.J. and Waterman, R.H. (1982) *In Search of Excellence: Lessons from America's Best Run Companies*. New York: Harper & Row.

Pfeffer, J. (1994) *Competitive Advantage Through People*. Boston, Mass.: Harvard Business School Press.

Pfeffer, J. (1998) *The Human Equation*. Boston, Mass: Harvard Business School Press.

Pieper, R. (ed.) (1990) *Human Resource Management: An International Comparison*. New York: Walter de Gruyter.

Poole, M. (1990) 'Editorial: Human resource management in an international perspective', *International Journal of Human Resource Management*, Vol. 1, No. 1, pp. 1–15.

*Prahalad, G. and Hamel, C.K. (1990) 'The core competencies of the corporation', *Harvard Business Review*, May–June, pp. 79–91.

*Purcell, J. (1995) 'Corporate strategy and its link with human resource management strategy', in Storey, J. (ed.) *Human Resource Management: A Critical Text*. London: Routledge, pp. 63–86.

Purcell, J. (1996) 'Human resource bundles of best practice: a utopia cul-de-sac?' Department of Management, University of Bath.

Purcell, J. (1999) 'Best practice and best fit: chimera or cul-de-sac', *Human Resource Management Journal*, Vol. 9, No. 3, pp 26–41.

Purcell, J. and Ahlstrand, B. (1994) *Human Resource Management in the Multi-Divisional Company*. Oxford: Oxford University Press.

Purcell, J. and Sisson, K. (1983) 'Strategies and practice in the management of industrial relations', in Bain, G. (ed.) *Industrial Relations in Britain*. Oxford: Blackwell, pp. 95–120.

Sisson, K. (1993) 'In search of HRM', *British Journal of Industrial Relations*, Vol. 31, No. 2, pp 201–210.

Storey, J. (1992) *Developments in the Management of Human Resources: An Analytical Review*. London: Blackwell.

*Storey, J. (1995) *Human Resource Management: A Critical Text*. London: Routledge.

Storey, J. (ed.) (1989) *New Perspectives on Human Resource Management*. London: Routledge.

Tyson, S. and Fell, A. (1986) *Evaluating the Personnel Function*. London: Hutchinson.

Ulrich, D. (1998) *Human Resource Champions*. Boston: Harvard Business School Press.

Walton, R.E. (1985) 'From control to commitment in the workplace', *Harvard Business Review*, Vol. 63, No. 2, March–April, pp. 76–84.

Watson, T. (1997) *The Personnel Managers.* London: Routledge.

West, M. and Patterson, M. (1997) *The impact of people management practices on business performance.* IPD Research paper No. 22. London: IPD.

Wood, S. (1995) 'The four pillars of HRM: are they connected?', *Human Resource Management Journal,* Vol. 5, No. 5, pp. 49–59.

Wood, S. and De Menezes (1998) 'High commitment management in the UK', *Human Relations,* Vol. 51, No. 4, pp 485–515.

2

Human resource management in context

Audrey Collin

OBJECTIVES

- To indicate the significance of context for the understanding of HRM.
- To discuss ways of conceptualising and representing the nature of context generally and this context in particular.
- To analyse the nature of the immediate context of HRM: the problematical nature of organisations and the need for management.
- To indicate the nature of the wider context of HRM and illustrate this through selected examples.
- To examine how our ways of interpreting and defining reality for ourselves and others construct and influence the way we understand and practise HRM: perception, epistemology and ideology.
- To suggest the implications for the readers of this book.
- To present a number of activities that will facilitate readers' understanding of the context of HRM.

INTRODUCTION

The significance and nature of context

An event seen from one point-of-view gives one impression. Seen from another point-of-view it gives quite a different impression. But it's only when you get the whole picture you fully understand what's going on.   (Copyright © the *Guardian*)

The classic, prize-winning, 'Points-of-View' advertisement for the *Guardian* newspaper in 1985 showed dramatically how we need to be aware of the context of human affairs in order to understand them. We can easily misinterpret facts, events and people when we examine them out of context, for it is their context that provides us with the clues necessary to enable us to understand them. Context locates them in space and time and gives them a past and a future, as well as the present that we see. It gives us the language to understand them, the codes to decode them, the keys to their meaning.

This chapter will carry forward your thinking about the issues raised in Chapter 1 by exploring the various strands within the context of HRM that are woven together to form the patterns of meanings that constitute it. As the last chapter explained, and the rest of the book will amplify, HRM is far more than a portfolio of policies, practices, procedures and prescriptions concerned with the management of the employment relationship. It is this, but more. And because it is more, it is loosely defined and difficult to pin down precisely, a basket of multiple, overlapping and shifting meanings, which users of the term do not always specify. Its 'brilliant ambiguity' (Keenoy, 1990) derives from the context in which it is embedded, a context within which there are multiple and often competing perspectives upon the employment relationship, some ideological, others theoretical, some conceptual. HRM is inevitably a contested terrain, and the various definitions of it reflect this.

You will recognise in the various models of HRM presented in Chapter 1 that this context is a highly complex one, not just because of its increasing diversity and dynamism, but also because it is multilayered, each of these layers affecting the others. The organisation constitutes the immediate context of the employment relationship, and the debate over how this relationship should be managed begins here. The nature of organisation and the tensions between the stakeholders in it give rise to issues that have to be addressed by managers: for example, choices about how to orchestrate the activities of organisational members and whose interests to serve. These issues of managerial control are of considerable significance for HRM, as subsequent chapters indicate.

Beyond the organisation itself lie the economic, social, political and cultural layers, and beyond them again the historical, national and global layers of the context. Considerable change is taking place within those layers, making the whole field dynamic. It is not the purpose of this chapter to register these many changes; you will become aware of some of them as you read the remainder of this book. However, we need to note here that the events and changes in the wider context have repercussions for organisations, and present further issues to be managed and choices to be made.

The various layers and the elements within them, however, exist in more than one conceptual plane. One has a concrete nature, like a local pool of labour, and the other is abstract, like the values and stereotypes that prejudice employers for or against a particular class of person in the labour market. The abstract world of ideas and values overlays the various layers of the context of HRM: the ways of organising society, of acquiring and using power, and of distributing resources; the ways of relating to, understanding and valuing human beings and their activities; the ways of studying and understanding reality and of acquiring knowledge; the stocks of accumulated knowledge in theories and concepts.

It is the argument of this chapter that to understand HRM we need to be aware not just of the multiple layers of its context – rather like the skins of an onion – but also of these conceptual planes and the way they intersect. 'Context' is being used here to mean more than the surrounding circumstances that exert 'external influences' on a given topic: context gives them a third dimension. The chapter is arguing, further, that events and experiences, ideas and ideologies are not discrete and isolatable, but are interwoven and interconnected, and that HRM itself is embedded in its context: it is part of that web and cannot, therefore, be meaningfully examined separately from it. Context is highly significant yet, as we shall see, very difficult to study.

Conceptualising and representing context

How can we begin to understand any subject that is embedded in a complex context? We seem to have awareness at an intuitive level, perceiving and acting upon the clues that context gives to arrive at the 'tacit knowledge' discussed later in Chapter 7.

However, context challenges our formal thinking. First, in order to be able to see a subject in its context, we need to be able to stand back to take in the wider picture (and to reflect upon it, as Chapter 7 suggests). It is not easy for HRM practitioners and theorists to obtain this perspective when they are also part of that picture. The context of HRM is theirs too. They are like the fish in water that 'can have no understanding of the concept of "wetness" since it has no idea of what it means to be dry' (Southgate and Randall, 1981: 54). Those who study HRM, therefore, have to stand back as far as they can to take the various interpretations of HRM into consideration, while recognising that they, too, may be part of the same context.

Second, we need the conceptual tools to grasp the whole (and dynamic) picture. To understand a social phenomenon such as HRM, we cannot just wrench it from its context and examine it microscopically in isolation. To do this is to be like the child who digs up the newly planted and now germinating seed to see 'whether it is growing'. In the same way, if we analyse context into its various elements and layers, then we are already distorting our understanding of it, because it is an indivisible whole. Rather, we have to find ways to examine HRM's interconnectedness and interdependence with other phenomena.

The study of context, therefore, is no easy task, and poses a major challenge to our established formal, analytical and detached ways of thinking. Nevertheless, as we shall discuss later in this chapter, there are ways forward that will enable us to conceptualise formally the many loops and circularities of these complex interrelationships in an often dynamic context.

Meanwhile, we shall try to conceptualise it through metaphor: that is, envisage it in terms of something concrete that we already understand. We shall use the metaphor of a tapestry, for this conveys interconnectedness and texture: tapestry is a 'thick hand-woven textile fabric in which design is formed by weft stitches across parts of warp' (*Concise OED*, 1982). This allows us to become aware of the different dimensions of context: the warp threads that run the length of the tapestry, the weft as the lateral threads that weave through the warp to give colour, pattern and texture. In terms of this metaphor, our ways of seeing and thinking about our world – the assumptions we make about our reality – are the warp, the threads that run the length of the tapestry contributing to its basic form and texture. They therefore play their part throughout the context of HRM. Ideologies and the rhetoric through which they are expressed – ways of defining reality for other people – are the weft threads that weave through the warp threads, and give the tapestry pattern and texture. Events, people, ephemeral issues are the stitches that form the surface patterns and texture of HRM. We see this in Figure 2.1. In the case of the context of HRM, this tapestry is being woven continuously from threads of different colours and textures. At times one colour predominates, but then peters out. In parts of the tapestry patterns are intentionally fashioned, while observers (such as the authors of this book) believe they can discern a recognisable pattern in other parts.

This metaphor again reminds us that an analytical approach to the study of context, by taking it apart to examine it closely, would be like taking a tapestry to bits: we would be left with threads. The tapestry itself inheres in the whole, not its parts. How, then, can the chapter begin to communicate the nature of this tapestry without destroying its very essence through analysis? The very representation of our thinking in written language is linear, and this undermines our ability to communicate a dynamic, interrelated complexity clearly and succinctly. We need to think in terms of the 'rich pictures', 'mind-maps', or 'systems diagrams' (Checkland, 1981; Senge, 1990; Cameron, 1997) devised to express systems thinking, which will be explained later.

Figure 2.1 HRM: the warp and weft of a tapestry

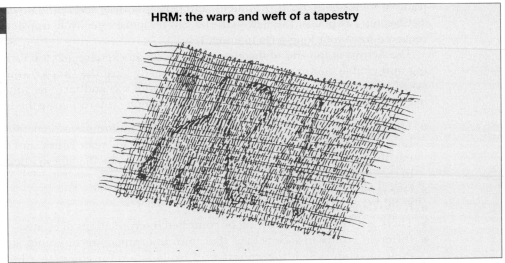

It is not feasible nor, indeed, necessary to attempt to portray the whole tapestry in detail; the chapter will focus instead upon a number of strands that run through it. You will be able to identify and follow them through the remainder of the book, and observe how their interweaving gives us changes in pattern and colour, some distinct, others subtle. Before beginning to read the exposition of the context of HRM, you will find it helpful to return to the various models that were presented in Chapter 1 in order to identify some of the elements of context and the relationships between them that we shall be describing. This will help you to keep the total picture in mind as parts of it are discussed. In this way you will develop some more appropriate mental 'hooks' upon which to hang your new understanding.

The chapter will thus shortly look at the immediate context of HRM and note how the nature of organisations presents their managers with choices over how to manage people. It will then examine a number of the choices that managers make and some of the interpretations that theorists make of them. It will then look briefly at the wider context of HRM, picking out a few elements to examine. It is when we turn to the outer layers of the world of ideas, philosophies and ideologies that we become fully aware of the need to represent context as a tapestry rather than as a many-skinned onion, for we find there various strands of meaning that managers and academics are drawing upon to construct – that is, both to create and to make sense of – HRM.

The concepts and language needed to understand context

To understand context, it has been suggested so far, we need to stand back as far as we can from it. We therefore need to move beyond description of the concrete world to the abstract world of ideas. Although the appropriate language to enable us to do this may be largely unfamiliar to you, you will find that you already have considerable understanding of the concepts it expresses. Your own experience in thinking about and responding to one aspect of context – the natural, physical environment – will have given you the basic concepts that we are using and a useful set of 'hooks' upon which to hang the new knowledge this chapter will give you. It would be helpful to your understanding of this chapter, therefore, if you examined some of the 'hooks' you are already using to think about the environment, and perhaps clarify and refine them. (In this way, as Chapter 7 explains, the new material can be more effectively transferred into and retrieved from your long-term memory.)

The Activity at the end of the chapter proposes an exercise that will focus your thinking and enable you to recognise that you already have the 'hooks' you will need to classify the material of this chapter in a meaningful way and increase your understanding of the nature of the context of HRM. For example, you recognise the following:

- The nature of the environment is multilayered, multidimensional, and interwoven. In it, concrete events and abstract ideas intertwine to create issues, and thinking, feeling, interpreting and behaving are all involved: it is like the tapestry described earlier in the section.
- Our understanding depends upon our perspective.
- It also depends upon our ideology.
- There are therefore competing or contested interpretations of events.
- Different groups in society have their own interpretations of events, stemming from their ideology, which incorporates an explanation for competing interpretations. They use the rhetoric of their own interpretations to express competing interpretations, thus suppressing the expression of competing views.
- There are powerful others who try to impose their interpretations of events, their version of reality, upon the less powerful majority: this is hegemony.

This subsection has perhaps given you a new language to describe what you already understand well. Later sections of this chapter will amplify the definitions of these concepts and use them in its exploration of the context of HRM.

THE IMMEDIATE CONTEXT OF HRM

Human resource management, however defined, concerns the management of the employment relationship: it is practised in organisations by managers. The nature of the organisation and the way it is managed therefore constitute significant threads that are interwoven to form the immediate context within which HRM is embedded, and generate the tensions that HRM policies and practices attempt to resolve. This section will introduce the theme of managerial control that recurs throughout this book, noting the ways in which it is exercised through the management of performance and the devolving of decision-making or empowerment. The deeper questions about managing people that such issues imply will also be noted here, and later traced through the outer layers of the context of HRM.

The nature of organisations and the need for management

At its simplest, an organisation comes into existence when the efforts of two or more people are pooled to achieve an objective that one would be unable to complete alone. The achievement of this objective calls for the completion of a number of tasks. Depending upon their complexity, the availability of appropriate technology and the skills of the people involved, these tasks may be subdivided into a number of subtasks and other people employed to help carry them out. This division of labour constitutes the lateral dimension of the structure of the organisation. Its vertical dimension is constructed from the generally hierarchical relationships of power and authority between the owner or owners, those employed to complete these tasks, and the managers employed to coordinate and control the workers and their working activities. Working on behalf of the organisation's owners or shareholders and with the authority derived from them, managers draw upon a number of resources to enable them to complete their task: raw materials; finance; technology; appropriately skilled people; legitimacy, support and goodwill from the organisation's environment. They manage the organisation by ensuring that there are sufficient people with appropriate skills; that they work to the same ends and timetable; that they have the authority, information and other resources needed to complete their tasks; and that their tasks dovetail and are performed to an acceptable standard and at the required pace.

The very nature of organisation therefore generates a number of significant tensions: between people with different stakes in the organisation, and therefore different perspectives upon and interests in it; between what owners and other members of the organisation may desire and what they can feasibly achieve; between the needs, capabilities and potentials of organisational members and what the environment demands of and permits them. Management (see Watson, 1994) is the process that keeps the organisation from flying apart because of these tensions, that makes it work, secures its survival and, according to the type of organisation, its profitability or effectiveness. Inevitably, however, as Chapter 10 discusses, managerial control is a significant and often contentious issue.

The need to manage people and relationships is inherent in the managing of an organisation, but the very nature of people and the way they constitute an organisation makes management complex. Although the organisation of tasks packages people into organisational roles, individuals are larger and more organic than those roles have traditionally tended to be. The organisation, writes Barnard (1938, in Schein, 1978) 'pays people only for certain of their activities . . . but it is whole persons who come to work' (p.17). Unlike other resources, people interact with those who manage them and among themselves; they have needs for autonomy and agency; they think and are creative; they have feelings; they need consideration for their emotional and their physical needs and protection. The management of people is therefore not only a more diffuse and complex activity than the management of other resources, but also an essentially moral one (again, see Watson, 1994). This greatly complicates the tasks of managers, who can only work with and through people to ensure that the organisation survives and thrives in the face of increasing pressures from the environment.

Owners and managers are confronted with choices about how to manage people and resolve organisational tensions. The next subsection examines some of these choices and the strategies adopted to handle them. Before then, however, it must be noted that as organisations become larger and more complex, the division of managerial labour often leads to a specialist 'people' function to advise and support line managers in the complex and demanding tasks of managing their staff. This is the personnel function, which has developed a professional and highly skilled expertise in certain aspects of managing people, such as selection, training and industrial relations, which it offers in an advisory capacity to line managers, who nevertheless remain the prime managers of people. However, this division of labour has fragmented the management of people: human resource management can be seen as a strategy to reintegrate it into the management of the organisation as a whole.

The approaches adopted by managers to resolve the tensions in organisations

The previous subsection suggested that there are inherent tensions in organisations. In brief, these are generated by:

- the existence of several stakeholders in the employment relationship;
- their differing perspectives upon events, experiences and relationships;
- their differing aims, interests and needs;
- the interplay between formal organisation and individual potential.

These tensions have to be resolved through the process of management or, rather, continuously resolved, for these tensions are inherent in organisations. Thus Weick (1979) writes that organising is a continuous process of meaning-making: 'organizations keep falling apart . . . require chronic rebuilding. Processes continually need to be re-accomplished' (p.44). A continuing issue, therefore, is that of managerial control: how to orchestrate organisational activities in a way that meets the needs of the various stakeholders. The owners of organisations or those who manage them on their behalf have explored many ways to resolve these tensions: the emergence of HRM to develop alongside, subsume or replace personnel management is witness to this. The strategies they adopt are embodied in their employment policies and practices and the organisational systems they choose to put in place (see also Chapters 5 and 10). They are also manifested in the psychological contract they have with their employees, the often unstated set of expectations between organisation and individual that embroiders the legal employment contract. (The notion of the psychological contract now in current use goes back to a much earlier literature – for example, Schein (1970) – and it is some of the earlier terminology that is used here.) This subsection will briefly outline some of the strategies that managers have adopted, while the next will discuss the interpretations by theorists and other commentators of those strategies. However, it must be kept in mind that managers are to some extent influenced by the concepts and language, if not the arguments, of these theorists.

In very crude terms, we can identify four strategies that managers have adopted to deal with these tensions. The first is represented by what is called scientific management, or the classical school of management theory. The second is the human relations approach, and the third could be labelled a contingency (or even a human resource management) approach. The fourth approach is perhaps more an ideal than a common reality. It must be emphasised that these brief pen-pictures cannot do justice to the rich variety of approaches that can be found in organisations. You can elaborate upon the material here by reading about these differing views in an organisational behaviour textbook, such as Buchanan and Huczynski (1997) or Clark *et al.* (1994).

The first approach addressed the tensions in the organisation by striving to control people and keep down their costs: the *scientific management* approach. It emphasised the need for rationality, clear objectives, the managerial prerogative, and the right of managers to manage, and adopted work study and similar methods. These led to the reduction of tasks to their basic elements and the grouping of similar elements together to produce low-skilled, low-paid jobs, epitomised by assembly-line working, with a large measure of interchangeability between workers. Workers tended to be treated relatively impersonally and collectively ('management and labour'), and the nature of the psychological contract with them was calculative, with a focus on extrinsic rewards and incentives. Such a strategy encouraged a collective response from workers, and hence the development of trade unions.

These views of management evolved in North America, and provided a firm foundation for modern bureaucracies (Clegg, 1990). In Britain they overlaid the norms of a complex, though changing, social class system that framed the relationships between managers and other employees (Child, 1969; Mant, 1979). This facilitated the acceptance of the outcomes, which Argyris (1960) saw as limiting, of the X-theory of management (McGregor, 1960): hierarchy; paternalism; the attribution to workers of childlike qualities, laziness, limited aspirations and time horizons. While this strategy epitomised particularly the management approach of the first half of the century, it has left its legacy in many management practices, such as organisation and method study, job analysis and description, selection methods, an overriding concern for efficiency and the 'bottom line', appraisal and performance management. Moreover, it has not been completely abandoned (see Clegg, 1990; Ritzer, 1996 on 'McDonaldization'; and current debates about employment in call-centres, for example, Davis, 1999 and Hatchett, 2000).

The *human relations* approach to the tensions in organisations emerged during the middle years of the century, and developed in parallel with an increasingly prosperous society in which there were strong trade unions and (later) a growing acceptance of the right of individuals to achieve self-fulfilment. Child (1969) identifies its emergence in British management thinking as a response to growing labour tensions. It tempered scientific management by its recognition that people differed from other resources, that – if they were treated as clock numbers rather than as human beings – they would not be fully effective at work and could even fight back to the point of subverting management intentions. It also recognised the significance of social relationships at work – the informal organisation (Argyris, 1960). Managers therefore had to pay attention to the nature of supervision and the working of groups and teams, and to find ways of involving employees through job design (see Chapter 5), motivation, and a democratic, consultative or participative style of management. The nature of the psychological contract was cooperative.

The third and most recent approach adopted by managers to address the tensions within the organisation has developed as major changes and threats have been experienced in the context of organisations (recession, international competition, the business success of the 'tiger economies', and more recently globalisation). It is a response to the need to achieve flexibility in the organisation and workforce (see Chapters 3 and 5) and improved performance through devolving decision-making and empowerment (see Chapter 13) and, as Chapter 7 indicates, requiring that employees become multi-skilled and work across traditional boundaries. Unlike the other two strategies, the third approaches the organisation holistically and often with greater attention to its culture, leadership and 'vision', the 'soft' Ss of McKinsey's 'Seven S' framework (Pascale and Athos, 1982: 202–206). It attempts to integrate the needs of employees with those of the organisation in an explicit manner: the psychological contract embodies mutuality. It recognises that people should be invested in as assets so that they achieve their potential for the benefit of the organisation. It also pays greater attention to the individual rather than the collective, so that these notions of developing the individual's potential have been accompanied by individual contracts of employment (see Chapter 10), performance appraisal and performance-related pay (Chapter 12).

The very title of *human resource management* suggests that this third approach to the management of organisational tensions is also an instrumental one. Although it differs greatly from the approaches that see labour as a 'cost', to be reduced or kept in check, it construes individuals as a resource for the organisation to use. The fourth, idealistic, *humanistic* approach aims to construct the organisation as an appropriate environment for autonomous individuals to work together collaboratively for their common good. This is the approach of many cooperatives. It also informed the early philosophy of organisation development (see Huse, 1980), although the practice of this is now largely instrumental, and it underpins the notion of the learning organisation (see Senge, 1990, and Chapter 8).

When we look more deeply into these four managerial strategies, we can recognise that they implicate some much deeper questions. Underlying the management of people in organisations are some fundamental assumptions about the nature of people and reality itself, and hence about organising and managing. For example, managers make assumptions about the nature of the organisation, many interpreting it as having an objective reality that exists separately from themselves and other organisational members – they reify it. They make assumptions about the nature of their goals, which they identify as the goals of the organisation. They make assumptions about the appropriate distribution of limited power throughout the organisation.

However, these assumptions are rarely made explicit, and are therefore rarely challenged. Moreover, many other members of the organisation appear to accept these premises on which they are managed, even though such assumptions virtually disempower or disenfranchise them. For example, many may assert the need for equal opportunities to jobs, training and promotion, but do not necessarily challenge the process of managing itself despite its gender-blind nature (Hearn *et al.*, 1989). Nevertheless, these assumptions inform the practices and policies of management, and hence define the organisational and conceptual space that HRM fills and generate the multiple meanings of which HRM is constructed. In terms of the metaphor used by this chapter, they constitute some of the warp and weft threads in the tapestry/context of HRM. They will be examined in greater detail in a later section.

Competing interpretations of organisations and management

When we stand back from the concrete world of managing to that of theories about organisations and management, we find that not only have very different interpretations been made over time, but that several strongly competing interpretations coexist. Again, this chapter can only skim over this material, but you can pursue the issues by reading, for example, Child (1969), who traces the development of management thought in Britain, or Morgan (1997), who examines in a very accessible way eight different metaphors or ways in which theorists as well as others have construed organisations. Reed and Hughes (1992: 10–11) identify the changing focus of organisation theory over the last 30 years, from a concern with organisational stability, order and disorder, and then with organisational power and politics, to the present concern with the construction of organisational reality. Some of these changing concerns are seen below, while a later section introduces the new perspective offered by postmodernism.

The reification of the organisation by managers and others, and the general acceptance of the need for it to have rational goals to drive it forward in an effective manner, have long been challenged. Simon (see Pugh *et al.*, 1983) recognised that rationality is 'bounded' – that managers have to make decisions on the basis of limited and imperfect knowledge. Cyert and March adopt a similar viewpoint: the many stakeholders in an organisation make it a 'shifting multigoal coalition' (see Pugh *et al.*, 1983: 108) that has to be managed in a pragmatic manner. Others (see Pfeffer, 1981; Morgan, 1997) recognise the essentially conflictual and political nature of organisations: goals, structures and processes are defined, manipulated and managed in the interests of those holding the power in the organisation. A range of different understandings of organisations has developed over time: the systems approach (Checkland, 1981), the learning organisation (Senge, 1990), transformational leadership and 'excellence' (Peters and Waterman, 1982; Kanter, 1983), the significance of rhetoric (Eccles and Nohria, 1992). This range is widening to include even more holistic approaches, with recent interest in the roles of emotional intelligence (Pickard, 1999) and of spirituality and love in the workplace (Welch, 1998).

The established views of managers are subject to further interpretations. Weick (1979) argues the need to focus upon the process of organising rather than its reified outcome, an organisation. Organising is a continuous process of meaning-making: 'organizations keep falling apart . . . require chronic rebuilding. Processes continually need to be re-accomplished' (p. 44). Cooper and Fox (1990) and Hosking and Fineman (1990) adopt a similar interpretation in their discussion of the 'texture of organizing'.

Brunsson (1989) throws a different light on the nature and goals of organising, based on his research in Scandinavian municipal administrations. He suggests that the outputs of these kinds of organisations are 'talk, decisions and physical products'. He proposes two 'ideal types' of organisation: the *action* organisation, which depends on action for its legitimacy (and hence essential resources) in the eyes of its environment, and the *political* organisation, which depends on its reflection of environmental inconsistencies for its legitimacy. Talk and decisions in the action organisation (or an organisation in its action phase) lead to actions, whereas the outputs of the political organisation (or the organisation in its political phase) are talk and decisions that may or may not lead to action.

> . . . hypocrisy is a fundamental type of behaviour in the political organization: to talk in a way that satisfies one demand, to decide in a way that satisfies another, and to supply products in a way that satisfies a third. (p, 27)

There are similarly competing views upon organisational culture, as we see in Aldrich (1992) and Frost *et al.* (1991). The established view interprets it as a subsystem of the organisation that managers need to create and maintain through the promulgation and manipulation of values, norms, rites and symbols. The alternative view argues that culture is not something that an organisation has, but that it is.

Just as many managers leave their assumptions unaddressed and unstated, taken for granted, so that their actions appear to themselves and others based upon reason and organisational necessity, so also do many theorists. Many traditional theorists leave unstated that the organisations of which they write exist within a capitalist economic system and have to meet the needs of capital. They ignore the material and status needs of owners and managers, and their emotional (Fineman, 1993) and moral selves (Watson, 1994). Many also are gender-blind and take for granted a male world view of organisations. These issues tend to be identified and discussed only by those writers who wish to persuade their readers to a different interpretation of organisations (for example, Braverman, 1974; Hearn *et al.*, 1989; Calas and Smircich, 1992).

The chapter has now examined some of the choices that managers make to deal with the tensions within organisations and some of the competing interpretations offered by theorists of those tensions and choices. Before inviting you to step back even further to become aware of the ways of thinking and of seeing that inform these assumptions, the chapter will first take an even wider look at the context of HRM.

ECHOES FROM THE WIDER CONTEXT OF HRM

Defining the wider context

The definition of the wider context of HRM could embrace innumerable topics (for example, from the Industrial Revolution to globalisation) and a long time perspective (from the organisation of labour in such constructions as Stonehenge onwards, perhaps). Such a vast range, however, could only be covered in a perfunctory manner in a book of this kind, which would therefore render the exercise relatively valueless. It is more appropriate, first, to suggest that you identify for yourself what you consider to be the most important sources of influence upon HRM; and, second, to explore a few of these influences in a little detail. This is how the section will proceed.

> **Activity**
>
> Go back to the models of HRM presented in Chapter 1 and, working either individually or in a group, start to elaborate upon the various contextual elements that they include. Look, for example, at the 'outer context' of Hendry and Pettigrew's (1990) model illustrated in Figure 1.4.
>
> 1 What in detail constitutes the elements of the socio-economic, technical, political-legal and competitive context?
>
> 2 What other influences would you add to these?
>
> 3 What are the relationships between them?
>
> 4 And what, in your view, has been their influence upon HRM?

Examples of influences upon HRM from the wider context

Here the focus will be on just two elements from this context and their impact on the field of HRM. The first example is of influence upon the management of the employment relationship from the socio-political sphere: the two world wars. This influence has already been exerted and, indirectly, is still being felt. The second example comes from the cultural sphere: the influence of modernism and the emergence of postmodernism.

Although what follows is not a complete analysis of these influences, it illustrates how the field of HRM resonates with events and ideas from its wider context.

The First World War and the Second World War

The two world wars, though distant in time and removed from the area of activity of HRM, have nevertheless influenced it in clearly identifiable and very important ways, some direct and some indirect. These effects can be classified in terms of changed attitudes of managers to labour, changed labour management practices, the development of personnel techniques, and the development of the personnel profession. This subsection will now examine these, and then note how the outcomes of the Second World War continue, indirectly, to influence HRM.

Changed attitudes of managers to labour
According to Child (1969: 44), the impact of the First World War upon industry hastened changes in attitudes to the control of the workplace that had begun before 1914. The development of the shop stewards' movement during the war increased demand for

workers' control; there was growing 'censure of older and harsher methods of managing labour'. The recognition of the need for improved working conditions in munitions factories was continued in the post-war reconstruction debates: Child (1969) quotes a Ministry of Reconstruction pamphlet that advised that 'the good employer profits by his "goodness"(p.49). The outcome of these various changes was a greater democratisation of the workplace (seen, for example, in works councils) and, for 'a number of prominent employers', a willingness 'to renounce autocratic methods of managing employees' and 'to treat labour on the basis of human rather than commodity market criteria' (pp. 45–46). These new values became incorporated in what was emerging as a distinctive body of management thought, practice and ideology (see later section on ways of seeing and thinking), upon which later theory and practice are founded.

Changed labour management practices

The need to employ and deploy labour effectively led to increased attention to working conditions and practices during both wars; the changes that were introduced then continued, and interacted with other social changes that ensued after the wars (Child, 1969). For example, the Health of Munitions Workers Committee, which encouraged the systematic study of human factors in stress and fatigue in the munitions factories during the First World War, was succeeded in 1918 by the Industrial Fatigue Research Board (DSIR, 1961; Child, 1969; Rose, 1978). During the post-war reconstruction period progressive employers advocated minimum wage levels, shorter working hours, and improved security of tenure (Child, 1969).

'The proper use of manpower whether in mobilizing the nation or sustaining the war economy once reserves of strength were fully deployed' was national policy during the Second World War (Moxon, 1951). As examples of this policy, Moxon cites the part-time employment of married women, the growth of factory medical services, canteens, day nurseries, and special leave of absence.

The development of personnel techniques

Both wars encouraged the application of psychological techniques to selection and training, and stimulated the development of new approaches. Rose (1978: 92) suggests that, in 1917, the American army tested 2 million men to identify 'subnormals and officer material'. Seymour (1959) writes of the Second World War:

> the need to train millions of men and women for the fighting services led to a more detailed study of the skills required for handling modern weapons, and our understanding of human skill benefited greatly . . . Likewise, the shortage of labour in industry led . . . to experiments aimed at training munition workers to higher levels of output more quickly.   (pp. 7–8)

The wars further influenced the development of the ergonomic design of equipment, and encouraged the collaboration of engineers, psychologists and other social scientists (DSIR, 1961).

The exigencies of war ensured that attention and resources were focused upon activities that are of enormous significance to the field of employment, while the scale of operations guaranteed the availability for testing of numbers of candidates far in excess of those usually available to psychologists.

The development of the personnel profession

Very significantly, the Second World War had a major influence on the development of the personnel profession. According to Moxon (1951), the aims of national wartime policy were:

(i) to see that the maximum use was made of each citizen, (ii) to see that working and living conditions were as satisfactory as possible, (iii) to see that individual rights were reasonably safeguarded and the democratic spirit preserved. The growth of personnel management was the direct result of the translation of this national policy by each industry and by each factory within an industry.

(p. 7)

Child (1969) reports how government concern in 1940 about appropriate working practices and conditions

led to direct governmental action enforcing the appointment of personnel officers in all but small factories and the compulsory provision of minimum welfare amenities.

(p. 111)

Moxon (1951) comments on the 'four-fold increase in the number of practising personnel managers' at this time (p.7). Child (1969) records the membership of what was to become the Institute of Personnel Management (and much more recently the Institute of Personnel and Development) as 760 in 1939, and 2993 in 1960 (p. 113). He also notes a similar increase in other management bodies.

The post-war reconstruction of Japan

This subsection has so far noted some of the direct influences that the two world wars had upon the field of HRM. It now points to an indirect and still continuing influence. The foundation of the philosophy and practice of total quality management, which has been of considerable recent significance in HRM, was laid during the Second World War. Edward Deming and Joseph Juran were consultants to the US Defense Department and during the Second World War ran courses on their new approaches to quality control for firms supplying army ordnance (Pickard, 1992). Hodgson (1987) reports that:

Vast quantities of innovative and effective armaments were produced by a labour force starved of skill or manufacturing experience in the depression.

(p. 40)

After the war, America 'could sell everything it could produce' and, because it was believed that 'improving quality adds to costs', the work of Deming and Juran was ignored in the West. However, Deming became an adviser to the Allied Powers Supreme Command and a member of the team advising the Japanese upon post-war reconstruction (Hodgson, 1987: 40–41). He told them that 'their war-ravaged country would become a major force in international trade' if they followed his approach to quality. They did.

Western organisations now attempt to emulate the philosophy and practices of quality that have proved so successful in Japan and, as you will read in this book, so influential in the preoccupations of human resource managers.

Modernism and postmodernism

It was in the fields of art and architecture, in which there had been early twentieth-century schools of thought identified as modernism, that certain new approaches became labelled 'postmodern'. Commentators upon culture recognised the relevance of the emerging concept of postmodernism to other fields. There followed in the 1980s a debate, which you can read about in Turner (1990), on the provenance, nature and direction of postmodernism: whether it is a continuation of or a disjunction with the past; whether it is the phenomena we experience or a critical approach to these phenomena.

The concept and ongoing debate have widened into the social sciences generally, into organisation studies (for example, Hassard and Parker, 1993; Morgan, 1997), and are now recognised in the HRM field. Fox and Moult (1990) suggest that they are as significant here as in other fields, and Connock (1992) included postmodernist thinking among the contemporary 'big ideas' of significance to human resource managers. Fox (1990) interprets strategic HRM as a self-reflective cultural intervention responding to postmodern conditions, while Legge (1995) deconstructs HRM as a 'postmodernist discourse' that serves the needs of its stakeholders (p. 312). This subsection therefore continues by outlining briefly some of the characteristics of postmodernism, a further source of influence upon HRM from its wider context.

Although, in the field of HRM, questions about postmodernism merge with others on post-industrialism, post-Fordism, and the present stage of capitalism (see Reed and Hughes, 1992 and other chapters in this book), postmodernism could be said to have the following influence. First, it is influencing the nature of organisations and HRM, as will be noted below. Second, it is influencing the nature of the individual. Although this, too, is relevant to the management of people in organisations, it will not be explored further here, but you can read of it further in Collin (1996) and Reed and Hughes (1992: 214). Postmodernism's third influence is upon our way of looking at and understanding organisations.

Clegg (1990: 180–181) discusses the possible existence of a 'postmodern organisation' and, by contrasting it with a 'modernist organisation', identifies its characteristics. For example, he suggests that modernist organisations (that is, the organisations that we have been familiar with until the last decade or so) were rigid, addressed mass markets and were premised on technological determinism; their jobs were 'highly differentiated, demarcated and de-skilled'. Postmodernist organisations, however, are flexible, address niche markets, and are premised on technological choices; their jobs are 'highly de-differentiated, de-demarcated and multiskilled'.

The postmodern critique of organisations has greater potential value than this classification of organisations as modernist or postmodernist. (A chapter of this kind is unable to do justice to Clegg's wider argument.) You will find that the differences between the postmodern way of thinking about organisations and what preceded it echo some of the issues discussed in the following main sections of this chapter. Here you will find Legge (1995) and Reed and Hughes (1992) helpful.

The postmodern critique leads to the recognition that there are multiple and competing views of organisations that are legitimate; that the significance of theory lies not in its 'truth' but in its usefulness for practice. (This, perhaps, is a significant issue for the learning organisation, which is discussed in Chapter 8.) Whereas the modernist discourse was premised on belief in a universal objective truth, knowable by means of rational, scientific approaches, postmodernism assumes that knowledge of reality is constructed and perspectival. Whereas modernism was premised on a belief in the possibility of social progress, for postmodernism everything is open to question, and there are always alternative interpretations; it is eclectic in its recognition and acceptance of diversity. Whereas modernism often ignored or, indeed, disguised ideologies (see the section on ways of seeing and thinking), postmodernism is aware of the significance of such perspectives, and so undermines the 'meta-narratives' that have constructed twentieth-century understanding, such as 'progress' and 'the value of science' or 'Marxism'. Whereas modernism treated language as a tool to reflect essential reality, postmodernism sees language as the means by which reality is constructed. Postmodernism encourages self-reflexivity and, therefore, a critical suspicion towards one's own interpretations, and an ironic and playful treatment of one's subject.

Because it is our current experiences to which postmodernism refers, we cannot yet fully grasp their nature, nor have a clear perspective upon them. However, we can now perhaps recognise from today's vantage point that the way in which we once conceptualised and managed the employment relationship was influenced by modernism. Moreover, it could now be argued that the emergence of HRM, with its ambiguous, or debatable, nature, discussed in Chapter 1, is consistent with the spread of postmodern phenomena and postmodern critiques. The recognition of multiple, coexisting yet competing realities and interpretations, the constant reinterpretation, the eclecticism, the concern for presentation and re-presentation – all of which you will recognise in this book – can be interpreted as a postmodern rendering of the debate about the postmodern employment relationship. But, with a true postmodern irony and playfulness, there are also other interpretations. . .

WAYS OF SEEING AND THINKING

The chapter will now step right back from HRM and its immediate context to pay attention to our ways of seeing and thinking about our world: ways that generate the language, the code, the keys we use in conceptualising and practising HRM. To continue the metaphor of the tapestry, these ways of seeing are the warp, the threads that, running the length of the tapestry, give it its basic form and texture, but are generally not visible on its surface. They are more apparent, however, when we turn the tapestry over, as we are doing now. It can present a very different appearance then; the pattern and colour may seem very different. This section can provide only a brief introduction to some of these very profound subjects that make up the warp, but if you return to the organisational and management contexts of HRM you will see how their interweaving gives us changes in pattern and colour, some distinct, others subtle.

Earlier it was noted how the very term 'human resource management' confronts us with an assumption. This should cause us to recognise that the theory and practice of the employment relationship rest upon assumptions. The assumptions to be examined in this section are even more fundamental than these for they shape the very way we think. Some are so deeply engrained that they are difficult to identify and express, but they nevertheless become embodied in the way we approach life, including the way we conceptualise, theorise about and manage the employment relationship. They therefore have important implications for our interpretation of HRM.

It will first be noted that perception, defence mechanisms and epistemological assumptions colour or, rather, construct our initial approach to reality. After that, the section will examine the social science philosophies and their impact on the ways we think; and lastly it will consider some of the different ideologies and rhetoric that come into play in the field of HRM.

Perceiving reality

Perception

Before discussing the ways in which people approach reality, it must be noted that human beings do not necessarily do so – perhaps cannot do so – in a completely detached and clinical manner. The barriers between ourselves and the world outside us operate at very basic levels:

> Despite the impression that we are in direct and immediate contact with the world, our perception is, in fact, separated from reality by a long chain of processing.
>
> (Medcof and Roth, 1979: 4)

Psychologists have identified that perception is a complex process involving the selection of stimuli to which to respond and the organisation and interpretation of them according to patterns we already recognise. In other words, we develop a set of filters through which we come to make sense of our world. Kelly (1955) calls these our 'personal constructs', which channel the ways we conceptualise and anticipate events (see Ribeaux and Poppleton, 1978).

Defence mechanisms

Our approach to reality, however, is not just through cognitive processes. There is too much at stake for us, for our definition of reality has implications for our definitions of ourselves and for how we would wish others to see us. We therefore defend our sense of self – from what we interpret as threatening from our environment or from our own inner urges – by means of what Freud called our 'ego defence mechanisms'. In his study of how such adaptive behaviour changes over time, Vaillant (1977) wrote:

> Often such mechanisms are analogous to the means by which an oyster, confronted with a grain of sand, creates a pearl. Humans, too, when confronted with conflict, engage in unconscious but often creative behaviour.
> (p. 7)

Freudians and non-Freudians (see Peck and Whitlow, 1975: 39–40) have identified many forms of such unconscious adaptive behaviour, some accepted as healthy, others as unhealthy and distorting. Without going to the lengths of the mechanisms of 'intellectualisation' and 'dissociation', which Vaillant (1977: 384–385) describes as 'neurotic' defences, a very common approach to the threats of the complexity of intimacy or the responsibility for others is to separate our feelings from our thinking, to treat people and indeed parts of ourselves as objects rather than subjects. The scene is set for the objective and 'scientific' approach to reality and, further, to the management of people.

Making assumptions about reality

Writing about personal construct theory, Bannister and Fransella (1971) argue:

> we cannot contact an interpretation-free reality directly. We can only make assumptions about what reality is and then proceed to find out how useful or useless those assumptions are. (p. 18)

However, we have developed our assumptions from birth, and they have been refined and reinforced by socialisation and experience so that, generally, we are not even aware of them. We do not, therefore, generally concern ourselves with epistemology, the theory of knowledge, and we find the discussion of metaphysical issues difficult to follow. Nevertheless, we are undoubtedly making significant assumptions about 'what it is possible to know, how may we be certain that we know something' (Heather, 1976: 12–13). These assumptions underpin thinking and contribute to the filters of perception: they therefore frame any understanding of the world, including the ways in which researchers, theorists and practitioners construe HRM. To understand something of HRM and its context we need at least to recognise some of the implications of these epistemological and philosophical issues.

In crude terms, we can distinguish some fundamentally different approaches, using Pepper's (1942) 'world hypotheses' constructed from two pairs of polarised assumptions. The first pair makes assumptions about the universe. The assumption at one pole is that there is an ordered and systematic universe, 'where facts occur in a determinate order, and where, if enough were known, they could be predicted, or at least described'

(Pepper, 1942: 143). At the other pole, the universe is understood as a 'flowing and unbroken wholeness' (Morgan, 1997: 251), with 'real indeterminateness in the world' (Harré, 1981: 3), in which there are 'multitudes of facts rather loosely scattered and not necessarily determining one another to any considerable degree' (Pepper, 1942: 142–143). Pepper's second polarity is between approaching the universe through analysis or synthesis: fragmenting a whole into its parts in order to examine it more closely or examining it as a whole within its context.

Western thinking appears to stand at the first pole in both pairs of assumptions above: it takes an analytical approach to what is assumed to be an ordered universe. Hence 'we are taught to break apart problems, to fragment the world' (Senge, 1990: 3); we examine the parts separately from their context and from one another, 'wrenching units of behaviour, action or experience from one another' (Parker, 1990: 100). These approaches, which shade into the positivism discussed in the next subsection, lead us in our research to examine a world that we interpret as

abstract, fragmented, precategorized, standardized, divorced from personal and local contexts or relevance, and with its meanings defined and controlled by researchers. (Mishler, 1986: 120)

By contrast, and of particular relevance to this chapter, Pepper's world hypothesis, which espouses the assumptions at the second pole of each of the two pairs above, is 'contextualism'. This regards events and actions as processes that are woven into their wider context, and so have to be understood in terms of the multiplicity of interconnections and interrelationships within that context. We can use further metaphors to grasp just how different this view is from our orthodox understanding of the world: the latter is like using a library, while the former is like using the Internet (Collin, 1997). The information in a library is structured and classified by experts in a hierarchical system according to agreed conventions; users have to follow that system, translating their needs for information into a form recognised by that system. The Internet, however, is an open-ended network of providers of information, non-linear, constantly changing and expanding. It presents users with a multitude of potential connections to be followed at will and, moreover, the opportunity to participate through dialogue with existing Web sites or through establishing their own Web page.

Differences as basic as those between Pepper's world hypotheses inevitably lead to very different ways of seeing and thinking about reality and, indeed, of understanding our own role in the universe. We rarely have reason to question our deepest assumptions. Not only does our orthodox approach itself impede our recognition of these epistemological issues, but the processes of socialisation and education in any given society nudge its members in a particular direction [although some may wander off the highway into the byways or, like the author of *Zen and the Art of Motorcycle Maintenance* (Pirsig, 1976), into what are assumed to be badlands]. It can be easier to discern these issues in the contrast offered by the epistemological positions adopted in other societies. We can, for example, recognise more of our own deeply embedded assumptions when we encounter a very different world view in an anthropologist's account (Castaneda, 1970) of his apprenticeship to a Yaqui sorceror. Of this, Goldschmidt (1970) writes:

Anthropology has taught us that the world is differently defined in different places. It is not only that people have different customs; it is not only that people believe in different gods and expect different post-mortem fates. It is, rather, that the worlds of different peoples have different shapes. The very metaphysical presuppositions differ: space does not conform to Euclidean geometry, time does not form a continuous unidirectional flow, causation does not conform to Aristotelian logic, man [sic] is not differentiated from non-man or life from death, as in our world . . . The central importance of entering worlds other than our own – and hence of anthropology itself – lies in the fact that the experience leads us to understand that our own world is also a cultural construct. By experiencing other worlds, then, we see our own for what it is . . . (pp. 9–10)

Most of the epistemological threads in the tapestry examined in this chapter reflect Western orthodoxy, but not all. And this orthodoxy itself may be gradually changing; some commentators have argued that it has reached a 'turning point' (Capra, 1983), that they can detect signs of a 'paradigm shift'. Indeed, over the last decade or so there have emerged new developments in the natural sciences (for example, the theory of chaos, quantum physics, the Gaia hypothesis: see Wheatley, 1992), and elsewhere (feminist thinking: Gilligan, 1982) that offer challenges to orthodoxy.

This chapter will now turn to a more accessible level of our thinking, easier to identify and understand, although again we do not customarily pay it much attention. The contrast between the several modes of thinking outlined in the following subsections draws attention to the significant way in which our thinking influences our everyday operations.

Defining reality for ourselves

The distinctions between the epistemological positions in the last subsection and the philosophical stances examined in this appear very blurred (Heather, 1976; Checkland, 1981). There is certainly considerable affinity between some of Pepper's (1942) 'world hypotheses' and the approaches noted below. The discussion here will be restricted to aspects of these approaches relevant to our understanding of concepts and practices like HRM.

Orthodox thinking

By orthodoxy we mean 'correct' or currently accepted opinions inculcated in the majority of members in any given society through the processes of socialisation and education and sustained through sanctions against deviation. In our society, for example, most people trust in rationality or 'orthodox medicine' and have doubts about the paranormal or 'alternative medicine'. We do not generally question our orthodox beliefs: they 'stand to reason', they work, everyone else thinks in the same way. By definition, therefore, we do not pay much attention to them, nor consider how they frame the interpretations we make of our world, nor what other alternatives there may be. This subsection will identify some characteristics of Western orthodoxy, and the next some alternatives to them.

The orthodox approach in Western thinking is based on positivism, which, very importantly, has informed most social science research, which in turn has reproduced, through the kind of new knowledge generated, this orthodoxy. It 'reigns' in much HRM research (Legge, 1995: 308). This positivist approach is characterised by 'a readiness to concede primacy to the given world as known through experimental evidence' (Checkland, 1981: 316). It forms the basis of scientific method, and applies the rational and ordered principles of the natural sciences to human affairs generally. It manifests itself (see Heather, 1976; Rose, 1978: 26) in a concern for objectivity, in the construction of testable hypotheses, in the collection of empirical data, in the search for causal relationships and in quantification. It is, at the same time, uneasy with subjective experience, and attempts to maintain distance between the researcher and those studied (called 'subjects' but regarded more as objects). For example, the Western view is that the individual has (rather than is) a self, which is a natural object, bounded, reified, highly individualised, and autonomous (see Collin, 1996). This has been challenged as a male world view (Gilligan, 1982; Spender, 1985); the feminist interpretation will be examined shortly.

We can perceive positivism's orthodox role in the contrast to which Kelly draws attention between the assumptions that underpin his personal construct theory to which we have already referred and those of orthodox science:

> A scientist . . . depends upon his [sic] facts to furnish the ultimate proof of his propositions . . . these shining nuggets of truth . . . To suggest [as Kelly does] . . . that further human reconstruction can completely alter the appearance of the precious fragments he has accumulated, as well as the direction of their arguments, is to threaten his scientific conclusions, his philosophical position, and even his moral security . . . our assumption that all facts are subject . . . to alternative constructions looms up as culpably subjective and dangerously subversive to the scientific establishment.
>
> (quoted in Bannister and Fransella, 1971: 17–18)

It will be clear from the earlier discussion of the immediate context of HRM that many managers and theorists of management espouse this orthodox approach. It underpins many organisational activities such as psychometric testing for selection and human resource planning models, as well as much of the research into this field (see Legge, 1995).

Challenging alternatives

This subsection will outline four of the several alternative ways of thinking that challenge orthodoxy: the phenomenological approach, social constructionism, feminist thinking, and systems and ecological thinking. You could read more about these alternatives in Denzin and Lincoln (1994). It is important to note that the forms of the latter two that have been chosen for inclusion here are those that espouse the constructionist or phenomenological approaches: in other words, there are also positivist versions. While these are four distinctive approaches, having different origins and, to some extent, values and constituencies, they also share some similarity apart from their express opposition to positivism.

The phenomenological and social constructionist approaches

The phenomenological approach stands in marked contrast to the positivist; it is characterised by 'a readiness to concede primacy to the mental processes of observers rather than to the external world' (Checkland, 1981: 315). It is not concerned to establish objective reality, but with how we experience it, our lived experience. Rather than analysing this into fragments, it addresses it holistically, and acknowledges the significance of subjectivity, which positivism subordinates to objectivity. Researchers who espouse this approach try to make explicit the conscious phenomena of experience of those they study, seeking access to these empathically, through shared meanings and inter-subjectivity.

This is not a commonplace approach in the field of HRM and management (Sanders, 1982), although it is sometimes discussed in qualitative research studies. However, with the development of postmodern thinking (see above, and Legge, 1995), social constructionism is gaining recognition. [You will recognise how it informs some of the competing interpretations noted in an earlier section – those of Brunsson (1989) and Weick (1979), for example – and become aware that this approach is colouring the message of this particular chapter.] Social constructionism holds that an objective reality is not directly knowable (and hence we cannot know whether it exists). The reality we do know is socially constructed: we construct it through language and social interaction.

Human beings in the social process are constantly creating the social world in interaction with others. They are negotiating their interpretations of reality, those multiple interpretations at the same time constituting the reality itself.
(Checkland, 1981: 277)

Knowledge is thus a social phenomenon (Hoffman, 1990), and language, rather than depicting objective reality, itself constructs meaning. Weick (1979) quotes a story that illustrates this nicely:

Three umpires disagreed about the task of calling balls and strikes. The first one said, 'I calls them as they is.' The second one said, 'I calls them as I sees them.' The third and cleverest umpire said, 'They ain't nothin' till I calls them.'
(p. 1)

To make sense of our experiences, we have to interpret and negotiate meaning with others. There can be no single objective meaning but, Hoffman (1990) suggests:

an evolving set of meanings that emerge unendingly from the interactions between people. These meanings are not skull-bound and may not exist inside what we think of as an individual 'mind'. They are part of a general flow of constantly changing narratives.
(p. 3)

As also suggested by Pepper's (1942) contextualism, discussed earlier, this view of the social construction of meaning implies that we cannot separate ourselves from our created reality: 'man [sic] is an animal suspended in webs of significance he himself has spun' (Geertz, 1973: 5). Again as with contextualism, this approach emphasises the significance of perspective, the position from which an interpretation is made (remember the *Guardian* advertisement at the start of this chapter?). Further, it also draws attention to the way in which some people contrive to impose their interpretations upon, and so define the reality of, others, with the result that less powerful people are disempowered, overlooked, remain silent, are left without a 'voice' (Mishler, 1986; Bhavnani, 1990). This is a point to which the chapter returns later.

Feminist thinking

Feminist thinking challenges what is increasingly becoming acknowledged as the male world-view of the positivist approach. This challenge stems from the recognition of differences between the world-views of women and men. Gilligan's (1982) landmark study concluded that women value relationship and connection, whereas men value independence, autonomy and control. Marshall (1989: 279) explores this further by means of the distinction between 'agency' and 'communion' made by Bakan (1966). Agency is 'an expression of independence through self-protection, self-assertion and control of the environment', whereas the basis of communion is integration with others. Bakan associates the former with maleness and the latter with femaleness.

The agentic strategy reduces tension by changing the world about it; communion seeks union and cooperation as its way of coming to terms with uncertainty. While agency manifests itself in focus, closedness and separation, communion is characterized by contact, openness and fusion.
(Marshall, 1989: 289)

Therefore, Marshall (1989) argues, feminist thinking 'represents a fundamental critique of knowledge as it is traditionally constructed . . . largely . . . by and about men' and either ignores or devalues the experience of women:

its preoccupation with seeking universal, immutable truth, failing to accept diversity and change; its categorization of the world into opposites, valuing one pole and devaluing the other; its claims of detachment and objectivity; and the predominance of linear cause-and-effect thinking. These forms reflect male, agentic experiences and strategies for coping with uncertainty. By shaping academic theorizing and research activities, they build male power and domination into the structures of knowledge . . .
(p. 281)

Calas and Smircich (1992: 227) discuss how gender has been 'mis- or under-represented' in organisation theory, and explore the effects of rewriting it in. These would include the correction or completion of the organisational record from which women have been absent or excluded, the assessment of gender bias in current knowledge, and the making of a new, more diverse organisation theory that covers topics of concern to women. Hearn *et al.* (1989) identify similar shortcomings in organisation theory in their discussion of the sexuality of organisations. For example, Tancred-Sheriff (1989) argues that women are located in organisational roles in which their sexuality can be utilised in the interface with workers and customers to effect 'adjunct control' in the difficult-to-manage space between employer and worker, producer and consumer, while managers remain in control of them through sexual domination (p. 55).

Systems and ecological thinking

Systems thinking offers particularly useful insights into the subject of this chapter, the nature of context. As with feminist thinking, there are both positivist and alternative views of systems, but the concern is with the latter, which pose a challenge to Western orthodoxy. Checkland (1981), for example, adopts a phenomenological approach in his 'soft systems methodology', employing systems not as 'descriptions of actual real-world activity' (p. 314), but as 'tools of an epistemological kind which can be used in a process of exploration within social reality' (p. 249). (Note that his later book – Checkland and Scholes, 1990 – updates the methodology but does not repeat the discussion of its philosophical underpinnings.) Like the feminist thinking noted above, systems thinking shifts our attention from what orthodox thinking allows us to see. In this case, it allows us to see the whole rather than just its parts, interconnectivity rather than isolated elements, and to recognise that we are a part of that whole. It registers patterns of change, relationships rather than just objects, a web of interrelationships and reciprocal flows of influence rather than linear chains of cause and effect.

The concept of system denotes a whole, complex and coherent entity, comprising a hierarchy of subsystems, where the whole is greater than the sum of its parts. Much of what has been written about systems draws upon General Systems Theory, a meta-theory that offered a way to conceptualise phenomena in any disciplinary area. Very importantly, the systems approach does not argue that social phenomena are systems, but rather that they can be modelled (conceptualised, thought about) as though they had systemic properties. The concept of system used in the social sciences is therefore a very abstract kind of metaphor. However, we can give only a brief outline of systems concepts here: you will find further detail in Checkland (1981), Checkland and Scholes (1990), Senge (1990), and Morgan (1997).

Systems may be 'open' (like biological or social systems) or 'closed' to their environment, like many physical and mechanical systems. As shown in Figure 2.2, the open system imports from, exchanges with, its environment what it needs to meet its goals and to survive, and converts or transforms these inputs into a form that sustains its existence and generates outputs that are returned to the environment and can be used to exchange for further inputs, along with waste products. The environment itself comprises other systems that are also drawing in inputs and discharging outputs. Changes in remote parts of any given system's environment can therefore ripple through its environment to affect it eventually. There is a feedback loop that enables the system to make appropriate modifications to its subsystems in the light of the changing environment. Thus the system constantly adjusts to achieve equilibrium internally and with its environment.

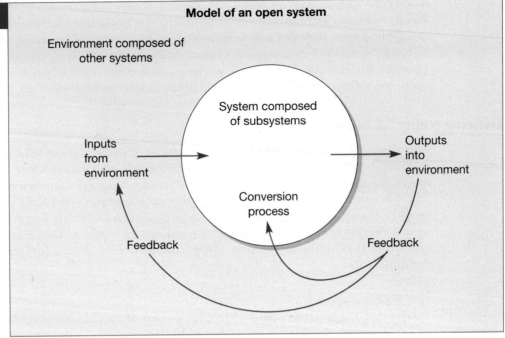

Figure 2.2 **Model of an open system**

Reflecting upon the management approaches identified earlier, we can now recognise that the scientific management, human relations and perhaps also the humanistic approaches treated the organisation as a closed system, whereas the human resource approach recognises it as open to its environment. Brunsson's identification of the 'action' and 'political' organisations could also be seen as an open system approach.

The significance of systems thinking, then, lies in its ability to conceptualise complex, dynamic realities – the system and its internal and external relationships – and model them in a simple, coherent way that is yet pregnant with meaning and capable of being elaborated further when necessary. This means that we can use it to hold in our minds such complex ideas as those discussed in this chapter, without diminishing our awareness of their complexity and interrelationships.

According to Senge (1990), systems thinking – his 'fifth discipline' – is essential for the development of the effective organisation – the learning organisation (Chapter 8):

> At the heart of a learning organization is a shift of mind – from seeing ourselves as separate from the world to connected to the world, from seeing problems as caused by someone or something 'out there' to seeing how our own actions create the problems we experience. A learning organization is a place where people are continually discovering how they create their reality. And how they can change it. (pp. 12–13)

Systems thinking should therefore help us in conceptualising an organisation in an increasingly complex and dynamic relationship with its complex and dynamic global environment. Changes in one part of the environment – the decline of the 'tiger' economies, global warming, poor harvests, international and civil wars – can change the nature of the inputs into an organisation – raw materials and other resources. This can lead to the need for adjustments in and between the subsystems – new marketing strategies, technologies, working practices – either to ensure the same output or to modify the output. The environment consists of other organisations, the outputs of which – whether intentionally or as by-products – constitute the inputs of others. A change in output, such as a new or improved product or service, however, will constitute a change in another organisation's input, leading to a further ripple of adjustments. Consider, for example, how flexible working practices and call centres have been developed. You will find an exercise at the end of the chapter to help you think this through.

Defining reality for others

This chapter has defined the warp of the tapestry of context as our ways of seeing and thinking. It will now examine some of the weft threads – the ways in which others define our reality (or we define reality for others): ideology, language and rhetoric, hegemony and discourse. These interweave through the warp to produce the basic pattern of the tapestry, but with differing colours and textures, and also differing lengths (durations), so that they do not necessarily appear throughout the tapestry. They constitute important contextual influences upon HRM, and in part account for the competing definitions of it.

Ideology

Gowler and Legge (1989) define ideology as 'sets of ideas involved in the framing of our experience, of making sense of the world, expressed through language' (p. 438). It has a narrower focus than the 'ways of thinking' we have been discussing above, and could be seen as a localised orthodoxy, a reasonably coherent set of ideas and beliefs that often goes unchallenged:

> Ideology operates as a reifying, congealing mechanism that imposes pseudoresolutions and compromises in the space where fluid, contradictory, and multivalent subjectivity could gain ground.
>
> (Sloan, 1992: 174)

Ideology purports to explain reality objectively, but within a pluralist society it actually represents and legitimates the interests of members of a subgroup. It is a 'subtle combination of facts and values' (Child, 1969: 224). What we hear and what we read is conveying someone else's interpretations. The way they express them may obscure their ideology and vested interest in those interpretations.

As you will recognise from earlier in the chapter, the organisation is an arena in which ideologies of many kinds are in contest: capitalism and Marxism, humanism and scientific approaches to the individual, feminism and a gender-biased view. For example, in contrast to the orthodox view of culture, Jermier argues that culture is:

> the objectified product of the labor of human subjects . . . there is a profound forgetting of the fact that the world is socially constructed and can be remade . . . Exploitative practices are mystified and concealed.
>
> (Frost et al., 1991: 231)

Child (1969) discusses the ideology embodied in the development of management thinking, identifying how the human relations approach chose to ignore the difference of interests between managers and employees and how this dismissal of potential conflict influenced theory and practice. Commentators such as Braverman (1974), Frost *et al.* (1991) and Rose (1978), and many of the readings in Clark *et al.* (1994), will help you to recognise some of the ideologies at work in this field.

Hegemony

Hegemony is the imposition of the reality favoured by a powerful subgroup in society upon less powerful others. Such a group exerts its authority over subordinate groups by imposing its definition of reality over other competing definitions. This does not have to be achieved through direct coercion, but by 'winning the consent of the dominated majority so that the power of the dominant classes appears both legitimate and natural'. In this way, subordinate groups are 'contained within an ideological space which does not seem at all "ideological": which appears instead to be permanent and "natural", to lie outside history, to be beyond particular interests' (Hebdige, 1979: 15–16).

It is argued that gender issues are generally completely submerged in organisations and theories of them (Hearn *et al.*, 1989; Calas and Smircich, 1992) so that male-defined realities of organisations appear natural, and feminist views unnatural and shrill. You could use the readings in Clark *et al.* (1994) to identify instances of hege-mony and the outcomes of power relations, such as the 'management prerogative'; Watson (1994) throws light on the manager's experience of these.

Language and rhetoric

Atkinson and Butcher (1999) write of the significance of the terminology used in effect-ing organisational change. Although it is recognised that rhetoric is 'the art of using language to persuade, influence or manipulate' (Gowler and Legge, 1989: 438), it would be generally assumed that language itself is neutral, 'the vehicle for communicating independent "facts"' (Legge, 1995: 306). The postmodern argument, however, is that this is not the case (see Reed and Hughes, 1992; Hassard and Parker, 1993). Language 'itself constitutes or produces the "real"' (Legge, 1995: 306). Moreover, it is 'ideological' (Gowler and Legge, 1989: 438): both the means through which ideologies are expressed and the embodiment of ideology. This can be seen in sexist and racist language, and in 'management-speak'. Ideology achieves its ends through language and rhetoric.

The 'high symbolic content' of rhetoric *'allows it to reveal and conceal but above all develop and transform meaning'* (Gowler and Legge, 1989: 439, their italics). It *'heightens and transforms meaning by processes of association, involving both evocation and juxtaposition'*. In other words, its artfulness lies in playing with meanings. In the 'eco-climate' of an organisation, where meanings are shared and negotiated, power and knowledge rela-tions are expressed rhetorically. For example, changes to structure and jobs are described as 'flexibility' rather than as the casualisation of work (see, for example, Chapters 3 and 4), and increased pressures upon employees as 'empowerment' (see Chapter 13). Moreover, Legge (1995) proposes that one way of interpreting HRM is to recognise it as 'a rhetoric about how employees should be managed to achieve competi-tive advantage' that both 'celebrates' the values of its stakeholders while 'at the same time mediating the contradictions of capitalism' (p. xiv). In other words, it allows those stakeholders to 'have their cake and eat it'.

Discourse

'Why do we find it so congenial to speak of organizations as structures but not as clouds, systems but not songs, weak or strong but not tender or passionate?' (Gergen, 1992: 207). The reason, Gergen goes on to say, is that our understanding takes place within a 'discursive context': discourse is an interrelated 'system of statements which cohere around common meanings and values' particular to a specific group (Hollway, 1983, in

Gavey, 1989: 463–464). It provides the language and meanings whereby the members of that group can interpret and construct reality. For example, academics have to learn

> a vocabulary and a set of analytic procedures for 'seeing' what is going on . . . in the appropriate professional terms. For we must see only the partially ordered affairs of everyday life, which are open to many interpretations . . . as if they are events of a certain well-defined kind.
>
> (Parker and Shotter, 1990: 9)

Of relevance to the argument of this chapter, Parker and Shotter (1990), in contrasting 'everyday talk' and academic writing, indicate that academic text standardises the interpretations possible by being divorced from any context:

> The strange and special thing about an academic text . . . is that by the use of certain strategies and devices, as well as already predetermined meanings, one is able to construct a text which can be understood (by those who are a party to such 'moves') in a way divorced from any reference to any local or immediate contexts. Textual communication can be (relatively) decontextualised. Everyday talk, on the other hand, is marked by its vagueness and openness, by the fact that only those taking part in it can understand its drift; the meanings concerned are not wholly predetermined, they are negotiated by those involved, on the spot, in relation to the circumstances in which they are involved . . . Everyday talk is situated or contextualised, and relies upon its situation (its circumstances) for its sense.
>
> (pp. 2–3)

Discourse, you will now recognise, provides the basis for the rhetoric that group members use to exercise and perpetuate their power. By interpreting competing positions in its own terms, the group's discourse shuts down all other possible interpretations but its own. It offers its members and others an identifiable position to adopt upon a given subject, thereby constituting their own identity, behaviour and reality (Gavey, 1989). Legge (1995), for example, offers an interpretation of HRM as 'a postmodernist discourse' (p. 312). There are many discourses in the field of organisation and management studies – managerial, humanist, critical, industrial relations – that offer their own explanations and rhetoric. You can explore them further in, for example, Clark *et al.* (1994), while remaining aware that academic discourse itself enables writers to exercise power over the production of knowledge and to influence their readers.

CONCLUSION . . . AND A NEW BEGINNING?

This chapter has examined something of the warp and weft that give the tapestry its basic form, pattern, colour and texture. To complete our understanding of the context of HRM we need to recognise that issues and people constitute the surface stitching that is drawn through the warp and weft to add further pattern and colour. You will be aware of examples from your own experience and the reading of this and other books, but we can instance the influences of recession, equal opportunities legislation, European directives, management gurus, Margaret Thatcher, 'new Labour', that resonate with the warp and weft to produce the pattern that has come to be known as 'HRM'.

The tapestry of which HRM forms a part is continuously being woven, but we can now become aware of the sources of the differing approaches to organisation and management and of the contesting voices about the management of people. We can now recognise that their contest weaves multiple meanings into the organisational and conceptual pattern which is HRM. However, this awareness allows us to recognise further that yet other meanings, and hence potentials for the management of the employment relationship, remain to be constructed.

By pointing to the need to recognise the significance of the context of HRM, this chapter is also acknowledging that you will find therein more interpretations than this book of 'academic text' (Parker and Shotter, 1990: see the previous section), shaped by its writers' own agendas and values and the practicalities of commercial publication, can offer you. The process both of writing and of publication is that of decontextualisation, fragmentation, standardisation, and presentation of knowledge as 'entertaining education', in bite-sized chunks of knowledge or sound bites. But by urging you to become aware of the context of HRM, this chapter is at the same time inviting you to look beyond what it has to say, to recognise the nature of its discourse or, rather, discourses, to challenge its assumptions (and, indeed, your own) and to use your own critical judgements informed by your wider reading and personal experience.

This, then, is why this book has begun its exploration of HRM by examining context. This chapter had a further aim (and this betrays this writer's 'agenda and values'). This is to orientate your thinking generally towards an awareness of context, to think contextually, for ultimately awareness of context is empowering. One of the outcomes may well be greater knowledge but less certainty, the recognition that there may be competing interpretations of the subject being considered, that the several perspectives upon the area may yield different conclusions. Attention to context, therefore, encourages us not to be taken in by our initial interpretations, nor to accept unquestioningly the definitions of reality that others would have us adopt (the 'hegemony' of the previous section). There are, however, no easy answers, and we have to make the choice between alternatives. Reality is much messier and more tentative than theory and, like 'everyday talk', it is 'marked by its vagueness and openness', its meaning open to interpretation through negotiation with others. The acceptance of this, however, as we shall later see in Chapter 7, is one of the marks of the mature learner: the ability to recognise alternative viewpoints but, nevertheless, to take responsibility for committing oneself to one of them.

By definition, one chapter cannot begin to portray the complexity and diversity of the context of HRM, but nor does it have a need to. It will have achieved its purpose if it causes you to recognise the significance of context and the need to adopt ways of thinking that enable you to conceptualise it. It can point you in some directions, and you will find many others in the chapters that follow, but there are no logical starting points, because context is indivisible; and you will never reach the end of the story for, from the perspective of context, the story is never-ending.

SUMMARY

● The chapter argues that the keys to the understanding of human affairs, such as HRM, lie within their context. Although context is difficult to conceptualise and represent, readers can draw on their existing understanding of environmental issues to help them comprehend it. Awareness and comprehension of context are ultimately empowering because they sharpen critical thinking by challenging our own and others' assumptions.

● Multiple interests, conflict, and stressful and moral issues are inherent in the immediate context of HRM, which comprises the organisation (the nature of which generates a number of lateral and vertical tensions) and management (defined as the continuous process of resolving those tensions). Over time, managers have adopted a range of approaches to their task, including scientific management; the human relations school; humanistic organisation development; and now HRM. Understanding of even this layer of HRM's context calls for the recognition of the existence of some significant assumptions that inform managers' differing practices and the competing interpretations that theorists make of them.

● The wider social, economic, political and cultural context of HRM is diverse, complex and dynamic, but two very different and unconnected strands of it are pulled out for examination. The two world wars left legacies for the management of the employment relationship, while emerging 'postmodern' experiences and critiques locate HRM within a contemporary framework of ideas that could eventually challenge some assumptions about the management of the employment relationship.

● The chapter, however, finds it insufficient to conceptualise context as layered, like an onion. Rather, HRM is embedded in its context. The metaphor of a tapestry is therefore used to express the way in which its meaning is constructed from the interweaving and mutual influences of the assumptions deriving from basic perceptual, epistemological, philosophical and ideological positions. The notions of 'warp' and 'weft' are used to discuss such key contextual elements as positivism, phenomenology, social constructionism, feminist thinking, systems thinking, ideology, hegemony, language, rhetoric and discourse. People, events and issues are the surface stitching.

● The nature of this tapestry, with its multiple and often competing perspectives, ensures that HRM, as a concept, theory and practice, is a contested terrain. However, the chapter leaves readers to identify the implications of this through their critical reading of the book.

Activity   **Drawing on your understanding of the environment**

The nature of our environment concerns us all. As 'environment' and 'green issues' have crossed the threshold of public awareness to become big business, we have become concerned about our natural environment as no previous generation has been. We are now aware of the increasing complexity in the web of human affairs. We recognise the interrelationships within our 'global village', between the world's 'rich' North and the 'poor' South, and between politics, economies and the environment, and at home between, for example, unemployment, deprivation and crime. Another feature of our environment that we cannot ignore is its increasingly dynamic nature. Our world is changing before our very eyes. Comparing it with the world we knew even five years ago, and certainly with that known by our parents when they were the age we are now, it has changed dramatically and in ways that could never have been anticipated.

1 You will have considerable knowledge, and perhaps personal experience, of many environmental issues such as the problems of waste disposal and pollution, BSE and genetically modified food, the impact on the countryside of the construction of new roads, or the threats to the survival of many species of animals and plants.
   Working individually or in groups, choose two or three such issues for discussion.

   (a) Identify those who are playing a part in them (the actors) and those directly or indirectly affected by them (the stakeholders). How did the event or situation that has become an issue come about? Who started it? How do they explain it? Will the situation change over time, and how long will it last? Who benefits in this situation? How do they justify this? Who loses in it? What do – or can – they do about it? Why? Who is paying the cost? How and why?
   (b) Look for concrete examples of the following statements.
      – 'We have an impact upon the environment and cause it to change, both positively and negatively.'

- 'The environment and changes within it have an impact upon us and affect the quality of human life, both positively and negatively.'
- 'The environment has a differential influence upon each of us, these differences being partly attributable to differences between us: each of us could therefore be said to have a different environment.'
- 'There are different levels of events and elements of the environment: some are local, others national or international.'
- 'They include both concrete events and abstract ideas.'
- 'The interrelationships between events and elements in the environment are so complex that they are often difficult to untangle.'
- 'It may not be possible or even meaningful to identify the cause of events and their effects; the cause or causes may have to be inferred, the effects projected.'
- 'Sometimes these effects are manifested far into the future, and so are not easily identifiable now, though they may affect future generations.'
- 'Our relationship with our environment therefore has a moral dimension to it.'
- 'Many significant environmental changes have not been accurately predicted – or predicted at all – or recognised for what they are.'
- 'To deal with some of the negative causes may be gravely damaging to some other groups of people.'
- 'The understanding of these events will differ according to the particular perspective of the observer, and will arise from interpretation rather than ultimately verifiable "facts".'
- 'These issues often involve powerful power bases in society, each of which has its own interpretation of events, and wishes others to accept its definition of them.'
- 'The actors involved in the events may have yet a different perspective, and so may other stakeholders.'
- 'The nature of our relationship with our environment challenges our traditional scientific ways of thinking, in which we value objectivity, analyse by breaking down a whole into its parts, and seek to identify cause and effect in a linear model.'
- 'It also therefore challenges our traditional methods of research and investigation, deduction and inference.'

2 The opening section of the chapter suggested such an examination of environmental issues would allow us to recognise that:
  - The nature of the environment is multilayered, multidimensional and interwoven, in which concrete events and abstract ideas intertwine to create issues, and thinking, feeling, interpreting and behaving are all involved: it is like the *tapestry* described in the section.
  - Our understanding depends upon our *perspective*.
  - It also depends upon our *ideology*.
  - There are therefore *competing or contested interpretations* of events.
  - Different groups in society have their own interpretations of events, stemming from their *ideology*, which incorporate an explanation for competing interpretations. They use the *rhetoric* of their own interpretations to express competing interpretations, thus often suppressing the authentic expression of competing views.
  - There are powerful others who try to impose their interpretations of events, their version of reality, upon the less powerful majority: this is *hegemony*.

Can you give concrete examples of these?

3 How would you represent the HRM activities of an organisation in a changing world in terms of the open systems model? Working individually or in groups, identify its inputs (where they come from, and how they could be changing), how it converts these, and what its (changing?) outputs might be.

QUESTIONS

1 In what ways does the conceptualisation of context adopted by this chapter differ from more commonly used approaches (for example, in the models of HRM in Chapter 1)? Does it add to the understanding they give of HRM and, if so, in what way?

2 What assumptions and 'world hypotheses' underpin those models, and what are the implications for your use of them?

3 What assumptions and 'world hypotheses' underpin this chapter, and what are the implications for your use of it?

4 Identify some recent events that are likely to play a significant part in the context of HRM.

5 This chapter has been written from a British perspective. If you were working from a different perspective – South African, perhaps, or Scandinavian – what elements of the context of HRM would you include?

6 The chapter has been written for students of HRM. Is it also relevant to practitioners of HRM and, if so, in what way?

EXERCISE

Having started to think in terms of context and to recognise the significance of our ways of thinking, you should be reading the rest of this book in this same critical manner. As you go through it try to identify the following:

● the assumptions (at various levels) underlying the research and theory reported in the chapters that follow;

● the implications of these assumptions for the interpretations that the researchers and theorists are placing upon their material;

● the possibility of other interpretations deriving from other assumptions;

● the assumptions (at various levels) that the writers of the following chapters appear to hold;

● the implications of these assumptions for the interpretations that these writers are placing upon their material;

● the possibility of other interpretations deriving from other assumptions;

● the implications of the various alternatives for the practice of HRM.

REFERENCES AND FURTHER READING

Those texts marked with an asterisk are particularly recommended for further reading.

Aldrich, H.E. (1992) 'Incommensurable paradigms? Vital signs from three perspectives', in Reed, M. and Hughes, M. (eds) *Rethinking Organization: New Directions in Organization Theory and Analysis.* London: Sage, pp. 17–45.

Argyris, C. (1960) *Understanding Organisational Behaviour.* London: Tavistock Dorsey.

Atkinson, S. and Butcher, D. (1999) 'The power of Babel: lingua franker', *People Management,* Vol. 5, No. 20, 14 October, pp. 50–52.

Bakan, D. (1966) *The Duality of Human Existence.* Boston: Beacon.

Bannister, D. and Fransella, F. (1971) *Inquiring Man: The Theory of Personal Constructs.* Harmondsworth: Penguin.

Bhavnani, K.-K. (1990) 'What's power got to do with it? Empowerment and social research', in Parker, I. and

Shotter, J. (eds) *Deconstructing Social Psychology*. London: Routledge, pp. 141–152.

Braverman, H. (1974) *Labor and Monopoly Capital: The Degradation of Work in the Twentieth Century*. New York: Monthly Review Press.

Brunsson, N. (1989) *The Organization of Hypocrisy: Talk, Decisions and Actions in Organizations*. Chichester: Wiley.

Buchanan, D. and Huczynski, A. (1997) *Organizational Behaviour: An Introductory Text*, 3rd edn. London: Prentice Hall.

Calas, M.B. and Smircich, L. (1992) 'Re-writing gender into organizational theorizing: directions from feminist perspectives', in Reed, M. and Hughes, M. (eds) *Rethinking Organization: New Directions in Organization Theory and Analysis*. London: Sage, pp. 227–253.

Cameron, S. (1997) *The MBA Handbook: Study Skills for Managers*, 3rd edn. London: Pitman.

Capra, F. (1983) *The Turning Point: Science, Society and the Rising Cultures*. London: Fontana.

Castaneda, C. (1970) *The Teachings of Don Juan: A Yaqui Way of Knowledge*. Harmondsworth: Penguin.

*Checkland, P. (1981) *Systems Thinking, Systems Practice*. Chichester: Wiley.

Checkland, P. and Scholes, J. (1990) *Soft Systems Methodology in Action*. Chichester: Wiley.

Child, J. (1969) *British Management Thought: A Critical Analysis*. London: George Allen & Unwin.

*Clark, H., Chandler, J. and Barry, J. (1994) *Organisation and Identities: Text and Readings in Organisational Behaviour*. London: Chapman & Hall.

Clegg, S.R. (1990) *Modern Organizations: Organization Studies in the Postmodern World*. London: Sage.

Collin, A. (1996) 'Organizations and the end of the individual?', *Journal of Managerial Psychology*, Vol. 11, No. 7, pp. 9–17.

Collin, A. (1997) 'Career in context', *British Journal of Guidance and Counselling*, Vol. 25, No. 4, pp. 435–446.

Concise Oxford Dictionary (1982) 7th edn. Oxford: Clarendon Press.

Connock, S. (1992) 'The importance of "big ideas" to HR managers', *Personnel Management*, June, pp. 24–27.

Cooper, R. and Fox, S. (1990) 'The "texture" of organizing', *Journal of Management Studies*, Vol. 27, No. 6, pp. 575–582.

Davis, R. (1999) 'Ring in the changes: smoother operators', *People Management*, Vol. 5, No. 9, 6 May, pp. 56–57.

Denzin, N.K. and Lincoln, Y.S. (eds) (1994) *Handbook of Qualitative Research*. Thousand Oaks, Calif.: Sage.

Department of Scientific and Industrial Research (1961) *Human Sciences: Aid to Industry*. London: HMSO.

*Eccles, R.G. and Nohria, N. (1992) *Beyond the Hype: Rediscovering the Essence of Management*. Boston, MA: Harvard Business School Press.

Fineman, S. (ed.) (1993) *Emotion in Organizations*. London: Sage.

Fox, S. (1990) 'Strategic HRM: postmodern conditioning for the corporate culture', in Fox, S. and Moult, G. (eds) *Postmodern Culture and Management Development*, Special Edition: *Management Education and Development*, Vol. 21, Pt 3, pp. 192–206.

Fox, S. and Moult, G. (eds) (1990) *Postmodern Culture and Management Development*, Special Edition: *Management Education and Development*, Vol. 21, Pt 3 (whole issue).

*Frost, P.J., Moore, L.F., Louis, M.R., Lundberg, C.C. and Martin, J. (1991) *Reframing Organizational Culture*. Newbury Park, Calif.: Sage.

Gavey, N. (1989) 'Feminist poststructuralism and discourse analysis: contributions to feminist psychology', *Psychology of Women Quarterly*, Vol. 13, pp. 459–475.

Geertz, C. (1973) *The Interpretation of Cultures*. New York: Basic Books.

Gergen, K.J. (1992) 'Organization theory in the postmodern era', in Reed, M. and Hughes, M. (eds) *Rethinking Organization: New Directions in Organization Theory and Analysis*. London: Sage, pp. 207–226.

Gilligan, C. (1982) *In a Different Voice: Psychological Theory and Women's Development*. Cambridge, Mass.: Harvard University Press.

Goldschmidt, W. (1970) 'Foreword', in Castaneda, C., *The Teachings of Don Juan: A Yaqui Way of Knowledge*. Harmondsworth: Penguin, pp. 9–10.

Gowler, D. and Legge, K. (1989) 'Rhetoric in bureaucratic careers: managing the meaning of management success', in Arthur, M.B., Hall, D.T. and Lawrence, B.S. (eds) *Handbook of Career Theory*. Cambridge: Cambridge University Press, pp. 437–453.

Harré, R. (1981) 'The positivist-empiricist approach and its alternative', in Reason, P. and Rowan, J. (eds) *Human Inquiry: A Sourcebook of New Paradigm Research*. Chichester: Wiley, pp. 3–17.

Hassard, J. and Parker, M. (eds) (1993) *Postmodernism and Organizations*. London: Sage.

Hatchett, A. (2000) 'Call collective: ringing true', *People Management*, Vol. 6, No. 2, January, pp. 40–42.

*Hearn, J., Sheppard, D.L., Tancred-Sheriff, P. and Burrell, G. (1989) *The Sexuality of Organization*. London: Sage.

Heather, N. (1976) *Radical Perspectives in Psychology*. London: Methuen.

Hebdige, D. (1979) *Subculture: The Meaning of Style*. London: Methuen.

Hendry, C. and Pettigrew, A. (1990) 'Human resource management: an agenda for the 1990s', *International Journal of Human Resource Management*, Vol. 1, No. 1, pp. 17–43.

Hodgson, A. (1987) 'Deming's never-ending road to quality', *Personnel Management*, July, pp. 40–44.

Hoffman, L. (1990) 'Constructing realities: an art of lenses', *Family Process*, Vol. 29, No. 1, pp. 1–12.

Hollway, W. (1983) 'Heterosexual sex: power and desire for the other', in Cartledge, S. and Ryan, J. (eds) *Sex and Love: New Thoughts on Old Contradictions*. London: Women's Press, pp. 124–140.

Hosking, D. and Fineman, S. (1990) 'Organizing processes', *Journal of Management Studies*, Vol. 27, No. 6, pp. 583–604.

Huse, E.F. (1980) *Organization Development and Change*, 2nd edn. St. Paul, Minn.: West Publishing.

Kanter, R.M. (1983) *The Change Masters*. New York: Simon & Schuster.

Keenoy, T. (1990) 'Human resource management: rhetoric, reality and contradiction', *International Journal of Human Resource Management*, Vol. 1, No. 3, pp. 363–384.

Kelly, G.A. (1955) *The Psychology of Personal Constructs*, Vols 1 and 2. New York: W.W. Norton.

Legge, K. (1995) *Human Resource Management: Rhetorics and Realities*. Basingstoke: Macmillan Business.

Mant, A. (1979) *The Rise and Fall of the British Manager*. London: Pan.

Marshall, J. (1989) 'Re-visioning career concepts: a feminist invitation', in Arthur, M.B., Hall, D.T. and Lawrence, B.S. (eds) *Handbook of Career Theory*. Cambridge: Cambridge University Press, pp. 275–291.

McGregor, D. (1960) *The Human Side of Enterprise*. New York: McGraw-Hill.

Medcof, J. and Roth, J. (eds) (1979) *Approaches to Psychology*. Milton Keynes: Open University Press.

Mishler, E.G. (1986) *Research Interviewing: Context and Narrative*. Cambridge, Mass.: Harvard University Press.

*Morgan, G. (new ed.) (1997) *Images of Organization*. Thousand Oaks, Calif.: Sage.

Moxon, G.R. (1951) *Functions of a Personnel Department*. London: Institute of Personnel Management.

Parker, I. (1990) 'The abstraction and representation of social psychology', in Parker, I. and Shotter, J. (eds) *Deconstructing Social Psychology*. London: Routledge, pp. 91–102.

Parker, I. and Shotter, J. (eds) (1990) 'Introduction', in *Deconstructing Social Psychology*. London: Routledge, pp. 1–14.

*Pascale, R.T. and Athos, A.G. (1982) *The Art of Japanese Management*. Harmondsworth: Penguin.

Peck, D. and Whitlow, D. (1975) *Approaches to Personality Theory*. London: Methuen.

Pepper, S.C. (1942) *World Hypotheses*. Berkeley, Calif.: University of California Press.

Peters, T.J. and Waterman, R.H. Jr (1982) *In Search of Excellence: Lessons from America's Best Run Companies*. New York: Harper & Row.

Pfeffer, J. (1981) *Power in Organizations*. London: Pitman.

Pickard, J. (1992) 'Profile: W. Edward Deming', *Personnel Management*, June, p. 23.

Pickard, J. (1999) 'Emote possibilities: sense and sensitivity', *People Management*, Vol. 5, No. 21, 28 October, pp. 48-56.

Pirsig, R.M. (1976) *Zen and the Art of Motorcycle Maintenance*. London: Corgi.

Pugh, D.S., Hickson, D.J. and Hinings, C.R. (1983) *Writers on Organizations*, 3rd edn. Harmondsworth: Penguin.

*Reed, M. and Hughes, M. (eds) (1992) *Rethinking Organization: New Directions in Organization Theory and Analysis*. London: Sage.

Ribeaux, P. and Poppleton, S.E. (1978) *Psychology and Work: An Introduction*. London: Macmillan.

Ritzer, G. (1996) *The McDonaldization of Society: An Investigation into the Changing Character of Contemporary Social Life*. Thousand Oaks, Calif.: Pine Forge Press.

Rose, M. (1978) *Industrial Behaviour: Theoretical Development since Taylor*. Harmondsworth: Penguin.

Sanders, P. (1982) 'Phenomenology: a new way of viewing organizational research', *Academy of Management Review*, Vol. 7, No. 3, pp. 353–360.

Schein, E.H. (1970) *Organizational Psychology*, 2nd edn. Englewood Cliffs, N.J.: Prentice Hall.

Schein, E.H. (1978) *Career Dynamics: Matching Individual and Organizational Needs*. Reading, Mass.: Addison-Wesley.

*Senge, P. (1990) *The Fifth Discipline: The Art and Practice of the Learning Organization*. London: Century.

Seymour, W.D. (1959) *Operator Training in Industry*. London: Institute of Personnel Management.

Sloan, T. (1992) 'Career decisions: a critical psychology', in Young, R.A. and Collin, A. (eds) *Interpreting Career: Hermeneutical Studies of Lives in Context*. Westport, Conn.: Praeger, pp. 168–176.

Southgate, J. and Randall, R. (1981) 'The troubled fish: barriers to dialogue', in Reason, P. and Rowan, J. (eds) *Human Inquiry: A Sourcebook of New Paradigm Research*. Chichester: Wiley, pp. 53–61.

Spender, D. (1985) *For the Record: The Making and Meaning of Feminist Knowledge*. London: Women's Press.

Tancred-Sheriff, P. (1989) 'Gender, sexuality and the labour process', in Hearn, J., Sheppard, D.L., Tancred-Sheriff, P. and Burrell, G. (eds) *The Sexuality of Organization*. London: Sage, pp. 45–55.

Turner, B.S. (ed.) (1990) *Theories of Modernity and Postmodernity*. London: Sage.

Vaillant, G.E. (1977) *Adaptation to Life: How the Brightest and Best Came of Age*. Boston: Little, Brown.

Watson, T.J. (1994) *In Search of Management: Culture, Chaos and Control in Managerial Work*. London: Routledge.

*Weick, K.E. (1979) *The Social Psychology of Organizing*. New York: Random House.

Welch, J. (1998) 'The new seekers: creed is good', *People Management*, Vol. 4, No. 25, 24 December, pp. 28–33.

Wheatley, M.J. (1992) *Leadership and the New Science: Learning about Organization from an Orderly Universe*. San Francisco: Berrett-Koehler.

PART 1 CASE STUDY

Retailer derided for 'moving the deckchairs' at a crucial time – fears of double-digit fall in sales

M&S to split into seven business units.
By **Susanne Voyle**

Marks and Spencer yesterday reshuffled its management and split the group into seven business units to improve its focus on customers.

M&S, which has suffered a dramatic fall from grace in the fiercely competitive UK retail environment, has changed the job description of three board members and appointed seven executives just below board level to head the new units.

The news came at the start of the crucial pre-Christmas trading week.

M&S is believed to be suffering a steep fall-off in sales as rivals slash prices. The group has refused to comment ahead of a trading statement due in January. But people close to the company believe the fall in like-for-like sales has hit double digits.

The group has yet to make its most eagerly awaited appointment – that of a chairman to replace Sir Richard Greenbury, who took early retirement in the summer.

Shares in M&S, currently the centre of bid speculation, rose $3\frac{1}{4}$p to $277\frac{3}{4}$. Last week, Philip Green, the retail entrepreneur, admitted he was considering a bid after the group's shares jumped on repeated rumours.

M&S yesterday stressed that the management changes were not a reaction to the possibility of a takeover. 'The changes are a continuation of the move to more customer focused, flatter structures which were announced with the interim results in November,' it said.

M&S said the new business units would each be fully profit-accountable. 'This means no one underperforming part of the business will be able to hide behind results of the group as a whole,' said one insider.

The biggest change comes for Barry Morris, formerly head of the food division, who has been put in charge of womenswear retail. Guy McCracken and Joe Rowe saw their roles changed slightly to reflect the devolution to buying power to the new business units.

The group has been split with immediate effect into retail units for womenswear, menswear, lingerie, children's wear, home, beauty and food. The heads of each unit will report directly to Peter Salsbury, chief executive.

Most of the unit heads are long-serving M&S employees, in line with the group's tradition of promoting from within. But there are two exceptions. Rory Scott, who heads lingerie, joined the group less than two years ago from logistics group TNT, while Jacqueline Paterson, at beauty, joined from Boots just four months ago.

The changes left some analysts unimpressed. 'In the middle of one of the most important trading weeks in the calendar they have decided to reshuffle the deckchairs,' said one. Another said: 'Most people don't know the insiders at M&S well enough to know whether changes like these will make any difference.'

Some institutional shareholders said the changes were unimportant while the chairmanship remains vacant. 'The only interesting news will be when they appoint a chairman, and we don't know when that will be,' said one.

M&S yesterday repeated that it had a preferred candidate and hoped to announce an appointment in the New Year.

Source: Financial Times, 22 December 1999.

This case describes the complex organisational issues facing Marks and Spencer. Assess the following HRM issues for the company.

1 What might be the strategic HRM issues facing the company in deciding to create business units?

2 To what extent does the company need to overhaul the relationship between HRM and its core businesses?

3 Using the styles and approaches to HRM outlined in this part, suggest a suitable HRM approach that Marks and Spencer might adopt for the medium term.

PART

2

RESOURCING THE ORGANISATION

Introduction to Part 2

This part deals with the internal and external human resourcing of organisations. The four chapters within it examine the operation of labour markets, manpower and human resource planning, job design, and recruitment and selection. Although each chapter deals with specific aspects of the processes of acquiring, deploying and extracting performance from employees, four main themes provide a common thread that links them to each other.

Our first theme is the relationship of HRM to the search for flexibility, the related development of production concepts such as just-in-time production and total quality management, and business process re-engineering. Chapter 3 outlines the various forces that have encouraged organisations to pay increased attention to cost reduction, productivity improvement and quality, and how this 'holy trinity' has been encapsulated, in theory at least, in the 'flexible firm'. Chapters 4 and 5 examine the implications of just-in-time, total quality management and business process re-engineering for human resource planning and job design. Likewise, Chapter 6 reflects on their implications for the recruitment and selection process. Chapters 4 and 5 also draw on recent theoretical and empirical literature that suggests that the concept of organisations as 'things', having permanence and stability and identifiable boundaries between the 'inside' and 'outside', is not only problematic in theoretical terms, but may also be beginning to be undermined empirically. This may have profound consequences for the nature of work and the employment relationship.

Following on from this, our second theme concerns how far and in what ways human resource management challenges older-established practices within organisations. Thus in Chapter 3 an economics perspective on HRM is developed, which argues that HRM can be understood as an attempt to modify the operation of internal organisational arrangements for acquiring, deploying, rewarding and managing the performance of employees. Chapter 4 examines the basis for distinguishing between traditional 'manpower' planning and human resource planning, with the latter claiming to pay more attention to qualitative aspects of human capital such as commitment and flexibility than traditional manpower planning, with its emphasis on measuring and forecasting quantitative flows of labour through the organisation. Chapter 5 explores innovations in work organisation and job design that have been claimed for and by HRM and which are often represented as being a rejection of the previously dominant Taylorist approach. Chapter 6 discusses how far HRM has led to a questioning of the procedures for recruitment and selection that are associated with traditional personnel management, as recruitment and selection come to be viewed as strategic rather than merely operational activities.

The third theme is the way in which organisations' policies for human resources are influenced by wider contextual influences. Generally, organisations may be seen to pursue the goals of cost reduction, productivity improvement and quality, but the relative emphasis attached to these goals, the ways in which they are defined, and the specific actions taken to attain them vary widely across organisations and even more widely across countries. These strategic choices are influenced profoundly by the product market strategy of the firm, the supply of skills available in the labour market, and the extent to which financial structures and public policy encourage or discourage long-term investment, not only in physical capital but also in human capital. These issues are discussed in each of the chapters, with reference to international comparisons.

Our final theme is the problematic nature of HRM, both in theory and in practice. In its insistence on strategic integration, HRM remains within the dominant approach to management, that of rational functionalism. That is, management is seen as an activity involving rational choices and planned actions aimed at achieving defined goals in the most efficient manner. However, this tends to imbue HRM with a unitarist perspective that pays insufficient attention to the contested nature of organisational relationships, the inevitability of conflict, the legitimacy of conflict, and the likelihood that all strategy is doomed to at least partial failure. This undermines HRM's claim to the status of theory. It also generates practical tensions, as evidenced by the concept of 'tough love' wherein employees are valued only as long as they are seen to be 'adding value' to the business. This may mean that employees experience HRM not so much as a humanising influence at work, but more as an onerous source of material and moral pressure to increase effort levels.

3

Human resource management and the labour market

Tim Claydon

OBJECTIVES

This chapter develops three economic perspectives on the labour market, and explains how they can be used to analyse HRM. In developing and presenting the theoretical arguments contained here, no prior knowledge of economics has been assumed. We have tried to present theory so that it is understandable on an intuitive rather than a formal level. Those of you who have some prior knowledge of economics and would like a more formal treatment of some of the arguments presented here are referred to the additional reading at the end of the chapter. King (1990) provides a useful treatment of labour economics.

- To introduce competing theories of the labour market.
- To examine how labour markets operate in practice, introducing the concepts of unemployment and wage rigidity.
- To introduce the institutional and radical theories of the labour market.
- To analyse labour market theories in relation to human resource management.
- To make a critical analysis of the debates surrounding 'flexibility'.

INTRODUCTION

Human resource management has emerged as a set of prescriptions for managing people at work. Its central claim is that by matching the size and skills of the workforce to the productive requirements of the organisation, and by raising the quality of individual employees' contributions to production, organisations can make significant improvements to their performance. However, as has already been shown in Chapter 1, different emphases are placed in the HRM literature on these two aspects of managing human resources. 'Hard' HRM emphasises the role of planned deployment of labour to reduce costs. 'Soft' HRM emphasises the importance of personnel policies aimed at motivating workers and obtaining their cooperation with management in the production process (Storey, 1987). We shall return to this distinction later in the chapter.

Following from this, a set of prescriptions have become commonplace in the human resource management literature:

- Human resource decisions should be integrated with other key business decisions at a strategic level within the organisation in order that the size, structure and deployment of the workforce are matched to market-led production requirements.
- Human resource policies, such as recruitment, selection and remuneration, are integrated with each other so that they cohere.
- Managerial action should aim to ensure that employees have high levels of organisational commitment and motivation.
- Line managers rather than personnel managers play the main role in developing and implementing human resource strategy and policy.

There is little doubt that considerable tensions exist between the different elements of this prescription: for example between 'hard' and 'soft' human resource management (Legge, 1995). HRM is almost certainly less unified and coherent in practice, and indeed in theory, than in popular prescription. Contingent factors exert a powerful influence on the way in which employment is managed in the real world.

This chapter is concerned with those contingencies that arise through the operation of the labour market. The policies associated with HRM can be seen as a particular set of responses to the way in which labour markets work, and the way this affects the employment relationship within organisations. As yet, however, little has been done to examine the economics of human resource management. While there is a burgeoning debate over how the labour market works, little attempt has been made to relate it to the HRM debate. This chapter aims to go some way towards filling that gap. The task is complicated by the fact that there is no single theory of labour markets, rather a number of differentiated and often competing approaches. Nevertheless, as the debate has evolved, more attention has been paid to the internal relationships and managerial processes of organisations. By tracing this evolution it is possible to develop a labour market perspective on HRM.

THEORIES OF THE LABOUR MARKET

The debate over how labour markets work has led to a proliferation of theoretical insights and approaches. However, a basic division exists between those approaches that see the labour market as an arena of competition between individuals and those that view it as being shaped and controlled by institutionalised forms of power. As we shall see, the pure competitive theory of labour markets has nothing to say about HRM, since it is not concerned with what goes on inside organisations. However, the concepts that underlie the theory also underpin the refinements of and amendments to it, so it is necessary first to set out its main features so that we can understand the subsequent evolution of the labour economics debate and its relevance to HRM.

The theory of competitive markets

The competitive theory of the labour market derives from neo-classical economics. The starting point is that our resources are scarce in relation to our wants, so that we have to make choices as to how to allocate them. In making these choices it is asserted that we act individually as rational economic maximisers. In other words, in making our choices we seek to maximise the economic satisfaction that we can obtain from our resources. The process of rational individual maximisation can be outlined as follows:

- We have an ordered set of preferences such that if we prefer A to B and B to C then we must also prefer A to C.
- We act so as to maximise our economic well-being in the light of our preference schedule.
- Our preference schedules are independent of those of other individuals: that is, we are not influenced by the preference schedules of others when we order our own preferences.

The condition for maximising the satisfaction that we can obtain from our scarce resources is that we will allocate them in such a way that no further reallocation can yield a higher level of satisfaction. As consumers, we will spend relatively more on satisfying our preference for A over C, but we will also allocate our expenditure so that the satisfaction we gain from the last penny spent on A is equal to that obtained from the last penny of expenditure on C. If this were not the case, and we were able to increase satisfaction by spending relatively more on A and less on C, or vice versa, then as rational economic maximisers we would do so.

As workers, our chief aim in work is to earn income to finance our consumption of goods and services. But that income itself carries a cost in the form of the leisure that we have to give up in order to earn it. As rational economic maximisers we allocate our time between work and leisure in such a way as to maximise the amount of satisfaction we can obtain given our preferences as consumers. This combination is different for different individuals, since some of us are money driven, with a relatively high preference for income relative to leisure, while others of us have a high leisure preference, which makes us willing to forgo income in favour of free time.

It is assumed that employing organisations also operate as maximising individuals. This means identifying a level of output and a combination of inputs to produce it that results in the maximisation of total revenues relative to total costs. For non-profit organisations such as charities or public sector services, maximising behaviour should aim to maximise the benefits to recipients of services generated from a given set of inputs. In either case, rational maximisers will seek out the least-cost combination of inputs to produce the desired level of output.

Private-sector firms operate in two sets of markets: factor markets – that is, markets for inputs, mainly labour and capital – and product markets, in which outputs are sold. The theory of competitive markets argues that the greater the degree of competition in both sets of markets, the greater will be the pressures for cost minimisation. Competition between firms in product markets encourages them to seek ways of reducing costs, and forces them to pass cost reductions on to consumers. Competition in factor markets prevents suppliers of inputs from increasing their own incomes at the expense of others by artificially raising the prices of inputs.

Market competition is therefore seen as producing efficient outcomes in two senses:

- It results in production being organised on the basis of least-cost combinations of inputs.
- It results in an efficient distribution of income in that each factor of production's share of total income equals its relative contribution to output. None can be made better off without making others worse off.

The desire to maximise economic well-being on an individual basis is often presented as a basic aspect of human nature: therefore the search for better economic efficiency is seen as a powerful inherent force among humans. From this it follows that market competition is a natural state since it is most consistent with individual maximising behaviour. While a particular group may have an interest in increasing their share of income above what is warranted by their contribution to output, competitive forces should prevent them from being able to do this except in the short run. Government policy can encourage or inhibit market competition. Within the neo-classical approach there is a preference for policies that support and encourage competition. In effect this means a preference for government non-intervention in markets unless it is to remove obstacles to their efficient operation. These arguments have been used to justify changes in government policy towards the public sector: for example, elimination of subsidies, privatisation and introduction of elements of market competition.

The basic competitive model of the labour market

In analysing the real world, economics, like other sciences, makes use of models. These are simplified versions of the real world. They are not meant to be realistic descriptions of it; rather they identify its key aspects in such a way as to enable us to make statements about how the real world works that can be tested against evidence. The starting point for the competitive analysis of the labour market is to build a model in which labour markets are perfectly competitive.

A perfectly competitive labour market is, by definition, perfectly efficient. Its characteristics are as follows:

- There are numerous small, independent employers competing for labour in the market, and also a large number of workers competing for jobs.
- New firms and new workers can enter the labour market at any time.
- Workers are perfectly mobile between jobs. All jobs require the same skills, and all workers are equally productive in that they possess the same skills and ability. Any worker can do any job within that labour market. Furthermore, the only benefit to the worker from the job is the wage. There are no non-wage benefits that attach to specific jobs that might lead workers to prefer them to other jobs available in the market.
- As well as being able to move freely between jobs, workers are also perfectly mobile geographically: there is no advantage in working in one place as opposed to any other, and there are no obstacles to movement from one place to another.
- The only cost to the employer of hiring labour is the wage. There are no 'fixed' costs of employment that may lead employers to prefer to retain existing workers rather than replace them with new ones.
- There is perfect information. All workers and all firms know the state of the market and are instantly aware of any changes in the market.

It follows from these conditions that there will be a single, uniform wage in the labour market. Wage differences between firms cannot exist, because, if they did, workers would know about them and move instantly from low-paying to high-paying firms. If the low payers wished to remain in business they would have to raise wages in order to retain workers, while high payers would reduce wages when faced with a queue of workers competing for jobs. The result is a single, uniform wage across all firms. It is therefore clear that, as individuals, employers and workers have no power to influence the market wage. They are all price-takers in the labour market. The only decision the firm has to take is how many workers to employ at the given wage. Two factors will determine this decision in the short run, the short run being defined as that period of time in which the firm is unable to alter the amount and/or type of physical plant used in production. These factors are:

- the law of diminishing marginal returns,
- the conditions for profit maximisation under perfect competition.

The law of diminishing marginal returns as applied to employment states that as successive units of labour are added to a fixed amount of capital equipment, the amount that each successive unit of labour will add to total output (its *marginal physical product*) will, at some stage, diminish. This is because, in the short run, firms are unable to increase their equipment or buildings, or introduce new technologies. The amount of capital is fixed in the short run. Any increase in demand for a firm's output will be met by increasing labour inputs. Labour is the variable factor in the short run. However, adding more and more units of labour to a fixed amount of capital yields diminishing returns after a time. Adding one further worker to the labour force may raise output and revenue significantly. By the time the fiftieth additional worker has been hired, the value of the resultant addition to output may only just cover that worker's wage. Any further workers hired would add less to the value of production than the cost of their wage.

Assuming that there is perfect competition, a firm's profit-maximising level of employment in the short run is the level at which the marginal *revenue* product of the last unit of labour hired equals its price (*marginal cost*). The marginal revenue product of labour is the amount that the last unit of labour adds to total revenue. Employers will hire successive hours of labour up to the point at which the addition to total revenue generated by the last hour of labour hired equals the hourly wage.

In the long run, organisations can vary the amount of capital equipment they employ and adopt new technologies. This means that, in the long run, organisations can replace labour with capital and vice versa. Such substitutions will occur in response to changes in the relative price of labour and capital. Should capital become cheaper relative to labour, there will be a long-run shift to more capital-intensive methods of production, since, by employing relatively more of the cheaper factor of production, costs are reduced. The optimum (least-cost) combination will be that for which the ratio of marginal product to marginal cost for each factor is the same, or, to put it another way, where the ratio of their prices is equal to that of their marginal products.[1]

Predictions of the competitive model

This model generates a number of statements or predictions about how real-world labour markets operate. The most important of these are as follows:

- The marginal revenue product of labour determines the level of the wage.
- The number of workers employed will vary inversely with the wage: that is, as wages rise, the quantity of labour employed will fall and vice versa.

This follows from the points made in the previous two paragraphs. Since the marginal revenue product of labour diminishes, and at the same time firms seek to equate the marginal product of labour with the wage, employers will only hire extra units of labour at progressively lower wage rates, assuming that other key variables such as the demand for output remain constant.

- The amount of labour offered in the market will vary positively with the wage. This is because an increase in the wage effectively raises the benefits that can be obtained from work relative to leisure. This leads to a rational decision to substitute extra hours of work for leisure.
- Since firms and workers adjust their demand and supply of labour in response to wage changes, it follows that the wage rate acts as the mechanism that 'clears' the market:

that is, brings the quantity of labour employed into equality with the quantity offered. A consequence of this is that the labour market operates like an auction, with firms bidding for labour. Should firms as a whole face a decline in demand for their output, fewer workers will be required in production. In this situation more labour is being offered than is needed at the current wage. Employers will therefore reduce their wage offers until the amount of labour offered is once more equal to that demanded. Conversely, if product demand rises, in the short run at least so will employers' demand for labour. Firms will compete with each other for the available pool of labour, bidding up the wage. This will encourage new workers to enter the market. It may also encourage existing workers to offer more hours of labour. Once again, this process continues until the quantity of labour supplied is equal to that demanded.

- There will be no unemployment at the market-clearing wage. By this we mean that nobody *who is willing to work at the market-clearing wage* will be without a job. While there may be some who are unwilling to work at that wage because of the nature of their leisure/income preference, by definition they will not be seeking work and therefore cannot be said to be unemployed except in the sense that they are voluntarily so. All those wishing to work at the market-clearing wage will be employed.

It should be clear that this model is a heroic simplification of the real world. It has nothing to say about the internal processes of managing people at work. Labour is hired up to the point at which marginal revenue product equals the marginal cost of hiring it: that is, the wage. Workers come equipped with necessary skills, and their productivity is not affected by anything other than the technology of production. There is no need for firms to train workers; there is no need for policies designed to motivate them. Labour is a simple commodity, like fish. The model has nothing to say about HRM since it does not recognise the key problems with which HRM is concerned. There is, however, a clear view that the ideal employment relationship is an individual rather than a collective one.

The controversy that exists among labour economists centres on how far this model can cope with the complexities of the real world. As we shall see, it is necessary to relax some of the assumptions of the basic model and add a number of refinements to it in order to explain the operation of labour markets in reality. Even then, a growing number of economists, as well as sociologists and students of industrial relations, have questioned the adequacy of the competitive approach to analysing labour markets. Two key criticisms are that even its most refined versions cannot explain the things that we actually observe satisfactorily, and that by adding refinements to the model in order to take the real world into account the competitive market approach actually changes into something else. The following section identifies some of the main ways in which real labour markets do not seem to conform to the predictions of our initial model. Later, we go on to examine the different attempts that have been made to explain these features and how they help us to understand the HRM phenomenon.

LABOUR MARKETS IN PRACTICE

Unemployment and wage rigidity

One of the first things that we observe in the real world is that unemployment exists. Contrary to the prediction of our initial model, not all of those seeking work can find a job at the prevailing wage rate. Moreover, we observe that unemployment can coexist with unfilled vacancies and rising wages for those in work. The wage adjustment mechanism does not seem to work, or if it does, only imperfectly.

One reason for unemployment is that the wage adjustment process does not operate in the way described in the basic competitive model. Employers do not immediately reduce wages as their demand for labour falls. Rather than adjusting the wage, employers will first cut back on recruitment, leave vacancies unfilled, cut overtime working, introduce short-time working, and ultimately lay off workers. When their demand for labour rises, the initial response is not to raise the wage but to demand increased overtime working and intensify recruitment. Employers initially go for quantity adjustments to changes in demand rather than wage adjustments. In severe recessions, when the demand for labour collapses, examples can be found of wage freezes and wage reductions. However, this is unusual, even in recessions as severe as those of the early 1980s and 1990s, as can be seen from Table 3.1. It is apparent that wages do not move flexibly in response to shifts in the demand for and supply of labour.

Not only do wages not instantly adjust in the face of changing demand and supply conditions, when they do move they do so asymmetrically. Specifically, wages move up more readily than they move down. Downward wage rigidity has been offered as a major

Table 3.1 **Unemployment rates and earnings movements, 1976–96**

Year	Seasonally adjusted unemployment, annual average (000s)	Average earnings index (1985 = 100)	Average weekly earnings, adult male workers (£)
1979	1312.1	53.8	96.9
1980	1611.2	65.0	111.7
1981	2481.8	73.3	121.9
1982	2904.1	80.2	133.8
1983	3127.4	87.0	143.6
1984	3158.3	92.2	152.7
1985	3281.4	100.0	163.6
1986	3312.4	107.9	174.4
1987	2993.0	116.3	185.5
1988	2425.7	126.4	200.6
1989	1841.3	137.9	217.8
1990	1664.5	151.3	237.2
1991	2291.9	163.4	253.1
1992	2778.6	173.3	268.3
1993	2919.2	179.2	274.3
1994	2636.5	185.5	_[a]
1995	2325.6	192.5	–
1996[b]	2158.1	200.7	–

[a] This series ceased to be published in 1994
[b] July figures only

Source: Employment Department /Department for Education and Employment, *Employment Gazette*, December 1980, 1984, 1986, 1991, 1993; *Labour Market Trends*, October 1996.

explanation for the large increases in unemployment during recessions. This is because when the demand for labour falls, wages do not fall. Therefore workers do not get the signal to reduce the quantity of labour they supply to the market, and employers do not get the incentive to hire more hours of labour as wage rates fall. Therefore there is an excess supply of workers. This suggests that competitive labour market forces are circumscribed, since the competition between workers for the reduced number of available jobs, which should bring about the wage reduction, does not appear to occur.

Inter-industry and inter-firm wage differences

The impression that competitive forces in the labour market are attenuated is reinforced by evidence of large wage variations across industries and even between firms in the same industry. From our model of perfect competition we predict that workers of the same ability doing the same job will be paid the same wage wherever they work. What we actually observe is very different. A study of a local labour market for engineering workers undertaken by Nolan and Brown (1983) found that there was a wage differential of more than 50% between the highest- and lowest-paying firms, with the remaining firms paying a variety of rates in between. Nor did these differences even out over time as we might expect if competitive forces were in operation. The range of pay and the relative position of individual firms in the pay dispersion remained much the same over a period of ten years. It seems that who you work for does make a difference to your pay. This impression is reinforced by research conducted by Routh (1989), who found that the dispersion of rates of pay within occupations was greater than that between them. Not only does it seem to be the case that who you work for affects your pay; it could be that who you work for is the most important influence on your pay!

Internal labour markets

Our simple model of perfect competition pictured a world in which labour was casually hired and fired as necessary. Workers acquired their skills outside the firm, and the wage rate was determined externally to the firm. We call this type of labour market an *external labour market*. In practice, however, many organisations operate differently, at least for certain sections of their labour force. Rather than relying on the external labour market to supply skills at an externally determined market rate of pay, many employers develop their own *structured internal labour markets*. Doeringer and Piore (1971) defined the main features of structured internal labour markets as follows:

- External recruitment is confined to junior and trainee positions, which serve as limited 'ports of entry' into the organisation. Other vacancies are filled through internal promotions and transfers. In this way current jobholders are shielded from direct competition from workers in the external labour market.
- Jobs are designed and arranged so as to provide career progression paths or 'job ladders'. Workers can climb job ladders by acquiring experience in lower-level jobs and undertaking appropriate firm-specific training.
- Rates of pay attach to jobs rather than to individual workers, contrary to the competitive model.
- Pay structures are rigid, and unresponsive to pressures from the external labour market. A study of firms employing professional engineers (Mace, 1979) found that they were unwilling to alter the salary structure even when faced with shortages of particular skills.

In summary, within internal labour markets rates of pay and the allocation of workers to jobs are determined by administrative rules rather than the market process. Thus in many organisations length of service (seniority) in one job remains the most important criterion for promotion to a higher position. Pay progression is also often organised on the basis of seniority. In Britain, pay structures are also frequently defined through job evaluation procedures, which try to link rates of pay to the responsibilities and skills required in the job.

In the light of this it should not be surprising that workers tend to remain with organisations for a long time. Studies of job tenure and worker mobility since the 1970s find that the majority of workers hold their jobs for long periods of time. For example, recent research has estimated that approximately 40% of male workers and 20% of female workers in Britain are in jobs lasting at least twenty years (Burgess and Rees, 1997). Across the European Union in 1996, 40% of men aged between 25 and 49 years had been in their current job for more than ten years, as had 32% of women in the same age group. A significant majority of both men (63%) and women (57%) had been in their current jobs for five years or more (European Commission, 1998a). Most job changing is concentrated among young workers. This is consistent with the idea that young workers move between firms in order to seek out the most advantageous job ladders within different internal labour markets. Older workers, having already progressed some way along job ladders, will be reluctant to move owing to the limited opportunities for entering other firms at a comparable point in their job hierarchies.

Historically, internal labour markets have been most highly developed in large Japanese and American corporations, where length of service rules often govern who is to be promoted or laid off. Within the UK, internal labour markets probably grew in importance with the growth in the size of businesses during the 1960s and 1970s. Studies of firms employing professional engineers and professional chemists found evidence of internal promotion, rigid wage structures and low labour turnover (Mace, 1979; Creedy and Whitfield, 1986). Stable wage structures were also found among manual workers in engineering (George and Shorey, 1985). However, job ladders and internal promotion opportunities for manual workers were very limited, suggesting that internal labour market arrangements are more highly developed for non-manual than for manual workers. Moreover, recent evidence that organisations are shedding layers of white-collar staff (thereby limiting opportunities for internal promotion), linking pay more closely to individual performance and employing more workers on part-time and temporary contracts raises the question of whether internal labour market structures are weakening.

Summary: limits to competition in the labour market

We have seen that actual labour market behaviour often deviates from the predictions of the competitive model. There is persistent unemployment, even when wages are rising. Wages are rigid downwards, and therefore do not act as the main means of adjustment to reductions in labour demand. Persistent wage differentials exist for similar types of labour. Structured internal labour markets are a feature of many organisations, especially for professional, technical and managerial personnel.

The features of labour markets outlined above suggest that the role of labour market competition in determining organisations' wage and employment decisions may be small. Organisations may be able to exercise considerable discretion in their employment policies. This raises some important questions. Is there more than one way to minimise costs? If so, why should this be the case rather than competition between firms defining the most economically efficient combination of inputs into the production process? Or does it mean that organisations do not maximise profits – that their goals, in so far as they can be identified, are more varied and complex? In the next section we look at different explanations for the features of real-life labour markets that we have identified here.

EXPLAINING THE REAL WORLD

Refining the competitive model: Labour market imperfections

One explanation for the apparent limitations of the basic competitive model is that the labour market is not perfectly competitive. Defenders of the competitive theory of labour markets argue that what we interpret as deviations from or contradictions of the model's predictions are in fact examples of individual maximising behaviour within the constraints imposed by market imperfections. Once we recognise the existence of market imperfections it becomes possible to explain unemployment and wage differentials within the competitive framework. In this section we examine the nature of so-called 'imperfections' in real-world labour markets. These 'imperfections', or limits to competition, arise from the following factors:

- Jobs and workers are heterogeneous rather than homogeneous. In other words, jobs have different characteristics and require different skills. Workers have different abilities and preferences. This is one factor that explains wage differentials between occupations and between different individuals in the same occupation.
- Neither employers nor workers have perfect information about the labour market. Labour market information is incomplete. The process of obtaining labour market information is known as labour market search: workers seek information about jobs and pay in order to make decisions about which job to take. Employers seek information about employees in order to be able to decide whom to hire. However, search is costly. Therefore labour market information is not equally available to all labour market participants.
- Costs associated with recruiting, selecting and training workers mean that labour turnover is costly to employers. Therefore they will try to encourage workers to stay with the firm. This takes these workers 'out of competition' by giving them a measure of job security.

Heterogeneous jobs and workers

Our initial model assumed that all jobs and all workers were the same. Clearly this is not the case. In reality there is not one homogeneous labour market but a number of sub-markets for different jobs and occupations. Mobility of labour between sub-markets is restricted because the skills that are tradable in one sub-market are not wanted in others. Also, to acquire new skills involves time and other costs. In other words, perfect general mobility of labour does not exist. Jobs require and workers possess different skills. It is therefore possible for unemployment to occur as some occupations shrink and others expand because of the time taken to rematch skills across sub-markets. This is compounded by obstacles to geographical mobility of labour, such as the costs of moving house.

Heterogeneity of jobs and workers also means that there will not be a single, uniform wage in the labour market. Instead there will be a pattern of *wage differentials*. The explanation for wage differentials advanced by Adam Smith as long ago as 1776 recognised the existence of differences between occupations, and argued that wage differentials compensated workers for the relative disadvantages attached to jobs. Some jobs involve more physical danger than others. Some involve unpleasant tasks or anti-social hours. Others carry a high degree of earnings insecurity. There are jobs that are seen to involve heavy responsibility and a high degree of accountability. Some require lengthy periods of training during which earnings are low or non-existent. Such jobs will have to offer higher pay compared with jobs that do not carry these disadvantages in order to attract sufficient workers to them. Pay differences between occupations or jobs therefore equalise their net advantages in relation to each other. Thus someone doing a safe, secure job with easy hours in a pleasant environment should not feel badly off when comparing themselves with a higher-paid worker undertaking dirty, dangerous work involving weekend and night shifts.

Competitive labour market theory suggests that wage differentials are the outcome of competitive market forces given the heterogeneous nature of jobs. They represent an efficient mechanism for allocating labour between occupations of varying disagreeableness. However, as noted above, we can observe large wage differentials between workers in the same occupation or sub-market. How can these be explained if, as competitive theory suggests, individual sub-markets operate competitively?

In order to explain intra-occupational wage differentials – that is, different wage rates for workers in the same occupation – in a way that is consistent with the basic competitive model, two arguments are advanced. The first is an extension of the compensating wage differentials argument. It has been observed that wage rates tend to be higher in large workplaces than in small ones. It is suggested that working in a large establishment is less pleasant than doing the same type of job in a smaller workplace. This is because large workplaces are alleged to more impersonal and bureaucratic, and more productive of stress. Workers in large establishments are therefore paid more than are comparable workers in small establishments.

The second argument allows for differences in worker quality within occupations. Rather than assuming that all workers within the occupational sub-market are of equal ability, differences in ability are assumed. These differences may be due to variations in natural ability, or they may be the fruits of experience in the job. Since more able workers will have a higher marginal productivity than less able workers they will also be paid more. Intra-occupational differentials are therefore consistent with the competitive model. The question that arises, however, is whether differentials of the size observed in the labour market are readily explicable in these terms.

Imperfect information and labour market search

We saw above that perfect information was one of the assumptions underlying the perfectly competitive model of the labour market. Once we relax this assumption to allow for imperfect information, it is possible to add to our explanations of unemployment and persistent wage differentials while remaining within the basic framework of the competitive approach.

When information concerning wage offers and job content is incomplete it is rational for workers not to accept the first job they are offered. Instead they engage in job search with a view to maximising their future income stream. Workers undertaking job search have to set the possible gains from continuing their search against the income forgone by not accepting the latest job offer. As the period of search lengthens, diminishing marginal returns to further search set in. This is because the worker will start by investigating the most promising job opportunities. Therefore there is a decreasing like-lihood that subsequent search will identify better offers. At the same time, the cost to the worker of further search will rise, since the longer he or she delays accepting an attractive job offer, the more likely it is that it will be taken by someone else. The worker will stop searching and accept the next job offer when the expected additional benefits of further search are equalled by the expected additional costs.

Two things follow from this. First, job search can explain why unemployment coexists with unfilled vacancies. Because search is costly, workers may not undertake sufficient search to enable all vacancies to be filled. Second, with imperfect information it is likely that some job-seekers will be luckier than others: that is, some workers will find rela-tively well-paid jobs while others of equal productive ability will find less well-paid jobs. Imperfect information and costly job search mean that inter-firm wage variations need not even out.

The problem with this is that it is not workers who usually decide on a job offer. More usually it is employers who select among workers in order to fill a vacancy. Employers' search behaviour can be analysed in a similar way to that of workers, since rational employers will seek to equate the marginal costs and benefits of labour market search.

Imagine an employer operating in a labour market where there are no variations in the quality of workers but where workers each have different reservation wages – that is, the wage level that must be exceeded if they are to accept a job offer. In this situation a high wage offer by the employer will increase the likelihood of getting vacancies filled and necessitate less search for suitable workers. Alternatively the employer can offer a lower wage and take longer to fill the vacancy, the cost of this choice being the resultant loss of output until the post is filled.

A different case arises if we assume that the quality of workers is variable. In this case organisations will employ various costly selection and screening procedures to identify workers of suitable quality. Organisations employing the most rigorous selection proce-dures will be those where an applicant's chances of being appointed are least – only the very best will be appointed. Therefore a relatively high wage will have to be offered to attract applicants. Organisations using less rigorous selection methods will be able to offer a lower wage. In this case wage differences reflect differences in the quality – that is, marginal productivity – of workers.

Labour as a quasi-fixed factor of production

In the simple competitive model of the labour market the only cost to the employer of hiring workers is the wage that has to be paid. Consequently, replacing workers who leave does not add to costs. This means that the current workforce is disposable, and the employer has no particular interest in retaining current workers. In practice, how-ever, labour turnover is costly. This means that employers may wish to retain existing workers and reduce labour turnover. We have already noted the existence of costs incurred by organisations searching for workers – that is, the costs of recruitment and selection. There are also costs involved in training workers, particularly in skills that are specific to the organisation. These costs mean that labour turnover is costly to the employer. The main costs of labour turnover are:

- losses of output due to unplanned reductions in the workforce resulting from work-ers quitting;
- financial costs of recruitment and selection;
- the cost of training new recruits: the direct cost of providing training, and the cost in terms of reduced output while the worker is being trained.

The fact that labour turnover is costly has important consequences for the management of labour and the operation of the labour market:

- The value of a worker's output has to cover costs of recruitment, selection and training as well as the wage cost. Therefore workers will be paid less than the value of their marginal revenue product.
- Employers will try to retain workers for at least as long as it takes the value of their output to cover the costs of recruitment, selection and training. This is particularly the case where workers receive large amounts of employer-financed training. From this it follows that employers are not indifferent as between 'insiders' – those currently employed – and the 'outsiders' who are their possible replacements. They prefer to retain 'insiders'.

To avoid the costs of high rates of labour turnover employers adopt a variety of employment policies, which, taken together, generate many of the key features of internal labour markets:

- Deferred benefits: that is, benefits that are contingent on the workers remaining with the organisation. Examples include entitlements to pensions, and holidays that become available only after a minimum period of service.
- Seniority wages, whereby pay rises with length of service, and therefore pay attaches to individuals rather than to jobs.
- Avoidance of layoffs during temporary downturns in production. Organisations will look first to non-replacement of workers who leave the organisation, reducing hours worked, for example by cutting back on overtime, before laying workers off.
- During upturns in production, employers will first look for ways of increasing the output of the current workforce, for example through overtime working, before hiring additional workers. This is because the higher costs of overtime premia may still be less than the additional costs of recruiting, selecting and training new workers.

Where organisations seek to foster long-term employment relationships, labour ceases to be a purely variable factor of production. It becomes instead a quasi-fixed factor, since the number of workers hired no longer varies directly with output. A consequence of this is that inter-organisational mobility of labour is reduced and so is the degree of competition among workers in the labour market. It becomes harder for unemployed workers to compete for jobs with those already in work because of the costs the employer will incur in replacing current workers with outsiders. This in turn means that there is less pressure on workers to accept wage reductions when the demand for labour falls. Conversely, when the demand for labour rises, employed workers are able to raise wages because non-wage employment costs initially deter employers from additional hiring. Costs of recruitment, selection and training, by making labour a quasi-fixed factor of production, are further explanations for persistent unemployment, asymmetry of wage movements and downward wage rigidity.

Organisation-specific human capital

An extension of the above argument is the concept of organisation-specific human capital. 'Human capital' refers to the investment in education and training that is embodied in the worker. Some types of training develop 'general' or 'transferable' skills that can be used equally productively across different organisations. Others provide 'organisation-specific' skills that enhance the worker's productivity within the training organisation only. These latter skills tend to be those best learned on the job. Workers having organisation-specific skills will be able to obtain a wage premium in respect of that skill only within the organisation where they were trained. To change employers would mean having to take jobs in which they were less productive and therefore less well paid.

Two things follow from this. First, there is an incentive for such workers to remain with the organisation in which they acquired their skills. This gives the employer a measure of monopoly power over those workers. Second, however, the loss of organisation-specific skills would involve the employer in costly training of new workers. This means that workers with organisation-specific skills are, in the short run, monopoly providers of those skills. There is thus a situation of *bilateral monopoly*. In such a situation the influence of competitive forces on wage rates is limited, at least in the short run, and the relative bargaining power of the two sides becomes a significant factor determining wages.

The significance of labour market imperfections

We can see that market imperfections restrict the amount of competition in the labour market. Contrary to the model of perfect competition, workers are not perfectly mobile between organisations because of recruitment, selection and training costs and organisation-specific skills. Market imperfections mean that employers or groups of workers can develop different degrees of bargaining power and use it to influence wages. To the extent that this results in wages that are higher than the 'market clearing' rate, there will be workers who wish to work at the going wage but who are unable to find a job: that is, there will be 'involuntary' unemployment. To the extent that varying degrees of relative bargaining power are important in determining the wages of different groups of workers, there will be wage differentials that cannot be explained in terms of productivity differences and the non-wage characteristics of jobs. Workers with strong bargaining power will be able to obtain wages higher than are necessary to reward productivity and compensate for the disadvantages of the job. Conversely, workers who lack bargaining power may be exploited by employers who use their own bargaining power to under-pay them.

Defenders of the competitive theory of labour markets argue in reply that, despite imperfections, competitive forces remain important, particularly in the long run. Since perfect competition is simply a model of the real world rather than a description of it, we can make it more complex by allowing for market imperfections without losing the essential features of the model itself. Therefore the refined version of the competitive model accepts that, because of market imperfections, labour markets will not function perfectly efficiently, and that there will be unemployment and persistent wage differentials that do not simply reflect differences in the nature of jobs or the quality of workers. Nevertheless, it maintains that competition between rational maximising individuals is still the main influence in labour markets, and labour market outcomes are consistent with this. Wages are still largely determined by the worker's marginal product, and wage differentials are mainly due to different job features and to variations in worker quality. This is particularly true in the long run, since this allows for technological change and the substitution of less expensive for more expensive inputs, for the acquisition of new or additional skills, and for the entry of new competitors into markets. For example, where bargaining power has raised the wage of an occupation relative to others, employers can, in the long run, substitute more capital equipment for labour. One effect of this will be to weaken the bargaining power of the workers, who now find that they are being replaced by machinery. Also, as long as wages remain relatively high in that occupation, more people will be encouraged to acquire the skills needed to enter it. This expands the supply of labour to that occupation, increases competition for the available jobs, and forces the wage rate closer to a level that reflects the 'disadvantages' of the occupation and the level of labour productivity within it.

Refining the competitive model: special features of the effort–reward bargain

So far we have explained deviations from the predictions of the basic competitive model of the labour market in terms of market imperfections. However, there are special features of the exchange of effort for rewards that make labour market transactions qualitatively different from others. Refined versions of the competitive theory of labour markets recognise this.

The most important distinguishing feature of the effort–reward exchange is that the worker's effort cannot be separated from the worker. Thus it is not disembodied 'effort' that the employer buys; rather it is the use of the worker's time, to be employed in production. While 'labour' is a commodity in the sense that it is bought and sold, labourers are not commodities but active, conscious individuals who can control their effort and who have an interest in the terms and conditions on which they are employed.

A further distinguishing feature of the effort–reward exchange is that the precise nature and amount of effort that the worker has to supply is not specified at the time of hiring – the employment contract is indeterminate. Thus the employment contract requires workers to subordinate themselves to the authority of management and obey all reasonable instructions. This enables management to vary hours of work, intensity of effort and the nature of the tasks performed by the worker, within reasonable limits. Clearly, what is reasonable is a matter of interpretation, and this can lead to managers and managed contesting what is a reasonable amount of effort in relation to the wage being paid.

In the rest of this section we consider how these distinctive features of the labour market are dealt with from the standpoint of competitive theory before going on to discuss other theories of the labour market.

Indeterminacy of the effort–reward bargain

In our initial model of the labour market, output varied directly with the quantity of labour inputs, the precise relationship being determined by the technology of production. The level of effort supplied by workers was taken as given and assumed to be non-problematic. In the real world, however, workers can exercise considerable control over their effort. When employers hire workers they are paying for productive potential rather than delivered output. Productive potential is converted into output in the production process. The extent to which productive potential is utilised – that is, the actual effort level supplied – cannot be specified in advance and is dependent on a number of factors, one of which is the worker's own motivation. This distinction between productive potential and actual effort provides the basis for the neo-classical analysis of the role of management in the employment relationship.

Alchian and Demsetz (1972) argued that in any kind of team production, in which individual rewards depend on team performance, there is a possibility that individuals will shirk, supplying less effort than their fellows in relation to the rewards obtained. This will be most likely in large teams where it is difficult to measure individual contributions to team performance. Management therefore performs a necessary role of supervision. This is in the workers' own interest as well as that of the employer, since shirking either reduces output and hence profits and employment, or else leads to inequities in the effort–reward bargain as between individual workers. From this view-point workers *want* to be managed.

Supervision, however, is itself costly. Costs of effective supervision will be greatest in large organisations and where measurement of effort levels is difficult, or where it is difficult for management to define appropriate effort levels. The implications of this have been analysed by Williamson (1975, 1985). Where workers possess knowledge of the production process that can only be acquired on the job, management is prevented from sharing this knowledge, and outsiders are no longer efficient substitutes for currently employed workers. Williamson argues that in these circumstances the effort–reward bargain is characterised by *idiosyncratic exchange* – that is, the terms on which workers are employed are influenced by the idiosyncrasies, or special features, of jobs and the specialised knowledge that attaches to them.

Idiosyncratic exchange means that there are limits to the extent of supervision that can be exercised without incurring disproportionate costs. In this situation it is possible for workers to behave opportunistically: that is, to mislead managers about what are appropriate effort levels or about what actual level of effort is being supplied. Also, labour market discipline on existing workers will be weak since they cannot easily be replaced. This provides currently employed workers with what Williamson refers to as 'first mover advantages': that is, bargaining power deriving from their position as 'insiders'. Once again we have a situation of bilateral monopoly.

Because of the limits to effective supervision and the high costs of supervising certain workers, it may be profitable for management to offer incentives for cooperation rather than relying solely on supervision. Such incentives might include commitments to providing employment security, wage progression and promotion ladders. Another variant of this approach is the *efficiency wage hypothesis*. Because monitoring workers' effort may be costly, it may be more profitable to pay them a wage higher than they could earn elsewhere so as to induce them to supply high levels of effort. In doing this, management tries to minimise *unit labour costs* – that is, total labour costs per unit of output (including costs of turnover and shirking) – rather than simply minimising wage costs per unit of output.

Once we acknowledge the possibility that workers may withhold effort from the employer we add to our explanation of observed labour market behaviour. First, paying a wage higher than the market wage generates unemployment as workers are attracted into the labour market. This queue of potential applicants acts as a disciplinary force on those already employed since, while employed workers may not be easily replaceable, failure to meet management standards may ultimately result in dismissal. The efficiency wage also helps to explain inter-firm wage differentials since the costs of supervision vary among firms. The efficiency wage hypothesis can therefore be seen as an alternative to the theory of compensating differentials in explaining why wages in large establishments tend to be higher than in small ones. Efficiency wages also explain downward wage rigidity because a reduction in wage rates in response to a downturn in labour demand would reduce employee morale and weaken the basis for worker–management cooperation.

Together with the quasi-fixed nature of labour inputs, the indeterminacy of the wage–effort bargain provides a basis for explaining internal labour markets, although they have been put forward as alternative explanations. Doeringer and Piore's (1971) approach to internal labour markets sees them as originating in the need for organisation-specific skills and training and the consequent attempt by employers to protect their training investment. Williamson (1985) emphasises instead the role of internal labour markets in reducing opportunistic behaviour by workers. Nevertheless, there is a lot of common ground between them, as the ability of workers to behave opportunistically stems from the specific nature of their skills, which in turn may be related to the technologies employed by organisations.

We may argue, therefore, that organisations seek to protect their training investments by deploying policies to retain trained workers. The same policies, for example promotion ladders and pay increments based on length of service, together with efficiency wages, may in certain circumstances be a less costly method of getting desired effort levels from workers than extensive supervision.

Rent-seeking by workers

Another way of looking at policies that offer high wages, job security and promotion based on seniority is to see them as the result of *rent-seeking behaviour* by workers. Given the imperfect nature of competition in both product and labour markets, it is possible for organisations to generate 'surplus' profits (rents). This ability stems from the market power that organisations can exert when shielded from the full force of competition in the product market. In essence, output can be priced more highly than it could be in a competitive market. This means that profits will be above the minimum necessary to keep the organisation in business: that is, there will be an element of rent. Where workers possess a measure of bargaining power, they can use it to gain a share of the rents of the organisation. This can take the form of wage increases and/or restrictions on management's freedom to hire and fire. Rent-seeking can also be seen as a source of inefficiency in labour and capital utilisation since it may take the form of limits on effort levels that are either imposed unilaterally by workers or agreed, informally or even formally, with management. Opportunistic behaviour can therefore be seen as a form of rent-seeking behaviour as workers use idiosyncratic job knowledge and first mover advantages to obtain a share of the rents of the organisation.

From a competitive labour market perspective rent-seeking behaviour by workers raises wages above the market-clearing rate and generates unemployment. It also distorts the pattern of relative wages so that too many workers are encouraged to seek work in some occupations and too few in others. This creates a situation in which there are, simultaneously, unemployment and unfilled vacancies. The 'solution' is to encourage a greater degree of competition between firms.

Implications for the competitive theory of labour markets

In developing theories of idiosyncratic exchange, bilateral monopoly and efficiency wages, how far have we moved away from a conception of the labour market based on competition between maximising individuals? It can be argued that internal labour markets and efficiency wages are ways in which managers maximise profits or minimise costs. Their aim is to minimise *labour* costs per unit of output rather than just wage costs per unit. It might be suggested that internal labour markets are in fact proxies for competitive external labour markets. When they set wages, organisations undertake wage surveys in the relevant section of the labour market. These surveys provide information about the market wage to which the internal wage structure can conform. Internal wage differentials represent rewards for different levels of productivity. By using wage surveys and job evaluation, organisations seek to ensure equitable wages that reflect performance. In this way it could be argued that internal labour markets are simply an institutional expression of competitive market forces. For this to be so, however, it has to be shown that the external influences on wage levels and wage structures within organisations are stronger than the internal ones. Evidence of large, persistent inter-firm wage differentials suggests that internal factors may often predominate, and that it is not obvious that internal labour markets simply replicate competitive forces.

The efficiency wage hypothesis also challenges the competitive model. While it may be argued that efficiency wages are consistent with cost minimisation, the main assumption underlying efficiency wages contradicts one of the main assumptions of the competitive model. Rather than the wage being determined by the productivity of the worker, the productivity of the worker is now determined by the wage. Firms may therefore be able to choose between alternative strategies regarding labour: a high-wage, high-productivity strategy, or a low-wage, low-productivity strategy.

Once we admit that employers may prefer to retain existing workers rather than treat them as interchangeable in the labour market, that workers may value current employment more highly than alternatives, that workers can to some extent control their own effort levels, and that terms and conditions of the effort–reward bargain may be influenced by bargaining power, we move well away from our initial model of competition. The employment relationship ceases to be simply an act of economic exchange and takes on social and political dimensions. It becomes necessary to examine how employment relationships are structured and perceived, and how they relate to outcomes such as pay and productivity.

INSTITUTIONAL THEORIES OF THE LABOUR MARKET

The refinements incorporated into neo-classical theory in order to explain institutional arrangements such as rigid pay structures and internal labour markets mean that there is considerable overlap with institutional theories of labour markets. However, institutional and radical theorists argue that the special features of the employment relationship mean that it is based more on the exercise of power than on market competition. Some analysts have gone so far as to question whether labour 'markets' really are markets at all (Marsden, 1986).

The main point of difference between competitive and institutionalist theories lies in institutionalism's rejection of the individual maximising postulate on which competitive theory rests.

Institutionalists argue that our preferences are not independent of those of others, but are interdependent. In other words, we formulate our own preferences in the light of those of others. This idea has strong intuitive appeal: 'keeping up with the Joneses' is an everyday way of saying that the satisfaction that we get from our income depends not only on its absolute value, but also on its relative value compared with others. The importance attached to pay differentials by workers and their unions or professional associations suggests that the force of inter-group comparisons is strong.

Institutionalists argue that such comparisons involve notions of fairness, and that these are important in establishing and maintaining pay differentials, which appear to remain stable over time. Concepts of fairness, such as 'a fair day's work for a fair day's pay', also provide a basis for work-group norms concerning appropriate levels of effort. Collective organisation with the purpose of enforcing such norms may develop within work groups. In this way the employment relationship is not simply an individual market transaction. Instead it is conditioned by sets of norms, customs and collective relationships.

Organisations' decisions are also seen to be interdependent. This is because competition in many product markets is not between a large number of small producers, but between a relatively small number of large ones. This means that, contrary to the assumption of the competitive model, an individual producer can, by its pricing and output policies and non-price strategies of competition such as marketing and advertising, influence the market conditions facing its rivals. Competition between producers then becomes like a game in which each player has to take into account the actions of others in deciding what strategy or tactic to adopt. They also have to consider how others will respond to the strategy or tactic adopted.

In such a situation simple profit maximisation is impossible. This is because the market situation facing each producer is indeterminate, since the outcome of any decision will depend also on the decisions made by others. Therefore goals other than profit maximisation may be pursued, for example market share, organisational growth or a target rate of return on capital employed. The inability to maximise profits means that a certain amount of inefficiency is present within organisations. This is manifested in the under-utilisation of capital and labour, referred to as X-inefficiency (Leibenstein, 1987). X-inefficiency also results from the limits to competition that result from the ability of large producers to exercise a degree of power in the market.

While institutionalists accept that employers' needs to retain skills and obtain desired levels of cooperation may play a part in explaining efficiency wages, rigid pay structures and internal labour markets, they place more emphasis on the role of group norms, custom and collective power. These may be present among employers as well as workers, but most attention has focused on the role of collective labour in influencing the labour market.

The starting point is the long-term nature of the employment relationship, which allows social bonds and a sense of collective interest and identity to develop among groups of workers. As we have seen, the emergence of group norms concerning 'fairness' in the effort–reward bargain is part of this process. Such norms include what is seen as an appropriate level of effort given the wage, how much any one group's wage rate should be relative to other groups, and what the limits are to the reasonable exercise of managerial authority.

The development of such norms or standards represents an attempt by workers to gain some control over the employment relationship in order to advance and defend their interests. There is no reason why these group interests should coincide with those of other groups, such as managers or shareholders. For example, workers' desire to maintain a given wage structure on grounds of 'fairness' may conflict with management's desire for change in the interests of 'flexibility'. The establishment and maintenance of norms may therefore require the exercise of power, and this encourages the development of collective organisation by workers. Therefore the terms of the effort–reward bargain are not simply the outcome of cost-minimising decisions by managers; rather they are negotiated outcomes that reflect the relative bargaining power of different collective interests.

The result of this analysis is that efficiency wages, rigid pay structures and internal labour markets are not simply the result of employers' attempts to minimise unit labour costs. Doeringer and Piore (1971), for example, argue that while internal labour markets may originate in attempts to reduce costs, the actual operation of internal labour markets generates rigidities and resistance to change. Any change or adjustment within the internal labour market means that the distribution of rewards as between groups of workers changes. Given that the existing distribution is partly grounded in group norms and custom, attempts to introduce change will produce conflict in the form of worker non-cooperation or more overt opposition organised through trade unions.

Other writers have questioned the extent to which the *origins* of internal labour markets can be explained in efficiency terms. Clark Kerr (1954) saw internal labour markets as the outcome of workers' and unions' attempts to improve conditions for insiders by limiting competition from outsiders. In this vein, Osterman (1984) has argued that certain features of internal labour markets in the United States, such as seniority rules relating to pay and lay-offs and formalised wage-setting arrangements through collective bargaining, were established in the face of strong resistance from managers, who saw such rules as a challenge to their prerogatives.

THE RADICAL APPROACH TO INSTITUTIONALIST ANALYSIS

The radical version of institutionalist theories of the labour market takes the class nature of capitalist society as its starting point. Capitalists are motivated not by the search for efficiency, but by the need to generate profits with which to finance the further accumulation of capital. The source of such profits is an exploited workforce that is paid less than the value of what it produces. Workers' resistance to exploitation threatens the accumulation of capital and hence the survival of the capitalist system. Capitalists therefore have a class interest in weakening workers' capacity to resist exploitation. This leads to forms of technology and work organisation and systems for the managerial control of labour that facilitate the continuance and even the intensification of the exploitation of workers. This is clearly a very different point of view from that which suggests that workers want to be managed (see above).

Workers' capacity to resist exploitation stems from:

● specialised job knowledge rooted in skill;
● a sense of solidarity and the development of collective organisation.

Therefore capitalists seek to:

● reduce the skill content of jobs – this makes incumbent workers more easily replaceable and also transfers knowledge and control of the production process from workers to management;
● structure the labour market in ways that divide the workforce and undermine its solidarity and collective organisation.

This approach has informed some influential studies of changes in the organisation and control of work during the twentieth century. Braverman (1974) argued that at the beginning of the twentieth century the move to mass production centred on the subdivision of jobs into narrow, standardised tasks, with work methods and work standards (such as pace of work) determined by management. Braverman argued that this development, known as Scientific Management, deskilled jobs and thereby reduced the amount of control over effort levels and the deployment of labour hitherto exercised by workers and their unions.

Others such as Edwards (1975) have argued that organisations set up internal labour markets based on jobs that are divided from each other vertically by means of narrow task specifications and also horizontally by means of job 'ladders' or job hierarchies. This differentiation deskills jobs and also divides the workforce into segments, undermining the capacity for solidarity and collective organisation.

Internal labour markets play a further role in radical theory, which is to segment the wider labour market into primary and secondary sectors. Workers in the primary sector enjoy relatively good pay, benefits and working conditions, receive training, may have opportunities for job progression, and have a degree of employment security. Workers in the secondary labour market are paid lower wages, enjoy few, if any, fringe benefits, receive little or no training, and have minimal employment security. Radical segmentation theorists argue that these differences are not explained by differences in the quality of workers in the two segments. Instead, workers of the same productive ability are rewarded differently in the two sectors. Internal labour markets are features of primary sector employment; the secondary labour market approximates to the casual external labour market of the competitive model. The secondary sector functions as:

- a pool of cheap labour on which primary sector employers can draw as required;
- a disciplinary device acting on primary sector workers. Since mobility between the internal labour markets of primary sector organisations is limited to low-level ports of entry, workers displaced from primary sector organisations run the risk of having to seek work in the secondary sector. This acts as a potential sanction against uncooperative behaviour by primary sector workers, particularly when managers seek changes that disrupt established internal labour market structures and procedures;
- a means of generating or reinforcing status divisions among workers – that is, between primary and secondary workers. In the case of primary sector workers, advantageous comparisons with those at the bottom of the 'heap' help to reconcile them to their own lot and reduce their sense of grievance and resistance to management control. In seeking to defend their relatively privileged position, primary workers will seek to differentiate themselves from those in the secondary sector rather than act in solidarity with them. This in turn means that the collective power of secondary sector workers is weakened, and with it the ability to resist their own exploitation.

While labour market segmentation is inefficient in that workers are not rewarded in line with their productivity, and consequently labour is inefficiently allocated between competing uses, it is consistent with profits since it weakens workers' solidarity and their ability to secure the full value of what they produce.

LABOUR MARKET THEORIES AND THE ANALYSIS OF HRM

It is evident that there is some overlap between the perspectives reviewed in the previous sections. Crucially, the refined competitive theory and both of the institutionalist approaches accept that there are special features of the employment relationship that make the conversion of productive potential of workers into actual effort problematic. This leads each of the perspectives to recognise that bargaining power plays a role in influencing labour market structures and the terms of the effort–reward bargain. However, the neo-classical view emphasises individual maximising behaviour as the main force underlying labour market behaviour, while institutionalist and radical theories stress the role of collective forces. The competitive analysis of structural features of the labour market, such as rigid wage structures and internal labour markets, sees them as rooted in cost-minimising behaviour – that is, efficiency-driven. Institutionalists argue that efficiency may not be the sole or even the main basis for such structures, and radical theorists argue that profit, not efficiency, drives employers' policies in the labour market. We now go on to ask what these different perspectives tell us about HRM, focusing on the following questions:

- What is the rationale for HRM?
- Is this rationale equally compelling for all organisations?
- What are the implied outcomes of HRM in terms of its effects on established labour market structures and the distribution of rewards, in the labour market and as between wages and profits?

The rationale for HRM

Whether we take the competitive approach or adopt the institutionalist or radical perspectives outlined above, HRM can be seen as a management-led challenge to existing institutional arrangements within the labour market, particularly the internal labour market arrangements of employing organisations. The competitive and institutionalist approaches identify changing conditions in product markets and changes in technology as the source of this challenge. The main currents of change can be summarised as follows:

- intensification of international competition;
- acceleration in the pace of both process and product innovation, with a consequent shortening of product lifecycles;
- the re-emergence of major recessions as part of the dynamic of capitalist development.
- As a consequence of the above, product markets have become more volatile as well as more competitive, with sharper and more frequent changes in the level and pattern of demand.
- Within the public sector, pressure to contain the level of public expenditure has led to increased attention being paid to cost control and resource allocation.

These changes have put organisations under pressure to reduce unit costs of production and raise product quality. They have also led to a search for ways of increasing the flexibility of organisations – that is, the ability to respond to and anticipate change. In terms of the management of labour this has meant reducing 'rigidities' and 'inefficiencies' in the allocation of labour and its utilisation.

As we have seen, much of what we observe about labour markets is explained in terms of the substitution of bureaucratic methods of allocating workers to jobs and determining the level and distribution of rewards in place of the competitive market mechanism. However, these methods, aimed at reducing costs of supervision by obtaining workers' cooperation and reducing the costs of labour turnover, are themselves costly. Moreover, changes in markets and technology mean that they may no longer be the most appropriate ways of minimising unit labour costs. This is because:

- The provision of promotion ladders as part of an internal labour market structure may create rigid job specifications that run counter to employers' needs for flexibility in the deployment of labour.
- Rigid wage structures, such as those based on seniority, run counter to employers' needs for greater wage flexibility – that is, the need to link pay to aspects of performance and to vary pay structures in line with changes in the pattern of demand for different levels and types of skill.
- The provision of incentives to effort through job security arrangements, promotion ladders based on seniority, and efficiency wages may not succeed in eliminating opportunism by workers as long as idiosyncratic exchange remains a feature of the effort–reward bargain.

● Where these incentives have resulted from workers using their collective bargaining power to gain a share of firms' rents, the weakening of that bargaining power during the 1980s and 1990s may have encouraged management to withdraw them.

The competitive labour market perspective

From the perspective of the competitive theory of labour markets we expect rational, maximising organisations to look for ways of reducing costs when faced with increased competition in their product markets. Reorganising work and introducing new systems of reward may also be necessary in order to maximise the effective use of new technology. Policies that minimised costs in the past may no longer do so once circumstances change. Moreover, if it is the case that those policies are the outcome of rent-seeking behaviour rather than being efficiency oriented, then the pressure for their modification will be all the stronger. This is because any intensification of competition will reduce the size of the rent that can be shared with the workforce.

In the light of this we can make some observations on the purpose of recent innovations in the management of labour that have been tagged with the HRM label:

● The decentralisation of pay bargaining within multi-establishment organisations and the vogue for individual performance-related pay are attempts to reduce rigidities in pay structures. Individual performance-related pay linked to appraisal can also be seen as an attempt to overcome problems of asymmetric information stemming from idiosyncratic job knowledge. By agreeing or setting performance targets for individual employees through appraisal, and linking pay reviews to performance outcomes, managers are seeking to gain greater control over the terms of the effort–reward bargain.
● The removal or relaxation of strict demarcations between jobs, and the associated interest among managers in developing teamworking, may represent a modification of the structure of the internal labour market that aims to make it compatible with the flexible deployment of labour. Job progression may continue to characterise the internal labour market; in fact opportunities for progression may be enhanced for some workers, but the criterion for progression is changed from length of service to the acquisition of bundles of skills through training.
● The reorganisation of work around quality control circles and work teams, and the replacement of supervisors with team leaders who are members of the work group, are consistent with management's interest in reducing information asymmetries and the scope for opportunism by workers. Quality control circles encourage workers to share their job knowledge with management and direct that knowledge towards improving productive efficiency. Team-based production with team leaders working as members of the group can be seen as providing management with access to detailed job knowledge, reducing information asymmetries in production.
● Selection procedures that emphasise a job applicant's personal values and attitudes as much as technical skills seek to ensure that selected employees are amenable and responsive to the systems of incentives and control, such as those outlined above, which are employed by the organisation.

These polices for managing labour within organisations can be seen as embodying both 'hard' and 'soft' HRM. For example, the emphasis on individual performance could be presented as embodying both 'hard' and 'soft' HRM. Setting targets and monitoring performance against them can be seen as the 'hard' face of HRM. Yet to the extent that this may also involve agreeing personal training needs and personal development plans it can also be presented as having a 'soft' aspect. The prime goal is efficiency, but this need not be inconsistent with meeting the needs of employees.

An institutionalist perspective

The points above can be admitted within the institutionalist perspective, but its main emphasis is on how HRM policies alter the nature of power within organisations and the distribution of power between different interests. Thus an institutionalist view of labour markets leads us to view HRM as a means of co-opting workers into the managerial vision of the organisation by establishing new norms of attitude and behaviour. 'Soft' HRM policies such as employee involvement seek to generate a 'commitment culture', sometimes centred round concepts of 'customer care' or 'total quality management'. To the extent that such policies are successful, they can be seen to substitute institutionalised patterns of high trust relations between workers and management in place of externally imposed discipline.

Policies such as these may be extended to collective industrial relations. This is most clearly exemplified by collective agreements in which companies have recognised a single union as representative of the workforce in return for a commitment by the union to cooperate with management in programmes aimed at enhancing labour flexibility, increasing productivity and improving quality. Alternatively, where co-opting of unions is seen to be impracticable or undesirable, HRM policies may be used to marginalise the union role and individualise the employment relationship. In general, however, institutionalist analysis tends to argue that HRM is not incompatible with trade union organisation, and that trade unions can facilitate policies aimed at generating high levels of employee commitment. Some evidence to support this has emerged from successive surveys of workplace industrial relations (Millward, 1994; Culley *et al.*, 1999).

On the other hand, some radical writers have suggested that the fact that HRM policies tend to be introduced in unionised workplaces is consistent with the argument that HRM is used to weaken trade union influence and organisation (Kelly, 1996). Yet others have argued that, while managers might not have made active use of HRM to weaken trade unions, they have taken advantage of union weakness to ignore traditional industrial relations machinery and focus instead on HRM initiatives, leaving unions to wither on the vine (Storey, 1992).

Radical perspectives

Taking a radical labour market perspective we might argue that policies such as those described above stem from capital's need to raise the rate of profit by increasing the surplus value extracted from workers. However, institutional features of labour markets, as we have seen, are not just the product of capitalists' efforts to control and exploit labour. Workers, in resisting exploitation, have also influenced the way in which they have developed. HRM represents an effort by capitalists to reshape labour markets so as to re-create the basis for the more effective exploitation of labour. While this may involve policies designed to co-opt certain sections of the workforce, others will be subject to work intensification, closer control by management, diminished employment security, and possibly lower pay.

From a radical perspective we would therefore extend the institutional approach to include the following aspects of HRM:

- policies to individualise the employment relationship, divide workers internally, and weaken the basis for their collective resistance to management;
- policies aimed at restructuring the workforce by reducing the proportion of 'core' or primary sector workers and expanding the 'periphery' or secondary sector of the labour market. Such policies are an intensification of divide-and-rule strategies across the labour market as a whole.

Radical theory also emphasises the role of state policy in the labour market and its relationship to patterns of exploitation at the organisation level. Examples are:

- the use of unemployment during the 1980s as a policy weapon to weaken the bargaining power of labour. This is diametrically opposed to the view of unemployment taken by proponents of the competitive view of labour markets, namely that unemployment is *caused* by the bargaining power of trade unions;
- policies of labour market deregulation as practised in the USA and the UK during the 1980s and most of the 1990s, for example withdrawal or curtailment of legal protections for workers in respect of minimum wages, employment protection and social security, and anti-union legislation.

From a radical perspective, the distinction between 'hard' and 'soft' HRM is somewhat illusory. This is because 'soft' HRM is seen as the 'velvet glove' concealing the 'iron fist' of 'hard' HRM. 'Soft' HRM initiatives such as employee involvement are seen as strategies to undermine independent trade union organisation and weaken workers' effective influence over terms and conditions of employment. This gives management greater freedom to determine pay, hours of work and effort levels, and to hire and fire as necessary. However, radical analysis also emphasises the tensions and contradictions within HRM that prevent such strategies from being fully realised. For example, management may not be able to take full advantage of this freedom, since by doing so it would destroy the credibility of the 'soft' HRM policies that are the basis for workers' acceptance of increased managerial control.

The incidence of HRM

The competitive viewpoint

Depending on which view of the labour market we adopt, is the rationale for HRM equally compelling for all organisations? From a competitive labour market perspective we would argue that cost-minimising organisations face a number of labour market decisions, among which the following are probably the most important:

- the amount of search to be undertaken in the labour market;
- how to acquire and retain skills in the workforce;
- how to obtain and maintain desired effort levels.

We have seen that there may be trade-offs in each of these areas:

- increasing search against raising the wage or trading off worker quality against the wage rate;
- accepting costs of labour turnover as against offering (costly) incentives to retain workers;
- the degree of (costly) managerial supervision against the provision of (costly) incentives to workers to supply desired effort.

We have also seen that HRM can be rationalised within the competitive model as a means of reducing unit labour costs, particularly those costs associated with the operation of internal labour market structures. However, we must remember that HRM policies are also costly. HRM will only be adopted by rational organisations where the ratio of benefits to costs exceeds that of other approaches to the management of labour. This implies considerable variety in organisations' labour market policies, since the costs and benefits associated with different policies will be contingent on numerous factors relating to the organisation and the labour market or markets within which it operates.

The classic external labour market policy is a casual 'hire and fire' regime. Labour turnover is high, and wages tend towards the market rate. In the light of the modified competitive theory of labour markets such a policy is most likely where the employer operates in the market for unskilled labour. This is because search costs are low, since the supply of unskilled labour is plentiful relative to that of skilled workers. There is also a minimal requirement for the firm to invest in training. Employers will therefore accept labour turnover in preference to relatively more costly employee retention policies.

Unskilled workers will also have little scope for opportunistic behaviour since they possess little idiosyncratic job knowledge. This makes it relatively easy for management to monitor effort rather than having to provide incentives through internal labour market arrangements or efficiency wages. This is even more likely to be the case where the size of the workforce is small. Therefore there is no need for HRM policies aimed at protecting training investments or reducing information asymmetries and opportunistic behaviour within the internal labour market. The prescriptions of 'soft' HRM are therefore unlikely to be put into practice in such organisations.

In contrast, structured internal labour markets are predicted where organisations operate in skilled labour markets. Employers often contribute to the costs of training of skilled workers so they have an interest in retaining them. It is also the case that skilled workers have the ability to behave opportunistically by virtue of possessing idiosyncratic job knowledge. Therefore managers are to some extent reliant on the willing cooperation of these workers. Employment security, seniority-based wage progression and opportunities for internal promotion, as well as efficiency wages, are more likely where skilled workers are employed. Indeed, the more discretion and individual responsibility workers are required to exercise in their jobs, and the greater the difficulty of exercising effective supervision, the greater will be the reliance on incentives to effort. Therefore HRM policies that are designed to reduce information asymmetries and tendencies to behave opportunistically within the internal labour market will be concentrated on skilled workers and workers required to exercise a high degree of discretion in their work roles. This may explain why HRM has been directed disproportionately towards management grades rather than lower-grade clerical and manual workers. However, there is an additional condition that must be met for HRM to be introduced: that HRM policies result in net cost reductions. Given that introducing HRM may involve significant costs, we would predict its implementation only where the perceived inefficiencies resulting from current internal labour market arrangements are considerable.

Institutionalist and radical views

Here we would argue that HRM policies are most likely to be developed in organisations where

- employee pressure has generated significant rigidities within the organisation's internal labour market, and
- there is a strong need for organisational and behavioural commitment from workers that makes co-option strategies necessary.

Again, this is most likely in organisations employing skilled workers who exercise significant discretion in their jobs. The first of the above conditions on its own is probably insufficient to encourage HRM policies. This is because the success of workers in establishing gains at the expense of organisational rigidity could simply reflect the insulation of the organisation from competition in its product market. Once exposed to these forces, organisations could opt to reduce labour costs and increase flexibility by exposing workers to competition in the labour market, as the following example shows.

Historically, unskilled workers in the public sector have enjoyed terms and conditions superior to those of workers in comparable jobs in the private sector. However, during the 1980s and 1990s Conservative governments introduced competition into large areas of the public sector by means of compulsory competitive tendering for a range of services, such as rubbish collection and hospital cleaning. Public-sector organisations were no longer allowed simply to employ their own workers to perform these tasks but had to offer contracts that private firms could bid for against the public-sector organisation. The lowest tender had to be accepted, subject in some cases to quality thresholds being met. This meant that competition from cheaper labour employed by private-sector firms forced managers in the public sector to insist that their employees raise effort levels and productivity and even accept pay reductions if work was to be kept in house.[2]

In this example the low skill content of jobs and the ready alternative supply of labour has meant that policies to elicit worker cooperation have been unnecessary, and the discipline of the market has been used to reduce labour costs.

HRM outcomes

From the competitive perspective, HRM outcomes must be viewed as positive since they are the products of efficiency-seeking behaviour. Unit costs will be lower where HRM is adopted, and pay will reflect worker productivity more accurately.

Institutionalist analysis might suggest that HRM is an efficiency-oriented response to the emergence of conflict between the external demands on organisations for flexibility and competitiveness on the one hand, and the 'rigidities' and 'inefficiencies' accumulated within their internal labour market structures on the other. While the successful implementation of HRM should therefore reduce inefficiencies in the allocation of labour and in the utilisation of both labour and capital, successful implementation cannot in itself be assumed. This is because institutionalist analysis stresses the role of different interests in the development and implementation of policies and their consequent impact on outcomes.

A perspective based on radical labour market theory sees HRM as being geared to profits rather than efficiency. HRM is depicted as extending managerial control over labour, even if in an indirect rather than a direct form, permitting the extraction of increased surplus value. However, the need to divide workers in order for this to happen means that some may gain in absolute and relative terms while others lose. Those most likely to gain are primary-sector core workers occupying high-discretion roles. However, these gains could be transitory. The co-option of high-discretion workers as part of a process of divide and rule based on segmentation of the labour market into primary and secondary sectors could be a precursor to the redesign and downgrading of high-discretion jobs. This is because labour market segmentation weakens the ability of both primary and secondary workers to resist attempts to redesign and restructure work in order to increase the rate of exploitation of labour.

Meanwhile the main losers will be workers who are displaced from the primary to the secondary sector as a result of work restructuring and the re-division of labour. Other losers may be workers who remain in the primary sector but who have nevertheless been exposed to increased competition from the external labour market. These workers may well experience work intensification and declining relative earnings. Some recent commentators have suggested that this is actually happening as employers are withdrawing from previous commitments to long-term employment security, even for 'core' workers, and the concept of employment security is being replaced by that of 'employability'. In other words, employees can no longer expect a secure job, but the employer will help to maintain the employee's value in the labour market by providing opportunities for training and updating of knowledge and skills. Thus:

> Security no longer depends on a job or an organisation, but on the employee's competences and willingness to learn and adapt to changes in the organisation and the labour market. Core employees, incidentally, pay a heavy price for their position within the organisation; in the present circumstances of persistent high unemployment, they are under constant pressure to improve their performance.
>
> (Van Ruysseveldt *et al.*, 1995: 3–4)

Essentially, this means a transfer of risk and responsibility from employer to employee, coupled with more intense exploitation.

The limits to HRM

What have been the actual outcomes? Over the last ten years research has pointed out the relatively low take-up of HRM. Thus at the end of the 1980s one leading writer pointed out that fully developed HRM was extremely rare in Britain or the USA (Guest, 1989). Significantly, he made the same point ten years later (Guest, 1998). The 1998 Workplace Employee Relations Survey (Culley *et al.*, 1999) found that while most organisations had 'relatively well-developed structures for managing employees' (p. 59), there was no compelling evidence that employers were acting more strategically than they had done in the past. 'For most employers, it might be best to characterise their approach as one of retaining control and doing what they can to contain costs' (p. 295).

At first sight the continued rarity of HRM in practice seems surprising in view of the advantages claimed for it by its proponents. Moreover, there is a growing body of evidence to suggest that where HRM policies aimed at achieving high commitment are in place, they have positive effects (Culley *et al.*, 1999). The limited take-up of HRM therefore requires explanation. As we stated above, HRM policies are costly. Policies that aim to generate high levels of worker cooperation and commitment and reduce the need for traditional forms of supervision involve considerable costs in terms of management time and resources as well as financial costs. Managers have to be convinced that the benefits of HRM will outweigh the costs of change. On this basis, we might hypothesise that an investment in HRM may not be warranted from a management point of view in a large number of cases because:

- Many organisations require low levels of skill and discretion from employees. Therefore conventional methods of controlling the effort–reward bargain are more cost-effective than HRM.
- Reductions in the size of employing establishments may have eased some of the problems of monitoring and control from management's point of view.
- Workers' ability to put pressure on the effort–reward bargain has been eroded by the rapid growth of unemployment during the early 1980s and 1990s, by legal restrictions on trade unions, and by the curtailment of legal protections for individual employees at work. These factors have had a disproportionate effect on the bargaining power of less skilled workers, but it may also be the case that managers can obtain compliance from skilled workers without having to pursue HRM policies aimed at securing willing cooperation. As one writer observed:

> Why should managers persist with complex, often delicate, schemes to involve workers in pro-
> duction systems, when the grim state of the market required swift and abrasive action. Far
> quicker and cheaper to play on employees' fears and kick a few arses, while trusting that the law
> has taken care of the unions.   (Dunn, 1993)

The evidence from a large-scale survey conducted during the early 1990s supports this point of view. It found that during the 1980s and early 1990s professional and managerial staff were given more discretion in their roles and were less subject to direct supervision, but the reverse was the case for manual workers, who were subject to closer supervision than before (Gallie *et.al.*, 1998). Fully developed HRM remains rare. Diluted and partial applications of HRM are probably more widespread, but a large number of organisations continue to pursue traditional policies that rely on unilateral managerial control to regulate the employment relationship.

Summary

So far we have viewed HRM from three different labour market perspectives. In each case, however, we have defined HRM as an attempt by employers to modify the operation of internal labour markets in response to changing external pressures. HRM has been presented as a means by which managers seek to reduce the costs that arise from perceived inefficiencies or obstacles to the exploitation of labour that are embedded in existing internal labour market structures.

This allows us to say something about why HRM so rarely appears in the fully developed form set out in so many textbooks. Briefly, we have argued that HRM is most likely to be attempted in organisations where bureaucratic mechanisms for the management of labour have replaced direct labour market competition. At the same time, HRM initiatives will be more likely to occur when the workforce is predominantly composed of skilled, high-discretion workers. This is because HRM is itself costly, and traditional forms of management may be more cost-effective than HRM in many organisational settings. Interestingly, these predictions remain broadly the same whichever theoretical labour market perspective we use as the basis for our analysis.

Regarding outcomes, the competitive approach suggests that HRM will result in efficiency gains. However, given the recognition of the relevance of bargaining power, which is implicit in some versions of this approach, such as asymmetric information and insider–outsider models, group processes and collective pressures may influence outcomes in ways not necessarily consistent with cost minimisation.

Institutionalist and radical approaches pay more attention to the processes by which the employment relationship is regulated. Indeed, an understanding of the various influences on processes is seen as essential to a proper explanation of outcomes. The subjects of HRM, the employees themselves, as well as their managers will influence HRM processes and outcomes in central rather than merely marginal ways. The force of this argument is illustrated in the following section.

CONTROVERSIES: THE FLEXIBILITY DEBATE

The central argument of this chapter so far has been that HRM involves the reshaping of organisations' labour markets so as to facilitate the more efficient use of labour or, alternatively, its more effective exploitation. The concept of flexibility has developed as a central theme in discussions of how to reshape organisations' labour markets. The search for labour flexibility has come to be seen as part of 'strategic' HRM with its 'hard' emphasis on the planned use of labour aimed at reducing unit costs of production. While labour is a valued resource, it has to be deployed as efficiently as possible. This approach has found popular expression in the term *lean production*, used to label production systems that minimise overhead labour costs by stripping out jobs that do not contribute directly to production, and by looking for ways to economise on the use of directly productive labour. Flexibility in this sense means the ability to adjust the size and mix of labour inputs in response to changes in product demand so that 'excess' labour is not carried by the organisation.

At the same time 'soft' HRM techniques, such as employee involvement and programmes for employee development, are represented as ways of achieving certain forms of flexibility at work. By involving workers in managerial decisions and plans for organisational change and by broadening workers' skills through training, HRM claims to create workforces that are *functionally* flexible. This means workers who are willing and able to acquire new or additional skills as production requirements change, and who accept the need for their periodic redeployment within the organisation. Taken together, the ability to 'flex' the amount of labour inputs and redeploy workers across tasks amounts to a restructuring of internal labour markets.

An important element of tension within HRM is how far the 'hard' emphasis on managing the size of the workforce and utilising labour more fully is consistent with the 'soft' emphasis on obtaining worker cooperation with management and raising performance through improved skills and motivation. This tension is clearly illustrated through the flexibility debate. This debate has been conducted on three interrelated levels. First, what is the best economic development path that countries can take in view of the fundamental changes taking place in the international economy? Second, how can European economies in particular escape from persistently high levels of unemployment that have plagued them for more than a decade? And finally, what kinds of flexibility should be sought at organisational level to ensure a combination of innovation, competitiveness and employee commitment?

Flexibility strategies for economic development

At the level of national development strategy, the question is: how can regional and national economies respond to the changes that have taken place in the international economy since the 1970s, often referred to as globalisation? Key aspects of these changes are:

- increasingly volatile and uncertain product markets;
- the accelerated pace of technological change;
- the emergence of newly industrialised countries since the 1970s such as Japan, Taiwan, Korea, other countries in the Far East and Pacific Rim and, latterly, Eastern Europe;
- the international mobility of capital that has resulted from liberalisation of financial markets, the application of information technology and the growing importance of multinational corporations. As a consequence there is a developing tendency for national governments to compete with each other for employment-creating international investment by offering flexible labour market conditions to prospective investors;
- a long-term rise in unemployment throughout most of Western Europe, linked to an inability to generate new jobs.

Two radically different strategies involving different types of labour flexibility have been put forward as alternative paths to future economic development. The first has been labelled a strategy of *defensive flexibility*.

Defensive flexibility

Defensive flexibility is an attempt to preserve existing patterns of comparative advantage in international trade by competing on the basis of cost and price. Mature industrial economies such as the USA and the major economies of Western Europe are characterised by high wages and, in Western Europe, a highly developed and costly system of social welfare benefits and employment rights for workers. Faced with the growth of competition from low-wage, newly industrialised parts of the world, the defensive flexibility strategy is one of reducing costs of production. Since labour costs are usually the most significant element of costs, and certainly the most variable, this means reducing wages in relative if not absolute terms and cutting non-wage costs of employment such as the level of financial contributions that employers have to make in order to fund welfare benefits. It also means enabling employers to reduce costs by giving them greater freedom to hire and fire as production requirements change. It has also been claimed that this strategy attracts direct foreign investment, since foreign-owned businesses will be encouraged to establish operations where labour costs are low in relation to the achievable level of labour productivity (see Chapter 16 for examples).

The emphasis in this approach is on labour market flexibility. It seeks to move closer to the competitive model of the labour market in which labour is a commodity pure and simple. Wages are flexible in that they are flexible downwards as well as upwards. Relative wages are free to change according to changes in the demand for different types of labour. Hire and fire means that employment levels are flexible in that they can be adjusted quickly in response to changes in the level of demand. Firms are also free to employ workers on 'non-standard' contracts, such as part-time, temporary, or fixed term, that may allow them to adjust labour inputs more easily as demand changes, as well as being able to offer such workers less in the form of wages and non-wage benefits. The emphasis then, is on *wage flexibility* and *numerical flexibility* of labour.

A number of criticisms can be levelled at the defensive flexibility strategy. First, the extent to which mature industrial economies face direct competition from newly industrialised, low-wage economies is limited. Most of the trade of advanced industrial countries is with other advanced industrial countries. Japan and Korea are no longer low-wage countries compared with much of Western Europe, including the UK. Therefore the extent of necessary cost reductions is probably exaggerated. Second, it is by no means certain that advanced industrial countries could cheapen labour sufficiently to compete with low-wage competition from newly developing parts of the world. If this is true, then defensive flexibility is a strategy of fruitless sacrifice. Third, it may undermine economic development and prosperity in the long run. This is so because, if employers are encouraged to employ cheap labour on a hire-and-fire basis, there will be little incentive for either employers or employees to invest in training. A lack of trained, skilled workers will mean slower rates of technical innovation, leading to increasing technological backwardness, relative underdevelopment and poor-quality, low-skilled jobs compared with technologically more progressive economies (Nolan, 1989; Dex and McCulloch, 1997).

Offensive flexibility

The alternative to defensive flexibility is a strategy of *offensive flexibility* based on 'diversified quality production' or 'flexible specialisation' (Lane, 1995: 151–152). This path to development seeks to develop new areas of competitive advantage by exploiting new technologies and new market opportunities rather than defend existing ones against low-cost competition. It is argued that by taking the lead in the development of new products and services, particularly those that embody high levels of research and development, creative design capability and high quality, economies pursuing this path will be able to maintain high wages and comprehensive social benefits for their populations. This implies that the country in question has the capacity to invent and innovate and to create as well as identify new opportunities in international markets. The kind of labour flexibility sought here will be the capacity of workers to acquire high-level skills, be adaptive to changes in technology and acquire further skills where necessary. It will also include the capacity of workers to undertake a range of skilled tasks rather than a single specialist task so that they can be redeployed easily and quickly to new tasks as technology changes and new products and production techniques are developed. Highly trained, multi-skilled workers are also seen as a source of new ideas for improvements in products and production processes. In other words, the emphasis is on *functional flexibility* of highly skilled labour. This strategy for flexible development surely sounds far more attractive than defensive flexibility, and seems more in tune with the ideals of HRM. However, the capacity for functional flexibility of this order may not be as widespread as we would like to think. It depends on a variety of factors. Some of the most important are:

- a highly skilled labour force and a highly developed, effective form of education and vocational training;
- a high degree of cooperation between workers and management;
- willingness among firms to make large long-term investments in capital equipment and training;
- security of employment for workers. This is generally seen as a condition for long-term investments in training and for the high levels of cooperation between workers and management that are seen to be central to flexible specialisation;
- a system of corporate governance that encourages firms to take a long-term view of their performance. Excessive attention to year-on-year profit and loss accounts biases firms against long-term investment since it figures as a negative item in the balance sheet.

These factors occur rarely in combination, and may not apply to all sectors of an economy. For this reason it may not be possible to avoid pressures for cost reduction, wage flexibility and numerical flexibility.

Labour market flexibility

The opposition between defensive and offensive flexibility is replicated in the recent debates over European labour market flexibility. Within Europe, concern over labour market flexibility, or rather the perceived lack of it, emerged as a result of the changes experienced by Western European economies during the 1970s and 1980s. These changes undermined what had come to be seen as a stable pattern of economic growth and rising living standards in the 1950s and 1960s. During the 1990s employment flexibility continued to be a central theme in debates over how Western Europe should respond to the changes in the international economy that have been summarised above.

At the level of the labour market the flexibility debate has been about the reasons for unemployment and low rates of job creation. Unemployment across the European Union has been on an upward trend since the early 1970s. Average unemployment across the European Union stood at 10% or more throughout 1992–98, with half of those unemployed being out of work for more than a year (European Commission, 1999). An important reason for this is Europe's inability to generate jobs. During the recession of 1991–94 there was a net loss of 4.9 million jobs across the EU. By 1996, after two years of recovery, there were still 3.5 million fewer people in work than in 1991 (European Commission, 1998a). This performance is seen to be in sharp contrast to that of the USA, where there has been little if any trend rise in unemployment, and where the level has been consistently lower than in Europe since the early 1980s.

Advocates of the free market have blamed so-called 'rigidities' within labour markets in Western Europe for high unemployment and low job creation. Legally enforceable employment rights for workers and trade union bargaining power have been presented as examples of rigidity: that is, obstacles that prevent the labour market from adjusting to the changes that have taken place in product markets and technology. For example, it is widely argued that restrictions on employers' rights to dismiss workers have prevented labour from being released from stagnant or declining sectors for employment in more dynamic areas of the economy. It is also argued that by making it more difficult for employers to dismiss workers, employment protection legislation has effectively raised the costs of employment to employers, discouraged them from creating new jobs, and led them in the long run to substitute capital for labour in production (Giersch, 1986). In addition, generous social welfare benefits have been blamed for discouraging the unemployed from undertaking job search. Trade unions have also been accused of preventing the wage adjustments needed to encourage the reallocation of labour in the economy and permit fuller employment (Hayek, 1984). A linked argument is that centralised bargaining over pay and conditions in some EU countries has prevented firms from being able to respond to the challenges of international competition and the opportunities presented by new technology by developing new pay and reward systems and reorganising work. This situation has been contrasted with that in the USA, where employers have freedom to hire and fire at will, social security benefits are minimal and conditional on recipients taking available jobs or undertaking training, union power is limited and collective bargaining is highly decentralised.

Labour market flexibility is achieved by removing rigidities so as to allow the labour market to approximate more closely to the competitive model. According to free market theorists, this implies a particular set of labour market policies:

- Reduce legal restrictions on the hiring and dismissal of workers.
- Remove state intervention in pay setting, for example, abolish minimum wage legislation.
- Make out-of-work benefits less generous and/or limit the duration of benefits and/or make them conditional on recipients actively searching for work.
- Increase the employability of the unemployed by providing them with training.
- Use the law and government policy to curb trade union influence over pay and employment.
- Decentralise collective bargaining to enterprise level.

Clearly this view, which guided British government policy on employment issues throughout the 1980s and much of the 1990s, can be seen to involve a bias towards defensive flexibility as a development strategy. As we have seen, the alternative vision is to develop a high-skills, high-wage response to changes in the world economy. This means developing high value-added products where competition is on the basis of quality rather than simply on price. This requires highly trained and highly skilled workers, willingness to invest long term, and high levels of management–worker cooperation within organisations. For the reasons outlined earlier in this chapter, it is widely held that these conditions are unlikely to be realised within a framework of hire and fire and downward pressure on pay and working conditions. A measure of labour market regulation is necessary in order to encourage employers to look for ways of achieving functional rather than numerical flexibility and promote high-quality training and employee participation in decision-making.

The debate between these two positions has been at the centre of recent European discussions on employment and unemployment. Some of the most important member states within the EU, such as France and Germany, have been reluctant to go down the path of labour market deregulation and have therefore espoused strategies of offensive flexibility. However, since the mid-1980s, largely owing to concern over the scale and persistence of unemployment, there has been a growing readiness within these countries, as in Europe generally, to relax certain forms of state regulation of labour markets and increase opportunities for wage and numerical flexibility. In practice this has chiefly meant reducing some of the administrative procedures that employers have to go through before dismissing workers, and easing the restrictions on shift working and part-time and temporary working. There has also been a tendency to limit the scope of centralised collective bargaining so as to allow more issues to be decided at the enterprise level (Ferner and Hyman, 1998).

Nevertheless, the European Union has not followed the simple course of labour market deregulation recommended by the free market economists. Most European Union member states and the European Commission have sought increased labour market flexibility within a reformed framework of regulation. While this has meant the relaxation of some regulations, there is a commitment to ensuring that so-called 'non-standard' workers, such as those on part-time, temporary and fixed-term contracts, enjoy the same employment rights as full-time, permanent workers (European Commission, 1999). The European Commission has also espoused the principle that in a more flexible, more decentralised and less closely regulated labour market, workers should have enhanced rights of representation and participation in decision-making (Gill et al., 1999). This is linked to the Commission's continued emphasis on the importance of competing on the basis of highly skilled, functionally flexible labour. In particular, the Commission is encouraging negotiation and consultation between management and worker representatives at enterprise level on ways of reorganising work and developing continuous learning within organisations.

In these respects it is possible to see some signs of convergence between the official European Union approach to the labour market and that of the UK under 'New Labour'. While the trend in mainland Europe is towards reducing the 'burden' of regulation on employers, in the UK the New Labour government has, since 1997, introduced a national minimum wage, strengthened employment protection, given trade unions the legal right to be recognised by employers,[3] and encouraged union–management 'partnerships' to improve productivity and raise the level of skills within enterprises.

The overall thrust of labour market policy in Europe as well as the UK has been to make it easier for organisations to develop their own employment policies. In theory this increases the opportunity for organisations to develop proactive employment strategies and determine terms and conditions of employment in line with their overall strategic aims. The next question to consider is how organisations are using this increased freedom to restructure their workforces and redefine employment relationships.

Organisational flexibility

At the organisational level, it is widely claimed that increased flexibility in the use of labour has been sought for the following reasons:

- Increased market volatility and uncertainty require that organisations should improve their ability to adapt to changes in markets. The implications for the management of labour are that organisations should be freer to vary the size and composition of their workforces in line with changes in demand.
- The acceleration of technological change, and the pervasiveness of applications of microprocessor technologies in particular, has eroded traditional job definitions and divisions between jobs. There is a need to reorganise work and redesign jobs in ways best suited to the efficient use of the new technology.
- The intensification of international competition has increased the importance of reducing unit costs of production and raising product quality. This, in turn, demands work reorganisation and job redesign to raise labour productivity and build quality into the production process.

However, the question of how far and in what ways organisations are reshaping their employment policies in the light of these factors has given rise to considerable debate. The key issues that have emerged in this discussion are:

- What forms of labour flexibility are being sought by organisations?
- What are the reasons for such changes? Is flexibility being developed as a strategic response to changes in market conditions? Is it an aspect of strategic HRM?
- What are the consequences of increased flexibility? Are they consistent with the emphasis on 'high commitment' within HRM?

We shall take the model of the 'flexible firm' as the starting point for our discussion of these issues.

The 'flexible firm' model

The model of the flexible firm was developed during the mid-1980s at the Institute for Employment Studies at the University of Sussex (Atkinson, 1984, 1985). It starts by identifying the different forms of labour flexibility that might be sought by organisations and how they might be achieved. These elements are then brought together in the model of the 'flexible firm'. Four types of flexibility are identified:

- *Numerical flexibility*, defined as the 'ability to adjust the level of labour inputs to meet fluctuations in output' (Atkinson and Meager, 1986: 3–4). This is achieved by altering working hours or by altering the number of workers employed.
- *Functional flexibility*, defined as 'the firm's ability to adjust and deploy the skills of its employees to match the tasks required by its changing workload, production methods and/or technology' (Atkinson and Meager, 1986: 4). Functional flexibility is obtained by training workers to perform a wider variety of tasks, and by breaking down barriers to the deployment of workers across tasks.
- *Distancing*, in other words replacing employees with subcontractors. Contracts of service (employment contracts), are replaced by contracts for services (commercial contracts). Distancing, or 'outsourcing', will be applied to functions that are not seen as being part of the core business: for example, for a manufacturing company, catering, cleaning, security, possibly even the personnel function! This reduces the firm's overhead and running costs since it can obtain these services at lower cost than it could provide them in house, partly because it does not have to bear the administrative costs of maintaining its own staff.
- *Pay flexibility*, 'concerned with the extent to which a company's pay and reward structure supports and reinforces the various types of numerical and/or functional

flexibility which are being sought' (Atkinson and Meager, 1986: 4). Flexible approaches to pay centre around linking pay to performance – of individuals, groups, or the enterprise as a whole. Pay can also be linked to the adoption of functionally flexible working practices.

Taken together, these elements amount to 'a reorganisation of firms' internal labour markets and their division into separate components, in which the worker's experience and the employer's expectations of him/her are increasingly differentiated' (Atkinson and Gregory, 1986: 13). The form of this reorganisation is illustrated in Figure 3.1. As we can see, the segmentation of the employed workforce is into 'core' workers and various categories of 'peripheral' workers.

The core workers deliver functional flexibility by virtue of training, retraining and re-deployment across tasks. The size and composition of the core will depend on organisational decisions on work organisation and the design of jobs, since core worker status applies mainly to those supplying firm-specific skills. Because organisations will have to invest in training core workers they will try to provide long-term employment security in order to protect their training investment. Moreover, continuity of employment is necessary for the build-up of skills and experience, which form the basis for

Figure 3.1 The 'flexible firm'

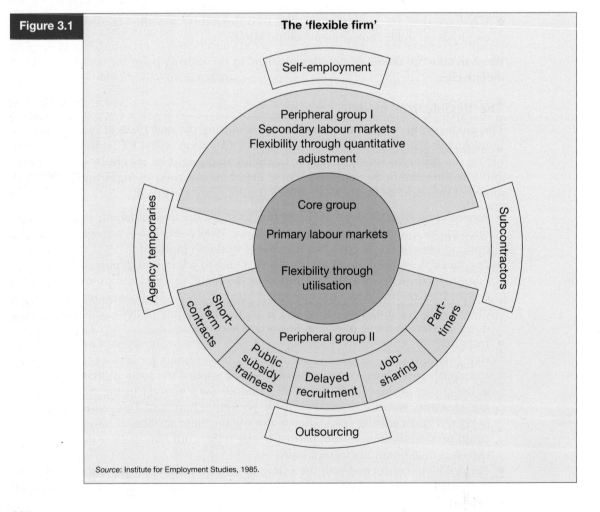

Source: Institute for Employment Studies, 1985.

functional flexibility. Additionally, management is reliant on the cooperation of core workers in implementing and adapting to change. Therefore the model predicts that policies of co-option based on 'soft' HRM will be directed at the core workforce.

Peripheral workers supply numerical flexibility. That is, they are subject to variations in hours and to lay-off and rehiring as required. Again, the size of the periphery will reflect the nature of skills sought by the organisation. Peripheral workers will supply skills that are easily obtainable in the external labour market, and their cooperation in the production process is not critical to organisational performance. The peripheral workforce is made up of:

- full-time employees having little prospect of secure, continuous employment;
- workers employed on 'non-standard' contracts of employment, such as temporary, part-time and casual workers;
- 'distance workers' – that is, workers not directly employed by the organisation but supplying their services as self-employed contractors or as employees of firms supplying services on a contract basis.

By providing numerical flexibility in this way, peripheral workers also act as a buffer between the product market and the core workforce. Numerical flexibility of the periphery supports employment security in the core. One of the predictions of the model is that peripheral workers will be 'exposed more and more to raw market forces'. In other words there will be a growing divergence in the work experience of core and peripheral workers in terms of pay, access to training, career progression and employment security (Atkinson and Gregory, 1986: 13).

The claimed benefits of the flexible firm to employers include the following:

- reduced labour costs from lower wage and non-wage employment costs in the periphery;
- the ability to tailor the size of the workforce to changing demand levels so as to reduce costs arising from carrying excess labour or, alternatively, from labour shortages;
- increased productivity from the core workforce.

From a radical perspective the further segmentation of the workforce represents an extension of divide-and-rule strategies for extending managerial control and increasing the effective exploitation of labour.

For workers, the claimed benefits are that functional flexibility provides better-quality, more highly skilled jobs that allow workers to exercise more discretion and responsibility in their work. The growth of numerically flexible jobs gives people a wider choice of types of work, and allows those who do not want full-time, permanent employment better opportunities to combine work with other aspects of their lives. From a radical perspective, however, it is argued that functional flexibility involves work intensification and work-related stress, while the discretion and control that employees are supposed to enjoy is largely illusory (Parker and Slaughter, 1988). Critics also claim that numerically flexible jobs are mainly low-status jobs offering low pay and few prospects, and that they reflect gendered patterns of discrimination because they are occupied disproportionately by women (Dex and McCulloch, 1997).

We can now summarise the ways in which the model of the flexible firm addresses the questions outlined at the beginning of this section. First, the model predicts that various forms of flexibility will be sought, ideally in combination with each other: numerical, functional and pay flexibility. Second, the flexible firm model is represented as a strategic response to the need to be able to respond quickly to changes in the level of demand, the pattern of demand, the need for faster rates of innovation, and the need to be competitive in terms of costs. Third, the model predicts that the effects of the flexible firm will be different for employers, core workers and peripheral workers. Employers gain in terms of cost savings and the ability to respond to changes in markets and technology. Core workers benefit from good pay, employment security and access to training, but the price they may have to pay for this is work intensification and more frequent redeployment. The majority of peripheral workers will lack employment security and access to training, although there will be a significant minority of highly paid workers who supply scarce technical or professional services as self-employed contractors or consultants.[4] The implication is that 'core' workers may be the recipients of 'soft' HRM policies aimed at fostering loyalty and commitment, while 'peripheral' workers represent the 'hard' face of HRM, since they are treated as disposable so that firms can match labour inputs to production requirements as closely as possible. A positive aspect of the expansion of part–time and temporary work, however, is that it provides employment opportunities for those who would like to take paid work but do not want full-time or permanent employment.

How valid are these claims? Does empirical evidence support the model's predictions that a combination of different forms of flexibility will be sought as part of a strategic response to new pressures on organisations? Does it support the prediction that 'core' and 'peripheral' workers will be subject to increasingly different treatment by management in terms of pay and conditions and employment status? What are the implications of workforce restructuring for HRM policies aimed at getting high commitment from employees? These questions are addressed below.

The flexible firm: empirical evidence

What forms of flexibility are employers and managers seeking?

Numerical flexibility
There is evidence of increased use of flexible forms of labour on an international scale. Across the EU, the 1990s saw a net decline in the number of full-time, permanent jobs. Employment growth has been the result of more part-time and temporary or fixed-term jobs. Part-time employment rose from 12.7% of total employment in the EU in 1985 to 16.9% in 1997. Employment on fixed-term contracts rose from 8.4% to 12.2% of the total. Moreover, a growing proportion of new jobs is both part time and temporary (European Commission, 1999: 46–47, 149). In addition, there has been a trend towards increased use of shift working and systems of annualised hours, which allow for greater flexibility in employers' use of workers' time. Some recent studies have also commented on the growth of numerically flexible forms of employment in the United States (Rosenberg and Lapidus, 1999).

The pattern of numerically flexible employment is highly variable across different countries. For example, Britain has a relatively high proportion of part-time workers (about 25% of total employment). Only the Netherlands has a higher proportion of part-time workers, at 38% of total employment (European Commission, 1999: 159, 164). Sweden also appears to be a heavy user of part-time workers, but in Sweden part-time work is defined as working fewer than 35 hours per week, compared with fewer than 30 hours in the UK (Dex and McCulloch, 1997: 159). On the other hand, the UK is one of the lowest users of temporary and fixed-term contract workers in Europe (7.4% of total employment). Only Belgium and Luxembourg have a smaller proportion of employees on fixed-term contracts. Spain is by far the greatest user of fixed-term employment, with one-third of all employees being on fixed-term contracts of employment (European Commission, 1999: 149–164).

There is considerable evidence that organisations in the UK are making more use of some forms of 'flexible labour', but it is less certain that this reflects a radical restructuring of employment in organisations. A study by Casey *et al.* (1997), based on data from the 1994 Labour Force Survey, found that overtime was still the most common way in which British employers obtained numerical flexibility, followed by the use of part-time workers, and that this gave employers only limited ability to vary total hours worked (p. 16). Part-time working has always been common in the UK, and it has grown steadily, if unspectacularly, as a proportion of total employment since the 1980s from 21.2% in 1985 to 24.9% in 1997 (European Commission, 1999: 164). Some of this growth can be attributed to the expansion of employment in sectors that have traditionally employed part-time labour, such as retail, and hotels and catering. The 1990s also saw a rapid rise in the number of workers employed on fixed-term contracts and 'zero-hours' contracts.[5] (Culley *et al.*, 1999: 35–36). However, although the proportion of workers in the UK who are employed on fixed-term contracts grew during the 1990s (from 5.2% in 1990 to 7.4% in 1997), this figure is only marginally higher than the 1985 figure of 7% (European Commission, 1999: 164).

Tele-working and freelancing by 'portfolio workers' – frequently hailed in the news media and popular management literature as the work patterns of the future – have as yet been adopted to only a limited extent. Only 13% of all workplaces covered by the 1998 Workplace Employee Relations Survey made use of freelance workers, and just 5% used home workers (Culley *et al.*, 1999: 35).

On the other hand, changes in the composition of directly employed workforces understate the extent to which organisations may have increased flexibility by contracting out certain functions to external suppliers. Ninety per cent of workplaces covered in the 1998 Workplace Employee Relations Survey had contracted out at least one function that was previously provided in house(Culley *et al.*, 1999).

Functional flexibility

There is also evidence that organisations have sought changes in working practices that involve reductions in demarcation between jobs and allow for easier redeployment of workers across tasks. Once again, patterns vary across countries. Most studies agree that, in Europe, functional flexibility is most highly developed and widespread in Germany. This has been attributed to the willingness of German firms to make long-term investments, the high quality of the system of vocational training in Germany, and a system of industrial relations that encourages cooperation in the workplace. These features of the German business system have underpinned Germany's espousal of an 'offensive flexibility' strategy based on 'diversified quality production' (Lane, 1995). Even so, Lane refers to rigidities in the organisation and management of German enterprises, and a recent comparative study warns against ignoring the continued importance of semi-skilled and unskilled labour in the German economy (Lane, 1995; Smith and Elger, 1997).

By comparison, other major European economies such as France and the UK have made more limited progress towards diversified quality production and hence the development of functionally flexible workforces. In France, employers have increased the rate of product and process innovation, increased training, and have also tried to achieve more flexibility in the use of labour. A recent study by Jenkins (1998) reports evidence of innovation in the organisation of work, including 'just-in-time' production, quality control circles and team working. These innovations have been most widespread in the machinery and equipment manufacturing industries and the energy and materials sector. Even so, cross-functional teams, which might be thought to embody functional flexibility, were present in just 34% of all companies surveyed in 1993 (p. 261). Moreover, in many cases, functionally flexible workers do not enjoy the pay and employment security envisaged for 'core' workers in the flexible firm model. Jenkins found that in car plants in particular, employees had limited skills, were not very well paid, and did not have employment security.

As far as Britain is concerned there is evidence to suggest that, despite claims of widespread increases in the skill content of jobs, there have been only limited increases in functional flexibility. The Employment in Britain Survey, carried out during the early 1990s, found evidence of 'very extensive upskilling of the workforce', particularly among 'skilled manual workers, technicians, lower non-manual employees, and professionals and managers' (Gallie *et al.*, 1998: 55–56). At roughly the same time, the third Workplace Industrial Relations Survey, conducted in 1990, found that 36% of all workplaces in the sample reported changes in working practices aimed at increasing flexibility (Millward *et al.*, 1992).

Despite these developments, the extent to which functional flexibility has been developed is limited. The ideal depicted by the proponents of the flexible firm was the 'multi-skilled craft worker' who was able to straddle hitherto discrete areas of work such as mechanical and electrical engineering operations. Generally, there has been little progress in this direction. A study carried out at the end of the 1980s found that where craft workers had developed some functional flexibility it was generally limited to carrying out relatively minor additional tasks linked to their main skill. The expansion of the work of machine and process plant operators had usually been restricted to very minor maintenance work only (Cross, 1988). Further studies during the early 1990s confirmed these results (Legge, 1995). Employers were not creating 'all-round craftsmen' but were seeking instead to equip craft workers with such additional skills as were 'necessary to progress specific tasks more quickly, by avoiding the need to call on other craftsmen' (Incomes Data Services, 1994: 1). The number of workers affected by even these modest developments was limited in 1990. The third Workplace Industrial Relations Survey found that changes in working practices affecting 'all non-managerial employees' had taken place in only 8% of establishments (Millward *et al.*, 1992). Even by the end of the 1990s only 23% of workplaces had a majority of workers who were functionally flexible in the sense of being formally trained to be able to do jobs other than their own, while 58% had none or just a few (Culley *et al.*, 1999: 35).

These findings give some support to the argument that British-owned manufacturing firms are seeking 'forms of functional flexibility that allow the employment of semi-skilled or unskilled labour' (Ackroyd and Procter, 1998: 174). This approach to functional flexibility can be seen to be concerned mainly with work intensification through job enlargement, rather than with a shift to diversified quality production on the basis of increased skills and job enrichment.

Is the use of flexible labour strategic?

Reasons for employing flexible labour

The model of the flexible firm sees flexibility of labour as a strategic response to changes in technology and markets. It is presented as a strategy that combines adaptability through multi-skilling and redeployment (functional labour flexibility) with the ability to vary the quantity of labour (numerical flexibility). Pay flexibility enables wage costs to be controlled and linked to performance. So to what extent have firms made conscious use of the flexible firm model when restructuring their workforces?

The idea that British firms might be acting strategically in their changing use of labour has been viewed with scepticism. A large body of research has found British management to be reactive and pragmatic in its approach to business decision-making in general and the management of employees in particular (Hunter and MacInnes, 1991; Storey, 1992; Sisson and Marginson, 1995). These characteristics have been attributed to the low quality of British management in terms of its technical expertise, and to the prevalence of short-termism in British business (Nolan, 1989; Lane, 1995; Sisson and Marginson, 1995).

During the late 1980s and early 1990s empirical research into the take-up of the flexible firm in Britain suggested that moves to increase the number of non-standard workers and improve the flexibility of working practices were not guided by a strategic model of the flexible firm. A major survey of employers who had made use of one or more types of non-standard labour found that the reasons for employing such workers were much the same as they had always been. Tasks requiring limited time to complete and the need to match staffing levels to demand were the main reasons for hiring part-time workers. Temporary workers were hired mainly to meet fluctuations in demand, deal with one-off tasks, and provide cover for absent permanent workers. There was no evidence that firms as a rule were using non-standard workers to provide employment security for a core of functionally flexible workers. Neither was there strong evidence to suggest that employers saw non-standard labour as a way of reducing wage costs by paying lower rates compared with full-time, permanent workers. In most cases hourly rates of pay were the same for all workers (McGregor and Sproull, 1992).

On the other hand, there were signs in the early 1990s that employers might be beginning to develop a more strategic approach to the use of non-standard, or peripheral, workers. Organisations that were *increasing* their use of non-standard workers were much more likely than others to give reasons for doing so that were more in line with the flexibility thesis: that is, reduced wage and non-wage costs and lower unionisation (McGregor and Sproull, 1992). This was partially confirmed by the 1998 Workplace

---

Activity   **Reasons for hiring temporary workers in 1999**

A paper manufacturing company reported that it used temporary workers because they were suited to low-skilled labouring occupations.

A National Health Service hospital trust reported increased use of temporary workers because of a shortage of nurses and other skilled workers.

Post Office Counters reported that some of its information technology posts are filled permanently by temporary staff because they could not recruit permanent staff to some specialist posts.

A city council reported increased use of temporary workers in response to reorganisation and contracting out, which had led to uncertainty about the number of permanent staff required.

A county council stated that temporary workers were being hired rather than permanent employees because of tight budgets.

Source: Industrial Relations Services, *IRS Employment Trends 677*, April 1999: 4–9.

1   Which, if any, of these cases can be described as a strategic use of temporary workers?

2   Explain why one organisation sees temporary workers as only suited to low-skilled jobs while others feel able to appoint them to skilled tasks.

Employee Relations Survey. Its findings are that private-sector employers appear to be adopting one or the other of two 'routes to flexibility' in their use of non-standard labour, both aimed at minimising labour costs rather than at developing flexible specialisation. The first aims at taking advantage of wider labour market flexibility and minimising wage costs through the extensive use of low-paid, low-skilled, part-time, female labour. The second aims at reducing wage and non-wage costs of employment through numerical flexibility, which is achieved by wide use of sub-contracting and other forms of non-standard labour (Culley *et al.*, 1999: 45). However, while there is evidence that firms may be making strategic use of numerically flexible labour, there is little evidence that they are dividing their workforces along the lines of 'core' and 'periphery'.

A core–periphery strategy?

Before addressing the empirical evidence, it is worth noting that the model of the flexible firm raises some conceptual difficulties. The core–periphery concept is central to the flexible firm model. However, critics have pointed to problems in making the distinction between core and peripheral workers. The model itself appears to use the nature of the skills required of the worker as its main basis. Atkinson and Meager (1986) suggest that workers will be included in the core where they possess organisation-specific skills, and their active cooperation with management is central to the production of the good or service. However, this ignores the question of how skill is defined, and the possibility that workers and their unions may use bargaining power to influence decisions as to who should be included in the core. It also ignores the possibility that workers who are numerically flexible carry out core functions. Do they then get included in the core? For example, a retail store employs part-time sales assistants. Because they are part time these workers fall into the 'peripheral' category. However, as front-line sales assistants, their efforts are central to the business. Does this make them 'core' workers? For a fuller development of these issues see Pollert (1988) and Legge (1995).

Empirical evidence does not support the prediction that firms are combining functional flexibility in the core with numerical flexibility at the periphery. Reality is more complex. First, and in line with the predictions of the flexible firm model, organisations that pursue functional flexibility do tend to contract out peripheral functions, such as cleaning, security, certain maintenance work, and training. This 'leaves them free to concentrate on developing the skills of the core workforce' (Culley *et al.*, 1999: 38). However, it is also the case that, where functional flexibility is being pursued, there is less likelihood that use will be made of non-standard *employees* to provide numerical flexibility (Culley *et al.*, 1999). This contradicts the flexible firm model, which predicts that firms will pursue both functional *and* numerical flexibility among their own direct employees as well as 'distancing'.

Second, where numerical flexibility is sought, it extends to core functions and is not confined to peripheral ones. The Employment in Britain Survey found that similar proportions of temporary workers as of permanent workers were employed in managerial and professional roles, lower non-manual and skilled manual jobs (Gallie *et al.*, 1998: 174–175). Similarly, the 1998 Workplace Employee Relations Survey found that when non-permanent workers are employed, they are most likely to be employed alongside and in the same functions as the largest occupational group within the workforce – that is, the 'core' workforce. The implication of this is that where numerical flexibility is sought, it is as likely to be in core functions as in peripheral ones (Culley *et al.*, 1999). This provides a further contradiction of the flexible firm model. Temporary workers in core functions do, however, provide a cushion that protects permanent workers from demand fluctuations, as argued in the original model of the flexible firm. Managers report that use of temporary and fixed-term contract labour in core activities is motivated by a desire to 'buttress' the core workforce and make 'short-term adjustments to the size of it' (Culley *et al.*, 1999: 38). However, the original distinction between core and periphery breaks down, since numerical flexibility is not confined to the 'periphery' but extends into the 'core'.

We can conclude that employers are making greater use of various forms of flexible labour, that in Britain the bias is towards numerical rather than functional flexibility, and that numerical flexibility extends to core functions. The available evidence suggests strongly that organisations are not pursuing functional and numerical flexibility of labour as a joint strategy; instead, numerical flexibility and functional flexibility offer alternative approaches to organisational flexibility. Where employers are seeking functional flexibility, it is of a more limited kind than that envisaged in the model of the flexible firm. In Britain and France it seems that so-called 'core' workers enjoy only limited employment security and career progression, and do not conform to the core worker stereotype in the flexible firm model (Ackroyd and Procter, 1998; Jenkins, 1998). The distinction between a highly trained, functionally flexible core workforce and a numerically flexible periphery is therefore problematic, conceptually and empirically.

Pay flexibility?

The argument that firms have been adopting a strategic approach to flexibility would be strengthened if there were evidence that flexible payments systems, in which pay is linked to performance or to greater flexibility of working practices, are in general use. Pay can be linked to different types of performance: individual performance, the performance of the work group or team, or the overall performance of the organisation. The large-scale survey evidence indicates that none of these forms of flexible pay was widespread during the early 1990s. Sixteen per cent of workers surveyed in the Employment in Britain Survey said that they received individual performance-related payments. Only 6% reported that they received any team bonus payment. Twenty-two per cent said that a proportion of their pay was linked to organisational performance.[6] Incremental pay scales were the commonest form of payments system reported, and a large majority of workers felt that pay rises were given to all workers, regardless of their performance (Gallie *et al.* 1998: 166–168).

More recent evidence of the limits to the use of pay as part of a wider strategic approach to organisational flexibility is provided in a study based on the Warwick University Industrial Relations Research Unit's Pay and Working Time Survey for 1997 (Arrowsmith and Sisson, 1999). This study, which covered engineering, printing, National Health Service trusts and retail, found that, while skill and qualifications were cited as an influence on pay by between 38% and 55% of respondents across these sectors, individual and group incentive payments were relatively uncommon. Moreover, while 'a sizeable minority' of respondents reported using appraisal and merit pay, this affected only a small proportion of the workforces concerned and involved 'relatively small sums' (p. 58). There was more widespread use of profit-related pay, but it seems likely that this was an opportunist response to the availability of tax advantages rather than being part of a strategic approach to pay. Finally, Arrowsmith and Sisson found only a very small number of cases – 25 out of 304 – where pay awards were 'linked to changes in technological or non-technological work organisation' (p. 61).

These findings on pay could mean that firms are not pursuing a strategic approach to flexibility. Alternatively, it could mean that greater flexibility of working practices and working hours is being achieved without having to link changes to pay. Either way, the evidence gives little support to the idea that managers are conforming to the flexible firm model.

The limits to organisational flexibility?

Limits to numerical flexibility

What are the prospects for further increases in the use of numerically flexible labour? It is true that both part-time and temporary employment have grown in recent years. However, to what extent is increased numerical flexibility constrained by the need to achieve and maintain high levels of employee commitment and motivation? The concept of employee commitment is one of the central planks of the HRM platform. Organisational commitment is generally seen as involving a sense of personal loyalty and attachment to one's employing organisation, although there is a large literature in which the meaning of the concept has been subject to much debate (Legge, 1995). Generally, however, it is argued that where employees develop high levels of commitment they express a strong desire to remain with the organisation, acceptance of and belief in the values and goals of the organisation, and a willingness to supply high levels of effort. The HRM literature suggests that there is a package of policies that generates high levels of employee commitment:

- provision of employment security;
- opportunities for training and promotion;
- attention to job design and work organisation so as to provide workers with opportunities to exercise discretion and responsibility and to have some control over their work;
- involvement of employees in decision-making.

The majority of non-standard workers are disadvantaged in most of these respects compared with full-time, permanent workers. The extent of insecurity among non-standard workers can be exaggerated, since most non-standard workers are part time, and 90% of part-timers are on permanent contracts. Part-timers appear to feel no more insecure in their jobs than full-time workers. However, part-time workers are concentrated in low-skilled, low-paid jobs (Gallie *et al.*, 1998: 144, 182; Legge, 1998: 288). Given the predominance of part-time workers among non-standard workers as a whole, we have to question the stereotype of the insecure peripheral worker. However, this also means that the majority of non-standard workers are in low-level, unrewarding jobs with few prospects of advancement. Temporary workers are less confined to low-level jobs than part-timers, but they do feel significantly more insecure in their jobs. Moreover, short-term temporary workers tend to feel trapped in jobs that they have little choice in taking, and are pessimistic about their chances of job advancement (Gallie *et al.*, 1998: 176–185).

Does this mean that non-standard workers cannot be relied upon to supply high levels of commitment, and if so, does it affect managers' willingness to employ them? Part-time workers on permanent contracts tend to be seen as reliable by managers, which might be taken to indicate a certain degree of commitment. However, they are also seen to be more difficult to manage than full-time workers are because they spend less time at work. This limits the flexibility with which part-timers can be deployed. Temporary workers are seen to be less committed and reliable than permanent staff, including part-timers. Studies in the early 1990s found that this was seen to be a sufficiently serious problem to cause some organisations to move away from fixed-term contracts. This was because the initial cost savings from hiring temporary workers were seen to be outweighed by additional costs arising from lower commitment (Hunter and MacInnes, 1991, 1992). While there was an increase in the use of temporary workers during the 1990s, there continue to be cases where managers are finding that this has created problems and are reducing their use of temporary workers, as the following example shows.

Activity **Problems with non-standard labour**

During 1998 two leading supermarket chains converted two-thirds of their temporary staff onto permanent contracts. Temporary workers had been hired to cope with seasonal peaks in demand or to enable the stores to adjust more easily under uncertain trading conditions. However, workers who remained on temporary contracts for too long lost motivation, and this had a damaging effect on the quality of customer service. Other problems associated with employing workers on temporary and zero-hours contracts that were identified by the stores' management were lack of training and difficulty of communication.

Source: People Management, June 1998:

1 Explain why workers on temporary contracts might become demotivated at work.

2 Why do you think temporary workers are likely to be less well trained than permanent staff?

Given that numerical flexibility appears to be sought in 'core' functions, we also need to consider how permanent, full-time workers respond to the introduction of numerically flexible workers. What is the effect of numerically flexible labour policies on 'core' workers' commitment? A study of a US-owned electronics plant in Ireland found that local managers were keen to minimise their use of temporary workers despite certain advantages they provided in terms of managerial control. In addition to the problems associated with employing temporary workers that we have already identified above, the use of large numbers of temporary workers was seen by managers to lead to lower levels of commitment from *permanent* staff. This was related to the occurrence of conflicts between permanent and temporary workers, and to a feeling that the employment of temporary workers on different – that is, inferior – terms and conditions was undermining the credibility of management's claim to be following enlightened HRM policies for all workers. This made it more difficult for managers to pursue their preferred goal of gaining control over workers on the basis of their willing cooperation and commitment (Geary, 1992).

In view of this it is perhaps unsurprising that managers view numerical and functional flexibility of labour as divergent rather than complementary approaches to flexibility.

Limits to functional flexibility

We have seen that while organisations have achieved increased numerical and functional flexibility, few conform to the model of the flexible firm. In particular, there is little evidence for a core of multi-skilled craft workers coexisting with a numerically flexible peripheral workforce. Functional flexibility falls short of multi-skilling, and might be better described as the multi-tasking of semi-skilled labour. How can we explain why the approach to flexibility that has been adopted in Britain is more limited than that envisaged in the model of the flexible firm?

Organisational considerations

A study by Clark (1993) provides a useful basis for explaining why functional flexibility has fallen short of full multi-skilling. It identifies six main reasons for this:

- Some employees are better suited to certain kinds of work than others. This may be partly due to their abilities as individuals, but it is also linked to different interests, and hence to what motivates individuals.
- In many cases management recognises that quality of effort depends on employees identifying with particular areas of work. Too much emphasis on multi-skilling and multi-tasking can undermine this.
- Some tasks require a high degree of specialist knowledge and ability for quality to be assured.
- The cost and availability of training may make it impracticable to develop multi-skilling for a large number of workers. This is particularly true of jobs that require a high level of specialised training. The costs of training in some areas may be high, so it is economically rational to develop trained specialists in those areas. Also, multi-skilling may be limited by shortages of suitable trainers.
- There is a potential for training investments to be wasted unless the newly acquired skills are put into practice soon after the training has been received. There is little point in investing in costly training for multi-skilling if workers are required to use additional skills only infrequently, since they are likely to forget what they have learned in training unless the learning is reinforced by frequent practice.
- Within 'lean' organisations, tight staffing may make multi-skilling difficult because staff cannot be spared from their existing tasks in order to undergo training.

Activity **Limits to functional flexibility**

Survey results from the 1998 Workplace Employee Relations Survey show that the lowest levels of functional flexibility are found in workplaces where scientific and technical workers are the largest occupational group. Functional flexibility is much more widespread in workplaces where sales workers are the largest occupational group.

Give an explanation for why this is the case. Bear in mind the different levels of specialised knowledge and the types of skill required by the different groups.

Wider historical and institutional constraints

The limited development of functional flexibility at organisational level may also be linked to the obstacles to taking an offensive flexibility pathway at national level. Lane (1995) has identified significant obstacles to the successful pursuit of diversified quality production incorporating functionally flexible labour in France and Britain. In France, rigid systems of job classification inhibit the functionally flexible use of labour. Although production workers' skills have been increased through training, they are underutilised. This is because production workers are still largely excluded from higher-level tasks by the continuing hierarchical division between production workers and technical and professional grades. This, in turn, is a symptom of deep-seated mutual suspicion and lack of trust between management and the shopfloor. Despite moves towards a greater degree of employee involvement in French firms in recent years, this continues to limit management–worker cooperation in achieving a greater degree of functional flexibility. Finally, the organisation of French firms still tends to be highly centralised and rigid, and this makes it harder for them to respond quickly to changes in markets.

Britain shares some of these difficulties. Low-trust relations between managers and workers are still widespread. On the other hand, the weakening of trade union influence in Britain has given employers a freer hand to do away with strict demarcation lines between jobs and extend task flexibility. More fundamental obstacles to flexible specialisation based on multi-skilling stem from an emphasis on short-term profits at the expense of long-term investment in equipment and training, and the consequent relatively low level of skill in the workforce (Lane, 1995). This has been a long-term feature of British economic history, and it can be linked to the structure of ownership of enterprises in Britain. In particular, the dominance of institutional investors looking to maximise the value of their portfolios on a day-to-day basis leads to a tight focus on short-term financial performance at the expense of longer-term innovation and growth. Over time this has led to British industry's failing to gain major shares of markets whose products are characterised by high levels of technological sophistication. Instead our comparative advantage has come increasingly to lie in the production of basic goods and services based on low-technology production and low-skilled labour. Progress towards greater functional flexibility has therefore been limited in the UK, and the emphasis continues to be on numerical flexibility and cost-cutting rather than functional flexibility.

Limits to flexibility: the 'new flexible firm'?

In the light of the evidence on the actual employment practices of organisations summarised above, Ackroyd and Procter (1998) have argued that, while the original model of the flexible firm is not supported by empirical evidence, a 'new flexible firm' is apparent in the manufacturing sector. The chief features of the 'new flexible manufacturing firm' are as follows:

- Production is organised on the basis of 'cell manufacture': that is, machines and workers are arranged so as to enable them to produce related components or products.
- There is little use of advanced technology in production.
- Limited functional flexibility of labour is achieved by having teams of semi-skilled workers performing 'a range of specific tasks and given (limited) training' (p. 171).
- There is no protected 'core' workforce. Employees 'compete with subcontracted labour and alternative suppliers' (p. 171).
- 'Production operations are considered as dispensable separate segments' (p. 171). These are subject to regular evaluation as to their cost-effectiveness. This provides the firm with ability to flex the size and shape of its operations.

This description is more consistent with what we have observed concerning the actual practices of management. It indicates that, with a few exceptions, organisational management has emphasised cost reduction rather than flexible specialisation as the goal of flexibility. This reflects the concentration on non-technologically advanced products and services that both results from and perpetuates the low level of skills in the labour force.

Summary: the practice of organisational flexibility

At the beginning of this section we asked the following questions:

- What forms of labour flexibility are being sought by organisations?
- What are the reasons for such changes? Is flexibility being developed as a strategic response to changes in market conditions? Is it an aspect of strategic HRM?
- What are the consequences of increased flexibility? Are they consistent with the emphasis on 'high commitment' within HRM?

We can now summarise our discussion of flexibility by answering these questions. First, regarding the forms of labour flexibility being sought, survey evidence shows that, instead of structuring their workforces in terms of 'core' and 'periphery', as advocated in the model of the flexible firm, employers are taking one of three approaches to labour flexibility, with a bias towards numerically flexible labour:

- To seek cost minimisation through the employment of so-called 'flexible' labour: that is, low-paid, part-time, female workers. This approach takes advantage of the relatively high degree of 'labour market flexibility' in the UK. Put simply, this means the relative absence of constraints on hiring and dismissal and, until recently, the absence of a minimum wage and the ability to pay part-time and temporary workers less pro rata than permanent full-time workers. However, recent changes in British and European Union legislation may make this cost-cutting route more difficult to pursue in future.
- To minimise costs by achieving numerical flexibility in 'core' as well as 'peripheral' functions. Extensive use is made of temporary workers and subcontracting.
- To combine functional flexibility in core functions with numerical flexibility in peripheral functions by contracting peripheral functions out to external agencies. However, functional flexibility is not developed to a high degree, and consists more in the multi-tasking of semi-skilled labour than in the multi-skilling of highly trained workers (Culley *et al.*, 1999).

Second, there has been scepticism as to how far the increased use of flexible labour can be seen as a strategic response by employers to changes in technology and markets. This reflects numerous studies that have emphasised the reactive nature of British management and its preoccupation with short-term financial pressures rather than longer-term plans. To the extent that a more strategic approach to labour flexibility has emerged during the 1990s, it is a strategy of cost minimisation based on cheap labour rather than one of flexible specialisation based on multi-skilled craft workers (Culley *et al.*, 1999). While this might be represented as embodying the 'hard' elements of strategic HRM, recent survey evidence suggests that the jury is still out on the question of whether employers are more strategic in their approach to the management of labour (Culley *et. al.*, 1999: 59, 295).

Third, we have seen that while, in theory, managerial strategies to enhance labour flexibility embody both 'hard' and 'soft' HRM, in practice the consequences of labour flexibilisation are not necessarily compatible with high levels of employee commitment. This is because:

- Certain categories of numerically flexible labour tend to have low commitment.
- Employing numerically flexible labour in core functions can reduce the commitment of 'core' workers.
- Excessive functional flexibility may reduce commitment because workers are unable to identify with and 'take ownership' of a defined role.

- Increased functional flexibility may be experienced mainly as work intensification. This *may* cause resentment and lower levels of commitment.

The emphasis on numerical flexibility and the limited level of functional flexibility in British firms reflect structural features of the British economy. These are: low levels of investment in technology and capital, which mean a generally low technological level in industry and therefore limited demand for highly skilled labour; and correspondingly low levels of investment in training, which mean a limited supply of skilled labour. These features have biased the UK towards defensive flexibility in its response to changes in world markets.

CONCLUSION: HRM, FLEXIBILITY AND THE LABOUR MARKET

It was stated at the beginning of this chapter that one of the main principles of human resource management is that human resources can be a key source of competitive advantage as long as they are managed strategically. However, different approaches to the strategic management of human resources are possible. They are expressed in the distinction between 'hard' and 'soft' HRM. The 'hard' version favours minimising labour costs by planned use of labour so that the quantity and quality of labour inputs are as closely matched as possible to production requirements. As Storey argues, it emphasises the 'quantitative, calculative and business strategic aspects of managing the headcount in as rational a way as for any other economic factor' (Storey, 1987: 6). This approach is consistent with the way firms are supposed to behave in refined versions of the competitive model of labour market. The 'soft' version sees employees as more than a passive resource to be managed and more as active contributors to competitive advantage on the basis of their capacities for innovation, problem solving and customer care. In order to develop and foster these capacities, however, it is necessary to generate employee commitment through 'communication, motivation and leadership' (Storey, 1987: 6). There is a strong emphasis is on building relationships of trust and reciprocity between workers and management. This is much more consonant with the types of organisational behaviour implied in institutionalist theories of labour markets.

Hard and soft HRM are combined in the model of the flexible firm. On the one hand, numerical flexibility, with its emphasis on the efficient deployment of labour, is an expression of the 'hard' strategic thrust within HRM. On the other hand, 'soft' HRM is a way of gaining the commitment of the 'core' section of the workforce to providing functional flexibility. This implies that different HRM policies will be applied, not only to different organisations but also to different groups of workers within the same organisation. This appears to be consistent with the perspectives on the labour market outlined earlier in this chapter. However, the empirical evidence on patterns of labour flexibility does not support this prediction. Numerical and functional flexibility are rarely combined within the same workforce and, where they are, the combination is not structured along core–periphery lines.

This raises the question of whether there is a contradiction within the flexible firm model and HRM. Is the existence of a peripheral workforce exposed to market forces consistent with a cooperative core? Can organisations operate different approaches to the management of workers without detracting from the very outcomes that the policies are designed to achieve? Are 'hard' and 'soft' HRM really compatible with each other?

Radical theory might suggest that these compatibilities do exist, since the aim is to divide workers and limit their ability to resist exploitation. However, Geary's study of an electronics plant in Ireland, referred to above, casts considerable doubt on this. The managers in his study felt that by applying different policies to different sections of their workers, they were generating low trust among 'core' workers, as well as conflict between them and temporary staff. If this was an attempt at 'divide and rule' it was counterproductive from management's point of view, since it actually resulted in management's having less control over the production process as a whole because of problems arising from low trust, inter-group resentment and conflict.

Refined competitive theory also suggests that employers can apply different policies to different sections of their workforce successfully. The argument is that rational policies aim to improve the efficiency with which the labour market works. Since one criterion of efficiency is that the market should meet the *various* needs of both buyers and sellers of labour, there is no reason why the efficient operation of one set of policies should interfere with that of the other. Yet it is also apparent from Geary's study that we cannot assume that different types of contract produce an efficient market outcome by meeting the needs of different groups of workers. The argument assumes that workers are simply intent on maximising their own independent utility functions, with no reference to other individuals or groups. Clearly this was not the case in Ireland, where comparisons between groups generated feelings of inequity and vulnerability and led to inter-group conflict and a poor climate of employee relations.

Both the radical and competitive arguments underplay the contradictory nature of management in the employment relationship. Management needs to be able to treat labour as a commodity, to be acquired and disposed of in line with the changing requirements of production. At the same time, however, management needs the active cooperation of workers in the production process (Edwards, 1995). Trust is a necessary condition for cooperation between workers and management. However, the need of managers to be able to treat labour as a commodity imposes an unavoidable limit to the trust and cooperation that they can rely upon from workers. This means that policies aimed at generating high levels of commitment are inevitably compromised by management's need to be able to dismiss workers when the need arises. Conversely, policies aimed at increasing management's ability to dispose freely of labour are constrained by the need to obtain a certain level of cooperation from workers.

What this shows is that HRM offers no escape from the contradiction involved in the management of the employment relationship. In fact the Janus-like features of HRM, with their opposite-facing 'hard' and 'soft' aspects, reveal that HRM is at least as much imbued with this contradiction as any previous approach to the management of labour.

SUMMARY

- This chapter has developed three economic perspectives on the labour market and the analysis of HRM: the competitive market, institutional and radical perspectives.

- The competitive market approach sees the labour market as an arena in which competing individuals – workers and employers – seek to maximise the benefits they can each obtain from the effort–reward exchange. The starting point is the model of perfect competition, but this is refined to allow for market imperfections that constrain maximising behaviour and lead to less than 'ideal' outcomes.

- Institutionalist approaches reject the concept of individual maximising behaviour on the grounds that individuals' preferences and decisions are not independent of those of others. They focus on the interdependence of choices made by individuals, and the role of collective influences on them. This approach emphasises the role played by group norms, custom and collective pressure in shaping labour markets and labour market outcomes.

- The radical perspective takes the class nature of capitalist society as its starting point, and argues that the condition for the accumulation of capital and the survival of the capitalist class is the exploitation of labour. Capitalist employers therefore seek to structure labour markets so as to weaken the ability of workers to resist exploitation.

- Each of these perspectives provides a particular focus on the HRM debate. The competitive market approach identifies HRM policies such as individual performance-related pay, relaxation of job demarcations and 'participative' approaches to work reorganisation as examples of flexibility that reduce inefficiencies in the employment relationship and lead to a closer approximation to competitive labour market outcomes.

- The institutionalist approach leads to an emphasis on the role of HRM in altering collective norms and customs and changing the distribution of power within organisations. HRM initiatives seek to promote acceptance of managerially defined goals and priorities throughout the organisation, either by incorporating potential sources of organised dissent into management, or, if this is seen to be unnecessary or undesirable, by marginalising their influence.

- The radical critique of HRM sees it as an attempt to reshape labour markets so as to further divide workers among themselves and create a more effective basis for the exploitation of labour.

- HRM seems most likely to be attempted where bureaucratic forms of labour management have replaced direct labour market competition. In addition, however, HRM will be more likely to occur where workers have a high degree of discretion in their jobs, or where management is seeking to increase the amount of employee discretion at work. These outcomes appear to follow from whichever theoretical perspective is used to analyse the labour market. It is in their evaluations of HRM in terms of the distribution of benefits between employers and employees and between different groups of workers that the three perspectives differ significantly.

- The limits to HRM in Britain are indicated by empirical evidence relating to the take-up of HRM policies and the limited extent to which functional flexibility has been sought and achieved. The reasons for the limited spread of HRM may be related to the lack of strategic awareness among managers, the costs of HRM initiatives relative to their benefits in many organisational settings, and changes in the labour market environment that have enabled management to reassert unilateral control at work.

- It has been argued here that a weakness of HRM theory lies in its lack of attention to the contradictory role of management in the employment relationship and the active role that workers may play in shaping the terms of the effort–reward exchange. A key question is how far HRM's emphasis on active worker cooperation with management is compatible with its other concern to maximise the efficient utilisation of labour as a resource. This issue is illustrated in the discussion of the debate over labour market flexibility and the flexible firm.

QUESTIONS

1 What are the grounds for arguing that the labour market is different from the markets for capital and goods and services.

2 What factors might an organisation's management bear in mind when deciding whether or not to adopt an HRM approach to the management of employees?

3 (a) What are the advantages of a development path based on highly skilled, functionally flexible labour?

   (b) Why, despite these advantages, might such a path not be followed?

4 What forms of compromise between EU-style labour market regulation and US-style deregulation might be emerging in Europe?

5 What factors have limited employers' use of numerically and functionally flexible employees?

6 In what main respects has empirical evidence led to a reconsideration of the 'flexible firm' model?

7 Explain (a) how a labour flexibility is an aim of HRM and (b) how labour flexibility might conflict with HRM.

CASE STUDY

Temp workers set for improved conditions

More than 7m European Union citizens are in line to win improved working conditions after employers agreed to negotiate with trade unions about temporary agency work.

The decision was welcomed by Etuc, the European trade union confederation. Emilio Gabaglio, the general-secretary, said: 'If we (the EU) want more flexiblity in labour markets, we need clear protection for workers.'

Unice, which represents private sector employers, has resolved to discuss a deal as part of efforts to end 'out-dated' restrictions on using agency workers and improve labour flexibility.

Negotiations will be the fourth set to take place under provisions established by the EU's 1992 Maastricht Treaty. These allow for employers and workers to reach agreements which governments can collectively adopt into national laws. Employers and unions have already agreed deals on parental leave, part-time working and fixed-term contract working.

Talks on temporary agency work, which public sector employers have already agreed, are the third in a series on 'atypical workers' after the part-time and fixed-term agreements. Tele-workers could be a subject for further negotiations.

Unice estimates that 2m temporary workers are assigned through an agency on any working day in the EU and that 7m undertake such work over a year.

George Jacobs, president, said employers were prepared to discuss how to avoid discrimination against agency workers providing unions recognised that temporary work was an integral part of a functioning market.

Temporary work was needed to deal with peaks of activity or to provide access to specialised skills needed for limited periods, he said. For job seekers, it increases employability and can provide a stepping stone to permanent jobs.

Unice wants an easing of restrictions on the lengths of contracts and their renewal.

Mr Gabaglio said temporary agency work appeared to be increasing all over the EU. In Spain, it had doubled between 1996 and 1998, and in France and Germany it had increased 30 per cent in three years.

Etuc want to ensure that any agreement sets limits on temporary work and that 'open-ended contracts remain the most common form of employment'.

'We are determined to see that temporary work does not lead to discrimination,' said Mr Gabaglio. 'You need to give value to new types of jobs if you are to successfully modernise labour markets.'

Source: Financial Times, 5 May 2000.

1 Discuss how far and in what ways protection for workers in the form of legislation and collective bargaining agreements helps to increase labour market flexibility.

2 Analyse the advantages and disadvantages of temporary forms of employment from employers', managers' and workers' points of view.

3 As teams of negotiators representing the ETUC (European Trades Union Congress) and UNICE (European Employers' Confederation) identify the key outcomes that you would want to achieve in negotiations over temporary working. Compare the sets of aims, and discuss where there is most likelihood of reaching agreement and where agreement will be most difficult to achieve.

REFERENCES AND FURTHER READING

Those texts marked with an asterisk are particularly recommended for further reading.

Ackroyd, S. and Procter, S. (1998) 'British manufacturing organisation and workplace industrial relations: some attributes of the new flexible firm', *British Journal of Industrial Relations*, Vol. 36, No. 2, pp. 163–183.

Advisory, Conciliation, and Arbitration Service (1988) *Labour Flexibility in Britain: the 1987 ACAS Survey*, Occasional paper 41. ACAS.

Alchian, A.A. and Demsetz, H. (1972) 'Production, information costs, and economic organization', *American Economic Review*, Vol. 62 (Papers and Proceedings), pp. 44–49.

Arrowsmith, J. and Sisson, K. (1999) 'Pay and working time: towards organisation-based systems?', *British Journal of Industrial Relations*, Vol. 37, No. 1, pp. 51–75.

*Atkinson, J. (1984) 'Manpower strategies for flexible organizations', *Personnel Management*, August, pp. 28–31.

Atkinson, J. (1985) *Flexibility, Uncertainty and Manpower Management*. Report 89. Brighton, Institute of Manpower Studies.

Atkinson, J. and Gregory, D. (1986) 'A flexible future. Britain's dual labour market', *Marxism Today*, Vol. 30, No. 4, pp. 12–17.

Atkinson, J. and Meager, N. (1986) *Changing Working Patterns: How Companies Achieve Flexibility to Meet their Needs*. National Economic Development Office.

Braverman, H. (1974) *Labor and Monopoly Capital*. New York: Monthly Review Press.

Burgess, S.M. and Rees, H.J.B. (1997) 'Transient jobs and lifetime jobs: dualism in the British labour market', *Oxford Bulletin of Economics and Statistics*, Vol. 59, pp. 309–328.

Casey, B. (1991) 'Survey evidence on trends in non-standard employment', in Pollert, A. (ed.) *Farewell to Flexibility?* Oxford: Blackwell, pp. 179–199.

Casey, B., Metcalf, H. and Millward, N. (1997) *Employers' Use of Flexible Labour*. London: Policy Studies Institute.

Clark, J. (1993) 'Full flexibility and self-supervision in an automated factory', in J. Clark (ed.), *Human Resource Management and Technical Change*. London: Sage, pp. 116–136.

Creedy, J. and Whitfield, K. (1986) 'Earnings and job mobility. Professional chemists in Britain', *Journal of Economic Studies*, Vol. 13, pp. 23–37.

Cross, M. (1988) 'Changes in working practices in UK manufacturing, 1981–1988', *Industrial Relations Review and Report*, No. 415, pp. 2–10.

Culley, M., Woodland, S., O'Reilly, A. and Dix, G. (1999) *Britain at Work: As depicted by the 1998 Workplace Employee Relations Survey*, London: Routledge.

Dex, S. and McCulloch, A. (1997) *Flexible Employment: The Future of Britain's Jobs*. Basingstoke: Macmillan

Doeringer, P.B. and Piore, M.J. (1971) *Internal Labor Markets and Manpower Analysis*. Lexington, Mass.: Heath.

Dunn, S. (1993) 'Hard times for workers' rights', *the Guardian*, 19 May, p. 18.

Edwards, P.K. (1995) 'The employment relationship', in P. Edwards (ed.) *Industrial Relations: Theory and Practice in Britain*. Oxford: Blackwell, pp. 3–26.

Edwards, R. (1975) 'The social relations of production in the firm and labour market structure', *Politics and Society*, Vol. 5, pp. 83–108.

European Commission (1998a) *Employment in Europe 1997: Analysis of Key Issues*. Luxembourg: Office of Official Publications of the European Communities.

European Commission (1998b) *Employment in Europe 1997*. Luxembourg: Office of Official Publications of the European Communities.

European Commission (1999) *Employment in Europe 1998*. Luxembourg: Office of Official Publications of the European Communities.

Ferner, A. and Hyman, R. (eds) (1998) *Changing Industrial Relations in Europe*. Oxford: Blackwell.

*Gallie, D., White, M., Cheng, Y. and Tomlinson, M. (1998) *Restructuring the Employment Relationship*. Oxford: Clarendon Press.

Geary, J.F. (1992) 'Employment flexibility and human resource management: the case of three American electronics plants', *Work, Employment and Society*, Vol. 6, pp. 251–270.

George, K. and Shorey, J. (1985) 'Manual workers, good jobs and structured internal labour markets', *British Journal of Industrial Relations*, Vol. 23, pp. 424–447.

Giersch, J. (1986) *Liberalisation for Faster Economic Growth*. London: Institute of Economic Affairs.

Gill, C., Gold, M. and Cressey, P., (1999) 'Social Europe: national initiatives and responses', *Industrial Relations Journal*, Vol. 30, No. 4, pp. 313–329.

Guest, D. (1989) 'Human resource management: its implications for industrial relations and trade unions', in Storey, J. (ed.) *New Perspectives in Human Resource Management*. London: Routledge, pp. 41–55.

Guest, D. (1998) 'Beyond HRM: commitment and the contract culture', in P. Sparrow and M. Marchington (eds)

Human Resource Management: The New Agenda. London: Financial Times/Pitman Publishing, pp. 37–51

Hayek, F.A. (1984) *1980s Unemployment and the Unions.* London: Institute of Economic Affairs.

Hunter, L.C. and MacInnes, J. (1991) *Employers' Labour Use Strategies: Case Studies,* Department of Employment Group Research Paper 87. London: Department of Employment.

Hunter, L.C. and MacInnes, J. (1992) 'Employers and labour flexibility: the evidence from case studies', *Employment Gazette,* June, pp. 307–315.

Incomes Data Services (1994) 'Multiskilling', *IDS Study 538,* July.

Jenkins, A. (1998) 'The French experience of flexibility: lessons for British HRM', in P. Sparrow and M. Marchington (eds) *Human Resource Management:The New Agenda.* London: Financial Times/Pitman Publishing, pp. 259–271.

Kelly, J. (1996) 'Union militancy and social partnership', in P. Ackers, C. Smith and P. Smith (eds) *The New Workplace and Trade Unionism.* London: Routledge, pp. 77–109.

Kerr, C. (1954) 'The balkanisation of labor markets', in Bakke, F.W. (ed.) *Labor Mobility and Economic Opportunity.* Cambridge, Mass.: MIT Press, pp. 92–110.

*King, J.E. (1990) *Labour Economics,* 2nd edn. London: Macmillan.

*Lane, C. (1995) *Industry and Society in Europe: Stability and Change in Britain, France and Germany.* Aldershot: Edward Elgar.

*Legge, K. (1995) *Human Resource Management: Rhetorics and Realities.* Basingstoke, Macmillan.

*Legge, K. (1998) 'Flexibility: the gift-wrapping of employment degradation?', in P. Sparrow and M. Marchington (eds) *Human Resource Management: The New Agenda.* London: Financial Times/Pitman Publishing, pp. 286–295.

Leibenstein, H. (1987) *Inside the Firm: The Inefficiencies of Hierarchy.* Cambridge, Mass.: Harvard University Press.

*Lindbeck, A. and Snower, D.J. (1988) *The Insider–Outsider Theory of Employment and Unemployment.* Cambridge, Mass.: MIT Press.

Mace, J. (1979) 'Internal labour markets for engineers in British industry', *British Journal of Industrial Relations,* Vol. 17, pp. 50–63.

Marginson, P. (1991) 'Change and continuity in the employment structure of large companies', in Pollert, A. (ed.) *Farewell to Flexibility?* Oxford: Blackwell, pp. 32–45.

*Marsden, D. (1986) *The End of Economic Man?* Brighton: Wheatsheaf.

McGregor, A. and Sproull, A. (1992) 'Employers and the flexible workforce', *Employment Gazette,* May, pp. 225–234.

Millward, N. (1994) *The New Industrial Relations?* London: Policy Studies Institute.

Millward, N., Stevens, M., Smart, D. and Hawes, W.R. (1992) *Workplace Industrial Relations in Transition. The ED/ESRC/PSI/ACAS Surveys.* Aldershot: Dartmouth.

Nolan, P. (1989) 'Walking on water? Performance and industrial relations under Thatcher', *Industrial Relations Journal,* Vol. 20, pp. 81–92.

Nolan, P. and Brown, W. (1983) 'Competition and workplace wage determination', *Oxford Bulletin of Economics and Statistics,* Vol. 45, pp. 269–287.

Osterman, P. (ed.) (1984) *Internal Labor Markets.* Cambridge, Mass.: MIT Press.

Parker, M. and Slaughter, J. (1988) *Choosing Sides: Unions and the Team Concept.* Boston: Labour Notes.

Pendleton, A. (1991) 'The barriers to flexibility: flexible rostering on the railways', *Work, Employment and Society,* Vol. 5, pp. 241–257.

Pollert, A. (1988) 'The flexible firm: fixation or fact', *Work, Employment and Society,* Vol. 2, No. 3, pp. 281–316.

*Rosenberg, S. and Lapidus, J. (1999) 'Contingent and non-standard work in the United States: towards a more poorly compensated, insecure workforce', in A. Felstead and N. Jewson (eds) *Global Trends in Flexible Labour.* Basingstoke: Macmillan, pp. 62–79.

Routh, G. (1989) 'Order and chaos, turbulence and strange attractors in labour markets'. Paper presented at the British Universities Industrial Research Association Annual Conference, Cardiff (unpublished).

Sisson, K. and Marginson, P. (1995) 'Management: systems, structures and strategy', in P. Edwards (ed.) *Industrial Relations. Theory and Practice in Britain.* Oxford: Blackwell, pp. 89–122.

Smith, C. and Elger, T. (1997) 'International competition, inward investment and the restructuring of European work and industrial relations', *European Journal of Industrial Relations,* Vol. 3, No. 3, pp. 279–304.

Storey, J. (1987) 'Developments in the management of human resources: an interim report', *Warwick Papers in Industrial Relations,* Vol. 17.

Storey, J. (1992) *Developments in the Management of Human Resources.* Oxford: Blackwell.

Van Ruysseveldt, J., Huiskamp, R. and van Hoof, J. (1995) *Comparative Industrial and Employment Relations.* London: Sage.

Williamson, O. (1985) *Markets and Hierarchies: Analysis and Antitrust Implications.* Glencoe: Free Press.

Williamson, O,. Wachter, M.L. and Harris, J.E. (1975) 'Understanding the employment relation: the analysis of idiosyncratic exchange', *Bell Journal of Economics,* Vol. 6, pp. 250–280.

NOTES

1. A formal demonstration of the conditions for profit maximisation in the short and long runs can be found in King, J.E. (1990) *Labour Economics*, 2nd edn, Macmillan, pp. 12–27.

2. The current government has changed this policy from compulsory tendering for the lowest price contract to an obligation on public-sector organisations to show that they are providing 'best value' in the way in which services are provided. This means that quality of service can be traded off more easily against cost. Nevertheless, this still means that there will be strong pressures on the public sector to contain and even reduce costs in the face of private-sector competition.

3. Where 50% of the relevant workforce are members of the union or where 40% of the total workforce vote in favour of union recognition.

4. For a view of the 'down side' of this kind of existence, see Sennett, R. (1998) *The Corrosion of Character: The Personal Consequences of Work in the New Capitalism*, New York: W.W. Norton.

5. Fixed-term contracts specify a fixed duration for the employment contract. This may vary from a few months to several years. Workers on fixed-term contracts are direct employees, unlike temporary workers hired through employment agencies. Employees hired on 'zero-hours' contracts are also direct employees, but they have no fixed hours of employment, being offered work as it becomes available.

6. Since employers can combine different forms of variable or incentive pay, the proportion of workers surveyed actually subject to some form of flexible payments system is considerably less than 44%. See Gallie *et al.* (1998) p. 166.

7. Readers may wonder how the evidence that non-standard workers are most likely to be employed alongside core workers can be reconciled with Gallie *et al.*'s finding that part-time and, to a lesser extent, short-term temporary workers tend to be assigned to low-skill jobs compared with standard workers. One possible explanation is that Culley *et al.* exclude part-timers from their definition of non-standard workers, and restrict the category to temporary agency workers, fixed-term contract workers, freelance workers, homeworkers and workers on zero-hours contracts (Culley *et al.*, 1999: 35). As Gallie points out, it is part-time workers in particular who are at a skill disadvantage compared with full-timers. Workers on fixed-term contracts, particularly those lasting for more than a year, are as likely to be employed in higher-level occupations as are full-time, permanent workers (Gallie *et al.*, 1998: 174).

4

Human resource planning: control to seduction?

Damian O'Doherty

OBJECTIVES

- To critically assess the transition from the quantitative regime of manpower planning to the more qualitative practice of contemporary human resource planning, a transition that we have characterised in terms of a move from *control* to *seduction*. Do not be seduced by this text.

- To impart a comprehensive understanding of the technical and prescriptive components of traditional 'scientific' manpower planning, from the measurement of labour turnover to the use of Markov models.

- To impart an understanding of the assumptions and metaphorical figures that underpin and support the traditional vision and practice of manpower planning. This will allow us to open up those domains of organisation that are typically excluded and neglected in the discourse of manpower planning.

- To stimulate a critical awareness of the tensions between order and disorder in organisation, tensions that fracture the integrity of the employment relation and which manpower planning, and latterly human resource planning, attempt to address. As we shall see, manpower planning often compounds and amplifies these tensions, tripping off further rounds of struggle and discord.

- To locate and identify areas of dissension within organisations that contest the objectives and practice of manpower planning, and to evaluate the extent to which the more radically 'unitarist' human resource planning succeeds in transcending divergent 'stakeholder' interests. The chapter seeks to advance an explanation of this dissension.

- To provoke critical self-awareness in the reading and writing of human resource planning. In effect we question the legitimacy of 'objectives' and the capacity of instrumental and linear-rational calculation to manage organisation. We do aim to be interesting and relevant even if it appears at times irreverent and irresponsible. At times perplexing, if not amusing, this might contribute to the adumbration of that space where organisation is given chance, where we are given chance, and where anything might happen next.

INTRODUCTION

Traditionally, manpower planning has been studied and taught from within a unitarist frame of reference. As a consequence, its practice is understood as a technical exercise performed exclusively by management. Consistent with this approach, management gets defined as a rational and politically neutral agent of organisation responsible for the execution of a series of business 'functions' in a perspective that abstracts management from issues of political struggle and negotiation (Cole, 1991; Torrington and Hall, 1995). Given this frame of reference, trade unions and shopfloor collective employee organisations were considered, at best, to provide a medium for securing managerial legitimacy. Outside personnel management departments, the activities of trade unions, for example, were generally looked upon as the antithesis of efficient manpower planning (Fox, 1985), deviant institutions that worked to prevent the most rational deployment and use of labour. By maintaining such things as customary norms, 'restrictive practices', and inefficient working routines, together with the publicity that certain manpower practices attracted in the public sector, in areas of manufacturing, and especially in the docks (Donovan, 1968; see also Turnbull, 1992; Turnbull and Sapsford, 1992), unions were seen as inimical to the 'acquisition, utilization, improvement and retention of an enterprise's human resources' (HMSO, cited in Bramham, 1990).

Where management was formally trained, this tended, in the main, to be a syllabus of neo-classical economics and 'organisation science' whose assumptions legitimised this sovereign and singular authority claimed by management (see Chapter 3). More commonly, however, the hegemony of neo-classical economics was established through the more informal processes of distillation and socialisation within work organisations, hegemony that finds only latent expression in the mundane assumptions and prejudices rehearsed in management discourse. The emergence of human resource management can be understood, to some extent, as a project to recover and extend the assumptions of unitarist management, especially in the domain of manpower planning. Following the collective challenge of labour and its prosecution of a pluralist agenda, pursued – in part successfully – through state institutions and the processes of social democracy, management seems to have been in need of a new discourse of legitimisation.

HRM is perhaps best seen as a complex hybrid product of its times (cf. Chapter 1) – the discourse of crisis (Eldridge *et al.*, 1991), Reagan economics, Thatcherism (see Hall and Jacques, 1983), and even the punk nihilism of the 1970s. In this chapter we shall explore the nature of this transition from manpower planning to 'human resource planning' in a way that seeks to restore the politics of the workplace as it is 'distilled' and 'socialised' through contemporary social relations and organisation.

Locating the technical procedures of manpower planning within the ambit of organisation struggle, we try, in a preliminary way, to open up an arena that mediates a whole force-field of order and disorder, a field of tension that embraces both the rational and the irrational, conscious organisation, unconscious organisation, and a complex series of heterogeneous struggles within power relations – including the economic struggle between capital and labour. We shall then be able to develop an understanding that attends to the co-implication of representational and practical dimension in manpower planning: that is, the *complicated* inter-articulation of theory and practice. Our chapter advances towards that boundary space **between representation and practice** where 'manpower planning' gets manifest as struggle, in perpetual self-crisis, internally and externally distracted. Manpower planning attempts to integrate this fractious tension in/of organisation, to bind the elements of manifold material and ideal phenomena and so render the world objective and utile.

Like the world of banking, manpower planning wants to secure confidence and credit. Manpower planning can be usefully thought of in terms of the analogy with banking: it 'banks' on prediction and control, anticipation and foresight; it banks on employees as currency and resource; stabilise-able as economic units of calculation; as an investment, employees are trained and developed, disciplined and shaped, bought and sold on the labour market, terminated or 'cashed in' at the most financially lucrative moment for an organisation. Manpower planning also banks on *making* organisation, on *making the whole*. It aims to secure a coherent *whole* out of the mobile heterogeneous *parts* of organisation/disorganisation (Cooper and Law, 1995), parts that move in agitated patterns, co-mingling and combining, assembling and disassembling in complex and unpredictable forms. From the recalcitrance of the subjects' will – 'I refuse to work hard today' and 'Sod it, I've had enough of this' – to dream of fantasy and escape, to gossip and rumour that spreads like wildfire to delay and suspend the seriousness of the working day. Economic calculation and efficiency in the use of manpower only ever achieves a precarious and partial outcome in organisation.

In order to approach these difficult issues, this chapter embodies a reflexive and ironic tone that, for many, might seem to mirror – or better *mimic* – contemporary practices in human resource management (cf. Taussig, 1993; O'Doherty and Roberts, 2000). Exploring what might appear inappropriate domains of study, the seemingly irrelevant, the out-of-bounds or off-limits, and mixing together texts from a dispersed range of disciplinary fields – industrial relations, personnel management, aboriginal folklore, the archive of functionalist prescriptive texts in manpower planning, labour history, and organisation studies – we invite you to read this text as a palimpsest. We want to catch you off your guard; juxtapose the unseemly and the unseen in-organisation; introduce strands of discourse that come from elsewhere and lead somewhere else, pathways and portals to other worlds and ways of being (see Burrell, 1997). Here, manpower planning can suddenly appear to take on the features of bank, a form of accountancy, or a military campaign, in a space where a unit of 'human resource' might become a 'wolf-man' (Freud, 1918/1991), and the employment relation a site of exploitation and the appropriation of surplus value.

Splicing the incongruous and the unexpected, the fragments of marginal phenomena, we illustrate, however, that manpower planning as 'banking' on the *whole* is not what it seems. As an introduction to human resource planning, this chapter represents an effort to think and write on manpower planning in novel and unconventional ways in order to stimulate *readerly* creativity (Barthes, 1977). For the successful human resource planner of the future, this ability to cope with the shock of the unexpected might well be mandatory. Moreover, the capacity to 'channel hop' – to negotiate and move across multiple domains of reality; to step through the classical marble banking hall and into the space of high finance, a world of *forked lightning* and the *Mae West* (Valdez, 1997: 242); to improvise and innovate – will prove invaluable. After all, isn't this how the discourse of what becomes 'traditional' manpower planning comes into being? It is *invented*. We are far from a calculation of the 'labour stability index' or a 'frequency distribution of leavers by length of service', a discourse we will need to leave behind and eventually abandon all together. Not that it offered anything real or enduring in the first place, or secured the (w)hole of organisation. As we shall see, *manpower planning as a banking hall is a knot-what of seams.*

This chapter can be watched, read alone in silence, or read aloud collectively in groups. It is not designed, however, for radio broadcast nor, unfortunately, is there any obvious musical accompaniment. In the first half of this chapter we shall mime an orthodox and incremental form of thinking in manpower planning that takes us through its basic 'functions'. Before the construction of a plan it is necessary to know where the need for manpower planning originates. Once we know this we can then address how one might go about creating a simple manpower plan. From the calculation of labour demand to an analysis of labour supply, manpower planning proceeds to reconcile demand and supply so as to secure equilibrium, harmony, and organisation. Following this we can work out some complications to the basic model that allows for dynamics and change. Then we shall explore the 'evolution' of manpower planning as it 'matures' towards *human resource* planning and the 'management of change'. In the second half of the chapter we unpack this linearity by opening up some of the definitions and assumptions that underpin resource planning. Here, we enter that field of tension that subverts the practice of manpower planning as rationality and organisation, a space of knots and seams where order becomes disorder and organisation – disorganisation. Before we think about 'who' it is that is said to conduct manpower planning within organisation, let's think about why there is a need for manpower planning.

THE NEED FOR MANPOWER PLANNING

For many years, the importance of manpower planning was seen to lie with the contribution it could make to reducing 'shocks' and 'disturbances' within the social relations of large organisations and, in the process, maintaining some kind of organisational stability and equilibrium. These shocks and disturbances might emanate from within the organisation, in response to changes in the outside world – in technology, the product, labour, and capital markets – or as the result of a complex interaction between the inside and outside.

Within the organisation wider corporate initiatives are seen to trigger off a number of manpower repercussions, and manpower planners are expected to respond in an appropriate manner in order to manage and contain its disturbance. While the kind of extensive productivity planning conducted at Fawley in the late 1950s and 1960s might have offered a model case study that illustrates the importance of involving specialist manpower planners (Flanders, 1964), in the main, manpower planning was conducted ad hoc within a system of industrial relations and personnel management that was 'largely informal' and 'largely fragmented'. Moreover, once we open up organisation and the employment relation more broadly, we shall see this informality and fragmentation writ large. So, for manpower planning it was more a case of 'muddling through' (Edwards *et al.*, 1992), rather than strategic direction and control.

Typically, one finds that issues concerned with personnel and specialist manpower planning are subordinate to the power of accountancy and finance within senior corporate management, a pattern of power relations and inequality that in recent years has become more hegemonic and disadvantageous for the pursuit of a distinctive set of values and ideals through personnel management (see Armstrong, 1995). In the past this has meant that when individual companies made plans for future product development, or drew up investment schedules for new technology, more often than not manpower planning was relegated to a relatively low status and downstream function. Left to pick up the pieces, manpower planning was preoccupied with 'firefighting', tackling the outbreak of consequences and repercussions arising from decisions taken within corporate management and other more powerful management specialisms.

This means that the need for manpower planning might be better thought of as a 'derivative need', something that followed and sought to correct for the mistakes and oversights of wider 'strategic' managerial decision-making. Subject to this wider pattern of organisational power relations, manpower planning then, has struggled to construct and promote an autonomous and distinctive set of practices and techniques. It has always found itself situated within the power politics of organisation and in competition with the claims of other management specialisms such that it is forced to adapt and modify, shape and develop its practices in an ongoing process of organisational negotiation and political lobbying. Subject to the winds of change, the 'need' for manpower planning remains an historically contingent phenomenon, and one partly constructed and promoted by manpower planners themselves.

When we unpack the functions and techniques of manpower planning we also find a whole series of tensions and problems that render its practice far less coherent and rational than commonly assumed, but which nonetheless contribute to this 'need' for manpower planning. In large organisations the understanding and measurement of even the most basic and simple numerical flows of individuals are tasks that quite clearly require detailed and careful monitoring. Over a number of years, it might well be expected that 'patterns' will emerge, reducing the anxiety and burden of persistent organisational monitoring. In many ways we can think of the role of manpower planning as one that involves a struggle to represent organisation and its 'movements' as a two-dimensional picture of resource flows. Manpower planning thought it was taking photographs (!?) – pull the trigger – flash – illuminate – bring the distant closer – capture movement as impression on a chemical surface – like those preparations, perhaps, for aerial bombing. Yet, as we shall see, the problems of 'time' and 'movement' – the processual dimensions of organisation – are complex, creating difficulties that are only partially amenable to the timeless abstractions, representation, and control of photography. Building up reliable long-term patterns of resource flows in organisation always remains a precarious and contingent accomplishment, an organisational exercise that can never relax, and one that is always subject to perturbation and mistake. Even with the so-called advanced sophistication of military hardware in the Gulf War, we know that bombs still missed their targets, and manpower planning mistakes were made in the calculation of civilian and NATO military casualties.

In the perpetual strife between movement/change in organisation and the representation/stasis of manpower planning, these mistakes and unintended consequences call out for further rounds of intervention, correction, and readjustment by manpower planning. This adds a further layer of 'need' for manpower planning, a vicious incestuous cycle that resembles the case of a dog chasing its own tail. Later in the chapter we delve into the organisation 'shadow' cast by the photographic illumination of manpower planning that opens up an irrecoverable space between the dimensions of movement and stasis, the body and head of organisation, and where the rationality of planning meets its limits. What we are concerned with here is how the 'need' for manpower planning emerges in part from the tension between the three-dimensional world of organisation and its two-dimensional representation in manpower plans.

In a stable environment, where the characteristics of product and labour markets might be expected to continue and persist in a predictable and orderly fashion, the conditions for modelling long-term patterns of employment within organisation are no doubt a little more propitious. This would allow the planner to calculate and predict such things as the number of retirements, the expected turnover of staff within departments, and the average number of staff leaving for 'involuntary reasons'. Yet models such as these provide a broad and rather crude picture of numerical turnover, providing only rudimentary information on things such as replacement times and rates. In other words, in order to maintain numerically stable employment over time, management requires more sophisticated and focused data on when, where, and how many employees need to be recruited.

The precise statistical and qualitative complexities and details that contribute to a manpower plan will be considered in more detail later in the chapter. At this stage it is important to appreciate that manpower planning is a critical managerial function because it provides management with information on resource flows that is used to calculate, amongst other things, recruitment needs and succession and development plans. This has been described above as an attempt to reduce shocks and disturbances. With detailed study of past and projected trends in 'employment loss', management can seek to minimise the shock of unexpected shortages of labour, inefficient and costly surpluses, and needless redundancies.

For example, if historically you have always recruited two junior members in the marketing department, a retrospection that leads you, once again, to seek the recruitment of two employees, management would be 'shocked' if they found the marketing department understaffed and unable to complete work on time. Upon further enquiry it might transpire that in that particular year there were more retirements, an 'unusual' number of sabbaticals, a large amount of maternity leave, an unexpectedly high degree of sickness leave, or indeed a higher than expected number of deaths! On closer analysis of relevant variables one might find that the marketing department was increasingly becoming a top-heavy and mature department. Furthermore, consider what might happen if British Airways were offering free around-the-world tickets for that year, child allowances had trebled owing to a rather generous restructuring of the Treasury under a Labour administration, and an epidemic of typhoid flu had been sweeping across Western Europe! Although this is a rather humorous example, it highlights the importance of manpower planning and the endless possibility of variables that one could possibly consider. This is partly why the task of manpower planning is such a difficult and time-consuming process involving a considerable amount of research and knowledge of current events that may shape and affect the availability of internal resources and indeed the current stocks of human resources available for recruitment in the local and national labour market.

How many variables is it sensible therefore to consider in a detailed manpower plan? If all variables are not considered then it may well be the case that at some stage management will be 'shocked' by 'disturbances' in organisational employment patterns in response to both internal and external environmental changes. It was well known, for example, that in certain British car factories in the 1960s and 1970s there would be a heavier than normal rate of sickness and absence on Fridays! Being aware of the variables that affect manpower supply is a crucial area of concern for professional manpower planners, and as the examples above show, it can prove critical for the success of the organisation. If management remains ignorant of the ebb and flow of organisation, the movement of employment patterns and the variables that lead to change, then severe operational difficulties will emerge as management finds itself with some departments overstaffed, other departments suffering from a chronic shortage of employees, and possibly some departments that cannot function on Fridays because of the absence of staff. The need for manpower planning arises therefore from the operational needs of an organisation, and its importance lies in maintaining a sufficient supply of employees, in the right place and time, and at the right cost. Only through detailed observation and planning of many variables, both internal to the organisation and external in the wider political socio-economic environment, can management ensure a reconciliation of labour supply and demand such that shocks and disturbances are avoided.

We can summarise the need for manpower planning as one that involves both a quantifiable and quantitative dimension leading to:

- *recruitment plans*: to avoid unexpected shortages;
- *the identification of training needs*: to avoid skill shortages;
- *management development*: in order to avoid bottlenecks of trained but disgruntled management who see no future position in the hierarchy, but also to avoid managerial shortages – this often requires careful planning;
- *industrial relations plans*: often, seeking to change the quantity and quality of employees will require careful IR planning if an organisation is to avoid industrial unrest.

In practice, 'manpower planning is concerned with the demand and supply of labour and problems arising from the process of reconciling these factors' (Tyson and York, 1989: 76). In sum, the need for manpower planning lies with the long-term and short-term practical operational needs of the organisation but also, critically, with the social, psychological, and financial needs and aspirations of individual employees within organisation. As we have seen, it also arises out of a complex process of political negotiation within organisation and is in part the self-serving product of what we might call a will-to-power by manpower planners. A basic strife between movement and representation in organisation compounds this paradox and contributes to the always unfinished ongoing need for manpower planning. Yet, who is it that does manpower planning? It seems an arduous and unenviable task, one that over time always ends in partial failure and incompletion.

WHO DOES MANPOWER PLANNING?

Traditionally in large organisations the function of manpower planning was normally carried out by the personnel department or by a specialist manpower planner employed within the personnel department. In many smaller organisations, often in the absence of any well-defined separate personnel department, the process of manpower planning would have been conducted by the general manager of the organisation. In small family-owned firms, for example, it may well be that the manpower planner would also have been the wages clerk, the financial manager, the marketing and distribution manager. It is really only in large-scale and often bureaucratic businesses that specialised personnel departments and manpower planners maintained a distinctive identity. Therefore, it is large-scale organisations such as the Civil Service, the National Health Service, the Royal Air Force, and the large high street retail banks that have provided the conventional empirical sites for the study and practice of manpower planning.

In the UK economy of the 1950s and 1960s, with full employment and an expanding dynamic international economy, the emphasis within manpower planning was one of employment growth and organisational expansion. Anticipating employee turnover, and identifying those areas of organisation that required additional 'manpower', constituted the principal responsibility of manpower planners. Recruiting and selecting cost-efficient employees in the context of difficult 'tight' labour markets, where inflationary pressures and wage rises were beginning to cause some concern over company profitability, combined to promote the virtues of 'good' manpower planning. Quick and efficient methods of replacing turnover through recruitment and selection were seen to be critical in securing and maintaining continued profitability.

In times of labour scarcity, the credibility and influence of manpower planning as a specialist domain of management expertise prospered. If a business suffered from a high turnover of staff in the 1960s, a series of organisation-wide consequences and repercussions would have created considerable operational difficulties for management. As a delicate eco-like system of relational phenomena, we know that organisations are vulnerable to a knock-on 'domino'-like effect of reverberation and complication in response to only small degrees of disturbance. So, what might seem a relatively minor change in one area of an organisation can rapidly spill over into other areas, aggravating and amplifying the initial agitation. Overworked departments and underresourced divisions within organisations might very quickly spark discontent and low morale amongst employees, pushing up rates of absence and sickness. Given the conditions of full employment in the 1960s and early 1970s, staff were difficult and costly to replace. As a consequence, large organisations sought to invest considerable resources in the management of manpower planning at a time when 'organisation structures were highly centralised and relatively stable, with the emphasis on promotion and upward mobility; and the main concerns were recruitment and retention' (Timperley and Sisson, 1989: 103). The scale at which such organisations were operating, both geographically and hierarchically, clearly necessitated some planning and coordination of human resources.

First of all, as manpower planners we would have needed to know where employees were in the organisation – which in the context of large complex organisations is not as simple as it first might appear. Once we have established the number of employees, and where they are currently being used, then we might be in a better position to think how they could be moved to where they are needed or where they could be more gainfully deployed. Yet the identification of 'shortages' and 'surpluses' is also not the simple technical exercise it might at first seem. Consider the difficulties involved, pre-computerisation, of establishing how many people are working within a large organisation.

An obvious answer might be employment records. Well, yes, this might give you a figure representing formal numbers employed. Yet how accurate are these records, and who maintains them? Within dockwork, the repercussions of 'welting' (Clegg, 1979:142) meant that while formal employment records might tell you how many people were employed, they didn't really tell you how many were actually *working*. In his highly influential study of manpower reorganisation and collective bargaining at the Esso Fawley plant, Allan Flanders notes that craftsmen's 'mates' worked at only about 40% of the productivity rate of the craftsmen they assisted (Flanders, 1964:170). So formal employment records might show that 216 employees worked as 'pipefitters' in 1960. Of these, however, 82 were 'mates' who worked, on average, only $3\frac{1}{2}$ hours a day. Therefore the formal record of numbers employed offers only a very limited reading of manpower utilisation. It doesn't really guarantee how many people are working, nor 'where' organisational resources are being deployed or used, let alone where they might be most efficiently employed.

When we think about who maintains these records we complicate the picture even further. For legal and tax reasons there are often incentives to overplay or underplay the number of employees. In transport for example, where the law restricts the numbers of hours a lorry driver can work, organisations might be tempted to fabricate employment records. 'Excessive' hours driven by one truck driver might reap wage benefits for the individual employee and avoid employment costs for the employer. In an effort to avoid legal proceedings the employer might create the 'illusion' that two drivers were working together in the cab. The 'strategic' use of multiple tachographs will allow one driver to work a 14-hour shift, while 'recording' only seven hours. The other seven hours are worked by another named driver, who exists only as a formal paper record. In order to 'distribute' the total number of driver hours among a larger population of drivers in an effort to avoid infringing legal requirements, formal records may show a far greater number of employees than is actually the case. In other companies, the creation of employment records might be a way of avoiding tax. This means that we always need to be cautious when approaching official company documents and published statistics, and ask who maintains the records and whose interests they serve.

Record keeping is an expensive administrative and managerial activity. We might even say that organisation needs to manpower plan for manpower planners! Before we know where we are, the risk is that manpower planning departments have sprung up, employing huge armies of statistical planners and record keepers. Paradoxically, keeping a tight control on the cost of maintaining such a large and diversifying workforce required considerable time and effort in the planning and control of manpower. Centralised within the apex of specialised head office departments, incumbent with its hierarchical vantage point, it was assumed that manpower planners could literally provide an 'overview' of manpower flows throughout the entire organisation. This is the manpower planner as the brains of the organisation, its heroic masculine 'author'. From its vantage point in the 'head' office, the stocks and flows of manpower could be monitored and recorded in a form that allowed its intellectual reprocessing by the 'head' so as to work the body of organisation more rationally and efficiently. This was an era of specialisation and the growth of management science, management as the 'science' of universal principles, techniques, rules and procedures. This was also the age of mechanised regularity and control, of organisation as machine (Morgan, 1986), where the formal-rational principles of modem organisation, or 'Weberian' bureaucracy (Weber, 1948), shaped the development of manpower planning. In the 1950s and 1960s, from national economic labour market planning to internal manpower planning audits and reviews – whether in the Civil Service, local government, or the banks – the rationalisation of manpower planning consolidated hierarchies of authority in organisation while contributing to the delineation of clear lines of command and control, the specialisation of function, and the cultivation of elite expertise.

The era of the specialist manpower planner, then, was one of growth, large complex organisation, record keeping, expanding bureaucracy, administration and control. In the main, manpower planning was a quantitative science officiated by white-collar technicians who traced their ancestry back to Taylor's time and motion study. The influence of Henri Fayol (1949), as mediated and popularised in the UK by Lyndall Urwick (1947), led to the increasing technical abstraction of manpower planning from the domain of the 'Taylorite' managerial struggle focused upon the point of production – that 'point' of day-to-day 'negotiation' and contestation in the employment relation between manager and worker over the substantive content of the wage–effort bargain (Armstrong, 1996). This was the 'white heat' of scientific and technological revolution – the onward march of science and man's ever greater mastery of the social and natural world.

In the context of the 1980s, traditional quantitative manpower planning fell somewhat out of favour as management, in response to product market crisis and international economic competition, sought to redevelop its employee resource and reduce staffing levels. With its associated bureaucracy and red tape, manpower planning was forced to reorientate its contribution to organisation in an era that saw large-scale rationalisations, redundancies and restructuring. It is said by some that manpower planning is becoming 'human resource' planning (Bramham, 1989), providing a more sensitive and qualitative approach to the acquisition, utilisation and development of employees, one that is not so fixated upon numbers and statistical calculation. In the 1987 report of the Manpower Services Commission, 'competence, commitment and the capacity to change' were deemed to challenge the quantitative traditions of manpower planning. As John Storey (1992) writes on the basis of his research of UK industry in the late 1980s, the 'mechanistic manpower-planning models have been superseded and there is very clear evidence of a type of planning which attends not only to regulating numbers but is proactive in respect of part-time work and annual hours contracts, and proactive in the realm of radically different forms of labour utilization' (p. 89).

We might think of this as the growth of a more 'open' authorship in manpower planning, in which manpower planners returned to the floor to make use of a more improvised and intuitive range of skills, tinkering with the 'culture' of organisation and the more qualitative aspects of the employment relation (Deal and Kennedy, 1982; Peters, 1993, 1994). If it was the growth of a more open authorship, it was also a period in which the identity and authorship of a specifically delimited elite practice of manpower planning was challenged. Manpower planning began to be devolved into the immediacy of the day-to-day employment relation, where it merged with other 'tacit' features of people management within expanded roles for first-line managers (Storey, 1992: 216–241). Now, while we say 'devolved' we should not forget that this was within a framework of tight budgetary control, more sophisticated performance monitoring, and the application of strict accountancy procedures in audit and control imposed by the centre – whether through the use of 'cash limits' in the public sector or through the diffusion of a logic of accountancy into the practice of shopfloor management (Armstrong, 1995; Brown et al., 1995).

There are further grounds for questioning whether manpower planning is simply becoming less 'quantitative' as it incorporates elements of a 'softer' and more qualitative form of management. The number of redundancies, early retirements, plant closures and reorganisations multiplied in the 1980s and 1990s, often accompanied by an organisational strategy that sought the replacement of full-time workers with novel forms of labour and labour contracts that maximised quantitative prediction and control. This might reflect, of course, the contradictions and tensions associated with 'hard' and 'soft' human resource management (Storey, 1987). Furthermore, during the late 1980s personnel managers were increasingly expressing concern over UK demographic changes, together with attendant fears over supply shortages and recruitment difficulties. For many there was the very real fear that there would be an insufficient number of young and qualified individuals, prompting management to seek new, and often controversial, forms of employment. This suggests a persistent obsession with numerical calculation and the abiding presence of a logic of quantification.

A more realistic interpretation of the state of contemporary manpower planning is one that is able to grasp the significance of **contradiction** and **paradox** in organisation and organisational change. To appreciate this, one needs to examine the role of organisational politics, the competition between the different management specialisms, and the networks of power-knowledge that build up across the domains of academia, business consultancy, the financial markets, the government, and the professional bodies that represent the various management disciplines (Cooper, 1998; Thrift, 1999). One needs to examine the growth of human resource management in the UK then, against the backdrop of the Conservative government (1979–97), the commercialisation of higher education, the rise of management consultancy, and the increasing power of the accountancy profession. This takes us beyond the scope of this chapter, but in tracing out the main lines of this analytical space we capture some sense of the importance of tactics, manoeuvring, and networking – between institutions, and across the social relations of organisation – by means of which the 'authorship' of manpower planning is achieved. Authorship becomes a derivative phenomenon, a contingent product of particular historical and social relations. We therefore de-centre the priority granted to the individual 'scientific' manpower planner by those studies that focus myopically upon the instruments and techniques of manpower planning (e.g. Bramham, 1990).

We might say then, that 'manpower planning' has been forced to reorientate its own values and reassess the contribution it makes – and the way in which it 'promotes' its contribution – to the regulation of employment relations. Qualitative and quantitative dimensions in manpower planning cannot be simply severed and organisational history assessed in terms of its predilection for one or the other. Any planning of manpower inevitably involves a complex of qualitative and quantitative features. Manoeuvring between the two represents a 'tactical' play of forces wherein the relations between manpower planners and the rising tide of human resource management, and those wider relations between HRM, other management professions, organisation more broadly, and the financial markets, are renegotiated and resettled. A history of capitalist enterprise would reveal that the tension between measurement-quantification and the demand to provide space for the less easily measured qualitative features of organisation and work is both indelible and potentially catastrophic for management.

In our assessment of who does manpower planning it is also worth noting the findings of a recent study, where it is reported that organisations 'prefer neither to use the term "manpower" nor to return to the large and elaborate planning documents produced by head offices a decade ago' (Cowling and Walters, 1990: 3). This means that when we try to assess *who* does manpower planning, we need to be aware that it is being increasingly performed in diffuse and complex ways by a heterogeneous range of agents, as formalised large-scale bureaucracies give way to the more disaggregated and experimental organisational configurations of organisation (Clegg, 1990; Hatch, 1997). This is taken up in greater detail later in the chapter. Here, it is necessary to stress that while many organisations are seeking to redirect the responsibility for manpower planning away from centralised specialised departments and towards 'empowered' production line managers, they do so by maintaining strategic hold and direction at corporate level (Marginson *et al.*, 1988, Storey, 1991, 1992; Salaman, 1992).

With the current emphasis on flexible manpower use, novel forms and new contractual modes of employment, together with innovative approaches to career and succession planning, one might be tempted to suggest that the decline of 'manpower planning' and the rise of 'human resource planning' (Bramham, 1989) captures the essence of contemporary human resource management. As Bennison and Casson (1984) suggest, in a somewhat cavalier fashion, manpower planning 'belongs to the world of calculation, computers and big bureaucracies' (p. ix). In its place, many theorists are recommending strategies and policies that address 'labour skill shortages and cultural change rather than hierarchical structures, succession plans, and mathematical modelling' (Cowling and Waiters, 1990: 3). This section has taught us to exercise some caution and critical scrutiny in the face of this kind of managerial self-representation. In the light of this we might say that this quotation from Cowling and Walters reflects an aspiration and a claim for relevance – a tactical manoeuvre within the changing composition of power relations and organisation politics – as much as it represents a factual state of affairs in the empirical world of organisation.

THE CREATION OF A MANPOWER PLAN

In this section we shall look more closely at those traditional techniques that contribute to the planning of manpower resources in terms of both internal considerations and external factors that influence the final outcome of the manpower plan.

Internal considerations

Wastage analysis

Initially the manpower planner will be concerned with the average number of employees that leave and therefore need replacing just in order to maintain a stable number of employees in the organisation. In large organisations, with many departments and complex demarcated lines of responsibility, this can become quite a difficult statistical task, one that requires considerable time and effort in the collection, synthesis and analysis of data. In smaller organisations it can often be calculated very simply. On a very simple level, everybody knows everyone else, and when someone leaves it is quite an important and visible event. In large organisations it is far more likely that an employee is simply seen as a payroll number, or a job code. The constant ebb and flow of 'numbers' within larger organisations requires a far more rigorous calculation of 'wastage' than the rule of thumb applied by management.

The simplest way of calculating wastage is through a turnover analysis. This can be calculated using the following simple formula:

$$\frac{\text{Number leaving in one year}}{\text{Average number of employees}} \times 100\% = x\%$$

However, this gives a somewhat crude and unrealistic picture of wastage. At its most basic it fails to locate *where* these people are leaving from. In general, though, it gives a broad picture of organisational turnover, where it is usual to consider a 25% turnover rate as perfectly respectable in modem large-scale businesses. Anything approaching 30–35% may well start alarm bells ringing. The cost of advertising, recruiting, and training of employees, for example, will be far in excess of the cost for those companies that are able to maintain a 25% turnover of employees, making the organisation uncompetitive and inefficient. However, as we suggested above, when the manpower planner comes to formulate plans and policies to address turnover, this figure does not provide much useful and practical information. For example, where are these people leaving from? What is the average age of the person who is leaving? It could be that your turnover figure has become distorted over the recent past because of the age profile of the organisation, and in any one year it may be that there are far more employees than on average reaching retirement age. As a consequence, it would be far more useful if we could disaggregate this figure in order to account for that proportion of turnover made up of retirements. In this way we might begin to identify that turnover which is 'voluntary' in nature and where 'better' management might be able to have an impact. Legally, there is very little management can do to prevent turnover on the basis of employees reaching the retirement age. What it can do is to isolate those areas of employee turnover in organisation where management *can* make a difference.

Furthermore, turnover might be limited to one particular category of employment, one department, a certain grade, or one geographical area. The variety of influences that affect employee turnover are far too numerous to be captured by one calculation such as the labour turnover ratio. Thus, for practical reasons, we need a more subtle index of turnover, which is more closely identifiable with factoral influences.

An alternative to the labour turnover ratio is the Labour Stability Index (Bowey, 1974), which is calculated from the following formula:

$$\frac{\textbf{Number of employees exceeding one year's service}}{\textbf{Number of employees employed one year ago}} \times \textbf{100} = \textbf{\textit{x}\%}$$

This calculation, by contrast, calculates and emphasises those who stay, and hence is known as a *stability index*. Its importance can be demonstrated through a calculation and comparison with the turnover ratio. Consider two companies:

- In January 2000 *Company* X employs 2000 assistants, but by January 2001 800 have 'voluntarily' left. This gives a turnover of $800/2000 \times 100 = 40\%$.
- *Company Y* by contrast employs 2000 assistants in January 2000. By January 2001 only 100 have actually 'voluntarily' left the company, although they have been replaced eight times during the year. This would, once again, give a turnover of 40%.

The Labour Stability Index by contrast would show that Company X has a stability rate of only 60%, whereas company Y has a far more impressive stability rate of 95%.

Far more sophisticated techniques than this have evolved in an attempt to more accurately plot and account for employee wastage. In recent years many companies have become interested in the 'length of service' of employees, and Figure 4.1 shows how it might be possible to develop a 'frequency distribution' of leavers by length of service.

From Figure 4.1 it is possible to identify three distinct phases in the analysis of turnover. Coming out of the work of the Tavistock Institute, Hill and Trist (1953, 1955), in two important papers reporting on the Park Gate Iron and Steel Company study, established the existence of a relationship between an initial 'induction crisis', a period of 'differential transit', and a concluding 'settled connection'. During the induction crisis it can be seen that the relationship between the individual and the organisation is unsettled and a little insecure. The frequency of leavers in this period was far greater in the first 18 months of service than during subsequent periods of employment. This is perhaps best seen as a 'trial period', where employees are not sure if they are going to stay. Moreover, the 'shock' of employment and its concomitant attention to discipline, hard work, and regular timekeeping takes some adjustment time. In the crisis period, therefore, there is likely to be a far greater incidence of inductees leaving than in subsequent periods.

Hill and Trist also found that other problems associated with manpower planning could be identified during this period. The rates of 'unsanctioned' absence and industrial accidents, for example, were found to be far greater during the induction crisis than during the period of settled connection. In attempting to explain and analyse this relationship the authors found considerable evidence to suggest 'that accidents are in part used, however unconsciously, as a means of withdrawal from the work situation' (Hill and Trist, 1955: 121). Over time the incidence of accidents would fall, and relatively 'sanctioned absences' would rise. This was explained as a result of the quality of the relationship established between the individual and the organisation. After the induction crisis a more stable and secure relationship was established such that a more positive relationship between the individual and the organisation helped to reduce accidents and transfer unauthorised absences to registered sickness leave:

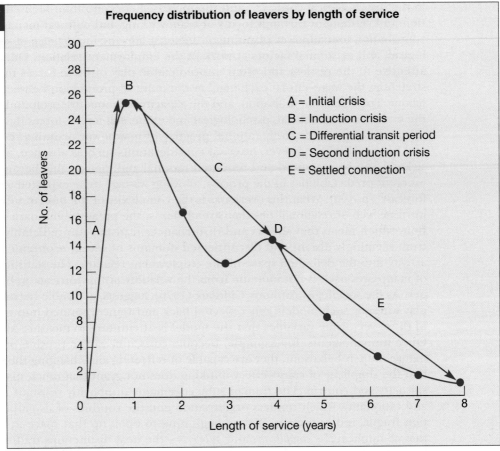

Figure 4.1   **Frequency distribution of leavers by length of service**

A = Initial crisis
B = Induction crisis
C = Differential transit period
D = Second induction crisis
E = Settled connection

Only sickness, therefore, remains; and the suggestion is that recourse is had to some kind of sickness when the individual, no longer able, in virtue of his [sic] improved relationship, to project his . . . bad feelings on to the firm as freely as he once did. (p.136)

Thus the authors conclude that employees internalise stress and dissatisfaction, and do not 'blame' the organisation after the induction crisis. The word 'blame' is used by the authors to denote a psychological reaction to the organisation such that the individuals are looking to punish or hit back at the organisation for the stress of employment by absenting themselves from work without authorisation. Accidents are also more likely to occur because of the same lack of commitment and dedication to the organisation. This also allows individuals to maintain the perception that it is the organisation which is at fault for their difficulties of adjusting to work rather than a problem for the individual employee. Therefore an overall fall in the level of absence after the induction crisis suggests 'a dynamic connectedness between sanctioned absence (in the form of sickness) and the phase of settled connection' (Hill and Trist, 1955: 136). Consequently the employee moves from being a victim at the psychological level to one who increasingly looks to him or herself for the cause of sickness or the need for absence.

The work of Hill and Trist is interesting because it suggests that manpower planning improves as individuals build up a positive working relationship with the organisation. Their work anticipates the interest among contemporary management in the 'psychological contract', and the increased concentration focused upon induction and settlement through forms of teamworking and cultural management. As a contribution to manpower planning, it demonstrates the importance of social, psychological, and existential factors at work in the employment relation. One needs to be attentive to the restless and often unpredictable play of these forces in pulling and stretching the wage–effort 'exchange' at the point of production between capital and labour. The retention, utilisation, and the capacity to labour are profoundly affected by the undercurrent of social, psychological and existential forces, forces that remain subterranean to the excessively rational practice of manpower planning. For Timperley and Sisson (1989), however, internal considerations such as absence, accidents and sickness can be measured and rendered rational and manageable because 'there are inherent predictabilities in the process, allowing wastage to be expected and therefore, forecast' (p. 109). What this overlooks is the complexity of the human subject, and the intricate web of relational ties that stretch across the putative boundaries of organisation, which mean that shocks and disturbances transmit unpredictably and rapidly from seemingly distant and disconnected domains of social, economic and cultural activity into the delimited space of the employment relation. The statistical modelling of manpower itself is not immune from the volatility of this intricate web of relational ties. As the sociologist Anthony Giddens (1976) suggests, a 'double hermeneutic' is in play whereby such models gets reflected back and reincorporated into the behaviour of those very same variables that the model is attempting to measure and formalise. Once human agents, for example, become conscious of the routine or predictable nature of their behaviour, they are capable of reflecting and changing their habits such that the simplicity of cause–effect thinking does not grant that much managerial perspicacity and control. The human subject remains stubbornly resistant to prediction and rationality, which renders organisation and the routines of its employment relation fragile and uncertain. We are beginning to open up that space in organisation that co-implicates – *complicates* and *subverts* – the neat distinctions traditionally made between 'theory' and 'practice', between re-presentation and the assumed a priori presence of organisation. Logic starts to break down in this space, and the procedural guidelines of rational manpower planning begin to sway and bend.

On one level, it is important to remember that rationality is 'bounded' (Simon, 1957), in part because there are far too many potential factors to incorporate and model. Manpower planners need not only accurate information on absence and turnover rates, but also statistical records and forecasts of retirements by department, sabbaticals, the average number of employees engaged at any one time in training and retraining, and even the fluctuating moods, sentiments and emotions of employees that affect performance and efficiency. This gives just a flavour of some of the factors that need to be taken into consideration in planning manpower, and we have already considered the difficulties involved in maintaining records. The work of Hill and Trist opens up the question of the human subject, and has stimulated us to think of the applicability and limitations of rationality and reason in explaining and accounting for its behaviour. Yet, if manpower planning is to be predictable and entirely accurate, rationality must observe no bounds!

Business objectives

It may be of course that stability in employee numbers is not what is required, as the business may well be expanding or contracting in response to product market pressures. If an organisation is experiencing rapid product market growth, as it launches a new innovative product for example, labour demand may well increase in order to respond and cover the extra workload. In the short term, organisations can adjust to unpredicted 'shocks' in the product market through making short-term adjustments to the supply of employees within the organisation.

The most obvious ways in which an organisation adjusts its manpower in response to growing demand include the increased use of overtime, the temporary extension in the hours of work of those employed, the use of subcontract labour, and the recruitment of short-term labour from temporary employment agencies. Of course, if manpower planning was integrated with business strategy and planning in a more 'human resource planning' mould, the launch of a new product and the projections for sales would have allowed manpower planners more time to make resourcing adjustments. One can never entirely predict the market response to new product launches. Who could have predicted the scale of success of the Rubik's cube? The film *Star Wars* was also widely expected to be a massive box office flop, and in order to secure the distribution of his film George Lucas was forced to sign an agreement that made him responsible for any losses incurred on merchandise. As we now know, not only was *Star Wars* one of the most successful films ever, it was precisely the merchandise that delivered the most profitability. The successful launch of a new product then often belies detailed planning and preparation. Even in more strategically integrated organisations professing to practise human resource management, the level of detailed resource planning that is needed to guarantee the elimination of 'shock' is almost impossible to calculate precisely. Indeed, it is this very unpredictability that provides the conditions for product market competition and the opportunity to make vast sums of money.

By contrast, organisations that are contracting or restructuring into new business areas may need to temporarily reduce the numbers of staff in old business areas. It may be that retraining and relocation packages are insufficient to resource the new plant or project, and consequently there will be a need to 'downsize' in one area of the business while expanding in other areas. This was the case for many UK organisations during the 1980s as they sought to respond to market and political pressures by restructuring their businesses. In the UK banking industry, for example, many of the old routine clerical and bookkeeping functions were being removed through the introduction of new technology while at the same time employment opportunities were increasing in the sales and insurance functions (Cressey and Scott, 1992; O'Doherty, 1993). Yet the limited scope of rationality and predictability is once again in evidence. A series of strikes in the financial services industry and rampant discontent and low morale spread deleterious effects in the capacity to utilise and develop manpower, while the reputation of the banks suffered further from a number of high-profile media stories. Alongside stories about overcharging customers and the withdrawal of local branch services, banks were also, perhaps unfairly, tainted by association with pensions and mortgage mis-selling within financial services more broadly. No amount of statistical modelling within the function of manpower planning could have forecast the compound and aggravated consequence attendant upon such rapid radiation and diffusion of effects across the complex interconnected web of social and political relations.

We have been arguing that it is undoubtedly necessary to take into account organisation-wide activity and wider business objectives during the process of manpower planning and in the creation of any competent manpower plan, but we have also illustrated the limitations of measurement and predictability. In the following section we take a look at so-called 'Markov' models, which offer an exceptional example of the role of calculation and prediction in the creation of a manpower plan.

Markov models

These models are often used by manpower planners in addressing the internal factors that need to be considered in the development of a manpower plan. The Markov model, and variants of it, attempts to model the expected life flow of individuals within an organisation. It states that organisations have predictable wastage patterns according to length of service, for example, and that this pattern can be discerned early on in an individual's career. Once 'survival' rates have been calculated, and barring no future shocks, a fairly stable pattern of career progression and replacement needs over time can be calculated. Furthermore, adaptations of the basic Markov model can be used to project recruitment on the basis of stable patterns of both wastage and promotion. From this a manpower planner can predict the probability and the likely time span of an individual progressing from one grade to another in the hierarchy.

From a consideration of these factors, important planning information can be acquired and used in the recruitment and selection process, but also more significantly in preparing the training of individuals so that the organisation does not suffer from quantitative or qualitative supply shortages in the future. If a planner knows with some certainty that an individual tends to spend only two years in a particular managerial grade before being promoted to some other department, contingent training and recruitment plans can be made so that shortages in that area can be eliminated. Thus if 'recruitment, promotion and wastage patterns of staff are stable over reasonable periods of time, . . . the probability that someone in a particular grade at any time will be in some other grade at a later time can be established from the detailed recent career histories of staff' (Timperley and Sisson, 1994: 156).

Markov models attempt to map the 'throughput' of human resources in an organisation by predicting the patterns of entry and exit: entry and exit from the organisation as a whole, and entry and exit from particular grades. Elaborations on the basic model allow for the behavioural effects consequent upon changes in the distribution and flow of employees through an organisation. This model presents a view of organisation as one of predictability and regularity, organisation as 'institutions' that 'pass through staffing cycles', as Timperley and Sisson (1994) note in their review. Markov models work best under conditions of organisational stability, but begin to lack predictive accuracy under conditions of uncertainty and change. One of the most volatile sources of disturbance and change is found to emanate from external sources – changes in labour markets, in global product markets, and in government legislation. We now turn to examine the importance of some of these external considerations in the development of a credible manpower plan.

External considerations

State legislation

One extremely important area that needs to be considered while formulating a manpower plan is the restrictions that are imposed on organisations by the government in areas of individual and collective labour law (see Torrington and Hall, 1989, and Chapter 10). The evolution of the industrial system in the UK has been characterised by successive governmental interventions to redress power inequalities between capital and labour, and shape the way in which labour is recruited, deployed, trained, promoted, and made redundant. It is a long time since managers and employers could simply 'hire and fire' according to their own whim. The responsibility for the welfare of employees has been increasingly assumed by national and European government and secured by means of state legislation, to such an extent that today many organisations and manpower planners have found it prudent to establish specialist legal advisory departments to assist them in the development and management of manpower planning.

Increasingly this legislation is of a European-wide nature, enacted and passed by the European Parliament in Brussels and Strasbourg. This has been the cause of some considerable friction between the directives and legislation of the European Parliament and the traditions of economic and industrial regulation in particular member states. In the UK, many of the legislative initiatives, including those within the Social Chapter of the Maastricht Treaty, are seen by a considerable proportion of UK management (as articulated most vociferously by the Institute of Directors and certain sections of the CBI) to be overly onerous and restrictive. The role of European legislation has become far more important in the day-to-day activities of UK organisations and in particular in the management of manpower planning. We have seen most recently legislation, with some industry-specific exceptions, prescribing a maximum working week of 48 hours. Co-determination, consultation, and information rights on matters relating to manpower planning and use, particularly as regards management procedure in redundancy, have been granted to European Works Councils. Although John Major's Conservative government negotiated and secured a UK opt-out from the Social Chapter at Maastricht in 1991, UK companies, in part by virtue of employing workers in other European economies, have been steadily adopting the regulations of the social protocol (Hall, 1992, 1994). The Blair Labour government, elected in 1997, has adopted a far more progressive approach to the developing European Community, and the signs are that greater integration and legislative harmony across nation states will have a significant impact on domestic UK manpower planning.

In the recent past it was in the areas of sex discrimination and race relations legislation where European policy has had most impact. In response to European policy and EC directives UK legislation imposes a responsibility on manpower planners to recruit, train and promote employees on an indiscriminate basis, such that religion, race and gender cannot by law be considered a basis for employing, promoting, training or redundancy. Of course manpower planners can discriminate on the basis of being able-bodied! This rather bizarre practice is rare, but in recent press advertisements some councils have advertised for the recruitment of handicapped people only. At first sight this might appear somewhat discriminatory, but in fact there is no legislation proscribing discrimination on the basis of being able-bodied. Thus for manpower planners seeking to maintain the recommended 3% of handicapped employees within the organisation, they are quite within their rights to insist that only those deemed handicapped may apply for the advertised post. Moreover, manpower planning in local councils is affected by the responsibility to secure a 'representative' workforce that can be expected to be sensitive and attentive to particular community and sectional group needs.

Legislation on the hours that people can be expected to work, the time that can be spent working in front of a VDU, rest periods, the provision of basic medical facilities, and recently the necessity to provide facilities for pregnant employees, all imposes some restriction on the managerial prerogative in manpower planning. Organisations cannot simply consider their own operational and internal organisational needs. They are channelled within certain guidelines on what they can and cannot do in the management and employment of individuals. As we have seen, this has important consequences for those who are responsible for manpower planning. Yet it is not just through the use of legislation that governments can make an impact on the conduct of manpower planning. A whole series of institutional mechanisms, and what are called 'supply-side' policies, can shape the development of company manpower planning, whether through changes to social security, unemployment benefits and taxation, or by means of company incentives, training schemes and regional development programmes. Manpower planners need to be aware of the interactions between the projects and institutions of national economic manpower planning conducted by the state and government and their company-specific manpower planning initiatives. We shall look at the use of regional development schemes in order to illustrate these connections between the wider political domain of manpower planning and company-specific management.

Regional development schemes

Successive UK governments have attempted to influence the direction and level of investment through offering tax and other financial incentives for companies to establish new plants and outlets in particular regions of the economy. This is an economic and often a politically motivated policy initiative to boost employment in recession-hit areas. The North-West and the North-East, for example, have suffered disproportionately in the post-1945 UK economy as a result of protracted industrial restructuring and the decline of the heavy coal, steel and shipbuilding industries. In an attempt to boost new employment in these areas companies have been offered a package of financial incentives to move and locate new factories, departments and retail outlets in these areas. The growth of part-time, casual, and temporary employment in the former industrial heartlands of the UK economy is a direct consequence of legislative and manpower planning initiatives developed by successive governments in collaboration with foreign capital and domestic UK businesses.

The importance for manpower planners is that in the development of manpower plans the organisation needs to know where it is likely to trade more profitably. So, for example, if the development of a new product is going to necessitate the construction of a new site and the creation of 2000 new jobs, it will be the responsibility of the manpower planner to provide information on the most profitable location for this plant. It may well be that as a result of regional development schemes the company would be far better locating its new plant in the North-East, where cheap local reserves of labour are available, together with tax privileges that reduce the costs of production relative to constructing the new plant more locally. In the creation of a manpower plan it is important that such 'external considerations' are fully evaluated so that the organisation's manpower plan can provide information on the most profitable alternatives (Lee Clark, 1993).

Micro-level factors

Finally, in the development of a credible manpower plan attention needs to be focused on the nature of the local labour markets. Successful manpower planning not only provides information on the immediate local labour market, but also needs to compare and contrast the age, skill and cost profiles of each local labour market. In this way the organisation plans the resource implications of organisational expansion, contraction and structural change in terms of quantity, quality and price. It may be the case, for example, that different local labour markets offer different average age profiles, which could be important for organisations seeking to recruit young employees. Alternatively, organisations might seek to locate new plants in areas where unemployment is high in order to guarantee the availability of sufficient employees and also to benefit from the likely wage cost advantages. If supply exceeds demand, as characterises depressed regional economies, economic theory would predict a tendency for wages to fall. Thus in comparing the South-East with the North-West in terms of wage costs it has been a well-observed phenomenon for a number of years that cheaper labour is to be found in the North-West.

We have now established that there are a range of important internal and external factors that contribute to the development of a successful manpower plan. The construction of the Japanese Nissan plant at Washington in the North-East of England, for example, was a decision informed by the logic of manpower planning, one that illustrates the play of a whole series of internal and external considerations. In part the region provides vast reserves of low-wage employees, who were not steeped in the traditions and experience of shopfloor car manufacture. These offered critical manpower planning incentives for the Nissan Corporation, who wanted to avoid both high-cost labour and the risk of shopfloor trade union militancy that had typified significant sections of the UK car industry (Beynon, 1973). However, as a number of recent studies of Nissan and Japanese car production suggest (Garrahan and Stewart, 1992; Delbridge, 1995), total manpower planning predictability and calculation cannot be achieved even in the context of sophisticated Japanese manpower planning and technology management. Low morale, poor commitment, unrecorded employee unrest and resistance, and health and safety abuses stand as testimony to the limitations of manpower calculation and prediction, and once again provide evidence that employment relations remain an unstable and partially unpredictable component of organisation.

ANALYSING DEMAND AND SUPPLY

Once the external and internal considerations have been brought together at the development stage of the manpower plan, our textbook manpower planner is held to be in a position to analyse the 'net demand' and 'net supply' of human resources. The manpower planner can then proceed to seek a reconciliation of demand and supply. This has been captured in Figure 4.2, which synthesises the major components of the human resource planning process.

From this diagram it can be seen that there are two distinct stages in the planning process: an analysis of the current state of play in the organisation's human resources, and an analysis of the future plans and requirements of the business.

It should be clear from the preceding section that manpower planning adopts a number of techniques that seek to predict and project the availability of current staff. Predictability arises because of the claim that manpower flows typically tend to follow a fairly orderly pattern when analysed and measured quantitatively. Thus a good manpower plan is able to locate those employees who are likely to leave, where they are likely to leave from, the rate at which they leave, and the training implications arising from the need to keep a constant flow of suitably qualified employees to fill vacant positions. Any change in this pattern should also be able to be predicted by the manpower planner, because at this stage they should have a fairly comprehensive understanding of the variables that impact on these patterns of employment. By carefully monitoring these variables, shocks should be avoided and adjustments made relatively slowly and smoothly in order to avoid difficulties in the conduct of the business. The science of manpower planning pursues the ideal of a self-regulating

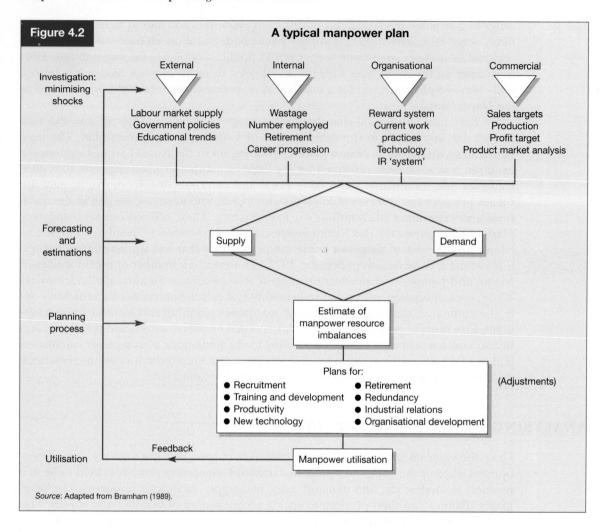

Figure 4.2   **A typical manpower plan**

Investigation: minimising shocks

External — Labour market supply / Government policies / Educational trends

Internal — Wastage / Number employed / Retirement / Career progression

Organisational — Reward system / Current work practices / Technology / IR 'system'

Commercial — Sales targets / Production / Profit target / Product market analysis

Forecasting and estimations — Supply / Demand

Planning process — Estimate of manpower resource imbalances

Plans for:
- Recruitment
- Training and development
- Productivity
- New technology
- Retirement
- Redundancy
- Industrial relations
- Organisational development

(Adjustments)

Utilisation — Feedback — Manpower utilisation

Source: Adapted from Bramham (1989).

organisation whole that automatically triggers a series of adjustments in response to signals and change in any one component of the organisation.

From the objectives of the business, the developmental, and relocation plans, the manpower planner has some basis within which to project the number of future staff that will be required by the organisation. At this stage the manpower planner is also in a position to advise on the strategic direction of the business in terms of what is possible strategically, given the constraints and opportunities in the internal and external labour market. For example, it is pointless to plan for organisational growth within a region that will be unable to supply the required number and skills of employees. In the absence of alternatives, organisational growth may be impossible given the future projection of labour supply availability. Good manpower planning can show how an organisation is best advised to develop and grow – where supply is available, the recruitment and training needs arising from growth, and the most profitable location for new plant and capital.

The third stage in Figure 4.2 shows the process of reconciliation. This arises because there is undoubtedly a mismatch between the quantitative and, importantly, qualitative demand for employees, based on future plans and projections, and what the current projections of employee availability are likely to be able to deliver. Initially, organisations would be interested in the numerical surpluses or shortfalls in staff that are likely to emerge in the future. A shortfall of staff will result if business growth and increasing product market success has not triggered compensatory plans to resource the organisation. This would result in the all-too-familiar scenario of departments being run at overcapacity, such that the increasing use of overtime, subcontract and temporary agency staff eventually leads to longer-term and more chronic operational difficulties. Orders may start to be processed late, and consequently deliveries to customers become erratic. If this persists, customers will begin to search for alternative sources of supply, and the organisation may well find itself losing market share. This highlights the critical role that manpower planning plays. If it is able to project future shortfalls and surpluses, adjustments and contingency plans can be developed to reconcile the mismatch between net demand and net supply.

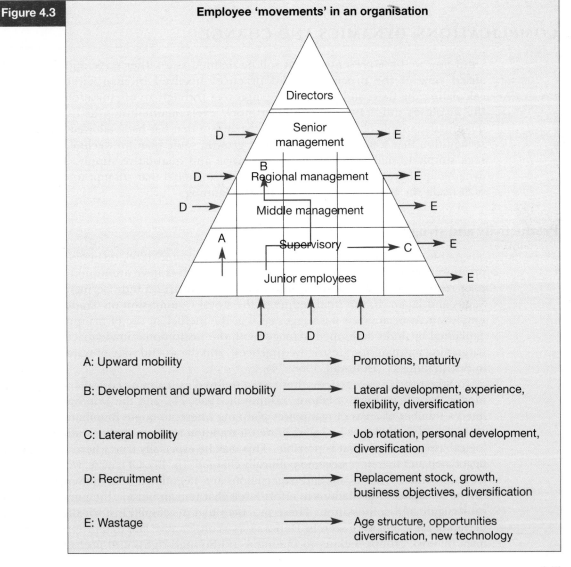

Figure 4.3   Employee 'movements' in an organisation

A: Upward mobility   ⟶   Promotions, maturity

B: Development and upward mobility   ⟶   Lateral development, experience, flexibility, diversification

C: Lateral mobility   ⟶   Job rotation, personal development, diversification

D: Recruitment   ⟶   Replacement stock, growth, business objectives, diversification

E: Wastage   ⟶   Age structure, opportunities diversification, new technology

The fourth stage in Figure 4.2 illustrates that function of manpower planning that is concerned with presentation and the evaluation of alternative policy routes in the management and reconciliation of shortfalls and surpluses. The final stage of the manpower planning process culminates in those changes that are made in the areas of recruitment and selection, training and development, redundancies and early retirements – in order to plug the gap between projected availability of staff and projected need. Figure 4.3 attempts to synthesise all the movements and flow of staff that typically exist in organisations. It reflects how difficult a task it is to track and monitor the complex movements of staff through an organisation, and at this stage we have not even really begun to consider the added complexity of the more qualitative dimensions of organisation.

In the next section of the chapter we address those factors that further complicate the process of manpower planning, factors that some would argue need to be taken into full account before the implementation of recruitment and selection plans.

COMPLICATIONS: DYNAMICS AND CHANGE

Until now we have presented what will be defined as a rather static and decontextualised view of the procedures and practices involved in manpower planning – calculating the flows and patterns of employees through an organisation, reconciling the surpluses and deficits of employee stock levels, maintaining the qualitative and quantitative supply of labour. The only dynamism that has been allowed has been the recognition that some companies project growth, some plan for decline, while others seek simply to maintain current quantitative and qualitative supply. A number of dynamic qualifications can be added to this basic model that attempt to capture more realistically the actual practice of manpower planning.

Productivity and struggle

Since at least the findings of the Donovan Commission in 1968, recurrent government pronouncements and periodic public policy initiatives have attempted to tackle the poor record of British industrial productivity in comparison with Germany, the United States and Japan. In the final report of the Royal Commission on Trade Unions and Employers Associations it was suggested that the inefficient use of manpower could be explained by underdeveloped management, the institutional inadequacy of collective bargaining mechanisms, 'restrictive practices', and the woeful state of training provision in British industry (Donovan, 1968: 74).

To take restrictive practices: these were defined as 'rules or customs which unduly hinder the efficient use of labour' (Donovan, 1968: 77), and the Donovan report outlined a number of areas of manpower planning where, to quote Bramham (1989), 'the standards of the job may be based more on tradition and expectation rather than on a logical assessment of what is possible. This may be especially true where standards are negotiated and therefore become politically charged' (p. 49). Of course, we might argue that all standards, workloads and expectations are 'negotiated' – in the sense that there can be no a priori foundations to effort levels that remain outside the purview of political struggle and contestation. These practices had developed historically over a long period of time, and were seen by Donovan as a conservative and inappropriate anachronism by work groups seeking to maintain 'traditional' rights and prerogatives in the context of changing economic circumstances and technological advance. The kinds of restrictive practices to which Donovan was drawing attention can be seen in a review of the work practices, work group norms, values and attitudes that persisted in the British docks and shipping industry. In a series of articles Peter Turnbull and his colleagues have studied the history of changing work practices in the British docks (Turnbull and Sapsford, 1991, 1992; Turnbull, 1992; Turnbull *et al.*, 1992), where the practice of 'welting' was common, for example, allowing workers on the docks to secure time and leisure when they should have nominally been working:

> dock workers were able to indulge in the practice of 'welting', where only half the gang works the cargo at any one time. The other half might be playing cards, drinking tea or coffee, or in extreme (well organised) cases working at the local market or driving a taxi.
>
> (Turnbull and Sapsford, 1992: 306)

It is precisely these kinds of practices that were deemed to be widespread throughout British industry during the 1950s and 1960s, and acted as a serious brake on the pursuit of productivity and competitive advantage.

The reform of the industrial relations system can be seen as an integral and important component in the evolution of 'formally rational' (Weber, 1964) methods of manpower planning. By 'formally rational' we mean those principles and techniques of organisation and order that seek to increase the efficiency of business operations. Now, this definition of rationality ignores the *ends* to which these techniques and procedures are being used. Thus it might be suggested that the 'politically charged' (Bramham, 1989) negotiations of manpower planning reflect some disagreement and political struggle over the precise scope and meaning of the term 'rational'. For manpower planning, the importance of formal rationality can be seen in the importance attributed to what is called 'efficient techniques' and procedures of calculation, forecasting, and the reconciliation of the supply and demand of labour. Its rationality is assumed by the ends that it serves – namely the maximisation of output, efficiency and productivity. The pursuit of these ends, however, might be secured at the expense of group norms, informal practices, and tacit agreements reached on the shopfloor between work groups and their representatives and immediate supervisors and managers. In the context of industrial relations more broadly, this is what Donovan referred to as the conflict between the *formal* and *informal systems* of industrial relations. For example, it was not uncommon for shopfloor line managers to allocate overtime more generously than was strictly justified by the formally rational techniques of manpower planning to strong, powerful, and perhaps militant work groups. Yet we can understand the 'rationality' of these allocations and concessions only if we look elsewhere within the capital–labour relations. For Edwards (1986), these informal and tacit unwritten agreements are an example of 'informal accommodation', a means by which managers can ensure that jobs get done without causing too much friction and disorder in their relationship with workers. Once we recognise the 'structured antagonism' that characterises the employment relation – that labour and capital both require each other in order to secure their ends, but at the same time pull in opposite directions – the meaning of what might be 'rational' changes.

For our purposes, what is important here is to recognise the implications of competing in product markets, implications that impel management to seek ways of improving the quantity and quality of output while at the same time reducing costs. As labour costs represent such a significant proportion of total costs, especially in traditional manufacturing and service industries, productivity provides management with ways of thinking how to increase labour output without incurring a concomitant increase in wage costs. The Donovan Commission was important because it identified the failings of British industrial competitiveness with the structure and conduct of management– labour relations. The pursuit of conflicting goals and values by labour and capital was the product of inadequate institutional means for bargaining and reconciliation. Productivity could be secured only within the framework of formal company-level collective bargaining. What Donovan recognised was that the need for change, which exists as an insatiable 'systemic' need in the context of free-market competition, interferes with the legacy of tradition and customary norms that congeal to form orderly and static arrangements in manpower use, deployment, and movement.

Those features of manpower planning that were considered in the sections on 'internal considerations' and 'external considerations' now need to be amended for the dynamic of productivity and its co-implication with the political struggle that wages over values and ends in the employment relation. If the basis for capital–labour antagonism runs deeper than the assumption made by the Donovan Commission – where the claim was that conflict and antagonism reflect institutional failures – productivity bargaining needs to be rethought in the terms of struggle. This assumption reflects the classic liberal-pluralist values of the authors of the Donovan report (Clegg, 1979). It may be that more recent moves to HRM reflect the failure of the institutional route to 'deliver' coherent 'political' integration and consensus in the employment relation. In other words, forms of productivity and efficiency in the conduct of manpower planning can be more effectively achieved in the absence of costly bureaucratic means of bargaining and negotiation.

This endemic and insatiable quest for productivity introduces a complex dynamic into manpower planning, one that raises a host of issues connected with politics, values, and struggle. In the study of manpower planning we open up one strand of its subject, only to find it weaves its way into a multiple set of relevancies. The productivity drive means that the performance of work accomplished through the day-to-day negotiations in the employment relation results in a situation where things are never stable for very long. We must expect change, upset and disturbance. Circumstances always change. A constant revolutionising of production, where 'all that is solid melts into air', as Marx once wrote (quoted in Berman, 1982: 15), characterises the dynamics of capitalist competition. It may be, for example, that a manpower assessment of the distribution of employees made five years previously, which had been used as a benchmark to guide future recruitment, training and succession needs, is no longer relevant or practical.

The rationalisations, redundancies, and restructuring of companies that have been witnessed throughout the public and private sectors over the past 15 years can be interpreted, in part, as a response to the persistence of outdated techniques, procedures and norms in the practice of manpower planning, norms that could no longer be sustained in the intensely competitive international economy of the 1980s and 1990s. Perhaps, in addition, this partly reflects the violence of what Foucault (1980) calls 'normalisation', or what we might call in the context of this chapter an increasing homogenisation of political values. In other words, where productivity might once have been seen as a contested political subject, it now appears to be an inviolable norm by which we all abide. Of course, it may well be that on the surface we submit to unitarist norms, but in the subterranean workings of organisation a whole series of tensions and repercussions are being played out, tensions that destabilise the functional stewardship of manpower planning.

Senior managerial initiatives seeking to drive productivity changes through are likely to seriously challenge, if not undermine, current manpower plans. It may be that an organisation's manpower plan dictates that in order to maintain demand and supply, three new employees are required each year in the accounts department to compensate for the anticipated turnover, promotions, and retirements. *Ceteris paribus*, if the department 'lost' three employees each year owing to turnover, promotions, or retirements, it would seem logical to seek to replace these employees. However, in the reality of manpower planning *ceteris paribus* can never really be assumed, and increasingly in the competitive environment of the 1990s and the new millennium, manpower plans are being constantly adjusted to satisfy productivity requirements and competitive needs. In the example above, although it would seem that the replacement of the three employees was required, management may seek to take advantage of the turnover to reduce costs, increase productivity, and hence increase market share and shareholder profitability. We might also expect the amplification of struggle and what some call 'dysfunctional' repercussion in response to these managerial initiatives.

Once again, we have begun to approach the limits of manpower planning as it is defined and understood by unitarism, to encroach upon the territory of politics, values and norms. In the section on the management of change below we seek to show that human resource planning, in contrast to manpower planning, is far more unitarist and unilateral in its planning and management of employee resource flows in an organisation, consistent with the 'unitarism' apparently characteristic of human resource management (Guest, 1989, 1990; Storey, 1995).

THE MANAGEMENT OF CHANGE: HRP AND FUTURE DIRECTIONS

For some the practice of human resource planning is entirely different to manpower planning:

> In HRP the manager is concerned with motivating people – a process in which costs, numbers, control and systems interact and play a part. In manpower planning the manager is concerned with the numerical elements of forecasting, supply – demand matching and control, in which people are a part.
> (Bramham, 1989: 147, emphasis added)

A 1988 IPM survey attempted to establish and survey the use of 'systematic human resource planning', defined as a long-term, strategic planning of human resources concerned more with the development of skill, quality and cultural change than with statistical numerical forecasting, succession planning and hierarchical structures. This survey was an attempt to assess the extent to which resource planning was being practised in response to the cutbacks and cost-cutting of the 1980s, which for many had reduced the input of traditional manpower planning:

> Manpower planning by then had come to be associated in many people's minds with growth, five year plans, and bureaucracy, at a time when firms were having to contract and become more flexible.
> (Cowling and Walters, 1990: 3)

The results suggested that of the 245 respondents, in excess of 60% claimed that they were now practising forms of human resource planning that were more attentive to qualitative factors concerned with the identification of future training, retraining and development needs. The least popular practices were those associated with the 'analysis of the labour costs and productivity of competitors', the 'communication of future HRP plans and intentions to employees', and the 'monitoring of HRP practices to ensure achievement of cost objectives' (Cowling and Walters, 1990: 7). Of course, they may have been unpopular but this doesn't mean that they were not being done, nor that they formed a significant part of the manpower planner's day-to-day responsibility. Of note is the finding that it was in the private sector that most of the practices associated with human resource planning were in evidence. It may be that the large and bureaucratic nature of most public sector organisations did not permit the exercise of radical and innovative techniques designed to develop the individual as a quality resource as counselled by human resource planning. Or that manpower planning in the public sector was pre-occupied with redundancies and simple cost control pursued through the channels of institutionalised collective bargaining. As Cowling and Walters go on to write:

> Modern style human resource planning, as outlined in the IPM guide, places considerable emphasis on a proactive strategy which anticipates and responds to changes in the environment, linked to a corporate strategy designed to enhance competitive advantage or quality of service. (p.7)

Far more emphasis was placed by personnel departments on the importance of personnel and line management working together in a coherent manner, where both cooperate to jointly determine the role, function and implications for HRP emerging out of new corporate strategy. Now, what management might say it does, and what actually happens in practice, may be two very different things. Yet this emphasis on the importance of the line manager seems consistent with our earlier definition of human resource planning. Human resource planning is supposedly distinctive on the basis of the devolution of operational responsibility down to line managers, where line managers are encouraged to assume 'ownership' of resource planning. In contrast to the rules and procedural bias of old-style personnel management and manpower planning, line managers are persuade to 'go it alone', to innovate and experiment, to learn to live without a dependence on traditions and rule books (Peters, 1994).

HRP is also distinctive in its attempts to generate commitment and the integration of organisational departments and resources. These ambitions are pursued through attempts to develop cultural awareness and homogeneity, rather than the imposition and control of rules and procedures. The assumed advantages of this form of management are deemed to lie in the stimulus of employee creativity, commitment and flexibility, all those characteristics of the human resource that are deemed to be of crucial importance to productivity and competitive success (Peters, 1993). In this way human resource planning has a far more *developmental role* to play, in terms both of planning for flexibility (Atkinson, 1985), and of developing the attributes of quality, skill and 'excellence' within employees. It has become somewhat of a consensus among management gurus, consultants, and many academics (Peters and Waterman, 1982; Kanter, 1984) 'that markets, machinery and the money are available to everyone: success goes to those organisations which are able to recruit and develop the right people and not just at the top' (Timperley and Sisson, 1989: 120). Within the context of market competition, where success depends on failure, and for every winner the market needs a loser, these kinds of assumptions, to say the least, seem problematic.

The two main issues that have concerned human resource planners over the past decade have been the implications of demographic changes and the need for flexibility.

Demographic changes

Towards the end of the 1980s many personnel departments began to express concern that demographic changes in the British economy meant that the number of young people coming onto the labour market was going to decline significantly. It is clear that in a mature industrialised economy such as the UK the average age of the working population is likely to increase as the numbers of births and deaths decrease. Eurostat figures forecast a decline of 1.7% per annum in the supply of labour in the age group 20–30 throughout Western Europe (Eurostat 1990). The median age of the UK population was 34.6 in 1980 compared with 35.9 in 1990 and a projected 37.7 for the year 2000. In the old Federal Republic of Germany the figures were even more striking, rising from an average of 36.7 in 1980 to 41.1 in the year 2000 (IRDAC, 1990). These projections are largely explained by the increasing proportion of retirements, which is not compensated for by an equivalent number of young people coming onto the labour market, so that:

> Even if the forecasts mentioned should be used with caution, they indicate that the starting base for the next decade is far from excellent. If no corrective action is taken, there is a major risk that Europe will lose some of its competitive strength because of a lack of sufficiently qualified manpower.
>
> (IRDAC, 1990: 8)

This so-called 'demographic time bomb' has forced employers to look to their manpower planners to seek new and innovative forms of labour so that the projected difference between labour demand and traditional labour supply may be breached. In part, these observations help to explain the increasing proportion of part-time labour-use strategies, labour that in the main is composed of married female returners to the labour market. A cursory read through the pages of recent editions of *Personnel Review, Personnel Management, People Management,* and the *International Journal of Manpower Planning* would illustrate the interest among personnel managers in developing innovative forms of labour contract, part-time labour, job-sharing, school term time only working, annualised hours contracts, temporary employment contracts, and forms of employment tailored for mature returners to the labour market. These developments are supplemented by prescriptions and advice for manpower planners and human resource managers on the best ways to plan, manage, motivate, remunerate and regulate these novel forms of employment use.

In addition, it is generally argued that industry and business are increasingly demanding more skilled labour, and that relatively unskilled manual blue-collar jobs are in terminal decline, to be replaced by more highly skilled computer programmers, professional technically qualified managers, and other service sector functions. A 1993 Institute for Employment Research review of UK employment and the economy predicted on the basis of trends established over the previous two decades that occupational change will continue to favour the growth of corporate management and professional services in health, education, science, and engineering. Craft and skilled manual occupations, and plant and machine operatives, by contrast, declined on average by 1.3% and 1.9% respectively each year between 1971 and 1991. High-level professional and managerial occupations constituted 35% of total employment in 1991, and this was expected to rise to 41% by the year 2000 (IER, 1993).

The Institute for Employment Research at the University of Warwick projected similar labour market changes in the demand for highly qualified people with social science degrees and graduates of science and vocational subjects. An increase of some 1.5 million jobs is expected for the highly qualified by the year 2001 in comparison with 1991 (IER, 1995/6). Employment in primary industries would continue to decline throughout the 1990s. Projections anticipated a decline of some 14% between 1991 and 2000: a loss of 520 000 jobs. Figure 4.4 attempts to represent those jobs affected by changes in numbers and skill levels.

Based upon the research of Rajan (1993) and the Centre for Research in Employment and Technology in Europe (CREATE), Figure 4.4 suggests the emergence of the so-called new 'knowledge worker'. In addition to an increasing demand for highly skilled occupational employees, organisations are seeking to develop and require more flexibility and adaptability from their employees. Technological, organisational and broader macroeconomic changes are creating a situation in which employees need to have a heightened awareness of their own skills profile and status. Increased 'reflexivity', and the importance increasingly being attached to 'self-development', remain controversial but arguably predictable outcomes of recent management initiatives as organisations expect employees to exercise and demonstrate their own 'entrepreneurial' worth (Garsten and Grey, 1997; O'Doherty and Roberts, 2000).

It is also interesting to note that Rajan projects an increased demand for *deskilled* jobs in secretarial, junior clerical and recreational occupations. Such jobs will increasingly be filled by part-time employees, or, indeed, even more insecure and casualised forms of employment. This may suggest a contradictory series of outcomes in the labour

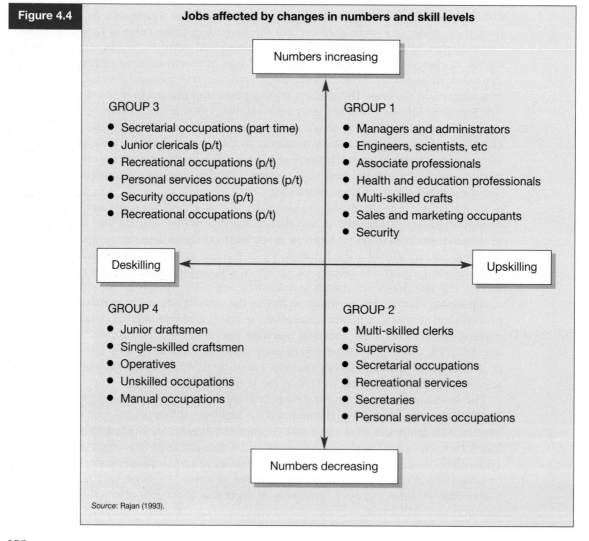

Figure 4.4   **Jobs affected by changes in numbers and skill levels**

Numbers increasing

GROUP 3
- Secretarial occupations (part time)
- Junior clericals (p/t)
- Recreational occupations (p/t)
- Personal services occupations (p/t)
- Security occupations (p/t)
- Recreational occupations (p/t)

GROUP 1
- Managers and administrators
- Engineers, scientists, etc
- Associate professionals
- Health and education professionals
- Multi-skilled crafts
- Sales and marketing occupants
- Security

Deskilling   Upskilling

GROUP 4
- Junior draftsmen
- Single-skilled craftsmen
- Operatives
- Unskilled occupations
- Manual occupations

GROUP 2
- Multi-skilled clerks
- Supervisors
- Secretarial occupations
- Recreational services
- Secretaries
- Personal services occupations

Numbers decreasing

Source: Rajan (1993).

market – highly trained and skilled professional employees, together with pockets of low-paid, 'ghettoised', deskilled employment, which offers few prospects for career progression or personal development. The complex relationship and causality between these contradictory labour market outcomes, and the emergence of 'hard' and 'soft' variants of human resource management, need to be carefully considered and researched. What contribution, therefore, does human resource planning make to the creation of low-paid and insecure temporary or part-time employment, which, we may note, tends to be filled by women workers? This remains an ethical and political question, but a question that nonetheless tends to be ignored by the majority of enthusiastic practitioner-based articles and writing, that celebrates the newsworthy and novel at the expense of careful scholarly research.

Nevertheless, even accepting an increased demand for professional and skilled employees, there remains the problem of supply (Keep, 1994; Keep and Rainbird, 1995). As economists have known for a long time, free markets have a tendency to fail in the provision of what are known as 'public goods'. A major problem facing UK organisations is that the free-market dynamic has a tendency to discourage investment in training by businesses operating in isolation. As one company unilaterally decides to invest in training another company will seek to reduce the costs of its training by buying in pre-trained employees. This cost-competitive dynamic operates to dampen down training investment as companies seek to pay slightly more for individuals who have been trained elsewhere and thus avoid the cost of training employees themselves. The market therefore fails. In recognition of this dynamic, governments often step in to support and counteract the deficiencies of pure market-based solutions to training and investment. This makes training and labour supply a macroeconomic and political problem, a domain of struggle and negotiation above and beyond those struggles that we have noted in the employment relation, but with implications and ramifications, nonetheless, for its conduct and management.

Unless educational opportunities are expanded in the UK, and the needs of training are seriously addressed at national level, it is argued that Britain will not only face a shortage of traditional sources of labour supply, but also a skills shortage will develop, creating a serious obstacle to future organisational growth and economic development (see Chapter 8). In response to these supply developments, and to cater for the increased demands placed on organisations to develop less bureaucratic and more responsible creative employees, manpower planners have sought to develop flexible manpower plans.

Flexibility

There is some debate within academic journals over the precise nature of flexibility within the UK labour market and over organisations' use of flexible labour. A significant feature of this debate focuses on the novelty and progressiveness of using part-time labour, female returners, casual labour and temporary employees (Pollert, 1988, 1992; Hakim, 1990).

Of less contention is the observation that during the 1980s most of the employment growth was in the area of part-time employment, and specifically female part-time employment. John Atkinson and his colleagues at the IMS have suggested, in a series of papers (Atkinson, 1984, 1985), that one of the responses to the demographic and competitive changes in the British economy has been a notable increase in the use of more flexible forms of labour. Atkinson suggests that this is becoming not only an increasingly popular form of manpower planning and practice but also one that needs to be seriously considered by other companies seeking to retain competitiveness in the market.

Essentially, flexible manpower plans have sought to introduce three forms of flexibility: numerical, financial and functional.

Numerical

Here, organisations in response to fluctuations in the business cycle have begun seeking a more numerically flexible labour force. For example, in organisations such as banks and retail stores there are predictable and stable patterns in the fluctuation of business activity. In banks, for example, the lunch-time period is particularly busy, and therefore a more flexible and cost-efficient manpower plan would seek to accommodate the peaks and troughs of business activity more accurately with available labour supply. By having pools of labour resources that can be called in at short notice, often called 'key-time labour' by the banks, manpower planning can cut waste and inefficiency by only having labour in the organisation, or at least only paying it, when it is needed and actually being used. Thus manpower planning uses its employees like a tap that can be turned on and off at will in response to demand cycles, customer arrival patterns, and the peaks and troughs of business activity.

Numerical flexibility is also achieved through the use of annualised hours contracts, which allows management to alter the number of employees at very short notice in response to operational and business needs.

Financial

Rather than paying individuals the 'going rate', or a collectively negotiated wage, companies are now seeking to pay employees and their labour a more flexible wage that, it is claimed, more accurately relates to their performance and productivity. In this way, manpower planning keeps cost under far greater control by using and deploying labour according to business needs and its measured contribution to output. This avoids the excessive rigidity in manpower plans that can arise when a fixed wage is paid for a set number of hours. This means that regardless of whether the employee resource is being used to full capacity or not, it is being paid. Financial flexibility therefore allows manpower planners to focus and contain the cost of employee utilisation. Performance-related pay and profit-related pay offer further examples of the way in which contemporary management is seeking to tie wage levels more accurately to the actual contribution that the employee makes to profit. The paradox here is that flexibility also decreases, in some sense, as reward is made ratio dependent on some measurement of addition to profit.

Functional

This form of flexibility is heralded as one of the most important developments in manpower planning, and provides a lot of the justification for the claims made by *human resource* planners for their distinctive approach to labour utilisation. Functional flexibility attempts to remove what are understood to be organisational rigidities and demarcations, which prevent employees from being moved from one section of the organisation to another, performing a range of tasks and exercising a polyvalence of skills. It is here that we encounter the developmental potential of human resource planning where employees are required, because of operational needs, to be moved through the shopfloor, or into other departments. This is often seen as part of the multi-skilling initiatives of many organisations, whereby employees are encouraged to develop a multiple range of skills and aptitudes so that they 'can be redeployed quickly and smoothly between activities and tasks. Functional flexibility may require multi-skilling – craft workers who possess and can apply a number of skills covering, for example, both mechanical and electrical engineering, or manufacturing and mainte-nance activities (Armstrong, 1992: 106). Whether these manpower, or rather, human resource plans amount simply to an extension of managerial prerogative, intensification and increased employee stress levels is a moot point (Wood, 1989; Elger, 1990). It is quite clear, however, that human resource planners have a vested interest in emphasis-ing the developmental potential and flexibility that these initiatives encourage.

One consequence of flexibility and flexible manpower planning is that with the attendant delayering of managerial hierarchies and the attempted breakdown in the typical pyramid structure of organisations, promotions and traditional hierarchical development may no longer be possible. Increasingly, human resource planners are having to develop alternatives to hierarchical succession planning in response to a rapidly changing business context that requires fluidity, rapid change and adaptability at the operational level. Hierarchies, therefore, and the functionally rigid structures of responsibility, seniority and status, can no longer be sustained because of the rapid change and flux in consumer demand, market fashion, and global product markets.

In order to resource this external volatility human resource planners are being forced to seek corresponding flexibilities and 'turnover' so that 'Workers, instead of acquiring a skill for life, can now look forward to at least one if not multiple bouts of deskilling and reskilling in a lifetime' (Harvey, 1989: 230). In the banking industry, for example, many of the traditional-style accountancy-biased branch managers are increas-ingly finding their skills redundant as banks seek to promote sales as the central focus of their business activities. The old-style paternalism in manpower planning, where employees were guaranteed, especially in the old large bureaucracies such as banks, 'cradle to grave' employment security, is being replaced by far more uncertainty and turnover. In terms of development, banks are now emphasising lateral development, or 'progression' *across* an organisation, rather than hierarchical promotion (Cressey and Scott, 1992; O'Doherty, 1993).

So far we have been following a fairly standard exposition of manpower planning. This programme has taken us through a number of stages, beginning with an explana-tion of the need for manpower planning, through to attempted identification of 'who' it is that actually does manpower planning, and then on to a discussion of the creation of a manpower plan that eventually took us on to a consideration of complication and complexity. Our discussion has challenged, at times, the scientific pretensions of man-power planning, illustrating the contested nature of the employment relation and the insecure nature of unitarist-style integration. What I want to do now is focus more explicitly on the assumptions, and what I call the 'field of vision', that inform the tradi-tional practice of manpower planning. Here we shall see that the pursuit of rationality, order, and control *borders* a domain or space of disorder, where the play of the irrational and the meaningless comes to wreak its damage on organisation. Paradoxically, the desire for order among manpower planners requires this very threat in order to consoli-date the need for its own existence. So this 'space' in organisation provides conditions of both possibility and impossibility for manpower planning. In recent years the fixation on control and regularity has subsided somewhat as manpower planning has evolved to assume the role of *human resource* planning. What we find here is that human resource planning yields to the space of the irrational and disorderly as it seeks to pursue management less by means of control than by 'seduction' (Bauman, 1992: 48ff.). Corporate culture, new forms of teamworking, the discipline of enterprise and entrepreneurialism, and the discourse of learning and development, all open up the psychology of the individual human subject where the passions, anxieties, and fears of the unconscious act in often unpredictable and disorderly ways. By seeking to work on these areas of the human subject, human resource planning is playing with fire. Seduction remains a fragile and unstable means of securing organisation, and as a management strategy aggravates the play of chance, unpredictability, and the risk that anything might happen next in the employment relation.

ASSUMPTIONS AND THE FIELD OF VISION IN MANPOWER PLANNING

The discourse of manpower planning has traditionally appropriated metaphors of 'stocks', 'flows', 'systems', 'state' and 'equilibrium' (Smith, 1976; McBeath, 1978), often directly from meta-sociological and economic theory. Such meta-theoretical work, and the values embodied in its discourse, remains at best contested and partial in contemporary social theory if not entirely discredited by developments and revisions in the understanding of the limitations not just of its theory but of all grand narrative 'catch-all' theoretical explanations (Lyotard, 1984).

Second-order business administration techniques and methodologies typically borrow indiscriminately from versions of Talcott Parsons' sociological model of structural functionalism (see Cole, 1991). This was contested within its own field in the 1950s and was subsequently subject to such revision and critique that contemporary students of social theory and the philosophy of social science may come across Parsons only in footnotes to textbooks (Game and Metcalfe, 1996). However, the husk of its discourse remains extant in the field of business administration, personnel management and the 'sciences' of marketing and accounting. This appropriation from social theory is forgotten, its contested nature suppressed, and its metaphors and methodology reified to an extent that it comes to take on the status of science and truth. The political and economic pressures that encourage this remain too complex to engage with here, but students should remain vigilant about the language, metaphors and world-views that are perpetuated in personnel management.

In George Cole's orthodox account of personnel management, this bias remains an integral, and even celebrated feature of his text in his claim that 'the approaches described throughout this book are firmly part of the functionalist approach, complete with managerial bias!' (Cole, 1991: 32). In terms of manpower planning, the assumptions of human behaviour and the human subject, the 'purposes' and values presumed to hold in something called organisation, and the nature of the employment relation, remain hidden if not actively suppressed.

If we consult the *Oxford English Dictionary* we appreciate the sense of divorce and *detachment* (Cooper, 1993) involved in many of the assumptions and practices of manpower planning. By divorce and detachment we mean that work of abstraction that is incarnate in the assumptions that enable orthodox manpower planning to proceed. To plan implies to *derive* or *contrive* by means and media to *control* and attempt to *tame* the active forces, energy, and agency of social relations at work, forces that remain only partially under the classificatory and designative capacity of 'planners'. To plan is also to construct an *imaginary* flat surface or plane, as in a perspective drawing, where 'several imaginary planes perpendicular to the line of vision form a grid within which the objects represented appear to diminish in size according to the distance between the viewer and the planes' (*Oxford English Dictionary*). Here one can clearly see the abstraction and detachment involved in the planning process, which deploys, as the organisational theorist Keith Hoskin (1995) writes, 'a fixed point of view' so as to 'retheorize the world as disembodied or mathematical space' (p. 147). The social and natural world is rendered mathematical. It doesn't pre-exist in the form of mathematics but gets translated and understood through a mathematical frame of mind.

Planning derives from the root *plano,* derived in turn from the Greek *planos,* which captures a richer and more ambiguous sense – of wandering, of 'free living' and 'mobility', as in planetary movement – than has survived in the everyday usage of the contemporary word 'plan'. Over time this conceptual ambiguity of planning has been lost as it becomes increasingly equated with the rational, interventionist construction of active self-centred human subjects who incessantly seek to order, classify and organise the world around them. Robert Cooper (1993) explores a similar conceptual emacia-tion that has taken place today in conventional accounts of 'technology' and 'representation'. The sense of 'technology' derives from the Greek *techne,* a concept that implied the art of bringing something forward or present to the senses of the human body – as in making something available for use and understanding. However, the root of *techne,* namely *tech,* derives from the Greek *tuche,* which named that which was *not* under the control of the human being – in particular, the accidental, chance, and fate. This *tuche* takes place in that area of organisation we have previously called the organisation 'shadow', that shadow cast by the photographic activity of manpower plan-ning. Therefore *techne* was that which controlled and ordered the vagaries of chance and accident, and hence that which *conquers* chance for the advantage of the human subject. Furthermore, *techne* was considered to be more detached from the interference of chance and accident:

> Human action expresses itself in relation to *tuche* in terms of attachment (at-tach-ment) and detachment (de-tach-ment). The more attached action is *tuche,* the more it is influenced by chance and vagary; the more detached it is, the more able it is to exert mastery and control.
>
> (Cooper, 1993: 279–280)

In modern uses of the word – technology – we tend to lose sight of this ontological relation as conceptually technology is confidently reduced by the human subject and equated solely with that which masters and controls.

This narrow rationalist frame of reference governs much of the manpower plan-ning tradition, and remains explicit in the work of those concerned with the planning of manpower resources in the Civil Service (see Smith, 1976). The tone of the con-tributors to this text is that of an unquestioned faith in the rational and abstract principles of statistical forecasting. It is assumed that if these techniques are rigor-ously adopted and exercised across sufficient domains that impinge on the planning of resources, regularity and control can be achieved in the movement and distribu-tion of labour. In reducing what is a complex and contradictory play of political, economic, and social-psychological relations, to one of quantified abstraction, where individuals appear simply as 'data' to be manipulated in a multivariable regression equation (Rowntree and Stewart, 1976), commits an analytical injustice upon the dif-ficulty and practice of management.

That such statistical techniques are assumed to remain neutral and without value bias appears naive in the extreme. Following the logic of Rowntree and Stewart (1976), we are informed that staff numbers can be correctly calculated and projected only if the manpower planner is able to 'de-correlate' the factors that are causally related to work-load levels. If, in calculating differing workload levels, for example L_1, L_2, L_3 and L_4, we fail to account for 'interrelated' forces that affect staffing requirements (p. 41), we fail to capture the underlying and essential factors that affect the workload level – and hence staff numbers. Manpower planning has a tendency to incorrectly isolate the contribution of forces x_1, x_2, . . . etc. by coefficients b_1, b_2, . . . etc., which results in a situation where the coefficient b_1 for example is not simply a measure of x_1 but picks up the influence of cross-correlated forces.

Here the adoption of multivariate regression in orthodox manpower planning takes account of a complex number of factors, which are positively or negatively related to staff requirements and which require both identification and measurement. So, for example, in a tax office processing tax claims, staffing levels will depend not only on the number of tax claims made (x_1) but on the complexity of the claims, which can be assessed, forecast and quantified by a variable (x_2) and the size of the claim (x_3). One member of staff may be required therefore for each 100 tax claims made of type i, and in a simplified regression analysis the b_1 coefficient would equate to 0.01. Staff numbers (y) would equal b_i, X_i, where b_i represents the coefficient of x that translates X_i into staff numbers. In the example here, where t = time period 1:

$$y^t = b_i X_i$$

Therefore:

$$y^t = 0.01(100)$$

and hence the calculation reveals we need one member of staff for each 100 tax claims made of type i. Cross-correlation would disturb our result if we calculated a figure for the numbers of individuals falling into a particular tax bracket, and then calculated this as a variable having an independent effect on staffing levels. There is likely to be a cross-correlation because an increasing number of individuals falling within a relevant tax bracket will affect the number of tax claims of X_i, and therefore the coefficient b_i will not be measuring an independent variable. By measuring one variable, one X, and assuming its independence, we may wrongly calculate the number of staff required to service this demand. Our calculation would be wrong because there is a strong cross-correlation between the variables. Hence, according to this analysis, we may overestimate or perhaps underestimate our calculation of staff levels. What is required, therefore, is this decorrelation of the factors in order to arrive at the underlying fundamentals that can be measured directly in terms of their impact on staff levels:

> In theory staff numbers can be expressed in terms of these underlying factors, which may be projected into the future and used to derive forecasts of staff. (Rowntree and Stewart, 1976: 43)

On the basis of such apparently rigorous statistical techniques for developing forecasts and trend analysis, we are led to believe that staffing levels appear as some fait accompli consequent upon the neutral tools of science. But it is the very abstraction and detachment of these techniques from power relations and contestation within social relations that belie its neutrality. Moreover, no matter what effort we make to decorrelate and measure underlying factors, if these underlying factors are not predictable, but irrational and subject to the caprice of accident, chance or contingency, our statistics necessarily border on that *tuche* as identified by Cooper (1993).

Although most orthodox approaches to manpower planning pay tacit recognition to the contribution of trade unions, in the negotiation over issues such as productivity, expectations, norms, standards, work organisation and acceptable staffing levels, the acknowledgement tends to be couched in terms of order and predictability. Trade unions are seen to simply add legitimacy, to offer a medium through which the neutral techniques of statistical forecasting must proceed. This extends the managerial prerogative by drawing unions into the logic of the neutrality of these techniques and the procedures that support a normative commitment to the values of agreement, resolution, and regulation (Clegg, 1975, 1979; Hyman, 1978). Unions may contest the relative weight ascribed to particular variables but not the principles or logic of rationality and measurement. Today, more unions accept the principles of efficiency and competitiveness. If redundancies need to be made, unions today are more likely to contest the numbers or the level of staff compensation, rather than the logic of a system that periodically requires unemployment, redundancy and economic crisis.

Staffing levels may reflect the solidification over time of contested, variable, and negotiable relations in the organisation, allocation and distribution of work. Thus the assumption of neutrality in the measurement of variables and forecasts of staffing levels is simply a projection from an assumed 'state of nature', a 'state' that may reflect simply a temporary consolidation or alliance in the struggles and caprices of human subjects and social relations. At any moment one could interpret this arrangement of relations and norms as only a temporary and partial condensation of what remains in tension, fractious, perhaps even chaotic. In the violent abstraction of planning, which detaches from these social relations and power inequalities, organisation is constructed and a 'balance of forces' regulated in the employment relation. Complexity gets diminished and disorder made orderly. The tradition of manpower planning is one that tends to construct analysis as if looking through an inverted telescope. Social relations and individual human subjects appear as 'entities' if we look this way through a telescope. Like a photograph we capture them as if like objects, timeless and abstract, with clear-cut lines of definition and boundary. As Foucault (1971) observes in his critique of the faith in the purity and singularity of origins in linguistic, conceptual and categorical thought, this represents almost a timelessness, a faith in the stable continuity of history. For Foucault, this commitment:

> is an attempt to capture the exact essence of things, their purest possibilities, and their carefully protected identities because this search assumes the existence of immobile forms that precede the external world of accident and succession. (p. 78)

The persistence of manpower planning techniques that maintain a commitment to the virtues of utilitarianism through the exercise of a singular, unitarist mode of rationality works to dim down those factors that cannot be subsumed within its logic. That which cannot be controlled gets relegated to a dustbin of error, deviance, and irrationality. Consider the work of McBeath (1978), who in discussing the necessity of control over recalcitrant subordinate managers urges the importance of vigilance in audit control (pp. 188ff). The rationality of the techniques of manpower planning are not called into question, and thus any deviance from the manning norms established by these methods must be the result of irrationality, a lack of understanding, or the irrational grandiose ambitions of managerial empire builders. The possibility that capitalist organisations are precisely about aggrandisement, growth, power, and empire building does not enter into his consideration. Deviance from prescribed standards must be punished and the managers 'red circled' (p. 189) for the convenience of the corporate gaze so as to enable it to quickly identify any likely future sources of transgression:

> Unfortunately, a few managers and supervisors are exceptionally able at maintaining their over strength establishments, somehow managing to get replacements even when someone does transfer or leave. It is these areas that the audit seeks to identify. (p. 189)

Such a perspective remains consistent with the command-and-control discipline of authority, hierarchy, and tradition, which perhaps until only recently governed the perspective and management of organisation. The manner in which discipline and authority are understood and the way in which it gets constructed in contemporary organisations may of course differ. Nonetheless, it is arguable whether the one-dimensional rationality (Marcuse, 1964) of technical utilitarianism is able to persist in the context of traditional and emergent corrosive forces and lines of division in contemporary organisation, forces that may have been unleashed by manpower planning and amplified through a more 'human resource'-style approach to planning.

The language of manpower planning also betrays this predilection for control and mastery. If we look at the texts of manpower planning we find a frame of reference that is predominantly masculine, with its discourse of 'power', 'efficiency', 'control' and 'man-power'. Organisation is synonymous with sobriety, control and exactitude. It is a kind of geometry, although one that can be disturbed and polluted, led astray, by the as yet unconquered, and perhaps unconquerable, forces of irrationality, conflict, deviance, and sheer bloody-minded stupidity. Thank a deity for stupidity?

Yet it is assumed that the exhaustive procedures and information-gathering techniques of manpower planning will eventually tend to order. A steady-state equilibrium is the natural state of affairs, which can be maintained in vitality and health, unified and coherent in order to allow further conquest and expansion. The language of 'conquest' pervades the texts on manpower planning – the conquest and control of nature we find in our assumption that precautionary contraceptive safeguards will guarantee 2.2 offspring together with the optimal allocation and distribution of domestic resources. This desire for completion and wholeness involves the repression and suppression of 'otherness' – whether competing frameworks, alternative rationalities, or novel modes of epistemology and ontology (see Inayatullah, 1990). That there may be different ways of being in the world is simply not entertained.

Let us consider the possibility that there *are* multiple ways of being in the world – a feminist mode of being, or an ecological mode, an aesthetic sensibility, or a queer way of being etc. To the native indigenous Australian population – what we have come to call 'aborigines' – there are *dream modes* of being in the world (Linstead and Banerjee, 1999) that offer access to understanding and truths closed off to the conscious daytime world. A greater sense of connectivity with the environment and with past and future family generations stimulates reflection on the limitations and potential dangers attendant upon the preoccupations of the ego-bound human subject. The human subject loses its sense of self-importance and is reminded of its temporary evanescent condition of transit through this world. Experience is enriched by the encounter with these shadowy domains, which exposes the constrictive bind imposed by our all-too-*modern* human rationality. Space and time lose their mundane, taken-for-granted presence; its defined and bounded state of coordination, which we routinely reify in the here and now, begins to unravel and dissolve. Consider the possibilities for alternative manpower planning – where the human subject might be 'distributed' across a range of space and time coordinates, some of which we might be conscious of, and others that remain unconscious. Do we slip across delimited boundaries in organisation while at work into reverie and dream time? A number of contemporary writers on organisation would seem to think so, including Gabriel (1995, 1997), Linstead (1993), Linstead and Benerjee (1999) and Sievers(1994).

How might manpower planning think about managing the transgression associated with these movements? Opening up these subterranean features of work organisation, where the fears and anxieties of employees are played out, and where the unpredictability and chance of human behaviour exact their toll, confronts management with a complex set of problems.

The unconscious organisation does not easily lend itself to the appropriating reach of meaning and reason. Our world begins to appear less solid, and all the numbers of manpower planning begin to flicker and dance. We literally become *numb*-er to numbers, as the world presents itself anew – more unstable, less meaningful, a little vulnerable, and strange. What might be the significance of 'banana time' and 'coke time' (Roy, 1958) in manpower planning, or where managers begin to take on the guise of magicians (Cleverley, 1973), medieval court barons (Jackall, 1988), or even God (Gabriel, 1997)? We are not just making reference to the recently well-publicised appointments of corporate court jesters, or Bill Gates's employment of actors to add life to corporate entertainment exercises. What is more interesting is when the distinctions between these different domains begin to break down.

It is has been well documented that secretaries often come to act as substitute office wives for male managers (Game and Pringle, 1983; Pringle, 1990), and male bosses can assume the role of a father figure among subordinate women workers; but what happens to the rationality of manpower planning when the boundaries around the world of dream and fantasy break down, and agents act upon impulses drawn from these domains? Employees might then drift through the multiple space and time of organisation, struggling to make coherent that which is fractious and chaotic, to 'still' the strife of ontological instability, where they might suddenly find themselves confronted with a sexually attractive young male one day instead of what they had always appeared to be – an agent of oppressive work discipline. What might happen next? What might happen to motivation and productivity? Now then, this word 'productivity' . . . ? (cf: Bataille, 1957/1987). What might happen if we are no longer sure whether or not we are dreaming? What might become of the difference between dream and reality (Castenada, 1971), especially given the prospect of virtual organisations, the 'virtual' worker, artificial intelligence, cloning, and the cyborg worker (see *Organisation*, 1999)? Will we be able to tell when we are – and when we are not – working? Might our dreams become utilisable as a form of labour?

No doubt the world of the Disney Corporation, the Las Vegas economy, and vast swathes of labour in the entertainment and leisure industries, constructed around the seductive exploitation of fantasy and the selling of alternative realities, already stand as testimony to this speculation. Manpower planning might then come to assume the role of 'reality engineer', regulating access to the multiple domains of reality in order to secure a more efficient use of organisational time. Isn't this what is already happening through the development of corporate culture programmes (Willmott, l993: Casey, 1995), where management seeks to tap into the existential insecurities of human subjects, to translate and re-bind – or 'cathect' as Freud would write – its energy into appropriate forms of corporate ritual and routine, myths and images, signs and symbols that stimulate excitation and passion in a careful regulation and deregulation of emotion?

In its traditions, manpower planning recognises none of this nonsense. When you're waging a war there is no time to entertain the extravagance of delusion and dream,

161

even if with all its mustard gas, chemical and biological weapons, our world might literally be disappearing. The metaphors of conquest and control that support the conventional perspective of manpower planning reflect and repeat the military and imperial history from which they derive. In fact, in many places in the manpower planning library, unashamed explicit reference is made to the linguistic roots of planning, recruitment, selection, training and regimen. It is not just linguistic roots, either. As Rose (1990) and Townley (1994) show, much of what has come to be the practice of personnel management finds its history in the military world of exercise and drill. According to Bartholomew and Forbes (1979), the 'statistical techniques of manpower systems must be as old as the planning of the military and building exploits of the ancient world' (p. 8). Acceptable statistical risks in trench warfare have been translated into the language of redundancy and wastage. Muscle, power, force, and productivity, a preoccupation with the physical body – 'put your back into it', 'how many hands have we got?' – provide the common currency of terms in manpower planning, mapping and constituting those human variables that come to form indispensable characteristics of employees and their social relations given the competitive nature of capitalist economies. The central planner at the apex of the organisation carefully calculates and calibrates, classifying and arranging, mapping movements and change, resolving the complexity of human relations by the application of the slide rule and mathematical calculation. As McBeath (1978) argues, manning systems require the constant attention and supervision of an elite of 'management':

> The regular attention of a systems man is essential, as much to ensure that some activities are discontinued or reduced in frequency, as to enable fresh demands to be made. (pp. 189–190)

This image of the white-coated male technician, omnipotent in his virility, rendering the world calculable for order (Kallinikos, 1995), seems today not only dangerous but in some ways rather sad. In the final section of our chapter we attempt to sketch some features of the contemporary workplace that are challenging some of these primordial assumptions and metaphors in manpower planning. One implication of the extension of interest in the management of the irrational and unconscious aspects of organisation and human interaction is the aggravation of the fragmentary tendencies inherent in the ongoing oscillation of organisation/disorganisation. This acts to limit the coherence and utility of the abstractions and techniques typically associated with manpower planning. We have seen how manpower planning remains an idealised abstraction from the struggle and contestation that characterise the day-to-day interaction of social and non-material relations. Now we shall find that the exercise of control by manpower planning is being made far more vulnerable by developments in post-bureaucratic, de-structured and networked organisation that amplify anxiety, insecurity and fear among employees.

NEW ORGANISATION, TEAMWORKING AND SELF-DEVELOPMENT: THE EMERGENCE OF HUMAN RESOURCE PLANNING

The fracturing and disintegration of formerly unified bureaucracies and hierarchies represents an attempt to reconstitute organisation, in part through the reworking and devolution of responsibility for the discipline and planning of resources. Still subject to the financial control of senior corporate management (Marginson *et al.*, 1988; Sisson and Marginson, 1995), these devolved 'business units' exercise far less autonomy, however, than some of the more enthusiastic management consultants and celebrants are likely to recognise. Yet there has been a discernible move in many sectors of the economy to shift the burden of day-to-day planning and management to 'empowered' team leaders and 'coaches' of small, team-based workgroups (Storey, 1992; IRS, 1995a, b, 1996).

According to Storey (1992, 1995), there has been a welter of HRM initiatives and restructuring programmes in an effort to reconstruct the balance of individual and collective forms of employment regulation, not simply in the new dynamic service sectors that emerged in the 1980s, but in the heartland of British industry. In an effort to encourage commitment and performance, much organisational restructuring has focused on the attitudes and expectations of the first-line supervisor–employee relation. From this point in the production process, organisational change seeks to remove the detailed layers of bureaucracy and management that service, monitor, discipline and plan from above. Those layers of middle management that hold in place the traditional command-and-control model of organisation have been eroded to refocus those activities in small workgroups or teams. The importance of the coach or first-line supervisor has been enhanced with added responsibilities, which now allow for a greater degree of middle-management delayering. In the place of these massed ranks of middle management, a more streamlined and flatter structure made up of supervisors, 'coaches', first-line managers, or 'heads' of shift, assumes responsibility for budgeting, planning and resourcing. This is the domain of that expanded supervisory role that Storey (1992) uncovers in his research, a role that 'embraced aspects of planning, scheduling, agreeing budgets, being responsible for a cost centre, ensuring quality and being the main managerial representatives in human resource management' (p. 239).

Research in human resource management has also discovered the importance attached to loyalty and commitment in generating motivation, but also coherence and meaning – given the fact that employees often work these days in smaller, more dispersed units of organisational activity. Teamworking provides an opportunity to foster communitarian values and commitment, which in conjunction with the adoption of performance appraisals, acts as a focus of a new disciplinary gaze. More extreme forms of devolution and empowerment have attempted to constitute the individual employee as a manager of themselves (Townley, 1994), in what Tom Peters has defined as the 'entrepreneurializing of every job' (Peters, 1994: 67). Ideally, those responsible for their own businesses will go anywhere, do everything, find anyone and break every barrier, procedure, and 'tradition' to get the job done and done well. Given the dispersal of work activity, binding more diffuse and heterogeneous elements might increasingly come to depend upon self-discipline and self-organisation. This is sold within the prescriptive literature as a means of generating new freedoms for individuals. By encouraging employees to continuously monitor and reflect upon their 'performance', in a context of team support and assistance, work becomes a preoccupation, a project of self-formation and mastery. The military overtones of manpower planning have not disappeared in human resource planning; they have simply refocused and reconstituted within organisation.

Some have noted that the type of organisational 'structure' that this kind of construction and management encourages (indeed Peters himself makes this observation) is one that comes to resemble the Jackson Pollock composition 'Autumn Rhythm'. Here, flexible lines of responsibility and authority continually shift and redefine, resting only temporarily to take form and shape before moving on. It remains difficult to identify a 'source' of manpower planning in these admittedly extreme, avant-garde and probably idealistic, if not terroristic, postmodern organisations (Clegg, 1991; Hassard and Parker, 1994; Hatch, 1997).

In the film and television industry, Starkey and Barratt (1994; see also Lash and Urry, 1994) have identified the emergence of similar 'vertically disaggregated' forms of organisation and planning. Planning takes place within a diffuse heterogeneous network, assembled by reputation and personal contact. To produce a new drama series, for example, involving the employment and cooperation of thousands of employees, or rather a temporary network of labour brought together under multiple and myriad forms of contract association, involves the mobilisation of new forms of manpower planning that we might associate with moves towards human resource planning. Manpower planning now takes place at multiple points of 'intersection' – boundaries if you like – between specialist agencies representing actors, technicians, studios, and distribution outlets. Budgets and 'financial constraints' are subject to a complicated series of 'spot contracts' involving negotiation and movement – albeit at the margins and within some 'tolerance' level acceptable to the investors and financiers of the project. Yet we know that the production of films is associated with spectacular examples of over-budget projects. The 'negotiations' never stop as funds are sought through complex circuits of 'wheeling and dealing'.

Lash and Urry (1994) discuss the growth in these forms of 'structure' in the broadcast media – film, television and music – and in publishing and tourism. The key feature of this form of organisation is the temporary coalescence of organisational form – its 'just-in-time' character – and the temporary and shifting draft of labour that come to assemble organisation. Figure 4.5 attempts to represent the nature and form of 'manpower planning' within this kind of organisation. In this example we represent the design, production and broadcast of a new television drama series.

The 'producer choice' strategy embarked on by the BBC over the past few years has further encouraged this form of planning and organisation. Instead of using in-house production and editing, and BBC-employed actors and actresses, all paid under terms and conditions negotiated by the structures of union–management collective bargaining, producers can now recruit from outside the walls of the BBC. They may presage the future possibilities for the 'empowered' first-line managers identified in the study by Storey (1992), increasingly responsible for planning, management and the allocation of financial and human resources. With the freedom to manage their own budgets they do not remain constrained in the same way as traditional BBC producers, who were obliged to draw on resources and facilities pre-funded and provided by their own organisation.

Foucault and power

Within these disaggregated and delayered, some would say *disordered*, organisations, teams of flexible and multifunctional alliances of labour, infrequently employees in the traditional sense, come to take on an increased responsibility and importance. Superficially, this might appear to resemble some utopian-empowered challenge to traditional hierarchical inequalities, with the planning and management of resources now performed closer to actual labour and the point of production. More extensive research, however, reveals the persistence of traditional forms of conflict, somewhat transformed, and the surfacing of many hitherto suppressed forms of antagonism and discontent.

Kondo (1990), and the work of Sewell and Wilkinson (1992), document the tremendous symbolic, discursive and material pressure that operate, often subliminally,

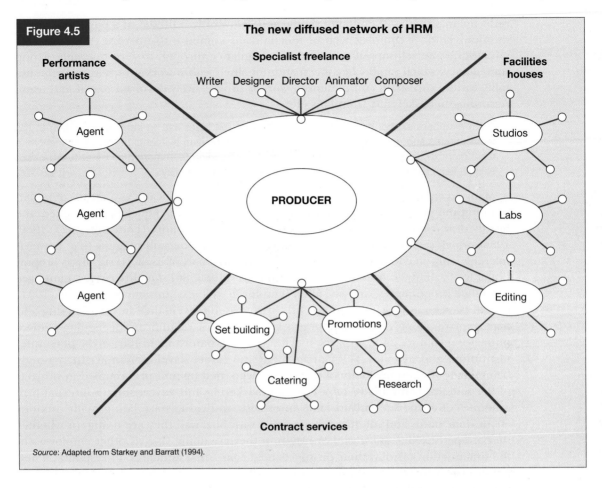

Figure 4.5

The new diffused network of HRM

Performance artists

Specialist freelance

Writer   Designer   Director   Animator   Composer

Facilities houses

Agent

Agent

Agent

PRODUCER

Studios

Labs

Editing

Set building

Promotions

Catering

Research

Contract services

Source: Adapted from Starkey and Barratt (1994).

through the discipline of manpower planning today, but the capacity for disruption and discontent is never far from the surface, and may actually have been aggravated by recent management initiatives. Given the decline of institutional regulation and the collective stability offered by trade union organisation, employment relations might well be expected to fracture and dissipate into a heterogeneous series of struggles throughout organisation. The imposition of new forms of discipline on workers 'can be expected – particularly if market conditions improve, or become accepted as the new normalcy', Hyman (1987) writes, to 'provoke unpredictable and disruptive forms of revolt' (p. 52).

The construction and constitution of team-based working brings with it new forms of vulnerability and volatility. While the intention of new forms of power-knowledge is to conscript individual employees as *objects* of discipline and control, the *seductive* aspects of these new forms of discipline work on cultivating *subjects* through the provision of 'opportunities' whereby individuals practise self-discipline and self-management. Empowered training regimes, through to performance appraisals, performance-related pay, and devolved schemes of career management, increasingly seek to turn work into a *reflexive project of self*. Employees are encouraged to reflect on their own performance, conduct, action and habits, to consider the ways in which they may benefit or hinder the performance of work. Increasingly, responsibility to one's self and one's team is reflected in attitudes of guilt and shame and, conversely, attitudes of a pious and sancti-monious kind. A complex web of mechanisms combine to nurture these kinds of emotions, from self-surveillance and team vigilance through to zero tolerance group surveillance, which rapidly become institutionalised within workgroups as the responsi-bility for the successful completion of work is progressively devolved to self and team. According to Barker and Tompkins (1994):

> Team members expect each other to identify with the team and to behave according to the team's norms and rules. By violating team norms or exhibiting elements of 'dis-identification', a team member risks punishment by the team. The offending teammate may be accused of not being a team player or of not being faithful to the 'team's personality'. (pp. 225–226)

Many recent commentators have turned to the work of Foucault as a means of under-standing the process and mechanisms of such discipline. As Foucault has argued, the beauty of this form of discipline is its subtlety and invisibility (Foucault, 1977, 1980, 1984), which serves to obscure the operation of power. Foucault suggests that 'power is tolerable only on condition that it masks a substantial part of itself. Its success is propor-tional to its ability to hide its own mechanisms' (1980: 86). Quality circles, employee assistance programmes, and so-called 'employee wellness' initiatives (Townley, 1994) can all be seen as new, more powerful forms of self-surveillance in the planning and management of one's own 'manpower'. They represent a significant deepening of disci-plinary mechanics in comparison with the old paternal, welfare-style personnel institutions and schemes. Self-management and career development are increasingly being made the responsibility of individuals who, tied up and preoccupied in projects of the self, are being made *subjects*. From marketing and advertising to internal pro-grammes of corporate culture and enterprise, individuals are being made anxious about their status and identity – concerned with how well they are doing, or whether they are perceived as successful or not, how they are doing vis-à-vis other employees in the organisation or what their prospects might be – that animates, in response, a des-perate quest for signs of confirmation and recognition (Grey, 1994). Individuals exercise only an illusory sense of freedom in their preoccupation with making them-selves subjects, a complete whole they can project and present to the world of organisation. Foucault's work tells us that individuals can no longer simply be thought of as *objects*, repressed by power, shunted about through the guidelines provided by the overarching governance of organisational structure, rules, or procedures. Power is pro-ductive and seductive; it turns self upon self, stimulating anxiety and reflexivity so that individuals feel compelled to shape and secure themselves through corporate-provided images, ideals, and role models. Power is diffuse through a complex 'micro-physics' of capillary networks that 'wires up' social relations through regimes of truth that is found extant in our language and norms, our bodies and gestures. Organisation, and the indi-viduals and collectives who compose it, can be usefully thought of as occupying a field of tension that is spread out across a series of negotiations and agreements, settlements and struggles, an unsteady balance of forces that never ceases looking for ways to sta-bilise itself, confronted, as it is, by the play of multiple lines of fracture. Power is not simply a form of repression, but offers ways of doing and being within these lines of fracture. We exercise power, albeit in asymmetrical relations of opportunity and restric-tion, in the everyday mundane activity of our employment relation, through the sanctions and norms we aspire to and pass on to others in the ever circling relays of quotidian social relations.

One of the distinctive features of human resource planning is precisely the exercise of this mode of discipline. Yet, with the attention it confers upon subjects and their psyche, it opens up new areas of fragility and vulnerability. Lasch (1978) talks about the emergence of pathological narcissism among individuals in late capitalist societies, a selfishness that is paradoxically amplified by the lack of a sense of self, of completion and wholeness, which stimulates individuals to seek forms of gratification and confirmation in efforts to compensate for their diminishing sense of self. Yet individuals never find satisfaction. They crave ever greater degrees of confirmation and recognition as they become volatile and anxious, easily bored and agitated. We become less tolerant of others, and seek their company only if they can make us feel good about ourselves. Teams at work suddenly become fractious and fragile, a space of infantile regression through which complex emotions and anxieties get played out, often to the detriment of disciplined production. Management is made difficult. It is literally playing with fire.

Interruptions, breakdowns, and conflicts

The 'directors' programme' at Royal Mail (IRS, 1995b) and the 'Development Partnership' scheme at the Trustee Savings Bank emphasise the importance of a shift in the conception of manpower and career planning. As one regional personnel manager at a large high street retail bank reported, 'We are moving away from a culture of "Do it to me" or "Do it for me" to one which emphasises self-development, empowerment, initiative and responsibility' (O'Doherty, 1994, 1996). In addition, the conception of a career as some progressive linear development through the ranks of middle management is now seen as anachronistic and redundant. In the fluid, delayered networks and alliances characteristic of contemporary organisational arrangements the old hierarchies are often no longer in place to the same extent or degree. Employees are being encouraged to broaden their understanding of career, to see a career as one that emphasises 'lateral development', which may be harnessed with the adoption of multiple and flexible forms of contract, exchange and relationship with the organisation. Temporary project work, part-time employment, job-sharing and service contracts across a range of business units, and even across different organisations, are seen by some to offer avenues for the future of career planning, development and management (Handy, 1989, 1994).

The entrepreneurial and Thatcherite rhetoric is barely disguised in the discourse of these new-style career-management strategies. In many ways this mirrors the withdrawal of institutional support and paternal welfare structures, the withdrawal of the 'nanny state', and the liberation of what is assumed to be a state of nature – competitiveness, entrepreneurialism, self-help, and the ideals of neo-classical economic liberalism. The Royal Mail 'directors' programme' is explicit in its efforts to encourage employees to view themselves as a project to be worked on and a self to be managed:

> The first aim of the directors' programme is to increase your awareness of who you are. What are your skills, strengths and abilities? What are your interests, weaknesses and values? One way of discovering where you want to go in the future is to look back at where you have been.
>
> (quoted in IRS, 1995b)

Most of the career planning initiatives of contemporary organisations remind employees, or contracted self-employed staff, that there are no guarantees: 'the only person that can make this work is you', and the only chance of success is a constant awareness and attentiveness to self and performance. This provides a clear example of the kind of disciplinary power that Foucault was talking about. Manpower planning becomes individualised and empowered, but individuals find themselves exposed far more immediately and directly to the vagaries and dynamics of market forces. Rather than eliminating the conflict and tensions associated with the traditional power structures – the hierarchy and inequalities of the capital–labour relation – these new forms of manpower planning and organisation simply shift the 'space' within which discontent is constituted and expressed. From stress, to anxiety and disorientation (O'Doherty, 1994), these forms of organisation and employment relations are subject to a range of interruptions, breakdowns and conflicts. This is perhaps different in form from the traditional organisation and expression of conflict and tension, but arguably no less debilitating in terms of the efficient functioning and reproduction of organisation, profit and capital.

Research finds considerable evidence to support the claim that power remains marked by tension, disruption, and breakdown within contemporary forms of work relations. Barker (1993) details how in small, self-managing teams, new rules, regulations and normative expectations emerge around things like attendance, performance and commitment. These far more insidious forms of discipline replace the traditional and formal managerial directives of the 'command-and-control' variety. Prominent team members soon arise from within these so-called self-governing democracies, democracies that soon reproduce familiar patterns of power, authority and hierarchy.

Team leaders are able to maintain their position only with the support of a majority of the team, support that remains, however, tenuous and fragile. These 'elected' team leaders seek to manage, guide and steer the rest of the group into conformity with extant rules and norms, but their status remains insecure, partial and contingent on the day-to-day alliances of political traffic. What Tomkins and Cheney (1985) define as *concertive control* operates to regulate and manage work teams far more perniciously through informal hierarchies and seniority. Paradoxically this form of control can be seen to be both tighter and more powerful, but also more fragile in terms of the work and effort that employees must routinely invest to maintain discipline and order. Barker's (1993) ethnography of ISE reveals how this discipline operates with the example of 'Stephi', a short-term worker seeking to gain full-time employment status with the team. She was considered by the team to have a bad attitude and failed to identify sufficiently with the team. In Stephi's words:

> When I first started I really didn't start off on the right foot, so I've been working to re-prove myself as far as a team player. My attitude gets in the way. I let it get in the way too many times and now I've been watching it and hoping they [her team] will see the change in me and I can prove to them that I will make a good ISE employee.
>
> (p. 425)

Of course, this may simply represent self-interested guile and instrumentalism on Stephi's behalf in an effort to secure a full-time position. Indeed, Barker details the expression of tension and conflict in the arguments that regularly attend team meetings. Rivalries, personalities, disputes – and what we may speculate to be nascent political cliques and alliances – emerge as the social relations within the team attempt to tackle the exigencies of performance and market competition. In their efforts to plan, organise and discipline human resources, teams begin to resemble the Lord of the Flies (Golding, 1954). The work of Catherine Casey (1995) is also illustrative of these divisions and contradictions, where loyalty to one's team, one's identity as a worthy and productive employee, and the pressures of effort and performance requirements, combine to generate unstable work 'organisation'. In an exemplary rich ethnographic study, Casey begins to expose the weaknesses and lines of division that accompany such corporate restructuring initiatives, which change the form and locus of manpower planning but not, it would seem, the inevitability of conflict and tension.

Stop and think

1 How does HRP attempt to 'smooth out' the complications associated with economic and political dynamics?

2 How convinced would you be as a human resources manager that effective HRP eliminates conflicting objectives?

CONCLUSIONS

We have found that traditional manpower planning attempts to present its practice as a pure scientific exercise. It is about statistical equations and differential calculus, and the belief that organisations can be made to resemble well-ordered machines. Derived from a history of warfare and murder, the discourse of manpower planning is a masculine prejudice, an illusion of quantitative mastery and representation that tries to translate the complexity and ambiguity of a three-dimensional world – and probably more than three, as we later discovered – into the flat cartography of two dimensions. As our chapter has evolved we have explored the ways in which this process of translation fails. The paper world of the scientific manpower planner is subject to continual dissolution by the encroachment of the material world, the world of work organisation and the employment relation. A constant relay between organisational presence and re-presentation gets continually interrupted and subverted and, almost like the dog chasing its own tail, the paper world of manpower planners and of those who write upon manpower planning spirals round and round in pursuit of ever greater representation and predictive accuracy. Yet the material world of organisation is nothing if not elusive, always just out of reach beyond the next horizon, and one step ahead. Perhaps manpower planners depend upon this elusiveness, this complexity, in order to provide a rationale for their own existence.

We have explored the categories of manpower planning and found them wanting. The idea that we can identify some heroic manpower planner occupied in an office at the apex of an organisation is another myth, an analytical convenience that fails to cultivate an awareness that it takes place everywhere – and therefore paradoxically nowhere – in organisation. This ontological problem has become more acute in the context of contemporary organisational form. We have tried to think of human resource planning as a method of restoring the discipline of manpower planning through new media and novel methods of organisational control. What we discovered was that the practice of human resource planning actually serves to aggravate tensions and conflict in organisation, adding to the antagonism that dislocates and disrupts the smooth economic exchange between capital and labour. Given the instability of many forms of organisation today, the fact that it mediates and generates a hypertrophy of realities – some that we remain conscious of and others that discharge their energy through subliminal and unconscious channels of existence – the hinges of order and disorder upon which organisation rests are made to oscillate more wildly and unpredictably. We see this in the dispersal of conflict and struggle among so-called empowered employees, who now increasingly work in teams, teams that resemble a viper's nest of accusation and counter-accusation, political back-biting, subterfuge, rivalry, and anxiety. Our chapter suggests that the warp and weft of human resource management (see Chapter 2 by Collin) is being pulled and stretched, its seams frayed and unravelling. Not *what* any more – organisation is becoming dematerialised, less tangible and solid, more temporary and evanescent. This creates a fractious space wherein employees play out a whole series of fears and anxieties in ways that challenge the integrative capacities of human resource planning and its efforts to render the world economic and utile. The parts of organisation might literally be spinning out of control such that we can no longer see its whole. Who knows these days where they are going, what they will be doing next week, where they might be headed, or whether there will even be a job for them next month (see Chapter 12)?

Yet organisation persists, outrageous fortunes are made, inequality spreads, and the blight of economic poverty scars ever greater tracts of inner city space (Lash and Urry, 1994: 145–170). Is there anybody left still asking what all this has got to do with our humble manpower planner and human resource management? In the face of unpredictability and uncertainty one might be able to hear the tension and suspense in organisation today. Something or someone is about to fly off the handle. Banking on the whole is a knot-what of seams.

SUMMARY

● This chapter has attempted to introduce students to the discursive, linguistic and theoretical suppositions that structure and inform traditional understandings in manpower planning. It was argued that a degree of suppression is evident in the myopic focus and reification of order. It was suggested that a process of undoing was simultaneously in play with the process of ordering through the practice of organisation and control.

● In seeking to reduce shocks and disturbances in the distribution and movement of human resources, planners traditionally seek to calculate manpower needs in the short, medium and long term. The devolution of aspects of manpower planning to the line manager, and indeed to the individual employee, associated with the practice of HRM, may lead to a situation where more diffuse lines of division undermine coherence and the strategic management of human resources.

● The traditional emphasis and faith in forecasting meant a considerable reliance on statistical methodologies. Only large organisations, such as the Civil Service and banks, seemed to pursue intricate statistical manpower planning. Perhaps this reflects the resources and expertise that they were able to invest in because of their insulation from the pressures and immediacy of market competition.

● The purported use of less mechanistic approaches to manpower planning, under the influence of human resource management, was seen to contain new lines of tension and division, that undermined a rational and coherent approach to the planning, organisation and distribution of resources.

● In the rhetoric of HRM we find a considerable emphasis on the 'needs' and aspirations of employees. However, there appears to be a serious potential conflict between the promise and expectations associated with HRM and the 'delivery' of responsibility, empowerment and career development.

● In the normative models of HRM (Legge, 1995) we find a considerable emphasis on strategic management and the importance of integrating human resource issues with business strategy. This chapter has argued for a holistic and contextual approach to human resource planning, one that recognises the interactions and contradictions associated with the play of economic, social and human relations.

Activity

Imagine that you are a regional personnel manager responsible for food retail stores in a growing regional economy. You have 36 stores in your area, ranging in size from small local grocery-style stores in which there are typically only about seven people employed, to large city centre superstores usually employing a store manager, two assistant managers, 12 line supervisors, 24 full-time employees working as check-out specialists, 45 full-time warehouse and stores staff, and 35 shopfloor assistants.

Over the last six months you have noticed a steadily increasing demand for your products within the region as a whole. Your chain is not renowned for paying particularly high wages relative to other employers in the area.

1 Carefully draw up an initial manpower plan for the organisation, indicating when and where staff are currently employed within the organisation, how long they are likely to stay in that position, and the future projections for staffing requirements. You can assume that within your region there are seven city centres in which you have two stores each. The remaining 22 stores are located in small to medium-sized peripheral towns.

2 Imagine now that you have been given the responsibility for designing an alternative method of planning and utilising labour. In your efforts to construct a new manpower plan and utilisation process you recognise that there are a number of aspiring career-minded individuals within the organisation. How are you going to reconcile the organisation's desire to maintain high productivity and low cost with individual employee requirements for progression and change?

3 How might the existence of a trade union affect the design and final outcome of a manpower plan?

QUESTIONS

1 What is the point in preparing detailed manpower plans when there is so much economic and business uncertainty?

2 In what ways are manpower planners responsible for maintaining staffing levels?

3 What are the advantages and disadvantages of constructing a labour turnover index?

4 Is it fair to suggest that employees experience an induction crisis when first joining an organisation? Which type of people do you feel this is likely to affect more, and are there organisations where this phenomenon is potentially more damaging for the operational needs of the business?

5 In what ways does human resource planning differ operationally from manpower planning? Is there a significant philosophical and strategic difference between human resource planning and manpower planning?

6 How and why is manpower planning increasingly seeking to construct flexible organisations?

7 In what ways could it be suggested that manpower planning in the UK political and economic context is at a significant disadvantage from its European competitors?

EXERCISES

1 Consider the reasons why the responsibility for manpower planning may have shifted away from head office personnel management. What is meant by organisational de-bureaucratisation, and in what ways may this interact with the supposed change from MP to HRP?

2 As a manpower planner in a large manufacturing firm producing components for television sets, prepare a report to senior management outlining the reasons for high turnover among recent inductees. Suggest methods and policies with which senior and line management may tackle this issue.

3 List those advantages and disadvantages that you associate with HRP in relation to MP.

CASE STUDY

Clarion call for a new social contract

Robert Taylor – What we expect from and are accountable for at work has drastically changed

The world of work is going through dramatic change but the institutions and policies that seek to support and govern it 'remain mired in the 1930s'. As a result the 'social contract' – what we expect from and are accountable for at work – has broken down'. Today's challenge in the US and elsewhere in the industrialised world is to update policies and institutions by the creation of a 'new social contract capable of meeting the needs and expectations of the workforce, economy and society of the new century'.

So argued Professor Thomas Kochan, outgoing president of the American Industrial Relations Association and a leading figure in MIT's institute for work and employment research, in a characteristically insightful address to last month's annual conference of the association in Boston.

He sees the term 'social contract' as a metaphor, which means 'the expectations and obligations that workers, employers and their communities and societies have for work and employment relationships'.

In his opinion, the 'good' employment relationship cannot be today's 'two-party instrumental exchange focused on only the narrow self-interest of the individual worker or their individual employer'. It must be enforceable, so that each party can be 'held accountable for keeping its part in the understanding'.

It also covers 'subjective principles and expectations that we bring to work as professionals, family members and community citizens'.

Kochan adds an ingredient that he describes as 'a uniquely American approach' reflecting its decentralising traditions which provide 'the parties closest to the workplace with the rights, power and capabilities needed to control their own destiny at work'.

Ever since Roosevelt's New Deal in the 1930s, US companies have had to balance competing responsibilities: to serve as agents for shareholders in maximising their wealth and to meet growing responsibilities focused on employment strategies.

In the US today, shareholder pressures have grown ever more intense but companies have discovered they need to recognise human capital, knowledge and learning as important critical assets for business success. We have also seen the transformation of the boundaries of the company, which have grown increasingly uncertain and blurred by corporate restructuring with an emphasis on core competencies.

Kochan argues that a 'new social contract' is needed that recognises companies now have 'multiple stakeholders to which they owe a fiduciary and social responsibility'.

Strategic partnerships between companies and their employees are one way forward, but few yet exist in the US. But in the dynamic and fluid US labour market he sees a possible advance by encouragement of a shift in employment policy away from a preoccupation with the individual enterprise to a focus on a wide network of intermediate labour market institutions and community bodies that facilitate employment mobility, and match people to jobs more efficiently.

Kochan pointed out in his Boston speech that there is evidence in the US that this is happening, with the creation of temporary help companies to meet recruitment needs in California's Silicon Valley and other tight labour markets; establishment of various family and work advisory services; and the formation of cross-company consortia.

But he would like to see much more experimentation in new forms of self-governance in workplaces.

Kochan's clarion call for action in workplace reform seems unlikely to interest any of this year's crop of US presidential candidates. But it deserves to be listened to and acted upon.

His demand for a national agenda on employment issues seems unlikely to meet with any favourable response. But it should. The breakdown between the world of work and the institutions and policies designed to provide employment with rules is not something that can be allowed to continue without adverse social and political consequences.

A recent elegantly written book by Professor David Marsden at the London School of Economics provides further evidence of the need for the closing of that perceived gap between work and how it is organised. He points out that, despite the hyperbole about the flexible labour market, as many as nine out of every 10 workers in the advanced industrialised world are still employed directly by companies under a relationship that gives them the right to determine the tasks their employees should undertake within specified but certain limitations.

However, those limits are vital for the durability of the open-ended and relatively stable employment relationship that remains the workplace norm despite the often-proclaimed arrival of the flexible labour

market with its temporary, short-term and contract employees. The scope for what Marsden terms the 'opportunism' of employees in their relationship with their employers is considerable. The economic nature of the employment exchange and the costs of job changing for employees as well as replacement of workers with the required skills make 'the conditions for opportunism ripe'.

This might be expected to ensure chronic instability but in practice flexible limitations are provided to management's authority over work assignments and to employee obligations over performance that ensure the employment relationship can work for mutual benefit.

The existence of 'horizontal coordination' between companies over skill development and job design helps to underpin the relationship. Prof Marsden points to 'occupational communities' such as inter-firm chambers of commerce in Germany, UK professional associations and industrial districts in the US. It is also evident that the more one-sided the relationship, the greater reliance on legal regulation and stricter enforcement of task-centred rules, but this inhibits the flexibility required for workplace modernisation.

Prof Kochan's paper can be found at: http://mitsloan.mit.edu/iwer *A Theory of Employment Systems* by David Marsden, Oxford University Press.

Source: Financial Times, 3 February 2000.

---

1 Carefully consider what might be implied by the 'adverse social and political consequences' that Kochan warns us of in employment relations characterised by an absence of rules and regulations. What role can human resource planners play in the consolidation of a 'social contract' between capital and labour?

2 The boundaries of companies are growing increasingly uncertain and blurred, so Kochan seems to be telling us. What do you think Kochan means by this, and in what ways might we extend his analysis?

3 How might we interpret those 'community bodies that facilitate employment mobility' through the frame of reference provided by Foucault and his understanding of power?

REFERENCES AND FURTHER READING

Those texts marked with an asterisk are particularly recommended for further reading.

Armstrong, M. (1979) *Case Studies in Personnel Management.* London: Kogan Page.

Armstrong, M. (1992) *Human Resource Management: Strategy and Action* London: Kogan Page.

Armstrong, P. (1995) 'Accountancy and HRM', in Storey, J. (ed.) *Human Resource Management: A Critical Text.* London: Routledge.

Armstrong, P. (1996) 'Productive and unproductive management', in Smith, C., Knights, D. and Willmott, H. (eds) *White Collar Work*, 2nd edn. Basingstoke: Macmillan.

*Atkinson, J. (1984) 'Manpower strategies for flexible organisations', *Personnel Management*, August, pp. 28–31.

Atkinson, J. (1985) 'Flexibility: planning for an uncertain future', *Manpower Policy and Practice*, Vol. 1, Summer.

Atkinson, J. (1989) 'Four stages of adjustment to the demographic downturn', *Personnel Management*, August, pp. 20–24.

Barker, J. (1993) 'Tightening the iron cage: concertive control in self managing teams', *Administrative Science Quarterly*, Vol. 38, pp. 408–437.

Barker, J. and Tompkins, P. (1994) 'Identification in the self-managing organisation: characteristics of target and tenure', *Human Communications Research*, Vol. 21, No. 2, December.

Barthes, R. (1977) 'From work to text', in S. Heath (ed.) *Image–Music–Text*. London: Fontana.

Bartholomew, D. and Forbes, A. (1979) *Statistical Techniques for Manpower Planning*. Chichester: John Wiley.

Bataille, G. (1957/1987) *Eroticism*. London: Marion Boyars.

Bauman, Z. (1992) *Intimations of Postmodernity* London: Routledge.

*Bennison, M. and Casson, J. (1984) *Manpower Planning*. Maidenhead: McGraw-Hill.

Berman, M. (1982) *All That is Solid Melts into Air*. London: Verso.

*Beynon, H. (1973) *Working for Ford*. London: Allen Lane.

Bowey, A. (1974) *A Guide to Manpower Planning*. London: Macmillan.

*Bramham, J. (1989) *Human Resource Planning*. London: IPM.

*Bramham, J. (1990) *Practical Manpower Planning*. London: IPM.

Brown, W., Marginson, P. and Walsh, J. (1995) 'Management: pay determination and collective bargaining', in Edwards, P. (ed.) *Industrial Relations: Theory and Practice*. Oxford: Blackwell.

Burrell, G. (1997) *Pandemonium: Towards a Retro-Organization Theory*. London: Sage.

Casey, C. (1995) *Work, Self and Society: After Industrialism*. London: Routledge.

Castenada, C. (1971) *A Separate Reality: Further Conversations with Don Juan*. London: Penguin.

Clark, J. (ed.) (1993) *Human Resource Management and Technical Change*. London: Sage.

Clegg, H. (1975) 'Pluralism in industrial relations', *British Journal of Industrial Relations*, Vol. 13.

Clegg, H. (1979) *The Changing System of Industrial Relations in Great Britain*. Oxford: Blackwell.

Clegg, S. (1990) *Modern Organizations: Organization Studies in the Postmodern World*. London: Sage.

Cleverley, G. (1973) *Managers and Magic*. London: Pelican.

Cole, R. (1991) *Personnel Management: Theory and Practice*. London: DP Publications.

Cooper, G. (1998) 'Simulating difference: ethnography and the relations of intellectual production', *British Journal of Sociology*, Vol. 40, No. 1, pp. 20–35.

*Cooper, R. (1993) 'Technologies of representation', in Ahonen, P. (ed.) *Tracing the Semiotic Boundaries of Politics*, Berlin/New York: Mouton de Gruyter.

Cooper, R. and Law, J. (1995) 'Organization: distal and proximal views', in S.B. Bacharach (ed.) *Research in the Sociology of Organizations*. Greenwich, Conn. JAI.

Cowling, A. and Walters, M. (1990) 'Manpower planning – where are we today?', *Personnel Review*, Vol. 19, No. 3.

Cressey, P. and Scott, P. (1992) 'Employment, technology and industrial relations in the UK clearing banks: is the honeymoon over?', *New Technology, Work and Employment*, Vol. 7, No. 2, pp. 83–96.

Deal, T. and Kennedy, A. (1982) *Corporate Cultures: The Rites and Rituals of Corporate Life*. New York: Addison Wesley.

Delbridge, R. (1995) 'Surviving JIT: control and resistance in a Japanese transplant', *Journal of Management Studies*, Vol. 32, No. 6, pp. 803–817.

Donovan, Lord (1968) *Report of the Royal Commission on Trade Unions and Employers Associations*. London: HMSO.

*Edwards, P. (1986) *Conflict at Work. A Materialist Analysis of Workplace Relations*. Oxford: Blackwell.

Edwards, P., Hall, M., Hyman, R., Marginson, P., Sisson, K., Waddington, J. and Winchester, D. (1992) 'Great Britain: still muddling through', in Ferner, A. and Hyman, R. (eds) *Industrial Relations in the New Europe*. Oxford: Blackwell.

Eldridge, J., Cressey, P. and MacInnes, J. (1991) *Industrial Sociology and Economic Crisis*. Hemel Hempstead: Harvester Wheatsheaf.

Elger, T. (1990) 'Technical innovation and work reorganisation in British manufacturing in the 1980s: continuity, intensification or transformation?', *Work, Employment and Society*, special issue, pp. 67–101.

Eurostat (1990) *Basic Statistics of the Community*. Luxembourg: Office for Official Publications of the EC.

Fayol, H. (1949) *General and Industrial Administration*. London: Pitman.

*Flanders, A. (1964) *The Fawley Productivity Agreement: A Case Study of Management and Collective Bargaining*. London: Faber & Faber.

Foucault, M. (1971) 'Nietzsche, genealogy, history', in Rainbow, P. (ed.) (1984) *The Foucault Reader*. Harmondsworth: Penguin.

Foucault, M. (1977) *Discipline and Punish*. Harmondsworth: Penguin.

Foucault, M. (1980) *Power/Knowledge* (ed. Colin Gordon). Hemel Hempstead: Harvester Wheatsheaf.

Foucault, M. (1984) *The History of Sexuality*, Vol. 1. Harmondsworth: Penguin.

Fox, A. (1985) *Man Mismanagement*. London: Hutchinson.

Freud, S. (1918/1991) 'The Wolf Man', in *Case Histories 2*, Vol. 9, The Penguin Freud Library. London: Penguin.

*Gabriel, Y. (1995) 'The unmanaged organization: stories, fantasies and subjectivity', *Organization Studies*, Vol. 16, No. 3, pp. 477–501.

Gabriel, Y. (1997) 'Meeting God: when organizational members come face to face with the supreme leader', *Human Relations*, Vol. 50, No. 4, pp. 315–342.

Game, A. and Metcalfe, A. (1996) *Passionate Sociology*. London: Sage.

Game, A. and Pringle, A. (1983) *Gender at Work*. Sydney: George Allen & Unwin.

Garrahan, P. and Stewart, P. (1992) *The Nissan Enigma: Flexibility and Work in a Local Economy*. London: Mansell.

Garsten, C. and Grey, C. (1997) 'How to become oneself: discourses of subjectivity in post bureaucratic organizations'. *Organization*, Vol. 4, No. 2, pp. 211–228.

Giddens (1976) *New Rules for Sociological Method*. London: Hutchinson.

Golding, W. (1954) *Lord of the Flies*. London: Faber & Faber.

Grey, C. (1994) 'Career as a project of self and labour process discipline', *Sociology*, Vol. 28, No. 2, pp. 479–497.

Guest, D. (1989) 'Personnel and HRM: can you tell the difference?', *Personnel Managment*, January, pp. 48–51.

Guest, D. (1990) 'Human resource management and the American dream', *Journal of Management Studies*, Vol. 27, No. 4, pp. 377–397.

Guest, D. (1991) 'Personnel management: the end of orthodoxy?', *British Journal of Industrial Relations*, Vol. 29, No. 5, pp. 149–177.

Hakim, C. (1990) 'Core and periphery in employers' workforce strategies: evidence from the 1987 ELUS survey', *Work, Employment and Society*, Vol. 4, No. 2, pp. 157–88.

Hall, M. (1992) 'Behind the European Works Councils directive: the Commission's legislative strategy', *British Journal of Industrial Relations*, Vol. 30, No. 4, pp. 547–566.

Hall, M. (1994) 'Industrial relations and the social dimension', in Hyman, R. and Femer, A. (eds) *New Frontiers in European Industrial Relations*. Oxford: Blackwell.

Hall, S. and Jacques. M. (1983) *The Politics of Thatcherism* London: Lawrence and Wishart.

*Handy, C. (1989) *The Age of Unreason*. London: Business Books.

Handy, C. (1994) *The Empty Raincoat*. London: Hutchinson.

Harvey, D. (1989) *The Condition of Postmodernity*. Oxford: Blackwell.

Hassard, J. and Parker, M. (eds) (1994) *Postmodernism and Organisations*. London: Sage.

Hatch, M.J. (1997) *Organization Theory: Modem Symbolic and Postmodern Perspectives*. Oxford: Oxford University Press.

Hill, J.M.M. and Trist, E.L. (1953) 'A consideration of industrial accidents as a means of withdrawal from the work situation, *Human Relations,* 6, November.

Hill, J.M.M. and Trist, E.L. (1955) 'Changes in accidents and other absences with length of service', *Human Relations*, 8, May.

Hoskin, K. (1995) 'The viewing self and the world we view: beyond the perspectival illusion', *Organization*, Vol. 2, No. 1, pp. 141–162.

Hyman, R. (1975) *Industrial Relations: A Marxist Introduction*. London: Macmillan.

Hyman, R. (1978) 'Pluralism, procedural consensus and collective bargaining', *British Journal of Industrial Relations*, Vol. 16, No. 1, March.

Hyman, R. (1987) 'Strategy or structure? Capital, labour and control', *Work, Employment and Society*, Vol. 1, No. 1, pp. 25–55.

*Inayatullah, S. (1990) 'Deconstructing and reconstructing the future: predictive, cultural and critical epistemologies', *Futures*, Vol. 22, No. 2.

Industrial Relations Services (1995a) 'Customer service drive at BT', *Employment Trends*, 579, March.

Industrial Relations Services (1995b) 'New directions at Royal Mail', *Employee Development Bulletin* , 67, July.

Industrial Relations Services (1996) *Employment Trends* 604, March.

Institute for Employment Research (1995/6) *Review of the Economy and Employment: Occupational Studies*. University of Warwick.

Institute of Personnel Management (1975) *Manpower Planning in Practice*. London: IPM.

IRDAC (1990) [Industrial Research and Development Advisory Committee of the Commission of the European Communities] *Skill Shortages in Europe*. Luxembourg: Office for Official Publications of the European Communities.

Jackall, R. (1988) *Moral Mazes: The World of Corporate Managers*. New York: Oxford University Press.

Kallinikos, J. (1995) 'Mapping the intellectual terrain of management education', in French, R. and Grey, C. (eds) *Rethinking Management Education*. London: Sage.

Kanter, R.M. (1984) *The Change Masters*. London: Allen & Unwin.

Keep, E, (1989) 'Corporate training strategies: the vital component?', in Storey, J. (ed.) *New Perspectives on Human Resource Management*. London: Routledge.

Keep, E. (1994) 'The transition from school to work', in Sisson, K. (ed.) *Personnel Management in Britain*, 2nd edn. Oxford: Blackwell.

Keep, E. and Rainbird, H. (1995) 'Training', in Edwards, P. (ed.) *Industrial Relations: Theory and Practice*. Oxford: Blackwell.

Kondo, D. (1990) *Crafting Selves: Power, Gender and Discourses of Identity in a Japanese Workplace*. Chicago and London: University of Chicago Press.

Lasch, C. (1978) *The Culture of Narcissism*. New York: Warner Books.

*Lash, S. and Urry, J. (1994) *Economies of Signs and Space*. London: Sage.

Legge, K. (1995) *Human Resource Management: Rhetorics and Realities*. Basingstoke: Macmillan.

Linstead, S. and Banerjee, B. (1999) 'Organizational dreaming: modes of being: modes of knowing, and modes of organizing', paper presented to *Critical Management Studies Conference*, Manchester School of Management, 14–16 July 1999. 1st Annual International Conference in Critical Management Studies, Helm Hall, Machester, UK.

Lyotard, J. F. (1984) *The Postmodern Condition: A Report on Knowledge*. Manchester: Manchester University Press.

Mackay, L. and Torrington, D. (1986) *The Changing Nature of Personnel Management*. London: IPM.

Manpower Services Commission (1987) *People: The Key to Success*. London: NEDO.

Marcuse, H. (1964) *One Dimensional Man*. London: Routledge & Kegan Paul.

Marginson, P., Edwards, P.K., Martin, R., Purcell, J. and Sisson, K. (1988) *Beyond the Workplace: The Management of Industrial Relations in Large Enterprises*. Oxford: Blackwell.

McBeath, G. (1978) *Manpower Planning and Control*. London: Business Books.

Morgan, G. (1986) *Images of Organization*. London: Sage.

O'Doherty, D. (1992) 'Banking on part-time labour' *Occasional Paper*, Leicester Business School, De Montfort University.

O'Doherty, D. (1993) 'Strategic conceptions, consent and contradictions: banking on part-time labour?,'paper presented to the *Organisation and Control of the Labour Process, 11th Annual Conference*, Blackpool.

O'Doherty, D. (1994) 'Institutional withdrawal? Anxiety and conflict in the emerging banking labour process, or "How to get out of it"', paper presented to *12th Annual International Labour Process Conference*, Aston University, Birmingham.

O'Doherty, D. (1996) 'Deflation and disappointment: the collapse of self and the failure of HRM in the banking industry', M*imeo, Department of HRM*, De Montfort University, Leicester.

O'Doherty, D. and Roberts, I. (2000) 'Career or slide: managing on the threshold of sense', in Collin, A. and Young, R. (eds) *The Future of Career*. Cambridge: Cambridge University Press.

Organization (1999) Thematic issue on organization as science fiction, Vol. 6, No. 4.

Peters, T. (1993) *Necessary Disorganisation in the Nano-second Nineties*. London: Macmillan.

Peters, T. (1994) *The Tom Peters Seminar: Crazy Times Call for Crazy Organizations*. London: Macmillan.

Peters, T. J. and Waterman, R. H. (1982) *In Search of Excellence: Lessons from America's Best Run Companies*. New York: Harper & Row.

Pollert, A. (1988) 'The flexible firm: fixation or fact?', *Work, Employment and Society*, Vol. 2, No. 3, pp. 281–316.

Pollert, A. (ed.) (1992) *Farewell to Flexibility?* Oxford: Blackwell.

Pringle, A. (1990) *Secretaries Talk: Sexuality, Power and Work*. London: Verso.

Quinn-Mills, D. (1985) 'Planning with people in mind', *Harvard Business Review*, July–August.

Rajan, A. (1993) *1990s: Where the New Jobs Will Be*. Centre for Research in Employment and Technology in Europe. CREATE, Tunbridge Wells.

Rose, N. (1990) *Governing the Soul: The Shaping of the Private Self*. London: Routledge.

Rowntree, LA. and Stewart, P.A. (1976) 'Estimating manpower needs II: statistical methods', in Smith, A.R. (ed.) *Manpower Planning in the Civil Service*, London. HMSO.

Roy, D. (1958) 'Banana time: job satisfaction and informal interaction', *Human Organisation*, Vol. 18, No. 1, pp. 158–161.

Salaman, G. (1992) *Human Resource Strategies*. London: Sage.

Sewell, G. and Wilkinson, B. (1992) '"Someone to watch over me": surveillance, discipline and the just-in-time labour process', *Sociology*, Vol. 26, No. 2, pp. 271–289.

Sievers, B. (1994) *Work, Death and Life Itself. Essays on Management and Organization*. Berlin: De Gruyter.

Simon. H. (1957) *Models of Man*. New York: Wiley.

Sisson, K. and Marginson, P. (1995) 'Management: systems, structures and strategy', in Edwards, P. (ed.) *Industrial Relations: Theory and Practice in Britain*. Oxford: Blackwell, pp. 89–122.

Smith, A.R. (1971) 'The nature of corporate manpower planning', *Personnel Review*, Vol. 1, Autumn.

Smith, A.R. (ed.) (1976) *Manpower Planning in the Civil Service*. London: HMSO.

Starkey, K. and Barratt, C. (1994) 'The emergence of flexible networks in the UK television industry', *British Journal of Management*, Vol. 5, No. 4.

Storey, J. (1987) 'Developments in human resource management: an Interim report'. Warwick Papers in Industrial

Relations, No. 17. Coventry: Industrial Relations Research Unit.

Storey, J. (ed.) (1989) *New Perspectives on Human Resource Management*. London: Routledge.

Storey, J. (ed.) (1992) *Developments in the Management of HRM*. Oxford: Blackwell.

Storey, J. (ed.) (1995) *Human Resource Management: A Critical Text*. London: Routledge.

Storey, J. and Bacon, N. (1993) 'Individualism and collectivism: into the 1990s', paper presented to the *East Midlands Work, Employment and Society Seminar*, Leicester.

Taussig. M. (1993) *Mimesis and Alterity: A Particular History of the Senses*. London: Routledge.

Thrift, N. (1999) 'The place of complexity', *Theory, Culture and Society*, Vol. 16, No. 3, pp. 31–69.

*Timperley, S. and Sisson, K. (1989) 'From manpower planning to human resource planning', in Sisson, K. (ed.) *Personnel Management in Britain*. Oxford: Blackwell.

Tomkins, P.K. and Cheney, G. (1985) 'Communication and unobtrusive control in contemporary organization', in McPhee, R.D. and Tompkins, P.K. (eds) *Organizational Communication: Traditional Themes and New Directions*. Beverley Hills, Cal.: Sage.

Torrington, D. and Hall, L. (1989) *Personnel Management: A New Approach*. Hemel Hempstead: Prentice Hall.

Torrington, D. and Hall, L. (1995) *Personnel Management: HRM in Practice*. London: Prentice Hall.

Townley, B. (1994) *Reframing Human Resource Management: Power, Ethics and the Subject at Work*. London: Sage.

Turnbull, P. (1992) 'Dock strikes and the demise of the "occupational culture"', *Sociological Review*, Vol. 40, No. 2, May, pp. 294–318.

Turnbull, P. and Sapsford, D. (1991) 'Why did Devlin fail? Casualism and conflict on the docks', *British Journal of Industrial Relations*, Vol. 29, pp. 237–57.

Turnbull, P. and Sapsford, D. (1992) 'A sea of discontent: the tides of organised and "unorganised" conflict on the docks', *Sociology*, Vol. 26, No. 2, May, pp. 291–309.

Turnbull, P., Woolfson, C. and Kelly, J. (1992) *Dock Strike: Conflict and Restructuring in Britain's Ports*. Aldershot: Avebury/Gower.

Tyson, S. and Fell, A. (1986) *Evaluating the Personnel Function*. London: Hutchinson.

Tyson and York (1989) *Personnel Management*. London: Heinemann.

Urwick, L. (1947) *The Elements of Industrial Administration*. London: Pitman.

Valdez, S. (1997) *An Introduction to Global Financial Markets*, 2nd edn. Basingstoke: Macmillan Business.

Weber, M. (1948) *From Max Weber: Essays in Sociology*. London: Routledge & Kegan Paul.

Weber, M. (1964) *The Theory of Social and Economic Organization*. New York: Free Press.

*Willmott, H. (1993) 'Strength is ignorance; slavery is freedom: managing culture in modern organizations', *Journal of Management Studies*, Vol. 30, No. 4, pp. 515–552.

Wood, S. (ed.) (1989) *The Transformation of Work? Skill, Flexibility and the Labour Process*. London: Allen & Unwin.

Job design: signs, symbols and re-signation

Damian O'Doherty

OBJECTIVES

- To outline and detail the traditional, but still widely influential, 'Taylorist' form of job design and work organisation. An appreciation of Frederick Taylor and his management principles will prove indispensable for those human resource managers employed or seeking to understand the nature of work and the opportunities there may be for job redesign in the growing service sectors of the economy: the hotel, catering, retail, tourism and leisure industries.

- To consider the expectations and impact of Taylorism on the modern work organisation. By 'expectations' we mean the explicit and latent managerialist assumptions that inform the work of Taylor and his followers.

- To facilitate an understanding of the motivation and contribution of the human relations of work approach to the design of jobs and the organisation of work. This is often thought to come after Taylorism as an enlightened reaction to the degradation of jobs entailed in the adoption of scientific management.

- To explore the idea that we are undergoing an epochal shift in management and work organisation, a shift that many claim is slowly eliminating the prevalence of Taylorist forms of job design and the relevance of human relations style thinking. HRM is often considered to be a part of these wide-ranging changes, variously thought of in terms of the flexible work organisation, the post-bureaucratic firm, a post-Fordist regime of accumulation, and a postmodern social and cultural milieu.

- To critically evaluate the meaning and scope of the concept 'job design'. This will help us to develop a more sophisticated understanding of job design, one that understands it in terms of a politics of struggle and contest rather than the simple linear-rational outcome of managerial initiative.

- To explore the ideas and practices associated with teamworking, post-bureaucratic design, and business process re-engineering. We need to connect an understanding of these developments with the confusion and anxiety experienced by employees subject to these practices. If we are to appreciate the complex forces and dynamics in organisation that shape job design, we shall be obliged to examine the nature of 'agency' in the employment relation.

- To locate human resource management and the HR manager *within* the context of these wider socio-political forces. In this analytical move we begin to explore the conditions of possibility and constraint that encompass attempts to design and redesign jobs.

INTRODUCTION

Is it worth the aggravation
To find yourself a job when there's nothing worth working for
It's a crazy situation
But all I need are cigarettes and alcohol

Noel Gallagher, 1994; Creation Records

Strange things are afoot in the field of job design. Making us slip. Kalashnikov rifles, murder, the Bacchic rites, Kevin Spacey, senility, and dandruff. Increasingly, practitioners are realising the limitations of the traditional prescriptive personnel management syllabus in allowing for a sophisticated understanding of the question of job design, an approach that in the main assumes that the design of jobs is the product of management initiative. Indeed, the very assumption that jobs can be 'de-signed' seems problematic today. This chapter explores these limitations. On one level it is exercised by the question of power and the complexity of social processes in organisation. On another, it begins to skirt deeper questions of rationality and meaning that permeate the subject of job design and the *writing on* the subject of job design. Job design is an inherently political subject. This is, then, the subject *of the subject* of job design. Many forget this. Or, perhaps it is more correct to say they wish to *repress* these difficult aspects of the subject. Let me explain.

Job design makes for hard reading. Now, I don't mean 'hard' in the sense that personnel managers will find contemporary developments in the understanding and practice of job design intellectually difficult or impenetrable. Far from it. Yet there are some of us who are worried that the technical training of traditional personnel managers has been or still is limited by the orthodox and provincial – limited by assumptions of modernity, science and rationality; assumptions that may no longer hold in contemporary work organisation. Consider recent developments in higher and management education as an exacerbation of these trends: financial poverty, student debts, working overnight in garages while attending university by day, modularity, semesterisation, accreditation, instrumental attitudes, broken classrooms, teachers moving from one class to the next without pause or breath. Remember, they no longer come out of their jobs feeling enriched – just knackered. Then think of the difference between education and training. A manager once said that he would rather employ a graduate of 'classics' than an MBA graduate, because at least the scholar of classics has been educated to *think* (Grey and Mitev, 1995). Is this not perhaps a little unfair?

So what is happening to the syllabus of personnel or human resource management? Is it more interesting than a rehearsal of how to recruit, how to select, how to train, how to develop, how to downsize, how to administer wages, the importance of fresh flowers in the restrooms? STRATEGY, STRATEGY, STRATEGY! declares the clarion call. We are probably now familiar with the mantras and litanies of the contemporary managerial sales pitch. Yet this is the syllabus that you probably will still be studying. However, HRM is spreading in weird and wonderful ways. Beware. Do you find it interesting? Is it relevant to you? Do you want a job? Are you in any position to tell? What would you rather be doing? Perhaps you have debts to pay off. You might want a mortgage and a more reliable car to shuttle you between your work and the mortgage. Casey (1995) reports that many managerial and white-collar employees employed at Hephaestus work 60–80 hour weeks, many priding themselves on being in seven days a week. Watson (1994) observes how managers would leave their offices for the night only to leave the lights on and their jackets slung over the back of their chairs so that colleagues leaving work would think that they were still in the office working. This is the discipline of a panoptic society, hidden cameras, saturated news reportage, remote monitoring, live CAM broadcasts, smart technology, artificial intelligence, databases that automatically record information, interactive television, silent surveillance, the 'interview society' (Silverman, 1993), voyeurism and street 'security' cameras. The truth is out there . . . as many will have it.

Yet many come to tolerate and even to like this state of affairs. Even more accept it as an unnoticed background condition of everyday mundane life. We *want* to work longer hours – to develop, improve ourselves, move on, be a success, 'be more desirable' as a recent Open University advert proclaimed; 'fitter happier more productive comfortable not drinking too much regular exercise at the gym (three days a week) getting on better with your associate employee contemporaries', as Thom Yorke (1997), of Radiohead, sings. How does it happen that many of us end up working such long hours? Presumably, in reading this, you will be saying, 'This sounds a bit extreme'. Paranoia perhaps, existential angst, the indulgent ravings of deviants and outsiders. If so, reflect a little further on the possibility or likelihood of 'healthy' job design. Alongside repetitive strain injury, eye strain, skeletal deformity and tinnitus, employees today complain of dandruff and nervous eye twitches, the result, many argue, of badly designed offices and equipment and the dependence on computers and VDUs. Consider the number of head teachers interviewed on television during the 1980s and 1990s. Can you remember how many of them seemed to have slurred speech, nervous ailments, odd twitches, discoloured bags under their eyes, and bad haircuts? How many of you are saying, 'That'll never happen to me'?

During the 1980s and the ascendancy of Japanese organisations it used to be a common refrain heard in many a classroom that the Japanese live to work, whereas the English work to live. Unfortunately these distinctions between work and life, home and work, and even leisure and work, might be breaking down today. Certainly one doesn't so often hear the complaint these days that the Japanese live to work. Are we becoming then a more competitive and disciplined workforce – one that enjoys work, able to find interest and stimulation in jobs? Or are we becoming more like Coupland's (1991) generation X – bored; disillusioned; staring with an odd mixture of boredom and fascination at the flickering images on our television screens; playing minesweeper and solitaire on our computers at work (when we should be working); considering the possibility of medication (as a lifestyle choice); or filling in an application for *Who Wants to be a Millionaire* while dreaming of illicit sexual liaisons and the television show *Gladiators*? Yet, if you are asking questions of this sort, you have begun to exercise some of the qualities that make the human subject so difficult and intransigent, and the processes of management so troublesome and complex. Indeed, you are beginning to think about the design of your jobs.

Now come on – how many of you are told that work is good for you; that one is obliged to work? The sociologist Max Weber famously talked about the influence of Protestantism and the work ethic (Weber, 1965). Christian Schumacher (1999), similarly, writes today on the possibility of 'finding God' and the realisation of harmonious universal perfection through better job design. So it might seem that not only is work universal and necessary but it has become the means through which we realise individual and collective salvation. But is it true that we have to work? We need to know our history. In Greek times, of course, it was only the slaves who had to labour; the free citizen was at liberty to pursue the finer questions of Platonic philosophy, the contemplation of aesthetics and poetry. More recently, the novelist Douglas Coupland has begun to talk about a 'slacker' generation, a generation 'X' who shun slavery and hard work, opting for low-responsibility jobs that do not interfere too much with their lifestyle pursuits – usually travel, drugs, music, video/television, shopping, and . . . well, more drugs. This has been explored more recently in the popular and Oscar-winning film *American Beauty*, in which the reformed slacker unfortunately gets murdered.

It would seem that questions of life and death surround the subject of job design. Is it possible that there is a relationship between the discharge of a Kalashnikov automatic rifle in a crowded McDonald's and the design of what Ritzer (1993) calls McDonaldized jobs and the Mcdonaldization of society? Open up any traditional introductory text-book on personnel management or human resource management and you won't find this being discussed. Nor will you find much in the way of cyborgs. Yet one of the most important developments in job design is the elimination of the 'human'. They're simply no longer needed. They cost too much. They're lazy. They are subject to inappropriate sexual impulses at work. They need to be fed, and need to sleep for 8 hours a day. Working conditions have changed too. This is not just a product of developments in e-commerce either. Think of the work of astronauts, off-world space engineering, deep sea divers, 'remote' medical operations, the NATO combat soldier, airline pilots, and the virtual worker – an example of which might be 'intelligent' software programs that filter information according to the user's needs and requirements as identified and established by the software program. All these designed jobs integrate the human and the non-human. In another sense it portents another kind of death for the individual human subject. They are beyond the simply human: hybrid jobs, part man, part machine – or, in other words, cyborgs (Featherstone and Burrows, 1995; Gray, 1995). Some now talk about the 'virtual organisation', the 'cyberorganisation', and the 'cyber-corporation', even the 'imaginary' organisation (Hedberg *et al.*, 1994). This goes way beyond a 'reconciliation' of those traditional categories used in the analysis of job design – the social and the technical – and the implications, far more profound.

To help us develop a critical appreciation of these issues, this chapter begins by dis-cussing the influence of Frederick Taylor and the principles of scientific management. We begin by locating our study within the analytical frame of reference provided by labour process study. Moreover, we shall study the contribution of Braverman (1974) and the rise of labour process analysis as a way of understanding the impact and impor-tance of deskilling on the nature of work organisation. One finds here that job design becomes a 'contested terrain', the contingent product of what some call a 'structured antagonism' (Edwards, 1986) between capital and labour. Rather than the determinist outcome of autonomous management initiative, the design of jobs is better thought of then as the precarious and unstable settlement of unequal power relations.

The negative implications associated with the impact of Taylorism prompted the study of human relations at work as a way of thinking about how jobs could be designed that secured some accommodation between the need for efficiency and indi-vidual 'needs', interest and motivation. In the main, the work of Mayo, Roethlisberger and Dickson, the UK-based studies emanating from the Tavistock Institute, and the var-ious movements addressing the quality of working life, arose in response to the perceived failures of Taylorism; yet we shall find that these approaches inherit many of its problematic assumptions.

The chapter then moves on to consider the theoretical contributions made by the flexibility debate (Atkinson, 1984; Pollert, 1988), flexible specialisation (Kern and Schumann, 1987; Hirst and Zeitlin, 1991), post-Fordism (Aglietta, 1976); and postmod-ernism (Jameson, 1991; Smart, 1993) in order to explore the idea that we are undergoing an epochal shift in management and work organisation. For many this is a systemic change that heralds the elimination of Taylorist forms of job design and the redundancy of human relations style thinking in the understanding and practice of job design. These theoretical proposals, however, operate at different analytical levels of abstraction and sophistication. Nevertheless, they all offer useful conceptual apparatus for assessing the development of human resource management and adjudicating the capacity of HRM to design jobs in innovative and novel ways. To extend our understanding of these issues we shall, following our discussion of the post-Fordist worker controversy, briefly read an etymology of 'design'. This allows us to unpack the conceptual assumptions that are built into the managerial understanding and use of job design. As an exercise in critical thinking this will further open up and extend our understanding of the tensions that exist between the nature of 'sign' and 'de-sign'. This adds further layers of complexity and struggle to the structured antagonism between capital and labour, an analytical move that works to further deflate and de-centre 'management' pretensions to rationality and control.

By locating our humble human resource manager *within* the context of these wider socio-political forces we can begin to explore the conditions of possibility and constraint that embrace attempts to design and redesign jobs. Seen as subject to forces over which they have little control or understanding, management and the process of job design begin to appear far less linear, rational and orderly. Even more, HRM may well prove to be part media and outcome of this growing irrationality or post-rational developments in management and organisation. Surrounded by the swarm of these cross-cutting tensions and struggles, the definition of a job – what it is, what it is composed of, where it 'starts' and 'finishes', and how it stitches in with other jobs in organisation – becomes vague and uncertain, stimulating further depths of confusion, struggle and anxiety.

We could extend this chapter by introducing an international dimension to the understanding of job design. For example, the German economy after the Second World War would offer an instructive example of nation state specificity in job design (Lane, 1989). This provides another way of thinking about the contextual location of management and the contingency of job design. We would find that global economic development is mediated by distinctive socio-political institutions and frameworks of governance, which place constraints on the 'freedom' and autonomy of management in the design of jobs. In many ways, Germany provides a useful contrast to the UK economy, illustrating how outcomes at the level of management and organisation can be shaped by wider political values and institutional structure. Given the limitations of this chapter we cannot develop a study of the other European economies other than to note that particular state institutions and legal frameworks in tension with an emergent pan-European series of coordinating regulations and institutions are likely to shape the development of very different patterns of job design. Nor can we, unfortunately, attempt to cover the burgeoning literature on gender, yet this too is of capital importance in any understanding of the thinking and practice of job design, a subject that has been dominated by masculine assumptions portrayed as universal.

TAYLORISM AND THE DEGRADATION OF LABOUR

Frederick Winslow Taylor (1856–1917) was in many ways the founder of modern rationalised management methods of organising and disciplining work and employees. It was Taylor who systematised the practice of work study, piece-rate schemes, and the use of time and motion studies in his drive towards redesigning jobs. What Taylor attempted to do was to break jobs down into their most basic and elementary components before reassembling them in more scientific and efficient ways. At least, this was the claim for rationality and science made by Taylor. Another way of looking at his work is to see the development of scientific management as part of a systematic attack by capital on the skilled craft traditions of organised labour. We first explore Taylor's life and early ideas before studying the ways in which he sought to secure management control over employment by means of the systematic deconstruction of work tasks. The role of financial reward occupied a central pillar in the system of scientific management, forming a major line of tension and disjunction in the employment relation, a medium through which its organisation was rendered fragile and insecure. Scientific management was to find its limitations attempting to repair and maintain organisation through this medium, generating tensions that prompted the development of 'human relations' study.

Taylor's life and early ideas

Taylor dropped out of his study of law and, against the wishes of his affluent bourgeois Philadelphia family, took up a job as a manual craft apprentice in a firm whose owners were close friends of his parents. Later, Taylor became a gang boss in a lathe department at the Midvale steel works, one of the most technologically advanced companies in the steel industry. In his youth, Taylor apparently displayed odd behavioural quirks, counting his steps, calculating his time in performing various duties and tasks, and studying his bodily motions while doing basic domestic chores (Kakar, 1970). This obsessive and compulsive type of behaviour was explained, by some, as an early example of Taylor's desire to cut down and minimise waste and inefficiency. Even at this early stage in his life he seemed to be searching for the one best way to carry out tasks that would eliminate excessive bodily movements and reduce mental and physical effort.

While employed at the Midvale steel works he became preoccupied with what he called 'natural' and 'systematic' soldiering. The practice of soldiering was the result of what Taylor assumed to be the natural tendency and desire of workers to take it easy, to control the speed and effort with which they performed their jobs, and to work no harder than was absolutely necessary. 'Systematic' soldiering was for Taylor far more inefficient and pernicious because this type of soldiering was controlled, regulated and supported by informal social groups of employees. A body of 'rules' and norms, supported by the close social networks and relationships on the shopfloor, acted to regulate the speed and output with which employees were 'allowed' to perform their jobs. As a worker, Taylor claimed he never once broke the agreed norms on work restrictions, but once he became responsible for output and productivity in his capacity as 'gang boss', he was determined to reorganise and maximise production. In his own words, Taylor claims:

> As soon as I became gang boss the men who were working under me and who, of course, knew that I was onto the whole game of soldiering or deliberately restricting output, came to me at once and said, 'Now Fred, you are not going to be a damn piecework hog, are you?' I said, 'If you fellows mean you are afraid I am going to try to get a larger output from these lathes,' I said, 'Yes; I do propose to get a larger output from these lathes'. (Taylor, 1912; quoted in Clawson, 1980: 212)

For Taylor, the strength of the workers lay in the fact that it was they who had far more knowledge and understanding of jobs. How tasks were performed, the tools that were used, and the precise way and speed with which jobs were done, lay primarily in the experience and the 'mysteries' of the 'craft' embodied in the work of the employees. We need to remember that the legacy of craft control was 'imported' into the early factories at the beginning of modern industry and the emergence of 'mass manufactures'. Under the craft system of production it was the workers themselves who organised the way work was to be done. Often this would extend to the management and control of recruitment and selection, training, development, and discipline – functions that were later colonised by management and appropriated within the terms of reference of the emerging specialist practice of personnel management. In many ways, what we have here is an example of semi-autonomous self-organisation. Jobs were designed and organised on the shopfloor by the employees themselves. Workers would deliberately keep management ignorant of the speeds that could potentially be achieved in the machine rooms and, as Taylor insisted, this was perfectly rational because of course as soon as management discovered the maximum potential speed of work tasks they would insist upon speed-ups and greater 'efficiency'. Systematic and natural soldiering are better thought of as rational attempts by workers to control the labour process, to control the speed and effort that they had to put into their jobs.

The management prerogative and the deconstruction of work tasks

Taylor emphasised the importance of acquiring and monopolising the knowledge of work tasks so as to grant management better control and improve its capacity to discipline employees. Management were told they had to impose themselves on the shopfloor, to get down into the actual material work process in order to observe, measure and calculate how tasks were done and how jobs could actually and potentially be improved through better design and coordination. Taylor embarked on a series of 'scientific studies' of shopfloor practice with the intention of redesigning jobs in ways that recovered all knowledge and expertise – and hence control – in the hands of management. Jobs were broken down and fragmented into their most basic components. This resulted in the extreme division of labour. It was held, following Adam Smith and Charles Babbage, that by breaking down tasks into their most elemental structures, workers would become more efficient and productive in performing one routinised and repetitive task. If discretion and decisions could be entirely eliminated from workers – so that all they had to concentrate on was the maximisation of output through the repetitive exertion of physical effort – then productivity and efficiency in the factory would increase.

The writings of Adam Smith had previously argued that as a consequence of greater familiarity with work tasks workers would become progressively quicker and more efficient in the execution of those work tasks. If jobs could be made far more rudimentary, and broken down further through a detailed division of labour, then workers could more easily master the movements and motions necessary to perform work. As a result of carrying out one simple repetitive task over and over again, manual dexterity would increase and workers became far quicker in a far shorter period of time. According to Charles Babbage this had the additional advantage that it would reduce costs so that previously skilled labour could be replaced by unskilled labour. As jobs became fragmented there would be no need to employ and pay skilled workers as these newly designed jobs could be performed by unskilled labour.

This extreme fragmentation and division of tasks created a series of mundane and repetitive jobs. Instead of employing one person to do a 'whole job', a number of employees would now be required to work on highly specialised, routinised and simplified jobs.

Furthermore, the design and knowledge of tasks were secured by management so that they could far better control the labour process. As Clawson (1980) observes, as long as workers knew more than managers about how to do the work, 'management would have to find a way to get workers' voluntary cooperation' (p. 214). It was this 'voluntary' cooperation that provided the point of insecurity and uncertainty in organisation and the management of employment relations, a zone of indeterminacy that modern management science claims to be able to eliminate.

This led Taylor to entirely revise the design of machine and hand tools. In his book *On the Art of Cutting Metals* he devised an entirely new set of standardised tool sizes and shapes to which, he insisted, all tools should comply. Taylor bestowed upon these tools obscure titles, symbols, and names, so that only he and his management colleagues would understand what tools were going to be used and allocated to specific jobs. As a consequence, far more detailed instruction cards and job details needed to be written and transferred from management to the shopfloor. In designing new symbols and titles it would be far quicker for management to write down and record which tools were to be used on which jobs. Equally it meant that workers were unable to challenge the instructions on the job card until the very last moment, by which time it would be too late to resist or organise protest about the way that management wanted the job to be done. For example, what had previously been known as a horizontal miller No. 7 would have been retitled as a 7MH. Far more obscure symbols were used in an attempt by Taylor to appropriate and control the knowledge of how tasks were to be performed. This effectively meant replacing the knowledge that workers had previously held in the labour process with managerial knowledge. Hence management was trying to learn what the workers themselves already knew: how precisely work was done.

A major consequence of the system that Taylor was trying to introduce, a system he later proselytised through lecture programmes, was a concomitant increase in the number of managerial and administrative staff. Taylor insisted that the conception of work, and the way work was to be organised and performed, should be placed in the hands of a planning department. It was the responsibility of the planning department to devise the 'one best way' of carrying out jobs. This divorce between the conception and the execution of tasks left the 'science of work' in the hands and minds of management, leaving only the physical execution of work as the responsibility of manual labourers. This led Taylor to claim that workers were not supposed to challenge managerial instructions on how tasks were to be performed, nor indeed the speeds upon which management insisted. In Taylor's scientific management workers were not 'paid to think' but simply to perform their tasks as prescribed in their instruction cards, written, devised and planned by management. It was management's 'right' to correct or modify the way work was to be done, through the careful calculation and analysis of job record cards, instruction cards etc., and through shopfloor time and motion studies.

The role of reward under the Taylor system: the 'rate busters'

In order to prove that jobs could be done far quicker, Taylor would often make use of what were known as 'rate busters' in his study of time and motion at work. The story goes that by offering a worker called Schmidt a higher rate to shift what would have been considered an impossible amount of pig iron, Taylor was able to show that effort and productivity could be improved through the combination of financial inducement and the detailed organisation of work by management. Essentially, Schmidt was offered more money to shift a greater amount of pig iron in a given period of time. In addition,

Taylor designed a new shovel with a scoop that was able to lift twice as much pig iron. Of course what was happening was that Taylor was extracting more effort and output than he was paying for – this is what made the system more 'efficient' – but, more importantly, by using Schmidt as an example, he was able to demonstrate that there was nothing natural, inevitable or sacrosanct in the work speeds that had been established by employee norms on the shopfloor. In this example, financial incentives were shown to complement and secure the control and monopoly of information and knowledge that management sought to gather and use in its control of the labour process. In Taylor's own words to Schmidt we read the commitment and importance that Taylor attached to the unilateral managerial design of jobs and the divorce in the conception and execution of work:

> Well, if you are a high-priced man, you will do exactly as this man tells you tomorrow, from morning till night. When he tells you to pick up a pig and walk, you pick it up and you walk, and when he tells you to sit down and rest, you sit down . . . And what's more, no back talk.
>
> (Taylor, quoted in Braverman, 1974: 105)

There are some who suggest that Schmidt later died tragically of a heart attack. One finds the history and contemporary practice of job design littered with similar tragedies and deaths. Taylor took the view that employees did not have the ability or intellect to be able to self-design and organise jobs effectively and efficiently. Therefore it needed to be left to a specialist elite of 'industrial engineers' in managerial planning departments. In the patronising and pretentious tone of Taylor's discussions with Schmidt, we catch a glimpse of this inherent elitism. This elitism seems to be further confirmed when we reflect upon his attempts to excuse his tone, claiming that this is the only kind of language that shopfloor employees are able to understand:

> This seems to be rather rough talk. And indeed it would be if applied to an educated mechanic, or even an intelligent laborer. With a man of the mentally sluggish type of Schmidt it is appropriate and not unkind, since it is effective in fixing his attention on the high wages.
>
> (Taylor, quoted in Braverman, 1974: 105–106)

For a man who was engaged in building his own house it is questionable whether this view of Schmidt, or indeed any manual employee, is justified.

In Taylor's ideal, therefore, workers should be left to perform those simple and routinised jobs for which they were inherently far better suited, leaving all 'possible brain work' in the hands of management. Taylor argued that efficiency and productivity could be guaranteed only if management took control over the design of and responsibility for the performance of jobs. This necessitated collecting all relevant information and knowledge over how jobs were traditionally done, and classifying, tabulating and restructuring work to prescribed rules, laws and formulae. Second, all possible brain work should be removed from the workers and the shopfloor and placed under the responsibility of the planning department. Finally, this knowledge and conception of work should be monopolised by management so that each stage of the production process is designed and controlled exclusively by management, who then simply give detailed instructions to workers. All pre-planning and pre-calculation is done by management at least one day in advance of its execution, so that all conception is removed from the imagination of the employee. In this way, according to Braverman (1974):

> Dehumanisation of the labour process, in which workers are reduced almost to the level of labour in its animal form, while purposeless and unthinkable in the case of the self-organised and self-motivated social labour of a community of producers, becomes critical for the management of purchased labour.
>
> (p. 113)

We have seen that scientific management seeks to redesign jobs in ways that reduce the exercise of initiative and discretion among shopfloor employees. It is perhaps a first attempt to design jobs that eliminate the human, and inaugurates a history that we find is strewn with corpses and bodily deformity – something Adam Smith (1982) was well aware of in *The Wealth of Nations*. We have also seen that financial reward provides the linchpin of the system. The work of Braverman allows us to extend and deepen our understanding of these developments in job design, exposing many of the tensions and antagonisms unleashed and exacerbated by this system, tensions that require considerable management attention and vigilance.

Braverman and the labour process

For Braverman (1974), the scientific management principles of Frederick Taylor and his attempts to simplify and fragment jobs expressed the essence of capitalist management and rationality. Braverman argues that Taylorism remains the dominant form of management and job design to which all industries and indeed all forms of organisation – whether in extraction, production, service or distribution – would eventually conform. In locating job design and the work of Taylor within the conceptual frame of the labour process, Braverman illuminates the inherently political nature of 'scientific' management, showing that its science is not neutral but developed and specifically applied for the purposes of greater capitalist efficiency, profitability, and the subordination of labour. The labour process understands the employment relation in terms of its mediation of contradictory and antagonistic pressures, forces that pit capital against labour. Labour sells a capacity to work, but not a fixed quantity. In competition with other units of capital, the inherently malleable nature of this 'capacity' provides management with a means of pursuing competitive advantage. Job design, then, becomes a tool in this managerial pursuit. Deskilling work is a way of cheapening labour, of reducing labour costs while maintaining or increasing output. This means that labour and capital are at some loggerheads with 'interests' that are likely to diverge.

In a manner reminiscent of Weber's ideal type concept and his conception of the inevitability of bureaucratisation, Braverman posited a similar 'trend' towards deskilling and degradation in the design and control of jobs. The central concern for management was the necessity to maintain control and discipline in the labour process, and Taylor theoretically and practically showed how he thought this could be achieved. In this assumption Braverman has been criticised and amended, both for his mechanical-like determinism, and for what has been called his 'over-structuralist' reading of Marx, from where he draws his inspiration and main theoretical assumptions (Storey, 1983; Thompson, 1989; Knights and Willmott, 1990). In brief, an 'over-structuralist' approach tends to ascribe too much machine-like determinism to the system of capitalist production, where it seems that individual and collective subjects have no scope to change or shape the logic of industrial development.

It will not be necessary in this chapter to rehearse the entire theoretical and empirical amendments, corrections and modifications that have been made to Braverman, primarily through the auspices of the annual international labour process conference and its attendant series of papers, articles and books. However, the influence and take-up of Taylor's ideas have been important in the development of assumptions that understand management as a science, and its impact on job design has been profound.

According to the work of Craig Littler (1982) and Littler and Salaman (1984), however, Taylorism was never as popular as Braverman has suggested. In its purest form it is difficult to find examples of the practice and successful application of concerted Taylorist deskilling and 'dehumanisation' of work tasks. In contrast to the USA, for example, Taylorism was far less popular in the UK and Japan. The existence of a stronger and more entrenched craft tradition in the UK and the paternalistic approach of many large-scale capital owners in the early twentieth century go some way to explaining the slow spread and unpopularity of Taylorism. In Japan the cultural traditions of teamwork and group fraternalism have acted both to resist Taylorist-style job design and to promote more participative and multi-skilled job design.

> Japanese factories depended on a tradition of work teams incorporating managerial functions and maintenance functions, with few staff specialists. There was a lack of job boundaries and continued job flexibility, unlike the prescriptions of Taylorism.   (Littler and Salaman, 1984)

This debate has been stimulated in part by the work of Andrew Friedman (1977, 1990), who has constructed an alternative approach to Braverman. Friedman questions the importance and centrality of deskilling and direct control. As Friedman argues, management itself is not primarily concerned with control, but with the profitability of business. If profit can be maintained or even enhanced through the continuation of skilled discretionary work then there will be little necessity or compulsion for management to seek to enhance control through deskilling and routinisation. Friedman goes on to develop a model that posits a continuum of job design and control structures. At one end of the pole we have direct control, deskilling, and low-trust employee relations; at the other we have high-skilled jobs based on flexibility and high-trust relations. Management is therefore assumed to have a choice, rather than the assumption made by Braverman, which sees management as inert pawns of an inevitable and predictable model of deskilling. The only historical role for management in the Braverman schema is to interpret correctly their role, which would anyway be difficult to interpret incorrectly because their job would ultimately depend on their ability to deskill and manage routinisation.

Friedman's work is important because it demonstrates both the *strategic choice* that management has and the constraints that partially 'guide' managerial practice. Direct control of the Taylorist type would be difficult to introduce in a situation where workers were currently highly skilled and discretionary. In these situations it would be better for management to seek a strategy of 'responsible autonomy', as the 'more complex and sophisticated the worker's knowledge and experience, the more difficult normally for management to prescribe tasks in detail and to monitor closely their performance' (Hyman, 1987: 39).

Management in these situations would be better advised to seek to manage and maintain a working relationship based on *trust,* where workers are not subject to intense direct control through detailed instructions, simplification and routinisation. Resistance is clearly going to be a problem if management looks to deskill workers who have previously been used to and socialised into high-discretion employment. Direct control is possible on work groups that are less central to the production process: those workers whom Friedman and others have called 'peripheral workers'. This form of labour can be more ruthlessly managed because they can be more easily replaced, and the insecurity associated with this form of employment does not bode well for collective organisation and resistance. Where this is the case management is likely to face less resistance in its attempts to impose deskilled low-trust work relationships. In the peripheral labour force, management may be able to pursue output maximisation and high volume intensity through repetitive and deskilled work tasks associated with the assembly line of car production (see also Fox, 1974).

Stop and think	1 How might the job of a BBC news presenter be 'Taylorised'?
	2 To what extent is this a realistic form of job design?
	3 How would Braverman have argued that the Taylorisation of the news media was inevitable?
	4 Do you think this is 'inevitable'? If not, why not?

Summary

There is a considerable amount of evidence that suggests that Taylorism was not adopted in its pure form. Where it was adopted, it was renegotiated, contested and modified by craft and work group resistance. Moreover, we have seen that there has been some awareness of the deleterious effects on individuals and their jobs, which has continued to promote academic and managerial interest in alternative forms of job design. Some of these developments have gone beyond simply seeking alternatives to deskilling to advance broader critiques of the assumed rationality of Taylorism as a system of management control and utilisation of labour. For example, if all work is inevitably deskilled then everyone becomes a routinised and dehumanised worker, simply acting as an adjunct to a vast technological automaton. In this situation workers are homogenised, and so there arises the risk that a collective consciousness and a collective sense of power will emerge as workers realise their common interest in the resistance of forces that seek to reduce them to non-thinking degraded functionaries. In what sense could Taylorism be considered 'rational' if its consequences lead, paradoxically, to its own demise? In disregarding these outcomes of Taylorism, Braverman is perhaps a little guilty himself of accepting and inadvertently confirming the 'scientific' status of Taylor's management principles. Braverman assumes an immense amount of knowledge, foresight and cunning in those he assumes are able to design and implement such production systems. Yet he does not recognise the possibility, and indeed arguably the logical conclusion, of resistance and conflict to this attempted appropriation and monopolisation of knowledge and discretion. Nevertheless, a strength of Braverman's work is that his labour process perspective opens up the question of job design to issues of power and control – that is, the inherently *politicised* nature of the subject.

In what follows we trace the emergence of the 'human relations' study of work, which builds upon a critique of what is called *alienation* at work. One of the central criticisms made in response to Taylorism is that it is inhumane. Through the process of deskilling, Taylorism generates work that is not stimulating or challenging. Some argue that this is more a feature of a capitalist system than something that more rational 'management science' can address, and that deskilling remains the major tendency in mature capitalist economies (Thompson, 1989; Warhurst and Thompson, 1998). However, if we understand the negative consequences of Taylorism by means of the concept of *anomie* instead of alienation, there may be room within the constraints of competition and capitalist accumulation for management to develop methods of working that suspend and divert resistance and the paradox of systemic collapse.

ALIENATION AND WORK

Blauner's thesis

The concept of alienation is often drawn upon in any discussion of Taylor. To suffer from alienation is to experience an *estrangement* from what is assumed to be one's own natural physical, mental and/or intellectual essence. It is argued that human beings have an inherent need to express and control their surroundings so that they may experience fulfilment and development. Where this 'need' is suppressed or prevented from being expressed, it is suggested, individuals will suffer from alienation. More fundamentally, alienation is also associated with the idea that while individuals and their society produce economic goods collectively, the proceeds of production are appropriated privately. It is worth remembering that it is a relatively peculiar social situation that leaves individuals with nothing to sell but their own labour, the result of the usurpation of common land and the expropriation of land from the people undertaken in the UK from the late fifteenth century. Now, while the first definition of alienation provides some hope that more effective management can ameliorate some of the worst excesses of modern job design, in the latter, more enduring social-historical forces and power inequalities render alienation inevitable and systemic. Here, management in itself can do little to remove alienating work from the employment relation through better job design.

Robert Blauner (1964) is more concerned with the impact of Taylorist-style technology and work organisation on the attitudes and orientation of employees than with a historical analysis of power, property relations, and alienation. Blauner sought to analyse the worker's 'relationship' to the technological organisation of work in order to determine

> whether or not he [sic] characteristically experiences in that work, a sense of control rather than domination, a sense of meaningful purpose rather than futility, a sense of social connection rather than isolation, and a sense of spontaneous involvement and self expression rather than detachment and discontent. (Blauner, 1964: vii).

To suffer from a sense of powerlessness, according to Blauner, is where an individual experiences a lack of control over the pace and method of work. For example, assembly line work in which the machine sets the pace of work allows for little control and involvement of the employee. There is very little autonomy granted to the individual employee in this work situation, as generally the quality of work, the techniques of work and the time allowed to perform it are dictated by the machine. Hence there is a sense of powerlessness because there is no subjective input by the employee. Instead the employee becomes simply an object, controlled and manipulated by what seems to be an impersonal and alien system. In performing highly specialised and simplified tasks employees may also experience a sense of meaninglessness because they have no conception of the end product. In situations where there is an extreme division of labour, with employees performing repetitive work cycles, the scope and size of the individual's contribution to the end product is small. It may not be a car that the individual is producing, even though they may be considered a car worker. For the individual concerned it may simply be screwing and tightening three bolts to a gearbox in an engine. Such fractionalised jobs may result in the situation where individuals achieve no sense of purpose or satisfaction from their tasks:

> Tendencies towards meaninglessness therefore stem from the nature of modern manufacturing, which is based on standardised production and a division of labour that reduces the size of the worker's contribution to the final product.
>
> (Blauner, 1964: 22)

Blauner also suggested that self-estrangement arises because the worker becomes 'removed from themselves'. By this Blauner means that the extreme division of labour, in which tasks are broken down into their most simplified components, provides work that is somehow unnatural for human beings. Whereas independent craftworkers would actually manufacture and produce an entire product, a table or a chair for example, in modern industry a worker may continually and repeatedly put headlights on the front of a car, or cheese slices on a burger. This provides work that is repetitive and incessant in its regularity. It is work that allows for no variety in pace, method, location, or discretion. Hence, quoting Marx, Blauner (1964) writes that the employee: 'In his work . . . does not affirm himself, does not feel content but unhappy, does not develop freely his physical and mental energy but mortifies his body and ruins his mind' (p. 27).

Although this concept of alienation has its roots in a Marxist critique of capitalism, it can be seen to enter the work of the human relations school of job design. It does this through the slightly different but related concept of *anomie,* as first developed and applied by Emile Durkheim (1984) at the end of the nineteenth century. Anomie is that state of moral confusion and purposelessness consequent upon the extreme fragmentation of roles and tasks in contemporary society. An exclusive emphasis on individualism, encouraged by the routinisation and fragmentation of tasks in Taylor's system, would, in the absence of the strong guiding principles, norms and values associated with *social regulation,* inevitably lead to the breakdown of the social fabric. This arises because as more and more individuals begin performing highly individuated tasks, in isolation and distance from other individuals, problems of social solidarity emerge. Individuals no longer feel a part of societal community. For the individual, cut off from interaction and social relationships, the maintenance of community values will be at risk as work tasks become increasingly meaningless. The Kalashnikov in the restaurant becomes a possibility!

Blauner draws on both anomie and alienation in his critique of monotony and the assembly line production system. Despite some weaknesses in his approach – his technological determinism and over-optimistic projection of the possibilities of future technology – his work provides an interesting and stimulating account of the problems and 'injustices' associated with Taylorism and the one best way of production of scientific management. Via the concept of anomie, management is directed towards the recovery and reconstruction of strong binding, collective meaning and norms. We begin to see here the foundations of cultural management and the importance of 'strong' cultures (Deal and Kennedy, 1982).

Elton Mayo's thesis

The human relations school of management, of which Elton Mayo is probably the best-known exponent and theorist, sought to attend to these anomic consequences of large-scale production and organisation. Mayo drew attention to the social needs of individuals. It is argued in this tradition that individual employees need a sense of social worth and satisfaction, which can only be developed if work is provided that allows for social interaction and communication. Furthermore, for Mayo, managers need to express a concern and interest in employees' personal problems, and to emphasise the importance of each individual for the organisation. Management needs to integrate the various elements of the organisation through the re-creation of those values and norms lost as a consequence of modern industry and Taylorism. A sense of community and 'belongingness' needs to be created and fostered by managerial intervention designed to increase communication and participation (see Chapter 13), together with a greater understanding of those variables that motivate and demotivate individuals, instead of a reliance upon the cash nexus and the economic incentives detailed by Taylor. Hence Mayo emphasised the need for Durkheimian-style 'moral communities'. As Watson (1987) writes, Mayo teaches that it is only with 'the integration of the individual into the [management-led] plant community' that 'systemic integration be maintained and the potential pathologies of the industrial society avoided' (p. 40).

Within the field of the human relations approach to job design there have been repeated attempts to recreate 'social man' (Schein, 1965). If read through the frame of reference provided by Durkheim and his concept of anomie, human relations thinking ignores the underlying economic and historical forces of alienation to concentrate on those variables at work that management can influence through things such as job design. The idea that employees were 'social' beings as much as they were economic actors was uncovered through a series of studies of human relations in work organisations. One of the most important of these was the Hawthorne studies.

Hawthorne studies: the informal work group

The Hawthorne studies in the mid-1920s appeared to show that informal work groups and associations were significant variables in explaining productivity and output performance. The Hawthorne studies were conducted in the Hawthorne plant of the United States Western Electrical Company, where 29 000 employees produced telephone equipment for the Bell system. Changing environmental variables such as the amount of lighting did not seem to have any consistent effects on the productivity of the work groups. Indeed, productivity would increase despite the contradictory changes in the degree of lighting and the number of rest pauses. This led the study to conclude that the work group was responding to the very act of being studied and analysed. Hence the result that paying attention and showing interest in work groups would itself lead to productivity increases: the Hawthorne effect.

In the later studies of the 'bank wiring room' the consultants and academics discovered, like Taylor, that work groups would systematically control and restrict output in order to maintain what they considered to be a fair day's work for a fair day's pay. Workers appeared to be responding to what in management's eyes were irrational sentiments such as 'fairness' and the 'right to work'. The recognition that informal groups, norms and attitudes could inhibit the efficient production and output of the enterprise led the leading authors of the study, Roethlisberger and Dickson (1939), to conclude that the best approach for management should not be to try and undermine and force the informal organisation to conform to the formal organisation. Rather, it was patently obvious that informal organisations would likely re-emerge and appear as a natural consequence of employees' needs for social solidarity, community and group association. The informal work groups in effect were substituting for the lack of social interaction and communication experienced in highly fragmented, individuated and specialised work tasks. Management were advised to attempt to engineer and channel sentiments and attitudes that prevailed in the informal work organisation. Through controlled participation, effective means and channels of communication, and socially skilled enlightened supervision, management could harness the strength and solidarity of the informal work groups to the productive needs of the 'formal organisation'.

Stop and think

1 How might an individual be alienated in their workplace yet not suffer from the condition of anomie?

2 How far did the Hawthorne studies demonstrate that management could only 'condition' the work *experience* of employees rather than materially re-design the employees' jobs?

The work of the Tavistock Institute

These studies led to a number of further programmes and initiatives designed to release and tap into the assumption that individuals had an inherent need for creativity and social interaction. In Britain the Tavistock Institute for Human Relations contributed a number of important studies into the productivity of work organisations. They found that in the coal-mining industry, for example, productivity fell after the introduction of mechanised technology. The formal and elaborate division of labour that this entailed reduced the amount of social interaction, teamwork, discretion and 'responsible autonomy' to which miners had become accustomed (Trist and Bamforth, 1951). Tavistock researchers were firmly committed to an approach that emphasised the importance of providing individuals with the satisfaction of completing a whole task, of being able to control their own activities, and of organising work tasks so that individuals can develop satisfactory social relationships (Trist *et al.*, 1963). In their conclusion to the study of the coal-mining industry in the late 1940s and early 1950s, Eric Trist and his colleagues emphasised that the technical reorganisation of work needs to pay careful attention to the social aspects of work and the features of social organisation that exist within work groups. The tendency for managers and industrial engineers to introduce the most technically efficient system of production would result only in a low productive response from employees.

These studies have been influential in the development of ideas in job design such as job enlargement, job enrichment, teamworking, and semi-autonomous work groups. Job enlargement basically means that more tasks are added to the one that an individual employee is currently doing to add a variety in task, pace and location. Job enrichment, by contrast, attempts to add responsibility and discretion to an individual's job so that not only do they experience a variety of tasks but they are also provided with an opportunity for development and realisation of 'self-actualising needs' (Maslow, 1954). Teamworking and semi-autonomous work groups (SAWGs) attempt to restore the opportunity for social interaction and communication. These schemes usually include measures that allow teams to establish their own patterns and routines of working, electing their own leaders, organising their own rest periods, and scheduling their own workloads. The recent collapse of the SAWGs at the Volvo plant in Kalmar highlights a significant problem with these schemes, notably productivity. Indeed, criticism has been made of the tokenistic nature of many of these schemes, and in one famous quote an employee claims that this simply means that:

'You move from one boring, dirty, monotonous job to another boring, dirty, monotonous job, and somehow you're supposed to come out of it all "enriched". But I never feel "enriched" – I just feel knackered.'
(quoted in Nichols, 1980: 279)

Yet we need to ask how robust some of these assumptions are in the work of the human relations school of job redesign. We move on in the following section to examine issues concerned with the 'socialisation' of employees – in other words to examine the conditions that might lead employees to accept and even welcome dirty, boring monotonous jobs. We find that, in many cases, employees adopt an 'instrumental' orientation to work, which means that they do not look to work for anything other than a wage, which then allows them to pursue gratification, meaning and fulfilment in areas outside the employment relation. We are beginning to enquire into what is called the *subjectivity* of employees – that is, the 'internal' existential and psychological processes common to the human subject – in our pursuit of an understanding of job design.

SOCIALISATION AND ORIENTATIONS TO WORK

A common assumption made by theorists and consultants working in the field of job redesign, and especially the quality of working life movement, is the inherent or essential needs that individuals possess for creative employment. Buchanan (1989), for example, in his work on job design has stressed the debilitating effects of Taylorist-style work regimes and the stultifying impact on the physical, emotional and psychological well-being of individuals:

> people have higher levels of ability and higher expectations of working life . . . they have a physio-logical need for sensory stimulation, for changes in the patterns of information that feed to the senses to sustain arousal.
>
> (p. 80)

Similarly Michael Cross (1990) in his uncritical and prescriptive 'advice' to management suggests that, because of an inherent need for creativity and self-fulfilment, jobs need to be designed that test the initiative and ability of individuals so that they 'seek to provide meaningful jobs which build upon and stretch people's abilities so that they can realise their potential' (p. 29).

This essentialism has been the subject of a sustained critique by radical social psychologists (Knights and Willmott, 1989; Knights, 1990; Willmott, 1990), and indeed we can look back to studies of plant sociology for examples where frustration and dissatisfaction have not arisen from the experience interpreted by some as the hallmark of conditions fostering the alienation of human nature.

Car workers

In their influential study of the Vauxhall car workers in Luton, Goldthorpe *et al.* (1968) discovered that, despite the machine-like Taylorist monotony of the work process, employees were neither militant nor sought to resist or renegotiate the content of jobs. The jobs themselves were the very ones that many in the school of human relations were arguing would lead to dissatisfaction and unrest because they denied the essential creativity and the self-actualising needs of human beings. Goldthorpe *et al.* found that certain groups of workers were not getting any intrinsic satisfaction from their work but equally were not prepared or inclined to do anything about it. This paradox was partly explained by what was identified as the employees' instrumental attitudes to work. This new class of affluent manual worker was prepared to labour on monotonous and intrinsically unrewarding work because they viewed employment as simply a means to pay for private housing, cars and other new consumer items proliferating during the 1960s. As the authors conclude, 'It is by no means those groups whose work-tasks and roles appeared least rewarding whose members had thought most often or most seriously about leaving' (p. 25). Furthermore, consumption and not production appeared as an equally important variable in employees' orientation to work:

> Workers within all groups in our sample tend to be particularly motivated to increase their power as consumers and their domestic standard of living, rather than their satisfaction as producers and the degree of their self-fulfilment in work.
>
> (Goldthorpe *et al.*, 1968: 38)

Studies such as these might suggest that deskilled jobs are not inherently frustrating or meaningless for employees. It prompts one to ask the question whether or not work necessarily has to be a source of fulfilment and meaning. Perhaps this is simply a modern bourgeois assumption. More than this, the Luton car workers study might suggest that organisation retains stability despite alienating conditions of work. In the work of Burawoy we are also offered ways of thinking how organisation is maintained and reproduced even where jobs are designed in traditional deskilled ways. The focus of Burawoy's work is, however, on the interaction of collective work groups with the existential forces that preoccupy individual subjects.

The work of Burawoy

Theoretical and empirical studies have shown that a deskilling-resistance/frustration model is far too simple, and does not adequately explain adaptation and habituation to routine and monotony. Michael Burawoy (1979, 1985), drawing on the pioneering work of Donald Roy and Tom Lupton, has developed empirical work that demonstrates that workers adapt to what may be perceived as intolerable low-discretion roles through ritualised engagement in *game playing*. The resistance that many theorists had predicted would emerge from a Taylorist-style work regime needs to be countered, according to Burawoy, by an equal tendency by management–worker relations to generate or 'manufacture consent'.

In the study of the Allied Corporation, Burawoy (1979) describes how workers would both ease the routinised nature of Taylorist-style job design and actively create time and space for themselves within the working day. Through a game of *'making out'*, workers would gain a relative amount of satisfaction from low-discretion deskilled work by manipulating output levels through the banking or 'gold-bricking' of finished goods. In this way, quotas could be more easily achieved by workers while generating a sense of control in when and how fast they worked. In essence there were two types of job on the shopfloor: jobs where it was difficult to achieve quota levels, and 'gravy jobs' where it was relatively easy to reach quota. In order to 'make out', workers needed to manipulate work schedules, cajoling and bargaining with other workers whose cooperation was essential for success in the game of making out. Close working and social relations needed to be fostered with the scheduling man, the crib attendant, the truck driver bringing stock to the workstation, and also the set-up man.

Informally the work groups studied by Burawoy also maintained a restriction on output of 140%. It was believed that if you were able to produce in excess of this, then management would reduce the rate for the job, as it would become apparent to management that the job was a 'gravy job'. Workers would therefore hoard work in excess of 140% in a 'kitty' and keep the work for times when they were employed on difficult jobs, therefore creating margins of time and space for themselves in the future. Also, workers would 'chisel', which meant that time would be redistributed so that workers could maximise the time they spent on the 'gravy jobs', where they could turn out work in excess of 100%.

As Burawoy comments, on first entering the shop individual employees may have perceived the game as being banal and 'mindless', but after a while this aloofness tended to recede as all employees became caught up and preoccupied with the game of 'making out'. Individuals would be evaluated by their peers and work group colleagues on their ability to make out, so that, as Burawoy writes, 'Each worker sooner or later is sucked into this distinctive set of activities' (Burawoy, 1979: 64).

This study of informal work groups and the restrictions and games in which they engage has long fascinated sociologists. At first sight it appears paradoxical. The game of 'making out' relieves the boredom of work, neutralises any discontent felt towards the job or towards management who were putatively 'responsible' for its design, and hence perpetuates the conditions for its ultimate survival. Employees appear to generate consent to the work process through this game of making out, ensuring profitability and the competitiveness of the organisation. For the employee:

> The rewards of making out are defined in terms of factors *immediately* related to the labour process – reduction of fatigue, passing time, relieving boredom, and so on – and factors that emerge from the labour process – the social and psychological rewards of making out on a tough job.
>
> (Burawoy, 1979: 64)

For the employer, production and output targets are maintained, and even, according to Burawoy, guaranteed, while deflecting concern over job content and work design. Conflict gets dispersed laterally to colleagues on whom individual employees are dependent in order to make out. Obstructive behaviour by other workers is likely to frustrate the ability to make out, and so potentially conflictual relations emerge among employees. The role of the foreman is seen as crucial in this respect, as it is he who 'referees' the game. Foremen can facilitate the game of making out by relaxing formal rules on health and safety – for example, running on the shopfloor may be overlooked – or they can obstruct the game by ensuring a strict adherence to formal rules and procedures. Hence conflict is dispersed down the organisation and laterally across the organisation, so that when 'the labour process is organised into some form of game involving the active participation of both management and worker, the interests of both are concretely coordinated' (Burawoy, 1979: 85).

Subjectivity and identity

The work of Burawoy has been outlined in some detail because it has reworked many classic assumptions in labour process and industrial sociology theory. From Braverman's work on deskilling it is easy to assume that workers would have no interest in the perpetuation of deskilled Taylorist-style jobs. The conditions are restrictive, the discipline is harsh, and the jobs are of little interest and variety. However, from the work of Goldthorpe *et al.* we can see that workers may adapt and habituate to deskilled work for a variety of seemingly rational reasons. Second, this body of work challenges the school of human relations in their assumption that jobs need to be provided that offer a variety of pace, skill and initiative in order to counter the danger of alienation. We might be prompted to ask: What is the essential self of human beings? According to some readings of Marx it may be assumed that the self-actualising and developmental needs of individuals cannot be met in a production system continually forced to seek cheaper and more productive ways of carrying out labour. This implies that individuals will always feel estranged from themselves and hence likely to resist. However, the adaptive and acquiescent behaviour of employees that Burawoy and others have charted can be explained by reference to the dynamic existential nature of individuals (Fromm, 1991). Instead of employees confronting an intolerable situation, they tend to adapt themselves to external circumstances, creating something new in their 'nature'. Given time, what might have appeared an impossible and degrading situation becomes familiar and is soon made second nature. Employees' identity – that sense of 'who' they are, what it means to be 'me', for example – is open and dynamic. Yet this can be an anxious experience. We therefore find ourselves compelled to seek some secure identity, to define ourselves as 'this' or 'that'. Over time we can even become attached to very boring routines because they offer a semblance of security and familiarity. We know what we have to do and what is expected of us in these routines; in fact we know who we 'are'.

In terms of personal identity this might mean that individuals may feel 'threatened' by a change in routine or habit. As Willmott (1990) suggests, although Marx stated that employees come to the factory simply expecting a 'tanning', they may actually come to experience the tanning as quite tolerable or even desirable. It is quite possible that individuals come to accept and enjoy the habits and security afforded by deskilled work: hence 'the extent to which such opportunities are valued for the sense of security associated with a confirmation of the social identity of self' (Willmott, 1990: 363). In Camus's *The Outsider* the character of Salamano and his 'ugly brute' of a dog demonstrate this attachment to routinised work and relationships. Twice a day for eight years the two were seen dragging and fighting with each other during a monotonous regular walk. Salamano would beat and drag his dirty dog round the walk; 'Then they'd halt on the pavement, the pair of them, and glare at each other; the dog with terror and the man with hatred in his eyes' (Camus, 1961: 35). As soon as the dog runs away, though, Salamano is distraught and 'lost', declaring the dog to be a fine breed with a wonderful coat, and would not consider a replacement as, 'reasonably enough, he pointed out that he'd become used to this one, and it wouldn't be the same thing' (p. 51).

Work by Collinson and Knights (1986) shows how female employees in the life insurance industry come to internalise, resign themselves, and ultimately accept their jobs and the lack of promotion opportunities. What at first sight might appear intolerable, prompting overt expressions of resistance, is then made tolerable as the individual comes to 'adapt' to employment situations. Conflict and frustration gets channelled and redefined through the medium of identity, which might then find expression in anxiety, neurosis, or conservative inhibition. Organisation is made stable not so much by the design of jobs, as by existential processes that habituate employees to their work conditions. In Collinson and Knights (1986) a sense of security and the pursuit of a secure social identity prevents the female clerical support staff from challenging the restrictive and monotonous nature of their jobs. Sales and clerical workers internalise the assumptions that are used to justify gender segregation, and hence it can be seen that individuals accommodate to routine and restriction:

> In the context of highly subordinated, poorly paid positions which provide few opportunities to 'advance', indifference, as a defensive mode of managing to retain a measure of dignity in the face of its erosion, is all pervasive within contemporary work situations.
>
> (p. 161; see also Cohen and Taylor, 1992)

Confirmation of one's self and one's own identity provides a degree of certainty and security that can tend to provoke conservative tendencies in our behaviour and assumptions. Collinson and Knights (1986) observe these processes in the character 'Lyn', who, despite initial resistance to sex typing and segregation, ultimately acquiesced to others' (read men, managers) definition and view of her and her 'essential' female nature. In response to her lack of promotion she claims:

> 'Being female, you see, I'd have to be that bit older.' (quoted in Collinson and Knights, 1986: 163)

196

We have been reviewing here a number of studies that challenge the idea that organisation is made vulnerable by Taylorist forms of job design. At first we have noted that Braverman's labour process framework adumbrates the political nature of job design. We then questioned the extent to which deskilling was as systematically determinist as Braverman argued. The work of the human relations school of job design both sought to address the negative consequences of scientific management and stood as some testimony to the argument that deskilling was an inevitable outcome of management and modern industry. In the latter part of this section we have begun to introduce ideas that open up the human subject in ways that help us to understand how organisation is maintained and reproduced even where overt deskilling and the degradation of work are evident. The politics of job design extends then to the question of subjectivity and identity. This prompts us to ask a series of questions: What is it that makes us what we are? What are the routines through which I might get ensnared? What is this work that I do? Is it what I want? What are the possibilities for change and personal growth offered in the job that I am currently doing? Do I want to be employed making weapons of mass destruction? Might I need to reach for my Kalashnikov?

HUMAN RELATIONS REVISITED: CHANGE PROGRAMMES AND JOB DESIGN

In recent years there has been a marked revival in thinking that emphasises the possibility not only of reconciling individual and organisational goals but of creating the conditions for an existential and spiritual fulfilment that transcends the divisions between the employee and his or her work organisation. Job redesign programmes developed through human resource management, at least on the level of rhetoric (Legge, 1995), seek to empower and devolve responsibility to individuals. Yet there is considerable diversity and ambiguity in practice and rhetoric. For some companies, empowerment, paradoxically, is something that is given to employees, a product of top-down engineering; others, perhaps more radically, withdraw centralised bureaucratic rules and procedures far more extensively, leaving employees to 'pick up the pieces', redesigning their jobs in collaboration with colleagues.

Yet we find that many of the human relations and humanisation programmes adopted by contemporary management, employ simplistic assumptions with respect to change and development. Not only is it assumed that there is a *need* to provide 'stimulating' and rewarding jobs to counter frustration and resistance to 'dehumanised' Taylorist-style assembly line work, but that change is a rational process, one that can be introduced relatively easily through cause–effect-style thinking and planning. So, with sufficient managerial sensitivity and communication, it is assumed that consent and commitment to managerially designed change can be fostered and secured.

In order to come to terms more effectively with organisational change and management intervention in job design, we shall need to address the politics of organisation. Moreover we shall need to rethink habitual understandings of 'change'. Change is far better thought of as non-rational and non-linear; often unplanned and chaotic, change programmes discharge a whole series of untold and unintended consequences. At times this threatens the very fabric of organisation. The fabric of organisation is being stretched in all kinds of ways. Since the demise of 'Taylor', organisations are becoming 'unstitched'. In organisations today, bereft of institutional or bureaucratic anchor, it might be thought that de-sign is being replaced by a dehiscence of signs – contradictory, uncertain, floating, and ambiguous – manifest in the explosion of management discourse and the whole plethora of buzzwords, fads and fashions. This is disorganisation, not organisation. More often than not what we are faced with today is not de-sign but re-signations. Like Kevin Spacey in the film *American Beauty*, there are many employees today quitting their jobs in search of something more meaningful. At one stage in the study of job design it was popular to ask the rhetorical question: 'If you won the lottery would you still do the same job?' Perhaps today a better question might be: 'If you didn't have a mortgage to pay would you still be in the job you are doing now?'

The prescriptive advice on change and job redesign

Prescriptive advice on change programmes (Cross, 1990; James, 1992) increasingly emphasises the need to gain employee commitment to the goals of the organisation through the creation of *common values*, beliefs and assumptions. The development of a unitary organisational culture is seen by many today as the sine qua non of successful economic performance. According to Cross (1990), it is essential that the process of job redesign moves logically though a series of well-defined stages, 'moving through the various stages of gaining commitment to change' (p. 29). However, to introduce this change it is assumed that only management can recognise what employees need. Moreover, it is often assumed that the fear of change can be overcome by reassurance and involvement. Yet, as we have seen, routines, habit and innate conservatism may run a lot deeper than just the surface-conscious fear of change. More problematic still are the assumptions of the prescriptive approach. Equally problematic is the understanding that management somehow has a monopoly on what the organisation 'is', what its values and assumptions are, and where it 'needs to go'.

Cross (1990) suggests that a dynamic culture can be introduced through managerially led education and 'normative re-education' (p. 11). Despite the somewhat Orwellian nature of this statement, Cross makes the mistake to which many prescriptive management job design manuals seem to fall prey. This can be summarised as the uncritical acceptance of that kind of humanistic-psychological theory associated with the work of Abraham Maslow (1943), and the assumption that a 'culture of change' can be successfully manufactured, imposed, and administered by management. This takes a rather simplistic and naive approach to culture, one that neglects the theoretical discipline and complexity of the subjects from which it borrows – anthropology and sociology. Culture cannot simply be imposed. Rather, it develops over time in response to a number of variables, some of which cannot be controlled and 'scientifically measured'. To a large extent, culture is an emergent and unpredictable phenomenon partly 'constrained' by routinised social interaction that gets produced and reproduced over long periods of time (Giddens, 1991; Lynn-Meek, 1992).

This has a complicated theoretical and disciplinary heritage, to which we cannot do justice in this chapter. Yet this complexity is scarcely acknowledged in much of the post-Peters and Waterman management literature on organization and culture change programmes (Schein, 1985). Suffice it to say that culture is not something that can simply be turned on and off at the behest of management in some unitarist manner. Culture is as likely to emerge from a conflict of values and beliefs, 'particularly when we consider organisations where management tends to belong to one social class and workers to another. In such organisations, values, norms and social meanings are constructed by "class structures" and are a constant source for dispute' (Lynn-Meek, 1991: 197). Gender, age, ethnicity, religion and sexuality complicate the divisions and patterns in the cultural fabric of organisation and impart even greater degrees of vitality, conflict, and dispute to the processes of cultural emergence in organisation.

Human resource management and job redesign

The enthusiasm with which HRM has been embraced by many working within the theory and practice of job (re)design is still founded on the prediction and promise that individuals need to be provided with stimulating and 'enriched' jobs, which tap those intellectual and cognitive domains left dormant by the traditions of organisation and management. Not only will individual employees perform far more varied and skilled jobs, but through the resulting quantitative and qualitative performance improvements organisations will become far more competitive. Hence one of the most important components of organisational effectiveness and economic prosperity is the attention and detail paid to the design of work tasks. It is proposed that 'multi-skilled' highly discretionary jobs will influence the critical psychological state of an employee, promoting a sense of meaningfulness, responsibility and value. Once an employee begins to experience a more positive psychological relationship with their job, their manager, the employer and organisation, it is expected that improved performance will follow (Hackman and Lawler, 1971; Hackman and Oldham, 1976).

In contrast to the rather jaded and in many ways discredited quality of working life movement in the 1960s and 1970s, it is argued that job design is back on the agenda as a critical component of organisational performance. This has emerged as a result of qualitative changes in product markets, communications and information technology, and trading conditions (Reich, 1983; Hirschorn, 1984). For many this promises, once again, to end the degradation and dehumanisation associated with the repetitive assembly line of mass production industries. A new utopia of management–worker consensus based on single-status empowered craft-style working practices is predicted within flatter, less hierarchical and autocratic organisational structures (Peters and Waterman, 1982; Deming, 1986). As Buchanan (1992) has claimed, acceptable worker control and autonomy have increased as a result of new environmental pressures, giving 'employees considerably more control over work activities, personal skills and development and career opportunities, and also offer[ing] significant opportunities for improved organisational performance' (p. 138). In contrast to the 'detailed' control of work tasks in the typical Western car factory, the contemporary worker is not only granted increased discretion and 'high trust' (Fox, 1974), but is also actually a functional prerequisite of successful economic performance (Piore and Sabel, 1984; Kern and Schumann, 1987).

Increased discretion and high-trust employment relations are often used as a justification for job redesign, a prerequisite it is claimed of competitiveness and market sustainability. However, the assumption remains that redesign initiatives remain the preserve of interventionist HR management. An assumption of linearity, even in those writers purporting to make a critical and interrogative examination (Buchanan, 1989, 1994) of job design, reduces change to something that HR order and channel into predictable and stable outcomes.

'Management' is seen in a relatively unproblematic manner – a delimited and well-defined 'category' of employee charged with the responsibility for the design, allocation, distribution and organisation of work. Given this assumption it then follows that change is formulated within the confines of this category and then filters down to have its effect downstream in the employment relation of shopfloor workers. The assumption remains that the high trust generated or granted to employees will be reciprocated by individuals. Work groups will now exercise vigilance and self-reflection in the conduct of their work, seeking continuous improvement through 'high performance work systems' (Buchanan, 1994). Subjectivity and the 'agency' status of employees is reduced to a level where it is assumed that they can only *respond* to higher managerial initiatives. Management is the primary change agent: only management has the capacity to intervene, restructuring and redesigning work. If it does this correctly, new structures and order in the organisation of employment can be established, which can then be sustained and reproduced more efficiently by the autonomy vested in high-performance work teams.

What this overlooks is that individual employees are continually negotiating and redesigning their work in continuous interaction and struggle with management and other agents. Not only subordinates but management too is often 'in search of itself', as Watson (1994) writes, wondering what might happen next, how they might respond, what they are 'about', and how to 'carry on' in the performance and accomplishment of their job. In the subtle fabric of work organisation, the precise content and nature of work are being contested and redesigned – day in, day out. It is amorphous, fluid, and unpredictable. It is also partly irrational and uncontrollable. Work has to be interpreted and redefined every day – indeed every hour and minute. For example, what for years might have seemed a reasonable job, researching the subatomic processes of nuclear fission, suddenly becomes unethical in the eyes of the employee, complicit with the military–state–industrial complex and in part responsible for genocide and vast ecological devastation.

In the main, human resource management and job redesign overlook these issues. They tend to maintain faith in the progressive enlightenment of managerial thinking, and shy away from what Corbett (1994) and Burrell (1997) identify as the *underbelly* or *darker side* of organisation. History is examined from the standpoint of today, which confines managerial practice such as Taylorism essentially to an unenlightened past, which is overcome by the undisputed progress assumed in management development. Liberal-Whig-style interpretations such as this see history as a movement from ignorance to enlightenment, where managers learn from the mistakes of the past, enabling them to develop and introduce improved remedies and methods in the organisation and design of work. From the rather crude Taylorism of mass production, management thinking has progressed through the humanisation initiatives of Elton Mayo, the work of the Hawthorne studies and the Tavistock Institute, to contemporary 'radical' and enlightened job design. Contemporary job redesign, it is claimed, seeks a systemic or organisation-wide orientation through just-in-time, cellular organisation forms, and systematic and coherent business process re-engineering (Buchanan, 1994), correcting for the deficiencies of earlier approaches.

Conflict and tension in job-redesign initiatives are seen to stem simply from contingency and irrationality, features of organisation that can be eliminated and restructured by enlightened management. The usual recipe for eliminating such contingency is careful strategic planning, projection and negotiation among all relevant parties. This builds coherence initially through a process of political lobbying by attempting to mobilise sufficient political interest among organisational cliques (Storey, 1992: 118–161). Corbett (1997) offers an interesting essay on the job design implications of advanced manufacturing technology that illustrates how complex and multiple 'spheres of influence' shape the constitution of the 'problem', which is then addressed by solutions negotiated between a host of interested parties. While a narrow engineering-technological frame of reference predominates in the design and introduction of new technology, the 'web of dependency' that exists between the producer, shopfloor user, management development team and board of directors pulls and stretches the implementation process in different directions. In the light of the research carried out by Corbett, together with the important work of the actor-network theorists (Callon, 1986;

Latour, 1987), and the subsequent review by Whittington (1993), we can conclude that strategy does not proceed in a linear and rational way but is only ever partially emergent, subject to fragmentation and readjustment, contestation, struggle, spin-off 'sub-strategies', recovery programmes and deviation. If we contextualise HRM as a subject and practice bound up with this complex of political machinations, job redesign becomes more like an element in the will to power of managerial expertise, yet a contested terrain that mediates a whole host of political groups and factions, technical expertise, trade unions, informal shopfloor organisation, and user groups.

The practitioners of contemporary job redesign also tend to assume that technology remains essentially a means of improvement. It can only be successfully introduced and implemented, though, by management. Management will need to give due consideration to the concerns and needs of employees who might expect a degree of discretion, interest, and involvement, but management as a function is retained as the privileged agent of change. In this formulation of change management there is a signal lack of consideration or critical reflection brought to bear on the 'instrumentalism' and 'abstraction' involved in organisation, features of management that reduce and confine rationality to one of perpetuating mastery and objectification (Heidegger, 1977). As a recent commentary in the tradition of such critical theory argues, this epistemological straitjacket works to

> mark and reproduce an attitude whereby society and nature are looked on as if they were things to be made and remade, changed and transformed, corrected, amplified, destroyed, reconstructed, etc.
> (Kallinikos, 1996: 37–38)

A corollary of this is a certain subjectification and closure in the constitution of the human subject that dims down critical reflection on the alternative futures and possibilities of social relations, organisation, and the human being. A narrow instrumental orientation to control that seeks the subjugation of nature requires an ontology of human beings that represents humans as the centre and measure of all things. A technological order that subjugates, aligns, and coordinates individual and collective subjects restricts enquiry and action to an inexorable egotistical drive for 'instrumental rationality' (Weber, 1964). Human relationships are reduced to impersonal exchanges as technology and organisation concentrate on the means to ends rather than on the ends themselves. In the summary of Marcuse (1964), technology acts to *reify* organisation and social relations whereby 'The world tends to become the stuff of total administration, which absorbs even the administrators' (p. 169), and thus it is only

> in the medium of technology [that] man and nature become fungible objects of organization. The universal effectiveness and productivity of the apparatus under which they are subsumed veil the particular interests that organize the apparatus.
> (p. 168)

The 'one-dimensional' mindframe of human resource management seeks to suppress questions of power and inequality, and denies the legitimacy of plural contested values. As we have seen in previous chapters, this reflects the unitarist aspirations of HRM, where particular interests are represented as universal and necessary: 'We're here to serve the customer', for example, or 'Profit is the bottom line, the judge and jury'. Part of the legitimacy for these claims to 'universality' and 'necessity' is the connections that are made between job design and the rise of the flexible firm, flexible specialisation, and the post-Fordist economy. At times these arguments have been used to support the argument that the future of job design is one of semi-autonomous skilled craft-workers and the end of Taylorism.

THE FLEXIBLE WORKER CONTROVERSY

Post-Fordism

An influential current body of theory and writing has sought to demonstrate the breakdown of production systems based on Fordist assembly line methods (Aglietta, 1976; Piore and Sabel, 1984; Boyer, 1988). Each writer shades a nuanced approach to what is causing the breakdown, ranging from the inherent productivity limitations of Taylorism, to theories that emphasise the collapse and saturation of mass markets: that is, where consumers are now demanding individualised 'niche' products that require a more flexible approach to production. Here, workers are required who can exercise sufficient self-responsibility and initiative so as to go 'beyond contract' in the pursuit of skills and knowledge that ensure product innovation and competitiveness. It is argued that workers are required to embody a 'customer focus', developing and redeveloping, continually retraining in order to acquire new skills so that they can contribute to the design and production of goods that respond to the rapidly changing tastes and styles demanded by the product market.

The so-called Fordist system of manufacture was premised upon the systemic consistency between the existence of a mass of consumers demanding mass-produced invariant products. The standard cliché offered during Ford's early car factories was that consumers could have any colour of Model T car they wanted, so long as it was black. Aglietta (1976), in probably the most significant contribution to this debate, suggests three reasons internal to the labour process of Fordism that place constraints on its development as a system (pp. 119–121):

- There exist technical limits to the further fragmentation of assembly line tasks.
- Simply intensifying this process of production will lead to concomitant increases in absenteeism, and deterioration in the quality of the product: for example, in 1913 Henry Ford was to experience a turnover rate of 380%, which continued despite his famous $5 day.
- It becomes increasingly difficult and more 'expensive' to motivate employees: the five dollar day that Ford introduced in response to the above failed to significantly counter labour problems.

This kind of theoretical analysis has been taken up in many accounts within the critical theory of job redesign (Kelly, 1985; Littler, 1985). Kelly (1985), for example, suggests that a breakdown between product markets, labour markets, and the organisation of the labour process was expressed through a *disarticulation* of these various spheres of capital accumulation. The restructuring of organisations in response to global product market reorganisation and the domestic Thatcher-driven recession provided both a need for and the incentive to restructure production systems. This level of analysis is far more subtle and satisfactory than some overly deterministic accounts of job design (Piore and Sabel, 1984; Atkinson and Meager, 1986), integrating political economy, organisation, management and the labour process within its explanation. Management is repositioned and contextualised here, in ways that illuminate the mutual influence and interrelationship that exist between organisation and the wider political economy. The interaction of interfirm relations, product markets, labour markets, the spheres of consumption and production – are all included in these vast abstract theories of post-Fordism, providing a holistic-integrated account of change.

Management is therefore made subject to conditions that delimit a framework of constraints and opportunities in the redesign of jobs. This is clearly one of the strengths of these theories. One of the disadvantages is precisely its level of generality and abstraction, operating a degree of abstraction that occludes and precludes the presence of divergence, contingency and contradiction. Operating at a slightly less generalised level of analytical endeavour is the theory of flexible specialisation.

Flexible specialisation

Piore and Sabel (1984) argue that a new system of flexible specialisation is emerging that demands a return to craft-style multi-skilled work. Flexible specialisation is seen as 'a new form of skilled craft production made easily adaptable by programmable technology to provide specialised goods which can supply an increasingly fragmented and volatile market' (Gilbert *et al.*, 1992). In order to make the best use of this programmable technology, workers are required who can be flexible, moving rapidly from one production set-up to the next, and capable of exercising greater levels of discretion in the monitoring and fine-tune adjustment of the technology. In a relatively early critical response to the promotion of flexible specialisation, Robin Murray (1985) argues that what is actually happening is that new technology is being used to further deskill work rather than reskill jobs. Instead of a return to the craft traditions of manufacturing and production, technology allows work to be outsourced to a host of small workshops, with a small central organising hub acting to coordinate production and exercise the strategic functions of management – in design, product development, marketing and investment.

This is what Murray calls the development of 'Benetton Britain'. So, in what might be thought of as an ideal-typical representation of flexible specialisation, Benetton organizations are assembled just in time, so to speak, combining and drawing upon a vast network of producer workshops. Flexible specialisation is accomplished by the temporary combination of different outsourced suppliers, who are able to provide particular products and styles. As fashion changes, the central coordinating hub drops individual outsourced workshops and draws upon others, reassembling organisation in response to market changes.

Like the Benetton product ranges, more and more products have a short lifespan today. Consider, for example, the pop music industry, where style and bands have a shelf-life approaching little more than three years. We now see a 'Greatest Hits' album hitting the shops after a group has been together in some cases for little more than two years. Moreover, like the Benetton 'organisation', the relationship between the product market and internal labour processes today is almost fully integrated and symbiotic, or de-differentiated, as Lash and Urry (1987) write. Sophisticated 'early warning' information technology connects up the central hub of these Benetton-style organisations with retail outlets, providing almost instantaneous feedback from current tastes and fashions located at the point of sale back to the internal labour process of Benetton. Within less than three days Benetton claim their production can respond to changing tastes and fashions. The design process is central to these production systems, where a high premium is placed on a quick 'turnover' in style and fashion. Companies increasingly compete on the basis of novelty and style, so that what was a fashionable item of clothing last week becomes an unfashionable garment this week. The role of marketing and advertising is obviously crucial in the promotion of this rapid style 'turnover'.

From this we can see how one might be led to suggest that the future for job design is based on flexibility and multi-skilling, a process of change driven by market imperative and fostered by intensive marketing and advertising. Alternatively, we might suggest that the future is one of insecurity and temporary employment, where increasing numbers of employees are condemned to work for subcontractors and outsourced suppliers subject to the beck and call of powerful multinational elites, who now have the technological capacity to shift sources of production from one part of the globe to the next (Burawoy, 1985). Either way, it seems the market decides. There is very little opportunity for choice in the development of job design. Management, then, becomes simply a cipher of broader market changes. It either interprets these changes 'correctly' or 'incorrectly': introduces the appropriate forms of job design, or makes mistakes that herald the onset of organisational collapse and insolvency. Perhaps what we are seeing is that management develops and preserves an elite workforce employed in the centre, who perform high-skilled and reskilled jobs, marketing, coordinating organisation, developing products, and exploring investment opportunities in new technology, while a mass of relatively unskilled labour is assembled as and when required. If we explore these subcontractors and suppliers we may find workshops that resemble, in many ways, the kind of deskilled Taylorist assembly lines to which we have become accustomed in our study of job design.

Walton (1985), in an influential account of forms of organisational restructuring that conform to the central tenets and philosophy of HRM, confirms that market necessity is prompting the restructuring, but that this was providing an opportunity to release and harness the frustrated but infinite potential of human labour rather than leading inevitably to deskilled and monotonous job design. Walton argues that workers respond best and most productively when they are not tightly controlled by hierarchical layers of management, and when they are provided with opportunities to move beyond narrowly defined and prescribed jobs. The influence of the early human relations philosophy and studies are clearly apparent here. We see this when Walton argues that workers *should be given* broader responsibilities, which will then harness commitment to the organisation, rather than nurturing conflictual relations at work that spiral into coercion and the adoption of regimes of direct control and harsh discipline. Walton seems to be able to find space in organisations where management is confronted with choice. Here, the market doesn't necessarily dictate outcomes at the level of job design. Moreover, management is using this space so that:

> Jobs are designed to be broader than before, to combine planning and implementation, and to include efforts to upgrade operations, not just to maintain them. Individual responsibilities are expected to change as conditions change, and teams, not individuals, often are the organisational units accountable for performance. With management hierarchies relatively flat and differences in status minimised, control and lateral coordination depend on shared goals.
>
> (Walton, 1985; quoted in Armstrong, 1992: 98)

The flexible firm

In a series of articles on 'flexibility', however, John Atkinson and his colleagues at the Institute for Manpower Studies have argued that firms are responding to changing external market circumstances by restructuring their internal labour markets in ways similar to our critique of 'Benetton Britain'. Flexibility is achieved by combining functional, numerical, and financial flexibility. Functional flexibility represents attempts by management to develop broad-ranged polyvalent skills among their workforce. This provides organisations with the requisite flexibility to adapt to changing technology and product market fashions and tastes. In the 1980s, companies sought to remove internal rigidities between craft union lines of demarcation where workers combined production with maintenance work. Of course, while this might be considered flexible working, for some it might represent simply an intensification of labour. Yet within this group of employees it is argued that skills and training are extremely important in ensuring the adaptability of organisation. Atkinson describes these employees as the *core group* or the *primary labour market* in work organisations. Promotion, skill development and favourable terms and conditions of employment are the rewards offered to highly valued employees in this category. In contrast the *secondary labour market*, the peripheral group of employees and quasi-employees, is made up of part-time labour, short-term contracts, public subsidy trainees, job-sharing and 'delayed' recruitment. This provides the organisation with numerical flexibility. The peripheral group of employees can be quickly called in and disposed of in response to fluctuations in the product market. They can be seen as 'labour on call', providing a buffer stock of resources enabling the organisation to 'organically' expand and contract (see Chapter 4).

The concept and practice of flexibility has generated much academic and business interest, both favourable and critical. Some have questioned the empirical validity of the studies conducted by the IMS (Pollert, 1988; Marginson, 1989), drawing attention to figures that suggest there was only a small growth in the number of peripheral and core employees during the 1970s and 1980s. Pollert and Marginson also questioned whether UK management could introduce flexibility with the kind of strategic integrity and intent that its advocates suggested. In addition, studies have shown that it was in the management of the public sector, often driven by a political logic, where many of the changes associated with flexibility were introduced, rather than the cutting edge of market competition leading the way. This is an unusual finding in that Atkinson and Meager stressed that flexibility is primarily a radical private sector strategy designed to meet the requirements of changing manufacturing technology and shifting product market patterns. Clearly, the argument that flexible production systems are based on high-quality job design emphasising multi-skilling and functional flexibility is clearly inadequate in terms of both its empirical validity and its explanatory utility. The so-called leading-edge examples of these new production systems, Benetton and the Emilia-Romagna region in northern Italy, would appear to be founded on exploitative subcontract relationships that use the familiar Taylorist methods of low discretion and intensive labour input (Pollert, 1988, 1991; Elger, 1990).

Furthermore, our discussion above should lead us to question the analytical determinism built into some of these accounts in ways similar to those revisions and criticisms made of Braverman's work. Braverman, as was shown, posited only one future and direction for job design, one based on deskilling and intensification. In the accounts of flexible specialisation and multi-skilled craft working proposed by Piore and Sabel and Robin Murray, we are likewise presented with an account that posits unilinearity. Yet here the determinism works in the opposite direction – towards reskilling and empowerment. Common to those accounts premised on analytical determinism is the assumption that in the restructuring of organisations management retains a considerable amount of foresight and ability. Management also tends to be presented as a politically neutral agent, a change agent of organisations that are held together by a common set of integrating norms and values. As Kelly (1985) suggests, any consensus is undoubtedly temporary and fragile. Recession has provided management with both an incentive and the rationale to drive through change in a situation in which individuals are glad just to have a job.

Many writers have attempted to account for the apparent contradiction in recent restructuring initiatives, which appear to be based simultaneously on reskilling and functional flexibility together with peripheralisation, intensification and deskilling (Shaiken *et al.*, 1986; Smith, 1989). This has been coined *neo-Fordism* in contrast to post-Fordism, and reflects a significant theoretical advance in moving away from overly deterministic 'uni-linear' accounts, which stress either deskilling or reskilling (Badham and Mathews, 1989; Lovering, 1990). As Batstone (1984) has argued, the development and form of labour relations outcomes must always be seen as provisional and contested, not simply between management and worker but within political struggles within management itself:

> Strategic change in organisations is accompanied by intra-management bargaining and micro-political struggles that make the outcome of the process of change uncertain and at the very least 'negotiable'. The ambiguities of the strategic process mean that the implications of strategy for labour relations are likewise uncertain, provisional and complex. (quoted in Hyman, 1987: 49)

Attempts by management to develop such production systems strategically are based on the simultaneous desire for commitment and consent from labour to work together with the retention of sufficient power within management to adjust the workforce numerically in response to market and technological developments. This contradiction has been usefully explored by Michael Burawoy (1979, 1985), who argues that *management simultaneously seeks to secure and obscure the power relations* in production. Ultimately management is responsible to the interests of capital, and if profitability is threatened management will need the power to preserve capital. The burden of adjustment to external market and technological shocks must fall asymmetrically on the quantitative and qualitative nature of labour. In our discussion of the flexible firm it can be seen that this contradiction has been partially 'managed' in organisations by obtaining numerical flexibility through peripheral labour and commitment and consent from a privileged core of employees.

Postmodernism, replicants and the end of job design

Like post-Fordism, theories of postmodernism operate at an equally abstract and at times obtuse level of analysis. The diversity of writing collected under the title of postmodernism makes it very difficult to present a brief overview. In general the study of postmodernism has derived from the fields of media and cultural studies, drawing on a range of French theoreticians including Jean Baudrillard, Gilles Deleuze, Michel Foucault, Jacques Derrida, and Paul Virilio. Many argue that postmodernism first came into prominence in the late 1960s and early 1970s through art and architecture, but it wasn't until the 1980s that the study of postmodernism became associated with organisational analysis and management studies. A brief look at some so-called postmodern architecture proves instructive, however, in delineating what postmodernism might have to say about contemporary job design (Venturi *et al.*, 1972; Jencks, 1987; Betsky, 1990). We find that these buildings often seek to problematise the distinction between the real and the fictional, borrowing styles from the past, and mixing genres of historical architectural codes in a disjunctive bricolage-hybridity of style. Consider the building of contemporary shopping centres and the architecture of places like Las Vegas. Irony, quotation, and pastiche run riot in these buildings, where we might find an exterior of 'fake' Greek temple-like pillars housing a three-year-old building, a surface that draws attention to itself as fake displaying its incongruity and artifice. If this marks the avant-garde in construction and design we might expect that contemporary work organisatioh will begin to follow its lead. It is increasingly being recognised in the field of job design that it is only in the presentation and packaging of ideas where there is anything new. Underneath the surface we find the persistence of Taylorised forms of job design. Yet one of the problems we might encounter in seeking to understand contemporary job design is where those distinctions between the authentic and fake, surface and depth, the real and the fictional, and/or objectivity and subjectivity no longer seem to hold. If we can no longer be sure what constitutes a 'job', or where its boundaries lie, and if the capacity of design is being overwhelmed by the explosion of 'signs' at work, we may be entering a period of postmodern employment where no one has a 'job', in that sense of a designed, delimited, bounded objective entity, and no one is sure any longer whether what they are doing constitutes something new or old, something 'skilled' or 'unskilled'.

There is a deconstructive impulse in the contemporary innovation and application of information and communication technology. Coupled with the growth in artificial intelligence and de-territorialising globalised trans-organisation, we seem to be threatened with a collapse in those spatial and temporal boundaries, borders and coordinates that we have traditionally used to orientate ourselves (Jameson, 1991). In work environments that are fluid and without geography, subject to perpetual construction and reconstruction, strange new evanescent forms seem to appear on the horizon. We are perhaps witness to the growth of 'virtual organisation': part workhouse, part shopping mall, part home, part slaughterhouse, Hybrid man–machine cyborgs (Haraway, 1985), and perhaps even the 'replicants' anticipated by science fiction writer Philip K. Dick, may be replacing the awkward, inefficient and recalcitrant bone–muscle–tissue– spirit that has evolved to take the form of the human body. Nexus 5 replicants, which for the moment remain only inhabitants of the fictitious world of science fiction and the films of Ridley Scott, may perhaps portent the future of contemporary movements in 'job design'.

These replicants are designed to work 'offworld' in basic engineering, maintenance and transportation employment in alien hostile conditions impossible for human subjects. Replicants are designed to perform with all the 'best' features of a human – intelligence, self-reflection, the capacity to learn from mistakes – but without the fallibilities and weaknesses of the human body. Whereas the human body 'naturally' gets tired and requires rest, occasionally questions the meaning and value of the work it is performing, gets hung up on the existential absurdity of it all, and remains subject to the inconvenience of emotional complexity and irrational interference, replicants are designed to work assiduously, efficiently, and without question. Does the future of job design entail the mass redundancy of traditional labouring subjects and their replacement by replicants and cyborgs, or does it perhaps spell the end of the human subject as we know it?

Strange questions to be asking in the context of a chapter on job design, but applications of new technology and organisational restructuring in manufacturing and engineering, and the emergence of the communications and education services, have led to job designs that not only disturb patterns of employment but also threaten the meaning of our categories 'job', 'technology', and 'human'. Contemporary education is not the exclusive preserve of lecturers and tutors who ply their trade in preparing weekly lecture and collective seminar material. Increasingly education takes the form of distant and isolated students surfing and interacting with other students on the

Internet, attending cyberspace courses and lectures from around the 'world'. The future student of job design theory and practice may attend a series of Internet workshops at the 'Virtual University' rather than sit in front of the ancient medium of a heavy 500-page textbook: a morning lecture at the University of California, lunch of Wiener schnitzel at a Viennese *Heurigen,* and an afternoon seminar organised by the Moscow Institute of Business Process Re-engineering. This would clearly have job design implications for the job of tutors and lecturers, but does it replace them? One can imagine self-selecting, structure and filtering software that designs courses of study for the student. Software programs may be designed to reflect and respond to academic text and articles, integrating and synthesising work in a field, summarising and even offering logical and 'intellectual' critique and beginning to produce text of its own (Woolgar, 1991). This may result in a situation where job design theory is split by the Warwick IBM 600 software dispute with the IBM 900 LSE program. One can imagine ideological hardware battles that may ultimately threaten Internet peace.

Applications of new computer and information technology are fundamentally redesigning jobs, in many cases blurring the distinction between organisational change and job design. In most academic texts on job design there is a signal lack of critical attention to and detail of the interaction between capital, technology and the complexity of social relations, complexity composed of centrifugal and centripetal forces. Job design, in the main, still tends to be seen in terms of a discrete and linear top-down intervention by representatives of some personnel department, which aims to restructure or transform the boundaries, allocation and distribution of job tasks. Yet deliberate and purposeful activity remains folded and shadowed by the accidental and contingent – what Cooper and Law (1995) call the proximal forces of organising. Management intention then, means what it says, that is 'in tension' – 'a pattern of actions that is distributed throughout such a field and which serves to maintain it or hold it together' (p. 246). Of course, this maintenance does not get reproduced unproblematically, but remains a contingent outcome of multiple and heterogeneous processes. In a remarkable and illuminating study, Yiannis Gabriel (1995) has illustrated one aspect of these processes, namely the marginal terrain he calls the 'unmanaged organization'. In this 'dreamworld', emotions, anxieties and desires find expression in stories, myths and fantasies, which refashion formal or official discourse and rhetoric for pleasure and perhaps simply for the 'kick'.

CONTEMPORARY JOB DESIGN: AN ETYMOLOGY

Design is derived etymologically from the Latin *designare* and the French *designer.* Reflecting on these terms opens up a rather richer understanding of the complexity latent to the concept design than that typically employed by personnel and human resource managers. In exploring this complexity we actually capture a better sense of the subtle and contradictory nature of job design today, where order and disorder are beginning to emerge as *mutually overlapping forces* present in employment relations.

Design encapsulates a range of understandings. In one sense it implies a 'marking out', or a tracing and denoting. The *Oxford English Dictionary* suggests that design provides for the sense of giving 'something form, an outline and definition'. For example, ideas and material are fashioned and 'de-sign-ated' by a title, a profession or trade. It also implies a deliberate calculation, 'a purpose, an intention, plot, ambition . . . an end in view, a goal'. Yet a rather more circumscribed sense of design has typically been understood and appropriated in the field of personnel management, reducing it simply to one of *purposeful* change and reconstruction in the objective content of jobs. Moreover, it secures a definition and unity for the practice of job design that is unwarranted. As we have seen, job design is a contested medium, a political subject, one that exists in a state of perpetual processual struggle. These limiting assumptions in traditional personnel management are perhaps better seen as an element of this struggle, part of an instrumental agenda pursued in the interests of normalisation and control, but they have cost us considerable versatility and subtlety in our understanding of job design. Let us take another look at the word 'design'.

The word also captures the sense of contemplation – to contemplate or project a plan, to lay a plot. As the Renaissance architect Moxon claimed, 'Tis usual . . . for any person before he begins to erect a building, to have Designs or Draughts drawn upon paper' so that each floor of the building is 'de-lineated' in a flat, geometric, two-dimensional projection. In its *materialisation* we find that the *intention* (in-tension) is marked by a series of 'limits' that are expressed across a multidimensional realm, a realm made up of complex and contradictory pressures, intransigent forces of composition and decomposition that 'work on' the abstract geometric projection. These multidimensional forces can be thought of in terms of 'signs' that de-sign attempts to rationalise and limit, to prescribe and contain. Signs are less conclusive, open to interpretation; they merely suggest, perceive or indicate in some representative form or medium something often beyond rational cognition and the intellect. Signs have to wait to be coded, and are subject to recoding and reinterpretation; as the *Concise Oxford Dictionary* defines it, signs are 'actions or gestures to convey information'. As we shall see, job design never manages to circle and enclose 'signs' with definitional precision, and in fact in many contemporary organisations and workplaces, the boundaries and content of 'jobs' remain ambiguous and subject to various pressures of destabilisation.

It is worth noting that design evokes notions of 'crafty contrivance', where people are said to have cunning designs on others, a plot or intrigue in medieval court society in which political forces are realigned by the ambitions and designs of cliques, cabals and gangs. As the well-worn adage states, 'They who ask relief have one design; and he who gives it another'. Those organisations studied by Robert Jackall (1988) reflect this understanding of design as management coteries plot and design the downfall of other management groups, which generates repercussions in coups and counter-plots, all of which add contingency and ambiguity in the evolution of roles and responsibilities:

> Because of the interlocking ties between people, they know that a shake-up at or near the top of a hierarchy can trigger a widespread upheaval, bringing in its wake startling reversals of fortune, good and bad, throughout the structure. (p. 33)

Finally, design contains within it an important aesthetic dimension. One fashions or designs with artistic skill or decorative device. In contemporary job design this aesthetic dimension comes to play a fundamental role in which the 'dressage' of costume, language, posture, customer interaction rituals, and the furniture and stage props of employment take on significance in the efforts to structure and organise efficient work (Hochschild, 1983; Austrin, 1991). As Featherstone's research in contemporary culture (1988, 1991) has shown, there has been a generalised process of 'aestheticisation' where design proliferates in signs, symbols, myths and images that have saturated the fabric of everyday life. Lash and Urry (1994), similarly, argue that objects in contemporary political economies lose their spatial and temporal referents, becoming progressively emptied of objectivity and materiality:

objects in contemporary political economies are not just emptied out of symbolic content. They are progressively emptied out of material content. What is increasingly being produced are not material objects, but signs. (pp. 14–15)

In contemporary work organisations the content of many people's jobs is arguably becoming more cognitive in nature and 'emptied out' as companies increasingly compete in the fields of information and ideas. Organisations often exist on the basis of networks of computer terminals that transcend the limitations of time, space and geography. The Californian advertising agency Chiat/Day, for example, offers its employees the option of working from home, and in any one day there are only 60% of staff on the premises. In addition, there are no private offices for employees of any status but rather collective 'living rooms', and for meetings, staff must book multi-purpose 'project rooms'. The accounting firm Ernst & Young has completely abandoned the traditional design and structure of jobs and offices, replacing its Chicago head office with a 'hotel'. A hotel coordinator books rooms, and arranges for special files or software to be available. Employees' jobs are designed to be mobile and flexible, 'out in the field', or in the relative peace of their home, where they can focus and study, complete reports, for example, in an environment they can better control. In giving employees more control and autonomy in the design of their own work routines, the quality of work, which in these sectors is increasingly of a cognitive nature, is likely to improve.

Oticon, the Danish hearing aid company, has abandoned offices and desks, taken out walls and barriers, erased job descriptions, and auctioned off all its office furniture to employees (Peters, 1994). Employees stow their effects in caddies or personal carts, and physically arrange themselves as they see fit and as the project or task demands. The plant is a completely open space, and employees have no fixed place but move around the interior of the plant as the job, which they themselves are responsible for organising and coordinating, changes and evolves. From a situation in which their market share had fallen by 50% in 1991, Oticon recovered and began to make record profits (Peters, 1994: 29). A similar idea of 'hot desking' has been introduced in many professional management service organisations. This removes all fixed furniture in a 'cordless office' designed with ponds and plants and infused by the Chinese philosophy of *feng shui* (Farmbrough, 1996). Workers become nomadic, equipped with their 'office in a briefcase', wired into the centreless organisation through mobile phones, car phones, paging systems, radio networks, portable fax machines, laptops and other portable technologies.

Organisational and job design initiatives in many sectors of the economy do not depend these days on centralised personnel management departments. In efforts to tap into the intangibles of ideas and imagination that now arguably fuel the competition in education, tourism, entertainment, management consultancies and services, job design becomes a less easily identifiable and delimited activity, but is diffused and decentralised so as to encourage networking, mobility and flexibility.

We can begin to see the relevance of this dematerialisation of work and the emptying out of objectivity when we look at the case of the Philip Morris company. When Philip Morris bought Kraft for $12.9 billion, the accountants were able to identify $1.3 billion of tangible assets. The remaining $11.6 billion dollars was defined as 'other', those intangibles including goodwill, brand equity, and ideas in the heads of the employees. Tom Peters (1994) calls this the 116/129 principle. Most management remains concerned with the 13/129 fraction, and the rest tends to get neglected. Peters also notes that only 6% of IBM staff actually work in the factory producing 'things'; the rest remain in design, servicing, product development, logistics and finance, in which the premium is on ideas and imagination. Even those in the factory mostly perform service tasks:

> Factory 'hands' (ah, words!) now spend much of their time working with outsiders in multifunctional teams that streamline processes, improve quality, or customize products. (Peters, 1994: 14)

In the final sections of this chapter we attempt to trace the development of contemporary job design techniques against the background of these theoretical concerns. In particular we focus on the sustainability, consistency and order of design and its relation to breakdowns, accidents, contingencies and incoherence. This extends our concern with the development of a critical study of technology that gives due attention to the interaction of capitalist forces of production with organisation, and social relations in production that allow us to draw out the tension in design/sign. In current efforts to restructure and *reform* work organisations this tension may be reaching a new crisis in which ontological categories – man/technology–machine – and the horizontal and vertical boundaries and definition of 'jobs' are subject to decomposition. Here we reach the limits of our chapter, where we can only raise the question whether a new form of composition and organisational assembly is emergent or imminent in contemporary social relations.

TEAMWORKING, BUSINESS PROCESS RE-ENGINEERING AND AESTHETICS: DISORIENTATION, SIMULATION AND RE-SIGN?

A relatively recent response to this putative crisis of modernity and Fordism has been the fervour surrounding the concept of business process re-engineering (BPR), sometimes peddled under the title 'business process transformation' or 'business process redesign'. The two key seminal articles propounding the miracle of BPR were published by Hammer in the July–August 1990 *Harvard Business Review*, and by Davenport and Short in the summer 1990 *Sloan Management Review*. Hammer and Champy's *Reengineering the Corporation: A Manifesto for Business Revolution* was published in the UK in 1993, and rapidly became a best-selling management text. The principles of BPR in themselves may not seem particularly revolutionary in the light of the above discussions, but the novelty seems to lie in the manner in which they are introduced, the holistic nature of the package, the synergy and coherence that the key principles are said to collectively deliver, and the inspirational and aggressive aesthetic of their texts. Tied in with these principles is the concomitant importance attached to human resource job design that drives through empowerment, devolution and autonomy. Managers are continually reminded of the market imperative that requires them to take a hammer, or an axe, to the structures and principles governing their organisation. Organisations require personality transplants; nothing less than a lobotomy will suffice, and employees who cannot and will not change need to be 'shot'.

Hammer and Champy claim that the origin of the problem is to be found in the propensity of capitalist organisations to develop large and unwieldy bureaucracies based on the separation of function, specialisation, hierarchy, long lines of authority relations, complicated structures of status, and layers of work task division and deskilling. Furthermore the products and services that organisations develop remain divorced from the customer, who gets easily forgotten, a remote element in this traditional supply-led and production-dominant system. According to Hammer and Champy (1993), employees need to 'deeply believe' that they are working not for bosses or to keep pace with targets, but simply for the customers (p. 14). Authority needs to be vested in small, multifunctional teams who can develop the capacity to respond rapidly and competently to the vagaries and whim of customer requirements. Grint (1995) offers a useful example of the approach BPR takes by looking at an organisation selling books:

> if the business is concerned with selling books by post then a customer wanting to buy books from different departments, pay for them by credit card, and have them delivered by special delivery, should not have to be switched through departments that deal with different categories of books, then be switched to a new section that deals with accounts, and then find themselves trailing through the telephone network in an attempt to have the books sent out. (pp. 92–93)

Organisational barriers need to be smashed to create self-guiding, team-based process units. Although sceptical of much of BPR, Tom Peters recommends a similar reorganisation of job design, one that enables employees to get 'closer' to the customer. Union Pacific Railroad was in many ways a classic example of the ordered and structured bureaucratic, functional organisation. If a customer or a track inspector reported a problem it would be passed on to the manager of that yard. The manager would report this to his or her boss who would then subsequently pass the problem on to the divisional superintendent for transportation. Then it would go to the general divisional superintendent to be passed on to the region, and finally to the apex of the management structure. From there it would make a horizontal shift to sales and marketing and pass back down this convoluted hierarchy to the district sales representative, who would liaise with the customer (as Tom Peters adds, if the customer is still alive!):

> Today, if a track inspector discovers a problem at a customer-owned rail siding, he informs the customer directly. If the customer disagrees with the track inspector . . . then the customer can call the track inspector's boss, the Superintendent for Transportation Services. But the super will say in effect, 'Look, I don't know anything about track. I'm just a boss. Keep talking to the track inspector.' (Peters, 1994: 31–32)

BPR seeks to integrate a whole set of practices (Hammer and Champy, 1993), from flattening hierarchies to effecting a shift from a mentality based on 'training' to one that emphasises 'education'. BPR attempts to incorporate into organisations pay systems that calculate *added value* rather than reward attendance. Managers are made coaches rather than supervisors in BPR-designed organisations in an attempt to devolve responsibility and facilitate lateral working relations. Perhaps its singular most innovatory component, however, is the *evangelism* of the BPR message combined with an aesthetic of masculinity and aggression. Managers are exhorted to see the world in a new way, as dangerous, unstable and subject to rapid shifts. They are warned of the vagaries of fashion and style, where customers will no longer tolerate organisations that do not have the capacity for rapid and immediate, rather than incremental, change.

One of the interesting features of BPR discourse is its emphasis on those organisations that have failed. The figure of 80% is widely documented as the number of organisations that have not been sufficiently radical in adopting the BPR package (Willmott, 1995), creating a climate more amenable to the exhortations of continual pressure and badgering. It seems that managers need to be subjected to continual pressure to encourage attendance at the weekly ecclesiastical sermon – to strengthen their commitment and moral fibre in order that they remain faithful to the cause in the face of pressures to deviate and temptations to seek an easy answer. Moreover, once we turn to examine the processes involved in job redesign through a reading of case study research, we find that design and implementation remain subject to a host of forces and pressures, all working to pull and stretch design in a multitude of directions. Once again, we are reminded of the clash of organisation/disorganisation, where the complex movements of social relations condemn the pursuit of design and stability to the space of a 'contested terrain'. Only ever partially realised or materialised, job design is forever in the process of 'becoming', fluctuating and oscillating in a constant movement between order and disorder. This is the terrain where anything might happen next, the accidental, contingent, and spontaneous – those features of organisation over which management has only partial control.

Teamworking at British Telecom

The recent customer service drive at British Telecom (IRS, 1995a: 579) seeks to develop team-based working that resonates with many of the job redesign implications of BPR. In the face of profound market changes – in the case of British Telecom, the product of political engineering, intervention, and state management – customers now have an increasing choice of suppliers for telephone equipment and maintenance. A BT marketing department survey found that 80% of customers wanted engineers to be available on Saturdays, and 25% of its customers wanted service availability on Sundays. Following a complicated and lengthy 18-month negotiation with the union, which ended in September 1994 with a union ballot returning an 85% rejection of the scheme, BT sought volunteers directly for their new attendance scheduling package. Engineers were offered the option of three different attendance patterns, ranging from intensive 12-hour, three-day working between Friday and Tuesday to a conventional five-day working week from Monday to Friday – but with evening work obligatory, and remunerated at standard rates. Management wanted to loosen up the rigid start and stop times that governed the traditional rostering system.

In addition to the change in attendance patterns, a vital component of the Customer Service Improvement Programme (CSIP) was the demand for flexibility that allowed management to call up engineers up to an hour before their scheduled shift start and insist upon their working, when required, an additional hour after the formal termination of their shift. This could be 'averaged out' and balanced over time by letting engineers go home early or start later as and when customer demand patterns dictated. As part of the CSIP, BT introduced a new Resource Administrative Management System (RAMS) that, able to store and load every individual engineer's roster in conjunction with derived data on customer orders, could automatically build work schedule rosters.

As part of this strategic programme BT sought to introduce small teams of field engineers who, instead of the traditional supervisory–management authority relations, would take on increased responsibility and initiative themselves. A major problem with the traditional structure was found to be the role of the first-line managers, who had increasingly become 'deskbound', tied up with administration and paperwork. BT wanted to get these managers back into the field, closer to the customer, and therefore they created a new role they designated as 'field manager'. This entailed a considerable effort in delayering organisational structure where the old supervisory grade had been made surplus to requirements. These new field managers were being trained to take on the role of 'coach' – managing, building, and developing teams through an attention to quality, workmanship and customer satisfaction. Field managers were not provided with dedicated office space, but were linked into a field support office by mobile phones and home-based faxes. While they take on the appearance of 'coach', in many ways field managers are being made into conduits for the channelling of new modes of 'silent' discipline; less structured and hierarchical, or rule-bound and proceduralised, discipline is nonetheless an integral element in these new forms of job redesign. As Barker (1993) shows, teamworking operates to delayer discipline and embed its practice in forms of peer surveillance and sophisticated methods of performance monitoring. Rules and procedures then take on a kind of 'virtual immanence'; discipline is present but also absent in jobs that are empowered but also monotonous, de-signed and un-signed, stimulating many employees into re-sign-ation.

Post-bureaucracy at W H Smith

WH Smith has embarked on a similar restructuring exercise following increased competition from supermarkets and petrol stations selling stationery, magazines and newspapers (IRS, 1995b: 596). A retail branch restructuring exercise sought a shift from a 'process' to a 'customer-driven' orientation, reducing unnecessary hierarchy, redefining job roles, rewriting job descriptions, and reducing the number of grades. The old paternal 'command-and-control' model that held the boundaries and structures of job design in place was deemed to be anachronistic given the present competitive climate. Departmental and assistant departmental managers were replaced with more flexibly defined customer service and support managers, with a team of customer support leaders responsible for coaching and developing their customer service teams. The guiding principles governing this change programme emphasised the importance of empowerment and flexibility:

> Managers and staff should feel a sense of personal ownership and accountability, making them quicker to respond to selling opportunities . . . We want to give people power to use their own initiative, make decisions and take responsibility.
>
> (IRS, 1995b: 6)

Similar to the changes taking place in the customer–employee interface in the high street retail banks (O'Doherty, 1994), employees are being refocused and reconstituted (Du Gay and Salaman, 1994) to service, satisfy and even 'excite' the customer, as Tom Peters has been proselytising throughout the 1980s and 1990s.

Ethnographies of work and organisation

Most accounts of job redesign tend to present only the formal, or official, version of events. Typically, empirical research that has examined new innovations in teamworking and BPR has tended to rely on surveys of management, or on interview-based case-study material that again relies wholly or primarily on the accounts of those who have formally 'designed' the change programmes. Detailed longitudinal and ethnographic research is far more rare. That research which has adopted the more qualitatively rich methodology offered by ethnographic tradition (including Jackall, 1988; Kondo, 1991; Collinson, 1992; Casey, 1995; Watson, 1994) tends to emphasise the precarious and partial nature of these 'deliberate' interventions and design programmes. The work of Tony Watson illuminates the ever-present climate of uncertainty and anxiety that attends managerial work, especially where management is engaged in the exercise of organisation change. Existential preoccupations, in combination with the struggles to secure definition and objectivity in organisation, tend to destabilise and subvert management efforts to execute its functions in the prescribed manner of a dispassionate agent of rational–

technical calculation. Recent efforts to tap into the hearts and souls of employees attempt to constitute and appropriate some of these irrational and emotional aspects of employee behaviour (Hochschild, 1983; Burrell, 1992), with the intention of redirecting its energy in a more instrumentally useful and purposive manner. However, the same instability, if not heightened instability, often accompanies such efforts, as employees attempt to make sense of the ambiguity of devolved responsibility.

Managers are seen to be preoccupied with a search for themselves; in effect they are concerned with the management of themselves. Managers are seen to confront ambiguity and dilemmas in situations where they have to negotiate some compromise or trade-off between their own sense of identity and the demands of work. This often challenges and impinges on assumptions of self and identity. Steve Loscoe, a technical manager at ZTC Ryland, the pseudonym that Watson (1994) adopts for his case-study organisation, reflects on this ambiguity and complexity in defining both himself and his role in the corporation:

> I really do wonder what my bloody job is sometimes. I say to myself 'I'm in charge of this office and this office and the office in Birmingham' but then I ask whether I'm really in charge of even myself when it comes down to it. I get told to jump here, jump there, sort this, sort that, more than I ever did before I was a section leader. (p. 29)

Catherine Casey (1995) reports similar findings in her research at the 'Hephaestus' Corporation, where the interrelation between work, self and identity continually disrupts the smooth functioning and reproduction of the formal and technical relations in production. An employee she calls Hal reflects on the turbulence of change and the uncertainty that attends the development of his role where occupational boundaries are being destructured to make way for multifunctional organic 'product teams' (p. 106). Knowledge and skills that were previously valued under the former locus of occupational identity are now being made redundant, as fluidity and change disrupt former certainties, demanding of employees a continual investment and reinvestment of skill acquisition. Employees are left to search for the 'signs' of what is required as they are brought nearer to what Karen Legge has called the 'indiscriminate deconstructive impact of "free" market forces' (Legge, 1995: 244).

One manager in the Watson (1994) study had to reprimand Watson for using the redundant language of 'jobs': 'To use the term "job" was to be slapped down by, for example, the injunction to "wash your mouth out"' (p. 115). On asking about job design the researcher was told 'For God's sake don't use that term; "job" is a dirty word here' (p. 115). Conventional job analysis assumes that there exists something stable called a 'job', which can be traced, marked and identified in terms of a stable set of tasks, responsibilities and knowledge. As one manager in the Jackall (1988) study comments, there are no rules, requirements or responsibilities that can be categorically defined as the boundaries of one's 'job'. Rather extreme, but perhaps reflecting the sentiments of those ambitious and desirous of success, is the following comment quoted in Jackall:

> The code is this: you milk the plants; rape the business; use other people and discard them; fuck any woman that is available, in sight and under your control; and exercise authoritative prerogatives at will with subordinates and other lesser mortals who are completely out of your league in money and status. (p. 97)

Where employees are 'positioned' in open and fluid skill grades, or in 'job clusters' in which the content and boundaries of jobs remain negotiable and subject to change, the security provided by status and identity, of knowing what is expected, is being slowly eroded. Employees can now expect continual bouts of reskilling and deskilling as the life expectancy of skills is reduced to one in which last week's knowledge and skill today become redundant. Hal comments on the nature of his job, for example:

> My job? Well, it just changed. Yesterday, I think. Principal Information Systems Consultant is what it changed to. And I used to be Manager Assistant Projects, I think it was called.

Specialisation and demarcation are rapidly dissolving, leading to a synthetic post-occupational culture of flexibility and generalisation, precariously held together by the glue of corporate culture. In the absence of traditional forms of solidarity and community, organisations are busy providing a surrogate corporate collectivity. Corporate culture, for example, attempts to engineer and foster team-based harmony through the manipulation of myths, symbols and stories through which employees can identify and cohere around common purpose and identity. Class-based and occupational affiliations are giving way to simulated families, which tap into individuals' needs for direction and purpose (see also Willmott, 1993). However, this remains a precarious and unstable form of design as the existential concerns and questions of individuals and collectives can never be indefinitely secured in the artificial cocoon of corporate culture and charismatic leadership (Hopfl and Linstead, 1993). As Bauman (1995) argues, passion, emotion and what he calls 'new forms of togetherness' in a mode of 'Being-for' – that is concern, empathy and emotional commitment – always threaten this 'courthouse' of instrumental reason:

> In the garden of Reason, sentiments are weeds – plants that seed themselves in unexpected and inconvenient spots. The spots are inconvenient because they have not been allocated in advance – they are random from the point of view of the master plan, and hence undermine the design because the design is, first and foremost, about the impossibility of randomness. (p. 54)

However, a major problem with this critical *existential humanism* is its foundational reliance on the traditional ontological features of a human being. There has been a plethora of innovative scholarship recently, exploring the historical and cultural contingency of what it is to be human. The critical work of the University of Keele's Social Theory and Technology group (see Law, 1991, in the first instance) has done much to examine the historical relationship between power, self and technology in the constitution of notions about what is and what it means to be a 'human-self'. This work seeks to incorporate post-structuralist advances in social theory into the understanding of contemporary technological and organisational design. One of its main concerns is the boundary or difference between humans and technology. As our introduction suggests, hybrid forms of man/machine cyborgs may portend the future of job design. As Law (1991) suggests, 'the very dividing line between those objects that we choose to call people and those that we call machines is variable, negotiable' (p.17). To capture a sense of this complex literature, consider your own helplessness once your Internet port breaks down, or the next time your car won't start, or the sense of a limb missing when your word processor won't work. In fact, if you walk to work, instead of driving, you may experience a whole new sense of self as the route and surroundings take on new dimensions of sensuousness, of topographical and temporal meaning. Perhaps you may reflect on the extent to which the body has become composed, constituted and assembled by material computer and information technology.

Corbett (1995) examines contemporary fears and possibilities as the advance of computer and information technology creates simulated environments of artificial intelligence and virtual reality that break down comfortable definitions of the real and the unreal. Machines that develop human characteristics and humans who increasingly resemble robots, as portrayed in the film *Bladerunner*, challenge the categorical divisions human/technology, reason/feeling and culture/nature. Is the future of job design one that undoes its own conceptual and practical foundations, where the notion of 'job' and 'design' as a top-down managerial delimitation and structure gives way to self-reflexive, quasi-organic cybernetic systems? Who (or what) remains in control here? Are we left with the rapid circulation of information bits, symbols and part-composed narratives, which float as 'signs' in an uncontrollable and unstable cyberspace (see Gibson, 1984)?

CONCLUSIONS

Our chapter began with a brief essay reflecting upon the limitations of the traditional syllabus and the orthodox frames of reference in studying the complex dynamics inherent in job design. It was argued that in order to come to terms with contemporary job design we need to find new ways of thinking and writing about organisation, ways that enable us to analytically prise open that space of chance, spontaneity, and disruption in the employment relation. We have made an initial attempt to broaden the focus of job design study by attending to issues of power, control and technology. In our concern to address subjective aspects of work, those existential processes that preoccupy employees, we have extended an exploration of the complex forces of organisation and disorganisation that seem to render management–employee relations quite unstable, precarious, and contingent. A subtext in this chapter has been the recurring analytical problem of structure–agency: the extent to which job design can be thought of as the product of structural determinism against the 'free will' of management.

Braverman, for example, stressed that deskilling was inevitable, a structural necessity of capitalism driven by the continual need to increase productivity and output. Braverman understood the system of scientific management developed by F.W. Taylor as the apogee and perfection of management rationality. This sought a progressive deskilling of labour so that control and direction of the labour process could be effectively monopolised by management and colonised more effectively in order to determine and maximise levels of output and efficiency. However, from the discussion in this chapter, we have seen how this somewhat crude and mechanical view of management and job design was far too determinist in its assumptions.

Debates around the flexible firm, flexible specialisation, and especially post-Fordism, impart a degree of sophistication to the understanding of job design, drawing attention to a heterogeneous range of subjects focused upon the level of political economy and the interaction of product and labour markets. Nonetheless, these developments remain governed by a formal logic still inhibited by the problem of reconciling the degree of determinism with the scope for management autonomy and choice in job design initiative. Towards the end of the chapter we began to explore the non-rational aspects of organisation: that space that seems to lie forever beyond the instrumental-calculative efforts of management design and control. It is in the processual dynamics of organisation, in the social relations that day in/day out produce and reproduce organisation, that we find the elusive and inchoate flux that permeates the fabric of employment relations. Given the growth of postmodern phenomena and its extension into work organisations, more and more aspects of the employment relation seem to be subject to an ontological ambiguity whereby it might not even be that clear any more whether the categories that we have traditionally used to study job design – 'job', 'design', the 'social', 'human', the 'technological' – are going to prove useful in a future driven by the speed of de-differentiation, amorphous hybridity (Latour, 1993), and the abnormal collision of signs, symbols and re-signations.

We have also established that job design does not take place in some neat, well-defined managerial enclave or elite. Nor is it a coherent activity, the contents of which consist of fixed, objective-like elements that proceed along a linear rational line from cause to effect within discrete and coherent functional organisations. When we locate our human resource manager in the context of this swarming vitality and turmoil the prospects for the rational implementation and administration of job redesign seem a little bleak, to say the least. However, what we do recover from this analysis is a sense of the complexity of organisational life; its trials and tribulations; the frustration of sub-verted and aborted plans; a world of interrupted meetings and the hastily prepared management report left unread and filed for future reference; the arguments and con-fusions of daily organisational life. It restores that paradoxical sense we have of boredom and fascination that, in equal measure, seem to co-mingle and combine to generate the peculiar miracle of organisation. It's enough to set you off in a search for that Kalashnikov.

SUMMARY

- The word and concept of 'job' is complex and ambiguous.

- The concept and practice of 'design' is multi-faceted and confusing.

- Issues of power, control and inequality are inextricably related to the practice of 'job design'. The practice of job design is therefore subject to interpretation, regulation and disagreement that renders 'organisation' precarious and at times unstable.

- Conflict and disorder are an ever-present feature of job design. These phenomena can be manifest, or latent and repressed – operating both within social relations and the individual psyche. The connections between these two sectors is usually considered the domain of social psychology.

- HRM is having a major impact on the sphere of resonsiblity and the content of jobs. We have tried to suggest that HRM is caught between contradictory demands or pres-sures. On the one hand, the practice of HRM is the 'object upon which' design is ultimately being directed. On the other, HRM is the subject that tries to indicate and exercise job design.

- The future of job design may well be one where both the terms 'job' and 'design' dis-appear. In some cases we might see the disappearance of the 'human' replaced by complex assemblages of man–machine hybrids. HRM is complicit with these historical tendencies, but may well turn out to be as much victim as perpetrator of those changes.

Activity Imagine that your group represents the large personnel department of a car manufacturing company. The research department has recently passed on the research and results of the 'Affluent Workers' study by John Goldthorpe and his colleagues. Senior management within the company feel that this research largely debunks the notion and validity of job redesign, which, as a department, you have been actively sponsoring as part of your overall philosophy that good job design is fundamental to the success of the company. For many years you have been encouraging senior management to consider the possibilities of restructuring jobs as a means of reducing turnover, increasing commit-ment and morale, and generally improving the climate of employee relations.

Divide the group into three specialist working parties. Group A is required to prepare and present a short summary of the research and results of the Affluent Workers study, paying particular attention to its strengths and merits as a piece of academic research with important practical implications for companies such as yours. Group B is to critically evaluate the Goldthorpe study, drawing attention to its defects, oversights and methodological weaknesses. Group C is requested to adjudicate between Group A and B by presenting a short summary of the strengths and weaknesses of the Affluent Workers study, concluding by drawing together what appears to be the long-term impact of this study for the approach taken to job design by your department.

QUESTIONS

1 Outline and define what is meant by a structuralist approach to job design and theory in contrast to an agency approach.

2 In what ways did Taylorism seek to 'degrade' workers?

3 In what ways may employees resist and/or consent to the deskilled nature of many of the jobs designed by Taylor and his methods of scientific management?

4 Do you think 'Taylorism' is justified in its claim to be a science? What is scientific about scientific management?

5 How might an 'essentialist' view of human nature lead one to the conclusion that job redesign is necessary?

6 What is meant by alienation and how does it differ from anomie?

7 Define what is meant by determinism in respect to job design. In what ways could it be suggested that theories of the post-Fordist worker are deterministic?

8 How may developments in the European Union actually promote UK companies to seek the redesign of their jobs?

9 How far are the claimed moves away from Fordism to do with technology and product markets in comparison to enlightened managerialism?

EXERCISES

1 Consider any recent employment you may have had, and list all the positive sides of the job that you particularly enjoyed and found rewarding. Then list all the negative aspects of the job, and the reasons why you found them tedious, repetitive or monotonous.

2 What would you like in an ideal job in the situation you have outlined above? Consider how realistic your ambitions for this job may be. For example, it may well be that what seems rational and ideal to you may seem impossible operationally for production and line managers.

3 Then prepare a report for personnel outlining the assumed benefits of job redesign and the importance both for employees and the organisation of restructuring jobs and responsibilities more in tune with the philosophy of human resource management.

4 Consider the validity of the reasons that are suggested for the assertion that workers 'learn to enjoy' monotony in their jobs.

5 As a member of a head office personnel department in a large British bank you have been asked to consider the recent work of David Collinson and David Knights. Prepare a brief report with the

help of three of your colleagues outlining the theoretical approach adopted by Collinson and Knights, and the results they obtained. Present this report with the help of visual aids so that as a group your personnel department can quickly digest the information so that they can consider and reflect on the impact the work of Collinson and Knights is likely to have in your approach to job design. The rest of the personnel department is largely suspicious of the approach taken in the work of Collinson and Knights, and have come prepared to give the group a hard time in what it is hoped will be a lively and stimulating debate.

6 Imagine that your group represents a highly successful firm of management consultants. Divide the group into three working parties. Group A has recently been sent on a fact-finding mission to Germany, where they have discovered that the approach taken to job design in medium-sized engineering firms is far more progressive and advanced than typically found in similar-sized UK firms. On your return you are asked to present a summary of your findings. Critically reflect on the reasons why management appear to be more proactive in job design initiatives and more successful in the outcomes they achieve.

Group B has been sent on a similar tour of French banks, where, among other things, it has been discovered that individual employees do not appear to spend the vast majority of their time specialised in the dedication to one task. Present your findings to the group, outlining the distinctiveness of French job design programmes.

Group C has been requested to reflect on the lessons for British management that the work of groups A and B seems to suggest. In your terms of reference you have been asked to delineate between what British management can do within British organisations and the limitations they face within the context of a different political and economic structure.

Consider the role that governments play in facilitating job design initiatives.

CASE STUDY

Divine model for the seven work commandments

A guru of job design and organisation has revealed an unexpected source of inspiration for succesful theories, writes **Steven Overell**

Secular success has come to Christian Schumacher in prodigious quantities. After arriving daunted and unqualified in the job of manpower research officer at the British Steel Corporation in the early 1970s, he embarked on a feverish stint studying job design and work organisation. From this he forged seven principles of how work should be organised and set about putting them into practice at vast steel plants during the 1970s industrial boom.

For the next 25 years, word of mouth alone propelled him on a tour of ailing factories across blue-chip Britain. He took in Philips, Imperial Chemical Industries, Unilever, Courage and Pilkington Glass. More recently he has extended his work to central government, health authorities and zoos.

What he saw everywhere dismayed him. People did tiny, mindless tasks, alienated and de-humanised –

what he soon learned to call 'deformed' work. It was inefficient, destructive and unsustainable.

Instead, he said, work should be based around a fundamental transformation in the product, so that people could see the results of their labour, so that it formed a 'whole' task. Workers should be organised into small groups with several different roles, with a leader taking responsibility for the team. The teams should be able to 'plan, do and evaluate' their own work, and participation in the wider organisation should be encouraged.

As invitations to install his new regime flooded in, he checked to measure and verify with the true empiricist's devotion.

The hard measures were impressive: plant efficiency, on-time deliveries, faults per unit. So too were the softer ones: fewer industrial troubles, lower absenteeism, better motivation. Best of all were the anecdotes: people were less bored, a sense of thoroughness and responsibility pervaded, natural leaders gradually emerged. Work organisation, he reflected, had the power to make people more sensitive to one another. Unlike so many management consultants, Mr Schumacher's ideas created no losers. They have brought him great success, made him one of the best-known work structure specialists and forced him to take on seven more consultants to his company, Work Structure Limited.

And yet all this is really only the froth of his story. For Mr Schumacher had a secret, to which only his wife and a few trusted friends were party: the real source of his inspiration.

His ideas about the best way to organise work came from long and profound reflection on the Christian Trinity: God, as embodied in the Father, Son and Holy Spirit. His principles of job design were arrived at through 'a synthesis of theology and science'.

This revelation in his book *God in Work* has left him, he says, 'expecting mockery, but hoping for a serious debate about the role of theology – at least among the religious'. Had his clients known his source, one wonders, would Mr Schumacher have been such a success? Is he even guilty of a metaphysical hoax? He does not think so. 'The point is that my ideas work,' he says, 'not necessarily where they come from. Their source is obviously very important to me, but it is not to my clients.'

As he remarks in his book: 'There is no need to make explicit their (the ideas') theological antecedents any more than a doctor has to go through the theory of penicillin to a patient infected with a disease-causing bacterium.'

A book about theology and management is probably many people's idea of a literary felony, a cocktail of abstracts that do not belong together.

Mr Schumacher's book is nothing of the kind. Written in the style of a personal odyssey towards his conclusions, it is clearly the product of a well-organised mind, comprising a consistently argued attempt to answer the age-old question of how Christians are to interact with the world. It is almost certainly the first to splice the wisdom of Saints Augustine and Bonaventure with that of the twitchiest American organisational psychologists.

Mr Schumacher argues that the Trinity contains the functions of God towards His creation, which broadly corresponds to planning, doing and evaluat-ing. The closer human beings can get to 'this divine exemplar', the better the result would be as 'good processes lead to good outcomes'.

God's relation to His 'work' would then be balanced by mankind's relation to work. Thus workers should 'plan, do and evaluate' as much of their work as is feasible. 'I honestly think,' he says, 'that many of the evils apparent in our society are rooted in job design – the loss of ownership, the task fragmentation, the de-skilling, the rendering of work psychologically meaningless to the worker.

'So when people see the results of my work reorganisation, they are always impressed by the compelling logic of the principles. If they asked, I could tell them the reason for that is that the relations they embody in the workplace are the same as the relations that exist in the Creator.'

Mr Schumacher – son of the late guru E.F. Schumacher of *Small is Beautiful* fame – describes himself as a 'very orthodox' member of the Church of England, and is anxious that no one think him 'fanatical or extreme'. He concedes that it is possible to stare at models of the Trinity and find all manner of distorted, sophistic reflections gawping back, but points out that the texts he has most relied on are those of the Medieval Church Fathers and that the theology is 'very mainstream'. It is the application that is radical.

The inspiration for Mr Schumacher's success in work organisation has not been heralded as a theological breakthrough. For six years he served on the snappily titled Industrial Committee of the Board of Social Responsibility of the Church of England, only to leave frustrated by colleagues' refusal to carry their belief beyond the level of individual consciousness and into the dimension of structures and systems. Mr Schumacher wanted to use theology directly as a model in that most worldly of worlds, business.

'The answers are actually there,' he says, 'but they have been overlooked because science and theology have drifted too far apart. Theology was once called the queen of the sciences.'

In contrast to the word of mouth that powered him through industry, interest in *God in Work* has been, he says, 'deep, but not wide. I may be wrong, of course, but my work is about synthesis and one part cannot be understood without the other.'

Source: *Financial Times*, 29 December 1999). Copyright © The Financial Times Limited. *God In Work*, Lion Books, 1999.

1 How important is the quest for 'meaning' in work organisations?

2 Discuss some of the theoretical sources that Schumacher draws upon to develop his ideas.

3 In the light of your reading in job design theory, what do you think of the likely success of this project? What are some of the obstacles that management may face if they try to introduce such a scheme?

REFERENCES AND FURTHER READING

Those texts marked with an asterisk are particularly recommended for further reading.

Aglietta, M. (1976) *A Theory of Capitalist Regulation: The US Experience.* London: Verso (English trans. 1979).

Armstrong, M. (1992) *Human Resource Management: Strategy and Action.* London: Kogan Page.

Atkinson, J. (1984) 'Manpower strategies for flexible organizations', *Personnel Management,* Vol. 16, No. 8, pp. 18–31.

Atkinson, J. and Meager, N. (1986) 'Is flexibility just a flash in the pan?', *Personnel Management,* September.

Austrin, T. (1991) 'Flexibility, surveillance and hype in New Zealand financial retailing', *Work, Employment and Society,* Vol. 5, No. 2, pp. 201–221.

Badham, R. and Mathews, J. (1989) 'The new production systems debate', *Labour and Industry,* Vol. 2, No. 2, pp. 194–246.

Barker, J.R. (1993) 'Tightening the iron cage: concertive control in self managed teams', *Administrative Science Quarterly,* Vol. 38, No. 3, pp. 408–437.

Batstone, E. (1984) *Working Order.* Oxford: Blackwell.

Bauman, Z. (1995) *Life in Fragments.* Oxford: Blackwell.

Betsky, A. (1990) *Violated Perfection: Fragmentation in Modern Architecture.* New York: Rizzoli International Publications, Inc.

Blauner, R. (1964) *Alienation and Freedom.* Chicago: University of Chicago Press.

Boyer, R. (ed.) (1988) *The Search for Labour Market Flexibility: The European Economies in Transition.* Oxford: Clarendon Press.

*Braverman, H. (1974) *Labor and Monopoly Capital.* New York: Monthly Review Press.

*Buchanan, D. (1989) 'Principles and practice in work design', in Sisson, K. (ed.) *Personnel Management in Britain.* Oxford: Blackwell.

Buchanan, D. (1992) 'High performance: new boundaries of acceptability in worker control', in Salaman, G. (ed.) *Human Resource Strategies.* London: Sage.

Buchanan, D. (1994) 'Principles and practices in work design', in Sisson, K. (ed.) *Personnel Management: A Comprehensive Guide to Theory and Practice in Britain.* Oxford: Blackwell.

Burawoy, M. (1979) *Manufacturing Consent.* Chicago: University of Chicago Press.

Burawoy, M. (1985) *The Politics of Production.* London: Verso.

Burrell, G. (1992) 'The organisation of pleasure', in Alvesson, M. and Willmott, H. (eds) *Critical Management Studies.* London: Sage.

Burrell, G. (1997) *Pandemonium: Towards a Retro-Organization Theory.* London: Sage

Burrell, G. (1995) 'Normal Science Paradigms, Metaphors, Discources and Geneologies of Analysis', in Clegg, S. Hardy, C. and Walter, R. Nord (eds) *Handbook of Organization Studies.* London: Sage.

Callon, M. (1986) 'Some elements of a sociology of translation: domestification of the scallops and fishermen of St Brieuc Bay', in Law, J. (ed.) *Power, Action and Belief: A New Sociology of Knowledge?.* London: Routledge & Kegan Paul.

Camus, A. (1961) *The Outsider.* London: Penguin.

Casey, C. (1995) *Work, Self and Society: After Industrialism.* London: Routledge.

Clawson, D. (1980) *Bureaucracy and the Labour Process: The Transformation of US Industry, 1860–1920.* New York and London: Monthly Review Press.

Cohen, S. and Taylor, L. (1992) *Escape Attempts: The Theory and Practice of Resistance to Everyday Life.* London: Routledge.

Collinson, D. (1992) *Managing the Shopfloor: Subjectivity, Masculinity and Workplace Culture.* Berlin: Walter de Gruyter.

Collinson, D. and Knights, D. (1986) 'Men only: theories and practices of job segregation in insurance', in Knights, D. and Willmott, H. (eds) *Gender and the Labour Process.* Aldershot: Gower.

Cooper, R. and Law, J. (1995) 'Organization: distal and proximal views', *Research in the Sociology of Organizations,* Vol. 13, pp. 237–274.

Corbett, M. (1994) *Critical Cases in Organizational Behaviour.* London: Macmillan Business.

Corbett, M. (1995) 'Celluloid projections: images of technology and organizational futures in contemporary science fiction film', *Organization,* Vol. 2, No. 3/4.

Corbett, M. (1997) 'Designing jobs with advanced manufacturing technology: the negotiation of expertise', in Scarbrough, H. (ed.) *The Management of Expertise.* London: Macmillan Business.

Coupland, D. (1992) *Generation X; Tales for an Accelerated Culture.* New York: St Martin's Press.

Cross, M. (1990) *Changing Job Structures: Techniques for the Design of New Jobs and Organisations.* Oxford: Heinemann Newnes.

Davenport, T.H. and Short, J.E. (1990) 'The new industrial engineering: information technology and business process redesign', *Sloan Management Review,* Summer, pp. 11–27.

Deal, T. and Kennedy, A. (1982) *Corporate Cultures: The Rites and Rituals of Corporate Life.* New York: Addison Wesley.

Deming, W. (1986) *Out of Crisis.* Cambridge: Cambridge University Press.

Du Gay, P. and Salaman, G. (1994) 'The conduct of management and the management of conduct: contemporary managerial disclosure and the constitution of the "competent' manager", Making up Managers Working Papers Series, No. 1, The Open University.

Durkheim, E. (1984) *The Division of Labour in Society.* London: Macmillan.

Edwards, P. (1986) *Conflict at Work: A Materialist Analysis of Workplace Relations.* Oxford: Blackwell.

Elger, T. (1990) 'Technical innovation and work reorganisation in British manufacturing in the 1980s: continuity, intensification or transformation?', *Work, Employment and Society,* Special Issue, pp. 67–101.

Farmbrough, H. (1996) 'Man's journey desk into space', *Voyager,* March/April, pp. 30–36.

Featherstone, M. (1991) *Consumer Culture and Postmodernism.* London: Sage.

Featherstone, M. (ed.) (1988) *Postmodernism.* London: Sage.

Featherstone, M. and Burrows, R. (eds) (1995) *Cyberspace, Cyberbodies, Cyberpunk.* London: Sage.

Fineman, S. (ed.) (1993) *Emotion in Organizations*. London: Sage.

Fox, A. (1974) *Beyond Contract*. London: Faber.

Friedman, A. (1977) *Industry and Labour*. London: Macmillan.

Friedman, A. (1990) 'Managerial strategies, activities, techniques and technology: towards a complex theory of the labour process', in Knights, D. and Willmott, H. (eds) *Labour Process Theory*. London: Macmillan.

Fromm, E. (1991) *The Fear of Freedom*. London: Routledge & Kegan Paul.

Gabriel, Y. (1995) 'The unmanaged organization: stories, fantasies and subjectivity', *Organization Studies*, vol. 16, No. 3, pp. 477–501.

Gibson, W. (1984) *Neuromancer*. London: Victor Gollancz.

Giddens, A. (1991) *Modernity and Self Identity*. Cambridge: Polity Press.

Gilbert, N., Burrows, R. and Pollert, A. (1992) *Fordism and Flexibility: Divisions and Change*. London: Macmillan.

Goldthorpe, J.H., Lockwood, D., Bechhofer, F. and Platt, J. (1968) *The Affluent Worker: Industrial Attitudes and Behaviour*. Cambridge: Cambridge University Press.

Gray, C. H. (ed.) (1995) *The Cyborg Handbook*, London: Routledge.

Grey, C. and Mitev, N (1995) 'Management education: a polemic', *Management Learning*, Vol. 26, No. 1: pp.73–90.

Grint, K. (1995) *Management: A Sociological Introduction*. Cambridge: Polity Press.

Hackman, J.R. and Lawler, E.E. (1971) 'Employee reactions to job characteristics', *Journal of Applied Psychology*, Vol. 55, pp. 259–286.

Hackman, J.R. and Oldham, G.R. (1976) 'Motivation through the design of work: test of a theory', *Organisational Behaviour and Human Performance*, Vol. 16, pp. 250–279.

Hammer, M. (1990) 'Reengineering work: don't automate, obliterate', *Harvard Business Review*, July–August, pp. 104–112.

Hammer, M. and Champy, J. (1993) *Reengineering the Corporation: A Manifesto for Business Revolution*. London: Nicholas Brealey.

Haraway, D. (1985) 'A manifesto for cyborgs: science, technology and socialist feminism in the 1980s', *Socialist Review*, No. 80, pp. 65–107.

Hedberg, B., Dahlgren, G., Hansson, J. and Olve, N.-G. (1994) *Virtual Organization and Beyond: Discover Imaginary Systems*. Chichester: John Wiley.

Heidegger, M. (1977) *The Question Concerning Technology and Other Essays*. New York: Harper & Row.

Hendry, C. (1990) 'New technology, new careers: the impact of company employment policy', *New Technology, Work and Employment*, Vol. 5, No. 1, Spring, pp. 31–43.

Hirschorn, L. (1984) *Beyond Mechanisation*. Cambridge, Mass.: MIT Press.

Hirst, J. and Zeitlin, J. (1991) 'Flexible specialization versus post-Fordism: theory, evidence and policy implications', *Economy and Society*, Vol. 20, No. 1, pp. 1–55.

Hochschild, A. (1983) *The Managed Heart: Commercialization of Human Feeling*. Berkeley, Cal.: University of California Press.

Hopfl, H. and Linstead, S. (1993) 'Passion and performance: suffering and the carrying of organizational roles', in Fineman, S. (ed.) *Emotion in Organizations*. London: Sage.

Hyman, R. (1987) 'Strategy of structure: capital, labour and control', *Work, Employment and Society*, Vol. 1, No. 1, pp. 25–55.

Iles, P. and Salaman, G. (1995) 'Recruitment, selection and assessment', in Storey, J. (ed.) *Human Resource Management: A Critical Text*. London: Routledge.

Industrial Relations Services (1995a) 'Customer service drive at BT', *Employment Trends*, 579.

Industrial Relations Services (1995b) 'Putting the customer first: organisational change at WH Smith', *Employment Trends*, 596.

Information Technology Skills Shortage Committee (1985) *Second Report: Changing Technology, Changing Skills*. London: Department of Trade and Industry.

Institute of Manpower Studies (1984) *Competence and Competition: Training and Education in the FRG*, Report for NEDO and the MSC. London: IMS.

Jackall, R. (1988) *Moral Mazes: The World of Corporate Managers*. New York: Oxford University Press.

James, G. (1992) 'Quality of working life and total quality management', *International Journal of Manpower*, Vol. 13, No. 1, pp. 41–58.

Jameson, F. (1991) *Postmodernism or the Cultural Logic of Late Capitalism*. London: Verso

Jencks, C. (1987) *Postmodernism*. London: Academy Editions; New York: Rizzoli International Publications.

Kakar, S. (1970) *Frederick Taylor: A Study in Personality and Innovation*. Cambridge, Mass.: MIT Press.

Kallinikos, J. (1996) 'Mapping the intellectual terrain of management education', in French, R. and Grey, C. (eds) *Rethinking Management Education*. London: Sage.

Kelly, J. (1985) 'Management's redesign of work: labour process, labour markets and products markets', in Knights, D. *et al.* (eds) *Job Redesign: Critical Perspectives on the Labour Process*. Aldershot: Gower.

Kern, H. and Schumann, M. (1987) 'Limits of the division of labour: new production and employment concepts in West German industry', *Economic and Industrial Democracy*, No. 8, pp. 51–71.

Knights, D. (1990) 'Subjectivity, power and the labour process', in Knights, D. and Willmott, H. (eds) *Labour Process Theory*. London: Macmillan.

Knights, D. and Willmott, H. (1989) 'Power and subjectivity at work: from degradation to subjugation in social relations', *Sociology*, Vol. 23, No. 4, pp. 535–558.

Knights, D. and Willmott, H. (eds) (1990) *Labour Process Theory*. London: Macmillan.

*Knights, D., Willmott, H. and Collinson, D. (eds.) (1985) *Job Redesign: Critical Perspectives on the Labour Process*. Aldershot: Gower.

Kondo, D. (1991) *Crafting Selves: Power, Gender, and Discourses of Identity in a Japanese Workplace*. London: University of Chicago Press.

Lane, C. (1989) *Management and Labour in Europe*. Aldershot: Edward Elgar.

Lash, S. and Urry, J. (1987) *The End of Organized Capitalism*. London: Sage.

Lash, S. and Urry, J. (1994) *Economies of Signs and Space*. London: Sage.

Latour, B. (1987) *Science in Action*. Milton Keynes: Open University Press.

Latour, B. (1993) *We Have Never Been Modern*. London: Havester Wheatsheaf.

Law, J. (ed.) (1991) *A Sociology of Monsters? Essays on Power, Technology and Domination,* Sociological Review Monograph 38. London: Routledge.

Legge, K. (1995) *Human Resource Management: Rhetorics and Realities*. Basingstoke: Macmillan.

Lipietz, A. (1987) *Mirages and Miracles: The Crisis of Global Fordism*. London: Verso.

Littler, C. (1982) *The Development of the Labour Process in Capitalist Society*. London: Heinemann.

Littler, C. (1985) 'Taylorism, Fordism and job design', in Knights, D. *et al.* (eds) *Job Redesign: Critical Perspectives on the Labour Process*. Aldershot: Gower.

Littler, C. and Salaman, G. (1984) *Class at Work: The Design, Allocation and Control of Jobs*. London: Batsford.

Lovering, J. (1990) 'A perfunctory sort of post-Fordism: economic restructuring and the labour market segmentation in Britain in the 1980s', *Work, Employment and Society*, May, Special Issue, pp. 9–28.

Lynn-Meek, V. (1992) 'Organisational culture', in Salaman, G. *et al.* (eds) *Human Resource Strategies*. London: Sage.

Marcuse, H. (1964) *One-Dimensional Man*. London: Routledge & Kegan Paul.

Marginson, P. (1989) 'Employment flexibility in large companies: change and continuity', *Industrial Relations Journal*, Summer, No. 20.

Maslow, A.H. (1943) 'A theory of human motivation', *Psychological Review*, No. 50, pp. 370–396.

Maslow, A.H. (1954) *Motivation and Human Personality*. New York: Harper & Row.

Mayo, E. (1949) *The Social Problems of an Industrial Civilisation*. London: Routledge & Kegan Paul.

Mintzberg, H. (1978) 'Patterns in strategy formation', *Management Science*, Vol. 24, No. 9, pp. 934–948.

Murray, R. (1985) 'Benetton Britain', *Marxism Today*, September.

Nichols, T. (ed.) (1980) *Capital and Labour*. Glasgow: Fontana.

O'Doherty, D. (1994) 'Institutional withdrawal? Anxiety and conflict in the emerging banking labour process or "How to get out of it"', *Paper to the 12th Annual International Labour Process Conference*, Aston University.

Peters, T. (1994) *The Tom Peters Seminar: Crazy Times Call for Crazy Organizations*. London: Macmillan.

*Peters, T.J. and Waterman, R.H. (1982) *In Search of Excellence: Lessons from America's Best Run Companies*. New York: Harper & Row.

Piore, M. and Sabel, C. (1984) *The Second Industrial Divide: Possibilities for Prosperity*. New York: Basic Books.

Pollert, A. (1988) 'Dismantling flexibility', *Capital and Class*, (34), pp. 42–75.

Pollert, A. (ed.) (1991) *Farewell to Flexibility?* Oxford: Blackwell.

Reich, R.B. (1983) 'A structuralist account of political culture', *Administrative Science Quarterly*, Vol. 28, pp. 414–437.

Ritzer, G. (1993) *The McDonaldization of Society*, Newbury Park, Cal.: Pine Forge Press.

Roethlisberger, F.G. and Dickson, W.J. (1939) *Management and the Worker*. Cambridge, Mass.: Harvard University Press.

Schein, E.H. (1965) *Organizational Psychology*. Englewood Cliffs, NJ: Prentice Hall.

Schein, E.H. (1985) *Organizational Culture and Leadership*. San Francisco: Jossey-Bass.

Schumacher, C. (1999) *God in Work*. Lion Books: London.

Shaiken, H., Herzenberg, S. and Kahn, S. (1986) 'The work process under flexible production', *Industrial Relations*, Vol. 25.

Silverman, D. (1993) *Interpreting Qualitative Data: Methods for Analysing Talk, Text and Interaction*. London: Sage

Smart, B. (1993) *Postmodernity*. London: Routledge.

Smith, A. (1982) *The Wealth of Nations*. Harmondsworth: Penguin.

Smith, C. (1989) 'Flexible specialisation, automation and mass production', *Work, Employment and Society*, Vol. 3, No. 2, pp. 203–220.

Storey, J. (1983) *Managerial Prerogative and the Question of Control*. London: Routledge & Kegan Paul.

Storey, J. (1992) *Developments in the Management of Human Resources*. Oxford: Blackwell.

Thompson, P. (1989) *The Nature of Work*. London: Macmillan.

*Trist, E.L. and Bamforth, K.W. (1951) 'Some social and psychological consequences of the Longwall method of coal-getting', *Human Relations*, Vol. 4, No. 1, pp. 3–38.

Trist, E.L., Higgin, G.W., Murray, H. and Pollock, A.B. (1963) *Organisational Choice*. London: Tavistock.

Venturi, R., Scott-Brown, D. and Izenour, S. (1972) *Learning from Las Vegas*. Cambridge, Mass: Institute of Technology, MIT Press.

Walton, R.E. (1985) 'From control to commitment in the workplace', *Harvard Business Review*, No. 63, March/April, pp. 76–84.

Warhurst, C. and Thompson, P. (eds) (1998) *Workplaces of the Future*. London: Macmillan Business.

Watson, T. (1987) *Sociology, Work and Industry*. London: Routledge & Kegan Paul.

Watson, T. (1994) *In Search of Management: Culture, Chaos and Control in Managerial Work*. London: Routledge.

Weber, M. (1964) *The Theory of Social and Economic Organization*. New York: Free Press.

Weber, M. (1965) *The Protestant Ethic and the Spirit of Capitalism*, London: Allen & Unwin.

Whittington, R. (1993) *What is Strategy and Does it Matter?* London: Routledge.

Willmott, H. (1990) 'Subjectivity and the dialectics of praxis: opening up the core of labour process analysis', in Knights, D. and Willmott, H. (eds) *Labour Process Theory*. London: Macmillan.

Willmott, H. (1993) 'Strength is ignorance; slavery is freedom: managing culture in modern organisations', *Journal of Management Studies*, Vol. 30, No. 5, pp. 515–552.

Willmott, H. (1995) 'The odd couple? Reengineering business process, managing human resources'. *Mimeo, Manchester School of Management*, UMIST.

Wood, S. (ed.) (1982) *The Degradation of Work: Skill, Deskilling and the Labour Process*. London: Hutchinson.

Wood, S. and Kelly J. (1982) 'Taylorism, responsible autonomy and management strategy', in Wood, S. (ed.) *The Degradation of Work: Skill, Deskilling and the Labour Process*. London: Hutchinson.

Woolgar, S. (1991) 'Configuring the user: the case of usability trials', in Law, J. (ed.) *A Sociology of Monsters: Essays on Power, Technology and Domination*. London: Routledge.

Recruitment and selection

Julie Storey and Mary Wright

OBJECTIVES

- To explore the external context in which recruitment and selection occurs.
- To examine recent developments in the systematic approach to recruitment and selection.
- To consider the effectiveness of recruitment and selection practices.
- To consider the impact of internal organisational factors on recruitment and selection.

INTRODUCTION

There can be few more important decisions made in the life of an organisation than ensuring the selection of the right people to join the workforce (IRS, 1999a). This has become particularly apparent with the growing emphasis on people as the prime source of competitive advantage, an idea that underpins much of the HRM literature. In the early 1990s, Beaumont (1993) identified three themes that appear to have enhanced the potential importance of the selection decision in individual organisations in the current operating environment' (p. 56), and which are still relevant at the start of a new century. First, demographic trends and changes in the labour market have led to a 'less homogeneous workforce', which has placed increasing pressure on the notion of fairness in selection. Second, the desire for a multi-skilled, flexible workforce and an increased emphasis on teamworking has meant that selection decisions are concerned more with behaviour and attitudes than with matching individuals to immediate job requirements. And third, the link between corporate strategy and HRM has led to the notion of strategic selection: that is, a system that links selection to the overall organisational strategy, and which aims to match the flow of personnel to emerging business strategies.

The contribution of effective recruitment and selection to enhanced business performance is also illustrated by the findings of empirical studies. For example, a recent study into small and medium-sized manufacturing establishments (Patterson *et al.*, 1997) found that the acquisition and development of employee skills through the use of sophisticated selection, induction, training and appraisals has a positive impact on company productivity and profitability. Thus the practice of recruitment and selection is increasingly important from an HRM perspective.

At the same time, the contemporary context in which organisations operate is challenging the accepted assumptions in recruitment and selection:

> These assumptions tend to have emerged from experiences based on organisation structures that have now passed. The future will involve far more complexity, greater ambiguity, more rapid change and a challenge to the methods that made sense to those managers who constructed the old organisations. This challenge will reduce the meaning and usefulness of traditional methods of recruitment and selection.
>
> (Sparrow and Hiltrop, 1994: 316)

This chapter discusses key contemporary approaches to recruitment and selection, and examines the influence of external and internal factors on the process. After clarifying what we mean by recruitment and selection we begin by describing the external context in which recruitment and selection occur. We then explore the systematic approach to recruitment and selection, and discuss recent developments at each stage of the process. Next, we turn our attention to the internal organisational context in order to examine factors that might account for variations in recruitment and selection practice. In the final section we emphasise the two-way nature of recruitment and selection, and consider ethical issues in the treatment of individuals. The chapter concludes with a summary and a number of self-test exercises.

Definitions

The recruitment and selection process is concerned with identifying, attracting and choosing suitable people to meet an organisation's human resource requirements. They are integrated activities, and 'where recruitment stops and selection begins is a moot point' (Anderson, 1994). Nevertheless, it is useful to try to differentiate between the two areas: Whitehill (1991) describes the recruitment process as a positive one, 'building a roster of potentially qualified applicants', as opposed to the 'negative' process of selection. So a useful definition of recruitment is 'searching for and obtaining potential job candidates in sufficient numbers and quality so that the organisation can select the most appropriate people to fill its job needs' (Dowling and Schuler, 1990); whereas selection is concerned more with 'predicting which candidates will make the most appropriate contribution to the organisation – now and in the future' (Hackett, 1991).

THE EXTERNAL CONTEXT

The processes of recruitment and selection take place within a framework of influential external and internal factors. Standardised approaches to recruitment and selection may be suggested by the external influences of relevant legislation and published codes of practice. However, critical dissimilarities in organisational and external contexts make this less likely. The overall context in which human resources are managed is well illustrated in Figure 6.1 (Schuler and Jackson, 1996). This section concentrates on the potential impact on recruitment and selection activities of factors in the external environment. A later section will consider the impact of internal organisational factors.

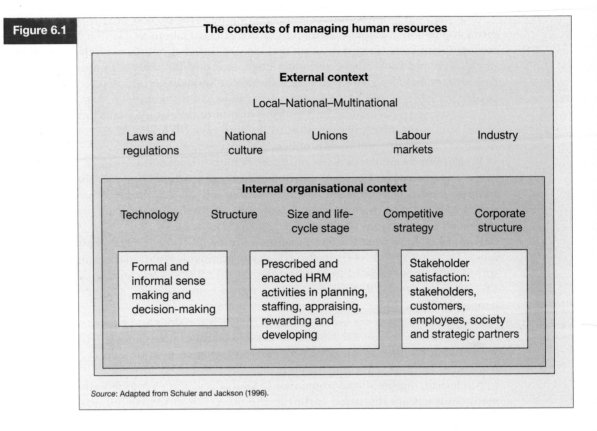

Figure 6.1   **The contexts of managing human resources**

External context

Local–National–Multinational

| Laws and regulations | National culture | Unions | Labour markets | Industry |

Internal organisational context

| Technology | Structure | Size and life-cycle stage | Competitive strategy | Corporate structure |

Formal and informal sense making and decision-making

Prescribed and enacted HRM activities in planning, staffing, appraising, rewarding and developing

Stakeholder satisfaction: stakeholders, customers, employees, society and strategic partners

Source: Adapted from Schuler and Jackson (1996).

External labour market factors

When organisations choose to recruit externally, as opposed to finding suitable candidates within the organisation itself, the search can take place in local, regional, national or international labour markets. The chosen market usually depends on the numbers, skills, competences and experiences required and the potential financial costs and benefits involved to the organisation concerned. External labour markets vary considerably in size, as Table 6.1 demonstrates.

Table 6.1 National comparisons of economically active populations 1998

Country	Million	Country	Million
China	710	South Korea	22
United States	137	Canada	15
Japan	68	Australia	9
Mexico	39	Sweden	4[a]
Germany	40[a]	Brazil	71
France	26[a]	Nigeria	45
Great Britain	28[a]	Indonesia	92

[a] Indicates 1997 figures
Source: Euromonitor plc (1999, 2000).

Both the population within a certain geographical region and the proportion of that given population available to form part of the external labour market vary considerably. Factors to consider when recruiting include age distribution, particularly the numbers of children and those above retirement age, and possible daily commuting distances. Age profiles may also give a potential indicator of 'trainees' as opposed to 'experienced' people available, as well as the proportion of those close to retirement age. Students are now considered a permanent and growing section of the nation's workforce (illustrated by De Montfort University's decision to set up its own 'WorkBank' to help students to find part-time work), and their numbers should also be considered.

Breakdown by gender is also important. A high proportion of women in the labour market might suggest a higher proportion of people seeking part-time or 'family friendly' contracts as opposed to inflexible and/or full-time hours. Women represent nearly half of those in employment, with 42% of them working part time to fill over 80% of all part-time jobs (Cully *et al.*, 1999: 25, 32).

Rates of unemployment affect the number of people potentially available for recruitment. Unemployment levels in the UK were running at a national average of 5.1% in spring 1999, ranging from the highest figure of 12.9% in Cleveland to Surrey at 1.8% (*Social Trends* 2000). Within this overall figure young people, disabled people and people aged over 50 have higher rates of unemployment.

The composition of the labour force, particularly the skills and experiences available, is as important as its size. Organisations need to consider how many potential applicants are available within a given labour market, and what competition an organisation has from other employers hunting within it.

Numerical, temporal and functional flexibility and the changing nature of employment contracts are discussed earlier in the book. Of particular interest here are the growth of recruitment to part-time jobs (which represent a quarter of employment generally in the UK), the growing incidence of employees on fixed-term contracts, and the widespread subcontracting of one or more services. Cully *et al.* (1999) found growth in teamworking, including the establishment of semi-autonomous teams.

National approaches to education, training and skills development

The availability of required skills and competences is influenced by the range and quality of learning experiences available to individuals within that market. Table 6.2 suggests that illiteracy levels still block potential skills development in the labour markets of a number of countries.

Similarly the number of young people remaining in full-time compulsory education in European countries varies considerably, as Table 6.3 demonstrates. Again, take-up of higher education limits the extent to which labour markets can become equipped with the higher-level skills required in contemporary society.

Within the UK there has been a long-standing debate about the relative roles and responsibilities of central and local government, employers and individuals in respect to skills training and qualifications. Historically, reliance has been placed on voluntarist approaches, with employers expected to achieve an adequate level of skill for the nation as a whole, the market supposedly ensuring that such provision is made. The issue of preparing current and future workforces through lifetime learning has resulted in government targets being set for young people and adults. In 1999 it was reported that 75% of 19 year olds, 54% of 21 year olds and 45% of adults had qualifications at NVQ level 3 or equivalent, with 26% of adults possessing NVQ level 4 or equivalent qualifications.

Table 6.2 Adult illiteracy rates (1995) as percentage of population

Country	Male illiteracy rate	Female illiteracy rate
Egypt	36	62
India	34	63
Nigeria	33	53
China	10	27
Turkey	8	28
Brazil	17	17
Indonesia	10	22
Mexico	8	13

Source: Adapted from Anon (1999a: 94), source UNESCO.

Table 6.3 Education/training participation rates 1995 (%)

	Aged 15–19	Aged 20–24
France	93.2	42.5
Germany	93.0	39.1
Ireland	83.7	30.1
Greece	80.0	29.2
Spain	79.1	41.8
UK	71.2[a]	23.6
Luxembourg	38.8	36.5

[a] By 1998 this had risen to 74% (*Social Trends*, 2000)
Source: Adapted from Leat (1998: 247).

Levels of investment and reinvestment in training appear critical, and government initiatives to reduce unemployment levels obviously affect the number of potentially suitable applicants. Contemporary initiatives include 'The New Deal' initially aimed at unemployed young people and now extended to target those over 50. Other initiatives include the expansion of the further education sector by 0.7 million students, the encouragement of life-long learning via the University of Industry, and the introduction of 1 million 'individual learning accounts' for people at work. Major initiatives in information technology and communication technology have also been announced (Twining, 1999).

A lack of appropriate investment can result in severe recruitment problems. Welch (1999a: 13) reports a shortage of talent at board level, and Whitehead (1999a) reports survey results that show that 'nearly three-quarters of companies were suffering severe labour shortages' due to lack of experience and technical skills, and 'one in three employers has faced an "absolute labour shortage", receiving not a single application for an advertised job' (p. 20.)

The degree of economic and other support given by national and regional authorities to the establishment of work opportunities can vary from country to country. The recent attraction of the UK for Asian, particularly Japanese, companies is based partly on the support given by national and regional government and assistance with costs. Fujitsu was one of several multinationals attracted to County Durham in the early 1990s as part of a development programme funded jointly by the European Union and local public interest groups.

Technological developments

A key change affecting organisations over the last five years has been advances in technology, particularly the growth and use of the Internet as a whole and organisation-specific intranets. Information once captured in paper format can now be effectively captured and communicated electronically. Expert systems replace and enhance individual decision-making. Knowledge management is made possible through information-sharing intranet developments, and assists in the quest for organisational competitive advantage.

Within existing organisations the potential for a growth in employment based away from the traditional office environment grows as technology allows individuals to communicate with others and be supervised at a distance. Homeworking and teleworking become possible through the use of email and video conferencing. The potential exists for wide-scale change from traditional classroom-based group learning to individual and ongoing computer-based training and development. Technological developments permit the constant (and sometimes covert) monitoring of employee behaviour.

As jobs are lost in manufacturing (as technological advances replace shopfloor employees with robots), traditional retailing (as a wide range of goods and services become available on the Internet), and the financial sector (as Internet and internal computer systems are introduced to enhance profitability and retain competitiveness), new employment opportunities are found in organisations supporting this technological growth.

These changes have a dramatic impact on the skills required by both existing job-holders and potential applicants and the recruiter has to be able to locate those with the skills or the potential to learn new skills and apply them effectively. Recently there has been a growth in those seeking work and applicants via the Internet, with specially designed expert systems and software having the potential to attract candidates, sift applications on-line and appraise and develop employees across the world.

Government policy and legislation

While organisations have considerable freedom of choice in the type of people they want to recruit, legislation plays a significant role in the recruitment and selection process, particularly in attempts to prevent discrimination on the grounds of sex, race or disability.

Sex and race discrimination

Two Acts are specifically designed to prevent discrimination in employment on the basis of sex or race. The Sex Discrimination Act 1975 makes it unlawful to discriminate against a person directly or indirectly in the field of employment on the grounds of their sex or marital status. The Race Relations Act 1976 makes it unlawful to discriminate against a person in the field of employment on the grounds of their race, colour and nationality, including ethnic or national origin.

Both Acts prohibit direct and indirect discrimination. Direct discrimination occurs when an individual is treated less favourably than another because of their sex, marital status or race. Indirect discrimination occurs when requirements are imposed that are not necessary for the job, and that may disadvantage a significantly larger proportion of one sex or racial group than another.

Although concerned with discrimination in a number of areas of employment, both Acts specifically prohibit discrimination during recruitment and selection. This includes advertisements, selection arrangements, interviews and terms offered as well as the actual offer or refusal of a job. Only the Equal Opportunities Commission or the Commission for Racial Equality can initiate proceedings relating to sex or race discrimination in advertisements, but individuals can complain of discrimination in all other aspects of the process.

Both Acts make it lawful for employers to take positive action to encourage applications from members of one sex or of racial groups who have been under-represented in particular work over the previous 12 months. However, positive discrimination is unlawful, which means that, although advertisements can explicitly encourage applications from one sex or particular racial group, no applicant can be denied information or be discriminated against in selection because they do not fit the 'preferred' category. Sex or race discrimination is permitted only where sex or race is a defined 'genuine occupational qualification' (GOQ). Examples of GOQs include those for models, actors and some personal welfare counsellors.

These Acts have had only limited success in achieving sexual and racial equality. The size of the task was recognised from the outset:

> Nobody believes that legislation by itself can eradicate overnight a whole range of attitudes which are rooted in custom and are, for that very reason, often unchallenged because unrecognised. But if the law cannot change attitudes overnight, it can, and does effect change slowly.
>
> (Select Committee House of Lords, 1972/3)

One could reasonably question whether changes are occurring too slowly. Nearly 30 years on there has been a removal of overt discrimination, particularly in recruitment advertising, but there is less evidence of eradication of discrimination in employment practices generally. National statistics indicate that, at a macro level, very little has changed in the distribution of employment on the grounds of gender or race.

Gender (Thair and Risdon, 1999; EOC Annual Report, 1998):

- 44% of all those of working age in employment are women, up from 42% in 1988.
- 81% of part-time workers are women.
- 53% of women in employment work in occupational groups in which more than 60% of workers are women – clerical/secretarial, service occupations and sales. These groups account for only 19% of employed men.
- 54% of employed men work in occupational groups in which more than 60% of workers are men – managers and administrators, craft and related occupations, plant and machine operatives.
- The average pay of women is 80% of the average pay of men.

Ethnic minorities (IDS, 1997a):

- People from ethnic minorities are two and a half times more likely to be unemployed than the white population. Unemployment among the under 25s averages 32% among ethnic minorities, nearly three times the rate for white youth.
- Unemployment statistics vary widely for different ethnic communities: for example, unemployment ranges from 28% for black males (African, Caribbean and others) to just over 12% for Indian men.
- Cultural diversity is also reflected in varying rates of labour market participation for women. Pakistani and Bangladeshi women have the lowest participation rate at 28% of working-age women compared with 56% for all women from ethnic minorities and 73% for white women.

Part of the problem is that the legislation requires an end to discrimination but 'does not actually require that employers do anything to promote equality' (Dickens, 1994: 275). This situation is now changing with regard to race, at least in the public sector. The Race Relations (Amendment) Bill currently going through Parliament includes a positive duty on public authorities to promote racial equality. Currently, equalising opportunity in employment is still dependent largely on initiatives undertaken voluntarily by organisations such as targeted recruitment, pre-recruitment training or participation in national initiatives such as Opportunity 2000 for women or the CRE's Leadership Challenge for ethnic minorities.

In order to attract more women and members of ethnic minorities, a number of organisations have adopted targeted recruitment through the design of advertisements and the media in which they are featured. Paddison (1990) suggests that job-seekers form a generalised perception of individual organisations and the people they employ, and so the gender and ethnic mix of applicants will tend to reflect the composition of the existing workforce, despite the ubiquitous slogan 'we are an equal opportunities employer'. A number of employers have recognised that this slogan has become less significant with overuse, and can seem particularly meaningless when attached to advertisements that give a different message through the use of male-dominated job titles, (such as 'salesmen'), or of pictures of a predominantly white, able-bodied, male workforce.

Targeted recruitment can go beyond the wording or appearance of advertisements. When Littlewoods opened a new store in Oldham in 1995 they made a special effort to increase the diversity of the workforce by contacting ethnic minority groups, religious groups and youth clubs. As a result the number of applications received was significantly higher than usual, the recruitment costs were lower, and extra sales were generated. 'Littlewoods now recruits in this way for all its new branches and has now improved on the initiative with the introduction of pre-employment training' (Pickard, 1999: 42).

Pre-employment training can help to increase the number of employees from previously under-represented groups, but is used by only a small number of organisations (Dickens, 2000). The idea is based on providing a 'level playing field' for all applicants. For example, the Metropolitan Police introduced a pre-recruitment course designed to increase the number of officers from ethnic minority communities by helping participants to 'compete on an equal basis with other applicants for places at the Met's training school at Hendon, north-west London' (Arkin, 1996: 10). These forms of positive action may be aimed at improving opportunities for previously disadvantaged groups, but they are not without their critics. Kandola (1995) suggests that such measures can be counter-productive because people who are perceived to have gained advantage through positive action are likely to be viewed negatively by others. Further, he states that women and ethnic minorities do not want extra training and help because this 'implies that they are deficient in some way and that consequently they are the problem . . . [when] invariably the problem lies not with the targeted group itself but elsewhere in an organisation's own processes or culture' (p. 20).

The effectiveness of recruitment and selection activities in improving the diversity of the workforce can be measured by monitoring the gender and ethnic origin of applicants and appointments. The results for the fourth Workplace Employee Relations Survey, WERS 4 (Cully et al., 1999), suggest that this does not happen as much as one might expect. Fewer than half of organisations with a formal equal opportunities policy collect statistics on posts held by men and women, or keep employee records with ethnic origin attached, and only a third review selection procedures to identify indirect discrimination.

Disability discrimination

The Disability Discrimination Act (1995) came into force at the end of 1996. The Act defines disability as a physical or mental impairment that has a substantial and long-term adverse effect on a person's ability to carry out normal day-to-day duties, and includes progressive conditions such as cancer and multiple sclerosis. The legislation makes it unlawful for companies with 15 or more employees to treat people with disabilities less favourably than they do others unless they can justify their actions. In addition, employers are required to make 'reasonable adjustment' to the workplace or to working arrangements where this would help to overcome the practical effects of a disability. The requirement for reasonable adjustment includes modifying the recruitment and selection procedure if required: for example, providing application forms in large print or accepting applications by audio tape. The use of testing during the selection process may present a potential problem for people with disabilities, and reasonable adjustments might include modifying test materials, allowing a disabled candidate assistance during a test, or flexibility in the scoring and interpretation of test results (IRS, 1999b).

Discrimination against disabled people has been unlawful only since 1996. Before then legislation relating to the treatment of disabled people at work was primarily to 'secure for the disabled their full share, within their capacity, of such employment as is ordinarily available' rather than preventing discrimination. It is therefore not surprising that disabled people still appear to be disadvantaged in the labour market. National statistics (Sly *et al.*, 1999) reveal that:

- 18% of the working-age population has a current long-term disability or health problem – of these 3.4 million are men and 3.1 million are women;
- 46% of disabled people are in employment compared with 80% of non-disabled people;
- the unemployment rate for disabled people is nearly twice that of non-disabled people of working age.

Discrimination against people with criminal records

People who have a criminal record are also likely to be disadvantaged in the workplace. IPD (1999a: 1) suggests that 'of all things likely to put an employer off, a criminal offence is the worst'. The Rehabilitation of Offenders Act (ROA) 1974 provides protection for certain categories of ex-offenders, as it enables offenders who have received sentences of 30 months or less to have their convictions 'spent'. This means that, after a specified period, they can reply 'no' when asked if they have a criminal record. Although it is unlawful for an employer to discriminate on the grounds of a 'spent' conviction, the candidate who is discriminated against has no individual remedy (IDS, 1992). In addition, a wide range of jobs and professions are exempt from the provisions of this Act, including teachers, social workers, doctors, lawyers and accountants.

Ex-offenders account for over 20% of the UK workforce (IDS, 1992). However, whether their ability to secure employment is based on the effectiveness of the ROA or ignorance on the part of employers remains unclear. At present there is no general obligation to disclose information relating to convictions, so it is up to employers to check if they consider it necessary. Dealing with the employment of people with a criminal record is likely to become a more immediate and overt issue in the near future when access to criminal records will be possible through the Criminal Records Bureau (IPD, 1999a). The establishment of this bureau is part of the 1997 Police Act, and it is expected to be operational by the end of 2000. The Police Act 1997 makes provision for three different levels of criminal record checks and three types of certificate. These are as follows:

- *Criminal Conviction Certificate (CCC)*: issued only to individuals who will be able to choose to show it to employers (or anyone else). A CCC will show all convictions held at national level that are not spent under the ROA.
- *Criminal Record Certificate (CRC)*: available for posts or purposes that are exceptions to the ROA. Groups include those involved regularly with children, young people, the elderly, sick or disabled, administration of the law and other sensitive areas. A CRC will include details of convictions, including spent convictions, and nationally held cautions. An application for a CRC must be countersigned by a registered person.
- *Enhanced Criminal Record Certificate (ECRC)*: available for those applying for positions involving regular care for, training of, supervision or sole charge of young people, for certain statutory licensing purposes and judicial appointments. An ESCR will contain similar information to the CRC and will include local police records, such as relevant non-conviction information. An application for an ESRC must be countersigned by a registered person (IPD, 1999a, pp.2-3)

Age discrimination

There is no legislation prohibiting discrimination on grounds of age, but in 1999 the UK government introduced a code of practice designed to promote age diversity in employment. The government argues that 'to base employment decisions on preconceived ideas about age, rather than on skills and abilities, is to waste the talents of a large part of the population' (DfEE, 1999). A survey commissioned by the Department for Education and Employment (McKay and Middleton, 1998) found that:

- 5% of those aged 45–69 believed they had been discriminated against on age grounds in making job applications;
- a higher proportion of men than women perceived themselves to have been discriminated against on the basis of their age;
- older workers were noticeably less likely than younger workers to have received any employer-paid training.

The code covers six aspects of the employment cycle: recruitment, selection, promotion, training, redundancy and retirement. Specifically in terms of recruitment the code recommends employers to recruit on the basis of skills and abilities necessary to do the job rather than imposing age requirements or making stereotypical judgements based on the age of the applicants. Similarly, for selection the code recommends that employers select on merit by focusing on application form information relating to skills and abilities and on interview performance. The government claims that the elimination of unfair age discrimination will enable businesses to reap a number of benefits including a greater ability to create a more flexible, multi-skilled workforce.

Other government initiatives

Other government policies recently announced by the Labour government, such as the National Childcare Strategy, might also be argued to increase the flexibility of the UK workforce. Family-friendly policies and their extension, work-life policies, are both aimed at increasing flexible options for work, especially attendance patterns. However others, such as the introduction of the National Minimum Wage and the Working Time Directive, could be seen to decrease that flexibility.

Professional codes of practice

The Institute of Personnel and Development has over 100 000 members, and is perceived as the body representing a large number of those involved in the recruitment and selection activities carried out in the UK. Members are expected to follow Institute policy and guidelines, and can in fact lose their membership for major breaches. The key document regulating their behaviour on recruitment and selection is the IPD guide on recruitment (1996). This prescribes expected behaviours in areas that include: policy communication; equality of opportunity; and training in and the use of fair, consistent and valid systems and selection tools. Other codes of practice relating to recruitment and selection are produced by the Equal Opportunities Commission and the Commission for Racial Equality. 'Best practice' is therefore both prescribed and expected.

DEVELOPMENTS IN THE SYSTEMATIC APPROACH TO RECRUITMENT AND SELECTION

Several personnel texts discuss an approach to recruitment and selection based on a systematic analysis of the requirements of an individual job (e.g. Armstrong, 1996; Torrington and Hall, 1995). The key stages of a systematic approach can be summarised as: defining the vacancy, attracting applicants, assessing candidates, and making the final decision. Another way of expressing this is as a series of questions:

- Who do we want?
- How can we attract them?
- How can we identify them?
- How do we know we have got it right?

In addition, a supplementary question that is increasingly asked is:

- Who should be involved?

Here we describe the main components of each stage, and indicate ways in which recruitment and selection activities may differ depending on whether an organisation adopts an HRM or a more traditional approach.

Who do we want?

Authorisation

Securing authorisation ensures that the need to start the recruitment process is agreed by management as being compatible with the organisational/departmental objectives: that is, necessary, timely and cost-effective. At the same time, it provides an opportunity to consider options other than recruitment and selection, for example:

- to debate the potential for restructuring workloads/departments and redeploying existing staff;
- to delay or eliminate expenditure on staffing and recruitment budgets.

Neither of these opportunities is risk-free: redeployment of surplus staff may mean that the incoming jobholder is not necessarily the 'best person for the job' and result in management resentment against the system; inadequately thought-through restructuring or short-term cost-saving measures may damage the department and organisation in the long term, as opportunities fail to be exploited for lack of suitable human resources.

HRM approaches emphasise the links to wider organisational strategy and effective human resource planning. Debates at this stage may consider long-term human resource development (HRD) objectives and succession planning alongside the immediate requirement to fill an operational post.

Defining the job and the person

The traditional approach involves writing a comprehensive job description of the job to be filled. This enables the recruiter to know exactly what the purpose, duties and responsibilities of the vacant position will be and its location within the organisation structure. The next step involves drawing up a personnel specification that is based on the job description, and which identifies the personal characteristics required to perform the job adequately. Characteristics are usually described within a framework consisting of a number of broad headings. Two frequently cited frameworks are the seven-point plan (Rodger, 1952) and the five-fold grading system (Munro Fraser, 1954), illustrated in Table 6.4. Both frameworks are somewhat dated now, and some headings can appear to be potentially discriminatory (e.g. physical make-up and circumstances), but nevertheless they continue to form the basis of many person specifications in current use. It is common to differentiate between requirements that are essential to the job and those that are merely desirable.

The person specification is a vital part of the recruitment and selection process as it can form the basis of the recruitment advertisement, it can help determine the most effective selection methods and, if applied correctly, can ensure that selection decisions are based on sound, justifiable criteria. However, the compilation of a person specification needs to be handled with care. Predetermined criteria can contribute to effective recruitment and selection only if full consideration has been given to the necessity and fairness of all the requirements, yet the techniques for translating information about jobs or organisations into personal attributes remain mysterious and ill defined (van

Table 6.4 Personnel specification frameworks

Rodger (1952)	Munro Frazer (1954)
Physical make-up: health, appearance, bearing and speech	Impact on others: physical make-up, appearance, speech and manner
Attainments: education, qualifications, experience	Acquired qualifications: education, vocational training, work experience
General intelligence: intellectual capacity	
Special aptitudes: mechanical, manual dexterity, facility in use of words and figures	Innate abilities: quickness of comprehension and aptitude for learning
Interests: intellectual, practical, constructional, physically active, social, artistic	Motivation: individual goals, consistency and determination in following them up, success rate
Disposition: acceptability, influence over others, steadiness, dependability, self-reliance	Adjustment: emotional stability, ability to stand up to stress and ability to get on with people
Circumstances: any special demands of the job, such as ability to work unsocial hours, travel abroad	

Source: ACAS (1983).

Zwanenberg and Wilkinson, 1993). Preconceived or entrenched attitudes, prejudices and assumptions can lead, consciously or unconsciously, to requirements that are less job-related than aimed at meeting the assumed needs of customers, colleagues or the established culture of the organisation. Examples of this might include insistence on a British education, unnecessary age restrictions, or sex role stereotyping.

Guidelines from the Institute of Personnel and Development state that 'all recruitment episodes should start with a job profile or person specification stating the necessary and desirable criteria for selection' (IPD, 1997a). Survey evidence on the use of job descriptions and person specifications is somewhat mixed. Torrington and Hall (1995) found that 'less than half of personnel departments use job analysis and its products for recruitment and selection, usually because they wish to avoid the close definition and inflexibility that careful specification often implies' (pp. 215–216). In contrast, a recent IRS survey of 111 employers (IRS 1999c) found that 95% of respondents used job descriptions and 98% used person specifications. This discrepancy might be attributable to differences in the composition of the surveys, but might also reflect more recent developments in the construction of job descriptions and person specifications to allow for greater flexibility.

Job descriptions can be perceived as inflexible in a number of ways. For example, there may be a lack of attention to potential changes in the job, or the list of duties and responsibilities may be too constraining, especially where teamworking is introduced. This concentration on 'the job' and its place in a bureaucratic structure may be detrimental to the development of the skills and aptitudes needed for the long-term benefit of the organisation. In response to this, a number of organisations have replaced traditional, highly specific job descriptions with more generic and concise job profiles, which consist of a list of 'bullet points' or accountability statements, and are often limited to one sheet of paper. Greater ambiguity and fluidity of job content reflect the shift from the 'careful delineation of written contracts' associated with a personnel and IR environment towards a 'beyond contract' approach associated with HRM (Storey, 1992).

The recognition that jobs can be subject to frequent change can also reduce the importance of the job description and increase the relative importance of the person specification. This approach has the potential for greater flexibility as it focuses 'more on the qualities of the jobholder and the person's potential suitability for other duties as jobs change' than on the job itself (IRS, 1999c). Findings from the latest Workplace Employee Relations Survey (Cully *et al.*, 1999: 60–61) show that skills, experience and motivation were the most common selection criteria used by employers.

In practice, a combination of the job-oriented and person-oriented approaches may be adopted, in order to recruit people who can not only do the job but also contribute to the wider business goals of the organisation. One way to achieve this is via the use of *competences*. The term has many definitions but most refer to 'the work-related personal attributes, knowledge, experience, skills and values that a person draws on to perform their work well' (Roberts, 1997: 6). Competence-based recruitment and selection involves the identification of a set of competences that are seen as important across the organisation, such as planning and organising, managing relationships, gathering and analysing information, and decision-making. Each competence can then be divided into a number of different levels, and these can be matched to the requirements of a particular job.

These competence frameworks can be used for more than just recruitment and selection. The application of the same competence framework to all areas of HRM can ensure consistency and aid vertical and horizontal integration (for further details on competences and competence frameworks see Whiddett and Hollyforde, 1999). The competence-based approach is frequently seen as being compatible with HRM initiatives such as flexibility, teamworking and multi-skilling: for example, Armstrong (1992) suggests that organisational requirements will include commitment and the ability to work effectively in a team. However, there is also a potentially sinister side to this approach, which may result in cloning or the creation of 'a workforce which would be more receptive to the broad span of HR philosophy' (Storey, 1992: 100).

Agree terms and conditions

Decisions on terms and conditions are made at various points in the process. Some of these are often not negotiated (e.g. hours, reward) until the final selection stages. There is a case for deciding the salary band (if not the specific amount) and other elements of the reward package before attracting candidates. This can take time (for example, if the position has to be processed through a job evaluation exercise), but potential candidates may fail to apply without some indication of the reward offered, as this often gives an indication of the level and status of the position.

The alternative is to wait and see who applies and then negotiate terms and conditions with the favoured candidate. This is a less restrictive approach, and may provide a better chance of employing high-calibre people who match the long-term aims of the organisation. However, the organisation may project a poor image by appearing to be disorganised and unsure of what is on offer. Additionally, the perception that the company is trying to take advantage of a weak labour market and pay 'what they can get away with' may damage its reputation in the long term.

The most appropriate approach is, at least partially, determined by the organisation's reward strategy, including the relative importance of internal pay equity and external competitiveness and the emphasis on individual and collective pay-setting.

How do we attract them?

> the actual channels or vehicles used to attract candidates . . . seem to influence whether the right kinds of applicants are encouraged to apply, and to persist in their application.
>
> (Iles and Salaman, 1995: 211)

Recruitment methods

The most effective recruitment method is one that produces the *best* results in terms of able candidates for the *least* cost (IRS, 1999c). Organisations can choose from a wide variety of methods, including the use of:

- informal personal contacts, such as existing employees, informal grapevine (word of mouth), and speculative applications;
- formal personal contacts, such as careers fairs, open days, and leaflet drops;
- notice boards, accessible by current staff or the general public;
- advertising, including local and national press, specialist publications, radio and TV, and the Internet;
- external assistance, including job centres, careers service, employment agencies, and 'head-hunters'.

The relative popularities of these different methods are shown in Figure 6.2.

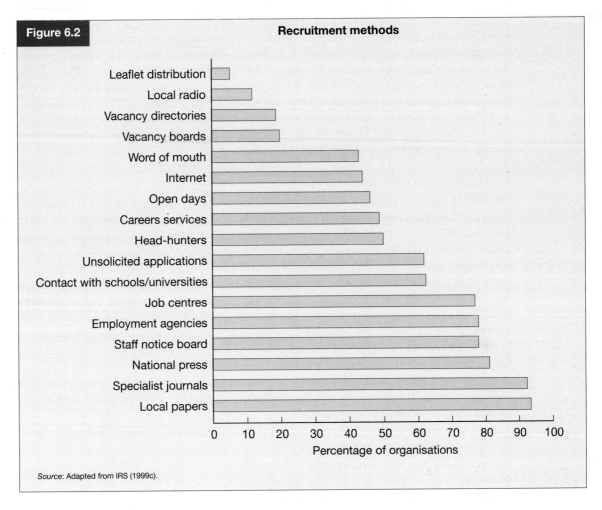

Figure 6.2

Recruitment methods

Source: Adapted from IRS (1999c).

Decisions about the most appropriate method (or methods, as many organisations will use more than one) are likely to be influenced by the level of the vacancy and its importance within the organisation. A recent IRS survey found that recruitment for managerial and professional posts was most likely to be via advertisements in specialist journals and the national press, whereas the local press was more popular for clerical and manual vacancies (IRS, 1999c). Other factors to be taken into account when choosing the most appropriate method include the resources available within the organisation (in terms of personnel and finance), the perceived target groups, and the organisation's stance on internal versus external recruitment. Human resource management literature emphasises the need to have well-developed internal labour market arrangements for promotion, training and career development, which would suggest that many openings can and should be filled internally (Beaumont, 1993). However, a number of organisations, particularly those in the public sector, have policies that require the majority of posts to be advertised externally.

Design of advertisements

The most popular formal recruitment method is press advertising. Good communication from the employer to potential applicants requires thought and skill, and many organisations use the services of a recruitment agency for the design of the advertisement and advice on the most effective media. The aim of the advertisement is to attract only suitable applicants, and therefore it should discourage those who do not possess the necessary attributes while, at the same time, retaining and encouraging the interest of those with potential to be suitable. Although there is some indication that selection is taken more seriously by organisations practising HRM (Storey, 1992), until recently there has been little fundamental challenge to common forms of recruitment advertising. However, the rapid growth of the Internet as a means of communication is now having an impact on recruitment and selection.

Recruitment via the Internet

The use of the Internet as a recruitment tool is increasing rapidly; 32% of respondents to the IPD recruitment survey are using the Internet as a recruitment tool, up from 14% in 1997 (IPD, 1999b). The challenge that the Internet poses to traditional recruitment is very variable. At one extreme the impact might be minimal: for example, advertising on the Internet can simply be used as an alternative or supplementary method to press advertising. Organisations can choose whether to advertise their vacancies on their own corporate web site or with a specialist provider. As with other recruitment methods this choice is likely to be contingent on a number of factors, including the nature of the job, the reputation of the organisation (people are more likely to browse the web sites of well-known corporations), and the resources available. At the other extreme, the impact of using the Internet might be more substantial, and might alter the recruitment process up to and including the shortlisting stage. Table 6.5 highlights the differences between the traditional approach to recruitment and a fully integrated Internet-based approach.

Recruitment documentation

The response to applicants should indicate the overall image that the organisation wishes to project. Some organisations prepare a package of documents, which may include the job description, the person specification, information about the organisation, the equal opportunities policy, the rewards package available, and possible future prospects. Some give candidates the opportunity to discuss the position with an organisational representative on an informal basis. This allows the candidate to withdraw from the process with the minimum activity and cost to the organisation. Much of this infor-

Table 6.5 Traditional verus Internet-based recruitment

Step	Traditional	Internet
1	A job vacancy is advertised in the press	A job vacancy is advertised on the Internet
2	A job seeker writes or telephones for more details and/or an application form	All the company and job details are on the web site together with an online application form
3	A job seeker returns the application form and/or CV by post	A job seeker returns the completed application form electronically
4	Personnel review the written application forms or CVs	Specialised computer software reviews the application forms for an initial match with the organisation's requirements

Source: IPD (1998a).

mation can now be supplied via the Internet: for example, the Greater Manchester Police web site holds information on the reality of being a police officer, plus details on who to contact for further information (IDS, 1997b). Other organisations provide little apart from a request for a letter, CV or completion of an application form.

The design of application forms can vary considerably, but the traditional approach tends to concentrate on finding out about qualifications and work history, and usually includes a section in which candidates are encouraged to 'sell' their potential contribution to the organisation. A recent development is the adoption of a competence-based focus, requiring candidates to answer a series of questions in which they describe how they have dealt with specific incidents such as solving a difficult problem, or demonstrating leadership skills. Some organisations, particularly in the retail sector, include a short questionnaire in which applicants are asked to indicate their preferred way of working.

A variant on the traditional application form, 'biodata' (short for biographical data), may also be used. Forms usually consist of a series of multiple-choice questions that are partly factual (e.g. number of brothers and sisters, position in the family) and partly about attitudes, values and preferences (Sadler and Milmer, 1993). The results are then compared against an 'ideal' profile, which has been compiled by identifying the competences that differentiate between effective and non-effective job performance. For example, a study of executives sent to foreign countries found that the more successful were more likely to have travelled voluntarily when young and to have learned a foreign language (Mitrani *et al.*, 1992).

How do we identify them?

The stages described above constitute recruitment, and are primarily concerned with generating a sufficient pool of applicants. The focus now shifts to selection, and the next stages concentrate on assessing the suitability of candidates.

Shortlisting

It is extremely unlikely that all job applicants will meet the necessary criteria, and so the initial step in selection is categorising candidates as probable, possible or unsuitable. This should be done by comparing the information provided on the application form or CV with the predetermined selection criteria. The criteria may either be explicit (detailed on the personnel specification) or implicit (only in the mind of the person doing the shortlisting). However, this latter approach is potentially discriminatory, and would provide no defence if an organisation was challenged on the grounds of unlawful discrimination (see discussion on legislative requirements earlier in this chapter). Potentially suitable candidates will continue to the next stage of the selection process. IPD guidelines state that unsuccessful candidates should be informed as soon as possible. In practice, written notification of rejection is increasingly less common, and many application forms warn candidates that if they have not had a response by a set date they can assume they have been unsuccessful.

The increased emphasis on personal characteristics rather than job demands may result in some changes to the way shortlisting is undertaken. For example, the use of biodata can provide a clearer focus than more traditional methods, as 'selectors can concentrate solely on those areas of the form found in the biodata validation exercise to be particularly relevant to the prediction of effective performance in the job concerned' (IRS, 1994). Other developments chiefly reflect a desire to reduce the time and effort involved in shortlisting from large numbers of applicants. One option is to use a computer software package that compares CVs with the selection criteria and separates the applications that match the criteria from those that do not. This has the advantage of removing some of the subjectivity inherent in human shortlisting, but does rely on the selection criteria being correctly identified in the first instance. Another option is to reduce large numbers of applicants via random selection. Although there is concern that this may operate against equal opportunities, it is also claimed that 'randomised selection may produce a better shortlist than one based on human intervention where the wrong selection criteria are used consistently or where the correct selection criteria are applied inconsistently' (IRS, 1994: 15).

Selection techniques

Various selection techniques are available, and a selection procedure will frequently involve the use of more than one. The most popular techniques are outlined here, and their validity and effectiveness are discussed later in the chapter.

Interviews

Interviewing is universally popular as a selection tool. Torrington and Hall (1995) describe an interview as 'a controlled conversation with a purpose', but this broad definition encompasses a wide diversity of practice. Differences can include both the number of interviewers and the number of interview stages. Recent survey data (IRS, 1999a) found that the number of interviewers varied from one to four (although two was the most popular number), and the number of interview stages varied from one to four or more. Interviews are mainly conducted face to face, but some organisations are now using telephone interviews as part of their selection procedure, particularly for jobs that involve a lot of telephone work, such as call centre operators. Advances in technology may facilitate 'remote' interviewing, for example by video link or via the Internet, but take-up is relatively low at present. Over the years interviews have received a relatively bad press as being overly subjective, prone to interviewer bias, and therefore unreliable predictors of future performance. Such criticisms are levelled particularly at unstructured interviews, and in response to this, recent developments have focused on more formally structuring the interview or supplementing the interview with less subjective selection tools such as psychometric tests and work sampling.

There are different types of structured interview, but they have a number of common features (Anderson and Shackleton, 1993: 72):

- The interaction is standardised as much as possible.
- All candidates are asked the same series of questions.
- Replies are rated by the interviewer on preformatted rating scales.
- Dimensions for rating are derived from critical aspects of on-the-job behaviour.

The two most popular structured interview techniques are behavioural and situational interviews. Both use critical incident job analysis to determine aspects of job behaviour that distinguish between effective and ineffective performance (Anderson and Shackleton, 1993). The difference between them is that in behavioural interviews the questions focus on past behaviour, (for example, 'Can you give an example of when you have had to deal with a difficult person? What did you do?'), whereas situational interviews use hypothetical questions ('What would you do if you had to deal with a team member who was uncooperative?').

Decisions about the number of interviewers, the type of interview and the number of interview stages are likely to take account of the seniority and nature of the post and the organisation's attitude towards equal opportunities. The number of interviewers and the number of interviews are likely to be highest for managerial and professional posts, and selection for these positions is most likely to involve situational interviewing (IRS, 1999a).

Tests

'Testing is essentially an attempt to achieve objectivity, or, to put it more accurately, to reduce subjectivity in selection decision-making' (Lewis, 1985: 157). The types of test used for selection are ability and aptitude tests, intelligence tests and personality questionnaires. Ability tests (such as typing tests) are concerned with skills and abilities already acquired by an individual, whereas aptitude tests (such as verbal reasoning tests or numerical aptitude) focus on an individual's potential to undertake specific tasks. Intelligence tests can give an indication of overall mental capacity, and have been used for selection purposes for some considerable time. Personality questionnaires allow quantification of characteristics that are important to job performance and difficult to measure by other methods (Lewis, 1985). The debate about the value of personality tests is ongoing, and centres around lack of agreement on four key issues (Taylor, 1998):

- the extent to which personality is measurable;
- the extent to which personality remains stable over time;
- the extent to which certain personality traits can be identified as being necessary or desirable for a particular job;
- the extent to which completion of a questionnaire can provide sufficient information about an individual's personality.

Despite these diverse opinions, the use of tests now appears firmly embedded within organisations as part of the selection process (IRS 1999a). Decisions about whether or not to use tests and, if so, what sort of test to use can be influenced by the nature of the vacancy. The IRS survey (1999a) found that only a tiny minority of organisations used tests for all positions. Ability, aptitude tests and personality questionnaires are used mainly for managerial posts, while literacy and numeracy tests are more popular for clerical and secretarial positions. Tests have the benefit of providing objective measurement of individual characteristics, but they must be chosen with care. Armstrong (1996) lists four characteristics of a good test:

- It is a *sensitive* measuring instrument which discriminates well between subjects.
- It has been *standardised* on a representative and sizeable sample of the population for which it is intended so that any individual's score can be interpreted in relation to others.
- It is *reliable* in the sense that it always measures the same thing. A test aimed at measuring a particular characteristic should measure the same characteristic when applied to different people at the same time, or to the same person at different times.
- It is *valid* in the sense that it measures the characteristic which the test is intended to measure. Thus, an intelligence test should measure intelligence and not simply verbal facility.

(Armstrong, 1996: 473)

Testing is likely to continue to be a fundamental part of the selection process, as the speed at which jobs can change has led to a concentration on flexibility and adaptability:

> The topic of selection and assessment has shifted from one based historically on matching past performance to a defined job which was held for life to the need to estimate a person's probable adaptability to learn new skills and tasks.
>
> (Sparrow and Hiltrop, 1994: 358)

This focus on potential rather than past employment record has also led to an increased use of assessment centre techniques.

Assessment centres

An assessment centre is not a place but rather a process that 'consists of a small group of participants who undertake a series of tests and exercises under observation, with a view to the assessment of their skills and competencies, their suitability for particular roles and their potential for development' (Fowler, 1992). There are a number of defining characteristics of an assessment centre:

- A variety of individual and group assessment techniques are used, at least one of which is a work simulation.
- Multiple assessors are used (frequently the ratio is one assessor per two candidates). These assessors should have received training prior to participating in the centre.
- Selection decisions are based on pooled information from assessors and techniques.
- Job analysis is used to identify the behaviours and characteristics to be measured by the assessment centre.

Assessment centre techniques are most often used for the selection of managers and graduate trainees. Their use increased rapidly through the 1980s and 1990s, but now appears to be stabilising. Successive IRS surveys report that 30% of organisations were using them in 1991 (IRS, 1991), 45% in 1997 (IRS, 1997), and 41% in 1999 (IRS, 1999a). However, the latest survey also found that a number of organisations have recently introduced assessment centre techniques, so the variation in number may be due to the different type and size of organisations responding to each survey. Assessment centre techniques are most likely to be used in the public sector and by larger private sector employers.

Job simulation/work sampling

A key component of an assessment centre is the job simulation exercise, which is designed to be an accurate representation of performance in the job itself. Candidates are placed in situations that they are likely to face if selected: examples include in-tray exercises and role-play interviews.

An extension of job simulation is work sampling: that is, giving the candidate the opportunity to perform in the role for a specified length of time. For example the selection process at the sandwich chain Pret a Manger involves a day's paid work experience (Mullen, 1997).

References

These are used to obtain additional information about candidates from third parties such as previous employers, academic tutors, colleagues or acquaintances. The accuracy of the information is variable; Armstrong (1996) suggests that factual information (e.g. nature of previous job, time in employment, reason for leaving, salary, academic achievement) is essential, but opinions about character and suitability are less reliable. He goes on to say that 'personal referees are, of course, entirely useless. All they prove is that the applicant has at least one or two friends' (p. 482).

References can be used at different stages in the selection process: some organisations use them only to confirm details of the chosen candidate after the position has been offered, whereas others will request references for all shortlisted candidates prior to interview. The format may also vary, with some organisations requesting verbal references by telephone and others requiring written references. In either case, organisations may require referees to answer specific structured questions or provide some general comments on the candidate's performance and suitability. Many employers consider references to be 'only marginally effective' (Industrial Society, 1994), yet there is little doubt that they remain a popular component of the selection process, with all respondents to the IRS selection survey (IRS, 1999a) using them.

Other methods

Two of the more unconventional and controversial selection tools include graphology and astrology. Graphology is based on the idea that handwriting analysis can reveal personal traits and characteristics. Although it is not widely used in the UK, its effectiveness as a selection tool continues to be the subject of considerable debate. Having reviewed the available data on graphology, the IPD concludes that 'the evidence in favour is inconclusive, anecdotal and therefore prone to bias and misinterpretation' (IPD, 1998b). If anything, astrology is even more controversial, and few organisations appear to use it in selection decisions. However, popularity may increase as access to astrological readings becomes easier: for example, a web site has been established that claims to produce detailed character analysis based on people's birth dates (Watson-Smythe, 1999).

Factors influencing choice of selection techniques

What determines the choice of different techniques? One could reasonably assume that a key factor in determining the type of method would be its ability to predict who is suitable and unsuitable for the position. In other words, whatever technique is used, people who do well should be capable of doing the job and people who do badly should not.

Accuracy

'None of the techniques, irrespective of how well they are designed and administered, is capable of producing perfect selection decisions that predict with certainty who is or who is not bound to be a good performer in a particular role' (Marchington and Wilkinson, 1996: 119). Figure 6.3 shows the accuracy of selection methods measured on the correlation coefficient between predicted and actual job performance, with zero for chance prediction and 1.0 for perfect prediction.

The increased use of more accurate methods such as assessment centres and selection testing can help to improve the effectiveness of the selection process. However, findings from the IRS survey (1999a) show that assessment centres are considered to be the most influential selection method in only 8% of organisations. In contrast, 76% of organisations consider interviews to be the most influential selection method. Nevertheless, doubts about accuracy appear to have encouraged employers to adopt more structured interview formats or supplement the interview with other selection methods such as tests or work simulation.

Statistics on the accuracy of different types of selection techniques mask wide variations within each technique. Two key criteria to be considered are reliability and validity. Reliability generally relates to the ability of a selection technique to produce consistent results over time or among different people, whereas validity relates to the extent to which the technique is able to measure what it is intended to measure. These

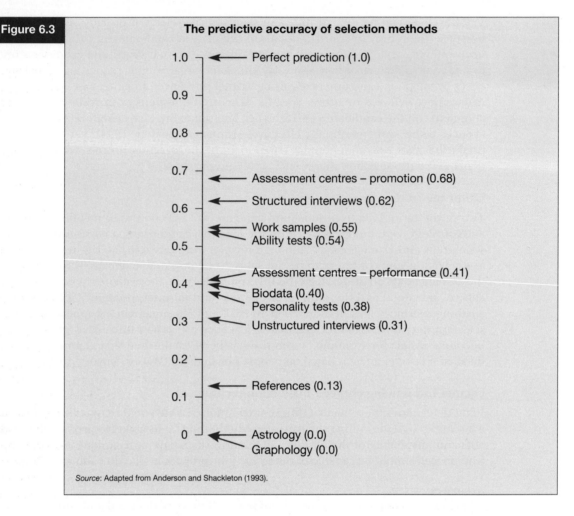

Figure 6.3 **The predictive accuracy of selection methods**

1.0 ← Perfect prediction (1.0)

0.9

0.8

0.7 ← Assessment centres – promotion (0.68)

0.6 ← Structured interviews (0.62)

← Work samples (0.55)
← Ability tests (0.54)
0.5

← Assessment centres – performance (0.41)
0.4 ← Biodata (0.40)
← Personality tests (0.38)

0.3 ← Unstructured interviews (0.31)

0.2

← References (0.13)
0.1

0 ← Astrology (0.0)
← Graphology (0.0)

Source: Adapted from Anderson and Shackleton (1993).

have already been discussed in relation to selection testing, but can be applied to other techniques too. For example, the reliability of interviews can vary if interviewers have differing levels of interviewing skills or different perceptions of the selection criteria. Reliability can also vary when just one person is involved in interviewing, as the conduct of the interview can be affected by the timing of the interview and by how many interviews have been conducted already.

In assessment centres, the effectiveness of the exercises in predicting job performance is dependent on the extent to which they represent the performance content and behavioural requirements of the job they are designed to sample. In practice, the standard of assessment centres can vary from organisation to organisation:

> Because properly designed and applied ACs work well, it does not mean that anything set up and run with the same name is equally good. A lot of so-called ACs in the UK use badly thought-out exercises and inadequately trained assessors; they probably achieve little other than to alienate candidates, who are usually quick to spot their shortcomings. (Fletcher, 1993: 46)

The same can be said of tests that are relevant only if the behaviours and attitudes they measure are those necessary for effective job performance. Additional problems are also associated with the use of tests. Both the British Psychological Society (BPS) and the Institute of Personnel and Development (IPD) have issued codes of practice on the use of tests, which stress that everyone responsible for the application of tests, which includes evaluation, interpretation and feedback, should be trained to at least the level of competence recommended by the BPS (IPD, 1997b). The guidelines also make it clear that 'the results of a single test should not be used as the sole basis for decision-making' (IPD, 1997b). However, a survey conducted by Newell and Shackleton (1993) found that, although companies used trained personnel to administer tests, the majority did not always give feedback of results to candidates, and some were using the tests to make definitive judgements about people. This latter point is also supported by the findings from the IRS survey (1999a), which reports that 2% of respondents consider personality, literacy and numeracy tests to be the most influential selection method.

Level of vacancy

IRS (1997: 16) argues that the type of job is 'the most significant influence on the choice of selection methods for any one vacancy'. In contrast, the IPD survey (1999b: 14) suggests that 'there is far less difference in the selection techniques used by organisations in respect of particular groups of workers than there is in the recruitment methods'. These different opinions may be due to the composition of the different surveys, but they are also due to the jobs being covered, as the IPD study concentrates on managerial, professional and skilled manual workers whereas the IRS survey also includes clerical, secretarial and unskilled manual workers. Assessment centres, in particular, are more likely to be used for managerial and graduate trainee posts and are rarely used for manual positions. This may indicate an organisation's willingness to invest more heavily in future managers than in other parts of the workforce, but may also be due to the candidate expectations and the organisation's need to attract the highest-quality applicants. It is possible to find examples of companies using assessment centre techniques for non-managerial appointments: for example, Häagen Dazs uses them to assess the customer service skills of front-line restaurant staff, but the process is 'noticeably shorter and cheaper than the one or two day models used by other employers' (IDS, 1995: 1).

Cost of selection techniques

There is no doubt that recruitment and selection can be costly activities, and the costs incurred by some selection techniques can make them prohibitive for all but a few 'key' vacancies in an organisation. For example, Barclays Bank estimates that its assessment centres usually cost about £15 000, including necessary materials (IDS, 1995: 5). However, in deciding on the most cost-effective methods, the 'up-front' costs need to be balanced against the costs of wrong decisions, which may include costs associated with labour turnover due to lack of ability. Jaffee and Cohen (cited in Appelbaum *et al.*, 1989: 60) suggest that consideration should include some or all of the following:

● the start-up time required by a replacement for the jobholder;
● the downtime associated with the jobholder changing jobs internally or externally;
● training and/or retraining for the replacement and the jobholder;
● relocation expenses;
● the shortfall in productivity between an effective and ineffective jobholder;
● the psychological impact on the 'failed' jobholder and the morale of others in the department.

Custom and practice

A possible explanation for the continued use of interviews is the simple fact that people are familiar with them. Although, at an academic level, the general consensus is that interviews are unreliable, invalid and provide ample opportunity for personal prejudice (Herriot, 1989), at a practical level many interviewers feel that they are good judges of people and can make effective selection decisions, and most of us would probably feel unhappy in starting a job without undergoing some form of face-to-face meeting with our prospective employer. It seems, then, that the appeal of interviews is universal, and they are 'both favoured and expected as an indisposable [sic] part of the selection process by organisations and applicants alike' (Anderson and Shackleton, 1993: 1).

Making the decision

The aim of the overall recruitment and selection process is to provide enough information to enable recruiters to differentiate between those who can do the job and those who can't. The prescriptive approach stresses that the final decision should involve measuring each candidate against the selection criteria defined in the person specification and not against each other (Torrington and Hall, 1995). The combination of a number of different selection methods can enhance the quantity and quality of information about each candidate, although Anderson and Shackleton (1993) warn of the dangers of information overload in selection.

Even the decision-making process might be affected by the contemporary situation and employers' increased desire for flexibility. Sparrow and Hiltrop (1994) suggest that the combination of technological change, low economic growth, low voluntary turnover rates and an increasingly legislated environment may lead to new employees having to perform a series of jobs over time with changes not necessarily linked to promotion, which may lead to a different approach to selection:

> Traditional 'go/no go' decisions, based on information and data relating to a specific job, will be replaced by decisions to manage a gradual entry of people into the organisation (via probationary periods, fixed term contracts, part time work and so forth).[1]
>
> (p. 316)

How do we know if we've got it right?

The final stage of the recruitment and selection process concerns measurement of its success, both qualitatively and quantitatively. ACAS guidelines suggest that any recruitment and selection system should be based on three fundamental principles: effectiveness, efficiency and fairness (ACAS, 1983). Effectiveness is concerned with distinguishing accurately between suitable and unsuitable candidates: Mayo (1995) suggests a number of ways in which this can be measured for recruits, including retention rates, promotion rates, and percentage of recruits perceived as having high potential after three to five years. However, these factors can also be influenced by working conditions and the emphasis on employee development within the organisation. Efficiency is concerned more with the costs of the exercise, and measures here may include average cost per recruit, average time lapsed between various stages, percentage of offers made, and offer-acceptance rate (Mayo, 1995). Fairness is concerned with dealing with all applicants fairly and honestly, but has often been taken to refer to equal opportunity monitoring, and has been limited to record keeping on the gender, ethnic origin and disability of successful and unsuccessful candidates.

In theory, the integration of recruitment and selection activity with other HR initiatives and business objectives should lead to more extensive evaluation. In practice there is little to indicate that this is happening:

> The ripple effects of recruitment practices on other HRM areas, such as . . . the effects of salary incentives offered to one group of recruits having a knock-on effect on salary claims of existing staff, or the effects of going outside to recruit staff on the aspirations and commitment of existing staff, are . . . often not considered.
>
> (Iles and Salaman, 1995: 214).

Who is involved?

Recruitment and selection have long been seen as two of the key activities of the personnel function. However, increasingly organisations are choosing to involve other parties such as line managers or specialist agencies, or to outsource the activity altogether.

Line managers

An expectation of HRM in academic literature is the increasing extent to which activities once seen as the remit of personnel specialists are devolved to others, particularly line managers and supervisors (e.g. Storey, 1992). Cully *et al.* (1999) throw interesting light on the contemporary degree of devolvement. Around 80% of managers within the survey considered they had responsibility for employment relations matters, with 94% of these including 'recruitment and selection of employees'. In workplaces (with supervisors and over 25 employees), 30% of private sector and 17% of public sector supervisors had the final say in decisions about taking on the people who worked for them, though relevant training was not given in the majority of cases. It appears therefore that the expectation of devolved recruitment and selection activities to managers and supervisors is reality in many UK organisations.

Specialist employment agencies

The specialist skills of the external recruitment advertiser have been used for many years by personnel departments looking outside the organisation for design skills and a contemporary knowledge of successful media. Employment agencies have also traditionally been used for the temporary recruitment of staff cover for periods when full timers have been absent on holiday or through unexpected illness.

Recently the reasons for using third parties in recruitment have intensified. The increasing use of non-permanent contracts increases the need for recruitment to temporary or fixed-term contracts. Cully *et al.* (1999) indicate that temporary workers are used in 28% of workplaces and that fixed-term contracts are now found in 44% of workplaces sampled. Survey results confirm that there have been significant shifts away from the traditional personnel function for executive recruitment and selection, graduate recruitment and temporary staff recruitment, as Figure 6.4 illustrates.

Agencies are also working with organisations where strategic decisions to resource large numbers of employees via a third party have been taken: for example the agency Manpower provided the staff and HR support for the Millennium Dome project at Greenwich (Manpower, 1999).

'Executive search and selection' is a phrase used to describe the recruitment of senior executives and specialists with an average compensation level of (usually) over $100000, (around £63000). The individuals targeted by executive search consultants work at senior levels, and have responsibility at international, national or regional level.

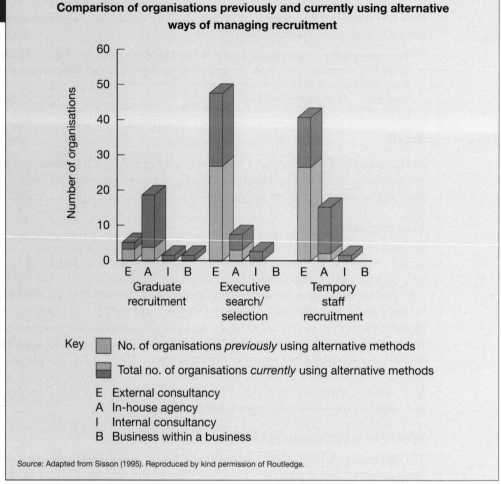

Figure 6.4 Comparison of organisations previously and currently using alternative ways of managing recruitment

Key

No. of organisations *previously* using alternative methods

Total no. of organisations *currently* using alternative methods

E External consultancy
A In-house agency
I Internal consultancy
B Business within a business

Source: Adapted from Sisson (1995). Reproduced by kind permission of Routledge.

Income generated from executive search in 2000 is estimated to exceed $10 billion, of which a third is generated in Europe. Within the world the top 15 multinationals are judged to have at least 25% of the market between them (Garrison-Jenn, 1998). Activities include both direct personal contact with potential employees (head-hunting) and executive selection (identifying candidates through advertising and shortlisting). Key reasons for using executive search and selection consultants include the need for confidentiality, a lack of in-house recruitment knowledge and skills at this level, and simply a lack of senior management time to devote to the activity. Figures 6.2. and 6.4 indicate growth rates and current use of specialist agencies.

Outsourcing

'Outsourcing' is the term used to describe the transfer of a distinct business function from inside the business to an external third party. Outsourcing of parts of the HR function has become more common. Lonsdale and Cox (1998) argue that outsourcing decisions can be classified under the following three headings:

- outsourcing for short-term cost and headcount reductions;
- core-competence-based outsourcing, where peripheral activities are passed to third parties and core activities are retained in-house;
- iterative and entrepreneurial outsourcing, where periodic reviews of critical market activities are undertaken, with subsequent decisions to retain or outsource.

If one considers that much initial recruitment is routinely administrative, outsourcing this activity becomes attractive because it can release time for the HR function to spend on more 'strategic' matters. BA, for example, outsources much of the recruitment process for cabin crew including recruitment telesales, processing applications and standard assessments. This is due to the sheer volume involved in handling 250 000 potential applications and 72 000 phone calls associated with its annual target of 15 000 recruits (Prickett, 1998). While BA chooses to outsource low-level activities, other organisations, particularly smaller ones unable or unwilling to afford professional in-house HR expertise, might consider outsourcing all recruitment and selection activity as part of their outsourcing of the total HR function.

INTERNAL ORGANISATIONAL CONTEXT

We have already discussed a number of factors that might influence the approach to recruitment and selection, such as the type of job, the accuracy of different techniques, and the costs involved. External factors such as legislation, government policy and labour markets also play a part. In addition, differences within organisations can affect the way recruitment and selection is handled. Variations can include an organisation's approach to HRM; the extent to which recruitment and selection activities are aligned with overall business strategy; size, industrial sector and financial position. This section also considers the approaches adopted by multinational corporations.

A soft or hard approach to HRM?

Organisations choose whether to fill a vacancy through the internal labour market (that is, in house) or through external labour markets. Some organisations prefer to fill as many vacancies as possible with existing employees. The opportunities for promotion and transfer can be perceived to be highly motivational and attractive in terms of personal development, with critical skills retained in house. Such an approach is consistent with 'soft' HRM, and has implications for human resource activities:

> Soft contracting implies an elaborate internal labour market, managed by a sophisticated HR function, with strong HR policies to govern relationships, pay, promotions, appraisal and development.
>
> (Storey and Sisson, 1993)

This 'soft' approach implies long-term commitment to investment in training and development and a rigorous appraisal scheme with an emphasis on identifying potential. Emphasis may well be on engendering commitment from employees, with organisational expectations of loyalty and retention.

Organisations pursuing a 'hard' HRM approach prefer to search for new employees in external labour markets. While this may suggest a short-term focus or unwillingness to invest in the human resource, it may also be seen as an approach that brings new skills, ideas and experiences into an organisation as they are needed. Rapidly changing competences may mean there is no time to develop the required competences in house, which must be bought in from outside (Schuler and Jackson 1996).

Reported examples of 'poaching' include the widespread acquisition of IT skills (Anon, 1999b) and more uniquely the 'wooing (of) entire teams from rival firms' by PriceWaterhouseCoopers, the management consultants 'as they aim to recruit 1000 professionals worldwide each week to meet client demands' (Welch, 1999b: 15)

Strategic fit?

The reasons for preferring certain approaches to the management of people received considerable attention in the 1980s as the influence of HRM grew. Within academic literature, normative models, based on a classical view of strategic decision-making, suggest that recruitment and selection policies should be aligned to a variety of organisational factors. Most illustrate the view that HR strategies and activities, including recruitment and selection, should be both vertically integrated with the organisation's position or preferred business strategy and horizontally integrated with each other. Parallel strategies in recruitment, selection, pay and development, in particular, are suggested.

A discussion of the following models can be found in Legge (1995). The Kochan and Barocci model, outlined in Table 6.6, argues that organisations have *life cycles*, and that recruitment, selection and staffing policies vary according to an organisation's perceived stage in the cycle. Other models attempt to link recruitment and selection to *product strategies* (e.g. Fombrun *et al.*, 1984) or overall *business strategy* (e.g. Miles and Snow, 1984).

Goold and Campbell (1987) consider human resource strategies, including recruitment and selection, depend on whether an organisation's *strategic management style* can be classified as one of *strategic planning* (maximum competitive advantage through the pursuit of ambitious long-term goals, with subsequent investment in the long-term development of employees), *financial control* (with an emphasis on short-term utilisation of, and minimal investment in, employees), or *strategic control* (a balance of the two).

The American writers Schuler and Jackson (1996) argue that the organisation's *competitive strategy* (cost reduction, quality improvement and customer focus, innovation or speed of response) is crucial:

Table 6.6 Kochan and Barocci's model of recruitment, selection and staffing functions at different organisational stages

Start-up	Attract the best technical and professional talent (through meeting or exceeding labour market rates)
Growth	Recruit adequate numbers and mix of qualified workers Manage succession planning and rapid internal labour market movements through meeting external labour market rates but also with due consideration for internal equality effects
Maturity	Less emphasis on recruitment. Encourage sufficient turnover to minimise layoffs and provide new openings, Encourage mobility, through 'controlled' compensation
Decline	Little recruitment and selection, rather planning and implementing workforce reductions and reallocation with very tight pay control

Source: Adapted from Legge (1995: 105).

These different ways of competing are significant for managing human resources because they help determine needed employee behaviors. That is, for competitive strategies to be successfully implemented, employees have to behave in certain ways. And for employees to behave in certain ways, human resource practices need to be put in place that help ensure that those behaviors are explained, are possible, and are rewarded.

(p. 64)

There is considerable debate about the extent to which a classical and rational approach to decision-making in organisations is either sensible or even exists. The problems include:

- the difficulties in agreeing what corporate strategy is, and the extent to which it is perceived as planned rather than emergent;
- a perception of critical time lag between 'strategic decision-making' and implementation of the policies deemed necessary to achieve corporate objectives;
- pressures to recruit and select in the short term via the external labour market to meet urgent needs, which may conflict with the chosen longer-term strategy of internal labour market development.

However, the models serve to highlight the variations in approach to recruitment and selection that may be found in organisations. Schuler and Jackson (1996) highlight an international insurance company where successful development has been through key competences in marketing, rapid response to new business areas, and creation of new products. Working in a 'highly decentralised manner through the creation of literally hundreds of new companies to attack new markets', it poaches experts with the skills needed in the industry, through offering much higher pay. When the market dries up or tough competition arrives these employees will be 'let go' to return to the labour market.

Littlewoods, the UK stores and leisure group, aims to become 'the UK's most admired consumer business' with equal opportunities in recruitment and selection a corporate objective that must be achieved for the aim to be achieved. By reaching out to minority groups they appear to have recruited a more effective workforce through 'fishing in the biggest possible pool', and to have increased profitability through widening the customer base (Pickard, 1999). Marks and Spencer, the high street retailer, adopted a recruitment and selection policy that targeted a wider potential labour market:

the policy was driven not only by the humanitarian values espoused by Michael Marks, but by hard-headed business imperatives. In a world where ethnic diversity was becoming an accepted reality, Marks and Spencer needed to lose its image as a white, middle-class, English department store and attract customers from the whole of society.

(Whitehead, 1999b).

In an attempt to increase profitability and finance anticipated growth, the strategic objectives of many of the growing number of call centres in the UK include reducing labour turnover (currently running at around 30% per annum) and waste in recruitment and training costs (currently estimated at over £100 million) (Davis, 1999). Of several suggestions made, one approach that appears to be having considerable success is the introduction of more rigorous selection techniques (such as competence-based interviews, psychometric tests, work sample tests and simulations) to identify the 'ideal person' for call centre work (which industry research suggests is 'rule conscious, dutiful, conscientious, perfectionist and introverted') (Whitehead, 1999c)

Financial position of organisation

The financial position of an organisation can have a great impact on recruitment and selection practices. Financial constraints limit the number and quality of recruitment methods available for use and the amount of cash available to fund the higher reward packages that might attract the highest-quality applicants. A constrained financial situation can also forestall the investment in training and development necessary to tap the potential of the internal labour market, or prevent the take-up of sophisticated (and costly) selection procedures.

Size, industry and cultural considerations

The recruitment and selection practices of an organisation can be further affected by issues of organisational size. Larger organisations may have established and regularly used policies and procedures for recruitment and selection. Within the largest organisations HR policy may be decided by a powerful central function, with individual business or service units expected to maintain strict adherence to written policy and procedure.

According to Cully *et al.* (1999) small organisations (25–49 employees) account for over half of UK workplaces. Within them, there may not be access to well-developed personnel functions or recruitment and selection systems. They may recruit irregularly, with a heavy reliance on informal methods of recruitment, especially if these have worked well previously. Responsibility for the recruitment activity, in particular, may be passed to enthusiastic 'amateurs' within the organisation, or outsourced to a third party. Support for small organisation recruitment and selection activity comes from government-funded organisations (Job Centres, TECS) and publications (e.g. DfEE, 1998).

Sector and industry also influence recruitment and selection norms. WERS 4 data (Cully *et al.* 1999) suggest that 72% of all workplaces in the UK are in the private sector, with financial services, manufacturing, wholesale/retail, hotels and restaurants almost totally within private ownership. The probable usage of third parties in recruitment appears high within this group, and the financial services and manufacturing industries are key users of executive search and selection. Conversely, public administration and education are firmly located in the public sector, where third-party recruitment has traditionally been very limited, with both recruitment and selection being maintained in house. Conservative government policy, which encouraged public sector organisations to contract out 'non-essential' activities, provided a challenge to this status quo.

Even within similar industries and sectors differences exist; those who hold power in organisations may have a strong preference for one particular recruitment method or a dislike of any selection method except one-to-one interviewing. Custom and practice in the approach to recruitment and selection may include a well-established routine, backed by written policies, procedures and monitoring systems, and an insistence on formal training for individuals in recruitment and selection. Deviation from the norm in such circumstances would not be usual. Alternatively recruitment may be seen as a marginal activity, undertaken as required in an ad hoc manner by some delegated employee. The roles (and training) of those engaged in recruitment and selection may vary from one business unit to another, and the extent to which divergence from organisational policy is permitted may vary considerably (Cully *et al.*, 1999).

Multinational perspectives on recruitment and selection

Earlier in the chapter we discussed differences that may occur in national labour markets because of levels of education and government support for training. Other international differences can include attitudes regarding the sourcing of recruits. In many areas of the world the main sources of recruits are relatives, friends or acquaintances of existing employees:

> in certain parts of Africa, where you studied is not as important as who you know, and the people you know may be more important than what you know.
>
> (Langtry, 1994)

This nepotistic approach may challenge our Western view of employee relations and equal opportunities:

> Much of the world still runs its organisations on a model of human relationships that is more akin to the traditional family than the functionally organised, formal, vision led type of organisation prevalent in the US and North West Europe.
>
> (Hall, 1995: 22)

However, even within the UK it is possible to find examples of organisations that recruit predominantly via word of mouth.

In some countries (such as Australia and Spain) a large proportion of organisations are in foreign ownership. In these companies recruitment and selection practices often reflect organisational rather than national values, especially where organisation culture is strong and recruitment and selection activity is carried out by those who are not host country nationals (Hollingshead and Leat, 1995). An examination of the WERS 4 data (Cully *et al.*, 1999) suggests that the growth of wholly foreign or partly foreign ownership in the UK is also on the increase. Private sector figures indicate that 6% of workplaces were partly foreign owned and 13% predominantly (that is, 51% or more) or wholly foreign owned. The larger the workplace, the more likely it is to be foreign owned. The result of a growth in multinational presence may include different approaches to recruitment and selection, different competences required in the workforce, and alternative recruitment methods and selection techniques.

> Variations in employment relations policies and practices within foreign-owned workplaces may reflect the cultures and management styles imported into, or adapted to fit in with, British industrial relations
>
> (Cully *et al.*, 1999: 19)

Four distinct approaches have been identified for recruitment in multinational companies. They imply different patterns of control over the 'overseas' activities', and have varying impacts on career development for the employees concerned:

- *Ethnocentric*, where all key positions are filled by nationals of the parent company. This is a typical strategy employed in the early days of the new subsidiary, and suggests that power, decision-making and control are maintained at parent headquarters.
- *Polycentric*, where host country nationals fill all key positions in the subsidiary. Each subsidiary is treated as a distinct national entity, though key financial targets and investment decisions are controlled by parent headquarters, where key positions remain with parent country nationals.
- *Regiocentric*, where decisions will be made on a regional basis (the new subsidiary will be based in one country of the region), with due regard to the key factor for success of the product or service. For example, if local knowledge is paramount, host country nationals will be recruited; if knowledge of established product is the key factor, parent country nationals are likely to be targets, though anyone from the geographical region would be considered.

- *Geocentric*, where the 'best people' are recruited regardless of nationality for all parent and subsidiary positions: for example, a national of a country in which neither the parent nor subsidiary is based could be considered. This results in a thoroughly international board and senior management, and is still relatively uncommon.

Increased internationalisation of business generates other issues of relevance when considering recruitment and selection. Hendry (1995) identifies an increasing number of managers and professionals affected by international assignments, leading to increased importance of managing international careers. PriceWaterhouseCoopers report growth of over 40% in expatriate, especially short-term, assignments throughout the world between 1997 and 1999 (PriceWaterhouseCoopers, 1999). Competence in language and technical skills are deemed to be key requirements, and many organisations provide language training for potential recruits. International awareness has been found useful in successful placements, as has an individual's ability to change his or her personal behaviour to fit with cultural requirements. Without international experience opportunities for individuals to develop career paths appear increasingly limited in multinational organisations.

Sparrow (1999) concludes, however, that there are 'no simple recipes that can be followed when selecting for international assignments. Rather there are choices to be made and opportunities to be pursued' (p. 40). He identifies three main resourcing philosophies. The first is a traditional, predictive approach, using psychometrics and competence frameworks to assess a person's suitability; the second is a risk assessment approach, which concentrates on cultural adaptability. His third philosophy involves reversing the process, and designing the assignment to match the skills of the manager.

Specific training and preparation become vitally important to ensure that such relocation is effective, and that high levels of expatriate failure are avoided. Likely interventions include pre-move visits to the proposed host country (often with family members), language and cross-cultural training for managers and families, and briefing by both host country and in-house representatives

Ethical issues in recruitment and selection

Up to now we have focused on recruitment and selection from an organisational perspective. We should not forget that recruitment and selection is a two-way process, and so our final topic for discussion concerns the extent to which any approach respects the rights of individuals participating in the process. Ethical issues arise concerning the treatment of people during recruitment and selection. To a large extent whether certain activities are perceived as ethical or unethical reflects the prevailing attitudes within the society or societies in which an organisation operates. However, differences in attitudes also reflect the judgement and positioning chosen by major stakeholders, and can be determined by traditional values inherent within the organisation itself.

Recruitment

Providing equality of opportunity for a diverse number of groups is considered important by certain organisations. However, opportunity to apply for positions can be restricted through the (sometimes unnecessary) insistence on previous experience, or prior development of skills and competences. 'Glass ceilings' exist in internal labour markets for women and minority groups. At the same time many organisations appear reluctant to widen the recruitment pool unless forced to by skills shortages. In the case of third-party recruitment, particularly executive search, opportunities to widen the net can be forestalled, with organisations frequently relying on the knowledge and networking of one consultant to deliver the chosen recruit, often to a specification that ensures that the status quo is maintained. The continued existence of such practices suggests a society in which those in power tolerate them as rational and sound, and where there is insufficient groundswell of opinion from society at large to insist on change. As Goss (1994) remarks:

> If HRM is to be serious in its commitment to the development of all human resources, it may need to face the challenge of wider patterns of social inequality. This means looking not only at disadvantage, but also addressing the issue of who benefits from the status quo. (p. 173)

In a similar vein, multinational and other organisations that have overseas supplier links have to consider their ethical position in relation to both employment conditions and more particularly targeted recruits. To some extent a similar discussion can be held concerning UK organisations where work is subcontracted to UK agencies and suppliers, on relatively poor conditions of employment, or where schoolchildren (already 'fully employed') are recruited in lieu of those already available in the external labour market.

The business decision may be difficult and involve weighing up important economic, financial, marketing and public relations considerations. While component costs may fall dramatically through the use of overseas subsidiaries and suppliers, bad publicity and loss of sales can ensue through dealing with an organisation where, for example, child labour is found to be extensively used, employment conditions are unsafe, or recruits are paid less than a living wage. Model codes of practice have been drawn up, but for many organisations the ethical issues in 'make or buy' decisions will continue to be debated.

Selection

Issues in selection revolve around areas of individual rights, the potential for abuse of power, issues of control and social engineering, use of certain assessment techniques, and the issues of equality of opportunity implied in the above.

The ownership of information about an individual passes in the recruitment and selection process from the individual to the organisation. While some protection is afforded by data protection legislation, the organisation is perceived to increase its power over the individual by holding such information and by accumulating more through the use of various selection techniques, the findings of which are not always made known to the candidate.

An individual's right to privacy is further challenged by the impact of scientific developments assisting the prediction of future employment scenarios. For example, tests now exist to enable organisations to conduct pre-employment medicals that predict the future health of candidates. In the USA, where most health costs are met by the employer, discrimination against apparently healthy people who have, or may have, a genetic defect is common, and health insurance has been found to be refused to one in five of this group (Thatcher, 1996). With genetic tests becoming increasingly available, will UK employers use them to screen out anyone whom they see as potentially expensive to employ? As certain genes occur more frequently in particular ethnic groups, the issues become even more complex.

Apart from questions about the technical effectiveness of various selection techniques, ethical questions remain about their use at all:

There are questions of a more ethical nature surrounding personality tests. It has been suggested that organisations have no right to seek to control access to jobs on the grounds of individual personality.

(Goss, 1994: 47)

Professional guidance in the area of occupation testing exists, both in specific codes of practice (IPD and BPS) and as part of ethical codes of practice within large organisations in particular. However, research has shown that, while selectors claim to recognise the rights of those being tested (for example to be fairly treated, to expect counselling where needed, to confidentiality of data, to know the tests used are valid), these rights are not always upheld in practice (Baker and Cooper, 1996). In addition, questions remain to be asked as to whether:

- the selection of one personality type leads to a weakened 'inbred' profile of employees in organisations, incapable of thinking or acting in original ways when the situation demands;
- an organisation has the right to enforce a unitarist perspective on employees – some selection tests, for example, are designed to filter out those who are 'prone to unionise' (Flood *et al.*, 1996), others to ensure that potential employees' values are in line with the organisation's thinking:

At the heart of these concerns seems to be a fear about the totalitarian possibilities of work organisations and the role of personality profiling as a form of 'social engineering' for corporate conformity.

(Goss, 1994: 47)

The use of interviews as a selection method has long been open to criticism on the grounds of subjectivity and stereotyping. Using biodata as a basis of selection has potential for misuse, discriminating against individuals and groups on factors that are beyond their control (education, social class and gender, for example). Graphology attracts criticism for similar reasons of social stereotyping and superficial judgements.

In conclusion, the use of both external and internal labour markets and associated selection techniques can raise ethical issues. Poaching experienced people from the external labour market implies an approach that only 'takes' from society, in terms of the costs of education and previous training and development, and the higher wages needed to attract applicants can be perceived as inflationary. Alternatively one can view the use of the internal labour market through in-house development around organisation-based objectives as somewhat menacing, tying the individual closely to the organisation from which escape is perceived as increasingly difficult and from which the measurement of individual freedom, and the quality of the conditions of employment enjoyed, become more difficult to judge.

CONCLUSIONS

The focus of this chapter has been to outline contemporary approaches to recruitment and selection, and to consider the influence of external and internal factors on the process. We conclude that the systematic approach to recruitment and selection still provides a useful framework for analysing activity. The key stages – defining the vacancy, attracting applicants, assessing candidates, and making the final decision – are applicable most of the time, but the way in which each stage is tackled can vary considerably. Key developments within the process itself include the increased use of technology. The Internet has emerged as a new recruitment medium, and its use is likely to continue to grow as an increasing number of households go on line. At the same time, the availability of software to aid the selection process is increasing. Developments in selection techniques appear to reflect growing awareness of the limitations of interviews, and so there is evidence of a growth in the use of more structured formats as well as greater use of supplementary tools such as tests and job simulations. For some organisations, however, it is business as usual and little has changed.

The current state of recruitment and selection is complex because a variety of internal and external factors continue to influence the process. The underlying philosophy regarding the management of human resources and the degree of adoption of technological advances affects the way work is organised and the resultant skills needed by employees. Externally, labour market conditions, legislation and government policy in training and education dictate who is available to fill contemporary jobs. Further complexity is added by the growth of multinational enterprises. These factors are constantly changing, and the environment in which the recruitment and selection process operates is uncertain and increasingly ambiguous. What is certain, however, is that there is no universal solution to this complexity – no 'one size that fits all' – and this is how one can account for the coexistence of both new and traditional approaches to the recruitment and selection of employees. Organisations tend to adopt a pragmatic approach to the attraction and selection of employees based on their assessment of current and future conditions and their response to the critical questions outlined in this chapter. Thus, one will find differences in approaches not only between organisations but also within organisations depending on the level of vacancies and organisational requirements.

Although this chapter has concentrated on recruitment and selection from an organisational perspective, readers should not forget that recruitment and selection is a two-way process. Not all the developments can be endorsed wholeheartedly. On the positive side, the use of more sophisticated techniques can be seen as an attempt to improve the quality of the selection decision, through increasing objectivity and reducing the scope for bias and prejudice. On the negative side, the emphasis on personality and behavioural characteristics can be used to create and manipulate a workforce that is more amenable to management initiatives. Ethical considerations continue to be important, and care must be taken in the use of these techniques, particularly in handling the increasingly large amount of information that can be gained about prospective workers.

The most appropriate recruitment and selection techniques will continue to be those that balance the requirements of organisations with those of current and prospective employees, and the approach adopted is likely to be determined, at least in part, by external circumstances. If predictions about the demise of 'jobs for life' and the growth of 'portfolio careers' are true, then the experience of recruitment and selection may become an increasing feature in all our lives, regardless of the techniques involved.

SUMMARY

The chapter began with four key objectives. Here we revisit those objectives and outline our key responses:

● The external factors most likely to affect recruitment and selection practices are conditions in external labour markets, national approaches to education and training, technological developments, and legislation and professional codes of practice. The

Chapter 6 • Recruitment and selection

combination of these factors can be contradictory: on the one hand, legislative requirements can suggest a common 'best' practice, whereas on the other hand variations in
labour supply and market conditions can indicate the need for a more diverse, pragmatic approach.

● The key stages of a systematic approach to recruitment and selection can be summarised as defining the vacancy, attracting applicants, assessing candidates, making
appropriate decisions, and evaluating the effectiveness of the process. Recent developments within this framework include greater use of the Internet for recruitment, and
increased adoption of more sophisticated selection techniques such as psychometric
tests and assessment centres. At the same time, more traditional methods such as press
advertising, interviews and references continue to be very popular. In addition, recruitment and selection activities are increasingly devolved to other parties both inside and
outside the organisation.

● There is considerable variation in the effectiveness of recruitment and selection
techniques. Although the use of selection methods with higher predictive validity is
increasing, the most widely used methods are not necessarily the most accurate at differentiating between people who can and cannot do the job. Effectiveness can also be
considered in relation to equal opportunity and ethical issues, such as the extent to
which employment of people from previously under-represented groups is encouraged,
and the existence of checks that selection methods are 'fair' – that is, discriminate only
on job ability. In measuring effectiveness, organisations need to balance the costs
involved in the actual process against the costs of selecting the wrong person.

● A range of internal organisational factors can influence approaches to recruitment
and selection. We have identified the key influences as the way in which the employment relationship is managed (soft or hard HRM) and the extent to which recruitment
and selection are perceived as strategic activities. Additional factors include industrial,
sectoral and size variation and the growth in multinational corporations. The combination of organisational diversity and pressures from the external environment can
account for variations in recruitment and selection practice.

Activity | **De Montfort Rail Enquiries Service (DMRES)**

De Montfort Rail Enquiries Service is an organisation that has recently won the contract to operate a 24 hour national rail enquiry service on behalf of the UK's passenger train companies.
Based in your area, the call centre will provide train information, general queries and ticket book-
ing services in a round the clock, 365 days a year operation. Although mainly UK enquiries are
anticipated, some overseas (and non-English speaking) calls may also be received.

The operation will require the equivalent of 200 FTE employees. A decision has been made to
offer full (35 hours) and part-time (15, 20 or 25 hours) contracts. Excess demand for staffed hours
above the 200 FTE will initially be met through the use of temporary agency staff. The whole situation will be reviewed in six months' time. Successful applicants will be offered contracts to work
weekends only, evenings only, night shifts, daytime hours or some combination of the above. The
core working hours for the whole operation are 8.00 a.m. to 6.00 p.m. every day.

The majority of recruits will be employed as customer service representatives, working within
teams of around ten, each headed by a team leader. Each customer service representative is

260

equipped with a computer screen and telephone headset. They are fed calls by an automated call distributor, which also sends information to an overhead 'scoreboard', which indicates the number of calls still waiting in the queue. The technology is also capable of providing immediate accurate information about individual performance. Pay rates are expected to be about average for the industry, and will consist of basic salary plus individual bonuses for achievement against predetermined targets. No overtime premiums are paid, although staff who work Bank Holidays get double time and a day off in lieu. Holidays are 23 paid days a year. Meals and refreshments are available at subsidised rates at all times.

The call centre industry has been identified as one where certain problems are found. Stress can be a major problem, and contributory factors include the lack of potential for individualised responses, surveillance through the electronic monitoring of work, little opportunity for social interaction, and payment systems, which depend to some extent on the achievement of targets. There are also very limited opportunities for promotion in the flat hierarchies. In addition, the technology involved provides scope for health and safety problems, with eyestrain and headaches frequently quoted. As a result, discontent among call centre staff may be widespread. These problems are often manifest in high labour turnover rates (sometimes as high as 30%) and very high levels of absenteeism, which may exceed 12%.

Measures taken to address these problems include effective induction training, the provision of focused training both to multi-skill call centre operatives (in telephone skills, customer care, telephone sales techniques and listening/note taking skills) and effective leadership guidance for team leaders (including running effective meetings, coaching and trainer skills). In addition the introduction of as much variety in work as possible, and the grouping of customer service representatives in some 'community' groups can help to overcome these statistics.

DMRES is familiar with the evidence, and is working towards ensuring that these figures are as low as possible for the industry. Bright offices with ergonomically designed workstations are being provided, and team leaders will be encouraged to provide positive feedback and support to supplement the quantitative measurements provided by the technology.

1 Design an appropriate recruitment and selection strategy, to attract a sufficient number of quality customer service representative candidates for the operation,

2 Identify the key criteria for evaluating the success of your strategy, and state how you would assess whether these criteria have been met.

QUESTIONS

1 To what extent can the Code of Practice *Age Diversity in Employment* (DfEE, 1999) reduce age discrimination in recruitment and selection? Justify your answer.

2 What are the advantages and disadvantages of devolving the recruitment and selection process to line managers?

3 'An organisation's desire to discover as much information as possible about prospective candidates in order to make sound selection decisions outweighs an individual's right to privacy.' Discuss.

CASE STUDY 1

Recruitment via the Internet

CORUS TELLS GRADUATES TO APPLY ONLY VIA INTERNET

Corus, the steel company, has told would-be graduate trainees they must apply for its scheme over the Internet.

Potential managers of the group – formed last October by a merger between British Steel and Hoogovens of the Netherlands – must send their details over the Net, then pass a telephone interview before attending a two-day conference.

To use pen and paper they must have a 'very good excuse', such as disability or lack of computer access.

British Steel commissioned WCN, the London software company, about a year ago to produce a tailor-made program. Now it is interviewing the first applicants for its 2000 intake, who have applied via the Web.

Many companies have electronic application forms, which they can print off and post to applicants, but Corus believes it is the first to process applications on line.

The steel group has been approached by Asda and Rolls-Royce to hear about the system. Other companies are likely to follow suit.

'We have been invited to speak at a number of seminars about it already, because we are the first company to take this fully interactive approach,' said Louisa Porter, personnel manager at Corus.

Corus said it was happy with the scheme. 'A lot of youngsters have said they have applied to us because it was such an innovative idea,' it said.

But Jeff Goodman, director of Bristol University's careers service, said it was too early to make Internet applications compulsory. 'A lot of companies are trying to do this because it makes their jobs easier, but most of them are keeping their options open for a very good reason, it is because they don't want to alienate those not using the Web', he said.

Source: Pickard (2000).

1 How appropriate is the use of the Internet for graduate trainee positions?

2 What are the advantages and disadvantages of exclusively using Internet-based recruitment?

CASE STUDY 2

The use of work sampling in selection

At Pret a Manger, the sandwich chain, candidates fill out an application form and then run through it with a member of the recruitment team in a structured interview to assess whether they would be a suitable employee. To pass this stage, applicants must be able to speak English fluently, possess a work permit (if appropriate) and have a combination of team orientation and friendliness. It also helps if they have cashier or catering experience and can show initiative, adaptability, energy, a sense of humour, interest in developing a career and a willingness to work hard.

Candidates passing this stage are then thrown in at the deep end, working as a paid employee at a shop for a day. At the end of this trial period, the manager and the shop staff decide whether they will be offered a permanent job in the shop.

Once accepted, the new recruits embark on a ten day induction programme of on-the-job training covering health and safety, hygiene, customer service and food preparation. This course culminates in two written tests (Mullen, 1997).

1 What are the benefits of including work sampling as part of the selection process?

2 What factors need to be considered before introducing work sampling?

REFERENCES AND FURTHER READING

Those texts marked with an asterisk are particularly recommended for further reading.

ACAS (1983) *Recruitment and Selection*, Advisory Booklet No. 6. London: Advisory, Conciliation, & Arbitration Service.

Anderson, A.H. (1994) *Effective Personnel Management: A Skills and Activity-Based Approach*. Oxford: Blackwell Business.

*Anderson, N. and Shackleton, V. (1993) *Successful Selection Interviewing*. Oxford: Blackwell.

Anon (1999a) 'The great learning', *The Economist*, 31 December, pp. 93–94.

Anon (1999b) 'IT managers happy to poach', *People Management* 11 March p, 23.

Appelbaum, S., Kay, F. and Shapiro, B. (1989) 'The assessment centre is not dead! How to keep it alive and well', *Journal of Management Development*, Vol. 8, No. 5, pp. 51–65.

Arkin, A. (1996) 'Haringey gives green light to police project', *People Management*, 7 March, pp. 10–11.

Armstrong, M. (1992) *Human Resource Management: Strategy and Action*. London: Kogan Page.

Armstrong, M. (1996) *A Handbook of Personnel Management Practice*, 6th edn. London: Kogan Page.

Baker, B. and Cooper, J.N. (1996) 'Beyond the rhetoric of good practice in psychological testing', paper presented to conference on Ethical Issues in Contemporary Human Resource Management at Imperial College, London.

Beaumont, P. (1993) *Human Resource Management: Key Concepts and Skills*. London: Sage.

*Cully, M., Woodland, S., O'Reilly, A. and Dix, G. (1999) *Britain at Work: As Depicted by the 1998 Workplace Employee Relations Survey*. London: Routledge.

Davis, R., (1999) 'Smoother operators', *People Management*, 6 May, pp 56–57.

Department for Education and Employment (1998) *Recruitment: Mind the Gap: How to Fill the Skills Gap and Improve Your Recruiting: A Guide for Small Businesses*. Nottingham: DfEE publications.

Department for Education and Employment (1999) *Age Diversity in Employment*. Nottingham: DfEE publications.

Dickens, L. (1994) 'Wasted resources? Equal opportunities in employment', in Sisson, K. (ed.) *Personnel Management: A Comprehensive Guide to Theory and Practice in Britain*. Oxford: Blackwell, pp. 253–296.

*Dickens, L. (2000) 'Still wasting resources? Equality in employment', in Bach, S. and Sisson, K. (eds) *Personnel Management: A Comprehensive Guide to Theory and Practice*, 3rd edn. Oxford: Blackwell, pp. 137–169.

Dowling, P.J. and Schuler, R.S. (1990) *International Dimensions of HRM*. Boston: PWS-Kent.

Equal Opportunities Commission (1998) *EOC Annual Report 1998*.

Euromonitor (1999) *European Marketing Data and Statistics 1999*. London: Euromonitor.

Euromonitor (2000) *International Marketing Data and Statistics, 2000*, Marketing Handbooks Series. London: Euromonitor.

Fletcher, C. (1993) 'Testing times for the world of psychometrics', *People Management*, December, pp. 46–50.

Flood, P.C., Gannon, M.J. and Paauwe, J. (1996) *Managing Without Traditional Methods: International Innovations in Human Resource Management*. Wokingham: Addison-Wesley.

Fombrun, C., Tichy, N. and Devanna, M. (1984) *Strategic Human Resource Management*. New York: Wiley.

Fowler, A. (1992) 'How to plan an assessment centre', *PM Plus*, December, pp. 21–23.

Garrison-Jenn, N., (1998) T*he Global 200 Executive Recruiters*. San Francisco, Cal: Jossey-Bass.

Goold, M. and Campbell, A. (1987) *Strategies and Styles: The Role of the Centre in Managing Diversified Organisations*. Oxford: Blackwell.

Goss, D. (1994) *Principles of Human Resource Management*. London: Routledge.

Hackett, P. (1991) *Personnel: The Department at Work*. London: IPM.

Hall, K. (1995) 'Worldwide vision in the workplace', *People Management*, May, pp. 20–25.

Hendry, C. (1995) *Human Resource Management: A Strategic Approach to Employment*. Oxford: Butterworth-Heinemann.

Herriot, P. (1989) *Recruitment in the 1990s*. London: IPM.

Hollingshead, G. and Leat, M. (1995) *Human Resource Management: An International and Comparative Perspective on the Employment Relationship*. London: Pitman Publishing.

IDS (1992) *Employment Law Supplement: Recruitment*, IDS Brief No. 64, April.

IDS (1995) *Assessment Centres*, Study No. 569, January.

IDS (1997a) *Racial Discrimination*, Study No. 625, May.

IDS (1997b) *Recruitment*, Study No. 634, September.

Iles, P. and Salaman, G. (1995) 'Recruitment, selection and assessment', in Storey, J. (ed.) *Human Resource Management: A Critical Text*. London: Routledge, pp. 203–233.

Industrial Society (1994) *Recruitment and Selection*, Managing Best Practice No. 4. London: The Industrial Society.

IPD (1996) *The IPD Recruitment Guide*. London: IPD.

IPD (1997a) *Recruitment*, Key Facts, March. London: IPD.

IPD (1997b) *Psychological Testing*, Key Facts, August. London: IPD.

IPD (1998a) *Recruitment on the Internet*, Information Note 12. London: IPD.

IPD (1998b) *Graphology*, Information Note 13. London: IPD.

IPD (1999a) *Employing People with Criminal Records*, Key Facts, October. London: IPD.

IPD (1999b) *Recruitment*, IPD Survey Report 5. London: IPD.

IRS (1991) *The State of Selection*, Recruitment and Development Report 19, July.

IRS (1994) 'Ensuring effective recruitment' and 'Random selection', *Employee Development Bulletin 51*, March, pp. 2–8.

IRS (1997) 'The state of selection: an IRS survey', *Employee Development Bulletin 85*, January, pp. 8–18.

IRS (1999a) 'The business of selection: an IRS survey', *Employee Development Bulletin 117*, September, pp. 5–16.

IRS (1999b) 'testing time for people with disabilities', *Employee Development Bulletin 113*, May, pp. 5–9.

IRS (1999c) 'Cost-effective recruitment: an IRS survey of employers' experience', *Employee Development Bulletin 115*, July, pp. 6–20.

Kandola, B. (1995) 'Firms must rework race bias policies', *Personnel Today*, 25 October, p. 20.

Langtry, R. (1994) 'Selection', in Beardwell, I. and Holden, L. (eds) *Human Resource Management: A Contemporary Perspective*. London: Pitman Publishing, pp. 230–263.

Leat, M., (1998) *Human Resource Issues of the European Union*. London: Financial Times Management.

*Legge, K. (1995) *Human Resource Management: Rhetorics and Realities*. Basingstoke: Macmillan Business.

Lewis, C. (1985) *Employee Selection*. London: Hutchinson.

Lonsdale, C. and Cox, A. (1998) 'Falling in with the out crowd', *People Management*, 15 October, pp. 52–55.

Manpower (1999) *2000 for 2000: The Complete Employment Solution*. In-house publication.

Marchington, M. and Wilkinson, A. (1996) *Core Personnel and Development*. London: IPD.

Mayo, A. (1995) 'Economic indicators of HRM', in Tyson, S. (ed.) *Strategic Prospects for HRM*. London: IPD, p. 34.

McKay, S. and Middleton, S. (1998) *Characteristics of Older Workers: Secondary Analysis of the Family and Working Lives Survey*, Research report No. 45, DfEE.

Miles, R.E and Snow, C.C. (1984) 'Designing strategic human resource systems', *Organizational Dynamics*, Summer, pp. 36–52.

Mitrani, A., Dalziel, M. and Fitt, D. (1992) *Competency Based Human Resource Management: Value Driven Strategies for Recruitment, Development and Reward*. Paris: Les Editions d'Organisation.

Mullen, J. (1997) 'Starring roles', *People Management*, 29 May, pp. 28–30.

Munro Fraser, J. (1954) *A Handbook of Employment Interviewing*. London: Macdonald & Evans.

Newell, S. and Shackleton, V. (1993) 'The use and abuse of psychometric tests in British industry and commerce', *Human Resource Management Journal*, Vol. 4, No. 1, pp. 14–23.

Paddison, L. (1990) 'The targeted approach to recruitment', *Personnel Management*, November, pp. 54–58.

Patterson, M., West, M., Lawthorn, R. and Nickell, S. (1997) *Impact of People Management Practices on Business Performance*, Issues in People Management No. 22. London: IPD.

Pickard, J. (1999) 'Equality counts', *People Management*, 11 November, pp. 38–43

Pickard, J. (2000) 'Corus tells graduates to apply only via Internet', *Financial Times*, 26 January, p. 7.

PriceWaterhourseCoopers (1999) *International Assignments: European Policy and Practice 1999/2000*. London: PriceWaterhouseCoopers.

Prickett, R. (1998) 'Outsourcing's strategic benefits beat cash gains', *People Management*, 11 June, pp.18–19.

*Roberts, G. (1997) *Recruitment and Selection: A Competency Approach*. London: IPD.

Rodger, A. (1952) *The Seven Point Plan*. London: National Institute of Industrial Psychology.

Sadler, P. and Milmer, K. (1993) *The Talent-Intensive Organisation: Optimising your Company's Human Resource Strategies*, Special Report No. P659. London: The Economist Intelligence Unit.

Schuler, R.S. and Jackson, S.E. (1996) *Human Resource Management: Positioning for the 21st Century*, 6th edn. St Paul: West Publishing Company.

Select Committee on the Anti-discrimination Bill (House of Lords) (1972/3) *Second Special Report from the Select Committee*. London: HMSO.

Sisson, K. (1995) 'Human resource management and the personnel function', in Storey, J. (ed.) *Human Resource Management: A Critical Text*. London: Routledge, pp. 87–109.

Sly, F., Thair, T. and Risdon, A. (1999) 'Disability and the labour market: results from the winter 1998/9 LFS', *Labour Market Trends*, September, pp. 455–465.

*Social Trends (2000) London: HMSO.

Sparrow, P. (1999) 'Abroad minded', *People Management*, 20 May, pp. 40–44.

Sparrow, P. and Hiltrop, J.–M. (1994) *European Human Resource Management in Transition*. New York: Prentice Hall.

Storey, J. (1992) *Developments in the Management of Human Resources*. Oxford: Blackwell.

Storey, J. and Sisson, K. (1993) *Managing Human Resources and Industrial Relations*. Buckingham: Open University Press.

*Taylor, S. (1998) *Employee Resourcing*. London: IPD.

Thair, T. and Risdon, A. (1999) 'Women in the labour market: results from the spring 1998 LFS', *Labour Market Trends*, March, pp. 103-114.

Thatcher, M. (1996) 'Contending with a genetic time bomb', *People Management*, 7 March, pp. 30–33.

Torrington, D. and Hall, L. (1995) *Personnel Management: HRM in Action*. London: Prentice Hall.

Twining, J. (1999) 'From dreams to reality', *Educa*, April, pp. 8–10.

van Zwanenberg, N. and Wilkinson, L. (1993) 'The person specification – a problem masquerading as a solution?', *Personnel Review*, Vol. 22, No. 7, pp. 54–65.

Watson-Smythe, K. (1999) 'Business aligns with astrology to match staff', *The Independent*, 8 November.

Welch, J. (1999a) 'Disappearing CEOs test City's faith', *People Management*, 23 April, p. 13.

Welch, J. (1999b) 'Market for consultants hotting up', *People Management*, 3 June, p. 15.

Whiddett, S. and Hollyforde, S. (1999) *The Competencies Handbook*. London: IPD.

Whitehead, M. (1999a) 'Employers face a drastic shortage of skills', *People Management*, 20 May, p. 20.

Whitehead, M. (1999b) 'A time for buy-in', *People Management*, 3 June, pp. 54–56.

Whitehead, M. (1999c) 'Churning questions', *People Management*, 30 September, pp. 46–48.

Whitehill, A.M. (1991) *Japanese Management: Tradition and Transition*. London: Routledge.

PART 2 CASE STUDY

Employment and the EU

By Robert Taylor

Many European employers believe they do not enjoy enough flexibility in existing labour markets to improve their competitiveness and productivity. In its submission to the European Union's social summit in Lisbon, Unice – the European employer federation – argued that companies need to 'adopt modern flexible work organisations and performance-related reward structures in order to harness the full creativity of people'. But Unice claimed 'Europe's regulatory and fiscal frameworks currently inhibit the development of modern high-performance workplaces'. Employers are particularly concerned at the social regulations designed to restrict working time, the use of outsourcing, recruitment and the use of temporary and fixed-term employment contracts.

In its memorandum to Lisbon Unice argued that such regulations, both at EU and nation state level, have slowed down the pace of innovation as well as the speed at which individual workers can find new employment. In addition, Unice is complaining that 'over-strict protection against dismissals discourages business start-ups to recruit'. It wants to see the removal of restrictions on employers to make more use of temporary workers to meet their business needs and a reduction in the level of indirect labour costs especially for small and medium-sized enterprises.

What employer associations would really like to see is the creation of a much more business-friendly environment for innovation and entrepreneurship inside the EU, especially for those involved in the creation of new information-based enterprises and small and medium-sized companies.

The more recent response of the European Commission to such arguments from employers indicates there is a growing sympathy in Brussels in response to their strenuous lobbying efforts, particularly in employer advocacy of more active labour market measures that encourage employment creation. But many of the EU's social regulations to which companies in general object, in areas such as parental and maternity leave as well as part-time and temporary employment, are the outcome of national rather than pan-European pressures, reflecting the strengths and weaknesses of the social partners across the countries of the EU.

Moreover, a number of them have resulted from detailed negotiations between employers and trade unions through the process of social dialogue.

However, many of those social regulations are seen by employers as a legacy from another age before the arrival of e-commerce and information technology. They argue today that employers require much more freedom to be flexible by being able to adapt their workplaces to meet the new challenges posed by industrial change and corporate restructuring. If this means either the dilution or even bypassing of existing social regulations, then this should not lead to a heavy-handed attitude by either the European Commission or others who have to enforce them.

Anna Diamantopoulou, the EU's social affairs commissioner, is keen to shift the emphasis of its employment strategy from social workplace rights to dealing with gender segregation, making health and safety at work measures more modern and simple and improving education and training to meet the requirements of the knowledge-based economy.

Most employers in Europe, however, are pragmatists, not ideologues. They have learnt to live with and make use in their own interests of national regulations that exist on the right to family leave and the use of atypical employment contracts.

Evidence – from the Organisation for Economic Co-operation and Development – does not suggest that the existence of wide-ranging workplace regulation in many western European countries has brought relatively poor levels of productivity and competitiveness. The UK productivity gap with its main European rivals remains between 20 and 30 per cent although the UK has fewer and minimalist legal rights for workers. Indeed, the OECD in its last employment survey saw a connection between the existence of robust social regulation in the workplace and better business performance.

It seems that, in practice, the provision of regulation to govern the treatment of part-time and temporary workers does not impede risk-taking and enterprise. But the European Commission's latest annual survey of structural reform underlines a new sense of urgency in modernising EU labour markets as much as those for capital, goods and services.

While it acknowledges 'increasing access to temporary employment contracts has helped to create more jobs for new entrants and people at the margins of the labour market in some countries', the commission also accepts 'no significant step has been taken to review job protection rules'.

But in its latest report the Commission points to the negotiation in Spain and Italy of agreements to encourage the promotion of part-time employment with reductions in social security contributions o encourage such modernisation. The regulation of fixed-term contracts has also been relaxed in Belgium, Germany, Italy, Sweden and the Netherlands to stimulate more employment creation. The cause of labour flexibility has been recognised across the EU by both employers, governments and trade unions.

The problem is there is not yet enough conclusive empirical evidence to focus specifically on the employment consequences of job protection regulation. The Lisbon summit communiquél called for a more in-depth examination and systematic monitoring of the labour market effects of such measures. However, until a set of comparative data has been agreed it will be hard to avoid the war of words between employers and unions on the pros and cons of regulation designed to ensure equity and social rights in the workplace without undermining job creation. Not for the first time the gap between the rhetoric and reality in employment practice remains substantial.

Source: *Financial Times*, 31 March 2000. Copyright © The Financial Times Limited

---

1 As a representative of UNICE, the European employers' confederation, explain in more detail the case for change in patterns of European social regulation.

2 As a senior representative of ETUC, the European Trade Union Congress, prepare a draft letter to the *Financial Times* in response to the main points made in the article above.

3 Debate the following issues:

(a) How compatible are the 'modern flexible work organisations' referred to in the article with the aim of harnessing 'the full creativity of people'?

(b) To what extent are high levels of social regulation responsible for unemployment and low job creation?

(c) Is social regulation a major obstacle to the effective use of labour by enterprises?

PART

3

DEVELOPING THE HUMAN RESOURCE

Introduction to Part 3

One of the main outcomes of the spread of human resource management (HRM) over the past decade has been increasing attention to what has become labelled *human resource development* (HRD). However, like HRM, this is a term that is often used loosely, and indeed poses problems of definition. Stewart and McGoldrick (1996), who write authoritatively in the HRD area, suggest that the question of what it is 'is not yet amenable to a definitive answer', but offer the following 'tentative' definition:

> Human resource development encompasses activities and processes which are intended to have impact on organisational and individual learning. The term assumes that organisations can be constructively conceived of as learning entities, and that the learning processes of both organisations and individuals are capable of influence and direction through deliberate and planned interventions. Thus, HRD is constituted by planned interventions in organisational and individual processes.
>
> (p.1)

This definition emphasises HRD of the individual and her or his relation to the organisation. HRD, however, can be viewed much more broadly than this. In Asian and African countries, for example, HRD encompasses government initiatives and policies to improve knowledge and skills to enhance economic growth. As Rao (1995) states:

> at the national level HRD aims at ensuring that people in the country live longer; live happily; free of disease and hunger; have sufficient skill base to earn their livelihood and well being; have a sense of belongingness and pride through participation in determining their own destinies. The promotion of the well-being of individuals, families and societies provides a human resource agenda for all countries the world over.
>
> (p.15)

We therefore need to recognise the role that the HRD that takes place in organisations plays in the overall economy and hence in the well-being of society. This concept is represented by the three concentric circles in Figure 1. The more overlap (the shaded area) there is between these three elements, the more likely HRD is to be mutually beneficial for the individual, the organisation and the economy as a whole. For example, support from government initiatives, such as legislation on vocational training, enhances the skills and knowledge of those seeking work in the labour market, which enhances the efficiency of organisations, which in turn enhances the growth and development of the economy. It is therefore not surprising that training and development are important issues, to which governments give careful consideration. For these reasons Part 3 looks beyond and beneath organisational HRD and examines both its national context and the basic processes that constitute it; where appropriate, it invites readers to reflect on their own individual learning and development.

HRD is also seen as having a significant part to play in achieving and maintaining the survival and success of an organisation. Managers have not only to acquire appropriate people to resource it, as discussed in Part 2, they also need to train and develop them, for the following reasons:

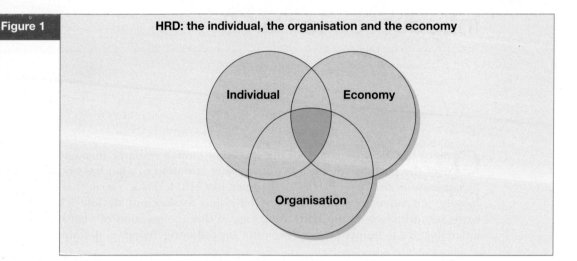

Figure 1 HRD: the individual, the organisation and the economy

Individual

Economy

Organisation

- New employees are, in some respects, like the organisation's raw materials. They have to be 'processed' to enable them to perform the tasks of their job adequately, to fit into their work group and into the organisation as a whole, but in a manner that respects their human qualities.
- Jobs and tasks may change over time, both quantitatively and qualitatively, and employees have to be updated to maintain adequate performance.
- New jobs and tasks may be introduced into the organisation, and be filled by existing employees, who need redirection.
- People need training to perform better in their existing jobs.
- People themselves change their interests, their skills, their confidence and aspirations, their circumstances.
- Some employees may move jobs within the organisation, on promotion or to widen their experience, and so need further training.
- The organisation itself, or its context, may change or be changed over time, so that employees have to be updated in their ways of working together.
- The organisation may wish to be ready for some future change, and require (some) employees to develop transferable skills.
- The organisation may wish to respond flexibly to its environment and so require (some) employees to develop flexibility and transferable skills.
- Management requires training and development. This will involve training for new managers, further development and training for managers, management succession, and the development of potential managers.

As the chapters that follow show, changes in the context of the organisation increase the need to train and develop its members to ensure effectiveness, quality and responsiveness. Because these changes are not being made once and for all, employees are having to adjust to continuous change, and their managers are having to pay greater attention to HRD than ever before. However, HRD does not take place in an organisational vacuum. To be effective, it presupposes effective selection, effective supervision and an appropriate management style, the opportunity to transfer learning to the workplace, career paths and promotion possibilities, appropriate incentives and rewards. It also presupposes some degree of planning and linkage to the strategy of the organisation, and is therefore implicit within organisation development. Indeed, for the organisation that espouses 'human resource management' and addresses the human resource implications of its strategic positioning, training and development become investment decisions and operations that are as important as investments in new technology, relocation or entry into new markets.

Chapter 7 identifies the need for HRD in the organisation, and considers the basic processes of learning and development involved and the ways in which they can be facilitated in the organisation. This chapter underpins the subsequent chapters of Part 3 and introduces some of the concepts they use. Chapter 8 examines, the processes and activities intentionally undertaken within organisations to enable employees to acquire, improve or update their skills, and then explores the nationational framework for vocational education and training, with some international comparisons, which is the context within which organisational HRD operates. Chapter 9 examines the development of managers, noting both their formal and informal modes of development, and relates management to organisation development.

As these chapters show, HRD takes several forms: the development of the employee both as an individual and as an employee; development of the employee by the employer or by self; training; education; career development; group development; staff development; professional development, management development and, even more widely, organisation development. These differ not only in terms of the hierarchical levels of the organisation but also in purpose and form. While recognising these different kinds of training and development in organisations, we have to understand that they are not necessarily easily distinguishable in practice, and that some activities contribute to more than one form of development. There is necessarily some overlap between the chapters of Part 3. Thus specific training to enable an employee to perform more effectively can now also contribute to that person's overall career development. What is intended as instrumental by the employer may be construed as empowering by the individual. This raises the question about who owns the individual's development, one of the controversial issues addressed in Chapter 7.

REFERENCES

Rao, T.V. (1995) *Human Resource Development*. New Delhi: Sage.

Stewart, J. and McGoldrick, J. (eds) (1996) *Human Resource Development: Perspectives, Strategies and Practice*. London: Pitman Publishing.

7 Learning and development

Audrey Collin

OBJECTIVES

- To outline some significant changes taking place in work and organisations.
- To indicate the learning and development that these changes demand of organisations and of individuals, and the implications for human resource managers.
- To discuss the nature of learning and development.
- To note the characteristics of different types of learners.
- To indicate the outcomes of learning.
- To outline the process of learning.
- To discuss the concept of development.
- To note the kinds of development and their implications for human resource managers.
- To examine the context of learning and development within and beyond the organisation.
- To identify how the organisation can facilitate learning and development through action learning, mentoring, and the development of the learning organisation.
- To pose some controversial issues for reflection and discussion.
- To offer some activities that encourage readers to review their own learning and development.

INTRODUCTION

Learning is 'the central issue for the 21st century', asserts Honey (1998: 28–29) when setting out the Declaration of Learning drawn up by some of the 'leading thinkers on learning in organisations':

> Changes are bigger and are happening faster, and learning is the way to keep ahead . . . to maintain employability in an era when jobs for life have gone. It enables organisations to sustain their edge as global competition increases. Learning to learn . . . [is] the ultimate life skill.

This makes human resource development a key activity in today's organisations, and lifelong learning crucial for individuals. The purpose of this chapter, which forms a foundation for Chapters 8 and 9, is to explain what learning and development are.

The chapter starts by identifying some of the ways in which work and organisations are changing, and why these changes demand continuous learning in individuals and organisations. It then explains the processes and outcomes of learning and development, identifies how their context influences them, and examines how they may be facilitated in work organisations.

THE CHANGING WORLD OF WORK AND ORGANISATIONS

By the end of the twentieth century, the firmly established nature of work and organisations was changing so dramatically that some observers had foreseen the 'end of work' (Rifkin, 1995) and workplaces without jobs (Bridges, 1995). These changes are being brought about through the new information and communications technologies, and through the way in which organisations are responding to the need to achieve and maintain their competitive edge in increasingly global markets. Castells (1996) argues that a new 'network society' is emerging. The new technologies are making economies interdependent, organised around global networks of capital, management, and information, and thereby are profoundly transforming capital and labour. While capital and information flow around the globe, unconfined in space and time, labour is local: individuals live and work in time and place. 'Labor is disaggregated in its performance, fragmented in its organization, diversified in its existence, divided in its collective action' (p. 475).

To be competitive, organisations have had to become more flexible, innovative, quality/conscious, customer orientated, constantly improving their performance. During the past 20 years or so they have undertaken what amount to massive experiments with various ways of achieving these ends. During the 1980s the imperatives were excellence, world-class and 'lean' manufacturing (a collection of techniques contributing significantly to organisational performance), and total quality management (TQM), resulting in downsizing, delayering, and breaking bureaucracies down into business units. During the early 1990s the new soft approaches were multi-skilling and the learning organisation, while the hard approach was business process re-engineering (BPR). In the later 1990s, attention turned to knowledge management and innovation, with a further emphasis on teamworking. Thus wave after wave of new approaches has brought about new tasks, new ways of working, new roles, relationships and skills, stimulating the need for human resource development.

For example, TQM (see also Chapter 13) holds that quality is achieved through continuous improvement in the processes, products and services of the organisation: Deming's 'journey of never-ending improvement' (Hodgson, 1987: 41). It requires new relationships between organisations and their suppliers and customers, and calls for the transformation of the management of people 'so that employees become involved in quality as the central part of their job' (Sheard, 1992: 33). Business process re-engineering, which radically restructured bureaucratic organisations by focusing on their lateral processes rather than their vertical functions, not only 'downsized' organisations, but also redesigned the nature of jobs within them:

> For multi-dimensional and changing jobs, companies don't need people to fill a slot, because the slot will be only roughly defined. Companies need people who can figure out what the job takes and people to do it, people who can create the slot that fits them. Moreover, the slot will keep changing.
>
> (Hammer and Champy, 1994: 72).

Whereas work had previously been packaged into jobs, Martin (1995: 20) argues, it now had to be reconstructed into the 'competences' needed to achieve customer satisfaction. 'The future will see a world based more on skills than on organisations' (Tyson and Fell, 1995: 45).

If TQM and BPR can be seen as natural heirs – in spirit if not in practice – of scientific management and Taylorism (see Chapters 2, 5 and 10), then knowledge management (see also Chapter 8) could be recognised as an echo of Trist and the Tavistock school (Pugh *et al.*, 1983). The working group is a socio-technical system: to be effective, the introduction of new technology has to take that into account. Fifty years later, it is once more being recognised (Malhotra, 1998) that it is people who make the difference. The wealth of information generated by information technology becomes meaningful and of competitive advantage to the organisation only when knowledge workers share, interpret and elaborate it. This enables them to anticipate challenges to the organisation's goals and practices, and thus adapt the organisation in appropriate and timely fashion. Knowledge management is still in its infancy, while the opportunities for e-learning are expanding rapidly (Masie, 1999). Organisations are beginning to understand that different kinds of knowledge have to be managed in different ways: some knowledge is explicit, and can easily be documented, whereas other knowledge is tacit. 'The knowledge needed to develop a new product is largely in people's heads . . . [it] cannot be written down, because an individual may not even know it is there until the situation demands a creative response' (Dixon, 2000: 37). Moreover, argues Scarborough (1999), HR managers need to have a direct involvement in this area.

It is now also recognised that, although the UK has shone in invention, it has lagged in innovation. '"the creation, successful exploitation and impact of new ideas at all levels – the economy, sector, enterprise, workplace and individual"' (Guest *et al.*, 1997: 1, quoting from the Economic and Social Research Council's Innovation Programme material). However, innovation is 'the source of sustained competitiveness in organisations':

> Creating, disseminating and embodying knowledge – tacit and explicit – becomes a key strategic resource to be leveraged. It holds the key to unlocking the organisation's ability to learn faster than its environment is changing. In summary, learning and development lie at the heart of innovation in organisations.
>
> (Guest *et al.*, 1997: 3)

For the future, according to Bayliss (1998), many of the traditional boundaries and distinctions – between organisations, between jobs, between employment and self-employment – will shift or become eroded. The relationship that individuals will have with employing organisations will change: individuals will move more frequently, have projects rather than long-term jobs, work in different locations and at different times, make their own work, no longer have fixed working lives. Many careers will be 'boundaryless', transcending traditional boundaries between organisations (Arthur and Rousseau, 1996). As the nature of careers changes, so also will the concept of career, from being a linear, future-orientated trajectory to becoming more of a collage of experiences (Collin and Young, 2000). To express these changes in metaphors: whereas during much of the twentieth century jobs were like pigeon-holes, or boxes piled up to form organisations, at the start of the twenty-first century they are more like nets and networks. To achieve flexibility, organisational structures and hierarchies are being dismantled, the boundaries between jobs and organisations are being eroded, and the organisational boxes are being opened up.

Such changes are of great significance for individuals and organisations, and demand new ways of thinking and working from employees. These include the ability to:

- break down traditional barriers and work outside the definition and security of traditional job descriptions;
- develop new working relationships that modify the organisation's hierarchical structure;
- deploy and develop these personal skills to the benefit of the working group and the organisation as a whole.

Moreover, according to Hamel (Arkin, 1998: 52), the 'question today is not: is the company built to last? But: is it built to change? That requires an ability to continually challenge deeply held beliefs and to ensure that the organisation contains an incredibly diverse array of voices and perspectives.' These new ways of thinking and working call for continuous learning and development on the part of individuals and organisations.

Activity   **Identifying contextual changes leading to HRD**

Before proceeding further, identify for yourself some of the changes taking place in organisations, in response to changes in its context, that are calling for human resource development and for employees to learn and develop.

The need for individual and organisational learning and development

It is evident that individual and organisational learning and development are of crucial and strategic importance. This is not just a matter of extensive training in task skills, but of completely new ways of thinking about work, and of working and relating with one another. Individuals at all levels need to be able to think and work 'outside the box'. They need to be able to do so without prior experience, clear guidelines, or close supervision. Overall, this amounts to the need for using high levels of cognitive skills, including learning how to learn. It also amounts to the need for managers to train and develop their existing workforce, facilitate their learning within a learning culture, and with appropriate resources, and train and develop new employees. And, beyond the organisation, it amounts to the need to develop a learning society.

The need for individuals to learn and develop

According to Barrow and Loughlin (1993: 198) organisations increasingly need their employees to have:

- a high level of education, possibly up to degree level, so that employees can operate new technology, understand the contribution of their role to the company, and take decisions appropriate to their jobs;
- the ability to learn new skills and adapt to changing circumstances – by taking responsibility for their own learning, keeping their skills up to date, learning new processes;
- the ability to work in organisations with flatter structures and fewer layers of management – to work without supervision, set their own objectives, monitor their own performance, correct failures;
- the ability to manage the interface with customers and between departments, requiring a good level of interpersonal skills;
- the ability to solve problems, thinking creatively about future possibilities, and contribute their own unique ideas.

For much of the industrial age, such abilities, when sought, were expected mainly in the upper echelons of organisations. In the twenty-first century, competitive organisations need to find these abilities much more widely in their workforce, in what Castells (1998: 341) calls the 'self-programmable' labour in the global economy. This has 'the capability constantly to redefine the necessary skills for a given task, and to access the sources for learning these skills'. Nevertheless, there will still be work that does not require those particular abilities – for example, 'flipping burgers' (see case study at end of chapter) – jobs that will be undertaken by what Castells calls 'generic' labour, which, lacking self-programmable skills, would be:

> 'human terminals' [which could] be replaced by machines, or by any other body around the city, the country, or the world, depending on business decisions. While they are collectively indispensable to the production process, they are individually expendable . . .   (Castells, 1998: 341)

(It should not be assumed, however, that all jobs giving personal service demand low-level skills: they may require high levels of social, emotional and other non-cognitive intelligences (Gardner, 1985, 1999; Pickard, 1999b).)

Whether employed within traditional organisations or not, individuals will need to be flexible, to be able to change and undertake new tasks. Moreover, they will also have to take responsibility for much of their own learning. It is now generally agreed (e.g. Arnold, 1997) that individuals have to develop their 'employability' as an investment against risk.

The need for organisations to invest in their employees' learning and development

Thus human resource management and development become essential to organisational survival and effectiveness. Indeed, the director-general of the IPD claims that 'staff management and development will become the primary weapon available to managers to generate success' (Rana, 2000). In the struggle to 'think global and act local', organisations need people who have 'a "matrix of the mind"'; sharing learning and creating new knowledge are among the key capabilities that organisations must have (Ulrich and Stewart Black, 1999).

Kanter (1992: 39) recognises these needs in her 'model company statement':

> Our company faces competitive world markets and rapidly changing technology. We need the flexibility to add or delete products, open or close facilities, and redeploy the workforce. Although we cannot guarantee tenure in any particular job or even future employment, we will work to ensure that all our people are fully employable – sought out for new jobs here and elsewhere. We promise to:
>
> - Recruit for the potential to increase in competence, not simply for narrow skills to fill today's slots.
> - Offer ample learning opportunities, from formal training to lunchtime seminars – the equivalent of a month a year.
> - Provide challenging jobs and rotating assignments that allow growth in skills even without promotion to 'higher' jobs.
> - Measure performance beyond accounting numbers and share the data to allow learning by doing and continuous improvement.
> - Retrain employees as soon as jobs become obsolete.
> - Recognise individual and team achievements, thereby building external reputations and offering tangible indicators of value.
> - Provide three-month educational sabbaticals or external internships every five years.
> - Find job opportunities in our network of suppliers, customers, and venture partners.
> - Tap our people's ideas to develop innovations that lower costs, serve customers, and create markets – the best foundation for business growth and continuing employment.

The need for a learning society

The need for learning and development is not just an issue for individuals and their employers. It is now widely recognised that we need to become a learning society, in which there is a culture of, and opportunities for, lifelong learning. To this end, the government has introduced a number of initiatives (see Chapter 8).

The need for higher-order skills

According to Wisher (1994: 37), among the 'competencies that occur frequently in the most successful clusters of different organisations' are conceptual, 'helicopter' and analytical thinking. Organisations are thus demanding more of their employees than new or enhanced task skills. They are requiring higher-order thinking skills that are not easily picked up within the constraints of existing jobs, or even, for many people, in everyday life.

However, there is a long way to go for many organisations. According to Myers and Davids (1992):

> workers are a resource which has not been well understood by management in the past. Blue-collar workers in particular have been regarded as a static commodity incapable of innovation and self-development. Consequently reservoirs of skill and ability remain untapped. (p. 47)

Cooley (1987) reports how the Lucas Aerospace Shop Stewards' Combine Committee, as long ago as 1975, recognised the value of human capital. It challenged the organisation not to lay its highly skilled workforce off when its market was failing, but to retain it by moving into new markets for 'socially useful' products:

> What the Lucas workers did was to embark on an exemplary project which would inflame the imagination of others. To do so, they realised that it was necessary to demonstrate in a very practical and direct way the creative power of 'ordinary people'. Further, their manner of doing it had to confirm for 'ordinary people' that they too had the capacity to change their situation, that they are not the objects of history but rather the subjects, capable of building their own futures. (p. 139)

'Ordinary people' have the capacity to learn and develop, but human resource managers need to understand the processes and nature of the learning of the higher-order and other task skills in order to be able to facilitate that learning and development. It is the purpose of this chapter to explain these.

LEARNING AND DEVELOPMENT

> Deep down, we are all learners. No one has to teach an infant to learn. In fact, no one has to teach infants anything. They are intrinsically inquisitive, masterful learners who learn to walk, speak . . . Learning organizations are possible because not only is it our nature to learn but we love to learn. (Senge, 1990: 4)

Learning is a natural process in which we all engage. It is not just a cognitive activity, and it affects the person as a whole. This section will first note these points, then define learning and development, and go on to identify some barriers to learning and development. It will then reflect on the fact that the learners in whom this chapter is interested are adults. It will continue by identifying some characteristics of different classes of learners within the organisation: older workers, whose learning capacities are frequently discussed, and women, disabled people and people from ethnic minorities.

From birth, humans, like all animals, learn and develop, and this learning and development lead to skilful and effective adaptation to and manipulation of the environment, which is one element in a much-quoted definition of intelligence (Wechsler, 1958, in Ribeaux and Poppleton, 1978: 189). Society fosters and facilitates these activities of its members, but also channels and controls them through socialisation and education so that they yield outcomes that contribute to and are acceptable to it.

People continue learning throughout life, whether encouraged or not, whether formally taught or not, whether the outcomes are valued or not. They learn at work and at home, in their hobbies and their social lives.

> Most of us have learned a good deal more out of school than in it. We have learned from our families, our work, our friends. We have learned from problems resolved and tasks achieved but also from mistakes confronted and illusions unmasked. Intentionally or not, we have learned from the dilemmas our lives hand us daily.
>
> (Daloz, 1986: 1)

However, although individuals have a lifetime's experience of being learners, some of their experiences (especially those in formal educational settings) may not have been happy ones, as some of those who responded to the Declaration of Learning (Honey, 1998) illustrated (Honey, 1999). They may be experienced learners, but not necessarily competent or confident learners.

Lifelong learning means continuous adaptation. Increased knowledge and improved skills enlarge the individual's capacities to adapt to the environment and to change that environment. As the systems model in Chapter 2 implies, such external changes will lead on to further internal changes, and hence new possibilities for the individual emerge. Moreover, these changes feed the individual's self-esteem and confidence, and enhance social status. Hence learning generates potentially far-reaching changes in the individual: learning promotes development. In his very warm-hearted and insightful book on 'the transformational power of adult learning experiences', Daloz (1986) draws on mythology to convey the nature of this development:

> The journey tale begins with an old world, generally simple and uncomplicated, more often than not, home . . . The middle portion, beginning with departure from home, is characterized by confusion, adventure, great highs and lows, struggle, uncertainty. The ways of the old world no longer hold, and the hero's task is to find a way through this strange middle land, generally in search of something lying at its heart. At the deepest point, the nadir of the descent, a transformation occurs, and the traveler moves out of the darkness toward a new world that often bears an ironic resemblance to the old.
>
> Nothing is different, yet all is transformed. It is seen differently . . . Our old life is still there, but its meaning has profoundly changed because we have left home, seen it from afar, and been transformed by that vision. You can't go home again.
>
> (pp. 24–26)

A later section will return to the nature of development, but meanwhile it needs to be noted that the facilitation of another's learning is a moral project: it has the potential to promote changes that may have a profound effect in the other's life. This, too, has implications for the debate about the ownership of learning, one of the controversial issues at the end of the chapter.

Your very reading of this book may itself represent some of these issues. Before proceeding further, therefore, it makes sense to identify and reflect on them so that you will then have ready in your mind the 'hooks' on to which to hang the information this chapter will give you. In the language of a learning theory to be noted later, you will be ready to decode these new signals.

Activity	**Your aims and motivation for learning**

List your reasons for reading this book, noting:

- both short-term and long-term aims;
- those aims that are ends in themselves and those that are means to an end;
- the most important and the least important;
- the aims that you can achieve by yourself;
- those that require others to facilitate them;
- what else you need to achieve these aims;
- what initiated your pursuit of these aims;
- who or what has influenced you during this pursuit.

This chapter will help you to understand the motivation for and influences on learning. It will also examine how people learn, and what helps or hinders them. Not only do human resource managers need to understand these processes, but so too do those individuals who want to become and remain employable. By paying attention now to how you are reading this book, you can begin to understand your own processes of learning. Later you will have the opportunity to identify who benefits from and who pays for your learning. This will help you to understand something of the problematical issues inherent in employee development.

Defining learning and development

To understand the processes of learning and development and use this understanding to good effect in developing people and their organisations, you have to be able to think clearly about the concepts you are using. The concepts 'learning' and 'development' are frequently used loosely and even interchangeably, so it is important to define how they are being used here. The following definitions will enable you to distinguish them and understand the relationship between them.

Learning is

a process within the organism which results in the capacity for changed performance which can be related to experience rather than maturation.   (Ribeaux and Poppleton, 1978: 38)

It is now widely recognised that intelligence is not just a cognitive capacity – note the theory of multiple intelligences (Gardner, 1985, 1999), and the recent interest in emotional intelligence (Pickard 1999b). Hence learning is not just a cognitive process that involves the assimilation of information in symbolic form (as in book learning), but also an affective and physical process (Binsted, 1980). Our emotions, nerves and muscles are involved in the process, too. Learning leads to change, whether positive or negative for the learner. It is an experience after which an individual 'qualitatively changed the way he or she conceived something' (Burgoyne and Hodgson, 1983: 393) or experienced 'personal transformation' (Mezirow, 1977). Learning can be more or less effectively undertaken, and it can be more effective when it is paid conscious attention.

Development, however, is the process of becoming increasingly complex, more elaborate and differentiated, by virtue of learning and maturation. (As will be noted later, it is sometimes assumed that development connotes progression and advancement.) In an organism, greater complexity, differentiation among the parts, leads to changes in the structure of the whole and to the way in which the whole functions (Reese and Overton, 1970: 126). In the individual, this greater complexity opens up the potential for new ways of acting and responding to the environment. This leads to the opportunity for even further learning, and so on. Learning therefore contributes to development. It is not synonymous with it, but development cannot take place without learning of some kind.

Development, whether of an organism, individual or organisation, is a process of both continuity and discontinuity. Quantitative changes lead to qualitative changes or transformations; development is irreversible, although regression to earlier phases can occur.

> The disintegration of the old phase of functioning . . . creates the conditions for the discontinuous 'step-jump' to a new phase. This succeeding phase incorporates yet transforms the repertoire of principles, values, etc., of earlier phases and adds to them. The new phase is therefore not entirely new – it is a transformation. Each succeeding phase is more complex, integrating what has gone before.
>
> (Pedler, 1988: 7–8)

It can be concluded from earlier sections that what organisations need of their members is development, for this is the process whereby a person (or any organism) through learning and maturation becomes increasingly complex, more elaborate and differentiated, and thereby better able to adapt to the changing environment. In an organism, greater complexity and differentiation among its parts lead to changes in the structure of the whole and in the way in which the whole functions (Reese and Overton, 1970: 126). In the individual, this greater complexity opens up the potential for new ways of acting and responding to the environment. This leads to the opportunity for even further learning, and so on.

The outcomes of a person's learning and development are the way they think, feel and interpret their world (their cognition, affect, attitudes, overall philosophy of life); the way they see themselves, their self-concept and self-esteem; and their ability to respond to and make their way in their particular environment (their perceptual-motor, intellectual, social, and interpersonal skills). Some of the experience of learning can be seen in the description that Daloz (1986: 24–26) gives of development, the journey that starts from the familiar world and moves through 'confusion, adventure, great highs and lows, struggle, uncertainty . . . toward a new world' in which 'nothing is different, yet all is transformed'; 'its meaning has profoundly changed'. Learning and development therefore are significant experiences for individuals and for organisations.

Learning and development are processes that we all experience, active processes in which we all engage: we do not have learning and development done to us. However, we rarely pay conscious attention to them and so may not fully understand them. This chapter therefore addresses you, the reader, directly, and in this section and elsewhere invites you to draw upon your own experience in order to understand and make use of the issues that it will discuss.

Barriers to learning and development

Although learning is a natural process, it is not necessarily easily undertaken, particularly – as noted above – when undertaken in formal settings such as school or work. People can experience significant barriers to their learning and development, and human resource developers need to be aware of these.

Writing primarily about managers, Mumford (1988) identifies significant blocks to learning. They are also relevant to other learners in the organisation, as the remainder of this chapter will demonstrate. They are listed in Table 7.1.

Table 7.1 Blocks to learning

Perceptual	Not seeing that there is a problem
Cultural	The way things are here . . .
Emotional	Fear or insecurity
Motivational	Unwillingness to take risks
Cognitive	Previous learning experience
Intellectual	Limited learning styles; poor learning skills
Expressive	Poor communication skills
Situational	Lack of opportunities
Physical	Place, time
Specific environment	Boss/colleagues unsupportive

Source: Mumford (1988: 26).

Anxiety and lack of confidence are frequently emphasised as significant impediments to learning. Barry (1988: 47), for example, notes that the considerable apprehension felt by the fitters and electricians who were returning to college after 20 years was an obstacle in the introduction of a multi-skilling programme. Their anxieties were dissipated once they learned that some of the tutors belonged to the same union and had the same craft background as themselves. Personality characteristics, such as an external rather than an internal locus of control (Rotter, 1966), may also make the individual less open to new learning.

Human resource developers need to recognise that other people and the organisation itself constitute the individual's learning environment, and that they may create barriers to effective learning. A later section will return to this context of learning.

Adult learners

What we know about learning and teaching derives mainly from the study of children and young people: pedagogy. The needs and experiences of adults are different: we need an androgogical model of learning (Knowles, 1984: 10–12). Knowles suggests that:

- The adult learner is self-directing.
- Adult learners have experience on which to draw, and learning events need to take this into consideration. They may have developed poor learning habits, and be defensive about their habitual ways of thinking. However, their former experience is a source of self-identity, so it must be approached sensitively and with respect.
- Adults are ready to learn when they become aware that they need to know or do something to make themselves more effective: they 'do not learn for the sake of learning' (p. 12). Learning experiences, therefore, have to be related to their needs and situation.
- What motivates them most are their needs for 'self-esteem, recognition, better quality of life, greater self-confidence, self-actualization' (p. 12).

Human resource development has to address these needs appropriately, as suggested in the later section on the organisation as a context for learning.

Learners in the organisation

Older workers

Older people have been widely discriminated against when seeking employment and when employed (Naylor, 1987; Dennis, 1988; Laslett, 1989; Waskel, 1991). They are commonly stereotyped as having failing cognitive and physical abilities, as being inflexible, unwilling and unable to learn new ways. However, the Carnegie Inquiry into the Third Age (Trinder *et al.*,1992) reports:

> There does seem to be a decline in performance with age . . . but such deterioration as there is, is less than the popular stereotype . . . Except where such abilities as muscular strength are of predominant importance, age is not a good discriminator of ability to work; nor of the ability to learn.
>
> (p. 20)

Trinder *et al.* (1992) also note that performance is influenced as much by experience and skill as by age: skill development in earlier years will encourage adaptability in later life.

Although older people are 'at a disadvantage with speedy and novel (unexpected) forms of presentation', Coleman (1990: 70–71) reports little or no decline with age in memory and learning, particularly 'if the material is fully learned initially'. (The role of rehearsal and revision in memory will be examined later in this chapter.) Pickard (1999a: 30), discussing changing attitudes to the employment of older people, and the possibility of retirement age rising to the upper 70s, quotes a 72-year-old Nobel prize-winning scientist as saying: 'You may forget where you were last week, but not the things that matter.' Coleman (1990) goes on to cite a study in which the majority of the 80 volunteers aged 63 to 91 years learned German from scratch, and in six months reached the level of skill in reading German normally achieved by schoolchildren in five years.

Until recently, there were few examples to cite of organisations that employed older people. The do-it-yourself retail chain B & Q was a notable exception, staffing one store solely by people over the age of 50. It was 'an overwhelming success . . . In commercial terms the store has surpassed its trading targets' (Hogarth and Barth, 1991: 15). In this trial these older workers were found to be willing to train, although initially reluctant to use new technology, and did not require longer or different training from other workers. Since then, as Pickard (1999a) reports, B & Q has been joined by other employers in giving employment opportunities to older people. These older workers demonstrate the ability to continue to learn through life; their learning will be facilitated if employers adopt appropriate approaches, which will be examined in the section on the organisation as a context for learning. This is likely to become more significant in the future as organisations raise their retirement age in order to retain key skills, and governments support their move as one response to the 'greying' of the population.

Other classes of employees

Three classes of people – women, disabled people, and individuals from cultural and ethnic minorities – are often socialised and educated in ways that do not advantage them in labour markets or organisations; they may develop correspondingly low expectations and aspirations. Negative stereotyping of them in employment is frequently discussed (Gallos, 1989; Thomas and Alderfer, 1989). This section will briefly note some aspects of their experience that will influence them as learners in the organisation: these need to be viewed in terms of the barriers to learning identified earlier.

Until recently, little seemed to have been written about disabled people in organisations. Moreton (1992) identified the role of the Training and Enterprise Councils in providing training programmes for them, and Arkin (1995b) summarised the implications for employers of the 1995 Disability Discrimination Act. Clearly, there is a wide range of disability, but in 1999 Whitehead was able to report on the employment of disabled people at Centrica, and Littlefield (1999) reported how some residents with learning disabilities accompanied staff at their community care home on training days, some achieving NVQ (see Chapter 8) level 1 qualifications.

As was noted in Chapter 2, there is now a considerable body of theory, including feminist critiques, that addresses the nature of women and their experiences in their own right, rather than as a subset of a supposed 'universal' (but often Eurocentric, middle-class male) nature. For example, Gilligan (1977: see Daloz, 1986: 134–135) argues that unlike men, who see their world as 'a hierarchy of power', women see theirs as 'a web of relationships'. The connected self interprets the environment differently, and so responds to it differently, from the separate self. These and other ways in which women may differ from men (Bartol, 1978) will influence their approach to, experience of, and outcomes from, learning. They may, indeed, advantage women in the development of some of the higher-order skills needed in organisations.

Different cultures imbue their members with different basic assumptions about the nature of reality and the values and the roles in social life. Cultural experiences differ, and hence the accumulated experience of the members will also differ. The concept of intelligence is not culture-free. Gardner (1985), who expounds a theory of multiple intelligences that include interpersonal and intrapersonal intelligence, recognises that

> because each culture has its own symbol systems, its own means for interpreting experiences, the 'raw materials' of the personal intelligences quickly get marshaled by systems of meaning that may be quite distinct from one another . . . the varieties of personal intelligence prove much more distinctive, less comparable, perhaps even unknowable to someone from an alien society.
>
> (p. 240)

Hence as women differ from men, so also may members of cultural and ethnic minorities have ways of learning that are dissimilar to those of the dominant culture, and also different outcomes from their learning. It is therefore important to assess such constructs as intelligence in as culture-fair a manner as possible (Sternberg, 1985: 77, 309), and to seek appropriate means to facilitate learning of the skills required in organisations. Learning through action may be particularly appropriate.

Understanding of and fluency with English are not the only language issues in organisations. As discussed in Chapter 2, language is ideological and can embody racism and sexism. Similarly, the construction of knowledge is a social and ideological process. Through the very nature of language and knowledge, these learners may be internalising constructions of themselves that ultimately undermine their self-esteem, alienate them from self-fulfilment, and erect barriers to their effective learning.

THE OUTCOMES AND PROCESSES OF LEARNING

If, as this chapter has argued, human resource managers are now charged with developing their employees, then they need to understand the nature of learning and development. This section will, therefore, examine the following:

- the outcomes of learning:
  - skill
  - competence
  - 'know-how' and tacit knowledge
  - employability
  - hierarchies of cognitive and other skills;
- the process of learning:
  - theories of the process of learning
  - elements in the process of learning
  - learning stages
  - cyclical models of learning and learning styles.

The outcomes of learning

This subsection will examine skill, competence, 'know-how' and tacit knowledge, hierarchies of cognitive and other skills, all direct outcomes of learning and development, and employability, an indirect outcome. These are all of concern to human resource managers.

Skill

> . . . the performance of any task which, for its successful and rapid completion, requires an improved organisation of responses making use of only those aspects of the stimulus which are essential to satisfactory performance. (Ribeaux and Poppleton, 1978: 53–54)

> . . . an appearance of ease, of smoothness of movement, of confidence and the comparative absence of hesitation; it frequently gives the impression of being unhurried, while the actual pace of activity may of course be quite high . . . increasing skill involves a widening of the range of possible disturbances that can be coped with without disrupting the performance. (Borger and Seaborne, 1966: 128–129)

These definitions are particularly appropriate to perceptual-motor skills, which involve physical, motor responses to perceived stimuli in the external world. Such skills are needed at every level of an organisation, from the senior manager's ability to operate a desktop computer to the cleaner's operation of a floor-scrubbing machine. High levels of such skills are particularly needed to operate complex and expensive technology. There are many other kinds of skills needed in organisations, such as cognitive, linguistic, social and interpersonal skills, that could also be defined in these terms. However, their complexity suggests that various levels of skill have to be recognised, which is what a later subsection will do in presenting some hierarchies of skills.

Competence

Competence – also referred to as competency in the literature – has been defined as

> an underlying characteristic of a person which results in effective and/or superior performance in a job. (Boyatzis, 1982)

> the ability to perform the activities within an occupational area to the levels of performance expected in employment. (Training Commission, 1988)

The core of the definition is an ability to apply knowledge and skills with understanding to a work activity.

Competences are now a major element in the design of training and development in Britain (Cannell *et al.*, 1999), and seem to fit well with what is happening in organisations. Martin (1995: 20) proposes that they are a means of 'aligning what people can offer – their competencies – against the demands of customers rather than against the ill-fitting and ill-designed demands of jobs'. Nevertheless, the notions of competence and competences are still matters of debate: from the confusion suggested by differences between the definitions above (Woodruffe, 1991) to the challenge of postmodern (see Chapter 2) thinking (Brittain and Ryder, 1999). Despite considerable variation in the number of competences being used in competence frameworks (one study suggested between 21 and 30 and 300–400), and often a lack of validation of such frameworks, there is claimed to be a 'dramatic increase' in the number of companies using them. 'Personnel professionals must stop dismissing competencies as fads' (Walsh, 1998: 15).

What needs to be noted at this point is that the concept of competence integrates knowledge and skill that are assessed via performance. This leads on to the distinction between 'know-how' and formal knowledge, in which tacit knowledge has a significant part to play.

'Know-how' and tacit knowledge

'Knowing how to do something' is a very different matter from knowing about 'knowing how to do something'. This truism is captured in the everyday suspicion and disparagement of 'the ivory tower': 'those who can, do; those who can't, teach'. It is also apparent in the reluctance of British employers to value higher education, evidenced in the small proportion of managers with degrees, documented in the Handy (1987) and Constable and McCormick (1987) reports (see Chapters 8 and 9). By contrast, 'can do' became a buzzword for pragmatic effectiveness in the 1980s.

Gardner (1985) makes the distinction between 'know-how' and 'know-that'. For him, 'know-how' is the tacit knowledge of how to execute something, whereas 'know-that' is the statement of formal thinking (propositional knowledge) about the actual set of procedures involved in the execution:

> Thus, many of us know how to ride a bicycle but lack the propositional knowledge of how that behaviour is carried out. In contrast, many of us have propositional knowledge about how to make a soufflé without knowing how to carry this task through to successful completion. (p. 68)

Tacit knowledge is an essential ingredient of 'know-how'. Sternberg (1985) recognises this in his definition of practical intelligence:

> Underlying successful performance in many real-world tasks is tacit knowledge of a kind that is never explicitly taught and in many instances never even verbalized. (p. 169)

The example that he gives is of the tacit knowledge relevant to the management of one's career. The individual also draws upon tacit knowledge in the fluent performance of perceptual-motor skills, as seen in the definition of skill above; indeed, Myers and Davids (1992) write of 'tacit skills'. Moreover, as you will have seen earlier, one of the purposes of knowledge management is to capture the tacit knowledge that employees have.

This tacit knowledge would appear to be acquired through experience rather than through instruction, and is embedded in the context in which this experience is taking place. This can be seen in Stage 2 of the model of Dreyfus *et al.* (see below), in which the learner becomes independent of instruction through the recognition of the contextual elements of the task, and thereafter develops the ability to register and 'read' contextual cues. However, unlike the formal knowledge that it accompanies, this tacit knowledge never becomes explicit, although it remains very significant. Myers and Davids (1992: 47) question whether 'tacit skills' can be taught, and identify that they are often transmitted in 'an environment of intensive practical experience' and in task performance: 'We may yet be able to learn much from "sitting next to Nellie"!' They also note the need to take account of both formal and tacit knowledge in selection. A later section will examine the concept of action learning, which contextualises learning and hence draws upon tacit knowledge.

Traditionally, practical knowledge tends to feature at a lower level in any representation of the social hierarchy of skills, and is thereby institutionalised in lower-level occupations. In discussing the public's understanding of science, Collins (1993) writes about:

> the all too invisible laboratory technician . . . Look into a laboratory and you will see it filled with fallible machines and the manifest recalcitrance of nature . . . Technicians make things work in the face of this . . . Notoriously, techniques that can be made to work by one technician in one place will not work elsewhere. The technician has a practical understanding of aspects of the craft of science beyond that of many scientists. But does the technician 'understand science'? (p. 17)

Cooley (1987: 10–13) draws attention to the way in which practical knowledge, craft skill, is devalued in the face of technological progress. This is the starting point for his reflections upon the way 'ordinary people' could achieve something extraordinary. He believes that technological systems

> tend to absorb the knowledge from them ['ordinary people'], deny them the right to use their skill and judgement, and render them abject appendages to the machines and systems being developed.

Myers and Davids (1992: 47) come to a similar conclusion after their discussion of the significance of 'tacit skills'. In contrast, it could be argued that knowledge management regards technology, rather than people, as the 'appendages'.

It is clear, however, that organisations need both 'know-how' and 'know-that': the concept of competence, therefore, as defined above is potentially a significant one for them. However, it can be argued that the institutionalised, transorganisational process of identifying and defining competences has wrenched them from their context and hence from the tacit knowledge that contributes so significantly to them.

Employability

An indirect outcome of learning and development is 'employability', a notion that has recently become current because of the proliferation of flexible contracts of employment and insecurity in employment during the 1990s. According to Kanter (1989a), employability is the 'new security': if individuals have acquired and maintained their employability then, should their job come to an end, they would be able to find employment elsewhere.

Employability results from investment in the human capital of skills and reputation. This means that individuals must engage in continuous learning and development, update their skills and acquire others that will be needed in the future by their current or other employer (Fonda and Guile, 1999). It is also argued that, as part of the 'new deal' in employment, good employers will ensure that their employees remain employable (Herriot and Pemberton, 1995) by keeping them up to date through training and development.

Hierarchies of cognitive and other skills

An earlier section concluded that today's organisations need their employees generally, and their managers in particular, to practise higher-order thinking skills. It was also pointed out above that not only a variety, but different levels, of skills should be recognised: a hierarchy of skills. This subsection presents several hierarchies, each with a somewhat different focus. They imply not just different levels but different stages: the individual can progress from the lower to the higher stages, but does not necessarily do so. The lower levels are prerequisites for, and subsumed by, the higher. The following subsection on the process of learning will return to the notion of the stages of learning, and outline what it calls the micro levels of the acquisition of learning. Each of these could be interpreted as needing to take place within each of the macro levels of the hierarchies here.

These hierarchies give insights into the higher-level thinking skills, which are clearly identifiable in higher levels of the hierarchies below: in the analysis, synthesis and evaluation levels of Bloom's taxonomy; in the characteristics of proficiency and expertise as defined by Dreyfus *et al.*; and in Perry's continuum. The human resource manager can therefore use these hierarchies, first to identify the prior learning that needs to take place before the higher-order skills can be attained, and then to plan ways of facilitating their learning.

Single- and double-loop learning

Single-loop learning refers to the detection and correction of deviances in performance from established (organisational or other) norms, whereas double-loop learning (Argyris and Schon, 1978) refers to the questioning of those very norms that define effective performance. Learning how to learn calls for double-loop learning.

The concepts of single- and double- loop learning do not actually constitute a hierarchy or stages of learning. Rather, they are two different approaches, and individuals do not necessarily progress from single- to double-loop learning, nor is the former an essential prerequisite for the latter. They are, however, important elements in learning, and it is convenient to present them here.

Bloom et al.'s taxonomy of cognitive skills

Bloom *et al.* (1956) identify the various levels of thinking skills at which learning can take place:

- knowledge (simple knowledge of facts, of terms, of theories, etc.);
- comprehension (an understanding of the meaning of this knowledge);
- application (the ability to apply this knowledge and comprehension in new concrete situations);
- analysis (the ability to break the material down into its constituent parts and to see the relationship between them);
- synthesis (the ability to re-assemble these parts into a new and meaningful relationship, thus forming a new whole);
- evaluation (the ability to judge the value of material using explicit and coherent criteria, either of one's own devising or derived from the work of others). (Fontana, 1981: 71)

Dreyfus et al.'s stage model of skills acquisition

Dreyfus *et al.* (1986, in Cooley, 1987: 13–15, and Quinn *et al.*, 1990: 314–315) set out a five-stage model of the process of acquisition of skill that moves from the effective performance of lower- to higher-order thinking skills.

- *Stage 1: the novice.* Novices follow context-free rules, with relevant components of the situation defined for them: hence they lack any coherent sense of the overall task.

- *Stage 2: the advanced beginner.* Through their practical experience in concrete situations learners begin to recognise the contextual elements of their task. They begin to perceive similarities between new and previous experiences.
- *Stage 3: competent.* They begin to recognise a wider range of cues, and become able to select and focus upon the most important of them. Their reliance upon rules lessens; they experiment and go beyond the rules, using trial and error.
- *Stage 4: proficient.* Those who arrive at this stage achieve the unconscious, fluid, effortless performance referred to in the definitions of skill given at the start of this subsection. They still think analytically, but can now 'read' the evolving situation, picking up new cues and becoming aware of emerging patterns; they have an involved, intuitive and holistic grasp of the situation.
- *Stage 5: expert.* At this stage, according to Cooley (1987), 'Highly experienced people seem to be able to recognise whole scenarios without decomposing them into elements or separate features'(p. 15). They have 'multidimensional maps of the territory'; they 'frame and reframe strategies as they read changing cues' (Quinn *et al.*, 1990: 315). With this intuitive understanding of the implications of a situation, they can cope with uncertainty and unforeseen situations.

Managers' levels of learning (Burgoyne and Hodgson)

A similar hierarchy has been proposed specifically for the learning of managers. Burgoyne and Hodgson (1983) suggest that managers have a gradual build-up of experience created out of specific learning incidents, internalise this experience, and use it, both consciously and unconsciously, to guide their future action and decision-making. They identify three levels of this learning process:

- **Level 1 learning**, which occurs when managers simply take in some factual information or data that is immediately relevant but does not change their views of the world.
- **Level 2 learning**, which occurs at an unconscious or tacit level. Managers gradually build up a body of personal 'case law' that enables them to deal with future events.
- **Level 3 learning**, when managers consciously reflect on their conception of the world, how it is formed, and how they might change it.

Perry's continuum of intellectual and ethical development

Perry's (1968) schema (see Daloz, 1986) emerged from his research into his students' experiences. He interpreted their intellectual and ethical development as a continuum, and mapped out the way in which individuals develop multiple perspectives while at the same time becoming able to commit themselves to their own personal interpretation. At one extreme is basic dualism, where everything is seen as good or bad. This moves through the perception of the diversity of opinion; of extensive legitimate uncertainty; through perception that all knowledge and values are contextual and relativistic; to the recognition of the need to make a commitment to a viewpoint; the making of the commitment; experiencing its implications; and, finally, to the affirmation of identity as this commitment is expressed through lifestyle.

The process of learning

Having identified what learning has to be achieved, we now need to examine the process by which it will be achieved. The following section therefore examines theories of the process of learning and elements within it. This is a very rich and complex field, to which the section cannot do justice here, and you are recommended to read a text such as Atkinson *et al.* (1993) or Ribeaux and Poppleton (1978).

Theories of the process of learning

Behaviourist approach to learning

The behaviourist approach has been one of the most influential in the field of psychology. It proposes that learning is the process by which a particular stimulus (S), repeatedly associated with, or conditioned by, desirable or undesirable experiences, comes to evoke a particular response (R). This conditioning can be of two kinds. Classical conditioning occurs when a stimulus leads automatically to a response. Dogs, for example, salivate at the presentation of food; Pavlov demonstrated that they could also be conditioned to salivate at the sound of a bell rung before food is presented. Operant conditioning (Skinner) takes place after a desired response, which is then reinforced, or rewarded, to increase the probability of the repetition of the same response when the stimulus recurs.

There has been much experimental research (including many animal studies) into such issues as the nature of the reinforcement (negative reinforcement, or punishment, is not as effective for learning as positive reward); the schedule of reinforcement (whether fixed or variable intervals: intermittent reinforcement is more effective than continuous reinforcement). This form of conditioning is also used to shape behaviour: that is, to continue to reinforce responses that approximate to the desired behaviour until that behaviour is finally achieved. We are familiar with this kind of approach to the encouragement of fairly simple forms of learning: we use it with small children, with animals, and in basic forms of training.

The S–R approach pays no attention to the cognitive processes whereby the stimulus comes to be associated with a particular response: it does not investigate what is in the 'black box'. Cognitive learning theory, however, offers a more complex understanding of learning, proposing, again on the basis originally of animal studies, that what is learned is not an association of stimulus with response (S–R), but of stimulus with stimulus (S–S). The learner develops expectations that stimuli are linked; the result is a cognitive 'map' or latent learning. Hence insightful behaviour appropriate to a situation takes place without the strengthening association of S–R bonds. Social learning theory also addresses what is in the 'black box'. It recognises the role in learning of the observation and imitation of the behaviour of others, but as seen in the debates over the influence of the media upon, say, young people's behaviour, there are clearly many moderating variables.

Information-processing approach to learning

This approach regards learning as an information-processing system in which a signal, containing information, is transmitted along a communication channel of limited capacity and subject to interference and 'noise' (Stammers and Patrick, 1975). The signal has to be decoded before it can be received, and then encoded to pass it on. In learning, data received through the senses are filtered, recognised and decoded through the interpretative process of perception; this information is then translated into action through the selection of appropriate responses. The effectiveness of learning depends on attention being paid only to the relevant parts of the stimuli, the rapid selection of appropriate responses, the efficient performance of them, and the feeding back of information about their effects into the system. Overload or breakdown of the system can occur at any of these stages.

Gagné (1974, in Fontana, 1981: 73) expresses this as a chain of events, some internal and others external to the learner. It begins with the learner's readiness to receive information (motivation or expectancy), and continues as the learner perceives it, distinguishes it from other stimuli, makes sense of it and relates it to what is already known. The information is then stored in short- or long-term memory. Thereafter it can be retrieved from memory, generalised to, and put into practice in, new situations. Its final phase is feedback from knowledge of the results obtained from this practice. Those concerned to facilitate learning in others can use their understanding of this chain to prevent failure to learn, which can take place at any one of these levels.

Elements in the process of learning

This subsection will deal briefly with other important elements in the process of learning that need to be taken into account when designing or facilitating learning. These are the need for feedback, the choice of whole or part learning, and the role of memory.

Feedback (or knowledge of results)

The feedback to learners of the results of their performance is recognised as essential to their effective learning. This is discussed in Ribeaux and Poppleton (1978) and Stammers and Patrick (1975). Feedback will be either intrinsic or extrinsic (or augmented). Learners receive visual or kinaesthetic feedback (intrinsic) from their responses to stimuli in the learning situation; they need to be encouraged to 'listen' to such bodily cues in order to improve performance. They may also receive feedback (extrinsic, augmented) from an external source while they are performing (concurrent feedback) or after it (terminal). Learners may also benefit from guidance given before their performance about what to look out for during it. The sources cited above set out the characteristics, advantages and disadvantages of these different kinds of feedback.

The notion of feedback is frequently discussed in terms of learning perceptual-motor or similar skills. It is also of considerable importance in the learning of the higher-order skills discussed in this chapter, but here it is very complex in nature, and difficult for the learner to be aware and make sense of it. However, by reflecting and engaging in the whole-loop learning discussed below, the learner will have opportunity to pay attention to both intrinsic and extrinsic feedback.

The choice of whole or part learning

Psychologists continue to debate the appropriateness of whole or part learning in learning to perform various tasks: that is, whether the task is learned as a whole, or in parts. Ribeaux and Poppleton (1978: 61) report on one approach that classifies tasks according to their 'complexity' (the difficulty of the component subtasks) and 'organisation' (the degree to which they are interrelated). Where complexity and organisation are both high, whole methods appear superior; where either is low, part methods are superior in most cases; when both are low, part and whole methods are equally successful. Stammers and Patrick (1975: 85–88), however, report on research that appears to draw opposite conclusions: where the elements of a task are highly independent the task is best learned as a whole, but where they are interdependent, they should be learned in parts.

It tends to be the whole method in operation when learning takes place during the performance of a job, through action learning, or through observing others.

The role of memory in learning

Memory plays a significant role in learning, and some understanding of it can therefore be used to make learning more effective. Once again, it is not possible to do more than present an outline here, but texts such as Stammers and Patrick (1975), Ribeaux and Poppleton (1978), Fontana (1981) and Atkinson *et al.* (1993) give further information.

Memory involves three kinds of information storage: the storage of sensory memories, short-term or primary memory, and long-term or secondary memory. Unless transferred to short-term memory, the sensory memory retains sense data for probably less than two seconds. Unless incoming information is paid particular attention or rehearsed, short-term memory holds it for up to 30 seconds and appears to have limited capacity, whereas long-term memory appears to have unlimited capacity and to hold information for years. What is therefore of concern for effective learning is the ability to transfer information to the long-term memory.

There are two aspects to such transfer. The first is 'rehearsal' – that is, paying attention to and repeating the information until it is coded and enters the long-term store; it is otherwise displaced by new incoming information. The second aspect of the transfer of information to long-term memory is coding: the translation of information into the codes that enable it to be 'filed' into the memory's 'filing system'. Information is largely coded according to meaning (a semantic code) or through visual images, but sometimes (where the meaning itself is unclear) according to sound.

The ability to retrieve information from long-term memory depends in part upon how effectively it has been organised ('filed') in storage (for example, words may be stored according to sound and meaning), but also upon having the most appropriate retrieval cue. We experience this when we are searching for something that we have lost: we think systematically through what we were doing when we believe we last used the lost object. Recognition is easier than recall from memory because it follows the presentation of clear retrieval cues.

Difficulty in retrieving information, or forgetting, occurs for several reasons apart from those concerning the degree of organisation in storage. Interference from other information can disrupt long-term as well as short-term memory (where new items displace existing items in the limited capacity). Interference may be retroactive, when new information interferes with the recall of older material, or proactive, when earlier learning seems to inhibit the recall of later information. Forgetting also takes place through anxiety or unhappy associations with the material to be learned, which may become repressed. Unhappy childhood experiences, for example, may be repressed for many years.

Finally, memory does not just operate as a camera recording what is experienced: it is an active and a constructive process. This is particularly so when learning the kind of complex material that constitutes the world of organisations and human resource management. As well as recording its data inputs, the process of memory draws inferences from the data and so elaborates upon them, filtering them through the individual's stereotypes, mind-set and world-view. What is then stored is this enhanced and repackaged material.

An understanding of the nature of memory suggests various ways in which it might be improved to make learning more effective. The transfer of new information to long-term memory is clearly crucial: attention, recitation, repetition and constant revision (known as *overlearning*) are needed. The coding and organisation of material to be stored are also important: this is helped by associating the new information with what is already familiar, especially using visual imagery, by attending to the context giving rise to the information to be learned, and by making the effort to understand the information so that it can be stored in the appropriate 'files'. Facilitators of learning need to ensure that the learning context or event does not provoke anxiety.

Learning stages

The previous subsection identified higher-order thinking skills within various hierarchies of skills. Here we shall note some of the micro stages through which, it may be inferred, the learner has to pass within each of the levels of those hierarchies. (See the next section on development for a further reference to stages.)

Fitts's stages of skills acquisition

Fitts (1962, in Stammers and Patrick, 1975) distinguished three stages of learning, in particular of perceptual-motor skills acquisition. It is recognised that they may overlap.

- **Cognitive stage**. The learner has to understand what is required, its rules and concepts, and how to achieve it.
- **Associative stage**. The learner has to establish through practice the stimulus–response links, the correct patterns of behaviour, gradually eliminating errors.
- **Autonomous stage**. The learner refines the motor patterns of behaviour until external sources of information become redundant and the capacity simultaneously to perform secondary tasks increases.

Gagné's classification of learning

Gagné (1970, in Stammers and Patrick, 1975) studied both the process of learning and the most effective modes of instruction, and has made several classifications of types of learning. For example, he identified the ability to make a general response to a signal; to develop a chain of two or more stimulus–response links, including verbal chains and associations; to make different responses to similar though different stimuli; to achieve concept learning and identify a class of objects or events; to learn rules through the acquisition of a chain of two or more concepts; and, finally, to combine rules and so achieve problem solving.

Gagné's classification allows us to identify the processes whereby skills of all levels are acquired, and hence suggests how to facilitate learning and prevent failure to learn at the various levels.

The learning curve

It is recognised that there is a relationship between the rate of learning and the passage of time: managers working on the introduction of a new system, for example, may say 'we are on a learning curve'. According to Hodgetts (1991), many psychologists 'feel that the S-shaped curve represents the most accurate description of learning' (p. 99). This is shown in Figure 7.1. However, since the shape of the curve must clearly depend on the nature and circumstances of the learning, this notion of a learning curve perhaps adds little of value to the understanding of learning.

Cyclical models of learning and learning styles

Here we examine a related, but more dynamic, notion of the process of learning: that of a cycle of learning. The recognition that learning is a process that may have different identifiable phases, and that more effective learning may be facilitated if methods appropriate to the various phases are used, has led to the development of models of learning as a cycle. (The assumptions here echo those underlying the concept of development, which is to be discussed in the next section.) As you will see, they offer a number of important insights to the human resource manager concerned to facilitate higher-order skills in the organisation. They draw attention to the significance of learn-

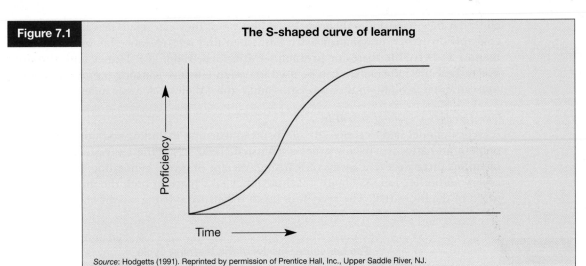

Figure 7.1

The S-shaped curve of learning

Proficiency

Time

Source: Hodgetts (1991). Reprinted by permission of Prentice Hall, Inc., Upper Saddle River, NJ.

ing through action and reflection, as well as through the traditional channels of teaching/learning. They recognise that individuals may prefer different phases of the cycle and have different styles: they offer means to identify those preferences; to engage in dialogue about them with individuals; and to identify means of helping individuals to complete the whole cycle.

Kolb's learning cycle

The best-known learning cycle in the field in which we are interested is that of Kolb. There are two dimensions to learning (Kolb *et al.*, 1984): concrete/abstract (involvement/detachment) and active/reflective (actor/observer). Learning is an integrated cognitive and affective process moving in a cyclical manner from concrete experience (CE) through reflective observation (RO) and abstract conceptualisation (AC) to active experimentation (AE) and so on (Kolb, 1983).

Effective learning calls for learners:

- to become fully involved in concrete, new experiences (CE);
- to observe and reflect on these experiences from many perspectives (RO);
- to use concepts and theories to integrate their observations (AC);
- to use these theories for decision-making and problem solving (AE).

However, many people have a preference for a particular phase and so do not complete the cycle: thus they do not learn as effectively or as comprehensively as they could. Kolb's Learning Styles Inventory identifies these preferences (Mumford, 1988: 27). The 'converger' (AC and AE) prefers the practical and specific; the 'diverger' (CE and RO) looks from different points of view and observes rather than acts; the 'assimilator' (AC and RO) is comfortable with concepts and abstract ideas; and the 'accommodator' (CE and AE) prefers to learn primarily from doing.

Honey and Mumford's learning styles

Honey and Mumford (1992) identify four learning styles similar to those of Kolb, and develop norms based on the results of those who have completed their Learning Styles Questionnaire. Their **activists** learn best when they are actively involved in concrete tasks; **reflectors** learn best through reviewing and reflecting upon what has happened and what they have done; **theorists** learn best when they can relate new information to concepts or theory; **pragmatists** learn best when they see relevance between new information and real-life issues or problems (Mumford, 1988: 28). Honey and Mumford discuss how this information can be used to design effective learning events. Individuals, too, can use it to build on their strengths and reduce their weaknesses in learning.

The Lancaster cycle of learning

A cyclical model said to represent 'all forms of learning including cognitive, skill development and affective, by any process' (Binsted, 1980: 22) is the Lancaster model. This identifies three different forms of learning: receipt of input/generation of output, discovery and reflection. As Figure 7.2 shows, they take place in both the inner and outer world of the individual. The receipt of input results from being taught or told informa-

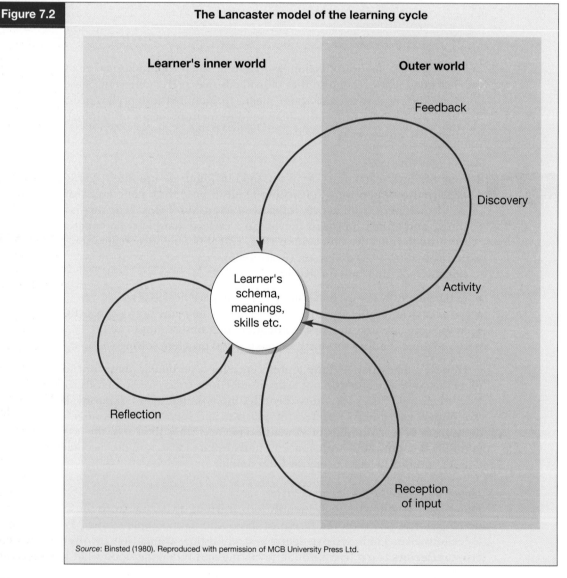

Figure 7.2 **The Lancaster model of the learning cycle**

Learner's inner world

Outer world

Feedback

Discovery

Learner's schema, meanings, skills etc.

Activity

Reflection

Reception of input

Source: Binsted (1980). Reproduced with permission of MCB University Press Ltd.

tion, or reading it in books. Learners follow the discovery loop (action and feedback) through action and experimentation, opening themselves to the new experiences generated, and becoming aware of the consequences of their actions. They follow the reflection loop (conceptualising and hypothesising) when making sense of the information they receive and the actions they undertake, and when, on the basis of this, theorising about past or future situations.

Each form of learning is cyclical, and the cycles can be linked in various ways (for example, learning in formal classroom settings links the receipt of input with reflection), but in effective learning the learner will complete the overall cycle.

THE PROCESS OF DEVELOPMENT

This section examines development, the process whereby, over time, the individual becomes more complex and differentiated through the interaction of internal and external factors. Learning plays a part in development. For example, the individual's innate tendencies towards growth and maturation are facilitated or constrained – shaped – by the influences in the individual's specific context, and by how the individual responds to them. (The systems thinking discussed in Chapter 2 helps to conceptualise this.) Life-span development, career development, continuing professional development, self-development, employee development, staff development, management and organisation development will now be briefly examined. Before then, however, consider the following question.

Stop and think	What is human resource **development**, and how does it come about?

Development is difficult to study, embracing as it does both the individual's (or organisation's) inner life and the changing nature of a complex world, with the lifespan as the time dimension. Researchers and theorists have therefore often focused upon segments of the lifespan and drawn implications for the remainder, or upon aspects, rather than the whole range, of development.

It has already been noted that 'development' – as in career development – is sometimes used to connote progression or advancement. Such use assumes that there are accepted norms against which an individual's development can be calibrated, and that those norms and the individuals' experiences can be clearly identified. If you recall the nature of various assumptions about social and personal reality discussed in Chapter 2, you will recognise that these are positivist assumptions. Positivist assumptions about individuals and the social and economic environment within which their lives are led (construed as an objective, orderly, stable framework) give rise to the definition of development in terms of sequential phases or stages, often with their own developmental tasks. Some theorists argue that their models represent universal, normative patterns of experience, that all individuals follow similar patterns of experiences, and that their models therefore allow some degree of prediction to be made about the basic outline of individual lives (for example Levinson *et al.*, 1978)). However, these models frequently interpret the experiences of women and black people in terms of those of white males.

Those working with these assumptions may also recognise that individuals have subjective experiences that cannot be studied in this scientific manner. They may therefore disregard them, although individuals base decisions about their life on their subjective experiences. However, as Chapter 2 outlined, there are alternative approaches. The phenomenological approach acknowledges the significance of a person's subjective experiences, and the social constructionist approach recognises that, because individual experiences are socially constructed, the context of the individual has to be taken into account. These alternative assumptions lead to a focus upon individual cases and the search for insights rather than generalisable conclusions. They also emphasise the significance of context, and the dynamic, intersubjective processes through which individuals interpret and make decisions about their lives and careers.

Lifespan development

Lifespan development embraces the total development of the individual over time, and results from the interweaving of the biological, social, economic and psychological strands of the individual's life. It is the framework within which individuals learn, and hence constitutes an important background to the development of the employee, of which the employer needs to be aware.

The influence of the sociocultural context

There are two perspectives in the literature upon the influence of the sociocultural context on the individual's lifespan experiences. The first interprets that there are tendencies towards common patterns in individual experiences resulting from socialisation. In any given social setting, whether culture, class or organisation, the members of that social group experience pressures to conform to certain patterns of behaviour or norms. Sometimes these pressures are expressed as legal constraints: the age of consent, marriage, attaining one's majority (becoming an adult); or as quasi-legal constraints such as the age at which the state pension is paid and hence at which most people retire from the labour force; or as social and peer group expectations. For example, Neugarten (1968) recognises how family, work and social statuses provide the 'major punctuation marks in the adult life', and the

> way of structuring the passage of time in the life span of the individual, providing a time clock that can be superimposed over the biological clock . . . (p. 146)

Organisations also have their own 'clocks'. Sofer (1970) writes of his respondents' 'sensitive awareness' of the relation between age and organisational grade, for they were:

> constantly mulling over this and asking themselves whether they were on schedule, in front of schedule or behind schedule, showing quite clearly that they had a set of norms in mind as to where one should be by a given age. (p. 239)

The other perspective, however, emphasises that the environment offers different opportunities and threats for individual lives. The process of development or elaboration takes place as the individual's innate capacity to grow and mature unfolds within a particular context, which in turn facilitates or stunts growth, or prompts variations upon it. For example, it is argued that there are significant differences in physical, intellectual and socio-economic attainments between children from different social classes (Keil, 1981). The interaction and accommodation between individuals and their environment therefore cannot be meaningfully expressed in a model that is cross-cultural or universal. Hence Gallos (1989) questions the relevance of many of the accepted views of development to women's lives and careers, while Thomas and Alderfer (1989) note that 'the influence of race on the developmental process' is commonly ignored in the literature.

Models of lifespan development

There are many different models of the lifespan: here you can see three that have been influential in lifespan psychology. It is important to be aware of the assumptions underlying these models, as discussed above. Their implications for human resource development will be noted below.

Erikson's psychosocial model

Erikson (1950) conceives of development in terms of stages of ego development and the effects of maturation, experience and socialisation (see Levinson *et al.*, 1978; Wrightsman, 1988). Each stage builds on the ones before, and presents the expanding ego with a choice or 'crisis'. The successful resolution of this 'crisis' achieves a higher level of elaboration in individuality and adaptation to the demands of both inner and outer world, and hence the capacity to deal with the next stage. An unsuccessful or inadequate resolution hinders or distorts this process of effective adaptation in the subsequent stages.

For example, the adolescent strives for a coherent sense of self, or identity, perhaps experimenting with several different identities and as yet uncommitted to one; entry to work and choice of work role play a part here. The choice, however, has to be made and responsibility assumed for its consequences: unless this occurs, there is identity confusion. Young adults have to resolve the choice between achieving closeness and intimate relationships, fusing identity with another without the fear of losing something themselves, or being ready to isolate themselves from others.

Erikson paid less attention to the remainder of the lifespan, but indicated that the choice for those aged 25 to 65 is between the stagnation that would result from concern only for self, indulging themselves as though they were 'their own only child' (Wrightsman, 1988: 66), and generativity. This is the reaching out beyond the need to satisfy self in order to take responsibility in the adult world, and show care for others, the next generation or the planet itself. The choice of the final stage is between construing life as having been well or ill spent.

The model of Levinson et al.

The research of Levinson *et al.* (1978) was into the experiences of men. They model men's lifespan in terms of alternating, age-related periods of stability and instability, as shown in Figure 7.3. In the stable periods, lasting six to eight years, a man builds and enriches the structure of his life: work, personal relationships and community involvement. The structure, however, cannot last, and during the transitional periods, of four to five years, the individual reappraises that structure, explores new possibilities, and sets the scene for adapting or changing it, which can be a painful experience. (You can read more about this model in Daloz (1986), and Wrightsman (1988).)

Kegan's model

Kegan (1982) examines individual growth in terms of the balance between self-centredness and other-centredness: he sees the **evolving self** as a helix spiralling upwards (see Daloz, 1986). Each transformation within this development involves risk, a move away from familiarity towards uncertainty. In the early **impulsive** phase, young children cannot distinguish their impulses from those of others, but as they get older they can get outside themselves and understand the value of reciprocity: their **imperial** phase. Teenagers move into an **interpersonal** balance as they redefine themselves through others. The **institutional** balance is achieved as individuals draw the boundaries around

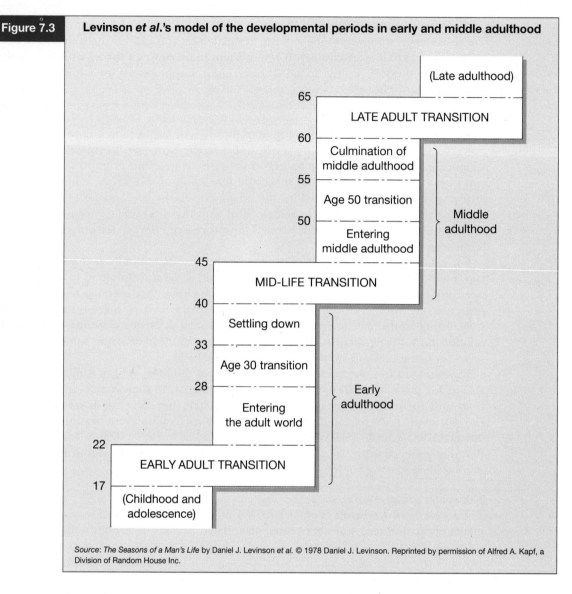

Figure 7.3 Levinson *et al.*'s model of the developmental periods in early and middle adulthood

Source: *The Seasons of a Man's Life* by Daniel J. Levinson *et al.* © 1978 Daniel J. Levinson. Reprinted by permission of Alfred A. Kapf, a Division of Random House Inc.

themselves more clearly, and define themselves in their own terms. The final stage sees individuals dissolving the boundaries of self again and reaching out to others in a new **interindividual** balance.

Career development

Individual development interacts with the organisation and its development through the individual's career. Career development therefore is of significance for both individual and organisation, and for human resource development. This subsection will look briefly at career development, although, like lifespan development, it is far broader than organisational experience.

Although the term 'career' is well understood in everyday language, the concept is a complex one with several levels of meaning, and is therefore open to several definitions (see Glossary, pp. 743–8, and Collin and Young, 2000). The core of the concept suggests the experience of continuity and coherence while moving through time and social space. Career, therefore, has two faces, the private world of the individual and the social structure, the subjective and the objective career.

As with development generally, the individual's career results from the interaction of internal and external factors. As individuals become more skilled and flexible, they gain more opportunities for promotion or other intra- or inter-organisational moves: their learning and development affect their objective career. This learning and development also influences the way they view themselves, the rewards they gain from their work, their relationship with their employer, and the role of work in their lives: their subjective career.

The theories of career development

Because of the assumptions commonly made about objectivity and subjectivity (see Chapter 2, and the discussion about the concept of development above), much of the literature emphasises the objective career, but the subjective is clearly also of relevance to human resource development. The theories of career development have similar characteristics to those of lifespan development. They:

- are more frequently formulated from a positivist than from a phenomenological or constructionist approach (see Chapter 2);
- focus upon objective rather than subjective experience;
- emphasise intra-individual rather than contextual factors;
- largely disregard the significance of gender, race and social class.

The theories (see Watts *et al.*, 1996) that have attempted to explain this rich concept of career can be classified into several families as follows:

- Theories concerned with external influences upon the individual's career:
  - economic and labour market theories
  - social class, social structure and social mobility
  - organisational and occupational structure and mobility.
- Theories concerned with factors internal to the individual:
  - factors such as age, gender
  - psychoanalytical explanations
  - lifespan development
  - implementation of self-concept
  - matching personality and occupation.
- Theories concerned with the interaction of internal and external factors:
  - decision-making
  - social learning.
- Theories concerned with the interpretation of the individual's subjective experiences.

It is not possible here to illustrate this wide range of theories of career, but the following indicate two different approaches. You can read more about careers, particularly careers in organisations, in Arnold (1997), Arthur *et al.* (1989), Herriot (1992), and Jackson (1999).

Career and lifespan development

The concept of lifespan development has been an important influence on career theories. For example, Cytrynbaum and Crites (1989) and Dalton (1989) relate career development to adult development, as does Evans (1986) writing about career management in organisations. His model of the stages of career development is very similar to those they cite, and is illustrated in Figure 7.4.

Career 'anchors' in organisations

Another influential, but very different, approach is that of Schein (1978) (see also Dalton, 1989). Schein identifies a number of 'career anchors' (self-perceived talents and abilities, motives and needs, and attitudes and values) that guide, constrain, stabilise and integrate individuals' careers. These are:

- technical-functional competence;
- managerial competence (analytical, interpersonal, emotional);
- security and stability;
- creativity;
- autonomy and independence.

He concludes that there is a need to examine the 'dynamics of careers' in order to achieve both organisational and individual effectiveness, and argues for a 'human resource planning and development system' (Schein, 1978: 243–256).

Forms of career

There are many different forms of career. Most would be regarded as elitist. However, the section first acknowledges the careers of blue-collar workers, ethnic minorities, and women, before looking at the bureaucratic, professional and entrepreneurial forms, and then finally at careers in the flexible organisations of the twenty-first century.

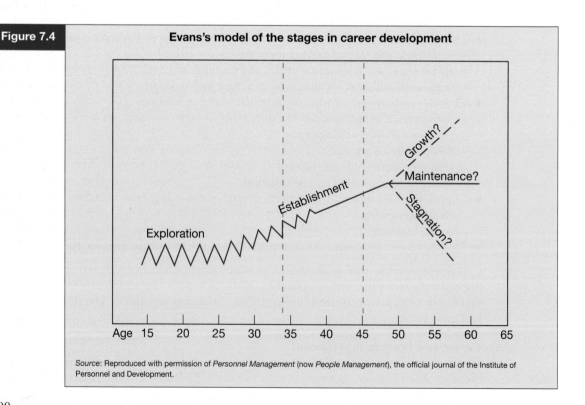

Figure 7.4 **Evans's model of the stages in career development**

Growth?

Maintenance?

Stagnation?

Establishment

Exploration

Age 15   20   25   30   35   40   45   50   55   60   65

Source: Reproduced with permission of *Personnel Management* (now *People Management*), the official journal of the Institute of Personnel and Development.

The careers of blue-collar workers, minorities, and women
The typical notions of career to date stem largely from the experiences of white middle-class males. There are, however, some challenges to the prevailing assumptions. For example, Thomas (1989: 355) recognises the existence of blue-collar careers, for 'blue-collar workers do indeed accumulate skills . . . over time and are concerned about the meaning of their work experiences'. He analyses the processes that shape their experiences, and discusses how social class, the organisational arrangement of occupations and labour market segmentation structure career opportunities. Thomas and Alderfer (1989) discuss the issue of race in career, noting, for example, that racial minorities often feel caught between two very different cultural worlds.

Some of the distinctive issues that arise in women's careers are: the construction of identity and the role of relationships; autonomy and control; partnership, pregnancy and children; social stereotypes, roles and socialisation; and the relationship between work and home life. Hence it is suggested that career theory, currently 'rooted in male values and based on disguised male psychology' (Marshall, 1989: 282), needs to be revised in order to take the needs of both women and men into account (Gallos, 1989; Marshall, 1989). According to Marshall (1989: 285), career theory could then have a more cyclical interpretation of phases, 'based in notions of ebb and flow, of shedding and renewal'. Further, it would allow the recognition of 'giving something up, letting achievements go, in order to create anew and differently'. This challenges some of the thinking behind the stage models of career, but offers a way of conceptualising change as renewal rather than destruction of the old.

Bureaucratic, professional and entrepreneurial forms of career
Kanter (1989b: 508) draws our attention to three different forms of 'organizing principle around which a career logic unfolds'. The 'bureaucratic' career, defined by a 'logic of advancement', is only one form of career but, she points out, it is the form that has come to colour our view of organisational careers generally. The 'professional' form of career (Kanter, 1989b: 516) is wider than that pursued by members of professional bodies. It is defined by craft or skill; occupational status is achieved through the 'monopolization of socially valued knowledge' and 'reputation' is a key resource for the individual. Career opportunities are not dependent in the same way as the 'bureaucratic' career upon the development of the organisation, nor is satisfaction as dependent upon the availability of extrinsic rewards. Some professional careers may be only weakly connected to employing organisations. The 'entrepreneurial' career develops 'through the creation of new value or new organisational capacity' (Kanter, 1989b: 516). Its key resource is the capacity to create valued outputs, and it offers freedom, independence and control over tasks and surroundings. However, while those with a 'bureaucratic' career have (relative) security, and 'professionals' can command a price in the marketplace, 'entrepreneurs' 'have only what they grow'. There is perhaps an affinity between the 'entrepreneurial' career and employability, self-development, and the new careers in flexible organisations.

Careers in the twenty-first century
This section has so far looked at career only as it has traditionally been understood. However, the flatter and more flexible forms of today's organisations, and the changing relationship between employees and employers ('the new deal', according to Herriot and Pemberton (1995)) could well change the nature of career dramatically. There are also some slow, deep-seated changes taking place in the context (see Chapter 2) of

career. Demographic changes and shifts in public and private values, for example, may over time have significant impacts upon individuals' opportunities, attitudes and aspirations. It is for this reason that questions are being asked not only about future careers, but also about the future of the concept of career itself (Collin and Young, 2000).

The possibilities, potentials and implications of some of these changes – for individuals, employers, educationalists, careers guidance practitioners and policy-makers of various kinds – are being discussed widely (see Jackson *et al.*, 1996). It has been suggested that it is the traditional 'onward and upward' form of career – Kanter's 'bureaucratic' form' (see above) – that is under threat, and that the 'professional' and 'entrepreneurial' careers could now become the predominant forms (Collin and Watts, 1996). However, 'don't write off the traditional career', advise Guest and McKenzie Davey (1996: 22), who have found little evidence of major organisational transformations in their own research.

Theorists are attempting to understand the nature of the twenty-first century career in increasingly flexible organisations. Weick and Berlinger (1989) argue that the focus will be on the subjective career in 'self-designing organizations' (the learning organisation of the next section). In the absence of the typical attributes of career such as advancement and stable pathways, 'the objective career dissolves' and the subjective career 'becomes externalized and treated as a framework for career growth' (Weick and Berlinger, 1989: 321), and a resource for the further organisational self-design. They liken career development in such organisations to what Hall (1976) described as the 'Protean career', in which people engage in 'interminable series of experiments and explorations'. Such a career calls for the acceptance of frequent substantial career moves in order to incorporate a changing, complex and multi-layered sense of self; the 'decoupling' of identity from jobs; the preservation of the ability to make choices within the organisation; the identification of distinctive competence; and the synthesis of complex information (Weick and Berlinger, 1989: 323–326).

Other theorists are pointing out other aspects of the new careers. Arthur and Rousseau (1996: 3) indicate that whereas careers traditionally took place 'through orderly employment arrangements' within organisations, they are now 'boundaryless', crossing traditional boundaries – between organisations, and home and work. Hall & Associates (1996: 2) suggest that, whereas it was customary to see career development in the individualistic terms of autonomy and 'mastery', it is now fruitful to recognise that it takes place in interaction with others within a 'context of connection and mutual influence and benefit'.

These new forms of career make demands of individuals, of organisations, and of those who manage them, that are very different from those of traditional careers. However, they accompany the changes in today's organisations identified at the beginning of the chapter, and highlight the significance of employability, discussed earlier, and the need for lifelong learning. The future of the concept of career, however, is still uncertain, and will be looked at as a controversial issue at the end of this chapter.

Continuing professional development

Continuing professional development (CPD) will now be briefly examined, because some of its principles and practices are relevant to human resource development in changing organisations.

Many professional institutions (see Arkin, 1992) require their members to undertake CPD because the changing environment is rendering obsolete some of their original skills and knowledge and demanding the development of others. However, CPD is more than updating: it calls for a continuous process of learning and of learning-to-learn, and so is likely to have considerable benefits for organisations employing professionals, especially when part of the overall corporate strategy (Young, 1996).

Likely to be of particular relevance to readers of this book are the requirements for CPD that the Institute of Personnel and Development (IPD) has introduced. Whittaker (1992) states that CPD is needed to ensure that professionals remain up to date in a changing world and that the reputation of the profession is enhanced, and to encourage professionals to aspire to improved performance and ensure that they are committed to learning as an integral part of their work. She identifies the following principles underlying CPD:

- Development should always be continuous, the professional always actively seeking improved performance.
- Development should be owned and managed by the learner.
- Development should begin from the learner's current learning state – learning needs are individual.
- Learning objectives should be clear, and where possible serve organisational as well as individual goals.
- Investment in the time required for CPD should be regarded as being as important as investment in other activities.

CPD for the IPD is undertaken through engagement in professional activities, formal learning, and self-directed and informal learning (see also Haistead, 1995).

The previous subsection referred briefly to the 'professional' form of career, and suggested that it might be more widely adopted in future. Continuing development, even where not required or monitored by a professional body, would be an important element of it. It should also be noted that the framework of vocational qualifications outlined in Chapter 8 is expected to accommodate the work of professionals at its level 5 (see Welch (1996) and Whittaker (1995) on the routes to the personnel and development profession).

Other forms of development within organisations

Some other forms of development within organisations will now be briefly noted.

Self-development

Self-development is the term used to denote both 'of self' and 'by self' types of learning (Pedler, 1988). People developing themselves take responsibility for their own learning, identify their own learning needs and how to meet them, often through the performance of everyday work, monitor their own progress, assess the outcomes, and reassess their goals. The role of others in self-development is not to teach or to train, but perhaps to counsel or act as a resource.

In the absence (or paucity) of the training and development of employees (especially managers) by their employers, the need for self-development has long been recognised. It has also been regarded positively as proactive and entrepreneurial, but for it to receive some form of accreditation it has often involved arduous part-time study, which can increase the pressures on and conflict between the individual's work and home roles. Such programmes of study have in the past been largely dictated by the traditions and values of the educational providers, rather than the specific needs of the learner.

This is now changing with the establishment of the Credit Accumulation and Transfer Scheme, the Accreditation of Prior Learning and of Experiential Learning (see Chapter 8). Moreover, the approach and framework of S/NVQs (see Chapter 8) is now allowing individuals to gain recognition for aspects of their work performance. The existence of employee development schemes (see below) should also help individuals in their self-development, whether systematic or sporadic.

What is now becoming widely recognised is that, with the increasing flexibility of organisations and their contracts of employment, individuals need to engage in lifelong learning – and many will find that they will not receive from their employers the continuous development they will need. The need for self-development, associated with the need for employability, is likely to be seen in the future as greater than ever.

Employee development

One definition of employee development is:

> . . . the skilful provision and organization of learning experiences in the workplace . . . [so that] performance can be improved . . . work goals can be achieved and that, through enhancing the skills, knowledge, learning ability and enthusiasm at every level, there can be continuous organizational as well as individual growth. Employee development must, therefore, be part of a wider strategy for the business, aligned with the organization's corporate mission and goals.
>
> (Harrison, 1992: 4)

The section earlier on the need for learning and development made clear the importance for the organisation of developing, or 'investing in', employees generally. Many British employers have traditionally neglected employee development, as seen in the quotations from Cooley (1987) used throughout this chapter. However, recent interest in the learning organisation and knowledge management (see start of chapter), and the establishment of the Investors in People award (see Chapter 8) are raising employers' awareness of the need to develop employees. Furthermore, those employers who have already recognised their own self-interest in their employees' continuous learning and employability are encouraging their employees to engage in learning activities for such self-development.

In employee development schemes, sometimes established by a consortium of TECs (see Chapter 8) and local employers, the employer provides some degree of financial or other activities that are not necessarily related to the needs of their jobs. A much-quoted example of this is Ford Motor Company's Employee Development and Training Programme (Corney, 1995). Moreover, many organisations have now established learning centres that often support learning opportunities beyond those needed specifically by the organisation. Others have set up corporate universities (such as Motorola and Unipart (Miller and Stewart, 1999; see also Coulson-Thomas, 2000).

Nevertheless, even though their employers may not formally 'develop' them or encourage them to develop themselves, people still continue to learn, as we shall note in the following section.

Staff development

This is similar to employee and professional development, but generally refers to the development of administrative, technical and professional staff in organisations, such as local authorities, in which such staff form a large proportion of those employed. Its aim is to enable such employees to perform their current and future roles effectively, but does not generally include their systematic development as managers.

Management and organisational development

It is not within the remit of this chapter to examine management development – this forms the subject of Chapter 9 – or organisation development, but they are included here for completeness. However, it can be noted here that organisations, like people, need to develop to become more flexible, differentiated and adaptable to their environment. Indeed, the very development of organisational members will contribute to the development of the organisation itself. For example, as Chapter 9 recognises, management development is both needed by the developing organisation and sets in train further organisation development.

Implications for human resource development

People develop through their lifespan, achieving greater degrees of complexity, even transformation. They are therefore continuously engaging in learning processes as they seek balance between changing self and changing environment. The theories and models of lifespan development have several implications for human resource development, for the organisation is one of the major arenas in which this adult development is taking place.

Those concerned with human resource development need to recognise that these developmental pressures could be exacerbated or compounded by work pressures. Managers need to be aware of the possible effects of developmental changes upon performance at work, some positive, others not. Young people entering adulthood, for example, may lack enthusiasm for or commitment to their job as they juggle with their potential various identities. Later the needs of their developing intimacy with another person may lead to conflicts with educational or organisational demands.

Opportunities for promotion, the mid-career plateau, training to ensure continuous improvement or cutbacks in training: these may influence the choice between generativity and stagnation. The outcome may influence the way in which supervisors and managers relate with their subordinates. Human resource development needs to harness the generativity and combat the potential stagnation of organisational members, by perhaps giving them the role of mentor (see the section on the organisation as a context for learning). Managers also need to be aware of the age clock (Neugarten, 1968), of individuals' vulnerability, and the possibility that they suffer when their roles in different social subsystems do not synchronise.

The career development of employees is one manifestation of human resource development, and those responsible for it will benefit from a knowledge of the theories of it and of lifespan development. Indeed, unless they construe the work of blue-collar workers and of women in terms of career, the development of these classes of employees may continue to be neglected. Managers will understand career development better with an awareness of, for example, the nature and effects of career anchors. They should pay attention to the nature of changes in blue-collar jobs incurred by quality management and similar initiatives if the organisation is to benefit from them. The ideas raised here about 'entrepreneurial' careers, careers in self-designing organisations and women's 'cyclic' careers offer starting points for effective human resource development in flexible and learning organisations.

Overall, having made themselves aware of the implications of these various forms of learning and development, human resource managers need to provide an environment in which the capacity to learn and adapt can be harnessed to benefit the organisation.

THE CONTEXT OF LEARNING

This chapter has examined how people learn and develop. This section now examines how individuals can learn and develop both within, and outside, organisations.

Learning and development *sans frontières*

The process of learning knows no boundaries; learning in one domain, such as employment, hobbies or maintenance of home and car, cross-fertilises that in another and thereby achieves a wider understanding and more finely honed skills. People bring the fruits of this naturally occurring and continuous process into their place of work and so, as Cooley (1987: 169) shows, 'ordinary people' have the potential to contribute the knowledge, skills, attitudes and creative thinking that organisations need for survival, flexibility and development. Moreover, their learning and development continues within the organisation. Employers benefit from – indeed, depend on – this. Some recognise this and encourage, facilitate and extend those aspects of their employees' learning that are essential for the organisation, and support them informally or undertake formal employee development activities (see, for example, Corney, 1995).

However, organisations themselves can sometimes make inhospitable environments for the learning and development individuals bring to them (e.g. Honey, 2000). As was noted in the section on the nature of the learner, learning involves the whole person, but as Chapter 2 identified, organisations are systems of roles, and these roles can distort or straitjacket individuals, as Argyris (1960) and McGregor (1960) argue. While they were both writing in a very different organisational era, and much has already moved in the directions they were advocating, nevertheless, the urgent calls for human resource development and for the development of the learning organisation hint that there still remain vestiges of those traditional assumptions and practices.

Some employers ignore the significance for the organisation of this learning, and do little either to overcome the way in which their organisation may thwart the development of their employees, or to foster that learning and development. In these cases, employee development is not a planned or systematic process. It takes place nevertheless: employees learn for themselves how to carry out their jobs, or improve their performance; how to make job changes or achieve promotions; how to become managers and develop others.

It must therefore be recognised in this overview of human resource development that much employee development may not be intended, planned or systematic; Chapter 8 indicates that this may be the case in the majority of organisations. Nevertheless, individuals may:

- learn how to carry out their initial and subsequent jobs through doing and observing, through trial and error, through the influence of and feedback from their peers and supervisors, through modelling themselves on others, and through informal mentors;
- develop themselves through their own more or less systematic analysis of their learning needs;
- take the initiative to acquire additional knowledge or understanding by attending educational and other courses.

Because of this, employee development is problematical. Employers will receive many of its benefits without effort on their part, while at the same time, unlike recruitment and selection, they cannot fully control or contain it. Some employers may feel threatened by the potential of their employees' learning and development, and not welcome significant changes in the people they had been at pains to select as employees. Through their work, employees may acquire knowledge and skills that make them marketable to other employers, and perhaps less than fully committed to their present employer. Equally, not exposed to best practice, they may learn poor lessons; they may also learn ineffectively and in an unnecessarily uncomfortable, effortful or wasteful manner. Thus they may not necessarily benefit from the learning and development they contribute to their organisation, although they will not be able to withhold some of its benefits from their employers.

To manage people effectively and fairly, and in a way that benefits the organisation, therefore, it is important, first, to be aware of these thorny and, at times, moral issues. (You will have the opportunity to consider them in greater depth in the section on controversial issues.) Then, it is necessary to understand how the processes of learning and development can be facilitated in the organisation and, indeed, how the organisation can itself learn. This is the subject of this section.

Influences upon learning and development outside the organisation

Many significant influences upon learning and development emanate from outside the organisation. Government-driven education and training initiatives and changes have contributed to the institutionalisation of competence-based education and training. The history, purpose and nature of these developments are discussed by Harrison (1992: 17–77). Within a comprehensive and continually updating national framework agreed across all sectors and occupations (see Chapter 8), elements in an individual's learning and development, whether achieved through formal education, training or experiential learning across the lifespan, are identified and assessed against nationally agreed standards. The language, philosophy and procedures of this framework are likely to shape individuals' perceptions of their learning and learning needs, and to influence how employers articulate the learning needs of their employees. Moreover, the Investors in People initiative (see Chapter 8 and Arkin, 1999) will also both prompt, shape and support human resource development practices.

Organising and managing to ensure learning and development within the organisation

Employees learn and develop through carrying out their jobs: this chapter has already noted the significance of action for learning. For example, the design of those jobs and the organisation structure, the degree to which it is centralised and bureaucratised, influence employees' learning opportunities. People may outgrow their jobs as they learn, and need to be able to grow in their jobs, or to move into new jobs that will allow them to continue the process of their development. An organisation that is growing or changing is more likely to offer these opportunities than one that is static or declining.

However, a 'world-class manufacturing' organisation, such as Oral-B Ireland, is a challenge to manage:

> When everyone participates in creating a quality culture, functional boundaries become fuzzy, and the 'seamless' organisation emerges. This culture makes people easier to lead, but difficult to drive.
> (Ryan, 1995: 41)

Here, then, some of the features of, first, organisation and then management that would facilitate learning and development will be examined.

The holographic organisation

In his metaphor of the organisation as a brain, Morgan (1997) offers us a new way of appreciating how the organisation itself can facilitate, constrain or repress the learning of its members. He suggests that both brain and organisation can be understood as holograms, 'where qualities of the whole are enfolded in all the parts so that the system has an ability to self-organize and regenerate itself on a continuous basis' (p. 100). Reminding us that the brains of employees and the brain-like capacities of computers and the Internet already have holographic features, Morgan considers how to design these features into organisations as well. He identifies five principles: the 'whole' built into the 'parts', redundant functions, requisite variety, minimum critical specification, and learning to learn.

Building the 'whole' into the 'parts'

One way of building the 'whole' into the parts of the organisation is through its culture. When this, Morgan suggests, embodies the organisation's 'vision, values, and sense of purpose', then it will act like a 'corporate "DNA"' (p. 102), which carries the holographic code of the human body in each of its parts. Another way is to network information throughout the organisation, so that it can be widely accessed, enabling organisational members 'to become full participants in an evolving system of organizational memory and intelligence' (p. 104). Further ways are to have the kind of structure that allows the organisation to 'grow large while remaining small' (p. 104), and to organise work tasks not into specialised jobs but into holistic teams of individuals having multiple skills.

Redundancy

Morgan suggests that the organisation needs an 'excess capacity that can create room for innovation and development to occur' (pp. 108–110). It therefore needs redundancy of functions rather than redundancy of parts (pp. 111–112). In the traditional mechanistic design of organisations, each part had a specific function, with additional parts for back-up or replacement. This allowed a degree of passivity and neglect in the system ('"that's not my responsibility"', p. 111); with the capacity for redesigning the system delegated to specialised parts, the capacity to self-organise is not generalised throughout the system. Where, instead, each part has additional functions – through multi-skilling and teamworking, for example – currently redundant but potentially available, the capacities for the functioning of the whole are built into the parts. Thus the system as a whole has flexibility, with the capacity to reflect on and question how it is operating and to change its mode of operating.

Requisite variety

The internal diversity of a self-regulating system must match the variety and complexity of its environment in order to deal with the challenges from that environment. All elements of the organisation should therefore 'embody critical dimensions' of the environment with which they have to deal; this variety can be achieved, where appropriate, through 'multifunctioned teams' (p. 112).

Minimum critical specification

Overdefinition and control, as in a bureaucracy, erode flexibility and stifle innovation. Hence the manager should define no more than is essential, but should instead have a role focusing on 'facilitation, orchestration and boundary management, creating "enabling conditions" that allow a system to find its own form' (p. 114). The challenge is to avoid the extremes of anarchy and overcentralisation.

Learning to learn

Finally, the organisation needs to engage in double-loop learning (see earlier), allowing its operating norms and rules to change as the wider environment changes.

Morgan concludes by noting that these five interconnected principles should not be regarded as 'a blueprint or recipe' (p. 115), but as a way of looking at how organisations could ensure that they remain adaptive.

Supportive management

Earlier sections have identified the need for learners to have self-confidence, and to receive feedback on their performance. The higher-order skills needed in organisations require the opportunity to take risks and hence to make mistakes. This presupposes not only a risk-taking and confident approach on the part of employees, but also a risk-taking and supportive management style. Effective learning and development in the organisation therefore call for a managerial style that is compatible with this need. The existence and nature of an appraisal scheme (see Chapter 12) could have positive or negative effects upon employees' learning (Thatcher, 1996). Essentially, organisations that want to develop these characteristics need also themselves to learn to learn, to become learning organisations.

Reporting on the results of research by the New Learning for New Work Consortium, Fonda and Guile (1999) set out the guiding principles for managing 'capable' organisations that seek to develop the learning of their employees. These are 'respect for the views of the workforce and clarity about the capabilities that the whole workforce will need; the creation of both challenge and support for developing and sustaining these capabilities; and an individualised approach to potential' (p. 41).

Informal and tacit learning

Other people are significant for an individual's learning and development, to provide instruction and feedback (see earlier), support and encouragement, confidence-building, perhaps even inspiration. They are also major actors in the context of the individual's learning. They may be, perhaps unknown to themselves, mentors, models or points of comparison for learners who learn not just from their formal instructors or supervisors, but also from peers and subordinates. This informal method of learning, 'sitting next to Nellie', may have its weaknesses, but it also has strengths. It offers whole rather than part learning, and the opportunity to apprehend tacit knowledge (see earlier).

Some organisations attempt to capture and use formally some of these informal ways of learning through people. Knowledge management (see earlier) and mentoring, to be discussed below, are examples of this. Shadowing is a method that gives the opportunity for a learner to observe the actions of a senior manager systematically and over a period of time. From this observation the learner can infer certain general principles, grounded in everyday organisational realities. However, as the novel *Nice Work* (Lodge,

1988) suggests, without feedback from the manager, the 'shadow' may misinterpret some of the situations witnessed.

THE FACILITATION OF LEARNING AND DEVELOPMENT IN ORGANISATIONS

This section will now examine how organisations can facilitate the learning and development of their members through learning resources, the design of learning, mentoring, action learning, and becoming a learning organisation.

Support and resources for learning and development

As well as specific training, individuals need encouragement, support, and resources to stimulate and sustain their learning and development. They will find these where the organisation has a learning culture and a learning centre (Coulson-Thomas, 2000).

The design of learning

The messages about how to design effective learning are very consistent. For example, the advice that Sternberg (1985: 338–341), a theorist of intelligence, gives on how intelligent performance can be trained includes the following: make links with 'real-world' behaviour; deal explicitly with strategies and tactics for coping with novel tasks and situations; be sensitive to individual differences and help individuals capitalise on their strengths and compensate for their weaknesses; be concerned with motivation. The implications of the androgogical model of learning introduced in an earlier section (Knowles, 1984: 14–18) are that the facilitator of adult learning needs to:

- set a climate conducive to learning, both physical and psychological (one of mutual respect, collaborativeness, mutual trust, supportiveness, openness and authenticity, pleasure, 'humanness');
- involve learners in mutual planning of their learning;
- involve them in diagnosing their own learning needs;
- involve them in formulating their learning objectives;
- involve them in designing learning plans;
- help them carry out their learning plans – use learning contracts;
- involve them in evaluating their learning.

Belbin and Belbin (1972) draw upon their experience of studying training in industry for this advice on training 40- to 55-year-old adults:

1 Reduce anxiety and tension in the adult learner:
   - provide social support and allow social groups to form;
   - use acceptable instructors;
   - offer a secure future.
2 Create an adult atmosphere.
3 Arrange the schedule:
   - appropriate length of sessions;
   - preference for whole rather than part method;
   - start slowly.

4 Correct errors:
 – at the appropriate time.
5 Address individual differences:
 – different instructional approaches;
 – effects of previous education and work;
 – spare-time interests.
6 Follow up after training.

The value of these approaches is illustrated in the lessons drawn from the adoption in Britain of the Deming-inspired quality and continuous improvement programmes (Hodgson, 1987):

> Train with extreme sensitivity – pick trainers who have operators' confidence, are alert to remedial training needs and people's fears about going back to class; minimise the gap between awareness, training and use; gear course contents to people's learning needs – don't impose blanket programmes. (p. 43)

Action learning

> There can be no action without learning, and no learning without action. (Revans, 1983: 16)

The role of action in learning, and the role of tacit knowledge in action, noted earlier, is now examined more closely here.

The competence movement's focus upon outcomes rather than inputs into learning, and the integration of knowledge and skill assessed via performance, appears to offer a route towards the development of learning through action, but the reservations about competences expressed earlier should be noted. However, there is an established approach that has been shown (Pedler, 1983) to achieve the kind of learning that organisations, and particularly managers, are seeking, action learning, and this is discussed more fully in Chapter 9.

Action learning offers a philosophy and a practice that human resource managers can adopt to help bring about the higher-order skills needed in an organisation. It is a greatly demanding process, one that will change the organisation and its members, but nevertheless one that could be carried out at all levels of the organisation, perhaps as a continuation of 'the restless searching for continuous improvement' and total quality management (see earlier). However, it demands commitment and support from the top, and would need to be cascaded down from higher learning sets.

Mentoring

Mentor was the friend to whom Ulysses entrusted the care of his young son before embarking on his epic voyages. In organisations mentors are more experienced employees (and often managers) who guide, encourage and support younger or less experienced employees, or 'protégés'. Their relationship is a developmental one that serves career-enhancing and psychosocial functions for the protégé while also benefiting the mentor.

The nature and purpose of mentoring

During the last 15 years or so many organisations have introduced mentoring programmes. You can read about this in Kram (1985), Collin (1988), Megginson (1988),

Bennetts (1995), Fowler (1998), Brockbank and Beech (1999), Clutterbuck and Megginson (1999) and Whittaker and Cartwright (1999).

Their experience suggests that mentoring facilitates the learning-to-learn of their employees and contributes to the process of meaning-making in the organisation (see Chapter 2) and hence to its responsiveness to its environment, while meeting the developmental needs of employees.

Organisations set up formal mentoring programmes for various reasons. These include supporting a graduate intake or training scheme and developing 'high fliers' or senior managers; encouraging career advancement of women or those from minority groups (see Crofts, 1995); nurturing employees with skills in short supply; stimulating and fostering innovation in the organisation; and supporting managers in training or other learners in the organisation. Examples are to be found in a wide range of private and public sector organisations in Britain, Europe and North America.

Protégés are not the only beneficiaries of mentoring: mentors also gain greatly from being challenged to understand their jobs and the organisation, and to find ways of helping their protégés share this understanding and work effectively. Mentors may also find that they, too, need mentoring. Mentors draw upon their own networks to give experience and support to their protégés, and encourage them to develop networks of their own. In this way, the practice and benefits cascade through the organisation.

The requirements for effective mentoring

This literature generally agrees on the following requirements for effective mentoring.

- *The status and characteristics of the mentor.* Mentors will generally be senior to protégés in status, experience and probably age. They should not have a line relationship with their protégé because the element of control inherent in it would conflict with the developmental nature of the mentoring relationship. It is highly desirable that senior managers act as mentors, and that top management be involved with the programme. Mentors should have the skills and qualities that protégés respect, good empathic and people-developing skills, good organisational knowledge and personal networks, and patience and humility to be able to learn from the protégé. Not all managers, therefore, would make appropriate mentors.
- *The protégé.* Protégés should have potential, and be hungry to learn and develop in order to realise it. There will be many more potential protégés in the organisation than can be mentored; it is therefore commonly noted that mentoring is elitist.
- *The relationship.* The relationship should be one of mutual trust, and will develop over time. Unless limits are set by the programme, it will continue until the protégé no longer needs its support. Sometimes it develops into a full friendship.
- *The activities.* Mentors encourage their protégés to analyse their task performance and to identify weaknesses and strengths. They give feedback and guidance on how weaknesses can be eliminated or neutralised. They help them recognise the tacit dimensions of the task skills, an important element in the development of competence and 'know-how'. Mentors act as a sounding board for their protégés' ideas, and support them as they try out new behaviours and take risks. They give honest, realistic but supportive feedback, an important element in learning generally and learning-to-learn in particular. They encourage their protégés to observe and analyse the organisation at work through their own and others' actions. Through this process the protégé begins to identify and then practise tacit knowledge and political skills.

Mentors help protégés to identify and develop potentials, question and reflect on experiences and prospects within the organisation, apply formal learning to practice, learn more widely about the organisation and develop networks. Overall, the mentor stimulates, encourages, guides, supports and cautions, acts as a role model, nurtures learning-to-learn, and encourages the adoption of a future orientation.

The development of higher-order skills through mentoring

These activities contribute to the development of the higher-order skills needed in the organisation. Daloz (1986: 209–235), for example, suggests that mentors offer their protégés support, challenge and vision. They support their protégés through listening, providing structure, expressing positive expectations, serving as advocate, sharing themselves with their protégés, and 'making it special'. They offer challenge by setting tasks, engaging in discussion, drawing attention to dichotomies, constructing hypotheses, and setting high standards. They offer vision by modelling, keeping tradition, offering a map, suggesting new language, and providing a mirror.

The learning organisation

It is evident that the human resource development argued for throughout this chapter would be achieved in a learning organisation. The holographic nature of the learning organisation (Morgan, 1997) provides the stimulus, prompts and cues for individuals to learn and develop the higher-order skills they need to sustain and develop the organisation in a changing world, and 'to develop a discursive, networking culture in which everyone constantly questioned their own assumptions' (Pickard, 2000: 39).

As Chapter 8 discusses, the concept of the learning organisation is open to criticism, not least because it is often expressed in theoretical terms. This is recognised by Senge (Pickard, 2000: 39), one of its early and influential proponents (Senge, 1990), who has now elaborated his thinking in more concrete terms (Senge *et al.*, 1998). Nevertheless, the learning organisation continues to be 'an aspirational concept' (Burgoyne, 1995: 24), a 'transitional myth' that makes sense both in the world that is passing and in the one that replaces it. Hence it enables people to bridge the gap – in this case as 'more emotionally involving, inclusive forms of organisation' emerge from the information-based organisation. However, Burgoyne (1999: 44), another early and key proponent, acknowledges that it has not 'delivered its full potential or lived up to all our expectations', and sets out what the characteristics of the second generation will have to be.

CONCLUSIONS

This chapter has identified the significance of learning and development for individuals and organisations. Many organisations have recognised this, and have invested in their human resource development, as *People Management* reports in its regular company profiles (e.g. Birmingham City Council, Bradford & Bingley Building Society, the Post Office, SmithKline Beecham, Stagecoach Holdings) and features on the National Training Awards (e.g. Clamason Industries, Dupont, Lloyds TSB). It is assumed that both organisations and their employees have benefited. However, as the Controversial issues and Case Study below suggest, the question that Legge (1995) asked of human resource management – rhetoric or reality? – should also be asked of human resource development.

CONTROVERSIAL ISSUES

This section presents a number of problematical or controversial issues for you to reflect upon and discuss:

● Who owns the individual's learning and development?
● Differing interpretations of human resource development.
● The future of career.

Who owns the individual's learning and development?

There are two routes to finding the answers to this question:

● reflecting on your own experience;
● identifying the stakeholders in the individual's learning and development.

You can then identify the implications for human resource development.

Reflections on your own experience

In order to recognise the significance of this question, complete the following exercise.

Stop and think

1 What is it costing you to learn? For example, take your reading of this book. What does this activity cost you?

2 Who pays the costs of your learning and development?

3 Who benefits from your learning and development? List the beneficiaries of your reading of this book.

The stakeholders in the individual's learning and development

When you examine the potential benefits of your learning, you can see that there are several beneficiaries, or 'stakeholders', in it. In the case of reading this book, you may have purchased it yourself and be reading this late at night in order to succeed in examinations for a qualification that will advantage you in getting a job, doing your present job better, or getting a better job. Because this learning is likely to enhance your job satisfaction and career, you may have initiated the process of development or even, if it was initiated by your employer, you may have been prepared to bear much of its costs (financial, opportunity cost, time, energy). Your employers, however, present or future, also benefit from your learning and development, and are therefore also stakeholders in it, and may or may not initiate the process and bear the cost (or part) of it.

There are, moreover, other stakeholders in your learning. Your family and dependants benefit from the increased income or status that this development may bring, but have to forgo time and money to achieve it. Government benefits from potential employees in training rather than unemployment, and pays for this through various state-sponsored training programmes, and society benefits from a skilled and satisfied workforce, and pays for it through the educational system.

The learner benefits in ways that spill over from the work situation. Much learning enlarges the individual, who gains not only knowledge and skills but a breadth and depth of understanding, and from this increased self-confidence and esteem. Learning, in other words, fosters development, so that through their learning people change: they are no longer the people they once were. As employees, they may become more demanding and less compliant. This enlargement of self may also be accompanied by an enhancement of status as learning enables individuals to move into more prestigious social roles or better-rewarded jobs.

The implications for human resource development

By reflecting upon your own motivation and experiences, you will already have an insight into some of the thorny issues inherent in human resource development (others are discussed by Rainbird and Maguire, 1993). These issues can be summarised as follows:

- Learning and development take place throughout life, and in every aspect of life, as well as through performance of the job.
- Employer-initiated and sponsored and delivered learning can constitute only a small part of an individual's total learning.
- Some of such activities are undertaken as part of planned development; some are random or opportunistic.
- The employer cannot ring-fence such employer-provided learning.
- Employer-provided learning will be infiltrated by learning from other arenas – from home or social life, but also from undertaking the daily job, or observing boss or colleagues. Such learning may influence, strengthen, challenge or undermine employer-provided learning.
- The processes of learning and development may work counter to the processes of matching and control in which some employers invest heavily in the selection process.
- Learning and development are difficult to evaluate, because they often need an interval of time for their outcomes to be manifested.
- It is not easy to apportion their benefits to either employer or employee.
- It is not easy to calculate their costs, nor apportion them between employer and employee.
- Some of the costs are not borne by either of these; partners, families and the state through the educational and vocational training systems also pay some of the price of employee development.
- Individuals expect reward for their training or development – they have put effort in, become more skilled – expect greater reward. This reward may be either extrinsic (promotion, increase in pay) or intrinsic (greater fulfilment through a more demanding or higher-status job).
- As employees learn and develop, they may become less compliant to their employer and more demanding of changes at work and further development.
- It may result in the employee's dissatisfaction with his or her present job or employer.
- Because of all the above, employers may be reluctant to pay to develop their employees.
- It is difficult formally to provide effective learning – it often seems false in comparison with the ongoing spontaneous learning from life in general, and there are often difficulties in transferring from formal learning situations to everyday work.
- Some of the processes, activities and benefits depend upon the individual's context (including the presence of significant others), age and stage of development in life.

The issue of the ownership of the learning and development of individuals, as employees, reminds us that managing people has a moral dimension – human resource management juggles with empowering and controlling. This is the unanswered (and unanswerable?) question at the heart of human resource development, and poses dilemmas to both employer and employee.

Differing interpretations of human resource development

The philosophy underpinning this chapter's presentation of its material is humanistic – learning and development have largely been interpreted as empowering of the individual. The chapter has not questioned whether the harnessing of individual learning and development by the organisation could not be interpreted in a very different way. The awareness that the ownership of individual learning is a matter of debate, however, presents the opportunity to look for other interpretations.

Consider this for yourself. What interpretations might the other chapters of this book have of human resource development? How idealistic or cynical are calls for activities such as mentoring and the learning organisation in today's flexible organisations? Is mentoring elitist or empowering? Is the learning organisation rhetoric or reality? Are there other possible interpretations? (You may find it helpful to return to the section on ideology and rhetoric in Chapter 2.)

Has the concept of career got a future?

Many have seen the traditional career as elitist, available to only a few, characterised largely by social background and education. The future career may also be elitist, available to a few, but perhaps a different few. At this point it is possible to identify some of the winners and losers from the changes that are taking place. So far the losers have included workers in manufacturing, unskilled workers of many kinds, clerical workers of many kinds, middle managers of many kinds, and full-time workers of many kinds (see also Chapters 3 and 4); many of these have been men. The winners have been the knowledge workers, those with the skills required by the new technologies, those with the attitudes and skills needed in service jobs, those who are able (or want) to work only part time; women seem to be benefiting from some of the changes. To be employable, employed and to have a career in the future – to be self-programmable (Castells, 1998, see earlier) – individuals will have to have, as this chapter has reiterated, the ability to learn new knowledge and skills, and above all to learn how to learn.

The changing nature of career is also of considerable significance for society as a whole, as well as for individuals and for the economy. For example, the future orientation that a career gives an individual is essential when making decisions about such key issues as starting a family, taking out a mortgage, changing one's occupation, re-entering education, or retiring from employment. Uncertainty about career could therefore over time affect the structure of the population or the housing market, while the effects of unemployment may be damaging the social fabric severely. The future of career, therefore, is of concern to us all.

Stop and think	1 Given these changes, has the present concept of career outgrown its usefulness? If so, how would it have to change in the future in order to reflect changing circumstances and experiences?
	2 How do you conceptualise your future career? How does it differ from the career of your parents' and grandparents' generations?
	3 What are the implications for your learning and development?

SUMMARY

- This chapter addressed the issue of why individuals generally and human resource managers in particular need to understand learning and development.

- It began with a series of definitions of learning that essentially rested on the view that the acquisition of knowledge and understanding facilitates change in perceptions and practice. These attributes are increasingly essential in the modern world of work, in which employees are expected to cope with change and new technology, take more responsibility, become more skilled and knowledgeable, and develop the ability for problem solving and creative thinking.

- The attributes that today's organisations need for their survival were examined – in particular, the need for quality and continuous improvement, flexibility, adaptability, and the exploitation of knowledge. Individual employees therefore must engage in a continuous process of learning how to learn, and managers must learn how to facilitate this.

- The nature of the learner in relation to work and career was examined; but it was also emphasised that learning is a lifelong process that means making continuous adaptations. In many senses it is a journey. In the process of learning, many barriers are thrown up, including anxiety and lack of confidence on behalf of the learner. Discrimination also exists and often creates barriers for certain groups such as older workers, women, disabled people and cultural and ethnic minorities. This may impair their ability to learn by undermining their confidence and/or preventing them from taking courses and training programmes that will lead to greater opportunities. Many in these groups belong to the most disadvantaged in our society.

- The outcomes of learning – the acquisition of new skills, competence, 'know-how', tacit knowledge and employability – were highlighted. It is equally important for managers to have an awareness of the hierarchies of learning, the various levels of learning through which learners proceed in the pursuit of knowledge and understanding. Each level adds a further layer of sophistication to this process, from the simple acquisition of knowledge of facts through to the ability to understand complicated analyses involving complex abstract processes. Such understanding will take the learner through the various stages of learning: novice, advanced beginner, competent, proficient and, finally, expert. Various theories and models of learning and learning styles were also examined in relation to these developments.

- The concept of development was explored. It is a process in which the learner 'becomes increasingly complex, more elaborate and differentiated, and thereby able to adapt to the changing environment'. A number of theories and models of lifespan, career and other forms of development were then examined and their implications for human resource development noted.

- Much learning and development takes place within the organisational context, itself influenced from outside by national training initiatives. Although learning knows no frontiers, organisations can often make inhospitable environments for the learning and development of individuals, and with this in mind it must be recognised that learning has to be supported by managers, mentors, and the overall learning climate of a learning organisation.

- The final part of the chapter examined three controversies for the reader to reflect on. These were who owns the individual's learning and development, the differing interpretations of human resource development, and the future of career. Rather than giving 'answers' the author posed a number of probing questions for the reader to develop their thoughts in pondering issues – a form of self-development in itself.

CASE STUDY

Offer of hope for Rover workers

The head of the taskforce helping Longbridge employees talks to **Jonathan Guthrie**

A furious row erupts between the government and BMW. Plans are hatched for a mass protest rally at Longbridge. It is all making life very difficult for Alex Stephenson, the affable, harassed head of a government taskforce set up to deal with estimated redundancies of more than 30,000 in the West Midlands, following the sale of parts of Rover by BMW. Mr Stephenson is fed up with recriminations at BMW's conduct: negotiating the sale of the huge Longbridge plant, even as the government was pressing the European Union to approve a £152m grant. 'It is time for both sides to say "what happened, happened", and to look for a way forward . . . BMW has been in a difficult position, running a company where things have not been going to plan. Pulling out is always going to look bloody terrible,' Mr Stephenson says. He is nevertheless sad about expected losses of up to 7000 jobs at Longbridge. He worked there for 10 years as Rover's head of engines and gearboxes. He still drives past it every day on his way to work as chairman of West Midlands Advantage, the regional development agency. Mr Stephenson's bluff bonhomie masks a shrewd mind that helped the West Midlands top league tables for inward investment in England last year. He clearly believes that Stephen Byers, the trade and industry secretary, will extract the most compensation from BMW by taking a conciliatory stance. The taskforce already has £152m to play with – the grant offered to BMW by the government, Birmingham City Council and the Department of Employment. The body, which includes representatives from industry, local government and unions, has three tasks to complete before it can make detailed spending proposals to government in four to six weeks. The first is to estimate the number of jobs that will be lost at Longbridge and its suppliers under plans by would-be buyer Alchemy Partners, the private equity firm, to concentrate on producing MGF sports cars. The second is to identify areas of the local economy where new jobs can be created. This dovetails with the third job: to think up uses for idle parts of the Longbridge site. Grants are likely to be available for companies setting up there, or at the nearby Birmingham Great Park industrial estate. Mr Stephenson regards the prospect of skilled men and women ending up flipping burgers as 'degrading'. A trained engineer, he hopes that new employment can be found at businesses where technical ability is at a premium. These include telecommunications, aerospace and transport. It could be tough, Mr Stephenson concedes, to retrain some of the mostly middle-aged Longbridge workers, in pure information technology work. But there is hope for the younger ones in businesses such as Specialist Computer Holdings, the Birmingham-based computing group. According to Mr Stephenson, another promising high-tech area is medical equipment. 'There are several hundred businesses of that kind here. We are trying to create a cluster around Birmingham University, which has expanded its research and development programme.' Despite the scale of the exercise, the taskforce head is optimistic. After all, he says, the West Midlands has already absorbed tens of thousands of job losses prompted by cutbacks at Rover since the mid 1980s. Mr Stephenson recently met Jon Moulton, the head of Alchemy, and found him 'personable'. He says the venture capitalist 'knows he has a big task ahead of him, and is clearly committed to the employees because he wants to create as many jobs as possible'. Thousands are expected to gather in Cofton Park beside Longbridge on April 1 to protest at its proposed purchase by Alchemy. Mr Stephenson will not be one of them.

Source: Financial Times, 22 March 2000

Working on your own or in a group, carry out the following exercises:

1 What comments would you like to make to Mr Stephenson about people's capacity to learn and develop through their lives?

2 Imagine that you are a middle-aged worker (in a company other than Rover) reading this press report.

What thoughts go through your mind about your own need for employability? What actions would you take?

3 Imagine you are a young person whose sole work experience has been 'flipping burgers'. What thoughts go through your mind about your own need for employability? What actions would you take?

QUESTIONS

1 Why do human resource managers need to understand the processes of learning and development?

2 What are the higher-order skills needed in organisations, and how may they be developed?

3 How may practical knowledge be developed in an organisation?

4 How may learning transform an individual? What are the implications of such transformation for an organisation?

5 What are the implications for an individual's career of new flexible forms of organisation?

EXERCISES

1 **Keep a learning diary**

Reflection is essential for effective learning. Systematically reflect upon what and how you learn by keeping a learning diary. It will also help you remember issues to discuss with your tutor, and may also contribute to your continuing professional development portfolio. Spend half an hour every week recording the following:

- the most meaningful or stressful events of the week;
- how they came about and who was involved;
- your interpretation of them;
- the emotions evoked by them;
- how you dealt with them;
- the outcomes of your actions;
- your evaluation of your actions;
- what you would do or avoid doing in future;
- what further skills, knowledge and understanding you need to perform more effectively;
- how you could acquire these;
- your action plan.

2 **Find yourself a mentor**

If you are not fortunate enough to have a mentor already, then find yourself one. Phillips-Jones (1982) suggests the following steps:

- Identify what (not who) you need.
- Evaluate yourself as a prospective protégé.
- Identify some mentor candidates.
- Prepare for the obstacles that may raise.
- Approach your possible mentors.

3 How can you make and keep yourself employable?

- Assess your present employability.
- What do you need to do to achieve, maintain or improve this?
- What would be the implications for the nature and quality of your life overall if your career proved to be flexible and/or fragmented?

4 Review and make plans for your career development

To make effective plans for your future development, you need to be aware of how you have arrived at where you are and become who you are.

- Write a brief story of your life and career to date. Why and how have you become who you are today? What are your strengths and weaknesses?
- Now write your story again through the eyes of people who know you well: your parents or partner; your best friend or boss. Would they have a different interpretation of your life and career from you? Does this tell you anything about yourself that you may not have noticed before?
- Are you content with yourself and your present life? What would you like to be different? Why? What are the opportunities and threats to your life and career? What would you have to do (and forgo) to bring this change about? Would it be worth it? And what would the effect(s) be?
- Who else would such changes affect? Who could help or hinder you in these changes? What resources would you need to effect them? In what sequence would these changes have to come about, and how do they fit into the other timetables of your life?
- Now draw up an action plan, identifying the actions you will have to carry out over the short, medium and long term.
- Take the first step in implementing it today. Commit yourself to it by telling someone else about it and enlist their support to keep you motivated.
- At the end of the first month and every three months thereafter review the progress of your plan and make any necessary adjustments.

REFERENCES AND FURTHER READING

Those texts marked with an asterisk are particularly recommended for further reading.

Argyris, C. (1960) *Understanding Organizational Behaviour.* London: Tavistock Dorsey.

Argyris, C. and Schon, D.A. (1978) *Organisational Learning: A Theory of Action Perspective.* Reading, Mass.: Addison-Wesley.

Arkin, A. (1992) 'What other institutes are doing', *Personnel Management*, March, p. 29.

Arkin, A. (1995a) 'Breaking down skills barriers', *People Management*, Vol. 1, No. 3, 9 February, pp. 34–35.

Arkin, A. (1995b) 'How the act will affect you', *People Management*, Vol. 1, No. 23, 16 November, pp. 20, 23.

Arkin, A. (1998) 'Profile of Gary Hamel: crash course', *People Management*, Vol. 4, No. 21, 29 October, pp. 50–52.

Arkin, A. (1999) 'Investors in future: above and beyond', *People Management*, Vol. 5, No. 3, pp. 40–41.

Arnold, J. (1997) *Managing Careers into the 21st Century.* London: Paul Chapman.

Arthur, M.B. and Rousseau, D.M. (1996) (eds) *The Boundaryless Career: A New Employment Principle for a New Organizational Era*, Oxford: Oxford University Press.

Arthur, M.B., Hall, D.T. and Lawrence, B.S. (eds) (1989) *Handbook of Career Theory.* Cambridge: Cambridge University Press.

*Atkinson, R.L., Atkinson, R.C., Smith, E.E. and Bem, D.J. (1993) *Introduction to Psychology*, 11th edn. New York: Harcourt Brace Jovanovich.

Barrow, M.J. and Loughlin, H.M. (1993) 'Towards a learning organization in Grand Metropolitan Foods Europe', in Wills, G. (ed.) *Your Enterprise School of Management.* Bradford: MCB University Press, pp. 195–208.

Barry, A. (1988) 'Twilight study sheds new light on craft development', *Personnel Management*, November, pp. 46–49.

Bartol, K.N. (1978) 'The sex structuring of organizations: a search for possible causes', *Academy of Management Review*, October, pp. 805–815.

Bayliss, V. (1998) *Redefining Work: An RSA Initiative.* London: The Royal Society for the Encouragement of the Arts, Manufactures and Commerce.

Belbin, E. and Belbin, R.M. (1972) *Problems in Adult Retraining.* London: Heinemann.

Bennetts, C. (1995) 'The secrets of a good relationship', *People Management*, Vol. 1, No. 13, 29 June, pp 38–39.

Binsted, D.S. (1980) 'Design for learning in management training and development: a view', *Journal of European Industrial Training*, Vol. 4, No. 8, whole issue.

Bloom, B.S. et al. (1956) *Taxonomy of Educational Objectives, Handbook 1: The Cognitive Domain.* London: Longmans Green.

Borger, R. and Seaborne, A.E.M. (1966) *The Psychology of Learning*. Harmondsworth: Penguin.

Boyatzis, R.E. (1982) *The Competent Manager: A Model for Effective Performance*. New York: Wiley.

Bridges, W. (1995) *Job Shift: How to Prosper in a Workplace Without Jobs*. London: Nicholas Brealey.

Brittain, S. and Ryder, P. (1999) 'A certain *je ne sais quoi*: get complex', *People Management*, Vol. 5, No. 23, 25 November, pp. 48–51.

Brockbank, A. and Beech, N. (1999) 'Mentor blocks: guiding blight' *People Management*, Vol. 5, No. 9, 6 May, pp. 52–54.

Burgoyne, J. (1989) 'Creating the managerial portfolio: building on competency approaches to management development', *Management Development and Education*, Vol. 20, Pt 1, pp. 56–61.

Burgoyne, J. (1995) 'Feeding minds to grow the business', *People Management*, Vol. 1, No. 19, 21 September, pp. 22–25.

Burgoyne, J. (1999) 'Better by design: design of the times', *People Management*, Vol. 5, No. 11, 3 June, pp. 39–44.

Burgoyne, J.G. and Hodgson, V.E. (1983) 'Natural learning and managerial action: a phenomenological study in the field setting', *Journal of Management Studies*, Vol. 20, No. 3, pp. 387–399.

Cannell, M., Ashton, D., Powell, M. and Sung, J. (1999) 'Training: auditory perceptions: ahead of the field', *People Management*, Vol. 5, No. 8, 22 April, pp. 48–49.

Castells, M. (1996) *The Information Age: Economy, Society and Culture. Vol. I: The Rise of the Network Society*. Oxford: Blackwell.

Castells, M. (1998) *The Information Age: Economy, Society and Culture. Vol. III: End of Millennium*. Oxford: Blackwell.

Clutterbuck, D. and Megginson, D. (1999) *Mentoring Executives and Directors*. London: Butterworth-Heinemann.

Coleman, P. (1990) 'Psychological ageing', in Bond, J. and Coleman, P. (eds) *Ageing and Society: An Introduction to Social Gerontology*. London: Sage, pp. 62–88.

Collin, A. (1988) 'Mentoring', *Industrial and Commercial Training*, Vol. 20, No. 2, pp. 23–27.

Collin, A. and Watts, A.G. (1996) 'The death and transfiguration of career – and of career guidance?', *British Journal of Guidance and Counselling*, Vol. 24, No. 3, pp. 385–398.

Collin, A. and Young, R. A. (2000) *The Future of Career*. Cambridge: Cambridge University Press.

Collins, H. (1993) 'Untidy minds in action', *The Times Higher Education Supplement*, No. 1066, 9 April, pp. 15, 17.

Constable, J. and McCormick, R. (1987) *The Making of British Managers*. London: British Institute of Management and Confederation of British Industry.

*Cooley, M. (1987) *Architect or Bee? The Human Price of Technology*. London: Hogarth Press.

Corney, M. (1995) 'Employee development schemes', *Employment Gazette*, Vol. 103, No. 10, pp. 385–390.

Coulson-Thomas, C. (2000) 'Carry on campus', *People Management*, Vol. 6, No. 4, 17 February, p. 33.

Crofts, P. (1995) 'A helping hand up the career ladder', *People Management*, Vol. 1, No. 18, 7 September, pp. 38–40.

Cytrynbaum, S. and Crites, J.O. (1989) 'The utility of adult development theory in understanding career adjustment process', in Arthur, M.B., Hall, D.T. and Lawrence, B.S. (eds) *Handbook of Career Theory*. Cambridge: Cambridge University Press, pp. 66–88.

*Daloz, L. A. (1986) *Effective Mentoring and Teaching*. San Francisco: Jossey-Bass.

Dalton, G.W. (1989) 'Developmental views of careers in organizations', in Arthur, M.B., Hall, D.T. and Lawrence, B.S. (eds) *Handbook of Career Theory*. Cambridge: Cambridge University Press, pp. 89–109.

Dennis, H. (1988) *Fourteen Steps in Managing an Aging Work Force*. Lexington, Mass.: D.C. Heath.

Dixon, N. (2000) 'Common knowledge: the insight track', *People Management*, Vol. 6, No. 4, 17 February, pp. 34–39.

Dreyfus, H.L., Dreyfus, S.E. and Athanasion, T. (1986) *Mind Over Machine: The Power of Human Intuition and Expertise in the Era of the Computer*. New York: Free Press.

Erikson, E. (1950) *Childhood and Society*. New York: W.W. Norton.

Evans, P. (1986) 'New directions in career management', *Personnel Management*, December, pp. 26–29.

Fitts, P.M. (1962) 'Factors in complex skills training', in Glaser, R. (ed.) *Training Research and Education*. New York: Wiley.

Fonda, N. and Guile, D. (1999) 'A real step change: joint learning adventures', *People Management*, Vol. 5, No. 6, 25 March, pp. 38–44.

Fontana, D. (1981) 'Learning and teaching', in Cooper, C.L. (ed.) *Psychology for Managers: A Text for Managers and Trade Unionists*. London: The British Psychological Society and Macmillan, pp. 64–78.

Fowler, A. (1998) 'How to run a mentoring scheme: guide lines', *People Management*, Vol. 4, No. 20, 15 October, pp 48–50.

Gagné, R.M. (1970) *The Conditions of Learning*, 2nd edn. New York: Holt, Rinehart & Winston.

Gagné, R.M. (1974) *Essentials of Learning for Instruction*. Hinsdale, Ill.: Dryden Press.

Gallos, J.V. (1989) 'Exploring women's development: implications for career theory, practice, and research', in Arthur, M.B., Hall, D.T. and Lawrence, B.S. (eds) *Handbook of Career Theory*. Cambridge: Cambridge University Press, pp. 110–132.

Gardner, H. (1985) *Frames of Mind: The Theory of Multiple Intelligences*. London: Paladin.

Gardner, H. (1999) *Intelligence Reframed: Multiple Intelligences for the 21st Century*. New York: Basic Books.

Gilligan, C. (1977) 'In a different voice: women's conception of the self and of morality', *Harvard Educational Review*, Vol. 47, pp. 481–517.

Guest, D. and McKenzie Davey, K.M. (1996) 'Don't write off the traditional career', *People Management*, Vol. 2, No. 4, 22 February, pp. 22–25.

Guest, D., Storey, Y. and Tate, W. (1997) *Opportunity Through People*. IPD Consultative Document, June. London: IPD.

Haistead, N. (1995) 'A flexible route to life-long learning', *People Management*, Vol. 1, No. 19, 21 September, p. 40.

Hall, D.T. (1976) *Careers in Organizations*. Pacific Palisades, Calif.: Goodyear.

Hall, D.T. & Associates (1996) *The Career is Dead – Long Live Career: A Relational Approach to Careers*, San Francisco, Calif: Jossey-Bass.

Hammer, M. and Champy, J. (1994) *Reengineering the Corporation: A Manifesto for Business Revolution.* New York: Harper Business.

Handy, C. (1987) *The Making of Managers: A Report on Management Education, Training and Development in the United States, West Germany, France, Japan and the UK.* London: Manpower Services Commission, National Economic Development Office and Institute of British Management.

Harrison, R. (1992) *Employee Development.* London: Institute of Personnel Management.

Herriot, P. (1992) *The Career Management Challenge.* London: Sage.

Herriot, P. and Pemberton, C. (1995) *New Deals: The Revolution in Managerial Careers.* Chichester: John Wiley.

Hodgetts, R.M. (1991) *Organizational Behaviour: Theory and Practice.* New York: Prentice Hall.

Hodgson, A. (1987) 'Deming's never-ending road to quality', *Personnel Management,* July, pp. 40–44.

Hogarth, T. and Barth, M.C. (1991) 'Costs and benefits of hiring older workers: a case study of B & Q', *International Journal of Manpower,* Vol. 12, No. 8, pp. 5–17.

Honey, P. (1998) 'The debate starts here', *People Management,* Vol. 4, No. 19, 1 October, pp. 28–29.

Honey, P. (1999) 'Not for the faint-hearted', *People Management,* Vol. 5, No. 21, 28 October, p. 39.

Honey, P. and Mumford, A. (1992) *Manual of Learning Styles,* 3rd edn. London: Peter Honey.

Jackson, C., Arnold, J., Nicholson, N. and Watts, A.G. (1996) *Managing Careers in 2000 and Beyond.* Brighton: Institute for Employment Studies.

Jackson, T. (1999) *Career Development.* London: IPD.

Kanter, R.M. (1989a) *When Giants Learn to Dance.* New York: Simon & Schuster.

Kanter, R.M. (1989b) 'Careers and the wealth of nations: a macro-perspective on the structure and implications of career forms', in Arthur, M.B., Hall, D.T. and Lawrence, B.S. (eds) *Handbook of Career Theory.* Cambridge: Cambridge University Press, pp. 506–521.

Kanter, R.M. (1992) 'Creating a habitat for the migrant manager', *Personnel Management,* October, pp. 38–40.

Kegan, R. (1982) *The Evolving Self: Problem and Process in Human Development.* Cambridge, Mass.: Harvard University Press.

Keil, T. (1981) 'Social structure and status in career development', in Watts, A.G., Super, D.E. and Kidd, J.M. (eds) *Career Development in Britain: Some Contributions to Theory and Practice.* Cambridge: CRAC, Hobson's Press, pp. 155–192.

Knowles, M.S. and associates (1984). *Andragogy in Action.* San Francisco Calif: Jossey-Bass.

Kolb, D.A. (1983) *Experiential Learning.* New York: Prentice Hall.

Kolb, D.A., Rubin, I.M. and MacIntyre, J.M. (1984) *Organizational Psychology: An Experiential Approach,* 4th edn. New York: Prentice Hall.

Kram, K.E. (1985) *Mentoring At Work: Developmental Relationships in Organizational Life.* Glenview, Ill.: Scott, Foresman.

Laslett, P. (1989) *A Fresh Map of Life: The Emergence of the Third Age.* London: Weidenfeld & Nicolson.

Legge, K. (1995) *Human Resource Management: Rhetorics and Realities.* Basingstoke: Macmillan.

Levinson, D.J., Darrow, C.M., Klein, E.B., Levinson, M.H. and McKee, B. (1978) *The Seasons of a Man's Life.* New York: Alfred A. Knopf.

Littlefield, D. (1999) 'Ormerod Home Trust: independence day', *People Management,* Vol. 5, No. 23, 11 November, pp. 52–54.

Lodge, D. (1988) *Nice Work: A Novel.* London: Secker & Warburg.

Malhotra, Y. (1998) *Knowledge Management for the New World of Business,* WWW Virtual Library on Knowledge Management, http://www.brint.com/km/

Martin, S. (1995) 'A futures market for competencies', *People Management,* Vol. 1, No. 6, 23 March, pp. 20–24.

Marshall, J. (1989) 'Re-visioning career concepts: a feminist invitation', in Arthur, M.B., Hall, D.T. and Lawrence, B.S. (eds) *Handbook of Career Theory.* Cambridge: Cambridge University Press, pp. 275–291.

Masie, E. (1999) 'Learning on demand: joined-up thinking', *People Management,* Vol. 5., No. 23, 25 November, pp. 32–36.

McGregor, D. (1960) *The Human Side of Enterprise.* New York: McGraw-Hill.

Megginson, D. (1988) 'Instructor, coach, mentor: three ways of helping for managers', *Management Education and Development,* Vol. 19, Pt 1, pp. 33–46.

Mezirow, J. (1977) 'Personal transformation', *Studies in Adult Education* (Leicester: National Institute of Adult Education), Vol. 9, No. 2, pp. 153–64.

Miller, R. and Stewart, J. (1999) 'U and improved: opened university', *People Management,* Vol. 5, No. 12, 17 June, pp. 42–46.

Moreton, T. (ed.) (1992) 'The education, training and employment of disabled people', *Personnel Review,* Vol. 21, No. 6.

*Morgan, G. (1997) *Images of Organization,* 2nd edn. Thousand Oaks, Calif.: Sage.

Mumford, A. (1988) 'Learning to learn and management self-development', in Pedler, M., Burgoyne, J. and Boydell, T. (eds) *Applying Self-Development in Organizations.* New York: Prentice Hall, pp. 23–27.

Myers, C. and Davids, K. (1992) 'Knowing and doing: tacit skills at work', *Personnel Management,* February, pp. 45–47.

Naylor, P. (1987) 'In praise of older workers', *Personnel Management,* November, pp. 44–48.

Neugarten, B.L. (1968) 'Adult personality: toward a psychology of the life cycle', in Neugarten, B.L. (ed.) *Middle Age and Aging: A Reader in Social Psychology.* Chicago: University of Chicago Press, pp. 137–147.

Pedler, M. (1988) 'Self-development and work organizations', in Pedler, M., Burgoyne, J. and Boydell, T. (eds) *Applying Self-Development in Organizations.* New York: Prentice Hall, pp. 1–19.

Pedler, M. (ed.) (1983) *Action Learning in Practice.* Aldershot: Gower.

Pedler, M., Burgoyne, J. and Boydell, T. (eds) (1988) *Applying Self-Development in Organizations.* New York: Prentice Hall.

Perry, W.G. (1968) *Forms of Intellectual and Ethical Development in the College Years: A Scheme.* New York: Holt, Rinehart & Winston.

Phillips-Jones, L. (1982) *Mentors and Protégés: How to Establish, Strengthen and Get the Most from a Mentor/Protégé Relationship.* New York: Arbor House.

Pickard, J. (1999a) 'Lifelong earning: grey areas', *People Management*, Vol. 5, No. 15, 29 July, pp. 31–37.

Pickard, J. (1999b) 'Emote possibilities: sense and sensitivity', *People Management*, Vol. 5, No. 21, 28 October, pp. 48–56.

Pickard, J. (2000) 'Profile: high-mileage meditations', *People Management*, Vol. 6, No. 7, pp. 38–43.

Pugh, D.S., Hickson, D.J. and Hinings, C.R. (eds) (1983) *Writers on Organizations.* Harmondsworth: Penguin.

Quinn, R.E., Faerman, S.R., Thompson, M.P. and McGrath, M.R. (1990) *Becoming a Master Manager.* New York: Wiley.

Rainbird, H. and Maguire, M. (1993) 'When corporate need supersedes employee development', *Personnel Management*, February, pp. 34–37.

Rana, E. (2000) '2000 predictions: Enter the people dimension', *People Management*, Vol. 6, No. 1, 6 January, pp. 16–17.

Reese, H.W. and Overton, W.F. (1970) 'Models of development and theories of development', in Goulet, L.R. and Baltes, P.B. (eds) *Life-Span Developmental Psychology: Theory and Research.* New York: Academic Press, pp. 115–145.

*Revans, R. (1983) *ABC of Action Learning.* Bromley: Chartwell-Bratt (Publishing and Training).

Ribeaux, P. and Poppleton, S.E. (1978) *Psychology and Work: An Introduction.* London: Macmillan.

Rifkin, J. (1995) *The End of Work: The Decline of the Global Labor Force and the Dawn of the Post-Market Era*, New York: Putnam.

Rotter, J. (1966) 'Generalized expectancies for internal versus external control of reinforcement', *Psychological Monographs*, Vol. 80, No. 1, pp. 1–28.

Ryan. J, (1995) 'Giving people the chance to sparkle', *People Mangement*, Vol. 1, No. 13, 29 June, pp. 40–42.

Scarborough, H. (1999) 'Science friction: System error', *People Management*, Vol. 5, No. 7, 8 April, pp. 68–74.

Schein, E.H. (1978) *Career Dynamics: Matching Individual and Organizational Needs.* Reading, Mass.: Addison-Wesley.

*Senge, P. (1990) *The Fifth Discipline: The Art and Practice of the Learning Organization.* London: Century.

Senge, P., Kleiner, A. Roberts, C., Ross. R., Roth, G., Smith, B. (1998) *The Dance of Change.* London: Nicholas Brealey.

Sheard, A. (1992) 'Learning to improve performance', *Personnel Management*, November, pp. 40–45.

Sofer, C. (1970) *Men in Mid-Career.* Cambridge: Cambridge University Press.

Stammers, R. and Patrick, J. (1975) *The Psychology of Training.* London: Methuen.

Sternberg, R.J. (1985) *Beyond IQ: A Triarchic Theory of Human Intelligence.* Cambridge: Cambridge University Press.

Thatcher, M. (1996) 'Allowing everyone to have their say', *People Management*, Vol. 2, No. 6, 21 March, pp. 28–30.

Thomas, D.A. and Alderfer, C.P. (1989) 'The influence of race on career dynamics: theory and research on minority career experiences', in Arthur, M.B., Hall, D.T. and Lawrence, B.S. (eds) *Handbook of Career Theory.* Cambridge: Cambridge University Press, pp. 133–158.

Thomas, R.J. (1989) 'Blue-collar careers: meaning and choice in a world of constraints', in Arthur, M.B., Hall, D.T. and Lawrence, B.S. (eds) *Handbook of Career Theory.* Cambridge: Cambridge University Press, pp. 354–379.

Training Commission (1988) *Classifying the Components of Management Competences.* Sheffield: Training Commission.

Trinder, C., Hulme, G. and McCarthy, U. (1992) *Employment: the Role of Work in the Third Age*, The Carnegie Inquiry into the Third Age, Research Paper Number 1. Dumfermline: The Carnegie United Kingdom Trust.

Tyson, S. and Fell, A. (1995) 'A focus on skills, not organisations', *People Management*, Vol. 1, No. 21, 19 October, pp. 42–45.

Ulrich, D. and Stewart Black, J. (1999) 'All around the world: worldly wise', *People Management*, Vol. 5, No. 21, 25 October, pp. 42–46.

Walsh, J. (1998) 'Competency frameworks give companies the edge', *People Management*, Vol.4, No. 18, 17 September, p. 15.

Waskel, S. A. (1991) *Mid-Life Issues and the Workplace of the 90s: A Guide for Human Resource Specialists.* New York: Quorum.

Watts, A.G., Law, B., Killeen, J., Kidd, J. M. and Hawthorn, R. (1996) *Rethinking Careers Education and Guidance: Theory, Policy and Practice.* London: Routledge.

Wechsler, D. (1958) *The Measurement and Appraisal of Adult Intelligence*, 4th edn. London: Baillière, Tindall & Cox.

Weick, K.E. and Berlinger, L.R. (1989) 'Career improvisation in self-designing organizations', in Arthur, M.B., Hall, D.T. and Lawrence, B.S. (eds) *Handbook of Career Theory.* Cambridge: Cambridge University Press, pp. 313–328.

Welch, J. (1996) 'HR qualifications get the go-ahead at last', *People Management*, Vol. 2, No. 11, 30 May, p. 11.

Whitehead, M. (1999) 'Centrica: energy efficient', *People Management*, Vol. 5, No. 22, 11 November, pp. 60–62.

Whittaker, J. (1992) 'Making a policy of keeping up to date', *Personnel Management*, March, pp. 28–31.

Whittaker, J. (1995) 'Three challenges for IPD standards', *people Management*, Vol. 1, No. 23, 16 November, pp. 30–34.

Whittaker, M. and Cartwright, A. (1999) *The Mentoring Manual.* London: Gower.

Wisher, V. (1994) 'Competencies: the precious seeds of growth', *Personnel Management*, July, pp. 36–39.

Woodruffe, C. (1991) 'Competent by any other name', *Personnel Management*, September, pp. 30–33.

Wrightsman, L.S. (1988) *Personality Development in Adulthood.* Newbury Park, Calif.: Sage.

Young, C. (1996) 'How CPD can further organisational aims', *People Management*, Vol. 2, No.11, 30 May, p. 67.

Human resource development: the organisation and the national framework

Len Holden

OBJECTIVES

- To examine the strategic nature of HRD and its relationship to the individual and to organisational development.
- To outline and explain a human resource development plan including the assessment of training needs, an outline of training methods, and the processes of monitoring and evaluating the plan.
- To examine the concepts of the learning organisation and knowledge management.
- To examine vocational education and training in the leading industrial nations, with an in-depth investigation of the training systems of Germany, Japan and France.
- To examine the implications of these international comparisons for the UK.
- To examine the national framework for vocational education and training in the UK.
- To outline possible future policy developments in vocational education and training.
- To identify some controversial issues in the field of vocational education and training.

INTRODUCTION

As we have seen from the previous chapter on employee development, it is difficult to arrive at a consensus definition of terms such as 'development', 'education' and 'training' because of the varied ways in which they are translated into work and life situations.

The Manpower Services Commission, set up by the 1973 Employment and Training Act but replaced in 1988, defined training as

> a planned process to modify attitude, knowledge or skill behaviour through learning experience to achieve effective performance in an activity or range of activities. Its purpose, in the work situation, is to develop the abilities of the individual and to satisfy the current and future needs of the organisation. (Manpower Services Commission, 1981)

This definition is no longer adequate or wide enough in a world where organisations are in a constant state of transformation in a turbulent and rapidly changing economic environment. Training was seen as a series of mechanistic interventions through which trainers poured knowledge into an employee's head, with the expectation of automatic improvement in individual and organisational performance.

Such a concept is too narrow for the modern organisation. First, the skills and knowledge that employees need are rapidly changing, and what is relevant now may not be relevant in the future. Second, there is an increasing need for employees to 'own' their learning. This means being aware of their own needs for both the organisation's requirements and their own long-term development. In other words, individuals also need to be aware of their own learning strategies. Third, increasing competition is forcing organisations to improve the quality of the products and services they provide, and this requires a closer relationship with the customer, empowerment of employees, and improved communication for exchanging knowledge and skills. Some commentators have suggested that this need to constantly improve knowledge and skill must lead to an environment where learning and sharing knowledge are at the centre of the organisation's operation – what has come to be called the *learning organisation* or the *knowledge-based organisation* (Senge, 1990; Nonaka, 1991; Pedler *et al.*, 1997; Dixon, 2000).

However, even in a learning environment there may be a conflict between developing the skills of employees and the future needs of the organisation. For example, many organisations prefer to train employees in firm-specific skills rather than transferable skills, and thus these two objectives may prove mutually exclusive or, at best, only partly achievable. A survey in the early 1990s concluded:

> Much of the training reported was for organisational rather than individual development, suggesting that many employees would not regard the training they receive as training at all, since it neither imparts transferable skills nor contributes to personal and educational development.
>
> (Rainbird and Maguire, 1993)

There is little to suggest that this situation has changed radically at the start of the new millennium. The loss of employees in whom considerable sums have been invested in training and development influences some employers to concentrate on training in areas that are specific to their organisation, while the 'poacher' organisations use money as an attractor and invest little or nothing in training their employees.

Other commentators believe that the idea of transferable skills is used far too widely, and that many processes are particular to organisations and their products and services. Even in a country such as Japan, whose training systems are much admired, the programmes involve a considerable proportion of training for firm-specific skills (Dore and Sako, 1989).

THE NEED FOR TRAINING

Until the 1980s, training and development in British organisations were inadequate compared with some other industrialised countries. This was confirmed by a number of surveys (Coopers & Lybrand, 1985; Industrial Society, 1985; Mangham and Silver, 1986; Constable and McCormick, 1987; Handy, 1987), which collectively had a considerable impact on the nation's consciousness. This added to an increasing awareness of the importance of change and the key role that training had played in helping that process.

Encouragingly, surveys in the early 1990s revealed that British companies seemed to be taking training more seriously (Saggers, 1994). The Price Waterhouse Cranfield Project Surveys indicate that training and staff development is the leading issue for most personnel departments across Europe, including the UK (Brewster and Hegewisch, 1993).

This growing awareness of the importance of training over the past decade was also supported by reports that employers were spending more in aggregate terms on training activities (Training Agency, 1989). However, the measurement of training expenditure is still controversial, and those figures that do exist are open to question, interpretation and political manipulation (Finegold, 1991; Ryan, 1991).

Thus there seems to be a gap between the perceived importance of training and the willingness to do something about it. The view strongly persists in the commercial and industrial culture of the UK that training is a 'cost' and not an 'investment.'

HRD and human resource management

Recognition of the importance of human resource development (HRD) in recent years has been heavily influenced by the intensification of overseas competition and the relative success of economies such as Japan, Germany and Sweden, where investment in employee development is emphasised. Technological developments and organisational change have gradually led some employers to realise that success relies on the skills and abilities of their employees, and this means considerable and continuous investment in training and development.

This has also been underscored by the rise in human resource management, with its emphasis on the importance of people and the skills they possess in enhancing organisational efficiency. Such HRM concepts as 'commitment' to the company and the growth in the 'quality' movement have led senior management teams to realise the increased importance of training, employee development and long-term education. There has also been more recognition of the need to complement the qualities of employees with the needs of the organisation. Such concepts require not only careful planning but also a greater emphasis on employee development. Indeed, some commentators have seen this aspect of HRM as so important that they see HRD as an equally important discipline in its own right (Hall, 1984; Nadler, 1984).

In HRM companies such as Hewlett-Packard, Xerox, IBM, Caterpillar and The Body Shop, HRD is seen as a major key to the success of the organisation, and is emphasised at all levels. HRD has also served as an agent for change or even survival in organisations such as Harley Davidson and Euro-Disney.

HRD programmes are continuous, and shaped to fit the culture changes in the organisation in relation to the needs of the individual. In this way training and HRD become tools for effecting change, and the policy ramifications can be wide ranging and strategic. As a result, HRD takes on a variety of forms and covers a multitude of subjects.

HRD is just one of the instruments at the disposal of the HR department and the organisation in creating HR strategy, and as Keep (1989) reminds us:

> The interrelationship between training and recruitment strategies is usually a very close one, not the least because if an organisation wishes to improve the skills of its workforce, it has the choice of either training its existing employees or recruiting pre-skilled labour that has been trained elsewhere.

Employee development needs

As noted in the previous chapter, HRD has significance for employees in fulfilling their own needs. One problem is that individuals are often unaware of those needs. It is important to help them towards some awareness, especially in terms of the emphasis on self-development, another important issue raised in the previous chapter.

Sadly, the further down the organisational ladder one descends the less money is spent on training. Thus managers and professionals generally receive more financial support for training than clerical and manual workers do (Price Waterhouse Cranfield Project, 1990; Brewster, 1999: 16). Given the need to encourage individuals to recognise their training needs and, more importantly, to seek ways to improve their knowledge and skills to advance their career prospects, the advantage seems to lie with individuals further up the organisational hierarchy.

The divide between professional and non-professional workers is increasing with the growing use of flexible work patterns, which emphasise core and periphery workers engaged on part-time or restricted contracts (see Chapter 3 and elsewhere). As a result of these changes, management is less likely to be committed to training periphery workers, and this is reflected in the time and money devoted to training and developing these groups (Syrett and Lammiman, 1994).

Another issue that further emphasises the status divide is that non-professional and non-managerial employees are less aware of the need for training and, more importantly, less able to do something about it, which places considerable barriers in the way of improving their working life prospects. Professionals are imbued with the value of education and self-development, which is often acquired in the routes to, and in, higher education. This need for continual self-development is becoming increasingly important throughout the working life of most professionals, who continue to embark on courses of varying kinds into their 40s and 50s.

Importantly, this process also helps them to cope with change. Awareness of the power of education and training leads to self-activation in meeting career changes and organisational change. By contrast, non-professional workers often rely heavily on the services of external agencies to help them cope with redundancy resulting from skills obsolescence. In the UK in the past agencies such as Employment Training have been less than adequate in dealing with the needs of the long-term unemployed and those wishing to retrain for employment that needs new skills, such as a redundant coalminer seeking to learn computer skills. Most importantly, once new skills are acquired there must be opportunities to practise them. This is difficult in areas undergoing structural change or industrial decay, such as mining and shipbuilding areas. This subject will be explored more fully later in the chapter.

CREATING A HUMAN RESOURCE DEVELOPMENT PLAN

There are no set procedures that organisations should follow in creating a human resource development plan, but the eight points listed in Table 8.1 should act as guidance. This can also be summed up diagrammatically as in Figure 8.1.

This has strong elements of the systems approach to training (SAT), but the mechanistic overtones of SAT should be moderated by recognising the human needs of employees and the changes (sometimes rapid) that can affect organisations. Therefore a more flexible or 'organic' approach is recommended: training schemes that are patently

Table 8.1 A human resource development plan

- Discern the training and development requirements from the organisational strategy and business objectives
- Analyse the training requirements for effective work performance in organisational fuctions and jobs
- Analyse the existing qualities and training needs of current employees
- Devise an HRD plan that fills the gap between organisational requirements and the current skills and knowledge of employees
- Decide on the apropriate training and development methods to be used for individuals and groups
- Decide who is to have responsibility for the plan and its various parts
- Implement the plan, and monitor and evaluate its progress
- Amend the HRD plan in the light of monitoring/evaluation and changes in business strategy

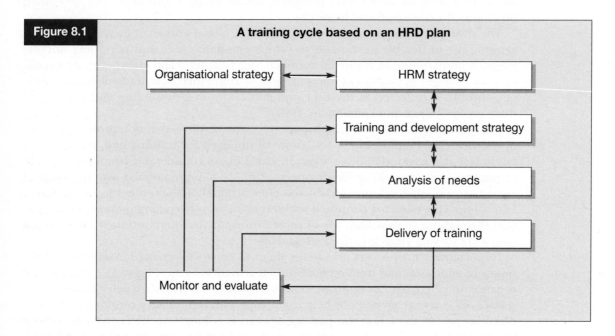

Figure 8.1 **A training cycle based on an HRD plan**

not working, perhaps because of changes in personnel, occupations, job specifications, personal relationships, business plans or economic performance, should be abandoned, or adapted to accommodate the change.

Analysing training needs

The first vital step in HRD is 'the identification of needed skills and active management of employees learning for their long-range future in relation to explicit corporate and business strategies' (Hall, 1984).

For training to be effective it is necessary to discern not only the training needs of the individual and the group, but also how their needs fit the overall organisational objectives. As we have already suggested, this may be more difficult to achieve than it appears.

Researchers and commentators doubt whether managerial hierarchies recognise the importance of these relationships in training initiatives or, if they do, doubt whether they have the will or the ability to carry them out. As Hall (1984) comments:

Many organisations invest considerable resources in training and development but never really examine how training and development can most effectively promote organisational objectives, or how developmental activities should be altered in the light of business plans.

Bernhard and Ingolis (1988), in studying training and its strategic implementation in US companies, believe that a considerable amount of money is 'thrown away' mainly because fundamental issues such as analysis of training needs in relation to the short- and long-term business plans have not been addressed.

A prominent French bank witnessed less than beneficial results after a huge investment in an extensive training scheme. This was seen to be primarily a consequence of the failure to analyse training needs within the organisation (Holden and Livian, 1992). Investors in People (IIP) schemes have been set up by numerous organisations in the UK in an attempt to align training needs to organisational strategy. However, as we shall see on examining IIP in greater depth later in this chapter, the results have been variable.

An integral part of analysing training needs is recognising what will 'fit' the company culture, as well as the company strategy and objectives. The training scheme that fits one company may not fit another, and these company differences can only be ignored at great cost. This is part and parcel of the organic approach to HRD, and a view shared by those organisations that claim to be (or on their way to being) learning organisations.

The training and development needs of the individual must be reconciled with those of the organisation. Conflicts here need to be resolved, for the benefit of both. Unfortunately, this may be easier to achieve for professional and managerial employees than for the workforce lower down the organisation. For example, many companies recognise the advantages of having managers with an MBA degree or a Diploma in Management Studies, a situation mutually beneficial to the individual and the organisation. Professionals such as accountants and lawyers have the advantage of transferable knowledge and expertise. But a shopfloor worker in a production company is much more likely to be trained in firm-specific skills that cannot be easily transferred to other organisational contexts.

For the job

Job description

Given the recent popularity of flexible work practices in many organisations, criticism has been levelled at job descriptions that are too highly structured. Critics claim that this narrows too strictly the perceived responsibilities of the employee, and can be counterproductive, by creating protectionist attitudes in employees towards their jobs, which could lead to demarcation disputes and other problems related to work roles.

Nevertheless, employees are usually hired to take a specific responsibility within the organisation (whether that be accountant, receptionist or cleaner), but they may have to take on other responsibilities in times of emergency, to enhance organisational efficiency. Therefore job descriptions are necessary in order to give employees a sense of purpose, and to enable their immediate superiors to appraise their performance, but a culture must prevail that enables employees to deal with problems that may be outside their immediate work domain.

Job analysis

Job analysis is a more sophisticated method of evaluating job functions, and is often used to discern the levels of skill necessary to do a job, primarily for the purpose of creating pay structures. Many modern organisations have rejected such techniques, as one executive of IKEA states: 'We reward individuals and not the job' (Pickard, 1992).

However, the information gleaned from such procedures can be useful in analysing the skill needs and requirement of jobs.

Interview with jobholders

This is one of the most commonly used methods: a manager, supervisor or member of the personnel department interviews the current jobholder about the duties and functions of the job. The interview can be structured, in the sense of having a series of questions framed to cover all aspects of the job.

Interview with managers and supervisors

Alternatively, a personnel manager or senior manager can interview the immediate supervisors of the job. Often descriptions arising are compared with the interview responses of the jobholder to act as a double check for discrepancies or elements missed by either party.

Performance objectives

The aim of increased quality, for example, will require performance objectives to be laid down. In doing so, assessment must take place as to whether current employees need training to reach these objectives. This has become increasingly popular in organisations that have adopted performance management programmes or *high-performance work systems* as they are known in the USA.

Analysis of competences

An analysis of competence requirements could be useful to match 'NVQ (National Vocational Qualification) or MCI (Management Charter Initiative) standards which are considered relevant to the various jobs involved. These can be compared with assessments of the current general levels of employee skills and abilities' (Fowler, 1991).

For the individual

Concomitant with an analysis of organisational needs is the analysis of the training needs of current employees. Much information about employees can be gleaned from organisational records, including original application forms and other databases.

Characteristics of people required (person specification)

In the effort to identify skills and competence requirements, the characteristics of the people required for the job are often forgotten. This will to some extent emerge in the competences analysis. For example, sales personnel would need an ability to deal with people, and this would undoubtedly be identified as an essential part of the job; but in other occupations and jobs, personal characteristics are often forgotten in the desire to isolate purely functional job requirements.

Personal profiles

Personal profile records are increasingly used in organisations, and useful for training needs analysis. They also include information on employees' career aspirations, which may well be of significance in creating training initiatives.

Appraisal

Appraisal has come in for much criticism recently, but a good appraisal can reveal much about the strengths and weaknesses of individuals in terms of their performance. Indications of areas where training and development programmes could improve performance are vital to both the individual and the organisation. Indeed the appraisal and variations of it are now used in many organisations as a central part of the learning organisation concept, whereby individuals can negotiate their training needs with their line manager. Some organisations have allocated training budgets for individuals to use for their own development in negotiation with their line managers. In this way an employee gains a sense of ownership of their development, with positive results for the organisation.

Assessment centre techniques

Though rather elaborate and expensive, assessment centres are the most thorough way of analysing individual strengths and weaknesses. Using a variety of methods including in-depth interviews and re-interviews, psychometric tests, team performance simulation exercises and other techniques, a detailed profile of employees can be constructed, which is useful for analysing training needs. Caution must be counselled, however, in terms of cost-effectiveness and an unrealistic expectation that infallible results are produced (Dulewicz, 1991).

Global review and training audits

The most wide-ranging method of training needs analysis is a global review, or more modestly a training audit. These are usually undertaken when far-reaching changes are planned within an organisation. Survey questionnaires and in-depth interviews are often used, together with all, or combinations of, the approaches previously mentioned.

Relating resources to the training objective

An across-the-board use of all these methods could be too expensive in terms of both time and money. Reid *et al.* (1992) point out that the global review could end up producing large amounts of paperwork, unjustified by the returns gained. It is therefore essential to assess the cost-effectiveness of training needs analysis in relation to the outcomes and returns expected.

Hirsch and Reilly (1998) warn that 'organisational structures and employee attitudes have an impact. Simply having appropriately skilled individuals does not automatically yield high performance' (p. 40). They give the example of the UK Post Office, where managers have learned that thinking through the skill implications of organisational change early enough gives them time to change the composition of the workforce. Hirsch and Reilly also stress that it may 'be important to design jobs and technology around the skills of the workforce, rather than to assume that the workforce will adjust to the new situation'.

Training methods

A careful use of training methods can be a very cost-effective investment in the sense of using the appropriate method for the needs of a person or group. However, many commentators have mentioned that organisations often use inappropriate methods, which can be both costly and time wasting and bring very little improvement in the performance of the employee. Storey (1991), in a comparative analysis of training in British and Japanese organisations, found that some British training is wasted as it is not embedded in the organisation as is the Japanese. British organisations also suffered from the 'bandwagon effect' and what he calls 'programmitis' – a constant series of newly launched programmes and initiatives which led to chopping and changing rather than consistently coherent long-term training initiatives.

In general, training can be divided into *on-the-job* and *off-the-job* methods. There is a place for both types, and each can be effective at meeting certain training requirements.

On-the-job training

On-the-job training (OJT) is probably the most common approach to training. It can range from relatively unsophisticated 'observe and copy' methods to highly structured courses built into workshop or office practice. Cannell (1997) defines OJT as

> training that is planned and structured that takes place mainly at the normal workstation of the trainee – although some instruction may be provided in a special training area on site – and where a manager, supervisor, trainer or peer colleague spends significant time with a trainee to teach a set of skills that have been specified in advance. It also includes a period of instruction where there may be little or no useful output in terms of productivity. (p.28)

'Sitting by Nellie' and learning by doing

These traditional methods are still very popular ways of teaching new skills and methods to employees, and they can be very effective. However, there are many acknowledged weaknesses that still persist in many organisational practices. Some people are better at it than others, and 'Nellie' may not be trained herself in the methods of transmitting knowledge and skills. There is often a lack of structure and design in the training given, which leads to the passing-on of bad or even dangerous working practices (Cannell, 1997).

Far more successful is to use a senior or experienced worker who has been trained in instruction or training methods and whose teaching skills are coordinated with a developed programme linked to off-the-job courses. Self-proclaimed learning organisations such as Analog Devices make very effective use of OJT, and claim that people learn and retain more of the training by performing the actual process at the place of work.

Mentoring

This is another version of the system, in which a senior or experienced employee takes charge of the training and development of a new employee. This suggests a much closer association than master–apprentice, and elements of a father–son or mother–daughter relationship can exist, whereby the mentor acts as an adviser and protector to the trainee. A study by Brockbank and Beech (1999) of mentors in the health sector reveals that overemphasis on the technical side of the mentoring process and an underestimation of the emotional side can have negative results. They recommend that appropriate support should be provided for mentors themselves. This dual role of providing professional and emotional support may clash, and it might be advisable for the two roles to be performed by different people.

Shadowing and job rotation

Shadowing is another oft-practised on-the-job training method. It usually aims to give trainee managers a 'feel' for the organisation by providing experience of working in different departments. It is an old technique, and has been criticised not so much for the concept itself as for the way it is often implemented. Trainees may feel it is time wasting, and people in the various departments in which they are temporarily working must also feel committed to and involved in the training if it is to work. Trainees are often not warmly welcomed, and are seen by supervisors and workers in the department as obstacles to the daily routines. However, if well structured, and planned with the cooperation of all departmental supervisors, this method can be a worthwhile learning experience.

Another version of training by switching roles is *job rotation*, which became popular in the 1970s to help relieve boredom and thereby raise the productivity of shopfloor workers. If appropriately implemented, it can be an excellent learning experience for workers, and it fits suitably with HRM concepts of teamworking and empowerment, whereby people are encouraged to take greater responsibility for their work and that of the team. On the negative side there have been criticisms that not enough structured training is given to enable workers to do these jobs well, and that it is also bound up with functional flexibility initiatives, often criticised for their deskilling and exploitative propensities.

Off-the-job training

Courses and other types of 'off-the-job' training have come in for much criticism, and are often viewed by both recipients and fellow employees as a waste of time and money. Yet off-the-job training is sometimes necessary to get people away from the hustle and bustle of the work environment. This enables the trainee to study theoretical information or be exposed to new and innovative ideas. The problem arises when those ideas or learning experiences do not appear to relate to the work situation. As we have seen from the research of Storey (1991), the predilection for sending employees on courses that do not appear to have much relevance to the employee or the job ('programmitis') only enhances the negative view of this type of training.

Perceptions of courses

Being sent on a course can be interpreted by the trainee as a sign of official approval or disapproval. For example, an approval sign would be that you are considered suitable for promotion, and the course is part of the training required for that position. A negative perception could be that the employee feels that they are being sent on a course because they are not very efficient in their job. Sending the correct messages to the trainees is also an important aspect of training initiatives.

A variety of methods

It is impossible to cover in depth in this book all the rich variety of approaches to training. Many of these the reader will have experienced before – sometimes with negative consequences. It is best to bear in mind that there may be nothing wrong with the methods, but that they may be utilised ineffectively by the trainer or the learner. In other words, the key is to make the appropriate match between the training requirements of the employee and the training methods available.

Active and passive learning

Much traditional training is a one-way learning process, in which the student is a passive learner receiving information from a lecturer, tutor or instructor. This can be an efficient way of imparting information, but all education theorists agree that the best form of learning is one in which the student is actively involved in the learning process.

Interactive learning methods

There are a wide variety of interactive learning techniques, some of them adaptations of one-way approaches:

- workshops;
- case studies;

- role play;
- simulations;
- interactive computer learning packages;
- video and audio tapes (interactively used);
- the Internet (web sites), intranet (organisational systems);
- problem solving.

For a fuller explanation of these techniques and others see Harrison (1997) and Barrington and Reid (1999).

Responsibility for and delivery of training

It is important to consider who is to be responsible for training, and who will deliver training.

Training departments

From the 1950s and (particularly) the 1960s, the responsibility for and delivery of training in many large organisations rested very much with specialist departments. By the 1980s and 1990s, however, training departments had come in for considerable criticism. They were accused of:

- being too rigid to respond to the changing needs of the organisation;
- being too much of an administrative expense;
- having lost contact with the changing skills needed on the shopfloor or at the place of work;
- being self-serving and bureaucratic;
- providing off-the-job training at their various centres that did not match up to 'on-the-job' needs;
- providing training that was too theoretical and not sufficiently practically based;
- not providing training and development that met individual needs – courses were too class/group based.

Despite these criticisms, training departments remain important in many organisations because they have personnel who have specialised knowledge and skills in the provision of training. As HRD becomes more important in the organisation the role of providers is becoming increasingly pivotal as facilitators of learning and the exchange of information and knowledge. The concepts of the learning organisation and the knowledge-based organisation place learning and HRD at the very heart of the organisation. HRD departments also act as internal consultants giving support to line managers alongside the HR department.

Training consultancies

Over the last decade the number of consultancies, many of them specialising in training, has burgeoned into an industry. While there are many excellent consultancies, there are also the inevitable 'cowboy' operations, which sometimes have unqualified, inexperienced and untrained staff, and at present there is no regulation to stop such operations from being set up. Some client companies and organisations have spent considerable sums on ineffective programmes, or to be told things they already knew. Of course, it is in the interest of the consultancy to push sometimes costly and unwarranted programmes on to unsuspecting clients, in order to drum up business.

It would be naive to believe that consultants are brought into organisations only to provide training programmes. They are also used to resolve political conflicts, to add kudos and status, to justify having larger budgets, to support political manoeuvring, and for other questionable reasons.

However, used carefully, reputable consultancies can provide invaluable specialist services and expertise that are often not available within client organisations, particularly small and medium-sized ones.

Training and the line manager

In order to counteract the perceived inflexibilities of training and personnel departments, there has been a notable trend to devolve many functions to line managers, including training policy. The justification is usually couched in terms of meeting the needs of people where it matters – at workplace level. Part of the line manager's brief is to discern the training needs of individuals in their department, and to suggest suitable training for them, usually in consultation with the personnel or training department. Training budgets have increasingly been devolved to line managers, in the belief that funding can be spent most effectively at the point where needs have been identified.

This can be very effective, because the assessment and delivery of training is more closely attuned to people in their working environment, but its efficacy depends very much on how it is carried out.

Research by the Price Waterhouse Cranfield Project team shows that there are many problems in splitting responsibilities between line managers and the personnel department:

> First there is often a dichotomy between the decentralised role and increasing responsibility of line managers, and the centralised role of the personnel/human resource function which must act as an interpreter of organisation-wide information and as a creator of human resource strategies. Secondly, the desire to empower the line manager may lead to sacrifices by the central personnel function in ensuring the relevant information is being relayed back. (Holden and Livian, 1992)

For example, 41% of personnel departments in the UK survey did not know how much money was spent on training, and 38% did not know the average number of training days allocated per person in the organisation (Holden, 1991; Holden and Livian, 1992).

Evaluation and monitoring of training

The penultimate stage in the training strategy is the evaluation and monitoring of training. It is one of the most important but often the most neglected parts of the training process.

This stage can be viewed as both simple and complicated. It is simple in that monitoring consists in gleaning information from the trainees and then amending the courses and programmes in the light of these comments. But it is also complex because there are other stakeholders in the process as well as the trainees: the designers of the courses, the trainers, and the sponsors. Each have their own purposes, aims and objectives, and these must be clearly identified before evaluation can proceed (Easterby-Smith and Mackness, 1992).

Another problem is that, while it is relatively easy to evaluate a formal off-the-job course, much on-the-job training often takes place in an informal way, which is usually subjective and open to interpretation (Holden, 1991).

Methods of evaluation include the following:

- *Questionnaires* (feedback forms) or 'happiness sheets' are a common way of eliciting trainees' responses to courses and programmes.

- *Tests or examinations* are common on formal courses that provide a certificate, such as a diploma in word-processing skills, and end-of-course tests can be provided after short courses to check the progress of trainees.
- *Projects* are initially seen as learning methods, but they can also provide valuable information for instructors.
- *Structured exercises and case studies* are opportunities to apply learned skills and techniques under the observation of tutors and evaluators.
- It is important to have the opinions of those who deliver the training. *Tutor reports* give a valuable assessment from a different perspective.
- *Interviews of trainees* after the course or instruction period can be informal or formal, individual or group, or by telephone.
- *Observation* of courses and training by those devising training strategies in the training department is very useful, and information from these observations can be compared with trainee responses.
- *Participation and discussion* during training must be facilitated by people who are adept at interpreting responses, as this can be highly subjective.
- Over the past decade *appraisal* has become an increasingly important method of evaluation. It has the advantage that the line manager and trainee can mutually assess the training undergone in terms of performance and employee development.

A combination of these approaches is advisable. It is also wise to receive feedback from the trainees and the tutors or trainers, and others involved in the assessment process.

Amending the HRD plan

While many organisations carry out excellent training programmes, the final and perhaps most vital stage is often ignored. As Easterby-Smith and Mackness (1992) wryly state:

> Training evaluation is commonly seen as a feedback loop, starting with course objectives and ending by collecting end-of-course reactions which are then generally filed away and not acted on.

Adjustments can be carried out after a small course to tighten up its effective operation, or when a training strategy cycle has been completed after six months or a year. At the end of such a phase it is essential to see whether training has effectively met the business objectives. Usually adaptations and changes are necessary, and the evaluation and monitoring process is invaluable in ensuring that these are appropriate.

Comment

In reading this section on training strategy two points need to be borne in mind:

- These training prescriptions can appear too simplistic, particularly in a textbook that has limited space to give to this complicated subject. The reality of creating training strategies is much more complex, and frustration and failure to achieve objectives are common, even in organisations that take such approaches seriously.
- There is limited evidence of a positive link between training and organisational efficiency and profitability, although there is a widespread belief that this is the case.

THE LEARNING ORGANISATION

The approach described above in the HRD strategy has been rejected by a number of organisations as far too mechanistic, controlling and inefficient. Writers such as Senge (1990) and Pedler *et al.* (1997) have put forward the concept of the *learning organisation*, in which learning and HRD are central functions of the organisation. In such an organisation the learning process is so embedded that learning and development become subconscious acts through which the business of the organisation operates. In this way its adherents claim that HRD becomes automatically strategic.

What is a learning organisation?

A clear definition of the learning organisation is elusive. Pedler *et al.* (1997) suggest that it is a vision of what might be possible when organisations go beyond merely training individuals towards developing learning at the whole organisation level. Their definition states:

> A Learning Company is an organisation that facilitates the learning of all its members and consciously transforms itself and its context.
> (p. 3)

Dixon (1994) added to the concept, suggesting that organisational learning, a key characteristic of a learning company, can be defined as

> the intentional use of learning processes at the individual, group and system level to continuously transform the organisation in a direction that is increasingly satisfying to its stakeholders.

Senge (1990) states that the basic meaning of the learning organisation is:

> an organisation that is continually expanding its capacity to create its future. For such an organisation it is not enough to merely survive . . . for a learning organisation 'adaptive learning' must be joined by 'generative learning', learning that enhances our capacity to create.
> (p.14)

Why the need for the learning organisation?

The concept has gained popularity in recent years because of the turbulent and increasingly competitive business environment. The impact of new technology and changing organisational forms that cater for customer needs mean dealing with continual change. This has led to what learning organisation (LO) adherents feel is *not* an add-on HRD system that is a lowly function driven by corporate strategy, but one that is central to the strategy of the organisation. The ability to respond swiftly to product and market developments is crucial. There has also been an increasing recognition of the importance of utilising not just the physical abilities of employees but also their mental powers. Senior managers are becoming aware that if their people are their greatest resource, they are also the source of any longer-term competitive advantage. This realisation has led to increased competition for skilled, flexible, adaptable staff, and to the development of organisational programmes that attempt to fully utilise the talents and knowledge of the workforce. It is also being recognised that international competitiveness means raising the standards of training to world-class levels. Failure to meet these pressures leads to organisational stagnation and ultimately organisational death.

Pedler *et al.*'s view of the learning organisation

A learning company is one that looks beyond mere survival. By developing an ability to constantly adapt its operations it is able to sustain market leadership. Such companies not only change with differing contexts but learn from their people and their environments while 'contributing to the learning of the wider community or context of which they are part' (Pedler *et al.*, 1997: 4). As leading-edge organisations they move beyond the visions of their founders or the conservatism of many companies formed in the same era or culture, evolving through an allegiance between internal and external environments.

Thus for Pedler *et al.* (1988: 4) a learning organisation is one that:

- has a climate in which individual members are encouraged to learn and develop their full potential;
- extends the learning culture to include customers, suppliers and other significant stakeholders;
- makes human resource development strategy central to business policy;
- is in a continuous process of organisational transformation.

While it is not possible to construct a model of a learning company, principally because there is no predetermined structure, Pedler *et al.* (1997: 15–17) identify 11 key characteristics that a learning company must possess:

- a learning approach to strategy;
- participative policy making;
- 'informating' (information technology is used to inform and empower people to ask questions and take decisions);
- formative accounting and control (control systems are structured to assist learning from decisions);
- internal exchange of ideas and knowledge;
- reward flexibility to promote performance and reward learning;
- enabling structures that remove barriers to communication and learning;
- boundary workers as environmental scanners benchmarking and using knowledge gained by sales staff and those who deal with the organisation's suppliers and customers. Seeing what rival oganisations are doing;
- inter-company learning;
- a learning climate;
- self-development opportunities for all.

Knowledge-managing organisation

Another concept that emerged in the 1990s was the *knowledge-managing organisation*. It is also known as the *knowledge-based organisation* or the *knowledge-creating company* (Nonaka, 1991). The process by which it is carried out is often known as *knowledge management* (Mayo, 1998).

A definition of knowledge management offered by Mayo (1998: 36) states that the following processes are essential:

- managing the generation of new knowledge through learning;
- capturing knowledge and experience;
- sharing, collaborating and communicating;
- organising information for easy access;
- using and building on what is known.

This list contains elements not greatly different from the learning organisation concept, and some observers claim that in effect they are the same phenomenon. Both concepts rely heavily on the exchange of knowledge and the desire of employees to be receptive to knowledge and learning – employees are the repositories of the organisation's knowledge and wisdom. As Tom Watson, former president of IBM, states: 'If you burnt down all our plants and we just kept our people and our files, we would soon be as strong as ever.' This underscores and adds to the strength of HRM and HRD departments, many of which have been preaching for years that 'our people are our greatest assets', often with the reality not living up to the slogan.

While the visionary concepts of knowledge management and the LO are inspiring, the reality is that, like most large-scale initiatives, implementation of such systems requires a massive change of attitude in most organisations that is not always easy to achieve. Success rests in creating a high-trust organisation where knowledge is readily exchanged. In practice there are many barriers. Knowledge is seen as power, and jealously guarded. Its possession and use can further ambitions. A culture of openness may be difficult to achieve, particularly in organisations where suspicion has been the norm. Knowledge management thus has serious implications for communication structures, employee involvement systems, reward systems and industrial relations.

There are many examples of companies that claim to be, or are on their way to being, learning organisations, including Anglia Water, Transco, IBM, Analog Devices, Nokia, GM, ICL, Xerox, and Hanover Insurance.

e-learning

A more recent concept of the informational and learning exchange environment is *e-learning*. This emphasises the use of new technology such as email, Internet, intranet and computer software packages to facilitate learning for employees whenever they need it. As one of its advocates (Masie, 1999) states:

> I expect to see an increasing alignment between e-learning and e-commerce. Information collected on the World Wide Web about product knowledge, for example, can be accessed in the same way for someone else to learn from. Organisations are even focusing on delivering knowledge and competencies to their whole supply chain by this method.
>
> (p. 32)

The adoption of on-line learning is attractive to organisations because the required data is available when learners want to learn. This will speed up the learning process and knowledge exchange. It also allows for 'granularisation' of learning. Until recently a unit of learning was expressed in terms of a three-day course, a morning course or a two-hour course. Granularisation can deliver a course in bite-sized chunks when the learner needs it. The e-learning forms can be formal (an actual course delivered via software or the Internet) or informal (exchange of information and knowledge via email or an intranet). The recently established University for Industry (UfI) in the UK will base a great deal of its approach to learning and delivery of courses on the use new technology, a trend that is increasing rapidly in universities and other educational institutions.

Criticisms of the learning organisation concept

Despite its relatively new entrance on the corporate scene there have already been a number of critical studies that have highlighted the weaknesses of LO. Garvin (1993) partly blames academics such as Senge, whose writings are often 'reverential and utopian (and) filled with near mystical terminology. Paradise, they would have you believe, is just round the corner.' He continues:

> Nonaka suggested that companies use metaphors and organisational redundancy to focus think-ing, encourage dialogue, and make tacit, instinctively understood ideas explicit. Sound idyllic? Absolutely. Desirable? Without question. But does it provide a framework for action? Hardly. These recommendations are far too abstract, and too many questions remain unanswered. How, for example, will managers know when their companies have become learning organisations? What concrete changes in behaviour are required? What policies and programmes must be in place? How do you get from here to there? (p. 49)

Sloman (1999) believes that 'the concept of the learning organisation should be redefined or declared redundant' (p. 31). The language and vocabulary of the learning organisation need to make sense to the hard-pressed line manager, and for these reasons alone the concept 'is in urgent need of review.'

An international study carried out by Chase (1997) for the *Journal of Knowledge Management* examined approaches to creating knowledge-based organisations. He found that while organisations acknowledge 'the importance of creating, managing and trans-ferring knowledge, they have so far been unable to translate this into need into organisational strategies. Mayo (1998: 38), cited in Chase's work, believes that 'most organisations are also struggling to use information technology to support implementa-tion' and a learning organisation. Chase's survey also pointed out that the biggest obstacles to creating a knowledge-based organisation were the existing company culture, lack of ownership of a problem, lack of time, inappropriate organisational structure, lack of senior management commitment, inappropriate rewards and recognition, and an emphasis on individuals rather than team work.

Lähteenmäki *et al.* (1999) have pointed to a number of criticisms that can be levelled at the concept:

- lack of clarity and multiplicity of definitions;
- lack of explanation of the detailed implementation of LO systems;
- lack of explanation as to how these systems are integrated;

(all these factors point to the need for a holistic model of the learning organisation, which should convincingly link theory and practice, bringing together 'pieces of theory')

- too much stress on learning by individuals and not by the organisation;
- a dearth of research on measurement of the learning process in organisations;
- a need to recognise the historical antecedents of the learning organisation;
- a need to recognise the relationship of the LO with organisational change literature;
- the need for further investigation of the link between HR strategy and change;
- the need for more research on LO in the international context, particularly the transfer of learning between units within multinational organisations, and the cul-tural barriers that may exist in that process.

The failure of LOs

Lähteenmäki *et al.* (1999), in summing up a number of research projects, emphasised these reasons for failure:

- failure to deal with feelings of uncertainty and insecurity in employees during peri-ods of intense competition and culture change;
- a work situation that lacks trust – this can only make failure more certain, because it inhibits the learning process, as employees recede into defensive coping styles;

- poor feedback, limited encouragement, insufficient discussion of mistakes and the lack of empowerment, which serve to further undermine the effectiveness of LO initiatives;
- failure to give all employees the responsibility for learning;
- failure to understand the linkages between the LO and HRM strategy.

They suggest some recommendations in moving towards a learning organisation:

- An environment of openness and trust, must be created.
- An atmosphere of certainty and security must be generated.
- This can be achieved by developing strategy from the bottom up, through building a shared vision, team learning, and developing core competences that are recognised and valued by all.
- It is essential to have objectives that are clearly and positively linked to HRM strategy.
- It must be recognised that measurement of learning can feed more positively into an evaluation of the effectiveness of the learning process.
- Finally, it is of paramount importance to create a learning atmosphere that all members of the organisation share.

There are no easy prescriptions for creating a learning organisation; it takes a considerable time to engender the right attitudes and conditions in the change process. Those organisations that can learn these lessons not only are well on the way to becoming learning organisations, but also are more likely to have the skills, competences and, above all, the right attitudes for survival in our increasingly competitive globalised environment.

HRD AND THE NATIONAL FRAMEWORK FOR VOCATIONAL EDUCATION AND TRAINING

Introduction

Learning and development are not solely matters of concern for individuals and their employers. An educated and skilled workforce is essential for the effective functioning of the economy, for the competitiveness and wealth of the nation, and for the overall well-being of society. Indeed, Tyson and Fell (1995) suggest that 'the future will see a world of work based more on skills than organisations' (p. 45). To ensure that a nation achieves the level of skills it needs, its government therefore puts in place the vocational education and training (VET) policies and systems that will facilitate their development. Such national strategies therefore form an important part of the context (see Chapter 2) of individual learning and organisational human resource development.

As new technology progresses, replacing jobs and changing skill requirements, there is an increasing need for a skilled and highly trained workforce able to meet these changing situations. Traditional skills, for example in the engineering and construction industries, are rapidly changing, and the type of economy in which a young person can receive an apprenticeship that would stand them in good stead for a lifetime career is dwindling.

This trend is international, and poses problems for the USA, Japan, Germany, France, Sweden and other industrialised nations. However, comparisons with competitor nations indicate that Britain is suffering from a severe skills shortage. Its 'first ever national audit of job skills', which the government published in 1996 to accompany its third 'competitiveness' White Paper, compares Britain with France, Germany, Singapore and the USA:

> Its findings confirm fears that Britain's skills are lagging behind those of Germany, which has had a policy of investment in vocational training for years. More worrying is the rapidly shrinking gap between the UK and Singapore in the league tables.
>
> (Welch, 1996c: 11)

Britain's greatest deficiency is in basic and level 2 skills, (low-level NVQ skills including numeracy and literacy) though 'Britain is ahead of its competitors both on quality and the quantity of its population' possessing degrees and vocational qualifications of a comparable level.

Many see the solution to be the investment of more capital in education and training, and the creation of an ever more skilled and knowledgeable workforce, partly because the industrialised countries can never compete with developing world economies in terms of cheap labour. The developments in VET in Britain, as elsewhere, have to be seen within this context. However, the efficacy of VET to achieve such national needs is not fully demonstrated. For example, the relative economic decline in Britain has led to much debate as to the adequacy of training in helping to arrest this trend. (This is a controversial issue that will be discussed in a later section.)

There has been considerable criticism of training policy in the UK at both national and organisational level (though other views are also now being expressed: see Harrison, 1995 and Merrick, 1995). As a later section will show, Britain has not compared favourably with Germany, Japan, Sweden or France in VET terms. Many surveys throughout the 1980s and 1990s have shown that employers regard training as being important, but the problem seems to be that, despite this recognition, not enough training has been done to meet the changing needs of the economy. What we have therefore seen is the British government tackling the training needs for the economy in an energetic way, and introducing many new policies and systems. These are having a major impact upon how learning individually and in organisations takes place by providing a framework of philosophies (such as competences), structures (such as the National Council for Vocational Qualifications), resources (such as the Training and Enterprise Councils), and incentives (such as the Investors in People award).

The purpose of this section is to outline some of the VET policies and systems currently in place in Britain, and to indicate possible future developments. However, it first recognises the key stakeholders in VET, and then sets British provision in the context of that of some of its major competitors.

Stakeholders in vocational education and training

Chapter 7 identified several stakeholders in the individual's learning and development, and it examined the needs and responses of the individual and the employer in particular. There are several stakeholders in VET too, and their values and actions constitute the framework within which individual learning and development and organisational HRD have to take place. The part the government plays in this field will be examined in some detail later in this chapter. Note that in Britain the departments concerned with education and employment have both been involved, and they were eventually merged to form the Department for Education and Employment.

Employers are also significant stakeholders in VET. This is apparent in the international comparisons in the following section. During the 1990s, the British employers' body, the Confederation of British Industry (CBI), played an influential role. For example, recognising the need for a 'skills revolution' (Confederation of British Industry, 1989), it proposed training targets (later adopted by the government) for the minimum standards needed to increase Britain's competitiveness.

The trade unions are further stakeholders in VET. At present the role of British unions in this regard is somewhat limited compared with that of their counterparts in France and Germany:

> where unions are involved widely at national, regional, sectoral and company levels in promoting and regulating the training process. This role is supported in France by law. In Germany it constitutes one part of the corporatist system of compromise and consensus between the 'social partners'.
> (Claydon and Green, 1992).

However, British trade unions have recently been examining their role in the economic system, particularly in the light of their decline over the past decade. One strategy they have begun to adopt is to advocate training as a collective bargaining issue other than in the narrow context of setting wages and conditions for apprentices (Kenney and Reid, 1988). Some unions, for example the EETPU, have advocated a policy of training their members to update their skills and improve their employability, in order to demonstrate to employers that the presence of unions can be beneficial (Lloyd, 1990). The TUC discussed training initiatives in *Skills 2000* (TUC, 1989) and *TUC: Joint Action over Training* (TUC, 1990), and has advocated greater 'involvement in the planning and provision of training and educational opportunities through participation at European, national and firm levels' (TUC, 1991; quoted in Claydon and Green, 1992).

Since the election of the Labour government in 1997, unions have been welcomed into a partnership with employers and the government, and have collectively been a large contributor to the National Skills Task Force (NSTF), which has investigated national skills shortages and has produced several reports and recommendations. Regional TUC organisations are also involved in implementing and operating Learning and Skills Councils, which replaced Training and Enterprise Councils (TECs) in April 2001.

VET IN THE LEADING INDUSTRIALISED NATIONS

This section compares and contrasts VET in six leading industrialised nations: Britain and five competitor countries. There are a number of similarities. All six countries have compulsory education of similar ages (Table 8.2) and therefore recognise the importance of at least a basic education in a modern industrialised society. All six countries experienced decline in the number of children of school-leaving age in the 1990s (Table 8.3); Germany experienced the most severe decline.

Table 8.2 Compulsory school education ages

Britain	5–16 yrs
Germany	6–15 yrs
France	6–16 yrs
Sweden	7–16 yrs
Japan	6–15 yrs
USA	6–16 yrs[a]

[a] Varies from state to state

Table 8.3 Indices of the 16 to 18-year-old population and participation in education rates

	16 to 18-year-old population indices (year)			16 to 18-year-old participation in education and training (%)		
	1980	*1990*	*2000*	*Full*	*Part*	*All*
Britain	121	106	94	33	31	64
Germany	125	83	72	47	43	90
France	100	103	90	66	8	74
Sweden	99	102	86	76	2	78
Japan	91	114	92[a]	77	3	79
USA	102	83	85[a]	79	1	80

100 = 1970

[a] 1996

Source: DES (1990). Reproduced by permission of the Controller of Her Majesty's Stationery Office.

Table 8.4 Proportion of salaries and wages spent on training 1990–91

	UK	*France*	*Spain*	*Sweden*	*Germany*
0.01–1.0%	21	4	33	9	20
4% and above	11	27	13	16	11
Don't know	41	2	25	48	47

Source: Price Waterhouse Cranfield Survey (Holden, 1991: 120).

Table 8.5 Proportion of salaries and wages spent on training 1991–92

	Switzerland	*Germany*	*Denmark*	*Spain*	*France*	*Italy*	*Norway*	*Netherlands*	*Sweden*	*UK*
0.01–2.0%	64	61	66	76	25	76	63	65	57	62
4% and above	11	16	13	10	32	9	19	16	25	18
Don't know	25	42	33	18	2	24	30	23	44	38

Source: Price Waterhouse Cranfield Survey (Holden and Livian, 1992: 15). Reproduced with permission of MCB University Press.

An examination of the statistics for 16- to 18-year-olds shows that the majority continue with some form of education or training, either full or part time (Table 8.3). Britain, however, has the fewest involved, being 10% below the comparable French figure, for example.

There are also significant differences between these countries in the amount of financial investment that their organisations make in training. This is demonstrated in Tables 8.4 and 8.5.

Germany has a thoroughgoing VET infrastructure, and Sweden has a well-established vocational system, which begins when children are 14 years old. These countries therefore, while having a large proportion of organisations ignorant of their training expenditure, have tried and tested systems of VET. The large UK 'don't know' figures are therefore all the more ominous given the unclear and contradictory approaches to VET.

VET policies and practices

An examination of the VET systems beyond compulsory school age for the same six countries reveals a varying, and sometimes widely varying, set of practices (see Table 8.6). They can be roughly divided into *voluntarist* and *directed*. By voluntarist is meant a

Table 8.6 VET policies and practices

Britain
- New Deal – Training for 18-24-year-olds out of work longer than 6 months, and training for over-24-year-olds out of work for longer than 2 years
- National Training Organisations (NTOs) – sectoral bodies whose function is to analyse skills gaps using international benchmarking, scenario planning and local focus groups
- National Skills Task Force (NSTF) – body composed of government, employees and union representatives investigating skill shortages nationally and recommending proposals
- Learning and Skills Councils – regional bodies set to replace TECs in April 2001
- National Vocational Qualifications (NVQ) levels 1 to 5
- Competence movement, e.g. Management Charter Initiative (MCI)
- Investors in People (IIP) – to encourage companies to attain a recognised level of strategic training
- New apprenticeships – set up in the early 1990s to encourage quality skilled training
- Colleges of higher and further education
- Universities (including the 'old polytechnics')
- Business schools, usually part of universities

Training culture – voluntarist: finance rather than industry orientated; class based; public/private education

Germany
- Dual system – in-company training (practical); vocational school (theoretical)
- Apprenticeships – 319 000 places, though demand is decreasing
- Technical colleges
- Universities

Training culture – directed: functionalist; industry orientated, particularly engineering

France
- Much VET in school system
- Apprenticeship places 300 000
- University institutes of technology
- Universities
- Grandes écoles
- Law requiring employers to spend 1.2% of total gross salaries on training employees

Training culture – directed: mathematical/engineering orientation; centralised; elitist, e.g. grandes écoles; the educational establishment attended often decides career prospects

Sweden
- Upper secondary school – large vocational content
- Technical and specialist universities
- Universities
- VET in most organisations is strong; heavy emphasis on HRD
- Retraining for unemployed
- Labour Market Training Board (AMU) is very influential
- Considerable free adult education
- Emphasis on 'self-development' and open learning systems

Training culture – directed: state will use training to affect labour market policy. Companies are strongly encouraged to train

Japan
- High schools take up to 90% of pupils up to 18 years
- Two-year college – vocationally specific training
- Four-year university courses
- Five-year college of technology courses
- Considerable continuous in-company training

Training culture – directed/voluntarist: central and local government set and enforce training standards; meritocratic – top companies will take from top universities etc.; lifetime employment and training in large companies; self-development emphasised

USA
- Junior or community college two-year associate degree course
- Technical institutes
- Vocational, trade and business schools
- 'GI Bill' federal loans/grants for four years' higher education after completion of four years' military service
- Private schools and colleges
- University courses
- Apprenticeships are increasingly less common and of low status
- Excellent training by leading companies but this is not universal

Training culture – voluntarist: anti-federalist in nature with wide variation; uncoordinated, with emphasis on individual effort and individual payment

Source: Dore and Sako (1989); Carnevale *et al.* (1990); Brewster *et al.* (1992), DfEE web page.

system that has little or no government interference, and effectively leaves training to the choice of the individual or the organisation. By directed is meant the existence of state legislation or regulation that has an element of compulsion for employers to train their staff.

Britain and the United States clearly have voluntarist systems and Germany, France and Sweden have directed systems, whereas Japan, while not having legislation that makes VET compulsory, has strong directives set by local and central government that enforce high-quality training standards (Dore and Sako, 1989). The Japanese also have a culture that values training and education highly, and such policies have a collectivist rather than an individualist imperative (Hofstede, 1984).

What can also be discerned is that in each country there are a considerable number of routes through vocational education and training, which vary from relatively low-grade schemes such as Training for Work in Britain to university graduate and postgraduate degrees. However, it is apparent that the British system lacks homogeneity and consistency in courses and standards of occupational qualifications compared with those of Japan, Sweden and Germany.

In Europe there are two main types of vocational training: the sequential and the dual systems. The *sequential system* is practised in France, Italy, Belgium, the Netherlands and Sweden, and is conducted in specialist vocational training colleges, which school leavers attend full time. The German *Berufsbildungssystem* is the main exemplar of the *dual system,* and is described below.

The German system of VET

The German 'directed' and dual system of vocational training has frequently been referred to as an example of excellent practice. A common misunderstanding is that the VET is funded and run by the state. In reality employers fund two-thirds of VET, and employers and trade unions have a considerable influence on the control of the system, together with central and local government. Laws and guidelines of VET regulate the system so that employers are duty bound to provide funding and resources for training. The institutions and procedures that operate the system are, however, administered jointly by employers, unions and the state.

There are three stages in the dual system (see Figure 8.2). The first begins in the latter years of school, where emphasis is placed on a high level of education for all. A good general education, it is recognised, provides the solid basis for later learning. Nearly all young school leavers enter apprenticeships, as do a quarter of youths with qualifications similar to A levels; the rest enter the college and university system (Rose and Wignanek, 1990).

The dual system stresses the strong relationship between theoretical and practical training; part of the apprentice's time is taken up in attending vocational college, and part in receiving structured training from a *meisterwerker* (skilled craftsman) in the workplace. The *meisterwerker*, it must be stressed, is also trained in instruction techniques (Thorn, 1988). On-the-job and off-the-job instruction is carefully coordinated to produce a vocational course that gives a thorough grounding in the skills of the apprentice's trade, and this, once acquired, is acceptable in all parts of the German labour market.

The costs of the dual system are shared by firms, government and youths. Firms pay for on-the-job training, youths accept relatively low wages, and the vocational colleges are paid for by public funds (Rose and Wignanek, 1990). There are approximately 319 000 apprenticeship places available in Germany compared with approximately

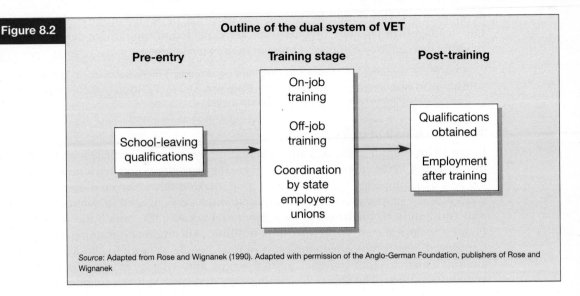

Figure 8.2

Outline of the dual system of VET

Pre-entry   **Training stage**   **Post-training**

School-leaving qualifications

On-job training

Off-job training

Coordination by state employers unions

Qualifications obtained

Employment after training

Source: Adapted from Rose and Wignanek (1990). Adapted with permission of the Anglo-German Foundation, publishers of Rose and Wignanek

13 000 in Britain. However, since 1986 young people in Germany have taken up only about 172 000 apprentice places, but that number may have declined with the advent of more difficult times in the 1990s (Gaugler and Wiltz, 1992).

Germany has three times more skilled workers than Britain, even though the labour force of each country is of similar size (Rose and Wignanek, 1990). Nevertheless, as will be noted in the section on controversial issues, Germany's much admired VET policies and practices are apparently no longer effective in reducing the number of the unemployed.

The Japanese system of VET

While the German system illustrates the comparative efficiency of its youth training programmes, an examination of the Japanese system of VET reveals the advantages of continuous development of employees throughout their careers. 'Lifetime employment' is a much referred to Japanese employment practice, although in reality '40% of new recruits leave within three years of entering their first job' (Dore and Sako, 1989). However, there is still a considerable proportion of lifetime employment in large-scale companies among the managerial and professional workforce in particular, who tend to form the core (those with relatively permanent positions and career structures) of company employees.

Lifetime employment allows for the long-term development of employees, and enables the creation of a structured succession programme that is mutually beneficial to the organisation and the individual employee. Decision-making is shared at all levels, there is a strong sense of collective responsibility for the success of the organisation, and cooperative rather than individual effort is emphasised, although achievement is encouraged. Training and development are an integral part of company policy in helping to reinforce these working practices, and in improving skills in technology and other related working practices. Training and development are thus 'embedded' in Japanese companies, rather than extraneous as in British organisations. A study of eight comparable British and Japanese companies recently revealed the inherent weaknesses of the British system (Storey, 1991). While the study concentrated on management development, the fact that the Japanese have no term for this was significant. They believe all workers should be developed, and this should be an ongoing part of systematic employee development. Line managers in Japanese organisations are expected to spend time developing their subordinates, and this is deeply imbued in their expectations:

> In the main, the Japanese treated training and development more seriously. In Britain, despite many good intentions and recent advances, there was a level of ambiguity about the real value of training and development that was not found in Japan.
>
> (Storey, 1991)

The French system of VET

In the 1970s training initiatives and expenditure were similar in Britain and France. In the 1970s and 1980s, however, successive French governments initiated a number of training laws that compelled organisations to train, making this a 'directed' system. The *taxe d'apprentissage* (apprenticeship tax) required employers engaged in commercial, industrial and handicraft activities to be subject to a tax of 0.6%, which was to be used to finance technical and apprenticeship training. An employee training tax was also introduced, which compelled employers of nine people or more to allocate a minimum amount equal to 1.2% of total annual wages and salaries to staff training (Price Waterhouse, 1989). The effects on training were dramatic. At first a considerable number of training consultancies came into existence to cater for the expected demand (Barsoux and Lawrence, 1990). Another longer-term factor was that, as companies were forced to train, many found that it brought benefits, and they began to spend above the 1.2% requirement, as Tables 8.4 and 8.5 indicate.

French organisations, in conforming to French law, have a much greater knowledge of their training expenditure compared with other European countries, as the Price Waterhouse data consistently show in both years of the survey, even when extended from five to ten countries (see Tables 8.4 and 8.5). Only 2% of French organisations did not know how much they spent on training, but well over 40% did not know this in the UK, Sweden and Germany. Similar figures can be found in the 1991–92 survey.

Overall, French organisations

> have been forced to pay more attention to training since under law they also have to draw up a training plan to be submitted and discussed with the *comité d'entreprise* [works council] [and] . . . gradually firms have begun to look on it [training tax] as an investment that can be integrated into the firm's strategy.
>
> (Barsoux and Lawrence, 1990)

The implications of these international comparisons for Britain

Statistics reveal that Britain has one of the lowest percentages of young people between the ages of 16 and 18 years of age staying on at school or undertaking vocational education schemes (see Table 8.3), compared with other industrialised countries of the European Union and the world (DES, 1990). A more recent report published by the OECD stated that of 14 countries studied in depth only Hungary and Portugal had a record as poor as the UK for smoothing the transition from school to work. Of those students staying on in full-time education 20% dropped out within one year, and an astonishing 10% could not be traced as in work or in education. It also stated that 40% of British young people aged 19–24 had not reached what the OECD considered to be a minimum-level qualification (Atkinson and Elliott, 2000: 6).

Concerns have also been raised regarding the relative decline of literacy and numeracy among school leavers and the relevance of the school curriculum to the world of work, for example the narrow and restrictive role of A levels. Moreover, there is also considerable concern about long-term unemployed people condemned to a life of inactivity because they have not been able to receive adequate training to create a suitable career. There has been disquiet regarding the role of training and education policy in helping to halt or reverse that trend. Yet despite high unemployment in some areas there are organisations experiencing difficulties in recruiting certain highly skilled positions. The comparisons made above between the British system of VET and those of some of its major competitors do little to allay such concerns. Recent nationwide skills audit reports show that Britain's workforce has slipped further behind its main economic rivals in training and education. In comparing Britain with France, Germany, Singapore and the United States, the report indicated that, while the number of young people staying on in full-time education in Britain had improved, it was still behind the other four nations. It was in VET, particularly in craft and technical skills, that the report stated that Britain still had much to do to equal its rivals (Targett, 1996: 3; Macleod and Beavis, 1996: 6).

Some critics claim that Britain is becoming a 'low-tech' (untrained and unskilled), cheap-labour economy, with an increasing proportion of the potential labour force condemned to a lifetime of economic inactivity. In the early 1990s Layard stated that 'two-thirds of British workers had no vocational or professional qualification, compared with only a quarter in Germany' (Anon, 1992a).

These issues raise many questions as to the scope and type of training that is needed. The following subsections outline some of the recent VET initiatives designed to improve Britain's competitiveness. It is too soon to judge their effects, but the conclusion that Britain lags behind its competitors is now being questioned: 'the UK system may eventually be seen as an example of how to create a more flexible workforce' (Merrick, 1995: 8).

VET IN BRITAIN

The involvement of government in VET in the UK

With its voluntarist system of VET, Britain has traditionally left the provision of training and employee development to employers, and has largely had an educational system that was geared to preparing young people as members of society rather than as workers. However, the experience of relative economic decline in Britain has raised a number of questions regarding the role of education and training policy in helping to halt or reverse that trend. It has become clear that employers by themselves cannot achieve the major investment needed by the nation in training and development. This is not only because they serve their own self-interest rather than that of the economy at large, but also because they have had to operate within a patchwork of complex and poorly integrated VET courses, standards and qualifications. The only way to deal strategically with the nation's shortfall in skills has been for the government to modify its voluntarist approach and develop an overall framework for VET. However, whether voluntarism should be abandoned entirely is being currently debated, although in February 2000 the Labour government stated that it will not be adopting a training levy proposal at present, an indication that the voluntarist approach will remain predominant (see the subsection on Labour government policies later in this chapter).

The recent history of government involvement

The history of government initiatives in training is a relatively short one. Not until 1964, when Industrial Training Boards (ITBs) were set up, was there an attempt by government to influence employer training behaviour. Subsidies were given to companies that were able to show that they were carrying out training programmes of a type approved by the Training Boards, and Boards were set up to oversee most sectors of the economy.

The ITBs did have some impact on popularising training by pointing to its benefits, which also helped to influence companies to set up training departments and improve their training methods (Manpower Services Commission, 1981).

The neo-liberalist Conservative governments from 1979 were directly opposed to any form of compulsion, and thus the voluntarist tradition was re-emphasised and bolstered. It is surprising, therefore, that more government policies directed at improving training were initiated than before. The Employment and Training Act 1981 abolished most of the ITBs, and the government stressed that 'it is for employers to make the necessary investment in training for the work that they require' (IMS, 1984).

During this same period the government introduced initiatives in education that were intended to generate an enterprise culture. Moreover, the new national curriculum for schools was designed expressly to meet the needs of employers. The merging of the Department for Education and Department of Employment into one ministry expressed how close the relationship between education and employment was deemed to be.

Government training initiatives

A further impetus for the government's increasing involvement in VET during the 1980s and 1990s was the dramatic rise in unemployment among young people and adults, with a high incidence of long-term unemployment. Consequently, a plethora of initiatives in the fields of education and training were introduced. These included schemes for training the unemployed, the establishment of bodies to initiate, foster and undertake training of direct relevance to employers (the Training and Enterprise Councils), the development of a comprehensive national framework of vocational qualifications, and national targets for training. The following subsections will outline the major elements of this context.

Youth Training Scheme and Employment Training

Increasing unemployment in the recession of the early 1980s forced the government to take action. In particular, youth unemployment, combined with the impact of the inner-city riots in 1981, led to the creation of youth schemes, and the Youth Opportunities Programme (YOP), introduced by the previous Labour government in 1978, was revived. This later became the Youth Training Scheme (YTS). However, there was considerable criticism levelled against YOPs and YTSs: that they were ineffective, and merely a way of relieving unemployment statistics by involving unemployed school leavers in poor-quality and, in some cases, exploitative work experience programmes.

The equally pressing need to help the adult unemployed back into the job market, particularly those who had been without work for a considerable time and those made redundant as a result of changing technology, led the government to set up Employment Training (ET) in 1988. ET was considered by critics as an even worse failure than YOP and YTS and by the end of 1992 ET 'had petered out through lack of cash and commitment' (Lowe, 1992). It was later merged with the Employment Action programme and retitled Training for Work. One review body stated:

> The concern is that both YT and ET (now Training for Work) are headed for low skill, low quality, low expectation, low takeup, and low prestige 'aid of last resort' position.
>
> (G10 Group of Training and Enterprise Council Chairmen, House of Commons, 1993: 4, quoted in Felstead, 1994: 1)

Training and Enterprise Councils

Another major Conservative government initiative was the setting-up of Training and Enterprise Councils (TECs) in England and Wales, and Local Enterprise Companies (LECs) in Scotland. Between 1991 and 1992, 82 TECs and 22 LECs were set up. Local business people were to be encouraged to sit on the TEC and LEC boards, as it was felt they would be in tune with local business needs and thus able to direct training schemes that would have relevance to local employers. The emphasis was put on closing the 'skills gap': that is, training people, such as the unemployed, to be able to fill jobs where there were shortages, which were often in skilled areas such as computer skills and electrical engineering skills. Training providers were not allowed to join the main board.

TECs and LECs have come in for a barrage of criticism, not only from political opponents but from the world of industry and commerce and those administering the schemes themselves (Milne, 1991; Anon, 1992b; Felstead, 1994). Many argue that leaving training to the voluntary decisions and exigencies of the business community cannot succeed, because it has repeatedly been shown that many business organisations will not train enough to suit the needs of the economy, but only their own needs. Critics further claim that voluntary systems have not worked, and that either a form of compulsion to force employers to train or an increase in direct government involvement is needed.

In addition, TEC board members have reproached the government for not providing enough funding to make the scheme viable and for leaving resources far too stretched to fulfil their aims (Graham, 1992; Wood, 1992).

There were also devastating criticisms of irregular practices by private training companies in collusion with TECs, leading to accusations of funding for jobs and training being given to people already about to be employed or even in employment. Felstead (1994) summed up the position by the mid 1990s:

> the prospect of TECs/LECs curing Britain's well known deficiencies in intermediate skills therefore looks bleak, the more likely outcome is the production of more and more workers with low level skills in business administration, community care and retailing. The 'skills revolution' that TECs/LECs were meant to prompt looks a long way off. (p. 21)

The Labour government has decided to replace TECs in April 2001, and their role will be taken over by the Learning and Skills Councils and National Training Organisations (see below).

Competences

Chapter 7 has identified competence as one of the outcomes of learning and development. Defined as the ability to apply knowledge and skills with understanding to a work activity and, importantly, assessed via performance, the notion has resonated with the values that have come to pervade the recent thinking of government policy makers on VET, with their increasing emphasis upon outcomes rather than inputs into education and training. During the later 1980s, therefore, competence and competency was adopted as a major building block in the new thinking about VET, and has now achieved wide currency in this field.

However, these notions are not universally accepted, and there has been considerable debate about the way they have been conceptualised and used in practice (Kandola, 1996). A key issue for those critical of this approach is the status given to the knowledge underpinning the performance of skills. The issue rumbles on in the various debates (e.g. Armstrong, 1996).

Nevertheless, the competency approach has been a major innovation in the field of HRD, and has permeated it widely during the 1990s. Although it may be applied in different ways (Kandola, 1996), there is no sense yet that it is fragmenting or fading. Buttressed by its adoption in various government-led VET initiatives (see below), it is likely that it will withstand its critics for some time yet, and will therefore continue to influence the format of and philosophy underpinning much individual and organisational training and development activity.

A national framework of vocational qualifications

The establishment in 1986 of the National Council for Vocational Qualifications (NCVQ) and the Scottish Vocational Educational Council (SCOTVEC) institutionalised the competency approach. These bodies provide a framework of National Vocational Qualifications (S/NVQs, or VQs), which accredit competencies across organisations so that an individual's performance at work can now be taken into account in an educational qualification. In addition, GNVQs are an alternative to academic A levels for those preparing for the world of work.

S/NVQs are statements 'confirming that the individual can perform to a specified standard' and that he or she 'possesses the skills, knowledge and understanding which makes possible such performance in the workplace' (Harrison, 1992: 28). There are five levels of S/NVQ: from the most basic level through craft, technician and lower-level professional skills to the higher professional levels. The standards of competence for particular occupations and professions are, after a lengthy analytical and consultative process, set by industry lead bodies, which include representatives of employers and trade unions, as Townsend (1992) illustrates in the work of the Personnel Standards Lead Body, to ensure that the standards are relevant to work and are valued by employers.

There is a wide range of lead bodies, such as the Small Firms Lead Body and the Guidance and Counselling Lead Body. The comparable body in the field of management is the Management Charter Initiative (MCI), the work of which is described in Chapter 9. Many occupational areas are therefore embraced in the new qualifications' framework: bouncers, caterers, translators, teachers etc. Awarding bodies such as City and Guilds, RSA and BTEC have changed their awards to meet S/NVQ criteria. The nature of the lead bodies has evolved, and some have formed themselves into occupational standards councils (OSCs) for particular sectors of employment. For example, the Personnel Standards Lead Body, the Training and Development Lead Body and the Trade Union Sector Development Body merged in 1994 to become the Employment OSC. This has not always been a smooth process, as Welch (1996a) indicates when reporting the eventual accreditation by NCVQ of the IPD's new qualifications in personnel, training and development.

The developments so far, however, have not been an unqualified success. There have been criticisms of definitions, purposes and methodology. There has been considerable frustration with their excessive bureaucracy and the 'jargon-ridden language' of the standards, and recognition of the need for the lead bodies or OSCs to provide external quality checks on the standard of assessment. The controversy and debate surrounding this issue will undoubtedly exercise the minds of the interested parties for some time to come.

Nevertheless, like the competency approach, the language and framework of VQs are influencing how individuals construct their own development, and how organisations approach and deliver HRD, and hence the nature of the learning environment they offer their employees.

Investors in People

Investors in People (IIP) was launched in 1991 and created out of the collaborative work of the National Skills Task Force (NSTF), CBI, Department of Employment, TUC and IPD. Since 1993 it has been a private company limited by guarantee – Investors in People UK (IIP UK, 1995; Taylor and Thackwray, 1995). Based on 'the practical experience of businesses that have improved their performance through investing in people' (Employment Department Group, 1990), IIP gives a national framework that specifies 'the principles which tie training and development activity directly to business objectives', ensures that the 'resources committed to training and development are put to the most effective use', and provides 'a clear benchmark of good practice . . . against which any organisation, large or small, can measure progress towards improved business performance' (IIP UK, 1995: 1).

The Employment Department Group's (1990) brochure *What is an Investor in People?* states:

An Investor in People makes a public commitment from the top to develop all employees to achieve its business objectives.

- Every employer should have a written but flexible plan which sets out business goals and targets, considers how employees will contribute to achieving the plan and specifies how development needs in particular will be assessed and met.
- Management should develop and communicate to all employees a vision of where the organisation is going and the contribution employees will make to its success, involving employee representatives as appropriate.

An Investor in People regularly reviews the training and development needs of all employees.

- The resources for training and developing employees should be clearly identified in the business plan.
- Managers should be responsible for regularly agreeing training and development needs with each employee in the context of business objectives, setting targets and standards linked, where appropriate, to the achievement of National Vocational Qualifications (or relevant units) and, in Scotland, Scottish Vocational Qualifications.

An Investor in People takes action to train and develop individuals on recruitment and throughout their employment.

- Action should focus on the training needs of all new recruits and continually developing and improving the skills of existing employees.
- All employees should be encouraged to contribute to identifying and meeting their own job-related development needs.

An Investor in People evaluates the investment in training and development to assess achievement and improve future effectiveness.

- The investment, the competence and commitment of employees, and the use made of skills learned should be reviewed at all levels against business goals and targets.
- The effectiveness of training and development should be reviewed at the top level and lead to renewed commitment and target setting.

By December 1999, 16 454 organisations (or units within them) had achieved the national standard as Investors in People, and almost 22 000 had made a commitment to gaining the award (IIP, 2000). Taylor and Thackwray (1995) report that organisations find considerable benefit in working for and achieving the standard. They quote a survey and case studies that suggest that the benefits derive from ensuring that training is strategic and relates to the organisation's business needs. In particular, organisations cite that working towards IIP helps to clarify and communicate business objectives, stimulates continuous improvement initiatives (see Chapter 7), increases the involvement of managers in individuals' development, brings together some seemingly unrelated activities, and gives attention to administrative staff who are often otherwise overlooked. Taylor and Thackwray (1995: 30) also note that some organisations believe that through IIP they have increased profitability, efficiency, sales and income, and reduced costs.

Alberga (1997) in a survey in 1996 warns that there could be difficulties over re-recognition as organisations seek to retain the reward after three years: 'The problem is that it enables people to let things slide and then drag them up just in time for the re-recognition process' (p. 32). The achievement of this standard calls for considerable effort, but it is becoming clear that its benefits lie in the diagnostic and reflective process that it sets in train rather than, perhaps, in the award itself.

New developments in education to increase flexibility

During the 1980s there were a number of developments that have made educational provision more flexible and the qualifications system more responsive to the needs of individuals. These are:

- the *Credit Accumulation and Transfer Scheme* (CATS) to help non-traditional entrants and eliminate unnecessary repetition of learning, by giving credit for learning achievements, the transfer of credits from one educational institution or programme to another, and so the possibility of exemption from relevant parts of a course;
- *Accreditation of Prior Learning* (APL) to give credit for previous learning, whether certificated or uncertificated;
- *Accreditation of Experiential Learning* (AEL) to give credit for learning from life and work experiences;
- *modularisation.*

National training targets

These various VET initiatives are pulled together by the setting of national training targets, first proposed by the CBI in 1989 to benchmark the UK's skills base against that of other nations, and launched in 1991. The National Advisory Council for Education and Training Targets (NACETT) came into being in 1993 to monitor and report on progress towards achievement of the targets. While targets were well received, Armstrong (1996) warned that the 'qualification cuckoo should not be allowed to push competence-based learning out of the nest' (p. 23). This is an issue for many commentators on the British VET policy. Welch (1996c) reports that 'a quarter of large British firms' do not see higher academic qualifications 'as reliable indicators of skills', and 40% do not consider that they indicate 'basic skills'.

The targets are ambitious, and despite wide consultation and updating in 1995 the revised targets for the year 2000 were not met. New targets have been set for 2002 to improve the UK's international competitiveness by raising standards and attainment levels in education and training to world-class levels through ensuring that:

1 All employers invest in employee development to achieve business success.
2 All individuals have access to education and training opportunities, leading to recognised qualifications, which meet their needs and aspirations.
3 All education and training develops self-reliance, flexibility and breadth, in particular through fostering competence in core skills (NACETT, 1996).

The National Learning Targets for the year 2002 are as follows:

1 Targets for 11 year olds – 80% of 11 year olds reaching the expected standard for their age in literacy and 75% reaching the standard for numeracy.
2 Targets for 16 year olds – 50% of 16 year olds getting five higher-grade GCSEs and 95% at least one GCSE.
3 Targets for young people – 85% of 19 year olds with a 'level 2' qualification and 60% of 21 year olds with 'level 3 'qualification.
4 Targets for adults – 50% of adults with level 3 qualification, 28% with level 4 qualification and 7% reduction in non-learners – the learning participation target.
5 Targets for organisations – 45% of medium-sized or large organisations recognised as Investors in People and 10 000 small organisations recognised as IIP. (DfEE, 2000)

(*Note*: At the time of writing Scotland, Wales and Northern Ireland were making their own separate arrangements, which had not been published.)

NACETT charts the progress so far. Again, there is speculation whether the targets will be achieved. However, these targets also serve the important purpose of directing, motivating and reinforcing the various other VET initiatives already referred to in this chapter, so that what is emerging in the UK is a systematic, self-reinforcing framework for VET rather than, as hitherto, a patchwork of piecemeal initiatives. A common characteristic of the elements of this framework is the emphasis upon observable, tightly defined and often measurable outcomes. This, in some respects, contrasts with other contemporary developments. For example, as noted in Chapter 2, in the fields of philosophy and the social sciences those (positivist) approaches that favour measurement are being increasingly challenged by those favouring interpretation; in organisations, multi-skilling and flexible working are to some extent eroding the traditional boundaries and definitions of jobs; while notions of total quality management and of the learning organisation are breaking down traditional internal and external organisational boundaries. This contrast prompts the question whether the underpinning philosophy of today's VET will remain unchallenged for long, and what would become of the VET framework if its philosophy were undermined.

RECENT VET DEVELOPMENTS

Industry is no longer drawn to the comparative advantage of abundant natural resources, but instead to pools of human skills. American – and British – governments neither provide the education nor the training in depth, nor the infrastructural foundations necessary for the post-electro-mechanical society.
(Ford, 1993; in Thurow, 1992)

Advanced economies of the future will not be based on a cheap and unskilled work-force. As we have noted, Britain and similar economies can never compete with Third World countries on these terms. If economies are to remain relatively prosperous, one of the policy imperatives for the future must be a considerable investment in education and training by both organisations (public and private sector) and governments.

There will have to be greater accessibility to universities for more of the population, a coherent system of VET in which harmonised qualifications are accredited and appreciated by all employees, and a commitment to lifelong learning. This implies an increase in funding for education. As noted in Chapter 7, the future organisation is a learning organisation, and future employees are those who are continually seeking to develop themselves.

Further developments in VET are therefore inevitable in the UK. The Labour government elected in 1997 strongly recognised this, and put in their election manifesto that one of their primary aims would be 'education, education education'. It is clear that further attention will be paid to education and VET in the UK for some time to come, although critics within the system at school, college and university levels claim that there is insufficient funding to meet all their needs.

Compulsory or voluntary VET?

One major issue will be whether training should be voluntary or compulsory. Observers and interested bodies are divided on the issue. The Liberal Democrats, the TUC, the Commission for Social Justice and, previously, the Labour Party have argued 'that the problem must be tackled with legislation. Employers should be compelled to provide training' (Harrison, 1995: 38). On the other hand, a strong case can be made for 'voluntarism' (Harrison, 1995). The Labour Party has now moved its position from one where organisations should be compelled to provide training (the levy system) to the most recent proposal, *learning accounts*, which backs away from elements of compulsion and retains the elements of persuasion (Littlefield and Welch, 1996). This approach has been reinforced recently with the rejection of a levy system, with its elements of compulsion, after the publication of the third report by the National Skills Task Force in January 2000. While welcoming the partnership approach, John Monks of the TUC expressed concerns about the emphasis on voluntarism (Rana, 2000:13).

The CBI, the Institute of Directors and the IPD have argued for 'carrot' rather than 'stick' measures, as levies or compulsory learning accounts could act as a tax on jobs. In the face of the failure of the Australian levy system and the fact that proposals for levy systems in New Zealand, Ireland and Sweden have not been taken up, it would appear that the Labour Party has seen these as precautionary tales (Beresford and Gaite, 1994; Harrison, 1995).

Labour government initiatives: building a VET framework

As we have already noted, the Labour government claims that one of its primary concerns has been education and training, and it visualises these as being fundamental tools to create a viable economic future for all in Britain in the twenty-first century. These are lofty but necessary ambitions, and – building on Conservative reforms – the Labour government has attempted to create a VET framework for all. We have already noted that training and education targets have been set for school pupils, students, young employed 16–21-year-olds, adults and organisations. Building on the Dearing Report's recommendations, attempts have been to harmonise diverse qualifications in the academic and technical worlds, with mixed results and some more development needed.

Since Labour has come to office VET initiatives have been abundant. The following section briefly describes the major initiatives that have been instituted to date.

The New Deal

This initiative is an attempt to provide training for 18–24-year-olds who have been out of work for more than six months, and 25-year-olds and over who have been unemployed for longer than two years. The idea behind the scheme is to make the unemployed more employable by providing them with skills. It offers four options (Pickard, 1997):

- a job subsidised for six months with an employer;
- six months' work with a governmental environment task force;
- six months' work with a voluntary sector employer;
- a year's full-time education and training for people who do not hold an NVQ level 2 or equivalent.

Scepticism has been expressed, partly because of the negative experiences of previous schemes such as YTS and ET, but also because of the failure of the Australian New Deal scheme, where employers were not enthusiastic about taking on the long-term unemployed because of 'low skills, poor attitudes to work and low levels of motivation' (Pickard, 1997: 34). These are concerns that remain in the minds of members of the CBI and other employer bodies, but nevertheless they are willing to cooperate with the TUC and other bodies. The government has made provisions to overcome these predicted difficulties by proposing the following:

- There will be a prolonged 'gateway' of up to four months' intensive counselling for the unemployed before being presented to an employer.
- Each individual will get an Employment Service case worker, who will stay with them throughout the programme.
- Each client will have a 'mentor' – someone from the community or local company but independent of the scheme's organisers – who can represent their interests.

The nationwide launch of the scheme took place in April 1998. Concerns have already been expressed about too much red tape, the low quality of the recruits, the lack of support from the Employment Service, and the fact that case workers have been overloaded with clients and do not have enough time to deal with individuals (Rana, 1999a: 14). Further criticisms are that the scheme has not met the needs of single parents, and has failed ethnic groups – claims rebutted by Andrew Smith, Minister of State for Employment (Smith, 1999: 33). A study of employers found that one in three have failed to train their New Deal recruits, and that 21% had no training planned for them. 'This is exactly what happened to YTS recruits and it discredited the scheme' claims Nick Isles, an IPD representative (Rana, 1999b: 18)

At present the jury is still out, with supporters such as Smith and David Blunkett, Secretary of State for Education and Employment, claiming that the New Deal has achieved far more than any previous scheme. If cooperation between the partners does break down, then the government may have to resort to more compulsory measures.

National Training Organisations

National Training Organisations (NTOs) were launched in May 1998 to replace Industry Training Organisations (ITOs). They are government-supported sectoral bodies, rather like the old ITBs, charged with the task of anticipating and analysing skill gaps using international benchmarking (comparing UK skills with other nations), scenario planning (plans to improve skills in given sectors of the economy) and local focus groups. The main idea is an 'investment framework' of voluntary measures that could be backed up by legislation if they failed to work. Among the more radical voluntary measures is the development of sector-based 'learning institutes' – physical or virtual – that would join forces with firms to allow workforce development (Pickard, 1998: 15).

With the demise of the TECs in April 2001, NTOs will take on some of their role. David Blunkett has made NTOs key players in the proposed reforms of post-16 education and training laid out in the *Learning to Succeed* White Paper (Rana, 1999c). It is suggested that the legal framework will encourage employers and employees to take up their training responsibilities rather than return to the old levy system. In 1999 85% of sectors reported recruitment problems, with acute shortages in manufacturing, but fewer than a third offered their workforce any training (Whitehead, 1999).

Learning and Skills Councils and the Small Business Service

From April 2001 TECs will be replaced by Learning and Skills Councils (LSCs), and the Small Business Service will replace Business Links (bodies that promised training and development of local companies). The role of LSCs will be to

> build a new culture of learning which will underpin national competitiveness and personal prosperity, encourage creativity and innovation and help build a cohesive society.   (DfEE, 1999)

The role of the Small Business Service will be

> to provide a single gateway for all government programmes directed primarily at mainly small business . . . and it will have the right to monitor all and existing proposals for business support.
>   (DfEE, 1999)

There will be 47 local LSCs and 45 Small Business franchises, their boundaries being co-terminous. These will be overseen by a national LSC that will, among other things:

- work to a three-year plan;
- assess national skills and learning needs;
- allocate budgets to local LSCs;
- set strategy on attainment of the National Learning Targets;
- secure information, advice and guidance for adults;
- develop national partnerships with local authorities and local education authorities, the Employment Service, the University for Industry, NTOs, trade unions, new support services for young people, major and multisite employers, and education and training providers.

These bodies, along with NTOs and the NSTF, will obviously play an important part in defining the role and structure of VET.

Other VET measures

A number of other initiatives are worth mentioning, although space does not permit extensive information. They include the following:

Modern apprenticeships

These are mainly for 16- and 17- year-old school leavers and training includes at least an NVQ at level 3, showing that the apprentice can do the job to the standard that industry and commerce require. Over 82 frameworks have been approved so far, from accountancy to warehousing.

National traineeships

These are aimed at a lower level than modern apprenticeships, and are for school leavers from 16 upwards. They offer quality training to industry standards at NVQ level 2. They are designed by employers for employers. Trainees, like apprentices, can earn while they learn.

Learning Card

The Learning Card is issued to young people in their final year of compulsory education. It acts as a reminder to young leavers of their right to further learning and careers information and guidance. The card entitles holders to discounts from a number of organisations, such as BT, YHA, National Express, Letts and BSM. It also gives access to a Career Bank to help in the choice of careers.

Lifelong learning

Lifelong learning is an ill-defined concept, although its name suggests the encouragement of continuous learning for all throughout their lives. Various initiatives have been set up by the government in collaboration with universities, local authorities and employers to examine the possibilities of regional lifelong learning projects and support mechanisms. Local authorities have been cast in the leading role, but they have been sluggish in taking the initiative (Pollock, 1999). By implication they will have to turn themselves into learning organisations, and one – Norwich, a pioneer in the initiative – calls itself a 'Learning City.' One of the problems is that the lifelong learning brief maybe too wide and thus too amorphous to manage effectively. If the idea is to create a learning climate for citizens in general, then there needs to be a considerable degree of coordination of existing support mechanisms in cooperation with the various partners and local bodies.

Learning accounts

The Labour government espouses the use of learning accounts rather than training levies. These will be 'targeted at people in most need of basic training. One million people will each be given £150 if they contribute £25 from their own pocket. This would allow individuals to take the first step up the learning ladder by enrolling on, say, an IT course for beginners or taking basic literacy skills' (Littlefield and Welch, 1996: 5). This 'Learn as You Earn' proposal 'is designed to give people the freedom to choose the training courses and skills which fit with their aspirations' (Butters, 1996: 2). It will also form the cornerstone for lifelong learning initiatives.

University for Industry

The University for Industry was proposed in 1996 by the Labour Party and came into being in November 1999. Its aim is to prepare individuals for the rapid economic and social changes in the modern, more flexible world of work, where there are 'weaker relationships between employers and employees' (Hillman, 1996: v). Among its aims are to:

- be the hub of a national learning network extending to workplaces, homes and local learning centres;
- provide access to user-friendly services on the Internet and create links with tutors, experts and other learners;
- commission new learning programmes in strategic areas;
- sustain an accessible system of support and guidance services;
- stimulate mass-marketing of learning opportunities.

It would also become a main support for lifelong learning. One of its principal aims to this effect is to widen accessibility of learning opportunities, in terms of time, place and pace. This obviously suggests the use of individualised programmes on the Internet, CD-ROMs and distance learning initiatives, combined with local learning support mechanisms. At the time of writing, 68 Learndirect centres had been set up across England that will work with UfI to develop a new approach to the delivery of flexible learning. Centres will also be set up in Wales, Northern Ireland and Scotland, and will be parallel but distinct organisations.

Conclusion

The Labour government hopes that these VET initiatives will provide a framework for the encouragement and development of a learning atmosphere in the nation as a whole. Whether this is the case or not depends on the enthusiasm, funding and continuing importance that the government places on the overall strategy and its individual programmes and institutions. It also remains to be seen whether these become a number of disparate schemes desperately operating to keep afloat despite lack of funding and support at national level. They will also be a test as to the success of the voluntarist system that the Labour government has continued from its Conservative forebears.

CONTROVERSIAL ISSUES

The contribution of training to national competitiveness

In the past, economic growth has been seen to have been bound up as much with the wealth of a nation's 'human capital' as with its material resources. Japan and Germany are two oft-cited cases. Both countries have relatively few natural resources, and both have relied heavily on the development of the skills, aptitudes and efforts of their people.

Both had suffered considerable wartime destruction by 1945, but had largely rebuilt their economies by the 1960s as a launch pad from which to challenge world markets.

The problem with training and education is that, although most observers acknowledge their importance, it is very difficult, if not impossible, to correlate directly their contribution to economic growth. Attempts have been made by some researchers to do this, albeit with questionable results (Prais and Steedman, 1986; Steedman, 1988; Prais and Wagner, 1988; Prais *et al.*, 1989). Comparative economic research by Freeman (BBC, 1996) finds that although the Philippines has increased and improved education, it is not doing as well economically as China, which has not significantly increased its education and training but is experiencing high economic growth. He warns that education and training alone are not a prescription for pulling a country out of low economic growth, and other writers from developing nations have also attested that the hopes invested in education in the 1960s and 1970s have not been realised in economic terms for many Asian and African countries (Halls, 1990).

However, Ashton and Sung (1994) cite the impressive economic growth of the Singaporean economy in recent years, and claim that much of this growth can be related to a comprehensive state-directed VET programme integrated into the Singaporean government's long-term economic aims. They claim that 'the relative autonomy of the state apparatus is the ability of the political elite to define long-term goals for political and economic action' (p. 5). From these examples we can at best conclude that the experience of developing economies is varied, and that the way VET policy is conceived and implemented is of utmost importance: this is an area of research that is receiving increasing attention.

Note also that in recent years the much vaunted German VET system has come under criticism, mainly because training for the unemployed is not affecting the labour market in the way it had done previously, and levels of unemployment are now equivalent to, if not greater than, those in Britain. It would seem that in certain areas of the economy training and retraining in practical skills are proving less effective, largely because of the changing nature of the economy, which is requiring fewer and fewer engineering, construction and other manual skills. As world competition increases, and new technology replaces many occupations that would once have absorbed the unemployed, retraining schemes appear increasingly out of date and ill equipped to help the 'new' unemployed (BBC, 1996). Unification has also had a negative economic impact on the new German state. The changing labour requirements of the economy in terms of numbers of employees and skills needed will be an increasingly pressing problem for the major economies, having ramifications for social as well economic policy making.

Similarly, while in-firm training has increased considerably in France, there remains the problem of what to do with the unemployed, particularly unemployed youth, in whom there has been a considerable increase. Long-term unemployment in France has also risen over the past decade, and labour-market policies have not been particularly effective in providing the skills-based training needed to help these people find jobs. France, like Britain, has not succeeded in bridging the skills gap, and this may be partly due to the low esteem in which vocational training initiatives are held (Bournois, 1992).

Training is also regarded as an instrument for solving specific economic problems such as unemployment, and for bridging the skills gap. Many advanced economies have pursued such training policies with, at best, mixed results and usually little long-term effect on the unemployment register. Social arguments seem to fare better, and according to Lord Young it is preferable to have unemployed youngsters on training schemes than out 'ram-raiding' (BBC, 1996). In addition, as we shall see in Chapter 15 on international HRM, factors such as the influence of national institutions, social attitudes and culture are also bound up with explanations of the economic success of these nations and their education and training systems. Nevertheless, comparative study can highlight weaknesses and strengths in national systems of training and education, from which we may learn some vital lessons.

SUMMARY

- This chapter examined the practicalities of human resource development, offering a definition and highlighting the problem of transferable and non-transferable skills. Although there has been a growing recognition of the need for training in organisations, controversy still exists as to the extent and quality of training required.

- Training is seen as a key instrument in the implementation of HRM policies and practices, particularly those involving cultural change and the necessity of introducing new working practices. Of equal importance in the training process is the recognition of individual needs. These may, however, clash with organisational needs, and it is crucial to harmonise these demands, to the mutual benefit of both parties.

- The first part of the chapter dealt with the practicalities of creating a human resource development plan. The first and most vital step in an HRD plan is to analyse the training needs of the organisation in relation to its strategy, and equate these with the needs of the individuals within it. Proposals were then made as to how this might be effected, including the use of various forms of analysis of job requirements and personnel performance. A choice of methods was then outlined, which fell into the basic categories of on-the-job and off-the-job training, followed by the equally important consideration of who was to deliver the training. The last and perhaps least well-performed part of the HRD plan is evaluating and monitoring the training. This section reviewed various methods by which this can be carried out, the results of which should be fed back into the HRD process to improve the effectiveness and increase the relevance of future programmes.

- The notion of the learning organisation and the knowledge-based organisation, and the difficulties in defining, modelling and implementing these concepts, were examined.

- The second half of the chapter examined the stakeholders in the individual's learning and development, concentrating on the role of the employer, the state and the trade union movement.

- An examination was undertaken of training in a comparative international context, which made an in-depth exploration of vocational training policies and practices in Germany, Japan and France, and outlined some of the lessons they might afford for the British experience.

- This was followed by an in-depth critical examination of the recent history of training in the UK context. Recent and past public policy training initiatives were examined such as the YTS, ET, TECs, the competency approach, vocational qualifications, Investors in People, national training targets, the New Deal, NTOs, and more recently the Learning and Skills Councils and the University for Industry.

- The chapter also examined the debate concerning whether or not training policies should be compulsory or voluntary, and the contribution of training to national competitiveness.

| Activity | **A debate on national vocational education and training** |

Divide the lecture group/class into groups.

One group is to assume the position of Secretary of State for Education and Employment and his/her supporters.

Another group is to assume the critical position of members of the parliamentary opposition.

A third group is made up of critics of the voluntarist approach to vocational education and training (VET): the TUC, for example.

By referring to this chapter, its references and further reading and other sources, each group must state its position. This should include a critique of the other two groups' case, and the reasons why you support your present views.

Elect a chairperson to order the debate.

QUESTIONS

1 The learning organisation is purely an aspiration, and can never be achieved in reality. How far would you agree with this statement?

2 What are the advantages of organisations adopting a learning organisation or knowledge-based approach to HRD? What difficulties could possibly develop in the implementation and operation of these systems?

3 Examine the experience of those countries mentioned in the international section, and comment on whether Britain can learn from their policies and approaches.

4 What are the potential effects of government initiatives such as National Training Targets, Vocational Qualifications (S/NVQs) or the Investors in People award upon the human resource development of an organisation?

EXERCISES

1 Divide into three groups. One group should identify the particular strengths of the French VET as compared with the British; the second should do the same for the German; and the third for the Japanese. Report back to the whole class.

2 Outline the strengths and weaknesses of the Investors in People programme. How does it fit in with government overall VET strategy? You may wish to contact your local IIP office or the national office: Investors in People UK, 7–10 Chandos Street, London W1M 9DE. Email: information@iipuk.co.uk

3 What steps would you follow if you were charged with devising an IIP programme for your company or organisation?

Below are two IIP case studies that may guide you. They are both actual case studies. The first shows how one organisation achieved IIP status and how it helped their organisation. The second sets the problem, and the *Lecturer's guide* that accompanies this textbook gives you the full report.

CASE STUDY 1

The Cumberland Hotel

The organisation

The Cumberland Hotel, Harrow, Middlesex, grew from a small guest house established in 1956 to its present size of 84 bedrooms with a capacity for over 140 guests, an award-winning restaurant and the recent extension of its conference and leisure facilities. This privately owned hotel employs 100 people, and has progressed to 4 Crown Commended status from the English Tourist Board for its facilities and quality of service, together with three-star AA and RAC rating.

The hotel serves the international business market for Wembley and the north-west London area, providing a service for visitors to the capital and, increasingly, for overseas guests from France, Germany, Japan and the United States. Investors in People has been crucial to the success of the Cumberland Hotel in what is, after all, a people-led business.

The hotel is unique in having recently won the prestigious London Regional Training Award for the exceptionally high standard of staff training: in 1996 it also won the Rubicon Award for Employer of the Year.

The challenge and the strategy

The principal elements of the strategy needed to meet defined business priorities required the following:

- hotel management and staff to perform to their maximum potential;
- the business to develop the ability to change and become more efficient and profitable;
- systematic sales and marketing activity, particularly regarding competition and the identification of new markets;

- a culture change for the recognition of the importance of new skills;
- the increasing amounts of new legislation covering health and safety and food hygiene to be understood and applied;
- improvement of personnel practices encompassing employee induction, ongoing training provision and performance appraisal;
- elimination of wastage, reducing operating overheads and preserving margins;
- improvement in continuity of action between departments and functions through better communication and interpersonal skills;
- consistent standards that met or exceeded the expectations of customers.

The results

Implementation of this strategy has resulted in significant business performance, including:

- increase in revenue of 50% in the past three years;
- growth in gross operating profit of 200%;
- reduction in labour costs and staff recruitment;
- savings used to invest in a £500 000 conference and banqueting suite.

Investors in People

The Cumberland Hotel was formally recognised as an Investor in People in 1993 and successfully reassessed in 1996. The hotel's recognition sets it apart from all competition in the area, and will continue to ensure high standards of customer service.

(Printed with the kind permission of Investors in People.)

CASE STUDY 2

Wealden District Council

The organisation

Wealden District Council was established as a local authority in 1974. Embracing 320 miles of East Sussex, it stretches from the Kent borders to the sea, and is the largest district council in the South East. Its 135 000 population is scattered among rural villages and four substantial market towns.

It provides a range of services, including planning and development, refuse collection, environmental health, housing and leisure services. A staff of 560 is divided between two offices, four leisure centres, two depots and 19 sheltered dwellings. The Council, with no overall control, has 58 elected councillors, serving on ten committees and subcommittees.

The challenge

The Council aims to offer the highest possible standard of service within the constraints of its budget, customer care being of paramount importance.

Particular challenges have continued to include:

- the introduction of compulsory competitive tendering, with the cost of services being tested in the open market against commercial operators;
- new legislation affecting large areas of the Council's work;
- the consolidation of Audit Commission performance indicators against which service performance is stringently measured;
- the requirement to work to constrained budgets, while delivering consistently high levels of service;

- introducing and developing new indicators for the benefit of the customer.

The objective continues to be to deliver a consistently high standard of service across an organisation widespread in location and function, with all the elements working harmoniously together, against a background of change.

(Printed with the kind permission of Investors in People.)

What strategy would you recommend Wealden District Council to follow in order to achieve its aims?

(A full answer to this question is given in the *Lecturer's Guide* that accompanies this textbook)

REFERENCES AND FURTHER READING

Those texts marked with an asterisk are particularly recommended for further reading.

Alberga, T. (1997) 'Investors in People: time for a check up', *People Management*, 6 February, pp. 30–32.

Anon (1992a) 'Call for training system reform', *Financial Times*, 11 December, p. 2.

Anon (1992b) 'TECs must get the resources to do the job, CBI director warns', *Personnel Management*, May, p. 6.

Armstrong, G. (1996) 'A qualifications cuckoo in the competency nest?' *People Management*, 16 May, p. 23.

Ashton, D. and Sung, J. (1994) *The State, Economic Development and Skill Formation: A New Asian Model?* Working Paper No. 3, Centre for Labour Market Studies. Leicester: University of Leicester.

Atkinson, M. and Elliott, L. (2000) 'UK fails to provide path from school to work', the *Guardian*, 11 February, p. 6.

*Barrington, H. and Reid, M.A. (1999) *Training Interventions: Promoting Learning Opportunities*, 6th edn. London: Institute of Personnel and Development.

Barsoux, J.-L. and Lawrence, P. (1990) *Management in France*. London: Cassell.

BBC (1996) 'Train and prosper', *Analysis*, BBC Radio 4, broadcast 11 April.

Beresford, K. and Gaite, J. (1994) *Personnel Management*, April, pp. 38–41.

Bernhard, H.B. and Ingolis, C.A. (1988) 'Six lessons for the corporate classroom', *Harvard Business Review*, Vol. 66, No. 5, pp. 40–48.

Bournois, F. (1992) 'France', in Brewster, C., Hegewisch, A., Holden, L. and Lockhart, T. (eds) *The European Human Resource Management Guide*. London: Academic Press, pp. 113–162.

Brewster, C. (1999) 'Who is listening to HR?' *People Management*, 25 November, pp. 16–17.

Brewster, C. and Hegewisch, A. (1993) 'A continent of diversity', *Personnel Management*, January, pp. 36–40.

Brewster, C., Hegewisch, A., Holden, L. and Lockhart, T. (eds) (1992) *The European Human Resource Management Guide*. London: Academic Press.

Brockbank, A. and Beech, N. (1999) 'Guiding blight', *People Management*, 6 May, pp. 52–54.

Butters, T. (1996) 'Labour's plans for a skills revolution', the *Guardian*, Careers Supplement, 27 April, pp. 2, 3.

Cannell, M. (1997) 'Practice makes perfect', *People Management*, 6 March, pp. 26–33.

Carnevale, A., Gainer, L. and Schulz, E. (1990) *Training the Technical Workforce*. San Francisco, Calif.: Jossey-Bass.

Chase, R. (1997) 'The knowledge based organisation: an international study,' *Journal of Knowledge Management*, Vol.1, No. 1, pp. 38–49.

Claydon, T. and Green, F. (1992) *The Effect of Unions on Training Provision*. Discussion Papers in Economics, No. 92/3, January. Leicester: University of Leicester.

Confederation of British Industry (1989) *Towards a Skills Revolution*. London: CBI.

Constable, J. and McCormick, R. (1987) *The Making of British Managers*. London: British Institute of Management.

Coopers & Lybrand Associates (1985) *A Challenge to Complacency: Changing Attitudes to Training*. London: MSC/National Economic Development Office.

Department for Education and Employment (1999) *Learning to Succeed: A New Framework for Post 16 Learning*. Nottingham: DfEE publications.

Department for Education and Employment (2000) *National Learning Targets for England for 2002*, DfEE web page, 1 March, dfee.gov.uk/nlt/targets.htm

Department of Education and Science (1990) 'International statistical comparisons of the education and training of 16 to 18 year olds', *Statistical Bulletin*, 1/90, January. London: DES.

Dixon, N. (1994) *The Organisational Learning Cycle*. London: McGraw-Hill.

*Dixon, N. (2000) *Common Knowledge*, Cambridge, Mass: Harvard Business School Press.

*Dore, R. and Sako, M. (1989) *How the Japanese Learn to Work*. London: Routledge.

Dulewicz, V. (1991) 'Improving assessment centres', *Personnel Management*, June, pp. 50–55.

Easterby-Smith, M. and Mackness, J. (1992) 'Completing the cycle of evaluation', *Personnel Management*, May, pp. 42–45.

Employment Department Group (1990) *What is an Investor in People?*, IIP 17, September. London: Employment Department Group.

Felstead, A. (1994) *Funding Government Training Schemes: Mechanisms and Consequences*. Working Paper No. 3, Centre for Labour Market Studies. Leicester: University of Leicester.

Finegold, D. (1991) 'The implications of "Training in Britain" for the analysis of Britain's skills problem: a comment on Paul Ryan's "How much do employers spend on training?"', *Human Resource Management Journal*, Vol. 2, No. 1, pp. 110–115.

Ford, G. (1993) 'Losing ground', *New Statesman*, 19 March, p. 41.

Fowler, A. (1991) 'How to identify training needs', *Personnel Management Plus*, Vol. 2, No. 11, pp. 36–37.

Garvin, D. (1993) 'Building a learning organisation', in *Harvard Business Review on Knowledge Management*. Cambridge, Mass: Harvard Business School Press, pp. 47–80.

Gaugler, E. and Wiltz, S. (1992) 'Federal Republic of Germany', in Brewster, C., Hegewisch, A., Holden, L. and Lockhart, J. (eds) *The European Human Resource Management Guide*. London: Academic Press, pp. 163–228.

Graham, A. (1992) 'YT funding and the TECs: a tragedy in the making', *Personnel Management*, February, p. 4.

Hall, D.T. (1984) 'Human resource development and organisational effectiveness', in Fombrun, C., Tichy, N. and Devanna, M. (eds) *Strategic Human Resource Management*. New York: John Wiley.

Halls, W. D. (1990) *Comparative Education: Contemporary Issues and Trends*. London: Jessica Kingsley Publishers for UNESCO.

Handy, C. (1987) *The Making of Managers: A Report on Management Education, Training and Development in the United States, West Germany, France, Japan and the UK*. London: NEDO.

Harrison, R. (1992) *Training and Development*. London: Institute of Personnel Management.

Harrison, R. (1995) 'Carrots are better levers than sticks', *People Management*, 19 October, pp. 38–40.

Harrison, R. (1997) *Employee Development*. London: Institute of Personnel and Devlopment.

Hillman, J. (1996) *University for Industry: Creating a National Learning Network*. London: Institute for Public Policy Research.

Hirsch, W. and Reilly, P. (1998) 'Cycling proficiency: how do large organisations identify their future skill needs among their thousands of employees?' *People Management*, 9 July, pp. 36–41.

Hofstede, G. (1984) *Culture's Consequences*. Newbury Park, Calif.: Sage.

Holden, L. (1991) 'European trends in training and development', *International Journal of Human Resource Management*, Vol. 2, No. 2, pp. 113–131.

Holden, L. and Livian, Y. (1992) 'Does strategic training policy exist? Some evidence from ten European countries', *Personnel Review*, Vol. 21, No. 1, pp. 12–23.

House of Commons (1993) *The Work of the Training and Enterprise Councils, Minutes of Evidence*, House of Commons Session 1992–93 (cited in Felstead, 1994).

Industrial Society (1985) *Survey of Training Costs: New Series No. 1*. London: Industrial Society.

Institute of Manpower Studies (IMS) (1984) *Competence and Competition: Training and Education in the Federal Republic of Germany, the United States and Japan*, MSC/NEDO.

Investors in People (IIP) UK (1995) *The Investors in People Standard*. London: Investors in People UK.

Investors in People (IIP) UK (2000) *Management Report 1999, No. 10*. London: Investors in People UK.

Kandola, B. (1996) 'Are competencies too much of a good thing?', *People Management*, 2 May, p. 21.

Keep, E. (1989) 'Corporate training strategies: the vital component?', in Storey, J. (ed.) *New Perspectives on Human Resource Management*. London: Routledge.

Kenney, J. and Reid, M. (1988) *Training Interventions*, 2nd edn. London: IPM.

Lähteenmäki, S., Holden, L. and Roberts, I. (eds) (1999) *HRM and the Learning Organisation*. Turku, Finland: Turku School of Economics and Business Administration, Series A-2.

Littlefield, D. and Welch, J. (1996) 'Training policy steals the political limelight', *People Management*, 4 April, pp. 5, 6.

Lloyd, J. (1990) *Light and Liberty: The History of the EEPTU*. London: Weidenfeld & Nicolson.

Lowe, K. (1992) 'End of the line for ET', *Personnel Today*, 8 December, p. 14.

Macleod, D. and Beavis, S. (1996) 'Britain trails rivals for want of skills', the *Guardian*, 14 June, p. 6.

Mangham, I.L. and Silver, M.S. (1986) *Management Training: Context and Practice*, ESRC/DTI Report. Bath: University of Bath, School of Management.

Manpower Services Commission (1981) *A Framework for the Future: A Sector by Sector Review of Industrial and Commercial Training*. London: MSC.

Manpower Services Commission (1981) *Glossary of Training Terms*. London: HMSO.

Mase, E. (1999) 'E-learning: joined-up thinking', *People Management*, 25 November, pp. 32–36.

Mayo, A. (1998) Knowledge management: memory bankers', *People Management*, 22 January, pp. 34–38.

Merrick, N. (1995) 'Moving up the class?', *People Management*, 30 November, pp. 8–9.

Milne, S. (1991) 'TECs failing to back training guarantees', the *Guardian*, 4 November, p. 6.

Nadler, L. (1984) *The Handbook of Human Resource Development*. New York: John Wiley.

National Advisory Council for Education and Training Targets (1996) *Skills for 2000: Report on Progress Towards the National Training Targets for Education and Training*. London: NACETT.

Nonaka, I. (1991) 'The knowledge creating company', in *Harvard Business Review on Knowledge Management*, Cambridge, Mass.: Harvard Business School Press, pp. 21–45.

Pedler, M., Burgoyne, J. and Boydell, T. (1988) *Learning Company Project Report*, Sheffield: Training Agency.

*Pedler, M., Burgoyne, J. and Boydell, T. (1997) *The Learning Company: A Strategy for Sustainable Development*, London: McGraw-Hill.

Pickard, J. (1992) 'Job evaluation and total management come under fire', *Personnel Management*, May, p. 17.

Pickard, J. (1996) 'Barriers ahead to a single currency', *People Management*, 21 March, pp. 22–27.

Pickard, J. (1997) 'The New Deal: just the job', *People Management*, 28 August, pp. 32–35.

Pickard, J. (1998) 'New training bodies focus on skills gap', *People Management*, 14 May, p.15.

Pollock, L. (1999) 'Upskill task,' *People Management*, 14 October, pp. 58–60.

Prais, S. and Steedman, H. (1986) 'Vocational training in France and Britain', *National Institute Economic Review*, No. 116, May, pp. 45–56.

Prais, S. and Wagner, K. (1988) 'Productivity and management: the training of foremen in Britain and Germany', *National Institute Economic Review*, No. 123, pp. 34–37.

Prais, S., Jarvis, V. and Wagner, K. (1989) 'Productivity and vocational skills in services in Britain and Germany', *National Institute Economic Review*, No. 130, November, pp. 52–74.

Price Waterhouse (1989) *Doing Business in France*. Paris and London: Price Waterhouse.

Price Waterhouse Cranfield Project (1990) *Report on International Strategic Human Resource Management*. London: Price Waterhouse.

Price Waterhouse Cranfield Project (1991) *Report on International Strategic Human Resource Management*. Cranfield: Cranfield School of Management.

Rainbird, H. and Maguire, M. (1993) 'When corporate need supersedes employee development', *Personnel Management*, February, pp. 34–37.

Rana, E. (1999a) 'Dim view of New Deal,' *People Management*, 3 June, p. 14.

Rana, E. (1999b) 'New Deal firms come under fire for training deficiencies', *People Management*, 19 August, p. 18.

Rana, E. (1999c) 'NTOs debate radical plans for voluntary investment', *People Management*, 16 September, p. 17.

Rana, E. (2000) 'National Skills Task Force rules out levy,' *People Management*, 20 January, p. 13.

Reid, M.A. and Barrington, H. (1997) *Training Interventions: Managing Employee Development*, 5th edn. London: Institute of Personnel and Development.

Reid, M.A., Barrington, H. and Kenney, J. (1992) *Training Interventions: Managing Employee Development*, 3rd edn. London: Institute of Personnel Management.

Rose, R. and Wignanek, G. (1990) *Training Without Trainers? How Germany Avoids Britain's Supply-side Bottleneck*. London: Anglo-German Foundation.

Ryan, P. (1991) 'How much do employers spend on training? An assessment of "Training in Britain" estimates', *Human Resource Management Journal*, Vol. 1, No. 4, pp. 55–57.

Saggers, R. (1994) 'Training climbs the corporate agenda', *Personnel Management*, July, pp. 40–45.

Sako, M. and Dore, R. (1986) 'How the Youth Training Scheme helps employers', *Employment Gazette*, June, pp. 195–204.

*Senge, P. (1990) *The Fifth Discipline: The Art and Practice of the Learning Organisation*. London: Century.

Sloman, M. (1999) 'Learning Centre: seize the day', *People Management*, 20 May, p. 31.

Smith, A (1999) 'Get with the programme', *People Management*, 3 June, p. 33.

Steedman, H. (1988) 'Vocational training in France and Britain: mechanical and electrical craftsmen', *National Institute Economic Review*, No. 126, November, pp. 57–71.

*Stewart, J. and McGoldrick, J. (1996) *Human Resource Development: Perspectives, Strategies and Practice*. London: Pitman.

Storey, J. (1991) 'Do the Japanese make better managers?' *Personnel Management*, August, pp. 24–28.

Syrett, M. and Lammiman, S. (1994) 'Developing the peripheral worker', *Personnel Management*, July, pp. 28–31.

Targett, S. (1996) 'Shepherd admits skills shortage', *Times Higher Education Supplement*, 14 June, p. 3.

Taylor, P. and Thackwray, B. (1995) *Investors in People Explained*. London: Kogan Page.

Thorn, J. (1988) 'Making of a Meister', *Industrial Society Magazine*, June, pp. 19–21.

Thurow, L. (1992) *Head to Head: The Coming Economic Battle Among Japan, Europe and America*. London: Nicholas Brealey.

Townsend, T. (1992) 'How the lead body sees it', *Personnel Management*, November, p. 39.

Trades Union Congress (1989) *Skills 2000*. London: TUC (quoted in Claydon and Green, 1992).

Trades Union Congress (1990) *TUC: Joint Action over Training*. London: TUC (quoted in Claydon and Green, 1992).

Trades Union Congress (1991) *Collective Bargaining Strategy for the 1990s*. London: TUC (quoted in Claydon and Green, 1992).

Training Agency (1989) *Training in Britain*. Norwich: HMSO.

Tyson, S. and Fell, A. (1995) 'A focus on skills, not organisations', *People Management*, pp. 42–45.

Welch, J. (1996a) 'HR qualifications get the go-ahead at last', *People Management*, 30 May, p. 11.

Welch, J. (1996b) 'YT alternative comes out of the shadows', *People Management*, 30 May, p. 12.

Welch, J. (1996c) 'Britain slipping behind in the race for skills', *People Management*, 27 June, p. 11.

Whitehead, M. (1999) 'Firms ignore staff needs in key areas of the economy', *People Management*, 11 February, p. 16.

*Wilson, D.A. (1996) *Managing Knowledge*. Oxford: Institute of Management/Butterworth Heinemann.

Wood, L. (1994) '"Urgent need" found for government to examine TECs funding', *Financial Times*, 25 March.

9 Management development

Mike Doyle

OBJECTIVES

- To explain the meaning and nature of management development in organisations.
- To recognise the significance of management development to organisational success.
- To contrast 'piecemeal' and open systems approaches to management development.
- To examine the methods, techniques and processes used to develop UK and international managers.
- To draw attention to some of the contemporary issues and controversies in management development.

INTRODUCTION

Within organisations there is now a growing awareness that the managerial role has become a 'critical' component in business strategies designed to deliver competitiveness, change and renewal (Kanter, 1982; Jackson and Humble, 1994; McClelland, 1994; Salaman, 1995). This has led organisations to review the nature of their managerial assumptions, attitudes and behaviours with a view to determining their 'fit' with strategic goals and desired levels of business performance (Fulop, 1991). This is giving rise to a new 'agenda' of organisational demands and expectations in respect of the manager's role. In effect, managers are being persuaded to change their existing values and behaviours and become 'new managers' (Rosenfeld and Wilson, 1999). In some cases it would appear as if management itself is being 'reinvented' (Salaman, 1995).

However, some management commentators are predicting that these changes will have complex implications for managers' roles and personal lives (Dopson and Stewart, 1993; Stewart, 1994). For some it means increased responsibility and reward, for others longer working hours and added stress.

You might consider it to be self-evident to state that organisational expectations in respect of managerial roles and levels of performance will be largely unmet if managers are not provided with the necessary level of training, commitment, resources, support, and encouragement. But it is only since a series of highly critical reports on the development of British managers were published in the late 1980s – *The Making of British Managers*, (Constable and McCormick, 1987), *The Making of Managers*, (Handy, 1987), and a more recent publication,

Management Development to the Millennium, (Cannon and Taylor 1994) – that we now see UK organisations beginning to discover and appreciate the significance of management development as a key process in delivering organisational transformation and renewal. This has led to the emergence of a range of organisational and national initiatives, all designed to raise the overall standards of management training and education (see Chapter 8 for a more detailed description of national frameworks and initiatives).

However, despite this growing awareness of management development as a strategic 'tool' (McClelland, 1994), all too often organisations have tended to view management development as a discrete and isolated process within the wider organisational 'system'. This has given rise to 'piecemeal' and fragmented approaches that prevent management development from making a significant contribution to organisational development and ends up wasting organisational investment, time and effort (Burgoyne, 1988; Mumford, 1993). Management development can therefore be seen to be 'failing' managers in the sense that it is unable to deliver the skills and knowledge needed to meet the requirements of the new agenda. Often this is because management development strategies and practices cannot deal with or come to terms with wider organisational influences such as organisational culture and politics (McClelland, 1994; Molander and Winterton, 1994). The outcome therefore is often an ineffective management development approach and considerable frustration and demotivation among the organisation's managers (Doyle, 1995; Doyle, 2000).

So the key issue for those who have responsibilities for, are involved in or affected by management development is how to integrate it with other organisational systems and processes to ensure that they deliver business goals efficiently (Cannon and Taylor, 1994). This is not just about reconciling and handling the complexity and diversity introduced by factors such as changing goals and priorities, new cultures and structures, new technology and new working practices. It must also involve consideration of the different rationales that justify the development of managers within a wider environmental, social, ethical and political context (Lees, 1992; Currie, 1999).

The main aim of this chapter is to assist you in exploring management development from within what is often constituted as an ambiguous, rhetorical and sometimes conflictual organisational context. In the first section of the chapter you will be presented with a brief summary of 'management': what it is or purports to be, how it is changing under the influence of a host of internal and external contextual factors, and not least how it influences HRM philosophies and practices. This will set the scene for a more detailed exploration of management development embedded within the wider organisational system. This exploration will begin with a discussion of management development: how it is defined, and how it might be differentiated from management training and education.

Consideration will then be given to the role and objectives of management development within the overall formulation of organisational policy and strategy. The aim here is to demonstrate how different conceptions of the role and significance of management development in relation to business strategy can give rise to contrasting approaches to developing managers within varying organisational contexts. This in turn raises a number of important issues for developers and the organisation, which have to be addressed if implementation is to be considered effective.

We then move on to the functional aspects of organising and implementing management development programmes. These are examined in some detail, beginning with a critical look at those who have responsibility for development, how that responsibility is shared, and the need for contingent and diverse approaches to meet varying contextual needs. We then examine the broader range of methods and techniques employed in the development of managers.

The chapter then adopts an international perspective. British and US models of management development are compared and contrasted with those from European and other countries, and the skills required to be an 'international manager' are examined.

Management development, like management itself, is now in a state of considerable flux. As you would expect, this is giving rise to considerable controversy and tension, and a number of current issues are discussed in the closing section of the chapter. It concludes with questions, activities and case studies. These will help you to review and consolidate what you have learned. There is also a list of recommended and further reading included for guidance and reference purposes.

DEFINING MANAGEMENT DEVELOPMENT

What is management?

Before we explore the way in which managers are developed, it is useful to have an understanding about 'management' and what managers do. Since the nineteenth century, rapid industrialisation and the growth of capitalism have given rise to organisational bureaucracies and functional divisions, which in turn have led to the 'separation, extension and dispersion of the management process' (Hales, 1993: 4). The outcome has been the emergence of 'management' as a discrete set of activities and responsibilities (Keeble, 1992; Reed and Anthony, 1992).

However, the concept of 'management' has evoked a variety of interpretations. In the early part of the twentieth century, management was highly rational and functional in orientation. This reflected a powerful classical economics, scientific view of organisations and the way they should be managed. Towards the middle of the century, this view of organisations was challenged by a group of social and behavioural scientists belonging to the *human relations* school. Theorists such as Elton Mayo, Douglas McGregor, Rensis Likert and others provided alternative perspectives rooted in an understanding of the social and psychological dynamics that govern the behaviour of people at work, and this led to new interpretations about the way they should be managed (Thomas, 1993; Mullins, 1996).

Child (1969) provides one of the most enduring contributions to the what-is-management debate. He views it from three perspectives:

- an economic resource performing a set of technical functions associated with the administration of other resources, e.g. the organisation of work;
- a system of authority through which policies and strategies are translated into the execution of tasks, e.g. defining roles and responsibilities;
- an elite social group that acts as an economic resource and maintains an associated system of authority, e.g. status, power and control over others.

Smith *et al.* (1980) describe management as 'making organisations perform', and claim it is concerned with:

- individuals who are delegated authority to manage others;
- activities for achieving goals;
- a body of knowledge represented by theories and frameworks about people and organisations.

More contemporary studies of management have been concerned less with theories or principles of management and more with the practice (some would say the art) of management itself. As Lupton (in Thomas, 1993) declares, 'management is what managers do during their working hours'. This concern about what managers *actually* do rather than what theorists *think* they do has formed the basis of studies such as Mintzberg's (1973) *The Nature of Managerial Work*, Kotter's (1982) *The General Managers*, and, more recently, ethnographic studies such as Watson's (1994) *In Search of Management*. Watson argues that:

> The image which has taken shape is one of management as essentially and inherently a social and moral activity; one whose greatest successes in efficiently and effectively producing goods and services is likely to come through building organisational patterns, culture and understandings based on relationships of mutual trust and shared obligation among people involved with the organisation.   (p. 223).

As well as pointing up the social, behavioural nature of management, these and other studies have revealed the complex, fragmented, dynamic nature of management, which is influenced by a whole host of contextual variables (Hales, 1993; Thomas 1993). In the past 'management' has often been defined in functional, *closed system* terms that revolve around tasks such as:

- forecasting;
- planning;
- organising;
- monitoring;
- motivating;
- controlling.

Such relatively narrow conceptions of the manager's job are now giving way to a more *open systems* orientation in which 'management' itself is seen as being socially constructed, given meaning and practised within the framework of interactions and relationships that exist between individuals, organisations and their environment (Whitely, 1989; Watson, 1994).

This more systemic orientation has begun to reveal a 'hidden' side to management, which to date has received little attention and in some organisational contexts remains largely 'undiscussable'. For instance, although modern theories and frameworks of management have highlighted the contextual complexity of the role, they have yet to provide adequate guidance and information to practitioners in areas such as:

- dealing with organisational politics;
- performing as an effective change agent;
- coping with ethical issues and dilemmas;
- how to support and develop women managers;
- invoking personal survival strategies and dealing with stress in rapidly changing contexts;
- adapting to the requirements of a new psychological contract.

Understanding and appreciating the complexity of management is therefore a vital prerequisite for understanding management development, for three reasons. First, different people, at different times, have different conceptions of what 'management' is about. This will shape their view about the way managers ought to be developed, and this can give rise to a number of tensions and contradictions that themselves have to be managed (Watson, 1994). Second, development itself has to be pragmatic, located, embedded and practised within what managers themselves consider to be *their* unique organisational context. It has to help them adapt and cope with the diversity and complexity that resides therein (Hales, 1993). Third, and linked to the second point, any development investment or action has to keep pace with and match the 'reality' of what managers do, and not (however well intentioned) be rooted in abstract or rapidly redundant models of what others might think they should do or used to do (Salaman, 1995).

We are in an era of rapid and far-reaching change. The use of rigid and inflexible approaches to management development can no longer be tolerated when they create frustration and disillusionment among managers, which leads to lower levels of morale and motivation and ultimately wastes resources and threatens future organisational success (Doyle, 1995). These are important issues to bear in mind as you read the rest of this chapter.

The need to develop effective managers

In earlier chapters of this book, the philosophical debate surrounding the management of the human resource was discussed. Implicit in the discussion was the growing recognition by many organisations 'that the quality of an organisation's human resources represents a critical success factor' (Coulson-Thomas, 1989).

But if the human resource is to become a 'critical success factor', organisations must be prepared to develop individual managers and management teams that are not only flexible, adaptable and innovative in technical, financial and business issues, but skilled in human resource management as well. To achieve this, organisations must be prepared to establish, as a strategic imperative, 'greater investment in continuous management education and development' (Coulson-Thomas, 1989: 14).

Organisations that fail to make this type of investment are unlikely to:

- exploit future opportunities and potential;
- adapt successfully in the face of major change;
- develop new markets and products;
- retain and motivate employees;
- create and sustain an effective management team;
- survive and prosper in an increasingly unstable and competitive global environment.

Management development must therefore be viewed as *a strategic imperative*. At the individual manager level, it can assist managers to unlearn their old ways, change attitudes, modify their management styles, and update technical and professional skills. At the organisational level, it can operate as a catalyst and a vehicle for change and development in organisations. Not only can it lend encouragement to managers to innovate in their area of responsibility, it can also provide them with the essential knowledge and skills to manage complex and radical change processes (Cannon and Taylor, 1994; Salaman, 1995; Newell and Dopson, 1996).

However, success depends largely on the way organisations *choose to approach* development. All too often, management development programmes fail to deliver effective managers because the approach selected was poorly coordinated, fragmented and with little linkage to strategic goals or the 'reality' of managerial work (Mumford, 1987; Woodall and Winstanley, 1998). What constitutes effective and ineffective approaches to development will be discussed later in the chapter.

Developing managers

Having briefly discussed management and the job of a manager, we can now begin to look at the way managers are developed. Before doing this, we need to take a closer look at some of the terminology that is used. It is not uncommon to find a degree of misunderstanding and confusion surrounding the terms *management education, management training* and *management development*. This is largely because these terms are seen by individual managers, and by those responsible for their development, as synonymous with each other.

In Chapter 7, the concepts of education, training and development were discussed. In practice, these terms are often seen as overlapping and interchangeable, and to some extent they are. However, problems arise when the development of managers is narrowly defined around some notion of 'sending managers on a course'. As we shall see later, this is a common perception and one of the significant factors leading to uncoordinated, fragmented, 'piecemeal' approaches and ineffective development.

Management education and training are *not* development

Management education and training are important components in a development programme but they do not, by themselves, constitute management development. When we educate managers, we seek to introduce, extend or improve their learning and increase their level of understanding about the managerial world they occupy. For example, managers on a postgraduate Diploma in Management Studies or a Masters in Business Administration will study and learn about the psychology of individuals and organisations. This will begin to raise their awareness and understanding of human behaviour and how to manage people more effectively in the 'reality' of the workplace, by for example raising their awareness of the psychology that underpins the processes of communication, motivation and teamworking.

Management training tends to be more specific and short term. It is primarily concerned with teaching managers the skills that they need to perform their jobs more effectively. For example, managers will attend short courses during their careers on a whole range of business topics such as financial planning, or improving communication skills.

Defining management development

Management development is defined variously in the texts as:

A conscious and systematic process to control the development of managerial resources in the organisation for the achievement of goals and strategies. (Molander, 1986)

An attempt to improve managerial effectiveness through a planned and deliberate learning process. (Mumford, 1987)

That function which from deep understanding of business goals and organisational requirements, undertakes (a) to forecast need, skill mixes and profiles for many positions and levels; (b) to design and recommend the professional, career and personal development programmes necessary to ensure competence; (c) to move from the concept of 'management' to the concept of 'managing'. (Beckhard, quoted in Storey, 1989)

Although such definitions represent useful starting points for discussion and debate, they tend to constrain the notion of development to processes that are seen as being formalised, planned and deliberate. It is true that many aspects of development are like that, but – as you will see later – development is also a continuous, ever-changing process in which managers often learn through informal, unplanned experience (Mumford, 1993).

To achieve a more comprehensive view of development, we need to incorporate additional aspects such as:

- frameworks for setting, linking and balancing individual and organisational objectives;
- systems for identifying and selecting managers;
- structures to support, motivate and reward;
- plans to enable career progression;
- mechanisms to measure and evaluate performance.

There is therefore a need to create a more holistic, integrated framework for developing managers, with an effective HR infrastructure at its core (Ready *et al.*, 1994). But in addition to an effective HR infrastructure supporting management development, those responsible for developing managers have to manage the complex and dynamic array of forces and influences that impinge upon the process. In other words, management development itself must be viewed as a subsystem within the overall organisational system, and be managed accordingly (Doyle, 1995; 2000). This wider perspective of management development will be a theme running throughout the rest of the chapter, and will be explored in more detail later.

MANAGEMENT DEVELOPMENT AND ORGANISATIONAL STRATEGY

Formulating a strategy

Major environmental shifts are now demanding a more strategic perspective from those who manage and lead in organisations. Organisations are 'globalising' in their quest for markets that will bring new opportunities for growth and prosperity. Developments in technology, especially in information technology and telecommunications, are leading to greater efficiencies, reduced costs and opportunities to launch new products and services. The nature of organisational life itself is changing. Organisations are becoming more complex and diverse. Change is becoming a dominant feature of organisational life. Adaptability and flexibility are the essential characteristics for survival and success. As a consequence, organisations are now espousing values that regard people not as costs to be minimised but as assets to be maintained and developed.

Such changes are setting new challenges for managers and employees alike. Managers are being challenged to respond with strategic leadership and perform in the role of change agent (Kanter, 1983; Salaman, 1995; Rosenfeld and Wilson, 1999). Their task is to establish a clear mission, linked to a set of strategic business objectives that enable organisations to acquire, control and allocate resources to maximise the opportunities available and to minimise any threats to their survival and success.

> In this respect, management development is attaining strategic significance because it ensures the right mix of management competences to secure current competitive position . . . it is a means to develop management competences to enable the organisation to maintain or shift its competitive position in the future.
>
> (Buckley and Kemp, 1989: 158)

The goals and objectives of management development

Storey (1989) points out that 'conceptualisations about what management development is are obviously closely wrapped up with what it is for because clearly it is not an end in itself' (p. 5). Increasingly, the goals and objectives of management development are becoming indistinguishable from the need for organisations to respond effectively to pressures and challenges of change and renewal. In this sense, management development has become a 'tool' in the pursuit of quality, cost reduction and profitability through excellence by equipping managers for new roles and responsibilities and supporting them in those roles (Storey, 1989). At the organisational level, there are examples to demonstrate how it is being used in an effort to facilitate and 'engineer' different forms of culture change in both the public and the private sector – often with mixed outcomes (Hopfl and Dawes, 1995; Simpson and Lyddon, 1995; Currie, 1999). Although the key strategic imperative is to use management development as a way of developing individuals and engineering change, there is a concern that a reliance on traditional, conventional approaches may be failing to deliver the anticipated outcomes. For instance, as one commentator observes:

> The firm had sent many managers to a variety of training and development programmes over the years with little direct pay off to the firm in terms of improved performance.
>
> (Pate and Nielson, 1987: 17)

Other commentators observe that the general status and perception of management development is not a good one:

> Without some initiative which helps build the role management development plays, this lacklustre perception of its value and poor utilisation will continue.　　　(Meldrum and Atkinson, 1998: 532)

The impression gained is that management development might somehow be 'failing' to deliver strategic and operational objectives. This view is not a new one. The reports of Handy (1987) and Constable and McCormick (1987) were highly critical of UK management development, which was held responsible for the relatively poor performance of UK industry in the 1980s. Since then, it would appear that organisations have increased their commitment to and investment in management development (Storey *et al.*, 1997). But while investment and commitment may have increased since the late 1980s, there are still reservations and doubts about the overall *efficacy* of management development and its ability to deliver increased performance and organisational success in a time of radical and far-reaching change (Doyle, 2000). In this regard, attention is now turning to the significance of *managing* development as well as *doing* development in unique organisational contexts. In practice, this means addressing the wider structural, political, social and cultural barriers that 'interfere' with the organisations' objectives of changing managerial attitudes and behaviours and improving organisational performance (McClelland, 1994; Molander and Winterton, 1994). However, there are also concerns that the formalised and highly structured approaches currently adopted may not be able to cope with the growing complexity and diversity that is becoming a characteristic of modern organisations (Woodall and Winstanley, 1998; Doyle, 2000).

What is required is a more contingent, holistic and systemic approach that links management development more firmly to a wider consideration of contextual influences and the unique context in which organisations are embedded (Doyle, 1995; 2000). The aim, as Pate and Nielson (1987: 28) conclude, is to evolve 'a system wide strategy'. Management development must therefore be integrated more closely with organisational development: they must be seen as 'complementary activities' (Vloeberghs, 1998: 650)

One organisation has produced a three-tier framework as a way of integrating its management development and business strategy.

Strategic management development at Thorn EMI Home Electronics

Corporate level
- Psychological environment for management development explicitly linked to key business characteristics:
  - Sector businesses strategically led
  - Competitively focused
  - Marketing oriented
  - People driven.

- Business performance measured and reviewed against management capabilities.

Strategic business unit (SBU) level
- Management development tailored to suit the specific business needs of SBUs.
- Strategy–manager matching model employed to identify and match available manager competences with job requirements.
- Development centre resource available to support SBUs.

Functional level
- Focused on bridging the gap between individual manager competences and business requirements.
- Linked to comprehensive appraisal system.
- Extensive use of short-term, individual specific programmes (self-awareness, planning, finance, problem solving, etc.).   (Buckley and Kemp, 1989)

Devising a management development policy

> Management development will fail if there is no clear policy.   (Margerison, 1991)

Developing effective managers begins with the formulation of a detailed management development policy. It is vital that when drafting a policy there is full consultation and involvement with all managers to achieve ownership and commitment to the subsequent development process.

Guidelines for preparing a management development policy

An effective and meaningful management development policy meets the following aims:

- It integrates development plans and activities to business strategies, human resource planning and employment policies.
- It determines who is responsible for developing managers, and the nature and extent of those responsibilities.
- It decides the characteristics for an effective manager within the unique organisational context.
- It identifies the managerial competences required to implement strategy.
- It 'maps out' the organisation's cultural philosophy with regard to required management behaviour.

- It communicates the organisation's strategic goals and objectives to managers and those involved in manager development to gain ownership and commitment.
- It ensures that development links to the reality of what managers do, not what the organisation thinks they do.
- It develops a flexible approach to management development that can accommodate both organisational and individual needs.

Policy statements are useful because they express an organisation's commitment to development, and set out clearly a framework within which it can take place. What is sometimes less clear is the extent to which organisations are prepared to implement them and how effective they are. Like other areas of management development, this is difficult to evaluate. Some of the reasons for these difficulties will be explored later in the chapter.

Extracts from a management development policy

- We accept that it is the Group's responsibility to provide every manager with the opportunity to develop his/her ability and potential so that he/she does their existing job effectively.
- We believe that people derive more satisfaction from working when they themselves have helped to establish and are committed to the objective of their job.
- The policy requires that through the Divisions we create an environment in which all managers contribute to the objectives of the business to their maximum ability.
- We have undertaken to support this policy by providing an organisational structure within which the responsibilities of each manager are clearly defined.
- We expect that increasing the influence and scope for initiative and self-motivation of managers and their subordinates will lead to increasing job satisfaction and to direct improvement in the Group's commercial performance.

(Mumford, 1993: 10. This extract is taken from *Management Development* (1993) by Alan Mumford and is reproduced by permission of the publishers, The Institute of Personnel and Development.)

Having determined its policy guidelines, the next step for the organisation is to consider how it should *approach* the development of its managers.

ORGANISATIONAL APPROACHES TO MANAGEMENT DEVELOPMENT

Why develop this manager?

In designing a management development programme, those responsible need to think through and be able to justify why they are developing an individual manager (or group of managers). The reasons for developing managers are varied. For example:

- to introduce new attitudes and behaviours to promote culture change;
- to encourage more empowerment and innovation;
- to develop the knowledge and the skills to seek new market opportunities;
- to develop the knowledge to maximise the use of new technology;
- to facilitate the introduction of new working practices.

You will note that many of these purposes overlap, but above all organisations must ensure that development is linked to the philosophies and strategic objectives of the organisation, while taking account of individual needs, expectations and aspirations. This can often be a difficult balance to achieve, and frequently becomes a source of tension.

Activity	**The bottom line**

Managers who are seeking to buy a new piece of plant or equipment, develop a new product, explore a new market, or build a new warehouse, will have to produce a well-researched, carefully drafted investment plan. Knowing that the plan will be submitted to rigorous examination by senior managers and financial experts, managers will prepare carefully their justification and response to the predictable question 'Why do you want to purchase/invest in . . . ?'

Suppose you were responsible for initiating a management development programme. What difficulties might you encounter in trying to prepare a supporting investment plan?

It is difficult to justify an investment in management development. There are problems in making the causal connections between (sometimes considerable) investment in management education, training and development, and evaluating future managerial performance and organisational success (Easterby-Smith, 1994). Some of the issues connected with the evaluation of management development will be discussed later.

Because management development is difficult to justify, it has often to rest on some notion of its being 'the right thing to do'. Senior managers who are seeking a quick-fix solution to a deep-rooted managerial or organisational problem will often consult with development 'experts', who are only too pleased to solve the problem by introducing them to the latest development fad. When the 'quick-fix' solution fails to produce the anticipated results or (worse) exacerbates an existing problem, management development is at risk of being undermined and discredited. It is therefore vital that organisations view management development as a long-term investment in a key part of their human resource, and select an approach that is suited to their specific needs and requirements. This again emphasises the need for a more holistic and systemic view of development.

Selecting the right approach

Management development can be approached in a number of different ways. Mumford (1993) describes three different types of approach that are broadly representative of current UK management development:

Type 1: 'Informal managerial' – accidental processes

Characteristics:
- occurs within manager's activities
- explicit intention is task performance
- no clear development objectives
- unstructured in development terms
- not planned in advance
- owned by managers.

Development consequences:
- learning real, direct, unconscious, insufficient.

Type 2: 'Integrated managerial' – opportunistic processes

Characteristics:
- occurs within managerial activities
- explicit intention is both task performance and development

- clear development objectives
- structured for development by boss and subordinate
- planned beforehand and/or reviewed subsequently as learning experiences
- owned by managers.

Development consequences:
- learning is real, direct, conscious, more substantial.

Type 3: 'Formalised development' – planned processes

Characteristics:
- often away from normal managerial activities
- explicit intention is development
- clear development objectives
- structured for development by developers
- planned beforehand or reviewed subsequently as learning experiences
- owned more by developers than managers.

Development consequences:
- learning may be real (through a job) or detached (through a course)
- is more likely to be conscious, relatively infrequent.

(This article first appeared in *Management Education and Development*, Vol. 18, Part 3 (1987).
We are grateful to the editor for permission to reproduce it here.)

Burgoyne (1988) argues that management development may be considered as progressing through different levels of maturity (see Table 9.1). At Level 1 there is no

Table 9.1 Levels of maturity of organisational management development

1 No systematic management development	2 Isolated tactical mangement development	3 Integrated and coordinated structural and development tactics	4 A management development strategy to implement corporate policy	5 Management development strategy input to corporate policy formation	6 Strategic development of the mangement of corporate policy
No systematic or deliberate management development in structural or developmental sense; total reliance on laissez-faire uncontrived processes of management development	There are isolated and ad hoc tactical management development activities, of either structural or developmental kinds, or both, in response to local problems, crises, or sporadically identified general problems	The specific managment development tactics that impinge directly on the individual manager, of career structure management, and of assisting learning, are integrated and coordinated	A management development strategy plays its part in implementing corporate policies through managerial human resource planning, and providing a strategic frame-work and direction for the tactics of career structure management and of learning, education and training	Management development processes feed information into corporate policy decision-making processes on the organisation's managerial assets, strengths, weaknesses and potential, and contribute to the forecasting and analysis of the manageability of proposed projects, ventures, changes	Management development processes enhance the nature and quality of corporate policy-forming processes, which they also inform and help implement

Source: Burgoyne (1988).

systematic approach to management development, and at Level 6 management development not only shapes and informs corporate strategy, it actually enhances the process of strategy formation. In practice, management development approaches for most organisations rarely extend beyond Levels 1 and 2. Those who reach Levels 5 and 6 find it is 'often precariously achieved and lost' (p. 44). Burgoyne argues that to progress through the levels of maturity to the point where management development is making the fullest contribution to organisation development demands a much more holistic approach to development, in which both 'hard' (roles, duties, technical competence, etc.) and 'soft' (career, quality of life, ethos, values, etc.) managerial issues are considered in framing the right approach.

A 'piecemeal' approach

Programmes that have characteristics similar to Mumford's Type 1 and Type 3 development and Burgoyne's Levels 1 and 2 tend to lead to *piecemeal* approaches, which in turn lead to inefficient and ineffective development.

Piecemeal approaches to development are characterised by the following:

- There is no management development infrastructure. Development is not linked to business strategy. Activities are unrelated, and lack overall direction or philosophy. They fail to reinforce each other, and reduce the potential for organisational effectiveness.
- Development often focuses on the needs of the organisation, and fails to meet the learning needs and aspirations of individuals and groups.
- Development is largely defined in terms of a range of universal, off-the-shelf internal or external courses.
- There is tacit support for management education and training because it is seen as a 'good thing to be doing' irrespective of organisational needs.
- There is a lack of common vision among those responsible for management development. For instance, some managers see development as a central part of their job, others see it as peripheral and a nuisance.
- Management development effort can be wasted because it is used as a solution to the wrong problem. Rather than developing managers, the correct solution may be to change aspects of organisation structure or systems.
- It is difficult to evaluate the effectiveness of a piecemeal approach that lacks clear direction and established objectives.

But there are a number of reasons why organisations might choose or be forced to adopt these approaches:

- resource constraints (in the case of smaller organisations);
- a lack of awareness on the part of those responsible for initiating or delivering development about linking management development to business strategy;
- groups who seek to exert control over development (personnel departments);
- a focus on formalised, intensive management training courses.

Sadly, piecemeal, fragmented and discrete approaches to management development are commonplace (Hitt, 1987; Roberts and McDonald, 1995). Such approaches are a significant contributor to the failure of management development to fulfil personal and organisational expectations (Temporal, 1990; Mumford, 1993). Not only do they waste investment, time and effort, there is also a risk of damage to existing levels of morale and commitment among managers as efforts to develop them founder on organisational barriers to change (Doyle, 1995, 2000). As Molander and Winterton (1994) argue:

> Where such conditions exist, what is required is an organisation-wide assessment of the elements in the culture which require changing, followed by an effective change programme. Focusing attention on individual managers . . . will not bring about required change. In this case the organisation itself should be the focus of change.
>
> (p. 89)

Example   **Evidence of piecemeal approach?**

An organisation spent a considerable amount of money running a series of in-house management training courses. It became concerned when the training produced no tangible results. The root cause of the problem became evident during a time-management module. The external consultant running the module realised from the reaction of the delegates that the structure and culture of the organisation would act as barriers to the implementation of time-management techniques. For example, managers had little flexibility to change existing rules and procedures to enable them to manage their time more effectively. The consultant informed the organisation that their management training would not produce the desired changes unless wider issues connected with existing culture, structures, rules and procedures were addressed.

After discussions with senior managers, the consultant was asked to design a long-term organisational development programme designed to tackle cultural and structural issues that were acting as barriers to management development. Measures were initiated to change the management style and promote a more participative, supportive culture. A more focused management development programme was established linked to the 'live' issues in the workplace and the organisation's business goals

---

An open systems approach

In Chapter 2, the *open systems model* was introduced as a way of conceptualising and making sense of the complexity of organisational life (Kast and Rosenweig, 1985; Morgan, 1997). If organisations can be persuaded to adopt an open systems perspective they are likely to overcome many of the problems created by a piecemeal approach to development. Instead of looking at management development in isolation, it becomes an integral part of a wider organisational system, and, more importantly, is linked to the context and 'reality' of managerial work (see, for example, Mumford's Type 2 development).

Viewing management development from an open systems perspective recognises and focuses attention on the following:

- Management development is both a *system* and a *process* (see Figure 9.1). It is composed of identifiable parts or components that act together in an organised way. Inputs are transformed by the management development process to produce a range of outputs. In some cases, the primary output will be increased organisational effectiveness. But in piecemeal approaches, we may find that reduced effectiveness is an output as the programmes 'fail' to meet expectations.
- Figure 9.1 also shows that in an open system the management development process *interacts with* and *is influenced by* variables from other environmental and organisational subsystems (structural, social, technological and cultural). Some of the main sources of internal and external influence are listed in Table 9.2.

Figure 9.1 **Developing the manager: an open systems view**

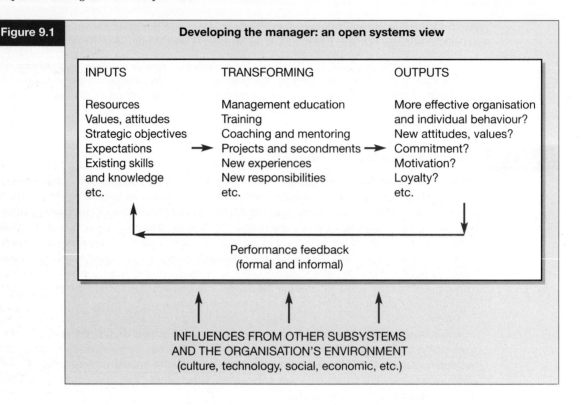

INPUTS

Resources
Values, attitudes
Strategic objectives
Expectations
Existing skills
and knowledge
etc.

TRANSFORMING

Management education
Training
Coaching and mentoring
Projects and secondments
New experiences
New responsibilities
etc.

OUTPUTS

More effective organisation
and individual behaviour?
New attitudes, values?
Commitment?
Motivation?
Loyalty?
etc.

Performance feedback
(formal and informal)

INFLUENCES FROM OTHER SUBSYSTEMS
AND THE ORGANISATION'S ENVIRONMENT
(culture, technology, social, economic, etc.)

Table 9.2 Internal and external influencers

Internal influencers	External influencers
Culture	Technology
Structure	Government/politics
Strategic goals	Macro-economic factors
Organisation size	Social change
Organisation growth	Market forces
Ownership	Demographic change
Power distribution and politics	Professional groups
Individual goals	Education sysem

● For example, prevailing ideologies, values and beliefs exist within the organisation as a *cultural subsystem*. Management development can be used as a way of reinforcing this cultural subsystem by shaping and moulding managers' attitudes and values and exerting pressure upon them to conform and display 'acceptable' behaviour patterns. The *technological subsystem* can have a profound effect upon managers. For example, information technology has transformed managerial work by removing layers of middle managers whose primary task was to receive and process information for management control and decision-making. Not only does management development become involved in developing new skills to cope with new technology, it also has to confront and adapt to changing career patterns and promotion pathways (Stewart, 1994; Newell and Dopson, 1996).

- Management development is therefore *integrated* with, and *mutually dependent* upon, other organisational subsystems, activities and processes. For example, the system for strategic planning and the setting of organisational goals must interact with a management development system that seeks to develop the managerial skills and knowledge to organise and implement the business strategy (Burgoyne, 1988; Ready *et al.*, 1994).

Adopting an open systems approach to management development offers the organisation a number of benefits:

- A broader set of strategies, policies and plans are developed that take fuller account of the organisation's unique situation and its specific requirements in respect of managerial skills and knowledge.
- The notion that *if you develop the manager, you develop the organisation*, and vice versa, becomes apparent (see Figure 9.2). An open systems view identifies the way management development contributes to overall organisational effectiveness. As the organisation changes and develops, so positive influencing 'loops' are created that lead to the further development of managers. Similarly, as managers are developed, positive influencing 'loops' lead to changes in the organisation that produce greater effectiveness. It can, of course, work the other way. Poor or ineffective development can create negative influencing 'loops' that undermine organisational or managerial effectiveness.
- By identifying, analysing and monitoring the complex network of influences and patterns of relationships in managerial work, development programmes can become more adaptable, flexible, responsive and proactive in the face of organisational change and turbulence.
- Viewing management development in open systems terms reveals the full extent of its influence on the organisation, and is likely to lead to more detailed and objective assessment of performance and overall effectiveness.

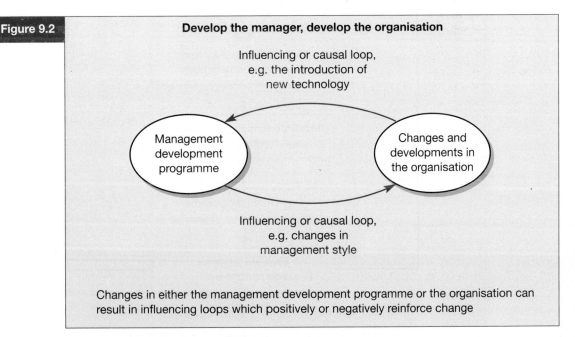

Figure 9.2

Develop the manager, develop the organisation

Influencing or causal loop,
e.g. the introduction of
new technology

Management development programme

Changes and developments in the organisation

Influencing or causal loop,
e.g. changes in
management style

Changes in either the management development programme or the organisation can result in influencing loops which positively or negatively reinforce change

A unified approach to management development

We saw in the previous section that an open systems approach can offer real benefits. But how can an open systems approach be translated into an effective management development programme? Figure 9.3 shows the example of a *unified management development programme* built on open systems principles.

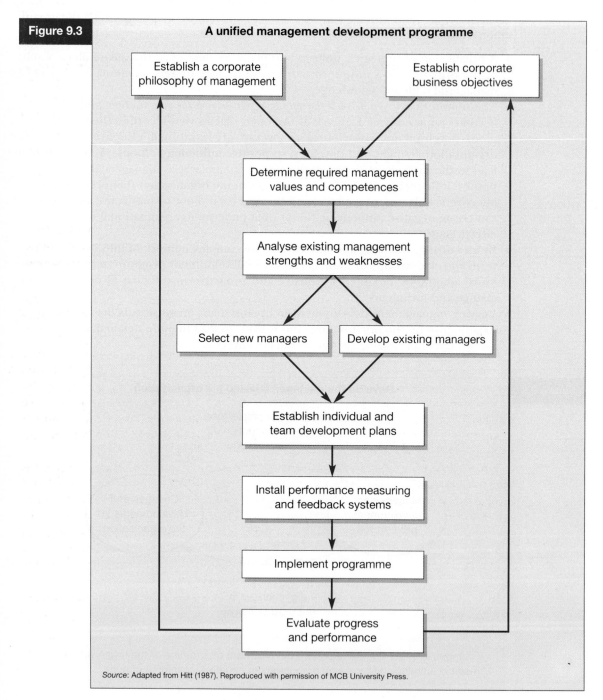

Figure 9.3   A unified management development programme

Establish a corporate philosophy of management

Establish corporate business objectives

Determine required management values and competences

Analyse existing management strengths and weaknesses

Select new managers

Develop existing managers

Establish individual and team development plans

Install performance measuring and feedback systems

Implement programme

Evaluate progress and performance

Source: Adapted from Hitt (1987). Reproduced with permission of MCB University Press.

In a unified programme, management development is located at the very heart of the organisation's philosophy, mission, business goals and human resource strategy. The process is integrated and coherent across all functions and hierarchies. Manager performance is measured, and development activity can be linked clearly to the organisational values and the achievement of strategic goals. As Hitt (1987) makes clear, 'effective management of the enterprise and development of managerial talent are a single integrated activity' (p. 53). Others reinforce this point. By adopting a unified, integrated approach to management development, 'all elements of the executive process are linked together to focus on the most essential outcome of the process – the development of a sustainable focus on organisational learning and ultimately competitiveness' (Ready *et al.*, 1994: 66). But an open systems approach to management development will have implications for the role of management development professionals, who have to move away from the role of needs assessor, programme coordinator and administrator to a role that is much more results and change orientated (Temporal, 1990). As Temporal rather pointedly remarks, they must 'get into the business of results or get out of the business of development' (p. 13).

Towards a more successful approach?

The main theme running through the whole of this section has been that management development cannot be viewed as a closed system. If it is, the likelihood is for a piecemeal, fragmented approach with adverse consequences for organisational development and renewal. As Mumford (1987) states:

> Any management development process which emphasises discrete activities, organised thinking processes, neatness and freedom of choice, is likely to be out of synchronisation with the *reality of management* that managers engage in. (p. 23)

But as we have seen, ineffective development may arise when managers encounter structural, cultural and political barriers to their development (Currie, 1995; Doyle, 1995). Faced with these wider contextual barriers managers may rapidly become disillusioned and frustrated, and create what Varney (1977) terms a 'counterproductive process'. The results can be catastrophic in terms of managers' morale and motivation as aspirations and expectations are not fulfilled (Hopfl and Dawes, 1995; Simpson and Lyddon, 1995; Currie, 1999).

What is needed is a more holistic, integrated perspective in which development is both *contingent* upon the interplay of contextual variables and embraces formal and informal learning opportunities and processes. This means shifting towards a more relational perspective that is concerned with managing the complex interactions between the management development subsystem and the organisational system and environment in which it is embedded (Doyle, 2000). However, such an approach will demand a radically different outlook and role from those with responsibilities for making sure that managers deliver business goals (Doyle, 1995; 2000).

In the next section we explore the way in which management development is organised and implemented.

ORGANISING AND IMPLEMENTING MANAGEMENT DEVELOPMENT PROGRAMMES

Organising management development programmes

With a clear set of policies, objectives and approaches established, the organisation is now in a position to consider the best way to organise and implement its management development programmes.

To organise an effective management development programme, even a modest one, requires considerable effort. This may partially explain why programmes have a tendency to become piecemeal and fragmented, and why line managers are tempted to leave them to personnel and training specialists to organise. Before development can be implemented, certain decisions will have to be made within the context of the organisation's strategic plans and environmental influences.

Determining who is responsible for management development

If a development programme is to be successfully planned and implemented, there has to be clear and unambiguous allocation of responsibility and a willingness to accept that responsibility by the parties involved.

Traditionally, responsibility for development has rested with the personnel function, with some input from the manager's boss. The individual manager was essentially passive in the process: they were only required to 'turn up and be developed'.

However, effective development demands the involvement of a range of stakeholders, each of whom will have an impact on the development process and its outcomes. Figure 9.4 identifies a number of key stakeholders who each share a measure of responsibility. At the core of the process, the main responsibilities are shared between the personnel specialist, the boss and the individual (Davis, 1990).

The effective development of managers requires the full involvement and participation of all of these three key parties. An active process of discussion and negotiation should ensure that they accept and own a share of the responsibility for setting development objectives, planning and implementing the process. However, although these three parties are central to the development process, other stakeholders may have an input (Mabey and Salaman, 1995). For example, the role of senior management is vital in terms of resourcing, commitment and establishing a supportive culture. Colleagues and mentors will advise and assist in overcoming particular problems and issues (Mumford, 1993).

Beyond the organisational boundary, national bodies such as the Institute of Management, NVQ lead bodies and TECs are influential in shaping management development policies and direction through mechanisms such as funding, reports, lobbying, and contact with industry representatives. Similarly, academic and vocational institutions are able to influence development methods and agendas through their research, teaching, awards and other activities (see Chapter 8). And finally it must be remembered that the individual's friends and family have a crucial role to play in providing support and encouragement (Mumford, 1993). As Mabey and Salaman (1995) point out, the linkages between each stakeholder are complex and each will 'help shape the ethos and practice of training and development within organisations' (p. 176).

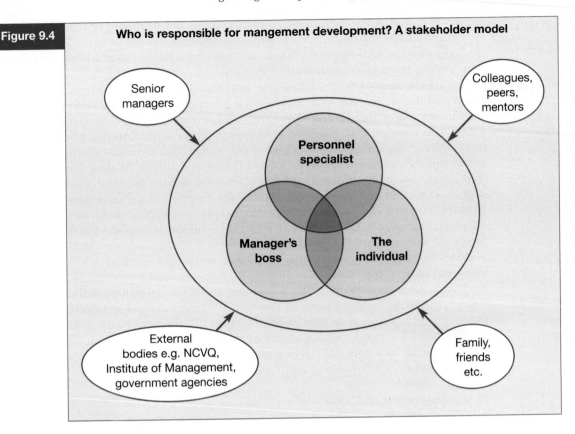

Figure 9.4 Who is responsible for mangement development? A stakeholder model

Ensuring the availability of suitable managers

To achieve their strategic objectives, organisations must ensure that they have the right numbers of managers, with the right skills, available at the right time. A core element of human resource planning is the assessment of existing managerial stock and, where necessary, the replenishment of that stock through the recruitment of new managers. A *managerial audit* is normally carried out, utilising information from sources such as assessment centres, performance appraisals, personnel files and discussions with bosses, to reveal the skills available to meet forecast demand. These skills are then compared with the organisation's HRM plan, and development objectives are established (Vineall, 1994; Woodall and Winstanley, 1998).

In certain cases, it may not be feasible or appropriate to develop the existing stock of managers, and organisations may choose or be forced to enter the marketplace to buy in the required skills.

Promotion and succession planning

Management development can only be effective if careful consideration is given to career paths and opportunities for promotion and progression (Mumford, 1993; Margerison, 1994a). This requires a well-prepared human resource plan that is future orientated (see Chapter 4).

As well as developing managers to step into the positions vacated by leavers and retirers, succession planning needs to consider the growth and future direction of the organisation. Plans should include the older, experienced, so-called 'plateaued' managers as well as the high fliers. As organisations downsize and restructure, vertical opportunities are fast disappearing, and innovative ways need to be found to set new challenges and provide opportunities to motivate managers through horizontal progression: leading projects, secondments, and so on.

Despite the opportunities offered by horizontally focused initiatives, some would argue that the picture for some managers is becoming increasingly bleak. While there are winners, there are also losers in career terms (Caulkin, 1994; Newell and Dopson, 1996). It is claimed that a lack of managerial career opportunities is increasingly a factor influencing the changing nature of the 'psychological contract' between the individual and their organisation (Herriot and Pemberton, 1996). As these authors remark, 'careers are becoming more complex sequences of actions based on choices and constraints which can take the individual from the core to the periphery and back again' (p. 338). This, it is claimed, is leading some managers towards a much more instrumental interpretation of their relationship with the organisation, captured in the notion of a 'new deal' (Herriot and Pemberton, 1995).

Predictions are therefore being made that, to survive, managers will have to take more and more responsibility for shaping their careers and ensuring their employability. With a more developed, professional and mobile management workforce there is every opportunity for them to do so (Stewart, 1994). And for those involved in developing managers, there is a new role emerging as the emphasis switches towards development for employability rather than for career progression. Their role will increasingly become one of enabling and facilitating rather than controlling development (Temporal, 1990; Cannon and Taylor, 1994).

Designing reward and appraisal systems

Since the 1980s, growing attention has been paid to the introduction of performance management systems to both motivate and reward those managers who contribute to strategic goals and objectives and, by implication, to exert sanctions on or to 'punish' those who fail to deliver anticipated performance levels.

Performance management can be conceptualised in the form of a cycle consisting of five elements (Mabey and Salaman, 1995):

- setting performance objectives;
- measuring outcomes;
- feedback of results;
- rewards linked to outcomes;
- amendments to objectives and activities.

Within the cycle, performance-related pay (PRP) and performance appraisal are key components: the former to produce the extrinsic financial rewards in the form of shares, income differentials, profit-sharing schemes and bonuses, and the latter to provide the essential mechanism for setting objectives and feeding back performance criteria (Hendry, 1995).

In terms of management development, there is a close interaction with performance management systems. First and foremost, performance management systems must be seen to reward personal development and achievement. This is leading a number of organisations to link their systems of reward more closely to the attainment of higher levels of competence, which is one way of overcoming 'the subjectivity and arbitrariness of assessment' (Hendry, 1995: 309). The achievement of objectives is also closely linked to management training and education, which act to provide the skills and knowledge required to meet objectives. Performance appraisal provides the forum for identifying development needs. It also serves as the mechanism for feeding back information to the manager about current levels of performance, enabling him or her to identify and negotiate adjustments or further development needs.

Although the focus of performance management is on extrinsic rewards, intrinsic rewards through praise, encouragement and reassurance are vital components in management development, particularly in the area of coaching and mentoring. For younger managers who may be on fast-track graduate programmes, continuous positive feedback during the early stages of the programme is vital to sustain motivation and commitment. Older, experienced managers also need regular praise, encouragement and above all reassurance that their skills and experience are still valued and appreciated, and that any investment in personal development is seen as being positive from the organisation's viewpoint (Mumford, 1993).

Provision of resourcing and support

To be successful, development requires adequate planning, resourcing and support (Vineall, 1994). Integrating management development with strategic planning clearly identifies the financial commitments that the organisation will undertake. Budgets can then be prepared in conjunction with those responsible for development. In smaller organisations, the physical resources to carry out development (trained personnel, training space and materials) are rarely available, and external resources in the form of consultants, academics and professional institutions are utilised.

In larger organisations, skilled training personnel are normally available, together with dedicated training and residential facilities. External resources may also be used if it is cost-effective to do so or if specialist skills are required.

Whatever the resources available, no development programme will succeed if it is not supported by senior and middle management (Margerison, 1991). One of the main strengths of the unified approach discussed earlier is in building that support from the outset. Development is integrated with strategic objectives, and senior managers can see clearly how development will benefit the organisation (Ready *et al.*, 1994). The main issue then becomes one of sustaining support for the duration of the programme, especially during a time of major change.

Acknowledging the diversity of management

We saw earlier that development has to be linked to the reality of managerial work. When organising development programmes, it is important to cater for the diversity of management skills, attitudes and experience that reside within the organisation. One example is given by Odiorne (1984), who advocates a *portfolio* approach to development to improve the overall efficiency of the process and ensure the optimal allocation of resources. This requires organisation to make a range of decisions and develop a 'mix' of objectives and techniques arranged to match the profile of the management team in the organisation.

A portfolio approach to development

'*Stars*': high-performing, high-potential managers

Aim:
- create challenge
- provide incentives and reward
- allocate adequate resources and effort.

'*Workhorses*': high-performing, limited-potential managers

Aim:

- emphasise value and worth of experience
- motivate and reassure
- utilise experience on assignments, projects, coaching.

'*Problem employees*': high-potential, underperforming managers

Aim:

- identify weaknesses
- channel resources to address weaknesses
- regular performance monitoring and feedback.

'*Deadwood*': low-performing, low-potential managers

Aim:

- identify weaknesses, resolvable?
- if not, consider release, early retirement, demotion.   (Adapted from Odiorne, 1984)

Furthermore, the diverse nature of management means that some key questions must be answered before development commences:

- *Who is being developed?*
  - Is it older managers seeking new challenges or younger 'high fliers' on a fast-track development programme?
  - Is it senior managers seeking to enhance their strategic skills, middle managers seeking to update and broaden existing skills, or junior-level managers looking to acquire additional managerial skills?
  - Is it technical specialists seeking to expand their cross-functional capabilities, or supervisors receiving training for the first time?

- *What is being developed?*
  - Does the programme seek to develop new attitudes and values, as in the case of a recently privatised public utility or a private sector company that has just undergone a takeover?
  - Does the programme aim to develop technical, financial, business or interpersonal skills? What are the priorities?
  - Does the programme seek to change existing managerial behaviours and styles to reflect an internal organisational restructuring, such as the introduction of new technology?

- *Where will the development take place?*
  - Should development be on-the-job in the office, factory or sales territory, or off-the-job in a residential hall, academic institution or individual's home, or a combination of both?

- *What are the most appropriate techniques to achieve the best fit between individual and organisational requirements?*
  - What are the most cost-effective/appropriate techniques available?
  - How much scope is there to accommodate individual learning needs and preferences?
  - How much choice is delegated to the individual over the choice of development techniques?
  - How is conflict resolved between individual and organisational needs?

It is only when these questions have been considered that the organisation is in a position to construct a framework of development that best fits its needs and the needs of its managers. In the next section some of the more commonly used development techniques are identified and discussed. It is important to reiterate the point made earlier in this chapter that a great deal of development takes place in unstructured and informal ways (Mumford, 1993).

Implementing management development programmes

Earlier, the question was posed: 'Why are we developing this manager?' In this section attention will turn to focus on the techniques and choices available to organisations when they implement development programmes. Implementation begins with a careful identification and analysis of individual development needs.

Development needs analysis

If managers are to be developed effectively, their individual development needs must be assessed in a careful and systematic fashion. There are several ways to do this. Traditionally, the diagnosis of development needs for managers has relied upon an often ad hoc and piecemeal process of observation and the 'constructive' but often subjective input of others in the organisation.

However, increasingly organisations are turning to performance appraisal as an effective way of identifying the skills and behaviours required to meet business objectives (Mumford, 1993; Woodall and Winstanley, 1998). During the appraisal process both the individual and their boss review performance against departmental/organisational objectives and other performance criteria to determine development needs. Once analysed, the development needs form the basis of a negotiated and agreed personal development plan, which is regularly reviewed and modified in the light of changing organisational and individual circumstances.

With a greater emphasis on performance management, in which individual reward is more closely aligned with and directed towards the attainment of business objectives, there has been a trend towards the greater use of assessment/development centres. Development centres are 'workshops which measure the abilities of participants against the agreed success criteria for a job or role' (Lee and Beard, 1994). It should also be borne in mind that the term 'development centre' relates to the process of identifying needs, not to a specific place (Munchus and McArthur, 1991).

The main aim of a development centre is to 'obtain the best possible indication of people's actual or potential competence to perform at the target job or job level' (Woodruffe, 1993: 2). Most development centres operate in the following way:

- There is careful selection of job-related criteria. These may be in the form of competences, dimensions, attributes, critical success factors, etc.
- A group of managers is identified and brought together in the form of a workshop of around six people for one or two days. In the workshops a series of diagnostic instruments and/or multiple assessment techniques are administered that aim to measure an individual's ability to perform against the job-related criteria. These can take the form of psychometric tests, planning exercises, in-tray exercises, interviews, games, or simulations.
- A team of trained assessors observe and measure performance, evaluate and provide structured feedback and guidance to individuals.

- After the workshop, line managers and/or trainers utilise the feedback to help the individual construct a personal development plan.

Although the use of development centres is growing, there have been a number of criticisms, which tend to revolve around: assessment techniques that do not relate to the task or job, poor organisation, poorly trained assessors, ineffective feedback and the lack of follow-up action (Dulewicz, 1991; Whiddett and Branch, 1993).

Whichever method or combination of methods is selected, it is vital that each manager's needs are carefully assessed before implementing a development programme, and that an effective system of providing feedback is established.

Competence-based development programmes

Recent years have seen something of a 'mini-revolution' in UK management education and development. The main catalyst for this was the publication in the late 1980s of two searching reports into the development of UK managers: *The Making of British Managers* (Constable and McCormick, 1987) and *The Making of Managers* (Handy, 1987). These reports examined the education and development needs of UK managers, and concluded that current provision and standards were wholly inadequate and that development had a low priority in many organisations. They identified an urgent need to develop managers more effectively and predicted that, if their recommendations were followed, standards and levels of performance would rise, ensuring that the UK economy was able to compete more successfully in an increasingly global market.

In response to these findings a number of initiatives emerged, beginning with the establishment of the National Forum for Management Education and Development and culminating in the Management Charter Initiative (MCI) (now in the process of being renamed the Management Enterprise and Training Organisation, METO). Since its inception in the early 1990s, MCI has commissioned extensive research into UK management development needs and approaches. The aim has been to focus on the development of managers through workplace activities. What matters is the manager's ability to perform and deliver predetermined outcomes rather than development being concerned with the acquisition of specific knowledge or academic qualifications.

MCI/METO is the Management Lead Body within the NVQ system (see Chapter 8). As lead body, its primary aim has been to establish a *generic set of standards and qualifications* based upon 'the areas of activity which the majority of managers would be expected to perform competently' (Miller, 1991). The original management roles to which the standards applied were:

- manage operations;
- manage finance;
- manage people;
- manage information.

Within each area of activity or role, there are associated *units of competence* derived from a functional analysis of what constitutes 'the manager's job'. For example, in the role of managing people, one unit of competence is to 'contribute to the recruitment and selection of personnel'. Having identified units of competence, there is a further subdivision into a series of *elements* against which there are established *performance criteria* and *range statements*. A standard is therefore established by which managerial performance can be assessed. Evidence can then be gathered and presented by the manager to a trained assessor, who will judge whether their performance is deemed to be 'competent' in their current position.

Currently, there are national standards of competence for supervisory, middle and senior managers that equate to NVQ levels 3, 4 and 5 respectively.

The standards were revised in 1997 to take account of concerns and reservations expressed about the administration and implementation of the original standards. The aim has been to produce a more flexible framework of mandatory and optional units from which managers can select the pathway of competence that best suits their circumstances and the qualification they wish to pursue. The new standards relate to the following key management roles:

- manage activities;
- manage resources;
- manage people;
- manage information;
- manage energy;
- manage quality;
- manage projects.

Competence-based development programmes for managers such as those set up by MCI have attracted considerable criticism, in both philosophical and practical terms. At the heart of the criticism is the belief that competence approaches such as that used by MCI are fundamentally flawed because they are too functional and behavioural in orientation (Stewart and Hamlin, 1992a). Some see them as bureaucratic and overly simplistic, unable to take account of the complex, contextual, contingent and ever-changing nature of the managerial role (Canning, 1990). Because of the growing significance of competence-based management development programmes, these and other criticisms will be explored more fully in the controversial issues section of this chapter.

Despite these criticisms, it would appear that the notion of competence-based development has now established itself within the framework of UK management development. However, there have been some interesting changes and adaptations. For example, in an MCI-sponsored survey, 20% of those surveyed reported that they were using the MCI framework, but within that figure 45% said they had customised the standards to suit their own purposes (MCI, 1993). More recent evidence supports this, and shows that many organisations are beginning to move away from the original generic model developed by MCI to a more contextually based approach. Rather than adhere to what they judge to be a somewhat costly, bureaucratic, prescriptive and rigid framework of national standards, organisations appear to be 'doing their own thing'. They are retaining the competence philosophy and principle, but devising their own competence framework for managers within the unique context of their organisational situation. They feel this is necessary if they are to respond to the complexity induced by rapid environmental change (Cockerill, 1994; Roberts, 1995). Evidence would also suggest that competence frameworks for managers are now becoming more fragmented and differentiated as they adapt to suit changing circumstances, for example shortened organisational lifecycles (Sparrow and Bognanno, 1994; Roberts, 1995).

Other adaptations of the original model include the growing use of competences to assess management behaviour and performance: 'the majority of organisations favour frameworks based on the development of behaviour rather than prescribed national standards' (Mathewman, 1995: 1). Management competences now form the basis for HR systems in areas such as development centres and performance management systems, and appear to be underpinning the drive towards more unitarist, behaviourist organisational cultures. More controversially, there is now a growing quest to identify higher-order, supra- or meta-competences that can be used to inform personality testing for selection and other 'judgements' about managerial behaviour and performance (Sparrow and Bognanno, 1994).

What appears to be happening, therefore, is a process of adjustment whereby NVQ/MCI frameworks of competences are being utilised for basic skills provision in a bottom-up approach, while new behavioural competences are being cascaded down to set behavioural patterns and cultural imperatives (Mathewman, 1995). This adjustment may be seen as an inevitable consequence of what some would judge to be inherent flaws in the national framework. But although this more pragmatic, flexible response is likely to be welcomed by many, it does raise a number of issues, not least how to maintain and guarantee a system of assessment and national accreditation for management qualifications with any measure of confidence.

Mainstream management education and training methods

While competence-based programmes continue to grow, they are still only part of the wider portfolio of frameworks and methods used in manager development. A great deal of management development is formalised, planned and structured. It can take place 'on-the-job' (in the workplace environment) or 'off-the-job' (away from the workplace) (Mumford, 1993). For example, a business studies graduate might leave university after four years of study and join a 'fast-track' development programme in a medium to large national or multinational organisation. The programme would typically last some 12–18 months, during which time the graduate would move through the different functional areas of the organisation. They would undertake carefully planned and supervised project-based tasks designed to stimulate and challenge their business and interpersonal skills. Performance would be carefully monitored at each stage. Towards the end of the programme, those graduates who are successful will negotiate and select a particular career path and begin to climb the 'managerial ladder', usually beginning with the acceptance of a junior managerial position.

Older, more experienced managers might attend short courses, either internally or externally, which are designed to 'top up' their managerial skills base. A number of them may embark on longer-term programmes of full- or part-time study at higher education institutions linked to promotion opportunities, career change or to maintain their employability in an increasingly insecure environment. For those managers who find it difficult to fit such programmes into their daily routines, distance learning schemes operated by institutions such as the Open University Business School and independent management colleges are available and are increasingly being seen as a flexible, cost-effective approach to education.

Within these and other programmes, we find a diverse range of formalised learning methods. These methods have tended to evolve through a pragmatic process of trial and error. Research by Burgoyne and Stuart (1991) reveals that the following methods are likely to be used (in order of predominance of use):

1 lectures;
2 games and simulations;
3 projects;
4 case studies;
5 experiential (analysis of experience);
6 guided reading;
7 role playing;

8 seminars;

9 programmed instruction (computerised/pa...

Although these methods are widely used in ...
detached and artificial nature can never comp...
everyday managerial problems and issues (Burgo...
the other weaknesses that have been identified in...
and training are:

- a clash between academic culture/expectations and...
  (Cunnington, 1985);
- difficulty in transferring and applying knowledge ...
  (Newstrom, 1986; Roberts and McDonald, 1996);
- the relevance of training course to the needs and wan............managers and
  organisations (Mumford, 1987).

Increasingly organisations are turning to experientially based techniques.

Action learning

In Chapter 7, the significance of experiential learning processes to the development of managers was identified. Much of the theory relating to experiential learning is drawn from the theoretical work of Kolb (1984) and Honey and Mumford (1986), who introduced the concept of a learning cycle in which managers learn through a process of:

- implementation;
- reflection;
- making changes;
- initiating further action.

Burgoyne and Stuart (1991) point out that a greater focus on experiential learning in the workplace, coupled to a reaction against the 'remoteness', complication and institutionalisation of management development, has encouraged organisations to adopt new methods of learning. Many of these new approaches are built around the principles of action learning pioneered by writers such as Reg Revans.

Revans' key principles of action learning

1 Management development must be based on real work projects.
2 Those projects must be owned and defined by senior managers as having a significant impact on the future success of the enterprise.
3 Managers must aim to make a real return on the cost of the investment.
4 Managers must work together and learn from each other.
5 Managers must achieve real action and change.
6 Managers must study the content and process of change.
7 Managers must publicly commit themselves to action.   (Margerison, 1991: 38)

Revans saw learning (L) as a combination of what he terms 'programmed knowledge' (P) and 'questioning insight' (Q): thus $L = P + Q$. When facing unprecedented changes, managers cannot know what programmed knowledge they will need. Instead, they need to 'understand the subjective aspects of searching the unfamiliar, or learning to pose useful and discriminating questions'. Therefore action learning becomes a 'simple device of setting them to tackle real problems that have so far defied solution' (Revans, 1983: 11).

that managerial learning has to embrace both 'know-how' and 'know-__' rooted in real problem solving, where 'lasting behavioural change is more ___ follow to reinterpretation of past experiences than the acquisition of fresh ___ledge' (p. 14). Managers will be more able to make their interpretations, which are 'necessarily subjective, complex and ill-structured' (p. 14), and reorder their perceptions by working with colleagues who are engaged in the same process, rather than with non-managers such as management teachers who are 'not exposed to real risk in responsible action'. In other words, managers form 'learning sets' (groups of four to six people) who, with the aid of a facilitator, work together and learn to give and accept criticism, advice and support. Margerison (1994b), citing Revans, likens this approach to 'comrades in adversity'. Managers will only 'learn effectively when they are confronted with difficulties and have the opportunity to share constructively their concerns and experiences with others' (p. 109).

Margerison (1991), drawing on case studies and personal experience of supervising action learning programmes, points out that managers learn a considerable amount

- about themselves,
- about their job,
- about team members, and most of all
- about how to improve things and make changes.

Experientially based development has led to new innovations in development such as learning contracts, learning communities and the learning organisation.

In a *learning contract*, there is a formal agreement between the participant (the manager being developed), the boss and the trainer. Not only does it reinforce responsibility for development, it also brings a number of benefits (Boak and Joy, 1990):

Participants:
- contracts are of their own choosing
- relevant to their needs
- improve their learning abilities.

Managers:
- become involved in training and development
- can influence the activities of trainer and participant.

Trainers:
- tackle a wide variety of real problems
- see real developments in skills and attitudes.

In *learning communities* managers are seen as self-developers who come together to share skills, resources and experiences, in much the same fashion as therapeutic self-help groups operate in the fields of social and psychiatric work.

In a *learning organisation* structures and processes are adapted to encourage managers to take responsibility for their own development. As they learn and improve, so the organisation is learning and improving with them (Pedler *et al.*, 1990).

Experiential learning methods such as action learning are gaining prominence in the field of management development. As organisations confront the growing uncertainty and instability brought about by far-reaching and radical change, they are discovering that management development is likely to be more effective when it is rooted in the everyday reality of what managers do and how they behave.

Coaching and mentoring

Coaching

To many managers, coaching and mentoring represent the most tangible, practical and, if carried out effectively, possibly most useful forms of on-the-job development.

Coaching is defined by Torrington *et al.* (1994) as 'improving the performance of somebody who is already competent rather than establishing competence in the first place' (p. 432). It is analogous to the sports coach who is seeking to improve performance by continually analysing and offering constructive criticism and guidance to an athlete or player. The coach (boss) must be willing to share tasks and assignments with the individual. Each task must have scope, responsibility and authority to challenge and test the individual. Coaching usually begins with a period of instruction and 'shadowing' to grasp the essential aspects of the task. There is then a transfer of responsibility for the task to the individual. Throughout the process there is a dialogue, with regular feedback on performance in the form of constructive criticism and comments. The effectiveness of this feedback is dependent upon a sound working relationship.

In most organisations, coaching is done on an informal basis and is dependent on the boss having the inclination, time and motivation to do it, as well as possessing the necessary expertise and judgement for it to succeed.

Mentoring

Mentoring was described more fully in Chapter 7. It differs from coaching in two ways:

- The relationship is not usually between the individual and his or her immediate boss. An older, more experienced manager unconnected with the individual's immediate workplace is normally selected or agrees to act as mentor.
- Mentoring is about developing and sharing relationships rather than engaging in specific activities.

Mentoring represents a powerful form of management development for both the parties involved. For the individual, it allows them to discuss confusing, perplexing or ambiguous situations, and their innermost feelings and emotions, with somebody they can trust and respect. They gain the benefit of accumulated wisdom and experience from somebody who is knowledgeable and 'street-wise' in the ways of the organisation, especially its political workings. For older managers looking for new challenges and stimulation in their managerial role, mentoring represents an ideal development opportunity. It gives them an opportunity to achieve satisfaction and personal reward by sharing in the growth and maturity of another individual.

Projects and secondments

Project management is increasing in prominence as the role and function of a manager changes within an increasingly turbulent, uncertain and often ambiguous world (Coulson-Thomas, 1989; Dopson and Stewart, 1990). Managers are developing new skills and having to take on board new values (Rosenfeld and Wilson, 1999). Research by Ashridge Management College (Buchanan and Boddy, 1992) highlights the need to develop the notion of the 'flexible manager' who has the ability to:

- understand and relate to the wider environment;
- manage in that environment;
- manage complex, changing structures;

- innovate and initiate change;
- manage and utilise sophisticated information systems;
- manage people with different values and expectations.

One way to develop these attitudes and competences is to delegate responsibility for managing a cross-functional team of people, tasked with achieving a specific organisational goal within a fixed timescale and to a set budget. This cross-functional project management role not only improves core management skills such as communication and motivation but is also effective at developing 'higher order' diagnostic, judgmental, evaluative and political skills (Buchanan and Boddy, 1992).

Secondments are also increasingly being used for manager development. Multinational companies have highly sophisticated management exchange programmes that are used not only to develop important language and cultural skills in managers, but also to reinforce the organisation's central belief and value systems. Exchange programmes also exist between public and private sector organisations to transfer knowledge and broaden understanding. Some larger organisations are seconding their managers to various initiatives designed to assist small business ventures and community programmes.

Outdoor management development

In a climate and environment of greater risk, challenge, change and ambiguity for managers, increasing attention is focusing on the benefits of outdoor management development (OMD) as a development tool. OMD has its roots in the Outward Bound movement founded by Kurt Hahn (Burnett and James, 1994). The aim is to provide opportunities for personal growth and for managers to realise the potential of their 'inner resources' (Irvine and Wilson, 1994). In OMD, managers are exposed to emotional, physical and mental risks and challenges in which skills such as leadership and teamwork become *real* to the individuals and groups concerned (Burnett and James, 1994) and where 'the penalties for wrong decisions are painful; the consequence of bad judgements can be as real as being lost in a cold rainstorm at the edge of a dark forest' (Banks, 1994: 11). Others have likened OMD to 'outdoor action learning' in which 'the physical tasks at the core of outdoor development courses, whether they be abseiling down a cliff, climbing a mountain peak or navigating rapids in canoes are real tasks which present real problems to real people in real time with real constraints' (Banks, 1994: 9).

However, OMD has received considerable criticism in recent years, a great deal of it stemming from a controversial 1993 TV documentary from the Channel 4 *Cutting Edge* series, which featured a group of managers being 'damaged in body and mind' while on such a course (Banks, 1994). Others are critical of the degree of risk and adventure that managers *actually* experience, and argue that many of the claimed 'benefits' of OMD can be attained within existing development frameworks (Irvine and Wilson, 1994). Jones and Oswick (1993) identify a plethora of claimed benefits for OMD, many of which are anecdotal and unsubstantiated; where they are evaluated, there is evidence of bias when the evaluation is carried out by those who provide the training.

Management team development

With growing complexity and interdependence between functions and departments, many organisations wish to see their managers working together as a management team. This has led to a range of techniques designed to instil a sense of team spirit or *esprit de corps* among managers. Activities range from outdoor training to intensive workshops and game playing at informal residential venues. This enables them to get to

know their management colleagues as 'peopl[
(Margerison, 1991: 88). The aim is to build up a cl
erness and cooperation in achieving organisational

However, the rhetoric of management teamwork i
ity (Critchley and Casey, 1994). The assumption tha
when managers work as a team may be questionable
with achieving their own personal and departmental ¡
their colleagues does not necessarily mean cultivating
common purpose. Indeed, such a team-based philosoph
cal culture that often permeates management teams.

On some occasions teamworking can be beneficial a   ..ample
during a time of maximum uncertainty where there has t   ..g of ideas and
resources to arrive at common perceptions and possibilitie   ..u enable the organisation to make strategic decisions. But on other occasions, pushing managers into a
sharing, open, team-based culture can be counter-productive and a source of disillusionment for managers (Critchley and Casey, 1994).

Activity | **Management team-building**

The management team in a medium-sized manufacturing company was not performing effectively. There was evidence of a lack of trust and confidence in the team, and relationships
between individuals were poor. The managers were brought together in a series of workshops
and asked to examine their managerial role and how it related to other managers and staff. They
explored key issues and 'blockages'. After a short time it was realised that there were a number
of misperceptions and misunderstandings. The workshops also revealed confusion over roles and
responsibilities. An action plan was implemented to tackle these problems.

---

1 As management development manager, what steps will you take to ensure that the action plan
   is successfully implemented?

2 How would you measure the effectiveness of the action plan?

Self-development

Organisations that invest in effective management development programmes are
encouraging their managers to take more responsibility and control of their own development. As Boydell and Pedler (1981) remark:

> Any effective system for management development must increase the manager's capacity and
> willingness to take control over and responsibility for events, and participating for themselves in
> their own learning. (p. 3)

If managers take responsibility for their own development they are likely to:

- improve career prospects;
- improve performance;
- develop certain skills;
- achieve full potential/self-actualisation.

Organisations also benefit if they are willing to support their managers in self-
development (Temporal, 1984).

include:

- ...eased individual participation and commitment;
- ...greater flexibility in the face of change;
- greater visibility of individual strengths/weaknesses;
- cost-effectiveness – 'the DIY approach'.

A range of techniques exist for self-development. Some involve managers helping each other by sharing experiences in self-managed learning groups. Other approaches are more personally focused, using techniques such as distance learning materials, computer-based training and interactive videos. (For a fuller discussion of the methods used, see Pedler *et al.*, 1990).

INTERNATIONAL MANAGEMENT DEVELOPMENT

Starting in the 1980s and continuing through the 1990s, many organisations have sought to 'globalise' in their quest for greater market and product opportunities. A number of factors were responsible for this trend:

- favourable changes and improvements in the world political and social situation (EU, Eastern Europe);
- advances in technology and transport (communication, computing, air travel);
- greater cooperation between countries (joint ventures, e.g. in aerospace);
- a range of incentives to encourage inward investment to create job opportunities (Japanese car and electronics production in the UK).

These and other changes have encouraged organisations to expand into areas previously not considered. As a result, a number have become truly multinational organisations. For example, 39% of Ford Motor Company's employees now work outside the USA, and 43% of ICI's employees work outside the UK (Phillips, 1992).

For managers working in these organisations, there has been a major transformation in managerial work and managerial careers. This gives rise to a number of questions:

- To what extent does the concept of management move easily across international boundaries?
- Are we seeing the appearance of the 'truly' international manager?
- What skills and knowledge do managers need to develop to enable them to work and survive in a global marketplace?
- How do you develop international managers?

Management as an international concept

In this section we shall examine the development of international managers. You should read and study this section in conjunction with Chapters 15–17, which deal with the topic of international HRM.

However, there are methodological and conceptual issues and controversies connected with studying HRM from an international perspective. Of particular relevance to this section are issues connected with the lack of accurate and longitudinally focused data; diversity in language and culture leading to variations in meaning and interpretation; and a tendency to generalise from specific data sources, which makes any comparison between countries difficult. For example, you might ask yourself how far it is feasible or sensible to consider management as a concept that can move freely across international boundaries. There is some evidence to suggest that certain aspects of management are starting to converge, for example a shared technical language, and certain HR practices such as job evaluation and staff appraisal (Brewster and Tyson, 1992). Phillips (1992: 40) describes the success of global teams using concepts derived from the USA.

However, others argue that it is *divergence* not *convergence* that is taking place. National cultural diversity (residual effects of history, beliefs, values, attitudes, religion and language) is a key determinant in influencing management behaviour, and 'these differences may become one of the most crucial problems for management – in particular, for the management of multinational, multicultural organisations whether public or private' (Hofstede, 1990: 392). This view is supported by others such as Hansen and Brooks (1994) who observe that, while structures and technologies may converge, 'cultural factors influence management models, thinking styles, career expectations, organisational culture, change efforts and instructional needs and development' (p. 70).

> A French manager working in a subsidiary of an American corporation that insisted upon an open-door policy may well leave his office door open – thus adjusting to the behavioural requirements of the corporate culture – without any modification whatsoever to his basic concept of managerial authority.
>
> (Laurent, cited in Hansen and Brooks, 1994: 57)

The issue of cultural diversity is an important one because management development itself must be considered to be 'embedded' in national cultural forms that, together with other social, economic and political factors, determine the nature, philosophy, practice, priorities and focus of management development in different national contexts. Some of these contexts will be explored shortly.

In a sense, it might be argued that diversity poses a challenge to some of the rhetoric that surrounds notions of 'global villages' and 'global market places'. For instance, in countries such as China, South Africa and those in Eastern Europe that have undergone major economic and social disruption and upheaval, the quest for growth and stability has seen the importation of Western concepts of business and management, especially those associated with management development. But as you will see shortly, although the demand for management development in these regions is becoming very strong, 'implanting' these Western concepts is often problematical for the host country. As the quality circles example below suggests, the problem of transfer is just as likely to be felt by Western countries.

Quality circles: a case of convergence or divergence?

A number of UK organisations 'imported' and adapted the concept of *quality circles* from Japanese organisations during the 1980s and used it as an HRM technique. (It is interesting to note that the Japanese developed quality circles from 'imported' American ideas about quality during the 1950s!)

What is a quality circle?

A group of four to twelve people coming from the same work area, performing similar work who voluntarily meet on a regular basis to identify, investigate, analyse and solve their own work-related problems. The circles present solutions to management and are usually involved in implementing and later monitoring them.

(Russell and Dale, 1989)

Proponents of quality circles claim that, although the idea was imported, it is not 'culture bound'. For instance, Russell (1983) quotes Dr Ishikawa, a Japanese authority on quality circles:

> I am convinced that quality circle activities have no socio-economic or cultural limitations. Human beings are human beings wherever they live, and quality circle activities can be disseminated and implemented anywhere in the world for human benefit. (p.3)

There is a case history of some success with quality circles in Western economies, especially among Japanese companies who have located in the UK and those that are competing with them, i.e. the UK car industry. However, there is also evidence of resistance and failure (Russell and Dale, 1989; Brennan, 1991; Miller and Cangemi, 1993; Redman *et al.*, 1995). One of the main factors seems to be 'cultural dissonance', where the underlying philosophy of quality circles (greater employee involvement, more responsibility and a reduction of managerial control) 'clashes' with countervailing UK managerial philosophies. The UK is not alone in experiencing difficulties; similar problems with quality circles have occurred in France (Barsoux, 1990).

How far such clashes are a result of a failure to adapt organisational cultures (that is, to develop management styles that are supportive to quality circles) and how far they stem from a more fundamental, deep-rooted rejection by managers on the grounds that such ideas are at odds with wider sociocultural values and belief systems is not clear. It may be that some UK managers are adhering to an 'elitist' view of management and a 'manager's right to manage' derived from their education and life experiences in a *national* rather than organisational culture. However, one thing is clear: if resistance is due to managerial attitudes and belief systems, then management development must respond with new ideas and approaches that tackle these deeper social and cultural impediments.

Some different perspectives on management development

International management development can be viewed from a number of different perspectives:

- global;
- international;
- European;
- Western imported.

Global

Some have argued that managers can be developed to overcome and transcend the barriers of national culture and identity through the creation of *microworlds* (McBride, 1992). Here, the focus is on creating a strong and influential organisational culture that can be transported across the world to operate within any national cultures, and into which managers of all nationalities can be developed. As Stumpf *et al.* (1994) observe, 'they must manage diversity *less* by appreciating and utilising national and cultural differences and more by establishing an organisational culture which *transcends* those differences' (p. 16). A good example of such organisations might be the McDonald's and Pizza Hut food chains. The development of truly global managers involves careful attention to behavioural simulations in which there is an effort to replicate real-life situations through the extensive use of analytical exercises, business games and discussions, which enable managers to develop 'shared visions and mental models' and equip them with appropriate 'culture shaping skills' (McBride, 1992; Stumpf *et al.*, 1994). However, such global approaches may run into problems when they fail to address the tensions that are created by corporate politics and the clashes between corporate and national cultures that emerge after takeovers or acquisitions (Ferner, 1994).

International

Much of the international management development literature is dominated by a Western international perspective. Here, the strategic goal of transnational/multinational organisations such as Philips and Unilever is to develop elite 'cadres' of international managers who are tasked with building efficient networks of organisations operating across national boundaries (Bartlett and Ghoshal, 1989; Handy and Barham, 1990; Barham and Oates, 1991).

Most organisations aim to develop one or more of the following types:

- local nationals to manage locally (host);
- managers who live abroad and run overseas divisions or companies (expatriates);
- managers or short missions or projects (sales teams, plant installation);
- managers who work across national boundaries (Euro-manager, Middle East).

Research has shown that, in the past, UK companies have tended to use expatriate managers to retain control and safeguard their investment (Rosenfeld and Wilson, 1999). However, more recent research suggests that many managers in the USA and UK are 'simply not global animals', and this may mean that a multinational's ability to disseminate its corporate strategy overseas is contingent upon its individual managers' propensity to adapt (Ferner, 1994: 91).

What, then, are the skills and knowledge required to operate as an international manager, and how might these be developed? Phillips (1992) argues that international managers must demonstrate skills in the following areas:

- technical skills and experience often beyond those normally required at home, for example the engineer who needs sound financial management skills;
- people skills – cultural empathy, team-building and interpersonal skills;
- intellectual skills – seeing the big picture, and thinking in a macro not micro way;
- emotional maturity – being adaptable, independent, sensitive, self-aware;
- motivation – drive, enthusiasm, stamina and persistence.

Successful development of the international manager is often predicated on the establishment of clear international management development policies supported by and integrated with an appropriate international manager selection, recruitment, appraisal, career and reward infrastructure (Harzing and Van Ruysseveldt, 1995). Development activities themselves are primarily based on education, language skills, secondments, exchanges, projects and action learning programmes, with a heavy emphasis on cross-cultural training that is designed to 'get beyond the home country mentality' (Handy and Barham, 1990) and engender a new level of cultural awareness: 'management development must contribute to the creation of a new corporate culture and a new managerial mind-set' (Barham and Oates, 1991). Increasingly, the evidence suggests that the failure of foreign assignments may be rooted in emotional and family circumstances rather than personal capabilities, and growing attention is now being paid to including partners and families in the preparation and training process to prepare them for life overseas (Harzing and Van Ruysseveldt, 1995: 221).

GrandMet's approach to management development is founded on an active interventionist approach to careers in which the individual must agree to 'mortgage' any short-term career considerations. Started in 1988, the 'cadre' programme aims to send young managers of high potential on international assignments before ultimately placing them in senior management positions in their home countries. At any one time there are 12–15 managers of 25–30 years of age sent on a maximum of four assignments each lasting 18–24 months. Selection is via a rigorous assessment process designed to detect 'international traits'. The process is designed to flush out any prejudices that might hinder a manager from adjusting to an unfamiliar culture.

(Barham and Oates, 1991)

European

As monetary, economic and social convergence and cooperation across Europe are seen to be growing, attention is now being focused on the 'Europeanisation' of management and, more recently, on how to develop what might be termed a *Euro-manager*. This is seen as an essential requirement if Europe is to be properly equipped to fend off the competitive challenges posed by the USA and Japan, and more recently by the 'tiger' economies of Taiwan, Singapore and Malaysia (Tijmstra and Casler, 1992).

However, any notion of a Euro-manager has to be located within Europe's rich and diverse set of social and cultural contexts. For the proponents of the Euro-manager concept, any lack of homogeneity created by such diversity need not necessarily represent a barrier. Indeed, it is argued that any barriers may be overcome through effective management development programmes that focus on and emphasise an understanding of the European business environment and European management dynamics (Tijmstra and Casler, 1992). Barriers may also be overcome through greater cooperation, sharing and integration in the field of management education and research (Easterby-Smith, 1992). And Fox (1992) argues that in the long term such a lack of homogeneity may be an advantage to European managers because it will develop cultural tolerance and understanding.

Others take a more cautious view. Hilb (1992) argues that there are major disparities in selection, appraisal and reward systems across Europe, and that management development is neither strategically orientated nor properly evaluated. Additionally, HRD practices in general are too heavily influenced by variations in national labour markets, cultures and legislative frameworks. Kakabadse and Myers (1995), studying 959 chief executives in Europe, found wide variations in terms of management orientation across a number of criteria that are predicted to have implications for management development. For Thornhill (1993) any move towards Europeanisation raises significant issues for management trainers, who have to contend with variations over job content, context, expectations, experiences and work-related values. Hilb (1992) reports the following statistics:

- Job rotation is used in 32% of Italian firms but only 8% of French.
- Career high-fliers are identified in 44% of French firms but only 22% of German.
- Assessment centres are used in 22% of UK firms but only 3% of Norwegian.
- In Swiss organisations 66% of promotions are internal but only 31% in Danish.

Thurley and Wirdenhuis (1991) also point out these cultural and other national variations, arguing that the concept of the Euro-manager will be relevant only in certain industrial contexts. Storey (1992) identifies managerial parochialism and the lack of a European 'mindset' as a barrier, concluding that:

The notion of the Euro-manager may not quite be a myth but the extent to which there is a clear conceptual and practical difference between this species and the international manager is open to question.

(p. 2)

Western imported

This final perspective refers to those countries that have sought to import Western and Japanese ideas and approaches to management development. There are a number of reasons for this. Management development may be seen as a vehicle for speeding up industrial development (China). It may be used to aid recovery after major social and political upheaval (Eastern Europe, South Africa) or, in the case of Third World countries (Latin America, Africa, India), it may be linked to geopolitical and economic efforts to survive in what for them is an increasingly competitive, even hostile world.

In summary, it is clear there are different perspectives on the way in which international management development is viewed. Thus, for those involved in the development of international managers, the issue remains a fundamental one: how to develop managers in a context where 'cultural factors influence management models, thinking styles, career expectations, organisational culture, change efforts, and international needs and development' (Hansen and Brooks, 1994: 70). Such considerations will become apparent in the next section when we review the development approaches in different countries.

Management development: a Cook's tour?

In this section you will embark on a brief tour of management development in different countries. You will recall the point made earlier, that any 'universal' comparison between the ways in which each country develops its managers is difficult, mainly because they cannot be separated from the cultural, social and economic context in which they are located. This will become even clearer as the 'tour' progresses.

United States/United Kingdom

In respect of management development, both the USA and the UK are very similar in their approach. Development is viewed as a separate, discrete and heavily individualised activity, aimed at correcting identified 'weaknesses' in skills and knowledge or 'deviances' in individual attitudes and behaviour. A rational-functional philosophy dominates, which views the main justification of any development programme as being its contribution to business strategy and performance (Lees, 1992). Increasingly, the aim is to develop generalist managerial rather than narrow specialist skills to improve mobility and the ability to take on new assignments and challenges (Heisler and Benham, 1992). Development in the past has often been synonymous with management education and/or short, intensive training courses. In both countries attention is now focused on competence-based approaches. In the UK such approaches are institutionalised and championed through initiatives such as the Management Charter Initiative (see Chapter 8 for more details). However, as we have seen in this chapter, there is now a growing emphasis on more holistic, contextual forms of development that are experientially based, such as action learning projects, coaching and mentoring.

Europe

In contrast to the Anglo-Saxon described model above, many continental European approaches have in the past been less concerned with management development as a discrete activity. In France, for example, the development of managers is linked more closely to its social and historical context. Rather than management being something that can be explicitly developed in individuals, it is perceived as 'more a state of being' (Lawrence, 1992). Those who become managers form part of a social elite (*cadre*), and much of their development begins within the higher education institutions (*grandes écoles*), where the study of natural sciences and mathematics predominates.

In Germany, the approach is much more functional, with specialist expertise, especially in engineering and science, being closely linked to the vocational system of education. Again, there is a weaker concept of management, which is less likely to be considered as something separate and instead is seen as part of the overall functional system. Managers have less mobility than in the USA/UK, tending to stay in their functional role much longer. There is therefore less need for generalist skills development. Discrete management development activity is seen as less salient, and does not flourish to the same extent (Lawrence, 1992). Where there is management teaching, Germans tend to favour 'structured learning situations with precise objectives, detailed assignments and strict timetables' (Hill, 1994).

Despite their relatively weak tradition in explicitly focused forms of management development, both France and Germany are beginning to establish institutions specifically aimed at developing managers. For example, there has been an apparent explosion of MBA activity in Germany and France (Easterby-Smith, 1992), and in France there is a belated emergence of US-style business schools (Hill, 1994). Additionally there are European initiatives such as ERASMUS designed to promote the exchange of European business and management students between educational institutions.

Japan

A great deal of attention has been focused on the prowess of Japanese management practice on the world stage. This success may have as much to do with social and cultural factors as it does with the way Japanese managers are developed, since the two are inextricably linked. For Japanese managers, the experience of development is much more likely to be a long-term affair rather than the short-term, 'sink-or-swim' approach that characterises the Anglo-Saxon countries. In Japan there is a strong foundation of individual loyalty to the organisation, and an emphasis on providing job security for employees. The approach to development is likely to be much more systematic, structured and carefully planned (Neelankavil, 1992). Whereas Anglo-Saxon models stress individualism and development through short, intensive bursts of training to prepare managers for assignments characterised by challenge and risk, Japanese development programmes are longer and more culturally reflective in focusing on collectivism and group/team effort. The influence of role models is also strong. Unlike the USA/UK, where management development is in the hands of specialists, the Japanese view the relationship between the individual and the boss as a significant factor in developing the manager. The aim is to nurture growth, loyalty, commitment and retention (Storey *et al.*, 1991).

Central Europe

The main force driving the development of managers in countries such as Russia, Poland, Hungary and Romania is the rapid transition from a centrally planned to a market-based economy. As Vecsenyi (1992) observes, there are no 'road maps' in respect of management development, and it is often carried out in an atmosphere of crisis. The aim has been to import ready-made Western models to provide know-how and practical skills. In Russia, for example, management education is booming, and demand massively outstrips supply as the country struggles to adapt to major economic, social and political upheavals. However, in a number of cases Western models have been found wanting as they have failed to adapt to local conditions, and there is a lack of infrastructure to support managers who wish to implement their newly acquired skills. Similarly, there is a lack of congruence between what is being taught and the state of the economy (Kwiatkowski and Kozminshi, 1992). Recent evidence suggests that, in general, Western 'recipes for success' fail because they do not take into account the context confronting them, they lack strategic credibility, and they have not responded to the variations in learning styles of Eastern European managers (Lee, 1995; Redman *et al.*, 1995). Interestingly, it has been suggested that Western-style management development may be at a crossroads. Taking a pessimistic outlook, Western-orientated business schools may be accused of contributing to rampant capitalism, engendering resentment, but if they can adapt they may contribute positively to a more sophisticated economic infrastructure, changing social attitudes, and new forms of political decision-making (Puffer, 1993).

Hong Kong and People's Republic of China (PRC)

In both countries, there are two concerns: the economic expansion of the PRC and the reintegration of Hong Kong with the PRC's rule since 1997. Strategically, management development has been concerned with meeting both concerns.

In China there is a massive shortage of managers, and management training has become a national imperative as the country opens itself up to global markets and Western capitalism. Like other countries, China has experienced the problems of discrepancies between the models of Western management development and Chinese culture and society. For example, many imported Western models of management development are based on techniques such as group discussion and classroom participation, with an emphasis on reflection and abstract reasoning and a free and open critique and challenge of ideas and assumptions. However, in Chinese culture there is a strong emphasis on collective ideals, conformity, social status, the need to preserve 'face' and self-esteem, the unchallenged position of the 'expert' and associative rather than abstract reasoning, all of which militate against the adoption of Western models (Bu and Mitchell, 1992). The preference is for more didactic development methods such as formal management courses. Experiential methods are almost unheard of (Kirkbridge and Tang, 1992).

In Hong Kong, the approach to management development is similar in many respects to that found in the PRC. However, in recent years, Western management education and know-how have been sought by managers in Hong Kong to provide them with the adaptive, flexible skills and knowledge they will require as they handle the transition to Chinese rule and the challenges of the Confucian, bureaucratic, centralising society that now confronts them (Chong *et al.*, 1993).

More recently, Far Eastern economies have had to cope with an unprecedented economic downturn that has forced them to shed labour and rationalise their organisational structures. This has posed a further challenge for management development, especially in how to develop managers to deal with the human resource issues raised by such events.

South Africa

In broad terms, the challenges facing those involved in management development in South Africa are not dissimilar from those found elsewhere. The country has undergone massive social and political upheaval in recent years. However, the issue currently confronting the country is how to use management development as a tool to overcome major societal gulfs in respect of the disadvantaged black majority and the well-educated white minority: for example, 50% of the black population is illiterate, and only 2–3% of middle managers and 1% of senior managers are black (Templer *et al.*, 1992).

The need therefore is to 'South Africanise' development through a more holistic, integrative approach that unifies the country by providing and sharing opportunities. This has involved a strategy of educating black managers and then coaching them and allowing them to practise their management skills in the workplace. However, there are problems in transferring newly acquired skills to the workplace, as existing structures and cultures deny black managers access to experiential learning opportunities. The situation is forecast to remain largely unchanged until there is a 'critical mass' of black managers who can take on the coaching role (Templer *et al.*, 1992).

Third World

For those countries in the Third World (Latin America, India, Africa) management development faces yet another set of challenges as it is used as a stimulus to growth and survival in a more competitive global marketplace. However, the barriers are invariably rooted in the multicultural, multiracial and multi-religious context that characterises many Third World countries. Again, the individualised Western model of management development may not be appropriate in those societies seeking greater synergy and cohesion, and where culturally attuned models are preferred – for example in Africa, where the need is for approaches that stress group solidarity rather than self-development (Srinivas, 1995). Although much use is made of Western ideas, their use requires sensitivity. There is also the issue of dependency, where decisions have to be made about when to cut the umbilical cord and allow managers in these countries to face the realities of global competition (Srinivas, 1995).

To conclude this section, you have seen that there is a considerable and growing interest in developing the skills and mindsets of the 'global' or 'international' manager. There is also a desire by many countries across the world to import Western (mainly Anglo-Saxon) conceptions and models of management development and utilise them as powerful tools in their quest for social and economic transformation and renewal. However, you will have noted that, although Western models are considered by many to be dominant across the world, efforts to import them by different countries have not been entirely successful. This reinforces a point made earlier, that there is growing evidence to suggest that management development cannot easily be removed or separated from the wider cultural, social, political and economic context in which it is embedded and which it shapes and is shaped by (Hansen and Brooks, 1994). It therefore becomes clear that any development policy, activity or programme is likely to be more effective if it is made *contingent* upon the unique set of circumstances that confronts it.

CONTROVERSIAL ISSUES

The development of managers, like so many aspects of organisational life, is surrounded by debate and controversy. If we accept the notion that managers play a pivotal role in human resource management in the sense that they contribute to the creation of its 'reality' and are a means through which it is shaped and enacted, then such debates and controversies cannot be ignored.

In this section, a number of the more significant contemporary issues and controversies will be reviewed. It is not intended to discuss them at great length, merely to illuminate important aspects of the debate. Further reading is indicated at the end of the chapter.

To what extent is management development a rational process?

Different attitudes and degrees of awareness with regard to management development will exist at different levels within the organisation and will influence the approach that is adopted. For instance, there might be a lack of knowledge, awareness or vision about the benefits of engaging in any management development, and it is therefore deemed a low-priority goal. There may be fear on the part of senior managers that by developing more skilled and knowledgeable middle managers they are somehow undermining their power and status (Hopfl and Dawes, 1995). Development may be constrained and attract little enthusiasm from middle managers because they cannot find the time, or – in a similar fashion to their senior manager colleagues – they may view the development of their junior managers as posing a threat to their own position and job security. Junior managers may have a very positive attitude to development, but development efforts focused on meeting their needs are often undermined by a lack of awareness or even hostility on the part of their boss about the need to create opportunities for them to transfer knowledge into the workplace to gain practical experience (Roberts and McDonald, 1995). In some cases, individual managers may simply fail to recognise or choose to ignore the need for learning, or they may see development as unnecessary for them. Such views often arise because of a lack of management education or the fear of implied incompetence if they seek development, especially with senior managers (Tovey, 1991: 69).

But resistance may also be generated by the different and often competing rationales that organisations and individuals use to justify their engagement in development activity. Thus far, this chapter has suggested that the primary rationale for developing managers is 'to directly improve managerial functioning and thereby corporate performance' (Lees, 1992). This requires a range of interventions to be employed by management development professionals in a systematic and logical fashion. For example, a range of pseudo-scientific techniques are devised to select managers, such as assessment centres. Formalised education and training programmes are used to impart theory and practical skills. Assessment of competence may be against a range of standardised academic and vocational criteria, often linked to a qualification. Performance management systems are used to provide feedback and to reward what are deemed the 'right' attitudes and behaviour patterns. Developing managers in this formalised, functional fashion offers a number of benefits. For instance, it enables organisations to maintain a clear focus on business objectives, and it provides a coherent framework of agreed standards and consistency of approach.

However, management development may be driven by rationales that relate to social, political, emotional, legitimatory, psychic or symbolic needs and motives. As Lees (1992) points out, these rationales

> are often given insufficient attention in management development being ignored or dismissed as insignificant. Yet their importance in making managers feel whole, rather than simply corporate functionaries with enhanced competencies, is immense. (p. 104)

Lees argues that any combination of rationales may operate at any given moment, which suggests that management development will mean different things to different managers at different times in different contexts. This is clearly demonstrated in

Salaman and Butler (1990), where managers were adopting seemingly irrational attitudes to their learning and development. For example, management learning was felt to be legitimate only if it enhanced their power, status and reward within a particular structure and culture, and had nothing to do with organisational strategies or goals. It is clear therefore that those responsible for development have to remain alert to the existence of different, often competing rationales, and this reinforces the need for managers and management development professionals to take a much more holistic, contextual approach in planning and implementing their programmes.

Developing political skills

Managers are employed by organisations to 'get things done through people' (Torrington *et al.*, 1994). Managers 'make things happen' (Lee, 1987). However, getting things done and making things happen within an organisation are rarely simple or straightforward tasks. As well as technical, human and administrative problems, managers are confronted by 'political' factors. They have to contend with 'obstacles' such as:

- competition for scarce resources;
- conflicting viewpoints and priorities;
- confrontation with coalitions of vested interests;
- managing ambitious and self-interested individuals.

There is a growing view that for managers to cope and, more importantly, to survive in an organisation they have to become 'politically competent'. As Baddeley and James (1987) point out, 'political and survival skills are likely to become increasingly prized amongst managers' (p. 4). Buchanan and Boddy (1992) argue that managers can only be effective if they engage in 'backstage' activities such as 'politicking and wheeler dealing' (p. 29).

To achieve political competence it is argued, managers must first understand the nature of power in organisations: the ability to make things happen (Lee, 1987). They must be aware of how power manifests itself, its sources, and how it is used. They need to understand the way political strategies and tactics are formulated and how they are used by various 'actors' (Ryan, 1989). They must develop an awareness of political context: the rules of the game, individual actors' power bases, relationships and coalitions, and political agendas (Lee, 1987).

But if political competence is required to get things done, why does the teaching of political skills scarcely feature on the majority of mainstream management development programmes? There are a number of possible explanations.

Lee (1987) suggests it may be because political behaviour carries connotations of being 'bad', 'dishonest', 'subversive', 'dysfunctional'. Baddeley and James (1987) point to different viewpoints about the need or practicality of developing political skills, or a link with the (sometimes distasteful) activities and behaviours of local and national politicians. Baddeley and James (1990) suggest that teaching organisational politics to managers is an admission that the 'rational' system of resolving problems and making decisions has failed.

Whatever the reason, there is now a growing realisation that managers require some measure of political competence and awareness (Buchanan and Badham, 1999). This absence of politics on development programmes, which tend to be politically neutral, is generating frustration and confusion in managers, who find difficulty in relating or applying what they learn to the 'reality' of managing back in the workplace (Baddeley and James, 1990). Political behaviour has implications for organisational effectiveness. However, there is often incongruity between 'acceptable' political behaviour and the nature and reality of political processes (Ryan, 1989).

In other words, a politically competent manager can contribute to organisational effectiveness. Equally, politically incompetent managers can hamper and 'damage' organisations as well as themselves.

To what extent can political skills be taught? A number of commentators suggest they can. Lee (1987) argues that managers can improve their political skills by analysing the process, tactics and the context of political activity. Kakabadse and Parker (1984) suggest a psychological approach that focuses on the differences in people and the way people interact. Baddeley and James (1987) identify key models of political behaviour around which role play and discussion can centre. Ryan (1989) and Lees (1992) suggest that conventional management development programmes are already 'political' in promoting certain ideologies and practices. For Buchanan and Badham, (1999) the management development agenda for developing political competence should comprise: first, the *skills and knowledge to implement change,* which may be qualitatively different from those required in an operational role; second, *a behavioural repertoire* that is focused on learning to play the 'turf-game', for example in deploying political strategies offensively and/or defensively; and finally, being able to bring to bear *a reflexive practitioner's perspective* that 'involves deploying a range of knowledge and experience in a creative, improvisatory, contextually appropriate and self-critical manner' (p. 227).

Activity   **A case of political incompetence?**

An experienced middle manager was seconded to manage a major project. The project team was effectively managed and a feasibility study carried out on time and within budget. The manager circulated copies of the team's report to the board of directors and arranged a presentation. During the presentation it became obvious that the feasibility study was being seen as a threat by certain directors, who criticised it heavily and successfully blocked its recommendations. Amid much recrimination and argument, it was decided to shelve the report and disband the project team.

Where do you think this manager went wrong politically?

Activity   **A case of political competence?**

A new finance director joined a large manufacturing company and brought with him an experienced credit control manager with whom he had worked closely at his previous organisation. The close relationship continued in the new organisation. They put together a detailed proposal for sweeping changes in the finance function, which were designed to improve its overall efficiency.

After a number of months it became apparent that the finance director was having problems persuading his senior management colleagues to accept the fundamental changes contained in the proposal, and it was rumoured that his position in the organisation was under threat.

The credit control manager heard the rumours and decided to distance herself from the proposal by letting it be known that she disagreed with many of the changes. She also took steps to reduce the number of informal meetings held with the finance director and to communicate through formal memos.

Do you think this manager was being politically astute?

The ethics of management development

Like power and politics, the ethical conduct of management and the ethical frameworks used by developers have begun to attract attention, as examples of ethically questionable behaviour by certain managers have attracted widespread publicity: for example the 'fat-cat' syndrome surrounding some senior managers in large corporations and privatised utilities. There is now growing pressure and a rhetoric urging managers to behave 'ethically'; to manage their responsibilities in what is deemed an ethical fashion; to build trust; to be fair and equitable in their treatment of employees; and to respect their rights as individuals. This is prompting various governing institutions to issue guidelines and codes of conduct to managers designed to influence their behaviour.

Activity **Quality of working life (QWL)**

As a philosophy, QWL views people as 'assets' capable of contributing skills, knowledge, experience and commitment, rather than as 'costs' that are merely extensions of the production process. It argues that encouraging involvement and providing the environment in which it can flourish, produces tangible rewards for both individuals and organisations.

(Source: ACAS advisory booklet No. 16, 1991: 7).

What ethical dilemmas might confront a manager adhering to a QWL philosophy?

The Institute of Management, in its *Code of Conduct* and *Guides to Professional Management Practice*, states:

> The discharge of one's duties as a professional manager also involves the acceptance and habitual exercise of ethical values, among which a high place should be accorded to integrity, honesty, loyalty and fairness. But the Institute recognises that . . . it is usual for managers to encounter circumstances or situations in which various values, principles, rules and interests appear to conflict . . . no ready answer can be given for such conflicts.

We may ask ourselves: Is ethical conduct rarely taught on development programmes because there is actually nothing to teach? In other words, managerial work is so complex, ambiguous, and at times confusing, that it is not possible to legislate or create an all-embracing framework of moral competences (Snell, 1990). Reed and Anthony (1992) point to the dilemmas facing managers who subordinate their moral values to the notion of 'corporate good', and claim that, in such instances, 'simplistic' ethical rules and codes of practice may not be helpful to managers and serve only to create 'managerial cynicism' (p. 606).

Indeed, they raise the question of whether management education can improve management behaviour. They argue that it can, but it requires a more critically reflexive stance on the part of managers and those who teach them. Can we conclude, therefore, that it is up to individual managers to define and review their own ethical code of conduct and behaviour within the context of a given situation?

Whether or not a manager defines his or her own ethical conduct according to their personal values, or adheres to some external code of business ethics linked to their profession or organisation, it cannot be ignored that ethical conduct is an output of, among other things, the ideology of management developers. So should there be an ethical code to cover the behaviour of developers? Snell (1986) argues against such a code because of the disagreements, contradictions and dilemmas that arise in trying to define what is 'good' or 'bad' ethical conduct for developers. He argues that managers and developers should 'catch' and confront each other's conduct as it occurs, and discuss its legitimacy. But such a strategy is likely to be uncomfortable, and will rely upon a close relationship between developer and manager.

Managerial competences

In Chapters 7 and 8 you were introduced to the concept of competence-based forms of training and development within the framework of National Vocational Qualifications (NVQs). You were also introduced to some of the controversies that surround the notion of competence in the workplace.

Earlier in this chapter we examined competence-based approaches as they apply in the field of management development, and focused on the Management Charter Initiative (MCI) and its framework of national standards. We now turn to explore some of the controversial issues that surround the notion of management competence, and – as you will discover – there is a lively debate generating considerable controversy.

Since competences were introduced into HRD, they have attracted much criticism, at both a philosophical and a practical level. Philosophically, there has been a long-standing, fundamental disagreement about the whole basis on which competences were conceived and the way in which they are enacted. Some have drawn attention to the rational, functional, behaviourist orthodoxy that underpins competence-based training and development, which, ideologically, grew from the 'social efficiency' movement in the USA, and represents a form of 'social engineering' in which habitual behaviour is a key principle (Hyland, 1994). In the case of management development, this objection is particularly relevant as such a philosophical stance seemingly precludes a consideration of the more complex, innovative, creative elements that underpin managerial work, especially in a time of radical change (Jacobs, 1989). As Jacobs observes, although competence-based forms of management training and development can introduce more structure and discipline, they can only ever be a partial solution because they fail to deal with the softer, qualitative aspects of managing. This is even more acute in the case of managers who have to rely heavily upon others to achieve their goals. However, the whole basis of developing competence is focused on the individual and the clear understanding of the manager as leader rather than on any notion of developing 'collective competence' (Kilcourse, 1994).

This seems somewhat paradoxical given the massive surge in team-based working arrangements and empowerment, but perhaps it accounts for some of the problems encountered in these areas and discussed earlier in this chapter, such as manager hostility to initiatives such as quality circles.

Others have challenged the functional, reductionist, mechanistic approach and the extent to which it leads to an 'abstraction of reality', and have questioned how far competences can be generalised from a particular context (Collin, 1989; Stewart and Hamlin, 1992a; Loan-Clarke, 1996). For example, can you provide managers with a set of generic competences that they carry around like a 'toolkit' as in the case of MCI's national standards, or should competences be more contextually based, reflecting the changing needs of the organisation and the individual (Canning, 1990; Donnelly, 1991)? As Kilcourse (1994) remarks: 'competencies thought to have general application will fit where they touch when it comes to specific organisations' (p.14). Managers may be competent in one contextual setting, but will they be judged competent when faced with new challenges if and when they leave to take up a post in another organisation?

413

In a related area, another issue emerges. Buchanan and Boddy (1992), with reference to managers in the role of change agents, have argued that if you develop a 'toolkit' of competences you must develop the diagnostic, judgemental capabilities to use the 'tools' in different contexts – what they term *expertise*. Linked to this last point a further question emerges: How far can a competence approach be 'taught' to managers (Donnelly, 1991)? How far, for example, can you derive, develop and measure competences in areas such as interpersonal skills, creativity and innovation, strategic thinking, and the cognitive processes linked to decision-making and problem solving (Donnelly, 1991)? Kilcourse (1994) goes so far as to argue that during a time of radical change, when innovation and creativity are at a premium, competence-based forms of development may be the 'antithesis of what is required'. However, others would appear to disagree. Cockerill (1994) argues that, on the basis of work done at NatWest Bank, it is possible to identify 'high performance managerial competences, relevant to rapidly changing environments and flexible forms of organisation' (p. 74).

Some have argued that there may be too much emphasis on assessment and not enough on learning (CNAA, 1992; Loan-Clarke, 1996). This might be interpreted as a way of saying that the focus on practical, workplace outcomes is subordinating learning and understanding to the extent that the competence approach might be seen as almost anti-theory/anti-academic. There may therefore be a case for reasserting the role of established methodologies within the existing and expanding educational and vocational framework (Stewart and Hamlin, 1992b). However, many managers might argue (and regularly do) that the gulf between learning and knowledge and its application in the workplace still remains. Theory, it would seem, does not travel easily into the workplace, and competence-based management development is presented as one attempt to overcome this problem.

Could it therefore be that the issue is not one of competence (however defined) but in finding a way of bridging the theory/practice 'gap'? Should there be a review of the whole basis of development itself? For example, should institutions such as business schools be teaching management theory at all? It could be claimed that much of it is too generic, difficult to transfer to unique contexts, and rendered virtually meaningless in a time of radical change. Perhaps the focus should shift to managers becoming their own 'practical theorists' (Thomas, 1993). Should managers be encouraged to develop the higher-order, reflective competences to analyse, synthesise, judge and reflect on situations and events that confront them? This means a shift from a narrow rational-functional way of thinking about their role to a broader mindset that takes account of the wider social, moral, cultural and political relationships and interdependencies that have consequences for their actions (Reed and Anthony, 1992; Roberts, 1996).

At an operational, practical level, there are major concerns in respect of the way competence-based approaches are seen to operate, and many of these concerns carry over into management development (Stewart and Hamlin, 1992a). Empirical research, examining the effects of NVQ levels 3 and 4 programmes in a recently privatised organisation, seemed to confirm a great deal of this anecdotal evidence, and echoes many of the earlier concerns (Currie and Darby, 1995). The main issues can be summarised as:

- the way management competences were defined;
- their generic nature;
- a lack of attention to softer qualities;
- bureaucracy and cost;

- a lack of future orientation;
- the approach was not seen by managers to be developmental.

This last point is of some concern when the managers involved viewed the approach as formalising and confirming current levels of competence and not developing new skills. According to Currie and Darby, after two years the organisation concerned reintroduced traditional methods to supplement its competence-based approaches. The authors concluded that 'competence-based development is not a panacea for all management development ills but is one approach which may be taken with others' (p. 17).

In summary, despite the criticisms, it would appear that competence-based approaches have raised the profile of management development and are proving to be a useful input to the portfolio of methods available to developers. Earlier efforts to introduce (some would say impose) a national framework appear to be giving way to a much more pragmatic and flexible stance. More and more organisations appear to be developing their own models of management competences tailored to suit their specific needs and shorn of the unacceptable bureaucracy and cost (Mathewman, 1995). But this raises a new set of issues, not least how to maintain the integrity of the national standards and present a coherent national approach to management development, if that is what is required.

Problems in evaluating management development

If management development is to be effective in meeting individual needs and delivering organisation goals, the process must be evaluated to make judgements about its cost-effectiveness and to aid organisational learning and improvement (Easterby-Smith, 1994). Traditionally, the literature on evaluation has focused heavily on the training and education 'components' of development (Warr et al., 1970; Rae, 1986). Evaluation is concerned with the immediate training or educational 'event': measuring the inputs to the event, the process itself and immediate outcomes (see Figure 9.5). Measurement is against identified development needs and training objectives within the framework of a systematic training cycle (Harrison, 1997). There is often less concern with the longer-term impact and effects of the event or activity (Rae, 1986).

There are different approaches to evaluation. Some may be regarded as being objective, rigorous and scientific, while others are much more pragmatic, subjective and interpretative in orientation (Easterby-Smith, 1994). In collecting data, a range of quantitative and qualitative methods are normally employed (Smith and Porter, 1990; Easterby-Smith, 1994).

Methods include:

- in-course and post-course questionnaires;
- attitude surveys and psychological tests before and after the event;
- appraisal systems;
- observations by trainers and others;
- self-reports and critical incident analysis.

Whichever method or combination of methods is chosen, it is important to realise that evaluation does not take place in a vacuum. Judgements about the outcomes of management development programmes must be viewed within the context in which they are embedded. This immediately raises a number of political, cultural and social issues, which in turn generate considerable controversy for those involved in developing managers.

415

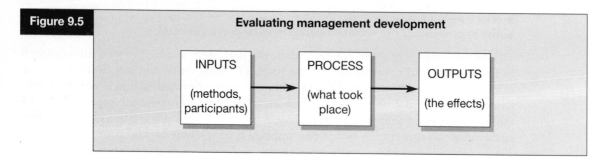

Figure 9.5　Evaluating management development

INPUTS
(methods, participants)
→
PROCESS
(what took place)
→
OUTPUTS
(the effects)

However, for some organisations, the proper evaluation of management development is rarely seen as a problem because they make little objective effort to carry it out anyway! Instead, it often becomes an act of faith for those involved. This may appear somewhat paradoxical if we assume that organisations are increasingly concerned about their cost base and overheads and yet fail to properly consider a significant bottom-line expenditure such as management development. It is even more paradoxical given that a failure to evaluate and justify such expenditure renders those who operate as development specialists vulnerable to cutbacks and job insecurity.

In attempting evaluation, a number of problems emerge. The first arises when the management development process itself becomes 'de-coupled' from the individual manager's unique context. This is often because providers are keen to find greater homogeneity and conformity in the way programmes and activities are designed and delivered (Mole, 1996). For the sake of efficiency and expediency, many providers are in the business of delivering programmes designed to provide off-the-shelf or 'canned solutions to organisational problems' (Roberts and McDonald, 1995). It therefore becomes the organisation's responsibility to select and utilise those programmes to meet both individual and organisational needs. In practice, a great deal of development activity then becomes 'commodified and standardised', with an almost mechanical reproduction of ideas and methods usually based upon the latest fad or flavour of the month. This gives rise to evaluation methodologies that are left striving to display some form of pseudo-scientific objectivity in an environment that is often highly complex and subjective (Smith, 1993; Mole, 1996). In other words, 'the complexity of management training and development demonstrates the point that measuring its effectiveness cannot be adequately accomplished by using a single, generic formula' (Endres and Kleiner, 1990).

A second set of problems emerges when the question is posed of what is being measured and how. In the case of management development, it is crucial that measurement incorporates emotional, attitudinal and behavioural changes alongside the measurement of harder aspects such as financial performance and technical competence. This necessitates the use of carefully constructed and focused methodologies incorporating ethnographic, interpretative techniques (Fox, 1989; Currie, 1994). But this presupposes that those tasked with evaluation have the time, commitment and skills to conduct research in these areas.

A third set of issues emerges to reflect the way in which management development is approached in organisations. Earlier in this chapter it was shown that a great deal of development is often isolated, fragmented, piecemeal and mechanistic, removed from the everyday reality of managing complex, rapidly changing organisations. It was argued that developers should adopt a more holistic, contextual approach in which internal and external influences such as structure, culture, politics and technology are considered to be integral features in the evaluation process, and, in effect, evaluation is seen to 'travel with the organisation' as it learns, adapts and renews itself (Smith, 1993). As Smith (1993) observes, 'management development programmes are not context free but dependent on the cultural baggage of the participants and the organisation' (p. 23).

This point is reinforced in another set of issues that revolve around the political dimension of evaluation. It is an inescapable fact of organisational life that, given its subjective and interpretative nature, evaluation will be rendered prone to bias and manipulation and become an arena for political 'games'. As Fox (1989) explains, 'because a pseudo-scientific approach does not deal with human issues and value judgements, it is not surprising that they fall into disuse or are simply done by token [then] politics takes over' (p. 192). Both Fox (1989) and Currie (1994) have examined the evaluation of management development programmes in the National Health Service and have concluded that political and cultural factors were influential: for example, there was a low value attached to management development, and responses were biased by people's fear for their positions. In the author's own experience of management development in the private sector, politics and culture do play a key role in evaluation: for example, efforts at 'impression management', 'eyewash' and 'whitewash' by external providers keen to secure future business; unsubstantiated and unsupportable claims for the 'success' of programmes; and evaluation findings that are 'doctored' to ensure that they meet senior management's expectations.

It therefore has to be assumed that the evaluation of management development will always be a difficult process so long as it involves human behaviour. In many organisations it is rarely carried out with any degree of enthusiasm or effectiveness, and so evaluation is often tagged on to development programmes, treated in a piecemeal fashion and concerned with immediate outcomes rather than examining wider systemic issues. A more systemic, holistic perspective of evaluation would examine the extent to which development activity fits with individual needs and organisational context; how far new behaviours can be applied in the workplace; and whether new behaviour corresponds with espoused organisational culture and values (Easterby-Smith, 1994; Mole, 1996). Questions must also be raised over the level of commitment to the evaluation processes shown by developers and sponsors alike, and to what extent they are perceived as capable or credible to conduct evaluation exercises. But are we asking too much? Is evaluation a chimera? As Easterby-Smith (1994) states:

> Thus attempts to evaluate development methods may fail to satisfy the purist, and much of this stems from the diffuseness of the target that is being examined and the difficulty of isolating procedures from the real constraints and politics of the organisations in which they are taking place.
>
> (p. 143)

Perhaps it is only if and when organisations wake up to the real and hidden costs of management development and its possible consequences for organisational learning and development that we shall see progress. Until then it is likely to remain an act of faith and a fertile playground for political games.

417

Activity	**Problems evaluating management development**

You are the personnel director of a medium-sized manufacturing company. You have had a hard task persuading your board colleagues that they should invest a considerable sum of money in a management development programme for middle managers to ensure succession and the continuing success of the business. However, they finally agreed to your request and the funds were made available a year ago.

The programme is now under way, and you have just reported progress to your colleagues. The operations manager, who fought against the programme a year ago because he wanted the money to install a new piece of plant, turns to you somewhat aggressively in a board meeting and says: 'This programme of yours has been running for a year now. In that time I could have saved this company considerable sums of money and increased both quality and revenue. What will you produce and when will we see some payback on our investment?' The rest of the board look expectantly in your direction.

How might you respond?

The progression and development of women managers

Women have traditionally been under-represented in UK management, but it is not easy to analyse the extent to which they are under-represented. The problem rests mainly with comparisons between different interpretations of the term 'manager' – defined in terms of work content and scope of responsibility (Davidson and Burke, 1994). In 1989 it was estimated that 44% of the UK labour force were women (this proportion was forecast to rise to some 50% by the year 2000), and yet only 11% of UK general management were women (Davidson, 1991). At chief executive level the picture was even bleaker, with only 1% senior management positions occupied by women (Davidson and Cooper, 1992).

More recent evidence seems to suggest an improving picture, with the proportion of women 'managers' approaching some 26% of the managerial workforce (Vinnicombe and Colwill, 1995). However, this figure appears to include all levels of management. Closer examination reveals a less rosy picture. Estimates vary, but it would seem that for middle managers the proportion is still around 8–10% of the managerial workforce (Woodall and Winstanley, 1998). And in respect of senior management positions, the situation has hardly improved at all since the 1980s. For example, a 1995 survey of some 300 enterprises in the UK revealed that only 3% of board directors were women, and in another cited study of 100 major companies it was estimated that only 4% of directors were women (International Labour Organization, 1997). It would seem that the so-called 'glass ceiling' seems stubbornly unbreakable at the higher levels of UK management.

A range of explanations are given for the increased proportion of women entering management in Western organisations. These include: better educational attainment; better access to training opportunities; and the removal of the more overt forms of gender discrimination in the workplace that have deterred or prevented women from entering management in the past (Larwood and Wood, 1995; Lewis and Fagenson, 1995). But there is less cause for celebration when we examine more closely the type of work that women managers are doing. Traditionally, women have suffered a degree of ghettoising in terms of their managerial roles. For example, women managers are concentrated mainly in the banking, retail and catering industries, at the lower managerial levels, and in the 'softer' areas such as personnel and customer service. Recent evidence suggests that this profile of roles has hardly altered, and progress out of the ghetto into more front-line, business-focused roles is slow (Ohlott *et al.*, 1994). Research also suggests a risk that women managers may find themselves caught in a vicious circle. Their very success in the softer roles may serve to stereotype them to remain in these roles. Where efforts are made to move them into front-line positions without adequate development there is a risk of creating a self-fulfilling prophecy. For example,

> putting a woman in a highly visible job she is unprepared for could result in visible confirmation of prejudice. The glass ceiling becomes real because in an effort to protect women, hiring managers do not give them the same challenges as men
> (Ohlott *et al.*,1994: 62)

What factors inhibit the development of women managers?

An early study by Ashridge Management College (1980) highlighted a number of key inhibitors:

- *Career factors and personnel systems*
  - Career paths to management are designed to fit the working life patterns of men (job mobility in early years, commitment to study and learning for advancement).
  - Many women were disqualified because of family commitments (career breaks to raise children).
  - Current selection, appraisal and training systems also inhibit women (asking for qualifications rarely held by women, no formal re-entry process after career breaks).
- *Women's attitudes and behaviour.* Women's lack of confidence in their perceived ability, and a belief that competence in their current job and technical ability were the sole criteria for advancement, were cited as significant inhibiting factors.
- *The attitudes of senior executives.* A 'kindly, protective' attitude by senior managers tending to concentrate women in jobs that were felt to be suitable for them (specialist roles and client contact roles).
- *Individual and organisational factors:* Prejudice, men seeing women as a threat, assumptions about women's capabilities, and organisations with poor management development systems.

Many of these inhibitors will be familiar to women managers, and are still commonly cited in the literature. More recent studies have added to the list. For example, Wentling (1992) highlights a lack of political 'savvy' and bosses who don't encourage development, while Grondin (1990) cites high expectations and misperceptions about career opportunities as barriers to women advancing in management. Flanders (1994) points to factors such as traditional work patterns, attitudes and prejudice, lack of role models and exclusion from the 'old boy network' as inhibiting women's progress.

What can be done to develop women managers?

Davidson (1991) makes the point that those organisations that fail to utilise the potential of women managers will be committing 'economic suicide'.

Apart from demographic and economic reasons, there are many potential benefits that women managers can bring to organisations, including participative, caring management styles (for an extensive list of costs/benefits see Fritchie and Pedler, 1984: 178).

Davidson (1991) argues that the first and perhaps the most important step that organisations can take is to encourage their managers (both male and female) to recognise and acknowledge masculine and feminine strengths and weaknesses and build these into development programmes. They should also realise that 'when comparing male and female managers in terms of managerial efficiency and performance, numerous cross-cultural studies and reviews have concluded that there are far more similarities than differences' (p. 8).

Other writers argue that organisations should aim for an increased cross-cultural perspective, where male and female managers learn to value each other's differences and aim to cooperate in their personal development to increase organisational effectiveness (Fischer and Gleijm, 1992; Whitaker and Megginson, 1992).

So what practical measures can be taken?

Much of the literature dealing with the development of women managers makes the point that the tasks facing men and women managers are similar but that women managers do face special difficulties. So what practical help/advice can be given? The literature contains many ideas and suggestions. The following list is by no means exhaustive:

- integrating women's development into mainstream HRD;
- mentoring/providing role models;
- reviewing childcare provisions;
- reviewing equal opportunities policies;
- auditing attitudes towards women;
- providing women-only training;
- encouraging women into management education;
- putting equality on the organisational agenda;
- reviewing selection/promotion/appraisal processes;
- promoting the networking of women;
- assertiveness training;
- moving women out of the 'ghetto' into front-line positions;
- career planning strategies for women;
- training before promotion.

It is clear from this list that the progression and development of women managers is complex, and will require a more strategic approach than has hitherto been the case. However, a cautionary note is sounded by Woodall and Winstanley (1998). They make the point that while these factors are indeed relevant, and a lack of attention to them may explain the underachievement of women in management, 'they are by no means universal'. Each factor may apply to different women in different organisational contexts at different times, and it is important that organisations carry out a 'prior analysis' before selecting any intervention. It is also important to ensure that any strategic approach to women's management development takes account of and deals with the wider structural and cultural impediments that continue to give rise to a more covert and often unconscious prejudice.

Paradoxically, and somewhat controversially, some commentators are beginning to argue that viewing women managers as requiring 'special' treatment may be exacerbating many of the problems they are experiencing. It is argued that while organisations should acknowledge the problems to which women managers are exposed, it should be in a less gender-focused way. Instead, development should seek to integrate women managers both socially and professionally with men in work-related activities (Snyder,

1993; Larwood and Wood, 1995). For Snyder, this means 'systematically and systemically attacking potential sources of segregation' (Snyder, 1993: 104). This suggests less concern with 'special' development arrangements such as women-only training courses – although these remain important. Instead, the focus should be on locating men and women as part of the organisation 'system' and analysing their strengths and weaknesses as individuals in the situational context in which they find themselves, irrespective of their gender, and developing them accordingly (Davidson and Burke, 1994). However, this will not be easy and, as Stead (1985) contends, will require a

> new and more comprehensive understanding [about development] . . . which can benefit both men and women. Business is finally realising that some areas of concern for women are also areas in which men have needed consideration all along. (p. 1)

SUMMARY

- The terms 'management' and 'manager' have different meanings within different contexts. The role and 'reality' of managing in organisations is often more complex, confusing and chaotic than many management texts would suggest.

- Management development is more than just management education and training. It involves the holistic development of the manager, taking account of such factors as: the needs, goals and expectations of both the organisation and the individual; the political, cultural and economic context; structures, and systems for selection, reward and monitoring performance.

- As part of an overall human resource strategy, management development is now identified by many organisations as a source of competitive advantage and one of the key ingredients for success. However, if management development is to be effective it must link to, and support, the organisation's business strategy. This enables those responsible for development to respond to the question, 'Why are you developing this manager?'

- Development programmes cannot be isolated from other organisational systems and processes in a series of 'piecemeal' approaches. An open systems perspective takes account of the interactions and dependences that exist between the organisation's context and management development programmes. An open systems approach offers a way of constructing a unified, integrated framework within which the organisation can organise and implement development programmes.

- Development is more effective when a stakeholder partnership exists between the individual, their boss and the organisation. A wide range of development techniques exist. The selection of the most appropriate techniques will depend upon the learning preferences and needs of managers. To be effective, development must reflect organisational context and the 'reality' of managerial work. An increasing reliance is being placed on the use of experiential techniques.

- Like many aspects of organisational life, management development cannot be isolated from controversy and debate. Areas of challenge, conflict, tension and ambiguity remain to be resolved.

Activity

The right approach?

As part of its strategic planning, an organisation decided to introduce a system of budgetary control to improve financial planning and control. A two-day course titled 'Finance for the Non-financial Manager' was arranged.

The course, although highly intensive, was delivered competently by an external consultant. However, some managers felt that the universal nature of the course meant that a lot of the content was not relevant to them. They were especially concerned because the course made only a passing reference to budgets. What they wanted was a course that would take them step by step through the process of preparing and administering a departmental budget.

Some managers pointed out that it would have made sense to consult them first and then develop a tailored course to suit both their and the organisation's needs. The course was therefore viewed as a waste of their time and the organisation's money.

1 What type of management development approach is indicated in this scenario?

2 Why might the organisation have approached management development in this way?

3 Imagine you are responsible for management development in the organisation. How would you respond to avoid the criticisms voiced by the line managers being repeated in the future?

QUESTIONS

1 What do you understand by the term 'management development'? Distinguish between management development, management education and management training.

2 To what extent does management development influence the human resource strategy in an organisation?

3 Who is responsible for management development? What are their roles and responsibilities?

4 What management skills and knowledge do international managers require? In what way do they differ from those required by UK managers?

5 'To survive in an organisation today, a manager must become a "political animal".' What are your views with regard to this statement?

EXERCISES

1 List the different methods and techniques used to develop managers. How would you judge and evaluate their effectiveness?

2 Organisations are increasingly turning to self-development as a management technique. Imagine you are the manager responsible for a group of young graduates about to embark upon your organisation's graduate development programme. Working in groups, discuss ways in which you might encourage them to adopt a self-learning culture.

Management Development in Mid-County NHS Trust

Introduction

Since the early 1990s, Mid-County NHS Trust has undergone radical and far-reaching change. The aim has been to improve the overall standard of patient care while at the same time increasing efficiency and reducing costs. To this end, the Trust set out to re-engineer its key structures, systems and processes. In 1994, it employed a firm of external change consultants who are acknowledged experts in the field of Business Process Re-engineering (BPR) and its BPR methodology was employed to act as a framework for change. It involved the systematic analysis, mapping and reconfiguration of key structures and processes to deliver cost and efficiency benefits.

To assist the consultants, the Trust identified staff from a range of professions across the organisation. These individuals were then seconded to work with the consultants on a full-time basis – acting in the role of internal change agents – and at any one time there were some 30 individuals in the re-engineering team. The team were coached and received extensive training in BPR from the consultants.

The implementation of redesigned processes and structures had a profound impact on the Trust. On a positive front, there were major improvements in the level of service and quality of patient care. But there were negative effects too. For a few individuals, change meant a loss of job. Others found their jobs radically redesigned, involving significant retraining – often for roles far removed from their existing jobs. Some individuals were demoted from their present roles.

Process management

One outcome of BPR was a radical reappraisal of the way the various Directorates were managed. To improve efficiency, the Trust created a new position of Process Manager. Process Managers as their name suggests were responsible for the patient care process from start to finish. Working alongside their clinical colleagues, their role was primarily to manage the operational and business elements of the process. Many of the newly promoted managers were ex-nursing staff or staff from occupational and support professions. Most had been involved as internal change agents in the BPR change process since its inception in 1994.

Shortly after occupying their new positions, it was clear that a sizeable minority of staff found coming to terms and dealing with managerial issues difficult. While most were competent in their profession, few had any prior managerial training. Areas such as strategic planning, budgets and finance, dealing with organisational politics and handling conflict were a burden and a strain. Some were also uncomfortable with the philosophy of their new role. They felt it took them away from their previously held 'caring' role.

Their views were communicated to the Trust's senior management who promised to initiate steps to improve the level of managerial capability among this key group.

Management development for process managers

The Trust found the resources and embarked on an urgent management development programme designed to develop the managerial skills required to operate in a more flexible and business-focused culture. It organised a series of in-house management training courses in core subjects delivered by a range of internal and external tutors. Details were circulated to the Process Managers and they were invited to put their names forward. The number of nominations received was lower than expected given the perceived scale of the 'problem'. When the courses were run, attendance was poor. When individuals were asked why they were not attending, most replied that they did not have the time. However, informally, a number questioned whether – given the changes they and the Trust had gone through – this was the right way to approach their management development. Few changes were made to the programme and eventually it was decided to terminate the programme and channel scarce resources into other training areas.

Recently, a firm of independent management consultants visited the Trust to review and evaluate the organisational change outcomes. They were highly critical of the management capabilities of some Process Managers. They felt that this lack of skills was severely hampering the anticipated benefits of the overall BPR change programme. They also commented unfavourably on the 'attitudes' of some managers whose view of their new role did not conform to the 'expected professional management behaviours'. They cited a lack of overall organisation ▶

and leadership, for example too much time spent concerned with non-managerial problems in a hands-on capacity.

Note: This case study is based on real events. Names have been altered to preserve confidentiality.

You are a member of the Trust's senior management team and have been asked by the Chief Executive to investigate this problem and design an overall strategy for improving the development of Process Managers.

1 Adopting a systemic view of the management development 'problem', what do you see as the main

issues to be explored in relation to the development of Process Managers?

2 How should the Trust address them?

Present your findings in the form of a short report/ presentation to your senior management colleagues.

REFERENCES AND FURTHER READING

Those texts marked with an asterisk are particularly recommended for further reading.

ACAS (1991) *Effective Organisations: The People Factor.* London: ACAS.

Ashridge Management College (1980) *Employee Potential: Issues in the Development of Women.* London: Institute of Personnel.

Baddeley, S. and James, K. (1987) 'Owl, fox, donkey or sheep: political skills for managers', *Management Education and Development,* Vol. 8, Pt 1, pp. 3–19.

Baddeley, S. and James, K. (1990) 'Political management: developing the management portfolio', *Journal of Management Development,* Vol. 9, No. 3, pp. 42–59.

Banks, J. (1994) *Outdoor Development for Managers,* 2nd edn. Aldershot: Gower.

Barham, K. and Oates, D. (1991) *The International Manager.* London: Business Books.

Barsoux, J.-L. (1990) 'Group behaviour in French business: quality circles à la française', in Wilson, D. and Rosenfeld, R. *Managing in Organisations.* London: McGraw-Hill.

Bartlett, C. and Ghoshal, S. (1989) *Managing across Borders: The Transnational Solution.* London: Hutchinson.

Boak, G. and Joy, P. (1990) 'Management learning contracts: the training triangle', in Pedler, M., Burgoyne, J., Boydell, T. and Welshman, G. (eds) *Self-Development in Organisations.* Maidenhead: McGraw-Hill.

*Boydell, T. and Pedler, M. (1981) *Management Self-Development.* Westmead: Gower.

Boydell, T. and Pedler, M. (1994) 'From management development to managing development: the changing role of the manager in the learning organisation', *Transitions,* Vol. 94, No. 9, November, pp. 8–9.

Brennan, M. (1991) 'Mismanagement and quality circles: how middle managers influence direct participation', *Employee Relations,* Vol. 13, No. 5, pp. 22–32.

Brewster, C. and Tyson, S. (1992) *International Comparisons in Human Resource Management.* London: Pitman.

Bu, N. and Mitchell, V. (1992) 'Developing the PRC's managers: how can Western Europe become more helpful?', *Journal of Management Development,* Vol. 11, No. 2, pp. 42–53.

Buchanan, D. and Badham, R. (1999) *Power Politics and Organisational Change: Winning the Turf Game,* London: Sage.

*Buchanan, D. and Boddy, D. (1992) *The Expertise of the Change Agent.* Hemel Hempstead: Prentice Hall.

Buckley, J. and Kemp, N. (1989) 'The strategic role of management development', *Management Education and Development,* Vol. 20, No. 1, pp. 157–174.

Burgoyne, J. (1988) 'Management development for the individual and the organisation', *Personnel Management,* June, pp. 40–44.

Burgoyne, J. and Stuart, R. (1991) 'Teaching and learning methods in management development', *Personnel Review,* Vol. 20, No. 3, pp. 27–33.

Burnett, D. and James, K. (1994) 'Using the outdoors to facilitate personal change in managers', *Journal of Management Development,* Vol. 13, No. 9, pp. 14–24.

Canning, R. (1990) 'The quest for competence', *Industrial and Commercial Training,* Vol. 22, No. 5, pp. 12–16.

Cannon, T. and Taylor, J. (1994) *Management Development to the Millennium.* Corby: Institute of Management.

Caulkin, S. (1994) 'Rewriting the rules', *Observer,* Sunday 25 September.

Child, J. (1969) *British Management Thought.* London: Allen & Unwin.

Chong, J., Kassener, M.W. and Ta-Lang Shih (1993) 'Management development of Hong Kong managers for 1997', *Journal of Management Development,* Vol. 12, No. 8, pp. 18–26.

Cockerill, T. (1994) 'The kind of competence for rapid change', in Mabey, C. and Iles, P. (eds) *Managing Learning.* London: Routledge.

Collin, A. (1989) 'Managers' competence: rhetoric, reality and research', *Personnel Review,* Vol. 18, No. 6, pp. 20–25.

Constable, J. and McCormick, R. (1987) *The Making of British Managers.* London: BIM/CBI.

Coulson-Thomas, C. (1989) 'Human resource: the critical success factor', *Leadership and Organisation Development Journal,* Vol. 10, No. 4, pp. 13–16.

Council for National Academic Awards (CNAA) (1992) *Review of Management Education.* London: CNAA.

Critchley, B. and Casey, D. (1994) 'Team-building', in Mumford, A. (ed.) *Gower Handbook of Management Development,* 4th edn. Aldershot: Gower Publishing.

Cunnington, B. (1985) 'The process of educating and developing managers for the year 2000', *Journal of Management Development*, Vol. 4, No. 5, pp. 66–79.

Currie, G. (1994) 'Evaluation of management development: a case study', *Journal of Management Development*, Vol. 13, No. 3, pp. 22–26.

Currie, G. (1999) 'Resistance around a management development programme: negotiated order in a NHS Trust', *Management Learning*, Vol. 30 No. 1, pp. 43–61.

Currie, G. and Darby, R. (1995) 'Competence-based management development: rhetoric and reality', *Journal of European Industrial Training*, Vol. 19, No. 5, pp. 11–18.

Davidson, M. (1991) 'Women managers in Britain: issues for the 1990s', *Women in Management Review*, Vol. 6, No. 1, pp. 5–10.

Davidson, M. and Burke, R. (eds) (1994) *Women in Management: Current Research Issues*. London: Paul Chapman Publishing.

*Davidson, M. and Cooper, C. (1992) *Shattering the Glass Ceiling: The Women Manager*. London: Paul Chapman Publishing.

Davis, T. (1990) 'Whose job is management development – comparing the choices', *Journal of Management Development*, Vol. 9, No. 1, pp. 58–70.

Donnelly, E. (1991) 'Management Charter Initiative: a critique', *Training and Development*, April, pp. 43–45.

Dopson, S. and Stewart, R. (1990) 'What is happening to middle managers?' *British Journal of Management*, Vol. 1, No. 1, pp. 3–16.

Dopson, S. and Stewart, R. (1993) 'Information technology, organisational restructuring and the future of middle management', *New Technology, Work and Employment*, Vol. 8, No. 1, pp. 10–20.

Doyle, M. (1995) 'Organisational transformation and renewal: a case for reframing management development?' *Personnel Review*, Vol. 24, No. 6, pp. 6–18.

Doyle, M. (2000) 'Management development in an era of radical change: evolving a relational perspective', *Journal of Management Development*, Vol. 19.

Dulewicz, V. (1991) 'Improving assessment centres', *Personnel Management*, June, pp. 50–55.

Easterby-Smith, M. (1992) 'European management education: the prospects for unification', *Human Resource Management Journal*, Vol. 3, No. 1, pp. 23–36.

Easterby-Smith, M. (1994) *Evaluation of Management Education, Training and Development*. Aldershot: Gower.

Endres, G. and Kleiner, B. (1990) 'How to measure management training and effectiveness', *Journal of European Industrial Training*, Vol. 14, No. 9, pp. 3–7.

Ferner, A. (1994) 'Multi-national comparisons and HRM: an overview of research issues', *Human Resource Management Journal*, Vol. 4, No. 3, pp. 79–102.

Fischer, M. and Gleijm, H. (1992) 'The gender gap in management', *Industrial and Commercial Training*, Vol. 24, No. 4, pp. 5–11.

Flanders, M. (1994) *Breakthrough: The Career Women's Guide to Shattering the Glass Ceiling*. London: Paul Chapman Publishing.

*Fox, S. (1989) 'The politics of evaluating management development', *Management Education and Development*, Vol. 20, Pt 3, pp. 191–207.

Fox, S. (1992) 'The European learning community: towards a political economy of management learning', *Human Resource Management Journal*, Vol. 3, No. 1, pp. 70–91.

Fritchie, R. and Pedler, M. (1984) 'Training men to work with women', in Hammond, V. (ed.) *Practical Approaches to Women's Management Development*. Brussels: European Foundation for Management Development.

Fulop, L. (1991) 'Middle managers: victims or vanguards of the entrepreneurial movement?' *Journal of Management Studies*, Vol. 28, No. 1, pp. 25–43.

Grondin, D. (1990) 'Developing women in management programmes: two steps forward and one step back', *Women in Management Review*, Vol. 5, No. 3, pp. 15–19.

Hales, C. (1993) *Managing Through Organisation*. London: Routledge.

Handy, C. (1987) *The Making of Managers*. London: MSC/NEDO/BIM.

Handy, L. and Barhan, K, (1990) 'International management development in the 1990s' *Journal of European Industrial Training*, Vol. 14, No. 6, pp. 28–31.

Hansen, C.D. and Brooks, A.K. (1994) 'A review of cross-cultural research on human resource development', *Human Resource Development Quarterly*, Vol. 5, No. 1, pp. 55–74.

Harrison, R. (1997) *Employee Development*, 2nd edn, London: IPM.

Harzing, A.-M. and Van Ruysseveldt, J. (1995) *International Human Resource Management*. London: Sage.

Heisler, W.J. and Benham, P. (1992) 'The challenge of management development in North America in the 1990s', *Journal of Management Development*, Vol. 11, No. 2, pp. 16–31.

Hendry, C. (1995) *Human Resource Management: A Strategic Approach to Employment*. Oxford: Butterworth-Heinemann.

Herriot, P. and Pemberton, C. (1995) *New Deals: The Revolution in Managerial Careers*. Chichester: John Wiley.

*Herriot, P. and Pemberton, C. (1996) 'A new deal for middle managers', in Billsberry, J. (ed.) *The Effective Manager: Perspectives and Illustrations*. London: Sage.

Hilb, P. (1992) 'The challenge of management development in Western Europe in the 1990s', *International Journal of Human Resource Management*, Vol. 3, No. 3, pp. 575–584.

Hill, R. (1994) *Euro-Managers and Martians*. Brussels: Euro Publications.

Hitt, W. (1987) 'A unified manager development programme', *Journal of Management Development*, Vol. 6, No. 1, pp. 43–53.

Hofstede, G. (1990) 'The cultural relativity of organisational practices and theories', in Rosenfeld, R. and Wilson, D. *Managing Organisations*. London: McGraw-Hill.

*Honey, P. and Mumford, A. (1986) *Manual of Learning Styles*, 2nd edn. Maidenhead: Peter Honey.

Hopfl, H. and Dawes, F. (1995) 'A whole can of worms! The contested frontiers of management development and learning', *Personnel Review*, Vol. 24, No. 6, pp. 19–28.

*Hyland, T. (1994) *Competences, Education and NVQs: Dissenting Perspectives*. London: Cassell Education.

International Labour Organization (1997) *Breaking Through the Glass Ceiling: Women in Management.* Geneva: ILO Publications.

Irvine, D. and Wilson, J.P. (1994) 'Outdoor management development: reality or illusion?' *Journal of Management Development,* Vol. 13, No. 5, pp. 25–37.

Jackson, D. and Humble, J. (1994) 'Middle managers: new purpose, new direction', *Journal of Management Development,* Vol. 13, No. 3, pp. 15–21.

Jacobs, R. (1989) 'Getting the measure of management competence', *Personnel Management,* June, pp. 32–37.

Jones, P. and Oswick, C. (1993) 'Outcomes of outdoor management development: articles of faith?', *Journal of European Industrial Training,* Vol. 17, No. 3, pp. 10–18.

Kakabadse, A. and Myers, A. (1995) 'Qualities of top management: comparisons of European manufacturers', *Journal of Management Development,* Vol. 14, No. 1, pp. 5–15.

Kakabadse, A. and Parker, C. (1984) 'The undiscovered dimension of management education: politics in organisations', in Cox, C. and Beck, J. (eds) *Management Development: Advances in Practice and Theory.* Chichester: John Wiley.

Kanter, R. (1982) 'The middle manager as innovator', *Harvard Business Review,* Vol. 60, No. 4, pp. 95–105.

*Kast, F.S. and Rosenweig, J.E. (1985) *Organisation and Management: A Systems Approach,* 4th edn. New York: McGraw-Hill.

Keeble, S.P. (1992) *The Ability to Manage: A Study of British Management, 1890–1990.* Manchester: Manchester University Press.

Kilcourse, T. (1994) 'Developing competent managers', *Journal of European Industrial Training,* Vol. 18, No. 2, pp. 12–16.

Kirkbride, P. and Tang, S. (1992) 'Management development in the Nanyang Chinese societies of S.E. Asia', *Journal of Management Development,* Vol. 11, No. 2, pp. 54–66.

Kolb, D. (1984) *Experiential Learning.* New York: Prentice Hall.

*Kotter, J.P. (1982) *The General Managers.* Glencoe: Free Press.

Kwiatkowski, S. and Kozminski, A. (1992) 'Paradoxical country: management education in Poland', *Journal of Management Development,* Vol. 11, No. 5, pp. 28–33.

Larwood, L. and Wood, M. (1995) 'Training women for changing priorities', *Journal of Management Development,* Vol 14, No 2, pp. 54-64.

Lawrence, P. (1992) 'Management development in Europe: a study in cultural contrast', *Human Resource Management Journal,* Vol. 3, No. 1, pp. 11–23.

Lee, G. and Beard, D. (1994) *Development Centres: Realising the Potential of Your Employees through Assessment and Development.* Maidenhead: McGraw-Hill.

Lee, M. (1995) 'Working with choice in Central Europe', *Management Learning,* Vol. 26, No. 2, pp. 215–30.

Lee, R. (1987) 'Towards an "appropriate theory" of organisational politics', *Management Education and Development,* Vol. 18, Pt 4, pp. 315–329.

Lees, S. (1992) 'Ten faces of management development', *Management Education and Development,* Vol. 23, Pt 2, pp. 89–105.

Lewis, A. and Fagenson, E. (1995) 'Strategies for developing women managers: how well do they fulfil their objectives?' *Journal of Management Development,* Vol. 14, No. 2. pp. 39–53.

Loan-Clarke, J, (1996) 'The Management Charter Initiative: critique of management standards/NVQs', *Journal of Management Development,* Vol. 15, No. 6, pp. 4–17.

*Mabey, C. and Salaman, G. (1995) *Strategic Human Resource Management.* Oxford: Blackwell.

Management Charter Initiative (MCI) (1993) *Management Development in the UK.* London: MCI.

Margerison, C. (1991) *Making Management Development Work.* Maidenhead: McGraw-Hill.

Margerison, C. (1994a) 'Managing career choices', in Mumford, A. (ed.) *Gower Handbook of Management Development.* Aldershot: Gower.

Margerison, C. (1994b) 'Action learning and excellence in management development', in Mabey, C. and Iles, P. (eds) *Managing Learning.* London: Routledge.

Mathewman, J. (1995) 'Trends and developments in the use of competency frameworks', *Competency,* Vol. 1, No. 4, whole issue supplement.

McBride, M. (1992) 'Management development in the global village: beyond culture, a micro world approach', *Journal of Management Development,* Vol. 11, No. 7, pp. 48–57.

*McClelland, S. (1994) 'Gaining competitive advantage through strategic management development', *Journal of Management Development,* Vol. 13, No. 5, pp. 4–13.

Meldrum, M. and Atkinson, S. (1998) 'Is management development fulfilling its organisational role?', *Management Decision,* Vol. 36, No. 8, pp. 528–532.

Miller, L. (1991) 'Managerial competences', *Industrial and Commercial Training,* Vol. 23, No. 6, pp. 11–15.

Miller, R. and Cangemi J. (1993) 'Why TQM fails: perspectives of top management', *Journal of Management Development,* Vol. 12, No. 7, pp. 40–50.

*Mintzberg, H. (1980) *The Nature of Managerial Work.* Englewood Cliffs, N.J.: Prentice Hall.

Molander, C. (1986) *Management Development.* Bromley: Chartwell-Bratt.

Molander, C. and Winterton, J. (1994) *Managing Human Resources.* London: Routledge.

Mole, G. (1996) 'The management training industry in the UK: an HRD director's critique', *Human Resource Management Journal,* Vol. 6, No. 1, pp. 19–26.

Morgan, G. (1997) *Images of Organisation,* 2nd edn. Beverley Hills, Calif.: Sage.

Mullins, L. (1996) *Management and Organisational Behaviour,* 4th edn. London: Pitman.

Mumford, A. (1987) 'Using reality in management development', *Management Education and Development,* Vol. 18, Pt 3, pp. 223–243.

Mumford, A. (1993) *Management Development: Strategies for Action.* 2nd edn, London: IPD.

Munchus, G. and McArthur, B. (1991) 'Revisiting the historical use of assessment centres in management selection and development', *Journal of Management Development,* Vol. 10, No. 1, pp. 5–13.

Neelankavil, J. (1992) 'Management development and training programmes in Japanese firms', *Journal of Management Development,* Vol. 11, No. 3, pp. 12–17.

Newell. H. and Dopson, S. (1996) 'Muddle in the middle: organisational restructuring and middle management careers', *Personnel Review*, Vol. 25, No. 4, pp. 4–20.

Newstrom, J. (1986) 'Leveraging management development through the management of transfer', *Journal of Management Development*, Vol. 5, No. 5, pp. 33–45.

Odiorne, G.S. (1984) *Strategic Management of Human Resources: A Portfolio Approach*. San Francisco, Calif: Jossey-Bass.

Ohlott, P., Ruderman, M. and McCauley, C. (1994) 'Gender differences in managers' developmental job experiences', *Academy of Management Journal*, Vol. 37, No. 1, pp. 46–67.

Pate, L. and Nielson, W. (1987) 'Integrating management development into a large-scale, system-wide change programme', *Journal of Management Development*, Vol. 6, No. 5, pp. 16–30.

Pedler, M., Burgoyne, J., Boydell, T. and Welshman, G. (1990) *Self-Development in Organisations*. Maidenhead: McGraw-Hill.

Phillips, N. (1992) *Managing International Teams*. London: Pitman.

Puffer, S. (1993) 'The booming business of management education in Russia', *Journal of Management Development*, Vol. 12, No. 5, pp. 46–59.

Rae, L. (1986) *How to Measure Training Effectiveness*. Aldershot: Gower.

Ready, D., Vicere, A. and White, A. (1994) 'Towards a systems approach to executive development', *Journal of Management Development*, Vol. 13, No. 5, pp. 3–11.

Redman, T., Keithley, D. and Szalkowski, A. (1995) 'Management development under adversity: case studies from Poland', *Journal of Management Development*, Vol. 14, No. 10, pp. 4–13.

Redman, T., Snape, E. and Wilkinson, A. (1995) 'Is quality management working in the UK?' *Journal of General Management*, Vol. 20, No. 3, pp. 44–59.

*Reed, M. and Anthony, P. (1992) 'Professionalising management and managing professionalisation: British management in the 1980s', *Journal of Management Studies*, Vol. 29, No. 5, pp. 591–613.

*Revans, R. (1983) *ABC of Action Learning*. Bromley: Chartwell-Bratt.

Roberts, C. and McDonald, G. (1995) 'Training to fail', *Journal of Management Development*, Vol. 14 No. 4, pp. 1–16.

Roberts, G. (1995) 'Competency management systems: the need for a practical framework', *Competency*, Vol. 3, No. 2, pp. 27–30.

Roberts, J. (1996) 'Management education and the limits of technical rationality: the condition and consequences of management practice', in French, R. and Grey, C. (eds) *Rethinking Management Education*. London: Sage.

Rosenfeld. R. and Wilson, D. (1999) *Managing Organisations: Texts, Readings and Cases*, 2nd edn, London: McGraw-Hill.

Russell, S. (1983) *Quality Circles in Perspective*, WRU Occasional Paper No. 24. London: ACAS.

Russell, S. and Dale, B. (1989) *Quality Circles: A Broader Perspective*, WRU Occasional Paper No. 43. London: ACAS.

Ryan, M. (1989) 'Political behaviour and management devel-opment', *Management Education and Development*, Vol. 20, Pt 3, pp. 238–253.

*Salaman, G. (1995) *Managing*. Buckingham: Open University Press.

Salaman, G. and Butler, J. (1990) 'Why managers won't learn', *Management Education and Development*, Vol. 21, Pt 3, pp. 183–191.

Simpson , P. and Lyddon, T. (1995) 'Different roles, different views: exploring the range of stakeholder perceptions on an in-company management development programme', *Industrial and Commercial Training*, Vol. 27 No., pp. 26–32.

Smith, A. (1993) 'Management development evaluation and effectiveness', *Journal of Management Development*, Vol. 12, No. 1, pp. 20–32.

Smith, A. and Porter, J. (1990) 'The tailor-made training maze: a practitioner's guide to evaluation', *Journal of European Industrial Training*, Vol. 14, No. 8, complete issue.

Smith, H., Carroll, A., Kefalas, A. and Watson, H. (1980) *Making Organisations Perform*. New York: Macmillan.

Snell, R. (1986) 'Questioning the ethics of management development: a critical review', *Management Education and Development*, Vol. 17, Pt 1, pp. 43–64.

Snell, R. (1990) 'Managers' development of ethical awareness and personal morality', *Personnel Review*, Vol. 19, No. 1, pp. 13–20.

Snyder, R. (1993) 'The glass ceiling for women: things that don't cause it and things that won't break it', *Human Resource Development Quarterly*, Vol. 4, No. 1, pp. 97–106.

Sparrow, P. and Bognanno, M. (1994) 'Competency forecasting: issues for international selection and assessment', in Mabey, C. and Iles, P. (eds) *Managing Learning*. London: Routledge.

Srinivas, K. (1995) 'Globalisation of business and the Third World: the challenge of expanding the mind-set', *Journal of Management Development*, Vol. 14, No. 3, pp. 26–49.

Stead, B. (1985) *Women in Management*, 2nd edn. Englewood Cliffs, N.J.: Prentice Hall.

*Stewart, J. and Hamlin, B. (1992a) 'Competence-based qualifications: the case against change', *Journal of European Industrial Training*, Vol. 16, No. 7, pp. 21–32.

*Stewart, J. and Hamlin, B. (1992b) 'Competence-based qualifications: a case for established methodologies', *Journal of European Industrial Training*, Vol. 16, No. 10, pp. 9–16.

Stewart, R. (1994) *Managing Today and Tomorrow*. Basingstoke: Macmillan.

*Storey, J. (1989) 'Management development: a literature review and implications for future research, Part 1: conceptualisations and practice', *Personnel Review*, Vol. 18, No. 6, pp. 3–19.

Storey, J. (1992) 'Making European managers: an overview', *Human Resource Management Journal*, Vol. 3, No. 1, pp. 1–10.

Storey, J., Mabey, C. and Thomson, A. (1997) 'What a difference a decade makes', *People Management*, June, pp. 28–30.

Storey, J., Okazaki-Ward, L., Gow, I., Edwards, P.K. and Sisson, K. (1991) 'Managerial careers and management development: a comparative analysis of Britain and Japan', *Human Resource Management Journal*, Vol. 1, No. 3, Spring, pp. 33–57.

Stumpf, S., Watson, M.-A. and Rustogi, H. (1994) 'Leadership in a global village: creating practice fields to develop learning organisations', *Journal of Management Development*, Vol. 13, No. 8, pp. 16–25.

Templer, A., Beatty, D. and Hofmeyer, K. (1992) 'The challenge of management development in South Africa: so little time, so much to do', *Journal of Management Development*, Vol. 11, No. 2, pp. 32–41.

Temporal, P. (1984) 'Helping self-development to happen', in Cox, C. and Beck, J. (eds) *Management Development: Advances in Practice and Theory*. Chichester: John Wiley.

Temporal, P. (1990) 'Linking management development to the corporate future: the role of the professional', *Journal of Management Development*, Vol. 9, No. 5, pp. 7–15.

*Thomas, A. (1993) *Controversies in Management*. London: Routledge.

Thornhill, A. (1993) 'Management training across cultures: the challenge for trainers', *Journal of European Industrial Training*, Vol. 17, No. 10, pp. 43–51.

Thurley, K. and Wirdenhuis, H. (1991) 'Will management become European? Strategic choice for organisations', *European Management Journal*, Vol. 9, No. 2, pp. 127–135.

Tijmstra, S. and Casler, K. (1992) 'Management learning for Europe', *European Management Journal*, Vol. 10. No. 1, pp. 30–38.

Torrington, D., Weightman, J. and Johns, K. (1994) *Effective Management: People and Organisations*, 2nd edn. Hemel Hempstead: Prentice Hall.

Tovey, L. (1991) *Management Training and Development in Large UK Business Organisations*. London: Harbridge House.

Varney, G. (1977) *An Organisation Development Approach to Management Development*. Reading, MA: Addison-Wesley.

Vecsenyi, J. (1992) 'Management education for the Hungarian transition', *Journal of Management Development*, Vol. 11, No. 3, pp. 39–47.

Vineall, T. (1994) 'Planning management development', in Mumford, A. (ed.) *Gower Handbook of Management Development*, 4th edn. Aldershot: Gower.

Vinnicombe, S. and Colwill, N. (1995) *The Essence of Women in Management*, London: Prentice Hall.

Vloeberghs, D. (1998) 'Management development in a context of drastic change', *Journal of Management Development*, Vol. 12, No. 9, pp. 644–661.

Warr, P., Bird, M. and Rackham, N. (1970) *Evaluation of Management Training*. London: Gower.

*Watson, T. (1994) *In Search of Management*. London: Routledge.

Wentling, R.M. (1992) 'Women in middle management: their career development and aspirations', *Business Horizons*, Vol. 35, No. 1, pp. 47–54.

Whiddett, S. and Branch, J. (1993) 'Development centres in Volvo', *Training and Development UK*, Vol. 11, No. 11, pp. 16–18.

Whitaker, V. and Megginson, D. (1992) 'Women and men working together effectively', *Industrial and Commercial Training*, Vol. 24, No. 4, pp. 16–19.

*Whitely, R. (1989) 'On the nature of managerial tasks and skills: their distinguishing characteristics and organisation', *Journal of Management Studies*, Vol. 26, No. 3, pp. 209–224.

*Woodall, J. and Winstanley, D. (1998) *Management Development: Strategy and Practice*. Oxford: Blackwell.

Woodruffe, C. (1993) *Assessment Centres: Identifying and Developing Competence*. London: IPM.

Transforming Anglian Water

The history

Anglian Water is geographically the largest of the ten regional water companies in the UK, delivering clean drinking water and removing sewage and waste-water from the homes and premises of some 5 million customers. Throughout the 1980s there were growing concerns over the standards and level of service delivery afforded by public sector organisations, and in line with the then government ideology and policy Anglian Water was privatised in 1989. Following privatisation, the company introduced a major reorganisation of its business, involving a rationalisation of existing structures and a diversification into new markets – many of them overseas operations. Between 1993 and 1995 the company reduced management layers from eleven to five, and 33% of white-collar jobs were eliminated, bringing a saving of £40 million. However, senior management were conscious that if the organisation was to transform itself into a successful, high-performing international company, a fundamental realignment of its existing culture was required.

Prior to privatisation, the company's culture could be described as 'militaristic' – and with some justification. The risks were high. Any mistake in delivering water to customers could prove disastrous, and the company abided by the principle that 'contaminated water cannot be recalled'. The management solution was to introduce strict rules and procedures that were to be followed to the letter and obeyed without question. Any diversion from routine procedures was alien to an organisation where small risks or mistakes could rapidly and seriously jeopardise health and safety. The result was a culture in which playing by the rules, obeying orders, the acceptance and non-questioning of procedures was (and in the eyes of many had to be) the norm.

Forging a learning organisation

Senior management were under no illusions: the company's future success and survival in an increasingly competitive and aggressive marketplace depended on replacing the company's command-and-control culture with a more outward-looking, entrepreneurial, customer-focused,

innovative approach to doing business. But how could this be achieved?

Philosophically, the company's approach was rooted in the need to reorientate and prepare its employees for continuing and radical change, and to do this meant creating a more flexible, empowering, learning culture. The need to move in this direction was highlighted by a series of employee attitude surveys carried out after the restructuring of the early 1990s. Among other things, the surveys highlighted a discontent with the existing management style and communication policies. This led the senior management of Anglian Water into a considered debate about the future cultural direction of the business and the decision to create what they termed a *learning organisation*.

As a learning organisation the company would move away from the old public sector, keep your head down, jobs for life, follow the procedure mentality towards an environment in which employee creativity, innovation and challenge would be encouraged and valued. Employees would be empowered to take the lead in change. Individually and in cross-functional teams they would involve themselves in continuous improvement, not only in the area of technological development but – more significantly for a highly rational, technical organisation – in the area of customer service to meet changing needs and demands.

Steps along the way

There were two central, interlocking components designed to transform Anglian Water into a learning organisation. The first was the *Transformation Journey*. The concept of the Journey evolved from a development programme for attitudinal and behavioural change among senior managers. Following its success, a decision was taken to roll it out to all employees. The Journey was not a training programme. Instead it was a holistic strategy designed to prepare and equip employees for the technical and emotional challenges of operating in a turbulent and uncertain environment. The Journey was aimed at changing mindsets and creating self-awareness. It sought to promote team-working and cooperation, and ultimately to have a direct bearing on operational effectiveness and business performance.

Any employee could 'sign up' for the Journey, and participation was entirely voluntary. However, clear signals were sent to the workforce that individuals were expected to participate, and enrolment on the Journey was regarded as an indication of their commitment to the company and its future.

Employees formed themselves into teams. Sometimes these were work related, but on other occasions individuals from disparate backgrounds came together. The only proviso was that any activity they engaged in was to benefit themselves, their group, and Anglian Water. There were four guiding principles for 'Travellers':

- a willingness to get to know myself;
- a desire to develop myself;
- a desire to realise my full potential with and through others;
- an ability to link my personal development to the development of Anglian Water.

A typical Journey lasted two years and was an essentially self-managed exercise. Each group was expected to acquire its own funding and sponsorship and to arrange its own support and skills development. Regular reviews along the way ensured that there was a basis for learning and reflection.

Journeys included groups who went outside Anglian Water, for example to build a toilet block on top of England's highest mountain, to refurbish a children's hospice, or to dig a well in Africa. Other groups focused on internal projects to improve overall business functioning and 'make things happen'. They involved themselves in more cross-functional teamworking, sought to improve their business knowledge and commercial awareness, became more creative and lateral in their thinking, conducted detailed research into business problems, and explored different options for change.

Between 1995 and 1997 3000 employees had enrolled on the Journey, with some 300 groups being formed. In a 1996 survey, 88% of respondents felt the Journey had benefited Anglian Water, and 99% said that participation in a Journey had been a 'good learning experience'. Coincident with this survey, it was reported that customer satisfaction ratings had risen from 70% in March 1995 to 90% in March 1996.

The second component in Anglian's strategy to transform itself into a learning organisation was the establishment of the *University of Water* (colloquially known as Aqua Universitas). Knowledge creation and sharing were seen as vital in promoting best-practice networks and better customer service, and

in enhancing commercial success. The University was aimed at acknowledging, integrating, supporting and accrediting all forms of learning taking place in the company. It's role was to define and develop the skills and competences – especially management skills – that were required to move Anglian into the twenty-first century and ensure its future as a global player. To this end, considerable resources were made available – for example a dedicated 'campus' on the shores of Rutland Water and the installation of an intranet to promote information exchange and communication.

Around these two central components throughout the 1990s the company introduced a raft of supporting initiatives including total quality management, leadership coaching, mass communication strategy development, change agent networks, new HR performance management policies, and vision and values statements designed to inculcate new attitudes and behaviours.

So have efforts to transform Anglian Water into a learning organisation culture been a success? Certainly there are considerable references to the 'old Anglian Water' and the 'new Anglian Water', reflecting a perception of behaviour and attitudinal change. And according to Clive Morton, ex-HR Director of Anglian, there is no doubt that a change in culture has occurred:

The combination of the Journey and the University of Water with its universal access has created the conditions for a learning business, helping to assure the future for Anglian Water and its stakeholders.

(Morton, 1998: 98)

The future

In 1998 Ofwat (the government's regulatory body for the water industry) recommended a price reduction of at least 17.5% (about £45 on the average bill) in 2000. This one-off cut in charges represented about £130 million loss of revenue, and compares with 1998 profits of £268 million on turnover of £850 million. 'Costs must come down', the company warned. During 1999 the company initiated a major cost-reduction strategy, and this has translated into 400 job losses (10% of the workforce).

References

Morton, C. (1998) *Beyond World Class*. Basingstoke: Macmillan Business Press.

Ciminero, S. (1990) *Anglian Water: Customer Service Transformation*. Boston, Mass.: Harvard Business School Publishing.

Extracts from *Anglian Water News*.

You are an external consultant(s) advising a company facing similar challenges to those experienced by Anglian Water. It has read an account similar to the one described above, and is interested in exploring the whole concept of the learning organisation as a way of helping it to transform and succeed in the face of radical change. However, the board is cautious, and slightly sceptical of the cultural transformation process that Anglian has undergone. It has asked you to make an assessment.

Specifically, they want you to report:

1 on the extent to which Anglian Water's claim to be a learning organisation can be justified. On what grounds should any claims or justifications be made?

2 against the backdrop of recent major job losses, whether or not Anglian can/should sustain the ideals and practices of a learning organisation. Are there any factors that might eventually undermine the concept and call into question the massive investment Anglian has made?

You are to prepare a report for the board of between 1000 and 1500 words, and follow this up with a short presentation (ten minutes).

PART

4

THE EMPLOYMENT RELATIONSHIP

Introduction to Part 4

The employment relationship is a key feature in the nature of managing employment. It brings together the sources of power and legitimacy, rights and obligations, that management and employees seek for themselves and apply to others. This Part is concerned with explaining this relationship and examining how it works out through a variety of applications such as the law, collective bargaining, performance and reward, and employee involvement.

Chapter 10 deals with the role and influence of the law in determining the nature of contract. The contract of employment is not simply a document that is presented to employees on appointment, but is a complex set of formal and informal rules which govern the whole basis of the employment relationship. Thus, the way employees and managers conform with, or break, those rules determines how that relationship works out in practice. Moreover, the nature of contract can have an important bearing on whether such newer concepts as human resource management can fundamentally change the nature of such a relationship that is so dependent upon the interaction of formal and informal legal regulation.

Chapter 11 introduces the concept and practice of collective bargaining. In recent years the collective determination of pay has reduced in scope and breadth in many market economies, but it still remains the most important single method of arriving at broad pay settlement for many employees and its impact and effect is often felt throughout economies. For these reasons its nature, structure and outcomes form the basis of analysis.

Chapter 12 discusses the processes that go towards settling pay for individuals when criteria which test their own performance are introduced. In recent years there has been an increasing use made of individualised pay, and this chapter examines some of the problems and issues in operating and evaluating such processes.

Chapter 13 is concerned with the development of employee involvement. This is a topic that has seen great interest recently, but there are contradictory elements within it which this chapter explores, among them whether involvement can genuinely bring employee and managerial interests together and whether involvement is a vehicle for 'empowerment' or simply a further way in which the managerial prerogative is asserted in the employment relationship.

Finally, Chapter 14 considers the particular issues involved in managing human resources in the public sector.

10 The employment relationship and contractual regulation

Ian Clark

OBJECTIVES

- To introduce the central significance of contract in the employment relationship.
- To introduce employment contracts and the legal regulation of economic activity within the labour market.
- To introduce the wider employment relationship as a process of socio-economic exchange through a discussion of the management function and its prescription, the role of management in the UK's industrial capitalism, and the role of management in the realisation of legal authority in the employment relationship.

INTRODUCTION

This chapter examines the employment relationship and its contractual regulation. In particular, it outlines the central significance of contractual regulation in the employment relationship, and how this legitimises the managerial prerogative. The employment relationship is visualised as a process of socio-economic exchange. That is, unlike other contractual relationships, for example something as mundane as the purchase of a railway ticket, the employment relationship is an open-ended contractual relationship. By this we mean that both parties intend the contract to continue until either party indicates a desire to terminate the relationship. Thus an employment contract is not an immediately closed relationship of exchange. The employment relationship contains an economic component – the exchange of work for payment – but also includes a sociological dimension centred on power and authority. The economic and sociological components of the employment relationship are structured by the contract of employment. In addition to this, the employment relationship is subject to a range of other processes, for example management competence and efficiency, work group control, management and worker motivation and the potential for workplace conflict and disagreement. These factors make the apparently rational process of economic exchange much more complicated and to some extent indeterminate – that is, a relationship in which the specific details are subject to ongoing negotiation and change.

The sociological dimension of the exchange relationship examines the issue of power in employment, and its central focus is on the management process. In contrast to this the economic dimension to exchange examines how the managerial process appears necessary in order to meet and sustain the efficiency criteria of market economies. For example, managers aim to raise productivity levels and reduce labour costs in order to improve competitiveness or meet the needs of market conditions. This chapter deals with this issue in two ways. First, the material locates the function of management within the context of market economies and examines the role of management and the managerial prerogative as an adjunct to contract. Second, we detail the limitations of contractual regulation in relation to operational control within organisations in market economies. Here we examine how management aims to control and structure the labour process: that is, how individuals who perform work interact with the means of production. In the UK the majority of the working population work within an employment relationship: thus individuals who work for somebody else – an employer – interact with the means of production through the employment relationship. For example, a textile worker who is employed as an overlocker works a machine (the means of production) owned by the employer.

The themes of contractual regulation in employment and management control provide a socio-economic structure within which the prescription, rhetoric and reality of HRM operate. This illustrates the contextual and operational difficulties that face managerial control strategies that aim to motivate employees to go beyond contract in the performance of their work. Equally, because much of the discussion is determined by the context of market economies, we ask the question: What does management do? Thus the function and role of management are examined through the context and dictates of a market economy.

The chapter is divided into three sections:

- We examine the central significance of contract in the employment relationship by discussing four issues: the concept of contract; the philosophical basis of contract; the capitalist requirement for the contractual regulation of employment within the market economy; and (in more detail) the employment relationship as a socio-economic exchange within the market economy.
- We discuss the contract of employment as the legal regulation of economic activity within the labour market by examining four issues: the regulation of employment through the legal process; the 'common law' duties of the employer and employee; the effects of 'statute' law on the contractual regulation of employment; and (briefly) HRM in terms of some of its practical effects on the nature and form of the contractual regulation of employment.
- We examine the employment relationship more conceptually and historically by discussing three issues: the process of management functions and their prescription; the role of the management function within the development of the UK's industrial capitalism; and the management process as the realisation of legal authority in the employment relationship.

The issues under discussion are general to industrial economies, but specific examples are drawn from British experience to explain particular points.

THE CENTRAL SIGNIFICANCE OF THE EMPLOYMENT CONTRACT

This section is divided into four parts. First, the concept of contract is examined. Second, the philosophical bases of contract are briefly introduced. Third, the contract of employment is examined within the context of the market economy. Last, the emergent nature of the wider employment relationship is introduced as a process of socio-economic exchange within which the contract of employment operates.

The concept of contract

In order to explain the concept of contract, it is useful to distinguish between commercial contracts and employment contracts, the area of our particular focus. Commercial contracts, for example something as simple as buying a bus ticket or something as complex as a house purchase, contain four elements:

- offer;
- acceptance;
- consideration;
- the intention to create legal relations.

To illustrate these four elements we can draw on the example of a house purchase. An individual may visit a particular house and decide they would like to buy it. As a result of this they decide to make an offer. The current property owner may decide to accept this offer – subject to contract. 'Subject to contract' will necessarily involve the person who wishes to buy the house – the offeror – receiving a satisfactory structural survey and acquiring the necessary purchase price either in cash or (more likely) through a mortgage. If these requirements are satisfactorily fulfilled, a contract can be drawn up. In consideration for the agreed purchase price the existing property owner – the offeree – agrees to give up their property rights to the house and exchange them through contract to the offeror. Thus consideration is the mechanism that validates the contract: that is, each party gives something to the contract, in this case a house for money by the offeror and money for a house by the offeree. If a contract contains offer, acceptance and consideration, the presence of these factors indicates that the parties to the contract wish to create a legally binding relationship.

A legally binding contract must also satisfy the following factors. First, the contents of the contract, to which the parties have agreed, must be reasonable. Second, the contract in itself must be legal, in terms of the prevailing law. For example, a contract to assassinate a person may contain offer, acceptance and consideration and an intention to create a legally binding relationship between the parties. However, conspiracy to murder is a criminal offence, thus any contractual relationship is void. Third, there must be genuine consent between the parties, and the parties themselves must have the capacity to consent to the agreement. For example, minors and bankrupts have only limited capacities in contract.

From this brief introduction we can now proceed to look at employment contracts, which are a very specialised form of contract.

A contract of employment is a *contract of service*, where an employee – the subject of the contract – is in the personal service of their employer. It is necessary to distinguish an employment contract of personal service from a commercial *contract for services*. As Wedderburn (1986: 106) makes clear, the law marks off the employee under a contract of service from independent contractors – the self-employed – who may provide services to an organisation under a commercial contract. For example, a commercial contract whereby catering or cleaning services are provided to one firm by a second firm is a contract for services, not an employment contract, even though the work is performed by labour. Catering staff may be employees in the offeror firm, but the offeree firm has bought their services under a commercial contract for catering services.

A contract of employment differs from a commercial contract for services in the sense that an employment contract of personal service to an employer is intended to be an open-ended relationship. It is a relationship that continues until either party decides to end it through due notice, whereas a commercial contract is more likely to be a precise exchange of services over a clearly defined period of time. Some employment contracts today are of a temporary or fixed-term nature, but nonetheless an employment relationship is created, whereas in commercial contracts of a long-term duration, for example computer or photocopier servicing, an employment relationship is not created. Equally, such commercial contracts are likely to contain clear and precise contractual duties for each party. Thus commercial contracts are a purely contractual relationship and, unlike employment contracts, are not subject to the *common law duties* of an employer and employee.

The common law refers to areas of law that are not covered by parliamentary or European Union legislation. The common law has been developed by the judiciary: that is, the common law is *judge-made law*. In the following section we detail the common law duties of both parties that are incorporated into contracts of employment.

Now that we have defined contract and distinguished between commercial and employment contracts, it is possible to proceed with a discussion of the underlying assumptions behind contract theory.

Equality and freedom of entry: market individualism

The philosophical basis of contract is derived from the principle of market individualism. Market individualism suggests that the individual is the best judge of his or her own interests. From this suggestion the notion of *freedom of contract* is introduced, which assumes that individuals are self-determining agents, who are primarily self-interested. Thus individuals are able to fulfil their own self-interest most effectively if they are free to enter into contracts between themselves within the market mechanism.

Freedom of contract suggests that individuals both freely enter into contractual arrangements and jointly determine the terms and conditions of the contract with equal status before the law. It follows from this assumption that the component elements of a contract – offer, acceptance and the consideration between the parties – are arrived at through a process of negotiation and then agreement to create legal relations. This may be the situation in the case of a house purchase, but in relation to employment the situation is somewhat different. As Fox (1985: 6) points out, contract theory alone, with all that it entails in terms of equality and references to adjudication by an outside body, cannot be an effective mode of regulation in the case of employment if the parties to the contract are in dispute. In the UK this is the case because the employment relationship remains one of *status*. The notion of status derives from paternalism in the master and servant relationship inherent to 'employment' prior to the rise of industrial economies. Examples of paternal employment include domestic service, and tied cottages for estate farmers and general agricultural labourers. In the nineteenth century domestic servants and agricultural labourers were not employees in the modern sense of the word; rather they were subject to a crude form of commercial contract whereby they provided their labour services to a master in return for board and lodgings. However, once employment became contractually determined in a formal legal sense it did not constitute a clean break with the past. By this we mean that the contractual process incorporates characteristics from pre-industrial 'paternal' employment: for example, the status bias of the master and servant relationship. Fox (1985: 3–5) identifies paternalism as the basis of status within employment. That is, although employment contracts provide employees with a degree of independence from their employer – for example, employees can terminate their employment through due notice – employees remain the subject of the employment contract. They are subject to the reasonable and legitimate authority of their employer, to whom they provide personal service.

Paternalism refers to a situation of subordination to legitimate authority. Prior to the contractual determination of employment the process of subordination to legitimate authority was entirely within the master–servant relationship. Within contractually determined employment, the employee subordinates him or herself to the greater legal authority of the employer, the superiority of which is derived from the status-based relationship of master and servant.

To further clarify the fusion of contract and status in employment two additional points are significant. First, the notion of freedom of contract between two consenting parties is present in relation to employment contracts, but only in terms of individual equality before the law. Second, equality before the law in employment contracts is not symmetrical because employer authority is derived from their paternal status that underpins the employment relationship. This is often referred to as the *managerial prerogative*. Thus in most contracts the agreeing parties are often the best judges of their own interests. However, in employment the status bias of the employer gives them the privilege of determining their self-interest and a partial say in the determination of employee interests. This privilege derives from the concept of *subordination*, which implies that the junior partner to the employment contract cannot perceive all their real interests. Kahn-Freund (1984) described the individually based contract of employment as an act of submission on the part of the employee:

> In its operation it is a condition of subordination, however much the submission and the subordination may be concealed by that indispensable figment of the legal mind known as the contract of employment.

An employer may determine the organisation of work, levels of payment and duration of working time. The employee is bound by such impositions if they are reasonable. Thus the notion of free employment contracts bears little resemblance to the real world (Hyman, 1975: 23). Relatedly, although all employees have an individual contract of employment, the terms and conditions of an individual's contract of employment are likely to be determined and regulated by means of a collective agreement, the details of which are normally incorporated in an individual's contract of employment. These agreements are often negotiated by a trade union through the process of collective bargaining. In the absence of a trade union and collective bargaining 'collective agreements' are unilaterally determined by management on behalf of the employer; they are not the subjects of negotiation. This point again illustrates that the notions of individual negotiation and freedom of contract exist at only a superficial level of relations between employer and employee. These points are clarified further in the next section of the chapter, which details common law and statutory provisions covering the determination of terms and conditions of a contract of employment.

Now that the philosophical trappings that underpin the concept of contract are clear we can proceed to examine the emergence of the employment relationship and its contractual regulation within the UK's capitalist economy.

Employment and its regulation: the emergence of the firm

In market economies commercial relations between individuals are governed by contract. Contracts are of two types: those where services are bought and sold (*a commercial contract*) and those where the service of individuals is the subject of the contract (*an employment contract*). In the second instance a contract of employment creates the employee who is in the service of the employer, whereas if a firm uses an independent subcontractor to perform work on its behalf a commercial contract exists between two independent firms. Their respective legal obligations and expectations constitute the critical difference between employment contracts and commercial contracts. In the case of employment it is a contract of subordination based on the service of the employee. In contrast, a commercial contract exchanges commercial services between independent individuals. This distinction is important because one feature of contemporary HRM is the strategic use of indirect labour sourced through commercial contracts. This use of subcontractors and independent traders/consultants constitutes part of a drive for greater flexibility in the management and deployment of human resources.

Institutional economists, for example Coase (1937) and in more contemporary vein Williamson (1975), argue that the market determines which type of contract will predominate in particular situations. Take the example of a house purchase by an individual. In this situation the individual is likely to require the personal services of a solicitor to convey the property. Thus the individual enters into a contract for the personal services of a solicitor to undertake this task. In a different situation where a property company is continually buying property, the market is likely to dictate that it is more efficient for the company to employ a solicitor to take responsibility for the large number of property purchases and sales in which it is involved. Thus an employment contract is created.

The central question at issue here is: Why are there not millions of independent contractors who sell their personal services to one another? Coase (1937) argues that this situation does not prevail because in many situations the details of what the supplier is expected to do are defined in very general terms. That is, the specific details are confirmed at a later date. For Coase, an entrepreneurial coordinator who directs production – an employer – can eliminate complex and repetitive market transactions that buy in materials and labour services.

Where direction of labour resources is dependent on the buyer, a relationship, which Coase terms the *firm*, will be created. A firm is likely to emerge when the use of short-term contracts would prove unsatisfactory, as is often the case with labour. Instead of a series of commercial contracts for the personal services of independent contractors, one contract, the employment contract, is substituted. This places the employee in the service of the employer. As we have already established, in employment contracts the employee agrees to obey the directions of the employer within the reasonable limits of the contract. The decision to use a commercial contract or an employment contract is balanced in terms of the costs of using the market price mechanism to create a commercial contract against the costs of organising an extra transaction – the creation of an employee, subject to an employment contract within the firm. Between 1979 and 1997 favourable government policies and extreme product market competition shifted this balance in favour of the market mechanism. Equally, deregulation of the employment relationship not only improved the managerial prerogative but also 'launched' *flexibility* as a central aim of management: see, for example, Atkinson (1984), where the notion of the flexible firm is presented in rational economic terms. Equally, see Hutton (1995) and Clark (1996) for more polemic and critical evaluations of a return to market principles over employment creation. The economic and legal rationale for the firm creates an employment relationship between employer and employee, when the use of one contract is more efficient than the use of many commercial contracts through the market mechanism. The pursuit of flexibility and the deregulation of the employment relationship during the 1980s reversed this rationale to promote the benefits of commercial subcontracts for labour services.

The employment relationship, although subject to contractual regulation and freely entered into, removes the freedom of action that an individual would have if they operated as an independent contractor. This is the case because, as the above discussion on the philosophical base of contract indicates, the theory of contract is fused with status in the specific case of employment. Hence, within the firm, the employment relationship is one of subordination to market authority relations that are in turn subject to the reasonableness of the contract of employment. The contract of employment defines the relationship of subordination between employee and employer that creates a legal duty to obey. It is important to emphasise that it is the reasonableness of the legally vested requirement to obey that can be challenged, not the overall requirement to obey. The past 30 years have witnessed a growing body of statute law that appears to reduce the imbalance in the employment contract referred to by Kahn-Freund. Significant pieces of the legislation are discussed in the next section of this chapter. At this stage we can summarise by suggesting that statute law aims to recognise that the employee has some property rights in their employment: that is, some say over how the contract may be terminated and some protection against unreasonable treatment during the course of the contract of employment.

Now that we have examined the emergence of employment within the firm it is clear that its contractual nature and regulation are derived in part from the concept of contract and in part from the status bias of traditional paternal employment in the UK.

The employment relationship: a socio-economic exchange

The term 'socio-economic exchange' suggests that the employment relationship has two dimensions. First, it is an economic exchange in which an employee, under an employment contract, receives monetary reward for the work they perform. Second, the employment relationship has a sociological dimension in that under a contract of employment a power relationship exists. While they are at work, employees provide their labour service to an employer and are therefore under a legal direction as defined in their contract of employment. In strictly economic terms an employee sells labour power to their employer, which the employer must transform into labour that produces value (in the form of goods and services) that the employer can then sell. The purchase of labour power is the subject of the employment contract and the economic dimension of the employment relationship.

'Labour power' refers to the capacity of an employee to perform work as detailed in the requirements of a job description and any person specification. Recruitment and selection exercises help employers to make informed judgements on potential employees. References, previous work experience as detailed in a CV, and the overall selection criteria indicate which candidate is best suited to an employment vacancy. The candidate, from a given shortlist of interviewees, who appears most qualified in terms of labour capacity to perform the requirements of the vacancy is likely to be employed.

Through the employment contract the employing organisation purchases the labour capacity of an employee. However, the organisation will, once employment is created, be necessarily concerned with employee performance. Efficient labour performance compels an employer to structure the employee labour process. This is necessary in order for the labour capacity of an employee to be transformed into effective labour performance. For example, supervisors in textile factories monitor employees in several ways. First, supervisors act as visual monitors, who check timekeeping and work rates. Second, supervisors inspect garments for quality faults. Third, supervisors are likely to structure work organisation in respect of competing orders by the use of target rates per worker, the use of overtime and bonus payments. In large firms supervisors and foremen do this on behalf of an employer: that is, they act as employer agents. In contrast to this, in smaller factories the owners of the business may fulfil these roles themselves.

If labour power were transformed into labour in a deterministic fashion as suggested by neo-classical economics, there would be no need for active management. Neo-classical economics, developed between the seventeenth and nineteenth centuries, aims to conceptualise the structure of civil society on the basis of society's economic foundation. Such theories abstract the individual and private property through the exchange mechanism of the market as regulated by contract. That is, civil society and the labour market in particular are visualised in terms of the *rational actor model*, whereby individuals enter into contracts determined on a free and individual basis on equal terms. Essentially labour is visualised like any other inanimate factor of production such as land or capital. In this visualisation management is merely an integrative process that coordinates the factors of production, as described in the neo-classical theory of the firm. However, this is not the case in operational conditions and illustrates the failure of purely economic conceptions of the employment relationship. Within market economies, where the majority of the labour force work within an employment relationship, the control, deployment and regulation of human resources are major management functions.

A central issue for the employer is the management of employees in order to get the maximum economic benefit from their economic control as vested in the contract of employment. This necessitates the creation of management systems. Inside an organisation the design of these systems aims to assist management in the process of transforming raw labour power into efficient labour performance in the form of goods and services that the employer can then sell through the market mechanism. This area is central to the evaluation of industrial relations and management strategies for control such as HRM.

Summary

This section has examined the central significance of the contract of employment in the management and regulation of human resources in four ways. First, a discussion of contract provided a distinction between commercial contracts and employment contracts. Second, the underlying philosophical assumptions behind the notion of a voluntary bargain illustrate that, while contracts are freely entered into in the case of employment, freedom of action within a contract is relative in the sense that an employee is subordinate to their employer. Third, a brief examination of the emergent character of the firm positioned the contract of employment within the wider employment relationship. Last, examining the employment relationship as a process of sociological and economic exchange illustrated that, while the contract of employment is central to the employment relationship, the legal control over employees that a contract provides to an employer does not automatically translate into operational control over the organisation and regulation of work. It follows from this that the employer or their agents must structure the employee labour process to extract an efficient labour performance from the labour potential that is bought under the contract of employment. Thus, the employment relationship is actively managed in order that the benefits of legal control derived from the contract of employment may result in orderly and efficient employee performance.

To amplify on this discussion of employment as a process of socio-economic exchange, the following section details the common law and statutory components of the contract of employment.

THE CONTRACT OF EMPLOYMENT

Now we turn to what could be described as a functional or legal explanation of the contract of employment.

This section is divided into four parts. First, the regulation of employment through the law is outlined. Here we distinguish between the common law and statute law. Second, we examine the common law duties of employer and employee in further detail. Third, we identify the effects of statute law on the contractual regulation of employment. Last, some of the practical effects of HRM on the regulation of the workplace are examined.

The contract of employment: common law and statutory regulation

There are two features to the English legal system that highlight the contexts within which all aspects of the law operate. First, the English legal system, unlike most other legal systems (for example those of other European Union states), does not operate in conjunction with a written constitution or a Bill of Rights. In the specific area of employment the absence of a written constitution or a Bill of Rights means that British subjects do not possess any specific inalienable rights as employees: for example, the right to strike. Second, and relatedly, the system is very conservative – some would say obsessed with the past. This conservatism explains why 'precedent' has so prominent a role in the common law. Precedent operates on the basis of decisions previously arrived at in a higher court. It is judge-made law that creates a rule for lower courts and/or subsequent future cases of a similar nature. Thus a precedent creates an example for subsequent cases or acts as a justification for subsequent decisions.

Advocates of Britain's unwritten constitution argue that its major benefit is adaptability over time, which contrasts with the rigid mechanism of a written constitution around which new developments have to be moulded. In matters of employment many of the rights held by British subjects result from case law and precedent and from trade union activity in collective bargaining. Equally, trade unions have a consultative role in the formulation of statutory protections and provisions such as the national minimum wage or the statutory procedure for trade union recognition under the Employment Relations Act 1999.

In employment common law rights are supplemented by various statutory rights, which bind contractual regulation. For example, under the common law a contract of employment can be verbal, implied by the conduct of the parties or written. However, the Employment Protection (Consolidation) Act (EPCA) 1978 as amended imposes certain statutory obligations on the employer, and introduces certain statutory rights for employees. For example, the employer must give employees itemised wage statements. Second, the ECPA gives employees the statutory right not to be unfairly dismissed and, in the case of job redundancy through no fault of their own, to be compensated by their employer. Both rights are subject to a qualification period: one year for unfair dismissal, and two years for redundancy. This qualification period illustrates the partial nature of an employee's statutory rights within the employment relationship. That is, protection against unfair dismissal and access to redundancy payment are not inalienable rights; they are acquired by continuity of employment in a particular organisation for a defined period of service. Hence employees with periods of employment service of less than one year can be 'fairly unfairly dismissed' and/or have no statutory redress to redundancy payments.

A third statutory requirement is covered by the Trade Union Reform and Employment Rights Act 1993 (TURER). TURER requires that all employees who work more than eight hours per week must be given a written statement of the particulars of their employment in one principal document within two months of the commencement of employment. These written particulars of an individual's contract of employment are referred to as the *express terms of the contract.*

Common law precedent acts in two ways. First, the common law regulates in disputes where there is no relevant Act of Parliament and thus has the status of an Act of Parliament. Second, common law precedent is independent of Parliament; judicial decisions represent an interpretation of common law principles or an interpretation of how particular statutory rulings should be interpreted by the judiciary in future cases. The common law duties of employer and employee are detailed in the next part of this section; however, before going on to that part we can make some brief reference to the effects of statute law.

A central feature of the English legal system operative in the common law and statute law is that of *reasonableness.* In employment contracts, the common law terms and conditions and statutory interventions both have to be reasonable in their effects on the employer and employee. Thus in many cases judgements on disputes between employer and employee often turn on the question of reasonableness. The notions of reasonable and unreasonable behaviour or instructions are questions of interpretation in the circumstances of particular cases. An express, implied or incorporated term in a contract of employment is reasonable if, in a matter of dispute, it is held that a similar employer would have done the same thing, for example discipline or dismiss an employee, in similar circumstances.

In relation to the contract of employment statutes have the effect of incorporating express or implied terms into an employee's contract. Statutory, express or implied terms can have a significant effect on the ordering and regulation of employees at the workplace and therefore are of central significance to human resource practitioners and researchers. The details of express, implied and incorporated terms of employment contracts are considered in further detail in the third part of this section. We now move on to discuss the common law duties of employer and employee.

Common law duties of employer and employee

The first section of this chapter introduced the concept of freedom of contract. This concept assumes that individuals are self-determining agents who are primarily self-interested. It follows from this that individuals both freely enter into contractual arrangements and jointly determine the terms and conditions of an employment contract. In the case of employment, the notion of freedom of contract operates in conjunction with the common law duties of employer and employee. That is, although contracts of employment may be entered into freely, the contract of employment itself incorporates the common law duties of employee and employer.

Common law duties of the employer

These are to:

- Provide a reasonable opportunity for the employee to work and be paid the agreed wages as consideration for work performed. It is a matter of some debate as to whether the employer has a common law duty to actually provide work; the issue appears to turn on the notion of reasonableness, which will depend on the details of any particular case.
- Take reasonable care to ensure that all employees are safe at the workplace, and indemnify any employee for injury sustained during employment. Employers have a vicarious common law duty to provide a safe working environment for their employees. Aspects of this liability are codified in statute under the Health and Safety at Work Act 1974.
- Treat all employees in a courteous and polite manner. That is, employers should not 'bully' or abuse their employees, or subject them to racist or sexist remarks. Aspects of this liability are codified in the Sex Discrimination Act 1975 (as amended) and the Race Relations Act 1976 (as amended). The common law duties of the employer contrast with those of an employee.

Common law duties of the employee

These are to:

- Be ready and willing to work for their employer.
- Offer personal service to the employer: that is, not hold a second job without agreement.
- Take reasonable care in the conduct of their personal service.
- Work in the employer's time, obey reasonable orders during that time, and undertake not to disrupt the employer's business on purpose.
- Not disclose any trade secret to their employer's competitors.

The common law duties of the employee and employer are not always detailed in the written particulars of a contract of employment, and may be implied terms in the contract derived from custom and practice or statutes.

In market economies the contract of employment is freely entered into; however, the terms and conditions, whether they are express or implied, are not jointly determined, and in terms of employee and employer obligations they are not equal in terms of their scope and coverage. In most cases the employer is in the dominant bargaining position because they are offering employment. Hence the employer is able unilaterally to determine how the common law duties of the employee are to be fulfilled. The common law duties of the employee, as listed above, are clear and precise but open to considerable interpretation. In contrast to this, the common law obligations of the employer are imbued with the tenet of limited reasonableness: that is, the obligations imposed on the employer should not be unreasonable. Thus the general concept of reasonableness can only be tested in individual cases. As Hyman (1975: 24) argues, the symmetrical equality within the concept of self-determining individuals freely entering into contracts of employment is really asymmetrical because of the form that the notion of equality (before the law) and freedom of entry actually take. Clearly, equality before the law belies the market power held by an employer. Individual equality before the law visualises firms that have access to necessarily expensive legal advice on the formulation of employment contracts and individuals bereft of such a capability on the same plane. As we pointed out in the first section of this chapter, within the contract of employment freedom and equality are fused with the traditional status bias of employment, and it is this that appears to reduce the equality of the employee and raise the equality of the employer. This dealignment of equality creates the asymmetrical situation described by Hyman.

The employment contract and statute law

All employees have a contract of employment; equally all employees receive some level of statutory protection against arbitrary and unreasonable treatment by an employer. Statutory protection can be framed in individual terms, for example protection against sexual and racial discrimination in the workplace; alternatively rights may be collective, for example the statutory procedure for trade union recognition introduced by the Employment Relations Act 1999. This discussion of the contract of employment details three issues that are of crucial significance to the human resource practitioner. First, we examine the different types of employment contract under which a worker may be employed. Second, we examine key statutory rights of employees under the contract of employment, distinguishing between 'day one' rights and rights that depend on an employee's length of service. Third, we examine new rights available to all employees under the Employment Relations Act 1999. Under each heading specific issues are listed and explained in general non-legal terms.

Contracts of employment

Every worker has a contract of employment. The contract is not always written down in one document, and sometimes the contract may not be written down at all.

There are several types of employment contract, as detailed below.

Permanent, ongoing or open-ended contracts

This type of employment contract is assumed to continue until either side gives notice of an intention to terminate the contract.

Temporary contract

This type of contract has a specified duration, but does not contain any restrictive fixed terms or waivers – for example the requirement that the employee waive their right to statutory protection against a claim for unfair dismissal or redundancy. A temporary contract may be made permanent, and in this case the clause that relates to the specified duration will be removed, and the time served under the temporary contract will constitute continuity of service. Hence in the case of employment rights that are based on an employee's length of service – for example unfair dismissal, which is currently set at one year's length of service – it would not be necessary for the employee to serve another full year to acquire this protection. However, although the general principle is clear, it is a complex area of law subject to the particular circumstances of individual cases.

Fixed-term contract

This type of contract has a specified duration: that is, a clear start date and a clear and unequivocal termination date. Examples of this might include situations where employment is subject to 'funding arrangements' that are not renewable, a specific one-off project or matters such as maternity and paternity leave. Both parties to a fixed-term contract should be aware that such a contract is not renewable. More significant than this, many employees who are subject to fixed-term contracts are required to waive their statutory protections against unfair dismissal and redundancy. The Employment Relations Act 1999 prohibits employers from using waiver clauses against unfair dismissal; however, redundancy waivers continue.

'Casual', 'spot' or zero hours contracts

Under this type of contract the employee must be available for work, but the employer does not have to guarantee work: for example, a retired teacher may be on call to cover for sick colleagues. Equally, banks use call staff to cover busy periods such as lunchtime, whereas the Post Office employs many casual workers at Christmas. In most situations this type of contract is mutually beneficial and not open to abuse; however, if a worker is required to be at work but clock off during slack periods – a practice common in many fast-food outlets – zero hours contracts are open to abuse. For example, such a worker could remain at the workplace for long periods yet have a very low rate of hourly pay owing to continual clocking off. In an effort to overcome some of the abuses of zero hours contracts a person employed on such a contract is now entitled to the national minimum wage whereas the Working Time Directive entitles the person to a paid holiday provided they worked during the preceding 13 weeks.

We have established that in the vast majority of cases the employer is the dominant party in the employment relationship. This dominance enables the employer to determine many terms and conditions contained within the employment contract.

There are three types of terms and conditions within a contract of employment.

Express terms and conditions

These form an explicit part of an individual contract of employment. They are often referred to as the *written* terms and conditions of the contract that are included in the written *statement of the contract*. Any employee, irrespective of the number of hours they work, must be given a statement of the written terms and conditions of their contract within two months – eight weeks – of starting work. The statement must include the following items:

- name and address of employer;
- date employment began;
- place or places of work;
- rate of pay or salary point;
- hours of work;
- holiday entitlements;
- sick pay arrangements;
- notice entitlements;
- pension rights;
- grievance procedure;

- discipline procedure;
- job title;
- period of employment if job not permanent;
- name of employee.

Implied terms and conditions

These are terms and conditions that are not explicitly stated in an individual contract of employment but which are assumed to be included in the contract: for example, work-place custom and practice arrangements and the common law duties of the employer and employee.

Incorporated terms and conditions of employment

These are terms and conditions that are incorporated into individual contracts of employment as either express or implied terms. Incorporated terms and conditions of employment include the provisions of collective agreements negotiated between an employer and a recognised trade union and statutory protections passed by Parliament or the European Union. In English law collective agreements negotiated between employers and trade unions through the process of collective bargaining are not legally binding. However, elements within collective agreements are legally binding if they are incorporated into individual contracts of employment: for example, working hours and pay rates.

Statutory rights relating to employment contracts

Since 1995 all workers, either full time or part time, have been subject to the same *day one statutory rights* irrespective of how many hours they work. Statutory day one rights provide a minimum level of protection to all workers. Some workers may have additional contractual rights negotiated by their employer and a recognised trade union. In addition to day one rights other rights depend on an employees' length of service.

Day one employment rights

Equal pay/equal value

The Equal Pay Act 1970 (EPA) as amended inserts an *equality clause* into contracts of employment that can be enforced by an employment tribunal. Under the EPA clauses within a contract of employment must be equal between the sexes. The equality clause enforces equal terms and conditions in the contracts of men and women employed in the same organisation. The clause covers pay and all other contractual terms of employment. The EPA is applicable in three situations:

- *Like work.* Where men and women are employed to perform like work that is the same work or work that is broadly similar men and women must receive the same rate of pay or be paid on the same salary scale. This is the case even if part-time men and women work fewer hours than full-time men and women, that is a part-time worker may compare themselves to a full-time worker and (although unlikely) vice versa.
- *Work rated as equivalent under an analytical job evaluation scheme.*
- Where work is of *equal value* even though it is not like work or work covered by a non-discriminatory job evaluation scheme in the same employment. Equal value is measured in terms of the demands upon the worker in terms of skill levels, effort and decision making. If different work is held to be of equal value under these criteria then the two groups of workers must have the same pay levels. Pay is constituted

in its widest sense and includes salary scales or pay rates, access to occupational pension schemes, redundancy protection, sick pay, travel concessions and other perks. In the 1980s, USDAW (the shopworkers' trade union) and the Equal Opportunities Commission successfully fought equal value cases on behalf of supermarket checkout workers, who are predominantly women, against delivery dock and warehouse workers who were predominantly men. An employer may defend an equal value case on the grounds that differences in pay between men and women are justified on the grounds of a genuine material factor that is both relevant and significant in the particular case. The fact that a particular group of workers who are predominantly women includes a male worker does not constitute a genuine material factor: that is, men who receive lower pay than other men employed in the same organisation are able to claim that their work is of equal value. For example, the presence of a 'token' male checkout worker or school lunch assistant appears insufficient to defeat a claim for equal value. In summary a claim to equal pay for work of equal value normally involves women in comparison to men; however, the presence of lower-paid men cannot undermine a claim because men are also protected in respect of equal pay for work of equal value.

Sex discrimination/harassment

It is unlawful to discriminate against an employee on grounds of their sex or marital status, or because of pregnancy. The EPA covers discrimination in respect of pay, whereas the Sex Discrimination Act 1975 as amended (SDA) covers discrimination in respect of selection, training, promotion, termination (e.g. selection for redundancy) or any other detriment in employment (e.g. sexual harassment). The SDA applies equally to men and women except with respect to pregnancy provisions, and defines discrimination in three ways:

- *Direct discrimination.* For example, denying a woman a job or promotion on the grounds that she is a woman, a married woman, a single woman, is pregnant and/or has children.
- *Indirect discrimination.* This category refers to apparently sex-neutral job requirements that have a disproportional effect on women, for example height requirements or age and length of service requirements for promotion that may preclude married women with children from having sufficient length of service to apply by an upper age limit. Some cases of indirect discrimination appear to be intentional, whereas other cases result from a failure to update personnel procedures in accordance with the law: for example dress codes that prevent women from wearing trousers. An employer may choose to defend a charge of indirect discrimination on the grounds that the apparently discriminatory provision is a necessary requirement of the job. For example, in selection exercises for the fire service candidates must be able to expand their lung capacity by a certain measurement. Many women applicants are unable to meet this requirement: hence it appears to have a disproportionate effect on women. However, many men are unable to meet the requirement. Lung expansion is a requirement of a firefighter's job because it plays a part in assessing whether or not a candidate would be able to escape from a variety of smoke-filled situations.
- *Victimisation.* This category covers verbal abuse or suggestive behaviour or harassment. It may also result from an employee's enforcing a statutory right.

Certain types of employment are exempt from the provisions of the SDA: for example, employment that is mainly or wholly outside the UK, photographic modelling, and some areas of social work such as child protection from child abuse and rape counselling.

Racial discrimination and harassment

The Race Relations Act 1976 (as amended) (RRA) follows the model set by the SDA and defines racial discrimination as direct, indirect and victimisation. Cases of direct racial discrimination in employment on the grounds that a person is black, Asian, or Afro-Caribbean are less in evidence than during the 1960s. However, examples of indirect racial discrimination in employment turn on the relevance of apparently race-neutral job requirements that have a disproportionate effect on ethnic minorities: for example, requirements that preclude candidates on the basis that their grandparents were not British, or English language requirements. If these requirements are unrelated to the job they may well be indirectly discriminatory. Racial victimisation in employment covers matters such as racial abuse, suggestive behaviour or harassment as a result of an employee's attempting to enforce a statutory right. Certain types of employment are exempt from the provisions of the RRA: for example, staff in specialised restaurants and community social workers who are required to speak particular ethnic languages.

Maternity rights

The rules and regulations in respect of maternity rights are very complicated. It is important that both the employer and the employee follow them carefully. Some employees have better maternity arrangements than the statutory arrangements; this is usually the result of collective bargaining arrangements in the workplace.

All women are entitled to basic maternity leave, which has recently been extended from 14 to 18 weeks under the provisions of the Employment Relations Act 1999. The entitlement is unrelated to the number of hours worked or length of service. A pregnant employee must conform to the following requirements:

- written notice of pregnancy and due date;
- a medical certificate if requested;
- the date the employee intends to begin leave – this cannot be before the 11th week.
- return to work within 18 weeks.

Maternity leave may be extended if the employee is sick or has an illness related to confinement. The day one employment rights listed above and below establish that employees who are either pregnant or on maternity leave cannot be dismissed or made redundant because of pregnancy or a pregnancy-related illness contracted or diagnosed as commencing before or after the birth of the child.

An employee who fulfils the following criteria is entitled to *statutory maternity pay*:

- Are their earnings equal to £66 per week – the lower earnings limit?
- The employee provides the employer with a maternity certificate giving the due date.
- They were employed up to and including the 15th week before the baby was due.
- They have stopped working.
- Have they given the employer 21 days' notice of their intention to stop working?
- At the end of the 15th week of confinement before the baby was due, did the employee work for this employer for 26 weeks?

Statutory maternity pay is calculated on the basis of 6 weeks at 90% of earnings plus 12 weeks at the basic rate of statutory sick pay. Employees who do not qualify for maternity pay may receive maternity allowance from the Department of Social Security. Awards for maternity allowance depend on an employee's National Insurance contribution.

Disability discrimination

The Disability Discrimination Act 1995 (DDA) makes it unlawful for an employer to discriminate against applicants for employment and employees who have a disability in relation to job applications, promotion, training and contractual terms and benefits. The provisions of the statute cover all employees from permanent to casual. In addition subcontract workers are also covered. The DDA is not universal in application. Currently, employers with less than 20 workers are exempt from its provisions. Small employers can discriminate against the disabled without the threat of legal sanction.

The DDA defines *disability* as mental or physical impairment that has a long-term and substantial adverse effect on the ability of an individual to perform normal daily activities. The legislation goes on to amplify this definition under several headings. First, the nature of impairment is broadly interpreted to include recognised medical conditions, for example HIV positive status, schizophrenia and other forms of mental illness. Second, the requirement for a substantial effect rules out minor complaints such as hay fever or colour-blindness. Third, and related, a condition of impairment must last at least a year or the rest of a person's life to qualify as a long-term effect. This requirement rules out impairments such as whiplash resulting from minor motor accidents and other temporary debilitating illnesses. Last, the ability to undertake normal daily activity covers issues such as the ability to hear and learn, comprehend the perception and risk of physical danger, continence, eyesight, hearing, manual dexterity, memory, speech and physical coordination.

The DDA outlines three tests for disability discrimination:

- *Less favourable treatment.* This situation arises when a disabled employee is able to demonstrate less favourable treatment – in comparison with an able-bodied person – that is related to their disability that cannot be justified by the employer. An employer can defend a claim for disability discrimination on the grounds of less favourable treatment if they can demonstrate a relevant or substantial reason for the treatment.
- *A duty to make reasonable adjustments.* A failure to make reasonable adjustments in the workplace may result in disability discrimination. It is likely to be unlawful and unreasonable where a disabled employee is substantially disadvantaged by work arrangements or the layout of the workplace when compared with an able-bodied employee. In this situation the employer is under a legal duty to make reasonable adjustments: for example, the installation of wheelchair ramps. An employer can justify the discrimination on the grounds that they were unaware that a job applicant or employee was disabled. Alternatively, an employer may justify discrimination with a substantial reason.
- *Victimisation.* It is unlawful under the DDA to victimise a person who alleges disability discrimination, enforces statutory rights under the DDA or gives evidence in a disability case.

Miscellaneous

In addition to the above day one rights all employees have the following day one rights where relevant:

- time off for trade union duties;
- protection against victimisation due to involvement in trade union duties – for example, unfair selection for redundancy;

- protection against victimisation due to involvement in health and safety activity;
- the right to itemised payslips;
- protection against unlawful deductions from wages;
- written reasons for dismissal during pregnancy and/or maternity leave;
- time off for antenatal visits;
- basic maternity leave, now at 18 weeks;
- sunday working rights, where relevant;
- victimisation for enforcing a day one or length of service statutory right.

Rights that depend on length of service

Access to the following statutory rights is dependent upon an employee's length of service, but is unrelated to how many hours they work.

- *Written statement of main terms and conditions of employment*: 2 months.
- *Extended maternity leave*: 1 year. Employees who have at least one year's employment service at the beginning of the 11th week before the baby is due are entitled to a longer period of maternity leave, termed extended maternity leave. This leave may extend up to 40 weeks starting 11 weeks before the birth and lasting up to 29 weeks after birth. As with basic maternity leave it does not matter how many hours the employee works. An employee who claims extended maternity leave has to follow several procedural rules:
  - work up to the 11th week before the baby is due;
  - give the employer at least 21 days' notice before the start of leave;
  - provide the employer with a statement that they are going on maternity leave and will return afterwards, and state the date the baby is due;
  - provide a certificate of due date signed by a GP or midwife if requested;
  - provide the employer with 21 days' written notice of the date they intend to return to work;
  - return to work within 29 weeks of the start of the week in which the baby is born.
- *Written reasons for dismissal* – 1 year
- *Protection against unfair dismissal* – 1 year
- *Protection against unfair dismissal due to 'whistleblowing', i.e. public interest disclosure* – 1 year
- *Unfair dismissal due to redundancy* – 2 years
- *Guaranteed lay-off pay* – 1 month
- *Medical suspension pay* – Absence or suspension from work on medical grounds – 1 month
- *Unpaid parental leave* – I year

Employers are required to provide employees with the periods of paid notice listed in Table 10.1. Employers must give employees full pay for the notice period even if the worker is off sick or on maternity leave.

New rights at work? The Employment Relations Act 1999 (ERA)

The ERA establishes many new rights, both collective and individual, that represent a significant improvement in workplace rights, bringing many into line with those found in other European Union states. The ERA complements other measures that aim to improve fairness at work, such as the Working Time Directive and the National Minimum Wage. The legislation aims to achieve decent minimum standards at work that will underpin a flexible labour market and facilitate good industrial relations in the workplace, via trade unions and collective bargaining where desired by employees.

The provisions of the ERA divide into four categories: new and improved individual

Table 10.1 Minimum notice periods

Length of service	Notice
4 weeks–2 years	1 week
2–3 years	2 weeks
3–4 years	3 weeks
4–5 years	4 weeks
5–6 years	5 weeks
6–7 years	6 weeks
7–8 years	7 weeks
8–9 years	8 weeks
9–10 years	9 weeks
10–11 years	10 weeks
11–12 years	11 weeks
Over 12 years	12 weeks

rights for all employees, new collective rights for all employees, maternity and paternity rights, and rights to representation in the workplace.

New rights for all workers

Improved protection against unfair dismissal

This protection is now available after one year's service rather than two years. Estimates suggest that up to 270 000 workers with between one and two years' employment services are dismissed each year. Some of these employees are 'fairly' unfairly dismissed, hence many will directly benefit from this new right. Moreover, the ERA increases top-level payments in cases of unfair dismissal from £12 000 to £50 000. Further, the ERA makes it automatically unfair to dismiss an employee taking part in lawfully organised industrial action for eight weeks. After two months, dismissal will be fair only if the employer can establish that they have taken all reasonable procedural steps to try to resolve the dispute.

Blacklisting

Blacklisting of individual employees for trade union membership or activity is prohibited. This provision relates to blacklists compiled by an employer or by an organisation such as the Economic League or the Freedom Association.

Unpaid parental leave

Employees with one year's employment service are entitled to parental leave (if named as a parent on a birth certificate) for any child born after December 1999 up to the age of 5 years or an adopted child below 18 born after the same date. A parent is entitled to 13 weeks for each eligible child, and this extends to multiple births. The employee remains 'employed' during the leave and on return the employee is entitled to their old job or – if this is unreasonable or impossible – a better job or one of the same standard in terms and conditions. Some employees had paid or unpaid parental leave clauses in their contracts of employment before the provisions of the ERA became effective. These arrangements, many of them arrived at through the process of collective bargaining, remain operative. On return from leave an employee must not have any seniority or pension rights denied as a result of taking leave. If a job is made redundant while an employee is on leave they must be treated as if they are working normally. In January 2000 the TUC, after taking legal advice, declared an intention to undertake a legal challenge to the December 1999 cut-off date. The TUC is advised that the Directive should be retrospective in covering all children under the age of 5 at the date of its implementation.

Personal contracts
The ERA makes it unlawful for an employer to dismiss, omit or otherwise act detrimentally towards an employee who refuses to sign a personal contract that excludes the employee from collectively negotiated terms and conditions of employment.

Prohibition of waiver clauses for unfair dismissal rights in fixed-term contracts
Under the provisions of the ERA it is no longer possible for employers to ask or compel employees on fixed-term contracts to waive the right to complain of unfair dismissal if the contract is not renewed. Waiver clauses in operation before the provisions of the ERA became effective can continue. Equally, the provisions within the ERA make no mention of redundancy rights waivers in fixed-term contracts: hence these waivers remain lawful.

Family emergencies
The ERA provides the right for employees to have reasonable time off work to deal with family emergencies such as accidents or illness to family members, bereavements and severe damage to property.

These new rights aim to provide workers with a more effective voice mechanism in the workplace where it was previously restricted or where they had none. Where employers are obstructive over access to new or extended individual employment rights the law will work in favour of employees in imposing trade union recognition where employees desire this.

Collective employment rights: trade union recognition.
ERA establishes that a claim for trade union recognition can be made with 10% membership and majority support. To demonstrate support for trade union recognition a union can call upon the findings of a survey or petition. Where a trade union already has over 50% membership within the proposed bargaining group, recognition will be automatic except on two grounds: first, where an employer appeals to the central arbitration committee for a secret ballot on the grounds that a ballot will be good for workplace industrial relations; second, where despite a high level of union membership a significant number of employees express the desire not be union members or to be represented by the union in collective bargaining, or where the central arbitration committee concludes either situation to be the case. The evidence suggests that where there is a majority of union members in a non-unionised workplace recognition is likely to be negotiated before the ERA becomes effective or employers offer guarded support for a recognition claim. Further, where the majority of union members is very high the evidence suggests that employers wish to avoid negative media coverage. For example, erstwhile anti-union employers such as Dixons Electrical Stores and Noons Foods, both of whom have very high union membership, have recently negotiated voluntary recognition deals with the AEEU and GMB unions respectively. In addition to this, survey evidence covering the period 1994–98 found that cases of trade union de-recognition fell significantly. In contrast, recognition agreements held constant at an annual level. This evidence demonstrates 44 cases of de-recognition involving 5000 workers and 157 cases of recognition involving 45 000 workers for the years 1997 and 1998 (Gall and Mackay, 1999). Further survey evidence for 1999 found 74 recognition agreements cov-

ering 21000 workers. Of more significance, almost 50% of the trade unions in the survey said that recognition deals resulted from an employer approach (TUC, 2000).

In situations where workplace ballots are necessary, a trade union will be able to address the workforce directly as well as mail information to employees. When recognition is won, the trade union acquires a legal right to negotiate terms and conditions to include hours, pay, and work allocation and discipline. Equally significant to these collective rights, recognition imposes a duty on the employer to inform and consult about training. In cases where an employer proves to be obstructive in establishing a bargaining procedure the ERA allows for one to be imposed upon them. In cases where a trade union is unable to prove 50% membership the statutory procedure for a recognition award will be made where there is majority support in a ballot with at least 40% of those eligible to vote taking part.

Maternity and parental leave

The above sections on day one rights and length of service rights establish that all employees are entitled to basic maternity leave, whereas those with at least one year's length of service are entitled to extended maternity leave. The ERA increased the period of paid basic maternity leave from 14 to 18 weeks and reduced the qualification period for extended maternity leave from 2 years to 1 year. The ERA also introduced the provision for parental leave that is discussed above under new individual employment rights.

The right to representation

The ERA establishes that whether a trade union is recognised or not, individual union members and non-union members alike have the right to be accompanied by a trade union official in disciplinary and grievance hearings. If the employer obstructs or denies this there is a compensatory penalty of up to 2 weeks' pay.

We can now relate the common law and statute law provisions of the contract of employment to the practice of HRM in the organisation in order to comment on how HRM initiatives might influence or be influenced by legal provisions relating to employment.

HRM and the contract of employment

As our starting point we take some of the issues and themes raised in Chapter 1. Arguably, the overriding message within prescriptive and practitioner approaches to HRM centres around the premise that a greater appreciation of how human resources are deployed and organised within an organisation can have a direct influence on its level of competitive performance. This is certainly the prescriptive message in Guest (1989, 1991). If we look at this assumption in another way it is possible to argue that HRM is concerned with (re-)asserting the managerial prerogative over industrial relations within the workplace, (Legge, 1995). Equally, Beardwell (1992) prescribes HRM as a mechanism to manage workplace industrial relations. Two questions of particular relevance to our discussion of the contract of employment and the employment relationship come out of this series of assumptions and presumptions. First, which elements of industrial relations are specifically and generally most accessible to HRM at the workplace? Second, what effects might this more managerially determined approach to job regulation have on the contract of employment? We can proceed to discuss both questions in relation to two models of HRM developed in the UK, those of Guest (1987) and Storey (1992). Both models are examined in Chapter 1. A feature common to both approaches is a desire to delineate HRM from traditional personnel management and its contribution to the management of industrial relations at the workplace.

Each model of HRM shares common elements in terms of central beliefs and assumptions and preferred systems of management structure. Both models stereotype personnel management and suggest that it centres around a highly bureaucratic system of designated work roles with job design based on the division of labour. These characteristics result in the creation of many separate job roles, many separate pay systems and conditions of work autonomy and work organisation. Hence contracts and work rules are clearly delineated, with management initiative bound and regulated within the procedures that this institutional framework creates.

In relation to the questions posed above, prescriptive models of HRM suggest that an alternative consideration of management roles and work rules can transform organisational performance through improved absence control, greater employee commitment (improved motivation), and higher levels of productivity. As a consequence, improved efficiency in the allocation of human resources may create a work environment where employees move beyond mere compliance and become committed to the goals of the organisation to improve financial performance.

It appears that the contract of employment is central to compliance-based systems of personnel management, whereas within the HRM strategies for management control its central significance is played down. In order to break the institutional bureaucracy of personnel management, line managers aim to exert their prerogative over work organisation rather than over pay and conditions. This is the case because if aspects of work organisation are removed from a negotiated order in employment relations other essential elements of job regulation will flow from it: for example strategic integration, fewer job categories, increased teamwork, and harmonised employment conditions.

The organisation of work is a key issue for firms that deploy control strategies that emphasise HRM. Kessler and Bayliss (1998: 275–277) suggest that changes in working methods and the pursuit of flexibility in the use of human resources were the main components of the managerial agenda during the 1980s. However, survey evidence in the fourth Workplace Employment Relations Survey (WERS4) points to little coherence in the take-up of these strategies, (Cully, et al., 1999).

Further, case study evidence provided by Purcell and Ahlstrand (1994) demonstrates that wider patterns of corporate governance associated with the multidivisional firm are likely to dissipate and fragment the transformational potential of HRM. The decentralisation of initiatives into separate business units results in disparate and financially separate cost centres that debilitate the potential of any central coherence in management strategy.

On the second question concerning the position of contract, both Guest (1987) and Storey (1992) suggest that HR strategies and HRM policies seek an employment relationship that is less contractually determined and less perfunctory in its performance. Guest concentrates on the psychological environment in his suggestion that the formality of personnel management and its associated bureaucracy create an air of compliance, whereas HRM seeks to generate an air of compliance that is in Storey's work termed 'beyond contract'. Guest (1987) and Storey (1992) examine issues first formulated by Fox (1974). Fox examined the notion of 'high trust/low trust' and discretion as a critique of traditional Taylorist control systems based on low trust and low discretion. Fox aimed to illustrate the limitations of low-trust work environments, where the effects of alienation and distrust between management and a workforce reinforce (contractual) regulation. The factor that distinguishes Fox from Guest and Storey is evident in the effects of low-trust management strategies. Fox illustrates the direct limitations of these strategies on motivation, absenteeism, labour turnover and productivity, whereas Guest and Storey illustrate how management aims to minimise these limitations via work restructuring, so as to play down the regulatory effects of contract.

The central question for the reader to consider is: What does this tell us about HRM? Is it about replacing existing forms of managerial regulation? Or is it a reconstitution of existing modes in an effort to raise worker performance and therefore improve organisational performance in terms of greater flexibility and higher productivity?

Within HRM-style organisations contracts of employment are more likely to be generally written and not carefully delineated. For example, job descriptions are more likely to be general in their make-up than highly specific. This is likely to be facilitated if work organisation is unilaterally determined, for example in workplaces that aim to exclude collective representation of employee interests. WERS4 material demonstrates that employers who exclude collective representation of the workforce may have high levels of management control and flexibility. However, the study finds that plural employers with employee representation by recognised trade unions operate more integrated and high-commitment work practices – strategic HRM – than do firms that exclude trade unions (Cully *et al.*, 1999)

HRM implies fewer job grades, fewer demarcated areas of responsibility, and therefore a greater use of teamwork. It is presumed that such innovations will encourage employees to improve their commitment to the organisation and go beyond contractual obligations. However, it must be emphasised that other components of the human resource strategies must be set in place in tandem with these innovations if competitive performance is to improve. For example, the dissemination and general pick-up of ideas and aims by general or line managers is necessary. Similarly, employees must have some effective voice mechanism within the organisation, whether through collective bargaining, collectively regulated works councils or managerially sponsored communication mechanisms such as briefing groups and appraisals. These mechanisms are necessary in order to maintain employee willingness to remain compliant and motivated beyond a framework of compliant contractual regulation.

In summary, the contract of employment enables employers to exercise a managerial prerogative in accordance with the common law duties of the employee. It appears that the prescription behind HRM, if not its deployment in the British economy, is ideally suited to this end. The job of human resource practitioners has two elements in this regard: first, to encourage and enthuse employees in a manner that avoids infringing employees' common law and statutory rights; second, to generate collective consent to the intensification of the employment relationship through willingness to go beyond what is contractually necessary. This is clearly a fine line, and any failure here can frustrate wider managerial objectives. For example, consider the long-running teachers' dispute in 1991–93 over National Curriculum testing and individual student assessment in GCSE examinations. John Patten, the then Secretary of State for Education, argued that industrial action undertaken by teacher unions in support of their grievance over workloads was not a trade dispute but a politically motivated dispute inspired by opposition to the new National Curriculum. Successive courts held that the teachers' grievance was a trade dispute and reasonable. Thus the efforts of the then Department for Education and Science to instil an air of flexibility and improved pupil, school and teacher performance were held to be an unreasonable intensification of teacher workloads. That is, they went beyond the requirements of teachers' contracts of employment in an unreasonable manner. More recently, pit deputies employed by RJB mining won a tribunal case over working time arrangements. Deputies had worked 48 hours in a particular week during the relevant test period, and refused to work further overtime. This action had a severe effect on pit opening owing to health and safety requirements. An employment tribunal held that when a group of workers have opted into the Working Time Directive framework, they cannot be compelled to work beyond the upper time limit. This is the case even where a refusal to work beyond 'normal hours' restricts the normal operation of the business.

OPERATIONAL CONTROL IN THE EMPLOYMENT RELATIONSHIP

In this section we consolidate our arguments, detailed in the previous sections, that the employment relationship is a process of socio-economic exchange. This section divides into three parts. First, we look at the issue of management and the management process. This discussion is pursued on two dimensions. Management functions and their prescription are examined, leading to a brief discussion of scientific management techniques. Beyond this initial introduction the process of management as a function within the UK's industrial capitalism is examined. This discussion leads to an examination of the effects of scientific management on the labour process. In addition we pose the question: What do managers do? This issue is further detailed in the second part of this section, which is a debate on the management process and the emergence of centralised workplaces. The final part of this section looks at management as the realisation of legal authority and control within the employment relationship. This discussion takes into consideration issues such as moral involvement, collective consent and participation. Additionally this discussion examines the emergence of organisation-specific employee relations policies that aim to assist the employer to realise legal control over employees as vested in the contract of employment. In this respect we pay particular reference to the use of HRM techniques.

Management and management functions

Management and the functions of management both appear to be so obvious that they do not need prescriptive or critical evaluation. People who work within the employment relationship are subject to management and may on occasions operate in managerial mode themselves. Thus the process of management is something that surrounds us all. As a consequence of this presence we all think we have a good idea of what management is all about and who is a good manager. However, management, like the 'state', contains many elements that are readily familiar but which many individuals find difficulty in explaining rather than explaining what managers do. For example, managers and supervisors structure works organisation and the labour process to extract an efficient performance from employees. However, many managers describe this as motivating employees in their team.

Management is defined as the administration of business concerns, and covers the persons engaged in this process, whereas a manager can be defined as someone who controls the activities of a person (*OED*, 1982). In order to fulfil the management role a manager must perform several functions.

The functions of management can be summarised under three main headings. First, management is concerned with *control*. The first two sections of this chapter quite clearly stated that, once a worker enters the employment relationship and offers their personal service to an employer, they are under the control and direction of that employer. Thus in order to work effectively an employee has to be directed and controlled in the delivery and performance of their work.

Direction and control are undertaken in a variety of ways. One is direct supervision, for example the use of supervisors and inspectors in textile factories. A second method, technical supervision, operates through methods of work organisation, associated job design, job descriptions and the use of technology to regulate and oversee the performance of work. Examples of the latter might be the use of scanners at supermarket checkouts or playback and conversation-monitoring devices in call centres. Lastly, control can be implemented through the use of bureaucratic measures such as the completion of time sheets, the use of appraisal schemes, quality circles, team briefings and the introduction of quality management systems. Essentially a controlled performance is required in order for an organisation, whether in the private or public sector, to be efficient and competitive within the wider framework of industrial capitalism – competitiveness and profitability in the private sector and working within fixed budgets in the public sector.

The second function of management is *coordination*. A central feature of the employment relationship in centralised workplaces is the division of labour. The division of labour examines productive benefits that are derived from the process of employee specialisation. Specialised employees are more productive in their work and at the same time have the opportunity to earn higher levels of wages, if their wage is related to the quantity of production. Adam Smith, who conceptualised the division of labour, argued that its internal benefits were potential advantages: that is, to realise potential benefits the division of labour requires management and supervision. Managers have to coordinate the number of workers required in order that the potential benefits of the division of labour are realised. Thus the second function of management is to coordinate human and capital resources in an efficient and productive manner.

The third function of management can be summarised under the heading of *motivation and compliance*. In the first section of this chapter we identified the difference between labour power and labour. To recap, an employer, via the contract of employment, buys an employee's labour power. The employer has then to transform this into effective performance by creating either goods or services that can be sold at a profit. This issue is central to the sociological dimension of the employment relationship. This is the case because the employer has to realise legally vested superiority: that is, power within the employment relationship, by controlling and coordinating employees. In addition, and more crucially, management must acquire the collective consent of employees to their subordinate position within the employment relationship whereby they are controlled and coordinated.

Although we have discussed the functions of management under several headings, at this stage we are still lacking a framework within which to locate and visualise the application of these functions. This is where we need to examine the prescription behind management science.

Management science

Management science aims to codify and rationalise a framework for the operation of management functions. In addition, management science is a quantitative academic discipline. In the functional sense management science is a prescription that legitimises the superior position of management within the employment relationship. It therefore emphasises the importance of the managerial prerogative. Thus property ownership in the form of a business gives the employer and their management agents the authority to direct factors of production. In respect of human resources this authority is clearly derived from the authority relation vested in the employer by the contract of employment.

The best-known theory of management science is that of Frederick Taylor (1911). Taylor argued correctly, if somewhat egotistically, that prior to his work no one had studied and visualised work in a scientific manner: thus he described all previous forms of management as 'ordinary' and distinguished them from his principles of scientific management. We have defined a manager as someone who controls the work of others. This definition appears to be very similar to that of scientific management: 'the science of the management of others' or 'work under capitalist employment relations'. In order to be able to do this an employee who operates in managerial mode must be able to fulfil the functions of management in three ways.

First, management must dissociate the labour process from skilled workers: in short, management needs to gather all necessary knowledge on the organisation and deployment of work. This enables those who operate in managerial mode to reduce work to a series of laws, procedures and rules that are arrived at and varied by systematic study. The objective of dissociation is to make the labour process dependent on management and reinforce the management prerogative vested in the contract of employment.

The first principle directly leads to the second one. If management is able to dissociate the labour process from employed labour this separates the conception of work from its execution. In other words, those who operate in managerial mode conceptualise work whereas other employees – shopfloor workers – execute it. Taylor argued that by separating the conception and execution of work the methods of work and their pace could be dictated by management. In both the first and second principles of scientific management Taylor implicitly follows the division of labour as formulated by Smith.

The third principle in Taylor's prescription was the monopoly of knowledge by management in order to control each step in the labour process. Taylor followed the arguments put forward by Smith, in particular the assertion that the division of labour would improve productivity via specialisation. Specialisation and improved productivity also give the employee the opportunity to earn high wages. Therefore the prescription of scientific management is in the interests of the employer as it facilitates effective work by employees, leading to maximum profits, as well as being in the employees' interest in the sense of improved earning potential.

The idea of scientific management as formulated by Taylor has been criticised on many levels. First, it treats labour as purely economic in the sense that all employees want from employment is an effective wage. Other management theorists, in particular the human relations school, have heavily criticised this assumption and argued that a preoccupation with economic return is short-sighted in terms of the effective realisation of all management functions.

Braverman (1974) has also been a notable critic of Taylor. Braverman argues that the prescription behind Taylor, while it might have an overall efficiency motive, has many degrading effects on labour. In summary, he argues that the primary motive behind Taylor's prescription is the need to deskill skilled labour. Another general criticism of Taylor centres on the overt rationality and simplicity of his prescription. In particular he fails to consider the likelihood of effective individual or collective worker resistance legitimised in trade union activity and collective bargaining. Equally, Taylor ignored the possibility that management may accept established spheres of worker control in the labour process such as those that prevailed in the printing industry, craft engineering or that which exists in the fire service. This point has been made with particular vigour in the case of the UK, where, even in the contemporary period unions that represent skilled workers still retain some control over their labour process from employers. What Braverman (1974) ignored was the need to contextualise his arguments by examining the specific development of industrial capitalism within particular market economies. In the UK, for example, in the period immediately after the Second World War skilled craftsmen maintained considerable control over their labour processes, which in some cases management had little interest in breaking down. For example see Clark (1999, 2000), where the effects of management reticence and failure as well as labour resistance are surveyed in relation to postwar reconstruction of British industry and its management.

In summary, the material in this section examines the notion of management as a set of functional skills that are necessary to legitimise and reinforce the authority of the employer. This authority is legally ordained in the contract of employment. Taylor codifies the functions of management within the techniques of scientific management, which aim to give employees who operate in management roles control over all aspects of the production process. In tandem the functions of management and techniques of management science assist management in turning labour power purchased through the contract of employment into useful and productive labour performance in terms of goods and services for sale in the market.

The management of industrial relations at the workplace by human resource techniques appears as one control strategy by which management can turn contracted labour power into productive labour. In the 1990s managerial control strategies such as HRM appeared to represent vogue methods by which management could transform organisational performance. However, survey material in WERS4 and case study evidence indicate two caveats. First, the prescription behind HRM is not always in evidence and where human resource initiatives are taken up they are disparate and disintegrated. For example, WERS material suggests that only 14% of workplaces have the necessary components of management strategy in place to generate what is currently termed a 'high performance' workplace. Moreover, the material demonstrates that the majority of personnel practitioners are involved in cost containment, rather than the development of human resource strategies that aim for high quality or innovation in the workplace (Cully et al., 1999).

A second caveat centres on mechanisms of corporate governance, such as the central power of the accounts function within the M-form (multidivisional) structure of corporate organisation. For the UK the evidence suggests that HRM appears as an adjunct to performance management, and has a marginal effect on economic performance as distinct from any scale effects. That is, a concentration on the reconfiguration of labour is likely to improve economic performance and competitive advantage on the margin at existing levels of capital investment and investment in human resources. In contrast to this, improvement in competitiveness and performance that is sustainable beyond the short term derives from improved capital investment and the upskilling of labour; see Purcell and Alhstrand (1994) for further case studies, Armstrong (1995), Gallie et al. (1998) and Purcell (1995) for general arguments. Each of the cited studies demonstrates that in most cases employers appear unwilling to entertain or sustain qualitative human resource measures beyond the short term unless they provide an early financial payback. Further, Clark (1998) demonstrates that, where an employer invests in promoting and resourcing the human resource function, internal conflict with line managers may reduce or impair any improvement in financial performance that results. This further impairs the contribution of strategic HRM to the 'bottom line', denting its empirical credibility yet further. We now expand our discussion of management by locating the function of management within the UK's industrial capitalism, and follow this with a discussion of management in relation to the labour process.

Management and the UK's industrial capitalism

The first section of this chapter demonstrates that contractual employment and its regulation occur because the emergence of the firm or centralised workplace necessitated the active management of work performed by employees. In this section we expand on this point to illustrate how the management process appears to regulate and structure employment by providing a framework to transform labour power into productive labour. The market process determines which form of contractual regulation governs the relations between individuals – that is, commercial or employment relations (Coase, 1937).

The Coasian argument is very influential at the level of general economic analysis; however, because economic theory is concerned with rationally defined efficiency it fails to consider the sociological dimension of the employment relationship. In short, the preoccupation with efficiency overlooks or belies any consideration of power within the employment relationship. This leads us to consider two questions of controversy and debate: Why did the centralised workplace emerge? And what is the relation of management to this emergence?

Controversies and debates: the centralised workplace and management

We can discuss the first question by reviewing the contrasting arguments of Landes (1986) and Marglin (1974). Marglin argues that the movement from pre-capitalist (and therefore pre-capitalist production relations) to centralised workplaces was largely inspired by a need for capitalists to acquire greater control over the production process by using the division of labour centrally as distinct from decentrally via cottage industry and the putting-out system. This argument contrasts strongly with the orthodox account of the movement to centralised workplaces as formulated by Landes (1969; 1986). Essentially Landes (1986) argues that the needs of the market and its scale of operation inspired the movement to the centralised workplace. To put it crudely, Landes argues that the dynamic of the UK's industrialisation process, and in particular technological change, became too big for existing forms of production relations such as cottage industry and putting-out. Thus the movement to centralised workplaces was motivated by the logic of economic efficiency as described by Coase. Movement to the factory system resulted in the extended use of the division of labour and eventually the deployment of scientific management techniques. Out of these two developments came the emergence of management and hierarchy within the employment relationship.

Landes and Marglin agree that movement to the factory resulted in the use of the division of labour in an extended fashion; however, they disagree on the basis of the movement and its effects. Marglin argues that the use of the division of labour was not motivated by efficiency considerations in the Coasian sense, but by a desire on the part of capitalists to gain greater control over the production process than would have been possible under existing production relations. Thus, in terms of our perspective that the employment relationship is a socio-economic exchange, Marglin concentrates on the sociological dimension of the employment relationship. In summary, Marglin emphasises the division of labour as a form of control and power. Improvement in both areas was motivated by a concern not for economic efficiency but for increased management control over the labour process.

Landes (1986) accepts some of Marglin's arguments but counter-argues that the extended use of the division of labour and new technology led to hierarchy and was itself inspired by efficiency criteria in the market. Landes concentrates on the economic side of the socio-economic exchange, and downplays considerations of power and control as initiators, but accepts that a power relation does exist.

A second theme particular to Marglin (1974) centres on the technical role of workplace management in the division of labour. Marglin argues that the role of management within the division of labour derives not from the pursuit of economic efficiency but from a desire to control the labour process of employees, which could not be satisfactorily undertaken through traditional work systems such as cottage industries, putting-out and subcontracting. This latter point is significant because the 1980s and 1990s witnessed the widespread use of putting-out and subcontracting in a more modern form of competitive tendering, self-employment and home working. One factor that might explain this process is the more developed protection that a large firm is able to obtain through improvements in contractual regulation of personal services. The prescription behind the notion of the flexible firm as popularised by Atkinson (1984) cites this development as one method by which firms can acquire greater flexibility. (See Chapter 3 for further discussion of flexibility.)

The pursuit of efficiency and the concentration on the economic side of the wider socio-economic exchange within the employment relationship causes economists to underplay the effects of the drive for efficiency on those who are employed and subject to management direction under a contract of employment. That is, the rational actor model views enterprise and labour as inanimate factors of production and therefore ignores the reality of workplace relationships, where management and employees act in less than a rational manner. We recall that management direction is concerned to actualise the legal control vested in the contract of employment and therefore centres on transforming labour power into productive labour performance. We discuss this by briefly examining the labour process, an area that is more comprehensively covered in Chapter 3.

The labour process and management

The term 'labour process' describes the process of work and how it seeks to satisfy the social needs of humans in their societal form. This process has three elements: first, how the activities of individual humans are directed to work; second, how work is performed – here the focus is on how natural objects or raw materials are transformed into a more useful state; and third, how technology is allied to the direction of work. Thus, essentially the labour process examines how individuals who perform work interact with the means of production within which their work or labour process operates.

Work occurs in all societal forms, whether they are tribal or industrial. The discussion and debate that surrounds the labour process focuses on how the means of production are controlled and organised. It is likely that the ordering of economic activity is particular to specific societal forms. In terms of market economies the arguments of Marx (1954) are of particular relevance.

In terms of the control and organisation of the means of production, Marx distinguishes between cooperative production and manufacturing production where the division of labour operates. The delineating factor between the two modes of production centres on the directed activity of workers. In cooperative production labour may be involved in holistic production, whereas in industrial economies individual labour units concentrate on the production of one component or element of a good. This delineation between the two production modes tells us something about the social relations of production. The social relations of production derive from the ownership and control of the means of production. In cooperative production, one group is likely to own the raw materials and means of production. In contrast to this, under conditions of industrial capitalism – the framework of manufactured production – the materials and the means of production are likely to be owned by a second smaller group. The capitalist entrepreneur may be an owner manager or, in larger organisations, is more likely to employ managers to realise the productive labour performance of employees in the form of profit. Marx made a valuable contribution to the evaluation of employment by locating work and its management in the context of market economies. In market economies a specific form of the social relations of production operates. This specific form centres around the contractual determination of the employment relationship described in the previous two sections.

Marx made two points of profound significance in this regard. First, the market mechanism within which work is constituted operates as a competitive anarchy. Second, in order for capital to reproduce itself it has to reproduce labour. As the market mechanism is based on profit, it puts all employers on a competitive basis within their defined market. This is one reason why productivity improvements and management control and motivation strategies aimed at controlling costs are central to work within market economies.

Marx therefore evaluated work as a socio-economic exchange. In terms of economic analysis Marx illustrates how the apparently docile market mechanism dictates the need for continual improvements in productivity in order that profits can be earned to enable capital to reproduce itself. In terms of the sociological side of work Marx illustrates the contradictory nature of its economic requirements. First, capital has to employ labour, pay it and therefore reproduce it. Second, Marx identified that the anarchy of the market mechanism forces employers to intensify work through improvements in productivity and better management control. In addition to this Marx argues that the economic requirements of the market will actually undermine capitalism. In particular, efforts to cheapen labour costs, the introduction of new technology and the growth of urban unemployment all inhibit the reproduction of capital because they inhibit the reproduction of labour. This situation leads to the overthrow of capitalism through a workers' revolution or more likely sees market economies in periodic crisis. Once in a crisis, market economies have to restructure themselves. HRM was one method by which management attempted to restructure employment in market economies during the 1980s and 1990s.

In summary, work is a universal activity that occurs in a variety of societal settings, each of which has its own social relations of production. These relations derive from the ownership of the materials and means of production, which in tribal and other non-industrial societies may be inclusive; however, within industrial society they are more likely to be exclusive. This is not to say that all societal types prior to industrial capitalism were without exploitation – for example, those based on slavery. The distinction between pre-industrial and industrial society centres on the mode of exploitation. In this chapter we are primarily concerned to illustrate the role of contract and management within the process of efficient and controlled production, which from the labour process perspective are mechanisms of exploitation.

Classical political economists such as Smith, Ricardo, Mill and Malthus were essentially concerned with the regulation of the employed class so as to create efficient market conditions. Marx, too, was a political economist; his point of departure was the perhaps undeveloped argument that employment was a socio-economic exchange. As a consequence of this Marx looked beyond the technical efficiency of the division of labour to its effects on labour who operate within the social relations of industrial capitalism: to this end it is essential to differentiate between labour power and labour performance.

The principal questions for our discussion centre on the extent to which the contract of employment facilitates management control over the labour process, and to what degree the management process is autonomous or predetermined in its effort to realise labour power bought through the contract of employment. This is really a question of interpretation and perspective. However, the central issue revolves around the degree to which one accepts or denies that employees who operate in management functions have autonomy and discretion on how they fulfil their roles – that is, the extent to which management and the deployment of management strategies and structures can enact strategic choice. The notion of strategic choice is central to human resource strategy, and suggests that managers are capable of responses to their competitive environment that are independent of historically and institutionally formed patterns of corporate governance, broader public policy enacted by the state and entrenched patterns of industrial relations management. In support of strategic choice, 'exemplar firms' are often generalised as the norm: for example, British Airways under Lord King, British Leyland under Michael Edwardes, British Coal and British Steel under Ian McGregor, Asda under Archie Norman, Burtons under Ralph Halpern, Tesco under Lord Mclorghlin and Ginger Productions under Chris Evans. Notwithstanding these exemplar firms, a key issue is the degree to which market opportunities and relations dictate choices made by firms as distinct from individual strategic choices.

We can examine management control by arguing that labour is animate and therefore cannot be considered in the same way as other factors of production. Therefore labour has to be managed, even though legally it is in a subordinate position within the contractually defined employment relationship. Notwithstanding this point, the management of employees operates within a variety of perspectives, for example pluralism and unitarism. The former recognises that employees have an interest in their labour process and its management; thus employers may recognise unions and in effect share the management process. Therefore the three types of work rule – simple, technical, bureaucratic – may in part be jointly determined. The unitary perspective emphasises unrestricted use of the managerial prerogative; employees are excluded from the management function and may only be consulted on management decisions.

In the period after the Second World War the central significance of the frontier of control at the individual workplace frustrated the systematic introduction and use of scientific management techniques without employee input. Thus, in relation to management control, it is clear that the contract of employment only facilitates management control over the labour process in the legal sense. To summarise, management failure and effective worker resistance, however sectional, cannot be overlooked as factors that frustrate the goal of management control (Clark, 1999).

The second question on management autonomy turns on the issue of how control is derived in the employment relationship. In some respects Braverman's arguments are reductionist in their view of the management process. The arguments may be correct at the general level of aims, but in terms of processes there may be other ways. Friedman (1977) argues that employers may derive operational control within the employment relationship by stimulating 'responsible autonomy', which is likely to play down some of the 'direct control' aspects associated with Taylorist work systems. This is precisely what human resource strategies attempt. The arguments developed by Guest and Storey on the prescription behind HRM make the same argument as Friedman. For Guest and Storey the focus is on how HRM aims to improve operational control by stimulating motivation, belonging and organisational culture. These processes seek to align the goals of the employee with those of the organisation, whereas Friedman is more concerned with the specific organisation of work rather than its organisational context.

In summary, the conclusion we draw is twofold. First, at the general level, managers within market economies seek a controlled and efficient performance of the labour process within the wider social relations of production. Second, and significantly, there are a variety of methods to achieve a controlled and efficient performance. These range from deskilling as emphasised by Braverman and utilised by organisations such as McDonald's and the food retailing industry, to the more sophisticated human resource strategies approaches employed by organisations such as Gent, IBM, Pedigree Pet Foods, Caterpillar and Bechtel. We now move on to discuss the notion of collective consent within the employment relationship and the contribution of HRM in this process.

Management and the realisation of legal authority and control

We have established that the legal authority to control the employment relationship, which is vested in the employer via the contract of employment, does not equate to operational control over the employment relationship. Management has to transform the purchased labour power into a productive labour performance that produces goods and services for sale through the market mechanism. Here we make some brief comments on the realisation of control within the employment relationship in order to produce a regulated labour performance.

As Fox (1985) points out, management strategy is a blend of coercion and consent. Both issues relate to the sociological dimension of the socio-economic dimension of the employment relationship. This blend occurs because both consent and control relate to power. Coercion represents the naked use of power to determine a situation. In the context of the employment relationship it may take the form of a highly controlled work environment, or the use of high-profile direct control by the employer or their agents, such as supervisors and team leaders. In a highly controlled work environment the social technology of a management structure conditions orderly workplace behaviour and workplace relationships. The social technology combines with material technology to create a disciplined regime of work – for example the use of barcoding in virtually all types of retailing, or the use of information technology within banks and work in call centres. The creation of a highly disciplined work environment is, in some respects, an expression of power in the management process. This does not mean to say that coercion is highly visible in these types of working situation. As stated above, management strategy is a fusion of coercion and consent.

By consent we mean voluntary agreement and compliance. Consent in an individual employment relationship refers to the individual employee agreeing to accept reasonable management authority. Managers appear able to generate collective consent over the entire workforce as a result of this individual contractual control, yet management has to legitimise its decisions to the employed labour force. At one extreme management can achieve this through total coercion, while at the other it can be derived through total consent; however, it is likely to be realised within a continuum between the two.

It is conceivable that management can legitimise its authority and get the workforce to consent to changes in the management of job regulation which may have the benefits described by Braverman without all the attendant negatives. This is partly the line developed by Friedman (1977) in his critique of Braverman, which highlights the notion of responsible autonomy. The degree and level of responsible autonomy given to workers may depend on the type of work they perform. 'High discretion' workers who have a professional standing or status may be subject to less overt control within the employment relationship. This type of control may be self-imposed or imposed by professional discipline or by vocational ethics. These forms of control are less related to the contract of employment and direct managerial supervision, but nonetheless are powerful controlling agents. Labour process theorists counter-argue that the control and organisation of the white-collar or professionalised labour process is different from that of the blue-collar or manual employees only in its form, not in its objective. For further elaboration of this position see Hyman and Price (1983) and Smith *et al.* (1991).

To minimise the coercive aspects of job regulation some form of participation within the employment relationship is necessary. Participation refers to the involvement of non-managerial employees within the decision-making process of an organisation. Employee involvement takes two forms: initiatives that pass information to employees, and initiatives that aim to tap the knowledge of employees. Thus participation may operate in a situation that accepts the presence of conflicting and differing views within an organisation; alternatively it can express the notion of a community of interests and common goals. In the post-war period the preferred form of participation in the UK was some combination of proceduralised personnel management and collective bargaining. Thus participation tended to operate on a collective basis through the employee voice mechanism of trade unions. The issue of collective bargaining is discussed in further detail in Chapter 11.

Two points need to be made in connection with participation in the employment relationship and its contractual regulation. First, the existence of participation in whatever form, be it collective bargaining, profit sharing or quality circles, represents attempts to realise managerial control and stimulate an effective work performance without a complete reliance on direct control mechanisms. Second, more individualised forms of participation may represent only a partial generation of consent. For example, they may not be subject to the process of negotiation but merely part of what the organisation 'gives' in terms of 'soft' HRM for the benefits of 'hard' HRM.

As part of the process of changing or supplementing the traditional form of employee participation in the UK and other European countries, we have seen the emergence of employee relations as an adjunct to the management of job regulation operating at the level of the organisation.

Marchington and Parker (1990) define the emergence of employee relations in three ways. First, it has arrived through slippage: that is, it may be the politically correct term to use when describing industrial relations. This position bears some similarity to that of Guest (1989) on the correctness of the term HRM vis-à-vis personnel management. Second, employee relations covers that part of the personnel function, as described by practitioners, that is concerned with the regulation of employees at organisation level. Such policies can be collective or individual in nature. Third, although employee relations is concerned with job regulation, which is the substance of industrial relations, its focus is less on the process and more on the management of employees or the managerial perspective on the employment relationship.

The aim of organisation-specific employee relations policies is to generate active employee involvement and consent in the process of change at the workplace as well as its general management. Within the HRM rubric this may take the form of seeking to create a high-trust working atmosphere that gives employees greater responsibility, or what Friedman refers to as *responsible autonomy*. These movements have two effects on the realisation of management control, both of which are significant to our discussion of contract and the employment relationship.

First, the newer forms of participation tend to be based around small work teams if not individuals. These modes of participation de-collectivise the labour process at the workplace, and as a result they appear to reduce the operational importance, if not the central significance, of any trade union presence.

Second, any moves to individualise employee participation have an effect on the organisation of work. In this respect we could argue that individualised employee participation is part of what the organisation gives in terms of 'soft' HRM for the benefits of 'hard' HRM. One such benefit is greater flexibility in the use and deployment of labour. The terms 'use' and 'deployment' represent work organisation, which, as Kessler and Bayliss (1998) argue, were major areas of the management agenda for change during the 1980s. This process often involves removing elements of work organisation from the collective bargaining process, thereby making employee participation in the regulation of a collective experience – employment – less collective and more individual – that is, subject to greater managerial control.

Our discussion of the management process and the realisation of controlled work performances illustrate that work has to be managed, monitored and regulated. By examining the issues of coercion, consent and participation in either collective or individual mode, it is clear that management aims to realise operational efficiency and control over the employed workforce in a variety of ways. The choice of methods may in part depend on the type of employee under consideration and the type of change that is sought. Human resource techniques are the latest or current vogue prescription to assist management in this process.

Summary

In this section we have consolidated our argument, developed in the first two sections, on the employment relationship as a process of socio-economic exchange. We developed this argument by examining the role and nature of the management function and process. The discussion was gauged in terms of the prescription behind management science, followed by critical evaluation that arrived at the conclusion that, while it appears correct in terms of economic analysis, its operation is more complicated and indeterminate.

We furthered these arguments by looking at the emergence of the centralised workplace and the technical role of management or otherwise in this process. Finally, we briefly commented on how the management process within the production relations of market economies seeks to realise economic efficiency and control in a less deterministic fashion than the way described by Taylor and criticised by Braverman.

CONCLUSION

The material contained in this chapter does three things. First, it establishes the central significance of contract within the management and regulation of the employment relationship. Within contract the employment relationship is visualised as an essentially private exchange between employer and employees. The second section of this chapter explains how the common law and parliamentary legislation confirms this visualisation. The third section broadens the discussion of the employment relationship into a process of a socio-economic exchange to illustrate the weakness of a purely economic and contractual visualisation of employment. We detail the emergent nature of the employment relationship in the UK's market economy to illustrate how the management of employees has become essential if employers are to realise their contractually vested authority.

Human resource strategies appear central to all three areas. As this chapter illustrates, contractual regulation and the wider employment relationship are derived in specific nation states over a long period of time. This derivation and its institutionalisation form the context within which human resource policies operate. Thus, although the prescription of HRM appears to be universal, its application and effectiveness are conditioned by the national context within which it operates.

SUMMARY

● The contractual relationship between the organisation and its employees regulates a sociological and economic exchange within a wider employment relationship. The concept of contract visualises an agreement between two or more parties that is enforceable by means of four elements: offer, acceptance, consideration and an intention to create legal relations. In the case of the contract of employment this is expressed in terms of an offer of engagement, an agreement to sign the terms of the offer, and the subsequent exchange of labour for wages as consideration. To be valid a contract must be reasonable, legal and between consenting parties.

● The philosophy of contract is based on market individualism, expressed as each individual's own best judgement of their own interests. Thus freedom of contract assumes that parties are self-determining individuals who are primarily self-interested. Employment contracts differ from other contractual forms because they are based on notions of authority, legitimacy and managerial prerogative. Thus the individual employee is not simply agreeing to a contract as a free agent but also accepts that managerial authority will be part of the contract. Employee acceptance of subordination to a superior marks the contract of employment as different from other contracts for services, where equality between the supplier and the purchaser is assumed. Further, employment is typified by one dominant mode of contract – the employment contract – rather than millions of independent contracts between firms and employees, because employers tend to buy 'labour' as a generic commodity from individuals.

● Both the common law and statutory regulation underpin this socio-economic exchange. The former provides the interpretative element that derives from judge-made rulings; the latter provides the regulative framework provided by Parliament. Both types of law are concerned with the concept of 'reasonableness'. European Union law now provides a further context in which UK law must operate.

● How far does the prescription of HRM, as a managerially derived agenda, change the nature of the contract? HRM is concerned with the managerial prerogative and the reorganisation of work, and clearly has a large impact on contract, in particular where employers use HRM to push employees 'beyond contract'. Thus HRM-style organisations may well have less specifically defined contracts in order to achieve greater fluidity and commitment in the way that tasks are performed. This becomes even more important in the context of debate over the labour process, where the role of management is viewed not simply as a partner in a contractual relationship, but as the prime mover in the control and organisation of work. The employment contract has, in these circumstances, to be evaluated against a background of the wider issues in managerial control and the employment relationship more broadly defined.

● The employment relationship is, in the UK, dominated by a tradition of voluntarism where the rights and responsibilities of and between employees and employers are subject to the vagaries of the contract of employment. That is, in comparison with other EU states, legal rights and responsibilities are recent developments and in many cases the subject of significant legal dispute. The increase in legal regulation – individual and collective employment rights – much of it inspired by EU Directives, may challenge the historically embedded employer preference for voluntary arrangements in employment regulation that is subject to a unilateral managerial prerogative. The labour process tradition establishes that HRM, like its predecessor personnel management, represents a series of bureaucratic controls that aim to stimulate and monitor work intensification and control labour costs. It remains to be seen whether legal regulation incorporated into the contract of employment can secure employee rights – individually or collectively – in the same way as collective representation in the workplace.

Activity   Buxford University

Buxford University has instituted the following 'contractual' agreement between staff and students governing the substantive and procedural organisation of tutorials.

Each week 2 of the 15 students in any tutorial group are required to present a paper on the topic for discussion that particular week. Students who are not presenting the paper are expected to read material appropriate to the discussion as directed in the course document and the prescribed course textbook. Lastly, all 15 students in a particular group are required to attend and positively contribute to the learning process in the one-hour class.

Each tutorial group has one student convenor who is responsible for liaising with staff on student concerns. The sanctions available to staff in the case of this contract being breached are rebuke, which can be followed by exclusion.

1 Assume you are the group representative. A student comes to you after having been excluded by the tutor. The particular student claims that they did not breach the collective agreement but merely chose not to contribute to the group discussion on subjects they found less interesting.

How would you go about representing this student? What measures would you need to take in order to clarify the situation and determine whether the contractual nature of the tutorial system had been breached?

2 In what ways do you think that the tutorial agreement described above gives the tutor operational control over the tutorial process? In what ways might it replicate the division between legal control and operational control over the employment relationship discussed in this chapter?

3 In what sense is the tutorial contract valid? In what way does its formulation 'shadow' the establishment of the terms and conditions within an employment contract?

QUESTIONS

1 How is a contract formed in the following situations?
   (a) Buying a magazine in a newsagent's.
   (b) An offer of full-time permanent employment.
   (c) The hiring of a subcontractor to perform maintenance work on a firm's computers.

2 How does employment protection legislation actually protect full-time and part-time employees?

3 Do you think that the employment protection legislation provides for effective and reasonable protection of employees?

4 How does contract assist management in the control of the labour process?

5 How would you interpret the Marglin/Landes debate in terms of:
   (a) the managerial prerogative;
   (b) the emergence of centralised workplaces?

6 Is Braverman correct, or are his views too general to be applied with any consistency to particular economies?

7 Is employment protection legislation necessary in an era of HRM?

EXERCISES

1 Outline what you think the central significance of contract is in relation to the management of human resources.

2 Discuss with your friends or work group colleagues the following proposition: 'The common law and statute law ensure the equality before the law of employers and employees.'

3 Outline how the emergence of an HRM-style culture within a firm may alter the way employees might be treated at work. Consider whether the emergence of an HRM culture and its attendant changes in the work organisation have to be contractually determined.

4 Coase (1937) suggested that economic efficiency criteria determine what type of contract a firm will use in any particular situation. If we accept the premise that HRM is all about making organisations more efficient, consider what factors will influence the decision to employ or not to employ labour.

REFERENCES AND FURTHER READING

Those texts marked with an asterisk are particularly recommended for further reading.

Armstrong, P. (1995) 'Accountancy and HRM', in Storey, J. (ed.) *HRM: A Critical Text.* London: Routledge, pp. 142–167.

Atkinson, J. (1984) 'Manpower strategies for flexible organisations', *Personnel Management*, August, pp. 28–31.

Beardwell, I. (1992) 'The new industrial relations: a review of the debate', *Human Resource Management Journal*, Vol. 2, No. 2, pp. 1–8.

Braverman, H. (1974) *Labour and Monopoly Capitalism.* New York: Monthly Review Press.

Clark, I. (1996) 'The state and new industrial relations', in Beardwell, I. (ed.) *Contemporary Industrial Relations.* Oxford: Oxford University Press.

Clark, I. (1998) 'Competitive pressures and engineering process plant contracting', *Human Resource Management Journal*, Vol. 8, No. 2, pp. 14–28.

Clark, I. (1999) 'Institutional stability in management practice and industrial relations: the influence of the Anglo-American Council for Productivity, 1948–1952', *Business History*, Vol. 41, No. 3, pp. 64–93.

Clark, I. (2000) 'The productivity race', review essay, *Historical Studies in Industrial Relations*, Vol. 9, No.7, pp, 137–140.

Clarke, S. (1991) *Marx, Marginalism and Modern Sociology*, 2nd edn. London: Macmillan.

Coase, R. (1937) 'The nature of the firm', *Economica*, No. 4, pp. 386–405.

Cully, M., Woodland, S., O'Reilly, A. and Dix, G. (1999) *Britain at Work: As depicted by the 1998 Employee Relations Survey*. Routledge, London.

Fox, A. (1974) *Beyond Contract*. London: Faber.

Fox, A. (1985) *History and Heritage*. London: Allen & Unwin.

Friedman, A. (1977) *Capital and Labour*. London: Macmillan.

Gall, G. and McKay, S. (1999) 'Developments in union recognition and derecognition in Britain 1994–1998', *British Journal of Industrial Relations*, Vol. 37, No. 4, pp. 601–614.

Gallie, D., White, M., Cheng, Y. and Tomlinson, M. (1998) *Restructuring the Employment Relationship*. Oxford: Clarendon Press.

Guest, D. (1987) 'Personnel management and industrial relations', *Journal of Management Studies*, Vol. 24, No. 5, pp. 503–521.

Guest, D. (1989) 'Personnel management and HRM: can you tell the difference?', *Personnel Management*, January, pp. 48–51.

Guest, D. (1991) 'Personnel management: the end of orthodoxy', *British Journal of Industrial Relations*, Vol. 29, No. 5, pp. 149–177.

Hutton, W. (1995) *The State We're In*. London: Jonathan Cape.

Hyman, R. (1975) *Marxist Introduction to Industrial Relations*. London: Macmillan.

Hyman, R. and Price, R. (1983) *The New Working Class? White Collar Workers and their Organizations*. London: Macmillan.

Kahn-Freund, O. (1984) *Labour and the Law*, 2nd edn. London: Stevens.

Kessler, S. and Bayliss, F. (1998) *Contemporary British Industrial Relations*, 3rd edn. London: Macmillan.

Landes, D. (1969) *The Unbound Prometheus*. Cambridge: Cambridge University Press.

Landes, D. (1986) 'What do bosses really do?', *Journal of Economic History*, Vol. 46, No. 3, pp. 585–623.

Legge, K. (1995) *The Rhetoric and Reality of HRM*. London: Macmillan.

Marchington, M. and Parker, P. (1990) *Changing Patterns of Employee Relations*. Hemel Hempstead: Harvester Wheatsheaf.

Marglin, S. (1974) 'What do bosses do? The origins and functions of hierarchy in capitalist production', *Review of Radical Political Economics*, No. 6, pp. 33–60.

Marx, K. (1954) *Capital*. London: Lawrence & Wishart.

Oxford Economic Dictionary (1992) 7th edn. Oxford: Oxford University Press, p. 614.

Purcell, J. (1995) 'Corporate strategy and its link with human resource management strategy', in Storey, J. (ed.) *Human Resource Management: A Critical Text*. London: Routledge, pp. 63–87.

Purcell, J. and Ahlstrand, B. (1994) *Human Resource Management in the Multi-Divisional Company*. Oxford: Oxford University Press.

Smith, C., Knights, D. and Wilmott, H. (1991) *White Collar Work: The Non-Manual Labour Process*. London: Macmillan.

Storey, J. (1992) *New Developments in the Management of Human Resources*. Oxford: Blackwell.

Taylor, F. (1911) *The Principles of Scientific Management*. New York: Harper & Row.

TUC (2000) *Trade Union Recognition*, London: TUC.

Wedderburn, W. (1986) *The Worker and the Law*. London: Penguin.

Williamson, O. (1975) *Markets and Hierarchies*. New York: Macmillan Free Press.

Establishing the terms and conditions of employment

Sue Marlow and Julie Storey

OBJECTIVES

- To define, examine and discuss the establishment of terms and conditions of employment through collective bargaining processes in organisations that recognise trade unions for bargaining purposes.
- To consider the influence of New Labour initiatives upon terms and conditions of employment, including social partnerships, works councils and the Employment Relations Act.
- To discuss the manner in which terms and conditions of employment are managed in the small firm sector.
- To examine and discuss the approach to establishing terms and conditions of employment in organisations that do not recognise trade unions or union bargained agreements.

INTRODUCTION

Critical to the structure of capitalist economies in the modern era has been the manner in which labour is rewarded for the effort made to produce goods and services – the 'effort–reward bargain' (Burawoy, 1979). As capitalism developed and began to mature, the foundations of a 'wage' economy were formalised. This led to contention regarding how work should be measured and valued. In response to the exploitative nature of early capitalism, trade unions developed as collective forces to protect employment conditions for skilled labour. The state, after some dissension, made union representation legal, and laid basic protective rights for labour on statute. Employers accepted such constraints upon their freedom, and so the concept of negotiating terms and conditions of employment with labour emerged into modern society (Coates and Topham, 1986). Regarding the establishment of, and improvement to, the terms and conditions of employment, it was determined that the most efficient and equitable manner in which the effort–wage bargain should be negotiated, for the majority of labour in society, was through the auspices of free collective bargaining (Webb and Webb, 1902: Brown, 1993), collective bargaining being a process of negotiation undertaken between employers' representatives and trade union representatives to determine the conditions under which labour should be employed. During the latter part of the nineteenth century and for most of the twentieth century, collective bargaining continued to be accepted as the most appropriate vehicle for establishing terms and conditions of employment and, to this end, was tacitly supported by the state and accepted by employers (Brown, 1993). However, with the election of a Conservative administration in 1979, this supportive stance, from both the state and employers, was actively dismantled. With a clear affiliation to a free market philosophy, successive Conservative governments since 1979 oversaw a calculated decline in the influence of trade unions in the UK. Along with the constraint and control of trade union power came a decline in the coverage of collective bargaining. This decline was recorded by successive workplace surveys undertaken during this period such that, in 1984, it was suggested that over 70% of employees were covered by collectively bargained agreements, but this figure had dropped to approximately 45% by 1998 (Cully *et al.*, 1999: 93), although it was noted that the majority of the largest firms in the economy, and the public sector, still utilised collective bargaining to establish and change the terms and conditions of employment.

So until recently, in any debate upon how the terms and conditions of employment are agreed, the critical focus would have been upon collective bargaining. However, it is now clear that while a substantial minority of employees still enjoy collective bargaining coverage, the majority do not. Bacon and Storey (1996) refer to the 'fracturing of collectivism' (p. 43) by the structural changes in the labour market and the pursuit of individualism by management. This is evident in the increasing number of firms that do not recognise unions as either employee representatives or bargaining agents (see the detailed discussion on such firms below). There is little evidence for a credible 'alternative model' of employee relations emerging to replace the collective bargaining approach, leaving what Beaumont (1995) describes as an 'institutional vacuum'. Towers (1997), meanwhile, suggests that there is now a 'representation gap' in the UK, where no formal method of articulation for employee voice has emerged with any coherence to effectively replace collective representation. There may be a role for HRM to fill this vacuum, but there is little indication that there is any wholesale, coherent and strategic adoption of HRM practices and policies by British management. Indeed, rather the opposite would appear to be evident in that where HRM initiatives *are* in evidence they have been adopted in an ad hoc opportunistic fashion, and are more likely to exist as a coherent policy strategy in unionised firms where collective representation persists (Mabey and Salamon, 1995).

It is undeniable that collective representation and bargaining have declined. Towers (1997) raises the pertinent question regarding union and bargaining decline: 'Does it matter?' (p. 64). If the modern economy has grown away from collectivity, and employees are not overtly resisting this trend, should there be concern over the demise of trade unions and collective bargaining? Based on two main issues, Towers argues that the decline of collectivity is a cause for considerable concern. Briefly, it is argued that employees are denied an independent representative channel within the naturally exploitative capitalist system, and that there are implications for national productivity, given that firms with a strong union presence are more effective at introducing change. Towers notes: 'It is more than arguable that collective bargaining can contribute positively toward the economic performance of individual enterprises and the economy as a whole' (p. 227). Supporting these points, Cully *et al.* (1999) found that investment in high-commitment management practices was concomitant with a strong union presence, while only a minority of workplaces without union representation offered employees opportunities for consultation over the organisation of the labour process. Brown (1993) explored the decline in collective bargaining, recorded in the

1992 workplace industrial relations survey (Millward *et al.*, 1992). Based on the 1992 evidence, Brown was pessimistic regarding the future of bargaining but noted: 'How much worse off are employees who do not enjoy the protection of collective bargaining. They are, on average, less favoured than their union brothers and sisters in terms of pay, health and safety, labour turnover, . . . consultation, communication and employee representation' (p. 198). It could be argued that periods of transition, such as that from collective representation to an alternative model, will be turbulent and lead to casualties. Yet this process of transition has been under way for some time, and, to date, the decline in collective representation would appear to have denied labour a democratic channel to articulate their rights; nor does it appear to have contributed to a sustained productivity growth in the UK (Nolan and O'Donnell, 1995). It would appear, furthermore, that the most innovative firms, in terms of employing new managerial strategies to effect change, are those with a union presence (Cully *et al.*, 1999). Overall, the decline in union representation and collective bargaining would appear to 'matter' and to be a cause for concern regarding the protection of labour rights, the introduction of change and improving productivity levels within the economy.

The extent of collective bargaining coverage in the UK does appear set to change. Gall and McKay (1999) note that current union recognition campaigns are aimed at over 300 companies with 235 000 employees. Indications are that many firms are planning to accept such agreements in advance of the statutory provision of the Employment Relations Act (1999). This will inevitably lead to an expansion in collectively bargained agreements. It is noted that by entering into voluntary recognition, employers are hoping to place some restrictions on the bargaining agenda, but unions can still apply to the Central Arbitration Committee for an extension of bargaining, even after recognition (Aikin, 2000). A future expansion in trade union recognition is also deemed likely by the CBI. The 1999 Employment Trends Survey found that from 830 companies currently without union recognition, 60% employing more than 5000 employees, and 50% of those employing 500 to 5000, were expecting a recognition claim. It is apparent that the collective bargaining model should not be   dismissed as an anachronism just yet.

The debate surrounding the contraction and expansion of bargaining coverage is set to continue, but it is clear that a majority of employees in the UK work in firms that do not recognise trade unions for bargaining purposes. Rather, a range of approaches from individual negotiation to unilateral management determination can be identified in this sector. Limited empirical evidence pertaining to such firms has led to descriptors such as 'black holes' (Guest and Hoque, 1994) and 'bleak house' (Sisson, 1993), implying that such firms are steeped in exploitation. This is somewhat simplistic; rather there are a range of approaches adopted by management in firms without union representation to reward, organise and innovate. These differing approaches will be explored at some length. To add to the complexity of the current debate surrounding organisations without union recognition, it is important to note the specificity of employee relations in the small firm sector. While the great majority of small firms do not recognise unions, it is acknowledged that they adopt specific tactics to managing labour, related to their size (Cully *et al.*, 1999). While the sector is heterogeneous in composition, it would appear that the close proximity of owner and employees, the restricted size of the management team and lack of professional personnel expertise within many firms lead to a particularistic approach to managing people (Marlow, 2000).

As there are a number of parallel processes regulating terms and conditions of employment in the contemporary economy, it is essential to explore all of these. In recognition of the critical role that collective bargaining has played in determining the labour process until relatively recently, and the likelihood that coverage will expand in the near future, this chapter will offer a comprehensive overview of the collective bargaining process. In recognition of the growing diversity in establishing terms and conditions of employment, there will be a discussion of the policies adopted within the small firm sector and an examination of practices employed by firms who do not recognise trade unions for bargaining purposes. The latter debate will explore whether the development of firms without union recognition is indicative of the adoption of an individualised approach based on the HRM premise.

Collective bargaining: history, definitions, analyses and criticisms

The term 'collective bargaining' was first utilised by Sidney and Beatrice Webb writing at the beginning of the last century (Webb and Webb, 1902). They believed that such bargaining was the collective equivalent to individual bargaining, where the prime aim was to achieve economic advantage. Bargaining had primarily an *economic* function, and was undertaken between trade unions and employers or employers' organisations. This 'classical' definition of collective bargaining has been subject to a number of critical analyses. In the late 1960s, Flanders (1968) argued that this view of collective bargaining was erroneous; rather, collective bargaining should be understood as a *rule-making process*, which established the rules under which the economic purchase of labour could initially take place. Further to establishing rules, collective bargaining outlines a framework for future negotiations regarding the buying and selling of labour. So collective bargaining is not a collective equivalent of individual bargaining, as nothing is actually bought or sold; only the rules under which the commodity of labour can be bought or sold are established.

Flanders argued that collective bargaining also entails a power relationship; the imbalance of economic power, status and security between the single employee and that of the management can, to some degree, be addressed by collective pressure such that agreements are compromise settlements of power conflicts. In consequence, collective bargaining is a political activity undertaken by professional negotiators, and this clearly differentiates it from individual negotiation.

Fox (1975) disputes Flanders' argument that an individual bargain is an economic exchange that always concludes with an agreement, whereas collective bargaining is essentially a process to establish rules for exchange. In fact there is no assurance that either process will achieve agreement on terms acceptable to the parties involved in negotiation. Moreover, Fox strongly argues that Flanders' view of collective bargaining as primarily political ignores the fact that 'the intensity of conviction, effort and feeling which many trade unionists appear to invest in pay claims hardly seems to be given sufficient recognition and weight in the Flanders analysis' (p. 170). Fox believes that the economic function of collective bargaining has not been afforded sufficient attention in the Flanders analysis.

Rather than isolating one major function of collective bargaining, Chamberlain and Kuhn (1965) offer an analysis that outlines three distinct activities, which interact to form the bargaining process:

● *Market or economic function.* This determines the price of labour to the employer: thus the collective agreement forms the 'contract' for the terms under which employees will work for the employer. The market or economic function establishes the *substantive terms* (see below) of the employment relationship.

- *Decision-making function.* In this role, collective bargaining offers employees the opportunity, if they wish, to 'participate in the determination of the policies which guide and rule their working lives' (Chamberlain and Kuhn, 1965: 130). Through union representatives, labour can influence management strategy on matters considered to be of joint concern, covered by the collective bargaining process.
- *Governmental function.* This is similar to the Flanders (1968) analysis, where collective bargaining establishes rules by which the employment relationship is governed. Thus bargaining is a political process as it establishes a 'constitution' (Salamon, 1992).

From the above points it is clear that collective bargaining is concerned with the establishment of:

- *Substantive rules.* These regulate all aspects of pay agreements and hours of work. These are all aspects of the market or economic function of the collective bargaining process. Substantive rules will be subject to frequent review as conditions of employment are renegotiated.
- *Procedural rules.* These establish the rules under which negotiation over the terms and conditions of employment can take place, and establish grievance and dispute procedures. They define managerial authority and trade union power, establishing a regulatory framework for the bargaining relationship.

Bargaining principles

The aim of collective bargaining is to reach negotiated agreements upon a range of issues pertaining to the employment relationship. From this range of issues, some will hold the potential for a conflict situation where the distribution and division of scarce resources are under negotiation (for example, division of profit as dividends or wage increase). Others, however, will have mutual benefit for employees and management, with the major debate focusing upon the most beneficial manner in which to implement change (for example, introduction of health and safety procedures). These differences were noted by Walton and McKersie (1965), who outlined two approaches to collective bargaining:

- *Distributive bargaining.* One party will seek to achieve gains at the expense of the other; the aim is the division of a limited resource between two groups, both of whom wish to maximise their share. Pay bargaining is distributive bargaining, as one party's gain is the other's loss.
- *Integrative bargaining.* This approach seeks mutual gains in areas of common interest with a problem-solving approach from the parties involved. Successful integrative bargaining depends upon a relatively high level of trust between parties and a willingness to share information.

Summary

Collective bargaining remains an important part of the contemporary employment relationship. In recent years it has been subject to substantial decline, but recent indications are for an expansion in union recognition for bargaining purposes. There has been considerable debate regarding the fundamental nature and purpose of the bargaining process, but any definition of collective bargaining must take account of the historical and contemporary influences that impinge upon those involved in bargaining practices.

THE COLLECTIVE AGREEMENT

At the end of the negotiating and bargaining process, collective agreements are reached. Traditionally, British collective bargaining has been notable for the informality with which agreements are recorded; as has been noted above, in the UK collective agreements are voluntary, and so are not legally enforceable on a collective basis. From the early 1970s, however, there has been a growing trend to establish formal written contracts to avoid any potential problems given the possibility of differing interpretations of negotiation outcome. The written agreement also contributes to a rationalisation and codification of industrial relations procedures, but the existence of formal written agreements will not prevent informal bargaining at local level. The extent to which this occurs will depend upon the nature of the existing power relationship between management and trade unions. There are several levels, outlined below, at which collective agreements can be reached.

Multi-employer agreements

Such agreements cover specific groups of employees (described within the contract) from a particular industry, and are negotiated by employers' associations or federations and full-time national trade union officials. Multi-employer agreements also form guidelines for employers who are not members of the industry association, and for firms that do not recognise unions. There is strong evidence that the incidence of multi-employer bargaining has been in decline for some time, with a growing preference for single-employer and more decentralised bargaining (Brown and Walsh, 1991; Cully, 1999).

Single-employer bargaining (organisational bargaining)

Organisational bargaining may occur at a number of levels, and has been characterised by a noticeable increase in recent years (Edwards, 1995; Ackers *et al.*, 1996):

- *Corporate.* All those employed by the organisation are covered by agreements bargained by the company and relevant trade union officials.
- *Plant.* The collective agreement is negotiated for a specific site or plant within the corporate structure, affecting only the employees of that location. These agreements may be totally independent of national terms or constructed upon an industry agreement.

Determinants of bargaining level within organisations

It is indicated that company-level bargaining is associated with large organisations and the presence of professional industrial relations specialists in corporate-level management (CBI, 1988). Site bargaining is associated with firms where labour costs are a high percentage of total costs and there are substantial numbers of workers on each site. At present, the choice of bargaining level falls within managerial prerogative influenced by a number of variables: for example, corporate-level bargaining may be favoured as one channel to neutralise potentially powerful plant-based union pressure and avoid inter-plant comparisons. Plant-based bargaining, however, will tie down labour costs to local conditions, bargained by negotiators who have a shared awareness of regional conditions, which may not always be to management's advantage.

THE DEVELOPMENT OF COLLECTIVE BARGAINING IN BRITAIN

Early development of collective bargaining

By the end of the nineteenth century collective bargaining had become established at local level for skilled labour, leading to demands for collective coverage from other groups of employees in semi- and unskilled trades. Despite considerable employer opposition, these groups formed and joined trade unions and won recognition for collective bargaining in the early years of the twentieth century. The system of local bargaining changed when the First World War acted as a stimulus to promote national procedure agreements. The greatest influence upon the growth of a national system of bargaining, however, came from the reports of the Whitley Committee in 1917 and 1918. The Whitley Committee was formed in response to major industrial unrest in the early years of the First World War and the growth of radical trade union action at local level [the 'first shop stewards movement'; see Hyman (1975) for an in-depth discussion]. The mandate for Whitley was to offer suggestions for improving contemporary industrial relations, and to establish a system whereby future employment issues could be evaluated and controlled effectively. The Committee suggested major changes to existing bargaining arrangements: first, to further develop the system of statutory wage regulation in poorly organised areas; second, to extend the powers already held by the government to conciliate and arbitrate during disputes; and finally, to establish joint employer/trade union councils known as Joint Industrial Councils (JICs). Such committees would meet at regular intervals for national bargaining purposes, but also to discuss wider issues such as labour efficiency. By the early 1920s the Joint Industrial Committees were in fact being used to negotiate wage cuts as the inter-war recession developed, and by 1938 there were only 45 JICs still operating (Jackson, 1991: 144). The advent of Whitley Committees did, however, make a significant difference to public sector workers where, for the first time, collective bargaining spread to white-collar staff. The system prevailed even during the inter-war depression years, but was subsequently subject to considerable revision by the 1979 Conservative government.

Developments in collective bargaining from the Second World War to the 1980s

During the Second World War there was a revival of national bargaining machinery. By 1945 15.5 million employees from a working population of 17.5 million (Palmer, 1983: 157) were covered by some type of national agreement. The influence of corporatism, where joint negotiations between employers and trade unions are encouraged by the state, ensured that industry-level collective bargaining became firmly established. The nationalisation programme and the advent of the welfare system ensured that the state became a major employer, and indeed, the post-war Labour government enacted legislation that obliged management in the newly nationalised industries to establish negotiating procedures for all employees.

It is incorrect, however, to presume that local or domestic bargaining ceased to be of relevance because of the formal establishment of national bargaining machinery for the majority of British labour by the early 1950s. Indeed, the conditions of full employment coupled with high demand offered considerable leverage for local bargaining by shop stewards, in the less bureaucratic private manufacturing sector.

Negotiation issues

Such local shopfloor bargaining increased wage drift, growth of short informal disputes and a growing tendency for national agreements to be utilised as a bargaining floor upon which local agreements were based, leading to inflationary pressures. This latter point generated concern from the then Labour government, given the problems of introducing and operating incomes policies in the face of informal, unregulated local bargaining and growing inflation. The growth and economic effect of domestic bargaining was deemed an 'industrial relations problem'.

Batstone *et al.* (1977), however, found that local shop stewards in the car industry were not in fact bargaining independently but remained in close contact with full-time officials. The Commission on Industrial Relations, established at the end of the 1960s, found many managers reluctant to move away from the intimate channels of negotiation they had established. Given that domestic bargaining was a problem for employers, who faced increasing international competition and found wage costs difficult to control, and was also a potential threat to government economic policy, a Royal Commission was established to examine industrial relations practices and procedures in both the public and private sector. The Donovan Commission reported in 1968, arguing that Britain had two systems of industrial relations, the formal and informal (Donovan Commission, 1968: 12). In private sector manufacturing the formal system was based upon national bargaining between employers' organisations and full-time trade union officials. The informal system was based upon local bargaining between management and shop stewards under the influence of full employment and buoyant demand for goods. Overall, the Donovan Commission argued that workplace bargaining had become of greater importance than national bargaining in the private manufacturing sector. This local level of bargaining, it was suggested, was 'largely informal, largely fragmented, and largely autonomous' (Flanders, 1970: 169), as it was based upon verbal agreements backed by custom and practice. Fragmented bargaining was undertaken by individual or small groups of stewards negotiating with individual or small groups of managers who did not consult with employers' organisations or full-time trade union officials, and did not respect national agreements.

The Commission argued that multi-employer bargaining at a national industry level could no longer effectively accommodate differentiated working practices throughout the private sector. The responsibility for introducing reform lay with management. The Commission did not denounce local informal agreements, but insisted that local agreements should achieve a level of formality such that they did not totally ignore and undermine national agreements. Moreover, the system of local informal bargaining effectively hampered the development of effective and orderly workplace bargaining: 'the objection to the state of plant bargaining at that time, therefore was its doubtful legitimacy and furtive character' (Clegg, 1979: 237). What was required was a rationalisation of the existing system that would effectively combine the two systems of industrial relations into one coherent, ordered process, which did not then undermine the formal rules in multi-employer agreements.

This reform of the content and structure of existing bargaining should be undertaken by senior management within their own companies. It was necessary to develop a framework of bargaining issues with extensive procedural agreements where management and trade unions could formally negotiate terms and conditions of employment. Changes in pay should be linked to changes in productivity, establishing a clear connection between formal domestic bargaining and enhanced profitability, with this tactic verified by the National Board for Prices and Incomes. In 1969, to encourage and advise upon the formalisation of domestic bargaining in corporate, nationalised and public industries, a Commission on Industrial Relations was established.

The reform of local-level bargaining

In consequence, most companies, encouraged by the Conservative government (1970–74) and the Labour government (1974–79) undertook voluntary reform of collective bargaining procedures. Using survey evidence from Brown (1981), it was apparent that by the late 1970s single-employer bargaining at establishment or corporate level had become the most prevalent level of bargaining for both manual and non-manual employees. The basis of this survey evidence indicated that significant changes had occurred in collective bargaining processes since the recommendations of Donovan. It was found that management had facilitated the formalisation of domestic bargaining by recognising shop stewards and supporting union organisation through closed shop agreements and check-off procedures (whereby union subscriptions are deducted by the company from wages and then paid to the trade union account). It was also noted that industrial sector and size of establishment affected bargaining level where, according to Deaton and Beaumont (1980: 201), single-employer bargaining was associated with larger firms, foreign ownership, multi-site operations and the existence of a professional tier of senior industrial relations management.

The reform of collective bargaining during the 1970s was initiated largely by management, with government support. Although there were clear benefits to trade unions from increased recognition and better facilities (for a critique of the incorporation of shop stewards into formal management/trade union bargaining hierarchy – the 'bureaucratisation thesis' – see Hyman, 1975), it is apparent that rapidly rising inflation, growing international competition and greater foreign ownership, combined with state intervention in industrial relations issues, created a climate favourable for management to press for reform. Although there was a trend towards decentralisation of bargaining and a growth in formal recognition of domestic bargainers, there remained considerable variation in collective bargaining processes within British industry during the 1970s.

Summary

In the post-war period there was a rapid expansion in domestic bargaining at local level in private sector manufacturing industry despite the existence of national agreements negotiated by multi-employer organisations and full-time trade union officials. The Labour government of 1964–70 was concerned that local bargaining was compromising its incomes policy programme, adding to inflationary pressure and adversely affecting Britain's competitive performance. The Donovan Commission was charged with investigating contemporary industrial relations, and concluded that Britain had two systems of industrial relations, one informal and one formal. The informal was conducted at plant level between shop stewards and management, the formal at industry level. The solution was to incorporate the two, establishing formal bargaining processes and procedures at the domestic level with an emphasis upon productivity bargaining. While it was recognised that the process of collective bargaining was creating economic and industrial relations problems during this era, there was no suggestion that the practice should be constrained or abandoned, but reformed. Governments throughout the 1960s and 1970s continued to support collective bargaining as the most appropriate and equitable manner in which to establish the terms and conditions of employment.

CHANGES IN COLLECTIVE BARGAINING SINCE THE 1980s

From the late 1970s to the mid 1990s the British economy suffered cyclical economic recession and volatile levels of unemployment. Although unemployment has, according to government figures, been generally falling since the late 1980s (note the increase in 1992 due to recession), the greatest increase in employment has been in part-time labour and low-paid, low-skill private sector work (Clark, 1998). Such structural changes, combined with the election of successive Conservative governments from 1979 to 1997, hostile to the ethos of collective action by trade unions, prompted substantial changes in the nature of collective bargaining in both the public and private sector. Such changes have resulted from joint pressures from industry, the government and trade union inability to rise to the attack upon their presence in the workplace. It was a combination of such factors that prompted substantial changes within the scope and influence of the collective bargaining process.

Recent workplace studies (Gregg and Yates, 1991; Cully *et al.*, 1999; Gall and McKay, 1999), while agreeing that the nature, scope and processes of collective bargaining have changed, found that collective bargaining remains the most important vehicle for fixing pay and conditions of employment in the public sector, and also remains important for a substantial minority of private manufacturing employees, but is of little importance for the private service sector. Overall, they agree that the following trends have emerged.

Decentralisation of bargaining

There has been a growing trend towards the decentralisation of collective bargaining away from multi-employer/industry level to organisation or plant level. This trend continued during the 1980s and 1990s. The pattern was encouraged by successive Conservative governments from 1979 to 1997, who, in the 1990 White Paper *Employment for the 1990s*, stated that plant- or company-level negotiations result in more 'realistic pay settlements' and thus avoid wage inflation. Support from government legislation during this period, constraining industrial action, also acted to dissipate further any union resistance to plant bargaining. There are no indications that the current Labour administration will take any action to reverse this trend, having declared that they will not be making any substantial adjustments to the labour legislation enacted by their Conservative predecessors (McIlroy, 1998)

From the corporate stance, decentralised bargaining offers the opportunity to link pay and productivity together at local level, where regional variations and conditions can be accounted for accurately by local management and trade union officials. The weakened state of contemporary trade unions ensures that they are less able to resist managerial strategy to utilise local bargaining to review labour costs and reform working practices – for example the introduction of new technology and flexible working practices (Sisson, 1987).

There is little doubt that regional variations in the labour market, and the growing preference for local profit centres, suggest that local bargaining is an appropriate step for many large companies. Survey evidence from Marginson *et al.* (1988) supports this argument, highlighting a number of cases where major corporate firms have withdrawn from national-level bargaining, including Sealink, Tesco and Midland Bank. Privatisation of the utilities in the 1980s also offered management the opportunity to decentralise bargaining structures.

There is a need for a note of caution regarding whether decentralised bargaining is a useful strategy for all corporate structures and also regarding the true extent of the 'decentralisation' process. Considering the issue of decentralisation in more detail, Kinnie (1990) finds a false image of local autonomy in bargaining, suggesting that local management are subject to head office directive even when there is an appearance of local autonomy. As Cully *et al.* (1999) comment, 'the pay setting process is often handled beyond the workplace and may be opaque to managers at a local level' (p. 106).

This clouding of autonomy between levels of management also raises more complex issues of employee access to decision-making processes. When local trade union officials enter into negotiation concerning pay and conditions at the domestic level, they are in fact entering a constrained process in which there is an illusion of autonomy for the bargaining team, whereas management are operating under restraint regarding their limits of concession. This has other implications in that local trade union negotiators are denied access to corporate decision-makers when in fact they are highly influential upon local management actions.

While there can be little doubt that there has been a shift in bargaining levels, which has complemented contemporary corporate strategies to downsize, focusing upon local profit centres, enabling employers to gain more control in the workplace (Sisson, 1987), the extent to which local management achieve independence and autonomy in the bargaining arena is questionable.

Activity — Local bargaining

A corporate enterprise has always undertaken centralised bargaining, with a specialised team of negotiators bargaining annually with full-time trade union officials. However, the corporation is considering a complete restructuring whereby local 'profit centres' would be developed as single business units. As part of this restructuring it has been suggested that collective bargaining should be devolved to local level, with outline directives issued from head office regarding acceptable bargaining agendas and final settlements.

As HRM consultants, outline the presentation you would make to the board to include the following issues:

1 the origins and extent of local bargaining;

2 the advantages and potential problems of local bargaining to both management and trade unions;

3 possible solutions to such problems;

4 recommendations concerning the move to local bargaining.

Flexibility issues

The introduction of flexible working has been made possible by the deregulation of the labour market, the weakness of trade unions to resist such change, and the growth of managerial prerogative (Pollert, 1988; Ackers *et al.*, 1996; Dex and McCulloch, 1997). Ackroyd and Proctor (1998) argue that flexible working is evident throughout all sectors of the workforce, and is not a phenomenon focused primarily upon the most vulnerable, but obviously the most skilled and secure labour will be more influential in determining the organisation of flexible working. Where changes aimed at the introduction of flexibility within the labour process are being negotiated, the following points have become evident. If a company introduces flexible working, not subject to statutory regulation, such changes usually form an overlapping agreement to become part of a complete package, which constitutes a flexibility agreement. The terms and conditions of contemporary flexibility agreements evidently will depend on such factors as the state of union–management relations, the bargaining environment, and the nature of technology employed.

The implications for collective bargaining of flexibility agreements are as follows:

- Trade unions are no longer bargaining terms and conditions for a specific craft or activity. Flexibility between tasks blurs lines of demarcation, so that the possession of a specific skill or talent is no longer exclusive as tasks are spread throughout the workforce. Thus, bargaining leverage is reduced.
- As employees undertake a wider range of tasks throughout the labour process, fewer 'core' workers are required, with an increasing dependence upon numerically flexible labour, leading to redundancies and a consequent fall in trade union membership and growth in unemployment.
- The growing links between flexibility bargaining and pay increases means that there is a growing trend to bargain around issues of exchange, for example for wage increases in exchange for changes in work organisation, manning levels and redundancies.

This last point is of some importance. This notion of exchange between improved pay and acceptance of changes in working methods is reminiscent of productivity bargaining during the 1960s. In return for accepting flexibility agreements, employees have been offered a range of benefits including pay increases, enhanced status and greater job security. Trade unions have been forced to bargain for better conditions on the basis of making concessions allowing significant changes in the labour process.

As with many other issues discussed, there is a robust critique of the ideas surrounding the flexible workforce idea. In a succinct, critical review of the flexibility debate, Pollert (1988) argues that this is not a new strategic attempt by employers to establish a labour force suitable to meet the needs of changing markets. Rather, employers have always made ad hoc attempts to make labour more flexible, but have been hampered by state and union regulation of terms and conditions of employment. Recently, employers have been able to take advantage of a weakened labour movement to introduce such changes, encouraged by a sympathetic government.

So, while there is some evidence concerning the development of flexible working and the inclusion of flexibility agreements in the bargaining forum, there is only a limited indication of a link between improved productivity and flexibility initiatives (Edwards, 1987). This, together with the critique of flexibility, suggests that, while flexibility issues are undoubtedly an important HRM initiative to effect change in the labour process, with implications for collective bargaining, caution is required in interpreting the extent of such change. This is particularly pertinent in respect to the degree to which the utilisation of flexibility represents a strategic or coherent approach to fragmenting the labour force, or to undermining collective coverage.

The Labour administration, 1997–, offers continued support for flexible working, but recognises the need to ameliorate the worst effects of such initiatives. This is to be undertaken by the statutory protection offered in the Employment Relations Act 1999, by the adoption of EU Directives such as that on working time, and by the recognition that flexible working can be used advantageously to form the basis of 'family-friendly policies'. Such policies are aimed at helping employees to meet domestic demands. It is recognised that statutory provision obviates the need for collective bargaining; however, such agreements may be used as a 'floor of rights' in some organisations while scope exists for unions to police the provision and ensure it is appropriately observed.

Contemporary bargaining initiatives

Single-union deals, single-table bargaining, no-strike clauses and pendulum arbitration are largely associated with Japanese management strategies, given their initiation within Japanese subsidiaries locating on greenfield sites in the UK. Single-union deals have posed difficult questions for the existing form and structure of the British trade union movement, having a number of implications for the collective bargaining process. The single-union agreement occurs where management grants recognition to only one trade union to represent employees in the bargaining process. This process was strongly opposed over the 1980s, with the main protagonist of such agreements, the (then) EETPU, being suspended from the TUC in 1988 for refusing to withdraw from such an agreement with Christian Salvesen and Orion Electric.

The major objection to single-union deals is the promotion of what Salamon (1992) describes as a 'beauty contest approach' between trade unions. Management outline the envisaged approach to industrial relations and a personnel strategy, inviting trade unions to state how they might measure up to the managerial view of employee relations – with the reward being a new pool of members during a time when trade unions are experiencing decline. Japanese firms employ management consultants to assess potential union candidates who wish to be considered as representatives within the firm (Ackers *et al.*, 1996). As such, the relationship between management and union becomes one in which unions must offer to fulfil the behavioural expectations of management, in order to be granted recognition, rather than prioritising the needs of the membership. Regarding the collective bargaining process, there will be some employees whose interests will not be best served by a union that has no history of representing them, and with which they feel no basis of affiliation. However, it could be argued that, given the labour process of organisations that adopt single-union deals (single-status working, flexibility, fewer separate job titles), the scope for a differentiated approach to bargaining is significantly narrowed. A further constraint upon the bargaining process in single-union firms is the association between single-union deals, no-strike deals and pendulum arbitration.

Obviously, a no-strike clause, once accepted by a trade union on behalf of the membership, effectively deprives union negotiators of the threat of strike action should bargaining break down and, moreover, denies employees the option of withdrawing their labour unilaterally. The controversial element relating to no-strike clauses is employees' forgoing the right to strike, where this is seen as the only positive right enjoyed by labour in the employment relationship; moreover, during the bargaining process it is the ultimate sanction. No-strike clauses are usually (but not always) accompanied by pendulum arbitration facilities, where a third party will arbitrate on behalf of the two principals should they fail to reach agreement. However, traditional arbitration, which draws from both sides of the negotiation stand-off, may encourage principals to hold back on their final stance as they believe the arbitrator will find middle ground between the two parties. Consequently, where both sides are aware that an arbitrator will adopt one side or the other's position, and this will represent a cost to the other party, they are more likely to bargain in good faith, making every effort to settle (Singh,

1986; Milner, 1993). The limited use of this practice in Britain makes it difficult to assess the impact upon the bargaining process.

The trade union movement has recognised that practices such as single-union deals and pendulum arbitration offer employers competitive advantage. Single-table bargaining is one alternative that offers employers similar benefits to single-union deals while maintaining a multi-union site. Bargaining takes place between unions to establish a negotiation proposal, which is articulated by one bargaining unit that negotiates for both manual and non-manual employees. However, for single-table bargaining to operate it is essential for all employees to share similar conditions of employment in respect of hours, holidays, pension and sick pay entitlements. A number of companies within the private manufacturing and service sector have adopted a single bargaining table, although the process is not widespread. Marginson and Sisson (1990) identify three incentives for favouring single-table bargaining:

- Multi-unit bargaining does not utilise management resources efficiently, and offers potential sources of inter-union conflict.
- The introduction of new working methods, for example flexible working, is most effectively achieved through single-table bargaining, bypassing the complexity of fragmented bargaining.
- It facilitates the introduction of single status or harmonises working conditions.

To achieve single-table bargaining, it is argued that there must be management commitment to the process, indicated by a willingness to discuss a wide range of issues. Marginson and Sisson also suggest that such bargaining will become more widespread as the impact of European Union Directives and legislation regarding information sharing, communication and collective bargaining encourages management to review bargaining processes. Recent evidence from Cully *et al.* (1999) indicates that this is indeed the case.

Summary

A number of bargaining initiatives emerged during the 1980s that have changed the level and structure of the collective bargaining process. These initiatives have facilitated the exercise of managerial prerogative in the bargaining relationship and further narrowed the scope of bargaining channels. Overall, where it persists, the collective bargaining function has remained intact but has been constrained in scope.

PUBLIC SECTOR BARGAINING

Public sector industrial relations can be differentiated from the private sector on a number of points:

- the persistence of historically established processes of national-level collective bargaining;
- the role of the government as employer, seeking to promote a specific model of industrial relations to the private sector, reflecting a political ethos;
- the problem of responding to market forces where the market is remote or a monopoly of service exists;
- the complex structure of bargaining arrangements consisting of local management and central government personnel;
- the continued high level of collective bargaining coverage within the sector.

The origins of public sector collective bargaining are to be found in the reports of the Whitley Committee (1917–18), which established national negotiating machinery and local consultative committees. Despite some resistance to the system from successive inter-war governments, by the end of the Second World War the Whitley system covered most public sector employees. With the advent of the National Health Service and an extensive nationalisation programme, the system of national-level, bureaucratic collective bargaining machinery was firmly established.

A further feature of public sector collective bargaining is that of comparability. Owing to the difficulty of establishing performance indicators based on market conditions, in 1955 the Priestly Commission recommended that the terms and conditions of employment for the Civil Service should be established through comparison with similar work groups in the private sector. Comparability agreements were then adopted as the most efficient manner in which to agree terms and conditions throughout the public sector, and indeed proved highly beneficial to employees, particularly in the mid-1970s. However, this formula for conducting collective bargaining – highly centralised, bureaucratic and detailed, comparability based – led to a number of difficulties. Linking pay to productivity or establishing local agreements became a major problem owing to the hurdles presented by national bargaining. Other difficulties arose in the late 1970s when, in response to growing inflation and falling competitiveness, the government introduced a series of incomes policies that restricted public sector pay. However, while the government was able to utilise incomes policies through highly centralised bargaining processes to control public sector pay settlements, this restraint was not reflected in the private sector. The growing differentials between private and public sector pay led to a series of major industrial disputes by public employees in the late 1970s, which the Labour government failed effectively to manage, or resolve. Consequently, after the General Election of 1979, the newly elected Conservative government focused upon industrial relations problems as a major source of economic disruption. The government determined to effect change in managing the employment relationship in the public sector, and this example, combined with a series of legislative acts to constrain trade union activities, would act to prompt similar change in the private sector.

From 1979, successive Conservative governments implemented a number of changes detrimental to the collective bargaining process and coverage. Independent pay review bodies were established for doctors, dentists, nurses, teachers and civil servants, which bypassed the collective bargaining process, with pay being index linked. Index linking has also been applied to the police and firefighters. Another noticeable trend during the period was an identifiable shift in public sector bargaining away from national-level to local-level collective bargaining. This was facilitated by successive Conservative governments' attempts to slim down the public sector through initiatives such as privatisation and opt-outs, while introducing market economy discipline to other areas through contracting-out and competitive tendering. Alongside attempts to reform established forms of collective bargaining, the government encouraged the introduction of performance pay indicators (Gospel and Palmer, 1993).

There has been opposition from public sector trade unions to decentralisation policies. The unions argue that the most vulnerable sections of the workforce are adversely affected by moves to local-level bargaining, while contracting services out to non-union, private sector service firms represents a loss of members for public sector unions. As the current Labour administration has stated that it intends to continue public spending constraints and observe the majority of industrial relations initiatives introduced by the previous governments, it is unlikely that the situation in the public sector will change to any considerable degree. Unions may feel a little more secure that their bargaining leverage will not be further constrained, but tensions are possible as expectations from employees to see pay differentials with the private sector addressed may be thwarted by the present government. This may place public sector unions in a tense position while attempting to both observe new partnership approaches with the government and appease membership calls for improved terms and conditions. There has already been discontent articulated by the nursing profession, while Royal Mail employees were involved in a series of disputes in 1998.

Summary

Traditionally, the public sector has enjoyed stable industrial relations, with a formally established system of national-level collective bargaining with a comparative ethos. Owing to intolerable pressure upon this formula during the 1970s, there was a series of wide-ranging bitter industrial disputes. Successive Conservative governments (1979–97) attempted to reform industrial relations in the public sector, with the dual aims of offering the example of the private sector as what they believed to be 'good practice' in industrial relations conduct, while also contributing to the control of public sector spending. There has been an identifiable trend towards decentralisation facilitated by the sale of publicly owned enterprises and other privatisation-type initiatives. The current Labour administration has not demonstrated that it wishes to radically alter the current approach to managing the public sector, preferring the decentralised somewhat remote practices already in place.

NEW LABOUR, COLLECTIVE BARGAINING AND SOCIAL PARTNERSHIPS

In May 1997 a Labour administration was elected to power. Under the auspices of New Labour, the Blair government presented a modernising agenda that moved away from social ownership to a support of private capital, private enterprise and a continuation of Conservative expenditure limits. The new government made it quite clear that the vast majority of the initiatives undertaken by the previous Conservative administration to reform the employment relationship would remain in place. There is some recognition of the vulnerability of the individual employee in the contemporary labour market and of the need to strengthen trade union rights: these issues have been partially addressed through the Employment Relations Act (1999). The Labour government has also committed itself to support the notion of a stakeholder society and social partnerships. In terms of stakeholding, the government recognises that, as members of an economic community, employers, employees and the state have a 'stake' in enterprise. In order for such stakeholders to be able to make an appropriate contribution to the enterprise it is necessary for them to act in partnership, and this is only possible in an environment of relative equity and fairness. In 1996, Tony Blair spoke of 'a vision of the company as a community or partnership in which each employee has a stake and where a company's responsibilities are more clearly delineated' (*Financial Times*, 9 January 1996). Notions of social partnership have been rather more nebulous, however. There is no suggestion of partnership on the European or 'Rhineland' model that would infer state support for unions, an affiliation to collective bargaining, and the establishment of long-term strategies between government and industry (Monks, 1996; Thompson, 1996). Rather, there remains a desire to retain flexibility, deregulation and competitiveness more in accord with the American model. In consequence, the current government refers to the mutual responsibilities between employers and employees, and is equally encouraging to both unions and management to engage in dialogue to introduce change, improve productivity and resolve dispute. Such ambiguity may also lie behind the recent trend of the government to refer to 'partnerships' rather than 'social partnerships'.

From unions, there has been support for the social partnership concept (Monks, 1996), although this may be to do with an element of pragmatism, recognising that the 'New Unionism' agenda must be seen to be moderate and conciliatory to maintain support from employers and the state (McIlroy, 1998). Support for partnerships from unions is, of course, not entirely based on pragmatism. In a number of polls commissioned by the GMB in the late 1980s and early 1990s it became apparent that employees had concerns relating to issues that were beyond the traditional remit of collective bargaining. These included job fulfilment, worthwhile work and job security, all of which were ranked above pay in importance. John Edmonds (1997), the GMB General Secretary, argued that such issues are most effectively addressed through partnership discussion rather than through collective negotiation. This union stance towards social partnerships has fuelled the contemporary debate surrounding the most appropriate strategies for unions to adopt in the workplace to ensure their continued relevance as both employee representatives and bargainers.

Kelly (1996; 1998) has developed a succinct critique of the social partnership approach and union moderation, stating: 'It is difficult, if not impossible to achieve a partnership with a party who would prefer that you didn't exist; the growth of employer hostility is a major objection to the case for union moderation' (1996: 88). Briefly, Kelly believes that, given the current state of management strength and the ambivalence towards unions from the current government, there is little rationale for employers to enter into true partnerships with unions when they can achieve their goals through flexing their prerogative. It is also argued that unions are not effective labour representatives when their policies are based on capitulation to employer perspectives. Kelly goes on to offer evidence that militant unionism is as effective in offering gains to employees through adversarial bargaining, as moderation. Critically, Kelly also believes that a partnership stance will undermine the role of collective bargaining and further narrow current agendas. Bacon and Storey (1996), however, describe the 'fracturing of collectivism' (p. 43), and instead argue that unions must find new ways of representing the individual in the workplace and engage with partnership channels, while recognising that partnership stances have been frustrated in a number of firms, owing to the lack of management commitment to the process, leading to a rhetoric of partnership. At the moment, it would appear that the stance of the TUC and the majority of member unions is to support the partnership approach, if with some caution.

Regarding collective bargaining, it is not yet evident how it will be affected by the notion of partnership, but a number of suppositions are possible. With the advent of the Employment Relations Act, signalling the current government's intention to tacitly support union recognition, it is certain that collective bargaining coverage will expand. To maintain union moderation and conform with the current government's desire for fairness and equity in employment, it is likely that employers may tolerate some expansion of the bargaining agenda. It is possible that organisations may be prompted to draw up new consultation agendas to promote partnership, in order to pre-empt unions attempting to include new issues within a bargaining framework. This may be unpalatable to unions, but if they are to be seen to support partnerships, they may have to accept a continued restriction of negotiation and expansion of consultation.

However, management will still have to enter into debate around the issue, and demonstrate progress, if partnerships are to be maintained. It may also be the case that, where unions are able to gain strong support for recognition, they are able to build new collective bargaining agendas in organisations which previously rejected a union presence. What is not in doubt is that partnerships are contentious, and their success will depend upon employer and employee representatives being able to demonstrate that they are reaching consensus through cooperation without one set of interests being consistently subordinated. From limited evidence based upon partnerships in the water industry in the UK and vehicle manufacturing in the USA, Towers (1997) comments that there is 'an essential need for equal partnership reinforced by collective bargaining which accepts the legitimacy of conflict of interests as well as encouraging and institutionalising cooperation' (p. 226). Further empirical evidence will be required to assess the impact and success of social partnerships.

Given that the Labour government has now signed the social protocol of the Maastricht Agreement, the European Works Council Directive has come into force in the UK. Since December 1999 all MNEs employing at least 1000 staff, with operations in more than one member state employing at least 150 people, have been required to establish councils for information and consultation purposes (EU.O.J. 1994). This will have some implications for existing representative channels. Hyman (1997) argues that the German model of works councils has created a dual system of representation, where the role of trade unions has been strengthened by the presence of works councils. This occurs as the councils have been dominated by trade union representatives, who then use this channel of communication to gain information to inform bargaining, which in turn further supports the efficacy of collectivism for the individual employee. While the German form of works councils is unlikely to be reproduced exactly in the UK, Streeck (1995) notes the trend for convergence in European representative consultation in the workplace, while Hyman observes that legimated works councils are a source of stability and resistance for trade unions. In the UK, unions have not embraced the notion of works councils with enthusiasm, fearing a further dilution of communication and negotiation channels. Based on European experiences, however, it does appear that, if strategically managed, there are substantial opportunities for unions to strengthen their representative logic through involvement with such councils and gain valuable information to inform the bargaining agenda.

CONTROVERSIES IN HRM AND COLLECTIVE BARGAINING

The early conceptual notion of HRM being focused upon, and only possible in, the unitary firm, has not emerged in the modern British economy. In contemporary usage, HRM is employed as a set of strategic initiatives focused upon the employee, with the aim of improving competitiveness, where any firm, depending on product and market demands, may utilise any number from a range of initiatives included under the HRM umbrella. However, there remains considerable debate concerning the strategic element, given the argument that the majority of British management are not able to employ strategic tactics (Mabey and Salamon, 1995). Yet introducing and managing HRM practices in a collective bargaining environment does raise a number of contentious issues, primarily whether a series of initiatives aimed at the individual employee can be compatible with the collective approach.

It appears that HRM initiatives are more evident in unionised firms, and this can be taken as evidence that the two practices – HRM and collective bargaining – are not mutually exclusive (Mishel and Voos, 1992). Guest (1989b) argues that the values underpinning HRM – strategic integration and the pursuit of quality – are not incompatible with collective representation, where bargaining channels can be effectively utilised to introduce change. Recent evidence from the 1998 Employment Relations Survey found 'high commitment management practices going hand in hand with a union presence' (p. 294) and also found this to be the case for high-productivity firms (Cully *et al.*, 1999). Storey (1989) argues that the two systems can co-exist in harmony where HRM initiatives are focused upon areas that do not pose a threat to the scope of collective bargaining, or where they do not attempt to bypass established bargaining channels. Consequently, it is not axiomatic that if HRM initiatives are to be utilised, collective bargaining must be removed from the agenda; the critical issue here is the motivation for the introduction of HRM. If individualised HRM practices are aimed at undermining union effectiveness, there is a real threat to existing procedures. However, if change is deployed after discussion or negotiation with existing unions, there is an opportunity for joint regulation of new working practices. This is not to argue that collective bargaining will be unaffected by the adoption of HRM. Storey (1992) found that while collective bargaining had become less of a management priority, new HRM practices and collective bargaining tended to exist as parallel arrangements. The emphasis was upon reducing the union role rather than replacing it. It is apparent that the social partnership agenda will also have an impact on the manner in which HRM initiatives are to be integrated into the organisation. It remains to be seen whether the development of partnership agreements in unionised firms will bring more HRM initiatives into the bargaining agenda or facilitate the growth of consultation channels.

Summary

The Labour government, elected in May 1997, has distanced itself from previous Labour administrations by adopting policies sympathetic to business interests and, critically, by not inviting trade unions to contribute to policy formation. To fulfil its ambition of 'fairness and equity' in the employment relationship the government has enacted the Employment Relations Act, which establishes a floor of rights for individuals at work, and affords statutory recognition rights for trade unions fulfilling a membership quota. The Act was constructed on the basis of consultation with both the TUC and the CBI to maintain the government's pledge of fairness to both employees and business. Offering statutory recognition procedures will certainly expand the coverage of collective bargaining within the economy. Further to legislative provision to promote fairness at work, the current government supports the notion of partnership at work. Such partnerships should be based on an employee's right to information and representation, which in turn will encourage a more consensual environment in the organisation, minimising conflict and employee resistance to change. Partnership agreements are to be encouraged in all firms, regardless of union presence. Trade unions have embraced the notion of moderation and partnership, believing this will strengthen their role in the workplace, reduce management opposition to a union presence, and so facilitate recruitment. The concept of partnership has been subject to criticism, notably from Kelly (1996; 1998), who perceives partnership as an ideological acceptance of moderation and capitulation to a capitalist agenda that seriously compromises the independence of trade union representation.

Britain has now accepted the EU Directive on works councils as an additional channel of communication between employees and management. While British unions have been suspicious that such channels could further narrow the scope for union influence and bargaining processes, this has not been the case in other European nations. Indeed, the German model depends upon a mutually reinforcing relationship between unions and councils. It is unlikely that the German model will be replicated in the UK. At the worst it is possible that such councils will become another communication channel where little of substance is disclosed. Yet, if unions are able to act strategically, they should be able to gain representation upon such councils to articulate the collective views of the workforce, while utilising information exchanged to inform and strengthen the bargaining process.

Considering the issue of HRM and collective bargaining processes specifically, it appears that the former can coexist with the latter, and indeed HRM initiatives may be introduced through bargaining channels. In established plants, while HRM initiatives are evident, they have not seriously challenged the main focus of collective bargaining upon pay issues, but the scope of bargaining has been narrowed, with consultation being employed as a preferred channel of communication.

ESTABLISHING TERMS OF EMPLOYMENT IN SMALL FIRMS

There are a number of differing definitions of a 'small' firm. In 1971 the Bolton Committee report referred to criteria of independence and a small market share, the Companies Act 1985 combined turnover and employment criteria, while the EU has the most comprehensive criteria of turnover, employees and independence. In the UK governments rely on the somewhat simplistic measure of the number of employees within the enterprise (DTI, 1997):

- small firm: 0–49 employees
- medium firm: 50–249 employees
- large firm: over 250 employees.

Given the heterogeneity of the sector, it is difficult to find a definition that adequately encompasses all relevant firms. Regardless of how the sector is defined, it is appropriate to consider small firms as a separate entity within the economy. For some time they have been recognised as being essentially different from their larger counterparts in their approach to management, markets and business outlook; it is no longer presumed that such firms are enterprises that have merely failed to grow to corporate dimensions (Storey *et al.*, 1987). As Cully *et al.* (1999) remark, 'small business occupy a distinct part of the lexicon in academic and policy debates' (p. 251); they have their own associations and government representative at ministerial level. This is not to suggest that small firms can be easily studied as a single entity. A significant challenge in analysing small firm behaviour is identifying common themes and trends in a sector noted for its heterogeneity. So any conclusions drawn and observations made must always be qualified with the caution that there will always be a substantial number of firms that refute established trends.

The number of small businesses in the UK economy has grown expeditiously since the early 1980s (for more discussion of such growth, see Storey, 1994). The DTI (1998) states that firms with fewer than 50 employees account for 99% of all businesses, 46% of non-government employment and 42% of turnover (excluding the financial sector)

(p. 2). It is apparent that small firms are significant employers in the modern economy, and so insight into how labour is managed in such firms is critical, but the study of employee relations in small firms has been largely neglected (Scase, 1995). The earliest evidence pertaining to the management of people of small firms initially indicated an environment where the close proximity of owner and worker could overcome the traditional tensions between labour and capital (Goss, 1991). In the late 1960s, a number of studies portrayed employment conditions in small firms as a relative haven of peace and harmony. It was recognised that financial rewards were lower in the sector, but this was more than compensated for by low levels of industrial unrest, teamworking with colleagues and low labour turnover (Ingham, 1970; Bolton, 1971). This image has since been dispelled by a number of empirical studies undertaken in the 1980s. These studies found that most small-firm employees would prefer to work in larger firms, that there were higher levels of job insecurity and labour turnover, and owner/manager strategies for labour control were largely authoritarian or based on benevolent autocracy. It was found that the perceptions of owner-managers regarding the employment environment in their firms differed significantly from that of their employees (Rainnie, 1989; Scott et al., 1989; Goss, 1991). Regarding the establishment of terms and conditions in small businesses, the empirical evidence indicated a high degree of informality. Scott et al. (1989) found that from initial recruitment and selection to point of dismissal, few formal systems or policies were in evidence. The preferred manner of employee recruitment was through the 'grapevine' – that is, someone known to an existing employee; for many employees, a contract of employment, or indeed any formal indication of tasks and duties, was non-existent. Discipline was relatively ad hoc, dependent more on the owner's perception of the problem than on any objective standard. Only a tiny minority of firms had union recognition or any form of negotiated terms. For the remainder, owners and management teams unilaterally decided upon payment rates and changes to working conditions. Other studies of the period (Rainnie, 1989; Goss, 1991) revealed similar findings, with the emphasis upon owner prerogative and informality.

When analysing such findings, it is simplistic to suggest that such informality and unitarism arise from a strategic goal to construct authoritarian power structures. Rainnie (1989) develops a somewhat deterministic analysis, arguing that the adverse competitive pressures, experienced by many small businesses, give the owner or management team little discretion in their approach to managing people. They are forced to minimise labour costs due to external market pressures. Ram (1999) disputes this thesis, suggesting that employees do negotiate social relations in small firms, but the relatively hidden and individualistic tactics employed somewhat obscure the process. It is also recognised that employers, whether in large or small firms, must have some degree of cooperation and consent from labour, and so cannot operate on the basis of absolute domination. Owners must be prepared to enter into some form of dialogue with employees. A further explanation for informality and owner prerogative in small firms is the relative absence of professional personnel managers (Wynarczyk et al., 1993). Finally, it is evident that many small firms work almost entirely in the short term owing to restricted and uncertain markets, volatile customer bases and uncertain financial strategies, so it is difficult for such businesses to develop structured or strategic approaches to managing their labour. For many firms there is a belief that they simply do not have the time for formal labour management (Storey, 1994). Such findings have prompted small firms to be described as part of the 'black hole' or 'bleak house' sector of firms within the economy (Sisson, 1993; Guest and Hoque, 1994), where employees have few rights, poor conditions and limited representation channels to address such issues.

Given the emphasis upon new managerial strategies in the 1980s and 1990s, it is important to ascertain whether these have filtered through to the small firm sector to address informality and relatively poor conditions of employment. Recent evidence suggests that there is still a dependence upon an informal approach to determining how work is organised and rewarded (Holliday, 1995; Cully *et al.*, 1999; Ram, 1999). When considering indications of formality in more detail, the Workplace Employee Relations Survey* (1998) noted that recruitment was still dominated by employee recommendation; there was some evidence for numerical flexibility, but few incidences of 'family friendly' policies and, critically, very few businesses employed a personnel professional. A clear preference persisted for direct owner or senior management control over the labour force. The survey indicates that few small firms have formal induction processes, and while many owners believed their firms to be engaged in teamworking, in fact very few firms met the survey remit for teamworking, which implied some employee autonomy and dilution of owner control. Regarding the determination of working terms and conditions, this was very unlikely to be undertaken through union representatives, with only a tiny minority of small firms recognising unions: therefore collective bargaining was not in evidence. Equally, there was no evidence to indicate alternative channels for employee interests, such as consultation committees. It was noted: 'The best way to characterise small businesses was by an absence of both recognised unions and consultative committees' (Cully *et al.*, 1999: 267). Rather than terms and conditions being jointly negotiated or discussed through consultation channels, they were set by the owner or management team, with some evidence that this unilateral process was complemented by individual negotiations. So overall this survey revealed a continuation of informality, with few opportunities for employee representation or voice. The research made no comment upon employee perceptions of their working conditions.

Taking a completely different methodological approach, in a series of ethnographic studies Ram (1994, 1999) again reveals patterns of informality and owner/managerial prerogative. However, the studies do reveal the scope for employees to engage in strategies to influence the social relations in the workplace. Employees may not enjoy the protection of collective bargaining but can utilise individual skills and awareness of personal relationships to protect and improve terms of employment; there is a positive advantage to being part of a small group, where each contribution can make the difference between firm viability and failure. Small firm owners and managers are aware of the value of their employees, so while they may organise the labour process unilaterally, this should not be equated with firm owners having freedom to treat labour as a renewable resource. Such detailed case studies of managing labour in small firms serve as a reminder that, as was initially noted in this discussion, the sector is highly heterogeneous. A range of tactics and strategies have emerged to manage labour in accordance with skill levels, market pressures, local employment conditions and owner preference.

In a study of 560 smaller firms in the Midlands, Bacon *et al.* (1996) did find some evidence for the utilisation of HRM policies that were sustainable over time. It was noted that a change in ownership was most likely to prompt new management initiatives, as this enabled the introduction of new ideas to the organisation. Business growth also ensured greater formality and a need to introduce new policies and systems to manage labour, as personal control became impractical. Another significant change trigger

---

* The Workplace Employee Relations Survey divides its sample of small firms into small multiples (subsidiary firms) and owner/managed firms. This discussion focuses upon the latter group as fulfilling the definition of a small firm, being independently owned and managed, and also being outside the direct influence of a larger organisation, as is likely to be the case in small multiples.

came from customer expectations and the desire to widen the customer base. It was recognised that quality was increasingly an issue: to meet customer requirements required more sophisticated approaches to production and labour management. Bacon *et al.* (1996) do not suggest that small firm owners and managers are familiar with theories of HRM, but they are aware of the implications of not introducing new management strategies within the labour process. It was also noted that the greatest impediments to introducing such changes in small firms were restricted finance and, critically, the limited business and management experience of many owners. Consequently, they found family firms to be most resistant to introducing new policies and practices, given their rather insular management construction, and that the ownership team were likely to have limited, if indeed any, other career experience prior to firm ownership. There is further evidence indicating that small firms are not averse to utilising HRM approaches. Based on a study investigating employee relations in the hotel industry, Hoque (1999) found that employers in the sector faced significant problems of labour turnover and gaining employee commitment to customer service. It was recognised that a major source of such problems was the traditionally poor terms of employment in the sector and the characteristics of the labour force willing to accept such working conditions. Firms who integrated an HRM approach and a focus on quality into their business strategy, however, were able to utilise labour to compete more successfully.

Summary

Although there will always be exceptions, it is apparent that establishing terms and conditions of employment in small firms is likely to be conducted on an informal basis, focused on the individual in a framework unilaterally devised by the firm owner. For some employees there will still be room to construct their own social relations of production and engage in mutual adjustment strategies, but for many there will be little opportunity to exercise any discretion over the manner in which they work and are rewarded. To some extent the Employment Relations Act will address the worst excesses in all firms within the economy, but this does depend upon employer awareness and observation of the legislation. As Earnshaw *et al.* (1998) found, increasing regulation and legislation is not a problem for many small owners because they simply do not know about it. Given the increasing number of employees within the small-firm sector, there is some cause for concern regarding the level of informality and ignorance that persists surrounding the management of labour. There is also a clear recognition gap (Towers, 1997) within the sector, in that employees are denied a collective voice to articulate their views upon labour management or express any opposition to management policies. However, this overview must again be qualified with the recognition of heterogeneity among small firms such that exceptions to these generalisations will be evident throughout the sector.

MANAGING LABOUR IN ORGANISATIONS WITHOUT UNION RECOGNITION

For many years, non-union workplaces were considered to be unworthy of industrial relations analysis because they were seen as an historical throwback to the nineteenth century and atypical in relation to the 'norm' of unionised industrial relations. This situation has changed steadily over the last 20 years, and non-union workplaces now account for the majority of all UK workplaces. In 1980 only 36% of workplaces were non-union, but the latest Workplace Employee Relations Survey, WERS 4 (Cully *et al.*, 1999), has found that 47% of workplaces have no trade union members at all and a further 8% have union members but do not recognise unions for collective bargaining purposes. The survey has also found that non-unionism is particularly evident in the private sector, where unions are not recognised for collective bargaining purposes in three-quarters of workplaces.

Assumptions about non-union workplaces

The relative lack of research into labour management in non-union firms means that we know little about what occurs within them. This lack of knowledge has led to two broad assumptions regarding such firms:

- There are clearly identifiable differences between labour management in unionised and non-union workplaces.
- Non-union workplaces can be divided into those that do offer good terms and conditions of employment and those that do not.

These differences have an impact on the quality of terms and conditions offered to employees, and the methods by which such terms and conditions are determined. Both assumptions overlap, to some degree, and this section will look at the basis of such assumptions, and empirical evidence to support or challenge them.

Unitarism and pluralism

One of the fundamental differences between unionised and non-union workplaces concerns the 'frame of reference' adopted by managers. Fox (1966) identified two principal frames of reference: *unitarist* and *pluralist*. The unitarist frame of reference assumes that everyone in the organisation has common goals, so conflict is pathological. From this perspective, trade unions are seen as unnecessary and unwelcome. In contrast, the pluralist frame of reference assumes that employees and managers have different goals and values, so that some conflict is inevitable. From this perspective trade unions have a legitimate role to play.

Within each of these frames of reference, industrial relations practices can vary considerably. Developing the work of Fox (1974), Purcell and Sisson (1983: 112–118) identify five ideal-typical styles: *traditionalists* and *sophisticated paternalists* (unitarist), *sophisticated moderns* (subdivided into *constitutionalists* and *consultors*) and *standard moderns* (pluralist). Traditionalists are perceived by Purcell and Sisson as somewhat akin to nineteenth-century sweatshops; their approach to trade unions is described as 'forceful opposition' and the treatment of employees as 'often overtly exploitative' (1983: 113). In contrast, sophisticated paternalists 'do not take it for granted that their employees accept the company's objectives or automatically legitimise management decision-making'. As a result they offer terms and conditions that 'ensure that individual aspirations are mostly satisfied, that collective action is seen as unnecessary and inappropriate' (p. 114).

Individualism and collectivism

The dimensions of individualism and collectivism have also been used to compare and contrast non-union and unionised firms. *Individualism* can be described as the extent to which employees are viewed as individuals 'with needs, aspirations, competencies and particular skills of their own'. *Collectivism,* on the other hand, relates to 'the recognition that employees have the right to form themselves into independent or quasi-independent organisations and to elect representatives to work on their behalf' (Purcell and Ahlstrand, 1994: 179). Thus the common assumption is that unionised firms embrace collectivism, while non-union firms are essentially individualist.

According to Purcell and Ahlstrand, these two dimensions are not mutually exclusive: organisations can have high individualism and high collectivism, or – equally – low individualism and low collectivism. 'Traditional' workplaces fall into this latter category; relatively poor terms and conditions suggest that they have minimal concern for the needs of individuals (low individualism) and that they resist union representation (low collectivism). 'Sophisticated paternalists', on the other hand, also have low collectivism, but they make use of HRM practices to enhance employee commitment and development (high individualism). Purcell and Ahlstrand include a third non-union category in their model, *paternalism* (low collectivism/moderate individualism). This style reflects a welfare-orientated image, with a strong emphasis on stability and employee loyalty, and thus offers a middle ground between the two more common extremes of non-unionism. However, Purcell and Ahlstrand (1994) suggest that paternalism is unsustainable, 'as markets impact more on organisations . . . *firms are required to move out of paternalism,* either towards high added-value policies of employee development or to cost minimisation' (pp. 207–208; emphasis added).

Non-unionism: deliberate choice or pragmatism?

The adoption of these frameworks has meant that non-union workplaces are generally thought to adopt one of two extreme positions, traditionalist or sophisticated paternalist. Both are perceived as 'atypical' in relation to the norm of unionised industrial relations. The standard modern style has been described as the predominant management style in Britain (Blyton and Turnbull, 1994), and so Purcell and Sisson's model not only highlights two extremes of approach to labour management in non-union firms but also emphasises the atypicality of industrial relations in a non-union setting:

> Non-union firms can be either exploitative and recalcitrant or innovative and flexible . . . but in both cases they are atypical in relation to the standard modern   (Beardwell, 1992: 3)

Assumptions about the atypical nature of non-union organisations also underpin the notion that non-unionism is a deliberate choice rather than a pragmatic approach to circumstance. The standard modern category includes all unionised organisations that do not appear to have a consistent or deliberate approach to industrial relations. The apparent exclusion of non-union firms therefore implies that any approach that does not recognise trade unions must be the result of a deliberate choice.

Beaumont (1995) interprets the different non-union styles as *union substitutionists* and *union suppressionists.* Substitutionists provide better-than-average terms and conditions, and adopt a variety of HRM practices 'to try to minimise employee job dissatisfaction, and hence any employee demand for union representation' (p. 172). In contrast, suppressionists offer relatively poor terms and conditions, few or no HRM practices, and 'rely largely on their small size . . . and recruitment/dismissal practices to avoid a union presence' (p. 172). However, the extent to which union avoidance is the key determinant of labour management practice is less clear in practice. Although there are undoubtedly many non-union firms where management are overtly or covertly anti-union, WERS 4 (Cully *et al.*, 1999) data suggest that the majority of managers are either neutral towards trade unions or do not see it as an issue.

The absence of deliberate management policy towards trade unions in non-union workplaces is apparent in a study of non-union firms in the high-technology sector. McLoughlin and Gourlay (1994) consider management styles in a non-union setting along two dimensions: *individualism/collectivism* and *level of strategic integration*. The first dimension relates to 'the balance between individual and collective methods of regulation in relation to particular substantive and procedural aspects of the employment relationship' (p. 36). The second dimension concerns both internal and external 'fit' – that is, the extent to which HR policies fit with each other and with the business strategy. The result is a four-fold categorisation of non-union workplaces:

- *traditional HRM* (high individualism/high strategic integration);
- *benevolent autocracy* (high individualism/low strategic integration);
- *opportunists* (high collectivism/low strategic integration);
- *strategic HRM* (high collectivism/high strategic integration).

The two management styles with high individualism might be expected to have something in common with earlier non-union models. Traditional HRM is similar to sophisticated paternalists or substitutionists because the absence of trade unions is 'a simple reflection of the absence of any need for them when rewards are high, working conditions good and even the redundancy package generous' (McLoughlin and Gourlay, 1994: 52). Benevolent autocracy falls somewhere between paternalism and sophisticated paternalism. The absence of unions was not due to deliberate policy as 'in most instances the issue appeared never to have arisen and no formal stance towards unions had ever been formulated' (p. 54). There is no reference to the traditional approaches identified in earlier models, but this is probably due to the focus on firms within the high-tech sector, which could be expected to be at the sophisticated end of the market.

The other two management styles challenge assumptions about the individualism and the atypical nature of non-union workplaces by suggesting that some non-union firms may adopt a primarily collective approach, for example through elected non-union representatives, or works councils. The management style of opportunists is described as reactive and fragmented, so these firms actually have more in common with standard moderns than they do with earlier models of non-union organisations. In the strategic HRM category the approach is a contingent one based on an assessment of 'best fit' with business strategy: in this instance all have chosen a predominantly collective approach, but this may not always be the case. The picture is a little muddled because many of the establishments in these two categories still have substantial links with unions. Many recognise unions for some elements of the workforce or are part of larger organisations that recognise unions in other establishments. So measures of high collectivism still appear to be centred on issues of unionisation even in a non-union context!

Testing non-union assumptions in practice

This section commenced by outlining two broad assumptions about non-union firms. Both are supported by empirical data to some extent but further exploration reveals a more complex picture.

Assumption 1: Non-union and unionised firms are different

One obvious difference between union and non-union sectors is the issue of union recognition, but the findings from WERS 4 (Cully *et al.*, 1999) suggest that there is some degree of overlap between the two sectors. The majority of non-union workplaces have no employee representation, but this is not true of all. Employee representatives are found in 11% of workplaces with no union members and in 19% of workplaces with union members, but no union recognition and health and safety consultative arrangements are similar in union and non-union workplaces. The study also found that the degree of joint regulation is no greater in workplaces with union representatives than in those with non-union representatives, and that there is actually greater consultation with non-union representatives. It is possible to make broad generalisations about differences between labour management practices in unionised and non-union firms, but the reasons for such differences may be many and varied, while there may be similarities, as well as differences, that require fuller investigation.

Assumption 2: Non-union workplaces can be divided into those that offer good terms and conditions and those that do not

At face value, the empirical evidence supports the distinction between sophisticated paternalists and traditionalists. However, the extent to which traditionalists deserve their sweatshop image is debatable. While there are undoubtedly firms that reflect the 'ugly' face of non-unionism, there is little hard evidence to suggest that this applies to most small to medium-sized non-union firms. Many of the studies equate an absence of HRM policies with exploitation and minimal terms and conditions, but this is not necessarily the case. A recent study into employee perceptions of 'black hole' workplaces found relatively high levels of job satisfaction, suggesting that 'even with the limited adoption of innovative human resource practices and without the pressure or support of a trade union some organisations are getting it right as far as their employees are concerned' (Guest and Conway, 1999: 386–387). Studies into new non-union workplaces (e.g. Guest and Hoque, 1994; McLoughlin and Gourlay, 1994) also illustrate the considerable diversity within the sector.

Part of the limitation of broad stereotypes is in the label 'non-union'. The non-union sector encompasses a broad range of companies that differ significantly in terms of size, sector, and product markets as well as in employee relations practices. 'Often the only characteristic these firms appear to have in common is that employees are not represented by unions: for this reason it is perhaps not appropriate to lump them all together in one category; referring to them all as non-unionised employers may seem to imply that their most important characteristic is the one that they have in common' (Mills, 1994).

Summary

We know little about labour management practices in non-union firms because for many years they were considered unworthy of industrial relations analysis. The situation has now changed, and the majority of UK workplaces are now non-union. In addition, the emergence of HRM and the initial assumptions that HRM practices would most likely be found in non-union workplaces has increased interest in this area. Comparisons between union and non-union workplaces have contributed to the perception that the two approaches are significantly different, but recent data about the degree of joint regulation suggest that there are substantial areas of overlap. Early analysis of management styles suggested that terms and conditions in non-union firms were likely to be very good or very bad depending on whether the firms were sophisticated paternalists or traditionalists. Subsequent investigations into labour management practices in non-union workplaces have shown that these extremes exist, but are not the only approaches adopted in the sector.

SUMMARY

- Collective bargaining has customarily been defined in Britain as the process of joint regulation of job control, undertaken by management and trade unions who negotiate to establish the terms and conditions that govern the employment relationship. Human resource management might be viewed as posing a threat to this joint process by its emphasis on the managerial dominance of the relationship, which requires that employees accept a managerially derived employment agenda.

- Contemporary developments in collective bargaining in the private sector have seen a narrowing of its coverage as a result of the decline in unionisation and managerial pressure to limit its scope among employees. In the public sector the government has limited collective bargaining by introducing pay review bodies for many classes of public employee, where pay is set without using bargaining processes at all. On a more general level, human resource management approaches are held to be inimical to collective bargaining, but it is still the case that many major organisations use a mix of both processes. There is some evidence from the Workplace Employee Relations Survey that mature collective bargaining environments are often the location of the very HRM policies that are held to be incompatible with traditional collective bargaining.

- The current Labour government is anxious to promote 'social partnerships' based on fairness, equity, information sharing, employee representation and consultation and a consensual approach to problem solving. Most trade unions and many employers have embraced the ethos of partnership. In becoming a full signatory to the Maastricht Agreement, the Labour government has committed the UK to the introduction of works councils by MNEs. It is unlikely that such councils will mirror the dual system evident in Germany; rather they are likely to form an additional consultation channel in firms with relatively sophisticated employee management policies. Again, it remains to be seen to what extent works councils will inform the bargaining process. The enactment of the Employment Relations Act will strengthen the rights of the individual at work, while the union recognition clause will ensure an increase in bargaining coverage.

- The number of small firms in the UK has grown rapidly in the last 20 years, such that the sector is now a significant employer in the modern economy. Until relatively recently there was a presumption that small businesses enjoyed harmonious industrial relations; this was based on the absence of overt conflict and a perception of greater teamworking due to the owner managers' close working proximity with labour. Recently this image has been questioned, with evidence suggesting that employees in many small firms have lower rewards, limited benefits and fewer prospects than those of most larger firms. It has also been revealed that agreeing terms and conditions of employment is likely to be undertaken unilaterally by owners or management upon an informal, ad hoc basis. It must be recognised that the sector is highly heterogeneous, and while certain trends, such as informality, can be identified as relatively common, there will be a considerable number of firms that do not reflect these approaches.

● There has been a significant increase in the number of organisations in the UK that have no form of union representation for employees. To date, there has been an assumption that such firms were either 'traditionalist' or 'paternalist' in nature, but this dichotomous analysis is now being challenged by contemporary research. Rather, it would appear that there are a range of policies and practices employed to establish the terms and conditions of employment for labour in organisations that do not have union representation.

CASE STUDY

An unlikely reunion

Companies are trying to attract 'friendly' trade unions in an attempt to pre-empt the government's legislation on union recognition, says **Robert Taylor**

A recent survey of unions carried out for the Trades Union Congress found as many as three-quarters of unions believe employers are reconciled towards the idea of union recognition, influenced by the prospect of the forthcoming legislation. John Cridland, director of human resource policy at the Confederation of British Industry, confirms the willingness by companies to look seriously at negotiating recognition agreements with trade unions. The CBI accepts this mood has been helped by the fact that the legislation is much more reasonable for companies than had once seemed probable. For example, the government has enshrined in the legislation the idea that union recognition should 'enhance competitiveness, prosperity and growth'. The more constructive mood among unions is also seen as important in calming employers' fears. Mr Cridland does not believe trade unions are out for revenge but are genuinely prepared to approach companies for recognition in the name of partnership.

By taking the initiative, employers are better able to shape collective arrangements in the way they want with their employees. Some companies are trying to select a preferred union for their employees or establishing so-called beauty contests between trade unions where they pick the one that can provide best value for their business. 'We are getting a lot of approaches from companies who like our partnership approach,' says the AEEU. But the tactic of selecting the friendliest union does not always succeed. Boxmore Plastics in Northern Ireland approached the TGWU for a recognition deal because it did not want a deal with the GPMU, the print union, but when the TGWU refused to negotiate it gave recognition to the GPMU. It is also clear that some companies are trying to establish no-strike clauses and other restrictions as the price for union recognition. Not all the agreements being signed reflect a mood of cooperation. It took a

long and often bitterly fought campaign lasting over seven months for the AEEU to gain recognition for its members at ADT, a fire and security company. A workplace ballot was held last October in which 67% of the bargaining group voted 'yes' in a 71% turnout.

Gregor Gall, industrial relations lecturer at Sterling University, argues in a forthcoming issue of *Labour Research* magazine that some employers are taking steps to try to avoid the legislation. This is seen as a particular tactic in the newspaper and printing industries where widespread derecognition of trade unions took place during the 1980s. Recent dismissals of union activists at the *Bolton Evening News,* part of the Newsquest group, and at Regional Independent Media suggest some employers are prepared to confront attempts by unions to recruit their employees and pursue recognition claims. A less aggressive tactic is to establish consultative committees or employee forums as an alternative to trade unions. Such bodies may not be independent but they could be used by a company for negotiations on pay and conditions as well as staff grievances. However, Mr Cridland accepts a 'small minority of companies' does exist which will resist what they see as a threat to their business from union recognition. But the CBI believes most employers will be keen to 'avoid litigation and interference by a legal body like the Central Arbitration Committee on recognition cases'. And at this early stage most trade unions seem keen to try and negotiate agreements rather than confront companies head on. 'I see no sign at the moment of any US-style union busting,' says Mr Cridland. The varied responses among employers to union recognition suggests it could become an integral part of an overdue modernisation of British industrial relations and not threaten a return to the trench warfare of 20 years ago that did such appalling damage to business performance.

Source: Financial Times. 4 March 1999.

1 Evaluate the advantages, and disadvantages, to an organisation of developing a 'partnership agreement', rather than retaining an adversarial relationship with trade unions.

2 If trade unions are adopting a stance of partnership and conciliation, discuss to what extent they can effectively represent the views and interests of the membership.

QUESTIONS

1 What have been the major developments in British collective bargaining since 1979?

2 'Collective bargaining processes contradict the basic assumptions of the HRM approach'. Discuss.

3 Why has there been an increase in the number of non-union workplaces?

4 Critically assess the effect the Employment Relations Act will have upon the extent of collective bargaining coverage in the UK.

5 Critically assess to what extent collective bargaining is the most appropriate manner in which to establish the terms and conditions of employment in the contemporary economy.

6 What are the major challenges facing small firms in establishing fair and equitable conditions of employment for their labour?

EXERCISES

1 Debate the proposition that 'collective bargaining is the most appropriate channel to redress the power imbalance within the employment relationship'.

2 Prepare a report in which you define 'social partnerships' and outline the advantages and disadvantages of such to management and employee representatives.

3 Prepare a workshop presentation that outlines the differing types of non-union firms in the contemporary economy, and the labour management strategies employed by such firms.

REFERENCES AND FURTHER READING

Those texts marked with an asterisk are particularly recommended for further reading.

Ackers, P., Smith, C. and Smith, P. (1996) *The New Workplace and Trade Unionism.* London: Routledge.

Ackroyd, S. and Procter, S. (1998) 'British manufacturing organisation and workplace industrial relations: some attributes of the new flexible firm', *British Journal of Industrial Relations*, Vol. 36, No. 2, pp. 163–184.

Aikin, O. (2000) 'Annus horribilis?', *People Management*, January 6th, p. 19.

*Bacon, N. and Storey, J. (1996) 'Individualism and collectivism', in Ackers, P., Smith, C. and Smith, P. (eds) (1997), *The New Workplace and Trade Unionism*. London, Routledge.

Bacon, N., Ackers, P., Storey, J. and Coates, D. (1996) 'It's a small world: managing human resources in small businesses', *International Journal of Human Resource Management*, Vol. 7, No.1, pp. 82–100.

Batstone, E., Boraston, I. and Frenkel, S. (1977) *Shop Stewards in Action.* Oxford: Blackwell.

Beardwell, I. (1992) 'Can management cope with the non-union firm?' Paper presented at British Academy of Management Conference, Bradford.

Beaumont, P.B. (1995) *The Future of Employment Relations.* London: Sage.

Blyton, P. and Turnbull, P. (1998) *The Dynamics of Employee Relations.* London: Macmillan.

Bolton, J.E. (1971) *Report of the Command of Inquiry on Small Firms*, Cmnd 0811. London: HMSO.

Brown, W. (1993), 'The contraction of collective bargaining in Britain', *British Journal of Industrial Relations*, Vol. 31, No. 2, pp. 189–200.

Brown, W. (ed.) (1981) *The Changing Contours of British Industrial Relations*. Oxford: Blackwell.

Brown, W. and Walsh, J. (1991) 'Pay determination in Britain in the 1980s: the anatomy of decentralisation', *Oxford Review of Economic Policy*, Vol. 7, No. 1, pp. 17–31.

Burawoy, M. (1979) *Manufacturing Consent*, Chicago: University of Chicago Press.

CBI (1988) *The Structure and Processes of Pay Determination in the Private Sector: 1979–1986*. London: Confederation of British Industry.

CBI (1999) *The 1999 Employment Trends Survey*. London: Confederation of British Industry.

Chamberlain, N.W. and Kuhn, J.W. (1965) *Collective Bargaining*. New York: McGraw-Hill.

Clark, I. (1998) 'Stakeholders in social partnership', Occasional Paper No. 26. Leicester: De Montfort University.

Clegg, H. (1979) *The Changing Systems of Industrial Relations in Great Britain*. Oxford: Blackwell.

Coates, K. and Topham, T. (1986) *Trade Unions and Politics*. Oxford: Blackwell.

*Cully, M., Woodland, S., O'Reilly, A. and Dix, G. (1999). *Britain at Work: As Depicted by the 1998 Workplace Employee Relations Survey*. London: Routledge.

Deaton, D.R. and Beaumont, P.B. (1980) 'The determinants of bargaining structure: some large-scale survey evidence for Britain', *British Journal of Industrial Relations*, Vol. 18, No. 4, pp. 201–220.

Department of Trade and Industry (1997) *Small and Medium Enterprise* (SME): *Definitions*. London: HMSO.

Department of Trade and Industry (1998) *Small Business Action Update*. London: HMSO.

Dex, S. and McCulloch, A. (1997) *Flexible Employment: The Future of Britain's Jobs*. Basingstoke: Macmillan.

Donovan Commission (1968) *Report of the Royal Commission on Trade Unions and Employers' Associations, 1965–68*, Cmnd 3623. London: HMSO.

Earnshaw, J., Goodman, J., Harrison, R. and Marchington, M. (1998) *Industrial Tribunals, Workplace Disciplinary Procedures and Employment Practice*, Employment Relations Research Series 2. London: DTI.

Edmonds, J. (1997) 'Unions and employers: how can partnership work?', in *Creating Social Partnerships*. Pamphlet published by Trade Unions. London: Unions21.

Edwards, P. (1987) *Managing the Factory: A Survey of General Managers*. Oxford: Blackwell.

*Edwards, P. (1995) *Industrial Relations Theory and Practice in Britain*. Oxford: Blackwell.

Ell, O.J. (1994) European Union Directive on Works Councils, Article Two, Directive 94/45.

Flanders, A. (1968) 'Collective bargaining: a theoretical analysis', *British Journal of Industrial Relations*, Vol. 6, No. 1, pp. 1–26.

Flanders, A. (1975) 'Collective bargaining: prescription for change', in *Management and Unions: The Theory and Reform of Industrial Relations*. London: Faber.

Fox, A. (1966) *Industrial Society and Industrial Relations*. Royal Commission Research Paper No. 3.

Fox, A. (1974) *Beyond Contract: Work, Power and Trust Relations*. London: Faber.

Fox, A. (1975) 'Collective bargaining, Flanders and the Webbs', *British Journal of Industrial Relations*, Vol. 13, No. 2, pp. 151–174.

*Gall, G. and McKay, S. (1999) 'Developments in union recognition and derecognition in Britain, 1994–1998', *British Journal of Industrial Relations*, Vol. 37, No. 4, pp. 601–614.

Gospel, H. and Palmer, G. (1993) *British Industrial Relations*. London: Routledge.

Goss, D. (1991) *Small Business and Society*. London: Routledge.

Gregg, P. and Yates, A. (1991) 'Changes in wage-setting arrangements and trade union presence in the 1980s', *British Journal of Industrial Relations*, Vol. 29, No. 3, pp. 361–76.

Guest, D.E. (1989a) 'Human resource management: its implications for industrial relations and trade unions', in Storey, J. (ed.) *New Perspectives on Human Resource Management*. London: Routledge, pp. 41–55.

Guest, D. (1989b) 'Personnel and HRM: can you tell the difference?', *Personnel Management*, January, pp. 48–51.

Guest, D. and Hoque, K. (1994) 'The good, the bad and the ugly: employee relations in new non-union workplaces', *Human Resources Management Journal*, Vol. 5, No. 1, pp. 1–14.

Guest, D. and Conway, N. (1999) 'Peering into the black hole: the downside of the new employment relations in the UK', *British Journal of Industrial Relations*, Vol. 37, No. 3, pp. 367–390.

Holliday, R. (1995), *Investigating Small Firms: Nice Work?* London: Routledge.

Hoque, K. (1999) 'Human resource management and performance in the UK hotel industry', *British Journal of Industrial Relations*, Vol. 37, No. 3, pp. 419–444.

Hyman, R. (1975) *Industrial Relations: A Marxist Introduction*. London: Macmillan.

Hyman, R. (1997) 'The future of industrial relations', *British Journal of Industrial Relations*, Vol. 35, No. 3, pp. 309–336.

Ingham, G.K. (1970) *The Size of Industrial Organisation and Worker Behaviour*. Cambridge: Cambridge University Press.

Jackson, M. (1991) *An introduction to industrial relations*, London: Routledge.

Kelly, J. (1996) 'Union militancy and social partnership', in Ackers, P., Smith, C. and Smith, P. (eds) (1997) *The New Workplace and Trade Unionism*. London: Routledge.

Kinnie, N. (1990) 'The decentralisation of industrial relations? Recent research considered', *Personnel Review*, Vol. 19, No. 3, pp. 33.

Mabey, C. and Salamon, G. (1995) *Strategic Human Resource Management*. Oxford: Blackwell.

Marginson, P. and Sisson, K. (1990) 'Single table talk', *Personnel Management*, May, pp. 21–22

Marginson, P., Edwards, P., Martin, R., Purcell, J. and Sisson, K. (1988) *Beyond the Workplace*. Oxford: Blackwell.

Marlow, S. (2000) 'People in the small firm', in Cartex. S. and Jones-Evans, *Enterprise and Small Business: Principles, Policy and Practice*. London: Addison-Wesley, pp. 300–22

Marsh, D. (1992) *The New Politics of British Trade Unionism*. London: Macmillan.

McLoughlin, I. and Gourlay, S. (1994) *Enterprise Without Unions: Industrial Relations in the Non-Union Firm*. Buckingham: Open University Press.

McIlroy, J. (1998) 'The enduring alliance; trade unions and the making of New Labour, 1994–1997', *British Journal of Industrial Relations,* Vol. 4, No. 36, pp. 537–564.

Mills, D. Q. (1994) *Labor–Management Relations,* 5th edn. New York: McGraw Hill.

Millward, N., Stevens, M., Smart, D. and Hawes, W.R. (1992) *Workplace Industrial Relations in Transition.* Aldershot: Dartmouth.

Milner, S. (1993) 'Dispute deterrence: evidence on final offer arbitration', in Metcalf, D. and Milner, S. (eds) *New Perspectives on Industrial Disputes.* London: Routledge.

Mishel, L. and Voos, P.B. (eds) (1992) *Unions and Economic Competitiveness.* New York: Sharpe.

Monks, J. (1996) 'Interview: John Monks', *New Statesman,* 6 September.

Nolan, P. and O'Donnell, K. (1995) 'Industrial relations and productivity', in Edwards, P. (ed.) *Industrial Relations Theory and Practice in Britain.* Oxford: Blackwell, pp. 397–433.

Palmer, G. (1983) *British Industrial Relations.* London: Unwin & Hyman.

Pollert, A. (1988) 'Dismantling flexibility', *Capital and Class,* Vol. 34, Spring, pp. 42–75.

Purcell, J. and Ahlstrand, B. (1994) *Human Resource Management in the Multi-Divisional Company.* Oxford: Oxford University Press.

Purcell, J. and Sisson, K. (1983) 'Strategies and practice in the management of industrial relations', in G.S. Bain (ed.) *Industrial Relations in Britain.* Oxford: Blackwell, pp. 95–120.

Rainnie, A. (1989) *Industrial Relations in Small Firms.* London: Routledge.

Ram, M. (1994) *Managing to Survive: Working Lives in Small Firms.* Oxford: Blackwell.

Ram, M. (1999) 'Managing autonomy: employment relations in small professional service firms', *International Small Business Journal,* Vol. 17, No. 2, pp. 2–16.

Salamon, M. (1992) *Industrial Relations: Theory and Practice.* Englewood Cliffs, NJ: Prentice Hall.

Scase, R. (1995), 'Employment relations in small firms', in Edwards, P. (ed.) *Industrial Relations: Theory and Practice in Britain,* Oxford: Blackwell, pp. 569–598.

Scott, M. Roberts, I., Holroyd, G. and Sawbridge, D. (1989) *Management and Industrial Relations in Small Firms,* Research Paper no. 70, London: Department of Employment.

Singh, R. (1986) 'Final offer: arbitration in theory and practice', *Industrial Relations Journal,* Winter, Vol. 15, No. 3, pp. 329–330.

Sisson, K. (1987) *The Management of Collective Bargaining: An International Comparison.* Oxford: Blackwell.

Sisson, K. (1993) 'In search of HRM', *British Journal of Industrial Relations,* Vol. 31, No. 2, pp. 201–210.

Storey, D.J., Keasey, K. Watson, R. and Wynarczyk, P. (1987) *The Performance of Small Firms.* London: Routledge.

Storey, D.J. (1994) *Understanding the Small Business Sector.* London: Routledge.

Storey, J. (1992) *Developments in the Management of Human Resources.* Oxford: Blackwell.

Storey, J. (ed.) (1989) *New Perspectives on Human Resource Management.* London: Routledge.

Streeck, W. (1995) 'Works councils in Western Europe', in Rogers, J. and Streeck, W. (eds), *Works Councils: Consultation, Representation and Cooperation in Industrial Relations.* Chicago: University of Chicago Press, pp. 262–293.

Thompson, N. (1996) 'Supply side socialism: the political economy of New Labour', *New Left Review,* Vol. 26, No. 216, pp. 194–210.

Towers, B. (1997) *The Representation Gap: Change and Reform in the British and American Workplace.* Oxford: Oxford University Press.

Walton, R.E. and McKersie, R.B (1965) *A Behavioral Theory of Labor Negotiations.* New York: McGraw-Hill.

Webb, S. and Webb, B. (1902) *Industrial Democracy.* London: Longman.

Wynarczyk, P., Watson, R. Storey, D. J. and Keasey, K. (1993) *The Managerial Labour Markets in Small Firms.* London: Routledge.

Reward and performance management

Ian Roberts

OBJECTIVES

- To explain the theoretical foundations of reward and performance management strategies in organisations.
- To examine the issues in designing a reward strategy and system.
- To examine the methods and aims of different forms of reward system.
- To critically examine contemporary issues and trends in reward and performance management strategies, techniques and philosophies.
- To analyse reward strategies in an international context.
- To highlight the relationship between reward and performance management and human resource management.

INTRODUCTION

The introductory chapter illustrated the extent to which human resource management seeks to achieve an integrated philosophy. This chapter explores the role played by performance and reward management in achieving human resource management outcomes and objectives (e.g. Beer *et al.*, 1984; Hendry and Pettigrew, 1990; Storey, 1992; Armstrong, 1996a).

As one writer states:

> . . . the pay package is one of the most obvious and visible expressions of the employment relationship; it is the main issue in the exchange between employer and employee, expressing the connection between the labour market, the individual's work and the performance of the employing organisation itself.
>
> (Hegewisch, 1991a: 28)

The design and operation of payment systems in many organisations have often been institutionalised by custom and practice, tradition and collective bargaining mechanisms, and as Smith (1992: 75–76) indicates, frequently as a result of simply 'muddling through'. Nevertheless, trends show that the movement towards human resource management has corresponded with the introduction of supposedly 'new' forms and strategies of reward management. Often termed 'new pay' (Lawler, 1990), contemporary developments in pay and reward concentrate on individual performance–reward contingencies in an unitarist framework. A strategic, integrative and flexible approach to pay is taken in order to address commercial and organisational realities, and adapt to changing employee expectations. 'New pay' is often contrasted with 'old pay', which reflects a pluralist approach and the use of job-evaluated grade structures, payment by time, and seniority-based financial rewards and benefits. (Heery 1996).

This chapter seeks to provide a sense of the historic development of payment systems, in order to paint a more realistic picture of the advantages and disadvantages of the methods currently in use.

THEORETICAL FOUNDATIONS

Due to competitive pressures, organisations are continually looking to increase the 'added value' of their employees by encouraging them to increase their effort and performance beyond that which is at a minimally acceptable standard, or by reducing labour costs to a minimum. Thus the study of employee behaviour and motivation has remained a constant managerial concern.

Content theories

Content theories help us to understand what people will and will not value as work rewards. They attempt to identify the specific factors that motivate people. The assumption is that individuals have needs that they seek to satisfy inside and outside of work. The following section discusses the most well-known need theories, and provides an indication of the different needs that individuals bring to the working environment. Managers should consider how they can create a working environment in which individuals have the opportunity to satisfy their important needs.

Maslow's hierarchy of needs

Abraham Maslow devised a theory of human nature that proposed that everyone is motivated to satisfy a series of instinctual needs:

- *Physiological needs* are basic biological needs essential for survival.
- *Safety and security needs* include protection from physical and psychological threats in the environment, such as freedom from fear, and a wish for certainty.
- *Social and belonging needs* include a need for love, affection, friendship, social interaction and acceptance of others.
- *Ego and esteem needs* include a need for self-respect, confidence, recognition, respect from others, status, power and competence.
- *Self-actualisation* includes self-fulfilment, achievement, individual growth, and the realisation of potential.

Maslow believed that once one level of needs had been satisfied they no longer motivated the individual and other needs would become prominent. Individuals would be motivated to progressively work their way up the hierarchy, satisfying each level until they reached the final level of *self-actualisation*. Thus in order to increase employees' motivation managers have to consider the higher levels of needs as well as the physiological and safety needs.

Herzberg's two-factor theory of motivation

Frederick Herzberg made the distinction between hygiene factors and motivators in the work environment. *Hygiene factors* were thought to be environmental, and prevented workers from becoming dissatisfied and demotivated. Herzberg believed, however, that hygiene factors did not motivate. Examples include pay, working conditions, supervision, company policy and administration, and interpersonal relationships.

A second set of factors were thought by Herzberg to be able to motivate individual employees. These *motivators* included such factors as interesting and meaningful work, achievement, recognition, responsibility, personal growth, and advancement. The lack of these factors at work would simply mean that employees were not motivated. Thus an organisation must be concerned with ensuring that both the hygiene factors and the motivators are to an adequate standard.

Porter and Lawler's expectancy model of motivation

Porter and Lawler (1968) modified and built upon Vroom's (1964) expectancy and Adams' (1963) equity theories of motivation. These theories can be termed *process* theories of motivation as they consider the dynamic relationship between effort, performance–reward for each individual.

Figure 12.1 illustrates the main variables in the Porter and Lawler model of motivation.

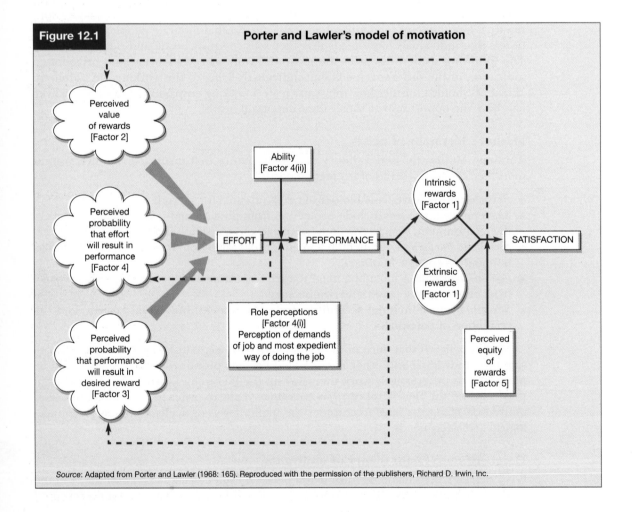

Figure 12.1 — Porter and Lawler's model of motivation

Source: Adapted from Porter and Lawler (1968: 165). Reproduced with the permission of the publishers, Richard D. Irwin, Inc.

Intrinsic and extrinsic rewards (Factor 1)

Intrinsic rewards are less tangible, originate from the person or job itself, and reflect Herzberg's motivators. Examples of such factors include:

- variety in job content;
- a sense of being part of the whole 'value adding' process;
- the belief that the person is a valuable member of a team;
- increased responsibility and autonomy;
- a sense of accomplishment;
- participation in setting targets, and opportunities to achieve them;
- feedback of information;
- recognition;
- opportunities to learn and grow.

Extrinsic rewards result from the actions of others such as supervisors, and are more easily controlled by managers. Examples include pay, fringe benefits, praise and promotion.

The Porter and Lawler model and management control

Managers are able to control employee behaviour by linking the occurrence of the desired behaviour to some form of reward, thereby ensuring predictability of behaviour. The intention is therefore to introduce and enforce agreed norms of behaviour on management's prescribed agenda. Thus management are able to control the workers when close supervision is not possible and/or workers' discretion is not possible. If an individual manager therefore has discretion as to which behaviour to reward and who to reward then he or she has power. See also Baldamus (1961: 91), Behrend (1961: 103–104), Etzioni (1961, 1964) and Flanders (1970: 73).

The Porter and Lawler model: summary of principles

By utilising this model the following principles can be stated:

- Employees must value the rewards (intrinsic or extrinsic) offered by the organisation (Factor 2).
- Employees will put in more effort if they believe that good performance will lead to the achievement of the desired rewards. Thus employees should perceive that higher performance will result in greater rewards (Factor 3).
- Employees must be able to engage in 'good' performance. They must have the opportunity, ability, resources, and effective management to carry out the tasks, and must believe that the quality of their work, and hence their reward, is directly related to and reflects the effort they put into the job. If these conditions do not exist then employees will not believe that working hard etc. will lead to the required level of performance, and the link between performance and desired rewards will be broken (Factor 4).
- Managers must communicate their expectations and objectives clearly, thereby ensuring that employees understand which behaviours are required.
- To increase expectations that desired performance will be rewarded, managers must make sure that rewards are clearly and visibly linked to performance.
- Managers must recognise the important role played by comparisons in determining employee satisfaction, and therefore the consequent levels of effort they will put into a task (Factor 5). See also the section on 'Distributive justice'.

Behaviour modification

Theories of behaviour modification also underpin many systems of payment that attempt to encourage new work habits. Theories suggest that individuals learn that the occurrence of certain behaviours will result in reward or punishment. Designers of reward strategies must therefore take into account Thorndike's *law of effect*:

> Of several responses made to the same situation, those which are accompanied or closely followed by satisfaction (reinforcement) . . . will be more likely to recur; those which are accompanied or closely followed by discomfort (punishment) . . . will be less likely to occur.
> (Thorndike, 1911: 244)

Thus behaviour modification explains motivation in terms of the external consequences of particular behaviours rather than previously discussed internal explanations such as satisfying needs (content theories) and the motivational pull of incentives (process theories). Concern here therefore is in the way organisation reward systems are administered: for example, the reinforcement/consequence (reward) should follow as soon as possible after the desired behaviour.

A STRATEGIC PERSPECTIVE ON REWARD

There are two different approaches to a strategic perspective on reward: an open or contingent approach, and a closed approach (see, for example, Mabey and Salaman, 1995). An *open approach* argues that the content of an HR strategy is contingent on the internal and external context and the type of business strategy. Thus the emphasis is on 'match' and 'fit' rather than on identifying one ideal type of HR strategy (e.g. Hendry and Pettigrew, 1990). It is argued that there should be a strategic fit between reward strategy and business strategy, to ensure that who or what delivers the critical skills, performance and behaviour with respect to business strategy and objectives is rewarded. In this way individuals will be motivated to put effort into reaching business goals, and will act in ways that are consistent with business strategy. Messages are provided on what the organisation values, the right people are retained in and attracted to the organisation, and therefore by applying leverage on employee performance business performance will be improved (Cokerton and Bevan, 1998). Furthermore, the design of a reward strategy should be 'appropriate' or 'integrated' with internal aspects of the organisation that affect employee behaviour such as organisational culture, structure and personnel, and the external environment in which the organisation exists (Mabey and Salaman, 1995). Hence reward strategy needs to fit with the existing organisational culture, structure and personnel or it can be used as a change lever to ensure fit between those factors. However, this approach simplifies the political and pluralistic nature of reward, and may overestimate the flexibility of a reward strategy to fit with a rapidly changing business strategy and external context. Moreover, it assumes an ability and desire to develop a coherent and planned reward strategy (Mabey and Salaman, 1995). Integration can also be achieved horizontally through ensuring that reward strategy fits with and supports other components of the HR strategy such as employee relations, resourcing, and development.

The *closed approach* argues that HR strategies should contain the same elements regardless of context and business strategy (e.g. Guest, 1987). For example, a reward strategy based on 'new pay' or 'contingent pay' is often believed to be a key component of strategic human resource management.

However, a particular reward strategy cannot operate as a single lever in creating and maintaining organisational change and long-term effective and harmonious human resource management. Although 'new pay' schemes are often assumed to lead to increased levels of employee commitment, Wood (1996) found little evidence to link 'high-commitment management' with payment schemes contingent on performance. In describing the views of the managers in his study, Wood (1996) reports:

> High commitment depends on more than fulfilling the money motivation, and to use the words of one manager, in a plant using individual bonuses, it 'is a much larger issue, involving enriching jobs, job satisfaction, and training.'
>
> (p. 65)

REWARD PHILOSOPHY

A useful way of conceptualising different reward philosophies is provided by Rajan (1997: 75). Figure 12.2 shows how reward can be categorised along two dimensions: identifying rewards that are money-related and non-money-related; and rewards that are group-related (available to all or most staff) or individual-related. Thus Rajan (1997) argues that there are four types of approach to reward.

Figure 12.2

Types of reward

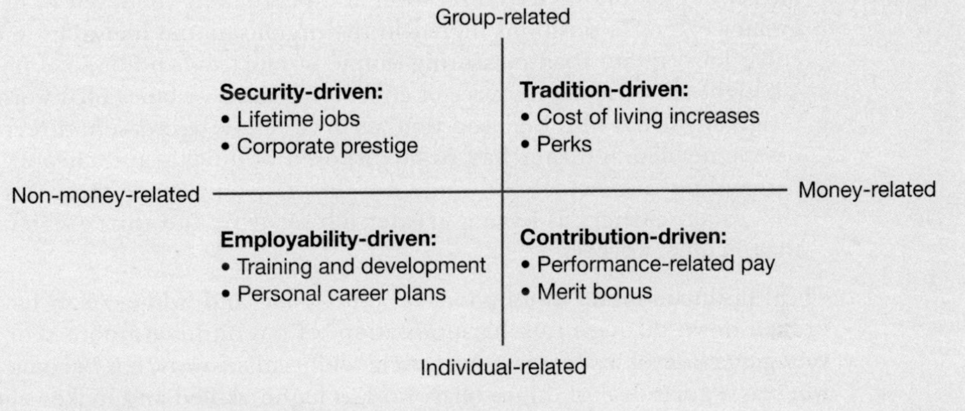

Group-related

Security-driven:
- Lifetime jobs
- Corporate prestige

Tradition-driven:
- Cost of living increases
- Perks

Non-money-related — Money-related

Employability-driven:
- Training and development
- Personal career plans

Contribution-driven:
- Performance-related pay
- Merit bonus

Individual-related

Source: Rajan (1997: 75). Reproduced with the permission of Eclipse Group Limited.

REWARD STRUCTURES AND SCHEMES

An individual's reward package is typically based around two components: a salary or wage component and an incentive-based component. The incentive-based component may contain several elements, and can vary in relation to results, performance or acquisition of skills. The balance between the salary and incentive components will vary for different occupational sectors, organisations, jobs and employees. In some cases an individual's reward package will contain only one component. Employee benefits may be performance linked or salary linked.

Salary structures

Salaries and wages

Historically there has been a separation in the methods of payment for blue-collar and white-collar employees. Manual, blue-collar employees have traditionally been paid a weekly wage based on a rate negotiated between the employer, or employer's national representatives, and the representatives of the employees. In some cases an hourly or weekly rate is unilaterally imposed by the employer. Wage earners are paid simply for the work they do and not for any personal characteristics or potential they bring to the employment relationship (Lupton and Bowey, 1983: 96). Salary earners are more likely to be paid monthly, and progress through a clearly defined career hierarchy based on factors such as age, seniority, qualifications, experience and performance.

The distinction reflects many historical assumptions. For example, Lupton and Bowey (1983: 97–99) draw out several explanations:

- Manual jobs in most cases do not constitute a basis for further career advancement. Companies traditionally have recruited graduates, technicians or professionals on a direct entry basis to provide the required skills, knowledge and attitudes to perform at high levels in the hierarchy. Furthermore: 'Family and social-class background not only inhibit educational progression, they condition expectations of advancement and a person's view of his own potential for advancement' (p. 97).
- Differences also arise because of the greater importance attached to and difficulty in measuring factors such as discretion and judgement (believed to be involved to a greater extent in positions higher in the organisational hierarchy and/or in white-collar jobs) rather than measuring simple productivity and 'innate' physical strength (thought to be the main source of effort for manual or blue-collar workers).
- Originally it was also believed that, as production decreased, direct labour would not be needed and thus had to be disposed of quickly and cheaply. However, the demand for indirect labour would not fluctuate and hence there was a tendency to view salary earners as having greater job security, and thus greater commitment, than manual workers.

These distinctions and assumptions of 'blue-collar' and 'white-collar' have more or less broken down through the 'harmonisation' of pay and conditions. For example, at a very general level we can see that much 'white-collar' work has become more routine, whereas a great deal of 'blue-collar' work is highly skilled and makes significant use of new technology.

Assumptions of a salary system

The rationale behind the use of salary schemes relies on certain assumptions. For example:

Deferred gratification

Commitment and loyalty to the organisation and therefore the use of initiative and discretion are thought to be encouraged through the 'promise of high future rewards in return for present efforts and achievement' (Lupton and Bowey, 1983: 122). It is hoped that competition for promotion encourages employees to increase their levels of effort. Indeed Flanders, writing in 1968 but pertinent for the contemporary flat or networked organisation, suggests that the prospect of promotion and future pay increases is an important part of the incentive system for managers, whereas '[t]he fact that the great majority of manual workers [have] little or no career prospects in their jobs [makes] it important to supply as far as possible more immediate and direct incentives' (p. 74). We can see that problems arise when the future rewards, such as promotion opportunities, are not forthcoming because of either a promotional blockage in the organisational hierarchy or a lack of opportunities. Furthermore, Williamson (1975) argues that stable wage hierarchies help to encourage a stable labour pool with firm-specific skills.

Prerogatives

Lupton and Bowey (1983) define these as 'those rewards or salary increments which are paid to an employee as of right, and which do not depend upon any appraisal of his (her) work'(pp. 122–123). Hence advancement in the salary structure would be perceived as an 'automatic right' on reaching a certain age or experience level. Again the intention is to encourage a high degree of commitment and loyalty to the organisation. Clearly a system based on prerogative rewards may lead to complacency and 'safe' attitudes, and employees may be discouraged to undertake risks, innovation and continuous improvement.

Meeting security needs and encouraging cooperation

Here there is a recognition of people's desire for a constant and predictable income (Shaw and Shaw Pirie, 1982: 300) and an assumption that alternative performance and individual-based schemes may be too hedonistic and conflictual.

Ensuring predictability and balance of labour costs

As incremental progression through grades is determined by predictable elements, and the payout associated with each grade is fixed, the total labour costs for an organisation are fairly predictable in a static labour market. Furthermore, the payment of labour costs for those with long service and who are at the top of the grade hierarchy will be 'subsidised' by those with shorter service who are at the lower end of the hierarchy. However, within a static labour market where there is little movement into or out of the organisation, the majority of employees 'creep up' the grade hierarchy and pay scales and create a significant financial burden for employers.

Managing conflict

It is recognised that employers and employees may have different expectations and perceptions of the wage–effort bargain, and possible conflict over pay is confined to structured and collective mechanisms such as collective bargaining, and to certain periods of the year. Furthermore Williamson (1975) argues that stable salary structures prevent opportunistic wage bargaining and minimise the transactional costs of individualised pay.

Designing a salary structure

A salary structure comprises a hierarchy of job grades with progressive levels of responsibility, status and authority with corresponding pay increments, and relates effort to these rewards through a system of rules and procedures (Lupton and Bowey, 1983: 102–103). The rules and procedures define what is required to move from one level to another level in the hierarchy and how that promotion decision will be made. Organisations, however, will differ greatly in the extent to which the pay and job hierarchy is formalised, and the extent to which managers have discretion in pay and promotion decisions or whether progression 'takes place automatically by the application of certain fixed rules' (Lupton and Bowey, 1983: 105).

Traditionally jobs are graded and grouped within fairly narrow pay bands or scales in the salary hierarchy. The grades and pay bands will normally overlap, and the number and scope of pay bands will vary between organisations. Each pay band will have a scale with maximum and minimum level of pay based around a midpoint. This midpoint could represent the median of market rates, or competitive positioning within that job market.

Organisations also have to take into account government interventions such as the National Minimum Wage, New Deal, and changes to the tax system, and the general economic outlook in terms of inflation and cost-of-living indexes.

Broadbanding

Broadbanding is the collapsing of a range of narrow and complex pay grades into fewer but wider pay bands. Pay flexibility within the bands can be based on individual performance, market rates, company performance and competences. The bands are normally overlapping, and can be composed of zones that reflect job families, competences or market rates. The intention is not only to create more flexibility in the delivery of pay, but also to enable and support lateral career movement, competence growth and continuous development. Clearly the focus is on the development and reward of the person rather than the job.

Importance of internal comparability

Internal comparability refers to assessments of differences and similarities between jobs and received reward within the organisation, and judgements of received reward in relation to the perceived worth or contribution of individual jobs. When designing salary structure, internal compatibility is addressed through five interrelated factors:

- beliefs about the worth of jobs – for example, this may be based on scope, level of responsibility, skill requirements, objectionableness of duties, commercial worth and strategic relevance;
- clustering of similar types of or similarly valued jobs;
- allocation of pay rates to bands or scales;
- relationships between the clusters;
- rules and procedures for moving to different levels of pay.

Typically, job evaluation schemes attempt to address these factors through the systematic collection of information and analysis of the relative worth of jobs through a 'pseudo-scientific' system. Although job evaluation has attracted much criticism, particularly in relation to inflexibility and subjectivity, such schemes can provide a defence against 'equal value' claims.

The criticism of inflexibility resides in the fact that job evaluation schemes are static, a snapshot of a job at a point in time. Thus schemes have to be constantly monitored and adjusted to ensure that they reflect what needs to be achieved: in other words there is a strong possibility that jobs within rigid schemes become an 'end' in themselves rather than a 'means to an end'. The subjectivity of job evaluation schemes has been well documented by many writers elsewhere (e.g Wootton, 1962; Bowey, 1980; Lupton and Bowey, 1983: 5–38; Fowler, 1996), and two main arguments seem to pervade the literature: the subjective selection of and weighting given to the pertinent factors thought to result in the successful accomplishment of the job; and the decoding of this factor analysis into a particular wage or salary. For example, if an analytical, factor-based scheme is used then the factors or weightings that are used can enable the organisation to emphasise specific competences:

When the national job evaluation scheme for a million local government workers was designed in 1987, the traditional emphasis on physical effort and working conditions was downgraded and more weight given to the skills involved in the caring for people. Consequently, the relative pay of refuse collectors and home-help workers was reversed, with the previously lower-paid home-helpers scoring 630 points against the refuse collectors' 272 points.   (Fowler, 1996: 43)

Furthermore, a possible conflict may develop between the introduction of a job evaluation scheme that attempts to scientifically 'discover' the fair rate for jobs, and mechanisms such as collective bargaining, which traditionally attempt to protect differentials and 'customary' relativities between the incomes received by different occupations (see, for example, Wootton 1962; Hyman and Brough, 1975: 32).

Importance of external comparability
A particular concern for organisations is the extent to which the amount and type of reward offered by the company is equitable relative to those offered by competitors. The level and composition of the reward package will be influenced by labour supply and demand either at national level or in response to the local labour market. Companies will have to match or exceed the median pay rates offered by their labour-market competitors in order to attract the staff they require and prevent existing employees from moving to other organisations.

Organisations can use several methods to formulate a competitive pay rate: for example, the use of job market surveys published by organisations such as Income Data Services and the DfEE; an informal exchange of information between organisations recruiting in the same labour markets; the monitoring of job advertisements; or information from exit interviews. Caution must be taken when using such sources because of problems of incompatibility of roles, and biased and outdated information. Companies may also remain competitive in the labour by a willingness simply to 'bump up' rates when the company is having difficulty in recruiting or retaining staff (White, 1982: 268).

Simplicity and rigidity versus complexity and flexibility?
There is an inherent tension between designing a differentiated pay structure that reflects diversity in needs, expectations and performance of individuals and encourages career advancement, and the objective of maintaining simplicity, predictability, and control through a standardised system (White, 1981: 37–39; Child, 1984: 179). Furthermore, flexibility in pay levels and the setting of 'competitive' pay rates in order to attract and retain certain categories of staff may violate the overall distribution of salaries and thus bear little resemblance to job requirements and job content. For example, see Daniel and McIntosh (1972: 156) and Lupton and Bowey (1983: 111).

Incentive-based schemes

The literature on remuneration abounds with confusing and conflicting labels and descriptions of different incentive-based payment systems. To attempt to clarify the situation the discussion below is based on the distinctions formulated by Casey *et al.* (1992). Thus incentive-based payment systems can be categorised into four broad types:

- *Individual payment by results.* Incentive schemes that directly reward the outcomes of the performance of an individual. Examples of such systems include piecework, output and target-based bonuses, and commission bonuses based on sales.
- *Collective payment by results.* Incentive schemes that directly reward the output or productivity of group, section, department or company.

- *Collective bonus schemes.* Incentive schemes based on company profits. Examples of this method include profit-sharing schemes, and employee share option schemes.
- *Performance-related pay.* Incentive schemes based on the assessment of performance and/or competence.

Payment by results (PBR)

As we have seen in the first section, the motivational impact of the linking of a financial reward to quantity and/or quality of employee outputs is recognised by many motivational theories. By paying employees for results, there is a direct and visible link between the outcomes of performance and financial reward. It is assumed that this relationship will lead the individual to try to continue or increase his or her level of performance in order to receive more financial rewards, and by implication increase their efforts.

Indeed the first systems that attempted directly to elicit increases in effort by increases in money were piecework systems that involved individual workers directly employed on a production process, undertaking simple, routine and repetitive manual work (see, for example, Webb, 1982: 289, 290). Piecework has a strong tradition in Britain, particularly in industries such as engineering, textiles, footwear and clothing, and still remains in use in one form or another in many firms in these industries (see White, 1981: 14; Cannell and Long, 1991: 58–60; Casey *et al.*, 1992).

PBR schemes relate either the whole or part of an employee's total pay package to the output produced by the individual or group to which he or she belongs. Schemes vary on several dimensions:

- the level of financial reward for each incremental level of output;
- the level of basic pay (i.e. the base rate of pay);
- the relationship between incremental pay and incremental output (i.e. is it symmetrical or is there an increasing or decreasing ratio between the additional output and the additional pay received?);
- the threshold of output for receiving PBR;
- the capping level of PBR.

These dimensions are illustrated in Figures 12.3–12.6. In Figure 12.3:

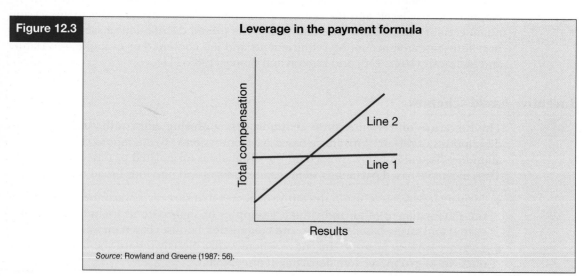

Figure 12.3

Leverage in the payment formula

Source: Rowland and Greene (1987: 56).

- *Line 1* refers to high base-rate pay and low payments for incremental outputs. Consequently reward and risk are low.
- *Line 2* refers to low base-rate pay and high payments for incremental outputs. Consequently risk and reward are high.

In Figure 12.4:

- *Linear.* A straight line represents a belief that each incremental level of output is as difficult to obtain or is as important as the previous incremental level of output.
- *Accelerating.* A curve upwards indicates that each incremental level of output is increasingly more difficult and/or more valuable.
- *Decelerating.* A curve downwards demonstrates the belief that each incremental level of output is easier to achieve and/or less valuable to the organisation.

Figure 12.5 outlines the decision of where to begin payments: that is, what sort of return or output the company should expect before paying out a bonus.

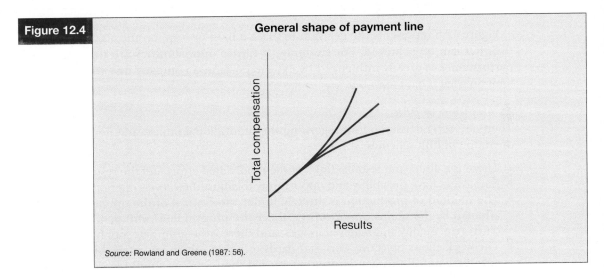

Figure 12.4 — **General shape of payment line**

Source: Rowland and Greene (1987: 56).

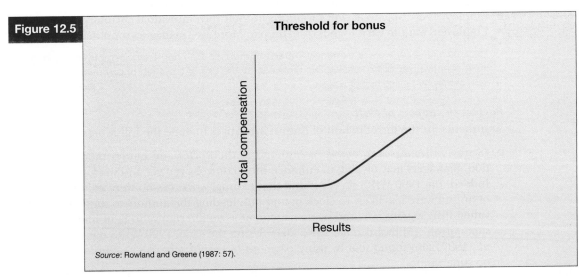

Figure 12.5 — **Threshold for bonus**

Source: Rowland and Greene (1987: 57).

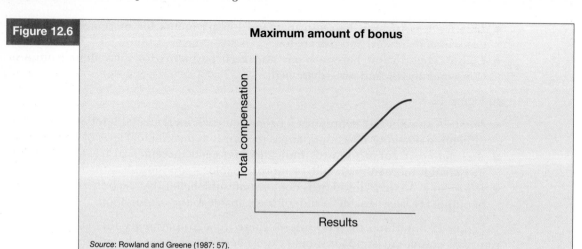

Figure 12.6

Maximum amount of bonus

Total compensation

Results

Source: Rowland and Greene (1987: 57).

Figure 12.6 represents the decision to place a limit or 'cap' on the amount of incentive that can be achieved. For example, if future opportunities are uncertain or if performance is greatly influenced by external events, a company may wish to place a limit on what it has to pay out.

Assumptions of PBR

There are several assumptions regarding the motivational impact and hence successful operation of PBR schemes:

- There is a direct and testable link between individual effort and the results obtained.
- Employees have the ability and opportunity to adjust their levels of effort.
- The method of production is directly under the control of the operator (or those affected by the bonus opportunity), there are no problems with maintaining standards (e.g. quality and material usage), and there is a continuous supply of work.
- The work allows objective work standards to be set, which are attainable and can be enforced, and if the standards are achieved then workers should believe that managers will not attempt to renegotiate a lower rate of payment.
- Employees are able to accept variations in their own individual earnings.
- Employees want to earn higher or extra pay. Moreover managers must believe that the:

financial motive for work is extremely important, more so than non-financial motives . . . [and] the most effective way of harnessing this motive is by the use of a system of payment by results . . . [not] simply by paying higher wages.   (Behrend, 1959: 140)

Factors in support of PBR

Arguments for the introduction of output incentives include the following:

- *Increase in management control.* As outlined in the Porter and Lawler model of motivation, managers may be able to enhance their control over pay and work performance. Indeed, the 1990 WIRS survey found that manual workers who were paid on the basis of output were less likely to clock in and out, leading the authors to suggest that 'individual PBR systems are used by management as an alternative to light monitoring and supervision' (Millward *et al.*, 1992: 261). Using the same 1990 WIRS data, Heywood *et al.* (1997) also found that by using payment by results schemes organisations can save on supervision.

- *Less supervision and greater freedom for employees.* There is, however, a somewhat contradictory proposition that PBR schemes can actually increase employees' discretion. For example, some PBR schemes place the responsibility for the methods and quantity of output at the feet of the workers: 'They can legitimately ask management to leave them alone to get on with their work as they see fit on the grounds that they will be the first to suffer if a high level of output is not attained' (Child, 1984: 193). Therefore the implication is that workers will take over some of the supervisory duties such as ensuring continuous and efficient production. Conversely time-based payment systems force supervisors into taking responsibility for ensuring high levels of effort and performance from workers (Child, 1984: 193). However, employees' discretion is clearly delimited as it is set within management's clearly defined parameters.
- *Opportunities to achieve high earnings.* Schemes that link performance to pay and do not have a cap in earnings are likely to give workers the opportunity to earn as much money as they choose: that is, workers decide for themselves how to balance the wage–effort bargain.
- *Create a joint appreciation of the necessity to increase profit so as to benefit both the company and workers.*

Criticisms of PBR

Many writers have described the problems and negative consequences associated with PBR schemes (e.g. Roy, 1952, 1953, 1955; Lupton, 1972; Brown, 1973; Haraszti, 1980; Herzog, 1980; Bowey *et al.*, 1982; Cavendish, 1982: 125–135; Edwards and Scullion, 1982: 167–199; Lupton and Bowey, 1983: 153–158; Thompson, 1992). For example, the relationship between effort and reward is too simplistic, and ignores factors such as the importance of social relationships, and the perceived fairness of the payment system. Such schemes also reflect the widely held assumption of the power of money to motivate sustained high performance.

Often payment by results systems fail to relate performance with pay, and therefore fail to motivate employees because of *erosion*. 'Erosion' has been defined by Lupton and Bowey (1983: 153) as the 'progressive loss of managerial control over the relationship between pay and productivity'. The introduction by managers of control techniques based on PBR may mean that workers develop routines of resistance that attempt to regain control of earnings and output.

Some of the symptoms of erosion are described below:

- One of the main problems of output incentive schemes, particularly piecework schemes, is workers' tendency to manipulate working procedures and falsify records of output. In order to ensure an unfluctuating level of income, employees may bank and cross-book work (that is, conceal work, restrict output, or exaggerate 'downtime' so as to stabilise the variations caused by 'loose' and 'tight' standards. As a consequence management will have inaccurate control information for the purpose of human resource planning, assessing individual and group performance, scheduling decisions, and general details on the cost of labour.
- Performance standards become 'slack' as employees receive pay for performance that is lower than originally envisaged, hence inflating unit labour costs. For example, workers may use the 'learning curve' to discover new ways of working, or may deliberately overstate the methods/effort required when standards were first drawn up.
- Workers are often directly or indirectly able to assert control over the process of work allocation to install their own notion of equity (for example, in the allocation of 'loose' and 'tight' jobs) rather than directed by management's ideas of efficiency.

- Management may deliberately relax standards and make it easier for workers to obtain bonuses when, for example, there is a shortage of labour. Alternatively, management may be forced to renegotiate wage rates continually in order to ensure that workers accept changes to the organisation of work.
- Workers may be reluctant to accept management's request for changes in working practices if their present job or task provides a high income and the change threatens their perceived ability to achieve high bonuses and receipt of other benefits.

Collective bonus schemes

Across-the-board collective bonuses can be differentiated between schemes based on the output, sales or productivity of a group, section and department, and those schemes based on the output, sales or productivity of the entire organisation.

Group, section or department bonus schemes

Incentive schemes based on the discrete performance of a particular work group attempt to encourage flexibility and cooperation among members of the group, and to some extent provide opportunities for the employees to decide for themselves how to achieve the required results.

Armstrong (1996b) defines team-based rewards as:

> payments or non-financial incentives provided to members of a formally established team and linked to the performance of that group. The rewards are shared among the members according to a formula, or on an ad-hoc basis for exceptional achievements. Rewards for individuals may also be influenced by assessments of their contribution to the team. (p. 22)

Such schemes, however, seem to be most effective when the work groups/teams are:

- stable, mature and naturally forming;
- clearly identifiable as a performing unit, and with performance that can be directly measured;
- have a significant degree of autonomy;
- composed of people whose work is interdependent;
- made up of individuals who are flexible, multi-skilled and good team players.

See, for example, Daniel and McIntosh (1972: 163), and Armstrong (1996b: 23).

The introduction of team-based payment schemes may lead to several problems. For example, pressures to conform and the requirement for consideration of others may lead to the reduction of effort to the lowest common denominator and the demotivation of high performers (see the classic study by Roethlisberger and Dickson, 1939). Employees may also resist the transfer out of high-performing teams because of the potential loss of individual earnings. Moreover, the move to a team-based reward strategy calls for a radical shift in the ways of working from an individualistic culture and a political environment, and an acceptance by individuals that their pay will not be wholly related to their own efforts.

Collective bonuses based on company output, sales or productivity

The central objective behind the introduction of plant- or company-wide schemes is to encourage involvement and interest in the operation and performance of the organisation as a whole rather than offering a direct financial inducement (Daniel and McIntosh, 1972: 164). The intention is to 'foster cooperation between all parts of the organisation so that corporate objectives may be better achieved . . . [and] . . . [t]heir motivational appeal is to the socially integrative rather than the self-assertive tendencies in human behaviour' (Wilson *et al.*, 1982: 321).

Collective bonuses based on generated profits

Profit-sharing schemes

> Profit-related pay is defined as a part of an employee's pay formally linked to the profits of the business in which the employee works.
>
> (IDS, 1992: 6)

Employees are usually rewarded at the end of the financial year with a cash bonus, which is normally on top of their basic pay. However, as Duncan (1988: 186) suggests, the term 'profit-related pay' can indicate that 'the profit-linked element of pay should replace some portion of previously fixed earnings so that "normal" pay will vary with profitability'. The interest in profit-sharing schemes was stimulated by the advent of enterprise culture and the encouragement of wider share ownership by the Conservative government during the 1980s, and was facilitated by several statutory enactments. However, the popularity of profit-sharing schemes has plateaued as the tax concessions for employees in registered schemes have been gradually removed.

The 1990 WIRS survey discovered that there had been substantial growth in profit sharing between 1984 and 1990, when the proportion of establishments in the industrial and commercial sector with such schemes rose from 18% to 43%. The 1998 Workplace Employee Relations Survey found that 47% of private sector workplaces had profit-related pay schemes (Cully *et al.*, 1999).

Non-cash-based profit-sharing schemes

At the end of the 1970s the incumbent Labour government introduced a piece of legislation to encourage the distribution of company profits to all employees in the form of shares. The trend towards wider share ownership was further encouraged by the incoming Conservative government through a series of legislatory enactments and highly publicised flotations of shares in companies such as British Telecom, British Airways and British Gas.

There are three main types of non-cash profit-sharing schemes (Anon, 1998a):

- *approved profit-sharing* – bonuses are paid in the form of shares;
- *savings-related share options* – employees are able to use tax-free savings to buy company shares at a discount;
- *company share option plans* – formerly called executive share option schemes, now used to allow the majority of staff to buy shares at current prices.

The 1990 WIRS survey found that from 1984 to 1990 the percentage of trading sector establishments with such schemes increased from 23% to 32%. The 1998 Workplace Employee Relations Survey found that 25% of private sector workplaces had employer share ownership schemes, and 6% had deferred profit-sharing schemes (profits are placed in a trust fund, and this is then used to acquire shares in the company for employees) (Cully *et al.*, 1999). Both profit sharing and employee share ownership schemes were more common in larger workplaces and in the privatised utilities and financial services industry sectors. It was also noted that within schemes where both managerial and non-managerial employees were eligible to participate in share ownership schemes, there was a significant gap between eligibility and purchase for the non-managerial employees.

Possible objectives for profit sharing and employee share ownership schemes include:

- to increase awareness and interest in the performance of the organisation, and possibly create an impression of ownership of the business. A sense of cooperation between management and the workforce is believed to emanate, thereby eliminating the conflictual distinction between 'them and us'. It is hoped that employees will identify more closely with the company and the pursuit of profit, thereby acting as an incentive for greater productivity and concern for cost control. Furthermore, it is also anticipated that employees will be more willing to accept changes in working practices and policies which will in turn improve the company's profitability;
- to encourage long-term commitment and loyalty to the company;
- to ensure that employees benefit from company profitability and share in the wealth they helped to create;
- to ensure that labour costs are responsive to the performance, and hence profits, of the company;
- to attract and retain employees;
- to reduce the role of, and therefore the need for, the trade unions;
- to allow employees and employers to take advantage of tax breaks;
- to use equity to reward good performance.

Although there is general support from both employees and managers for the concept of profit sharing, there is little comprehensive evidence that such schemes have any significant impact on the performance, motivation or attitudes of employees. (For example, see Ramsay and Haworth, 1984: 320; Bell and Hanson, 1985: 6–8; Ramsay *et al.*, 1986: 25–26; Poole, 1987, 1988; Duncan, 1988: 189; IDS, 1992: 7.)

Poole and Jenkins (1988) succinctly sum up the difficulties in determining employees' attitudes towards profit sharing:

> interpretation of widespread approval of cash based awards should be tempered with the thought that some employees felt they were being asked if they preferred a free gift . . . as against nothing.
>
> (p. 32)

Problems associated with collective incentive schemes include the following:

- Most schemes do not reward the differential contribution of individuals in terms of effort.
- The motivational impact is limited, as there is a fragile and vague relationship between individual effort and company profit through either remoteness or the intrusion of external factors that are beyond the control of either party.
- A seemingly minimal and infrequent financial reward, and the long timespan between individual effort and receipt of bonus, also serve to erode any motivational force.
- Schemes may be introduced without a supportive participatory and consultative culture, management style or structures.
- These are problems with calculating and allocating profit accurately and fairly.
- The widening rather than the closing of the gap between 'them and us'. This is due to factors such as the distribution of bonuses on a pro rata basis, which results in higher income groups receiving a bigger bonus and the exclusion of part-timers and new recruits.

Reinvention of PBR schemes

With the move towards human resource management, traditional PBR schemes have tended to be subsumed under the general term of *performance-related pay* or indeed incentive pay. However, the experiences of managers and subordinates as discussed above help greatly in the analysis of the issues associated with contemporary payment schemes. The rationales, implications and experiences evinced within the literature on performance-related pay resonate strongly with the existing body of research on PBR.

Nevertheless there does appear to be a resurgence of the use of payment by results schemes through the payment of bonuses that are tied closely to tangible results (IDS, 1999b: 14). Within periods of low inflation, costs are controlled and more of a motivational impact is made by PBR schemes than by the automatic inflation-linked pay rise (IDS, 1999b: 14). For example, Easyjet is reported to have recently changed the pay scheme for call centre staff:

> They receive the fixed sum of 80p for each seat they sell. They have no 'fall back' rate (although in fact the minimum wage would provide one) and work at their own pace. Originally Easyjet paid its sales people a fixed salary plus a small commission, but the company found itself having to pay supervisors to chivvy staff to do the work. The switch to piecework has eliminated this completely. Staff largely supervise themselves, and the motivating effect of the payment system is clear: walk round the call centre at Luton Airport and you can see staff totting up their sales on pads and notebooks next to their computer terminals. (p.14)

PERFORMANCE-RELATED PAY

The interest in remuneration schemes that attempt to link the assessment of individual performance to pay shows no sign of abating. Performance-related pay (PRP) can be defined as: 'a system in which an individual's increase in salary is solely or mainly dependent on his/her appraisal or merit rating' (Swabe, 1989: 17). This rating may take into consideration generalised indicators of performance such as customer service, quality, flexibility and teamworking, as well as output measures.

Possible reasons for introducing PRP

To increase the motivation of employees

It is often argued that incremental salary scales are too static and inflexible to financially reward and recognise differential levels of performance. Furthermore, within flat or network-based organisational structures there will be fewer opportunities to reward performance with promotion to higher grades. The expectancy theory of motivation argues that there is little direct incentive for employees to increase their effort when there is no direct link between effort and a valued outcome. Thus PRP schemes posit that financial reward is a valued outcome, and that by directly and explicitly linking that financial reward with performance, employees will increase their efforts. Employees must expect that higher levels of performance will lead to higher levels of financial reward.

Murlis (1996) makes an important distinction between the use of PRP to manage performance directly through the motivational incentive of financial rewards, and the use of PRP to recognise different levels of performance. Hence an objective of a PRP scheme could be to differentiate clearly and visibly between high-achieving employees and those who are 'doing no more than they need to' (IDS, 1998). PRP may also help to maintain the motivation of employees who have limited opportunities for promotion or salary growth (IDS, 1998).

To encourage certain behaviours

For example, in a survey by Poole and Jenkins (1998), organisations had linked rewards to performance in order to encourage, recognise and reward employees for customer service and quality, innovation and creativity, productivity, and the individual's development of skills and knowledge.

To help in recruitment and retention

For example, one of the reasons that local authorities have for introducing PRP is to try to improve the attractiveness of salaries in order to improve recruitment and retention (Heery, 1992: 9). Furthermore, as Kessler and Purcell (1992) observed in their study: 'In terms of retention, PRP was viewed as sending the "right messages" in rewarding highly those the organisation wanted to keep and lowly those it was happy to lose' (p. 20).

To facilitate change in organisational culture

The introduction of PRP can be seen as a key lever in creating a 'performance orientated' culture in the organisation by emphasising 'flexibility, dynamism, entrepreneurial spirit and careful allocation of resources' (Kessler and Purcell, 1992: 21). This has been particularly evident in the introduction of PRP in the public sector or privatised public companies (Fowler, 1988).

PRP may also have a symbolic impact, rather than acting directly on employees' incentive motivation. For example, PRP schemes clarify and reinforce certain expectations of employee performance, attitudes and values, and make it clear that 'old securities' are obsolete and that continued employment is 'contingent upon individual contribution' (Harris, 1997).

To encourage the internalisation of performance norms

PRP can encourage the internalisation of the organisation's goals or norms of behaviour among the employees of the organisation (Geary, 1992: 42) by endorsing congruous work efforts by way of PRP increases, and by punishing incongruous performance through the withholding of pay increases. Thus, as Townley (1989) indicates, management are able to install a system of control over those aspects in the workplace that are not covered by rules and close supervision. Thereby through a pattern of 'implicit expectations' and 'shared norms of understanding' managers can control workers' increased flexibility and discretion within managerial parameters.

To weaken trade union power

In assessing the impact of PRP on trade unions, one personnel director has been quoted:

> There is going to be a lot more focus on the individual; the individual's worth and the talents he or she has and the contribution they make to the business; involving them in that part of the business they work in and that really involves being far more open; involving people far more in what they do; moving people down the track to change the way in which we reward people. All this begins with cutting the power of Trade Unions in the traditional collective bargaining sense off at the knees.
> (Kessler and Purcell, 1992: 22)

Heery (1992) has summarised the main possible negative consequences for trade unions:

- the instrumental value of union membership may decline because pay is determined through individual performance, rather than collective bargaining;
- collective interests may be fragmented and rivalry generated among employees, thus eroding the basis for the collective discipline;
- schemes may be perceived as indicating reduced management support for collective negotiation and so may indirectly discourage union membership;
- where schemes satisfy employee aspirations for recognition and reward, they may lead to the removal of grievances and a consequential collapse in support for unions. (p. 4)

Furthermore, if part of employees' pay is determined at management's discretion then the scope of collective bargaining may contract (Guest, 1989: 44; Heery, 1992: 3) and fundamentally change the role of trade unions from bargaining to personal support such as during appeals (Hegewisch, 1991a: 34) and legal advice (e.g. Pickard, 1990: 43). Nevertheless, there is little evidence of a direct attempt by managers to dismantle collective bargaining mechanisms (e.g. Batstone, 1984; Millward and Stevens, 1986; Edwards, 1987; Storey, 1987, 1992; Marginson et al., 1988; Millward et al., 1992; Thompson, 1992).

Increased role of the line manager

PRP and appraisal schemes demand more from line managers in terms of providing feedback to and evaluating their subordinates. They are forced into taking 'quality time' to discuss their subordinates' performance, progress and development. Additionally, line managers have to clarify the role and outline the expectations of not only their subordinates but themselves (Kinnie and Lowe, 1990: 46; see also Storey, 1992).

As indicated previously, by linking reward to performance management control is increased. The subjectivity and discretion as to which people or behaviours are rewarded will give line managers more authority or power to enforce managerial prerogative. Line managers are then likely to be asked to justify their decisions and the performance of their subordinates in their own appraisal.

Greater financial control and 'value for money'

Greater financial control is thought to result from the proposition that those employees who are performing to or above standard should receive pay increases, rather than rewarding those employees who are not contributing to the performance of the organisation through an across-the-board pay increase. Hence pay awards to employees are self-funding through increases in performance and consequently higher profits.

A moral justification

It is possible to argue that PRP schemes are inherently more 'moral' than other pay schemes. The basis of this argument is that it is 'fairer' for organisations to reward people on the basis of effort, performance or contribution to the organisation rather than as a result of egalitarian values, status or salary structures and processes that are independent of management judgement or not unilaterally determined by management. For example, Armstrong and Murlis (1994) state 'it is right and proper for people to be rewarded in accordance with their contribution', but do not provide clear reasons why this should be the case. Interestingly there is also some evidence to suggest that managers significantly overestimate the extent to which their employees perceive PRP schemes as being fair (IPD, 1998).

Encouragement of flexibility

By linking rewards to particular types of performance, companies can encourage a wider range of working practices and skill deployment. Furthermore, the general competence of 'flexibility' and the acquisition of skills can be directly rewarded and therefore encouraged. For example, a production manager in Geary's study outlined the effect of having flexibility as an assessment criterion:

> People are very much aware that it is going to cost them if they aren't flexible . . . people can see written down for the first time, if you don't do A and B, come your next review it will cost you in money terms. It's both a penaliser and a motivator.   (Geary, 1992: 42)

Possible problems with PRP

Expectancy theory of motivation

As discussed earlier in the section on payment by results schemes, the notion of there being a clear and direct relationship between effort and reward is rather simplistic. Indeed, the expectancy theory of motivation proposes that motivation is influenced by two other factors besides simply linking outcomes (rewards) to performance (P-O): the relationship between effort and performance (E-P) and the perceived value of the outcome.

Hence the relationship between effort and performance (E-P) and therefore motivation is influenced by many factors such as:

- social and political pressures;
- individual and group goals;
- perceptions of the most expedient and appropriate ways of carrying out the task and performing at the required level;
- the skills and knowledge required to carry out the task and perform at the required level;
- the opportunity to carry out the task and perform at the required level;
- the confidence in one's ability to carry out the task and perform at the required level.

It may also be the case that financial reward is simply not valued by the employee, or more realistically there are other outcomes that are more greatly valued. Factors that may influence whether financial rewards are seen and experienced as a valued outcome include self-set goals, needs and personal values. For example, Richardson (1999) makes the point that many employees may accept the principle that paying better performers more is fairer, yet deny the incentive effect of PRP. Employees may believe that the amount of work they do and how they do it are determined by other factors, such as professional or personal standards.

Displacement of objectives

The assessment of performance for pay award purposes relies on the use of proxy measures of the quality of that performance, and employees will behave in ways that maximise their score on those proxy measures in order to maximise their rewards. However, the proxy measures may not closely or fully reflect 'actual' quality of performance, and the proxy measures may become ends in themselves. Indeed, being 'seen' to be a high performer may not reflect higher actual levels of performance (Randle, 1997). Employees may focus on achieving certain stipulated objectives (for which they will be assessed and hence rewarded on) and overlook or ignore other less tangible aspects of their job. Furthermore, employees may be reluctant to engage in innovation or act on their own discretion in case their efforts are not acknowledged or their progression towards their set objectives for assessment purposes is adversely affected.

In effect employees may determine that the basis of their psychological contract has changed from relational to transactional, and therefore act in relation to a transactional type of contract. There is also some evidence that performance-based pay schemes can discourage behaviour that is not directly financially rewarded and 'extra' to their formal role but crucial to the smooth functioning of the organisation (Morrison, 1996; George and Jones, 1997). This behaviour has been termed *organisational citizenship* (Bateman and Organ, 1983), and Organ (1988) sees it as being composed of altruism, conscientiousness, courtesy, sportsmanship and civic virtue.

Steven Kerr (1975) highlights how reward schemes in organisations that are designed to affect one type of behaviour can in actuality encourage another undesirable type of behaviour. Some examples of this type of behaviour include the following:

- Staff suggestions, on improving work procedures may be encouraged by the organisation, yet the implementation of those suggestions may be 'rewarded' with the displacement of jobs and extra workload.
- Employee openness may be desired, but when someone states an opinion that is different from that of management, he or she may be labelled as having an attitude problem or as a 'troublemaker'.
- An organisation's desire to encourage teamwork and cooperation may be discounted by a payment system and management style that 'rewards' individual success and promotes 'friendly competition'.
- An organisation 'hopes' that all employees will consider long-term costs and opportunities, but the reward system is likely to be geared towards short-term results, which are often achieved at the expense of long-term growth and profits.

Kerr (1975) believes that reward schemes often ignore the simple 'law of effect', and suggests four possible reasons for this:

- *Fascination with 'objective' criteria.* The scoring of performance on certain concrete and measurable outputs such as productivity and then linked rewards to that score.
- *Over-emphasis in highly visible behaviours.* Some aspects of performance are simply more obvious and easier to identify.
- *Hypocrisy.* In some cases management may actually be getting the behaviour that they desire despite their public claims. For example, management may publicly state that certain behaviours are valued by the organisation or individual manager, whereas the reward strategy encourages other behaviours. Through a deliberate strategy, management may therefore 'secretly' obtain the behaviours that they desire.
- *Emphasis on morality or equity rather than efficiency.* Sometimes the consideration of other factors means that the desired behaviours are not rewarded. For example, we may feel that it is fairer to reward someone on the basis of some measure of performance through the introduction of a PRP scheme, yet the resultant behaviours may not be the ones that we desire.

Undermining *esprit de corps*

By rewarding some employees and not others, and through the individualisation of the wage–effort bargain, the *esprit de corps* and cohesion of the work group, section, department or company may be undermined, and dysfunctional conflict and excessive competition be encouraged. An employee's performance does not happen in isolation from the behaviours of others, and almost always depends on the cooperation of others within the organisation. This individualisation of effort and pursuance of individual advantage may ultimately hinder the cooperation needed to achieve corporate, rather than individual, goals.

To attempt to mollify the adverse effects of individualism, some schemes incorporate factors such as 'contribution to teamworking' or 'contribution to corporate objectives'. But these factors are also proxies for something else that may not reflect the 'actual' communal behaviours.

Reinforcement of status, control and power differences

When pay is contingent on performance indicators as measured and determined by management, status and power differences are made visible and reinforced. The message is clear: the control of the work processes and determination of rewards lie in the hands of management, but the ultimate responsibility for achieving performance levels and securing rewards rests with employees.

Problems with the assessment of individual performance

There are many difficulties associated with the assessment of performance, including subject and problems of reducing the complexity of a multi-factor appraisal into a single overall rating for pay awards (Fowler, 1988: 33). See section on Performance Management.

Financial constraints

Financial constraints may mean that the PRP element of a pay increase will be small or '[t]he expectations raised by positive feedback from a performance review may simply not be translated into a significant pay increase' (Kessler and Purcell, 1992: 28). Any incentive to increase effort will be extinguished, and employees may in fact feel 'insulted by the low level of extra pay they receive' (Fletcher and Williams, 1992: 47). Furthermore, companies worried about escalating costs may enforce quotas or forced distributions to limit the number of employees who can be awarded payments (Fowler, 1988: 34). The 1998 IPD performance pay survey found that almost three-quarters of respondents felt that their performance awards were to some extent 'too small to act as a motivator' (Anon, 1998b: 5).

'Crowding out' intrinsic motivation

Frey (1997) argues that intrinsic motivation may be 'crowded out' by financial rewards, and this may 'spill over' to other tasks. For example:

> For a considerable number of years patients in old age homes and psychiatric asylums were believed to be motivated to at least partially care for themselves if they were given tokens which they could redeem for various goods at the asylum store. It has, however, turned out that such 'token economy' programmes had limited success and that the high hopes did not materialize . . . The offer of tokens for making the bed, or keeping the room clean, promoted a general attitude that the patients were not responsible for anything per se. Only if they received a payment in the form of tokens were they prepared to do any work at all. For the rest of the wide-ranging activities in such asylums, the patients actively transferred the task and responsibility to the staff. As tokens can only be given for a limited number of well-defined tasks (not least because of the transaction costs involved), the increased involvement and participation of the patients proved to be largely futile, so that in most asylums, the token economy systems have either been discontinued or never introduced.
>
> (Frey, 1997: 16)

Rhetoric or reality?

Evidence of the effects of PRP on employees' motivation, attitudes, performance and productivity is limited and inconsistent: see Thompson (1992: 19) for a summary of studies. Indeed, very few companies have formal monitoring and evaluation procedures for their own schemes (see Thompson, 1992; IPD, 1998).

The study of the Inland Revenue by Marsden and Richardson (1991) provides some concrete evidence of some of the possible implications of PRP. Although most respondents supported the principle of PRP, the introduction of the scheme had very little impact in practice upon motivation and performance levels, and in some cases had led to demotivation (Marsden and Richardson, 1991). This conclusion has been supported by Heery (1992: 10), who found that while personnel managers were very enthusiastic about PRP, 'The survey of individual employee attitudes . . . provided less support for the effectiveness of PRP . . . suggesting the incentive effects of schemes are typically modest.' (See also Kinnie and Lowe, 1990; Fletcher and Williams, 1992.) The IPD 1998 performance pay survey found that only 4% of respondents thought that their schemes had a major impact on poor performers. This may lead us to the conclusion that PRP reflects natural differences in performance, and rewards high performers, but does not lead to an overall increase in levels of performance.

There is some evidence for the decline in popularity of PRP schemes. In a review of pay surveys it was found that: 'The trend towards all-merit reviews seems to have altered, and may even have gone into reverse' (IDS, 1999b: 12).

Competence-based pay

Competence-based pay reflects an intention by the organisation to reward the use or development of job-related competences. Competences can be 'behavioural characteristics that are necessary for the satisfactory performance of each job' or items that 'each employee acquires – whether these are of immediate use in the current job or not' (Fowler, 1996: 43). The latter would suggest the introduction of payment for potential.

Possible reasons for introducing competence-based pay schemes include the following:

- Competences are already in place for development purposes (Sparrow, 1996).
- There is a move away from job-based pay to person-based pay (Sparrow, 1996).
- There is a need to stimulate and reward horizontal career moves.
- There is a need to develop and encourage flexibility and empowerment.
- Such schemes are less judgemental and more flexible than traditional PRP.
- There is a need to acknowledge and reward more intangible aspects of working, such as initiative, teamwork, and customer-orientation.
- There is a need to acknowledge and reward the way in which objectives have been reached, not just the achievement of the objective.
- There is a need to ensure that organisations have the right competences and people with those competences for the future.
- They communicate the message that 'change is happening, and you are expected to change with it, but we will help and reward you'.

It is important for organisations to correctly identify what competences are needed to meet the business strategy, and exactly how those competences lead to improved individual and business performance. Indeed, focusing on task-related skills and knowledge rather than personality-based abstract and generic competences may be more appropriate for pay awards (Lawler, 1996). Care must be taken to ensure that the competences identified and rewarded are relevant to the content and scope of employees' roles, as there is a clear danger that organisations will significantly increase their overall salary bill without any improvements in organisational performance.

THE IMPORTANCE OF FAIRNESS

Judgements of the fairness of pay schemes are based around two key criteria:

- evaluations of distributive justice;
- evaluations of procedural justice.

Distributive justice

Individual judgements of the fairness of outcomes in relation to what employees believe they should have received and what others have received will partly determine their reaction to a pay scheme. Equity theory of motivation (Adams, 1963) focuses on the importance of distributive or outcome-based justice. Adams argues that individuals have a need to be treated fairly and make comparisons between two variables: inputs and outcomes. *Inputs* are what an individual brings to the employment relationship, such as effort, experience, skills, training and seniority. *Outcomes* are those factors that an individual receives in return, such as pay, recognition, fringe benefits, status symbols and promotion.

Equity theory argues that employees will subconsciously formulate a ratio between their inputs and outcomes and compare it with the perceived ratios of inputs and outcomes of other people in the same or a similar situation. For example, Blau (1994: 1253) refers to five possible pay referent categories:

- social (e.g. family, friends, relatives);
- financial (i.e. the extent to which one's current income meets one's current financial needs);
- historical (i.e. one's current income in comparison to income received in the past);
- organisation (i.e. pay comparisons within the company);
- market (i.e. pay comparisons outside the organisation).

Equity theory proposes that if the two ratios are not equal then the individual will take action to attempt to restore a sense of equity and maintain motivation. Adams (1963) suggests that individuals may:

- change inputs (they can reduce effort) if underpaid; or
- try to change their outcomes (ask for a pay rise or promotion); or
- psychologically distort their own ratios or those of others by rationalising differences in inputs and outcomes; or
- change the reference group to which they compare themselves in order to restore equity.

Deckop (1992) makes the useful distinction between organisational pay satisfaction/dissatisfaction and career pay satisfaction/dissatisfaction with regard to employees' behavioural responses. Behaviours that are associated with organisational pay dissatisfaction include reduced effort, complaints, union activity and intra-occupational turnover, whereas career pay dissatisfaction is more likely to result in behaviours such as increased effort, retraining, or actually leaving the occupation (Blau, 1994: 1252).

In summary we can say that reward satisfaction and motivation are influenced by perceived differentials rather than by absolutes, and this perception of equity is determined by the cognitive selection of comparison points and reference groups.

Procedural justice

Individual judgements of the fairness of the process of allocating rewards are the second key determinant of an employee's reaction to a pay scheme.

Research suggests that understanding of how pay is determined affects an employee's satisfaction with both the processes and the outcomes of the pay scheme (Dulebohn and Martocchio, 1998; Lee *et al.*, 1999).

Bringing together the work of Leventhal (1976), Lind and Tyler (1988), and Folger *et al.* (1992), we can propose that procedural justice within pay schemes is enhanced by the following factors:

- Decisions should be based on complete, accurate and timely information.
- Decisions should be transparent to all concerned.
- Procedures should be consistent across time and people.
- Procedures should be neutral – free from bias, the pursuit of self-interest and dishonesty.
- Parties to the decision should treat each other with politeness, dignity and respect.
- Decisions should be compatible with prevailing moral and ethical standards.
- Procedures must reflect the concerns, values and interests of all parties.
- The relationship should be based on trust – beliefs of intention to treat people in a reasonable and benevolent manner.

In summary we can state that judgements of procedural justice and distributive justice can affect motivation and satisfaction, organisational commitment and judgements of the effectiveness of the pay scheme (Lind and Tyler, 1988; McFarlin and Sweeney, 1992; Dulebohn and Martocchio, 1998).

In crude terms, most reward schemes make some people happy and others unhappy. Unless organisations give all their staff every possible discretionary bonus or promotion, people will be unhappy (Rogers, 1995), but doing this defeats the objective of such schemes and would prove impossibly expensive. Thus organisations must ensure that although employees may be dissatisfied with the outcomes of a pay scheme, they perceive the procedures leading up to the allocation as 'fair'.

Importance of equity for employers

Equity and fairness issues are also key to understanding the wage–effort bargain. Many writers have argued that labour for employers is a cost of production, and employers will therefore attempt either to maximise the contribution of an employee relative to a level of wage or, achieving the same ends of reducing unit labour costs to minimise wage costs with respect to a level of effort (e.g. Hyman and Brough, 1975: 14). However, human resource management portrays labour as a resource to be invested in and developed. The basic proposition remains the same, however: management are simply concerned with maximising the contribution of workers relative to the rewards given. Thus equity for employers can be seen in terms of receiving maximum desired input from employees (e.g. in terms of productivity, performance, skill, and flexibility) in relation to the rewards offered. Human resource management, however, does not consider that there may be differences in perceptions of equity between employees and employers, and therefore assumes no possible conflict in expectations and objectives.

Performance-related pay and performance – Conclusion

As mentioned previously, there is little research evidence to indicate that PRP schemes have a significant positive impact on employee performance and motivation, and in some cases the impact has been negative. Moreover the direct and indirect costs of running such schemes may outweigh any possible gains, and make the vast majority of the workforce unhappy (Pfeffer, 1998). Some observers blame the tool. For example, Duncan Brown of the management consultants Towers Perrin on the problems of PRP:

> They don't stem from fundamental philosophical weaknesses, or conceptual motivation issues, but typically relate to unclear objectives, bad design, and very poor implementation. Most of all, I think, merit pay systems are badly managed.
>
> (Anon, 1998b: 7)

However, it may be a false diagnosis that these problems are a result of faulty implementation or design of the PRP scheme or appraisal schemes. PRP schemes may have an inherent inability to improve the levels of motivation and hence the performance of the whole workforce, and may lead to distrust and a lack of commitment. For example, do PRP schemes simply reflect indigenous individual performance differences, rewarding the certain few highly rather than continuously improving the performance of all employees? (See, for example, Fowler, 1988: 34; Kinnie and Lowe, 1990; Marsden and Richardson, 1994; Institute of Personnel Management, 1992; Scott, 1994; Stewart and Walsh, 1994; Clark, 1995.)

EMPLOYEE BENEFITS AND RECOGNITION SCHEMES

This section considers the remaining aspects of the reward package, such as 'employee benefits' and forms of recognition that do not depend directly on money or promotion.

In terms of motivation and perceptions of fairness, a crucial distinction can be made between benefits that operate as 'incentives' and are linked to assessments of performance or achievement of targets, and those benefits that are salary based and are seen as 'entitlements'. We can also observe a change in the concept of benefits – away from a narrow 'welfare' commitment (IDS, 1999a) towards a key lever in a strategic reward strategy.

Types of benefit

There are numerous different types of employee benefit that can be offered, and successful schemes tend to be those that meet the specific needs of the workforce and are imaginative. With some benefits, however, there tends to be a 'sting in the tail' in that they tend to be taxable and may attract VAT and National Insurance contributions (Curry and Prickett, 1996). The situation is further complicated by different rules and regulations across countries. Possible employee benefits include:

- Company cars – Britain seems to be unique in the provision of cars as a managerial status symbol (Hegewisch, 1991b: 5), where even the specific make, specifications, colour and opportunity to 'upgrade' to a superior car are crucial factors in motivation (Brown, 1996: 62; Vavasour and Vignali, 1999). However, the company car has been heavily taxed by the British government as a 'perk of the job', and therefore to avoid the car being a 'taxable benefit' some schemes pay a cash sum or annual subsidy instead (IDS, 1999a; Vavasour and Vignali, 1999).
- Flexible hours and working patterns.

- Teleworking.
- Subsidised meals, canteen facilities and free drinks.
- Travel passes and car breakdown cover.
- Extra holiday entitlements.
- Foreign travel, conferences and 'lifestyle experiences'.
- Telephone and IT costs.
- Casual dress.
- Discounted, or the provision of, insurance.
- Private health care, dental treatment and eye tests.
- Shopping, travel and entertainment vouchers.
- Financial planning and legal advice.
- Crèches.
- Payment of graduates' debts.
- Office accommodation and facilities.
- Career breaks and sabbaticals.
- Sports/social facilities which can encourage identification with the company.
- Discount and company purchase plans, where employees can purchase goods at a favourable price.
- Assistance with housing, i.e. company-owned houses, house-moving expenses and assistance with house purchase.
- Help with educational courses.
- Pension schemes.

The different types of pension schemes include (Braithwaite and Hoey, 1999; Hopegood, 1999):

- *Final salary pensions.* These are based on length of time in the scheme and how much the employee earns. The employee is guaranteed a minimum level of pension, and contributes a fixed part of the cost, with the employer picking up the balance. Employees can only contribute up to 15% of earnings but are guaranteed a certain level of benefit, and the scheme contains extras such as widow's pensions and life insurance. They are not particularly attractive to mobile employees, but are valuable for employees who stay with one company for many years. The employer must meet the costs if there is not enough money in the scheme, and has an open-ended and expensive liability and must be able to demonstrate a solvency margin at all times. Employers therefore take on the investment risk. The scheme is run by trustees, who are sponsored by the employer but legally bound to act in the best interests of the employees.
- *Group money purchase schemes.* These schemes build up a pot of cash over time, which is then used to buy a pension income at retirement. The contributions of both parties are defined, and the employee receives whatever the accumulated fund will buy. The level of pension is dictated by stock market growth, thereby limiting employer liability and putting the investment risk on to the employee. As the scheme pays out only two-thirds of salary, employers can reward employees with a lump sum payment. This type of scheme is run in a similar manner to final salary pensions.
- *Group personal pensions.* This type of scheme is a collection of individual personal pension plans, which are owned by the individuals concerned but administered as a group. The schemes do not burden the employer with any guarantee, and their contribution and involvement are minimal. Employees have a choice of how much to put into their schemes, and if they decide to leave the company they simply take their plan with them.

- *Stakeholder pensions.* Stakeholder pensions are due to be introduced in April 2001, and are to be targeted at people on average earnings who do not have a pension plan. It is proposed that they will be low cost, and employers may also have to set up payroll facilities for employees to pay their contributions through direct debit.
- *Additional voluntary contributions.* These are top-up schemes that normally run aside final salary schemes in order for employees to make extra contributions to move their pensions towards the maximum amount.

Companies are likely to prefer 'group' schemes or private plans (Terry and White, 1998) as they provide more flexibility for the company and the employee, and are less of a fixed financial burden. These types of pension plan are also characteristic of the more strategic approach of HRM, and are less paternalistic (Terry and White, 1998).

Companies need to recognise what they want to achieve from the provision of each benefit and understand the motivational characteristics of each benefit for their *own* employees. For example, fringe benefits such as company cars, parking spaces and large offices will address social status motives, whereas the provision of pensions and private health care attempts to satisfy more security-based motives. From a European perspective the Price Waterhouse Cranfield Survey found that the provision of certain benefits in different countries will reflect 'tradition and cultural preference'. For example, tax constraints and an inclination towards cash-based rewards limits the popularity of fringe benefits in France (Hegewisch, 1991b: 4–5).

Companies must not underestimate the symbolic value of providing a well-thought-through benefits package: it gives the impression of caring, concern and value. However, it is important for companies to systematically and regularly to monitor the costs of providing each benefit and the total costs of the benefits.

Reasons for using employee benefits

- Some benefits do not attract tax and therefore can be advantageous for both employer and employee, particularly the high earner.
- Some benefits can be provided cheaply through economies of scale.
- Some benefits are needed to facilitate the execution of the job duties of the employee, for example company cars for sales representatives, and special equipment or clothing.
- Some companies may be able to offer discounts on their own products or services, for example banks and building societies, retailers, car manufacturers.
- The provision of certain benefits may ensure long-term commitment to the company and 'inhibit turnover by imposing a relatively large economic cost on leavers . . . Thus, management use fringe benefits as a deterrent against quitting by making them the particular vehicle through which seniority benefits are obtained' (Green *et al.*, 1985: 263). Examples could include pension rights and several status-linked benefits such as company cars and opportunities for foreign travel.

Flexible benefits

Flexible benefits schemes are sometimes known as 'cafeteria benefits'. Such schemes 'allow employees, within certain limits, to make their own choices or to construct their own benefits package . . . the employer determines both the budget allocated for indirect compensation and the choices offered, but it is the employee who decides which of the benefits offered he or she wishes to receive' (Tremblay *et al.*, 1998: 668). Furthermore, employers have to determine the relative worth of each benefit in order to allocate the appropriate 'benefit credit'.

Possible reasons for employers introducing flexible benefit schemes include the following:

- to ensure flexibility in the reward package to improve retention and recruitment;
- to help create an 'employer brand';
- to offer employees the rewards they desire and thereby increase their motivation;
- to support empowerment, personal responsibility and the individualisation of the employment relationship;
- to help employees meet lifestyle needs and maintain a healthy work/life balance;
- to raise employees' awareness of the total value of their reward package and the costs of particular benefits;
- to increase transparency of reward mechanisms;
- to maintain 'value for money' and monitoring of cost for both employees and employers;
- to reflect increased diversity in the workplace;
- to create single-status employment.

Companies in the UK have been slow to adopt flexible benefits schemes, but such schemes are becoming increasingly common (Arkin, 1999). Typical concerns with introducing such schemes include problems with explaining the scheme to employees, complex tax implications and the additional administrative burden, especially in the short term while schemes are being 'bedded-down'. However, the use of interactive HR software, company intranets and outsourcing may allow flexibility and simple explanations without the administrative burden placed on employees or employers (Mullen, 1998). Creating excitement, engaging publicity and momentum and involving the whole family in the selection of benefits may also help to make a flexible benefits scheme a success (McLuhan, 1999). Such schemes are perhaps best suited to those employees who have generous benefits allowances (IDS, 1999a).

Employee recognition schemes

The importance of recognition is well documented. Companies are becoming aware of the importance of formally and visibly recognising the efforts of their employees. Recognition schemes tend to be based on public acknowledgement of out-of-the-ordinary effort or customer service. Types of award vary, but include medals, dinners, award ceremonies, articles in company newspapers, photographs advertising achievement, holidays, jewellery, gift vouchers, business accessories, clothing and cash prizes. Companies must periodically review their schemes to ensure that they remain relevant and that interest is maintained.

One American vice-president whose company uses such schemes states:

Recognition must speak to the employee receiving it, and awards are only one aspect of this. The symbolism, meaning and intrinsic value attached to the reward are equally important.

(Cited in Rawlinson, 1988: 141)

It must be noted that recognition does not have to come from awards with monetary value. Recognition schemes should remind managers that recognition of employee efforts should be a part of their day-to-day activities, and may involve simple and spontaneous verbal or written 'thank you's' (IDS, 1999c).

CONTINGENCY THEORY

Some writers have argued that there is no one 'best way' to design a payment system, but that effectiveness depends on a match between the scheme and the particular circumstances of the company. Managers need to take into account structural factors such as sector, size, structure, culture, competitive market, technology, internal and external labour market, and whether the company is expanding or contracting (White, 1981; Lupton and Bowey, 1983; Poole and Jenkins, 1998; Armstrong, 2000). Furthermore, reward strategies and schemes can reflect and support the strategic choices made by the organisation, the role of human resource management in the enterprise, and other people management policies and procedures (Poole and Jenkins, 1998; Armstrong, 2000).

It has also been suggested that the effectiveness of the payment system depends more on the *method* of selecting and implementing the system – that is, the extent of employee participation in the process – than on the actual *choice* of payment system (Bowey and Thorpe, 1989; Geary, 1992: 40). The key determinant of the effectiveness of reward schemes may therefore be the match to the expectations of the employees involved in such schemes.

Competence-based pay and contingency theory

Sparrow (1996) argues that competence-based pay schemes may be appropriate when accredited professional qualifications are important, or where there is a clear link between inputs and outputs: that is, the possession of competences directly leads to higher performance. An output-based approach is more appropriate than a competency based approach where (Sparrow, 1996):

- competences are difficult to identify;
- there is no clear link between the possession of competences and higher levels of performance;
- roles offer little scope for the development of competences;
- it is difficult to judge performance against competences;
- there is flexibility in the way of carrying out a role;
- each role has its own set of unique skills.

PRP and contingency theory

PRP schemes are more likely to be effective in the following circumstances:

- The principle and objectives of PRP are accepted and supported by all employees.
- PRP is a component of an integrated performance management process.
- There are clear reasons and objectives for using PRP, which are not contradictory or conflictual.
- Employees accept the set goals and the goal-setting process.
- Employees perceive the assessment of performance to be fair and efficient.
- Differences in individual performance can be clearly identified, and reflect differences in effort.
- Organisational culture is supportive of PRP, with high levels of trust between employees and the organisation.
- Rewards consistently and accurately reflect differences in individual performance.
- All employees have opportunities to be rewarded for their performance.

EXECUTIVE PAY

The issue of executive pay often makes headline news, and is a very contentious issue. There has been discernible public discomfort with regard to the large salaries, bonuses and share options that chief executives receive, often when their companies underperform.

Research has failed to identify a clear and systematic relationship between the compensation of chief executives and company performance (Jensen and Murphy, 1990; Barkema and Gomez-Mejia, 1998). Barkema and Gomez-Mejia (1998: 140) provide a useful framework for analysing the determinants of executive pay (Figure 12.7; see Gomez-Mejia, and Wiseman, 1997 for a full discussion).

Stock options should in theory ensure that the chief executive's interests are aligned with those of the shareholders. The chief executive should be motivated to direct the company in such a way that the stock price will rise, and both the shareholder and the chief executive will benefit (Walters *et al.*, 1995). However, in most cases the chief executive risks no loss of money because nothing is paid for the option, and if the value of stock falls the option is not exercised (Walters *et al.*). Moreover, the chief executive will

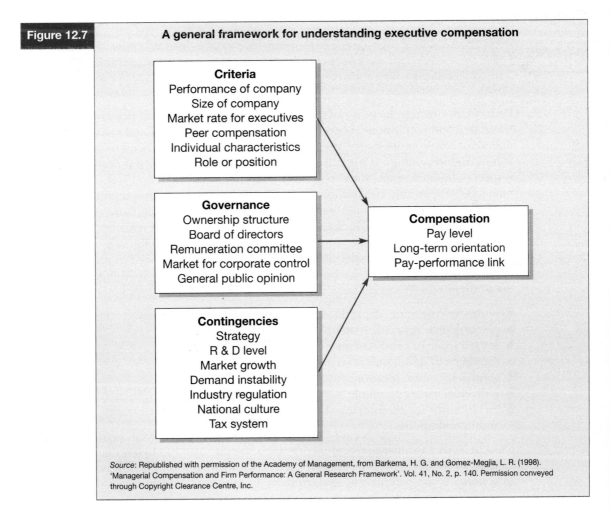

Figure 12.7 A general framework for understanding executive compensation

Criteria
Performance of company
Size of company
Market rate for executives
Peer compensation
Individual characteristics
Role or position

Governance
Ownership structure
Board of directors
Remuneration committee
Market for corporate control
General public opinion

Contingencies
Strategy
R & D level
Market growth
Demand instability
Industry regulation
National culture
Tax system

Compensation
Pay level
Long-term orientation
Pay-performance link

Source: Republished with permission of the Academy of Management, from Barkema, H. G. and Gomez-Mejia, L. R. (1998). 'Managerial Compensation and Firm Performance: A General Research Framework'. Vol. 41, No. 2, p. 140. Permission conveyed through Copyright Clearance Centre, Inc.

be in a 'privileged' position to act in ways that deliberately inflate share prices at the expense of other possible indicators of performance, such as long-term profit, stability and survival, and employee satisfaction and loyalty. Nevertheless, share option schemes can be very effective in attracting talented people to small start-up firms which have high potential profits but limited current financial resources.

Indeed, the issue may be that society, investors and employees want to see executives' awards linked to their real contribution to value creation as compared with competing companies. For example, a rise in share prices is influenced by many factors, and is only one definition of 'performance'. WPP's chief executive Martin Sorrell has come up with a performance-related pay scheme that may offer one solution:

> In essence Sorrell is rewarded with shares for performing better than his competitors in the industry. Sorrell and the other senior executives have to put their own money into the compnay through 'investment shares', and therefore there is the possibility that they will lose money. Sorrell has been quoted as saying: 'This is about making sure WPP is an entrepreneurial business . . . To be that we have to have significant stakes in the company'.
>
> (Lynn, 1999: p.7)

PERFORMANCE MANAGEMENT

> Performance management can be defined as 'a strategic and integrated approach to increasing the effectiveness of organisations by improving the performance of the people who work in them and by developing the capabilities of teams and individual contributors', and also can be seen as a 'continuous process involving reviews that focus on the future rather than the past, . . .'
>
> (Baron and Armstrong, 1998: 38–39).

Performance management is not simply the appraisal of individual performance: it is an integrated and continuous process that develops, communicates and enables the future direction, core competences and values of the organisation, and helps to create an 'horizon of understanding'. It identifies who or what delivers the critical performance with respect to business strategy and objectives (Hendry *et al.*, 1997), and ensures that performance is successfully carried out. Effective performance management ensures that employees and managers understand each others' expectations, and how corporate strategy and objectives impact on their own context – their roles, behaviours, relationships and interactions, rewards and futures. It also ensures that all employees and managers know how to meet those expectations and goals, and are supported in doing so. Hence performance management is a holistic process that ensures that the following are developed and effectively carried out:

- setting of corporate, department, team and individual objectives;
- performance appraisal system;
- reward strategies and schemes;
- training and development strategies and plans;
- feedback, communication and coaching;
- individual career planning;
- mechanisms for monitoring the effectiveness of performance management system and interventions.

Thus performance management incorporates the effective day-to-day management and support of people, and is not simply concerned with appraisal forms, procedures and interviews, or the paternalistic evaluation by a superior of a subordinate's performance.

Employee commitment and performance are secured through a mutually supportive strategy of reward-driven integration, developmental integration and culture management.

Figure 12.8 outlines the steps of systematic and integrated performance management. It is argued that for performance management to be effective these activities should be carried out throughout the year as a normal part of the interaction between employee and manager, and not simply through the annual performance appraisal. All these activities should involve joint problem solving and the acceptance of joint responsibility for action.

Setting direction and planning:
- identifying business strategy and the performance and behaviours critical to the achievement of that strategy;
- developing individual objectives and identifying the required individual behaviours and/or competences to meet these objectives;
- resolving the fit between individual goals and department and organisational goals;
- developing joint action plans to meet individual objectives;
- developing personal development plans to address performance weaknesses, future roles and performance demands, and future career aspirations.

Coaching and support:
- providing continuous feedback to motivate and improve performance (employees are more likely to accept suggestions for improving performance if given in a less concentrated form);
- ensuring the provision of training and development opportunities and resources when needed;
- providing the necessary resources when needed;
- encouraging and supporting employees to monitor themselves and take responsibility for their learning.

Reviewing:
- evaluating actual performance against expected performance;
- identifying the reasons for good and bad performance;

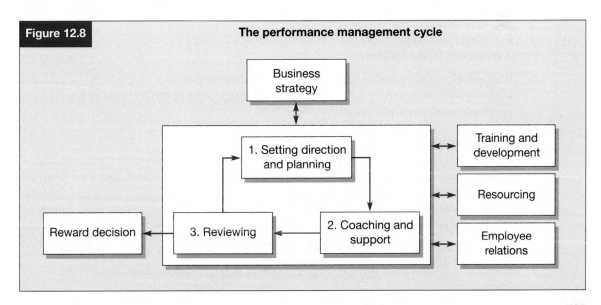

Figure 12.8   **The performance management cycle**

- identifying strengths and weaknesses of employees and managers;
- identifying training, development and support needed to improve performance;
- using periodic formal appraisals in the most effective way to summarise key issues and maintain motivation.

Key principles in the design of performance appraisal schemes

Employees and line mangers may meet performance appraisal schemes with distrust, suspicion and fear, but an integrated and effective process can lead to increased organisational performance and employee motivation. It is important for employees to be genuinely involved in the design of an appraisal scheme, the evaluation of performance, and the objective-setting process. An appraisal scheme should be set up in an atmosphere of openness, with agreement between management, employees and employee representatives of the design of the scheme (Grayson, 1984: 177). Employees need to have a clear understanding of the purpose of the process (evaluative or developmental). The following are key principles in the design of a performance appraisal scheme:

- It creates motivation to change or improve behaviour.
- It provides recognition for successful performance.
- It provides valid and reliable information for pay decisions.
- It provides guidance on what skills, competences and behaviour are required to meet expectations.
- It needs to be simple, clear, and written in accessible language.
- It must be seen as providing business benefits and to be relevant to day-to-day tasks and local needs.
- It must make realistic demands on employees' and managers' time and other resources.
- It must be perceived to be fair.

Types of performance outcomes and criteria

A distinction can be made between *input-* and *output-*based criteria:

- *Input-based criteria* relate to the personal traits, competences and skills that an employee brings to a company or job.
- *Output-based* criteria are concerned with individual performance objectives or goals to be met by the employee.

Performance management can provide the link between 'whats' (objectives, targets and performance standards) and 'hows' (behaviours, competences and processes) of employee performance.

Performance objectives

Figure 12.9 shows how, in a performance management system, departmental-level objectives will be derived from business strategy and objectives, which will then be translated into team and individual objectives.

Objectives (frequently termed *targets* or *goals*) are generally agreed upon jointly by the employee and manager, and used to measure and assess employee performance. Indeed, information from the process of setting goals at each level can prove useful when setting up the objectives of the next level.

Often companies use the acronym SMART to help set effective objectives:

S Specific or Stretching
M Measurable
A Agreed or Achievable
R Realistic
T Time-bounded.

However, there are difficulties in setting objectives for certain types of job and activity (R&D, medicine, teachers and lecturers for example (Townley, 1990/1991; Randle, 1997). Indeed, we must question whether it is possible, or desirable, to reduce the intangible to 'score-cards', and the complexity of organisational life to single dimensions. Moreover, is it possible to set objectives or measures that are sufficiently wide and vague to cover all eventualities and encourage initiative, but sufficiently tight and clearly defined to avoid subjectivity?

Competences

Competences are the knowledge and skills that employees require to perform a job satisfactorily. Examples include commercial/customer awareness, commitment and contribution, teamwork, initiative, productivity, leadership, concern for quality, and developing and empowering others. Performance throughout the year is then judged against these competences during the appraisal process. Alternatively, employees may be assessed and rewarded on their acquisition of new skills and competences required to perform future jobs.

The use of competences within the performance management process can enable change to take place, communicate shared values and perceptions, provide a language for proving feedback, and clarify exactly what is expected. However, a competence approach can become excessively complicated and an administrative burden to design and carry out. For example, the process of design of the competences, the collection of evidence of individual performance, and difficulties of measuring actual performance against competence descriptions may mean that organisational resources are directed away from actually contributing organisational performance. Furthermore, Sparrow (1996) notes the possible negative effects on motivation: 'To some people, a negative assessment of personal skills is more damaging than being told you have not achieved a certain target' (p. 27).

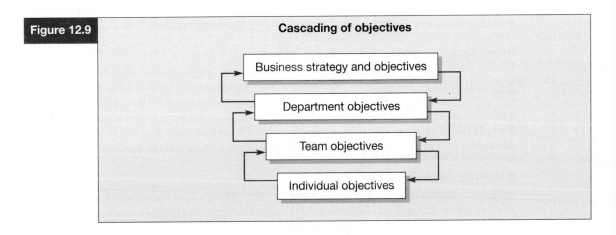

Figure 12.9 Cascading of objectives

Reviewing performance

The review of performance should be a joint process in which both parties review performance, provide feedback to each other, and identify what support is needed to improve performance.

Performance assessment methods

Some methods and techniques of reviewing the performance of employees are listed below.

Comparative methods

- *Paired comparisons.* A manager assesses the performance of pairs of individuals, until each employee has been judged relative to each other employee, or until every possible combination of individuals has been considered. A rating scale is then produced from the number of times for which each individual was rated as better.
- *Ranking.* Individuals are assessed with reference to a single measure of effectiveness or merit and placed in a hierarchy (from best to worst).
- *Forced distribution.* Again, individuals' performances are given single ratings, but this time they are allocated, usually by percentage, to categories or ranked performance levels according to some predetermined distribution.

Absolute methods

Individuals are assessed with reference to some standard(s) of performance, and not to other individuals.

- *Narrative approach.* The appraiser describes in his or her own words the work performance and behaviour of the employee during a given period. The report may be in the style of an essay, or a controlled written report that asks for answers to certain headings or guidelines. Written feedback, although time consuming, can be invaluable for personal development and justification of evaluations.
- *Rating scales.* This method lists a number of factors such as job-related qualities or behaviours, or certain personality traits, and then the individual is rated on the extent to which they possess these factors. The rating scale can either be numerical or alphabetical, or graphically represented on a continuum, from 'very high' to 'very low'.

Critical incident techniques

The appraiser records incidents of the employee's positive and negative behaviour that have occurred during a given review period. Thus this form of appraisal is based upon specific examples, not subjective assessments (e.g. Drummond, 1993).

Behaviourally anchored rating scales (BARS)

Numerical, alphabetical and single adjectival anchors such as 'average' and 'above average' may be difficult to define, and ambiguous for assessors. Thus BARS are designed to replace or, in some cases, add to these scale anchor points, with descriptions of specific examples of actual job behaviours. The first stage is to define specific activities required for successful performance in a job. Specific job behaviours that correspond to high, moderate and low performance are then identified within this dimension.

Results-orientated methods

Objectives and standards are set to assess specific results and outcomes arising from job performance and not job behaviour. The appraisal process then examines the extent to which these objectives have been attained.

Self-assessment

Self-assessment is used mainly to identify training and development requirements. But Margerison (1976) has argued that self-assessment appraisal systems are the only way to give a complete picture of the performance of the employee, and to avoid a 'criticise–defend' scenario. Furthermore, it can be argued that it is the appraisee who 'knows – or can learn – more than anyone else about his [sic] own capabilities, needs, strengths and weaknesses, and goals' (McGregor, 1957: 92).

360-degree appraisals

As the name suggests, 360-degree appraisals require a wide range of people to give feedback on an individual's performance. Combined with the traditional source of information from the direct superior and the individual themselves, 360-degree feedback schemes are designed to give a more complete and comprehensive picture of the individual's performance and contribution. For example, managers might be assessed by their employees on 'softer' people issues such as communication and support, and their peers on issues such as teamwork. Indicators of both internal and external customer satisfaction may be used, and suppliers and subcontractors may also be asked to give feedback on the individual manager's performance and demonstration of competences. It is generally acknowledged that 360-degree appraisals can be a valuable development tool, but they require very careful design and implementation if they are to be used for continuous evaluation, and perhaps reward, of performance.

Responses may be confidential, especially upward appraisals, or alternatively contributors may be identified and therefore held accountable. The selection of people to complete 360-degree appraisals should be made by the appraisee in consultation with the appraiser, and objective criteria such as interdependency and opportunity to observe behaviour should be used to justify the choice of respondents (Antonioni, 1996). As a 360-degree appraisal tends to provide extensive, often conflicting, information, both appraisers and appraisees need to be trained in interpreting the information, setting improvement targets and dealing with feelings associated with receiving unexpected feedback (Antonioni, 1996). Antonioni (1996) provides a useful framework for processing 360-degree appraisal feedback (Figure 12.10). For example, reactions to types 1 and 2 feedback are positive, reactions to type 3 feedback are normally neutral because it is expected, but reactions to type 4 feedback can range from confusion to defensiveness. Reactions to feedback can be influenced by differences in information, perceptions, values, goals, comparison points and standards, and defensive emotional reactions.

360-degree feedback schemes may provoke defensive reactions and some resistance. For example, some managers may feel that their management is under question, and may feel nervous that their weaker areas will be exposed (Goodge and Watts, 2000). Furthermore, subordinates may be reluctant to provide honest feedback on managers because of a fear of adverse consequences if they provide negative feedback, or the possibility that the feedback will be misinterpreted (Fletcher, 1998).

Possible difficulties with the assessment of performance

Subjectivity

The inherent subjectivity of the assessment process may lead to claims of favouritism, bias and arbitrariness. For example, one of the employees studied by Geary (1992) exclaimed:

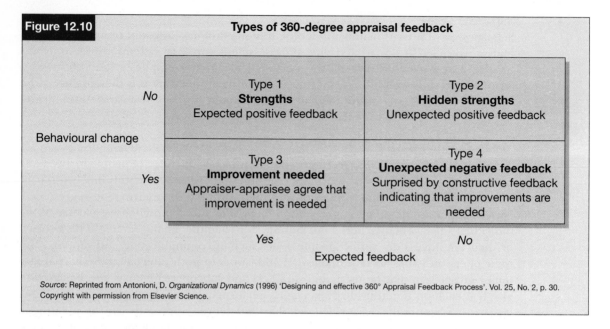

Figure 12.10 — Types of 360-degree appraisal feedback

Source: Reprinted from Antonioni, D. *Organizational Dynamics* (1996) 'Designing and effective 360° Appraisal Feedback Process'. Vol. 25, No. 2, p. 30. Copyright with permission from Elsevier Science.

> Your appraisal depends on your supervisor. If you are liked or socialise with him you're more likely to get a good review!
>
> (p. 46)

Appraisers may allow the evaluation of a single observed trait, characteristic, objective or competence to influence their ratings on all subsequent factors. If the appraiser judges the employee positively on one factor, he or she may give high ratings to all other areas of performance even though the appraisee's actual performance in these aspects may be weaker or unobserved. This is known as the *halo* effect. Conversely, a negative rating in one aspect could lead to other performance factors being evaluated negatively. This is called the *horns* effect.

Problems of subjectivity are particularly evident when non-quantifiable criteria are being used for assessment purposes.

Judging contribution

Appraisers may find it difficult to identify and measure, the distinct contribution of each individual (Kinnie and Lowe, 1990: 47). This may be exacerbated by staff (appraisers and appraisees) constantly moving from one project to another project (Howell and Cameron, 1996: 28).

There may be many external factors beyond the control of the individual employee that affect their performance, such as resources, processes, technology, corporate and HR strategy, working environment, external business context and management. In terms of expectancy theory, for rewards to act as an incentive the attainment of rewards must be tightly linked with individual performance.

If there is a long timespan between appraisals, managers may place greater importance on more recent performance (the *recency effect*), thereby possibly ignoring incidents that had occurred earlier.

Management's resistance to appraisals may be due to a perception of being placed in the 'embarrassing' situation of having to pass judgements on and criticising their fellow workers. As McGregor (1957) states:

> Managers are uncomfortable when they are in the position of playing God. (p. 90)

This is particularly the case when their judgements are formalised, written down and linked to some form of reward (see also Rowe, 1964: 19–20; Margerison, 1976: 30). One of the consequences of this tension is the reluctance to rate their subordinates at the extremes of the rating scale, particularly negatively (Carlton and Sloman 1992: 87–88; Kessler and Purcell, 1992: 25).

Role of line manager

Line managers/supervisors may lack the required technical skills and people management skills to be able to conduct an effective appraisal.

Furthermore, a lack of time and resources may hinder line managers in providing comprehensive and effective performance reviews and objective setting. Moreover, managers may perceive the appraisal process as a bureaucratic nuisance and form-filling exercise (e.g. Long, 1986: 65). This would be particularly evident in small companies.

Development vs Reward Conflict

There is a conflict in the nature of performance review procedures that attempt to assess performance for both training and development purposes and pay purposes. For example, Randell (1973) has argued that the reward review should be completely separate in terms of operation and documentation from performance, potential and organisation reviews.

Demotivation consequences

An appraisal outcome that labels an employee as simply 'average', or determines that he or she is not a 'high flier', may lead to demotivation. To state the general principle:

> When one person begins to make a judgement on another, unless that judgement is favourable, reaction and resistance begin to set in. (Margerison, 1976: 32)

Interpretation 'spin'

The 'cascading' approach of progressive levels of management setting objectives for the level below and consequently being assessed themselves by the attainment of these objectives can result in the manipulation and 'fudging' of standards. Furthermore, managers must be aware that the impact of the company's strategic pay policy may be reduced or diverted by lower levels of management pursuing alternative goals and objectives (Bowey and Thorpe, 1989: 17). Thus senior managers must install adequate monitoring systems and controls in order to ensure that their policy or objectives are implemented as designed (see also Murlis and Wright, 1993: 33).

PSYCHOLOGICAL CONTRACTS

The concept of the psychological contract is a useful tool in helping us to understand more about the employment relationship (Herriot and Pemberton, 1996; Kessler and Undy, 1996). Sims (1994) defines the psychological contract as:

> the set of expectations held by the individual employee that specify what the individual and the organization expect to give to and receive from each other in the course of their work relationship. (p. 375)

A more specific definition is provided by Spindler (1994):

> the bundle of unexpressed expectations that exist at the interfaces between humans . . . (which) are greatly influenced by the personal history and individual self-image of the parties to the relationship . . . (and) creates emotions and attitudes which form and control behavior. (pp. 326–327)

Whereas a short yet perceptive view is given by Guzzo and Noonan (1994):

> a part of the glue that binds employees to organizations. (p. 448)

The interest in psychological contracts is perhaps a consequence of the uncertainty in the working environment as the 'old' employee psychological contract is seen to have been unilaterally violated by management, leaving employees feeling disorientated, weak and betrayed (e.g. Kissler, 1994; Sims, 1994). The 'old' contract was predictable, and seemed to be known to both employees and employers alike; now both sides to the bargain are searching for an understanding of the new set of employee and employer expectations.

The 'old' contract lay in individual reward being determined by hierarchical structure and a socially constructed set of rules and rituals. The bargain seemed to be based on an 'entitlement' culture where hard work and loyalty were given in exchange for job security, stable career progression, and steady and predictable rewards.

It appears that the 'new' psychological contract asks the individual employee to accept risk, ambiguity and uncertainty, which has previously been borne by the organisation (Rousseau and Greller, 1994: 391). The trends outlined in the chapter with regard to reward and remuneration have supported this displacement of risk: individually rather than collectively determined reward, pay determination based on the evaluation of the person rather than the job, variability in pay, subjectively defined and evaluated performance measures, and performance indicators that are influenced by factors outside the individual's control. Furthermore, employees' anxiety is encouraged by the omniscient and omnipotent web of performance management measures, which may lead to the impression of Orwellian or Kafkaesque technologies and practices of surveillance and control (Burrell, 1988; Barlow, 1989; Townley, 1993a, 1993b, 1994). Thus an employee's motivation may be centred around the need to reduce uncertainty rather than a simple equation of reward–performance based on behaviourist theories.

The HR profession will have a significant role to play in the management and balancing of the general or specific psychological contracts of employees. The HR function can act as a focal point for helping to discover employees' expectations through collective channels or individual mechanisms, while seeking to provide for the meeting of employees' expectations (e.g. Sims, 1994). The HR professional must make sure that different facets of human resource management, such as recruitment, selection, training and reward, and different managers, shape and support the psychological contracts in a consistent, integrated and balanced manner (Rousseau and Greller, 1994). Human resource management interventions can discretely and accumulatively affect employees' psychological contracts over time, while a drastic or significant intervention or event such as redundancy or relocation may break or significantly disrupt the psychological contract in one go (Guzzo and Noonan, 1994; Herriot and Pemberton, 1996). If employees feel that their psychological contract has been breached, then they may withhold or withdraw from the relationship, consciously or unconsciously (Spindler, 1994: 326–327).

The psychological contracts of all employees are therefore an important consideration in an organisation's reward and remuneration strategy and policy. A clearly defined, balanced and equitable psychological contract is essential if the employment relationship is one that is to be based on mutual trust, commitment, stability and cooperation (Sims, 1994; Herriot and Pemberton, 1996). When considering concepts such as reward management, performance management and psychological contracts in the (post)modern world, the student and practitioner would be wise to note the observations of Spindler (1994):

> The commitment of a free people can only be freely given. It cannot be obtained by trickery, bribery, or coercion. One can be committed only if he or she is free to withhold commitment.
>
> (p. 331)

INTERNATIONAL REMUNERATION POLICIES

Many companies are responding to the globalisation of business and, more specifically, the integrated European market by designing a single international remuneration policy.

When designing a reward strategy for employees who are taking up overseas appointments many factors have to be taken into consideration:

> Knowledge of the laws, customs, environment, and employment practices of many foreign countries; familiarity with currency relationships and the effect of inflation on compensation; and an understanding of why special allowances must be supplied and which allowances are necessary in what countries – all within the context of shifting political, economic, and social conditions.
>
> (Dowling and Schuler, 1990: 116)

Indeed, consideration must also be given to the variations in the traditional method of payment in the host country.

Design of an international reward package

The main method of drawing up a compensation package is known as the *balance sheet* approach (Figure 12.11). This is defined by one writer as:

> A system designed to equalise the purchasing power of employees at comparable position levels living overseas and in the home country, and to provide incentives to offset qualitative differences between assignment locations. (Reynolds, 1986, cited in Dowling and Schuler, 1990: 118)

An example of this type of approach, with certain modifications, is provided by Willmore (1992: 22). The author describes how BT designed its expatriate remuneration policy:

BT uses the biannual comparative cost-of-living tables, produced by consultancy Employment Conditions Abroad, and its accompanying taxation tables to calculate a net salary for each employee due to start work overseas. This is equivalent to his or her salary at home. This is later split between spendable income and a housing and savings element, the latter intended to reflect UK financial commitments and therefore not adjusted for cost-of-living differences.

The sorts of expenses incurred by expatriate families and thus the types of allowances offered in the international compensation package can be categorised as follows (Dowling and Schuler, 1990: 122–129):

● *Income taxes* incurred in both home and host country. Ensuring effective and favourable tax return administration and tax equalisation is an important but costly and complex requirement of companies.

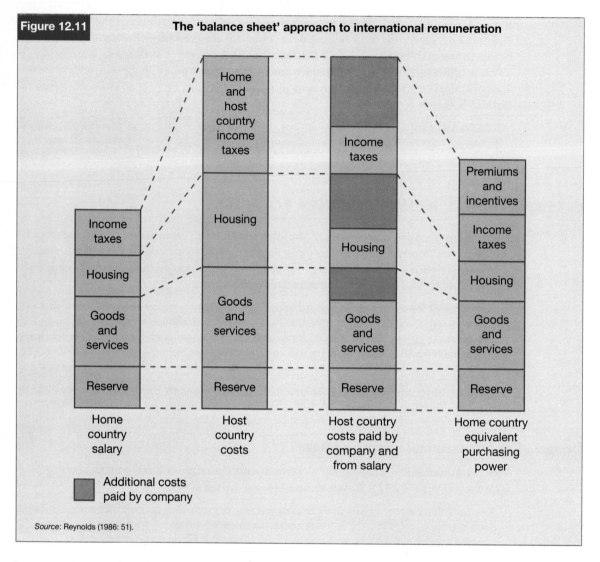

Figure 12.11   The 'balance sheet' approach to international remuneration

Source: Reynolds (1986: 51).

- *Housing allowances* range from providing financial assistance, so that employees can maintain their home country housing standards, to company housing or help in the sale or leasing of an expatriate's former residence.
- *Cost-of-living allowances* help to make up the differences in prices between the home and foreign country (for example, to take account of different inflation levels).
- *Reserves* include contributions to savings, pension schemes, investments, etc.
- *Relocation allowances* include the moving, shipping and storage of personal and household items, and temporary living expenses.
- *Education allowances* for expatriates' children are an important part of the remuneration package for medium/long-term assignments. For example, language tuition and enrolment fees in the host country or boarding school fees in the home country may be paid for by the company.
- *Medical, emergency and security cover* for expatriates are often overlooked by companies, but are very important (Brewster, 1991: 74).

In many companies the view that an overseas assignment has to be suffered by unlucky individuals is increasingly becoming obsolete, as is the traditional 'hardship allowance' for everyone going to work in a different country. However, some observers are unconvinced of this notion, believing that 'hardship payments' are hidden in other benefits, and parochial views of employees working in foreign countries still exist (e.g. Willmore, 1992: 23).

To conclude this section, it is perhaps worthwhile to err on the side of caution when we talk of less differentiated global, and especially European, markets. When formulating remuneration policies companies have to be aware that harmonisation of terms and conditions of employment, pensions, social security and taxation requirements does not exist currently.

CONCLUSION

In this chapter it has been suggested that the developments in reward management indicate a move towards 'new pay'. The characteristics of 'new pay' are a response to the need for a flexible organisational form and a constantly changing business environment. These characteristics include the integration of the reward strategy with business strategy in order to achieve business objectives, performance-related pay schemes based on a range of different indicators, flexible benefits schemes, the individualistic nature of the effort–reward bargain, and the unitary nature of the employment relationship based on the principles of 'help yourself by helping the organisation' and 'partnership'. The trend towards 'new pay' does seem to reflect Guest's (1987) four tenets of human resource management – the encouragement of commitment, flexibility, quality and strategic integration – but we have yet to see any clear evidence of these initiatives achieving Guest's rhetorical objectives. Thus there is increasing interest in alternative forms of reward management: competence-based pay, team-based pay, and non-financial rewards.

There is often an unquestioned assumption that employees will be highly committed, and thus motivated and productive, if the reward strategies of an organisation match the corporate and the human resource strategy and are carefully implemented. Furthermore, it is often hoped that the reward strategy will support other management techniques such as empowerment and teamwork, to blur the distinction between 'workers' and 'management'.

The belief that payment by time systems simply encourages 'minimally acceptable performance' has caused many firms to introduce payment schemes that incorporate a financial incentive to perform consistently at a high standard. Schemes such as piecework, payment by results, measured daywork, management by objectives, merit pay, team and individual bonuses, profit sharing and performance-related pay have been introduced in companies in many different guises in the belief that the main method of motivation is through direct financial incentives.

However, researchers such as Roy (1952, 1953, 1955) and Roethlisberger and Dickson (1939) writing over 40 years ago discovered that the relationship between economic incentive and effort is not simple, and is influenced by many factors. Indeed, the problems encountered through the introduction of more 'modern' payment-by-results schemes perhaps originate from a persistent attempt by workers to regain control over work output, methods and earnings. Practitioners, academics and employees alike are questioning whether 'in vogue' payment schemes such as performance-related pay are the most effective way of increasing and harnessing the motivation of employees, and whether it is wise to ignore the lessons from history. We appear to be very reluctant to believe that most employees are not simply and solely driven by the 'cash nexus' and behavioural modification techniques, and that most employees wish to improve their performance, learn, develop and are committed to doing a good job (see also Kohn, 1993).

There is very little evidence to suggest that performance-related pay schemes increase the overall performance of the organisation, and indeed they may lead to dysfunctional outcomes (e.g. Kinnie and Lowe, 1990; Marsden and Richardson, 1991; Institute of Personnel Management, 1992; Scott, 1994; Stewart and Walsh, 1994; Clark, 1995). Indeed, many professionals find it absurd, objectionable and possibly insulting that it is expected that they will work harder and more effectively because of an element of performance-related pay.

It can be argued that motives are not simply external forces that bear down on us but exigencies only in relation to our 'stance' towards the world (Cooper, 1990: 152).

Sartre, for example, believed that the explanation of behaviour was 'hermeneutical' not causal (Cooper, 1990: 152):

> We should attempt to disengage the meanings of an act by proceeding from the principle that every action, no matter how trivial, is not the simple effect of the prior psychic state and does not result from a linear determinism but rather is . . . in the totality which I am.   (Sartre 1958: 459)

Indeed, as an individual's motivation is determined by complex interaction of influences so is one's attitude towards appraisal. Fisher (1995), for example, outlines how the language used by appraiser and appraisee suggests different ways in which they interpret and make sense of the 'theatre' of performance management and appraisal schemes. Thus there can be no objective 'truth' of one's motivation and performance, only a reality created through language (Grint, 1994: 69) and social construction. As Leiper (1994) indicates:

> There are a variety of approaches and systems which have been developed for evaluation in recent years. However, methods and materials are of less consequence than the frame of mind in which evaluation is undertaken. It requires the development of a spirit of enquiry and conditions which provide the security necessary for learning from experience, especially containing anxiety, both organizational and personal.   (p. 204)

Literature on performance management is dominated by the consideration of the design, mechanisms and procedures of such schemes (e.g. Fletcher, 1993) rather than critique of the principle and outcomes of performance management such as an obsession with measurement, control and rationality (Alvesson, 1984; Brunsson, 1985; Watson, 1994: 138–140). Individuals within organisations have to operate within the constraints provided by resources, processes, technology, corporate and human resource strategy, the working environment and management, and may therefore not be able to improve their actual performance to any great extent without significant changes to the work system. (For example, the 'quality' guru Deming argues that about 80% of improvement requires management effort and major change in the work system, while only 20% of improvement can be actioned by front-line employees.)

It is possible, therefore, that the role of a performance management system that is driven by evaluation and judgement will be reduced to that of the site of a political game. Authority and dependency relations are defined and reinforced (Bowles and Coates, 1993: 8), and the apportionment and avoidance of blame can very easily predominate. Leiper (1994), for example, states:

Any system of evaluation can all too easily come to feel like an accusation of inadequacy: it then comes to represent a critical 'parental' voice . . .
(p. 201)

Predictably, employees' levels of motivation and commitment to work will be reduced (Bowles and Coates, 1993: 8) and their self-esteem will be shattered. Thus the 'image of performance', and the management of that image, become the overriding motivating factor for employees (Bowles and Coates, 1993: 5), and the appraisal process thereby becomes an end in itself rather than a means to an end (e.g. Watson, 1994). For example, Caulkin (1997) states:

Take, for instance, university departments, whose financial fortunes depend on the grades they get in never-ending rounds of research and teaching assessments. As most academics now complain, a disproportionate amount of their effort – including hiring specialist consultants – now goes into achieving the secondary outcomes of wowing their assessors, rather than into the primary one of making their students more effective or their research more useful.
(p. 8)

We may have to accept finally both the inevitability of subjectivity in performance appraisal systems and a pluralistic conception of organisational life. The practice and discipline of human resource management must fundamentally be based on an acceptance and consideration of different stakeholders in the organisation, and the contentiousness and opaqueness of concepts such as quality, efficiency, effectiveness, value for money, profit and, indeed, performance.

This chapter has also outlined an alternative to an approach to performance management that is driven by control, financial reward and single-loop learning. This alternative approach focuses on the development of all employees, and views financial reward as only one possible way to increase performance, motivation and commitment. A strategic, holistic and developmental approach offers hope for organisations seeking to develop a mutually supportive and trusting working environment based on commitment and continuously high performance.

QUESTIONS

1 How can companies and managers help employees to satisfy the needs in Maslow's hierarchy?

2 What are the main implications for employee reward of Herzberg's two-factor theory of motivation?

3 Identify the differences and similarities between content theories, Porter and Lawler model and behavioural modification theories of motivation.

4 To what extent is money motivating?

5 What is the relationship between Porter and Lawler's model and Performance Related Pay?

6 Outline the business strategies and circumstances in which each type of reward philosophy is appropriate.

7 Your tutor has set a group assignment. Do you believe everyone should receive the same group mark? Do you think individual group members should be rewarded on the basis of their contribution to group discussions and writing? If so, how can the tutor decide what mark to give to each group member? How are these problems similar to those experienced in other organisations? How can they be overcome?

8 Outline the circumstances in which a group incentive scheme should be used. When should an individual-based scheme be used?

9 How would you assess the performance of your lecturer/tutor?

10 What are the advantages and disadvantages of introducing Performance Related Pay for teachers, tutors and lecturers?

11 What are the advantages and disadvantages of Competency-Based Pay compared to Performance Related Pay?

12 Do you believe it is fair to reward everyone equally? Why? Do you believe it is fairer to reward employees on the basis of the evaluation of performance rather than across-the-board increases? Why?

13 How can companies and managers prevent 'inequity' problems?

14 How can companies and managers ensure procedural justice within reward and performance management strategies?

15 What are the possible management objectives for using employee recognition schemes? In what circumstances are employee recognition schemes inappropriate?

16 Compare performance management to traditional performance appraisal schemes in ensuring a mutually supportive and trusting working environment.

17 Suggest SMART objectives for the following types of people:
- police officers
- dentists
- doctors and nurses
- social workers.

18 What are the possible advantages and problems with using 360 degree appraisals?

19 Which methods of performance assessment are most suitable for linking the assessment of performance to pay increases?

20 How can PRP schemes lead to discrimination against women and ethnic minorities?

CASE STUDY 1

BT hit by first strike for 13 years: call centres union takes action over 'oppressive working conditions'

British Telecommunications suffered it first strike for 13 years yesterday when the Communications Workers Union protested at what it dubbed 'oppressive working conditions' at 37 call centres around the UK.

The strike disrupted repair and billing calls, and fuelled the prospect of further industrial action next month and early in the New Year.

Yesterday, a union official said the strike had been an 'overwhelming success' with 95 per cent of its 4,000 members employed in the call centres refusing to cross picket lines. Ten days ago, 1,507 union members against 339 voted in favour of going on strike in a 50 per cent turnout. BT, which employs 8,000 at its call centres, claimed the stoppage had had 'minimal impact'.

The union said later that BT had agreed to hold talks, probably later this week, to try to resolve the dispute. 'Members have shown their concern for all the issues we have raised on their behalf. If management will now treat the matter with equal seriousness, today will be an important one in shaping a new atmosphere and conditions at BT call centres,' a union official said.

The strike is ostensibly over what the union claims are inadequate staffing levels and intimidating performance targets. But it also focused on BT's policy of recruiting agency staff with fewer pay, pension and redundancy rights than those held by the permanent unionised employees.

It is in this group that union officials have identified a potential fertile ground for future recruitment. The significance of the strike lies in the message it is sending to other call centres where pay and conditions are far worse than those at BT.

The industrial action by the CWU follows a speech aimed at white-collar unions last month from John Monks, TUC general secretary, in which he urged them to recruit more members in a sector he described as 'new mills of the 21st century Britain'.

It is estimated 480,000 people will be employed in 5,000 call centres within three years. With 350,000 now employed at more than 4,000 sites, the UK is home to more than half of Europe's call centres. The sector is fast replacing traditionally more unionised manufacturing industries as a source of jobs, particularly in areas of high unemployment.

Despite allegations that a lot of call centres are the 21st century equivalent of the sweat shop, companies such as BT claim to have consciously fought off being branded as such.

Patricia Vaz, BT managing director responsible for UK customer service, said in a letter to staff last week that she wanted 'a new spirit of partnership . . . that will give a satisfying and enjoyable environment for us all to work in'.

According to some industry analysts, the high turnover rate for many employees in call centres is forcing companies to take the complaints of staff more seriously than they once did.

Source: Financial Times, 23rd November 1999, p. 8.

1 To what extent are call centres the 'new mills of the 21st century Britain'?

2 What are the main issues with regards to employee motivation, reward and performance management within call centres?

3 Develop an appropriate reward and performance management strategy for BT's call centres to ensure 'a new spirit of partnership . . . that will give a satisfying and enjoyable environment for us all to work in'

CASE STUDY 2

Barclays defends chief's pay package

Barclays yesterday defended itself against allegations of 'fat cat' salaries, saying its share price would have to rise so much to pay the maximum bonus that shareholders and customers would not begrudge Matt Barrett, Barclays' chief executive, his top £30m payout.

The bank, which is embroiled in a political row after shutting 171 branches, said its share price would have to reach £170 within three years for Mr Barrett to make £30m from his share options. This is a 10-fold rise on yesterday's £17 price – although last year Barclays shared topped £20.

'If he can get the share price up to £ 170 in the next three years 1 would be delighted to tell him he will get £30m,' said Cathy Turner, executive compensation director, who drew up the scheme.

She added: 'It would be good for our shareholders and our customers, because we would have to please them so much to get (that) much business.'

Ms Turner said a more typical payout to Mr Barrett might be £3m, assuming the bank performed well but not astonishingly well. Had Mr Barrett – appointed last year – had the same scheme since 1996, the three-year bonus would have been options worth just under £1m, less than the scheme in place at the time. She calculated that if the bank were nearly to triple its share price Mr Barrett would get £6m worth of options, while the market capitalisation would rise £41bn. The share options come on top of his basic pay of £850,000, plus substantial pension contributions and other benefits, including £15,000 for accountancy fees to help minimise tax. Last year he also received a cash bonus of £638,000 for three months' work.

The bonus scheme has provoked anger among lobby groups and MPs. 'I find it quite incredible that people are being made overnight multimillionaires in return for providing an even worse service to customers,' said Martin Salter, the MP who led a campaign against the branch closures. However, Barclays said the bonus scheme, was at the cutting edge of corporate governance, providing no share options at all if the bank performs badly. 'We want a heavily skewed risk pay profile for this plan that is penal and delivers zero when we perform badly,' said Ms Turner. If the bank's preferred profit measure, economic profit, rises less than 8 per cent a year the first tranche of options will be cut in half, while if it rises more than 15 per cent the 500 staff covered by the scheme get twice as many options.

Top executives awarded more than 10,000 options – now worth £56,000 – will have the excess tested against 12 rival banks' share prices. Depending on how Barclay's shares perform the options could be cancelled or increased up to four times. Stuart Cliffe, chief executive of the National Association of Bank Customers, said pay awards at Barclays were 'upsetting customers' already worried by branch closures. 'Managers are awarding themselves for damaging the company in the long term,' he said. 'Banks need to rejoin the real world,' he said.

Source: Financial Times, 14th April 2000, p. 6.

1 Using the 'General Framework for Understanding Executive Compensation', evaluate the reward package of Barclay's chief executive.

2 What are the main difficulties in designing the reward packages of senior executives? To what extent are these difficulties different or similar to those in designing reward packages for all employees?

3 Who should decide on the pay of senior executives? How should companies reward senior executives?

4 Do you believe that senior executives are generally paid too much? Do you believe it is fair for executives to receive such large amounts of money?

REFERENCES AND FURTHER READING

Those texts marked with an asterisk are particularly recommended for further reading.

Adams, J.S. (1963) 'Toward an understanding of inequity', *Journal of Abnormal and Social Psychology*, Vol. 67, pp. 422–436.

Alvesson, M. (1984) 'Questioning rationality and ideology: on critical organization theory', *International Studies of Management and Organisation*, Vol.14, No. 1, pp. 61–79.

Anon (1998a) 'We're in this together: profit sharing schemes', *Pay and Benefits Bulletin*, No. 444, March, pp. 2–8.

Anon (1998b) 'There is merit in merit pay', *Pay and Benefits Bulletin*, No. 445, April, pp. 4–7.

Antonioni, D. (1996) 'Designing an effective 360-degree appraisal feedback process', *Organizational Dynamics*, Vol. 25, No 2, pp. 24–38.

Arkin, A. (1999) 'Supple difference', *People Management*, 16 December, pp. 43–45.

*Armstrong, M. (1994) *Performance Management*. London: Kogan Page.

Armstrong, M. (1996a) *Employee Reward*. London: IPD.

Armstrong, M. (1996b) 'How group efforts can pay dividends', *People Management*, 25 January, pp. 22–27.

Armstrong, M. (2000) 'Feel the width', *People Management*, 3 February, pp. 34–38.

*Armstrong, M. and Murlis, H. (1994) *Reward Management: A Handbook of Remuneration Strategy and Practice*, 3rd edn. London: Kogan Page.

*Bach, S. (2000) 'From performance appraisal to performance management', in Bach, S. and Sission, K. (eds) *Personnel Management*. Oxford: Blackwell, pp. 241–263.

Baldamus, W. (1961) *Efficiency and Effort*. London: Tavistock.

Barkema, H.G. and Gomez-Mejia, L.R. (1998) 'Managerial compensation and firm performance: a general research framework', *Academy of Management Journal*, Vol. 41, No 2, pp. 135–145.

Barlow, G. (1989) 'Deficiencies and the perpetuation of power: latent functions in management appraisal', *Journal of Management Studies*, Vol. 226, No. 5, pp. 499–517.

Baron, A. and Armstrong, M. (1998) 'Out of the box', *People Management*, 23 July, pp. 38–41.

Bateman, T.S. and Organ, D.W. (1983) 'Job satisfaction and the good soldier: the relationship between affect and "citizenship"', *Academy of Management Journal*, Vol. 26, pp. 587–595.

Batstone, E. (1984) *Working Order*. Oxford: Blackwell.

Beer, M., Spector, B., Lawrence, P.R., Quinn Mills, D. and Walton, R.E. (1984) *Managing Human Assets*. New York: Free Press.

Behrend, H. (1959) 'Financial incentives as a system of beliefs', *British Journal of Sociology*, Vol. 2, pp. 137–147.

Behrend, H. (1961) 'A fair day's work', *Scottish Journal of Political Economy*, Vol. 8, pp. 102–118.

Bell, D.W. and Hanson, C.G. (1985) 'Profit sharing and employee shareholding attitude survey', *Topics*, Vol. 21, March, pp. 6–8.

Blau, G. (1994) 'Testing the effect of level and importance of pay referents on pay level satisfaction', *Human Relations*, Vol. 47, No. 10, pp. 1251–1268.

Bowey, A.M. (1980) 'Coming to terms with comparability', *Personnel Management*, February, pp. 28–33.

Bowey, A.M. and Thorpe, R. (1989) 'Payment systems and performance improvement', *Employee Relations*, Vol. 11, No. 1, pp. 17–20.

Bowey, A.M., Thorpe, R., Mitchell, F.H.M., Nicholls, G., Gosnold, D., Savery, L. and Hellier, P.K. (1982) *Effects of Incentive Payment Systems: United Kingdom 1977–80*, Research Paper No. 36. London: Department of Employment.

Bowles, M.L. and Coates, G. (1993) 'Image and substance: the management of performance as rhetoric or reality?', *Personnel Review*, Vol. 22, No. 2, pp. 3–21.

Braithwaite, N. and Hoey, C. (1999) 'Contributory factors', *People Management*, 15 July, pp. 50–52.

Brewster, C. (1991) *The Management of Expatriates: Issues in Human Resource Management*, Monograph 5, Cranfield School of Management. London: Kogan Page.

Brown, M. (1996) 'Britain's longest love affair', *Human Resources*, May/June, pp. 60–66.

Brown, W. (1973) *Piecework Bargaining*. London: Heinemann.

Brunsson, N. (1985) *The Irrational Organization*. New York: John Wiley.

Burrell, G. (1988) 'Modernism, post modernism and organisational analysis 2: the contribution of Michel Foucault', *Organisational Studies*, Vol. 9, No. 2, pp. 221–335.

Cannell, M. and Long, P. (1991) 'What's changed about incentive pay?', *Personnel Management*, October, pp. 58–63.

Carlton, I. and Sloman, M. (1992) 'Performance appraisal in practice', *Human Resource Management Journal*, Vol. 2, No. 3, pp. 80–94.

Casey, B., Lakey, J. and White, M. (1992) *Payment Systems: A Look At Current Practice*, Research Series No. 5. Department of Employment: Policy Studies Institute.

Caulkin, S. (1997) 'League tables? A restaurant guide is a lot more use', *The Observer Business*, 6 April.

Cavendish, R. (1982) *Women On The Line*. London: Routledge & Kegan Paul.

Child, J. (1984) *Organisation*, 2nd edn. London: Harper & Row.

Clark, J. (1995) *Managing Innovation and Change: People, Technology and Strategy*. London: Sage.

Corkerton, S. and Bevan, S. (1998) 'Paying hard to get', *People Management*, Vol. 4, No. 16, pp. 40–42.

Cooper, D.E. (1990) *Existentialism*. Oxford: Blackwell.

Cully, M., Woodland, S., O'Reilly, A. and Dix, G. (1999) *Britain at Work: As Depicted by the 1998 Workplace Employee Relations Survey*. London: Routledge.

Curry, L. and Prickett, R. (1996) 'Rewards without a sting in the tail', *People Management*, 18 April, pp. 40–42.

Daniel, W. and McIntosh, N. (1972) *The Right To Manage?* London: Macdonald.

Deckop, J. (1992) 'Organizational and career pay satisfaction', *Human Resource Management Review*, Vol. 2, pp. 115–129.

Dowling, P.J. and Schuler, R.S. (1990) *International Dimensions of Human Resource Management*. Boston, Mass.: PWS-Kent.

Drummond, H. (1993) 'Measuring management effectiveness', *Personnel Management*, March, pp. 38–41.

Dulebohn, J.H. and Martocchio, J.J. (1998) 'Employee perceptions of the fairness of work group incentive pay plans', *Journal of Management*, Vol. 24, No. 4, pp. 469–488.

Duncan, C. (1988) 'Why profit related pay will fail', *Industrial Relations Journal*, Autumn, pp. 186–200.

Edwards, P.K. (1987) *Managing the Factory: A Survey of General Managers*. Oxford: Blackwell.

Edwards, P.K. and Scullion, H. (1982) *The Social Organisation of Industrial Conflict, Control and Resistance in the Workplace*. Oxford: Blackwell.

Etzioni, A. (1961) *A Comparative Analysis of Complex Organizations*. New York: Free Press.

Etzioni, A. (1964) *Modern Organizations*. Englewood Cliffs, NJ: Prentice Hall.

Fisher, C. (1995) 'The differences between appraisal schemes: variation and acceptability – Part II: rhetoric and the design of schemes', *Personnel Review*, Vol. 24, No. 1, pp. 51–66.

Flanders [...]
analysis [...]
pp. 1–26.

Flanders, A. [...]
Reform of In[...]

Fletcher, C. ([...]
London: IPM [...]

Fletcher, C. (19[...]
1 October, pp. [...]

Fletcher, C. and [...]
mance managen[...]
pp. 42–47.

Folger, R., Konovsky[...]
due process metaph[...]   ...staw,
B.M. and Cummings, [...]   ...*ganizational*
Behavior, Vol. 13. Green[...]   ...ess, pp. 129–177.

Fowler, A. (1988) 'New [...]ons in performance pay', *Personnel Management*, November, pp. 30–34.

Fowler, A. (1996) 'How to: pick a job evaluation system', *People Management*. 8 February, pp. 42–43.

Frey, B.S. (1997) *Not Just for the Money: An Economic Theory of Personal Motivation*. Cheltenham: Edward Elgar.

Geary, J.F. (1992) 'Pay, control and commitment: linking appraisal and reward', *Human Resource Management Journal*, Vol. 2, No. 4, pp. 36–54.

George, J.M. and Jones, G.R. (1997) 'Organizational spontaneity in context', *Human Performance*, Vol. 10, pp. 153–170.

Gomez-Mejia, L.R. and Wiseman, R.M. (1997) 'Reframing executive compensation: an assessment and outlook', *Journal of Management*, Vol. 23, No. 3, pp. 291–374.

Goodge, P. and Watts, P. (2000) 'How to manage 360-degree feedback', *People Management*, 17 February, pp.50-52.

Grayson, D. (1984) 'Shape of payment systems to come', *Employment Gazette*, April, pp. 175–181.

Green, F., Hadjimatheou, G. and Smail, R. (1985) 'Fringe benefit distribution in Britain', *British Journal of Industrial Relations*, Vol. 23, No. 2, pp. 261–280.

Grint, K. (1994) 'What's wrong with performance appraisals? A critique and a suggestion', *Human Resource Management Journal*, Vol. 3, No. 3, pp. 61–77.

Guest, D. (1987) 'Human resource management and industrial relations', *Journal of Management Studies*, Vol. 24, No. 5, pp. 503–521.

Guest, D. (1989) 'Human resource management: its implications for industrial relations and trade unions', in Storey, J. (ed.) *New Perspectives on Human Resource Management*. London: Routledge, pp. 41–55.

Guzzo, R. and Noonan, K.A. (1994) 'Human resource practices as communications and the psychological contract', *Human Resource Management*, Vol. 33, No. 3, pp. 447–462.

Haraszti, M. (1980) 'Piecework and looting: payment systems and productivity', in Nichols, T. (ed.) *Capital and Labour*. London: Fontana, pp. 290–301.

Harris, L. (1997) 'When high commitment personnel policies create low commitment and uncertainty'. Paper presented at 12th Annual Employment Research Unit Conference, Cardiff Business School, 11–12 September (unpublished).

Chapter 12 • Reward and performance [...]
Heery, E. (1992) 'Divided we fall? Paper [...]
Heery, E. related pay', (unpu[...]
mance, 19 March (1996) 'Ris[...]
Seminar, E. (1996) [...]
Personnel Review, A[...]
Hegewisch, A. [...]
ing: Eur[...]
No. 6[...]
He[...]

...rade unions and perfor-
...r LSE/TUC Trade Union
...lished).

..., representation and the new pay',
...l. 25, No. 6, pp. 54–65.

...(1991a) 'The decentralisation of pay bargain-
...pean comparisons', *Personnel Review*, Vol. 20,
..., pp. 28–35.

...gewisch, A. (1991b) 'European comparisons in rewards policies: the findings of the first Price Waterhouse/Cranfield Survey', SWP 65/91. Paper presented at the 6th EIASM workshop on International HRM, St Gallen, Switzerland, March (unpublished).

Hendry, C. and Pettigrew, A. (1990) 'Human resource management: an agenda for the 1990s', *International Journal of Human Resource Management*, Vol. 1, No. 1, pp. 17–43.

Hendry, C., Bradley, P. and Perkins, S. (1997) 'Missed a motivator?', *People Management*, 15 May, pp. 20–25.

Herriot, P. and Pemberton, C. (1996) 'A new deal for middle managers', *People Management*, 15 June, pp. 32–34.

Herzog, M. (1980) *From Hand To Mouth: Women and Piecework*. Harmondsworth: Penguin.

Heywood, J.S., Siebert, W.S. and Wei, X. (1997) 'Payment by results systems: British evidence', *British Journal of Industrial Relations*, Vol. 35, No. 1, pp. 1–22.

Hopegood, J. (1999) 'Package tour', *Personnel Today*, pp. 34–35.

Howell, K. and Cameron, E. (1996) 'The benefits of an outsider's opinion', *People Management*, 8 August, pp. 28–30.

Hyman, R. and Brough, I. (1975) *Social Values and Industrial Relations*. Oxford: Blackwell.

IDS (1992) *'PRP Grows as Tax Relief Doubles'*, IDS Study 520, December.

IDS (1998) *Performance Related Pay*, IDS Study 650, June.

IDS (1999a) 'Employee benefits', *IDS Focus 89*, March.

IDS (1999b) 'Motivation without money', *IDS Focus 92*, Winter.

IDS (1999c) *Employee Recognition Schemes*, IDS Study Plus, Winter.

IPD (1998) *Performance Pay Survey: Executive Summary*, January, London: Institute of Personnel and Development.

IPM (1992) *Performance Management in the UK: An Analysis of the Issues*, London: IPM.

Jensen, M.C. and Murphy, K.J. (1990) 'CEO incentives: it's not how much you pay, but how', *Harvard Business Review*, May–June, Vol. 68, No. 3.

Kerr, S. (1975) 'On the folly of rewarding A, while hoping for B', *Academy of Management Journal*, Vol. 18, No. 4, pp. 769–783.

*Kessler, I. (2000) 'Remuneration systems', in Bach, S. and Sission, K. (eds) *Personnel Management*. Oxford: Blackwell, pp. 241–263.

Kessler, I. and Purcell, J. (1992) 'Performance related pay: objectives and applications', *Human Resource Management Journal*, Vol. 2, No. 3, pp. 16–33.

Kessler, I. and Undy, R. (1996) *The New Employment Relationship: Examining the Psychological Contract*. London: IPD.

Kinnie, N. and Lowe, D. (1990) 'Performance related pay on the shopfloor', *Personnel Management*, November, pp. 45–49.

Kissler, G.D. (1994) 'The new employment contract', *Human Resource Management*, Vol. 33, No. 3, pp. 335–352.

Kohn, A. (1993) 'Why incentive plans cannot work', *Harvard Business Review*, Sept–Oct, Vol. 71, No. 5, pp. 54–60.

Lawler, E.E. (1990) *Strategic Pay*. San Francisco: Jossey Bass.

Lawler, E.E. (1996) 'Competencies: a poor performance for the new pay', *Compensation and Benefits Review*, Vol. 28, No. 6, pp. 20–25.

Lee, C., Law, K.S. and Bobko, P. (1999) 'The importance of justice perceptions on pay effectiveness: a two year study of a skill-based pay plan', *Journal of Management*, Vol. 25, No. 6, pp. 851–873.

Leiper, R. (1994) 'Evaluation: organizations learning from experience', in Obholzer, A. and Roberts, V.Z. (eds) *The Unconscious at Work: Individual and Organizational Stress in the Human Services*. London: Routledge, pp. 197–205.

Leventhal, G.S. (1976) 'Fairness in social relationships', in Thibaut, J.W., Spence, J.T. and Carson, R.C. (eds) *Contemporary Topics in Social Psychology*. Morristown, NJ: General Learning Press, pp. 211–240.

Lind, E.A. and Tyler, T. (1988) *The Social Psychology of Procedural Justice*. New York: Plenum.

Long, P. (1986) *Performance Appraisal Revisited: The Third IPM Survey*. London: Institute of Personnel Management.

Lupton, T. (1972) *Payment Systems*. Harmondsworth: Penguin.

Lupton, T. and Bowey, A.M. (1983) *Wages and Salaries*. Aldershot: Gower.

Lynn, M. (1999) 'Midas Martin', *The Sunday Times Business*, 22 August, p. 7.

Mabey, C. and Salaman, G. (1995) *Strategic Human Resource Management*. Oxford: Blackwell.

Margerison, C. (1976) 'A constructive approach to appraisal', *Personnel Management*, July, pp. 30–34.

Marginson, P., Edwards, P., Martin, R., Purcell, J. and Sisson, K. (1988) *Beyond The Workplace*. Oxford: Blackwell.

Marsden, D. and Richardson, R. (1991) 'Performing for pay? The effect of "merit pay" on motivation in a public service', *British Journal of Industrial Relations*, Vol. 32, No. 2, pp. 243–262.

McFarlin, D.B. and Sweeney, P.D. (1992) 'Distributive and procedural justice as predictors of satisfaction with personal and organizational outcomes', *Academy of Management Journal*, Vol. 35, No. 3, pp. 626–637.

McGregor, D. (1957) 'An uneasy look at performance appraisal', *Harvard Business Review*, Vol. 35, May/June, pp. 89–94.

McLuhan, R. (1999) 'Hidden extras', *Personnel Today*, 29 April, pp. 38–39.

Millward, N. and Stevens, M. (1986) *British Workplace Industrial Relations 1980–84*. Aldershot: Gower.

Millward, N., Stevens, M., Smart, D. and Hawes, W.R. (1992) *Workplace Industrial Relations in Transition: The ED/ESRC/PSI/ACAS Surveys*. Aldershot: Dartmouth.

Morrison, E.W. (1996) 'Organizational citizenship behaviour as a critical link between HRM practices and service quality', *Human Resource Management*, Vol. 35, pp. 493–512.

Mullen, J. (1998) 'Booth opportunities', *People Management*, 16 April, pp. 50–51.

Murlis, H. (1996) *Pay at the Crossroads*. London: Institute of Personnel and Development.

Murlis, H. and Wright, V. (1993) 'Decentralising pay decisions: empowerment or abdication?', *Personnel Management*, March, pp. 28–33.

Organ, D.W. (1988) *Organizational Citizenship Behavior: The 'Good Soldier' Syndrome*. Lexington, Mass. Lexington Books.

Pfeffer, J. (1998) 'Six dangerous myths about pay', *Harvard Business Review*, Vol. 76, No. 3, pp. 108–119.

Pickard, J. (1990) 'When pay gets personal', *Personnel Management*, August, pp. 41–45.

Poole, M. (1987) 'Who are the profit sharers?', *Personnel Management*, January, pp. 34–36.

Poole, M. (1988) 'Factors affecting the development of employee financial participation in contemporary Britain: evidence from a national survey', *British Journal of Industrial Relations*, Vol. 26, March, pp. 21–36.

Poole, M. and Jenkins, G. (1988) 'How employees respond to profit sharing', *Personnel Management*, July, pp. 30–34.

Poole, M. and Jenkins, G. (1998) 'Human resource management and the theory of rewards: evidence from a national survey', *British Journal of Industrial Relations*, Vol. 36, No. 2, pp. 227–247.

Porter, L.W. and Lawler, E.E. (1968) *Management Attitudes and Performance*. Homewood, Ill.: Irwin.

Rajan, A. (1997) 'Employability in the finance sector: rhetoric *vs*. reality', *Human Resource Management Journal*, Vol. 7, No. 1, pp. 67–78.

Ramsay, H. and Haworth, N. (1984) 'Worker capitalists? Profit-sharing, capital sharing and juridicial forms of socialism', *Economic and Industrial Democracy*, Vol. 5, No. 3, pp. 295–324.

Ramsay, H., Leopold, J.W. and Hyman, J. (1986) 'Profit sharing and share ownership: an initial assessment', *Employee Relations*, Vol. 8, No. 1, pp. 23–26.

Randell, G.A. (1973) 'Performance appraisal: purposes, practices and conflicts, *Occupational Psychology*, Vol. 47, pp. 221–224.

Randle, K. (1997) 'Rewarding failure: operating a performance related pay system in pharmaceutical research', *Personnel Review*, Vol. 26, No. 3, pp. 187–200.

Rawlinson, H. (1988) 'Make awards count', *Personnel Journal*, October, pp. 140–141.

Reynolds, C. (1986) 'Compensation of overseas personnel', in Fanularo. J.J. (ed.) *Handbook of Human Resource Administration*, 2nd edn. New York: McGraw-Hill, pp. ?

Richardson, R. (1999) *Performance Related Pay in Schools: An Assessment of the Green Papers*, Report prepared for the National Union of Teachers. London: London School of Economics and Political Science.

Roethlisberger, F.G. and Dickson, W.J. (1939) *Management and the Worker*. Cambridge, Mass.: Harvard University Press.

Rogers, R. (1995) 'The psychological contract of trust – Part 1', *Executive Development*, Vol. 8, No. 1, pp. 15–19.

Rousseau, D.M. and Greller, M.M. (1994) 'Human resource practices: administrative contract makers', *Human Resource Management*, Vol. 33, No. 3, pp. 385–401.

Rowe, K.H. (1964) 'An appraisal of appraisals', *Journal of Management Studies*, Vol. 1, No. 1, pp. 1–25.

Rowland, D.C. and Greene, B. (1987) 'Incentive pay: productivity's own reward', *Personnel Journal*, March, pp. 48–57.

Roy, D. (1952) 'Quota restriction and goldbricking in a machine shop', *American Journal of Sociology*, Vol. 57, March, pp. 427–442.

Roy, D. (1953) 'Work satisfaction and social reward in quota achievement: an analysis of piecework incentive', *American Sociological Review*, Vol. 18, pp. 507–514.

Roy, D. (1955) 'Efficiency and "the fix": informal intergroup relations in a piecework machine shop', *American Journal of Sociology*, Vol. 60, pp. 255–266.

Sartre, J.-P. (1958) *Being and Nothingness: An Essay on Phenomenological Ontology* (translated by Barnes, H.E.). London: Methuen.

Scott, A. (1994) *Willing Slaves? British Workers under Human Resource Management*. Cambridge: Cambridge University Press.

Shaw, A.G. and Shaw Pirie, D. (1982) 'Payment by time systems', in Bowey, A.M. (ed.) *Handbook of Salary and Wage Systems*. Aldershot: Gower, pp. 297–308.

Sims, R.R. (1994) 'Human resource management's role in clarifying the new psychological contract', *Human Resource Management*, Vol. 33, No. 3, pp. 373–382.

Smith, I. (1992) 'Reward management and HRM', in Blyton, P. and Turnbull, P. (eds) *Reassessing Human Resource Management*. London: Sage, pp. 169–184.

Sparrow, P. (1996) 'Too good to be true?', *People Management*, 5 December, pp. 22–27.

Spindler, G. (1994) 'Psychological contracts in the workplace: a lawyer's view', *Human Resource Management*, Vol. 33, No. 3, pp. 325–333.

Stewart, J. and Walsh, K. (1994) 'Performance measurement: when performance can never be finally defined', *Public Money and Management*, April–June, pp. 45–49.

Storey, J. (1987) *Developments in the Management of Human Resources: An Interim Report*. Warwick papers in Industrial Relations No. 17. IRRU, School of Industrial and Business Studies, University of Warwick.

Storey, J. (1992) *Developments in the Management of Human Resources*. Oxford: Blackwell.

Swabe, A.I.R. (1989) 'Performance-related pay: a case study', *Employee Relations*, Vol. 11, No. 2, pp. 17–23.

Terry, N.G. and White, P.J. (1998) 'Occupational pension schemes and their interaction with HRM', *Human Resource Management Journal*, Vol. 8, No. 4, pp. 20–36.

Thompson, M. (1992) 'Pay and performance: the employer experience', *IMS Report*, No. 218. Brighton: Institute of Manpower Studies.

Thorndike, E.L. (1911) *Animal Intelligence*. New York: Macmillan.

*Thorpe, R. and Homan, G. (2000) *Strategic Reward Systems*, London: Pearson.

*Townley, B. (1989) 'Selection and appraisal: reconstituting "social relations"?', in Storey, J. (ed.) *New Perspectives on Human Resource Management*. London: Routledge, pp. 92–108.

Townley, B. (1990/1991) 'The politics of appraisal: lessons of the introduction of appraisal into UK universities', *Human Resource Management Journal*, Vol. 1, No. 2, pp. 27–44.

Townley, B. (1993a) 'Performance appraisal and the emergence of management', *Journal of Management Studies*, Vol. 30, No. 2, pp. 221–238.

Townley, B. (1993b) 'Foucault, power/knowledge, and its relevance for human resource management', *Academy of Management Review*, Vol. 18, No. 3, pp. 518–545.

Townley, B. (1994) *Reframing Human Resource Management: Power, Ethics and the Subject at Work*. London: Sage.

Tremblay, M., Sire, B. and Pelchat, A. (1998) 'A study of the determinants and of the impact of flexibility on employee benefit satisfaction', *Human Relations*, Vol. 51, No. 5, pp. 667–687.

Vavasour, P. and Vignali, C. (1999) 'Research into the motivational aspects of the company car: examined specifically in Calsberg-Tetley – Scotland', *Career Development International*, Vol. 4, No. 1, pp. 19–25.

Vroom, V.H. (1964) *Work and Motivation*. New York: John Wiley.

Walters, B., Hardin, T. and Schick, J. (1995) 'Top executive compensation: equity or excess? Implications for regaining American competitiveness', *Journal of Business Ethics*, Vol. 14, pp. 227–234.

Watson, T.J. (1994) *In Search of Management: Culture, Chaos and Control in Managerial Work*. London: Routledge.

Webb, G.H. (1982) 'Payment by results systems', in Bowey, A.M. (ed.) *Handbook of Salary and Wage Systems*. Aldershot: Gower, pp. 285–296.

White, M. (1981) *Payment Systems in Britain*. Aldershot: Gower.

White, M. (1982) 'Selecting a salary system', in Bowey, A.M. (ed.) *Handbook of Salary and Wage Systems*. Aldershot: Gower, pp. 265–281.

Williamson, O.E. (1975) *Markets and Hierarchies*. New York: Free Press.

Willmore, N. (1992) 'Is the grass always greener?', *Personnel Today*, 13 October, pp. 22–23.

Wilson, F., Haslam, S. and Bowey, A.M. (1982) 'Bonuses based on company performance', in Bowey, A.M. (ed.) *Handbook of Salary and Wage Systems*. Aldershot: Gower, pp. 321–347.

*Winstanley, D. and Stuart-Smith, K. (1996) 'Policing performance: the ethics of performance management', *Personnel Review*, Vol. 25 No. 6, pp. 66–84.

Wood, S. (1996) 'High commitment management and payment systems', *Journal of Management Studies*, Vol. 3, No. 1, pp. 53–77.

Wootton, B. (1962) *The Social Foundations of Wage Policy*. London: Allen & Unwin.

13

Employee involvement and empowerment

Len Holden

OBJECTIVES

- To examine the relationship of employee involvement and empowerment.
- To examine the relationship of employee involvement and human resource management.
- To explore the relationship between employee involvement and issues of control.
- To provide a definition of employee involvement, and examine its recent historical development, including cycles and waves and other discernible patterns.
- To examine the various types of employee involvement schemes practised in organisations.
- To critically examine the concept and practice of empowerment.
- To examine other employee involvement initiatives such as business process re-engineering (BPR) and total quality management (TQM).
- To investigate employee involvement practices in Sweden, Germany and Japan and other countries, and make a comparative evaluation of them.
- To examine recent developments in the European works council issue.

INTRODUCTION

In recent years there has been an enormous growth in the popularity of various employee involvement (EI) schemes under the umbrella of *empowerment*. In the light of these developments this chapter could equally have been called 'Empowerment' but, like TQM and quality circles before it, there is no way of telling whether this is a stepping stone on the way to another EI fad or a permanent fixture as a generic term that will supersede EI, just as EI superseded the term 'participation', and 'participation' superseded the term 'industrial democracy.' A starting point in answering this will be to differentiate the terms.

Employee involvement or empowerment?

Employee involvement is a term that has a history, and as Foy (1994: xvii) points out, '*empowering* people is as important today as *involving* them in the 1980s and getting them to *participate* in the 1970s.' But as Lashley (1997) comments:

> Such statements reveal little of the environmental, economic and industrial circumstances which have led to differences in focus and terminology. Nor do they consider the continuity of concerns which they reveal about employing organisations.
>
> (p. 10)

It is important to consider not only the economic and industrial context, but also the social and political context and, as Foy suggests, the historical context. In differentiating EI from empowerment it is clear that EI initiatives are support mechanisms for other managerial strategies such as TQM, business process re-engineering, high-performance work systems and the learning organisation. Empowerment is an initiative in its own right, which can be all-pervasive in organisational terms. In addition, both EI and empowerment can be seen to be managerially inspired, with circumscribed powers given to employees. They have also been strongly associated with the introduction of HRM strategies. Participation and, to a greater degree, industrial democracy allow greater autonomy to employees and their representatives, such as trade unions, who decide their own policies in reaction to organisational changes and managerial policy. A generic term is required for all forms of participation and most contemporary writers use the term *employee involvement* (EI). To differentiate the generic term EI from employee involvement associated with HRM schemes, the latter will be labelled *HRM EI* in this chapter.

Human resource management and employee involvement

As we have already noted, employee involvement is not a new concept. It has a rich and varied history, but in recent years many managerial initiatives have sprung up in its name. The best known of these have been quality circles, team briefing, teamworking and empowerment, which are often connected with organisational culture change schemes such as total quality management, customer service initiatives, business process re-engineering, and the learning organisation. This is the type of employee involvement that we have called HRM EI. It is likely to be part of an overall culture change, which may involve delayering, the creation of flatter organisational structures, and improvements in communication. Nevertheless, the language surrounding these initiatives has generated debates that are central to HRM. To involve employees is to gain their commitment to the organisational goals, and this has often been couched in terms of empowering employees to take responsibility for their roles and function within the organisation.

This resonant rhetoric has been used freely within the more popular managerial literature, often without thought or knowledge of how it translates into day-to-day situations, but in recent years studies have begun to examine these issues more closely. Can employee involvement exist only in unitarist frameworks, in which employee compliance is the main objective? How much responsibility can be given to employees? If one of the objectives of EI is to release employees' creative energies, what are the boundaries between creativity and responsibility? Are such schemes merely new attempts at reinforcing managerial control? What other factors impinge on the process? This chapter will attempt to answer some of these questions. The first part deals with the concept of employee involvement, and the second part examines more closely the concept of empowerment.

HRM AND EMPLOYEE INVOLVEMENT

HRM EI began to flourish in the 1980s in the guise of managerial policy initiatives inspired by the new 'excellence' movement and the rise of human resource management. Management gurus such as Tom Peters and Rosabeth Moss Kanter began to preach that people are the most valuable resource of an organisation, and that training and developing them, adequately rewarding their performance and involving them in organisational policy making, particularly at customer interface level, could only enhance employee motivation and thus performance. In this context there was a need for management to direct employees' efforts 'in pursuit of organisational goals to ensure that tasks are performed in cost-effective and market effective ways' (Hyman and Mason, 1995: 52). Successful companies carrying out such policies were lauded as exemplars of the new managerial approach (Peters and Waterman, 1982; Kanter, 1983).

Much of this rediscovery of the intrinsic worth of the employee was driven by the relative decline in US economic performance, particularly compared with Japan. A considerable literature was generated analysing the key to Japanese success, and one oft-cited element was the involvement of employees in work groups such as quality circles (Lawler, 1986).

Employee involvement was also expounded as a key instrument in the creation of HRM strategies, and the influential Harvard Business School HRM programme proposed by Beer *et al.* (1984) put 'employee influence' firmly in the centre of this approach. The Harvard HRM programme casts employees as one of the main 'stakeholders' in the organisation, and therefore 'it is critical that managers design and administer various mechanisms for employee influence' (Beer *et al.*, 1984: 11). They continue: 'Not only will their [the employees'] interests be heard, but there will be mechanisms to help shape their company's HRM policies' (p. 41).

This recognition of employees' and other stakeholders' interests raises a number of important questions for policy makers in the organisation:

> How much responsibility, authority, and power should the organisation voluntarily delegate and to whom? If required by government legislation to bargain with the unions or consult with workers' councils, how should management enter into these institutional arrangements? Will they seek to minimise the power and influence of these legislated mechanisms? Or will they share influence and work to create greater congruence of interests between management and the employee groups represented through these mechanisms? (Beer *et al.*, 1984: 8)

These questions raise further concerns about the inexactitude of the language of HRM EI. Terms such as 'influence', 'involvement', 'empowerment' and 'commitment' are blithely used by writers on HRM, without any attempt at definition or even clarification. Of the Harvard Business School academics, Walton has had the most to say on the subject. In his view, employee influence is most effective when employees have commitment to the organisation, and this can only be achieved if there is congruence between the HRM and general management policies of the organisation. Walton (1984a) calls this a 'high commitment' work system, and he proposes that 'high commitment is the essential ingredient in the future pattern of HRM' (p. 4). Walton (1984b) sees the HRM conception replacing previous systems 'because the common denomination among systems being replaced is the emphasis on imposing control' (p. 36). In other words, there is a move from 'control to commitment' (Walton, 1985: 36).

These arguments contain a number of non sequiturs. There is no guarantee that mutuality will 'elicit employee commitment', or that it will lead to increased economic effectiveness and human development, although this may be more likely to happen in organisations with positive HRM policies than in those that have negative employee relation policies. In essence, what is happening here is what Keenoy calls a reconstruction of the employment relationship through rhetoric and metaphor (Keenoy, 1990: 371; Keenoy and Anthony, 1992: 235).

As Goss (1994) states, 'the evidence suggests that commitment is a complex phenomenon that operates in different directions and at different levels. It is not something that can easily be generated or sustained, neither does it necessarily lead to improved performance' (p. 101). Noon (1992), in exploring these criticisms further, comments: 'Employees may resent the dissonance created between commitment to the task (encouraged by the individually based performance management mechanisms) and commitment to the company (encouraged through the rhetoric of culture and the rewards of promotion and employment security)' (p. 23).

The economic downturn in the early 1990s led some commentators to ask whether HRM is 'recession proof' (Beardwell and Holden, 1994: 686). Storey (1989: 8) has identified 'hard' and 'soft' types of HRM, which may sit well with different types of organisational culture and, we posit, different economic climates. Legge (1989: 33) has alluded to 'tough love' HRM in such contexts, and this is readily witnessed in the experience of such 'HRM companies' as IBM, with its forced redundancy programme (Noon, 1992: 24). It is pertinent to ask, therefore, how human resource management changes under such circumstances, and how employee commitment and involvement are affected. Marchington (1995) proposes that EI will be considerably different in nature, or may not exist at all, in organisations that practise forms of hard HRM, compared with those that practise soft HRM. In organisations that practise hard HRM:

> EI may not be seen as important by senior managers, given the emphasis on tight cost control, deskilled jobs, and a lack of investment in training. In others, EI may be little more than one-way communications channels, designed merely to convey the latest news to employees and indicate to them the merits of management's decision. In these cases, if EI is practised, it is likely to take a rather diluted and marginal form. (p. 280)

HRM can also be affected by changes in the economic climate, and Holden (1996) cites the experience of an organisation in the banking and finance sector. This company was an early convert to HRM, and initiated policies that contained mechanisms to increase employee influence. In the boom economy of the late 1980s 'soft' policies were emphasised, including for example training for TQM and other EI measures. In the harsher climate of recessional Britain in the 1990s, downsizing and retrenchment became the order of the day. Survival meant a move to hard HRM policies. In this climate the soft mechanisms of EI tended to be overlooked and even ignored.

Control and employee involvement

One important element in the EI equation is the degree of control given to managers and non-managerial employees. For example, informational, communicational and consultational types of participation tend to come from management initiatives, and are more likely to be controlled by management. However, the term 'control' itself is problematic. For example, a worker can feel in control of his or her work process (the day-to-day operations), but have little control or say in the running of the organisation in terms of influencing overall policy or strategy. Second, various issues at workplace level will allow more control and influence by the workforce than others.

These problems have long been recognised in the vast literature generated around this important subject (Edwards, 1987: 90). Drucker (1961), for example, states that 'control is an ambiguous word. It means the ability to direct oneself and one's work. It can also mean domination of one person by another' (p. 128). These positive and negative views of control have spawned a parallel literature rooted in the acceptance and rejection of capitalist values, of which the latter is represented strongly by the *labour process* theory school inspired by the work of Braverman (1974) (see also Chapters 3, 5 and 10).

Control according to the labour process school of thought postulates that technology controls the work process in its drive to help fulfil the requirements of the capitalist organisation (i.e. profits) in response to intensive competition. This obviates the necessity to control the work process in order to extract the maximum output in relation to labour cost and the ability of labour to resist control (Salaman, 1979). According to Braverman (1974), the ability to resist control and exert greater autonomy is higher among workers whose skills are in great demand, and less among workers in unskilled or deskilled situations. Thus deskilling has considerable implications for control and the way it is applied and viewed by participants (employees, managers, employers) and hence for participation schemes, especially in institutions such as banks, which have undergone intensive technological change and reorganisation in the past five years.

Since Braverman's work there have been a number of refinements and challenges to his thesis, many sharing the Marxian perspective. Edwards (1979) focuses on the move away from more coercive methods rooted in new technology, with its associations with Fordist and Taylorist managerial control mechanisms, to bureaucratic control systems aimed at the dual goals of dissolving class solidarity and maximising commitment to, and dependence on, the firm. 'Promotion, pay, security and other benefits go to employees who are good corporate citizens, who are loyal to the company, share its values and integrate themselves and their families into the enterprise community' (Lincoln and Kalleberg, 1990: 9). Such managerial initiatives fit particularly well with HRM conceptualisations.

Friedman (1977) has divided managerial control systems into direct control and responsible autonomy. *Direct control* is associated with rules, regulation, work organisation and technology that directly control the behaviour and work rate of the employee. This is strongly associated with the Fordist–Taylorist approach. *Responsible autonomy* allows the worker and the work team a degree of control over the work process, and

> attempts to harness the adaptability of labour power by giving workers leeway and encouraging them to adapt to changing situations in a manner beneficial to the firm. To do this top managers give workers status, authority and responsibility. Top managers try to win their loyalty, and coopt their organisations to the firm's ideals (that is, the competitive struggle) ideologically.
>
> (Friedman, 1977: 78).

This again has strong resonances with developments in HRM in the 1980s and 1990s, particularly in terms of participation schemes such as TQM, which aim to enhance commitment to the organisation by allowing the workforce a degree of autonomy. Edwards (1992: 390) points out, however, that HRM apologists such as Walton (1985), who speak of a move from control to commitment, partly by means of employee involvement and participation policies, should perceive that commitment 'is still a form of control'.

Burawoy (1979) has also developed a dual perspective of management regimes that rely on coercion or consent. Earlier capitalist systems relied heavily on the former approach, and adopted autocratic methods of workforce control, particularly in response to intensive capitalist competition. Latterly the adoption of more subtle approaches to the employment relationship has emphasised policies designed to induce commitment in the employee. This has been caused to some degree by the softening of overt autocratic systems by state regulation and welfare policy. Burawoy (1983) sees such new approaches as creating a hegemonic regime under which coercive compliance is replaced by normative control, as managers make concessions in order to persuade employees to cooperate in furthering the success of the organisation. Once again we can discern echoes of HRM policy initiatives in such hegemonic systems.

We shall return to some of these questions later in the chapter, but at this point it is appropriate to examine some of the mechanisms and definitions of employee involvement, beginning with communication.

EMPLOYEE INVOLVEMENT AND COMMUNICATION

All organisations need communication systems to function, whether these are overtly recognised or subconsciously taken for granted. In the 1990s it was increasingly recognised by many employers and managers that the creation of effective communication is an extremely important aspect of the efficient running of organisations. Communication is a complex series of processes operating at all levels within organisations, ranging from the 'grapevine', heavily laden with rumour, to formalised systems such as joint consultative committees (JCCs) or works councils. These can operate at the localised level of the shopfloor or office between supervisor and staff and the staff themselves, or at a distance by means of representatives such as union officials or messages from on high from the boardroom or the chief executive, to various branches or subsidiaries of large and complex organisations. They can be one way or two way, top down or bottom up and both top down and bottom up, as well as across the organisation.

It is being increasingly recognised that messages to and, equally important, from the workforce have considerable significance. They are important for conveying the organisation's mission, business aims and objectives, and its general ethos or culture. They are needed to enable the thoughts and feelings of the workforce to be expressed and, of equal significance, heeded and acted upon. Such policies are being heavily influenced and underscored by HRM practices.

Communication systems also carry implicit messages about the mediation of power within organisations. Employee involvement communication systems are processes that enable the workforce to have a greater say in decision-making to varying degrees, with the concomitant loss of managerial prerogatives – an issue that can create conflict, as well as attempting to allay it.

However, even the simplest message can be misunderstood or misconstrued because of the complex influences that act on the communication process. Equally important, and potentially disastrous, is the fact that communication channels can send conflicting messages. An oft-cited case is the company that encouraged employees to take up share options which entitled them to attend the annual shareholders' meeting, where they were told how successfully the company had performed over the previous year. Many of these same employees were also in the union, to which management communicated later that because of the company's poor performance over the previous year, the pay increases requested could not be met!

Employee involvement: history and development

The idea of involving the workforce may seem self-evident, as employees must be involved in order to do their job. It has long been recognised, however, that doing a job does not necessarily mean being interested in it or doing it well. The school of human relations promoted by thinkers in the field such as Mayo, Vroom, Likert and Maslow, among others, has drawn conclusions from their various studies that positive motivational factors engendered by such methods as employee involvement may develop a more creative, interested and therefore more productive workforce.

Even though employee involvement is just one aspect of organisational communication it is, nevertheless, wide ranging and diverse in its forms. Types of EI also evolve and change with managerial vogues, which are governed by political, economic and social pressures. For example, the First World War witnessed a considerable growth in worker militancy together with an increased popularity of left-wing ideologies, many of which espoused various forms of workers' control, one example being Guild Socialism (Cole, 1917). The Bolshevik revolution in Russia in 1917 also had a significant impact on work relationships, as Marxist ideology is based on an analysis of how capitalism exploits the proletariat in the workplace. These influences had, and still have, a considerable impact on arguments surrounding work-related issues. One attempt to mollify these forces in Britain was to acknowledge legally, in the form of Whitley Councils, that employees and their representatives (trade unions) had some say in negotiations over pay and working conditions. Despite good intentions from some parties on both sides of industry, these arrangements largely fell into disuse once recession hit the British economy after 1921 and the threat of workforce militancy receded.

It was not until the Second World War that a popular revival occurred in EI schemes. The need for huge productivity increases to meet the war effort led workers to demand something in return – a greater say in the operation of the workplace. Works committees or joint consultative committees were set up in many factories. Some continued in existence after the war, but management and unions lost interest in them in the 1950s, and many fell into decline when there was a preference for direct collective bargaining via unions, employer organisations and employers. Nevertheless, there was a considerable revival in the atmosphere of industrial democracy in the 1960s and 1970s, and shop stewards were to be found filling delegational positions (Marchington et al., 1992). Debates concerning the extent to which these committees existed, and the real power they afforded the workforce, still engage social and economic historians.

In the 1970s the Bullock Committee Report (1977) echoed an increased interest in industrial democracy. There was a growing consciousness that, while politics and society were increasingly being 'democratised', the world of work did not reflect this trend. In addition, British membership of the European Community influenced the Bullock Committee to examine forms of industrial democracy among its European partners, such as co-determination in Germany and Sweden, and some societies where more radical forms of employee involvement were being undertaken, such as the worker self-management practised in Yugoslavia and at Mondragon in Spain. These practices attracted considerable interest, as did worker-director schemes and the formation of workers' cooperatives, which often happened in UK companies under threat of liquidation (Broekmeyer, 1970; Brannen et al., 1976; Eccles, 1981; Thomas and Logan, 1982).

The political climate that had engendered industrial democracy swiftly changed under Thatcher's Conservative government, which tarred such policies with the brush of left-wing ideology, and in the economic and political climate of the 1980s managerial EI schemes associated with HRM became popular.

Cycles and waves of participation

It is apparent from even this brief history that numerous influences have a bearing on the type, strength and sustainability of various participation schemes and trends. Unsurprisingly, therefore, commentators have attempted to discover patterns of EI and to place them into a theoretical framework.

For example, the relationship between the introduction of profit sharing with a high level of employment and industrial unrest down to the First World War has been indicated by Church (1971). Ramsay (1977, 1983) has argued that there are cycles of participation:

> Managements have been attracted to the idea of participation when their control over labour has been perceived to be under pressure in some way. This perception has coincided with experience of a growing challenge from labour to the legitimacy of capital and its agents. In Britain these challenges have coincided with the impact and aftermath of two world wars, and with the rise of shop floor union organisation at the same time as squeezed profit margins in the 1960s and 1970s. In each case mounting pressure, including demands for 'industrial democracy' from sections of the labour movement, helped to precipitate management response.   (Ramsay, 1983: 204)

Marchington *et al.* (1992) have pointed to 'waves' of employee involvement within organisations, which respond to external trends and cause the institution of new schemes and the revamping of old existing ones. For example, a quarter of organisations in their survey sample had introduced their current schemes (survey period 1989–91) between 1980 and 1984, 'and several of these were share ownership schemes which appear to have been stimulated by legislative changes from 1978 onwards' (p. 25). Other schemes such as team briefing were introduced in the early 1980s' recession to communicate 'gloom and doom' messages such as pay freezes and voluntary severance. Over half of the schemes of their survey group had been introduced within the previous five years, and tended to be TQM programmes of various types. The 'wave' concept, they point out,

> is analytically more useful than cycles, in that it does not presuppose any automatic repetition of events in an historical pattern, or any all embracing theory of waxing and waning which applies in the same way across all workplaces. On the contrary waves come in different shapes and sizes and last for different lengths of time in different organisations.   (p. 26)

Thus the importance of EI can be understood only if it is viewed as being central to the organisation, and not necessarily prominent. For example, a joint consultative committee may achieve a central position in an organisation over time, although the most prominent new measure may be team briefings. If the JCC becomes less important or dies out, another scheme may replace it and attain the status of centrality. Whether schemes are retained, reformed or dropped depends on multifarious influences within organisations, for example the values and beliefs of managers, which interact with other influences in complex ways.

Poole has attempted to construct a theoretical framework to explain these influences. He sees workers' participation and control as being understood as a specific manifestation of power. This is linked with 'underlying or latent power resources and a series of values that either buttress particular power distributions or facilitate their successful challenge' (Poole, 1986: 28). The relationship of power sources is illustrated in Figure 13.1.

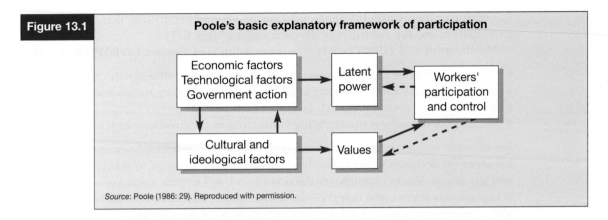

Figure 13.1   **Poole's basic explanatory framework of participation**

Source: Poole (1986: 29). Reproduced with permission.

Poole (1986) postulates that:

> Workers' participation and control are reflections of the latent power of particular industrial classes, parties or groups and the 'value' climate which may or may not be favourable to participation experiments. These values thus mediate between certain structural factors associated with latent power and their realisation in the form of workers' participation and control. It will also be seen that the principal structural factors associated with the latent power of the main industrial classes, parties or groups are economic factors, such as the levels of employment, the profit margins of particular companies, the levels of competition, the degree of industrial concentration and periods of economic 'disintegration'; technological factors, such as the approximation of the technology of a company to a given point on the 'technical scale', the degree of complexity and education involved in any given task and the effects of the micro-electronic revolution; and finally, various forms of government action such as legislation on labour issues, its intervention in the workings of the economic system and so on.
> (p. 28)

Finally, 'values about participation and control are shaped by the existing levels of workers' participation and control, latent power, government action and ideologies' (p. 29).

While this framework pinpoints the main factors influencing the types and styles of employee participation and control, it cannot clearly demonstrate how these factors interact to produce such systems. Nevertheless, it is a useful model to aid understanding of these complex processes.

Definitions of employee involvement

There is an enormous range of employee involvement schemes, varying from those that are informational mechanisms to full-blown democratic systems where employees have as much say in the decision-making processes as does management. This makes an all-encompassing definition problematic. In addition, different labels have been attached to these processes, such as employee or worker participation, industrial democracy, organisational communications, co-determination, and employee influence, each of which has its own definitions.

Wall and Lischerson (1977) state that there are three elements central to the concept of participation: influence, interaction and information sharing. Marchington *et al.* (1992) divide definitions into three categories: those that refer 'to employees taking part or having a say or share in decision making, with no attempt to quantify their impact on the process'; those that 'refer to participation as concerned with the extent to which employees may influence managerial actions'; and those that 'link together participation and the control over decision making' (pp. 6, 7).

Marchington *et al.* (1992) believe that these definitions also need to take into account:

- the *degree* of involvement (the extent to which employees influence the final decision);
- the *level* of involvement (whether at job, departmental or organisational level);
- the *forms* of involvement (direct, indirect and financial);
- the *range* of the subject matter being considered in the involvement scheme.

For example, quality circles may have a high degree of direct employee involvement and influence on decisions at workplace level, but be limited in range to matters of teamwork and job design. Works councils, on the other hand, will involve employee representatives at organisational level, and may consider a wide range of areas such as business and industrial relations strategies, in joint decision-making with the management.

One problem with this tabular representation (Table 13.1) is that some EI schemes may pervade many or all levels of the organisation, for example financial participation. Others may cascade through many levels, such as team briefings (Ramsay, 1991). Team briefings could also fall into both the 'informational' and 'communicational' categories. Another problem is that the degree of participation with one scheme could differ from one organisation to another. For example, JCCs could vary in power from merely rubber-stamping management decisions to forming joint consultational mechanisms covering a rich variety of organisational topics.

Marchington *et al.* (1992: 13) divide EI schemes into four categories:

- *Downward communications* (top down), for example from managers to other employees. This includes forms of EI such as house journals, company newspapers, employee reports and regular briefing sessions, often with videos as well.

Table 13.1 Some types, levels and degrees of employee involvement

Degree	Levels of involvement		
	Local (workplace level)	Both local and distant	Distant (company or organisational level)
Control (by workers or workers and management together)	Worker self-management		Worker self-management of cooperatives
Co-determinational	Union shop steward representation		JCCs; works councils; worker directors; representation union–management negotiations
Consultational (two-way communication)	Quality circles; job enrichment; suggestion scheme; appraisal	Attitude survey; customer care; TQM, email, Internet, intranet	Video conferencing, email, Internet, intranet
Communicational	Team briefings; department or group meetings	Email, Internet, intranet	Mass meetings, email, Internet, intranet
Informational (top down)	Noticeboards, email, Internet, intranet	Memos; briefs, email Internet, intranet	Company newspaper/ magazine; bulletin

- *Upwards, problem-solving forms,* which are designed to tap into employees' knowledge and opinion, either at an individual level or through the mechanism of small groups. This includes practices such as suggestion schemes, attitude surveys, quality circles and total quality management and customer care programmes.
- *Financial participation* via schemes that attempt to link rewards of individuals to the performance of the unit or the enterprise as a whole. This includes schemes such as profit sharing, employee share ownership, and value-added or establishment-wide bonus arrangements.
- *Representative participation,* in which employees are involved through representatives drawn from among their number, often – though not always – on the basis of union membership, for example JCCs, advisory councils, works councils, co-determination, and collective bargaining.

In many organisations a combination of these forms of communication and EI schemes will exist, hopefully supporting and complementing each other.

In a book of this nature it would be impossible to examine all of these approaches, but a closer study of some of the more popular and recent schemes in each category may serve to illustrate current trends.

Downward communications

The company magazine or newspaper

One of the most common methods of downward communication, which has witnessed a considerable increase over the past 20 years, is the company newspapers or magazine (CBI, 1989). Reviewing methods of communication in six surveys of organisations conducted between 1975 and 1983, Townley (1989) indicates that most put the company newspaper or house journal as either the most popular or the second most popular form of communication. The problem is that they can vary in quality from amateur desktop-published affairs produced by employees in their 'spare' time, to the lavish glossy productions that have been part of the communications systems of many large companies for a number of years.

There is also the question of editorial control, which may restrict the messages conveyed to the workforce. Continual glowing reports of the company successes or anodyne and meaningless information may have negative results in the long run. Genuine expressions of employee feelings via letters pages or forthright quotes from employee representatives, even of a negative nature, may show the management's desire to achieve fairness. Of course, the judgement of the editor will come into play in deciding the content of the newspaper or journal, which in turn will be affected by the organisational culture and management views.

For example, during a dispute a militant shop steward called the managing director a 'fascist', which the personnel director urged the editor to expunge as being insulting. The editor defended the decision to retain the quote on the grounds that he had sought a comment from the shop steward, and not to print it would look like corporate censorship. In addition, such a quote was so patently absurd that it would have a negative effect. In the event the quote was left to stand, and the prediction of the editor proved true when the shop steward was spurned by his fellow employees and the union felt moved to apologise publicly for the comment (Wilkinson, 1989). Unfortunately, many company journal editors are still unable or unwilling to follow such boldly democratic policies, and the workforce often regards publications as a conduit for managerial views. Given their primarily one-way nature and editorial control, this is not surprising.

Team briefings

There has been a considerable increase in team briefings in the past five years, although they have been in existence in some organisations for longer (Marchington *et al.*, 1992). They are often used to cascade information or managerial messages throughout the organisation. The teams are usually based around a common production or service area, rather than an occupation, and commonly comprise between 4 and 15 people. The leader of the team is normally the manager or supervisor of the section, and should be trained in the principles and skills of how to brief. The meetings last for no more than 30 minutes, and time should be left for questions from employees. Meetings should be held at least monthly or on a regular pre-arranged basis.

Surveys often reveal considerable satisfaction with team briefings by both employers and management (e.g. CBI, 1989) as they are effective in reinforcing company aims and objectives at the personal, face-to-face level. However, Ramsay (1992a) urges caution in accepting this rosy picture, because success depends on 'context to a significant extent' (p. 223). For example, briefings might be postponed or cancelled at times when business is brisk, which may lessen commitment to holding them at all in the long run. If the intention is to undermine union messages, the success will very much depend on the strength of the union and the conviction of the management. A sceptical and undertrained management and supervisory force can do much to undermine the effectiveness of team briefings.

Upwards, problem-solving forms of communication

These schemes can also be described as two-way communication, and are most associated with 'new' managerial concepts such as HRM. They are clearly aimed at increasing employee motivation and 'influence' within the organisation, but usually at a localised level – workshop, office or service area. They also aim to improve employee morale, loyalty and commitment, with a view to increasing service and efficiency. Another facet of these types of schemes is that they facilitate acceptance of changes in work practices, functional flexibility and new technology, as well as engendering an atmosphere conducive to cooperation and team-building (Ramsay, 1992a).

Quality circles

One of the first methods identified with the 'new' involved approach to management was the quality circle (QC). This first arrived in Britain via the USA from Japan, although the concept was implanted in Japan in the years after the Second World War by two US consultants, W. Edwards Deming and J.M. Duran (Clutterbuck and Crainer, 1990).

QCs are made up of 6–10 employees, with regular meetings held weekly or fortnightly during working time. Their principal aim is to 'identify problems from their own area and, using data collection methods and statistical techniques acquired during circle training, analyse these problems and devise possible solutions; the proposed solutions are then presented formally to the manager of the section who may decide to implement the circle's proposal' (Brennan, 1991).

Tremendous interest was shown in QCs by British managers in the early 1980s, but within a few years they began to decline in popularity. A number of reasons have been identified for this decline, but principal among these was the attitude of middle managers. For example, it is crucial that a manager or supervisor with the requisite qualities and training leads the circle. Technical competence alone is not enough, and studies began to highlight the need for interpersonal skills. Some managers also felt that their power and authority were undermined by the QC, and others lacked commitment in the initial stages, which had the effect of making the circles difficult to develop effectively. There were also difficulties from overenthusiastic facilitators who deliberately gave an overtly positive but false impression of the circle's operation, possibly for career progression reasons. This made it difficult to identify problems within the circle or improve its effectiveness (Brennan, 1991). Suspicion of circles could be engendered if they were seen as a way of undermining trade union functions. Lack of consultation with the union, particularly when setting up QCs, often bred suspicion that this was another anti-union management ploy, and the initiative was therefore effectively undermined by non-cooperative attitudes.

Other circles failed because suggestions by the workforce were not in fact applied or even considered, thus rendering them a waste of time in the minds of the participants. Finally, many circles simply 'ran out of steam' after the initial burst of enthusiasm. The need for continual reinforcement of their function and purpose was evident (Collard and Dale, 1989; Ramsay, 1992a).

Teamworking

Teamworking is one of the most recent initiatives in EI; like QCs it originated in Japan. As yet it is not as widespread as TQM, but its influence is gradually spreading. It emphasises problem solving in a teamworking situation, and in order to function effectively it must be bound up with policies of task flexibility and job rotation (Price, 1989). Teams vary in size from seven to ten people, or even more, and large elements of training are necessary to ensure that workers, team leaders, supervisors and managers have the requisite skills to enable the team to function efficiently. A large part of such training is of a managerial or interpersonal skill and communicational nature, as well as of a technical nature.

Financial participation

Financial participation differs from other forms of employee involvement in that it is less likely to involve employees in consultational or decisional processes. The general aim of such schemes is to enhance employee commitment to the organisation by linking the performance of the organisation to that of the employee. Thus, it is argued, employees are more likely to be positively motivated and involved if they have a financial stake in the company through having a share of the profits or through being a company shareholder. Although such schemes are by no means new – early profit-sharing schemes were in operation in the nineteenth century (Church, 1971) – their recent popularity has been partially spawned by the Conservative government's philosophy of creating a property-owning democracy in an attempt to individualise work and societal relationships, and also by the rise in human resource management initiatives (Schuller, 1989).

In addition, legislation has been introduced to bolster and lay down legal parameters for such schemes in the form of the Finance Acts 1978, 1980, 1984, 1987 and 1989. Evidence suggests that most managers' aims in introducing forms of financial participation are for positive reasons associated with employee motivation, rather than attempts to undermine trade union influence (although this is an objective in some organisations), and schemes were indeed welcomed by most employees in the organisation (Badden *et al.*, 1989; CBI, 1989; Poole and Jenkins, 1990a, 1990b; Marchington *et al.*, 1992).

Types of financial participation

Schuller (1989: 128) categorises financial participation schemes on a scale that ranges from individualism to collectivism. Towards the individual end there are personal equity plans, profit-related pay, profit-sharing and employee share option schemes; at the collective end there are workers' cooperatives, management buyouts, pension fund participation and wage earner funds.

Of these categories, individual forms of financial participation are the most common, especially profit-related pay and share option schemes (CBI, 1989; Marchington *et al.*, 1992). Given the controversy in recent years concerning the maladministration of pension funds, most notably that of the Maxwell organisation (although this is by no means a rare example), it would be logical to expect to see increased demands by employees for some representation on the boards that oversee these funds (for a more detailed examination of pension funds see Schuller, 1986, 1989).

Profit-related pay and employee share options

As already noted, profit-related pay schemes have a long pedigree, and were stimulated by the Finance Act of 1978. In essence, profit-sharing or profit-related pay schemes are those 'where a cash bonus or payment is made to employees based upon the share price, profits or dividend announcement at the end of the financial year' (Marchington *et al.*, 1992: 11).

Employee share options are schemes 'using part of the profits generated or earnings of employees to acquire shares for the employee in the company concerned, or discounted shares on privatisation or public quotation' (Marchington *et al.*, 1992: 11).

There are four main types of scheme (Poole and Jenkins, 1990b):

- profit sharing – with cash rewards;
- profit sharing – through shares in the company (approved deferred share trust, ADST);
- save-as-you-earn share option schemes (SAYE);
- executive share schemes.

There is a degree of overlap in these schemes: for example, ADST and SAYE both concern share options, but the former is often bracketed with profit sharing, where shares are part of the reward, and the latter with employee saving schemes, which lead to the purchase of shares. A considerable amount of financial legislation, and the fact that successive chancellors of the exchequer have made over ten concessions in successive budgets since 1978, bear testimony to the importance that the government gives to such schemes. Between 1978 and 1990 the Inland Revenue approved, for tax purposes, 6500 schemes, which are made up of 909 ADSTs, 919 SAYEs and 4521 executive share option schemes (Dunn *et al.*, 1991: 1).

How effective are these schemes, given their apparent popularity? In general terms, commentators and researchers divide into two basic camps – the optimists and the more sceptical. The optimists are backed by a plethora of positive literature emanating from consultants and the more popular business journals. The question of success, however, rests on the criteria by which they are judged, and here opinion is much more mixed, but even in-depth studies differ in some of their conclusions (Badden *et al.*, 1989; Poole and Jenkins, 1990b; Dunn *et al.*, 1991; Marchington *et al.*, 1992).

Poole and Jenkins (1990a, 1990b) represent the more optimistic view, but they still distinguish between the effect of such schemes on employee attitudes and the effect on employee behaviour. They believe that employee attitudes are favourably affected in the sense that employees have increased their identity with company goals, feel more involved, and have a more positive attitude towards the company. 'Indeed, the most important impact of profit sharing is almost certainly to improve organisational identification and commitment and hence, indirectly, to enhance industrial relations performance' (Poole and Jenkins, 1990a: 96).

Ramsay *et al.* (1986) are less optimistic in their view, and claim that many surveys play down the negative effects; while Dunn *et al.* (1991: 14), using evidence from their longitudinal survey, claim that there is not even a correlation between improved employee attitudes and the introduction of such schemes. Both studies point to the fact that the 'them and us' attitude that the schemes attempt to break down may well reinforce the status quo, because executives and older workers tend to be the majority of employee shareholders as younger and less senior employees cannot afford shares.

Marchington *et al.* (1992) and Dunn *et al.* (1991) also state that a number of internal and external factors affect employee attitudes and behaviours, and these are difficult to disentangle from perceptions of financial participation schemes. Marchington *et al.* (1992) state that employees viewed the scheme much more negatively in one company that was unable to pay out dividends on shares because of market pressures, than in another company that was relatively financially buoyant.

A problem with all the surveys to date is that they suffer from unrepresentativeness and a lack of comparative time-series data. Some surveys choose a qualitative in-depth approach and others a quantitative wide-survey approach; only one survey has conducted a longitudinal survey, but this was in only one company.

Representative participation

Joint consultative committees

Apart from collective bargaining, the most common form of representative participation in the UK is joint consultative committees. As already noted, these received a considerable impetus in the Second World War, declined somewhat in the 1950s and 1960s, and witnessed a revival in the 1970s, which – according to various surveys – has continued. According to Badden *et al.* (1989) one-third of companies had consultation machinery, and the CBI (1989) survey puts this figure at 47%, though both stress that such mechanisms are more likely to exist in larger organisations. Shop stewards also tend to be employee representatives in unionised firms, indicating a retreat from the view held by many unionists that JCCs were mere talking shops without power, set up to dupe the employees and undermine union presence.

In examining JCCs it soon becomes evident that they operate differently in various organisations and sectors, at different levels within organisations and with different degrees of power (Marchington, 1989b). Thus in one organisation they could be rubber-stamping bodies for management initiatives, discussing at the most 'tea, toilets and trivia', and in other organisations they could be genuine conduits for the expression of employees' views, with some degree of decisional power.

According to Marchington *et al.* (1992) joint consultation is defined as

a mechanism for managers and employee representatives to meet on a regular basis, in order to exchange views, to utilise members' knowledge and expertise, and to deal with matters of common interest which are not the subject of collective bargaining. (p. 11)

Organisations with a strong union presence attempt to keep issues such as pay bargaining off the JCC agenda, leaving them to collective bargaining issues. This has led some commentators to the view that management in organisations that encourage employee participation may see JCCs as a less important channel of communication. This relative powerlessness may 'often leave JCCs with a marginal role in labour management relationships' (Ramsay, 1991). Marchington (1989a; Marchington *et al.*, 1992) is, however, more optimistic, and sees their role as often complementing and supporting other channels of communication and EI, such as collective bargaining.

All commentators agree that if JCCs are given only unimportant issues to deal with, then employees themselves will view them as ineffectual, and they will be marginalised.

Ramsay (1992a) recommends that for the joint consultation medium to be effective it needs to be consulted in advance of decision-making, to have a representative range of issues to discuss, to be adequately resourced with proper administrative back-up and to have an effective feedback mechanism to employees; management representation should be seen to be of the requisite level (that is, senior managers); action on proposals should be carried out quickly; and unions should be kept officially informed.

Other forms of consultation are types of co-determination such as works councils, often backed by government legislation as in Germany, Belgium and the Netherlands. These will be considered later in the chapter.

EMPOWERMENT

Empowerment is a concept that gained immense popularity in the 1990s, and looks set to continue as a popular organisational initiative in the twenty-first century. It is a managerial ideology in its own right as well as being used with other initiatives and strategies such as BPR, TQM and the learning organisation. It is strongly associated with culture change initiatives, delayering and restructuring, and usually involves devolving power and responsibilities to teams at workplace or customer level (Arkin, 1995).

Defining empowerment

Various one-dimensional definitions of empowerment have emanated from the practitioner literature. Typical of this view is Cook and Macaulay's (1997) definition of empowerment as 'a change-management tool which helps organisations create an environment where every individual can use his or her abilities and energies to satisfy the customer' (p. 54). Its all-embracing nature skirts over issues of how employees use their abilities, and whether there are boundaries to responsibilities, the degree and type of power employees enjoy, power relations between employee, managers, individuals, teams, customers and the context of empowerment. Both Wilkinson (1998) and Lashley (1997) have commented that empowerment is influenced by historical, economic, social and political factors, and in attempting a definition the context in which it is practised must be considered. Wilkinson (1998) defines empowerment as a managerially led initiative:

> Unlike industrial democracy there is no notion of workers having a right to a say: it is employers who decide whether and how to empower employees. While there is a wide range of programmes and initiatives which are titled empowerment and they vary as to the extent of power which employees actually exercise, most are purposefully designed not to give workers a very significant role in decision making but rather to secure an enhanced employee contribution to the organisation. Empowerment takes place within the context of a strict management agenda.
>
> (p. 40)

Empowerment is thus a managerially controlled phenomenon operating at a work-based rather than a strategic level within the organisation. Honold (1997) implicitly acknowledges this by seeing empowerment as 'control of one's work, autonomy on the job, variations of teamwork, and pay systems that link pay with performance' (p. 202). She further divides empowerment into five groupings: leadership, the individual empowered state, collaborative work, structural or procedural change, and the multidimensional perspective that encompasses the other four categories.

The leader's role in creating an empowering context

In Honold's first category the leader must set the context and cultural climate for the implementation of empowerment schemes. If by implication power is to be delegated then employees need the requisite training, development and support mechanisms and processes (such as team building) to enable this to happen. As an initiative this conforms strongly to Wilkinson's (1998) concept of empowerment – that is, being managerially led.

The individual perspective of empowerment

Honold (1997) reminds us 'that if power is not taken by those it is bestowed upon then, there is no empowerment' (p. 204). In other words individual employees must feel that it is a worthwhile process for them, for example the satisfaction of gaining influence over events. Menon (1995) surveyed 311 employees in a company and found that greater job autonomy and meaningfulness of the job led to greater perceived control and greater empowerment. He found that the greater the empowerment the greater was the motivation to work among employees. This also led to less job stress and increased employee commitment to organisational goals.

Collaborative work as empowerment

The individual usually has to work with others, and the element of empowerment combining collaborative efforts has to be acknowledged, such as via quality circles or teamworking measures. This means developing the ability of employees to work together and cooperate, and using this sharing process to empower themselves further (Rothstein, 1995).

Structural and procedural change as empowerment

This is concerned with the nuts and bolts of the empowerment process, associated for example with TQM systems. Ward (1993: 4) believes that such systems have three crucial components:

- clarity and consistency of the organisation's overall production and development goals, and an alignment of all systems and management and employee levels towards those goals;

- ongoing evaluation and development of the professional needs of the employees, with preparation for a greater sense of process ownership and accountability;
- assurance of congruence between corporate goals, management goals and the goals of the organisation's employees.

Such goals can be achieved only by improving internal and external organisational communications. The use of electronic channels such as email, Internet and intranet systems has important ramifications for the effective operations of such systems.

Multidimensional perspectives on empowerment

Honold's (1997: 206) final category shows that one approach is insufficient for empowerment to be effective. Others believe that combining education, leading, mentoring and supporting, providing and structuring is more likely to enable empowerment systems to be successful. Human resource systems should also be fully supportive of these components, providing a contextual framework within which empowerment systems are able to operate. This means linking the empowerment process to the vision, goals and aims of the organisation, through HRD, reward systems and employee relations systems combined with adequate feedback measures.

The benefits of empowerment to the individual and the organisation

Table 13.2 outlines the proclaimed benefits of empowerment for individual employees and for the organisation. It can be deduced from this table that the benefits to the organisation outweigh those to the staff. However, before embarking on a critique of empowerment it would be apposite to see how it fits into HRM systems as a whole.

Empowerment and 'soft' and 'hard' systems of HRM

Claydon and Doyle (1996) distinguish between forms of empowerment in 'soft' and 'hard' HRM systems. The 'soft' aspect can 'provide enhanced opportunities for involvement in decision making' and 'employees will gain those feelings of control, personal efficacy and self-determination which constitute the state of being empowered' (p. 3). They also point out a second but extremely important aspect of the 'soft' system, in that empowerment connects with organisational learning. 'More open communication, shared problem-solving geared to continuous improvement, and a related willingness to expose existing organisational arrangements to critical scrutiny imply more democratic, less authoritarian and bureaucratic work relations' (p. 4). Empowering employees also means that managers lose some control, and must learn to accommodate a more ques-

Table 13.2 Benefits of empowerment to the individual and the organisation

Benefits for organisations	Benefits for employers
• Greater awareness of business needs among employees	• Increase in job satisfaction
• Cost reduction from delayering and employee ideas	• Incease in day-to-day control over tasks
• Improved quality, profitability and productivity measures	• Ownership of work
• Organisation able to respond more quickly to market changes	• Increase in self-confidence
• Enhanced loyalty and commitment	• Creation of teamwork
• Decrease in staff turnover	• Acquisiton of new knowledge and skills
• More effective communication	

tioning and risk-taking workforce, a problem of which many empowerment schemes fall foul (Arkin, 1995).

The 'hard' aspect of empowerment signifies the exercise of a sense of responsibility, and implies elements of monitoring and accountability: it therefore poses contradictions in its implementation and practice. These elements of 'responsible autonomy' are overseen by forms of surveillance via set objectives, customer reports, the policing by fellow members of autonomous work teams, and other controls. 'Empowerment [like BPR, see below] is also closely linked to organisational restructuring, job cuts and moves towards increasingly fragmented and unstable and contingent employment relationships' (Claydon and Doyle, 1996: 4).

Here we see some of the contradictions inherent in capitalist enterprise and therefore in processes such as empowerment, BPR and TQM, which are related to HRM issues. Is it possible to gain commitment when employees perceive themselves as being merely disposable units of production? These and other controversial questions will continue to exercise the minds of both practitioners and academics in the continual search for congruence between the aims of companies, employees and society.

Criticisms of empowerment

Writers cited in the preceding text have already implied considerable criticism of the empowerment movement: its imprecise definitions; the fact that it remains, for all its good intentions, a managerial tool to gain employee compliance; and the fact that empowerment as such is restricted to workplace issues, allowing little or no employee voice in strategic organisational concerns.

Most criticism of empowerment can be divided into two categories: reasons for operational failure, and wider ideological critiques.

A number of studies have pointed to practical reasons for the failure of empowerment schemes. These do not tend to take issue with the concept of empowerment as such but are critical of the way in which it has been applied. A study by Rothstein (1995) showed that an empowerment scheme in an American company failed because of management incompetence. Senior management, including the company president, failed to give adequate support, and employees felt they lacked authority to make meaningful decisions. Training in empowerment was cursory, and communication systems were inadequate to deal with the feedback necessary between employees and managers at different levels and across the organisation. Senior management also expected success to be immediate, a situation that would inevitably lead to feelings of thwarted expectations.

Wilkinson (1998) makes the point that empowerment schemes often fail because they are regarded too simplistically in the sense that 'empowerment has different forms and should be analysed in the context of broader organisational practice' (p. 53). Buchanan and Preston's (1992) research into high-performance teams (in which empowerment is central to the operation) showed that management was ever mindful of how the cell team operations fitted with the broader business strategy. HRM strategy in terms of reward systems, flexitime systems, training and development were also crucial in enabling empowerment to operate effectively. Many schemes fail because senior management has not recognised that the implementation of empowerment schemes usually means a wholesale organisational culture change, which affects all corners of the organisation. Honold (1997) also emphasises that culture change implies a change from a low- to a high-trust culture, including the 'tolerance of risk taking'

(p. 208). It is often difficult to prescribe where the limits of risk taking and employee responsibility lie; such issues are not directly confronted in many organisations until a serious problem arises, and then it is often too late. Babson's (1995) research into car plants showed that responsibilities transferred to employees were more symbolic than substantive, relegated to handing out pay cheques on pay day, for example.

Ideological criticisms are often couched in terms that empowerment systems are just another management ruse to exploit the workforce more effectively, and that in reality employee empowerment is limited and ultimately does not 'free' the workforce from the shackles of forms of control, arguments rehearsed earlier in this chapter. This has echoes of Friedman's concept of 'responsible autonomy', in which the perception is given that employees have control over the work process but in reality this is limited and very much contained within the parameters of set performance targets. It is management that usually set the targets, not the employees.

Babson (1995) has raised a recurring concern within the EI literature, that empowerment schemes can undermine and destroy the legitimate and independent voice of the workforce – that is, the trade unions. This may be a deliberate ploy to undermine union presence and power, or to create a climate where the union presence is deemed superfluous as its role in mediating between management and workers is redundant. A European Union-wide study by Wood and Fenton O'Creevy (1999) found that companies which depend on direct employee involvement that bypasses trade unions involved their employees less than those companies that recognised and involved unions. 'This was because they involved workers in fewer issues and, when they did, they were less likely to consult or negotiate rather than simply inform them' (p. 44). Interestingly, they also found that the exclusive use of direct involvement schemes, such as those associated with empowerment, correlated with lower labour productivity.

Another feature of the exploitation argument is that empowerment schemes reduce workforce levels. This follows the logic that as productivity increases fewer staff are needed. In other words one is empowered out of a job! This is often associated with forms of lean production. Parker and Slaughter (1995) also believe that this creates 'a management by stress approach that pushes people and systems to the breaking point by increasingly forcing workers to do more with less' (Honold, 1997: 209).

Business process re-engineering

Business process re-engineering (BPR) is one of the latest 'fads', and has been hailed as the big solution to the problems facing companies and organisations in the 1990s (Peppard and Rowland, 1995). Its American advocates, such as Michael Hammer, claim that quality in production and service must now be accompanied by efficiency in process – that is, the way that groups and departments function interactively (Hammer and Champy, 1993). BPR has enormous implications for employee involvement as its supporters advocate stripping away unnecessary layers of management and empowering the workforce to seek better process solutions in the drive towards greater efficiency.

There have been studies that relate its successful application in a number of organisations (Buchanan, 1996), but 'emphasis on the ability of re-engineering to reduce employee numbers shows how messages tend to get distorted as they are passed on. Unfortunately, the message wanted and received by most of US industry was not improvement through reorganisation, but reduced costs through staff cuts' (Mumford and Hendricks, 1996: 22). Given such experiences, it is not surprising that these schemes are viewed with an air of cynicism and fear by employees who may well become the next 'victim' in the drive towards efficiency.

Lumb (1996) has defended BPR as being 'about changing the way people think and behave. It means investing employees with the power to make decisions and encouraging them to take risks.' All laudable aims, but the *raison d'être* of companies is to operate profitably; if the confusion of message and intent is responsible for the growing cynicism that sees reduction of costs (BPR's aim) as also incorporating not only efficient processes but reduction of staff levels, then messages of trust, commitment and empowerment could be radically undermined.

CONTROVERSY: DOES EMPLOYEE INVOLVEMENT WORK? THE CASE OF TQM

Whether employee involvement works or not depends on the aims and objectives of the EI scheme. In addition, there are times when certain schemes will work successfully and other times when they will be unsuccessful, and this is why EI, like many other HRM policies, goes through fashion changes. The economic, political and social context influences the type and success of the scheme that organisations adopt (Ramsay, 1992a). Further influencing factors are the type, size and sector of the organisation. What may work in a small firm, for example, may not work so well in a large, bureaucratic organisation. What may work in a democratic organisational culture will probably be unsuccessful in a more authoritarian one (Wilkinson, 1989).

The aims and objectives of an organisation in increasing the number and intensity of communication channels may be specifically 'political'. For example, in times of dispute with the union, the management may feel they need to put their side of the case more effectively to the workforce. In the past many companies found themselves at a comparative disadvantage in disputes, as the unions had a virtual monopoly of the informational channels to the workforce. This was no fault of the unions but more a reflection of the incompetence of management, who were incapable of creating effective communication channels, which they suspected could be used at other times for what might be perceived as more negative purposes (Monks, 1989). In other words, management can themselves suffer from their own ideology of operating 'mushroom systems' (keeping the workforce in the dark and piling 'manure' on them), which maintains a climate of distrust and attitudes of 'us and them'. Fortunately, surveys indicate that in many organisations such ideas are becoming less popular (CBI, 1989; Marchington *et al.*, 1992).

Even schemes such as TQM, which begin life for the most positive reasons – for example the enhancement of employee commitment, motivation and empowerment – may become distorted by factors, both internal and external, that turn them into something more unworkable and, from the employee point of view, into a sinister attempt to gain more commitment, work and productivity, without the concomitant reward, control or empowerment given to employees.

Total quality management has been increasing in popularity in many organisations in recent years, and is often bound up with culture changes and other HRM and managerial initiatives such as customer service programmes. TQM operates at both a local and an establishment-wide level, and pervades the whole organisation. It is concerned with concepts such as culture change, which in turn engender attitudinal changes in the workforce. At workplace level emphasis can be placed purely on improving the quality of the product or service and, like customer service schemes, this can also be the implementation of more efficiency between internal departments (which can be seen as internal customers) and external customers themselves. Like quality circles, the idea stems from the writings of Deming, Juran, and more recently Crosby (1979, 1984). It has also been linked to British Standard BS 5750 and ISO 9000 approaches, although many claim that this is more suitable for production-oriented rather than service sector work.

Wilkinson *et al.* (1992: 5) point out clearly the differences between QCs and TQM (and their implications) (Table 13.3). The compulsory nature of TQM, with its top-down overtones, suggests a system in which worker empowerment is very much restricted within the boundaries set by management. In its operation in production companies Sewell and Wilkinson (1992) also propose that it has an air of surveillance, whereby the performance of individual workers is monitored so as to control their work to conform to the group norm – a norm set by management.

They describe how, in an electronic components factory, the teams who make the components, especially the team leader, 'have a great deal of discretion in the way labour resources are deployed across the cell [the unit of manufacture]' (Wilkinson and Sewell, 1992: 104). Multi-skilling is encouraged, and work rotation is allocated by the team and team leader. Within the team, individuals are encouraged to improve personal performance, and innovations should be made to improve productivity and product quality. Team meetings provide the forums where such issues are debated and information shared. Quality is controlled by a visual inspection and electronic tests, which also trace the individual responsible for the fault. This information, together with data on absenteeism, conformity to standard times and production planning targets, is prominently displayed for all the team to see. Naturally, the information forms the basis of much discussion between team members. In turn this creates a situation where the team will 'discipline' those whom they feel are not conforming to the norms. This is a form of what Friedman (1977) called *responsible autonomy*, a situation in which the group acts as the controller of the individual and therefore the team. Thus managers can clearly claim that the workforce is being 'empowered'. This delegation of power, however, has a dual nature, which according to Muetzfeldt (quoted in Sewell and Wilkinson, 1992), 'can actually increase the power of the delegating agency, so long as it can legitimate and retain its authority, and undermine it if the obedience of the delegated agents cannot be assured' (p. 106).

Sewell and Wilkinson see this system of TQM as an analogy of the work of Foucault, who stressed the importance of tracing the loci of power in organisations in order to understand its importance and how it is used, like the panopticon, the hub of the surveillance system in Victorian prisons. The electronic quality-recording mechanisms in the operation of TQM in the electronics factory they dub the *information panopticon*, a device used in the control of team norms set by management.

Table 13.3 Ideal types of quality circle and TQM

	Quality circles	*TQM*
Choice	Voluntary	Compulsory
Structure	Bolt-on	Integrated quality system
Direction	Bottom-up	Top-down
Scope	Within departments or units	Company-wide
Aims	Employee relations improvements	Quality improvements

Wilkinson *et al.* (1992), in their research into EI for the Department of Employment (see also Marchington *et al.*, 1992), visited 25 organisations, of which the majority had TQM programmes in operation. In examining these practices it was evident that TQM operated in a wide variety of forms and, like HRM, was open to a variety of definitions and interpretations. In a close examination of TQM in three typical British companies in engineering, finance and marketing, the researchers discovered several problems in its implementation and operation. All of the schemes were difficult to sustain for four basic reasons.

First, the schemes were narrow in conception and 'bolted-on to rather than integrated in, key management policies' (Wilkinson *et al.*, 1992: 14). As a result some schemes looked very similar to quality circles and thus had many of their faults. Companies tended to look for immediate gains rather than long-term cultural changes. 'If these are not forthcoming TQM is short lived' (p. 15). In turn this created an obsession with 'the cost of quality and immediacy of return, concepts which are totally different from Japanese thinking' (p. 15).

Second, the role of middle managers became unclear and confused, and was looked upon as one group of managers imposing itself on another. This had the effect of creating conflicts. Because TQM was carried out in a highly centralised framework in most organisations, teams were reliant on the services of other departments, with which they were competing for resources, and each department was often in ignorance of how they were affected by each other. The competition thus militated against mutually cooperative solutions.

Third, industrial relations, while affecting TQM programmes, are rarely considered by employers. Thus there was usually neglect in obtaining union agreement or establishing a positive working climate before implementing TQM schemes, a situation almost guaranteed to create suspicion in either the unions or the workforce. TQM has a strong impact on such issues as job control, working practices and reward, all of which can, if not handled sensitively, create problems, as unions and workers may place obstacles in the way of the system's operation.

Fourth, employee involvement in TQM schemes can have contradictory elements. Similar to the findings of Sewell and Wilkinson, it was discovered that there was a contradiction in the language of employee involvement (empowerment of the workforce, etc.) and the actuality of the work situation, in which power very much rested in the hands of management.

Recent critical studies of the 'quality' movement have drawn attention to its wider implications. Wilkinson and Wilmot (1995) state that it is relevant to place the quality movement 'in the wider context of pressures from shareholders upon managers to organise the work of employees in ways that are more profitable' (p. 13). They continue by stating that 'quality initiatives are often imposed upon an unprepared and hesitant, if not hostile, management by the intensity of (global) competitive pressures'. They also draw attention 'to the strength and depth of the participation promoted by TQM. It is striking that participation does not extend to key decisions relating to the ownership and control of companies' (p. 20). In a recent comparative study of employee involvement in the banking sector in Britain and Sweden, Holden (1996) has concluded that most participation mechanisms, particularly those related to recent HRM initiatives such as TQM, do not encourage participation by the workforce in strategic issues. Most are confined to workplace areas, and therefore tend to be restricted in their sphere of control. This is particularly surprising when much HRM literature advocates the strategic nature of HRM policy in relation to employee influence.

These studies point to a number of problems in the implementation of TQM. Ramsay (1992a) has noted, with some laconic interest, the rise and fall of fads and fashions in employee involvement, and speculates about what might be next on the agenda if TQM does not succeed! What is certain is that easy solutions do not exist, and the implementation of new systems has to be viewed within a long-term framework and reviewed constantly with the full consent and approval of the workforce.

INTERNATIONAL ASPECTS OF EMPLOYEE INVOLVEMENT

In many countries in Europe and the rest of the world, trade unions still act as one of the most important communication channels, despite indications that there has been a decline in membership worldwide over the past ten years (ILO, 1993). Their importance is central in Scandinavian countries, especially Sweden, and they still carry considerable weight in Germany and Britain, though the rise in long-term unemployment and the decline in the old staple industries such as shipbuilding, coal, iron and steel and engineering, where unionism had a strong traditional base, have tended to erode their power.

Employee involvement rooted in industrial democratic processes has witnessed a surer growth over the past 30 years in legislatively supported systems such as co-determination in Germany and Sweden. The operation of these two contrasting styles of industrial democracy is also reflected by the relative union strength in each country – 85% in Sweden and 35% in Germany in 1988 (OECD, 1991).

Swedish co-determination

In many respects Sweden has the most advanced forms of participation in the world, at both organisational and workplace levels (Wilczynski, 1983). The basis of industrial democracy in the country stretches back to 1948 with the setting up of the National Labour Market Board. This was composed of representatives from labour, employers and government, and participated in economic planning.

In the economic and political climate of the 1970s, demands were made for the extension of industrial democracy, which led to the passage of a body of legislation, most notable of which was the Co-determination at Work Act (MBL) passed in 1977. The aim of the Act was to extend the scope of collective bargaining to areas of management policy, including organisational and technical change. It required all employers to allow consultation with employees and the participation of their representatives in decision-making at both board and shopfloor levels. For example, one of the central provisions of the Act requires that, when employers are contemplating making major changes in their operations or working conditions of employment, they are required to negotiate with employee representatives before the final decisions are taken and changes are introduced (Edlund and Nyström, 1988).

In reality, employee representatives in the co-determination system tend to be union representatives, and it was the unions in Sweden that gave the impetus for much of the drive towards industrial democracy. The union strategy was to focus on issues of health and safety, and 'this created a political climate in which new laws and regulations in support of industrial democracy could be introduced . . . these laws were supplemented by financial support for training and research which to a large extent was channelled through the unions' (Hammarström, 1987). The crucial role of unions, not only in bar-

Figure 13.2

Co-determination: not a drag but a motive force

Source: Edlund and Nyström (1988).

gaining structures but in the co-determination system, meant that they would always be an important element in Swedish employee relations.

Companies have also enhanced the reputation of Swedish employee involvement. Volvo in particular introduced job enlargement and job enrichment, 'quality of working life' techniques to its Kalmar plant in the 1970s, and became the focus of much attention worldwide as an alternative to the mass-assembly Fordist systems of production (Sell, 1988).

While these systems have been admired, they have also received criticism. The neo-liberalists have seen the corporatist state pay too heavy a price in terms of high wages and high taxes for a regulated labour market that is seen as being heavily influenced by the ability of the workforce to impede management prerogatives in policy creation. Conversely, left-wing critics have attacked the system for not addressing the real needs of the workforce, which have been emasculated by the unions in collusion with the Social Democratic Party in attempts to maintain the corporatist status quo. 'Kalmarism', as one French observer has dubbed the EI initiatives in Volvo (Lipietz, 1992), has also been attacked for being no more than a public relations exercise. Many of the EI initiatives are seen as untypical, and a number have been dropped recently as being uneconomic and inappropriate.

A recent trend in Sweden has been seen to be bound up with managerial HRM initiatives, which have shifted from formal to more informal models of participation and decentralised practices. Some observers suggest that these trends might eventually undermine the formal system of participation (Cressey, 1992).

What is certain is that the change in the economic climate in the early 1990s as a result of recession, raising unemployment from 1.5% in 1990 to 8.5% in 1993, has had an enormous impact on the Swedish collective psyche, challenging many of the assumptions that were generally acceptable in the agreeable economic environment of the 1980s (Holden, 1996).

The balance of power between state, unions and employers changes continually with each economic phase, but there is no reason to believe that the essence of the system will not survive. Despite the fact that management prerogatives in Sweden still outweigh those of the employee, the culture of involvement is still very well developed compared with most other countries.

German co-determination

Given the embodiment of the concept of consultation and participation in the EU Social Charter and the draft European Works Council Directive, it is not surprising that the German system of co-determination and works councils has been seen by some observers to be a model for the rest of the Union:

> In contrast to other countries, the system of co-determination in Germany is very extensive, and involves the participation of employees and their representatives in nearly all decisions relating to personnel and many aspects of company policy.
>
> (Gaugler and Wiltz, 1992)

Co-determination is legally embodied in the work system by four key Acts: the Montan Co-determination Act 1951, the Workplace Labour Relations Act 1952, the Workplace Labour Relations Act 1972, and the Co-determination law of 1976. Co-determination operates basically at company and plant levels, although there are three methods by which workers can participate: works councils, supervisory boards and management boards. In places of work that have five or more employees the workforce elects a works council, consisting of workers' representatives only. The works council has a right to information concerning:

- health and safety;
- the organisation of work;
- the working environment and jobs;
- the hiring of executives;
- planned changes in the company that could result in considerable disadvantages to employees.

In addition, the works council has the right to make suggestions (Gaugler and Wiltz, 1992):

- during the formulation and implementation of personnel planning;
- regarding vocational training (apprenticeships, etc.);
- about other training and development measures.

The views of the works council must be considered by the employer, although there is no compulsion to accept them. For larger companies (not family owned) employing more than 500 people, representatives elected by the workers sit on the supervisory board, where they make up one-third to a half (depending on size) of the policy-making body. Other board members are elected by the shareholders, and a neutral chairperson is appointed. In companies over 2000 employees in size trade union representatives are guaranteed places on the board. German workers tend to believe that in general the works councils and co-determination system represent them adequately, and there has been a reluctance to join unions (35% as opposed to Sweden's union density of 85%), although the recession in the early 1990s witnessed a revival of trade union militancy.

The supervisory board meets four times a year, and also appoints members to the management board, a full-time executive body that oversees company policy in its day-to-day operations. (For a fuller explanation of the history and detailed operation of the co-determination system, see Lawrence, 1980; Lane, 1989; Gaugler and Wiltz, 1992.)

Co-determination: an evaluation

In evaluating co-determination one must be aware of the diversity of positions from which views emanate. These are of course influenced by political ideology, position in the organisation (whether management or worker etc.), whether one is a shareholder, and the type of organisation. Lane (1989), in her survey of research analysing the influence of co-determination in Germany, points to the diversity of findings depending on the level (whether workplace or enterprise), company size, sector and managerial style.

Not surprisingly, co-determination at enterprise level has had relatively little impact on the everyday work of employees, but, it can be argued, has had the long-term positive effect of engendering a spirit of cooperation between management and labour. Labour representatives perceive more clearly the reasons for managerial policy initiatives, and conversely the management have more understanding of the concerns of the workforce.

At workplace level there has been a wide variety of research. For example, Wilpert and Rayley (1983) showed that there was a large discrepancy between formal rights and actual rights of participation. They also state that, while participation rights in Germany are high compared with most other European countries, so too is formal and actual managerial control.

Lane (1989) posits the view that 'faced with a strong and control-oriented management and forced to prove themselves *vis-à-vis* their electors by concrete achievements, works councillors may decide to pursue only those issues on which they are confident to get concessions' (p. 232). Thus the degree of participatory influence could also vary with each issue.

Not surprisingly, there are German employers who share the view of recent British Conservative governments that the co-determination system undermines the employer's right to manage. Survey evidence suggests, however, that works councils are supported by the overwhelming majority of employers, except in the smallest of firms (Mauritz, 1972, quoted in Lane, 1989: 233).

Works councils bolstered by legislation also exist in Belgium, France, Italy, Luxembourg, Spain and the Netherlands, but the range of issues and decisions submitted for employee approval is smaller than in Germany. The operation of the councils is also affected by employee and management attitudes bound up with the institutions and culture of the country.

For example, the Auroux Laws 1982 extended workers' participation rights in French companies, but research reveals that the consultation process has been ignored or undermined by management accustomed to the hierarchical and often autocratic ways strongly emphasised (although changing) in many French organisations (Lane, 1989: 240). In Sweden there has been much criticism of the relatively weak position of unions in the co-determinational process, particularly in time of recession (Korpi, 1981;

Kjellberg, 1992). Unions often do not receive adequate information, and in the recent bank crisis had much less influence than management on the restructuring and downsizing exercises (Holden, 1996).

Works councils and the European Union

The Works Council Directive was embodied in the Social Charter and was formally adopted by the European Union (EU) in 1994. This requires any company with over 1000 employees in the EU and with at least 150 employees in two different countries to set up a council for the purpose of informing and consulting employees. In December 1999 the UK government embodied this in British legislation. In previous years UK Conservative governments and employer organisations had strongly resisted any attempts by the EU to impose a works council directive, but the Blair Labour government has signed up to the Social Charter and consequently fully subscribes to the principle of works councils. Employers will have ten months from the passage of this legislation to set up works councils voluntarily, after which they will have to conform to the legislation requirements.

There are also proposals to force companies to consult with employees at national level. This has received continued opposition from the UK government and employer associations, a stand supported by their German counterparts. The European Social Partners failed to agree on this issue in 1998, and Dirk Hudig, secretary-general of the employers' confederation in Europe (UNICE), 'predicts that any definite movement on the proposals, which would force companies to set up works councils at national level, is unlikely' (Rana, 1999: 13). Employers fear that national and pan-European works councils could interfere with their national and international policies, such as downsizing or closing company subsidiaries in other European countries.

Nevertheless, recent evidence shows that the number of works councils (and similar bodies) is on the increase in Britain. More than half are in French and German-owned subsidiaries such as Renault, Crédit Lyonnais, Grundig and Bayer, although increasing numbers are coming from Scandinavia (such as Electrolux and Norsk Hydro). British companies are also creating their own works councils, most notably BP, Coats Viyella and United Biscuits (Carley, 1995). The presence of a works council does not, however, guarantee employee consultation or indeed a voice in managerial policy, as the experience of job losses at Coats Viyella in 1996 clearly displayed. This lack of consultation has outraged unions and employees throughout the company's British and European concerns (Littlefield, 1996). Nor is such behaviour confined to British-owned companies. In 1998 Renault closed its Vilvoorde plant in Belgium without adequately consulting or informing its employees. Union protests led to a French court ruling that Renault did not act in accordance with the European Works Council (EWC) Directive about the proposed plant closure. Obviously this retrospective censure has not returned those Renault jobs to Belgian workers, and the European trade union movement (ETUC) has demanded amendments tightening the EWC legislation, so far without success.

Such incidents clearly indicate that social dialogue progress remains limited. Nevertheless, research by Marginson *et al.* (1998) shows that companies in France, Germany, the UK and even the USA found a widespread preference for joint employer–employee bodies, be it only at plant level.

Japanese employee involvement

Japan is often cited as an exemplar of employee participation practices, particularly giant corporations such as Komatsu, Hitachi, Nissan, Honda, Mitsubishi and Toyota. The most commonly emulated participation technique has been quality circles, which we have already noted were conceived in the USA by Deming and Juran, and were implanted in Japanese organisations in the 1950s. Since then employee involvement techniques such as QCs and teamworking have been part and parcel of the working practices of Japanese companies in the UK, such as Nissan in Sunderland and Toyota in Derby. Many studies have been made of Japanese organisations in order to discover the secrets of their economic success, and teamworking techniques have received much attention as a perceived key to efficient work practices.

Pascale and Athos (1982) emphasise that the work group is the basic building block of Japanese organisations: 'Owing to the central importance of group efforts in their thinking, the Japanese are extremely sensitive to and concerned about group interactions and relationships' (p. 125). They liken the Japanese worker's view of the group to that of a marriage that rests on commitment, trust, sharing and loyalty, and while power ultimately rests with management, the group leader handles the interaction within the group carefully. This 'participation assumption' is also related to a lifetime employment assumption, which ensures that the worker has a strong stake in the firm and its success. Finally, and perhaps most importantly, participation is backed up by training of both group leaders and workers in the skills of group participation (Dore and Sako, 1989). Employee involvement, like training, is thus embedded in Japanese organisations.

A number of observers (including Klaus and Bass, 1974) have pointed out that employee involvement should not be confused with decision-making, particularly at the higher levels within the organisation: 'The reality is that not all employees wield real power . . . [and] when it comes to making the decision, workers feel under great pressure to agree with supervisors and unpopular decisions are simply ignored' (Naoi and Schooler, 1985, quoted in Briggs, 1991: 40). Briggs sees this paradox of employee involvement and emasculation of power as being explained by the split between opinion and behaviour. In a number of surveys Japanese workers have rated themselves low on job satisfaction and yet they work far more hours for less reward than their US and British counterparts. This cannot be explained by coercive methods alone; Briggs points to the extent of unionisation, albeit organised around large corporations, and finds this view untenable. Her explanation is based on cultural factors in that the Japanese have 'a deep felt desire to keep the realm of duty separate from the realm of personal feeling . . . duty must come first and must exist totally separate from the domain of personal feelings' (Briggs, 1991: 41).

If this is the case, it has ramifications for the export of such EI practices to other countries, most notably Britain, which has received enormous amounts of Japanese investment. Wickens (1987), in his exposition of how Nissan implanted Japanese practices into its Sunderland factory, strongly believes that people are capable of change and that the institution of Japanese-style working practices was partly effected by a watering-down process to meet British attitudes, combined with a process of education and training to enable newly hired (often novice) workers in car manufacturing to be imbued with Japanese-style practices. This was reinforced by a greenfield culture with workers who had predominantly been recruited from regions where high unemployment meant an eagerness to gain and retain employment.

A number of observers have pointed out that control and the mechanisms of employee involvement in Japanese-owned British organisations still reside firmly in the hands of management. Lewis (1989), in his study of employee participation in a Japanese-owned electronics factory, found that, while a board was set up (a kind of JCC) to represent employee interests, employees were not quite sure what was meant by involvement. Most of the issues raised were not about the overall running of the operation but more parochial shopfloor concerns, and the real aim in setting up the board was to introduce unitarist principles in the company such as single-status terms and conditions, no-strike arrangements and flexible work practices. All were reinforced with powerful symbols of unitarism such as the brightly coloured jackets that everyone wore, replete with the owner's forename. This sent messages of egalitarianism and that the organisation was one happy family. The single-status restaurants and toilets were also part of this symbolic reinforcement of unitarism. Oliver and Lowe (1991) endorse this unitarist view of Japanese-style management. In comparing styles of HRM in Japanese, US and British computer companies based in the UK, they found that the Japanese emphasised consensus and collectivism with 'a thin dividing line between the public and the private and a strong sense of mutual support and awareness'.

In essence, the implementation of EI, even in Japanese organisations that have strong commitments to such systems, is not as a decision-making instrument per se or even as a conduit of employee criticism, but as a mechanism that reinforces common aims and goals within the unitarist organisational context.

Ramsay (1992b) has also pointed out that few non-Japanese-owned British organisations have adopted Japanese EI measures in the long term. The use of quality circles, after an initial flurry of interest, dropped from 63% in 1980 to 10% in 1989 in British organisations. He concludes: 'No matter what the degree of genuine autonomy or control Swedish or Japanese work group experiments, the greater constraints on the prospect for worker influence came from the institutional settings and – even more critically – the broader social and cultural contexts' (p. 40).

Comparative aspects of employee involvement

Comparative research of a statistical and analytical nature into EI is relatively sparse, although there have been numerous international surveys of institutional and legal aspects of employee involvement (Poole, 1986). Studies in the 1980s and 1990s revealed a diversity of trends influenced by a multiplicity of organisational, economic, political and technical factors. The Price Waterhouse Cranfield Survey into International Strategic HRM investigated trends in employee communications in five countries (the UK, Sweden, the then West Germany, Spain and France) in 1990, and ten countries in 1991 (the original five plus the Netherlands, Norway, Denmark, Italy and Switzerland), with subsequent surveys in 1995 and 1999. These surveys reveal a marked increase in attempts at communicating with the workforce, both via staff representative bodies, such as trade unions, and by more direct methods associated with HRM initiatives (Holden, 1990; Price Waterhouse Cranfield, 1990 and 1991). Parallel to overall increases via staff representative bodies were even larger increases in verbal and written communication in all countries. This obviously indicates a greater desire by employers to increase communication, probably inspired by HRM trends, which spread in the 1980s. France and the UK show particularly large increases in both verbal and written communication, which parallel the rise in team briefing and other teamwork methods, as well as increases in the more traditional written forms of communication.

It would seem that communication with and from the workforce is increasing at workplace level, but the more established forms of communication and EI such as unions, works councils and JCCs are still important in those organisations where they are established. The survey conducted by Marchington *et al.* (1992) in UK organisations would seem to confirm this.

Nevertheless, these surveys do not indicate the degree of participation by employees in organisations. Research by Fröhlich and Krieger (1990), Cressey and Williams (1990), Boreham (1992) and Gill (1993) has tried to address this issue in comparative contexts. Fröhlich and Krieger (1990) examined the extent of employee participation in technological change in five EC countries – the UK, France, Germany, Italy and Denmark. They discovered that of the four phases of introducing new technology (planning, selection, implementation and subsequent evaluation) workers were more likely to be involved in the latter stages, and that full participation, particularly in decision-making, remained relatively low for all countries and for all stages. Cressey and Williams (1990), in a similar survey but covering all of the then 12 EC countries, found comparable results and posed a 'paradox of participation'. As the scope for influence by employees over the processes of technological change decreased, so the intensity of participation increased. In other words, there was more scope for participation in the implementation stage (the latter stage) when participative influence concerning fundamental decisions was reduced, and less participation in the crucial earlier planning stages in the introduction of new technology.

Gill (1993), using the same 12-country EC data analysed by Cressey and Williams (1990), perceives differences in attitudes between Northern European and Mediterranean countries, which result in a wide diversity in levels of participation. Denmark, Germany, the Netherlands and Belgium have much greater employee participation than do Portugal, Spain, Italy, Greece, France, Luxembourg and the UK. In France and the UK, however, Gill argues, 'there is a dependence by management on the skills and problem solving abilities of the labour force' (p. 346). Nevertheless, he claims that 'in the United Kingdom there has been a shift away from negotiation towards more consultation during the last decade and management has become increasingly paternalistic in their style' (p. 346). These differences are caused, he argues, by the diverse industrial relations practices in each country, shaped by historical and cultural factors.

In all three studies managers were of the view that increased participation was effective for the efficient implementation of new technology, but this may have the effect of compromising their prerogatives.

Boreham (1992) investigated the degree of employee control over labour processes in seven countries (Australia, Britain, Canada, Germany, Japan, Sweden and the USA). He was particularly interested to know whether employee control was enhanced by the introduction of new practices associated with post-Fordist systems such as flexible working linked to quality improvement and greater response to market conditions. The assumption here was that efficiency was improved by decentralisation and democratised decision-making practices. The findings clearly indicated that 'the nearer one approaches the core of status and power in the enterprise the more likely it is that one be allowed discretion over one's work arrangements' (p. 18). He also found that there was little evidence 'to support the view that management will cede its decision making prerogatives in the interests of more rational production methods' (p. 21). This pattern was generally true of Japanese and Swedish organisations, which are associated with employee involvement styles of management.

These surveys clearly indicate a contradiction in managers' perceptions that employee involvement is an effective way of increasing work efficiency, but is outweighed by the challenge to their prerogatives over decision-making. Thus employee involvement is very limited, and is more likely to take the form of information dissemination to, and consultation with, the workforce, which is not the same as the 'empowerment' to which many HRM textbooks allude.

Boreham (1992) also stresses the significance of flexible employment patterns and involvement. In a world where increases in part-time, fixed-contract and short-term working are becoming more pronounced, he shows that these employees have even less involvement in workplace decisions, and that core groups, particularly in management categories, still hold far greater sway over the organisation and control of work. Such evidence casts huge question marks over growing trends – for example 'zero hours contracts' alongside involvement schemes aimed at motivating workers.

What can we learn from these studies?

The findings of these pieces of research are replicated to some degree by earlier and more recent research by IDE in 1981 and 1993.

In essence, it seems that there is a contradiction in what employers and managers want from EI and what they are prepared to allow to the workforce in terms of empowerment and control. In ideological terms, the control of the organisation rests in the hands of the upper realms of the hierarchy, either the board or within the senior management teams, and there will be resistance to attempts to extend significant power to workers lower down the organisation. Thus the concept of 'industrial democracy' per se is perceived as a power challenge, even in societies that allow considerable autonomy to the workforce and have in place sophisticated structures of co-determination, such as those that exist in Sweden and Germany. This power 'balance' will also shift with changing economic and political climates, and management will allow considerably more concessions in times of labour shortage than in times of recession, when worker power is much weaker.

The ideas of 'empowerment' and 'employee influence' at workplace level have greater justification for management in HRM terms, as the rationale for the introduction of EI policies is ultimately to increase the efficiency of the organisation. The perception of management poses a dilemma in terms of how much power to extend to the workforce while harnessing their creative energies, and at the same time not undermining managerial prerogatives. This conundrum is in many ways a central one to the whole debate concerning HRM and modern organisational practices such as delayering of middle management structures, the introduction of new technology, TQM, the creation of flatter organisations, culture change and empowerment initiatives. Perhaps the working out of these power balances is a continuing part of the managerial process, until, that is, the structure of ownership in society radically changes. Equally important is the relationship between middle management and senior management, which to some extent can be seen as similar to that between workforce and middle management, but overlaid with elements of status and role strain, i.e. squashed between senior management and the workforce.

Another factor at both organisational and workplace levels is the influence of cultural values, to which many commentators on EI ultimately allude. Writers such as Hofstede and Laurent have attempted to examine these influences, and concede that much research has still to be completed before our understanding of these complex issues is clearer (see Chapter 15). Even then, 'culture' is in a state of permanent flux, and our concept of it is ever changing, often in subtle ways. Yet observers would have us believe that British adaptations to Japanese work practices are possible despite the different cultural values of British workers. Others have stated that the practices become palatable because of the environment into which they are introduced: greenfield sites with single-union deals and no-strike clauses, and a compliant workforce conscious of the lack of alternative employment in high unemployment areas.

Several factors emerge that make the proper working of EI mechanisms possible:

- a willingness by management to concede some of their prerogatives;
- the need to train managers in EI initiatives such as teamworking;
- the need for a clear policy regarding the role and prerogatives of line managers in relation to senior management and the workforce under their supervision;
- the need to train workers in group skills such as presentation, leadership, assertiveness and problem solving;
- the need for providing proper feedback mechanisms that clearly indicate that the workforce is being listened to, and not in a purely lip-service fashion;
- the need for action to implement group decisions, which reinforces the view among he workforce that their contributions are well received;
- the need for conflicting views to have a place in developing initiatives.

SUMMARY

- This chapter began by exploring definitions of employee involvement and empowerment as generic (EI) and specific terms (HRM EI). This was followed by an examination of EI practices in relation to HRM, and EI and forms of control within organisations.

- Employers' increasing recognition of the significance of communications in organisations was acknowledged. Over recent years employee involvement has been recognised as one important communication instrument.

- The history of employee involvement was traced, including forms of industrial democracy, and more recently the fashion for recognition of the centrality that employee involvement has begun to assume in HRM trends. Patterns of EI were investigated, ranging from theories of cycles and waves of participation, proposed by Ramsay and Marchington respectively, to an explanatory framework of participation suggested by Poole.

- Definitions of EI were summarised, with an outline of the types and levels of participation within organisations. These included two broad categories of EI at macro and micro levels: macro level being types of EI at organisational or enterprise level, such as works councils or joint consultative committees (JCCs), and micro level being at the workplace, such as quality circles and team briefings. Types of EI were examined under four basic headings: downward communication from managers to employees, such as company journals, newspapers, videos, briefing sessions; upwards, problem-solving forms, such as quality circles, suggestion schemes, TQM and customer care programmes; financial participation, such as profit sharing and share ownership schemes; and representative participation, such as JCCs, works councils, co-determination and collective bargaining. The various strengths and weaknesses of the most popular forms of EI were analysed.

● The term 'empowerment' was examined, providing some definitions of the concept. This was followed by some discussion as to how empowerment benefits the individual and the organisation. Empowerment was also examined in relation to HRM initiatives, and this section concluded by proposing some critiques of the concept and practices, revealing its confinement to workplace levels, rather than strategic policy-making levels within the organisation.

● The concept of business process re-engineering (BPR) was briefly examined, and this was followed by an in-depth analysis of total quality management, based on various studies that pointed to common pitfalls in its implementation.

● International aspects of EI were considered, beginning with a review of the Swedish system, noted for its advanced EI practices, particularly the co-determination system and the quality of working life movement. The German co-determination and works council system was also examined in the light of suggestions that it might act as a possible European model. An evaluation of co-determination was then undertaken, followed by an exploration of the European works council issue in the context of the European Union.

● A review of influential Japanese EI methods was undertaken, outlining the difficulties in cross-cultural transfers of work practices. The international section ended by evaluating some comparative surveys of employee involvement, highlighting similar trends as well as common problems in different countries, for example the mediation of power and control in the implementation of EI systems.

● Finally there was some advice as to which factors should be taken into consideration in implementing EI schemes.

Activity **Company newsletter**

The Public Relations and Human Resource Management departments of Flexible Printing Services Ltd oversee 300 workers on 12 different sites, and are conscious of the need to keep their employees aware of new developments within the company. They have therefore decided to produce a small company newsletter for this purpose. There is a relatively small but active number of union members within the company on most of the sites.

---

1 In groups, role-play the members of the editorial team in the first editorial meeting to discuss the new company newsletter. Decide upon the policies and practices for the newsletter to ensure that it is a genuine communication, reflective of the organisation as a whole.

2 Write a report on the meeting to the Public Relations and Human Resource Management departments describing the issues that were dealt with by the editorial committee.

QUESTIONS

1 How is the concept of empowerment different from that of employee involvement and industrial democracy?

2 What forms of managerial control operate in the practice of employee involvement schemes?

3 What forms has employee involvement (EI) taken over the past 50 years? In your answer, give examples from both micro and macro levels in the organisation. What evidence is there to suggest that EI develops in waves according to economic cycles?

4 What are the main issues under discussion at present concerning European works council schemes and participation generally in the European Union?

5 What evidence is there to suggest that schemes of financial participation rarely achieve their goals?

6 Why are empowerment schemes popular at present? What criticisms can be made of such schemes?

EXERCISES

1 As editor of a company newspaper, what policies and practices would you follow in order to make it a genuine communication reflective of the organisation as a whole?

2 A prominent British bank is interested in setting up a works council. Write a report recommending the policies in terms of aims, objectives and implementation that should be considered in its foundation.

3 Divide the class into pairs. Ask one group of people to devise reasons why there should be greater participation by employees in the workplace, and ask the other group to put the case against extending participation. Each group should evaluate their reasons from the viewpoint of employers, managers and employees. Then ask the whole group to debate the question of employee participation from each side's viewpoint.

CASE STUDY 1

Total quality management

Precision Tool Engineering is a company producing machinery and machine tools and some other related engineering products for specialist production companies. It employs a total workforce of 400, two-thirds of whom work in the production departments.

In late 1993 the company's management decided to introduce a total quality management scheme to increase efficiency and quality control. In 1990 more flexible arrangements had been introduced, accompanied by a breakdown of old work demarcation lines. Machines were now built by flexible teams of workers employing different skills (e.g. fitters, electricians, and hydraulic engineers). In 1994 the first moves towards TQM were made with the introduction of BS 5750. Workers were asked to inspect the quality of their work, with the result that the need for specialist inspectors was greatly reduced, and both time and money were saved. Agreements were negotiated with the union for extra pay as result of the increase in worker responsibility.

In early 1995 the management decided to introduce a full-blown TQM scheme on the basis of the success of the introduction of BS 5750. Problem-solving groups were formed based on work groups with voluntary participation. Group leaders, who were mainly supervisors, were trained in how to run a

group and in problem-solving techniques. The aims of the groups were to:

- identify problems inside their work area;
- propose solutions;
- identify problems outside their work area;
- refer external problems to a review team.

The review team was made up mainly of managers with one representative from each group, usually the group leader. The unions were lukewarm towards the scheme, and some shop stewards were directly against it.

Within the space of nine months the TQM scheme was reviewed, and senior management came to the conclusion that it had not lived up to expectations, some board members calling it a failure. Some of the areas they identified were that team leaders had felt uncomfortable in their role, and there had been considerable scepticism from some groups of workers.

---

1 Why do you think the BS 5750 scheme was successful but the TQM scheme failed in Precision Engineering?

2 What suggestions would you make to a similar company that was thinking of introducing TQM, in order to make it a success?

CASE STUDY 2

Emplowerment at Semco

Semco, an engineering company in Brazil, caught the attention of the world in the 1990s by the claims of its CEO, Ricardo Semler, that it was a democratic and profitable organisation. On returning from studying for an MBA at Harvard, Semler was convinced that the way to increase the productivity of the workforce was to empower them and involve them in the operation of the business. Since undertaking his empowerment initiatives the company has increased in size 11 times and, in the first half of the 1990s, became one of the fastest-growing companies in Latin America. How did he achieve such impressive results?

According to Semler (1993), 'Democracy is the cornerstone of the Semco system' (p. 249). There is representative democracy through factory committees. All employees excluding management elect representatives to serve on these committees. The union is also represented. The committees meet regularly to discuss workplace issues and policy. 'They are empowered to declare strikes, audit the books, and question all aspects of management' (p. 249). Employees have a vote on all important decisions such as plant relocations. There is also a suggestion scheme.

Semler describes Semco as a 'circular organisation'. Bureaucracy has been drastically cut by reducing 12 layers of management down to three. There are only four titles in the company: Counsellors, who are similar to vice-presidents and coordinate general policy and strategy; Partners, who run the business units; Coordinators, senior managers in charge of sales, marketing, production and assembly area foremen; and Associates, who are the rest of Semco employees.

Semco also practises what it calls 'reverse evaluation', which includes what is now generally known as 360-degree appraisal. Every six months managers are evaluated by their employees. This is done anonymously by multiple choice questionnaire, and the grades are publicly displayed. Before any one is hired or promoted they must be evaluated by all the people who will work with them.

Work is organised in manufacturing cells, with work teams that are given responsibility to create a whole product. This avoids assembly line production

boredom and alienation, and increases employee control over their work process. This 'makes them happier and our products better' (Semler, 1993: 250). Semco has reduced barriers between departments and encourages 'management by wandering around'. Offices do not have walls, and workplaces are demarcated by plants. Employees can adapt and change their working space as they please.

There is also profit sharing, but with a difference. Management does not decide unilaterally what profit is to be shared; that decision is made after negotiations with the workforce. Semler also allows the workforce to 'self-set pay' – a policy whereby employees decide their own salaries. This is done through negotiations with the unions, comparing local pay rates and consulting with both management and the team. Individuals can also choose how much of their earnings can be basic pay and how much bonus. Employees can also choose when they work, flexitime is encouraged and time punch clocks have been removed. Home working is also encouraged if possible.

There is a high union presence, and Semco encourages union membership as well as carrying out negotiation and discussion with the unions. There are disagreements, and some have led to strikes, but the strikes are far less than under the old regime.

The ultimate aim is 'transparency': all information within and about the company is available to all employees. Workers are even given training by trade union officials on the company premises and in the company time on issues such as understanding the company balance sheets, to enable more effective participation. All employees are encouraged to have a voice and express their concerns.

1 Can Semco be rightly regarded as an empowering organisation? Give reasons for your answer.

2 Why can't Semco be a truly democratic organisation?

3 Where is the locus of control in Semco?

4 How could Semco be more democratic in its human resource and managerial policies?

REFERENCES AND FURTHER READING

Those texts marked with an asterisk are particularly recommended for further reading.

Arkin, A. (1995) 'The bumpy road to devolution', *People Management*, 30 November, pp. 34–36.

Babson, S. (1995) *Lean Work: Empowerment and Exploitation in the Global Auto Industry*. Detroit, Mich.: Wayne State University Press.

Badden, L., Hunter, L., Hyman, J., Leopold, J. and Ramsay, H. (1989) *People's Capitalism: A Critical Analysis of Profit and Employee Share Ownership*. London: Routledge.

Beardwell, I. and Holden, L. (1994) *Human Resource Management: A Contemporary Perspective*. London: Pitman Publishing.

Beer, M., Spector, B., Lawrence, P., Quinn Mills, D. and Walton, R. (1984) *Managing Human Assets*. New York: Free Press.

Boreham, P. (1992) 'The myth of post-fordist management: work organisation and employee discretion in seven countries', *Employee Relations*, Vol. 14, No. 2, pp. 13–24.

Brannen, P., Batstone, E., Fatchett, D. and White, P. (1976) *The Worker Directors: A Sociology of Participation*. London: Hutchinson.

Braverman, H. (1974) *Labour and Monopoly Capital: The Degradation of Work in the 20th Century*. New York: Monthly Review Press.

Brennan, B. (1991) 'Mismanagement and quality circles: how middle managers influence direct participation', *Employee Relations*, Vol. 13, No. 5, pp. 22–32.

Briggs, P. (1991) 'Organisational commitment: the key to Japanese success?', in Brewster, C. and Tyson, S. (eds) *International Comparisons in Human Resource Management*. London: Pitman, pp. 33–43.

Broekmeyer, M.J. (ed.) (1970) *Yugoslav Workers' Self-Management*. Pordrecht: Reidel.

Buchanan, D. (1996) *The Re-engineering Frame: An Assessment*, Occasional Paper Series. Leicester: Leicester Business School.

Buchanan, D. and Preston, D. (1992) 'Life in the cell: supervision and team in a "manufacturing systems engineering" environment', *Human Resource Management Journal*, Vol. 2, No. 4, pp. 55–76.

Bullock Committee Report (1977) *On Industrial Democracy*, Hendon: HMSO.

Burawoy, M. (1979) *Manufacturing Consent: Changes in the Labour Process Under Monopoly Capitalism*. Chicago: University of Chicago Press.

Burawoy, M. (1983) 'Between the labour process and the state: factory regimes under advanced capitalism', *American Sociological Review*, Vol. 48, pp. 587–605.

Carley, M. (1995) 'Talking shops or serious forums: works councils', *People Management*, 13 July, pp. 26–31.

CBI (1989) *Employee Involvement: Shaping the Future Business*. London: Confederation of British Industry.

Church, R. (1971) 'Profit sharing and labour relations in England in the nineteenth century', *International Review of Social History*, No. 14, pp. 2–16.

Claydon, T. and Doyle, M. (1996) 'Trusting me, trusting you? The ethics of employee empowerment', paper presented at the Conference of Ethical Issues in Contemporary Human Resource Management, Imperial College, London, 3 April.

Clutterbuck, D. and Crainer, S. (1990) *Makers of Management: Men and Women who Changed the Business World*. London: Macmillan.

Cole, G.D.H. (1917) *Self Government in Industry*. London: Bell and Sons; 1972 edn, London: Hutchinson.

Collard, R. and Dale, B. (1989) 'Quality circles', in Sisson, K. (ed.) *Personnel Management in Britain*. Oxford: Blackwell, pp. 356–377.

Cook, S. and Macauley, S. (1997) 'Empowered customer service,' *Empowerment in Organisations*, Vol. 5, No. 1, pp. 54–60.

Cressey, P. (1992) 'Worker participation: what can we learn from the Swedish experience?', *P+ European Participation Monitor*, Vol. 3, No.1, pp. 3–7.

Cressey, P. and Williams, R. (1990) *Participation in Change: New Technology and the Role of Employee Involvement*. Dublin: European Foundation for the Improvement of Living and Working Conditions.

Crosby, P. (1979) *Quality is Free*. New York: McGraw-Hill.

Crosby, P. (1984) *Quality Without Tears*. New York: McGraw-Hill.

Dore, R. and Sako, M. (1989) *How the Japanese Learn to Work*. London: Routledge.

Drucker, P. (1961) *The Practice of Management*. London: Mercury.

Dunn, S., Richardson, R. and Dewe, P. (1991) 'The impact of employee share ownership on worker attitudes: a longitudinal case study', *Human Resource Management Journal*, Vol. 1, No. 3, pp. 1–17.

Eccles, T. (1981) *Under New Management: The Story of Britain's Largest Cooperative*. London: Pan.

Edlund, S. and Nyström, B. (1988) *Developments in Swedish Labour Law*. Stockholm: The Swedish Institute.

Edwards, P.K. (1987) *Managing the Factory*. Oxford: Blackwell.

Edwards, P.K. (1992) 'Industrial conflict: themes and issues in research', *British Journal of Industrial Relations*, Vol. 30, No. 3, pp. 361–404.

Edwards, R. (1979) *Contested Terrain*. New York: Basic Books.

Friedman, A. (1977) *Industry and Labour: Class Struggle at Work and Monopoly Capitalism*. London: Macmillan.

*Foy, N. (1994) *Empowering People at Work*. Aldershot: Gower.

Fröhlich, D. and Krieger, H. (1990) 'Technological change and worker participation in Europe', *New Technology, Work and Employment*, Vol. 5, No. 2, pp. 94–106.

Gaugler, E. and Wiltz, S. (1992) 'Federal Republic of Germany', in Brewster, C., Hegewisch, A., Holden, L. and Lockhart, T. (eds) *The European Human Resource Management Guide*. London: Academic Press, pp. 163–228.

Gill, C. (1993) 'Technological change and participation in work organisation: recent results from a European survey', *International Journal of Human Resource Management*, Vol. 4, No. 2, pp. 325–348.

Goss, D. (1994) *Principles of Human Resource Management*. London: Routledge.

Hammarström, O.L. (1987) 'Swedish industrial relations', in Bamber, G. and Lansbury, R. (eds) *International and Comparative Industrial Relations*. London: Allen & Unwin, pp. 224–248.

*Hammer, M. and Champy, J. (1993) *Reengineering the Corporation*. London: Nicholas Brealey.

Holden, L. (1990) 'Employee communications in Europe on the increase', *Involvement and Participation*, November, pp. 4–8.

Holden, L. (1996) 'HRM and employee involvement in Britain and Sweden: a comparative study', *International Journal of Human Resource Management*, Vol. 7, No. 1, pp. 59–81.

Honold, L. (1997) 'A review of the literature on employee empowerment', *Empowerment in Organisations*, Vol. 5, No. 4, pp. 202–212.

Hyman, J. and Mason, B. (1995) *Managing Employee Involvement and Participation*. London: Sage.

IDE (1981) *Industrial Democracy in Europe*. International Research Group, Oxford: Clarendon Press.

IDE (1993) *Industrial Democracy in Europe Revisited*. Oxford: Oxford University Press.

ILO (1993) *World Labour Report*. Geneva: International Labour Organization.

Kanter, R.M. (1983) *The Change Masters: Innovation and Entrepreneurship in the American Corporation*. New York: Simon & Schuster.

Keenoy, T. (1990) 'Human resource management: rhetoric, reality and contradiction', *International Journal of Human Resource Management*, Vol. 1, No. 2, pp. 363–384.

Keenoy, T. and Anthony, P. (1992) 'HRM: metaphor meaning and morality', in Blyton, P. and Turnbull, P. (eds) *Reassessing Human Resource Management*. London: Sage, pp. 233–255.

Kjellberg, A. (1992) 'Sweden: can the model survive?', in Ferner, A. and Hyman, R. (eds) *Industrial Relations in the New Europe*. Oxford: Blackwell, pp. 88–142.

Klaus, R. and Bass, B. (1974) 'Group influence on individual behaviour across cultures', *Journal of Cross Cultural Psychology*, Vol. 5, pp. 236–246 (quoted in Briggs, 1991).

Korpi, W. (1981) 'Workplace bargaining, the law and unofficial strikes: the case of Sweden', *British Journal of Industrial Relations*, Vol. 16, pp. 355–368.

Lane, C. (1989) *Management and Labour in Europe*. Aldershot: Edward Elgar.

*Lashley, C. (1997) *Empowering Service Excellence: Beyond the Quick Fix*. London: Cassell.

Lawler, E. (1986) *High-Involvement Management*. San Francisco Calif.: Jossey-Bass.

Lawrence, P. (1980) *Managers and Management in West Germany*. London: Croom Helm.

Legge, K. (1989) 'Human resource management: a critical analysis', in Storey, J. (ed.) *New Perspectives on Human Resource Management*. London: Routledge, pp. 19–40.

Lewis, P. (1989) 'Employee participation in a Japanese owned British electronics factory: reality or symbolism?', *Employee Relations*, Vol. 11, No. 1, pp. 3–9.

Lincoln, J. and Kalleberg, A. (1990) *Culture, Control and Commitment*. Cambridge: Cambridge University Press.

Lipietz, A. (1992) *Towards a New Economic Order: Post Fordism, Ecology and Democracy*. Cambridge: Polity Press.

Littlefield, D. (1996) 'Works council snub infuriates employees', *People Management*, 2 May, p. 5.

Lumb, R. (1996) 'BPR: not a fad, not a failure', *People Management*, 2 May, p. 26.

Marchington, M. (1989a) 'Joint consultation in practice', in Sisson, K. (ed.) *Personnel Management in Britain*. Oxford: Blackwell, pp. 378–402.

Marchington, M. (1989b) 'Employee participation', in Towers, B. (ed.) *Handbook of Industrial Relations Practice*, 2nd edn. London: Kogan Page, pp. 162–182.

Marchington, M. (1995) 'Involvement and participation', in Storey, J. (ed.) *Human Resource Management: A Critical Text*. London: Routledge, pp. 280–305.

Marchington, M., Goodman, J., Wilkinson, A. and Ackers, P. (1992) *New Developments in Employee Involvement*. Employment Department Research Series No. 2. Manchester: Manchester School of Management.

Marginson, P., Gilman, M., Jacobi, O. and Krieger, H. (1998) *Negotiating European Works Councils: An Analysis of Agreements under Article 13*. Dublin: European Foundation for the Improvement of Living and Working Conditions.

Mauritz, W. (1972) '10 Jahre Betriebsverfassungsgesetz aus der Sicht des Eigentümer-Unternehmers', in Lezius, M. (ed.) *10 Jahre Betriebsverfassungsgesetz*. Spardorf: R.F. Wilfer (quoted in Lane, 1989: 233).

Menon, S. (1995) *Employee Empowerment: Definition, Measurement and Construct Validation*. McGill University, Canada.

Monks, J. (1989) 'Trade union role in communications', in Wilkinson, T. (ed.) *The Communications Challenge: Personnel and PR Perspectives*. London: IPM, pp. 29–34.

Mumford, E. and Hendricks, R. (1996) 'Business process re-engineering RIP', *People Management*. 2 May, pp. 22–29.

Naoi, A. and Schooler, C. (1985) 'Occupational conditions and psychological functioning in Japan', *American Journal of Sociology*, Vol. 90, No. 4, pp. 729–752 (quoted in Briggs, 1991).

Noon, M. (1992) 'HRM: a map, model or theory?', in Blyton, P. and Turnbull, P. (eds) *Reassessing Human Resource Management*. London: Sage, pp. 16–32.

OECD (1991) *OECD in Figures: Statistics on the Member Countries*. Paris: Organization for Economic Cooperation and Development.

Oliver, N. and Lowe, J. (1991) 'UK computer industry: American, British and Japanese contrasts in human resource management', *Personnel Review*, Vol. 20, No. 2, pp. 18–23.

Parker, M. and Slaughter, J. (1995) 'Unions & management by stress', in Babson, S. (ed.) *Lean Work: Empowerment and Exploitation in the Global Auto Industry*. Detroit, Mich: Wayne State University Press.

Pascale, R. and Athos, A. (1982) *The Art of Japanese Management*. London: Allen Lane.

*Peppard, J. and Rowland, P. (1995) *The Essence of Business Process Re-engineering*. Hemel Hempstead: Prentice Hall.

Peters, T. and Waterman, R. (1982) *In Search of Excellence: Lessons from America's Best Run Companies.* New York: Harper & Row.

Poole, M. (1986) *Towards A New Industrial Democracy: Workers' Participation in Industry.* London: Routledge & Kegan Paul.

Poole, M. and Jenkins, G. (1990a) *The Impact of Economic Democracy: Profit Sharing and Employee Shareholding Schemes.* London: Routledge.

Poole, M. and Jenkins, G. (1990b) 'Human resource management and profit sharing: employee attitudes and a national survey', *International Journal of Human Resource Management*, Vol. 1, No. 3, pp. 289–328.

Price, R. (1989) 'The decline and fall of the status divide?', in Sisson, K., (ed.) *Personnel Management in Britain.* Oxford: Blackwell, pp. 271–295.

Price Waterhouse Cranfield Project on International Strategic Human Resource Management (1990) *Report.* London: Price Waterhouse.

Price Waterhouse Cranfield Project on International Strategic Human Resource Management (1991) *Report.* Cranfield: Cranfield School of Management.

Ramsay, H. (1977) 'Cycles of control', *Sociology,* Vol. 11, pp. 481–506.

Ramsay, H. (1983) 'Evolution or cycle? Worker participation in the 1970s and 1980s', in Crouch, C. and Heller, F. (eds) *International Yearbook of Organisational Democracy*, Vol.1. Chichester: John Wiley.

Ramsay, H. (1991) 'Reinventing the wheel? A review of the development and performance of employee involvement', *Human Resource Management Journal,* Vol. 1, No. 1, pp. 1–22.

Ramsay, H. (1992a) 'Commitment and involvement', in Towers, B. (ed.) *The Handbook of Human Resource Management.* Oxford: Blackwell.

Ramsay, H. (1992b) 'Swedish and Japanese work methods: comparisons and contrasts', *P+ European Participation Monitor,* Vol. 3, No. 1, pp. 37–40.

Ramsay, H., Leopold, J. and Hyman, J. (1986) 'Profit sharing and employee share ownership: an initial assessment', *Employee Relations,* Vol. 8, No. 1, pp. 23–26.

Rana, E. (1999) 'Europe split on issue of worker consultation plans', *People Management,* 11 November, p. 13.

Rothstein, L.R. (1995) 'The empowerment effort that came undone', *Harvard Business Review,* January–February, pp. 20–31.

Salaman, G. (1979) *Work Organisations: Resistance and Control.* London: Longman.

Schuller, T. (1986) *Age, Capital and Democracy: Member Participation in Pension Scheme Management.* Aldershot: Gower.

Schuller, T. (1989) 'Financial participation', in Storey, J. (ed.) *New Perspectives on Human Resource Management.* London: Routledge, pp. 126–136.

Sell, R. (1988) 'The human face of industry in Sweden', *Industrial Society Magazine,* March, pp. 30–32.

Semler, R. (1993) *Maverick: The Success Story Behind the World's Most Unusual Workplace.* London: Century.

Sewell, G. and Wilkinson, B. (1992) 'Empowerment or emasculation? Shopfloor surveillance in a total quality organisation', in Blyton, P. and Turnbull, P. (eds) *Reassessing Human Resource Management.* London: Sage, pp. 97–115.

Storey, J. (ed.) (1989) *New Perspectives on Human Resource Management.* London: Routledge.

Thomas, H. and Logan, C. (1982) *Mondragon: An Economic Analysis.* London: George Allen & Unwin.

Townley, B. (1989) 'Employee communication programmes', in Sisson, K. (ed.) *Personnel Management in Britain.* Oxford: Blackwell, pp. 329–355.

Wall, T.D. and Lischerson, J.A. (1977) *Worker Participation: A Critique of the Literature and Some Fresh Evidence.* London: McGraw-Hill.

Walton, R.E. (1984a) 'The future of human resource management: an overview', in Walton, R.E. and Lawrence, P.R. (eds) *HRM: Trends and Challenges.* Boston: Harvard Business School Press, pp. 3–11.

Walton, R.E. (1984b) 'Towards a strategy of eliciting employee commitment based on policies of mutuality', in Walton, R.E. and Lawrence, P.R. (eds) *HRM: Trends and Challenges.* Boston: Harvard Business School Press, pp. 35–65.

Walton, R.E. (1985) 'From control to commitment in the workplace', *Harvard Business Review,* March/April, pp. 76–84.

Ward, P.J. (1993) 'A study of organisational variables affecting worker empowerment,' *Educational and Psychological Studies,* Miami, Florida: University of Miami.

Wickens, P. (1987) *The Road to Nissan: Flexibility, Quality and Teamwork.* Basingstoke: Macmillan.

Wilczynski, J. (1983) *Comparative Industrial Relations.* London: Macmillan.

Wilkinson, A. (1998) 'Empowerment: theory and practice', *Personnel Review,* Vol. 27, No. 1, pp. 40–56.

*Wilkinson, A. and Wilmot, H. (1995) *Making Quality Critical: New Perspectives on Organisational Change.* London: Routledge.

Wilkinson, A., Marchington, M., Ackers, P. and Goodman, J. (1992) 'Total quality management and employee involvement', *Human Resource Management Journal,* Vol. 2, No. 4, pp. 1–20.

Wilkinson, T. (ed.) (1989) *The Communications Challenge: Personnel and PR Perspectives.* London: IPM.

Wilpert, B. and Rayley, J. (1983) *Anspruch und Wirklichkeit der Mitbestimmung.* Frankfurt: Campus (quoted in Lane, 1989: 232).

Wood, S. and Fenton O'Creevey, M. (1999) 'Employee involvement: channel hopping', *People Management,* 25 November, pp. 42–45.

14

Human resource management in the public sector

Trevor Colling

OBJECTIVES

● To consider shifting public policy contexts and their ramifications for the employment relationship.

● To examine the concept of 'model employer' practice.

● To outline current developments in employment and working time, pay and performance, and employee representation and involvement.

● To debate whether these constitute 'new model employer' practice.

INTRODUCTION

For much of the period following the Second World War, public sector employment relationships were distinctive, and designedly so. Managers were held accountable through political and administrative mechanisms, rather than through the market, and links between management practice and public policy were viewed as obvious and entirely legitimate. Public organisations were required to exemplify 'model employer' practice. Employment procedures were prescribed explicitly, sometimes by statute, and were subject to informal ministerial influence. Collective bargaining and consultation with trade unions were well established. National bargaining forums sat atop complex local and regional structures, and set uniform national pay rates and conditions of service.

In recent years, public sector employment relationships have been subject to two distinct shifts in overall policy. Conservative administrations during the 1980s and early 1990s developed programmes of market-based reforms designed to 'roll back the frontiers of the state'. Influenced by the philosophy and economics of the 'New Right', ministers diagnosed inherent weaknesses and inefficiencies in the public provision of goods and services, and held that these provided cumulatively a drain on the national economy. Enterprises and utility services were transferred to the private sector, and quasi-market disciplines were introduced into the remaining public services. Reducing public expenditure became a cardinal objective of public policy. New funding mechanisms pressed service managers to reduce employment and contain wage costs, and price became the predominant basis for competition.

With the election of a Labour government in 1997, market relationships were de-emphasised and a process of 'modernisation' embarked upon. Some elements of market structures were retained, including organisational divisions between purchasers and providers, and private sector involvement in service delivery remained important. Purchasing decisions, however, were placed firmly within policy frameworks and targets established by ministers and their departments. Importance was attached to performance against these targets rather than simply shifting provision to the private sector. Investment in public services was promised, but was targeted to secure improvements in specified areas. Benchmarking against best practice, the creation of bodies charged with spreading innovation, and ever more elaborate mechanisms for measuring and reviewing performance are becoming the hallmark of modernisation.

What ramifications have these changing policy regimes generated for 'model employer' practices? Market-based approaches were fundamentally antithetical to the concept. New Right policy makers had difficulty with specific elements of prevailing practice, particularly the importance accorded to trade unions, which they identified as unnatural impediments to the free operation of markets. But the very idea of prede-fined principles of employment practice sustained little credence in contexts where the ability to match terms and conditions to prevailing 'market' conditions was considered the hallmark of efficient management. For these reasons, the concept was de-empha-sised and its key tenets overturned. This does not mean, however, that government interest in employment matters diminished. In the previous edition of this text, it was argued in this chapter that the rhetoric of organisational change masked continuing fiscal and political direction (Colling, 1997). Sustained difficulties in reducing public expenditure kept control of public sector pay at the forefront of government policy. Developing and maintaining 'free market' reform required not a diminished state but the determined intervention of a strong one (Gamble, 1988). Attempts to establish public service cultures based on attention to customers, rather than workforces, and improved performance created structures dedicated to target setting, data collection and organisational review.

Such an argument is built on in this chapter, which seeks to incorporate preliminary assessment of the current programme of 'modernisation'. It is argued that current developments amount to the introduction of 'new model employer' policies even if they are not heralded in these terms. Government responsibility for the strategic develop-ment of public services is explicit again. The importance of national frameworks and of dialogue with trade unions has been asserted once again. These elements, resonant of public sector management in the formative post-war period, have been combined with sustained quests for flexibility in grading structures and an emphasis on 'performativity' (Webb, 1999). Employee effort is subject to measurement against targets, and this informs decisions about pay and career progression.

Discussion begins with an examination of the 'golden era', the period between 1945 and 1979 when the public sector grew in size and importance. Particular attention is paid to the principles and development of 'model employer' practice. Attention then turns to recent programmes of reform. Market-based reform pursued by Conservative governments between 1979 and 1997 is examined first. The main contours of the Labour Party's 'modernisation' agenda are then outlined, and the implications of these changes for public sector employment relationships are examined.

THE 'GOLDEN ERA': MORRISONIAN ORGANISATIONS AND MODEL EMPLOYMENT

Much of what was until recently recognised as the public sector developed in the immediate post-war period. Between 1945 and 1950, the Labour government took into public ownership a number of basic industries including coal, steel and the railways. Together these accounted for approximately 10% of the country's total productive capacity (Dearlove and Saunders, 1984: 268). Services that were to constitute the welfare state, including health and social security, were established under public administration and expanded rapidly. By 1959, almost a quarter (23.9%) of the labour force worked in the public sector (Fairbrother, 1982: 3). Over the next 30 years this diverse range of enterprises, utility industries and services was gradually restructured more or less according to the principles of public corporations established by the Labour politician, Herbert Morrison. During this 'golden era', there was little doubt that employment practice in the public sector was different from that prevailing elsewhere in the economy, and designedly so.

Morrisonian principles were derived from management structures established for the London Passenger Transport Board (Pendleton and Winterton, 1993: 2). These were informed by two policy objectives: first, to ensure that the priorities pursued by key industries and services were consistent with macroeconomic, industrial and social policy; and second, to provide within this framework some autonomy for professional managers. These large, integrated organisations were managed, therefore, through independent industry boards that had responsibility for day-to-day operational matters. But these boards were accountable directly to the relevant ministers, who were also empowered to give 'general direction' (ibid).

Differing contexts meant that the model could not be implemented uniformly, and some variation was apparent. Given the constitutional position of local government, for example, accountability to central government had to operate through different kinds of mechanisms. But the principles by which management operated were shared widely. An ethos of public service, founded upon accountability, impartiality and commitment to communitarian values, was fostered deliberately and became a primary motivating factor for employees (Pratchett and Wingfield, 1995). In the interests of equality of treatment, uniform standards of product or service were a priority, and departments would be deployed to ensure consistency across the organisation. Guaranteeing probity in the public interest required complex internal control systems and hierarchies of management and committee structures. Public sector organisations also tended to be structured according to functional expertise, with relatively rigid demarcations between professional groups. There was little, if any, requirement for general management. Rather, managers developed through the ranks of their specialism: engineers were managed by engineers, nurses by nurses, and so on (Stewart, 1989).

The public sector as a whole was also assigned a particular industrial relations mission: to be a 'model' employer and implement 'a range of practices which today constitute good management' (Priestly Commission, 1955, cited in Farnham and Horton, 1995: 8). The state sector's role in macroeconomic policy was important in this regard. Though the depth of the post-war consensus can be exaggerated, commitments to full employment and the welfare state structured the programmes of both of the key political parties for as long as they could be combined with economic growth (Hills, 1990). The public sector was assigned a key role in job creation, 'mopping-up' under-employment created by restructuring in the broader economy. Expanding public sector employment enabled managers to offer meaningful job security. Market notions of efficiency were generally alien to the public sector, and public expenditure planning mechanisms permitted public employers to pass on increasing labour costs to central government (Winchester, 1983).

'Model employer' practice also implied a range of procedures intended to set an example to organisations across the economy. Given the strategic importance of public industries in particular, great emphasis was attached to the collective involvement of employees as a means of identifying and resolving grievances, and thereby avoiding potentially costly disruption. The requirement on public enterprises 'to consult with organisations which appear to them to be representative' was legally specified in their respective nationalisation acts (Kelf-Cohen, cited in Pendleton and Winterton, 1993: 3). Elaborate, formal and bureaucratic systems for negotiation and consultation, often referred to as 'Whitleyism', developed across the public services too. Created with the brief to establish viable industrial relations systems following the end of the First World War, the Whitley Committee advocated centralised bargaining through joint industrial councils with a view to securing 'cooperation in the centre between national organisations' (Whitley Committee, cited in Clegg, 1979: 31).

Employee relations were marked consequently by a significant degree of centralisation. Most key employment decisions in the Civil Service were taken directly by national negotiators and handed down to local managers in the *Code and Guide*, 'a works handbook of monumental proportions' (Jary, 1991: 4). But there were important variations in this general picture (Fogarty and Brooks, 1986). Traditions of local bargaining in some of the nationalised industries (such as coal, docks and steel) remained entrenched long into the 'golden era', and local government employers came to full national bargaining relatively late in the day (Kessler, 1991: 7). By the mid-1950s, however, trends towards centralisation were apparent even here, and these conditioned a generally limited role for local management and trade union organisation:

> The principal tasks of local, traditional personnel departments were to act as monitors of policy and to maintain staffing establishments. There were few local variations in interpreting national policies and personnel management locally was essentially advisory and administrative, with line managers having a relatively passive role in managing people. (Farnham et al., 1994: 4)

As in operational matters, the prominent influence of central government made the management of public workforces particularly distinctive. The extent of political intervention, and the form that it took, varied between different parts of the sector. The constitutional position of local authorities, though weak by European standards, offered some protection from ministerial direction. Services with a more direct interface with government departments were much more susceptible, as Clegg (1979: 106) noted of the National Health Service:

> The rules negotiated by the joint councils are supplemented by a great many regulations laid down by the Department [of Health] on its own authority, and on the councils themselves the unions effectively negotiate, not with their employers, but with representatives of the government.

Government influence was often brought to bear to ensure the minimisation of conflict (Ferner and Colling, 1993). But cost constraint, and its ramifications for the management of the public sector, were more prominent features of the 'golden era' than is often acknowledged. Ministerial responsibilities for containing public expenditure generated a compelling interest in the outcome of collective bargaining. As early as the 1950s, government departments intervened to veto agreements in health and public transport that set precedents potentially which were deemed undesirable

(Crouch, 1979; Thornley, 1994). Repeated attempts to ensure that Civil Service pay awards were 'offset by corresponding economies' prompted shrill protests from the historically placid Civil Service unions:

> The National Staff Side sincerely trusts that there will be no interference in collective bargaining in the Civil Service . . . or any action which might bring into question the impartiality of the Civil Service arbitration tribunal or any refusal to honour awards of the tribunal.
>
> (cited in Mortimer and Ellis, 1980: 197)

Model employer principles developed during the period, then, resulted in relatively coherent frameworks for bargaining and consultation and a prominent role for trade unions in the management of change. But it is important to maintain an appropriately nuanced perspective. Exhortations to 'good management' were laced intermittently with cost pressures backed by ministerial pressure. While public employment was secure, low pay and discriminatory employment procedures remained characteristic of large parts of the public sector (Thornley, 1994). Proclaimed aspirations to industrial harmony were pursued selectively and, increasingly, with only moderate success. As ambivalent as these pressures may have been, both they and their effects rendered public sector employment relationships distinctive throughout the Morrison era.

CHANGING POLICY CONTEXTS: MARKETS TO MODERNISATION

Industrial relations literature has long recognised that the environment in which organisations conduct their operations influences the development of internal relationships. Legal frameworks established by national governments, and increasingly by supra-national bodies, regulate aspects of employment, corporate governance, and the terms on which companies engage in trade. In the private sector competition in product markets, and for investment from capital markets, may have significant implications for employment relationships. An appreciation of the context in which public sector workforces are managed is similarly critical. The following sections outline the broad phases of public policy development since 1979. Market-based reform pursued under recent Conservative administrations through the 1980s and early 1990s marked the abandonment of the organisational principles that had built the public sector. Production of goods and services was transferred to the private sector wherever possible, and remaining functions were subject to tight fiscal and performance criteria. The focus on modernisation, apparent since the election of a Labour government in 1997, suggests some acknowledgement of the positive role of public services and some corresponding muting of market pressures.

Markets

When economic growth faltered, the viability of large-scale state investment came to be questioned. Attempts to rein back public expenditure and to control inflation through incomes policies destabilised public sector employment relationships. Between 1969 and 1973 disputes in the public sector increased sevenfold, and contributed substantially to the defeat of the Heath Conservative government in 1974 (Coates, 1989: 66). At the height of the public sector disputes in 1978, dubbed the 'Winter of Discontent', the Labour Prime Minister is reputed to have told senior officials from the Trades Union Congress, 'We are prostrate before you – but don't ask us to put it in writing' (cited in

Taylor, 1993: 258). Out of this pervasive sense of crisis emerged a series of radical Conservative governments, committed to reducing the size and influence of the state sector and reconstituting employment relationships.

Finance was initially the principal tool of reform. Discarding the macroeconomic policies that had shaped the 'golden era', governments from 1979 focused upon the control of inflation (rather than the maintenance of employment levels), and public expenditure restraint became a primary objective. Limits on capital spending – inherited from the previous Labour government – were intensified, and volume planning, by which finance for existing commitments was merely increased in line with price movements, was replaced by cash limits. The discretion of local authorities to maintain spending by raising supplementary local income was cut back progressively, culminating in the wholesale revision of local authority finance and the introduction of the Community Charge and, subsequently, the Council Tax (Travers, 1989; Cochrane, 1993). This legislation removed the right of local authorities to levy rates on non-domestic/business premises and further limited the amount of revenue that could be retained from the domestic tax. As a consequence, 'the new system [reduced], by about half, the level of local revenue which may be decided locally' (John, 1991: 64).

These domestic commitments were reinforced by preparations for European Monetary Union (EMU). Convergence criteria established by the Maastricht Treaty include limits on public expenditure. Britain's short-lived membership of the Exchange Rate Mechanism (ERM), the precursor to full EMU, ended in 1995 with the loss of several billion pounds spent trying to defend the value of sterling against massive sales in the currency markets. Discretion to invest in public services available to the incumbent Conservative government, or the subsequent Labour one, was reduced significantly, and the requirement to constrain or reduce public expenditure was reinforced. These pressures carried particular implications for employment. Reducing the aggregate level of spending proved difficult in practice. In the face of cyclical increases in unemployment and the greater demand for pension payments stemming from an ageing population, quests for savings in social security spending repeatedly ran into the buffers of political reality. Public sector labour costs, particularly increases in the wage bill, are a relatively soft area to control and to justify. Governments inclined to reduce expenditure were bound therefore to review employment and wage costs as a priority.

Financial stringency was augmented increasingly by organisational restructuring to admit, or emulate, market forces. With the exception of the postal services, all of the major industries and utilities in public ownership in 1979 were privatised via flotation on the Stock Exchange or, in the case of the railways, through franchising agreements. The programme started in piecemeal fashion with the sale of relatively small stockholdings in companies such as ICL, Cable & Wireless and British Aerospace. Following the successful sale of British Telecom in 1984, plans rapidly gathered pace, and the large-scale privatisations of British Gas, British Airways and the water and electricity industries followed (Colling and Ferner, 1994). Though less well publicised, elements of the public services were also privatised via trade sales, such as the Property Services Agency and the Skills Training Agency (PSPRU, 1994).

Competitive pressures were released in the remaining public services. Competitive tendering was introduced into local government (1980) and the National Health Service (1983). Focused initially on ancillary services, such as cleaning, laundry and housing maintenance, competitive tendering required public authorities to test the cost of existing provision by allowing private companies to bid for the work. Having proved successful in reducing costs (though the size of savings is a matter of dispute), such regimes were made compulsory in local government (hence the acronym CCT for compulsory competitive tendering) and extended to cover a broader range of functions including computing, architectural and personnel services. Similar mechanisms, referred to as 'market testing', were introduced into the Civil Service. In contrast to the NHS and local government, where the vast majority of work was retained in house, the common practice of prohibiting in-house bids in the Civil Service resulted in the simple transfer of operations to private companies (PSPRU, 1994: 9).

Finally, various forms of quasi-markets were constructed. In education and health, service providers (that is, schools and hospitals) were ostensibly released from regulation by local policy networks to compete in internal markets for status and resources. Hospitals were vested as trusts and contracted with health care purchasers (principally the health authorities) to provide services for their local area. Restructuring in the Civil Service devolved operational responsibility to executive agencies, separated from their government departments, who retained responsibilities for overall policy and strategy. Though the forces of competition were more muted here, comparisons of performance across agencies and with the private sector introduce them by proxy.

These pressures altered the framework within which the public sector was managed. At the extreme, managers in the former public enterprises now operated entirely in the private sector, where competitors, regulatory bodies and shareholders provided new influences (Ferner and Colling, 1991). Following marketisation of the remaining public services, managers had to accommodate a range of similar pressures. Private sector management practice was extolled repeatedly by government ministers. Efficiency reviews were led by prominent businessmen, such as Lord Rayner (of Marks and Spencer) and Roy Griffiths (of J Sainsbury). Bodies such as the National Audit Office and the Audit Commission were established to promote business values of efficiency, economy and effectiveness (the 3Es) in the public services. Management consultants played a significant role in inculcating business perspectives. One conservative estimate suggests that the public sector spent over £250 million on consultants between 1994 and 1995 alone (*Investors Chronical*, May, 1995: 17).

From this maelstrom, some observed an emerging management style dubbed the 'New Public Management' (Dunleavy and Hood, 1994). What set this apart from traditional conceptions was the emphasis on the 'right' , and later the obligation, to *manage* in ways stereotypically associated with the private sector. Whereas previous traditions of professions managing themselves had given rise to introspective and collusive management systems, the importance attached to general management skills was intended to enable managers to take heed of constituencies other than employees alone (Stewart, 1989). Operational priorities were re-focused around cost and performance rather than equity and social impact as in the past. These two imperatives were to be harnessed to a revitalised 'customer culture' (Harden, 1992; Heery, 1992). Though some parts of the public sector had an honourable history of developing customer service programmes independently, the requirement to do so was codified through initiatives such as the Citizen's Charter and the plethora of performance indicators, targets and complaints procedures spawned subsequently.

Thus the assumptions underpinning public sector management practice through the 'golden era' were dismantled or eroded as a consequence of the primacy given to 'markets' during the 1980s and 1990s. Notions of affordability, flexibility and organisational efficiency largely displaced those of consistency, probity and accountability as the guiding principles of public administration.

Modernisation

Writing three years into the first period of Labour government in nearly two decades, full *evaluation* of the current modernisation programme would be premature. The early pace of initiatives has been rapid, however, and the skeletal proposals apparent during the election in 1997 have been fleshed out considerably. Following a comprehensive White Paper (Cabinet Office, 1999) and several service-specific announcements (DoH, 1997, 1999a, 1999b; DETR, 1999; NHS Executive, 1999; Wilson, 1999b; DfEE, 2000b), it is possible to identify the main contours of likely reform.

The current agenda appears distinguishable from market-driven reform in both tone and form. The explicit and sustained denigration of public service, and of public servants, has largely gone. Though the Prime Minister has complained famously of the 'scars on his back' sustained trying to reform public services, such rhetoric has not found its way into formal proposals. Stemming from the government's key election pledges, the role played by public services in a modern economy has been recognised, and the intention to invest in them adequately has been articulated repeatedly. Continuing innovation in the 'knowledge economy', for example, has been linked to raising attainment levels in schools and opening up opportunities for 'lifelong learning'. The contrast with previous priorities of 'rolling back the frontiers of the state' seems obvious in this light. Indeed, a critique of the misapplication of market principles in public service contexts underlies current policy. Competitive behaviour between fragmented public services is said to have led to confused areas of responsibility, uncoordinated management initiatives, and inadequate lines of accountability. As the Head of the Home Civil Service has conceded:

> I would not claim that the manner in which we implemented . . . reforms over the years was a model to emulate. There was not enough overall vision or strategic planning. Too often it was uncoordinated, with different parts of the centre of Government launching initiatives simultaneously or at a pace which long suffering managers in departments found hard to handle.
>
> (Wilson 1999b: 2)

Current proposals for 'modernisation' cohere around key themes and principles (Cabinet Office, 1999). First, incentives to *competitive* behaviour are removed or dampened. Dismantling the internal market between hospital trusts was an early priority, for example. Second, public and government interest in management behaviour is acknowledged once again. Though Morrisonian models are eschewed emphatically, the principle of political accountability is strengthened by cascaded target-setting. Objectives established for ministers and government departments are adapted and extended as appropriate to agencies, suppliers and service providers. Thus:

> In the new NHS all those charged with planning and providing health and social care services for patients will work to a jointly agreed local Health Improvement Programme. This will govern the actions of all the parts of the local NHS to ensure consistency and coordination. It will also make clear the responsibilities of the NHS and local authorities for working together to improve health.
>
> (DoH,1997: para. 2.11)

Similarly, Annual Framework Agreements, which governed the activities of Civil Service agencies, have been replaced by longer-term Public Service Agreements (PSAs). By 1998, over 350 new performance targets had been set by 28 new PSAs (Theakston, 1998). Finally, previous emphasis on establishing for public servants 'the right to manage' is tempered now by requirements for managers to work in 'partnership' once again. Collaborative rather than entrepreneurial behaviour is supposed to manifest itself in managers' relationships with other agencies (as in joint initiatives between health and social services, for example), with service users and citizens (such as increased consultation over economic regeneration and expenditure priorities in local government), and with workforces (as discussed below).

Rebuttal of previous practice is far from complete, however. Key elements of 'market-based' reform are retained and developed further within the modernisation agenda. Expenditure targets set by the previous government were retained for the first half of Labour's first term of office. New investment planned for thereafter has been targeted closely on new technologies and funds to meet key service targets. Inevitably, cost reduction has remained a key management objective in large parts of the public services. Market structures remain to some extent. Divisions between service purchaser and provider functions, for example, were subject to inter-party agreement under the Major government, and remain now that Labour is in government. Private sector involvement looks likely to increase if anything. Opposed vehemently in opposition, privatisation is now firmly on Labour's policy agenda, and is being considered actively for the national air traffic control system, for example. Under the Private Finance Initiative (PFI), commercial companies are invited to build, equip and maintain public service outlets (such as hospitals and schools) in return for payments phased over long contract periods. Greeted with scepticism when first introduced by the Major government (not least by the private sector companies, whose enthusiasm and readiness was presupposed), the scheme has been driven forward by Labour in government. Finally, the emphasis on measuring performance against targets has been retained and intensified by Labour in government. The seven 'challenges' issued to civil servants by the Labour government within 18 months of assuming office built on the six 'Whitehall Standards' of customer service established by the Major government immediately prior to the election in 1997 (IRS, 1999c: 6). Various forms of benchmarking performance against public and private sector bodies have been introduced. In the Civil Service, benchmarking entails measuring Civil Service agencies against the Business Excellence Model (now renamed the EFQM Excellence Model; DETR, 1998: 51), which comprises nine criteria developed by 200 private sector organisations (Corby and White, 1999: 12). Where public service managers fail to perform on any of these criteria, services are to be transferred to alternative providers from the public or private sector. Support services provided by education authorities have become a particular target following unfavourable reviews by the schools inspectorate, OFSTED (e.g. DfEE, 2000a).

Modernisation in practice: 'best value'

Because it combines each of these elements, 'best value' (Labour's replacement for CCT) illustrates how modernisation may work in practice (DETR, 1999; Unison, 1999). The new regime represents a shift away from competition as the main guarantee of service quality. Yet it simultaneously maintains cost pressures, widens the scope for private sector involvement, and intensifies performance pressures. New procedures require service reviews, and these are to proceed according to the four Cs: *challenge* (why and how services are being provided); *compare* (performance with that offered by analogous organisations); *consult* (local taxpayers); and, finally, *compete* where necessary (by inviting tenders from alternative providers). Flexibility is offered to authorities through the removal of prescriptive and proscriptive statutory measures, but best value is still expected to contribute to efficiency savings of 2% per annum (Unison, 1999). Pressures to extend private sector participation are extensified and intensified. The requirement to demonstrate 'best value' is extended beyond those services subject to CCT, and new duties are placed on authorities to sustain markets for business services where they exist and to build them where they do not. Finally, performance reviews via benchmarking are seen as providing stiffer and more regular tests for authorities than competitive tendering exercises alone. The Department of the Environment, Transport and the Regions will establish national performance indicators, in consultation with authorities and the Audit Commission, and these will be monitored eventually by a Best Value Inspectorate. Authorities will be expected to set *quality* targets consistent with the upper quartile of performers, and *cost* and *efficiency* targets consistent with the upper quartile of performers in specified regions.

> This framework of targets will put most pressure on those authorities who are currently performing poorly on both the quality and the efficiency with which they deliver services. However, it is likely to exert pressure on nearly all authorities because very few authorities score very highly on both aspects of performance at the same time.
>
> (DETR 1998b: para. 7.14)

Summary

The scope and depth of public sector activity grew dramatically during the 'golden era' from the 1940s to the late 1970s. Principles established by Herbert Morrison underpinned management structures and behaviour. A key feature was the need to ensure some degree of congruence between the goals of particular public organisations and espoused public policy. Organisations were highly integrated, characterised by bureaucratic procedures, and managed by professional specialists subject to general direction by the relevant government ministers.

From 1979 to 1997 the focus shifted to market-based approaches. Expansion was halted by public expenditure constraints and then reversed, as 'rolling back the frontiers of the state' became a priority. Public enterprises were transferred to the private sector, and market mechanisms and competitive pressures were introduced into the remaining public services. Organisations were fragmented as distinct roles were created for service purchasers and providers.

The modernisation agenda, developed and pursued since 1997, reveals a 'third way' based on combining elements from planning and from market-driven approaches. The denigration of public services has ceased, and their contribution to national economic and social priorities is acknowledged to a greater degree. Some market-driven pressures have been removed, including the internal market in health and CCT in local government, and organisations have been re-integrated. Explicit target-setting has reintroduced elements of planning by ensuring compliance with national policy priorities within and across public services.

Obvious as these policy changes might appear, closer examination reveals that important continuities as well as departures have marked them. Decentralisation pursued under the period of market reform was accompanied by the early development of performance reviews (Carter and Poynter, 1999). Control and direction from national centres, a characteristic of the planning era, was reconstituted through such mechanisms, rather than abandoned as the rubric of devolution might suggest (Talbot, 1997). While reining back the rhetoric of decentralisation to some degree, moderniser have developed further just such an approach. Service managers are offered greater flexibility, but control and accountability are ensured through organisational change, performance review, and continuing financial constraint.

What implications have these pressures had for employment practice? This question is now addressed through detailed discussion of three key themes: employment and working time; pay and performance; and employee representation and involvement. In each case, attention focuses on those employees who continue to provide public services in the health and in central and local government departments. Though subject still to quasi-governmental regulation, employees in the former public enterprises now work in quite distinct contexts, and cannot be considered part of the public sector in any meaningful sense.

THE CHANGING NATURE OF THE 'MODEL EMPLOYER'

The deliberate diffusion of 'model employer' practice has become a less prominent feature of public policy. Conservative ministers from 1979, and the New Right thinkers who influenced them, were inclined to view trade unions as an impediment to the effective operation of markets. At a more pragmatic level, they recognised too that public sector unions had become a potent source of opposition to government policy, and had contributed in no small measure to the downfall of the 1974–79 Labour government. Promoting national collective bargaining and trade union organisation became somewhat less of a priority, therefore. More important perhaps, the very notion of a single set of employment principles was not attractive to policy makers who regarded as the hallmark of effective management the ability to tailor terms and conditions of employment to specific trading contexts. During the period of market-based reform, the emphasis shifted from promoting model employment to providing the space in which managers could assume the *right* to manage.

The extent to which this philosophy was reflected in changed management practice is a different matter. As argued in the previous edition of this text (Colling, 1997), government's interest in employment levels and pay remained undiminished and constrained the extent to which decision-making could be left entirely to local actors. Paradoxically, promoting market pressures in these and other areas often required government to intervene more determinedly rather than stand back. Alongside measures promising greater discretion, therefore, initiatives were developed to test performance and to set targets for change and improvement.

Human resources issues arising from this approach emerged only partially, and were not implemented with particular success. Meaningful reform of pay structures, for example, grounded on the twin rocks of expenditure restraint and an ideological allergy to dealing effectively with continuing trade union opposition. The modernisation agenda, however, develops an explicit approach to precisely such issues. Though important aspects of policy towards the public services have changed, current emphasis on employment flexibility and performance can be traced back in linear fashion to previous governments. In this context, it is possible to argue that the notion of the model employer remains with us – it is the model that has changed. Where the focus was provided once by due process and comparability, 'performativity' is the objective of current employment reform. Such issues are now addressed through consideration of employment and working time, pay and performance, and employee representation and involvement.

Employment and working time

Given the high-profile policy stance of rolling back the frontiers of the state, it is possibly surprising that public sector employment remains significant. Key areas, including health and education, have barely shrunk at all. These aggregate patterns, however, should not obscure important changes in the composition of the public sector work-force or the flexibility in contractual forms and working time that is an increasingly prominent characteristic. Current policy objectives are likely to develop flexibility initiatives, not least in response to the promotion of 'family-friendly' working practices and the wish to secure further 'diversity'.

In the two decades since 1979 the public sector workforce shrank by just over a third (see Figure 14.1) yet it still employs 5 million people, one in five of the total workforce and over 1 million more than the combined manufacturing sector (Pierson, 1994; NIESR, 1995; MacGregor 1999). Health and education, the two largest public services, each employed over 1 million people in 1998, almost exactly the same as in 1979.

Central government saw the most significant decline, principally because of the government's ability to drive through reductions in Civil Service employment in contrast to other areas where it is not the direct employer. Even here change was complex. First, it was episodic rather than incremental. Reductions gouged from the Civil Service between 1979 and 1985 effectively halted until 1993 (Hogwood, 1998). Reductions resumed from this point can be attributed reasonably to programmes of market testing, which commenced simultaneously. This raises a further complication discussed below. Second, central government employment has embraced both industrial and service-based employment, and their experience has differed markedly. Employment in the industrial Civil Service has declined steeply, but service-based employment levels have been more 'sticky', particularly in policy-sensitive areas such as social security. Finally, as the earlier point about market testing highlights, it is difficult to disentangle genuine employment reductions from employment *transfers* within the public sector and between public bodies and the private sector. The marked fall in central government employment since 1990 is partly explained by the transfer of NHS staff from central government payrolls to the individual trusts. Trusts are now recorded as public corporations: hence the corresponding rise in employment in this category. Transfers of staff in the education sector have been similarly interpreted. In 1989, universities, polytechnics,

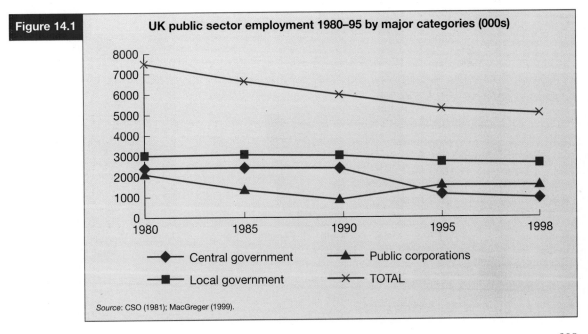

Figure 14.1 **UK public sector employment 1980–95 by major categories (000s)**

Source: CSO (1981); MacGreger (1999).

higher education colleges and schools opting out of local authority control were reclassified within the national accounts as private sector, non-profit-making bodies.

It was employment patterns, rather than headcount, that changed significantly. Three related but distinct aspects need to be noted. First, the ratio of non-manual to manual jobs increased as a consequence of marketisation and the decline of industrial employment. The NHS was able to cut its ancillary workforce in half between 1983 and 1991 (Winchester and Bach, 1994). But cuts here were offset by increased recruitment of professional, administrative and managerial posts. Employment in social services increased throughout the 1980s, and new technology generated the need for new skills across all organisations. Second, principally as a consequence of the rationalisation of traditional manual jobs, the public sector workforce became increasingly feminised. Figure 14.2 compares gendered employment data from 1980 and 1996. Women's presence in the public sector workforce increased from 45% to 57% over the period. Women's employment overall declined marginally by 12%, while the male workforce was nearly halved.

Finally, so-called 'non-standard' working arrangements spread across organisations and professions. In the context of long-term downward trends in employment, fixed-term or temporary working became significant. Over half of all employees on fixed-term contracts currently work in the public services (Hegewisch, 1999: 117), and almost three-quarters of public sector workplaces have staff on fixed-term contracts, compared with just one-third of private sector companies (Cully *et al.*, 1999: 35). Part-time working, always a part of public sector employment, has become an especially prominent feature. Also illustrated in Figure 14.2 are employment trends categorised by full-time and part-time hours between 1980 and 1996. Job cuts focused on full-time employment, while part-time employment for both women and men increased by small

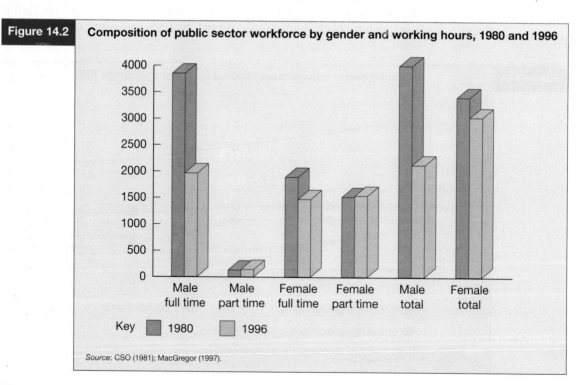

Figure 14.2 Composition of public sector workforce by gender and working hours, 1980 and 1996

Key ▮ 1980 ▮ 1996

Source: CSO (1981); MacGregor (1997).

margins. The proportion of the workforce working part time increased from less than a quarter to around a third as a consequence (Hogwood, 1992). Nearly all public sector workplaces (95%) have some part-time employees, and they comprise over half of the workforce in 30% (Cully *et al.*, 1999: 32). It is a particular feature in health and education, where it accounts for nearly half of the total workforce (Pierson, 1994; GSO, 1996). Feminisation and part-time working are strongly associated. Nine out of every ten part-time employees in the public sector are women, and the ratio is higher still in some specific services (GSO, 1996: 16).

Modernisation policies are likely to intensify these kinds of trends. Continuing expenditure constraints rule out increased employment except possibly in areas identified as having recruitment difficulties such as nurses and teachers. Employment transfers look set to continue, both within the public sector and across to the private and voluntary sectors as a consequence of best value and PFI. Flexible working looks set to increase as a consequence of two related initiatives. To the extent that commitments to extend 'diversity' in the Civil Service include increasing the number of women employees, employers may find it necessary to extend the availability of part-time working to levels long apparent in local government and the NHS (Cabinet Office, 1999). Where such provisions are already established, they may be extended across occupational groups and possibly to senior levels in grading structures.

Pay and performance

Reform of the centralised bargaining and consultation structures, characteristic of the Morrison era, has been one of the most tangible indicators of changing employment practice. Market orientations fostered an approach to pay determination founded on aligning pay with local labour markets and affordability considerations at the level of service providers. Decentralisation was thus the primary motif of Conservative governments through the 1980s and 1990s. It was pursued pragmatically (rather than strategically), however, and was held in tension by a contending desire to maintain central control of the overall pay bill. The resulting confusion is cleared to some degree by the modernisation agenda. Initiatives coordinated across the public services are intended to reform bargaining arrangements and reconstitute workforces.

The growth of indexation and independent pay review mechanisms played a significant role in reducing the scope of collective bargaining. Where they have been introduced, pay issues are decided through either predetermined formulae, in the case of indexation, or the deliberations of a panel following the submission of evidence from managers, unions and government. While some argue that the latter amounts to 'quasi-bargaining forums' (Winchester, 1996: 10), the removal of formal collective bargaining, and notionally thereby the threat of strike action, was a common element. Although it was reserved initially for judges, doctors and the armed forces, other significant occupational groupings were incorporated gradually. The fire and police services were surprisingly late additions at the end of the 1970s, and schoolteachers, nurses and midwives were added subsequently. One-third of public sector employees were no longer affected by collective pay bargaining by the end of the period of market-based reform (Bailey, 1996: 136).

Throughout the 1980s centralised bargaining structures came under informal pressure through changes to public sector financial procedures. The switch to cash rather than volume planning (mentioned earlier) required employers to balance increases in pay against levels of service. From the late 1980s managers in the NHS used discretion

available to them to vary starting salaries and job descriptions for ancillary and administrative staff (Grimshaw, 1999). The creation of market relationships, such as those
stemming from competitive tendering, provided additional impetus. Decisions about
the allocations of service contracts were based primarily on price, of which labour costs
are usually a substantial element. Quests for savings thus prompted service managers
locally to redesign work organisation and terms and conditions of employment
(Colling, 1993). Ad hoc adjustments to employment packages became common, irrespective of whether or not the work was retained by public sector employers. In local
government, for example, reform of bonus payments and working hours disorientated
pay and grading structures, increasing pay inequalities, particularly between women
and men (Escott and Whitfield, 1995; Colling, 1999).

From the early 1990s attempts were made to extend decentralised bargaining
across and up grading structures to include professional and technical staff whose pay
and conditions remained subject usually to national negotiations. This required a
more direct approach to reform. The 1992 White Paper *People, Jobs and Opportunity*
promised to

> encourage employers to move away from traditional, centralised collective bargaining towards
> methods of pay determination which reward individual skills and performance; respond to the
> wish of individual employees to negotiate their own terms and conditions, and take full account of
> business circumstances.   (cited in White, 1994: 7)

The government's determination in this area was illustrated by the escalation of pressure on NHS trust managers. Local managers, aware of the considerable opposition of
the unions and professional associations, sought initially to innovate through job
redesign and to maximise the grading flexibility offered by existing national agreements
rather than negotiate locally for professional groups (Bach and Winchester, 1994).
Following the 1992 election, however, burgeoning entrepreneurial spirit was galvanised
by increasingly explicit exhortations from ministers and the NHS Executive and, after a
protracted stand-off with the unions, the 1995 pay settlement eventually permitted some
element of local bargaining for health service staff with the exception of doctors.

Pressures for decentralisation were held in tension by the contending objective of
retaining control of the overall public sector pay bill. The Civil Service provides a particularly marked, though not unique, example of this Janus-faced approach to reform.
Responsibility for pay bargaining was delegated to the newly created executive agencies
by the Civil Service (Management Functions) Act 1992 (Massey, 1993; Bailey, 1994;
Marsden and Richardson, 1994). Central controls remained extensive, however. The
annual settlement on running costs provided continued opportunities for Treasury officials to control agency expenditure, including staffing and payroll costs (Talbot, 1997).
Controls were implemented rigidly to ensure that efficiency savings were not vired into
increased rewards for staff. They were also extended beyond budgets to cover matters
such as negotiating priorities and tactics. Talbot (1997) illustrates colourfully the experience of supposedly decentralised negotiations in the Vehicle Inspectorate Agency
(VI). VI's initial submissions to the Treasury were rejected firmly on the grounds that
the agency's staff would still be covered by the grading structure used in their host
department. Treasury officials required VI to formulate independent plans, to set out a
business case for them, and to submit a negotiating remit. Treasury approval was
required on each of these elements in advance, and the negotiating remit had to detail
the opening stance, the extent to which negotiators would vary their proposals and
identify precise fall-back positions (Talbot, 1997: 23).

Decentralisation and market-based reform contributed significantly to changing expectations surrounding public sector pay. Comparability gave way to affordability, and earnings growth in the public sector now lags considerably behind the private sector (Elliot and Duffus, 1996: Winchester, 1996). They also generated difficulties of their own. Disorientation of pay structures, and the inequalities that emerged subsequently (Escott and Whitfield, 1995), arguably did little for morale, and provided the basis for substantial legal challenges. The Acquired Rights Directive and its UK variant, the Transfer of Undertakings (Protection of Employment) Directive (TUPE), provide rights to consultation and prohibit changes to pay and conditions when staff are transferred from one employer to another (e.g. from the public sector to a private contractor). Equal pay legislation makes it illegal to pay different rates to women and men when they carry out similar work, work rated as equivalent by a job evaluation scheme, or work that is of equal value in terms of effort or skill. Though the extent and security of such protections have been far from total (Napier, 1993; Dickens, 2000), unions became adept at selecting test cases to inhibit or reverse market-driven reform of pay systems, and won some notable victories in both domestic and European courts (Colling, 2000). The threat of further proceedings underpinned subsequent bargaining strategies, particularly in health and local government, where potential equal value cases became intertwined with union demands for coordinated reviews of pay and grading.

The resulting confusion was cleared to some degree by approaches adopted subsequent to the 1997 election. The modernisation agenda includes a desire to reintroduce coordination into public service employment. Fundamental reviews of pay, grading and bargaining arrangements are planned for health and the Civil Service (Cabinet Office, 1999). Policy on the matter built on models provided by the Single Status agreement signed by local government employers and unions in 1997. Experimentation with local pay bargaining in the NHS was ended formally: 'The current mix of national and local contracts is divisive and costly. The Government's objective for the longer term is therefore to see staff receive national pay' (Department of Health, 1999a: para. 6.28).

Continuities from the previous period of market-based reform are striking, however. First, though pay rates will be established by national frameworks, existing local flexibility will be retained and extended. In health, for example, trust managers have exercised discretion over starting salaries and job descriptions for ancillary staff since 1986, and for administrative and clerical staff (since 1989) (Grimshaw, 1999: 289). Comprehensive local reviews envisaged currently will further extend functional flexibility within and across a broader range of occupational groupings (NHS Executive, 1999).

Second, commitments to link pay with performance have also been sustained and intensified:

> A person's pay should reflect their ouput, results and performance. This means the best performers, both individual and teams, and those who contribute most, should be rewarded. We should challenge systems which give automatic pay increases to poor or inefficient performers.
>
> (Cabinet Office, 1999: para. 20)

Existing performance-related pay (PRP) schemes in the Civil Service are to be reviewed and reformed. PRP has been limited to senior managers in other services, but longstanding plans to extend it have been driven forward by Labour in government. Head teachers were assimilated on to new scales incorporating performance elements in 1999. Pay review body recommendations that classroom teachers should be included from 2000 were subject to consultation at the time of writing (IRS 1999a: 2; DfEE, 2000b). Significantly, training programmes for head teachers on the issue were rolled out by the DfEE in parallel with consultation exercises, rather than by local education authorities – an indication of the government's determination to drive change forward and to circumvent passive opposition at local level.

Third, overall pay levels remain subject to tight constraints on public expenditure. Above-inflation settlements were agreed for those areas experiencing recruitment difficulties, and pay review body recommendations have been implemented in full, following several years of staged implementation. In health, nurses and professions allied to medicine received an average 4.7% increase in 1999 (IRS, 1999a). Controls remain tight, however. The Treasury committed the government to contain expenditure growth to no more than 2.25% per annum for the first three years in office and an inflation target of 2.5% over the same period. The consequent restraint on public sector pay was made explicit in government evidence to pay review bodies who were required to construct awards consistent with fiscal targets (Bolger and Timmins, 1998: 9). As the Comprehensive Spending Review progressed through 1999, the Chancellor announced higher than expected general settlements for health and for education, but pressure on pay was sustained. New money was tied explicitly to funding new capital projects, such as improved information technology, and meeting previously established service targets, such as hospital waiting lists. Interventions by the Prime Minister made it clear that government did not expect to see pay levels increasing at the same rate as general expenditure unless they were 'linked to results' (Peston and Timmins, 1999: 1).

This funding context leaves little scope for general increases in pay sufficient to recover the comparability with private sector occupations demanded by unions. Performance management systems will receive additional monies separate from core spending. Systems for teachers are to be funded to the tune of £1 billion over the first two years' operation, for example. Where such innovations are not planned, or where employees are ineligible or decline to participate, increases in core pay and allowances will still have to be balanced against existing budgets and investment needed to meet other performance targets.

Employee representation and involvement

Model employer policies pursued in the post-war period promoted collective employee relations. Union growth was stimulated directly (through the promotion of trade union membership) and indirectly (through the promotion of union involvement in collective bargaining). Gradual growth was followed in the 1970s by ballooning memberships as public sector workforces expanded and unions sought to recruit within them more aggressively. Membership in NUPE and NALGO increased by 78% through the period, for example (Fryer, 1989: 23). Growth coincided with declining employment in manufacturing industries, and therefore trade union membership, and the intensifying pressures on public sector pay discussed earlier. During the closing stages of the planning era, public sector trade unionism emerged as the focal point of the British Labour movement and a major source of opposition to prevailing government policy. Disarming and undermining trade union strength became a priority for governments committed to market-based reform. Approaches to public sector unions during this period can be characterised in four ways: confrontation, exclusion, disorientation, and fragmentation.

Ushered into government on waves of anti-union sentiment following the Winter of Discontent, Conservative ministers encouraged managers to confront unions, albeit selectively. Strikes in the Civil Service and the Health Service were early features of the period, but the year long stand-off with the National Union of Mineworkers, ending in their defeat in 1985, assumed particular symbolic importance. Civil Service unions were excluded from GCHQ, the national intelligence-gathering centre in Cheltenham. Direct derecognition remained relatively rare. Instances in hospital trusts were primarily rationalising arrangements, aimed at unions with very small memberships, rather than excluding unions in general. Competitive tendering provided some hawkish local authorities with an indirect means of derecognising unions. Prior to awareness of the Acquired Rights Directive, tendering exercises permitted the transfer of public sector workforces to employers with no union recognition arrangements (Ascher, 1987). More important has been the selective removal of groups of staff from collective bargaining. Senior technical and professional staff in the Health Service and Civil Service have been put on to managerial grades that are not covered by collective agreements, thereby weakening the rationale for trade union membership. A few employers also began to tighten time-off arrangements for union activists (Corby, 1998). Others specified more closely those they were prepared to deal with. Employers have excluded full-time officers in some instances or lay representatives not directly employed by them (Bryson *et al.*, 1995). Managers sought to secure ongoing organisational change through extra-union forms of involvement, including total quality management and business process re-engineering (Davies and Hinton, 1993; Morgan and Murgatroyd, 1994).

For organisations that had grown around the pergola of national bargaining, decentralised negotiating arrangements were disorienting – and intentionally so. Important aspects of decision-making remained centralised, or became more so, such as setting of performance and financial targets. Combined with residual central bargaining frameworks, these required continuing coordination at national level. But devolution of budgets, managerial authority and aspects of collective bargaining often exposed the need also to invest in local organisation, which circumstances had allowed unions to neglect previously. Weakness was not manifest evenly across all services or all issues. In areas such as local government, with relatively recent traditions of local bargaining, the shock effects generated by decentralisation were not as great as elsewhere. Union influence over some aspects of bargaining remained relatively robust even where local negotiations were more novel. Thornley's (1998) assessment of local negotiations in health leads her to dispute the image of local union activists as 'passive and powerless agents' (p. 428). Union organisation was one factor muting variation in pay awards following decentralisation (IRS, 1999a). Given the funding climate described earlier, however, union demands at local level have been hamstrung by 'ability to pay' arguments and the consequent requirement to balance pay increases against efficiency savings (meaning job loss in most instances). The size of pay awards, as distinct from their variation, has been affected as a consequence, and unions have had to respond to ad hoc reform of work organisation and employment patterns (Lloyd and Seifert, 1995; Thornley, 1998). Performance reviews, extension of fixed-term contracts in line with peaks and troughs in contracted business, and the development of outsourcing/competitive tendering – all became common gambits, and put local organisation on the back foot. As Carter and Poynter (1999: 503) note:

> In this context, the continuance of traditional forms of consultation and negotiation with local union representatives in many Trusts represented a continuity in form which thinly disguised an important shift in the management of local management/union relations.

The disorienting effects of decentralisation have been compounded by organisational fragmentation. In addition to cost-questing managers, local organisers in areas subject to outsourcing have had to come to terms with memberships spread over several employers. Unison's larger local government branches, for example, can now deal with over 100 different local voluntary and private sector employers, all providing local authority services through one contractual arrangement or another. These workforces are dispersed in more than the geographical sense; their interests and sense of identity can diverge in important respects. Servicing their needs is therefore a demanding and expensive business, and uneven patterns of representation have been noted as a consequence (Waddington and Kerr, 1999; Colling and Claydon, 2000).

Public sector workforces remain predominantly collectivised despite these substantial challenges, and continued rapid decline in other sectors of the economy means that public sector unions still constitute the core of the labour movement. Data from the Workplace Employee Relations Survey (WERS) indicates that there is a recognised union in almost all public sector workplaces (95%), but in only a quarter (25%) of private sector ones (Cully *et al.*, 1999: 92). There is some variation in union density – that is, in the proportion of the workforce in union membership. Nearly two-thirds of civil servants are union members compared with fewer than half (43%) of NHS employees (Cully *et al.*, 1999: 88). Overall density remains markedly higher, at 61%, than elsewhere in the economy, however. Labour force changes have taken their toll on membership figures for some unions, particularly in the Civil Service and those with large manual workforces affected by competitive tendering. Others have grown substantially, notably the Royal College of Nursing (RCN) and the National Association of School Masters/Union of Women Teachers (NASUWT) (Colling, 1997; Mathieson and Corby, 1999).

The modernisation agenda appears to offer a platform for unions from which to rebuild. In contrast to the emphasis on individualising employment relationships and union exclusion, the emphasis on partnership *working* depicts unions as legitimate stakeholders in the public services (Cabinet Office, 1999: para. 40). Guidance on revising pay systems in the NHS, for example, points to the work likely to be required of local negotiators in the future (DoH, 1999a). It advises employers to assist staff side representatives in developing negotiating expertise: 'this would include arrangements to promote good employment relations and a social partnership approach to training and implementation' (para. 9). Subsequent and separate advice on establishing employment procedures in new primary care trusts (PCTs) refers to the need to 'encourage trade union representation by nominated members of staff who are employees of the same organisation' (DoH, 1999b: para. 56).

Trends towards fragmentation are not halted either, but unions are offered a more influential role. This stems in part from the framework of rights to recognition established for unions generally by the Employment Relations Act 1999. Unions' efforts to secure recognition for private companies bidding for public sector contracts have become more active and successful. Gall and Mckay (1999) report agreements with major private contractors for manual services including ServiceTeam, Onyx, Brophy, Ecovert, Compass and SitaGB (p. 607). Some professional and white-collar services are also beginning to sign up. CSL recognises Unison and PCS for bargaining and representation purposes (IRS, 1999: 5). The full negotiating and consultation structure proposed features a groundbreaking national forum for bargaining purposes. Representatives elected from business sites sit alongside national officers from the two unions and negotiate with CSL representatives including the director of personnel, two general managers and a client manager. In business sites where one or other union has more than 40% of membership, the local representative must be a union member. Where membership falls below that threshold, a non-member may be elected. Agreements reached nationally will cover all employees, including the 65% who have taken up CSL terms and conditions of employment, rather than the TUPE-protected local government or Civil Service ones.

Regulations relating to the processes and procedures through which contracts are offered also provide important rights for unions that were lacking previously. Since April 1998, NHS unions have had the right to interview prospective bidders for PFI projects on their employment practices, equal opportunities and health and safety records. Similar rights were extended to Civil Service unions in October of the same year (Unison, 1998: para. 6.3). Best value guidelines emphasise repeatedly the need to involve staff in reviews of service provision. This falls short of explicit reference to union representation, but unions have indicated their readiness to use TUPE legislation to secure rights similar to those available in PFI contexts (Unison, 1999: para. 17).

CONCLUSIONS

The central task of this chapter has been to evaluate the changing nature of public sector employment relationships. Contextual change during the 1980s and 1990s strained the models of employment and employee relations that had prevailed for most of the period after the Second World War. Large, integrated bureaucracies associated with Morrisonian models of public administration were eschewed during the period of market-based reform between 1979 and 1997. Approaches to employment practice developed pragmatically, rather than strategically. They were characterised by attempts to stiffen the sinews of management (and by corollary to confront public sector unions), and to decentralise bargaining and decision-making to allow for flexibility and affordability considerations at lower levels within organisations. Such preferences for locally tailored solutions implied a need to jettison aspects of 'model employer' practice, and the concept fell into virtual disuse.

But tensions were apparent in such approaches (Colling, 1997). Political responsibility for public services could not be atomised and transferred simply to the private sector. Indeed, dissatisfaction with the level and quality of public services became a key factor in electoral performance. Equally, while devolving responsibility for the utilisation of budgets, government interest in the level of expenditure was retained. Aspirations to join the single currency extended it further, and inclined ministers to intervene to control expenditure. Decentralisation, the leitmotiv of market solutions, was accompanied consequently by an increasing array of policy and financial controls. Objectives of increasing responsiveness to local labour market pressures were displaced by the perceived need to reassert control over public sector pay.

Modernisation consequently builds on the central controls over organisational performance and expenditure developed through the 1980s, and locates political responsibility for public service provision at the governmental centre. The consequences for employment have followed in like fashion. Coordination of pay and pay determination is re-established through national framework agreements reached centrally. Approaches to change management based on confrontation with workforces and their representatives have ostensibly given way to partnership working. But the flexibility agenda has been developed further and facilitated through local reviews of work organisation and grading structures. Systems of performance management linked to pay have been extended, heightening service delivery pressures on organisations and individual employees. In this context, it could be argued that the role of the model employer has returned, but that the model has changed. Where due process and comparability were the hallmarks in the Morrisonian era, the accent is now on 'performativity'and partnership (Webb, 1999).

The model, and the proposals stemming from it, is an ambitious one. Evidence from the Workplace Employee Relations Survey (WERS) suggests that the legacy of employee morale left by market-based approaches to reform provides shaky foundations (Cully *et al.*, 1999; 167–190). Comprehensive surveys conducted in 1998 found labour turnover in health markedly higher than other sectors except hotels and restaurants. Absenteeism was above average in public administration and health. Public sector employees appeared the most susceptible to work-related illness, with the highest rates per 100 employees recorded in health, education, and public administration (Cully *et al.*, 1999: 132). Public sector workers were more likely than others to report feeling stressed at work. Nearly half reported they had too little time to get work done. Workers in education were consistently the highest scorers on three measures: 82% said they had to work very hard; 56% said they had insufficient time to get work done properly; and 37% worried a lot about work outside working time (Cully *et al.*, 1999: 173). Attempts to improve organisational performance in such contexts require genuine innovation and investment in the human resource infrastructure of the kind that market-based approaches failed to deliver.

The overall context and aspects of the modernisation agenda auger relatively well. To start with the least positive, the costs of failure are high indeed. At the mid-point of the current government's term, comments from a senior medical consultant, mildly critical of prevailing health service policy, were enough to provoke a media furore and immediate promises from the Prime Minister of still further increases in investment (Riddell, 2000). Expectations of credible reform can only increase as the next election looms, heightening pressure on ministers to deliver for citizens and employees alike. More positively, governments committed to securing change in public organisations, as opposed to their extinction, are surely well advised to pursue it in 'partnership' with employees and their unions rather than through conflict with them. Judicious approaches to new framework agreements in health and local government have already provided better prospects for reform than were achieved previously, even if their tone has yet to be tested fully against actual negotiations at local level.

Success depends arguably on a demonstrable break in the lineage of 'performativity', and a willingness to think more laterally than budget headings have allowed heretofore. Prospects in this area are not yet that encouraging. The criteria against which organisational performance are to be judged, for example, are far from imaginative in the senses required. A continuing preoccupation with outputs rather than outcomes has been noted in guidance on the achievement of best value through benchmarking (Boyne, 1999). Measurements focus on the administration of the service – time taken responding to customers, for example – rather than on the impact of that service on recipients. Where this is the case, benchmarking may permit employers to continue squeezing physical productivity, increasing pressure on employees without bringing any job satisfaction benefits in terms of tangible improvements in service quality. Individual performance-related pay schemes have also focused so far on the physical productivity of employees. Comparisons within the Benefits Agency, for example, were founded upon the numbers of benefit applications processed by offices and by individual employees within them (Foster and Hoggett, 1999). Resentment at the increased pressures this generated for employees was compounded by the under-recognition of team-based initiatives and perceived inequalities in reward arising from the scheme (Foster and Hoggett, 1999). Current reviews in the Civil Service have acknowledged problems of this kind and may even presage a shift towards team-based bonuses (Wilson

1999a; Timmins 2000). In education, however, the focus remains firmly on individual teachers. Concerns have been raised here that school ethos, which is essentially a collective, whole-school activity, will be damaged as individual teachers come to prioritise those individualised aspects of their work over which they have control and for which they receive rewards (Richardson, 1999).

A second set of issues revolves around the extent to which change is seen as legitimate and a process in which employees' views have been heard and acted upon. Public sector unions are well placed to respond to overtures to partnership working offered by government and employers nationally. Real benefits might be envisaged for unions, for their members and for employers where these arrangements develop effectively, but limits might be reached quickly. Government proposals for performance-related pay for teachers have been amended (for example, requirements to sign new contracts of employment have been dropped), but fundamental objections to the individualised nature of schemes and to criteria based on pupil performance were still being ignored six months prior to implementation of the scheme. Circumstances may be still less propitious at local level. Unions have faced their stiffest organisational challenges here. Workforce restructuring and employment transfers within and beyond the public sector have fragmented memberships. In the context of tightening budgets, employers taking the opportunity to expand local bargaining have sought concessions from unions, creating primarily defensive rather than innovative approaches to change. Such a context obviously conditions responses to new initiatives such as best value. Despite encouragement from employers nationally to harness employee involvement, the GMB found only a minority of councils establishing training or briefing sessions on best value for employees (IRS 1999b: 671). Where employee involvement has been developed, it has not necessarily meant union involvement – a point on which national guidance remains ambiguous (Unison, 1999).

Finally, the funding context is critical to the prospects for restructuring. Trust in devolved pay setting and performance management systems has been compromised in the past where employees have perceived that governments have intervened to control costs or direct expenditure (Talbot, 1997; Bach, 1999). Funding also constrains the ability to 'buy change': that is, to compensate employees who may be affected detrimentally and to reward those developing genuinely innovative approaches. The failure of local pay setting in health has been attributed to just such pressures (Thornley, 1998; Bach, 1999; Grimshaw, 1999) and, in education, evidence that schools have not received additional funding has prompted concern from the School Teachers Pay Review Body (STRB, 1999). They concluded that uncertainty over funding

> constrains action on pay and conditions which schools might otherwise want to take now and in the future. It is vital that the promised extra funding does reach schools so that they can recruit and retain the staff they need, use existing pay flexibilities to the full, and support whatever new pay structure emerges from the Green Paper. (para. 33)

Whether the 'new model employers' in the public services can deliver the changes expected of them, and on the scale hoped for, must remain an open question for the time being. The agenda is ambitious and the costs of failure are high. Developments in the next few years will be important for all those who rely on public organisations, both service users and employees.

Acknowledgement
The author is grateful to Duncan MacGregor at the Office of National Statistics for supplying the data used in Figure 14.2.

SUMMARY

● The objectives set for this chapter were to explore shifts in policy towards the public sector and how these have affected relationships between government, managers and the large workforces employed there. Specific attention was to be paid to the notion of the 'model employer' and how this has changed over time.

● Three distinct phases covering the post-Second World War period were identified. First, during the 'golden era' from the 1950s through to the late 1970s, the public sector expanded rapidly in terms of its scope and its employment needs. A comprehensive welfare state was developed, including health, education and social security, and a range of basic industries, such as steel and rail transport, was taken into public ownership. These operated in very different contexts but organisational principles attributed to Herbert Morrison were shared widely. These included a division between operational and political control (though the latter remained manifest); a public service ethos; and management by professionals rather than by generalists. The market-based reforms pursued during the second period, from 1979 to 1997, were antithetical to this culture, which they associated with inefficiency and even corruption. Market environments were thought to foster more effective and efficient management and to be intolerant of waste. Wherever possible, public sector organisations were privatised through asset sales or transfer. Where this was not possible, market pressures were introduced through competitive tendering, through performance pressures, or through organisational change. But market approaches did not resolve the issues faced by the public services and a third period, begun with the change in government in 1997, has preferred 'modernisation'. Fragmentation and duplication have been associated during this period with the market reforms pursued previously. While elements of these remain, and some have been extended, the emphasis overall has been on establishing policy frameworks within which public service managers are to work and performance targets against which they are to be held accountable.

● The notion of the 'model employer' is associated primarily with the first of these periods. Employment procedures were prescribed explicitly, sometimes by statute, and public employers were expected to demonstrate best practice. Collective bargaining and consultation with trade unions were well established with complex local and regional structures ascending usually to powerful national negotiating forums that set uniform national pay rates and conditions of service. But the notion fell into disuse during the market-based era. The cause was partly philosophical: universal employment standards sit uneasily with the belief that efficiency is delivered primarily by unfettered responses to specific market circumstances. There were political overtones too, however. A government determined to weaken opposition to its policies emanating from public sector unions was bound to undermine the collective bargaining and consultation procedures from which they derived their strength. 'Model employment' has hardly been mentioned by modernisers but concerns about recruitment and retention in the public sector have made employment strategy a more prominent issue than it was once and it is possible to see some consistency emerging in government responses. Pay and conditions are set increasingly through framework agreements that establish minimum and key standards nationally while leaving substantial leeway for local discretion. This in itself offers a fillip to unions concerned about previous attempts to decentralise bargaining and their position is strengthened further by the emphasis on 'partnership working' that is also widespread. At national and employer level, support for trade union organisation and an emphasis on consultation are apparent once again. But there are continuities from the previous period too. In particular, intense political pressures to deliver service improvements are manifest in the continued preoccupation with the performance of employees. Arguably there is a 'new model employer' in the public services – it is merely the model that has changed. Where once the concern was with due process and comparability, the focus is now on 'performativity', that is, making additional investment, including pay, conditional upon demonstrable increases in efficiency and effectiveness. Whether such a model can deliver the changes expected must remain an open question for the time being.

Case Study

Primary school

Formed into small groups, put yourself in the position of the senior management team responsible for a medium-sized primary school in an inner city area.[1] You have approximately 370 pupils on role, 37% of whom qualify for free school meals and 27% of whom are additional language learners (that is, their first language is not English). You have a staff group of 13 classroom teachers, not including the headteacher, with additional support and ancillary staff.

As in all schools, your headteacher will shortly be charged with implementing performance management for classroom teachers.[2] Teachers opting voluntarily to cross a threshold at the top of their pay spine will receive an additional £2000 per annum and be subject to individual performance management annually thereafter. Teachers wishing to progress further through the pay spine will have to demonstrate their contribution to raised levels of pupil attainment. The school's governing body is required by law to manage the performance of the headteacher. It also has to adopt a performance management policy for classroom teachers and it has done so following consultation with staff. Detailed implementation and administration of the policy, however, is the responsibility of your headteacher, subject to scrutiny and advice from specified external advisers appointed by the government.

Seven members of teaching staff have applied to cross the threshold. Two have expressed their opposition to individual performance management and the remainder are not yet eligible to apply to cross the threshold.

What do you think about these developments? Will performance management for teachers lift morale? Will it lift attainment levels for pupils?

- Consider first the role that you will have as a senior management team. Do you have one at all? What implications does this have for the way that the school is managed more broadly? You might want to reflect here on the authority vested in the headteacher, which is increased further by performance management. The headteacher is responsible initially for deciding which teachers can proceed to cross the threshold and subsequently for setting targets and monitoring performance against them. Is this individualised model of management, in which one capable and professional individual is held accountable for the success, or otherwise, of his/her decisions, appropriate in a school setting?

- What expectations would you have of the impact on relative pay? Think first about pay in your school relative to others. A significant proportion of your pupils speak English as a second language. A larger proportion qualify for free school meals, which is taken as a proxy measure of poverty. Does this context impact upon the ability of your staff to demonstrate improved levels of pupil attainment, and thereby increase their pay? Would this be more or less hard than in a similarly sized school in an affluent area where the majority of pupils speak English as their first language? Note that it is *improvement* in attainment levels that is important here, not levels of attainment per se.

  Consider also relative pay *within* school. Half your teaching staff may have access to accelerated pay progression while the remainder will not; what implications might this have for motivation and morale, and thereby for pupil attainment? Your answer may depend upon your conception of

621

'performance'. If an individual teacher is harder working or more talented, then it makes sense to reward them for their effort relative to others. But how do you measure this? Can you be confident that improvements in one year group are attributable to the staff who taught them or are other factors involved? Can you be confident that your headteacher has the time, expertise, perhaps even the inclination to make fairly such complex judgements?

● Finally, consider the extent to which these judgements are made particularly complicated by the sector context. As Ian Roberts' chapter in this volume makes clear, considerations like these are part and parcel of remuneration policies everywhere. What, if anything, makes performance-related pay in the public services distinctive? You might want to think here about the manner in which it has been introduced, the policy implications and outcomes, and the extent to which law, and authorities beyond the organisation, influence decision-making.

Notes:

[1] Though the details are hopefully sufficiently plausible for an exercise of this kind, they and the case study are entirely fictitious.

[2] The details of the scheme were in abeyance at the time of writing following a court judgement sought successfully by the National Union of Teachers challenging the process through which the reforms were introduced by the Secretary of State for Education. Most commentators thought it likely that PRP for teachers would still proceed in some form, however.

QUESTIONS

1 Identify the traditional characteristics of public sector employment relationships in the United Kingdom.

2 What were the main consequences of the shift to market-based organisations and policy for employee relations?

3 To what extent has restructuring and changing employment practice weakened trade union influence in the public sector?

ACTIVITY

In July 2000, the government announced the outcome of the Comprehensive Spending Review. This marked a historic turning point since, following several years of sustained pressure on public expenditure that extended into the first two years of the 1997 Labour administration, budgets for health, education, and transport are to receive substantial real terms increases. The significance and complexity of the issues attending the review are summarised neatly by Nicholas Trimmins in the article reproduced below.

New Labour stakes everything on service

The comprehensive spending review is the government's make-or-break chance to fulfil its centre-left responsibilities

Tomorrow is not just a defining moment for this Labour government. It is perhaps the defining moment for the whole idea and purpose of centre-left government. The results of tomorrow's comprehensive spending review, as seen over the next four or five years, linked to what happens in the US presidential election this November, could well shape British politics for the following decade. It is Labour's reward and could potentially be its nemesis. In its first two years in office, Labour battened down the hatches. For reasons as much to do with politics as economics it pledged to stick to Conservative party spending plans – a final proof together with its tax pledges, that Labour would be fiscally responsible in government. Thanks as much to luck as judgment, it got away with it.

Social security spending, which for decades has risen faster than the rate of growth of the economy as a whole, undershot remarkably. Forecasts of its likely rise for once proved pessimistic. The economy remained strong. There were some favourable demographics. Combined with Labour's changed rhetoric – "work for those who can" – and its new deals for the jobless, the outcome was a saving of several billion pounds that helped keep health and education on the road.

Then came the first comprehensive spending review. Its effects started to be felt last April. But the sums involved were hyped hugely by the chancellor, raising expectations sky-high about the scale of change in education, health and elsewhere. Labour is now having to live these inflated expectations. Tomorrow will be different. Health spending will be a third higher in real terms by 2004 compared with last year. Education – which chiefly means schools – will do roughly as well.

Transport is to receive a significant boost, while law and order, defence and much else look likely to receive genuine and sustained increases in real terms.

But with this has come the promise – the government's promise, not the media's spin – of a "transformation" of public services.

In one sense, this is hardly surprising. Politicians have given up so much else that running public services is virtually all they have left to do. Under the Conservative they ceased to-run ports, railways, steel, coal, gas, electricity, water, cars and much else – all privatised. Under Labour they no longer run interest rates. Soon they won't run air traffic control, or the projects arm of the Treasury's private finance task force, or nuclear fuel reprocessing – privatisations that continue to shift the very definition of what a public service is. They do, of course, regulate, negotiate and legislate beyond mere services, but chiefly they run public services – which Labour has promised to "transform". Failure, therefore, may carry a far higher price than in the past, when not quite delivering on what was less extravagantly hoped for would not necessarily kill off all prospects of re-election.

And this comes when the age-old wisdom of political pundits – neatly summed up by Bill Clinton's "It's the economy, stupid" back in 1992 – that it is chiefly people's sense of current and future financial well-being that decides elections, may be ceasing to hold true. In the US, there is a real chance that a Republican challenger will see off the Democrat who is effectively the incumbent – despite the strongest economy ever. There are already signs that the brief experience of three years of Labour has produced the glib assumption in the UK that governments of whatever colour can run the economy effectively these days.

A victory for George W. Bush in November and a Labour one next year, combined with continued stability and some saner economic policies from the Tories, could make a reasonable economic performance seem simply a given and no longer a battleground. This helps explain the fear of failure behind the government's bold rhetoric of public service transformation – and thus its centralising tendencies. With so much at stake, it scarcely dare trust anyone to run these services for it. Hardly a penny leaves Whitehall without a target, a carrot (although-more-often a stick) and an inspector attached to it. Public sector managers can barely be trusted – and they know it, a fact that means their enthusiasm for Labour's reforms runs lower than it should. Local councillors certainly can't be trusted – witness the fact that if most of what is currently being mooted in Whitehall for school funding, housing, housing benefit and care of the elderly is fulfilled, in five years local government will be left doing little more than emptying bins and grappling with child abuse.

Yet at the same time, the government knows that if it tried to run everything by command and control from Whitehall, it would fail. The tension between its desperate desire for real change in the way public services are delivered, its determination to get value for money, its terror that the public services won't deliver, and its understanding that it has to enthuse people on the ground – and release them to innovate – is palpable. And it is easy to see why. By celebrating its responsibility for public services, the government is also centralising blame. If this project fails, the question will be not just "should more become privatised", but "what is centre-left government for any more?"

By Nicholas Timmins

Financial Times 17 July 2000

1 Discuss the tensions apparent in current policy making related to the public services, between centralisation and decentralisation, between investment and cost-control, for example.

2 How are these are apparent in aspects of current HR policy and practice?

3 What implications for the future development of HR policy might be drawn from the scenario that is painted by Timmins?

REFERENCES AND FURTHER READING

Those texts marked with an asterisk are particularly recommended for further reading.

Anon (1995) *Investors Chronicle*, May, p. 17.

Ascher, K. (1987) *The Politics of Privatisation: Contracting Out Public Services*. London: Macmillan.

Bach, S. (1994) 'Restructuring the personnel function: the case of NHS trusts', *Human Resource Management Journal*, Vol. 5. No. 2, pp. 99–115.

*Bach, S. (1999): 'Personnel managers: managing to change?', in Corby, S. and White, G. (eds) *Employee Relations in the Public Services: Themes and Issues*. London: Routledge, pp. 177–199.

Bach, S. and Winchester, D. (1994) 'Opting out of pay devolution? Prospects for local pay bargaining in the UK public services', *British Journal of Industrial Relations*, Vol. 32, No. 2, pp. 263–284.

Bailey, R. (1994) 'Annual review article: 1993', *British Journal of Industrial Relations*, Vol. 32, No. 1, pp. 113–136.

Bailey, R. (1996) 'Public sector industrial relations', in Beardwell, I.J. (ed.) *Contemporary Industrial Relations: A Critical Analysis*. Oxford: Oxford University Press, pp. 121–151.

Bolger, A. and Timmins, N. (1998) 'Public sector pay: government sets out tighter guidelines'. *Financial Times*, 15 July. p. 9.

Boyne, G. (1999) 'Processes, performance and best value in local government', *Local Government Studies. Special Issue on Managing Local Services From CCT to Best Values*. Spring, Vol. 25, No. 2, pp. 1–15.

Brown, G. (1995) Speech to Labour Party Conference 1995. Text issued by Labour Party Conference Media Office, Brighton, October.

Brown, W. and Rowthorn, B. (1990) *A Public Service Pay Policy*. Fabian Pamphlet 542. London: Fabian Society.

Bryson, C., Jackson, M. and Leopold, J. (1995) 'The impact of self-governing trusts on trade unions and staff associations in the NHS', *Industrial Relations Journal*, Vol. 26, No. 2, pp. 120–133.

Cabinet Office (1999) *Modernising Government*, Cm4310. London: HMSO.

Carter, B. and Poynter, G. (1999) 'Unions in a changing climate: MSF and Unison experiences in the new public sector.' *Industrial Relations Journal*, Vol. 30, No. 5, 499–513.

Central Statistical Office (CSO) (1981) *Economic Trends*, No. 338, December. London: HMSO.

Clegg, H. (1979) *The Changing System of Industrial Relations in Great Britain*. Oxford: Blackwell.

Coates, D. (1989) *The Crisis of Labour: Industrial Relations and the State in Contemporary Britain*. Oxford: Philip Allan.

Cochrane, A. (1993) *Whatever Happened to Local Government?* Buckingham: Open University Press.

Colling, T. (1993) 'Contracting public services: the management of CCT in two county councils', *Human Resource Management Journal*, Vol. 3, No. 4, pp. 1–15.

Colling, T. (1997) 'Managing human resources in the public sector', in Beardwell, I, and Holden, L. (eds) *Human Resource Management: A Contemporary Perspective*. London: Pitman, pp. 654–679.

Colling, T. (1999) 'Tendering and outsourcing: Working in the Contract State' in Corby, S. and White, G. (eds) *Employee Relations in the Public Services*. London: Routledge, pp. 136–156.

Colling, T. (2000) 'Personnel Management in the extended organisation'. in Bach, S. and Sisson, K. (eds) *Personnel Management: A Comprehensive Guide to Theory and Practice*. Oxford: Blackwell, pp. 70–91.

Colling, T. and Claydon, T. (2000 Forthcoming) 'Strategic review and organisational change in Unison'. in Terry, M. (ed) *Unison Five Years On*. London: Routledge.

Colling, T. and Ferner, A. (1994) 'Privatisation and marketisation', in Edwards, P.K.E. (ed.) *Industrial Relations: Theory and Practice in Britain*. Oxford: Blackwell, pp. 491–515.

Corby, S. (1998) 'Industrial relations in civil service agencies: transition or transformation?', *Industrial Relations Journal*, Vol. 29, No. 3, pp. 194–206.

Corby, S. and White, G. (1999) 'From the New Right to New Labour', in Corby, S. and White, G. (eds) *Employee Relations in the Public Services: Themes and Issues*. London: Routledge, pp. 3–27.

Crouch, C. (1979) *The Politics of Industrial Relations*. London: Fontana.

Cully, M., Woodland, S., O'Reilly, A. and Dix, G. (1999) *Britain at Work: As Depicted by the 1998 Workplace Employee Relations Survey*. London: Routledge.

Davies, K. and Hinton, P. (1993) 'Managing quality in local government and the health service', *Public Money and Management*, Vol. 13, No. 1, pp. 51–55.

Dearlove, J. and Saunders, P. (1984) *Introduction to British Politics*. Cambridge: Polity Press.

DETR (1998) M*odernising Local Government – Improving Local Services through Best Value*. Consultation Paper, London: DETR.

DETR (1999) *Local Government Act 1999: Part 1 – Best Value*. DETR Circular 10/99. London: Department of the Environment, Transport and the Regions.

DfEE (2000a),' Contract signed for Islington's Education Service,' Press release, 14 January. London: Department for Education and Employment.

DfEE (2000b) *Teacher's Pay in 2000–2001*, DfEE 0006/2000. London: Department for Education and Employment.

Dickens, L. (2000) 'Still Wasting Resources'. Equality in Employment'. in Bach, S. and Sisson, K. (eds) *Personnel Management: A Comprehensive Guide to Theory and Practice*. Oxfrd: Blackwell, pp. 137–171.

DoH (1997) *The New NHS*, Cm.3807. London: HMSO, for Department of Health.

DoH (1999a) *Agenda for Change: Modernising the NHS Pay System – Joint Framework of Principles and Agreed Statement on the Way Forward*. London: Department of Health.

DoH (1999b) *Working Together: Human Resources Guidance and Requirements for Primary Care Trusts*. London: Department of Health.

Dunleavy, P. and Hood, C. (1994) 'From old public administration to new public management', *Public Money and Management,* Vol. 14, No. 3, pp. 34–43.

Elliott, R. and Duffus, K. (1996) 'What has been happending to pay in the public services sector of the economy? Developments over the period 1970–1992'. *British Journal of Industrial Relations.* Vol. 34, No. 1, pp. 51–85.

Escott, K. and Whitfield, D. (1995) *The Gender Impact of Compulsory Competitive Tendering in Local Government.* Manchester, Equal Opportunities Commission.

Fairbrother, P. (1982) *Working for the State,* Studies for Trade Unionists, 8.29. London: Workers Educational Association.

Farnham, D. and Horton, S. (1995) 'The New People Management in the UK's public services: a silent revolution?', paper presented to the International Colloquium on Contemporary Development in HRM, École Supérieure de Commerce, Montpellier, France, October.

Farnham, D., Horton, S. and Giles, L. (1994) 'Human resource management and industrial relations in the public sector: from model employer to a hybrid model', paper presented to Employment Research Unit Annual Conference, The Contract State: The Future of Public Management, September.

Ferner, A. and Colling, T. (1991) 'Privatisation, regulation and industrial relations', *British Journal of Industrial Relations,* Vol. 29, No. 3, pp. 391–409.

Ferner, A. and Colling, T. (1993) 'Electricity supply', in Pendleton, A. and Winterton, J. (eds) *Public Enterprise in Transition.* London: Routledge, pp. 100–131.

Flynn, N. (1993) *Public Sector Management.* Hemel Hempstead: Harvester-Wheatsheaf.

Fogarty, M. and Brooks, D. (1986) *Trade Unions and British Industrial Development.* London: Policy Studies Institute.

*Foster, D. and Hoggett, P. (1999) 'Change in the Benefits Agency: empowering the exhausted worker?', *Work, Employment and Society,* Vol. 13, No. 1. pp. 19–39.

Fryer, B. (1989) 'Public Service Unionism in the twentieth Century'. in Mally, R. Dimmock, S.J. and Sethi, A.S. (eds): *Industrial Relations in the Public Services.* London: Routledge, pp. 17–68.

Gall, G. and McKay, S. (1999) 'Developments in union recognition and derecognition in Britain, 1994–1998'. *British Journal of Industrial Relations.* Vol. 37, No. 4, pp. 601–614.

Gamble, A. (1988) *The Free Economy and the Strong State: The Politics of Thatcherism.* London: Macmillan.

Government Statistical Office (GSO) (1996) *Economic Trends,* No. 508, February. London: HMSO.

*Grimshaw, D. (1999), 'Changes in skills-mix and pay determination among the nursing workforce in the UK', *Work, Employment and Society,* Vol. 13. No. 2. pp. 295–328.

Harden, I. (1992) *The Contracting State.* Buckingham: Open University Press.

Heery, E. (1992) 'Industrial relations and the customer', paper presented to the British Universities Industrial Relations Association (BUIRA) Annual Conference, July.

Hegewisch, A. (1999) 'Employment flexibility: push or pull?', in Corby, S. and White, G. (eds) *Employee Relations in the Public Services: Themes and Issues.* London: Routledge, pp. 114–136.

Hills, J. (1990) *The State of Welfare: The Welfare State in Britain since 1974.* Oxford: Clarendon Press.

Hogwood, B. (1992) *Trends in British Public Policy.* Buckingham: Open University Press.

Hogwood, B. (1998) 'Towards a new structure of public employment in Britain?', *Policy and Politics,* Vol. 26, No. 3, pp. 321–341.

Industrial Relations Services (IRS) (1999a) 'Public sector pay in 1999–2000', *Pay and Benefits Bulletin,* 486, December, pp. 2–11.

Industrial Relations Services (IRS) (1999b) 'The progress of best value in Brighton and Hove Council', *Employment Trends,* 671, January, pp. 11–16.

Industrial Relations Services (IRS) (1999c) 'Managing high performance in the public sector', *Employment Trends,* 690, October, pp. 5–11.

Industrial Relations Services (IRS) (1999d) 'The new partnership at CSL', *Employment Trends,* 693, December. pp. 4–10.

Jary, S. (1991) 'Decentralisation in the civil service: the implications for industrial relations', paper presented to symposium on Public Sector Employee Relations in the 1990s: Continuity and Change, University of Greenwich, November.

John, P. (1991) 'The restructuring of local government in England and Wales', in Batley, R. and Stoker, G. (eds) *Local Government in Europe.* London: Macmillan, pp. 58–73.

Kerr, A. and Sachdev, S. (1992) 'Third among equals: an analysis of the 1989 ambulance dispute', *British Journal of Industrial Relations,* Vol. 30, No. 1, pp. 127–143.

Kessler, I. (1991) 'Workplace industrial relations in local government', *Employee Relations,* special issue, Vol. 13, No. 2, complete issue.

Lloyd, C. and Seifert, R. (1995) 'Restructuring in the NHS: the impact of the 1990 reforms on the management of labour', *Work, Employment and Society,* Vol. 9, No. 2. pp. 359–378.

MacGregor, D. (1999) 'Employment in the public and private sectors', *Economic Trends,* 547, June. London: Office for National Statistics.

*Marsden, D. and Richardson, R. (1994) 'Performing for pay? The effects of merit pay on motivation in a public service', *British Journal of Industrial Relations,* Vol. 32, No. 2, pp. 243–261.

Massey, A. (1993) *Managing the Public Sector: A Comparative Analysis of the United Kingdom and the United States.* Aldershot: Edward Elgar.

Mathieson, H. Corby, S. (1999) 'Trade Unions: The Challenge of Individualism'. in Corby, S. and White, G. (eds) *Employee Relations in the Public Services.* London: Routledge, pp. 199–255.

Millward, N., Stevens, M., Smart, D. and Hawes, W. (1992) *Workplace Industrial Relations in Transition.* Aldershot: Dartmouth.

Morgan, C. and Murgatroyd, S. (1994) *Total Quality Management in the Public Sector.* Buckingham: Open University Press.

Mortimer, J. and Ellis, V. (1980) *A Professional Union: The Evolution of the Institution of Professional Civil Servants.* London: Allen & Unwin.

Napier, B. (1993) *CCT, Market Testing and Employment Rights: The Effects of TUPE and the Acquired Rights Directive*. London: Institute of Employment Rights.

National Institute of Economic and Social Research (NIESR) (1995) *The UK Economy*. London: Heinemann.

NHS Executive (1999) *Agenda for Change: Modernising the NHS Pay System. Joint Framework of Principles and Agreed Statement on the Way Forward*. Health Service Circular 1999/227.

Nichol, D. (1992) 'Unnecessary conflict: NHS management's view of the 1989–90 ambulance dispute', *British Journal of Industrial Relations*, Vol. 30, No. 1, pp. 145–154.

Office for National Statistics (ONS) (1997): *Economic Trends*, March.

Pendleton, A. and Winterton, J. (1993) 'Public enterprise industrial relations in context', in Pendleton, A. and Winterton, J. (eds) *Public Enterprise in Transition*. London: Routledge, pp. 1–22.

Peston, R. and Timmins, N. (1999) 'Brown to boost NHS and schools', *Financial Times*, 13 July, p. 1.

Pierson, C. (1994) 'Continuity and discontinuity in the emergence of the "post-Fordist" welfare state', in Burrows, R. and Loader, B. (eds) *Towards the Post-Fordist Welfare State?* London: Routledge.

Pratchett, L. and Wingfield, M. (1995) *Reforming the Public Service Ethos in Local Government: A New Institutional Perspective*, Leicester Business School Occasional Paper 27. Leicester: De Montfort University.

PSPRU (1994) *Private Corruption of Public Services*. London: Public Services Privatisation Research Unit.

*Richardson, R. (1999) *Performance Related Pay in Schools: An Assessment of the Green Paper*, Report prepared for the National Union of Teachers. London: London School of Economics.

Riddell, M. (2000) 'The New Statesman interview: Robert Winston', *New Statesman*, 17 January, pp. 14–15.

School Teachers Pay Review Body (STRB) (1999) *Report of the School Teachers Pay Review Body*, January. London: Department for Education and Employment.

Stewart, J. (1989) 'The changing organisation and management of local authorities', in Stewart, J. and Stoker, G. (eds) *The Future of Local Government*. Basingstoke: Macmillan, pp. 171–185.

*Talbot, C. (1997) 'UK Civil Service personnel reform: devolution, decentralisation and delusion', *Public Policy and Administration*, Vol. 12, No. 4. pp. 14–34.

Taylor, R. (1993) *The Trade Union Question in British Politics*. Oxford: Blackwell.

*Theakston, K. (1998)' New Labour, New Whitehall?', *Public Policy and Administration*, Vol. 13, No. 1. pp. 13–34.

Thornley, C. (1994) 'Nursing pay policy: chaos in context', paper presented to Employment Research Unit Annual Conference, Cardiff Business School, September.

Thornley, C. (1998) 'Contesting local pay the decentralisation of pay in the NHS'. *British Journal of Industrial Relations*, Vol. 36, No. 3, pp. 413–435.

Timmins, N. (2000) 'PRP: Team bonuses for civil servants'. *Financial Times*, February 12th, p. 11.

Travers, T. (1989) 'The threat to the autonomy of elected local government', in Crouch, C. and Marquand, D. (eds) *The New Centalism: Britain Out of Step in Europe?* Oxford: Blackwell, pp. 3–21.

Unison (1998) *A Step by Step Guide to the PFI process*. London: Unison.

Unison (1999) *Unison's Response to Implementing Best Value: A Consultation Paper on Draft Guidance*. London: Unison.

*Waddington, J. and Kerr, A. (1999) 'Trying to stem the flow: union membership turnover in the public sector', *Industrial Relations Journal*, Vol. 30, No. 3. pp. 184–196.

Webb, J. (1999) 'Work and the new public service class', *Sociology*, Vol. 33, No. 4. pp. 747–766.

White, G. (1994) 'Public sector pay: decentralisation versus control', paper to Employment Research Unit Annual Conference, The Contract State: The Future of Public Management, September.

Wilson, R. (1999a) *Report to the Prime Minister*, 15 December. London: Cabinet Office.

Wilson, R. (1999b) *The Civil Service in the New Millennium*. London: Cabinet Office.

Winchester, D. (1983) 'The public sector', in Bain, G.S. (ed.) *Industrial Relations in Britain*. Oxford: Blackwell, pp. 155–179.

Winchester, D. (1996) 'The regulation of public services pay in the united Kingdom', paper to the Industrial Relations in the European Community (IREC) Network Annual Conference, Industrial Relations in Europe: Convergence or Diversification? University of Copenhagen: FAOS.

Winchester, D. and Bach, S. (1994) 'The state: the public sector', in Edwards, P.K.E. (ed.) *Industrial Relations: Theory and Practice in Great Britain*. Oxford: Blackwell, pp. 314–337.

Malone Superbuy Ltd

Malone Superbuy is a large food retail company that has been established since the beginning of the twentieth century. Over the last 100 years the organisation has built a reputation for quality foods, and so depends on relatively discerning shoppers for its market; most of its outlets are in the South-West and South-East of Britain. The organisation is a large employer (more than 4000 employees); it is highly dependent upon part-time, female labour and casual student workers for shopfloor employees, with full-time management staff consigned to given stores. The firm does experience costly medium-to-high labour turnover, largely because of the unsocial hours to which all employees are rostered, and the transient nature of student labour. Wage rates are average for the sector, and were unaffected by the Minimum Wage Regulation. The organisation has never recognised trade unions, but has had a fairly informal system of local employee representation committees, many of which have fallen into disuse in recent years.

The food retail sector has recently experienced growing competition between the market leaders as attention has been drawn to the differentials between the price of food in the UK and in other European countries. British farmers have also been active in publicly denouncing the profiteering that has been evident in the retail food sector. Consequently, the big firms are engaged in 'price' wars' and are actively increasing the quality and variety of goods on offer while also focusing on the level of service offered within their stores. Malone Superbuy is not in the top league, but nevertheless has been affected by increasing competition in the sector. To add to its troubles, the TGWU is actively recruiting employees, and it looks as if Malone's will be presented with a recognition claim for bargaining rights in the near future. To remain competitive in the market the firm must:

- improve the quality of service offered to customers throughout the organisation;
- find ways of cutting labour costs.

Further to developing a strategy for change to deal with market pressures, the firm must also decide whether it intends to:

- accept a trade union presence and attempt to build a partnership agreement;
- adopt a substitution or suppressionist approach to union recognition.

As part of an external team of HR consultants employed by the company to develop a strategy to achieve competitiveness and change, your recommendations will encompass issues pertaining to employee resourcing, employee development, the physical contract and industrial relations.

1 Outline and discuss the strategies you would recommend to address:

(a) The labour turnover problem

(b) Engendering a new approach to customer service from all staff

(c) Saving on labour costs.

2 Having considered appropriate strategies to strengthen the competitive position of the firm, evaluate the advantages and disadvantages to the organisation of accepting or rejecting the trade union's bid for recognition for bargaining purposes.

PART
5
INTERNATIONAL HUMAN RESOURCE MANAGEMENT

Introduction to Part 5

Since the last edition of this book there has been a considerable growth of interest in international human resource management (IHRM). This flows from increased globalisation as a result of the growth in world trade, foreign direct investment, worldwide mergers and acquisitions and a considerable burgeoning of telecommunications, faster and cheaper transport and rapid technological change. Globalisation has also been considerably enhanced by the integration of markets both worldwide and at regional level, as well as witnessing the rise of new and potentially powerful markets in China and Central and Eastern Europe. The trend towards privatisation and deregulation has led to an increase in cross-border integration in areas such as telecommunication, energy and finance.

The 1990s witnessed a rapid economic growth particularly associated with the activities of multinational companies (MNCs), reflected in the considerable increase in foreign direct investment (FDI). There are 53 000 MNCs that control 450 000 subsidiaries, and these MNCs account for approximately a quarter of output in the developed economies (Kozul-Wright and Rowthorn, 1998). More importantly, FDI is of immense importance to world economic growth, and the 1990s witnessed a strong expansion of FDI flows. OECD countries set a new FDI record in 1998 with inward investment reaching $465 billion (a 71% increase over 1997), and outflows reached an unprecedented $566 billion (Miyake and Thomsen, 1999).

As companies and organisations expand their cross-border activities there has been a concomitant increase in business activity together with an increase in cross-border integration of their production and services. This in turn has created an increasing interest in the processes by which international management coordination and control can be exercised.

The United States still remains dominant in the global economy, and over a quarter of the 100 largest MNCs are American owned. Although the considerable expansion of Japanese companies overseas in the 1980s caused the USA to briefly lose its premier position as the world's leading foreign direct investor, by the latter part of the 1990s the USA had regained its former position while the Japanese banking and financial crisis had taken its toll. Such economic hegemonies influence labour market and management trends. As Hyman (1999) states:

> After two decades in which the superior performance of such 'institutionalised economies' as Germany and Japan was widely recognised, the conventional wisdom of the 1990s has been that dense social regulation involves rigidities requiring a shift to market liberalism. (p. 93)

Such shifts in the managerial climate influence approaches to the employment relationship and ultimately to HRM. However, IHRM is still very much in its infancy, its parameters are still being set. The problem with examining HRM in a global context is that it raises far-reaching and complex questions, and the present state of research and theory is a long way from producing satisfactory explanations.

Globalisation has taken place against a backcloth of social and political turbulence in the twentieth century, and has continued in the wake of the fall of communism in Eastern Europe and the resulting economic and political problems. There has been a huge and continuing growth of the world's population, which has intensified the problems of poverty for many poor nations. Pollution has brought green issues to the forefront of the consciousness of political and business policy makers. We have witnessed a challenge to Western economic supremacy with the rapid growth of the Asia Pacific states, led by the 'tigers' – Japan, China, South Korea, Taiwan and Hong Kong – as well as Singapore and Malaysia.

The chapters in this section cannot do justice to these massive changes within the narrow context of HRM, and they will serve, therefore, merely to give the reader a flavour of some of the developments in the field and some of the major debates that are now emerging.

The section begins with an examination of some definitions of international HRM. This is followed by a chapter reviewing some of the developments of HRM in a European context, including both the European Union and recent developments in Eastern Europe.

The last chapter examines trends in the Asia Pacific rim, especially in Japan, China and the other 'tiger' economies. We have not included a chapter on the United States in this edition, mainly because much of the ideas and literature on human resource management emanate from there, and thus a general discussion of it is by implication a reference to its American origins and influence.

REFERENCES AND FURTHER READING

Hyman, R, (1999) 'National industrial relations systems and transnational challenges: an essay in review', *European Journal of Industrial Relations*, Vol. 5, No. 1, pp. 80–110.

Kozul-Wright, R. and Rowthorn, R. (1998) 'Spoilt for choice? Multinational corporations and the geography of international production', *Oxford Review of Economic Policy*, Vol. 14, No. 2, pp. 74–92.

Miyake, M. and Thomsen, S. (1999) 'Recent trends in foreign direct investment', *Financial Market Trends*, No. 73, June, pp. 109–126.

15

International human resource management

Len Holden

OBJECTIVES

- To define and distinguish between international HRM and comparative HRM.
- To examine the debate over whether HRM systems are converging or will remain divergent.
- To examine comparative HRM models, and to review some international and comparative surveys.
- To explore country of origin and host country effects on international HRM.
- To examine mechanisms used by multinational corporations to control and coordinate HRM activities in and between their subsidiaries.
- To investigate expatriation management issues.
- To examine some models of international HRM.

INTRODUCTION

There is increasing recognition of the importance of human resources in international competition. Porter (1990) states that the most important factors that influence national competitiveness are skilled human resources and the scientific base. He asks: Why does a nation achieve international success in a particular industry? Switzerland, for example, is a landlocked nation with high-cost labour, strict environmental law, and few natural resources – least of all cocoa. Yet it is a world leader in chocolate, not to mention pharmaceuticals, banking and specialised machinery. Similarly, Japan has few natural resources and yet from a shattered post-war position has built itself up into one of the most formidable economies in the world, rivalling, and in some industries, surpassing the United States. What both Switzerland and Japan lacked in natural resources they compensated for strongly in human resources, nurturing the education, skills and abilities of their populations. Porter (1990) claims that for nations wishing to achieve competitive advantage understanding these lessons is vital.

Similarly, multinational companies (MNCs) are beginning to understand the strategic importance of the resourcing and deployment of their human resources. Initially much of this concern has been with the development of expatriate managers, but increasingly there is concern about the export of managerial

633

systems, and how local subsidiary managers and staff can be induced to cooperate and absorb these ways of working. It is being increasingly recognised that the malfunctioning of managerial and HRM systems can have far-reaching consequences for the effective operation of MNCs in an overseas context.

INTERNATIONAL HRM: SOME ATTEMPTS AT DEFINITION

The recognition of the significance of human resources to organisational and national productivity has led to a surge of interest in international human resource management (IHRM), but there is still some confusion as to what it means. IHRM can be studied in an organisational and a comparative context. Definitions would therefore need to recognise the locations of, and the approaches to, IHRM. Boxall (1995) arrives at similar conclusions, and defines international human resource management as being 'concerned with the human resource problems of multinational firms in foreign subsidiaries (such as expatriate management) or, more broadly, with the unfolding HR issues that are associated with the various stages of the internationalisation process' (p. 5). This accords with Dowling *et al.* (1994: 2) and Briscoe (1995: 9), and also Torrington (1994) who sees IHRM as 'simply HRM on a larger scale' (p. 6).

Comparative HRM, on the other hand, has much wider significance both in terms of the HRM role, which Boxall (1995) states 'should be interpreted as the comparative study of labour in its broadest sense' (p. 6) and in the national contexts in which it exists. He points out that HRM as such was initially perceived in mainly Anglo-American terms, but the comparative label would suggest a move beyond this 'into an intellectual and cultural terrain where there may well be diverse notions of management itself and of labour management institutions and practices' (p. 6).

Here he suggests an examination of the richer vein of comparative industrial relations and comparative labour market theory, incorporating the historical development of management labour systems, as for example in the work of Gospel (1992), which attempts to offer explanations of poor British productivity throughout the preceding century by an examination of internal and external labour markets.

Boxall also notes the lack of rigour in the theoretical development of the subject, and comparative studies that have been conducted to date tend to lack depth of analysis as a result. Other commentators have suggested that a move towards the comparative case study approach may prove more fruitful. Clark *et al.* (1999), in examining a wide variety of IHRM and comparative HRM and contingent literature, lament the lack of progress in theoretical, conceptual and research methodological terms. We shall return to some of these themes later in this and subsequent chapters.

APPROACHES TO INTERNATIONAL AND COMPARATIVE HRM: CONVERGENCE AND DIVERGENCE, THE STUDY OF COMPARATIVE HRM

In studying comparative and international HRM from a number of perspectives, writers have borrowed freely from theories of various philosophies and academic disciplines, and these approaches can be categorised into four main areas:

- the convergence or contingency perspective;
- Marxist theory;

- the cultural approach;
- the institutionalist perspective.

These categories follow closely those of Lane (1989, 1995). Each approach attempts to examine the relationship between social settings and organisational forms, and the similarities and differences that would point to convergence or divergence. One main problem with each approach is that it tends to exclude or play down factors that other perspectives emphasise. This results in a less rounded and thus less satisfactory analysis of the forces influencing IHRM. Cultural theorists are thus inclined to play down or ignore institutional or economic factors. Those advocating a contingency approach and those coming from a Marxist perspective are often suspicious of the dangers of national and racial stereotyping that could emanate from the cultural approach. Institutional theorists, while acknowledging the influence of cultural values, are wary about becoming too involved in examining the 'black box' of culture, given the difficulties in defining and researching it.

A synthesis of approaches

Each of the four approaches listed above has its weaknesses and limitations, which many adherents as well as critics acknowledge. A synthesis of the major ideas and approaches that have influenced the scope, direction, and ideological interpretation of international and comparative HRM may prove a useful way forward.

The four approaches to the employment relationship in a comparative context can be placed in convergent and divergent categories as illustrated in Table 15.1. Most observers have to come to the view that in an evolving and globalising world economy both convergent and divergent forces have considerable impact. Child (1981) claims that there is evidence for both convergence and divergence; Child and Tayeb (1983) emphasise the evolutionary nature of managerial and HRM development and the fact that, while culture may be regarded as a contextual contingency, over time cultural differences are of diminishing importance. Prentice (1990) goes so far as to say that there will be a best management style for the future. The problem with this view is: How far in the future will that be? Evidence seems to suggest that while some aspects of employee relations are converging, the influence of culture and national institutional factors remains strong. Kidger (1991), Sparrow and Hiltrop (1994), Sparrow and Wu (1999) and others have come to the view that separating these influences out is the present concern of research. This will be examined in more detail in the sections dealing with international HRM, but at this point it is worth examining each of the convergent and divergent perspectives in more detail, and exploring some of their weaknesses.

Table 15.1 **A synthesis of theoretical approaches to comparative HRM**

Convergent

Convergence or contingency perspective: Kerr *et al.*, Purcell and Mueller, McLuhan

Marxist theory: Braverman, Friedman, Edwards, Burawoy, regulationist school (Aglietta, Boyer and Lipietz)

Divergent

Cultural theorists: Hofstede, Laurent, Trompenaars, Hall, Tayeb

Institutional perspective: Aix school (Maurice *et al.*), Lane, Sorge and Warner, Dore, Whitley, Crouch, Sisson, Fulcher

Convergence approaches

Convergence or contingency perspective

This perspective on industrialisation and its influence on management and labour relation systems originated from the writings of Kerr *et al.* (1960). They posited the view that technological change ultimately creates similar industrial systems. These systems are rooted in the industrial organisation, where technology imposes the need for similar structures and work forms. This growth in similarity of organisational structures over time Kerr *et al.* called *convergence theory.*

An argument of the convergence school claims that, when organisations reach a certain scale, defined by the numbers of employees, it becomes necessary to introduce functional specialisation. To coordinate and control these functions results in a more formalised system of organisation, with rules, regulations and hierarchies. More staff are thus needed to perform these roles, with parallel development of more centrally controlled systems. Probably the most overt example of convergence has been Fordist systems, where the logic of the assembly line controls and constrains the ability of workers to take initiatives in the work process.

In this manner ways of working in countries throughout the world become similar when influenced by the same technologies and organisation of production. For example car plants, whether in Brazil, South Africa, Britain or the United States, will have similar production lines, which in turn influence the kind of human resource and work policies each nation will tend to follow, for example speed of the line, control over the work process and payment systems. Mueller and Purcell (1992) for example, claim that in the automobile industry 'convergent forces in the shape of globalisation of markets, European legislation and common product standards, as well as the easing of cross border shipments of components or half finished products, have led to the emergence of remarkably similar operational requirements in management policies in various countries' (p. 15).

A more recent interpretation of convergence theory has been proposed by Ritzer (1998) in what he calls the *McDonaldization thesis.* Here we can see the application of Fordism to the growing service sector, in which attempts are made by global organisations such as McDonalds, to achieve homogeneity not only of product but also of service. Close controls are created through training employees to perform a given script when customers enter the restaurant. In this way the consumers are also controlled and conditioned by the dialogue with the server, and by the way the restaurant is designed for fast turnover of customers. Thus

> Europe and the rest of the world are moving towards business and cultural worlds dominated by the principles of efficiency, predictability, calculability, and control through the substitution of non-human for human technology. In other words, we are moving towards a world in which business and culture in one region will be indistinguishable from the business and culture of every other.
>
> (Ritzer, 1998:75)

Cultural and institutional theorists would take issue with such a unidimensional view of how management and HRM operate in different national contexts. Even Kerr *et al.* (1971) revised their views on convergence theory, and claimed that they had been far too simplistic in explaining how technology influences organisational structure and behaviour. Other critics claimed that the convergence approach considers only the formal structures, and remains insensitive to informal structures within organisations. Another problem with the convergence approach as posited by Kerr *et al.* is that there is an assumption that only technology, work organisation and organisational forms drive convergence. The work of Mueller and Purcell (1992: 15) shows clearly that the globalisation of markets, regional legislation such as in the European Union, and common product standards also affect convergence. To this can be added the cross-border integration of products and services within MNCs and the influence of 'Japanese' methods across the globe, such as lean production and just in time. Convergence thus can take a number of forms and emanate from a number of sources. Nevertheless, it has enjoyed some revival in a revised form in recent years, and globalisation provides some compelling reasons for this.

Marxist theory

Another form of convergence theory emanates from the ideas of Karl Marx and his view of the development of capitalism. Like the convergence perspective this view ignores cultural and other informal influences on organisational development.

Essentially, this view sees capitalism as a mode of production in which the primary features are private ownership of capital, and competition between capitalist enterprises. The need for profit drives the system, and this is achieved by appropriation of surplus value from labour – that is, paying a wage that is lower than the value of the goods. Therefore in order to be competitive there is a need to exploit labour for ever-higher productivity for comparatively less reward.

A relatively recent development of the Marxist view of capitalism was advanced by Braverman (1974). The Marxists, unlike the convergence theorists, shift the emphasis from the structure of the organisation to the relationship between management and labour. In other words, there is a focus on the actors in relation to the processes of production. Braverman and his followers stress the importance of managerial control over the workforce, deskilling, and the cheapening of labour. They emphasise the importance to management and owners of the necessity of breaking down skill processes by the use of new technologies and the implementation of flexible work practices. The variety of management–labour relations throughout the world merely reflects the various stages of capitalism through which economies are passing. As developing economies grow they will pass through similar stages to advanced ones, with, presumably, the development of similar management–labour systems.

This deterministic view has been reinforced by writers positing what has become known as the *Fordist* view of capitalist development in terms of the organisation of production. This 'regulationist' school of Marxist theorists (Aglietta, Boyer and Lipietz) believes that developments of economic growth through periods of boom and slump lie in 'the rise and decline of a particular form or regime of economic organisation and regulation' (Meegan, 1988:138). The era of Fordism up to the 1960s and 1970s was the main form of industrial organisation upon which Western capitalism was built. The slumps in the 1970s and 1980s witnessed a crisis of capitalism and consequently a breakdown in the Fordist system. Fordism is predicated on mass production, often on an assembly line system, which enables the fragmentation of the labour process (job tasks etc., which each worker can perform, usually with little training). It is mostly heavily associated with car and vehicle production – hence the term 'Fordism' – and latterly with white goods and electrical appliance manufacture. Like the convergence theorists, the regulationists assume that the mode of production will create similar systems of control through machine pacing, and there will be less need for supervisors or foremen and a greater need for managers. Using 'scientific' methods such as those advocated by

Frederick Taylor, managers would seek ways of increasing employee productivity. The assumption was that these scientific methods would be applicable in all work contexts.

Marxists believe that the competitive world of capitalism will eventually lead to a crisis in production whereby too many goods will be produced for the market to absorb. However, while there have been crises in capitalism they have not led to its breakdown. They claim that the adoption of neo-Fordist or post-Fordist techniques of manufacture that emphasise customer differentiation in an attempt to meet individual customer needs through flexible specialisation has created new forms of work organisation that have given capitalism a new lease of life. This means giving greater autonomy to the workforce by introducing measures such as teamworking, job enrichment, cellular manufacture and forms of functional flexibility. In the 1980s and 1990s HRM strategy and policy has been used to support these forms of flexible specialisation. In this way another regime or regulationist paradigm has been created in the intensive search for markets, by lowering costs and increasing quality of product or service. These work forms have been increasingly extended beyond those industries associated with mass production, particularly as there has been considerable restructuring of advanced economies, shifting the emphasis of labour force employment to the service sector. In this way the new work forms and management systems that emanate from them become widespread globally.

Divergence approaches

The cultural approach

Writers who emphasise divergence in managerial and HRM forms tend to view convergence theories as being overly simplistic in their applicability to all work contexts. The cultural approach is one of the most important schools that criticises convergent theories, and one of the most notable writers in the field is Geert Hofstede, who believes 'that there is no evidence that the cultures of present-day generations from different countries are converging' (Hofstede, 1991:17). He believes that cultural influences play an enormous part in the way employees behave in organisations, and that the introduction of technology produces only superficial similarities.

Culture is in itself notoriously difficult to define. It can mean many things, ranging from expression through the arts and other creative media to societal perceptions of history and spirituality. The most commonly accepted definition is the one put forward by Kluckhohn (1951) after studying over a hundred definitions:

> Culture consists of patterns, explicit and implicit of and for behaviour acquired and transmitted by symbols, constituting the distinctive achievement of human groups, including their embodiment in artefacts; the essential core of culture consists of traditional (i.e. historically derived and selected) ideas and especially their attached values; culture systems may, on the one hand, be considered as products of action, on the other as conditioning elements of future action. (p. 86)

Even with this definition the multiplicity of meaning makes social investigation using empirical tools very difficult.

The work of Hofstede

Hofstede's research into IBM is one of the most groundbreaking and important pieces of research into the cultural influences on the management process. Using the responses of managers from 66 different countries produced some interesting if controversial evidence on cultural differences. He found that managers and employees vary on four primary dimensions, which he called: *power distance, uncertainty avoidance, individuality* and *masculinity* (Hofstede, 1980).

Power distance

By power distance (PDI) Hofstede means 'the extent to which the less powerful members of institutions and organisations within a country expect and accept that power is distributed unequally' (1991: 28). For example, in democratic societies the distance between the government and the governed is narrower than in dictatorships. In other words a worker in the Philippines will have far less chance of influencing the decisions of the government than would a worker in Sweden; and the same applies in the workplace. There is thus a high PDI in the Philippines and a low PDI in Sweden. Such work attitudes, Hofstede believes, are culturally determined and are liable to be accepted as much by the workforce as by the managers.

Uncertainty avoidance

The definition of uncertainty avoidance involves, *inter alia*, the creation of rules and structures to eliminate ambiguity in organisations and support beliefs promising certainty and protecting conformity. In simple terms, this means that human beings try in various ways to avoid uncertainty in their lives by controlling their environment through predictable ways of working. For example, France and Germany are much higher in uncertainty avoidance than Britain and Sweden. In other words, the Germans and French feel a much greater need to adhere to rules and regulations than do the Swedes and British.

Individualism

Individualism describes the relationship between the individual and the group to which he or she belongs, or the preference for living and working in collectivist or individual ways. Not surprisingly, the USA and Britain score high on the individual index, and South American and Asian countries score low. In the latter there is much more reliance on the extended family and the subsuming of the individual identity within the group, whereas in countries with high individual indexes, such as the USA and the Northern European countries, there is a tendency to revere individual achievement.

Masculinity

Hofstede's last and perhaps most controversial index of culture is masculinity. This pertains to societies in which social gender roles are clearly distinct: that is, men are supposed to be assertive, tough and focused on material success. Femininity pertains to societies in which women are supposed to be more modest, tender and concerned with the quality of life (Hofstede, 1991: 82). In his index, masculine and feminine values can apply to both men and women. Thus we find that in Sweden, the least masculine country in the index, feminine values apply also to men. However, in the most masculine country, Japan, women seem to retain their feminine values.

Some commentators have pinpointed feminine values as being those most required in management practices in the organisation of the future. If that is the case, then some cultures will have considerable problems in adapting to those values immediately, if we are to believe Hofstede's masculinity index. The Netherlands comes very low on the masculinity index (MAS score 14) and the USA quite high (MAS score 62). Naturally, managerial practices could pose cultural misunderstandings between managers and workforces from the two countries.

The research of Trompenaars

Trompenaars has also examined cultural differences in a world context. He uses seven dimensions of culture, each of which has within it a tension as exemplified by two opposite or polarised values. These measures are:

- **Universalism–Particularism**, in which individuals from a 'universalist' culture would focus on rules, and from a 'particularist' culture on relationships (Trompenaars, 1993: 29). For example, he asked respondents to state whether they would tell the truth to the authorities if they were accompanying a friend who, driving at 35 mph in a 20 mph speed-restricted zone, knocked down a pedestrian. In universalist cultures the respondents would feel a greater obligation to state that the friend had been travelling at 35 mph, but in a particularist culture respondents felt a greater obligation to the relationship by protecting the friend from a possible serious conviction.
- The **Analysing–Integrating** dimension examines the tension between the tendency to 'analyse phenomena into parts i.e. facts, items, tasks, numbers, units, points, specifics, or . . . to integrate and configure such details into whole patterns, relationships, and wider context' (Hampden-Turner and Trompenaars, 1994: 11).
- **Individualism–Collectivism** is the 'conflict between what each of us wants as an individual, and the interests of the group we belong to' (Trompenaars, 1993: 47).
- The **Inner Directed–Outer Directed** scale ranges from individuals who are influenced to action by 'inner directed judgements, decisions and commitments, or signals, demands and trends in the outside world to which we must adjust' (Hampden-Turner and Trompenaars, 1994: 11).
- **Time as Sequence–Time as Synchronisation** is the preference for doing 'things fast, in the shortest possible sequence of passing time, or to synchronise efforts so that completion is coordinated' (Hampden-Turner and Trompenaars, 1994: 11).
- **Achieved Status–Ascribed Status** examines the view that 'the status of employees depends on what they have achieved and how they have performed, or on some characteristic important to the corporation, i.e. age, seniority, gender, education, potential, strategic role' (Hampden-Turner and Trompenaars, 1994: 11).
- **Equality–Hierarchy** asks the question: 'Is it more important that we treat employees as equals so as to elicit from them the best they have to give, or to emphasise the judgement and authority of the hierarchy that is coaching and evaluating them?' (Hampden-Turner and Trompenaars, 1994: 11). This dimension has similarities to Hofstede's power distance index. Table 15.2 indicates where some major industrial powers would be located on Trompenaars' scale of cultural measures.

The work of André Laurent

André Laurent of INSEAD in France has also achieved considerable recognition through his research on work-related values. He studied the attitudes of managers in Western European countries, the United States and two Asian countries, Indonesia and Japan (Laurent, 1983). He asked managers from these countries to describe their approaches to over 60 normal work situations. He discovered that managers of each of these countries fitted four clear groupings concerning perceptions of the organisation as a political system, authority system, role formulation system and hierarchical relationship system.

For example, when he posed the statement, 'The main reason for hierarchical structure is so that everybody knows who has authority over whom,' there were a variety of responses. Americans tended to disagree with the statement, believing the purpose of

Table 15.2 **The position of some major industrial countries on Trompenaars' cultural dimensions**

Universalism	Britain, Sweden, USA, Germany, the Netherlands
Analysis	Britain, Sweden, USA, the Netherlands
Individualism	Britain, Sweden, USA, the Netherlands
Inner direction	Britain, USA, Germany
Time as sequence	Britain, Sweden, USA, Germany, the Netherlands
Status by achievement	Britain, Sweden, USA, Germany, the Netherlands, Japan
Equality	Britain, Sweden, USA, Germany, the Netherlands
Particularism	France, Japan
Integration	France, Germany, Japan
Collectivism	Germany, France, Japan
Outer direction	Sweden, the Netherlands, France, Japan
Synchronised view of time	France, Japan
Status by ascription	France
Hierarchy	France, Japan

Source: Hampden-Turner and Trompenaars (1994: 301). Reprinted from *The Seven Cultures of Capitalism* by permission of Piatkus Books.

hierarchy is to organise tasks to assist in problem solving. The Americans tended to appreciate an organisation with as few levels of bureaucracy or hierarchy as possible. By contrast many Southern European and most Asians managers strongly agreed with Laurent's statement. These managers regard hierarchy as important in making sense of work structures and thus work itself. The structure being distinct enables them to know more clearly where they fit in and what their role is in the work process.

In response to the statement 'In order to have efficient work relationships, it is often necessary to bypass the hierarchical line' cultural differences were also revealed.

On this index the Swedes scored the lowest, which is consistent with the Swedish style of working, in which employee involvement is emphasised and many responsibilities are given to the workforce compared with other countries. However, cultural theorists would regard it as being simplistic and unjustified to place a value judgement on these attitudes, as they are rooted very much in the values of a society. In Italy, for example, it would be considered disrespectful and even challenging to bypass the boss, even to solve a problem advantageous to the organisation. This would be regarded as a challenge to the boss's authority.

In other words, while employees in different countries outwardly appear to be carrying out the same type of work processes, the cultural values that each individual carries shape both their perception and understanding of the workplace and their preferences for certain styles of working.

High and low context cultures

Hall (1976; Hall and Hall, 1990) has made a comparative study of national attributes in the setting of *high context* and *low context* cultures.

> Low context people appreciate explicit, clear written forms of communication, as provided by computers, books and letters. In contrast high context peoples, such as the Japanese, Arabs and Southern Europeans, divulge less information officially in written forms, but tend to be better informed than low context people, since they tend to develop extensive informal networks for exchanging information verbally face to face or by telephone. High context people are also more adept in interpreting non-verbal aspects of communication, and seeing the significance of what is implicit or not said, pauses, silence, tone, and other subtle signals.
> (Leeds *et al.*, 1994: 12)

641

One could say that the British 'old boy network' falls very much into this high context category, as does the felt need for exclusive clubs and societies, providing an entrée into various influential networks, which pervades British society. See Table 15.3.

Table 15.3 **Locating low and high context cultures**

Country	High context	Low context
West Germany		XXXX
German Swiss		XXXX
Scandinavian		XXX
North American		XXX
Belgium, the Netherlands, Denmark		X
France		X
Britain	XX	
Southern Europe	XXX	
Middle East	XXX	
Asia, Africa, Latin America	XXX	
Japan	XXXX	

Source: Leeds *et al*. (1994: 13).

Criticism of the cultural approach

Attempts at measuring attitudes in human beings are difficult enough (as the wealth of research work in the social sciences testifies), but the application of numerous cultural values to the equation makes the work of disentangling one value from another extremely difficult, if not impossible. The cultural values of the researcher must be considered, and how much they are embodied in the research, from its conception to the analysis of the findings.

The cultural approach to HRM has received considerable criticism from academics working in HRM and related fields. Research such as that of Hofstede, Trompenaars and Laurent, which uses a positive approach, has been attacked for being too narrow in focus, and that using ethnographic approaches as often being too nebulous (Hollinshead and Leat, 1995: 3). Altman (1992) sums up the dilemma of the positive approach:

> Hofstede's strength lies in a finely tuned and rigorously applied research design. This is also his limitation. His approach can be likened to a powerful torch – sending a concentrated and bright, extremely sharp, ray of light, but, necessarily, leaving much in the dark. (p. 36)

In addition, the focusing of cultural values on bipolar dimensions has its difficulties. Individualism, for example, can have widely differing interpretations from one society to another, and may not necessarily mean the opposite of collectivism. Both Sweden and the USA are seen as high in individualism, but they do not have the same type of individualism. Swedish individualism resides very much within a welfare society, and American individualism within a neo-liberalist one. This begs the question of what these indices are actually representing.

Hofstede and Trompenaars also tend to assume clear relationships between attitudes and behaviours. There is an assumption that certain cultural attitudes will automatically lead to specific types of behaviour. They also ignore the wider context of culture, and their work suffers from being a static analysis in that it does not locate values in real historical development patterns and relationships between social groups and institutions –

an approach that the institutional perspectives attempts to address. Other critics claim that not all important value dimensions are represented, and that 'the structure of those four dimensions . . . can be challenged. The Masculinity/Femininity dimension is perhaps misnomered; it invites interpretation in terms limited to sexism' (Mead, 1994: 74).

There is also the problem of ascribing one culture to a whole national context. Very few societies are culturally homogeneous (Clark *et al.*, 1999: 521). For example, it would be difficult to sum up culturally what Englishness is, given the variety of regions and classes within England. Summing up Britishness will have greater problems given the diversity of Welsh, Scottish, English and Irish cultures.

In addition Sparrow (1995) astutely points out that

> The 'culture bound' perspective runs the gauntlet between generalizability and stereotyping and fails to consider the equally pervasive impact of both individual differences and organisational choice over its resource development. We need to know how all the operationalised dimensions relate to each other, and to the different levels and concepts of culture? Which dimensions have the greatest utility in shaping or influencing HRM when translated to the work of organisations?
>
> (p. 949)

Thus while many observers point to the importance of culture and the understanding of cultural differences in the HRM context, there are still considerable problems concerning definitions and approaches to meaningful and applicable research.

The institutional perspective

A more wide-ranging divergence perspective on international HRM emanates from institutional theory. This view essentially sees the business environment as socially constituted. In other words, the influence of national and regional institutions and the historical traditions from which they have emerged is important in understanding why institutions differ throughout the world.

This perspective on the employment relationship suggests not only that business systems vary, but also that there are different models of capitalism. Until the 1980s much emphasis was placed upon four business systems or modes of industrial organisation: the American, European, Japanese and Soviet systems. Work by Sisson (1987), Lane (1989, 1995), Fulcher, (1991), Whitley (1992), Crouch (1993) and others has shown the complexity of industrial systems rooted in national institutional frameworks. For example, to speak of a 'European model' is patently absurd given the wide-ranging differences within the European Union alone, let alone the whole of what may qualify as Europe and indeed the world. In addition, since the collapse of the Soviet system another hybrid form of capitalism has emerged rooted in Soviet and Russian pre-existing systems and thus possessing unique characteristics of its own.

Such influential factors as the role of the state, financial systems, systems of education and training, national labour markets, culture, employment relations and systems of industrial bargaining, for example, have evolved in diverse ways in different national contexts that in turn affect the way organisations develop. These factors create a variety of configurations of institutional systems that have a considerable impact on the way human resource management is conducted. Given such diversity of national institutional frameworks Whitley (1992) has argued that creating a European system of HRM will prove virtually impossible, certainly for the foreseeable future.

The corporatist systems of Sweden, Germany and France, for example, are not only radically different from the neo-liberalist systems of the United States and the UK but also have considerable differences between themselves. These differences originate in the way in which each nation's institutions have historically evolved, affected not only by the changing economic structure but also by historical events that impact on the national psyche at crucial points in institutional development. For example the Ådalen Strike in Sweden in 1931, in which a number of workers were killed by government troops, came to symbolise the old conflictual industrial relations. This had a considerable impact on the Saltsjöbaden Agreement 1938 between employers and unions, which implemented controls over the use of the strike weapon and the lockout in the resolution of disputes (Martin, 1984). This in turn had an impact on the creation of the Swedish Model in the 1950s, one of the main purposes of which was to resolve disputes and subsequently avoid such drastic incidents (Hadenius, 1988).

Lane (1989, 1994, 1995) has compared the industrial orders of Britain, Germany and France, and points to five institutional effects on business systems: the state, the financial system, the system of education and training, trade associations and chambers, and the system of industrial relations. For example, Lane (1992) shows that the state has a much higher profile in Germany than in Britain by endeavouring to provide 'a stable economic environment as well as uniform regulatory frameworks resulting in considerable national homogeneity of structural arrangements' (p. 67). State regulation of the British industrial order is much less than in Germany, particularly where the state acts as a coordinator for the integration of local and national policy with local government and other relevant regional bodies. The German and British financial systems are also structured differently. There is a heavy reliance on the stock market for large capital investment in the UK compared with Germany, with the result that short-termism predominates as investors desire to see immediate gains, and the capital markets are more prone to fluctuations. By contrast the German stock market is less developed. The role of capital provider is filled by large universal banks that maintain close links with industry. This interconnected system of mutual support makes events such as a hostile takeover rare, and viewed with suspicion if not hostility, as illustrated by the attempt by Vodafone to take over Mannesmann in early 2000.

In Germany there is strong structural support for training by government, although the costs are borne mainly by employers. By contrast, in the UK, structural supports, while existing, have emerged from different sociopolitical traditions, and the emphasis at present is on a voluntarist approach, which relies on organisations being willing to participate in government-inspired schemes. Vocational education and training (VET) has greater prestige in Germany, and the institutions (government, local government, private and public sector organisations, unions and educational institutions) that will benefit from such arrangements readily cooperate in providing support. The result is a high level of technical competence within the German workforce which is able to cope with forms of functional flexibility, and the productivity of German workers is thus much higher than that of their British counterparts.

In Germany, trade associations and chambers of industry and commerce also perform a crucial role in maintaining the craft tradition of high skill that keeps abreast of modern technical developments. Their importance is underscored by legislative support, and as statutory bodies they can impose levies on firms. In Britain, chambers of commerce do not have statutory status, and therefore have a more marginal role in the institutional framework of the industrial order.

The systems of industrial relations in the two countries also have different structures and influence. The German system is nationally homogeneous, with considerable legal underpinning. There is employee representation through works councils, the right to join unions and engage in collective bargaining is legally supported, and the system is geared towards conflict resolution at all times rather than shaped by the determinants of market forces as in the UK. The British system has emerged through custom and practice over a long period of time, and has experienced intense conflict at certain periods. This has been partially explained by the lack of strong employer associations and the practice in the past of backing up demands by industrial action. However, over the past 20 years there has been a considerable shift in collective bargaining from national to organisational levels, with a subsequent decline in union influence at national level. Legislation has also had the effect of curbing union power, and while union density remains relatively high militant activity has receded considerably. The lack of national bargaining arrangements compared with the German system has served to undermine British trade union power further. We can thus see that while both countries are European and ultimately subscribe to capitalist values each system is substantially different from the other in the way in which it deals with employment relation issues.

Supporters of the institutional perspective claim that it avoids the controversial issues associated with cultural theory, which can be heavily laden with culturally based value judgements. However, significant work using an institutional perspective does rely to some extent on the interpretation of culture. Dore's work comparing a British and a Japanese corporation shows how the Japanese employment system is 'partly an adaption of earlier pre-industrial patterns, partly a conscious attempt to create new arrangements consonant with dominant cultural values, and partly the result of borrowing elements from industrialised nations' (Dore, 1973, quoted in Lane, 1989: 32). He finds, for example:

- adaption of earlier pre-industrial patterns – that is, European and US;
- adaption of Japanese values – 'Bushido spirit', loyalty, group work, respect, duty;
- elements borrowed from other industrialised nations, such as Deming's ideas on total quality management.

Another perspective on the institutional approach has been provided by Whitley (1992), in what he calls *business systems*. He views economic systems as being socially constructed in that 'major differences in dominant institutions result in different kinds of leading firms becoming established and following different growth patterns in different European economies' (p. 1). To understand its management structures, industrial and employment relations and HRM, an understanding is also needed of how the market is organised and of the nature of firms, and how this influences their authority, coordination and control systems. The way these three elements interact results in the unique business system of each national economic entity.

Convergence or divergence?

Despite the simplicity of the convergence perspective and the limitations of the Marxist view there is some evidence to support increased convergence. Sparrow *et al.* (1994) conclude that there is a convergence in the use of HRM for competitive advantage, although they counsel caution in the interpretation of their findings, and still believe that cultural and institutional differences have some influence on divergent practices. Similarly, the Price Waterhouse Cranfield Surveys (Cran E net) reveal similar trends within corporations operating in different national settings: for example, greater use of flexible employment policy, the devolvement of HRM to line managers, an increase in spending on training and management development, and a greater strategic use of HRM initiatives (Brewster and Hegewisch, 1994). McGaughey and De Cieri (1999) have also taken up the theme of convergence recently, and have refined convergence to macro-level variables in HRM and divergence to micro-level ones, focusing on individual attitudes, performance and behaviours. These are generally variables that are psychological and behavioural.

Another support for the convergence view is the widespread dissemination of managerial practices that has had the effect of creating a degree of managerial homogeneity (Celestino, 1999). The export of American managerial practices and ideas has been under way since the Second World War, and since the 1970s Japanese managerial styles have had a considerable influence on managerial theory and practice. The ubiquity of the Masters in Business Administration (MBA) has also witnessed the spread of ideas, together with popularity of managerial fashions such as TQM, quality circles, empowerment schemes, performance management and numerous other initiatives propagated by the 'business and management industry' and the media. These have been extensively disseminated through business sections in newspapers, the proliferation of managerial journals, consulting practices and the growth in popularity of business and management courses worldwide.

This archetypal form of modernism, some claim, has been superseded by postmodernist work forms in which decentralisation and flexibilities pervade the new working environment (Harvey, 1989). Others have refuted this postmodernist view and believe that this flexibilised world hides types of Fordism, which remains strongly influenced by the capitalist organisation's compulsion to produce profit.

This limited evidence does not really disturb the view that divergence remains strong in cultural and institutional terms throughout the world. The recognition of this has been acknowledged with the growth of expatriate management training and development programmes, the increasing popularity of which in MNCs and other overseas organisations is clearly evident in the cultural, societal and institutional barriers that can create huge problems for companies operating in a foreign context. (See below in the expatriation section for a fuller discussion). There is also considerable evidence that the transposition of a management system that has worked well in one national setting will not work in others. The work of Dore (1973) and more recently Broad (1994) has clearly shown the difficulty of implanting Japanese management systems even within the same company from one national sociocultural context to another – from Japan to Britain, for example. Research on quality circles and TQM in the 1980s and 1990s also illustrated that a wholesale adoption of an imported approach from Japan can have even less success when adopted by companies that have little or no connection with the country where they originated (see Chapter 13 for an in-depth discussion of such initiatives). Subsequently such systems survive only when considerable adaptations are made to accommodate the customs and practices of the indigenous country.

Blyton and Turnbull (1996), in reply to Warhurst's (1995) article (on HRM convergence in European airlines in seeking competitive advantage), point to the limitations of the convergence versus divergence approach. They argue that comparative analysis should focus on modes of labour regulation rather than institutions of industrial relations. In doing so, a more profitable approach to understanding the dynamics of comparative HRM would be the exploration of how 'different choices are open to management (and) how they might interact with, rather than simply be determined by the external environment, and how this might affect industrial relations' (p. 14). In a sense this is an application and extension of the business systems approach advocated by Whitley (1992).

Whatever comparative method or combination of methods we choose to use, uncertainty and inexactitude will remain important weaknesses in all approaches. With so many influential factors playing on the employment relationship and the relationship of organisations to governments, there will always be considerable room for debate and controversy.

COMPARATIVE HRM

The separation of international HRM and comparative HRM is a useful way to untangle the various debates that surround the area of international HRM as a whole. International HRM we have defined as the creation and implementation of HRM strategy and policies and issues of international organisations, and comparative HRM as dealing with HRM concerns in national and regional contexts. Comparative HRM encompasses a wider area, and can range from comparing national employment systems rooted in ideologies, to aspects of HRM and related subjects such as training systems, pay systems, and the extent of the spread of flexible work systems. Comparative HRM can also vary in its approaches and meanings. One approach is to compare one nation state's HRM advantage with another. This approach often rests on a comparison of predominant national economies such as USA and Japan.

Economists and labour market theorists have undertaken considerable research into the essential properties that these regional and national contexts possess as drivers for successful economic growth. Unsurprisingly, the more successful these economies are (the USA and Japan, for example,) the more likely they are to be imitated or held up as exemplars of managerial efficiency. The US origin of HRM has been alluded to by a number of writers, who have attributed American values and even ideology to its theory and practice. This has led to a consideration of the transferability of HRM, both ideologically and as a set of employment issues, to other national and regional contexts, and whether other nations and global regions have HRM characteristics separate from American ones (Guest, 1990; Brewster, 1994; Clark and Mallory, 1996).

Another approach to comparative HRM is to draw a number of variables together into an analytical framework or model to help understanding of a nation's uniqueness in terms of its employment structure, industrial relations system and deployment of human resources. This poses many difficulties. Nevertheless, there have been some attempts to construct models to help understand these processes in a comparative context, and in this limited work we shall examine three: Poole's adaptation of the Harvard model, Brewster and Larsen's European model of HRM, and Sparrow and Hiltrop's comparative model of European HRM.

Comparative HRM models and frameworks

The growth of interest in international HRM issues has led observers to attempt to systematise its processes and influences. The first attempts to create a coherent framework were extensions of already existing models rooted in Anglo-American experience. Thus Poole (1990) in the first issue of the *International Journal of Human Resource Management* begins the process by examining the Harvard model for its suitability for international application. The Harvard model of Beer *et al.* (1984) is very much reflective of its North American origins. Nevertheless, Poole argues that the Harvard model lends itself readily to international HRM because of its pluralist nature, in that it accepts differing approaches and attitudes to the employment relationship. While Poole's model may be seen to be comparative, the fact that it is rooted in the Harvard model, which tries to explain HRM in an organisational context, also suggests that there is some confusion as to whether it is a comparative or an international model. In this sense it reflects the early stages of research in the subject, and in some senses it is a hybrid. Nevertheless it is a useful model, as it sets out the key elements in the study of comparative (and international) HRM.

Poole's adaption of the Harvard model

Because some of the key features of the Harvard model reflect its North American origin, Poole (1990: 3) believes three key modifications are necessary for it to be accommodated into a new framework of international HRM:

- the global development of business;
- the power of different stakeholders;
- the more specific links between corporate and human resource strategies.

Taking his cue from writers on other aspects of the international employment relationship, including his own work on comparative industrial relations (Poole, 1986), Poole emphasises the notion of strategic choice in international HRM. The main areas of strategic human choice he sees as:

- employee influence;
- human resource flow;
- reward systems;
- work systems.

Employee influence
The concept of empowerment of the workforce has long been recognised as an important in employee relations, and it has taken many forms in national and organisational cultures, including quality circles, job enrichment, union representation, works councils, co-determination, producer cooperatives, and self-management. Not all of these forms of participation will fit into HRM frameworks, but 'most are (a) relevant and (b) are the subject of vibrant comparative research' (Poole, 1990: 5).

Human resource flow
This is divided into *inflow* (recruitment, assessment and selection, orientation and socialisation), *internal flow* (evaluation of performance and potential, internal placement, promotion and demotion, education and training), and *outflow* (termination, outplacement and retirement). Each of these policy levers is governed by the government legislation, educational institutions, unions, societal values and public policy of each national and regional context.

Reward systems
These would include in the framework not only the traditional methods of rewards such as pay, but also intrinsic rewards such as employee satisfaction and motivation to work.

Work systems
The aim of all organisations is to gain high commitment from employees, and the various ways of achieving this reflect work-related value systems that need to be recognised and integrated.

Apart from these additions and adaptions to the Harvard model, Poole emphasises the need to recognise the role of globalisation, power and strategy in the evolution of international HRM.

The transcendence of national boundaries by multinational enterprises* (MNEs) and their relation to supranational bodies such as the European Union are becoming crucially important in the HRM process. Intertwined are the power structures of such bodies, which may conflict strategically and politically at company, country or regional level. The creation of strategies to take account of these possibilities becomes crucial in shaping the strategy of human resources. New technologies, the economies of large markets and market competition are other important factors to add to this strategic melting pot.

Poole sums up this process by quoting Adler and Ghadar (1989): 'the central issue of MNEs is not to identify the best international HRM policy per se, but rather to find the best fit between the firm's external environment, its overall strategy, and its HRM policy and implementation.'

As an early model it was useful in conceptualising some of the major issues that confront organisations in framing IHRM strategy, and acted more as a pointer towards research and theory building rather than being an end in itself.

Brewster and Larsen's model of European HRM

The uniqueness of Brewster and Larsen's model of comparative HRM is that it is rooted in, and has emerged from, an extensive comparative research data bank. The Price Waterhouse Cranfield Surveys (Cranet -E) compared HRM practices initially in five countries (France, Germany, Spain, Sweden and the UK) in 1989–90, and then ten countries (the original five plus Denmark, Italy, the Netherlands, Norway and Switzerland) in 1990–91. The survey was extended to 16 countries in 1995 with the addition of Finland, Ireland, Turkey, East Germany, Greece and Belgium, more recently has been expanded to Eastern European states, and there are plans to extend it beyond Europe.

Brewster claims that his European model attempts to break away from American-influenced conceptualisations of HRM (Brewster and Bournois, 1991; Brewster, 1993). One major problem, however, is the lack of homogeneity of European employment systems (despite the attempts of the European Union social action programme), which creates considerable difficulties for model building. Yet European HRM systems are different from American ones, and this difference and diversity requires a distinctly different model.

The Brewster/Larsen model, like later ones developed by Brewster, emphasises the strategic positioning of HRM in the organisational context. HRM is considered part of the strategic apparatus, and it should also inform the business strategy and not be merely a tool to enact HRM aspects of the business strategy. The model rests on two dimensions that they argue are crucial to HRM being strategic: the integration and devolution of HRM. By integration is meant 'the degree to which HRM issues are considered part of the formulation of business strategy' (Brewster and Larsen, 1992: 411). HRM is thus integrated with technological, financial and human considerations of strategy implementation. Devolution concerns the transference of HRM functions to line managers and others at the operational levels within the organisation. HRM policy and functions are thus shared between the HRM department and line managers. The two dimensions are placed on a matrix, allowing an analysis both of the roles of the HRM department and of HRM as a general management activity (Figure 15.1).

* The terms MNE (multinational enterprise) and MNC (multinational company) are interchangeable.

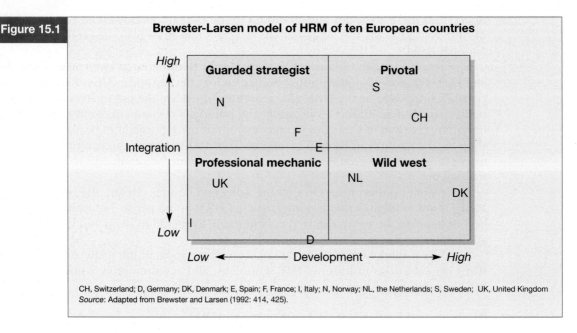

Figure 15.1   **Brewster-Larsen model of HRM of ten European countries**

CH, Switzerland; D, Germany; DK, Denmark; E, Spain; F, France; I, Italy; N, Norway; NL, the Netherlands; S, Sweden; UK, United Kingdom
Source: Adapted from Brewster and Larsen (1992: 414, 425).

Within the matrix are four types of HRM. The bottom left box indicates that business strategy is low, and there is little devolvement of HRM to the line. They have called this the *Professional mechanic* 'to emphasise the specialist, but limited skills and interests of practitioners' (Brewster and Larsen, 1992: 414). The professional role of the HRM department is emphasised, cherishing its HRM expertise and viewing it as not transferable to the line to any great extent. It thus has an increasing distance from strategic interests. The bottom right-hand box is called the *wild west*, because while a considerable amount of HRM is devolved to the line, the integration of HRM with business strategy remains low. In the top left-hand box is the *guarded strategist,* where integration of HRM with the business strategy is high, but devolvement to the line is low. This type of HRM is usually found in large and influential departments. The top right-hand box, the *pivotal,* represents the situation where HRM is fully integrated with business strategy and there is a high degree of devolvement to the line.

The UK, Germany and Italy emerge as professional mechanics, the Netherlands and Denmark as wild westers, Norway, France and Spain as guarded strategists, and the most integrated with the business strategy and the most devolved are Sweden and Switzerland in the pivotal box.

While presenting an interesting analysis of European HRM this does also pose a number of problems. First, these findings need to be put in the context of the national institutional environments in which HRM operates. These factors have a considerable impact, and it is hard to accept that the UK, Germany and Italy are similar in their HR practices because they appear in the same box based on only two dimensions. Institutional theorists would argue strongly how different HR is in these countries in terms of labour law, VET systems and collective bargaining, which could have a strong bearing on integrational and devolutional approaches to HRM. Second, these countries are very different culturally, and although the authors make some attempt to place the findings against the cultural dimensions of Hofstede and Laurent this has limitations. Third, there is always a methodological question mark over postal surveys and the drawing of wide generalisations based on them. Only personnel/HR managers were asked to complete the questionnaire, and large staff sections of the organisation were excluded. There are also ontological and epistemological limitations to the final analysis. Without other data, for example qualitative research, these results must be viewed with some scepticism. The authors do acknowledge some of these limitations, and we must also bear in mind that this is the only Europe-wide survey that has been conducted consistently over a period of a decade. It would be interesting in future works emanating from the Cran E survey material to attempt to contextualise the findings more deeply.

In later works Brewster (1994, 1995) has tried to address some of these concerns, and has developed models that attempt to give explanations of the influence on HRM of factors external to the organisation, such as culture, legislation, patterns of ownership, sector, size, trade union representation, employee involvement and communication, bargaining arrangements, labour markets, education and training. European organisations operate with restricted autonomy owing to the constraints of the European Union (for those member countries) and, at national level, the constraints of legislation and culture. These features, he claims, need to be integrated into the concept of HRM.

Clark and Mallory (1996) have criticised these models on the grounds that there cannot possibly be a European model of HRM given the diversity of European cultures. They also accuse Brewster of being Anglo-American in that he takes the parameters of the HRM debate purely from the literature of the UK and USA without due regard to writings in related areas in European organisations. While these criticisms have some validity, Brewster would claim that they are by no mean perfect models but merely steps in our thinking towards devising better ones.

The Sparrow and Hiltrop model

Sparrow and Hiltrop's model also aims to differentiate European HRM from its American origins. They state 'that if European management exists it is in terms of greater cautiousness, sophistication of methods, and pursuance of elitist reward and career systems' (Sparrow and Hiltrop, 1997: 201). They suggest that a European perspective needs to take these factors into account:

- more restricted levels of organisation autonomy in HRM decisions such as recruitment, dismissal and training;
- a history that has produced a lower exposure of organisations to market processes;
- a greater emphasis on the role of the group over the individual;
- the increased role of social partners (trade unions and employee representatives) in the employment relationship;
- higher levels of government intervention in the management of business and the people within it.

In examining comparative HRM their aim is to make a dynamic model that is orientated towards the process of change, as they claim that the field hitherto has been 'long on description but short on analysis' (p. 202). The subject of their model centres on the factors that result in distinctive national differences; unlike Brewster's model it does not try to place emphasis on HRM practices in the organisation. The *force field* framework that they develop (Figure 15.2) is constructed around four sets of factors:

- cultural factors, such as national understandings of distributive justice and the manager–subordinate relationship;

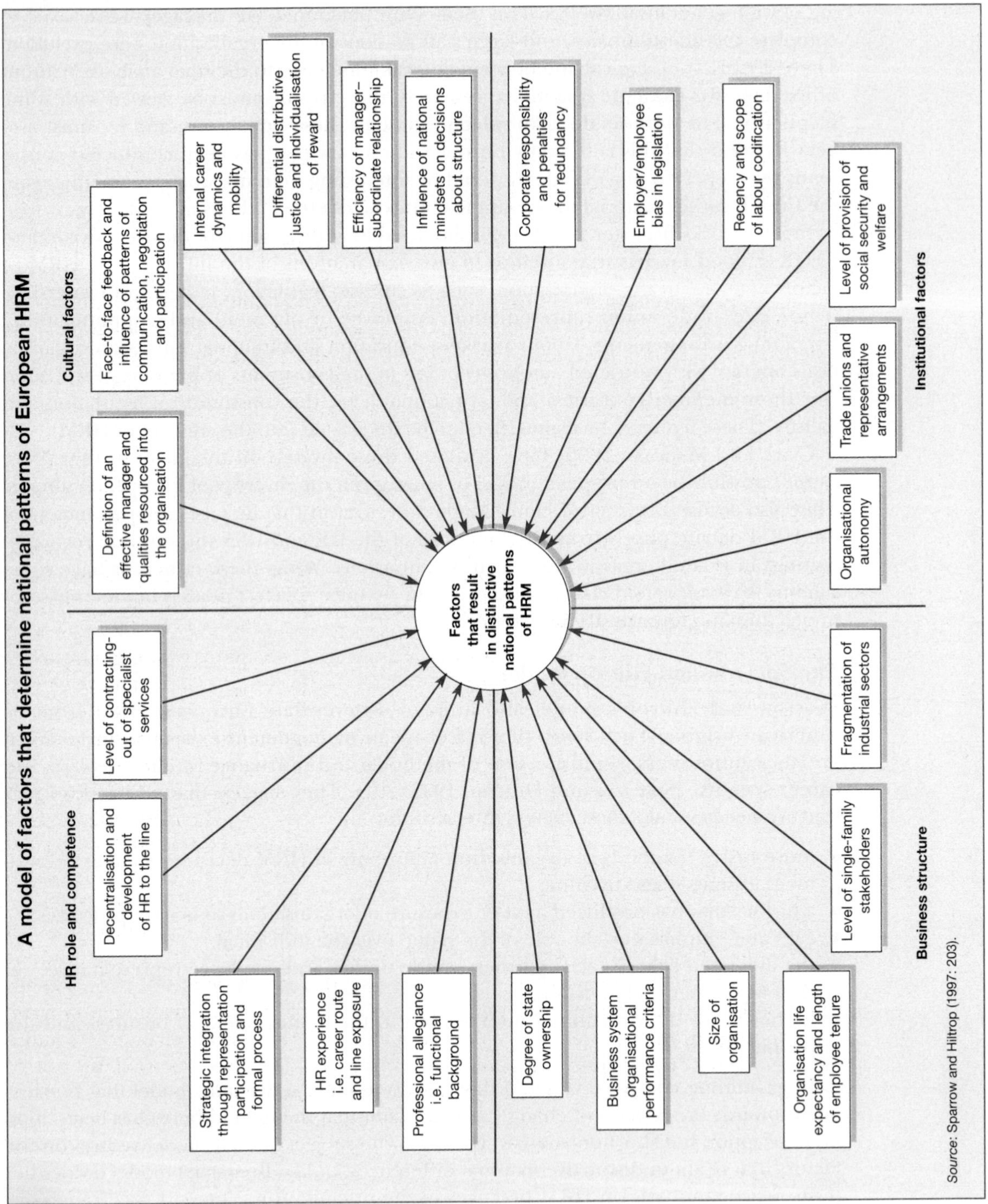

Figure 15.2

A model of factors that determine national patterns of European HRM

HR role and competence

Strategic integration through representation participation and formal process

HR experience i.e. career route and line exposure

Professional allegiance i.e. functional background

Decentralisation and development of HR to the line

Level of contracting-out of specialist services

Definition of an effective manager and qualities resourced into the organisation

Cultural factors

Face-to-face feedback and influence of patterns of communication, negotiation and participation

Internal career dynamics and mobility

Differential distributive justice and individualisation of reward

Efficiency of manager-subordinate relationship

Influence of national mindsets on decisions about structure

Factors that result in distinctive national patterns of HRM

Corporate responsibility and penalties for redundancy

Employer/employee bias in legislation

Recency and scope of labour codification

Level of provision of social security and welfare

Institutional factors

Trade unions and representative arrangements

Organisational autonomy

Fragmentation of industrial sectors

Level of single-family stakeholders

Organisation life expectancy and length of employee tenure

Size of organisation

Business system organisational performance criteria

Degree of state ownership

Business structure

Source: Sparrow and Hiltrop (1997: 203).

- institutional factors, including the scope of labour legislation and social security provisions, and the role of trade unions;
- differences in business structures and systems, such as the degree of state ownership and fragmentation of industrial sectors;
- factors relating to the roles and competence of HRM professionals.

Organisations respond to their immediate business environments, and thus economic activities are controlled and coordinated differently in each national business system setting. For example, the impact of social and economic legislation of the European Union will be mediated by differing organisational strategies in the context of the national business system. Factors such as the degree of state ownership, the way public sector organisations connect to the business environment, and the number of small family-owned businesses are crucial to understanding different national business systems. For example, the preponderance and influence of small family-owned businesses in Italy has a powerful impact on the way HR issues are dealt with. In large organisations a greater number of employees tend to create more formalised HR structures compared with the informal practices of small businesses.

Institutional factors provide a second force field framework in their model. The role of the state, financial sectors, national systems of education and training and labour relations systems create unique 'logics of action' in each country, which guide different management practices (Whitley, 1992). The impact of national cultures (the third force field framework) shapes behaviour and perceptions, and there is a wide diversity of culture within Europe. The variations in culture will thus give widely differing approaches to management and HRM in terms of attitudes and definitions as to what makes an effective manager. HRM practices such as recruitment, selection, training, employee involvement, feedback, negotiation, communications, reward and performance will be perceived differently in divergent cultural settings.

The final force field framework relates to HR roles and competence and how these are interpreted at organisational levels in different national contexts. The levels of competence, career paths and the professional background of European HRM managers vary considerably. Thus the 'German HR professional with their strong legalistic background will have a very different mindset when compared to their less formal Anglo-Saxon colleagues, while the financial backgrounds of many Dutch and Italian HRM professionals produce yet a different focus' (Sparrow and Hiltrop, 1997: 208).

These force field frameworks are themselves open to different pressures from an ever-changing business environment that is experiencing rapid and discontinuous change as a result of the globalisation of markets and production and service systems. This in turn leads to choices within nations as to levels of taxation, investment in training and education, degrees of regulation or deregulation of labour markets and a number of other decisions. Sparrow and Hiltrop believe that the working out of responses to these changes will be most immediately felt at organisational level, perhaps by the adoption of 'best practices' in management and HRM. MNCs often act as a conduit for Anglo and Japanese approaches to HRM for example. In this sense a degree of convergence begins to overlay national HRM and managerial settings.

The Sparrow and Hiltrop model is a useful theoretical advance in aiding our understanding of comparative HRM, but in this short exposition of their work we cannot do justice to its complexity. They also clearly point to the sterility of strategic models of HRM, which do not consider the importance and influence of wider contextual factors. Strategic models that have emerged particularly from the American context embody

American values either explicitly or implicitly, and in many ways are inapplicable to other national and regional contexts. The strength of this model, given the fact that it has not been rigorously tested in the field, is that there is a recognition of the influence of cultural and institutional factors peculiar to business environments within which organisations have to operate.

Some comparative HRM studies

Comparative studies into international aspects of the employment relationship have been carried out for a number of years and in their widest sense cover an enormous area of research, from an industrial relations and labour market perspective (Wilczynski, 1983; Bean, 1985; Poole, 1986; Bamber and Lansbury, 1987, 1998; Lane, 1989; Baglioni and Crouch, 1990; Hyman and Ferner, 1994; Ferner and Hyman, 1992, 1998; Ruysseveldt, *et al.*, 1995; Ruysseveldt and Visser, 1996; Cooke and Noble, 1998) to a broad raft of managerial issues including management development (Handy *et al.*, 1988; Randlesome, 1990; Kakabadse, 1991; Storey *et al.*, 1991; Storey, 1992; Lawrence, 1992; Brewster *et al.*, 1993). While such studies inform aspects of the employment relationship, human resource management is not their central concern.

Other studies have taken aspects of the employment relationship and have compared policy and practice in a number of national or regional contexts: for example, comparisons of employee involvement systems (Poole, 1986; Lincoln and Kalleberg, 1990; Gill, 1993; IDE, 1993; Holden, 1996). However, there is still a dearth of research that examines overarching HRM strategy and various HRM-related issues in a comparative context. There are many single-country studies, and while these may be informative, collectively they lack the unifying research methodology that allows rigorous comparability. Purcell (1993: 508–509) made a plea that comparative HRM research should examine different industry settings, and the extent to which capital markets and accounting practices affect HRM, as well as the impact of organisational size and ownership. This research agenda still remains relevant.

There have been studies of comparative and contrasting aspects of personnel management, management, management styles, international business and organisational behaviour, but in many ways they illustrate the hybrid nature of the relatively new discipline of HRM. There have been a number of single-nation surveys of aspects of HRM (Brewster and Tyson, 1991; Tyson *et al.*, 1993), and various dual or multiple-country qualitative studies and case studies, but there have been few internationally comparative quantitative surveys. One such survey is the Price Waterhouse Cranfield Survey on international strategic human resource management, referred to earlier.

Price Waterhouse Cranfield Survey of International HRM

The research team were confronted with many methodological problems, and so the results have to be handled with care. For example, the creation of a questionnaire that would be completely compatible in all national employment settings posed enormous difficulties. Meanings of words change in context and in translation. For example, in France three general staff categories are used:

> Cadres, referring to managers and some professional employees, ETAM who are administrative, technical and advisory staff and ouvriers or operatives. These are not only the customary definitions but are also defined in law. There is little point therefore in trying to force French personnel managers into the customary British fourfold division of: 'management'; professional/ technical; 'clerical', and 'manual'.
> (Brewster et al., 1991)

Meanings of work typologies alluded to earlier in this chapter also presented problems of interpretation. Another restricting factor was that the survey dealt only with organisations in European countries, although a number were owned by American, Japanese and other non-European based companies.

The survey questionnaire was also directed at personnel managers, and therefore responses could well be flavoured with their interests and biases. Despite these and other methodological problems, observable trends were in evidence. Strategic HRM, as we have noted in Chapter 1, is concerned with the view that the creation of HRM policy is aligned to, and is an important part of, business strategy. In companies employing over 200 people the survey revealed that the HRM function seems to be becoming a more important part of organisations, as indicated by the high percentages of HRM managers or their equivalents with places on the board of directors.

The survey also revealed that the Scandinavian countries (Denmark, Norway, Sweden) had the highest percentage of organisations (over 60%) that had written personnel or HR strategies, and the Netherlands and Switzerland had over 50%, while the rest, including the UK, had less than 50%. Of those that had a personnel/HR strategy, only half to three-quarters translated these into work programmes, and 'this raises a substantial question mark over the extent of strategic human resource management in Europe' (Price Waterhouse Cranfield Project, 1991: 8).

The survey, however, confirmed a number of trends, including the continuing devolution of some aspects of HRM to line managers, particularly in recruitment and selection. Training is also tending to be devolved much more, albeit with consultation from the HR function. Industrial relations, however, remains typically within the personnel department's purview, which clearly indicates some of the differences between American organisational autonomy and the more centralised and coordinated European systems of collective bargaining. This, of course, is reflected in pay bargaining, which, while indicating a drop at national level in Britain and France, still remains relatively strong in these countries, and very strong in the rest of the survey countries, particularly Scandinavia (Price Waterhouse Cranfield Project, 1991; Brewster and Bournois, 1991). Trade union strength, while showing a relative decline in some countries, still retains a strong influence, and even low-density figures in France and Spain belie the considerable political power that the trade union movement can exert in these countries (Segrestin, 1990; Estevill and de la Hoz, 1990).

As we have noted in Chapter 13, employee communication is one of the central tenets of HRM, and the survey indicates a significant increase in its use; but in many European countries it is supported by legal requirements (and EC Directives) to consult and inform the workforce, another element that does sit well with American views of HRM (Brewster and Bournois, 1991: 9).

Atypical working or forms of flexibility (e.g. part-time workers) have increased in recent years, and have significance both for organisations that practise 'soft' HRM, associated with unitarist concepts aligned to internal labour markets, and for 'hard' HRM, associated with the core–peripheral external labour market model. Evidence from the survey shows a distinct increase in part-time working, and to a lesser degree fixed-term contracts. 'There is some evidence from the survey that Germany approximates more to the internal labour market model and Britain to the external' (Brewster and Bournois, 1991:10). 'Currently, however, there are indications here that support the view that European organisations are looking to create a more controlled external labour market for themselves' (Brewster and Bournois, 1991:11).

The survey gives credence to the views of Guest, Poole and others that HRM trends in Europe must be put in context against many different working practices (both internal and external to organisations) resting on different legal requirements and national assumptions, which contrast strongly with American HRM. Only further research will make it possible to develop and refine an international model and a European model.

The Towers Perrin survey

Another survey conducted by Towers Perrin and analysed by Sparrow *et al.* (1994) looked at 12 countries worldwide. They asked the question: Do firms in different parts of the world practise HRM for competitive advantage differently? Data gathered from a questionnaire postal survey of chief executive officers and human resource managers revealed after analysis that there was convergence in the use of HRM for competitive advantage. These included:

- changes in organisational culture to create greater empowerment and equality of employees and greater diversity in their roles;
- organisational restructuring to reduce the number of vertical layers (delayering) and increase employee flexibility;
- an increase in the number and variety of performance management policies;
- improvements in resourcing – acquiring personnel and training and developing them;
- improvements in communication and corporate responsibility.

There were divergences in the way that specific aspects such as culture, work structuring, performance management and resourcing were utilised, but these, they claimed, differed more in degree than in kind (Sparrow *et al.*, 1994: 295).

It would seem that the influence of HRM and management trends is beginning to have a global impact on organisations, and that there is a degree of convergence of practices and approaches.

Easterby-Smith *et al.* (1995), using a case study approach in conducting a comparative piece of research between Chinese and UK companies, also found a convergence of approaches. However, they associated this convergence with 'hard' HRM policies such as manpower planning, and they noted divergence in 'soft', culture-sensitive areas, bound up with motivational issues such as remuneration and reward.

The research findings in the above surveys seem to suggest that the impact of managerial education, through international management programmes such as the MBA, and the increase in the worldwide popularity of management issues with an ever-increasing profile in the media, is influencing a convergence of policy and practice in HRM. Equally, however, we must recognise that these practices are not implemented in the same way in each country and organisational context.

Problems of international research

The astute and experienced observer will note that there are considerable problems confronting the researcher of comparative aspects of HRM. Apart from the expense and communicational problems involved in conducting such undertakings there are considerable methodological mountains to climb. We have alluded to some problems already in examining the Price Waterhouse data. Although research is increasing there is still a considerable lack of reliable information, and that which does exist poses problems of interpretation. These include the following:

- There is a *lack of data*. It is only relatively recently that many countries have begun to keep detailed records of their economic performance, such as GNP, growth rate, unemployment, trade balances, and workforce statistics.
- Even though advanced industrial nations have been keeping such statistics for many years, there is still a *lack of comparative data*: for example, trade union statistics, GNP and unemployment can all be measured quite differently in different countries.
- *Statistics and similar data are highly political and open to manipulation and bias*, both in the way they are collected and in the way they are presented for public consumption.
- Another difficulty is to find a *series of figures that do not have a break in consistency*. For example, is it possible to meaningfully compare unemployment statistics of the 1930s with those of the 1980s?
- International statistics are also noted for having *time lags where one economy is behind in furnishing statistics*. Thus one country may be giving data pertaining to a period as much as one year behind another country's data on the same subject.
- *Language and meaning can be diverse*: even though the same words are often used they can cause confusion. Job titles vary widely from country to country. For example, the equivalent term for 'management' in France is 'cadre', although the meanings are not the same. In consequence the English term 'manager' is increasingly being used in French organisations. Japanese corporations have no concept of management development; they prefer what can only be described as 'capability development', and this includes all employees.
- Some national economies emphasise *some aspects of economic performance* rather than others, because these are the areas in which they are strong – agriculture, new technology or engineering for example – and this can skew comparisons.
- *Cultural differences can give quite differing approaches to the same data*. This can affect interpretation and meaning.
- *Generalisation is necessary but leads to dilution to the point where the interpretation of the data can become meaningless*. For example, regional differences could be ignored because they do not fit the national pattern closely.

Thus the area of comparative study is fraught with many pitfalls and difficulties.

INTERNATIONAL HRM

At the beginning of this chapter we made a distinction between comparative HRM and international HRM in that the latter exists primarily in multinational companies (MNCs) and the former has a wider contextual setting. This section will explore developments in international HRM. There is a considerable overlap between international and comparative HRM in that both examine aspects of HRM policy and practice in a world or regional context. Comparative HRM is concerned more with examining trends in HRM practice and comparing HRM and business systems between nations. International HRM is concerned with how HRM is carried out purely within the international organisational context: for example, how international HRM strategy is conceived and implemented in an MNC, and how the parent company relates to the overseas subsidiaries in terms of the amount of control it exercises over them and the amount of autonomy it gives them. It is concerned with what kind of HR policies should be adopted and how they should be implemented. It is also concerned with the strategy makers and the implementers themselves – that is, the attitudes and approaches of the parent company's HR managers and overseas subsidiary staff, including expatriate managers and host country staff. It is also concerned with how HR policy and practice will vary within different organisational parameters such as size, sector and ownership (public, private and non-governmental organisations).

Despite the burgeoning literature concerning international HRM, comparatively little is known about how such firms manage their human resources, particularly across national borders. The literature to date has concentrated largely on MNCs and mainly on issues of expatriation (Scullion, 1995), though the subject is now receiving increasing attention from researchers. However, MNCs have been increasingly aware of the growing need to have not only international business strategies but also international human resource strategies (Pucik, 1984). Attention has been focused on HRM by such issues as global management succession planning, recruitment, selection and training for the expatriation process, recruitment from the indigenous population, and awareness of labour and human resource practices in different countries and regions.

Expatriation

Expatriation has been a dominant theme in the literature of IHRM, and an understanding of the reasons for this is an appropriate point to start an examination of IHRM. MNCs are now recognising that internationally minded management teams of expatriate managers with international skills and experience are becoming a major competitive advantage. Increasingly, multinational corporations are expecting their senior executives to have had international experience. The implications for management training and development are enormous (see Chapter 9), a fact that nations and companies ignore at their peril (Pucik, 1984: 404).

Brewster and Scullion (1997) have identified a number of key reasons why expatriates are used extensively by MNCs. The first is the transmission of technical and management skills from the parent to the subsidiary. Often this takes place in the early stages of international development particularly in countries that lack these skills. Expatriates thus perform not only a management and technical operational role but often also a training and development role in which they pass on these skills to the indigenous workforce. Second, expatriates are used as a control mechanism to ensure that the company strategy, policies and procedures are being correctly followed by the subsidiary. Edström and Galbraith (1977) identified three types of control mechanism, two of which have expatriate managers in a pivotal role.

- *Bureaucratic.* Bureaucratic control is indirect and impersonal. This allows some discretion at the local level, where procedures and processes (such as financial) are put in place to monitor activities, and therefore decisions can be delegated to lower levels locally.
- *Geocentric.* Control is through expatriate managers. The advantage is increased communication between HQ and the subsidiary. The approach is personal, allowing face-to-face communication. It can make company policy more acceptable at local levels, and it allows local discretion and responsiveness while maintaining a level of control from the centre.
- *Socialisation.* This is achieved through expatriate managers building social networks for informational and communicational interaction between HQ and subsidiaries

and between subsidiaries. Functional behaviours and rules determining them are learned by individuals. This obviates the need for procedures, hierarchical communication and surveillance. This approach emphasises loyalty to a person as well as to the organisation (Edström and Galbraith, 1977).

Organisations will not necessarily use only one of these control mechanisms, but are more likely to use a combination of some or all of them. Ethnocentric organisations (high parent company control – see below for a fuller explanation) seeking greater degrees of control may well use combinations of all. Polycentric organisations (high subsidiary company control – see below for fuller explanation) may be seeking to keep a lower ownership profile for political reasons, and may be more inclined therefore to use bureaucratic control mechanisms perhaps setting financial or production targets. If the subsidiary meets them then it is allowed to sustain a large degree of autonomy. But as Adler and Ghadar (1990) suggest, organisational HQs are more than likely to emphasise different aspects of control at different periods in the organisation's development.

Expatriation failure and its prevention

Considerable attention in the literature on expatriation has been concerned with the failure of expatriate assignments and with methods to prevent this (Brewster, 1991). Support for expatriate managers is expensive for companies. They are often required to pay high salaries, and additional costs are incurred such as relocation costs for the expatriates and their families involving travelling expenses, accommodation, schooling and other factors not directly paid for in the parent company environment. If an assignment fails then the company stands to lose considerable money and has to replace the repatriated manager. There has recently been a debate as to the extent of failure rates, and Harzing (1995) has claimed that the figures have been considerably inflated and based on dated and limited research that has been repeated in the literature without being examined or questioned. While Forster (1997) agrees with Harzing's critique he nevertheless believes that the definition of failure has been too narrow, and must include 'the stresses and strains experienced by a minority of staff who are under performing; the poaching of successful managers by other companies while they are abroad . . . ; the often negative outcomes of the repatriation experience . . . ; the negative (and largely unreported) effects on some families and their career prospects of partners and negative views about the prospect of overseas postings in the future' (p. 414). Indeed, a growing subsidiary but, nevertheless, equally important concern is the high failure rate of assignments associated with the unhappiness of the spouse and the family (Black and Stephens, 1989).

Failure of assignments has also focused significantly on the difficulties of acculturation in terms of a 'culture clash' between expatriate managers and the host country environment and employees (Torbiörn, 1982). Failure to understand a foreign culture can lead to feelings of alienation and depression in the expatriate manager and his or her family.

As a result of these concerns there is a considerable literature concerned with expatriate selection, training, development and career succession (Brewster, 1991). Torbiörn (1982) has made a close examination of the adjustment process that expatriate managers experience in postings abroad, and as we have already noted, Hofstede (1980) and Laurent (1983) have examined cultural differences of managers.

Considerable attention has therefore been given to recruitment, selection and training of potential expatriate managers and acculturation and acclimatisation issues (Dowling et al., 1994, 1999). There is also a growing body of research on repatriation issues, particularly the re-acculturation of expatriates who have spent considerable time abroad (as many as 10 or 20 years) and the problems of 're-entry' into not only their home country culture, but also their HQ organisational culture (Black and Gregersen, 1991; Forster, 1994). Another area of growing interest is the experience of the international woman manager (Adler and Izraeli, 1994).

In recent years there has been speculation that expatriate managers are being used less in MNCs because of their high cost, the increasing levels of education and technical expertise in foreign countries, and the increase in communications making contact between parent and subsidiaries much easier. However, research by Scullion (1992) shows that the majority of the British and Irish MNCs in his study used expatriate managers, and the shortage of such managers was of considerable concern to them. These findings are similar to research into American MNCs (Dowling *et al.*, 1994, 1999).

Kobrin's (1994) research also emphasises the importance of expatriates and claims that their training, development and experience are essential for creating a geocentric mindset (a global perspective of the organisation and its goals). Kobrin proposes a tentative hypothesis that the need to transmit knowledge and information through the global network may lead, through increased interpersonal interaction, to organisational geocentrism in terms of attitudes and IHRM policies. The latter point is interesting in that his research reveals a growing interest in IHRM among major MNCs as it is perceived to have a crucial link to effective policy implementation.

Globalisation and the effects of country of origin and host country on HRM

As globalisation proceeds apace, MNCs and other cross-national organisations are becoming increasingly important, and one of the chief concerns of observers of the globalisation phenomenon is the key role played by MNCs in influencing change. Where MNCs locate production plants can have considerable impact on employment at home and abroad. Critics have pointed to the power that MNCs have in persuading national governments to be amenable in their labour practices in return for large investments in their economies (Hirst and Thompson, 1996). With the increase of globalisation there has been a growth in the number of transnational companies. These are companies that have no national adherence that are globally free floating, with the ability to switch resources to different global arenas to gain competitive advantage. A number of observers have noted that this argument has been considerably exaggerated, and that the transnational is still a rare phenomenon. Having examined the evidence, some writers believe that national economies are still important in shaping MNCs' strategies (Porter, 1990; Ruigrok and Van Tulder, 1995; Hirst and Thompson, 1996) and most MNCs are strongly rooted in their country of national origin, but nevertheless pay particular attention to host country influences such as laws, customs and practices (Whitley, 1992).

The country of origin of most MNCs is still a powerful influence on the strategy, structure and managerial and HRM policy implementation worldwide. The major assets as well as the key strategic decision-making groups reside, in the overwhelming majority of cases, with the parent company. While there has been some interest in the way in which companies control and manage their subsidiaries from headquarters there has been little in the way of research conducted into the effects of country of origin on organisational and HRM issues (Ferner, 1997). This perspective emphasises the way in which developments in HRM are informed by trends within the parent company and its national context. The United States has had the most significant impact in promoting innovative HRM, but this raises questions as to the exportability of HRM policy and practice from one national socio-economic context to another – a theme touched on in the section on comparative HRM above. Early literature tended to ignore these questions, and there was an assumption that convergence would readily take place between the parent company policy and practice and that of the subsidiary – the view that international HRM was HRM 'writ large.' Researchers working from cultural and institutional perspectives have clearly indicated the complexity of transposing HRM policy and practices from one national context to another, even within the same organisational culture. The variety of influences on the creation and implementation of strategic IHRM is thus one of the major themes demanding the attention of researchers in the field.

There has also been recognition that subsidiaries can play important and varied roles in HRM strategy formulation and implementation. Strategic HRM becomes increasingly complex as companies expand overseas, and it would be naive to assume that once HQ decisions are made they are automatically implemented as intended. Thus the influence of subsidiaries in interpreting and implementing becomes an important element in the internationalisation of the HR process; and the way subsidiaries execute HR policy is also conditioned by host country environmental factors. Seminal writers in the field of international management have recognised that the pressures for global integration and the forces for national differentiation are the two major environmental factors in the practice of international management and HRM processes (Bartlett, 1986; Hedlund, 1986; Bartlett and Ghoshal, 1989; Doz and Prahalad, 1991). The balancing of these forces is thus a pivotal element in the management of international HRM. An understanding of the headquarters–subsidiary relationship has therefore become the focus of considerable research (Hedlund, 1980; Ghoshal and Nohria, 1989; Forsgren 1990; Nohria and Ghoshal, 1997).

This raises questions of power and control in the implementation of strategy – how much power and control reside in different parts of the organisation. Simplistic conceptualisations assume that control is automatically imposed by HQ on the subsidiary, but Perlmutter (1969) has created a typology that proposes that the subsidiary role can vary widely in organisations.

Perlmutter's headquarters–subsidiary orientations in MNCs

Four approaches have been identified to describe the way MNCs conduct their international HRM policies: ethnocentricism, polycentricism, geocentricism and regiocentrism.

The ethnocentric approach

This approach has all key positions in the host country subsidiary filled by parent company nationals. It therefore offers the most direct control by the parent company over the host country subsidiary, when there is a felt need to maintain good communication between the subsidiary and the MNC HQ. This is common in the early stages of internationalisation, when the MNC is establishing a new business process or product in another country. It may also be used because there is a lack of qualified host country nationals.

The polycentric approach

This is directly opposite in approach to ethnocentricity: host country nationals are recruited to manage the subsidiary in their own country. This allows the MNC to take a lower profile in sensitive economic and political situations, and to avoid intercultural management difficulties.

The geocentric approach

This approach utilises the best people for the key jobs throughout the organisation, drawing on all parts of the world MNC operation. This makes it possible to develop an international executive team.

The regiocentric approach

In this approach an MNC divides its operations into geographic regions and moves staff within these regions, such as Europe, America, or the Asia Pacific rim. Some see such regionalisation as an effective way of developing management succession programmes.

An MNC may pass through several of these stages depending on its familiarity with the host country setting, the calibre and quality of its host country national staff, and the degree of direct control that is felt necessary to impose on the subsidiary. These decisions are all bound up with wider economic, political and social concerns.

While this approach provides a useful framework for conceptualising managerial approaches in MNCs, it lacks explanations of change and fails to take into account the dynamics of turbulent changes in the global environment. Perlmutter acknowledges that companies could change from an ethnocentric to a polycentric orientation (and vice versa) but he offers no explanation as to why or how this is accomplished.

Adler and Ghadar's phases of internationalisation

Adler and Ghadar (1990) have attempted to develop a framework to explain the changing nature of international HRM by relating HRM strategy and policy changes to product life cycles. As companies expand their activities from domestic to overseas markets and operations they concentrate on different aspects of organisational development. They perceive this organisational development moving through four phases (summarised in Table 15.4).

Phase I: Domestic

Phase I concentrates mainly on the home market, with some overseas sales through agents, and as a result international HRM is non-existent.

Phase II: International

The international phase witnesses a definite commitment to overseas markets, marked by the creation of subsidiaries or joint ventures. Expatriate managers are assigned positions overseas, and bring with them managerial and technical expertise and financial control. This phase is characterised by the passing on of skills and knowledge to locally recruited employees, some of whom may assume managerial positions in running the operation at a later time. Human resource issues become important in terms of recruiting, selecting, training, developing and rewarding expatriate and host country staff. The expatriate managers will need language and cultural awareness training, among other things, and the host country staff will need to learn the skills and knowledge of the business.

Phase III: Multinational

In the multinational phase the organisation seeks to gain competitive advantage by high sales and low cost. The emphasis in this phase is on creating cohesion through the spread of the organisation's aims and values and inculcating them into a developing

Table 15.4 Globalisation and human resource management

	Phase I Domestic	Phase II International	Phase III Multinational	Phase IV Global
Primary orientation	Product or service	Market	Price	Strategy
Strategy	Domestic	Multidomestic	Multinational	Global
Worldwide strategy	Allow foreign clients to buy product/service	Increase market internationally, transfer technology abroad	Source, produce and market internationally	Gain global strategic competitive advantage
Staffing expatriates	None (few)	Many	Some	Many
Why sent	Junket	To sell control or transfer technology	Control	Coordination and integration
Whom sent		'OK' performers, salespeople	Very good performers	High-potential managers and top executives
Purpose	Reward	Project 'To get job done'	Project and career development	Career and organisational development
Career impact	Negative	Bad for domestic career	Important for global career	Essential for executive suite
Professional re-entry	Somewhat difficult	Extremely difficult	Less difficult	Professionally easy
Training and development	None	Limited	Longer	Continuous throughout career
For whom	No one	Expatriates	Expatriates	Managers
Performance appraisal	Corporate bottom line	Subsidiary bottom line	Corporate bottom line	Strategic positioning
Motivation assumption	Money motivates	Money and adventure	Challenge and opportunity	Challenge, opportunity, advancement
Rewarding	Extra money to compensate for foreign hardship		Less generous, global packages	
Career 'fast track'	Domestic	Domestic	Token international	Global
Executive passport	Home country	Home country	Home country, token foreigners	Multinational
Necessary skills	Technical and managerial	Plus cultural adaption	Plus recognising cultural differences	Plus cross-cultural interaction, influence and synergy

Source: Alder and Ghadar (1990).

management cadre. Managers may be drawn not only from the country of origin and from host country staff, but also from third country staff (staff from neither the home or host country moved from one subsidiary to another in a different country). In HRM terms emphasis will be placed on career development, management development and management succession.

Phase IV: Global

In the global phase the company will become a truly international player, operating worldwide in a wide variety of countries and regions. Management cadres will reflect this approach by creating strategies to gain advantage from global integration with local responsiveness. Differentiation will be welcomed as staff become increasingly skilled and knowledgeable. They will be able to utilise their local knowledge in coordination with their company skills to create competitive advantage. Human resource management issues will be continued from phases II and III, and ideally forums will be created to facilitate the exchange and development of knowledge, transforming the company into a learning and knowledge organisation on a global scale.

One of the problems with this conceptualisation is that it makes huge assumptions about what constitutes an MNC or an international organisation in general. Such organisations could take many forms in terms of size, ownership, distribution or sectoral characteristics, all of which could defy the developments predicted in the framework outlined.

Adler and Ghadar's phases of internationalisation also do not address issues of HRM beyond expatriation, and there is no attempt to explain the linkages between parent and subsidiaries in terms of HRM strategy and its implementation. Some observers have attempted to do this by building models, and the next section explores this.

Models of strategic international human resource management

The difficulties of attempting to create a model of HRM have already been noted even within the cultural context of one country, the United States, and the further complexities of attempting to apply such models to other national settings. This is also compounded by the variety of organisational and managerial styles that abound within different organisations in different sectors depending on the products they make and the services they perform within the diversity of national and regional cultures. A further drawback is the relative lack of research that has taken place in the field of IHRM. Research emphasis has been very much in the realm of expatriation, while questions of IHRM strategy and its operationalisation have been relatively neglected. Thus model building has tended to lean towards theoretical considerations, resting on prescriptions rather than rooted in research. Other writers, most notably Pieper (1990), hold the view that no universal model of HRM is possible. Pieper bases this argument on the fact that the variations are too wide in terms of institutions and working practices between nations.

Since Pieper wrote this a decade ago there have been some significant developments in international HRM. It has also become clear from comparative surveys available that there have been, if not degrees of convergence in HRM practice, at least trends that indicate the adoption on a worldwide basis of many managerial initiatives associated with HRM.

Schuler *et al.*'s integrative framework of international HRM

The most comprehensive model in the field to date is that proposed by Schuler *et al.* (1993) (Figure 15.3). They have linked human resource management with organisational strategy into a framework of strategic international human resource management (SIHRM), that they hope will be useful to both academics and practitioners alike. They claim that a considerable amount of the research literature has concentrated on the problems of expatriation, and that the 'next task for researchers is to examine the influence of exogenous and endogenous factors on strategic international HRM and to consider the consequences of these influences and interrelationships' (p. 753). By exogenous factors they mean those external to the MNE, such as industry characteristics and country/regional characteristics. By endogenous factors they mean those internal to the MNE, such as the structure of international operations, headquarters international orientation, competitive strategy and the experience in managing international operations.

These endogenous and exogenous factors influence the organisation's strategic IHRM, which in turn affects the MNE's competitiveness, efficiency, local responsiveness, flexibility and transfer of learning. Of vital importance in the creation and enactment of strategic IHRM is the way units within MNEs link and how they can be integrated, controlled and coordinated. This concerns how much autonomy can be granted to

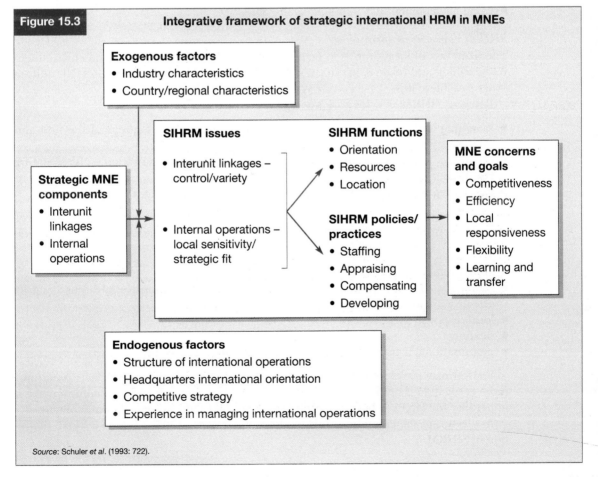

Figure 15.3 — Integrative framework of strategic international HRM in MNEs

Exogenous factors
- Industry characteristics
- Country/regional characteristics

Strategic MNE components
- Interunit linkages
- Internal operations

SIHRM issues
- Interunit linkages – control/variety
- Internal operations – local sensitivity/ strategic fit

SIHRM functions
- Orientation
- Resources
- Location

SIHRM policies/ practices
- Staffing
- Appraising
- Compensating
- Developing

MNE concerns and goals
- Competitiveness
- Efficiency
- Local responsiveness
- Flexibility
- Learning and transfer

Endogenous factors
- Structure of international operations
- Headquarters international orientation
- Competitive strategy
- Experience in managing international operations

Source: Schuler *et al.* (1993: 722).

local units, how they are coordinated and controlled, and how much control the MNE will exercise over internal operations. It also involves decisions on whether to export people or the HR function.

SIHRM concerns at headquarters

Schuler *et al.* state that SIHRM functions at HQ level will have three areas of concern:

- the MNE's HR orientation;
- the time, energy and financial resources devoted to operating the human resource organisation in the MNC;
- the location of those resources and the human resource organisation – centralised or localised, or a combination of both.

Policies and practices will be designed in accordance with the way individuals will be managed and the way specific practices are developed – for example, how performance is rewarded, and how staffing, appraising and developing are carried out. This will also mean that the HQ will be concerned with three issues:

- maintaining a mix and flow of parent country nationals (PCNs or expatriates), host country nationals (HCNs) and third country nationals (TCNs – managers and employees from neither host or parent country);
- systematically developing HR policies and practices;
- using management development as the glue.

SIHRM concerns at local level

The main task of local units is to be responsive to and effective in the local environment yet be willing and ready to act in a coordinated fashion with the rest of the MNE units in order to achieve this.

Relevant SIHRM policies and practices are:

- matching and adopting HR practices with the competitive strategy of the unit and the local culture and legal system;
- creating a modus operandi whereby HR practices can be modified to fit changing conditions;
- developing global HR policies flexible enough to be adapted for local HR practice.

Throughout the balancing and coordination of these processes a number of concerns must be kept in mind in the practice of HRM within the organisation's worldwide context:

- global competitiveness – a main concern;
- efficiency – HRM is increasingly seen as a source of competitive advantage and its effective use as crucial;
- local responsiveness (sensitivity);
- flexibility;
- organisational learning (the transfer of information across units).

SIHRM may travel well, and policy and practice may actually transfer across cultures more easily than is often assumed, but local conditions such as laws and culture make it imperative for MNEs to be aware of the need to adapt their human resource practices.

As a result of the creation of this model Schuler *et al.* (1993) came to a 'final' definition of SIHRM:

developing a fit between exogenous and endogenous factors and balancing the competing demands of global versus local requirements as well as the needs of coordination, control and autonomy. (p. 753)

The model is highly complex, and space dictates that we cannot do justice to it here, but it points a way forward to further refinements to future models and theorisation. However, critics have pointed to its still highly prescriptive nature, and the fact that it does not explain the political micro processes that take place between HQ and the subsidiaries (Quintanilla, 1998). Ferner (1994) has also pointed out that that it is primarily concerned with senior management, and not the workforce as a whole.

Taylor *et al.*'s integrative model of strategic IHRM

Taylor *et al.*(1996) build on previous work on IHRM by drawing on concepts from the resource-based view of the firm to develop a theoretical model of the determinants of SIHRM systems in MNCs (Figure 15.4). Resource-based theory adds to prior models of SIHRM the fundamental notion that, in order to provide value to the business, the SIHRM system of global firms should be constructed around specific organisational competences that are critical for securing competitive advantage in a global environment (Pucik, 1992). The resource-based framework helps to identify those situations in which MNCs will exercise control over the SIHRM system of their affiliates. The authors define SIHRM as

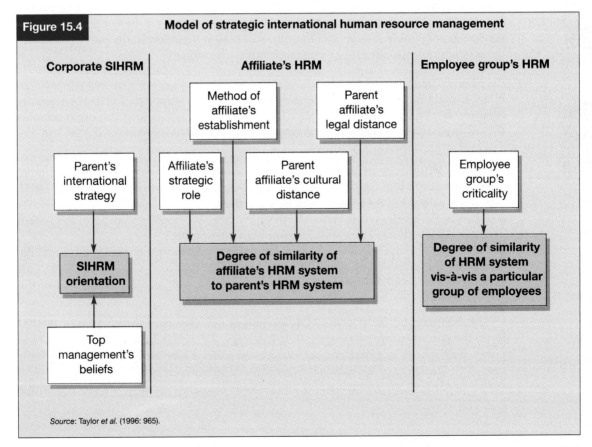

| Figure 15.4 | Model of strategic international human resource management |

Corporate SIHRM

Affiliate's HRM

Employee group's HRM

Method of affiliate's establishment

Parent affiliate's legal distance

Parent's international strategy

Affiliate's strategic role

Parent affiliate's cultural distance

Employee group's criticality

SIHRM orientation

Degree of similarity of affiliate's HRM system to parent's HRM system

Degree of similarity of HRM system vis-à-vis a particular group of employees

Top management's beliefs

Source: Taylor et al. (1996: 965).

human resource management issues, functions and policies and practices that result from the strategic activities of multinational enterprises and that impact the international concerns and goals of those enterprises.

(Taylor *et al*,. 1996: 961)

They quote Lado and Wilson's (1994) definition of the resource-based view of HRM:

The resource-based view suggests that human resource systems can contribute to sustained competitive advantage through facilitating the development of competencies that are firm specific, produce complex social relationships, are embedded in a firm's history and culture, and generate tacit organisational knowledge.

(p. 699)

HRM competence is viewed as both the *tangible* resources (e.g. HR planning systems, selection tests) and *intangible* resources (e.g. shared mindset, ability to attract qualified employees) that allow a firm to outperform its competitors. Using the resource-based theory approach, they distinguish between resources at three levels in the MNC:

- parent company *resources* developed from a particular configuration of economic, cultural, human and other resources in a country – not differentiated domestically, but can give an MNC an advantage when competing outside its home country (e.g. German apprenticeship system);
- parent company *unique bundle of assets and capabilities* developed over its lifetime;
- affiliate *resources,* which may provide a competitive advantage at the local, regional or global levels (e.g. developing HRM selection policies to deal with high labour market mobility).

The origin of the resource (national, firm or affiliate) is likely to affect its usefulness in other locations. Resources, including HRM competence, can be context specific or context generalisable. The model examines SIHRM at three levels: the parent company, the affiliate, and specific employee groups within the affiliate.

Corporate SIHRM

SIHRM orientation is defined as the general philosophy or approach taken by top management in the design of its overall IHRM system. This will reflect the organisation's overall approach to managing the *differentiation vs integration dilemma.*

Three orientations are identified:

- *Adaptive.* HRM systems are designed for affiliates that reflect the local environment. Differentiation is emphasised. Reflects a polycentric approach in all aspects of HRM, with virtually no transfer of policies and practices.
- *Exportive.* An ethnocentric approach in which there is complete transfer of the parent firm's HRM systems. The emphasis is on high integration.
- *Integrative.* Attempt to take the 'best' approaches and use them across the organisation in the creation of a worldwide system (Bartlett and Ghoshal, 1989). This approach incorporates substantial global integration, with an allowance for some differentiation.

The orientation will be decided as a result of two factors at the corporate SIHRM level: the parent company's international strategy, defined here after Porter (1986) as either *multidomestic* or *global;* and *top management beliefs.* These attitudes can change over time. The influence of the *national origin of the MNC* is also seen to affect choices, especially where there are strong institutional pressures.

Affiliate's HRM system

The degree of similarity of an affiliate's HRM system is assessed via its strategic role using the resource-based approach – that is, how reliant the subsidiary units are on the parent company's unique resources. Under this approach, the strategic role of an affiliate can be defined by the amount and direction of the resource flows between the parent company and the overseas affiliate. Four types of role are distinguished:

- *global innovator*, with high outflow of resources to the parent company and low inflow of resources to the affiliate;
- *integrated player*, with a high outflow and high inflow;
- *implementer*, with low outflow and high inflow;
- *local innovator*, with low outflow and low inflow.

As the resource flows between the affiliate and the parent company increase, the resource dependence and hence the need for control will also increase. The resource dependence of the parent company on its affiliates is greatest for global innovators and integrated players.

Three other factors constrain the exercise of control of the parent company over the affiliate. The first is the method of affiliate establishment, with affiliates established as greenfield operations being seen to have a greater degree of similarity in their HRM patterns than those that were acquired or established as shared partnerships. The second and third constitute the cultural and legal distances of the affiliate from the parent company. The authors propose that the greater the cultural distance between the host country of the affiliate and the home country of the MNC, the less similarity between the parent and affiliate's HRM system. Likewise the greater the legal distance between the host country of the affiliate and the home country of the MNC, the lower the degree of similarity between the parent and affiliate's HRM systems. Once again, it is acknowledged that such relationships evolve over time.

The final part of the model, focusing on *employee group's criticality*, again adopts the resource dependence perspective, and argues that the HRM system will be different depending on the nature of the employee groups within the affiliates. It is proposed that the highest degree of similarity between a parent company's HRM system and an affiliate's HRM system will be in relation to the groups of employees who are most critical to the MNC's performance.

Implications of the model

The authors see the following main implications from their model. First, it acknowledges the critical role that the HRM competence of the parent firm plays in the transfer of HRM policies to affiliates and how this can contribute to competitive advantage. Second, it recognises the pivotal role of top management in SIHRM. The authors see a key research area in an analysis of the factors that influence top management's ability to perceive an MNC's HRM competence and those factors that lead management to decide whether the firm's HRM competence is context specific (that is, cannot be transferred) or context generalisable and hence, transferable. Third, there is a need to reconsider the assumption that the critical groups of employees at affiliate level are either expatriates or white-collar workers. On a more general level, Taylor *et al.* argue that further research is needed into the determinants of the context generalisability of a resource and the ways in which managers can judge whether a particular resource is useful beyond the context in which it was created. However, the authors dismiss country of origin as a determinant without saying why, and omit to state what is actually transferred in strategic international HRM.

While these frameworks and models are ways forward in helping us towards an understanding of the complexities of IHRM, there is also a need for research on operational issues.

Issues in international HRM

As we have already noted, an increasingly important concern in the IHRM literature is how it is operationalised. Much of this research has centred on which aspects of HRM are exportable from the parent country and which are not exportable, a question tentatively explored in examining the host country influence on IHRM, and examined more fully in the work of Rosenzweig and Nohria.

Rosenzweig and Nohria and the influence of local isomorphism

Rosenzweig and Nohria (1994) explore a key concern in IHRM – the tension between the pressures for internal consistency and local isomorphism (the influence of local culture, institutions and working practices on MNCs' HRM policies). From a research base of 249 US affiliates of foreign-based MNCs they argue that, of all organisational functions, HRM tends to most closely adhere to local practices as they are often mandated by local regulation and shaped by strong local conventions. Within HRM, they see the order in which six key practices will most closely resemble local practices as:

- time off;
- benefits;
- gender composition;
- training;
- executive bonus;
- participation.

This order is predicated on the assumption that HRM practices for which there are well-defined local norms and which affect the rank and file of the affiliate organisation are likely to conform most to practices of local competitors.

Three other factors are identified as being important in determining the extent of internal consistency or local isomorphism. The first is the degree to which an affiliate is *embedded* in the local environment. This refers to its method of founding and its age, as well as its size, its dependence on local inputs, and the degree of influence exerted on it from local institutions. The second is the strength of the flow of resources, such as capital, information and people, between the parent and the affiliate. The third relates to characteristics of the parent, such as the culture of the home country, with a high degree of distance between cultures being predicted to lead to more internal consistency (that is, an ethnocentric approach). Two final characteristics relate to the parent organisation's orientation to control and the nature of the industry, with greater local isomorphism in a multi-domestic industry as opposed to a global industry (Porter, 1986; Prahalad and Doz, 1987).

Other areas of international HRM are related to issues concerning the management and motivation of host country staff by expatriate managers, and issues of compensation and staff promotion. For example, a performance-related pay scheme that works in the USA (a highly indivdualistic culture) may well prove disastrous in Indonesia (a highly collectivist culture). Thus the way in which HRM policies are transferred and translated into subsidiary host country contexts can prove crucial to their success.

Training and development has been emphasised by many writers as an important aspect in the implementation of HRM strategy and as helping to create an 'organisational glue' in terms of binding subsidiary units into the aims, objectives and values of the company as a whole. Training is not only essential in imparting technical know-how, it is also crucial in enabling employees to imbibe the organisational culture as well as providing forums for the imparting and exchange of information. Some writers conceptualise forms of an international learning organisation or a knowledge-based organisation (Kamoche, 1997; Bonache and Fernández, 1999) in which the creation of a learning climate for the sharing and transfer of knowledge is crucial in the international context. This is a move away from the goal-measuring orientations that have become popular in recent years under the guise of performance management, but which have encountered considerable problems in the domestic context let alone within the complexities of the international context.

In addition HRM impacts more widely on the international organisation than the individually prescribed subjects of recruitment, selection, training and development, management development, reward, outplacement, employee involvement might suggest. As we have seen in other chapters in this book HRM is also concerned with organisational change and the implementation of new work practices that have important strategic implications. The work of Broad (1994), Tayeb (1998), Muller (1998), Martin and Beaumont (1998, 1999) and others has illustrated how difficult this process can be. Their work also reveals how simplistic, and even primitive, the models and frameworks that have emerged so far are as a tool in aiding analysis of the transference of HRM from one national context to another.

CONCLUSION

The forces of globalisation have clearly created convergences of more flexibilised systems of work and employment, although these will be operationalised in differing ways in different institutional and cultural settings. Research and theory building still have some way to go, but developments of the global economy in the 1990s saw much more attention from researchers to the importance of international and comparative HRM as part of the equation that gives companies and economies their competitive edge.

Limited space forbids an in-depth examination of individual aspects of HRM such as recruitment, selection, reward, training and development, employee involvement and industrial relations. For more detailed aspects of international and comparative HRM the following chapters will be of value:

- human resource planning: developments in the UK and Europe: Chapter 4;
- multi-skilling and European developments: Chapter 5;
- international perspectives on recruitment and selection: Chapter 6;
- vocational education and training in the leading industrial nations: Chapter 8;
- international management development: Chapter 9;
- variable pay – results from across nations and international remuneration policies – remuneration and reward: Chapter 12;
- international aspects of employee involvement: Chapter 13;
- HRM and Europe: Chapter 16;
- HRM and the Asia Pacific Rim: Chapter 17.

SUMMARY

- This chapter examined the increasing importance of human resource management in an ever-changing competitive international environment and the growth of multinational corporations. The distinctions between comparative HRM and international HRM were examined: this saw international HRM located in multinational organisations, and comparative HRM being concerned with the comparison of HRM systems within the context of countries and regions.

- Various major theories relating to comparative HRM were explained: convergence theory, which poses the view that technological developments create homogeneous global work practices; Marxist theory, with its class-based view of the processes of work in capitalist organisations; cultural theory, which emphasises the differences in work practices influenced by cultural values; and the view of how work practices in different national settings are influenced by institutional aspects such as legal and political structures, which are in turn affected by social factors. An attempt was made to synthesise these convergent and divergent approaches to comparative HRM.

- Comparative HRM models by Poole, Brewster and Larsen, and Sparrow and Hiltrop were outlined and critiqued. A review of the quantitative survey conducted under the banner of the Price Waterhouse Cranfield Project revealed the similarity of a number of trends across Europe, such as moves towards atypical working, decentralisation and devolvement of HRM practices, particularly to line managers, increases in direct communication channels to the workforce, the decline in influence of trade unions, and the increasing decentralisation of pay bargaining. The survey researchers warn, however, that practices still vary widely and are still heavily influenced by national employee relations laws and practices. The Towers Perrin survey analysed by Sparrow *et al.* concluded that there was a convergence in the use of HRM for competitive advantage.

- Problems of international research were outlined that often hinge on differing practices in collecting data and varying interpretations based on cultural and linguistic influences.

- Within the international HRM part of the chapter the effects of globalisation on MNCs were examined, as were the effects of country of origin and host country on HRM strategy and policy formulation. Perlmutter's typology of headquarters–subsidiary orientations was also outlined, with comment on its shortcomings. Adler and Ghadar's phases of internationalisation were explained in the context of HRM. The use of a variety of mechanisms to control subsidiaries within MNCs was then discussed.

- Expatriation issues such as assignment failure were also examined, and suggestions made as to how organisations could make provisions to prevent this happening.

- Two international HRM models were explored in detail: Schuler *et al.*'s integrative framework of SIHRM, and Taylor *et al.*'s integrative model of SIHRM. Each was critiqued from both theoretical and practical positions.

- The last section dealt briefly with the difficulties of the practical applications of IHRM policy. Rosenzweig and Nohria's local isomorphism model was taken as a starting point in considering which HRM practices were exportable and which were not.

- Given the relative infancy of IHRM the chapter indicates the need for more research and theorising if our knowledge of this increasingly important subject is to be extended.

QUESTIONS

1 In what ways does international HRM differ from HRM?

2 What problems are expatriate managers liable to find in a foreign assignment, and how could these problems be prevented in future?

3 Is there increasing convergence in human resource management practices worldwide?

4 How much do parent company culture and strategy influence the practice of HRM in overseas subsidiaries?

5 What control mechanisms can MNCs use to ensure that their aims and objectives are being fulfilled across the organisation?

6 Of the models of international HRM examined in this chapter which seem the most feasible as a guide to the formulation and implementation of IHRM?

EXERCISES

1 A British expatriate manager undertakes an assignment at a UK-owned subsidiary in Malaysia. Given the following Hofstede cultural indices, with what problems is he likely to be confronted and why? In the light of this information what management approaches would you advise him to adopt in the subsidiary?

	UK	Malaysia	Difference
Power distance	35	104	69
Uncertainty avoidance	35	36	1
Individualism	89	26	63
Masculinity	66	50	16

2 Devise a training and development programme for expatriate managers and their families for pre-departure, overseas assignment experience and re-entry. How could the experience of expatriate managers be utilised by the company for future training and development?

CASE STUDY

Pharmco International

Hugo Bradshaw is a senior executive of Pharmco International, a large multinational pharmaceutical company. He has just returned from a fact-finding tour of its operations in the Asia Pacific Rim (Hong Kong, Taiwan, Japan and Malaysia). He presents his report to the board, and it makes sobering reading. Sales are down in some areas and not progressing in others. Hugo believes that the company is not using its local personnel effectively.

The products have proved to be of a high standard but have failed to penetrate the market deeply. Hugo believes there is too much control from HQ and not

enough initiative allowed to the local workforce.

The Head of HRM, Carol Johnson, has proposed areas that would help the company to fulfil its new strategy: a new HRM strategy including recruitment initiatives, training and development, reward, management development policies and team building and communicational and networking structures.

How would you suggest Carol Johnson implements these policies? Could you make any other suggestions that might help Pharmco International to create an effective HRM strategy to help solve their problems?

REFERENCES AND FURTHER READING

Those texts marked with an asterisk are particularly recommended for further reading.

*Adler, N. (1997) *International Dimensions of Organizational Behavior* 3rd edn. Cincinnati, Ohio: South Western College Publishing.

Adler, N. J. and Ghadar, F. (1989) 'International business research for the twenty first century: Canada's new research agenda', in Rugman, A. (ed.) *Research in Global Stratgic Management: A Canadian Perspective*, Vol. 1. Greenwich, Conn.: JAI Press.

Adler, N.J. and Ghadar, F. (1990) 'Strategic human resource management: a global perspective', in Pieper, R. (ed.) *Human Resource Management: An International Comparison.* Berlin: De Gruyter, pp. 235–260.

Adler, N. and Izraeli, D. (1994) *Competitive Frontiers: Women Managers in a Global Economy.* Cambridge, Mass.: Blackwell.

Altman, Y. (1992) 'Towards a cultural typology of European work values and work organisation', *Innovation in Social Science Research*, Vol. 5, No. 1. pp. 35–44.

Baglioni, G. and Crouch, C. (1990) *European Industrial Relations.* London: Sage.

Bamber, G. and Lansbury, R. (eds) (1987) *International and Comparative Industrial Relations: A Study of Developed Markets.* Sydney: Allen & Unwin.

Bamber, G. and Lansbury, R. (eds) (1998) *International and Comparative Industrial Relations: A Study of Industrialised Market Economies.* London: Sage.

Bartlett, C. (1986) 'Building and managing the transnational: the organisational challenge', in M. Porter (ed.) *Competition in Global Industries.* Boston Mass.: Harvard Business School Press, pp. 367–404.

Bartlett, C. and Ghoshal, S. (1989) *Managing Across Borders: The Transnational Solution.* London, Hutchinson.

Bean, R. (1985) *Comparative Industrial Relations.* London: Croom Helm (reprinted by Routledge, 1994).

Beer, M., Spector, B., Lawrence, P.R., Quinn Mills, D. and Walton, R.E. (1984) *Managing Human Assets.* New York: Free Press.

Black J.S. and Gregersen, H. (1991) 'When Yankee goes home: factors related to expatriate and spouse repatriation adjustment', *Journal of International Business Studies*, Vol. 22, No. 4, pp. 671–694.

Black, J.S. and Stephens, G. (1989) 'The influence of the spouse on American expatriate adjustment and intent to stay in Pacific rim overseas assignments', *Journal of Management*, Vol. 15, No. 4, pp. 529–544.

Blyton, P. and Turnbull, P. (1996) 'Confusing convergence: industrial relations in the European airline industry – a comment on Warhurst', *European Journal of Industrial Relations*, Vol. 2, No. 1, pp. 7–20.

Bonache, J. and Fernández, Z. (1999) 'Strategic staffing in multinational companies: a resource based approach', in Harris, H. and Brewster, C. (eds) *International HRM: Contemporary Issues in Europe.* London: Routledge, pp. 163–182.

Boxall, P. (1995) 'Building the theory of comparative HRM', *Human Resource Management Journal*, Vol. 5, No. 5, pp. 5–17.

Braverman, H. (1974) *Labour and Monopoly Capitalism.* New York: Monthly Review Press.

Brewster, C. (1991) *The Management of Expatriates.* London: Kogan Page.

Brewster, C. (1993) 'Developing a European model of human resource management', *International Journal of Human Resource Management*, Vol. 4, No. 4, pp. 765–784.

Brewster, C. (1994) 'European HRM: reflection of, or challenge to, the American concept?', in Kirkbride, P. (ed) *Human Resource Management in Europe: Perspectives for the 1990s.* London: Routledge, pp. 56–92.

Brewster, C. (1995) 'Towards a "European" model of human resource management', *Journal of International Business Studies*, 1st quarter, pp. 1–21.

Brewster, C. and Bournois, F. (1991) 'Human resource management: a European perspective', *Personnel Review*, Vol. 20, No. 6, pp. 4–13.

Brewster, C. and Hegewisch, A. (eds) (1994) *Policy and Practice in European Human Resource Management: The Price Waterhouse Cranfield Survey*. London: Routledge.

Brewster, C. and Larsen, H. (1992) 'Human resource management in Europe: evidence from ten countries', *International Journal of Human Resource Management*, Vol. 3, No. 3, pp. 409–434.

Brewster, C. and Scullion, H. (1997) 'A review and agenda for expatriate HRM', *Human Resource Management Journal*, Vol. 7, No. 3, pp. 32–41.

Brewster, C. and Tyson, S. (eds) (1991) *International Comparisons in Human Resource Management*. London: Pitman.

Brewster, C., Hegewisch, A. and Lockhart, T. (1991) 'Researching human resource management: methodology of the Price Waterhouse Cranfield Project on European trends', *Personnel Review*, Vol. 20, No. 6. pp. 36–40.

Brewster, C., Lundmark, A. and Holden, L. (1993) *A Different Tack: An Analysis of British and Swedish Management Styles*. Lund: Studentlitteratur.

Briscoe, D. (1995) *International Human Resource Management*. Englewood Cliffs, NJ: Prentice Hall.

Broad, G. (1994) 'The managerial limits to Japanization: a manufacturing case study', *Human Resource Management Journal*, Vol. 4, No. 3, pp. 39–51.

Celestino, M. (1999) 'Graduate education programs with international vision: how graduate business schools are transcending borders', *World Trade*, Vol. 12, No. 7, pp. 86–92.

Child, J. (1981) 'Culture, contingency and capitalism in the cross-national study of organizations', in Staw, B. and Cummings, L. (eds) *Research in Organizational Behaviour*. Vol. 3, London: JAI Press.

Child, J. and Tayeb, M. (1983) 'Theoretical perspectives in cross-national organizational research', *International Studies of Management and Organization*, Vol. 7, Nos. 3–4, pp. 23–70.

Clark, T. and Mallory, G. (1996) 'The cultural relativity of human resource management: is there a universal model?', in Clark, T. (ed.) *European Human Resource Management*. Oxford: Blackwell, pp. 1–33.

Clark, T., Gospel, H. and Montgomery, J. (1999) 'Running on the spot? A review of twenty years of research on the management of human resources in comparative and international perspective', *International Journal of Human Resource Management*, Vol. 10, No. 3, pp. 520–544.

Cook, W. and Noble, D. (1998) 'Industrial relations systems and US foreign direct investment abroad', *British Journal of Industrial Relations*, Vol. 36, No. 4, pp. 581–610.

Crouch, C. (1993) *Industrial Relations and European State Traditions*. Oxford: Clarendon Press.

Dore, R. (1973) *British Factory–Japanese Factory: The Origins of National Diversity in Industrial Relations*. London: Allen & Unwin (quoted in Lane, 1989: 32).

Dowling, P., Schuler, R. and Welch, D. (1994) *International Dimensions of Human Resource Management*. Belmont: Wadsworth.

*Dowling, P., Welch, D. and Schuler, R. (1999) *International Human Resource Management: Managing People in a Multinational Context*. Cincinnati, Oh.: South Western College Publishing.

Doz, Y. and Prahalad, C. (1991) 'Managing DMNCs: a search for a new paradigm', *Strategic Management Journal*, No. 12, pp. 145–164.

Easterby-Smith, M., Malina, D. and Yuan, L. (1995) 'How culture sensitive is HRM? A comparative analysis of practice in Chinese and UK companies', *International Journal of Human Resource Management*, Vol. 6, No. 1, pp. 31–59.

Edström, A. and Galbraith, J.R. (1977) 'Transfer of managers as a coordination and control strategy in multinational organisations', *Administrative Science Quarterly*, Vol. 22, June, pp. 248–263.

Estevill, J. and de la Hoz, J. (1990) 'Transition and crisis: the complexity of Spanish industrial relations', in Baglioni, G. and Crouch, C. (eds) *European Industrial Relations*. London: Sage, pp. 265–299.

Ferner, A. (1994) 'Multinational companies and human resource management: an overview of research issues', *Human Resource Management Journal*, Vol. 4, No. 2, pp. 79–102.

Ferner, A. (1997) 'Country of origin effects and HRM in multinational companies', *Human Resource Management Journal*, Vol. 7, No. 1, pp. 19–37.

Ferner, A. and Hyman, R. (eds) (1992) *Industrial Relations in the New Europe*. Oxford: Blackwell.

*Ferner, A. and Hyman, R. (eds) (1998) *Changing Industrial Relations in Europe*. Oxford: Blackwell.

Forsgren, M. (1990) 'Managing the international multi-centred firm', *European Management Journal*, No. 8, pp. 261–267.

Forster, N. (1994) 'The forgotton employees? The experience of expatriate staff returning to the UK', *International Journal of Human Resource Management*, Vol. 5, No. 2, pp. 405–426.

Forster, N. (1997) 'The persistent myth of high expatriate failure rates: a re-appraisal', *International Journal of Human Resource Management*, Vol. 8, No. 4, pp. 414–433.

Fulcher, J. (1991) *Labour Movements Employers and the State: Conflict and Cooperation in Britain and Sweden*. Oxford: Clarendon.

Ghoshal, S. and Nohria, N. (1989) 'Internal differentiation within multinational corporations', *Strategic Management Journal*, No. 10, pp. 323–337.

Gill, C. (1993) 'Technological change and participation in work organization: recent results from a European Community survey', *International Journal of Human Resource Management*, Vol. 4, No. 2, pp. 325–348.

Gospel, H. (1992) *Markets, Firms and the Management of Labour in Modern Britain*. Cambridge: Cambridge University Press.

Guest, D. (1990) 'Human resource management and the American dream', *Journal of Management Studies*, Vol. 27, No. 4, pp. 377–397.

Hadenius, S. (1988) *Swedish Politics During the 20th Century*. Stockholm: The Swedish Institute.

Hall, E. (1976) *Beyond Culture*. New York: Anchor Press Doubleday.

Hall, E. and Hall, M. (1990) *Understanding Cultural Differences.* Yarmouth: Intercultural Press.

Hampden-Turner, C. and Trompenaars, F. (1994) *The Seven Cultures of Capitalism.* London: Piatkus.

Handy, C., Gordon, C., Gow, I. and Randlesome, C. (1988) *Making Managers.* London: Pitman.

Harvey, D. (1989) *The Condition of Postmodernity.* Oxford: Blackwell.

Harzing, A.-W. K. (1995) 'The persistent myth of high expatriate failure rates, *International Journal of Human Resource Management,* Vol. 6, No. 2, pp. 457–474.

*Harzing, A.W. and Van Ruysseveldt, J. (eds) (1995) *International Human Resource Management.* London: Sage.

Hedlund, G. (1980) 'The role of foreign subsidiaries in strategic decision making in Swedish multinational corporations', *Strategic Management Journal,* No. 1, pp. 23–36.

Hedlund, G. (1986) 'The hypermodern MNC: a heterarchy, *Human Resource Management,* pp. 9–35.

Hirst, P. and Thompson, G. (1996) *Globalisation in Question.* Cambridge: Polity Press.

Hofstede, G. (1980) *Culture's Consequences: International Differences in Work Related Values.* Beverly Hills, Calif.: Sage.

Hofstede, G. (1991) *Cultures and Organisations: Software of the Mind.* London, McGraw-Hill.

Holden, L. (1996) 'HRM and employee involvement in Britain and Sweden: a comparative study', *International Journal of Human Resource Management.* Vol. 7, No. 1, pp. 59–81.

*Hollinshead, G. and Leat, M. (1995) *Human Resource Management: An International and Comparative Perspective.* London: Pitman.

Hyman, R. and Ferner, A. (eds) (1994) *New Frontiers in European Industrial Relations.* Oxford: Blackwell.

IDE (1993) *Industrial Democracy in Europe Revisited.* Oxford: Oxford University Press.

Kakabadse, A. (1991) *The Wealth Creators.* London: Kogan Page.

Kamoche, K. (1997) 'Knowledge creation and learning in international HRM', *International Journal of Human Resource Management,* Vol. 8, No. 3, pp. 213–225.

Kerr, C., Dunlop, J.T., Harbison, F. and Myers, C.A. (1960) *Industrialism and Industrial Man.* Cambridge, Mass.: Harvard University Press.

Kerr, C., Dunlop, J.T., Harbison, F. and Myers, C.A. (1971) 'Postscript to industrialism and industrial man', *International Labour Review,* 103.

Kidger, P. (1991) 'The emergence of international human resource management', *International Journal of Human Resource Management,* Vol. 2, No. 2, pp. 149–164.

Kluckhohn, C. (1951) 'The study of culture' in Lernex, D. and Lasswell, H. (eds) *The Policy Sciences.* Stanford, CA: Stanford University Press, pp. 61–90.

Kobrin, S.J. (1994) 'Is there a relationship between a geocentric mind-set and multinational strategy?', *Journal of International Business Studies,* 3rd quarter, pp. 493–511.

Lado, A. and Wilson, M. (1994) 'Human resource systems and sustained competitive advantage: a competency-based perspective', *Academy of Management Review,* Vol. 19, pp. 699–727.

Lane, C. (1989) *Management and Labour in Europe.* Aldershot: Edward Elgar.

Lane, C. (1992) 'European business systems: Britain and Germany compared', in Whitley, R. (ed.) *European Business Systems: Firms and Markets in their National Context.* London: Sage, pp. 64-97.

Lane, C. (1994) 'Industrial order and the transformation of industrial relations: Britain, Germany and France compared', in Hyman, R. and Ferner, A. (eds) *New Frontiers in European Industrial Relations.* Oxford: Blackwell, pp. 167–195.

Lane, C (1995) *Industry and Society in Europe: Stability and Change in Britain, Germany and France.* Aldershot: Edward Elgar.

Laurent, A. (1983) 'The cultural diversity of Western conceptions of management', *International Studies of Management and Organisation,* Vol. 13, Nos. 1–2, pp. 75–96.

Lawrence, P. (1992) 'Management development in Europe: a study in cultural contrast', *Human Resource Management Journal,* Vol. 3, No. 1, pp. 12–24.

Leeds, C., Kirkbride, P. and Durcan, J. (1994) 'The cultural context of Europe: a tentative mapping,' in Kirkbride, P. (ed.) *Human Resource Management in Europe: Perspectives for the 1990s.* London: Routledge, pp. 11–27.

Lincoln, J. and Kalleberg, A. (1990) *Culture, Control and Commitment: A Study of Work Organization and Attitudes in the United States and Japan.* Cambridge: Cambridge University Press.

Martin, A. (1984) 'Trade unions in Sweden: strategic responses to change and crisis', in Gourevitch, P., Martin, A., Ross, G., Bornstein, S., Markovits, A. and Allen, C. (eds) *Unions and Economic Crisis: Britain, West Germany and Sweden.* London: George Allen & Unwin, pp. 190–342.

Martin, G. and Beaumont, P. (1998) 'Diffusing "best practice" in multinational firms: prospects, practice and contestation', *International Journal of Human Resource Management,* Vol. 9, No. 4, pp. 671–695.

Martin, G. and Beaumont, P. (1999) 'Co-ordination and control of human resource management in multinational firms: the case of CASHCO', *International Journal of Human Resource Management,* Vol. 10, No. 1, pp. 21–42.

McGaughey, S. and De Cieri, H. (1999) 'Reassessment of convergence and divergence dynamics: implications for international HRM', *International Journal of Human Resource Management,* Vol. 10, No. 2, pp. 235–250.

Mead, R. (1994) *International Management: Cross Cultural Dimensions.* Oxford: Blackwell.

Meegan, R. (1988) 'A crisis of mass production', in Allen, J. and Massey, D. (eds) *The Economy in Question.* London: Sage.

Mueller, F. and Purcell, J. (1992) 'The Europeanisation of manufacturing and the decentralisation of bargaining: multinational management strategies in the European automobile industry', *International Journal of Human Resource Management,* Vol. 3, No. 1.,

Muller, M. (1998) 'Human resource and industrial relations practices of UK and US multinationals in Germany', *International Journal of Human Resource Management,* Vol. 9, No. 4, pp. 732–749.

Nohria, N. and Ghoshal, S. (1997) *The Differentiated Network: Organizing Multinational Corporations for Value Creation.* San Francisco, Calif.: Jossey-Bass.

Perlmutter, H.V. (1969) 'The tortuous evolution of the multinational corporation', *Columbia Journal of World Business,* Vol. 4, pp. 9–18.

Pieper, R. (ed.) (1990) *Human Resource Management: An International Comparison.* New York: Walter de Gruyter.

Poole, M. (1986) *Industrial Relations: Origins and Patterns of National Diversity.* London: Routledge & Kegan Paul.

Poole, M. (1990) 'Editorial: Human resource management in an international perspective', *International Journal of Human Resource Management,* Vol. 1, No. 1, pp. 1–16.

Porter, M. (1990) *The Competitive Advantage of Nations.* London: Macmillan.

Porter, M. (ed.) (1986) *Competition in Global Industries.* Boston, Mass.: Harvard Business School Press.

Prahalad, C.K. and Doz, Y.L. (1987) *The Multinational Mission: Balancing Local Demands and Global Vision.* New York: The Free Press.

Prentice, G. (1990) 'Adapting management style for the organisation of the future', *Personnel Management,* Vol. 22, No. 6, pp. 58–62.

Price Waterhouse Cranfield Project (1991) *Report on International Strategic Human Resource Management.* Cranfield: Cranfield School of Management.

Pucik, V. (1984) 'The international management of human resources', in Fombrun, C.J., Tichy, N.M. and Devanna, M.A. (eds) *Strategic Human Resource Management.* New York: John Wiley, pp, 403–419.

Pucik, V. (1992) 'Globalisation and human resource management', in Pucik, V., Tichy, N. and Barnett, C. (eds) *Globalising Management: Creating and Leading the Competitive Organisation.* New York: John Wiley, pp. 61–84.

Purcell, J. (1993) 'Developing research in comparative human resource management', *International Journal of Human Resource Management,* Vol. 4, No. 3, pp. 507–510.

Quintanilla, J. (1998) 'The configuration of human resource management policies and practices in multinational subsidiaries: the case of European retail banks in Spain', Unpublished PhD Thesis, University of Warwick.

Randlesome, C. (ed.) (1990) *Business Cultures in Europe.* London: Heinemann.

Ritzer, G. (1998) *The McDonaldization Thesis.* London: Sage.

Rosenzweig, P. and Nohria, N. (1994) 'Influences on human resource management practices in multinational corporations', *Journal of International Business Studies,* No. 25, pp. 229–251.

Ruigrok, W. and Van Tulder, R. (1995) *The Logic of International Restructuring.* London: Routledge.

Ruysseveldt, J. and Visser, J. (eds) (1996) *Industrial Relations in Europe.* London: Sage.

Ruysseveldt, J., Huiskamp, R. and van Hoof, J. (eds) (1995) *Comparative Industrial and Employment Relations.* London: Sage.

Schuler, R., Dowling, P. and De Cieri, H. (1993) 'An integrative framework of strategic international human resource management', *International Journal of Human Resource Management,* Vol. 4, No. 4, pp. 717–764.

Scullion, H. (1992) 'Strategic recruitment and development of the "international manager": some European considerations,' *Human Resource Management Journal,* Vol. 3, No. 1, pp. 57–69.

Scullion, H. (1995) 'International human resource management', in Storey, J. (ed.) *Human Resource Management: A Critical Text.* London: Routledge, pp. 352–382.

*Scullion, H. and Holden, L. (2001) *International HRM: A Critical Perspective.* London: Macmillan.

Segrestin, D. (1990) 'Recent changes in France', in Baglioni, G. and Crouch, C. (eds) *European Industrial Relations.* London: Sage, pp. 97–126.

Sisson, K. (1987) *The Management of Collective Bargaining: An International Comparison.* Oxford: Blackwell.

Sparrow, P. (1995) 'Towards a dynamic and comparative model of European human resource management: an extended review', *International Journal of Human Resource Management,* Vol. 6, No. 4, pp. 935–953.

Sparrow, P. and Hiltrop, J.-M. (1994) *European Human Resource Management in Transition.* Hemel Hempstead, Prentice Hall.

Sparrow, P. and Hiltrop, J.-M. (1997) 'Redefining the field of European human resource management: a battle between national mindsets and forces of business transition?', *Human Resource Management,* Vol. 36, No. 2, pp. 201–219.

Sparrow, P. and Wu, P.-C. (1999) 'How much do national value orientations really matter? Predicting HRM preferences of Taiwanese employees', in Lähteenmäki, S., Holden, L. and Roberts, I. (eds) *HRM and the Learning Organisation.* Turku School of Economics and Business Administration Publication, Series A-2, pp. 239–284.

Sparrow, P., Schuler, R. and Jackson, S. (1994) 'Convergence or divergence: human resource practices and policies for competitive advantage worldwide', *International Journal of Human Resource Management,* Vol. 5, No. 2, pp. 267–299.

Storey, J. (1992) 'Making European managers: an overview', *Human Resource Management Journal,* Vol. 3, No. 1, pp. 1–11.

Storey, J., Okazaki-Ward, L., Gow, I., Edwards, P.K. and Sisson, K. (1991) 'Managerial careers and management development: a comparative analysis of Britain and Japan', *Human Resource Management Journal,* Vol. 1, No. 3, pp. 33–57.

*Tayeb, M. (1996) *The Management of a Multicultural Workforce.* Chichester: John Wiley.

Tayeb, M. (1998) Transfer of HRM practices across cultures: an American company in Scotland', *International Journal of Human Resource Management,* Vol. 9, No. 2, pp. 332–358.

Taylor, S., Beechler, S. and Napier, N. (1996) 'Toward an integrative model of strategic human resource management', *Academy of Management Review,* Vol. 21, No. 4, pp. 959–985.

Torbiörn, I. (1982) *Living Abroad: Personal Adjustment and Personal Policy in the Overseas Setting.* Chichester: John Wiley.

Torrington, D. (1994) *International Human Resource Management: Think Globally, Act Locally.* Hemel Hempstead: Prentice Hall.

Trompenaars, F. (1993) *Riding the Waves of Culture.* London: Nicholas Brealey.

Tyson, S., Lawrence, P., Poirson, P., Manzolini, L. and Soler, C. (1993) *Human Resource Management in Europe: Strategic Issues and Cases*. London: Kogan Page.

Warhurst, R. (1995) 'Converging on HRM? Change and continuity in airlines' industrial relations', *European Journal of Industrial Relations*, Vol. 1, No. 2, pp. 259–274.

Whitley, R. (ed.) (1992) *European Business Systems: Firms and Markets in National Contexts*. London: Sage.

Wilczynski, J. (1983) *Comparative Industrial Relations*. London: Macmillan.

16

Human resource management and Europe

Len Holden

OBJECTIVES

- To examine the origins, development and operations of the European Union and the Social Charter.

- To highlight the difficulties in framing, interpreting and enforcing social legislation in the European Union.

- To examine the controversy over the effects of the implementation and non-implementation of the Social Charter and the Amsterdam Treaty.

- To examine HRM and labour market trends in Western Europe.

- To examine the degrees of convergence of HRM practices within Europe.

- To survey the recent history of and contemporary developments in Eastern European management and labour relations.

INTRODUCTION

Most of the nation states of Europe, as we know them, have emerged over the past 150 years, and many of these have experienced considerable changes in borders and ethnic composition since then. This process has radically continued with the break-up of the former Soviet Union and its satellite states, and the former Yugoslavia.

Thus the concept of a unified Europe begs many questions, which must fundamentally include an answer to 'What is Europe?' and 'How unified can it be?' The latter question has already caused considerable controversy over the ratification of the Maastricht Treaty, and the former over whether Eastern European states, as well as Turkey, should be included in the European Union. Answers to these basic but essential questions have a fundamental influence on the shaping of economic, political and social policy.

This chapter will examine Europe from the perspective of HRM, but as we have noted in the previous chapter on international HRM the concept itself has a number of interpretations depending on the context in which it is used, which include: exploring the European Union social dimension (Gold, 1993; Wise and Gibb, 1992; Leat, 1998); trends in industrial relations systems and individual European countries (Baglioni and Crouch, 1990; Ferner and Hyman, 1992, 1998; Hyman and Ferner, 1994; Ruysseveldt and Visser, 1996); labour market trends across Europe (Adnett, 1996; Addison and Siebert, 1997); under the banner of

HRM of individual countries (Brewster *et al.*, 1992; Clark, 1996); and in analysis of HRM trends (Lane, 1989; Hegewisch and Brewster, 1993; Brewster and Hegewisch, 1994; Kirkbride, 1994; Sparrow and Hiltrop, 1994). Some of these surveys confine themselves to EU countries only and others to a wider range of European nations including the former Soviet Union and its satellites. Thus the field is wide, and a chapter on this subject can only hope to give a general picture of the major issues and trends.

There are a number of issues that have been the subject of discussion and debate over the past decade and longer, and some that have emerged more recently. The aim of this chapter is to divide issues into those that are relevant to the European Union and those that have wider significance for all European countries, and concern general trends in HRM and HR-related issues.

EUROPEAN UNION ISSUES

Within the European Union the central platform for HRM issues has been the Social Charter and the Social Action Programme to implement it. The main concerns here have been the debates over the form and content of the Social Charter, how to integrate its provisions within the existing employment relations systems of member states, and how to harmonise aspects of the Charter's provision across the Union. These debates have taken place in the context of ideological positions within and between member states concerning degrees of regulation.

The main issue to the forefront of the European Union (EU) social agenda has been unemployment, which increased considerably across the Union in the 1990s. It is particularly high among certain social groups, such as young people, ethnic minorities and women, and in regions undergoing structural change.

Other issues have concerned 'social dumping' (see section on 'the regulationists') and recently the impact of European Monetary Union. Single issues such as the minimum wage in the British context provoked some controversy when adopted by the Labour government in 1998 along with the UK's signing up to the Social Charter. There has also been the long-festering issue of TUPE (the Transfer of Undertakings (Protection of Employment) Directive: see later in this chapter), and more recently the debates over degrees of employee voice that include, more importantly, the issue of the form and powers of works councils.

There has also been considerable work on general labour market trends and a concern with issues such as trends in flexibilisation, decentralisation of bargaining, the role and strength of unions, the changing nature of corporatism and collective bargaining generally, and the growth in size and influence of multinational corporations. We shall deal with these issues later under the heading of HRM and labour market trends. Most of these issues have been debated within the ideological context of deregulation and regulation, which will also be examined in greater depth later in this chapter.

The European Union: origins and development

It is neither possible nor appropriate to cover the historical origins of the EU in detail in this book, but a brief outline of the relevant events should help students new to the subject to put into context some of the factors that influence European human resource issues.

The European Union arose out of the wreckage of the Second World War. There was a consensus among most politicians that the devastation wreaked upon Europe should never be repeated, and that cooperation between nations was one important way to prevent conflict. Partly towards this end, and to help war-torn economies to revive, the European Coal and Steel Community (ECSC) was set up between France, West Germany, Belgium, the Netherlands, Italy and Luxembourg in 1952. The general aim was to dismantle tariff barriers between these nations, affording a single market for iron, steel and coal. Robert Schuman, one of its prime architects, anticipated that one day the ECSC would broaden into a movement towards economic and even political unity.

The success of these early attempts at cooperation led to the forging of stronger links, and after a number of preliminary reports and meetings the six ECSC countries formed the European Economic Community (EEC) under the Treaty of Rome 1957. The aim of the Treaty was to create a 'common market' among its members, although it was accepted at this time that political union was a long way away. The Treaty of Rome also established the European Atomic Energy Community (EURATOM), which still influences many aspects of EU legislation.

The positive progress of the EEC influenced other European states to become members, and Britain, Denmark and the Republic of Ireland joined in 1973. In 1981 Greece joined, and in 1986 Spain and Portugal. In 1995 Sweden, Austria and Finland were granted membership of what by then had become the European Union (EU), although after a referendum Norway decided to stay out of the Union. Another 12 countries have applied for membership: Cyprus and Malta in the Mediterranean area, and Bulgaria, the Czech Republic, Estonia, Hungary, Latvia, Lithuania, Poland, Rumania, Slovakia and Slovenia in Central and Eastern Europe. Turkey has also been given time to meet the requirements for membership within the next five years. Such an enlargement will constitute a much more representative bloc of European states.

A chronology of the EU

1952 European Coal and Steel Community founded (Belgium, France, Italy, Luxembourg, the Netherlands and West Germany)

1957 Treaty of Rome sets up the European Economic Community or 'Common Market' (Belgium, France, Italy, Luxembourg, the Netherlands and West Germany)

1957 Treaty of Paris sets up European Atomic Energy Community (Belgium, France, Italy, Luxembourg, the Netherlands and West Germany)

1958 EEC and EURATOM come into being

1972 Paris Summit gives commitment to action in social field

1973 UK, Denmark and Republic of Ireland join EC

1974 Commission's 'Action Programme' comes into being

1981 Greece joins the EC

1986 Spain and Portugal join the EC

1987 Single European Act passed

1989 Social Charter ratified by 11 states except the UK

1991 Austria, Norway and Sweden apply to join the EC

1992 Hungary, Poland and the former Czechoslovakia express a desire to join

1992 Maastricht Treaty signed but UK insists on separate protocol for the Social Charter (Chapter). The European Community is renamed the European Union

1995 Austria, Finland and Sweden join the EU

1997 Treaty of Amsterdam incorporates the Social Charter into four pillars of employment policy: employability, entrepreneurship, adaptability, equality of opportunity

1997 Agenda 2000 reviews the criteria for membership of aspiring states

1999 European Monetary Union

1999 Treaty of Amsterdam comes into force 1 May

The institutions of the EU

There are five main institutions that govern the European Union:

- the European Council;
- the Council of Ministers (based in Brussels);
- the Commission (based in Brussels);
- the Court of Justice (sits in Luxembourg);
- the Parliament (based in Strasbourg).

The European Council
The European Council consists of the heads of each member state, who usually meet twice a year to give overall direction to the EU's programme.

The Council of Ministers
The Council of Ministers is made up of one representative, usually a government minister or highly placed politician, from each member state, and is presided over in turn by each state for a six-month period. The Council is the EU's main decision-making body; it acts on proposals by the Commission. Decisions are taken on a unanimous vote, although majority voting was introduced via the Single European Act for some issues.

The Commission
The Commission is composed of 20 members or commissioners, and is made up of two representatives from each of the larger countries (France, Germany, Italy, Spain, the UK) and one from the rest. Commissioners are appointed for four years, and act only in the interests of the Union. The President serves for a four-year period on a renewable basis. The Commission proposes and executes EU policies, and acts as a mediator between the 15 governments of the Union. It also has the power to bring legal action via the Court of Justice against member states that it deems to have violated EU laws. It is ultimately subservient to the Council of Ministers.

The European Court of Justice
The European Court of Justice comprises one judge from each member state assisted by advocates-general, who rule on questions of community law. Judgments are by majority vote, and directly binding on all parties. This is the final court of appeal for member states, and is often used by individuals, groups and organisations to challenge national laws or rulings that are perceived as being in contravention of EU law. It has become increasingly important in enforcing EU regulations by adjudicating individual, group and company cases brought before it, such as interpretations on the application of TUPE (see below).

The European Parliament
The European Parliament has 626 members: 99 from Germany, 87 each from France, Italy and the UK, 64 from Spain, 31 from the Netherlands, 25 each from Belgium, Greece and Portugal, 22 from Sweden, 21 from Austria, 16 each from Denmark and Finland, 15 from Ireland and 6 from Luxembourg.

Members of the European Parliament (MEPs) are directly elected by citizens of their countries for a five-year term. The last election took place in June 1999. The European Parliament does not have the same power as the Council of Ministers or a national Parliament, but very few proposals can be adopted without its opinion being sought. It also has the power to dismiss the Commission on a two-thirds majority vote.

Other institutions concerned with human resource issues

Economic and Social Committee

This is an advisory body that is consulted by the Commission and Council. It is made up of representatives of employers, trade unions, and other interests including consumers, small firms and professions. It provides detailed information and advice in the following areas:

- agriculture;
- transport and communications;
- energy and nuclear questions;
- economic and financial questions;
- industry;
- commerce, crafts and services;
- social questions;
- external relations;
- regional development;
- protection of the environment, public health and consumer affairs.

European Foundation for the Improvement of Living and Working Conditions

This is a body set up primarily for investigating and disseminating information on living and working conditions in the EU, including health and safety, environmental protection, industrial relations, restructuring working life and assessing new technologies and the future of work. It is based in Dublin.

Employer and Employee Representative Groups

EU-wide groups were set up to represent the interests of employers and employees. These included the European Trade Union Confederation (ETUC), the Union of Industrial and Employers Confederations of Europe (UNICE), and the European Centre for Public Enterprise (CEEP), which represents public sector employer interests. Talks between employer and employee representatives of member countries concentrated on examining macroeconomic policy and employment, and new technology and work. From these talks two committees were formed, which deal with training and labour market issues. In recent years there has been concentration on examining flexibility and adaptability of the workforce.

These meetings also led to the creation of the European Framework Agreement, which proposed that the Commission would consult the social partners at European level before putting proposals forward. This could have important ramifications in creating controversy between those states that have relied on negotiations at the workplace (Denmark, Ireland and the UK) and those that rely on centralised regulation in their industrial relations systems (Germany and Sweden) (Lockhart and Brewster, 1992).

The legislative process

In simplistic terms, legal proposals emanate from the Commission and are sent for consideration to the Council, which seeks approval from the Parliament and advice and information from the Economic and Social Committee. The Commission then has the right to amend the proposal in the light of these opinions and return it to the Council for acceptance or rejection.

There are four types of EU legislation, as follows:

- *Regulations* are binding on all member states without any further process of confirmation by national parliaments.
- *Directives* are binding on all member states, but leave to national discretion how these laws are to be complied with. Target dates are also set for implementation.
- *Decisions* are binding on those to whom they are addressed (member states, enterprises, individuals).
- *Recommendations and opinions* are not binding. These are not laws as such, but may help to encourage particular responses. 'The Commission places emphasis on using such Recommendations to achieve "convergence", i.e. to move towards harmonisation of policy and practice' (Hughes, 1991).

Regulations are generally used when an identical law is required across the Union, often where none has existed in member states previously. Directives are more appropriate as a mechanism where the method of implementation may vary at national level and has to be related to existing laws. This incorporates the principle of 'subsidiarity', that is, that legislation should be passed by the lowest level of government competent to enact it.

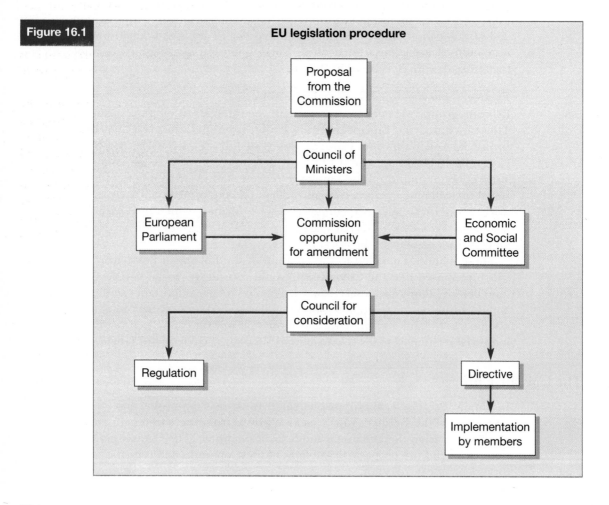

Figure 16.1 EU legislation procedure

THE SOCIAL CHARTER

In terms of human resource management the Social Charter is the key indicator of EU legislation, as its proposals will have considerable impact on employee relations at international, national and local levels.

Origins and development

Much of the Social Charter is an amalgam and extension of the articles embodied in the various treaties that jointly created the EU: the Treaty of Paris, which set up the ECSC in 1952, and the Treaties of Rome and Paris, which created the EEC and EURATOM respectively in 1957.

At the Paris summit in 1972 it was agreed that as much importance should be attached to reducing disparities of living conditions and improving the quality of life within the community concerning issues of economic and monetary union. This resulted in the creation of an 'Action Programme' in 1974, which became committed to the promotion of employment, upward harmonisation of living conditions, and the increased involvement of management and labour in the decision-making processes of organisations. This was to be achieved by coordinating provisions in the treaties with new initiatives. A number of economic problems were besetting the community, and the reaction by member states at the time was, at best, mixed. In this period of 'Europessimism', however, it can be argued that incremental agreements, particularly in areas such as equal opportunities, witnessed the foundation of what is still the most effective part of legislation embodied in the Social Charter (Lockhart and Brewster, 1992).

A revival of interest in the 'social dimension' occurred in the 1980s as a result of the debate over, and the subsequent agreement to, the creation of a single European market (SEM) under the Single European Act 1987. The creation of a unified market across 12 European states would have deep implications for the labour market and employment relationships, and therefore under the influence of Jacques Delors, the President of the Commission (1985–95), it was proposed that policies that addressed employment relations issues should be created. In December 1989 the Social Charter was finally adopted by the Council of Ministers (with the exception of the UK), and a Social Action Programme was set up to implement it. The UK eventually signed up to the Social Charter in 1997, when New Labour came to power.

The Social Charter provisions

The Social Charter states that:

> the completion of the internal market must offer improvements in the social field for workers of the European Community, especially in terms of freedom of movement, living and working conditions, health and safety at work, social protection education and training.
>
> Whereas, in order to ensure equal treatment, it is important to combat every form of discrimination, including discrimination on grounds of sex, colour, race, opinions and beliefs, and whereas in a spirit of solidarity it is important to combat social exclusion.

The 12 main provisions are as follows:

- *Free movement.* All workers have the right to free movement within the Union.
- *Employment and remuneration.* All employment should be fairly remunerated. Workers should have an equitable wage – that is, a wage sufficient to enable them to have a decent standard of living (often interpreted as a minimum wage). Workers subject to atypical terms of employment (such as part-time work) should benefit from an equitable reference wage – that is, a wage in line with full-time employee remuneration.
- *Improvement of living and working conditions.* The process must result from an approximation of conditions, as regards, in particular, the duration and organisation of working time and forms of employment. The procedure must cover such aspects of employment as collective redundancies and bankruptcies. Every worker must have a weekly rest period, annual paid leave, and a contract of employment.
- *Social protection.* Every worker in the Union shall have a right to adequate social protection and shall, regardless of status, enjoy an adequate level of social security benefits. Persons outside the labour market (those unable to work, e.g. retired, ill) must receive sufficient resources and social assistance in keeping with their particular situation.
- *Freedom of association and collective bargaining.* Employers and employees have the right of association (that is, employers' associations and trade unions) to protect their social and economic interests. There is also the right *not* to join. There shall be the right to negotiate and conclude collective agreements, and the right to collective action (such as strikes and lock-outs), subject to national legislation.
- *Vocational training.* Every worker must have access to and receive vocational training, with no discrimination on grounds of nationality.
- *Equal treatment for men and women.* This applies in particular in regards to access to employment, remuneration, working conditions, social protection, educational training and career development.
- *Information, consultation and participation of workers.* These must be developed along appropriate lines, taking account of the practices in force in the various member states. This shall apply especially in companies or groups of companies with establishments in several member states. These processes must be implemented: when technological change occurs that has major implications for the workforce; in connection with restructuring operations or mergers; in cases of collective redundancy; and when trans-frontier workers in particular are affected by the employment policies of the undertaking where they are employed.
- *Health protection and safety in the workplace.* Every worker must enjoy satisfactory health and safety conditions in the workplace. Appropriate measures must be taken to achieve further harmonisation of conditions in this area.
- *Protection of children and adolescents in employment.* The minimum employment age must not be lower than school-leaving age, and neither of these can be lower than 15 years of age. The duration of work must be limited, and night work prohibited under 18 years of age. After compulsory education young people must be entitled to receive initial vocational training of reasonable duration.
- *Elderly persons.* Every worker must, at the time of retirement, be able to enjoy resources affording him or her a decent standard of living, and those not entitled to a pension must be provided for.
- *Disabled persons.* All disabled people must be entitled to additional measures aimed at improving their social and professional integration. These measures must address vocational training, ergonomics, accessibility, mobility, means of transport and housing.

Difficulties of implementation and interpretation

The implementation of the Social Charter has proved to be more controversial than the debate over what it should contain, although these processes are inextricably intertwined (Hughes, 1991). Implementation hinges on the influence and interpretations of:

- political parties and groupings;
- national governments;
- employers and employee bodies;
- multinational corporations;
- the economic and political climate;
- the ambiguities and imprecisions of Charter policies.

Deciding on the provisions of the Social Charter was, and still is, a difficult process given the varied opinions within the EU in terms of political and economic ideology.

Margaret Thatcher's Conservative government was the most prominent and vocal opponent. Given her neo-liberalist position she was never happy with the Social Charter per se, and raised many objections to proposals, ultimately refusing to ratify it in 1989 – the UK being the only government of the 12 member states to do so. John Major, her successor, continued this policy and demanded that the Maastricht Treaty should have a separate protocol for the Social Chapter, as the Social Charter is also called, upon which member states vote separately. However, Tony Blair's Labour government has completely reversed this position: it has subscribed to all the provisions of the Social Charter, and finally ratified the treaty on behalf of the UK when elected in 1997. Nevertheless, Mr Blair has continued to advocate some of the deregulatory policies of the previous Conservative administrations.

The process of amendment and change is still continuing, and past and present efforts to please Margaret Thatcher and other critics have meant that the original proposals from the mid-1980s have been watered down, some considerably. The implementation of the Charter under the Social Action Programme has also been significantly revised, and the biting recession of the early 1990s had another slowing effect on its implementation. Thus Jacques Delors, and other parties of the opinion that a strong social dimension is an important part of the Single European Market, have had to revise their views on the timetable for implementation. It is now agreed, even by its strongest advocates, that the full Charter will take a very long time to complete, if at all (Piachaud, 1991; Goodhart, 1992; Milne, 1992b.)

Although a great deal of the Social Action Programme has been accepted, the consultation process has ensured that many of the original proposals have been diluted, and some have been blocked entirely. Even if the Social Charter had been accepted in principle by all member states, interpretation of the directives is problematic. Directives rather than regulations were deliberately used in framing the Charter in order to allow for national differences and the accommodation of existing laws. As one commentator accurately notes, 'responsibilities for such implementation often rests with national governments who have a reputation for giving variable priority both to implementation and enforcement' (Butt Philips, 1988).

In addition, some of the directives are so vague that they are open to wide interpretation. The provision for 'information, consultation and participation of the workforce' has many varied interpretations, ranging from works councils in Germany, Belgium and the Netherlands to multifarious practices in the UK, covering schemes as representative as works councils to organisations that give the workforce the bare minimum of information. Yet the CBI claimed that British organisations already adequately conform to the provisions of this directive.

Another directive, the Transfer of Undertakings (Protection of Employment) or TUPE, has caused considerable controversy over interpretation in the UK. This directive (77/187) protects employees' pay and conditions when an undertaking is transferred as, for example, when privatisation of government and local government services takes place. 'If the directive applies a successful bidder must take over staff on their existing terms and conditions which will reduce scope for saving through lower pay or staff cuts' (Willman, 1993). This would in effect

> put an end to private contractors depressing their pay and conditions to lower bid costs when competing for contracts against the public sector. Contractors are increasingly jittery about the lack of clarity and are reluctant to bid for contracts without knowing the extent of their liabilities.
>
> (Weston, 1993)

UK governments under Major and Thatcher argued that the directive did not apply to contracting out, but the European Court of Justice has forced the government to amend the existing law that covers this situation, the new wording of which, trade unions believe, extends protection to cover many public sector and former public sector activities.

There is also the problem of enforcement. The EU has no inspectorate, and relies heavily on member states to enforce directives, which, as we have already noted, can vary widely. The most common way is through legal action by individuals or groups via the Commission. These actions take time to investigate, prepare and process through the Court of Justice. Leaving the enforcement to individuals or groups often means that such contraventions of directives depend on the strength of mind of individuals and groups in bringing the action, who may be subject to pressures not to protest, particularly if it is against their employer. However, as Singh (1999) states: 'there is little doubt that the European Court of Justice continues to give rulings in employment law cases which have a profound impact on national legal systems' (p. 385).

Labour market trends in Europe

Along with the difficulties of implementing the social agenda are the problems associated with a constantly changing labour market. As we have seen in the previous chapter on international HRM there have been numerous influences on the way that economies and organisations are developing, thanks to – among other things – the increasing intensification of world competition for global markets and the impact of new technology.

In addition, demographic changes have witnessed declining birth and falling mortality rates, with the consequent effect that the EU population is ageing and so too therefore is the workforce. This has considerable implications for future labour supply. Will there be enough young people to fill employment positions in the future? This looks not to be a problem at present, given the high percentage of youth unemployment across Europe. Another effect of these changing demographics is that social welfare measures such as pensions and health will take up increasing resources of the member states.

There have also been significant sectoral shifts over the past 20 years with a continuing decline in agriculture and the old 'smoke stack' industries such as coal, iron and steel, textiles, shipbuilding and traditional engineering. This in turn has caused high unemployment in regions where these industries once thrived. In contrast new 'high tech' industries (such as computer technology and communications) have arisen, along with a considerable increase in financial services and the service sector generally. The demand for the old traditional skills has thus been in deep decline, while demand for skills relevant to the newly predominant sectors has witnessed a steep rise. Technology has also reduced the demand for unskilled and semi-skilled workers as many of these jobs become automated.

In attempts to maintain competitiveness, employers have increasingly introduced new work forms and contracts of employment. Flexibility, not only in job functions but in numerical terms and hours of work, has witnessed a considerable increase across Europe. Atypical work has also increased significantly, with more part-time, short and fixed-term and temporary contracts.

There have also been increasing levels of unemployment among women, the young and ethnic minorities, as well increases in the long-term unemployed, especially in depressed regions and among workers aged over 50. This general picture is complex and while, for example, there is a rise in female unemployment there has also been a percentage rise in women participating in the labour market. But as some observers have pointed out, women are much more likely to be employed in less well-paid and less secure jobs than men (Rees, 1998). The picture is also complicated by the variations between EU regions. The *La Dorsale* regions (London, Belgium, Frankfurt, Luxembourg and Milan), the *East–West core* regions (Paris, Frankfurt and Berlin) and the *Arc Mediterranean* (Barcelona, Marseilles and Rome) are characterised by high growth and low unemployment. By contrast, low growth and high unemployment zones are on the periphery of the EU: for example, most of the UK, excluding the South East, Midlands and East Anglia, Southern Italy, Greece and Southern Spain (Sapsford *et al.*, 1999). The European Social Fund has tried to compensate for these divergences in the past by directing funds to those areas with particularly high unemployment rates, especially among the long-term unemployed.

The regulation–deregulation debate

These problems and how to resolve them are part of a wider debate that emerged strongly in the 1980s, rooted in the differing ideological viewpoints concerning degrees of regulation of labour markets. Essentially, two main opinions predominate: the *deregulationists* or *neo-liberals*, and the *regulationists* or *interventionists*. These two stances are a polarised simplification of varied political positions. There are prominent trade unionists who view some of the provisions as undermining collective bargaining by a greater emphasis on individual rights and consultative arrangements (Gospel, 1992). There are some employers who believe that the full adoption of the Social Charter will bring order and the advantage of homogeneity to a European-wide market. Nevertheless, the argument to date has been based on the regulatory and deregulatory schools and median positions.

The deregulationists or neo-liberal school

The minimalist or deregulatory school was strongly advocated by Margaret Thatcher in the 1980s and John Major in the 1990s, as well as many employer groups and conservative or right-wing political parties. It posited the view that government and legislative interference prevents the efficient operation of the labour market.

In political terms the minimalists see the Social Charter as a 'socialists' charter' and Delors, its past champion, as an 'old-fashioned bureaucratic socialist'. Deregulationists believe that 'prosperity, progress and liberty presuppose economic freedom' (Marsland, 1991). Economic freedom means freedom from any regulatory influences that might hinder the industrial and commercial competitive process and therefore the operation of the market.

In economic terms, the neo-liberals see the provisions of the Charter as creating the conditions for 'Eurosclerosis', a hardening of the free flow of labour-market arteries. The Eurosclerosis view emanated from the 1970s and 1980s, when the EU states were perceived as doing less well economically than the United States. 'Reaganomics' (the policies of Ronald Reagan, US Republican President 1980–88) argued that abolishing or moderating regulatory restrictions had freed up the labour market and had lowered unemployment by enabling the creation of more jobs. 'Thatcherism' (the policies of British Conservative Prime Minister Margaret Thatcher, 1979–91) had attempted similar deregulatory measures in the UK with comparable success in the 1980s, or so claimed her supporters. Such Social Charter proposals as a minimum wage would create a rigid high-wage economy with small differentials where workers would be priced out of a job. 'Furthermore, legally based labour rights and employment protection schemes have gone too far, leading to high labour costs which in turn cause redundancies and discourage hiring' (Teague, 1991: 4).

The cost to employers of implementing this and other provisions would have the effect of decreasing jobs and slowing the labour market. For example, the UK Conservative government claimed that 100 000 jobs would be lost in Britain in implementing maternity rights for women and safeguards for working hours and part-time working contained in the Charter.

Other critics believe that the imposition of a Europe-wide Social Charter would not benefit those for whom it was intended – the poorer workers (Addison and Siebert, 1991, 1992). They argue that 'it will not succeed in making the desired transfer to disadvantaged groups. Since mandated benefits work at the level of the firm, rather than at the level of the tax transfer system, firms will tend to make countervailing moves which frustrate the redistributive aims of the policy' (Addison and Siebert, 1992: 511). They also claim that the unskilled will lose out as a result of better safety protection because 'they were the ones doing the unsafe jobs for high pay; now the unsafe jobs have been removed, wages have been reduced but the skill gap remains' (p. 511). In addition, the attempts to impose uniformity on nations with diverse systems of social legislation will impede competition (p. 495).

Most minimalists do support some of the measures in the Social Charter to varying degrees, namely:

● freedom of movement of workers;
● provision of training;
● harmonisation of qualifications;
● pensions to become portable;
● help to the less favoured regions through the Social Fund;
● schemes to help the long-term unemployed.

They remain, however, strictly against measures to regulate the labour market, which they believe should be made freer by clipping the power of trade unions, reducing the government role in industrial relations, and increasing forms of flexibility.

The regulationists

The regulationist or interventionist position is generally held by those who believe that if the single European market is to create a free market in terms of a competitive 'level playing field' for goods, industry and services, then the same principle should apply to the social dimension to prevent the exploitation of various work groups or giving one organisation or economy an advantage over another in the naked drive towards profit. Unregulated markets would lead to poorer countries and employers holding down 'wages and social benefits to limit imports from richer member states and at the same time increase their exports to those countries. Such a strategy would amount to exporting domestic unemployment . . . Such action would inevitably force richer countries to check real wage growth and streamline existing labour market regulations triggering a price and cost reducing war inside the community. (Teague, 1991:7) From this would ensue redundancies and high unemployment. This is one version of what has come to be called *social dumping*.

A second and concomitant view of social dumping envisages

a sizable shift in production from Northern to Southern Europe as companies chase after low wage investment sites. It is feared the combination of these two processes would destabilise European economies by shifting the concern of governments and managers away from product and process innovations, towards cost reducing strategies. In this scenario of social dumping the main casualties of the competitive regime would be workers and their families who would experience a lowering of their incomes. (Teague, 1991:7)

An example of this was the exposure by a television documentary of the high incidence of illegal child labour in Portugal, which had the effect of removing manufacturing jobs from the UK shoe industry as labour costs were so much cheaper in Portugal. Consequently, many British companies choose to manufacture there rather than in the UK (Twenty Twenty Television, 1993).

Another recent example seized on by the regulationists to illustrate their argument was the decision by the Hoover Company to transfer its production facilities from Dijon, France to Cambuslang, near Glasgow, Scotland. Hoover president, William Foust, claimed that the prime motive for moving the company's whole production facilities was that non-wage labour costs were only 10% in Scotland as opposed to 45% in France (Goodhart, 1993). Another example is Bowater, the UK-based packaging group, which shifted production of some of its cosmetic packaging to the UK from Italy and France. 'The company has calculated national ratios for average employment costs at its plants, from managing director down to apprentice. If the UK is 100,' says Michael Hartnell, Bowater's Finance Director, 'Italy is 130, France 140 and Germany 170' (Jackson, 1993).

The regulationists claim that such practices play off one national workforce against another in an attempt to bid down labour costs. The deregulationists point out that companies will be attracted by cheap labour costs because they reflect maximum efficiency in terms of productivity. However, despite the examples referred to above, by the end of the 1990s there was not a great deal of evidence that social dumping is widespread in Europe. There have been more significant shifts globally from Europe and North America to Asian and South American states, thus reinforcing the view that Europe is part of a global economy.

Some also claim that these ideological tensions are reflected in the differences between the Commission, served with the responsibility of implementing the social agenda, and the European Parliament, representative of the national interests of member states (Towers and Terry, 1999).

By the latter part of the 1990s the power balance in many European states and in the European Parliament had shifted to the centre left as conservative and right-wing governments were replaced by parties of a more social democratic orientation. Consequently there was a re-emphasis on the idea of social partnership and what the Blair government in the UK has called the 'Third Way', a 'position between the Old Left and the New Right (Pierson *et al.*, 1999). Thus while social concerns and welfare measures have been revisited it is in accordance with the need to create proactive labour markets that do not create barriers to entrepreneurship and job creation. This emphasis on creating a social dialogue between the social partners of the EU (trade unions, employer associations, governments and EU agencies) led, through a series of meetings, to the Amsterdam Treaty.

The Amsterdam Treaty, 1997

The Amsterdam Treaty was an attempt to prepare the EU labour force to deal with a world where work design, organisational forms and labour markets are constantly changing and, most importantly, in the process to decrease levels of unemployment. By the mid-1990s the social affairs agenda of the EU was in need of a fresh impetus. As Padraig Flynn (Commissioner for Employment, Industrial Relations and Social Affairs, 1995–99) stated:

> There was a number of moribund proposals and a general lack of interest in the Member States in dynamically pursuing the social agenda. In addition, DGV (Directorate-General V for Employment, Industrial Relations and Social Affairs) badly needed to improve its image. In far too many instances, there was too much emphasis on drawing down budget funds rather than making effective use of them.
>
> (European Commission, 1999: 3)

White Papers were published, and a number of meetings of member states were held at the instigation of Flynn to hammer out a social affairs strategy in an attempt to move the process forward. Major mistakes were pinpointed in past attempts to implement social policy. First, there was an absence of coordinated economic policies, which have failed to keep pace with European integration. Governments have operated independently of one another and so fiscal and monetary policies were not integrated at EU level. This was sometimes damaging to in social and economic terms. Second, there has been an inability to modernise the labour market to keep pace with the changing conditions of modern economies.

The response to the first mistake was to establish European Monetary Union (EMU), establishing convergence and coordination of economic policies, in order to prevent fluctuations in exchange rates and reduce shocks to the European economy. The response to the second problem was the creation of the European Employment Strategy to promote convergence and coordination in employment policies. This strategy derives from the Amsterdam Treaty in 1997, of which the general aims are:

- to create a realistic strategy for social affairs;
- to make the process of convergence of social policy more effective across the EU;
- to have more effective monitoring based on national action plans with specific objectives and targets;
- to place emphasis on an integrated approach 'across a number of policy fields instead of isolated measures and "quick fixes"' (European Comission, 1999: 7).

The four pillars upon which this new strategy is based are designed ultimately to provide solutions to the high levels of unemployment among the young, ethnic minorities, women and the long-term unemployed as well as the unemployed in general by preparing people for economic and labour market changes. These pillars are:

- *Employability.* This is concerned with investment in human resources within a new active policy: how to cover the skills gap in Europe and create attachments to the world of work for the young and long-term unemployed and other groups who are less competitive in the labour market so that they do not drift into exclusion. Equally important is the enhancement of the skills and motivation of people in order to deal with the rapidly changing world of work, and to create in turn successful industries and a successful EU economy. Emphasis is placed on active rather than passive support.
- *Adaptability.* This is concerned with how to strengthen the capacity of workers to meet the challenges of change and how to change the organisation of work in such a way that structural adjustment can be managed and competitiveness maintained. This means also investment in lifelong learning, and reforming contractual frameworks to take into account new emerging work forms, but maintain the right balance between flexibility for enterprises and security for workers.
- *Entrepreneurship.* This is concerned with how to create a new entrepreneurial culture and spirit in Europe by encouraging self-employment, cutting red tape, reforming taxation systems, and identifying new sources of jobs, especially at local level and in the social economy. This encapsulates a series of measures to make it easier to start and run a business, to develop new jobs, and tap the employment potential of the information society.
- *Equal opportunities.* This is concerned with how to create conditions where men and women have equal responsibility and opportunities in family and working life, and how to respond to the demographic challenges that require us to maintain conditions of growth through high female participation in the labour market.

Unemployment

The main aim of the treaty was to deal with unemployment by not just advocating welfare support and funding but actively closing the gap between job vacancies and the unemployed. Unemployment in the EU has compared unfavourably with the major economies and the G7 average, as Table 16.1 illustrates.

Table 16.1 **Unemployment in the EU and the major economies (percentages)**

	1996	1997	1998
EU Average	10.8	10.4	9.8
G7 Average	6.8	6.5	6.4
USA	5.3	4.7	4.3
Japan	3.3	3.4	4.0
UK	7.7	6.4	6.2

Source: *Labour Market Trends* (1998, 1999).

These figures clearly indicate that the combined EU economies have been less successful in tackling unemployment than the USA, Japan and the G7 nations, and critics of regulationism have pointed to the better performance of economies such as the USA and UK. They strongly advocate deregulationist policies in order to facilitate job creation and bring unemployment down.

The question of what approaches to take to tackle unemployment has divided the social democratic governments that came to power in the EU in the 1990s. However, Tony Blair's government in the UK has advocated a 'Third Way' that emphasises social partnership and the pursuit of deregulationist policies that do not hinder the operation of the labour market. This is seen to be in keeping with the spirit of the four pillars of the Amsterdam Treaty, which advocates more proactive strategies in tackling unemployment by encouraging a more entrepreneurial approach in terms of helping the workless to be employable and adaptable to changing labour market conditions. Employability rests on skill formation through education and training and adaptability in the promotion of flexible forms of employment.

Social partnership or 'social dialogue' to date has had a mixed record, with those member states that have subscribed to a corporatist approach for some time, Germany and Sweden for example, happy to continue with that system and seemingly performing well in labour market terms (Crouch, 1996; Traxler, 1999). At EU level the picture is less rosy, with only two of the seven proposed directives having been agreed to by the social partners (state governments, employer associations and employee associations, e.g. trade vendors) by the end of 1998, although a number have been adopted without the social partners' agreement, the Works Councils Directive for example (Keller and Sörries, 1999). Another cause for concern for employment strategy is the negative effect of European Monetary Union.

European Monetary Union

The possible adverse effects of EMU on employment policy have caused these two issues to rise to the top of the EU agenda. In general two positions have been taken: that of the optimists, and that of the pessimists. The third stage of EMU, leading to full monetary union, was completed in 1998 with 11 of the 15 member countries joining. Convergence criteria required participating member states to preserve price inflation within certain limits, to restrict national debt to 60% of gross domestic product (GDP), and to confine budget deficits to no more than 3% of GDP. Optimists see this as another opportunity for further convergence and harmonisation of economic and social policy in the wake of the single European market of 1992 and in the spirit of the Amsterdam Treaty.

Pessimists believe that, in striving to maintain these criteria, economies will create higher unemployment 'by eliminating exchange rate flexibility as a means of adjustment' (Towers and Terry, 1999):

> The continuing absence of good, secure, reasonably paid work for large segments of the working population could then have major adverse political consequences for the progress or even cohesion of the EU.
> (p. 274)

While there are built-in monitoring processes in the operation of EMU it also has a deregulatory dimension, and this could clash with EU social aims. Barnard and Deakin (1999) see these developments as

> an attempt to lock member states into a path of economic development based on economic convergence around tight budgetary controls and the maintenance of price stability. Labour flexibility . . . is the corollary of this process. Some of these reforms, it is clear would be deregulatory, in the sense of removing indirect labour costs through reforms to employment protection legislation and the tax benefit system.
> (p. 363)

In other words such measures could benefit employers more than workers by removing protections. It is not surprising therefore that the EU employers' association UNICE, as one of the social partners, has been more cooperative than in the past in participating in the social dialogue. Up to early 2000 the more pessimistic prognostications have not been fulfilled, mainly because the monetary convergence criteria have been maintained without undue stress. However, if economic difficulties were to arise, then there could well be serious implications for European social and employment policy.

Equal opportunities

As we have noted, equal opportunities (EO) is one of the pillars of the Amsterdam Treaty proposals. It is concerned with eliminating the gender gaps and the development of a social infrastructure to enable better reconciliation between family life and working life. It is also concerned with developing a framework to respond to the demographic changes that shape economic and social life.

Equal opportunities is a complex issue: merely making it a pillar of EU social policy will not necessarily resolve all the questions about gender differences in the labour market. The principle of equal treatment for men and women was embodied in the Treaty of Rome 1957, and is one the 12 provisions of the Social Charter (see above). While some progress has been made on these issues, the situation within the EU varies widely between member states, with the Scandinavian countries having the most progressive legislation and Greece, the least.

As Leat (1998) states there are three types of equality, each of which varies in terms of progress towards implementation:

- *Equality of opportunity* may encompass pre-work experience and circumstance as well as opportunities to compete for work and for advancement within a particular employment organisation.
- *Equality of treatment* may encompass such issues as the allocation of tasks, working conditions, issues of harassment and conditions governing dismissal.
- *Equality of outcome* is likely to encompass issues of pay and other substantive terms and conditions of employment, as well as quotas of the working population.   (p. 172)

Each of these types of equality has had varying degrees of implementation across the EU, and some member states will have to make considerable progress if harmonisation is to be achieved. Recently, emphasis has been placed on the concept of *mainstreaming*, which 'involves the incorporation of EO issues into all action programmes and policies from the outset. It moves beyond equal treatment and positive action approaches to EO' (Rees, 1998: 4).

One of the key actors in the field in forging EO initiatives has been the European Court of Justice (ECJ), which has become involved in resolving individual cases that in turn set precedents for future judgments across the EU. For example, indirect discrimination was demonstrated in the *Bilka-Kaufhaus* judgment. This deemed that the exclusion of part-time workers from a company pension scheme (made up mainly of women workers) was indirect discrimination. The *Hill and Stapleton* judgment concerned women who moved from job sharing to full-time work but were placed on a lower pay scale despite the fact they had worked at the company as long as full-time workers, who were paid more (Barnard and Deakin, 1999: 365).

Women were also helped indirectly by the UK government's recent adoption of the minimum wage, which helped many female workers to raise their salaries. The preponderance of women in atypical and lower-paid work has considerable implications for the satisfactory operation of the EO provisions of the Amsterdam Treaty. If the entrepreneurial agenda is overtly deregulatory, in that it is seeking the removal of social charges and other potential restrictions on business start-ups, this could well clash with attempts to maintain and improve protective legislation.

Rees (1998), however, argues that

> While the legal framework for EO is essential, it is inevitably limited in its effectiveness. Positive action projects, while creating spaces for women and being laboratories for the development of good practice, appear to be precariously funded, provision is *ad hoc*, and there are few linkages to mainstream providers. It is mainstreaming which is likely to have the most significant impact on developing women's skills and the rigidities of gender segregation in the labour market. It also has the potential capacity to move beyond gender into other dimensions of equality, such as race and disability.
>
> (p. 4)

Vocational education and training

In order to fulfil the Amsterdam Treaty's pillars of employability, adaptability and entrepreneurship considerable reliance has been placed on vocational education and training (VET) as tools to enable the creation of a more skilled and educated workforce, able to respond and adapt to the demands of a rapidly changing and increasingly competitive world. The Social Commission has emphasised the active nature of VET proposals, in contrast to the passive measures associated with the Social Charter. The need to create a more employable workforce and in turn reduce unemployment places a huge emphasis on the ability of VET initiatives to equip people with the requisite skill and knowledge for a world of high technology, increased communication, and growth in the service sector, as well as enabling them to deal with the forms of flexibilisation demanded by neo-Fordist systems.

How this is achieved depends on initiatives to help the individual, the organisation and the economy – a theme running through Part 3 of this book. Such initiatives may come from the EU, from national governments, from organisations or from individuals themselves. The role of the EU and national governments often rests on political positions. Britain has strongly advocated a neo-liberalist position over the past 20 years: successive governments have adopted a voluntarist approach, which encouraged rather than compelled organisations and individuals to train. Germany, Sweden and France, by contrast, have advocated more compulsory initiatives, including legislation to increase levels of training. Neo-liberalists claim that the persistence of high unemployment levels in many European countries testifies to the failure of these compulsory initiatives (Addison and Siebert, 1991; Marsland 1991).

Success has been mixed in the past, with the much-vaunted German dual system (see Chapter 8) receiving a considerable degree of praise and attention, but Leat (1998) suggests that 'attempts to directly transpose the German member states with different traditions, cultures and maybe even different production systems and strategies may not be at all successful' (p. 239).

The dual system in Germany, and the reliance on internal markets in French and Italian companies, have been successful but only for those who have employment. The core problem of moving the unemployed, and in particular the long-term unemployed, into work has proved more problematic in these economies. Provision of the requisite skills for them to gain employment has been no easy task, and even if the skills *are* acquired there is no guarantee of work in regions where traditional industries have declined and little new industry has replaced it.

Regini (1995) has drawn attention to the diversity of strategies that companies use to gain competitive advantage, ranging through forms of flexible mass production (or mass customisation) to flexible specialisation, neo-Fordism, diversified quality production and the traditional small firm. Each will require its own mix of skills, and will in turn impose its own particular demands on the labour market, but at the same time will be subject to the characteristics of the existing supply of labour nationally and locally (Leat, 1998: 240). Institutional theorists would add that historical, cultural and institutional forces will also serve to shape the particular nature of a country or region's VET.

All this makes for considerable difficulties in meeting the aim of harmonisation of EU social policy, and given these constraints it is unlikely to see convergence within the near future. The Amsterdam Treaty's proposals imply a mix of approaches, finding a marriage point between EU suggested policy, local prevailing conditions, and responses to a rapidly changing global competitive environment.

Employee participation and involvement

A significant part of the social dialogue ardently advocated by the European Commission has been the strengthening of employee participation, and the European Works Council (EWC) has been seen to be a major institution to promote it. An important aim behind the social dialogue is that if a forum can help the major partners (Germany, France, the UK, Italy) to agree on proposals then it is more likely that the social agenda will be adopted, leading to a greater harmonisation of social policy across the community.

Experience suggests that this is stretching logic too far. Like many of the social proposals it is adhered to more in theory than in practice. The question of adopting EWC proposals has been contentious since the framing of the Social Charter, and the Directive was adopted in 1994 in the face of strong opposition from the employers' association UNICE. It was adopted by the Commission by a majority vote, but the closure of the Renault plant at Vilvoorde in Belgium has shown that its application in terms of the spirit intended still has some way to go. Subsequently a French court ruled that management should have informed employees and consulted about the proposed closure in advance.

The ETUC (European Trades Union Confederation) responded by demanding amendments to the EWC Directive that would tighten employees' rights by strengthening the terms on which information is given and consultation takes place. UNICE has made it clear that it would resist such proposals (Gilman and Weber, 1999).

The ETUC has pointed to five major areas of weakness in framing its proposals for amending the EWC Directive:

- a lack of clarity on the type of information and consultation, to be provided to employee representatives;
- a lack of recognition of the important role played by trade union representatives;
- insufficient resources for translations and preparatory meetings;
- prevalence of management control of the agenda of meetings;
- the limited competence of the EWCs.
  (Gilman and Weber, 1999: 424).

The last point has also been emphasised by Miller and Stirling (1998), who have highlighted the specific need for training for participants in transnational meetings of EWCs.

The picture is not entirely pessimistic, however, and research by Marginson *et al.* (1998) shows that multinational companies of French, German, British and American origin operating in the EU have a widespread preference for joint employer–employee bodies. While this points to a more hopeful future for works councils and by implication the social dialogue it does not really attest to a dialogue between equals.

Human resource management and the European Union

While speculation on the influence of the Social Charter on labour markets has fuelled a major debate, there has been little research into its actual influence on organisations. Research carried out by Wood and Peccei (1990) on the preparation of personnel strategies for the single European market (SEM) in British organisations showed that most firms did not perceive this as a critical issue. The minority of companies that did have some sort of human resource strategy were those already involved in EU trading, with more awareness of the need for policies for the SEM. However, many of these HR initiatives were business led, and 'more often than not are developed downstream from corporate strategy and are treated as "third order" within the strategic planning process' (Wood and Peccei, 1990: 84).

The Price Waterhouse Cranfield Project (1991) surveyed human resource initiatives in organisations across ten countries in Europe. While concern was expressed about the effects of the SEM, few organisations had developed a conscious strategy for the SEM, and even fewer had a human resource strategy for it. Most had positive policies on the Social Charter directives associated with equal opportunities and health and safety, but many of these policies had been established long before by national legislation. It would seem from these studies that most organisations will respond to the influences of the Social Charter and the SEM only when it is necessary to do so. Many HRM policies are still influenced by the attitudes of national governments towards enforcement of directives, which in turn rest on varying interpretations of the subsidiarity process.

However, despite a picture of relative parochialism in terms of organisational responses to the Social Charter and the SEM, the Price Waterhouse Cranfield Survey revealed many similar human resource trends taking place across Europe, despite the varying employee relations systems at both macro and micro levels. There are strong trends towards the decentralisation of human resource functions in terms of the devolvement to line management of recruitment and selection, training and development and other functions. However, in such areas as pay bargaining and industrial relations responsibility still resides very much in the personnel function and is strongly influenced by national bargaining structures, particularly in Germany and Sweden. Nevertheless, 'decentralisation in the level of decisions within the organisation and devolution to line management continues apace. Line management responsibility is increasing in all countries and for all subjects with the single exception of Italian industrial relations' (Price Waterhouse Cranfield Project, 1991: 8).

This seems to suggest that it is premature for EU initiatives to have had an influence on personnel and HR policies in organisations. It seems that organisations are still influenced more by their own particular markets and global trends in HRM than by regional initiatives. Thus local, national and international organisations have been influenced by many trends in HRM emanating from, in particular, the USA and Japan, but the extent and the ways in which these strategies are adopted depend on the size, sector, geographical distribution of the market, industrial relations and bargaining systems in which organisations are placed.

EASTERN EUROPE

Employee relations in the Central and Eastern European states (CEE) have been undergoing enormous change in the post-communist era since 1989. Two predominant views have emerged. The first perceives that most CEE countries are wedged in the transitional phase between the former Soviet system and a market economy (Blanchard *et al.*, 1991; EBRD, 1999). The second view, held by Martin and Cristesco-Martin (1999), holds that there is diminishing confidence in such a vision, and in some CEE countries 'the hybrid public/private ownership structures are assuming a continuing organisational form rather than a brief intermission between socialism and capitalism' (p. 387).

Changing nature of the CEE economies

In the post-communist collapse there was a widespread assumption that free market capitalism would bring the benefits so transparently obvious in the West: consumer products, full shops, a higher standard of living, and economic and political freedom. This was reinforced by a huge initial interest from Western businesses and governments, who saw the potential for cheap labour and ultimately a large new market to exploit. The immediate repercussion, however, was a steep rise in unemployment, accompanied by inflation and the undermining of currencies. The early 1990s witnessed a fall in standards of living for many people, and the emergence of poverty. Thousands of enterprises went into liquidation, unable to compete in open markets after being confronted with their inefficiencies (Blanchard *et al.*, 1991).

Responses to these changes have varied considerably throughout CEE countries, influenced by cultural and historical factors. The former Czechoslovakia and Hungary, which had developed industries before the advent of communism, have been able to use these pre-communist memories and experiences in the process of adaptation and change. Bulgaria, Romania, Albania and the newly constituted states of Yugoslavia, coming from peasant pre-communist conditions, had and are still having greater difficulties in constructing a modern economy (Smith and Thompson, 1992; Holden, 1993).

Channon and Dakin (1995) believe that the former Soviet states can now be divided into three regions according to geography, responses to and experiences of the post-communist world:

● Central Europe – the Czech Republic, Poland, Slovakia, Hungary and Slovenia, the Baltic States (Latvia, Lithuania and Estonia);
● Russia and the former Soviet Union;
● South-central region (the Balkans) – Romania, Bulgaria, Albania and the former Yugoslavia.

The Central European states have fared the best, partly because they have proved most attractive to foreign capital investment. The South-central region has been less attractive to capital investors, partly because of the rise of nationalist turbulence in the former Yugoslavia, but also because of the relatively underdeveloped nature of their economies.

Russia has in many ways proved the most difficult for foreign companies to deal with, because of the deep-rooted nature of the old communist system and its greater historical isolation from Western Europe:

> There was autocratic government and a peasant culture, with a strong tradition of collectivism and mutual support or patronage mechanisms in the face of a harsh external climate. This is a far more difficult culture in which to establish an operation, because there are no deep seated traditions of private enterprise or private property.
>
> (Channon and Dakin, 1995: 26)

The economic crisis that hit Russia in the late 1990s has also served to further undermine confidence, and there is a widespread view that privatisation has led to profiteering by the 'Mafiosi', leading to the plundering of state property and the widening of inequalities. Even the best performers of the CEE economies, the Czech Republic and Poland, were affected by the Russian crisis. Unemployment remains generally high, and is probably higher than the unreliable official statistics indicate. Wage levels, compared with the West, remain relatively low (Martin and Martin-Cristesco, 1999).

Employee relations in the 'new' economies

Trade union density is generally high but is in decline. Levels remain high partly because of the backlash against the hardships wrought by free market policies. As early as 1992 the old 'official' unions had fared the best, 'partly because of organisation, habit and resources, partly because they are the more consistent opponents of the new power' (Milne, 1992a). In the former Czechoslovakia unions have adapted to the changes comparatively well, and although membership fell immediately after the 'Velvet Revolution', it increased once again because of the fear of redundancies (Brewster, 1992). Subsequent rises in unemployment have, however, caused membership to fall, although not to previous levels, but the efficacy of the unions has not been aided by the attitude of the government, which is perceived by union officials to be hostile to the point of wishing them to be non-existent (Brewster, 1992).

In Poland, OPZZ, the old 'official' union organisation, while experiencing some decline, has been relatively successful in the long term compared with Solidarnost, which has witnessed a fall in membership from 10 million to below 2 million (Milne, 1992a). In Hungary the main union organisation, MSZOSZ, has fared less well, 'and is now less than half of its [communist government-controlled] predecessor SZOT' (Gill, 1990; Brewster, 1992). In Bulgaria a large independent trade union, Podkrepa, was created in the aftermath of the fall of the communist regime. Initially born out of the desire to defend workers' rights against communist abuse, it joined forces with a united front of anti-communist groups under the banner of the Union of Democratic Forces (UDF), but in the post-communist Bulgarian state has threatened and initiated strikes in protest at the undermining of its members' living standards (Holden, 1991).

In Russia the old unions remain the most important organisation representative of the workers. The Soviet All Union Council of Trade Unions (AUCTU) had 142 million members in 32 branch unions in 1990, although since then its membership has witnessed some decline (Lloyd, 1990). As one Moscow worker stated, 'most of us belong to the official trade unions, because there is no serious alternative' (Weir, 1992). As with many of the new non-communist governments in Eastern Europe, trade unions are not encouraged. In the initial desire to copy Western government practices many anti-union laws have been passed. For example, the draft law on collective agreements states that groups other than trade unions can participate in collective bargaining. As one Russian trade unionist states, 'Of course it undermines the position of the union. At any workplace or enterprise, the manager can say to the workers "Why do you need to join the union in order to have a collective agreement?"' (Cathcart, 1992).

Nevertheless, the unions have expressed dissatisfaction with government and organisational policies: strikes have occurred in Russia, Poland, Bulgaria and the former East Germany, and there was a particularly bitter coal strike in Romania in 1998–99. Government responses have not been encouraging, and the argument is regularly stated that industrial unrest will have the effect of discouraging foreign investment.

The future for trade unionism is not particularly optimistic, although the experience across CEE states has varied. Increased privatisation has helped to undermine union membership, and evolving industrial relations legislation by many governments has curbed trade union powers (Blanchard *et al.*, 1991; Smith and Thompson, 1992; Weir, 1992). Trade union influence at company level remains weak (Mason, 1995; Standing, 1997), and Western companies seek to exclude them, particularly on greenfield sites (Martin and Cristesco-Martin, 1999).

The rise of the tripartite system

Despite the difficulties that have faced the CEE economies, a form of tripartitism has emerged, with the state continuing to have a major influence on employment relations. This is partly because the state still remains a major employer, and it also sets the agenda for policy reforms. Martin and Martin-Cristesco (1999) define tripartitism as 'the institutional expression of the concept of social partnership' (p. 392). Under a tripartite system the government, employers and trade unions negotiate issues related to employment relations, such as wage bargaining, in order to come to some consensual agreement. Such systems create a forum for discussion, and reduce the potential for conflict and damaging disputes.

While trade union density remains high its influence at company level is limited. At national level trade unions have had more impact, particularly by the use of strikes to defend employees against redundancy when restructuring has taken place. Employers' associations, by contrast, remain weak, but management prerogative is strong at company level where collective bargaining takes place. This dichotomy is also one cause of the decline in union membership, as employees do not perceive their trade union representatives as being effective in collective bargaining. This is partly because trade unions in CEE countries have emerged from the old communist organisations, and have found difficulties in adapting to the free bargaining system, which requires their officials to have skills in negotiating and employee representation.

While tripartitism does not seem to serve employers and employees very well in the short term, it is a framework within which employment policy can be forged in the long term, and it can help to frame protections for both employees and employers. Sceptics, however, see it as 'a political shell for a neo-liberal economic strategy (Thirkell *et al.*, 1998: 166) – a guise for the introduction of anti-union legislation.

Tripartite institutions are stronger in some countries than in others. East Germany has unsurprisingly adopted it and adapted to it well, whereas in Hungary the industrial relations system is more decentralised and less likely to serve its members' interests (Frege and Tóth, 1999). Other observers are sceptical about the survival of tripartitism owing to the weakness of employer and employee associations and the decentralisation of economic management from the state to the enterprise (Mason,1995).

HRM and management in Eastern Europe

One of the main problems facing both economies and organisations is the change not only in organisational structures but also in management attitudes, which in many organisations remain locked in the old bureaucratic ways (Holden and Peck, 1990; Watts, 1991; Elenkov, 1998).

Attempts at reform in management practices were already under way in many Eastern European states before 1989, with patchy results. Management in post-communist society was seen as gaining the right to manage, unfettered by the shackles of the Communist Party, state and trade unions, and hence creating an efficient human resource capable of competing with Western countries (Landa, 1990). Not surprisingly, there has been a considerable emphasis on management development, with many Eastern European managers and academics forging links with Western business schools, universities, companies and organisations to set up business management courses of various kinds. There have been considerable problems, largely because of differences in attitudes and perceptions. Though many senior managers lost their positions after 1989 because of their associations with the communist system, others have thrived in the new atmosphere, holding on to their positions and making full use of their connections and networks built up under the old regimes (Meyer, 1990; Pieper, 1990; Elenkov, 1998; Kelemen, 1999).

Personnel and HRM continue to have a low priority in most CEE organisations; many training and recruitment functions are still entrenched in practices associated with the former regimes, although attempts to bring in payment systems linked to performance have been more successful (Landa, 1990; Koubek and Brewster, 1995; Kelemen, 1999). HRM practices are making headway, however, in foreign-owned subsidiaries that can operate fairly autonomously. In state-owned enterprises, and even in joint ventures, new management approaches remain relatively rare, although changes are beginning to take place.

Recently companies have given much more emphasis to HRM issues since initially having had their 'fingers burnt' by underestimating personnel problems. A survey conducted by the School of Slavonic Studies at London University and a corporate language training company, Communicaid, found that 'almost all HR directors and managers of 30 British companies questioned agreed that Western companies had generally underestimated cultural differences and their impact on the establishment of operations and the nature of the local workforce' (Channon and Dakin, 1995: 24). As a result, a number of recommendations are beginning to emerge for companies setting up and operating in Eastern Europe. Training of staff has become a high priority, and this includes not only training in work skills but also attitudinal training. Another problem is poaching: as some companies train, other companies will attract away workers with desirable skills by offering larger wages and salaries. This means that the compensation package also becomes important in retaining staff.

Another consideration is succession planning and the takeover of operations by host country staff from expatriate staff. Considerations of when and how this should take place are also important. It is vital to have 'connections' (someone who can 'fix' things, and who has contacts to smooth operations), especially in Russia and the South-central region (the Balkans). The system of patronage can cause difficulties in removing staff who may appear to no longer fit the job. In this respect recruitment and selection will prove crucial, but the criteria used in Western companies may not always be appropriate.

With the passage of over a decade since the fall of the Soviet systems in the CEE countries a diverse pattern is emerging based much more on the individual strengths of economies and their previous development. This trend will continue, and employment relations institutions and practices will vary increasingly between states. For example, the fragile tripartite system may survive in some countries but not in others. This will depend on the continuing strength of trade unions, the effectiveness of state interventions at macro level in the economy, the continuing weakness of employer organisations, and the way HRM practices are filtered through the back door of foreign companies at micro level.

SUMMARY

- Human resource management is a concept that is slowly becoming absorbed into the language of European models of personnel management, but within different institutional structures from those that obtain in the UK, the USA or Japan. Within many Western European countries there is a strong tradition of employee rights incorporated into state provision and the nature of the employment relationship. This explains the move towards social integration that dominated the EU agenda in the early 1990s. The advent of the single European market stimulated a debate about the proper role of a 'social dimension' in the operation of EU and the Maastricht Treaty, committing the EU to ever-closer monetary and political union.

- By the mid-1990s the debate within the EU concerning the pursuit of regulation or deregulation was set against the backdrop of a moribund Social Charter. The Amsterdam Treaty 1997 is an attempt to rejuvenate the social agenda through the adoption of a 'Third Way'.

- This has been reinforced by the recognition that the intensification of global competition has created the need for a much more proactive labour market to solve the problems of unemployment and skill shortages. This view has been embodied in the Amsterdam Treaty in terms of the four pillars: employability, adaptability, entrepreneurship, and equal opportunities.

- Nevertheless there is evidence that some common HRM developments are occurring across Europe within EU members as well as in those economies that are not as yet members. Among the more notable HRM shifts are those connected with the decentralisation of decision-making and the devolution to line managers of decisions relating to the management of employees, as well as increases in forms of flexible working.

- In Eastern and Central Europe the agenda for change has been sudden and large: the replacement of highly centralised state-run economies with the 'shock treatment' of market forces has led to vast upheaval in terms of unemployment.

- A form of tripartitism has emerged in most CEE states but in varying degrees of strength. Despite high union membership union influence is relatively weak, particularly at company level.

- Management attitudes in former communist countries have equally felt the stress of reform and the difficulty of transition to more market-orientated and less bureaucratic modes of operation. In these circumstances the very nature of HRM is a concept that has little currency. Most HRM innovations are being implemented in fully foreign-owned subsidiaries.

Hotel group in Poland

Kotel is a British-based hotel group that has recently acquired a group of five hotels in Poland. The board of the company is divided over which human resource strategy it should pursue. One board group, represented by the finance director and marketing director, wants to go for a policy whereby labour is recruited from other hotels at the cheapest possible price. The other group, represented by the human resource director and operations manager, desires a full HRM strategy based on careful recruitment and selection, with full training and development policies, and remuneration policies based on performance and quality of service.

1 Divide into three groups, two of these representing the two strategies proposed for the Kotel Group. Role-play a board meeting, with each group putting forward its views, backed by rational argument as to why their strategy should be adopted. A person should be selected to act as managing director to chair the meeting. The third group will act as neutral observers, with the power to question members of each group on their views. At the end of the meeting the third group will decide by vote which is the most convincing strategy to adopt.

2 Draw up a list of problems, particularly related to human resource and employment relationship issues, which would face the Kotel Group setting up its company in Poland.

QUESTIONS

1 What difficulties might there be in the operation of the principle of subsidiarity in enforcing the provisions of the Social Charter?

2 What are the main arguments for and against the regulationist and deregulationist views of labour market policy in the European Union?

3 How effective do you think the Amsterdam Treaty will be in producing solutions to unemployment in the European Union?

4 Can a tripartite system of employee relations survive in the former Soviet Central and Eastern European states?

CASE STUDY

A human resource strategy for Europump Ltd

Background

Europump is a UK-based engineering company specialising in hydraulic and pumping equipment. It was founded as a partnership by John Wall, an engineer, who has responsibility for research and development and the production side of the company; Bill Hodges, an accountant with managerial experience; and Paul Marceau, a manager experienced in the engineering business. The company was founded in 1976, saw considerable growth in the earlier years, and although experiencing some difficulties in the 1980s' recession survived to prosper in the late 1980s.

The board members have cultivated a profile of looking to the future, and with the imminence of the European Single Market in 1992 decided on expansion into continental Europe. A small subsidiary was set up in Lyons, France, in 1987, the founding of which was greatly facilitated by Paul Marceau, who speaks fluent French as a result of having a French father. The company quickly expanded and, influenced by this success, the UK board decided to set up another subsidiary in the Netherlands. Because of the specialised nature and excellent marketing of its products it was able to establish a successful medium-sized company in Groningen, which, while not enjoying the same degree of success as the UK and French companies, has managed to establish a market niche.

Structure of the company

The UK-based Northampton operation is situated on a greenfield site in a business park on the edge of the town, and employs 340 people, 35% of whom are in unions. Pay is in line with national trends in the engineering and related industries. There is a personnel department with three full-time and two part-time staff. The production department employs 295 people, making up the majority of the workforce.

The research and development department (R&D) employs 5 people, and the finance and marketing department 35 people. Some extra services in these areas are purchased on an agency or consultancy basis.

The French operation in Lyons, Europump (France), employs 200 people, with a composition in a similar ratio to that of the UK company in regard to departmental size and functions, although there is no R&D department. It has a French director, who is ultimately responsible to the UK board. Only 10% of the workforce is unionised, but pay reflects national standards. There is, however, a works council that conforms to French law.

The Dutch operation (Europump AB) employs 175 people with a similar composition to the French organisation in terms of size and function; 25% of the workforce is unionised, and there is a works council in operation.

Developments since 1990

In 1993 Europump opened a subsidiary near Barcelona employing initially 20 workers, and since 1996 the workforce has increased to 50. They are paid in line with local engineering pay rates. While Europump Ltd as a whole enjoyed considerable success in the 1990s, the recession in the early part of the decade affected sales badly, particularly in the UK. As a result, redundancies occurred in all the European operations but particularly so in Northampton. In the post-redundancy period from 1996 on, the UK HQ has increasingly introduced various forms of flexibility. It has pursued functional flexibility backed by considerable training and development for employees. But it has also introduced atypical working in the form of short-time and temporary contracts and the increasing use of agency staff.

While this has brought down production costs and has greatly helped in increasing company profits, it has not pleased the union, which views this as a threat to its membership and, it claims, has had a derogatory effect on its members' conditions.

Performance management has also been introduced, with the result that there are now varied pay packages based much more on individual effort. Again, the unions are not happy with this situation.

The UK board decided to invite the directors and personnel managers to an international board meeting in a London hotel to hammer out an HRM policy for the organisation as a whole. While all the board are 'good' Europeans, John and Bill hold the view that EU social policy can be detrimental to the company's future. Paul, however, believes that following EU social policy will pave the way for more harmonised and harmonious working conditions within the company. At the end of the meeting it was decided to ask Jane Lawson, the UK HRM manager, to prepare a report for the extension of the British HR policy to the European subsidiaries.

1 What problems might Jane Lawson, the UK HRM manager, envisage in extending the proposals for flexible working practices and performance management to the company's subsidiaries in France, the Netherlands and Spain?

2 What suggestions could she make to overcome these difficulties, given the high union density and existence of works councils in these countries?

REFERENCES AND FURTHER READING

Those texts marked with an asterisk are particularly recommended for further reading (but bear in mind that books on
the European Union quickly become out of date). The issues
covered in this chapter are also addressed in Chapters 3, 8,
13 and 15.

Addison, J.T. and Siebert, W.S. (1991) 'The Social Charter of
the European Community: evolution and controversies',
Industrial and Labor Relations Review, Vol. 44, No. 4, 597–625.

Addison, J.T. and Siebert, W. S. (1992) 'The Social Charter:
whatever next?', *British Journal of Industrial Relations*,
Vol. 30, No. 4, pp. 495–513.

*Addison, J.T. and Siebert, W. S. (eds) (1997) *Labour Markets
in Europe: Issues in Harmonisation and Regulation*. London:
Dryden.

*Adnett, N. (1996) *European Labour Markets: Analysis and
Policy*. London: Longman.

Baglioni, G. and Crouch, C. (eds) (1990) *European Industrial
Relations: The Challenge of Flexibility*. London: Sage.

Barnard, C. and Deakin, S. (1999) 'A year of living danger-
ously? EC social right, employment policy and EMU',
Industrial Relations Journal, Vol. 30, No. 4, pp. 355–372.

Blanchard, O., Dornbusch, R., Krugman, P., Layard, R. and
Summers, L. (1991) *Reform in Eastern Europe*. Cambridge,
Mass.: MIT Press.

Brewster, C. (1992) 'Starting again: industrial relations in
Czechoslovakia', *International Journal of Human Resource
Management*, Vol. 3, No. 3, pp. 555–574.

Brewster, C. and Hegewisch, A. (1994) *Policy and Practice in
European Human Resource Management*. London: Routledge.

Brewster, C., Hegewisch, L., Holden, L. and Lockhart, T
(eds) (1992) *The European Guide to Human Resource
Management*. London: Academic Press.

Butt Philips, A. (1988) 'Management and 1992: illusions
and reality', *European Management Journal*, Vol. 6, No. 4,
pp. 345–350.

Cathcart, R. (1992) 'Struggling to survive in the "free"
market', *Morning Star*, 16 May, p. 3.

Channon, J. and Dakin, A. (1995) 'Coming to terms with
local people', *People Management*, 15 June, pp. 24–29.

Clark, T. (ed) (1996) *European Human Resource Management*.
Oxford: Blackwell.

Crouch, C. (1996) 'Revised diversity: the neo-liberal decade
to beyond Maastricht', in Van Ruysseveldt, J. and Visser, J.
(eds) *Industrial Relations in Europe: Traditions and
Transitions*. London: Sage, pp. 337–357.

EBRD (1999) *Transition Report, 1998*. London: European
Bank for Reconstruction and Development.

Elenkov, D. (1998) 'Can American management concepts
work in Russia? A cross-country comparative study',
California Management Review, Vol. 40, No. 4, pp. 133–156.

European Commission (1999) 'Forum special: 5 years of
social policy', *Employment and Social Affairs*. Brussels:
European Commission.

Ferner, A. and Hyman, R. (eds) (1992) *Industrial Relations in
the New Europe*. Oxford: Blackwell.

*Ferner, A. and Hyman, R. (eds) (1998) *Changing Industrial
Relations in Europe*. Oxford: Blackwell.

Frege, C. and Tóth, A. (1999) 'Institutions matter: union solidarity in Hungary and Eastern Germany', *British Journal of
Industrial Relations*, Vol. 37, No. 1, pp. 117–140.

Gill, C. (1990) 'The new independent trade unionism in
Hungary', *Industrial Relations Journal*, Vol. 21, No. 3,
pp. 14–25.

Gilman, M. and Weber, T. (1999) 'European industrial relations in 1998: chronicle of events', *Industrial Relations*,
Vol. 30, No. 4, pp. 387–404.

Gold, M. (ed.) (1993) *The Social Dimension: Employment Policy
in the European Union*. Basingstoke: Macmillan.

Goodhart, D. (1992) 'Community's social action plans
succumb to sabotage and recession', *Financial Times*,
19 November, p. 8.

Goodhart, D. (1993) 'Social dumping: hardly an open and
shut case', *Financial Times*, 4 February, p. 9.

Gospel, H. (1992) 'The Single European Market and industrial relations', *British Journal of Industrial Relations*, Vol. 30,
No. 4, pp. 483–494.

Hegewich, A. and Brewster, C. (eds) (1993) *European
Developments in Human Resource Management*. London:
Kogan Page.

Holden, L. (1991) *Bulgaria, Perestroika, Glasnost and
Management*. Cranfield School of Management Working
Paper SWP 14/91.

Holden, L. (1993) 'Bulgaria: economic and political
change', *Critique: Journal of Socialist Theory*, No. 25,
pp. 133–143.

Holden, L. and Peck, H. (1990) 'Perestroika, glasnost, management and trade', *European Business Review*, Vol. 90,
No. 2, pp. 26–31.

Hughes, J. (1991) *The Social Charter and the Single European
Market*. Nottingham: Spokesman.

Hyman, R. and Ferner, A. (eds) (1994) *New Frontiers in
European Industrial Relations*. Oxford: Blackwell

Jackson, T. (1993) 'Footloose across Europe's frontiers',
Financial Times, 9 March.

Kelemen, M. (1999) 'The myth of restructuring "competent"
managers and the transition to a market economy: a
Romanian tale', *British Journal of Management*, Vol. 10,
No. 3, pp. 199–208.

Keller, B. and Sörries, B. (1999) 'Sectorial dialogues: new
opportunities more impasses?', *Industrial Relations Journal*,
Vol. 30, No. 4, pp. 330–343.

Kirkbride, P. (ed) (1994) *Human Resource Management in
Europe*. London: Routledge.

Koubek, J. and Brewster, C. (1995) 'Human resource man-
agement in turbulent times: HRM in the Czech Republic',
International Journal of Human Resource Management, Vol. 6,
No. 2, pp. 223–247.

Labour Market Trends (1998) London: The Stationery Office,
106, 2, S40.

Labour Market Trends (1999) London: The Stationery Office,
107, 3, S46.

Landa, O. (1990) 'Human resource management in
Czechoslovakia: management development as the key
issue', in Pieper, R. (ed.) *Human Resource Management: An*

International Comparison. New York: Walter de Gruyter, pp. 155–176.

Lane, C. (1989) *Managment and Labour in Europe.* Aldershot: Edward Elgar.

*Leat, M. (1998) *Human Resource Issues of the European Union.* London: Financial Times/Pitman.

Lloyd, J. (1990) 'Trade unions: a tough transition', *Financial Times,* Soviet Union Supplement, 12 March, p. 10.

Lockhart, T. and Brewster, C., (1992) 'Human resource management in the European Community', in Brewster, C., Hegewisch, A., Holden, L. and Lockhart, T. (eds) *The European Human Resource Management Guide.* London: Academic Press, pp. 6–41.

Marginson, P., Gilman, M., Jacobi, O. and Krieger, H. (1998) *Negotiating Works Councils: An Analysis of Agreements Under Article 13.* Dublin: European Foundation.

Marsland, D. (1991) 'The Social Charter: rights and wrongs', *The Salisbury Review,* June, pp. 16–18.

Martin, R. and Cristesco-Martin, A. (1999) Industrial relations in transformation: Central and Eastern Europe in 1998', *Industrial Relations Journal,* Vol. 30, No. 4, pp. 387–402.

Mason, B. (1995) 'Industrial relations in the unstable environment: the case of Central and Eastern Europe', *European Journal of Industrial Relations,* Vol. 1, No. 3, pp. 341–367.

Meyer, H. (1990) 'Human resource management in the German Democratic Republic: problems of availability and the use of manpower potential in the sphere of the high qualification spectrum in a retrospective view', in Pieper, R. (ed.) *Human Resource Management: An International Comparison.* New York: Walter de Gruyter, pp. 177–194.

Miller, D. and Stirling, J. (1998) 'European works council training: an opportunity missed?' *European Journal of Industrial Relations,* Vol. 4, No. 1, pp. 35–56.

Milne, A. (1992a) 'The past with a punch', the *Guardian,* 13 March, p. 14.

Milne, A. (1992b) 'Delors' social Europe is workers' paradise lost', the *Guardian,* 14 November, p. 13.

Piachaud, D. (1991) 'A Euro-Charter for confusion', the *Guardian,* 13 November, p. 12.

Pieper, R. (1990) 'The history of business administration and management education in the two Germanies: a comparative approach', *International Journal of Human Resource Management,* Vol. 1, No. 2, pp. 211–229.

Pierson, C., Forster, A. and Jones, E. (1999) 'Politics of Europe 1999. Changing the guard in the European Union: in with the new, out with the old?', *Industrial Relations Journal,* Vol. 30, No. 4, pp. 277–290.

Price Waterhouse Cranfield Project (1991) *Report on International Strategic Human Resource Management.* Cranfield: Cranfield School of Management.

Rees, T. (1998) *Mainstreaming Equality in the European Union:*

Education, Training and Labour Market Policies. London: Routledge.

Regini, M. (1995) 'Firms and institutions: the demand for skills and their social production in Europe', *European Journal of Industrial Relations,* Vol. 1, No. 2, pp. 191–202.

Sapsford, D., Bradley, S., Elliott, C. and Millington, J. (1999) 'The European economy: labour market efficiency, privatisation and minimum wages', *Industrial Relations Journal,* Vol. 30, No. 4, pp. 291–312.

Singh, R. (1999) 'European Community employment law: key recent cases and their implications for the UK', *Industrial Relations Journal,* Vol. 30, No. 4, pp. 273–386.

Smith, C. and Thompson, P. (1992) *Labour in Transition: The Labour Process in Eastern Europe and China.* London: Routledge.

Sparrow, P. and Hiltrop, J.M. (1994) *European Human Resource Mangement in Transition.* Hemel Hemptead: Prentice Hall.

Standing, G. (1997) 'Labour market governance in Eastern Europe', *European Journal of Industrial Relations,* Vol. 3, No. 2, pp. 133–159.

Teague, P. (1991) 'Human resource management, labour market institutions and European integration', *Human Resource Management Journal,* Vol. 2, No. 1, pp. 1–21.

*Thirkell, J., Petkov, K. and Vickerstaff, S. (1998) *The Transformation of Labour Relations: Restructuring and Privatization in Eastern Europe and Russia.* Oxford: Oxford University Press.

Towers, B. and Terry, M. (1999) 'Editorial: Unemployment and social dialogue', *Industrial Relations Journal,* Vol. 30, No. 4, pp. 272–275.

Traxler, F. (1999) 'Employers and employer organisations: the case of governability', *Industrial Relations Journal,* Vol. 30, No. 4, pp. 345–354.

Twenty Twenty Television (1993) 'The secret children', in the *Storyline Series* for Carlton Television.

Van Ruysseveldt, J. and Visser, J. (eds) (1996) *Industrial Relations in Europe: Traditions and Transitions.* London: Sage.

Watts, S. (1991) 'Clasping the competitive nettle', *The Times,* 1 August, p. 22.

Weir, F. (1992) 'When thunder roars', *Morning Star,* 9 May, p. 3.

Weston, C. (1993) 'Whitehall farce over EC job directive row', the *Guardian,* 23 March, p. 8.

Willman, J. (1993) 'EC laws "will not delay tendering", *Financial Times,* 12 March, p. 4.

Wise, M. and Gibb, R. (1992) *A Single Market to a Social Europe.* London: Longman.

Wood, S. and Peccei, R. (1990) 'Preparing for 1992? Business-led versus strategic human resource management', *Human Resource Management Journal,* Vol. 1, No. 1, pp. 63–89.

17

Human resource management in Asia

Len Holden and Linda Glover

OBJECTIVES

- To explore the extent of convergence of HRM practices in the Asia region.
- To examine the origins of and recent developments in Japanese human resource management.
- To explain the developments of human resource management in the People's Republic of China and Hong Kong.
- To explore the developments in human resource management in Singapore and South Korea as examples of the growing 'tiger' economies.

INTRODUCTION

This chapter will examine the growth of some of the main Asian economies and in particular explore their human resource practices. Japan has become an exemplar of and model for HRM practices, and is the subject of so many published works that the observation of its organisational working practices has become an industry in itself, despite recent severe setbacks to the Japanese economy. Hong Kong has also witnessed extraordinary growth over the past 20 years, and has become a major centre in Asia for commerce and finance despite its absorption into the communist mainland regime. The People's Republic of China (PRC) has potentially the largest market in the world in terms of population, and foreign investors have been keen to gain a foothold there. Foreign companies have set up manufacturing bases and established joint ventures, and the export of Chinese goods has seen a huge expansion. This is an economy with an enormous potential. Its management processes have not been scrutinised to the same extent as the Japanese systems, but there is a burgeoning literature on management and HRM in China.

In addition Singapore and South Korea are examined here as examples of other 'tiger' economies in the region, although space limits further investigation of important Asia Pacific economies such as Australia, India, Indonesia, Malaysia, New Zealand, the Philippines, Taiwan and Thailand.

Convergence or divergence in the Asia Pacific Rim?

The assumption in the past was that management and employee relation practices could be transposed to any international context with requisite training and the implementation of proper systems of management, usually American. Another assumption by many Westerners was that Asian cultural influences on management could largely be ignored. This was a perspective strongly informed by imperialist attitudes that assumed that what was good for Western economies could automatically be transplanted into any sociocultural context. As has already been noted in Chapter 15 on international HRM, these convergence assumptions have been rigorously challenged by divergence theorists from a cultural and institutional perspective, as well as by Whitley (1992) and his followers, who believe that each national context throws up its own unique business system. However, more recently there has been a return to the convergence view, much influenced by the phenomenon of 'globalisation' (a concept still largely ill defined and subject to much misunderstanding) and the relative decline of Japan in relation to the United States in the latter part of the 1990s. Separating and analysing the relative strength of convergent and divergent variables of international HRM has become the main focus of a number of studies in the Asia Pacific region (Warner, 1993; Easterby-Smith *et al.*, 1995; Leggett and Bamber, 1996; Paik *et al.*, 1996; Rowley, 1997; Sparrow and Wu, 1999; Warner, 2000).

Recent studies that have examined the specific question of divergence and convergence in the Asia Pacific region have come to the general conclusion that divergence of HRM practices remains predominant (Leggett and Bamber, 1996; Rowley, 1997; Warner, 2000). This is due to sociocultural differences, varied investment patterns and financial institutional practices, and political and historical factors that have led to different stages of economic development. Leggett and Bamber (1996) claim that despite enormous growth, high investment from foreign companies and closer cooperation through the Association of South East Asian Nations (ASEAN) and the Asia-Pacific Economic Cooperation (APEC) forum, Asia Pacific economies diverge into three tiers or levels of development. The top tier, led predominantly by Japan, also includes Australia, Hong Kong, New Zealand, Singapore, Taiwan and South Korea. The non-Anglo-Saxon countries are generally known as the *Asian tigers*, and are made up of what has come to be called *newly industrialised economies* (NIEs). These have witnessed impressive growth rates in their economies over the past 20 years, and are moving into a second phase of development where the reliance on cheap labour is being superseded by investment in high technology and service industries.

The second tier is a second generation of tigers, comprising Malaysia, the PRC and Thailand. They reflect the earlier experience of the older tigers, and are at present at the stage of being 'caught in a "sandwich trap" of cheap labour competition from below and exclusion from higher value-added markets from above' (Deyo, 1995: 23).

The third tier, made up of Burma, India, Indonesia, the Philippines and Vietnam, comprises a diverse range of economies that have not reached the overall developmental stages of the first two tiers. Sections of the Indian economy, however, have experienced enormous growth in the past ten years, albeit from a comparatively low base, and some sectors are highly developed. What characterises this tier is the availability and abundance of cheap and unskilled labour. Nevertheless, to put these economies into one all-embracing category does not do justice to the diversity of their cultures, nor the political and social structures that create their unique business systems. As Warner (2000) states: 'There is hardly any evidence to support the classic convergence hypothesis . . . it is hard to argue that Asian HRM is fast converging to a common model' (p. 177). In separating forms of convergence into 'hard' and 'soft' ('hard' being labour market and economic influences exemplified by deregulation and privatisation and institutional structures, and 'soft' being more concerned with sociocultural variables) Warner (2000) concludes that

> the Asia-Pacific model is far from homogeneous [and that there is] a vast range of geographical and demographic variation. The economic systems range from emerging from a communist planned economy to fully fledged liberalised market-based ones. The political systems also differ greatly, as do the social arrangements. There is probably less cultural variation but more variety than acknowledged by many writers in the field. There is in this sense a fair degree of residual cultural diversity in the Asia-Pacific region that is likely to continue into the new millennium. On the other hand, if there is a common direction in which the HR systems are moving, it is most likely to be towards business restructuring, deregulation and liberalisation vis-à-vis the challenges of globalisation.
>
> (p. 181)

In studying the management practices of the five Asian countries in this chapter we are also studying the uniqueness of each business system – the factors that make Chinese systems in Hong Kong different from those of the PRC and of Japan. We begin by examining the Japanese business system from the perspective of its human resource management practices.

JAPAN: ECONOMIC GROWTH AND HRM

In the 1970s and 1980s the Japanese economy and its managerial and working practices came under intense investigation, mainly because of the phenomenal growth in its economy led by a number of Japanese multinationals in the vehicle and electronic industries. Incursions were made into previously dominated European and US markets, and by the 1980s according to Vogel (1980) Japan had become 'number one nation' by outstripping American growth. The Japanese phenomenon generated an entire literature devoted to understanding and explaining this miracle, ranging from prescriptive eulogistic texts such as Ouchi's (1981) *Theory Z* to more critical analyses rooted in careful research (Dore, 1973; Gerlach, 1992). Much of this literature concentrated on the role of human resource management in creating higher Japanese employee productivity, product quality and company expansion. This has usually been encapsulated in the pattern of employee relations in the form of the *three pillars*: lifetime employment, the seniority system (*nenko*) and enterprise unionism. However, this simplistic view of the Japanese system of employee relations has been criticised by numerous observers from various positions including historical, cultural, economic and labour market perspectives (Berggren and Nomura, 1997; Sako and Sato, 1997).

The classical Japanese model: the three pillars

The basis for the three-pillar approach has been described by Abegglen and Stalk (1987) thus:

> First, the employee is hired directly from school, rather than from an open job market. Second, he [sic] is hired for his general characteristics and abilities, rather than for a particular skill or a particular job. Third, he is expected to remain with the company for a lifelong career and in turn expects not to be laid off or discharged.
>
> (p. 199)

The establishment of enterprise unionism

The company is also the basic unit for employee representation through company unionism, which forms the third pillar of the Japanese employee relations system, together with lifetime employment and the seniority wage system. While industrial unions exist in Japan, most large corporations allow only one union based around the enterprise itself.

The origins of enterprise unionism date back to the 1920s (Gordon, 1985), although the system as we recognise it today stems from the period after the Second World War. The American occupation enacted a trade union law allowing trade unions the right to exist with full legal rights, and by 1949 trade union density had risen to 56%, but by the late 1980s had fallen to 27% (Tsuru and Rebitzer, 1995).

There are two major controversial reasons for this growth and decline in trade unions. Growth took place after the Second World War. First, workers wanted to safeguard their rights amid the collapse of the industrial structure and wholesale inflation. Second, for the first time blue-collar and white-collar workers cooperated in controlling production for the sake of their own living standards. It therefore made sense to combine into one enterprise union. Third, the unions demanded a number of conditions:

- removal of the old grades and status;
- job security;
- reform of management organisation;
- the setting up of participation systems;
- recognition of the unions;
- the right to negotiate and conduct labour agreements;
- the democratisation of management;
- expansion of workers' rights.

The best way for the two groups of workers (white and blue collar) to cooperate to gain and maintain these initiatives was at the enterprise level.

Employers also encouraged enterprise unions, primarily because in the 1950s there was high employment and high demand for labour in a rapidly expanding economy. However, employers also saw the advantages of promoting enterprise unionism, and they ensured that labour relations were conducted vertically, thus weakening the horizontal solidarity of the workers. It also emphasised cooperation in the workplace: supporting the desire for consensus made it easier to remove workers who propagated radical ideas and were aggressive towards management. This also had the effect of creating a unitarist style of organisation.

However, the path of industrial relations was not always smooth, and up to the 1960s there were often disputes, sometimes of a violent nature. The cooperative industrial relations that have been identified with Japanese management style only began in, and developed after, the 1960s. Thus the so-called 'traditional model' is really quite a recent phenomenon.

The decline in union density began after 1975, and a number of reasons for this have been put forward by Tsuru and Rebitzer (1995). First, and most important, has been the inability of unions to organise in new firms. Second, unions have had a limited effect on wage levels. This perceived lack of influence limits the attractiveness of union membership. The non-effectiveness of unions, particularly in times of crisis, as in the recessions of the 1970s and the 1990s, has shown the unions to be 'overly accommodating' to the employer's position rather than rigorously protecting their members.

Community consciousness

Enterprise unionism has thus been seen to be synonymous with unitarist HRM practices, reinforcing company objectives and allowing for only limited independent action on behalf of the workforce. This paternalist nature of large Japanese corporations creates an understanding between employer and employed. Sako (1997) describes this relationship as existing within a community – that is, the corporation:

> For a community to be viable, there has to be a two way process between management and workers. In particular not only should the firm offer employment security and a career to its employees, the employees must also expect employment security and identify with the firm. The boundary of a firm as community, and hence the criterion for full membership in the community, are defined by the matching in mutual expectations between the firms and its employees. (p. 4)

Sako (1997) believes that this mutual interest between employer and employee cannot be expressed in terms of the psychological contract, which has elements of instrumental bargaining rather than shared values, or even common interest (p. 5). A more apposite description he believes is the term *community consciousness*, in that employees identify closely with the organisation, and the 'community' extends beyond the firm into shaping individual identity, and influences life beyond the workplace itself. In return for this employment security the company expects worker commitment and flexibility.

This community consciousness is reinforced by internal labour markets that encourage the development of employees through training and development, mentoring, and teamworking, leading to progression through the organisation, until 55 or 60 years of age when the intensity of work is reduced in preparation for retirement. Promotion is based heavily on seniority, as are wages and salaries and other forms of remuneration. However, *nenko* is not just about seniority; it is also increasingly about merit. Within the first 10 or 15 years of employment each employee cohort will move together, but after that promotion is based on merit. This gives management a long period to screen people for selection to senior positions.

This community consciousness is also reinforced by employee participation at workplace levels. This form of participation (*ringi*) is less about workplace democracy in the Western sense and more about reaching consensus (*nemawashi*) and harmony (*wa*) in the decision-making processes.

Perspectives on Japanese HRM

This view of the classical Japanese model of HRM is, of course, simplistic, and critics of the system have challenged the outward appearances of harmony and cooperation, particularly in the light of the economic crisis that began in the 1990s and is continuing into the new millennium. In 1999 unemployment had risen from a consistently low level to 5% and probably double that for young workers, and the percentage of temporary and part-time workers rose to 7% (Japan Labour Bulletin, 1999d). Before examining some of these criticisms it is appropriate to explain how the Japanese classical model originated and developed.

Analytical approaches to understanding the Japanese system of HRM

In general four approaches have been to taken in analysing the origins, influences and development of Japanese HRM: history and tradition, the influence of culture on work attitudes, industrialisation as bound up with the 'late developer' thesis, and politico-economic arguments (Stam, 1982). Others might describe these influences as cultural, institutional and politico-economic influences, or attribute developments to the unique business system of Japan that incorporates most of these factors (Whitley, 1992).

The historical view

This view emphasises the unique historical context within which Japanese HRM has emerged, and highlights the pre-industrial influences of the Samurai as an elite group in a feudal society, with its emphasis on fealty (duty and loyalty) and a strict code of conduct, the *Bushido* – the way of the warrior. In a sense the continuity through history lies in the development of large family-owned companies, the *zaibatsu*, which acted as small fiefdoms that emphasised these historical values.

This feudal form of managerial 'familyism' (the organisation perceived as one big family) was a means of integrating employees into the quickly expanding enterprises. After the First World War this was extended to include *welfare corporatism*, in which the enterprise provided protection through welfare measures as befits family duty.

The cultural view

The cultural view incorporates some of the concepts of the historical perspective, and in reality they cannot be separated.

Geographical and commercial isolation until the late nineteenth century, and racial and linguistic homogeneity, have resulted in a unique culture in which the Japanese strongly value the social nexus or social structure in which they function. This can be in either the family, a circle of school friends or the company where one works. Such bonding groups provide certainty and security.

Second, there is a strong emphasis on anti-individualism. In other words the group has a strong priority over the individual. This can be associated with Hofstede's and Trompenaars' forms of collectivism as the opposite characteristic to individualism. These relations are structured through hierarchy in the enterprise. However, while different grades of status exist, all members of the organisational community are valued.

Third, and as we have already noted, harmony and consensus are significant in Japanese culture. The importance of preserving these values is reflected in the intensive informational and communication networks within and between groups in the organisation. Nothing is acted upon until consensus has been reached (see Chapter 13 on employee involvement for further reference to this). Group orientation and consensus support loyalty to the enterprise and further act to underpin lifetime employment and collective responsibility.

The late developer view

This is often associated with the institutional and business systems perspective of HRM. The work of Dore (1973) proved seminal in developing this perspective in his examination of the origins of national diversity in industrial relations in a comparative analysis of Britain and Japan. In essence this view maintains that countries that start to industrialise late show a number of specific institutional and organisational characteristics caused by the fact that they can benefit from the experiences of their industrial predecessors. The state's role in helping to foment the conditions favourable for enterprise growth is also significant. The Meji governments of the late nineteenth century set up the core of Japanese industry, transferred it to private interests, and provided these enterprises with government contracts. These eventually developed into the *zaibatsu*, such as Mitsui, Mitsubishi and Sumitomo. Companies formed after the Second World

War, such as Matsushita, Sony and Honda, in having to adapt quickly to expansion adopted the models of corporate structure that already existed, and became part of the mutual nurturing growth mechanism between the state and large private corporations.

These large enterprises allow no direct personal relationships to develop, instead of which an extensive administrative apparatus is required. Standardisation and formalisation in the Japanese enterprises have led to precise relations, ranging from a clear-cut career structure based on *nenko* (seniority) to a diversity of benefits such as allowances for housing, family and study. From the 1920s this developed into a form of welfare corporatism in which the company performs many of the welfare functions that in other industrial economies are performed by the state. This has the effect of binding the workforce into the objectives, values and culture of the company. The nurturing relationship of the state and companies is thus important in the late developer's view of how corporate HRM systems develop in Japan.

The politico–economic view

As with the historical and cultural views there is a considerable degree of overlap between the late developer view and the politico-economic view. Both emphasise, for example, the importance of the role of the state in developing privately owned capitalist enterprises. This form of development has often been called *alliance capitalism* (Gerlach, 1992; Berggren and Nomura, 1997). Another feature of alliance capitalism is the weaker control of shareholders over managerial decision and company strategy formulation compared with American and British companies. Whereas US and UK companies are conscious of the requirement to provide high dividends for their shareholders in the short term, Japanese corporations have been less subject to these immediate financial pressures, and can consequently indulge more effectively in long-term strategy making.

This in turn enables them to take a long-term view in considering HRM policy and practice, and two of the three pillars – lifetime employment and the seniority system – could only exist within such a politico-economic national context.

Criticisms of the Japanese system

There have been many observers who have been sceptical of the Japanese miracle and its ability to last. These views command a wide breadth of opinion in the politico-economic spectrum.

Left-wing critics tend to the view that the Japanese system has been strongly bolstered by American capital since the Second World War as a bulwark against communism, especially in the wake of the fall of China to Mao Zedong's forces in 1949. American wealth in essence nurtured and sustained the 'miracle' for essentially political reasons.

Other commentators in a similar vein have criticised the three-pillar model as being only partly representative of the workforce of Japan as a whole, as it excludes peripheral workers, many blue-collar workers, women, and those who do not work for large corporations, where the model predominantly operates. Small-firm suppliers, it is claimed, bear the exploitative costs of the system, where workers lack the security of the large corporations, and are often the first to be made redundant in times of restructuring. Chalmers (1989) also found clear divisions between core and peripheral workers. Peripheral workers tended to be segmented by age, gender, education and skill, and they were most likely to exist in small firms. Recent critics have claimed that Japanese companies cannot sustain the expensive three-pillar model in the face of recent financial and economic disasters. Benson (1996) believes that limiting the core of workers in corporations, emphasising the greater number of peripheral workers, and operating

714

lean practices with smaller supplier firms, is a labour strategy to offload the high costs of lifetime employment and the seniority wage system. One extreme American critic, Kroll (1993), claims that the 'final, frantic climax of capitalism without cost' ended with the collapse of the 'bubble economy' in 1986–90. He also claims that the low-cost capital that accounted for Japan's unique HRM systems could not be sustained after this period, and that Japanese companies will have to compete on Western terms – another slant on the convergence view.

Other commentators believe that this view is a gross exaggeration. Kawakita (1997) claims that while Japanese companies have been adapting their strategies to changes in the economy, with for example increases in peripheral workers, this must be seen in context. The high cost of the three-pillar system has been recognised by employers for a long time, but there is still a strong belief that companies do not lay off redundant workers as this would destroy the whole psychological basis of the high-trust work system that has been so painstakingly built up. Companies thus proceed with caution even in times of crisis, and resort to large-scale redundancies and restructuring only when no other course can be taken. Berggren and Nomura (1997) also believe that the system with adaptations is still resilient.

Free-market critics emphasise the obstructive forces posed by Japanese governments to free trade: the imposition of barriers on foreign imports, while Western economies accept Japanese goods, and also welcome Japanese investment. This lack of free trade reciprocation came under fire by US critics in the 1980s when Japan overtook the US lead in terms of growth.

Recent trends in Japanese HRM

There has been an awareness for some time of the negative influence of demographic trends and increased globalisation on the Japanese economy and labour market. The population is ageing, and this is having and will continue to have enormous implications for human resource policy and practice in Japanese companies.

As Table 17.1 indicates, there is an older labour force and fewer young people entering the labour market. This is putting, and will continue to put, a strain on the pensions system and the *nenko* system as remuneration rises with age. There is a shortage of senior positions. There has also been a significant increase in female labour participation, and new technology has replaced a considerable number of jobs. The rise of the service sector and relative decline of the older industries has also had an impact on the economy (Sano, 1993). Highly educated younger workers are less likely to stay with one company for long periods, thus creating greater fluidity in the labour markets.

There is also a significant and growing number of female workers who are seeking senior positions and a career structure. There has been a considerable increase of women in the expanding service sector such as banking, retailing, insurance, especially

Table 17.1 The Japanese population and labour force

	Population			Labour force		
Year	1980	1990	2000[a]	1980	1990	2000[a]
Age 55 or over (%)	17.7	23.6	28.7	16.1	20.2	23.6
Age 65 or over (%)	9.1	12.0	16.3	4.9	5.6	8.0

[a] Estimates
Source: Sasajima (1993).

in the 25–29 age group. Women's rising level of education, the drive for equal opportunities, and female take-up in employment have increased pressures for equal opportunities policies. This was backed by equal opportunities legislation in 1985, and companies are now required to provide equal opportunities in recruitment, employment, work assignments and promotion. The law also forbids sexual discrimination with regard to training and education, employee welfare benefits, retirement age, resignations and dismissals. This is further supported by the provision of child care leave.

The traditional internal labour markets of large Japanese corporations are at a turning point, and some characteristics that were considered unique to Japanese companies may be disappearing. The hierarchical structure of companies has been considerably flattened, and formerly bureaucratic organisations have become more flexible units, with project teams working with subsidiary and subcontracting companies. The compensation system is also changing to cope with these influences. Shibata (2000) states that 'generally it appears that employees' age and seniority have become less important while their performance has become more influential in Japanese wage determination' (p. 312). As Table 17.2 indicates, Sano (1993) has systematised these changes.

A solution to the problem of the ageing work force has been raising the pensionable age. In 1985 the retirement age was raised to 60 years, with the possibility of its being raised to 65 years in the future. As we have already noted, there have been modifications to the seniority wage system. Many companies have now set an age where wages start decreasing, or at least increasing at a rate less than average. There have also been revisions to the retirement benefits policy – for example, reducing the proportion of salary that makes up the lump sum received on retirement.

Because there are not enough senior positions for the 'baby boomer' generation (those born after the Second World War and now aged 40 and over) many companies are beginning to emphasise ability and other factors besides age and service for promotion. Many companies are requiring resignation from a senior position at a certain age to make room for younger managers.

Some observers believe that, as a result of these changes, it will spell the end of the classic Japanese model based on the three pillars. Many authoritative writers (Berggren and Nomura, 1997; Sako and Sato, 1997; Kuwahara, 1998), however, while accepting

Table 17.2 Changes in HRM patterns in large Japanese firms

Past	Present
Internal labour markets	Enlargement of related internal labour markets (related firms)
Hierarchical pyramid-type organisation	Flat organisation
Lifetime employment	Variety of employment contracts
Job segmentation	Flexible job categories
In-house on-the-job training	Emphasis on out-of-house interaction
Manual skilled orientated	Conceptual skill orientated
Internal human network	External human network
Firm-specific skills	Firm-specific culture
Systematic job rotation	Failure of internal career development plan
Manufacturing factory model	Flexible unit model
Mass production orientated	Value-added orientated
Long-range evaluation of performance	Short-range evaluation of human resource performance
Money value of work for employees	Non-pecuniary value of work for employees
Bureaucratic control	Partnership relations

that change is inevitable, still believe that the ingredients and uniqueness of the Japanese system remains largely intact. As Sako (1997) states: 'The principle of lifetime employment continues to be upheld by management because without it, the motivational basis of workers' and unions' cooperation would falter . . . but in order to maintain the lifetime employment principle, pressures are placed elsewhere in the system' (p. 11).

While the employee relations system will evolve and change slowly, there is no sign that it is converging towards the American model.

CHINA: ECONOMIC GROWTH AND HRM

Introduction

China has an area of 9 561 000 square kilometres, and had an estimated population of 1242 million people in 1998 (*Financial Times*, 1999a). Its capital is Beijing, which had a population of 12 200 000 in 1997 (*Financial Times*, 1999a). China has experienced rapid economic, political and social development in the past two decades. The death of Mao Zedong in 1976 heralded the beginning of a period of economic reform led by Deng Xiaoping. During this period China adopted an 'open door' policy for encouraging trade and technology transfer. The management of the economy moved from a centrally planned *command economy* to a *socialist market economy* (CCCC, 1993). The annual economic growth has averaged 9% since 1978. Domestic spending rose by five times in the 1990s. There has been a rapid increase in the number of foreign-invested enterprises in China (Ding *et al.*, 1999). Foreign investment in early 1996 was US$ 7.74 billion. This had risen to record levels of US$ 46 billion by 1998. This meant that China was the largest recipient of foreign investment after the United States. The levels of China's foreign currency reserves were second only to those of Japan in 1999 (Kynge, 1999).

The speed of economic development slowed down slightly after 1998. While China was not severely affected by the economic crisis in Asia during 1997–98, it was exhibiting certain institutional weaknesses. The World Bank highlighted three main problems in its report 'China: Weathering the Storm and Learning the Lessons' (1999). These were:

- weaknesses in corporate governance, and a poor definition of ownership and accountability;
- government interference in investment decisions;
- a lack of speed in terms of setting up satisfactory mechanisms by which to regulate the financial sector.

In conjunction with these institutional weaknesses, there were associated problems of corruption within the system. It was estimated that one-fifth (Rmb 117bn) of central government revenues had been misused in the first eight months of 1999 (Kynge, 1999). The lack of legal regulation meant that foreign businesses often experienced problems when setting up businesses within China (Murray, 1994; Peng, 1994). These included dealing with broken contracts, incurring bad debts, and completing property developments. Foreign direct investment fell by 10% in the first half of 1999, which led to speculation that the 'gold rush' mentality towards China was subsiding (Barber, 1999). China is now facing a changing climate of industrial restructuring, downsizing and unemployment. Later in this section we provide an overview of some of the key business and HR issues that are impacting upon China today.

The 'iron rice-bowl' to 'socialism with Chinese characteristics'

An historical overview serves to provide a framework for understanding some of the contemporary human resource issues that are impacting upon China. The historical review begins by focusing upon the period during which Mao Zedong was in power. Child (1994: 36–38) suggests that one can categorise four main phases of industrial governance during this period. These are summarised below.

Phase 1: Central planning 1953–56

Mao Zedong came to power in 1949. He advocated that China should move to an economy based upon socialist ownership. The *Five Year Plan* was launched in 1953. This included moves towards centralised planning and control from the state. Trade unions did exist, but their role was confined to dealing with welfare issues. Complicated piece-rate systems were used to reward many workers.

Phase 2: Decentralisation and the Great Leap Forward 1957–61

The system of industrial governance that developed as part of the five-year plan was influenced by the Soviet system. Child argues that this tended to be very hierarchical, and as such was not in sympathy with a Chinese culture in which collectivism was a central feature. The Great Leap Forward was a period within which many of the collectivist values came to the fore. During 1957–61 control for much of industry passed from central to provincial government. However, a great emphasis was placed upon allegiance to the Communist Party, and factory directors had to report to party committees. The system of bonus payments was reduced.

Phase 3: The period of readjustment 1962–65

The 1959–61 period saw a drop in agricultural output, followed by a famine. This was partly caused by an overemphasis on expanding the manufacturing sector during the Great Leap Forward. The period of readjustment saw moves back towards more centralised planning; however, factory directors were given more control over day-to-day production issues.

Phase 4: The Cultural Revolution 1966–76

The Cultural Revolution was a distinctive period, during which politics and ideology were the predominant concerns. There was a great emphasis upon allegiance to the Party. Factories moved away from hierarchical control towards using factory revolutionary committees as the management mechanism. In terms of rewards, 'competitive, individual and material incentive was rejected in favour of cooperative, collective and moral incentive' (Child, 1994: 37). Therefore, a context of collectivism and control developed. Child comments that

> The Cultural Revolution was seen to have dissipated incentive and responsibility for economic performance through egalitarianism, the weakening of management, the general devaluation of expertise and the claim that ideological fervour and inspired leadership could substitute for technical knowledge . . . The xenophobia of the period had denied the country opportunities for inward investment and technology transfer.
>
> (p. 39)

Child's summary of the *four phases of industrial governance* gives an insight into the context that developed during the rule of Mao Zedong. The role of the state was central throughout. The state managed the economy, and increasingly enforced its ideology upon the citizens. China was relatively undisturbed by foreign influence during this period. Child notes that social and political discipline was used as an effective force for controlling the Chinese people.

One of the legacies of Mao's rule was the system that became known as the *iron rice-bowl*. This related to the provision of lifetime employment and cradle-to-grave welfare structures (Ding *et al.*, 2000). The enterprise played both an economic and a social role, and would provide its employees with housing, medical support and education provision. Central to the enterprise were work units (*danwei*). The *danweis* formed the core of the community. Ding *et al.* (2000) comment that a number of writers have suggested that the iron rice-bowl encouraged a high degree of 'organisational dependency' (p. 218). They argue that organisational dependency is a deep-seated feature of the Chinese system, and that it has encouraged attitudes and behaviours that are difficult to change. The implications of organisational dependency interlinked with many of the HR issues that are discussed below.

China's industrial production was dominated by state-owned enterprises (SOEs). These accounted for 80% of industrial production in 1978 (Warner, 1997). Under the full employment system that emerged, the dismissal of workers was allowed only if a worker had committed 'gross negligence', but this term was open to interpretation, and the sanction was rarely used even if the individuals concerned were undisciplined. In order to avoid the problems that are associated with unemployment, a system of 'featherbedding' was used, which resulted in enterprises that were overstaffed, with low levels of productivity (Child, 1994). Wages were based on seniority, and there was no real incentive for employees to strive for promotion. There was no concept of a labour market, and individuals were not allowed to move within China to 'follow work'. Trade unions existed, but had a different role from those of their in Western counterparts:

> The All China Federation of Trade Unions (ACFTU) were assigned two functions: by top-down transmission, mobilisation of workers for labour production on behalf of the State, and by bottom-up transmission, protection of workers' rights and interests. (Chan, quoted in Warner, 1997: 37)

Therefore the union role centred upon production and welfare issues. They would not be involved in negotiations on pay and conditions, as would be the norm in Western countries.

After the death of Mao Zedong in 1976, Deng Xiaoping assumed power in China. Under his leadership China embarked on an economic reform programme. This included the commencement of an 'open door' policy in which international trade and the influx of foreign technology were encouraged. The term 'socialism with Chinese characteristics' was first used by Deng Xiaoping in 1982 to describe the approach to economic reform. China allowed joint ventures to operate from the early 1980s onwards. From this point, foreign invested enterprises (FIEs) became widespread. Foreign companies provided technology and managerial knowledge (Ding *et al.*, 2000).

In 1999 the government amended the constitution to formally recognise the concept of private ownership. Employment in the private sector rose from 150 000 to 32.3 million in the period from 1980 to 2000 (Montagnon, 1999a). Therefore FIEs were important in terms of providing employment, technology and modern management techniques.

However, the process of modernisation has not been painless. One of the key problems was that the SOEs were overmanned and underinvested. Workers in the SOEs had been socialised into the iron rice-bowl mentality, in which they expected that the organisation would provide cradle-to-grave employment and welfare. One of the aims of the modernisation programme was to move away from this. In 1992 personnel legislation

Table 17.3 Summary of the differences in characteristics of the labour–management reforms

System characteristic		Status quo	Experimental
1	Strategy	Hard-line	Reformist
2	Employment	Iron rice-bowl	Labour market
3	Conditions	Job security	Labour contracts
4	Mobility	Job assignment	Job choice
5	Rewards	Egalitarian	Meritocractic
6	Wage system	Grade based	Performance based
7	Promotion	Seniority	Skill-related
8	Union role	Consultative	Coordinative
9	Management	Economic cadres	Professional managers
10	Factory party-role	Central	Ancillary
11	Work organisation	Taylorist	Flexible
12	Efficiency	Technical	Allocative

Source: Warner, (1996: 33).

was introduced that became known as the *three systems reforms*. The three key areas were: the introduction of labour contracts, performance-related rewards, and social insurance reforms. Warner (1996) provides a useful summary of the key differences between the traditional system and the emerging system of labour reforms within China (see Table 17.3).

The 1994 Labour Law provided a further spur to the modernisation. It aimed to provide regulation for 'a labour system compatible with a social market economy' (Warner, 1997: 33). The law covered a variety of issues, including the right for workers to choose jobs, equal opportunities, minimum wage levels, directives on working hours, and provisions for dispute handling and resolution. Warner comments that one of the implications of the 1994 Labour Law was that the distribution of power would be readjusted so that the trade unions could have more autonomy from the state.

The process of modernisation has meant that there is no longer a 'job for life'. Other aspects of the iron rice-bowl are also beginning to wane. From 1998 the *danweis* were no longer allowed to allocate subsidised housing, and allowances for education and medical support were slowly being reduced (Kynge, 1999). The modernisation programme led to SOEs being restructured and downsized. However, it is estimated that SOEs currently have 20 million employees excess to requirements (Montagnon, 1999a). There is a concern that the workers involved cannot be passed easily into the labour market, and a fear that mass redundancies could lead to social unrest. The government has set up a system of social security. The cost of the social security bill rose by 23% in 1998, and unemployment rose from 3.1% in 1998 to 5.5% in 1999 (Montagnon, 1999a). Clearly, unemployment will remain as a key concern for some time to come, especially given the huge levels of surplus labour within the SOEs. A process of modernisation is taking place, but the size and historical development of China mean that this is a slow process. The legacy of the iron rice-bowl is still apparent, and complete reform is still a long way off.

HRM with 'Chinese characteristics'?

Economic reforms in China have allowed the influx of foreign interests, and have set a new context in which both indigenous Chinese and foreign invested companies manage the employment relationship. There is a debate as to whether employment systems in the Asian block are converging towards common approaches to HRM or, alternatively, whether they are becoming more divergent as time goes by. Some have argued that an Asian model of HRM exists. The Asian model has been characterised by: non-adversarial relationships; low union density, or unions (as in China) that are closely controlled by the state; and low instances of overt industrial conflict. However, as we have already noted, academics are now beginning to appreciate that the Asian block is far from homogeneous, and differences in IR/HRM systems reflect different national histories and cultures (Leggett and Bamber, 1996; Rowley, 1997; Warner, 2000). Part of the remit of this section is to explore the extent to which employment systems in China are becoming more 'Westernised'. This seems possible for two main reasons: first, the high levels of foreign investment in the country, and second, the fact that the modernisation programme has increasingly subjected the SOEs in particular to the logic of the market.

The debate regarding the extent to which Chinese enterprises are adopting HRM is a problematic one. Academic perspectives on this issue relate back to the wider debate about the nature of HRM itself. Child (1994) questions the extent to which one can utilise the term 'HRM' as a descriptor for the management of personnel in Chinese enterprises:

> Although definitions of personnel management and human resource management vary considerably, modern Western thinking tends to be predicated upon assumptions such as the primary contribution of competent and motivated people to a firm's success, the compatibility of individual and corporate interests, the importance of developing a corporate culture which is in tune with top management's strategy for the firm, and the responsibility of senior management rather than employees' own representative bodies for determining personnel practices. It attaches importance to systematic recruitment and selection, training and development (including socialisation into corporate culture), close attention to motivation through personal involvement and participation in work and its organisation, appraisal and progression procedures and incentive schemes . . . This concept of human resource management is not found in Chinese enterprises. (p. 157)

Therefore authors such as Child believe that the term 'HRM' is unsuitable as a model for analysis to be used within the Chinese context. Others however are explicitly using mainstream HRM models in order to analyse human resource issues within China. Benson and Zhu (1999) use Storey's model of HRM, which categorises four key elements of HRM (beliefs and assumptions, strategic aspects, management role, and key levers), in order to evaluate the extent to which six SOEs were adopting HRM practices. They refute Child's assertion that the concept of HRM is not found within Chinese enterprises. By reference to the Storey model, they conclude that there were three models of HRM within their sample. The first model was a minimalist approach, in which two of the SOEs had made few attempts to adopt an HRM approach. The second model was one in which two companies had attempted to adopt an HRM paradigm. Part of this was related to the fact that both of these companies were relatively small, and had strong connections with foreign companies via joint ventures or contracting arrangements. The third model represented a transitional stage between the old and the new. Benson and Zhu argue that there is evidence that some enterprises had developed the concept of and practices associated with HRM, and the extent to which this had happened depended upon factors such as market forces and changes in legislation. Their evidence does not however suggest that HRM is the dominant paradigm, and they acknowledge that factors such as China's historical development and cultural traditions can act as a barrier to the development of a Western model of HRM.

Clearly, the extent to which China is adopting an 'HRM' approach is a matter of some debate. The evidence seems to suggest that some enterprises may be adopting some of the practices that are associated with Western models of HRM, but it is unlikely that full-blown models are widespread. The following sections will review some of the evidence regarding different aspects of contemporary HR/personnel practice within China.

Employment contracts, surplus labour and social insurance

Part of the modernisation process has included the shift to a more decentralised and flexible labour market. The employment contract system was formally implemented in 1986, and it gave employers the ability to hire employees on contracts that specified the terms of employment. Under this system, enterprises were able to downsize and remove problematic employees (Ding and Warner, 1999). The drive to modernise the labour market was further progressed by the provision of subsequent legislation such as the personnel legislation of 1992 and the 1994 Labour Law. This meant that both individual and collective labour contracts could be set up. The collective contracts would cover employees belonging to an enterprise, and would be arranged via the trade union. Collective contracts would cover areas such as pay and conditions, working hours, holidays and welfare (Ding and Warner, 1999: 249).

One of the outcomes of the reform programme has been that a substantial number of redundancies have been made. Seventeen million employees of SOEs had been laid off by the end of 1998 (Benson and Zhu, 1999). The enterprise took responsibility for welfare issues such as pensions and medical cover, prior to the economic reforms. It would usually provide free or subsidised housing as well. Since the reforms and the gradual move away from the iron rice-bowl, the government has had to set up a system of social insurance. The funds for social insurance are contributed to by the state, the enterprise and individual employees (Ding and Warner, 1999). Social insurance is designed to act as a safety net, particularly for employees who are made redundant. As reported in the discussion above, one of the issues that China will have to deal with is the rising cost of social insurance (Montagnon, 1999a). In conjunction with this is the fear of social unrest that could result from mass redundancies.

Recruitment, selection and training

One of the impacts of the reforms has been that there is now greater mobility within the labour market. Prior to the reforms, workers were assigned to firms from labour bureaus. This often meant that workers were assigned even when they did not hold the requisite skill and knowledge for the job. While there is the possibility for greater labour mobility now, evidence suggests that mobility remains fairly low, especially in the shopfloor workers category (Tsang, 1994; Ding and Warner, 1999; Benson *et al.*, 2000). Table 17.4 demonstrates the continuing role of external agencies in the recruitment process.

Evidence suggests that mobility is higher within the managerial ranks. There are reports, however, that joint ventures continue to find it difficult to recruit employees of SOEs (Tsang, 1994). This is due to a number of reasons including SOEs retaining employee files, which means that the employee can be cut off from a range of benefits. Overall, China has a large pool of unskilled and semi-skilled labour from which to draw, but there is a dearth of managerial employees and engineers with the skills and knowledge that modern industry and commerce require (Ding and Warner, 1999).

One of the HR problems confronting China is the huge scale of training and development that is needed to ensure that industry and commerce can continue to develop. Warner (1992) suggests that this relates back to two key factors. First, education and development were severely disrupted during the Cultural Revolution. For example,

Table 17.4 Multiple recruitment methods in state-owned enterprises (SOEs) and joint ventures (JVs)

	SOEs N = 12	JVs N = 11
Sources for recruiting workers		
Secondary/technical school	11 (92%)	7 (64%)
Allocated by labour bureau	9 (75%)	2 (18%)
Labour market	7 (58%)	9 (82%)
Transferred from Chinese partner firm	NA	3 (27%)
Internal recruitment	2 (17%)	NA
Sources for recruiting managers		
Promoted from within the firm	12 (100%)	11 (100%)
Appointment by superior government body	7 (58%)	11 (100%)
Open recruitment	4 (33%)	7 (64%)
Appointed by parent firm	0	3 (27%)
University graduates	0	1 (9%)

Source: Ding and Warner (1999: 247).

management development and training were banned during this period. The lack of effective training and development meant that there was a lack of educated managers and engineers, and the legacy of this still remains today. Second, the speed of economic development in China has meant that there is a great demand for educated, skilled staff. The state has responded by encouraging the development of an infrastructure for management development and training (Child, 1994). However, there remains a lack of systematic training within companies. Foreign investors in joint ventures (JVs) can find that Chinese partners often request an enormous amount of overseas training for indigenous employees. FIEs can also experience problems in retaining staff they have trained, especially given the tight labour market for skilled managerial and technical employees (Tsang, 1994). Training and development issues are likely to remain as continuing concerns for the future within China (Glover and Siu, 1999).

Reward systems and employee relations

The review above has highlighted some of the changes in relation to reward systems. The seniority-based flat rate system is now being replaced by systems that often have some link to performance. Wages were determined by legislation and regional agencies until the mid-1980s, and seniority was the most important factor in terms of employee earnings, but other aspects were entering the equation by the mid-1990s. Factors such as responsibility and qualifications have started to be taken into account (Benson *et al.*, 2000). However, the evidence remains that SOEs are often unwilling to increase wage differentials. State enterprises have tended to pay equal bonuses to all employees regardless of the performance of individual employees. They have also retained a great degree of harmonisation of work conditions (Benson *et al.*, 2000). This appears to be an example of the way in which the principle of equality has endured post-Mao.

Ding and Warner (1999) carried out a study that compared the average monthly wages of SOE and JV employees. Their evidence demonstrated that while SOEs and JVs tended to adopt the same basic wage structure – a basic salary plus bonuses and allowances – the JVs tended to pay much more on average. The results are summarised in Table 17.5.

Table 17.5 Average monthly wages (RMB) 1994–96

Type of employee	SOEs (N=12)	JVs (N=12)
1994		
Workers	610	763
Section heads	745	933
Middle managers	758	1731
Senior managers	928	2479
1995		
Workers	722	933
Section heads	878	1103
Middle managers	894	1994
Senior managers	1048	2765
1996		
Workers	741	1098
Section heads	867	1294
Middle managers	930	2300
Senior managers	1150	3144

Source: Ding and Warner (1999: 251).

Therefore, there have been overall moves to increase flexibility within reward systems and linkages between pay and performance. However, some aspects of the old system endure, including the reluctance of SOEs to penalise poor performers (Benson *et al.*, 2000).

The discussion will now turn to employee relations. The role of trade unions has been highlighted above. Trade unions have in the past tended to play a different role within Chinese enterprises, tending to concentrate on welfare issues and assist in production issues. This situation remains much the same today. Benson *et al.* (2000) comment that while trade unions currently seem to be 'relegated' to the role of 'watchdog' over issues such as health and safety and workers' rights, they could potentially play a role in securing better conditions for their members in the future. However, they point out that the traditional role of assisting management in achieving optimum performance could eventually create conflicts, and that,

> workers can become the victims of reform rather than the vehicle for change. Chinese workers are therefore in a similar situation to workers in most other countries   (p. 193).

The preceding review has given an overview of the current situation in key areas such as employee resourcing, development and relations. It seems that China is beginning to use techniques that are derived from Western and Japanese practices. However the full-scale adoption of Western-style techniques is unlikely, at least in the short term, as these would be incongruent with Chinese culture and the historical development of their business traditions. The following section will highlight some of the issues that impact upon the management of people in China.

Issues influencing HRM in China

Culture

This section will provide an overview of some of the issues that influence the management of people in China. These include the impact of culture, the lack of managerial skills, problems of labour discipline, and dealing with low motivation. Warner (2000) has noted that a great deal of divergence remains within the Asian block, and that one of the explanatory variables for this is the impact of national cultures upon human resource systems. Culture is a notoriously difficult concept to define, and it is hard to make broad generalisations that would fit all individuals and groups within a particular country. China, for example, comprises a huge land mass, and many argue that one can find differences in culture between people from the North compared with those of the South (Fairbank, 1987). For example, Northern Chinese tend to speak Mandarin, while many southerners speak Cantonese. However, it is useful to outline some of the features that are associated with Chinese culture, in order to understand some of the HR issues that are affecting both SOEs and FIEs.

Child (1994: 28–32) provides an overview of some of the key aspects of Chinese culture. He points out that there is a degree of agreement that Confucianism is the basis for many Chinese traditions. An understanding of Confucianism does help one to understand certain values, attitudes and behaviours within the Chinese context. Fan (1995) suggests that Confucian ideologies are relevant to contemporary studies for four main reasons:

- Confucian ideology has become firmly rooted as an 'undeniable' system that governs many aspects of Chinese lives.
- Thousands of years of a feudalistic system have dominated the Chinese view of themselves and the world.
- To gain acceptance in China, new ideas have to be proved to be compatible with classics and tradition.
- The current economic reforms are not necessarily changing Chinese people's fundamental mentality or behaviour.

Kong Fu Ze (551–479 BC) was called Confucius by Jesuit missionaries. His philosophy on life became popular some 300 years later. The fifth Han Emperor, Wu, found that Confucian ideologies fitted well with the need to create a strong, centralised monarchy. Confucianism emphasised a respect for elders and the family, order, hierarchy, and a sense of duty. Confucius believed that individuals had a fixed position in society, and that social harmony could be achieved when individuals behaved according to rank (Jacobs et al., 1995). There was an emphasis upon the 'correct and well-mannered conduct of one's duties, based upon a sound respect for the social conventions of a patrimonial society' (Child, 1994: 29). Age was respected, particularly in the case of male elders.

Child quotes Lockett (1988), who identified four values that are central to Chinese culture, and which are based upon Confucian ideologies:

- respect for age and hierarchy;
- orientation towards groups;
- the preservation of 'face';
- the importance of relationships.

'Face' is an important concept, and it relates to a person's social standing, position and moral character. Child (1994: 30) comments that the Chinese attach great importance to how they are viewed by others. 'Face' means that conflicts within a group would be kept private, as the group would be demeaned in the eyes of the wider community if conflict were overt. The importance of relationships is captured in the concept known as *guanxi*. Luo and Chen (1997) note that '*guanxi* refers to the concept of drawing on connections or networks to secure favours in personal or business relations' (p. 1).

Guanxi relates to relationships that are outside the person's immediate family (Child, 1994: 30). The concepts of *guanxi* and face are intertwined, and some have argued that they can act as inhibitors to the modernisation programme (Chen, 1995)

The preceding paragraphs have given a short overview of a complex subject. There is much evidence that FIEs often find it difficult to operate within China, and that some of the problems are caused by a lack of appreciation of Chinese culture. The examples quoted have highlighted some of the underlying tensions that have developed between foreign and Chinese partners. Peng has commented that foreign investors have complained that Chinese managers lack initiative, are unwilling to delegate, and are perceived to be unsystematic. Lockett (1988) argues that such behaviours reflect aspects of Chinese culture: for example, he reminds us that during the Cultural Revolution managers were promoted according to Party allegiance rather than on the basis of merit. He argues that this legacy has hampered the level of management skill in China. The tendency towards collective rather than individual orientation often leads to behaviours that clash with the behaviours expected by foreign counterparts. Chinese managers will often avoid taking individual responsibility, and Child (1994) argues that this is due to a combination of Chinese traditions and the Cultural Revolution.

Jacobs *et al.* (1995) argue, however, that there is too much emphasis upon the negative implications of Chinese culture. They argue that Confucian-based philosophies can lead to positive outcomes in the workplace, because of the emphasis upon 'diligence, responsibility, thrift, promptness, cooperation and learning' (p. 33). More research is needed in order to evaluate the impact of Chinese culture upon business performance.

Management skills, labour discipline and motivation

One of the issues affecting China today is a dearth of appropriate management skills. Tsang (1994) argues that the lack of skills relates to four main factors. First, the Cultural Revolution severely disrupted education, training and development. Second, central planning meant that managers had little autonomy. For example, all products were sold to the state at a predetermined price. Therefore managers did not have the scope to develop entrepreneurial skills. Third, mistakes were severely penalised, but achievements were not rewarded. Fourth, important decisions were made by collective consensus, and that managers saw themselves as an 'information conduit' and that individuals were unwilling to take risky decisions (relating back to the danger of losing face). Again, these behaviours relate back to a combination of Confucian ideology and the legacy of the Cultural Revolution. The development of adequate levels of managerial skill is likely to remain as a key issue for the future.

Two linked issues are the problems of labour discipline and low motivation. Evidence suggests that Chinese managers are often unwilling to discipline staff, as they prefer to avoid overt conflict and maintain harmony (Tsang, 1994). While Chinese culture emphasises the importance of hard work and diligence, the system of featherbedding in SOEs meant that the enterprises were overstaffed and productivity was low. Tsang quotes from the *China Daily:*

> Labour discipline in our enterprises is very lax. Some workers don't work eight hours a day, a few are absent for a long time to engage in speculation and profiteering. Others even turn to street brawling and stealing of state property. There are also technically incompetent people who do not seek improvement, but just drift along, wasting their own and other people's time. (Tsang, 1994: 5)

This comment reflects the fact that China is going through the equivalent of an industrial revolution, in that many workers are being drawn from agricultural work to factory work. The problems highlighted above are reminiscent of those that faced nations such as America, Japan and the United Kingdom as they went through their own industrial revolutions and sought to find ways in which to control and motivate agricultural/migrant workers (Zuboff, 1988; Buchanan and Huczynski, 1997).

Glover and Siu (1999) have pointed out that FIEs based in Southern China often employ migrant workers from the North of China. Their case study evidence suggested that the main aim of the migrant workers was to accumulate money and return home as soon as possible. For this reason, they were not motivated by the prospect of career development. As a result of this, they had a purely instrumental attachment to the company, and no real stake in the long-term prosperity of the firm. It is also important to point out that part of the attraction of the joint venture was that the company could take advantage of the low pay levels in China. In other words, the company itself was operating in an instrumental way in respect of its use of manual labour in China. Glover and Siu identify a range of problems that were being encountered by the company, many of which were related to human resources issues rather than equipment failures. Burrell (1997) describes such workers as the 'peasantariat', and argues that

> they retain much if not all of their deep-seated social and political characteristics. They remain 'peasants who travel'.
> (p. 14)

Burrell argues that although many of the world's workers are in fact peasants, traditional organisational theory has ignored this and has essentially led to a lack of knowledge and understanding about the motivations and aspirations of a numerically significant group of workers. More research is needed in this area.

HONG KONG: ECONOMIC GROWTH AND HRM

It is relevant to refer to Hong Kong here, as it has a different history from that of mainland China. Hong Kong has a relatively small land mass of 1095 square metres. It has an estimated population of 6 687 200. It enjoyed rapid economic growth until the Asian crisis of 1997–98. This section will give a short review of Hong Kong's historical development, and will highlight some of the issues that face the territory after its reunification with China.

Hong Kong became a British colony in 1843. The British wanted to secure a base from which to trade. Initially, one of the key exports to China was opium, which proved to be a lucrative business for the British. Drug taking was illegal, but there was a high demand for opium within China in the mid to late 1800s. The Japanese invaded China and subsequently Hong Kong in the Second World War, and occupied Hong Kong between 1941 and 1945. They surrendered in 1945. The Communist Party came to power in China in 1949, and this provoked a wave of immigration from China to Hong Kong. Many of the immigrants were traders and businessmen. Many had fought against the Communists during the civil wars in China, and tensions remained between the two factions. Hong Kong became wealthy in the period after the Second World War. Central to its success were the Asian 'tycoons', many of whom were immigrants who had left mainland China in 1949–50. The tycoons preferred to work with family members or close contacts, relating back to the Chinese concept of *guanxi*. However, there is an argument that Hong Kong will slowly move away from its patriarchal culture. Four main reasons have been highlighted. First, the first generation of Chinese businessmen are preparing to hand over to their children, many of whom have been educated in the

West. Second, the financial crisis of 1997–98 made the businesses more reliant on Western capital. Third, the Internet may pose a threat to more traditional businessmen. Finally, Asia's maturing legal and financial framework may undermine the influence of Chinese networks overseas (Anon, 2000a).

Hong Kong was ruled under British sovereignty until 1997. As a result, it developed a capitalist business system that was influenced by Chinese culture and traditions. Sovereignty was handed back to mainland China in 1997. Hong Kong became a Special Administrative Region (SAR), and the agreement was that it would maintain its legal system and capitalist approach for at least 50 years. There were many concerns that the agreement would not protect the democratic rights of the people of Hong Kong, or that reunification would affect the economic progress of Hong Kong. In the event, the hand-over appeared to run smoothly. Hong Kong now has an executive-led, non-elected government and a legislative council (elected by universal suffrage). The system has not been without its problems, and Hong Kong must decide in 2008 whether or not it wishes to move to a fully elected government (*Financial Times*, 1999b). The main problem that has faced the government since 1997 is how to respond to the Asian economic crisis.

Hong Kong's economy was badly hit by the Asian economic crisis. GDP growth fell by 5.1% in 1998 and by 1.5% in 1999. Unemployment levels rose from 4.7% in 1998 to 7% in 1999 (*Financial Times*, 1999b). Indeed, when South Korea, Singapore and the Philippines began to emerge from the Asian crisis, Hong Kong's GDP continued to fall. After 1997, Hong Kong began to be regarded as having an uncompetitive cost base. Several factors have been cited as contributing to Hong Kong's problems, and three key issues emerged. First, property values were too high. Second, property rental was too high. Third, service charges levied at ports and airports were too high (Lucas, 1999a). A fourth key problem related to wage levels within the territory. Prior to 1997, wage levels were spiralling without concomitant increases in productivity. After the onset of the Asian crisis, some large companies cut salaries and others moved operations abroad (Lucas, 1999a). Hong Kong has been used as a gateway to China, but China is increasingly shipping direct from its own ports (Lucas, 1999a).

Some believe that the future for Hong Kong's economy will lie in high technology. For example, it may be used as a base for developing China relevant software (Lucas, 1999b). However, there are concerns that it is less advanced in this sphere than countries such as Singapore. In common with Hong Kong, Singapore has also been used as a small open economy that is a springboard to less developed economies. However, Singapore has been more aggressive in terms of offering incentives to attract preferred industries such as banking, technology and the media (Lucas, 1999b). Hong Kong has not offered the same degree of incentives to potential businesses. In terms of technology, in particular, there is also a concern that there could be a lack of skills to service the fast-growing technology sector within the local labour market (Lucas, 1999b). Therefore, although Hong Kong was a fast-growing market, it is now faced with a number of potential problems. Some of these are contributing to the fact that economic growth is forecast to fall by 0.4% in 2000, whereas economic growth in other Asian nations such as South Korea and the Philippines is expected to rise (Lucas, 1999a).

Hong Kong has acted in recent years as 'a "half-way" house between a modern Western business society and the mainland China context' (Selmer *et al.*, 2000: 237). However, this role may diminish as the process of modernisation and openness in China continues to develop. Some of the specific HR issues include the fact that Hong Kong has strictly limited the importation of labour. Businesses are allowed to import construction workers and domestic help, but it has been more difficult to import potential managers (Fields *et al.*, 2000). Some studies have suggested that labour turnover of educated workers and managers tends to be high, and can pose a problem for Hong Kong businesses. Some companies are placing more emphasis upon internal development and promotion to try to alleviate this problem. Fields *et al.* (2000) have found retention rates are higher in these cases. However, an adequate supply of skilled managers will be critical for Hong Kong's future, especially in the information technology sector.

Training is also likely to be a key issue. Fields *et al.* (2000) have found, for example, that some companies are reluctant to invest in training, and this is possibly linked to the problem of 'job-hopping' in Hong Kong. The issue of wage rises has been dealt with above. Wage rises prior to 1997 tended to run ahead of productivity, so contributing to the fact that it is expensive to operate from Hong Kong. These were reigned in after 1997, and some employees had their salaries cut. This caused conflict in some industries. For example, Cathay Pacific cut the salaries of its pilots, and this led to 17 days of disruption in 1999, which cost the company between HK$400m and HK$700m (Anon, 1999b).

This short review has highlighted some of the key differences in the historical and economic context of Hong Kong. It is clear that there are substantial differences between the system in Hong Kong and that of its mainland counterpart. It is also clear that Hong Kong's role of 'middle-man' between the West and the East may be further compromised if China continues to modernise.

SOUTH KOREA: ECONOMIC GROWTH AND HRM

South Korea (referred to hereafter as Korea) has an area of 99 313 square kilometres and an estimated population of 46.4 million people (*Financial Times*, 1999c). Its capital is Seoul, which has an estimated population of 10.5 million (*Financial Times*, 1999c). Korea is a relatively new industrialised country, which experienced rapid economic growth from the 1960s to the early 1990s (Anon, 1995). It was affected by the Asian crisis in 1997–98. The percentage GDP growth fell by 5.8% in 1998 (*Financial Times*, 1999c). However, this was quickly reversed, and Korea's GDP rose by almost 11% in 1999 (Anon, 2000b). Inflation rose by 7.5% in 1998 and then fell back to 1.3% in 1999. Similarly, industrial production fell by 7.3% in 1998 and then rose by 16% in 1999. The unemployment rate was 6.8% in 1998 and is expected to fall to 5.5% by the end of 2000 (*Financial Times*, 1999c). However, Korea's position is not universally sound. One of the biggest shocks to hit the economy after 1998 was the financial crisis within Daewoo. Daewoo was one of the influential *chaebols*, which are large, family-owned conglomerates that dominate Korea's economy. The five leading *chaebols* prior to the collapse of Daewoo were Hyundai, Samsung, Daewoo, Lucky Goldstar and the SK group. The discussion that follows will discuss the role of the *chaebols* and their importance to Korea in more detail.

As highlighted above, Korea's economy performed well after the Asian economic crisis. However, concerns remained about the long-term future of the economy. Burton (1999a) suggests that Korea risks being 'squeezed economically' as it occupies a middle ground between China's low-wage economy and Japan's high-technology economy. Burton argues that Korea will have to find a new industrial model that is capable of taking it forward in the long term. In order to understand some of the contemporary economic and HR issues that are impacting upon Korea, it is useful to give a brief review of its history. This allows an insight into the way in which the business context has developed and the legacy that this has created.

In comparison with other Asian countries such as Japan, relatively little has been written about general business and HR issues in Korea. Whitley (1999) provides one of the most useful insights into the business context in Korea. He provides an overview of Korea's history that is summarised below. Whitley argues that the dominant institutions in Korea can be understood by reference to pre-industrial society, the period of Japanese colonial rule and the Korean war. He argues that the present structures for governance and business reflect three key aspects from the past. First, there has always been a tendency towards a high degree of political centralisation. Second, there is a continuing Confucian influence in terms of the importance attached to superior authority and moral worth, and these are linked to examination success. Third, there has been a history of factional struggles among the aristocracy, and aristocratic status and ancestry have always been viewed as important (Whitley, 1999: 152). These will now be expanded upon.

Korea was ruled by the Yi or Chosun dynasty between 1392 and 1910. Confucianism was predominant during this period. In particular, political power was highly centralised, and success in examinations was prized. There was a sharp division between the aristocratic elite and others. Within the aristocracy, success in examinations tended to secure senior posts. Although the monarch was revered, the aristocratic bureaucracy that developed ensured that the monarch would never achieve despotic power. There was much competition between different factions, which was encouraged by the monarch, so that local power bases would not develop. Another related aspect was that the

> private accumulation of wealth was officially regarded as an indicator of corruption and Confucian rulers established it as their ethical right to prevent it as part of their duty to preserve harmony and frugality
>
> (Whitley, 1999: 154).

This meant that there was a relatively small merchant class, and they were regarded with suspicion. While there were factional struggles, the society did not disintegrate owing to the 'finely tuned mechanisms of checks and balances' (p. 154). Collectivism was never a central feature of Korean society, and there was always a great distance between rulers and the ruled.

Japanese colonial rule spanned from 1910 to 1945. While the Japanese made some changes, Whitley argues that many of the aspects of Korea's pre-industrial past were sustained. This included the 'capricious and unpredictable behaviour of the executive' (1999: 155). Korea was awarded its independence again in 1948. Power was centralised among the elite once more. The entrepreneurs of the 1947–57 period were men who were favoured by the president. The president virtually gave away businesses that had been owned by the Japanese. These firms form the basis of the *chaebols* that are central to the Korean economy today. The state continued to play a key role in terms of the development of the *chaebols*. It offered cheap credit to them via the banking system, and as the president controlled access to the credit, he maintained a strong position. The family members that owned the *chaebols* continued to operate on a factional basis. The Korean War raised the power of the military elite. Korean management style is often described as authoritarian, and this reflects the influence of the military after the Korean War.

Whitley argues that the growth and diversification of the *chaebols* was influenced by the requirements of the state. The state offered subsidised credit, and in return the *chaebols* developed in accordance with state priorities. These included a desire to expand rapidly and to 'catch up' with Japan, and as a result the *chaebols* grew and diversified rapidly. Second, the *chaebols* developed heavy engineering and chemical production in the 1970s because of the military threat from North Korea. Certain key themes have been sustained through to the present: political centralisation and the president's influence upon the business context; good personal relationships between the owners of the *chaebols* and the president; rivalry between the *chaebols*.

Education and qualifications continued to be prized, to the extent that there was a dearth of workers with manufacturing skills in the 1990s (Robinson, 1991). The authoritarian management style was, as we have said, influenced by the military, and subordination was reinforced by Confucian traditions. While trade unions exist in Korea, the state has acted to limit their power – for example, by intervening in disputes. A considerable distance between the business-owning elite and the masses persists, and *chaebol* owners have had little need to harness the support of trade unions or workers. All these themes reflect Korea's historical development, and they continue to impinge upon business relationships in Korea today.

The contemporary business and human resource context

This historical overview has offered an insight into some of the contemporary business and HR issues that face Korea as it enters the twenty-first century. The economy continues to be dominated by the *chaebols*. They operate in heavy engineering, car production, electronics, construction, transport, insurance and finance. However, there are concerns that Korea must reform its economy, and move the emphasis away from the *chaebols*, which are regarded by some as large and inefficient (Burton, 1999a). There is an argument that the economic environment has not supported the development of small, entrepreneurial businesses, but an explanation for this can be found in the historical overview above. The South Korean president Kim Dae-jung (appointed in 1998) has begun a programme of reform that was spurred by the Asian crisis of 1997–98.

The economic crisis in Korea was at least partly related to the actions of the *chaebols*. The government has recently attempted to put measures into place to stem those practices of the *chaebols* that have had negative consequences for the economy. The *chaebols* had over-invested in production facilities, which had created huge debts (Burton, 1999a). Another related problem has been that stronger businesses within *chaebol* empires have supported weaker ones. When the government eased restrictions on cross-shareholding for the *chaebols* in an attempt to encourage consolidation, many *chaebols* used this as an opportunity to rescue weaker businesses, by using money from the stronger businesses to purchase shares in them (Burton, 1999b). This meant that internal shareholdings often represented as much as 34% in 1998 (Burton, 1999b). However, the *chaebol* leaders have resisted many of the economic reforms. They have argued that Korea needs its conglomerates in order to secure growth in the future.

The economic crisis was also closely linked to the debt-ridden banking sector. The government injected Won 64 trillion into the banking sector during the economic crisis. This was equivalent to approximately 16% of the GDP (Montagnon, 1999b). Of 33 commercial banks, five were closed and four were merged. This led to a wave of redundancies, which many argue was necessary given the fact that the banks were over-staffed. However, there is evidence that many employees have been rehired on short-term contracts (Montagnon, 1999b). The government encouraged foreign investment after the economic crisis, partly to try to bring more discipline into the banking sector in particular. Foreign investment reached a record $8.9 billion in 1998, and $15 billion was expected in 1999 (Burton, 1999a). However, there is a continuing reluctance to allow foreign investors to take control at operating level (Montagnon, 1999b).

Therefore there are a number of issues that are affecting the Korean economy. The economy has recovered in the short term, but many commentators argue that continued reforms are necessary in order to secure its long-term prosperity.

Human resource issues

This section will give a short overview of some of the HR issues that are affecting contemporary Korea. One such issue has been highlighted in the historical review above. Some commentators have argued that the predominantly authoritarian, military-influenced management style is likely to prove unsuitable for the long term (Burton, 1999a). The preferred style tends to be reminiscent of a scientific management approach, within which subordinates are closely controlled by supervisors. The approach encompasses low levels of trust between managers and subordinates. Work is often organised such that surveillance of subordinates is made possible. In common with the principles of scientific management, jobs tend to be broken down into narrowly defined tasks. Workers in manual grades are not promoted, and tend to stay in initial jobs (Whitley, 1999). This is especially the case within smaller *chaebols*. The situation is different for white-collar workers. They tend to be moved around, and are often transferred across subsidiaries either within Korea or abroad. This is reflective of the historical development of Korea, in which educated employees were regarded as superior and those with technical and manual skills as inferior. Finally, roles and responsibilities were often defined more in terms of authority relations rather than in terms of formally documented job descriptions (Whitley, 1999). Therefore the traditional approach to management tended to be informed more by scientific management than by 'modern management techniques'. Modern management techniques such as quality management and human resource management emphasise worker involvement as a route to quality enhancement and increased performance. Burton (1999a) has argued that the authoritarian management style of the Korean *chaebols* could limit their development as global players in the future.

Kim and Briscoe (1997) provide an overview of some of the traditional and new human resource practices used by the *chaebols*. They recruit and select college graduates twice a year. Graduates from the top universities are preferred. The graduate trainees undergo four weeks of training, in order to turn them into 'warrior workers' for the *chaebols* (p. 299). During this period the graduates are socialised into the history, norms and behaviours required by the *chaebols*. Interestingly, there is less emphasis upon technical skills, which again reflects the historical development of Korea. Rewards were traditionally based upon seniority. Posts tended to have a minimum tenure before an employee could be promoted to the next level. *Chaebols* would normally offer a bonus that was linked to the overall performance of the company. Performance appraisals were not widely used, partly because managers preferred not to give critical feedback. Most employees would retire by the age of 55.

Kim and Briscoe (1997) also provide some evidence of the modernisation of some of the HR practices. They use the example of Samsung, which is generally regarded as a *chaebol* that has attempted to restructure after the Asian crisis. Kim and Briscoe argue that Samsung had to respond to a new paradigm of domestic and international competition. They outline three key areas of modernisation in terms of HR policy and practice: job hierarchy and promotion, compensation, and performance appraisals. The key differences are summarised in Table 17.6.

Table 17.6 Samsung's 'new HR policy'

HR practice	Traditional approach	New approach
Job hierarchy and promotion	• Based on seniority • Younger employee could not supervise older employee	• Promotion linked more tightly to performance • Minimum tenure for each position abolished
Compensation	• Compensation had three main elements: basic salary (50%), allowances (10%), and a bonus (40%) • Lack of individual performance measurement/problems of 'free riders'	• Compensation has two main elements: base pay (related to position and seniority), and performance pay (related to individual performance). The percentage of performance pay is highest for senior managers (68%)
Performance appraisal	• No history of performance appraisal	• Performance pay related to performance ratings. Appraisal has four key aspects: – Supervisor keeps a diary recording performance – 360-degree appraisal introduced – Appraisal interview introduced – Forced distribution of performance ratings

Source: Adapted from Kim and Briscoe (1997)

There is some evidence that *chaebols* are beginning to modernise their human resource practices.

Korean trade unions are often described as weak, but strikes and stoppages do occur, and the state often intervenes to dissipate them. There was a significant increase in strike activity during 1996–97. Morden and Bowles (1998) suggest that this was related to four key factors. First, the government had passed new labour laws, which were aimed at increasing the flexibility of the labour market. This included removing the provisions for lifetime employment and as a result, making workers redundant. Second, the International Labour Organization (ILO) and the OECD had called for a reduction in statutory curbs on trade union activities. Third, the state had recognised the Federation of Korean Trade Unions (KCTU), which was more vocal than its predecessor, the Federation of Korean Trade Unions (FKTU). Finally, the ban on multiple workplace unions was not to be lifted until the year 2000. More recently, strikes have been sparked by the Daewoo crisis. Workers in both Daewoo and Hyundai walked out in April 2000 to protest against plans to sell Daewoo in an international auction. The police arrested 20 trade unionists during the dispute, and this sparked a further strike within Daewoo (Burton, 1999c). In addition to conventional strike activity, workers at Daewoo Motor blocked attempts by Hyundai officials to carry out due diligence in respect of a possible takeover of the car division. This is an example of continuing factionalism between the rival *chaebols* (Burton, 1999c).

SINGAPORE: ECONOMIC GROWTH AND HRM

As we noted earlier in this chapter Singapore is one of the first-tier economies in South East Asia, along with Japan and others. It has witnessed remarkable growth in the past 35 years, and between 1965 and 1980 its GDP growth rate averaged 10%. Since 1980 the GDP growth rate has fallen slightly below 10%, although the recessions in the mid-1980s and recently have hit the economy hard. Much of this long-term growth has been put down to the economic strategies of the government of Singapore (Aryee, 1994; Teen and Phan, 1999).

Singapore is a small state with a population of 2.8 million, and is located on the southern tip of the Malaysian peninsular. Until 1965 it was a British colony and briefly part of the Malaysian state until it gained independence. As Singapore lacks natural resources, including land, the People's Action Party, which has been in power since 1959, decided that economic survival and prosperity rested on the abilities of its people. In attempting to understand Singapore's economic development, an analysis of human resource development in relation to national strategy is pivotal.

The development of Singapore's economy

Singapore's institutional structures are heavily underpinned by government support, and the role of the state has been crucial in its development. From the 1960s to the present, economic policy and national economic strategy formulation have gone through three stages. In the first stage, in the 1960s, the government decided that economic growth rested on the development of industry, the attraction of foreign capital, and the promotion of Singapore as a centre of trade in the region. This form of alliance capitalism, while underpinned by a socialist (or social democratic) philosophy, also encouraged free enterprise. As the Prime Minister, Lee Kuan Yew, stated concerning Singapore's initial independent state:

> The sole objective was survival. How this was to be achieved by socialism or free enterprise was a secondary matter. The answer turned out to be free enterprise tempered with the socialist philosophy of equal opportunities for education, jobs, health and housing.   (Vickers da Costa, 1983:14)

In this first phase economic strategy was focused on developing low added value and labour-intensive industries – a mixture of steel mills, shipyards, oil refineries and electronics. This development coincided with a boom in the world economy and MNCs that were seeking competitive advantage through reduced labour and running costs by opening subsidiaries in developing countries such as Singapore.

By the end of the 1970s that advantage was no longer so apparent as other less developed economies began to offer even lower labour and production costs, and so a second economic strategy was formulated in the 1980s. This concentrated on high-tech industries, and moved away from labour-intensive industries. High-tech industries focus on science, technology, skill and knowledge, and to realise this strategy the government set about attracting foreign high-technology companies through high tax breaks and other inducements, and embarked on a massive, long-term human resource development programme.

The government itself also provided a considerable amount of capital and became a major shareholder in and owner of many of the new industries, though in the 1990s many were subsequently privatised (Teen and Phan, 1999). This approach is similar to the alliance capitalism that created the *zaibatsu* in Japan. Ashton and Sung (1994) describe this model as one where 'the political need to secure long-term survival of the society meant that the short-term interests of the class-based groupings such as landowners or capitalists were subordinated to the wider goal of collective economic growth' (p. 4). Ayree (1994) sees the government's role in human resource terms as an allocator within the labour market and also as a developer of unique human resource capabilities and competences to enable Singapore to have a critical competitive edge.

Considerable money was poured into high-tech research and development and the building of science parks. The success of this strategy is evidenced by Singapore's continuing high economic growth rates in the 1980s and 1990s, by when it had become, for example, the leading world producer of hard disk drives. It had also developed a thriving stocks and securities market and had become a regional leader in this area. There was considerable investment in education, particularly in the tertiary sector, and human resource development became a central focus of the government manpower development programme (Low *et al.*, 1991).

In the 1990s the Singapore government launched a third economic strategy to take the economy well into the twenty-first century. This was precipitated by a sharp downturn in growth in the mid-1990s, caused by the impact of the financial crisis and consequent recession in South East Asia and the slowdown in global electronics demand. The manufacturing sector was further weighed down by excess capacity and keen regional competition in the non-electronics industries. In the light of these developments Singapore's Economic Development Board (SEDB) created a 'blueprint' for the future grounded in a knowledge-based economy. Singapore will become 'a vibrant and robust global hub of knowledge-driven industries. Singapore's manufacturing and service sectors will be further developed with a strong emphasis on technology, innovation and capabilities' (SEDB, 2000). To sustain economic growth Singaporean companies are being strongly encouraged to move out into the Asia Pacific region and form a 'second ring'. Advantage would then be taken of the abundance of cheaper labour in these surrounding economies, and Singapore would become the hub of this ring as a powerful international economic centre (Low, 1993). The main aim of the blueprint is for the people of Singapore to achieve the same living standard as the Swiss by the year 2020 or 2030.

In human resource terms there are two main consequences of these strategic changes in the light of increased global competition: first, the continuing development of the Singaporean education and human resource development systems to high levels; and second, the restructuring of the labour markets between the declining old industries and the rising new ones. The latter development is having and will continue to have negative effects, especially on marginalised elements in the labour force, who lack the skills, knowledge and youth to adapt to these changes.

Human resource development in Singapore

Central to Singapore's economic strategies has been the development of the educational and knowledge levels of the population. Ashton and Sung (1994) believe that advanced NIEs such as Singapore are significant examples of a new model of skill formation and economic development in which changes in education policy are linked directly with the current and future demands of the economy. As late-developing countries they have had the advantage of learning from the examples and mistakes of the older, established economies. This can take the form of transferring specific skills and knowledge directly through education and training programmes, through gaining knowledge and skills from and through foreign-based companies, and through sending students to foreign countries to learn. An important factor is that the whole population is encompassed as well as groups within the economy such as unions, companies and employer groups. This will often mean that individual and separate group interests have to be subordinated to the long-term aims of the nation, and that some elements of freedom may be sacrificed. For example in the first economic phase, dating from the 1960s to the 1980s, the government acted to contain labour costs by repressing labour organisations, and in the recent crisis wage costs have been cut to bring them in line with 1994 levels (SEDB, 2000).

The centrality of human resource development has been emphasised at all stages: in the first phase by developing the basic education level and skills of the population, and in the second phase by raising them to the more sophisticated level required by an advanced, high-tech economy. This required the upgrading of the education system and the creation of a training infrastructure coordinated by the Vocational and Industrial Training Board.

The Ministry of Trade and Industry and the Investment Board define the vision of the national economic strategy and then set the goals. The Ministry gathers information on the future skill and knowledge needs to fulfil the strategy, and these are compared with estimates of present skills. The Economic Development Board then calculates targets to achieve the set goals, which are then given to the Council for Professional and Technical Education to implement. They in turn set targets for schools, colleges, polytechnics, universities and other educational and training establishments.

In the third phase much emphasis has been placed on work-based learning, because the new organisational forms require not only technical skills but also the ability to work flexibly and with a greater degree of group autonomy within a problem-solving context. Studies have been made of the best systems, perceived to be Japanese, German and Australian on-the-job training. The German dual system has been particularly admired, and elements of it were borrowed in developing Singaporean apprenticeship systems in the early 1990s.

The successful growth of the Singapore economy has been ascribed to the role of the state and the institutions it has developed to enhance the knowledge and skills of its people to meet the challenges of the twenty-first century. This has taken place in the context of a mixed economy where foreign investment and subsidiaries of MNCs have been welcomed. However, the need to achieve a balance between state and private capital interests within a unitarist HRM state means that individual and group freedoms have had to be curtailed from time to time in the long-term interests of the economy. Thus at times trade union and individual rights have been side-stepped, as have the short-term profit motives of individual companies, and while the model has been eulogised by some observers there are doubts as to its applicability to economies outside the Asia Pacific region.

SUMMARY

- The chapter began by briefly examining the controversy of whether Asian business systems and practices were converging and conforming more to an American managerial approach. The consensus among observers is that while elements of Western HRM practices are more prevalent, divergences of practices remain marked owing to socio-cultural differences, varied investment patterns and financial institutional practices, and the political and historical factors that have led to different stages of economic development.

● The origins and development of the Japanese employment relations system were examined from four perspectives: the historical view, the cultural view, the late developer view and the politico-economic view. An examination was then made of the 'three pillars' (lifetime employment, seniority system, and enterprise unionism) that underpin the employment system in large Japanese corporations. This was followed by a critique of this simplified version of the Japanese employment system, which emphasised its narrow application in organisational and working population terms. The section finished with an examination of recent trends in Japanese HRM, exploring the problems of an ageing population, the effects of increased global competition and changing patterns of HRM in Japanese companies in response to these pressures.

● The section on the People's Republic of China discussed key issues relating to human resource management, and outlined some of the key points in China's historical development under Mao. It illustrated the way the system known as the 'iron rice-bowl' continued to exert some degree of influence over contemporary practices. While China has enjoyed rapid economic growth, it is now confronting a number of problems, including restructuring, downsizing and unemployment. In response to this, it is having to develop a system of social insurance. There is a debate as to the extent to which HR practices within China are converging with Western approaches. This section concluded that while there is some degree of similarity, full-blown Westernised models of HRM are unlikely to take hold because of cultural and institutional differences. There are a number of issues that are impacting upon people management in China, including skills gaps, problems of labour discipline, and low motivation.

● The short review of Hong Kong highlighted the clear and substantial differences from the PRC, its mainland counterpart. It is also clear that Hong Kong's role of 'middle-man' between the West and the East may be further compromised if the PRC continues to modernise.

● Four key issues were highlighted in the development of South Korea's HRM systems. First, there has been a historical tendency towards the centralisation of power. Second, Confucian influences were important, particularly in relation to superior authority and moral worth and the importance attached to examination success. Third, there is a history of factional struggles among the elite. Finally, the *chaebols* are central to the Korean economy and are closely linked to the state via the control of cheap credit. There has been relatively little foreign investment within Korea. Some key HR issues were highlighted. These included: the continuation of an authoritarian management culture; the predominance of white-collar, educated workers; the role of trade unions; and the moves toward modernisation within some of the *chaebols*. While some convergence towards Western models of HRM is apparent, it is likely that historical traditions will continue to impact upon HRM both within Korea and within the foreign subsidiaries of the *chaebol* empires. However, the decline of Daewoo served to highlight that the *chaebols* cannot ignore domestic and foreign competition.

● The section on Singapore noted the impressive growth of the economy from the 1970s, and the various stages of and adjustments to its national economic strategy in the light of changing external influences. An examination of the vocational and training system was seen as one of the key policies in creating a vibrant economy. Raising the skill and knowledge levels of the population was seen as pivotal in the twenty-first century in order to meet the challenges of a high-growth economy based on high-technology industries and services.

Activity China

As a member of the human resource development department of a large multinational corporation you have been given responsibility to devise a programme to prepare managers and other parent company employees who will be working in China.

Prepare a presentation that you might give to these employees including general information on the country, history, culture, language and customs and work-related attitudes. Use anecdotes and solid examples to illustrate your presentation.

Activity Japan

Divide the lecture group into four smaller groups and give each group the task of preparing a presentation on the origins of the Japanese employment system from the perspectives given in the section on Japan:

- the historical view
- the cultural view
- the late developer view
- the politico-economic view.

Emphasise that material in addition to that presented in the Japan section of this chapter will be given extra credit.

QUESTIONS

1 To what extent would you agree with the contention that existing models of HRM fail to recognise cultural differences, and that this is a weakness given the rapid rate of globalisation?

2 Outline the similarities and differences in terms of the approaches to the management of people in the Asian countries outlined above.

3 To what extent would you agree with the view that there is an 'Asian model of HRM'?

4 Describe the employment polices in large Japanese companies. How have these changed over the last few years and why?

CASE STUDY

Yummee biscuits

Yummee Biscuits is a large UK-based snack manufacturer that was set up in the nineteenth century. It is now one of the largest snack manufacturers in the UK. Over the past two decades it has been internationalising its operations, and has acquired companies in the USA and Australia. In 1995 it became involved in a joint venture in the south of the People's Republic of China (PRC). The Chinese partners were local businessmen who had no prior experience in biscuit-making. Yummee pumped in money and resources, and the Chinese partners set up the land deal. The biscuit factory was built on a greenfield site, and was equipped with state-of-the-art machinery. Work was organised on scientific management (Taylorist) lines, with strictly demarcated jobs and close supervision. Yummee took the view initially that it would be best to employ local Chinese managers to run the factory. However, in the following two years numerous problems occurred within the factory. These included problems of quality control, stock control, and failing to deliver orders to customers on time.

Yummee sent out a delegation of senior managers to investigate the problem. They found that many of the problems were related to a lack of managerial skill and poor coordination between different departments. They realised that it had been a mistake to assume that the indigenous Chinese managers could run the factory to British standards with little support or training. They put all managers through management development training. This included topics such as leadership skills, communication skills, time management skills, and dealing with conflict. The training

programmes were adapted from programmes that were delivered in the UK. Individual training needs were not assessed. The managers said that they had enjoyed the training, but the trainer felt that there could be an element of politeness involved. There was little improvement in the performance of the subsidiary one year later.

A senior executive from Yummee travelled to the subsidiary to inspect the plant. He sent a report outlining the key problems in the factory. These were the main points of his report:

Shopfloor problems

- There were low levels of motivation within the shopfloor ranks. Most of the shopfloor workers were from the north of China.
- Shopfloor workers seemed unwilling or unable to take on any level of responsibility.
- There seemed to be little interest in promotion or development opportunities.
- There was no appreciation of hygiene rules and regulations.

Management problems

- Many managers seemed unwilling to take responsibility.
- Managers would often prefer to hire members of their family rather than the best person for the job.
- Managers were often unwilling to discipline subordinates.
- Interdepartmental communication was poor.
- Managers seemed to spend a lot of time dealing with the personal problems of subordinates.

---

1 Does a knowledge of the historical and cultural development of China help you to understand the problems experienced in the PRC subsidiary? Give examples.

2 You have been asked to take over the running of the PRC subsidiary. What managerial initiatives would

you implement to help resolve the above problems? What barriers would you face and how would you deal with them?

3 To what extent could a Western model of HRM be applied to the context of this factory? If not, why not? Give specific examples.

REFERENCES AND FURTHER READING

Those texts marked with an asterisk are particularly recommended for further reading. The issues covered in this chapter are also addressed in Chapters 8, 13 and 15.

There are also regular articles on Asian countries in the *International Journal of Human Resource Management* and the *Asia Pacific Business Review*. These two journals and the *Human Resource Management Journal* have had special editions on HRM in the Asian region in recent years. There are also occasional articles on Asian HRM in the many other journals that cover HRM subjects.

Abegglen, J. and Stalk, G. (1987) *Kaisha: The Japanese Corporation.* Tokyo: Charles F. Tuttle.

Anon (1995), 'The economic growth of Korea', *Asian Wall Street Journal*, 15 September, p. 3.

Anon (2000b) 'Let the good times roll', *The Economist*, 18 April.

Anon (2000a) 'The end of tycoons', *The Economist*, 29 April.

Aryee, S. (1994) 'The social organisation of careers as a source of sustained competitive advantage: the case of Singapore', *International Journal of Human Resource Management*, Vol. 5, No. 1, pp. 67–88.

Ashton, D. and Sung, J. (1994) *The State Economic Development and Skill Formation: A New Asian Model?* Working Paper 3, Centre for Labour Market Studies, Leicester University, May.

Barber, L. (1999) 'A palpable shift in sentiment', *Financial Times*, 1 October, p. 10.

Benson, J. (1996) 'Management strategy and labour flexibility in Japanese manufacturing enterprises', *Human Resource Management Journal*, Vol. 6, No. 2, pp. 44–57.

Benson, J. and Zhu, Y. (1999) 'Markets, firms and workers in Chinese state-owned enterprises', *Human Resource Management Journal*, Vol. 9, No. 4, pp. 58–74.

Benson, J., Debroux, P., Yuasa, M. and Zhu, Y. (2000) 'Flexibility and labour management: Chinese manufacturing enterprises in the 1990s', *International Journal of Human Resource Management*, Vol. 11, No. 2, pp. 183–196.

*Berggren, C. and Nomura, M. (1997) *The Resilience of Corporate Japan: New Competitive Strategies and Personnel Practices.* London: Paul Chapman.

Buchanan, D. and Huczynski, A. (1997) *Organisational Behaviour: An Introductory Text.* Hemel Hempstead: Prentice Hall.

Burrell, G. (1997) *Pandemonium: Towards a Retro-Organisation Theory.* London: Sage.

Burton, J. (1999a) 'Economic squeeze calls for change', *Financial Times*, 20 October.

Burton, J. (1999b) 'The chaebol: the empire strikes back', *Financial Times*, 20 October.

Burton, J. (1999c) 'Banking: still reluctant to change', *Financial Times*, 20 October.

CCCC (1993) *The Work Report of the 14th Conference of the Central Communist Party.*

Chalmers, N. (1989) *Industrial Relations in Japan: The Peripheral Workforce.* London: Routledge.

*Chen, M. (1995) *Asian Management Systems: Chinese, Japanese and Korean Styles of Business.* London: Thunderbird/ Routledge Series in International Management.

*Child, J. (1994) *Management in China in the Age of Reform.* Cambridge: Cambridge University Press.

Deyo, F. (1995) 'Human resource strategies in Thailand' in Frenkel, S. and Harrold, J. (eds) *Industrialization and Labor Relations: Contemporary Research in Seven Countries.* Ithaca, New York: ILR Press, pp. 23–36.

Ding, Z. and Warner, M. (1999) 'Re-inventing China's industrial relations at enterprise level: an empirical field-study in four major cities', *Industrial Relations Journal*, Vol. 30, No. 3, pp. 243–260.

Ding, Z., Goodall, K. and Warner, M. (2000) 'The end of the "iron rice-bowl": whither Chinese human resource management', *International Journal of Human Resource Management*, Vol. 11, No. 2, pp. 217–236.

*Dore, R. (1973) *British Factory – Japanese Factory.* London: Allen & Unwin.

Easterby-Smith, M., Malina, D. and Yuan, L. (1995) 'How culture sensitive is HRM? A comparative analysis of practice in Chinese and UK companies', *International Journal of Human Resource Management*, Vol. 6, No. 1, pp. 31–59.

Fan, X. (1995) 'The Chinese cultural system: implications for cross-cultural management', *SAM Advanced Management Journal*, Vol. 60, No. 1, pp. 14–20.

Fields, D., Chan, A. and Akhtar, S. (2000) 'Organisational context and human resource management strategy: a structural equation analysis of Hong Kong firms', *International Journal of Human Resource Management*, Vol. 11, No. 2, pp. 264–277.

Financial Times (1999a) 'Country survey of China', 1 October.

Financial Times (1999b) 'Country survey of Hong Kong', 30 June.

Financial Times (1999c) 'Country survey of Korea', 20 October.

Gerlach, M. (1992) *Alliance Capitalism: The Social Organisation of Japanese Business.* Berkeley, CA: University of California Press.

Glover, L. and Siu, N. (1999) *The Human Resource Barriers to Managing Quality in China*, Leicester Business School Occasional Papers Series, Number 55.

Gordon, A. (1985) *The Evolution of Labor Relations in Japan.* Cambridge, Mass.: Council on East Asian Studies, Harvard University.

Jacobs, L., Gao, G. and Herbig, P. (1995) 'Confucian roots in China: a force for today's business', *Management Decision*, Vol. 33, No. 9, pp. 29–35.

Japan Labour Bulletin (1999d) August.

Kawakita, T. (1997) 'Corporate strategy and human resource management', in Sako, M. and Sato, H. (eds) *Japanese Management and Labour in Transition.* London: Routledge, pp. 79–103.

Kim, S. and Briscoe, D.R. (1997) 'Globalisation and a new human resource policy in Korea: transformation to a performance based HRM', *Employee Relations*, Vol. 19, No. 4, pp. 298–308.

Kroll, J. (1993) 'From capitalism without cost towards competitive capitalism', *Nikkei Weekly*, 25 October, pp. 9–10.

Kuwahara, Y (1998) 'Employment relations in Japan', in Bamber, G. and Lansbury, R. (eds) *International and Comparative Employment Relations.* London: Sage, pp. 249–279.

Kynge, J. (1999) 'Reflections on half a century', *Financial Times*, 1 October.

Leggett, C. and Bamber, G. (1996) 'Asia Pacific tiers of change', *Human Resource Management Journal*, special issue: *HRM in the Asia Pacific Region*, Vol. 6, No. 2, pp. 7–19.

Lockett, M. (1988) 'Culture and the problems of Chinese management', *Organisation Studies*, Vol. 9, No. 4, pp. 475–496.

Low, L. (1993) 'From entrepot to a newly industrialising economy', in Low, L., Heng, T.M.H., Wong, T.W., Yam, T.K. and Hughes, H. (eds) *Challenge and Response: Thirty Years of the Economic Development Board.* Singapore: Times Academic Press.

Low, L., Toh, M.H. and Soon, T.W. (1991) *Economics of Education and Manpower Development: Issues and Policies in Singapore.* Singapore: McGraw-Hill.

Lucas, L. (1999a) 'Still lingering in negative territory', *Financial Times*, 30 June.

Lucas, L. (1999b) 'Tiger rivalry: jury still out on best methods', *Financial Times*, 15 September.

Luo, Y. and Chen, M. (1997) 'Does guanxi affect company performance?' *Asia Pacific Journal of Management*, Vol. 14, No. 1, pp. 1–16.

Montagnon, P. (1999a) 'Agonising choices accompany change', *Financial Times*, 1 October.

Montagnon, P. (1999b) 'Banking: still reluctant to change', *Financial Times*, 20 October.

Morden, T. and Bowles, D. (1998) 'Management in South Korea: a review', *Management Decision*, Vol. 36, No. 5, pp. 316–330.

Murray, G. (1994) *Doing Business in China.* Kent: China Library.

Ouchi, W. (1981) *Theory Z.* New York: Avon.

Paik, Y., Vance, C. and Stage, D. (1996) 'The extent of divergence in human resource practice across three Chinese national cultures: Hong Kong, Taiwan and Singapore', *Human Resource Management Journal*, Vol. 6, No. 2, pp. 7–19.

Peng, F.C. (1994) 'China: managers can learn from the methods of venture partners', *South China Morning Post*, April, Vol. 13, No. 15.

Rowley, C. (1997) 'Conclusion: reassessing HRM's convergence', *Asia Pacific Business Review*, special issue: *Human Resource Management in the Asia Pacific Region: Convergence Questioned*, Vol. 3, No. 4, pp. 197–210.

Sako, M. (1997) 'Introduction: forces for homogeneity and diversity in the Japanese industrial relations system', in Sako, M. and Sato, H. (eds) *Japanese Management and Labour in Transition.* London: Routledge, pp. 1–28.

*Sako, M. and Sato, H. (eds) (1997) *Japanese Management and Labour in Transition.* London: Routledge.

Sano, Y. (1993) 'Changes and continued stability in Japanese HRM systems: choice in the share economy', *International Journal of Human Resource Management*, Vol. 4, No. 1, pp. 11–28.

Sasajima, Y. (1993) 'Changes in labour supply and their impacts on human resources management: the case of Japan', *International Journal of Human Resource Management*, Vol. 4, No. 1, pp. 29–44.

SEDB (2000) 'EDB launches economic blueprint for the 21st century', Singapore Economic Development Board, web site: www.sedb.com.sg/home.html

Selmer, J., Ebrahimi, P. and Mingtao, L. (2000) 'Personal characteristics and adjustment of Chinese mainland business expatriates in Hong Kong', *International Journal of Human Resource Management*, Vol. 11, No. 2. pp. 237–250.

Shibata, H. (2000) 'The transformation of the wage and performance appraisal system in a Japanese firm', *International Journal of Human Resource Management*, Vol. 11, No. 2, pp. 294–313.

Sparrow, P. and Wu, P.-C. (1999) 'How much do national value orientations really matter? Predicting HRM preferences of Taiwanese employees', in Lähteenmäki, S., Holden, L. and Roberts, I. (eds) *HRM and the Learning Organisation*, Turku, Finland: Turku School of Economics, pp. 239–284.

Stam, J.A. (1982) *Human Resource Management in Japan: Organisational Innovation in Three Medium Sized Companies.* Rotterdam: Erasmus University.

Teen, M.K. and Phan, P.H. (1999) 'Corporate governance in Singapore: current practice and future developments', Paper to OECD conference on Corporate Governance in Asia: A Comparative Perspective, Seoul, South Korea, 3–5 March (unpublished).

Tsang, E.W.K. (1994) 'Human resource management problems in Sino-foreign joint ventures', *Employee Relations*, Vol. 15, No. 9, pp. 1–14.

Tsuru, T. and Rebitzer, J. (1995) 'The limits of enterprise unionism: prospects for continuing union decline in Japan', *British Journal of Industrial Relations*, Vol. 33, No. 3, pp. 459–492.

Vickers da Costa (1983) *Singapore's High Technology Future.* Singapore:

Vogel, E. (1980) *Japan as No. 1.* Tokyo: Charles Tuttle.

Warner, M. (1992) *How Chinese Managers Learn: Management and Industrial Training in China.* London: Macmillan.

Warner, M. (1993) 'Human resource management with Chinese characteristics', *International Journal of Human Resource Management*, Vol. 4, No. 1, pp. 45–65.

Warner, M. (1996) 'Human resources in the People's Republic of China: the "three systems reforms"', *Human Resource Management Journal*, Vol. 6, No. 2, pp. 32–43.

Warner, M. (1997) 'Management–labour relations in the new Chinese economy', *Human Resource Management Journal*, Vol. 7, No. 4, p. 3.

Warner, M. (2000) 'Introduction: the Asia-Pacific HRM model revisited', *International Journal of Human Resource Management*, Vol. 11, No. 2, pp. 171–182.

*Whitley, R. (1992) *Business Systems in East Asia.* London: Sage.

Whitley, R. (1999) *Divergent Capitalisms: The Social Structuring and Change of Business Systems.* Oxford: Oxford University Press.

World Bank (1999) 'China: weathering the storm and learning the lessons', *Country Studies*, 8 January, p. 114.

Zuboff, S. (1988) *In the Age of the Smart Machine: The Future of Work and Power.* Oxford: Heinemann Publishing.

Global and local: the case of the inoperable HRM strategy

Medical Precision Systems (MPS) is an American-owned company based on the outskirts of Birmingham, Alabama, USA. It has been producing medical precision tools used in surgery since 1972, and has built up a well-respected business in the USA with a turnover of $150 million annually. Its Birmingham plant employs 2000 staff made up of skilled and semi-skilled workers. Most staff are employed in production process work, but a significant number work in research and development and other highly skilled and knowledge-based areas.

There are no unions and the Human Resources Department has consciously followed a policy of best-practice HRM to keep out union influence. There is a an excellent pensions scheme, a successful profit-sharing scheme, and a share options scheme whereby employees can choose to have bonuses in the form of company shares if they have worked at MPS for more than two years. Laying employees off is avoided as much as possible during slack periods in order to retain staff loyalty.

However, a performance management culture is strong at MPS, and there is an astringent appraisal system linked to remuneration and promotion. Target setting for groups and individuals has been strongly implemented for the past 20 years and refined over that time. A total quality management (TQM) programme has been in operation for the past 15 years, and work areas or cells are operated by teams. Under the TQM system groups of ten workers are allowed to elect a leader, who organises feedback sessions and reports to senior production managers. Annual staff opinion surveys are conducted on a range of employment and production issues. Training is taken seriously, and all employees attend sessions to train in teamworking and people skills, as well as sessions and courses of a more technical nature. MPS prides itself on its strong culture, and likes to communicate its values and vision clearly and frequently to the workforce. The mission statement 'MPS – working for the health of America' is printed on all pay packets and slips, and most communication bulletins.

There are excellent canteen and recreational facilities, the employees have a number of sports teams, and social events take place regularly.

Expanding overseas

Since the early 1990s MPS has decided to set up plants overseas, but in doing so is conscious that it needs a fairly educated workforce that can cope with the highly technical nature of the work. In addition it has recognised that its major markets are in Europe, where it has been exporting since the early 1980s. The MPS board thus decided to open subsidiaries in the UK initially, followed by Sweden and later France.

The UK operation was acquired by taking over a medical engineering company in 1991 near Bath and initially employed 150 people rising to 350 by the end of the decade. The Swedish subsidiary was set up on a greenfield site in a business park on the outskirts of the university city of Uppsala in 1994, employing 50 and then 250 staff by the end of the decade. A new plant was set up in Lyons, France, in 1997 that employs fewer than 200 staff

In 2001 the MPS HQ in Alabama was revamping its strategy in line with its global developments and commitments. The production and marketing side of the business were doing well, and there had been steady growth in the UK subsidiary in Bath and the Swedish subsidiary at Uppsala. Preliminary reports also indicated that the French subsidiary had enormous potential. However, the Director of Human Resources, Jim Grant, commissioned a full report on the overseas HRM operations as there had been difficulties experienced in HRM. Jim wanted to create an HRM strategy that would complement the new business strategy and at the same time solve the problems in the overseas subsidiaries.

The existing international HRM strategy

Using Perlmutter's typology MPS's international HRM strategy can only be described as ethnocentric (see Chapter 15). It attempts to exert strong controls over its subsidiaries through the extensive use of expatriate managers in both technical and managerial areas of the business. Its goals in financial and production terms have been set by the parent company, and the local subsidiaries have little say. The feedback mechanisms have been implemented from the USA, backed with training programmes for all employees.

Expatriate managers have been told to either keep the unions out or ensure that their influence is as minimal as possible. Loyalty schemes such as profit sharing have been introduced, and it is planned that the company share scheme will be introduced in 2002 across all subsidiaries. Annual staff opinion surveys have been implemented, and communication is emphasised as being fluid and as frequent as possible between expatriate managers, host country managers and employees.

TQM programmes have also been introduced, and are run with the teamworking systems and workplace feedback and improvement mechanisms. The strong MPS culture has been effectively reinforced through regular staff bulletins, and local company magazines in the language of the subsidiary company country. The mission statement is widely displayed, and a strong public relations image also supports the company culture.

While many of these initiatives have had success there has been some reluctance and even opposition to others in the three European subsidiaries. In 2001 Jim Grant carried out a full review, and was able to make the following points in a report to the US HQ board.

HRM overseas in MPS: Report by Jim Grant
One of the problems we have faced is the diversity of conditions in the subsidiaries, and the practices we follow in the USA do not always translate well in the local context. These problems concern expatriate managers, industrial relations, management style and the degree of control that subsidiaries believe is being exerted over them. Expatriate managers faced a considerable degree of difficulty when given assignments, particularly in the European subsidiaries. While all the senior managers in France and Sweden spoke excellent English there were considerable communication barriers between the American expatriates and their subsidiary workforces. Common problems were incomprehension of each other's culture and working practices.

Expatriate manager feedback, Bath, UK
Joe Mendes, who runs the English operation, also commented that, despite the common language, he didn't always understand the British mentality. There was considerable resentment when it was suggested that weekend working be brought in to fulfil some emergency orders.

He also said the plant we inherited was highly unionised, with several technical and other unions

operating. When he suggested having one union for negotiating purposes there was nearly a mass walk-out, and union officials became very obstructive. Another problem was the performance management system, which met with considerable initial difficulties in being set up. The unions and many employees felt the targets were too harsh and divisive, and they also felt that they had little control over them.

Expatriate manager feedback, Lyons, France
Andy Smith, who runs the French operation, had no problems in regard to the unions, as it was a greenfield site and it was relatively easy to exclude unions by recruiting new staff, although some of the technical staff had union membership. The major problem concerned management style. While there were some initial difficulties in setting up the performance management system, the main problem was with the feedback mechanisms. The French workforce could not see the point of the cellular feedback mechanisms, and preferred to have a line manager with an authoritative air, technically proficient and capable of directing the workforce towards work tasks.

Andy also had problems in getting the workforce to work extra hours, and he felt there were excessive holidays in France. 'Every time production seemed to be up running perfectly, another saint's day holiday would put out our schedule,' he said.

A works council was set up in accordance with French law, but in the eyes of most of the French workforce did not operate very effectively.

Expatriate manager feedback, Uppsala, Sweden
Gary Alder, head of the Swedish operation, reported that despite the subsidiary being a greenfield site start-up operation the workforce very soon joined unions, and by the end of the first year over 65% of employees were union members. As in France and the UK the Swedish workforce baulked at the targets set under the performance management scheme. However, there was considerable enthusiasm for the feedback mechanisms in the cellular manufacturing processes, and many interesting ideas and innovations emerged as a result of this.

The Swedes, like the French and the British, were not impressed by the attempts by American management to engender a 'gung ho' culture through culture training and attitudinal orientation sessions. Most employees in all three countries paid lip service to these sessions.

Under Swedish and EU law a works council had to be set up for management and employees, but the Americans, although having to conform to European and national laws, resented these meetings and tended to treat them with less than enthusiasm. They appeared in the eyes of one Swedish union organiser at times to be almost non-cooperative.

The general conclusion that Jim drew was that some HRM policies had been more successful than others.

1 Given the report, what would you advise Jim to recommend to the board in drawing up a new international HRM strategy?

2 How could this strategy be locally responsive and yet global in its scope?

Glossary of terms and abbreviations

ACFTU The All China Federation of Trade Unions.

AEL Accreditation of Experiential Learning.

Androgogy 'The art and science of helping adults learn' (Knowles, 1984: 60).

Annualised hours contract Relatively novel form of employment contract that offers management, and sometimes workers, a considerable degree of flexibility. The hours that an employee works can be altered within a very short time frame within a day, a week, or even a month. So long as the total hours worked do not exceed the contractually fixed annual amount an employee can be asked and expected to work from 0 up to anything in excess of 80 hours in any one week.

APL Accreditation of Prior Learning.

Attitude survey Survey, usually conducted by questionnaire, to elicit employees' opinions about issues to do with their work and the organisation.

BMA British Medical Association.

BS 5750 British standard of quality, originally applied to the manufacture of products but now also being used to 'measure' quality of service. Often used in EI as a way of getting employees to self-check their quality of work against a standardised norm.

BTEC Business and Technology Education Council.

Bushido Japanese term meaning 'the way of the warrior'.

Business process re-engineering (BPR) System that aims to improve performance by redesigning the processes through which an organisation operates, maximising their value-added content and minimising everything else (Peppard and Rowland, 1995: 20).

Career 'The evolving sequence of a person's work experiences over time' (Arthur *et al.*, 1989: 8); 'the individual's development in learning and work throughout life' (Collin and Watts, 1996: 393).

CATS Credit Accumulation and Transfer Scheme.

CBI Confederation of British Industry. Powerful institution set up in 1965 to promote and represent the interests of British industry. Financed by subscription and made up of employers associations, national business associations and over 10 000 affiliated companies. Works to advise and negotiate with the government and the Trades Union Congress.

CCT Compulsory competitive tendering.

CEEP European Centre of Public Enterprises.

Chaebols The large, family-owned conglomerates that dominate Korea's economy. The five leading *chaebols* prior to the collapse of Daewoo were Hyundai, Samsung, Daewoo, Lucky Goldstar and the SK group.

Closed system System that does not interact with other subsystems or its environment.

COHSE Confederation of Health Service Employees.

Collective bargaining Process utilised by trade unions, as the representatives of employees and management, as the representatives of employers, to establish the terms and conditions under which labour will be employed.

Competence 'The ability to perform the activities within an occupational area to the levels of performance expected in employment' (Training Commission, 1988)

Competences Behavioural repertoires that people input to a job, role or organisation context, and which employees need to bring to a role to perform to the required level.

Cooperatives Organisations and companies that are collectively owned either by their customers or by their employees.

CPSA Civil and Public Servants Association.

Culture The prevailing pattern of values, attitudes, beliefs, assumptions, norms and sentiments.

Danwei Central to the state-owned enterprises in China were work units or *danweis*.

DES Department of Education and Science, now renamed the Department for Education and Employment (DFEE).

Design Interventions in the social and natural word that attempt to reduce the fleeting, fluctuating, and ambiguous signs of its life by the establishment of limits and boundaries that define reference and meaning. Like the sculptor, the process of design expresses the efforts of man to carve out and stabilise 'form' from that which is unformed.

Deskilling The attempt by management to appropriate and monopolise workers' knowledge of production in an effort to control the labour process. To classify, tabulate, and reduce this knowledge to rules, laws and formulae, which are then allocated to workers on a daily basis.

DETR Department of the Environment, Transport and the Regions.

Development The process of becoming increasingly complex, more elaborate and differentiated, by virtue of learning and maturation, resulting in new ways of acting and responding to the environment.

Development centres Normally used for the selection of managers. They utilise a range of intensive psychological tests and simulations to assess management potential.

DfEE Department for Education and Employment

Double hermeneutic Concept developed and worked by a number of sociologists including Anthony Giddens to describe the relation between theoretical and lay knowledge. Sociology invents secondary concepts to supplement or replace those inexact and informal concepts that agents use in their understanding and 'negotiation' with the world. Over time, social scientific concepts get reappropriated by agents and enter into everyday discourse, so that there is a relay between everyday language use and that language developed by social scientists.

Double-loop learning *See* single-loop learning.

Dual system German system of vocational training for apprentices, which combines off-the-job training at vocational colleges with on-the-job training under the tutelage of *meister* (skilled craft) workers.

EC European Community. The term superseded the EEC after the SEM, as describing more than purely economic union. Since 1992 has been renamed European Union (see below).

ECSC European Coal and Steel Community, founded in 1952.

EEC European Economic Community. A term used to describe the Common Market after the Treaty of Rome 1957.

EI Employee involvement; a term to describe the wide variety of schemes in which employees can be involved in their work situation.

e-Learning Use of new technology such as email, the Internet, intranets and computer software packages to facilitate learning for employees.

Employability The acquisition and updating of skills, experience, reputation – the investment in human capital – to ensure that the individual remains employable, and not dependent upon a particular organisation.

Empowerment Recent term that encompasses EI initiatives to encourage the workforce to have direct individual and collective control over their work processes, taking responsibility for improved customer service to both internal and external customers. Generally confined to workplace level issues and concerns.

EMU European Monetary Union.

Enterprise unions Japanese concept of employee unions associated with only one enterprise and the only one recognised by the company. One of the 'three pillars' of the Japanese employment system.

EPU European political union.

ESOPS Employee share option scheme, whereby employees are allowed to purchase company shares or are given them as part of a bonus.

ET Employment Training.

ETUC European Trade Union Confederation.

EU European Union, so named in 1992 (formerly EC).

EURATOM European Atomic Energy Community.

FIEs Foreign invested enterprises.

Firm-specific skills Skills that can be used in only one or a few particular organisations.

FKTU Federation of Korean Trade Unions.

Forked lightning, the Mae West Language and concepts used by city financiers working on the international currency and commodity markets. Used to describe the patterns formed by fluctuating price movements as they get represented on dealers' screens.

GDP Gross domestic product.

GNVQs General National Vocational Qualifications.

Guanxi Chinese term that refers to the concept of drawing on connections or networks to secure favours in personal or business relations.

HMSO Her Majesty's Stationery Office. Publishers of parliamentary proceedings, official government documents and reports.

Holistic Treatment of organisations, situations, problems as totalities or wholes as opposed to a specific, reductionist approach.

HRD Human resource development.

Human relations Associated with the pioneering work of Roethlisberger and Dickson, Elton Mayo and others, who studied the importance of community and collective values in work organisations. These studies first identified that management needed to attend to the 'social needs' of employees.

IIP Investors in People.

ILO International Labour Organization.

IMS The Institute of Manpower Studies. Located at the University of Sussex.

Institutional vacuum/representation gap Situation in which collective bargaining is no longer the dominant form of establishing terms and conditions of employment, but no recognisable or regulated channel of employee representation or employee voice has emerged to replace it.

IPD Institute of Personnel and Development.

IRDAC Industrial Research and Development Advisory Committee of the Commission of the European Communities.

IRS Industrial Relations Service. A data gathering and publications bureau that collects and analyses movement in key variables of importance to the study and practice of industrial relations.

ITBs Industrial Training Boards. Set up in 1964 to monitor training in various sectors of the economy. Most were abolished in 1981, but a few still survive.

JCC Joint consultative committee; body made up of employee representatives and management, which meets regularly to discuss issues of common interest.

Job enlargement Related to job rotation, whereby a job is made bigger by the introduction of new tasks. This gives greater variety in job content and thereby helps to relieve monotony in repetitive jobs such as assembly line working.

Job enrichment Adds to a cycle of work not only a variety of tasks but increased responsibility to workers. Most associated with autonomous work groups introduced into Volvo's Kalmar plant in Sweden in the 1970s.

Job rotation Originally introduced in the 1970s for members of a team to exchange jobs to enliven work interest, but also used recently to promote wider skills experience and flexibility among employees.

JV Joint venture.

KCTU Korean Federation of Trade Unions.

Knowledge-based organisation One that manages the generation of new knowledge through learning, capturing knowledge and experience, sharing, collaborating and communicating organising information and using and building on what is known.

Labour process The application of human labour to raw materials in the production of goods and services that are later sold on the free market. Labour is paid a wage for its contribution, but capital must ensure that it secures value added over and above what it is paying for. Some call this efficiency. Others prefer the term 'exploitation'.

Learning Complex cognitive, physical, and affective process that results in the capacity for changed performance.

Learning cycle Learning seen as a process having different identifiable phases. Effective learning may be facilitated if methods appropriate to the various phases are used.

Learning style Individuals differ in their approaches to learning, and prefer one mode of learning, or phase of the learning cycle, to others.

Learning organisation (LO) 'A Learning Company is an organisation that facilitates the learning of all its members and consciously transforms itself and its context' (Pedler *et al.*, 1997: 3).

LECs Local Enterprise Companies. Scottish equivalent of TECs. There are 22 in existence. (*See* TECs.)

Lifetime employment Japanese concept whereby in large corporations employees are guaranteed a job for life in exchange for loyalty to the organisation. One of the 'three pillars' of the Japanese employment system.

LMS Local management of schools.

LSC Learning and Skills Council.

Maastricht Protocol Part of the Maastricht Treaty dealing with the Social Chapter (Social Charter), allowing Britain to sign the treaty without signing the Maastricht Protocol or Social Chapter.

Maastricht Treaty The content was agreed at a meeting at Maastricht in the Netherlands and signed in a watered-down form in Edinburgh in 1992. It was rejected and then accepted by the voters of Denmark in two referendums. It concerns extending aspects of European political union (EPU) and European and Monetary Union (EMU).

Management gurus Phenomenon of the 1980s, when academics, consultants and business practitioners began to enjoy celebrity status as specialists on the diagnosis of management problems and the development of 'business solutions'. Includes people such as Tom Peters, Rosabeth Moss Kanter, John Harvey Jones, and M.C. Robert Beeston.

McDonaldization The reduction of organisation to simple, repetitive, and predictable work processes that make the labour process more amenable to standardised calculation and control.

MCI (Management Charter Initiative) Employer-led initiative with the aim of developing recognised standards in management practice.

Mentor More experienced person who guides, encourages and supports a younger or less experienced person.

MSC Manpower Services Commission. Previously had responsibility for training but was abolished in 1988.

NACETT National Advisory Council for Education and Training Targets.

NALGO National and Local Government Officers Association.

NASUWT National Association of School Masters/ Union of Women Teachers.

National curriculum Obligatory subjects of the UK's school system, introduced via the Education Reform Act 1989.

NATO North Atlantic Treaty Organization. Western defensive alliance set up originally in 1949 to promote economic and military cooperation among its members. The original members were Belgium, Britain, Canada, France, Italy, Norway, Portugal and the Netherlands. Greece and Turkey joined in 1952, and the former West Germany in 1955.

NCU National Communications Union.

NCVQ (National Council for Vocational Qualifications) Government-backed initiative to establish a national system for the recognition of vocational qualifications.

Nemawashi Japanese term for consensus.

NHS National Health Service.

Nenko Japanese term meaning seniority and/or age. One of the 'three pillars' of the Japanese employment system.

Networking Interacting for mutual benefit, usually on an informal basis, with individuals and groups internal and external to the organisation.

New Deal Government initiative that provides training for 18–24-year-olds who have been out of work for more than six months, and 25-year-olds and over who have been unemployed for longer than two years.

NSTF National Skills Task Force.

NUCPS National Union of Civil and Public Servants.

NUPE National Union of Public Employees.

NUT National Union of Teachers.

NVQs National Vocational Qualifications. An attempt to harmonise all VET qualifications within the UK by attributing five levels to all qualifications, from level 1, the lowest, to level 5, the highest.

Open system System that is connected to and interacts with other subsystems and its environment.

OSC Occupational Standards Council.

PFI Private Finance Initiative.

Pluralism Theoretical analysis of the employment relationship that recognises inequality between capital and labour where each of the interest groups has some conflicting and some common aims. To address these issues, pluralists argue that employees should be facilitated to act collectively, usually as a trade union, to redress such imbalances. Management, as the representatives of employers, should engage in collective bargaining with trade unions to establish consensual agreements on issues of conflict and commonality.

Post-Fordism A claimed epochal shift in manufacturing that sees a move away from mass production assembly lines and the development of flexible systems that empower and reskill line workers. Associated with the move towards niche products and volatile consumer demand.

PRB Pay review body.

Profit sharing Scheme whereby employees are given a bonus or payment based on a company's profits.

Psychological contract The notion that an individual has a range of expectations about their employing organisation and the organisation has expectations of them.

Psychological (psychometric) testing Specialised tests used for selection or assessing potential. Usually in the form of questionnaires. They construct a personality profile of the candidate.

Quality circle (QC) Group made up of 6–10 employees, with regular meetings held weekly or fortnightly during working time. The principal aim is to identify problems from their own area.

RCN Royal College of Nursing.

Ringi Japanese form of employee involvement.

SCOTVEC Sottish Vocational Education Council.

SEA Single European Act 1987. Proposed the creation of a single European market for trade on 31 December 1992.

SEDB Singapore Economic Development Board.

SEM Single European market, also known as '1992' owing to the date it was set up. See SEA.

Single-loop learning Detection and correction of deviances in performance from established (organisational or other) norms. Double-loop learning is the questioning of those very norms that define effective performance. (Compare efficiency and effectiveness.)

Single-table bargaining Arrangement under which unions on a multi-union site develop a mutually agreed bargaining agenda, which is then negotiated jointly with management.

Single-union deal Arrangement under which one trade union operates to represent all employees within an organisation; this is usually a preferred union sponsored by management.

Social Chapter Another name for the Social Charter, which emerged from the Maastricht meeting in 1989.

Social Charter A programme to implement the 'social dimension' of the single market, affording rights and protection to employees.

Social partnership Process whereby employers and employees establish a framework of rights based upon minimum standards in employment, flexibility, security, information sharing and cooperation between management and employees' representatives.

Social relations in production The patterns and dynamics produced and reproduced in action by individuals and collectives employed in the labour process.

Sociotechnical The structuring or integration of human activities and subsystems with technological subsystems.

SOE State-owned enterprise.

Stakeholder society One in which individuals recognise that only by making a positive contribution to contemporary society can they expect a positive outcome from society.

Stakeholders in social partnership Those groups with an interest in promoting strong social partnerships at work, i.e. the state, employers and their organisations, employees and their organisations.

Suggestion scheme (box) Arrangement whereby employees are encouraged to put forward their ideas for improving efficiency, safety or working conditions. Payment or reward is often given related to the value of the suggestion.

SVQs Scottish Vocational Qualifications.

System Assembly of parts, objects or attributes inter-relating and interacting in an organised way.

Systemic Thinking about and perceiving situations, problems and difficulties as systems.

Tacit knowledge Knowledge that is never explicitly taught, often not verbalised, but is acquired through doing and expressed in know-how.

Team briefing Regular meeting of groups of between 4 and 15 people based round a common production or service area. Meetings are usually led by a manager or supervisor and last for no more than 30 minutes, during which information is imparted, often with time left for questions from employees.

TECs Training and Enterprise Councils. These operate in England and Wales, and there are 82 at present. They are made up of local employers and elected local people, to create local training initiatives in response to local skill needs.

TQM Total quality management, an all-pervasive system of management-controlled EI based on the concept of quality throughout the organisation in terms of product and service, whereby groups of workers are each encouraged to perceive each other (and other departments) as internal customers. This ensures the provision of quality products and services to external customers.

Transferable skills Skills that can be used anywhere in the economy.

TUC Trades Union Congress

TUPE Transfer of Undertakings (Protection of Employment) Regulations.

UNICE Union of Industrial and Employers Confederations of Europe.

Unison Public service union formed following merger of COHSE, NALGO and NUPE.

Unitarism Theoretical analysis of the employment relationship based on managerial prerogative, valuing labour individually according to market assessments, and which views organised resistance to management authority as pathological.

VDU Visual display unit – a computer screen for example. That component of a computer that transmits often dangerous levels of radiation.

VET Vocational education and training.

VQs Vocational qualifications.

Wa Japanese term for harmony.

Weberian bureaucracy Associated with the research and writing of the sociologist Max Weber (1864–1920), who observed and studied the growth of vast organisational bureaucracies. Notable for the extreme degree of functional specialisation, formal rules and procedures, and long lines of command and authority. Staffed by professional full-time, salaried employees who do not own the resources and facilities with which they work.

Welting Unofficial form of manpower planning used by dockers in order to maximise the opportunities for overtime, when wage rates were higher. A practice reported by the Devlin Committee in their 1967 final published report to be widespread in the Liverpool docks. Essentially, work teams would split into two so that half the gang worked for 30 minutes while the other half drank cups of tea, had a smoke, or played cards. After half an hour the gangs would swap over. There were reports that in some docks this practice was organised by the half day and even half week. When not working on the docks workers might work on a fruit and vegetable market or even take additional employment as a taxi driver.

Works councils Committees made up either solely of workers or of joint representatives of workers, management and shareholders, which meet, usually at company level, to discuss a variety of issues relating to workforce matters and sometimes general, wider-ranging organisational issues. Usually supported by legislation, which compels organisations to set them up.

Works council Consultative body consisting of management and labour representatives, which meets at regular intervals to share information pertinent to the performance and future development of the organisation.

YOPs Youth Opportunities Programme. A programme initially set up in 1978 and revived in 1983 to help unemployed youth to gain employment skills.

YT Youth Training (formerly Youth Training Service, YTS).

Zaibatsu Large, diversified Japanese business groups, which rose to prominence in the early twentieth century, such as Mitsubishi, Mitsui and Sumitomo.

Index

Index

tacit knowledge 285–6
tacit learning 309–10
Talbot, C. 612
Tancred-Sheriff, P. 52
'tapestry' 34–5, 40, 46, 54, 56
targets, training 354–5
Tavistock Institute for Human Relations 192–3, 200
tax evasion 131–2
Taylor, Frederick 177, 180–8, 217, 461–2, 638
Taylor, Robert 172–3
Taylorism 180–8, 189–91, 197, 200, 205, 466, 563
    trust 457
Taylor's model 667–70
team briefings 460, 566, 568, 570
team leaders 91, 168
teamworking 163–8, 192, 211–16, 571, 580
    collective bonuses 520
    management development 398–9
TEC *see* Training and Enterprise Councils
technology 203, 207–8, 216
    see also information technology
    changes 103, 157
    developments 230
television industry 164–5
temporary workers 102, 105–6, 109–13, 116, 118, 142, 153, 249
tension resolution 38–40
    contingency approach 38–9, 53
    human relations approach 38–9, 53–4
    humanistic approach 39–40, 53
    scientific management 38–9, 53
terms and conditions of employment 448–9, 474–505
tests, types 243–4
Thatcherism at Work (MacInnes) 4
"Third Way"
    Treaty of Amsterdam 1997 694
    UK government 692
Third World, management development 408
Thorndike, E.L. 510
Thornley, C. 615
three pillar approach, Japan 710–15
three systems reforms, China 720
tiger economies 39, 53
    see also newly industrialised economies
Timmins, N. 623
Timperley, S. 138, 140
Tompkins, P. 166
total quality management (TQM) 92, 560–3, 566, 575–82, 593, 646, 742–3
Towers, B. 475, 491
Towers Perrin Survey 656
Townley, B. 162, 524, 569
TQM *see* total quality management

trade unions 10, 15, 19, 38, 92, 101, 115, 125, 159, 343
    see also enterprise unionism
    blacklists 454
    BT case study 552–3
    China 719, 724
    collective bargaining 440, 449, 474–93
    communication channels 579
    empowerment schemes 578
    international comparisons 582–3, 585, 586
    Japan 711
    labour process control 461
    "new" economies 700–1
    performance-related pay 524–5
    recognition 455–6, 458, 476, 490, 500
    South Korea 733
    statutory protections 444, 452
trade-offs 93
training
    China 722–3
    compulsory 356
    evaluation 335–6
    Hong Kong 729
    methods 331–4
    national approaches 228–30
    national competitiveness 360–1
    national targets 354–5
    needs 130, 144, 325–6, 328–31
    responsibility 334–5
    youth schemes 350–1
Training and Enterprise Councils (TECs) 351
Transfer of Undertakings (Protection of Employment/TUPE), European directive 688
transformational leadership 41
transport 131–2
Treaty of Amsterdam 1997, European labour force 692–7
tripartite system, Central and Eastern European states 701
Trist, Eric 136–8, 192
Trompenaars, F. 640, 642
trust 457
TUPE *see* Transfer of Undertakings (Protection of Employment)
Turnbull, Peter 147
turnover 130–1, 135, 155, 203
    jobs affected diagram 152
Tyler, T. 531

UfI *see* University for Industry
Ulrich, D. 7
uncertainty avoidance 639
unemployment 74–6, 78–80, 93, 100, 228, 693–4

768

China 719
women 689
unfair dismissal 445, 447, 453, 454, 455
unified approach, management development 384–5
uniform wages 72
unions *see* trade unions
unit labour costs 84
unitarism 19, 149
United Kingdom
 banking industry 139, 154–5
 collective bargaining 476, 479
 economy 130
 employee involvement 586, 589
 Japanese companies 587, 588
 labour process 461–2
 management 109
 small firms 493–4
 works councils 491
United States, Medical Precision Systems 742–4
University for Industry (UfI) 359–60
upward communications 569, 570–1
Urry, J. 164, 209
USA, economy 17–19
'utilitarian instrumentalism' 6–7
utilitarianism 159–60

Vaillant, G.E. 47
Varney, G. 385
Vehicle Inspectorate Agency (VI) 612
VET *see* vocational education and training
VI *see* Vehicle Inspectorate Agency
virtual organisations 161, 180, 207–8
vocational education and training (VET) 341–3
 Britain
  competencies 351–2
  government involvement 349–51
  Investor in People 353–4
 building framework 356–60
 industrialised nations 343–8
 policies and practices 344–8
 recent developments 355–60
 Treaty of Amsterdam 1997 696–7
Volvo 583
Voyle, S. 63
Vroom, V.H. 508

wages 72–3, 82–4, 512
 adjustments 75
 China, average monthly 724
 differentials 76–9
 flexibility 99
 market-clearing 74
 rigidity 74–6, 81

rises, Hong Kong 728, 729
structures 77, 90
surveys 85–6
Wall, T.D. 567
Walters, M. 134, 149–50
Walton, R.E. 16, 27, 204, 478, 561, 563
Ward, P.J. 575
wastage analysis 135–8, 140, 145
Watson, T. 178, 191, 214–15, 371
Wealden District Council 364–5
Webb, Beatrice 477
Webb, Sidney 477
Weber, Max 179, 186
Weberian bureaucracy 132
Wedderburn, W. 438
Weick, K.E. 38, 41, 51, 302
'welting' 131, 147
WERS *see* Workplace Employee Relations Survey
Western Europe, economies 99–100, 106–7
Western thinking 48–9
WH Smith 214
white-collar work 512
Whitley, R. 643–5, 709
'Whitleyism' 601
Whittaker, J. 303
Wickens, P. 587
Wilkinson, A. 574–5, 577, 580, 581
Williams, R. 589
Williamson, O.E. 84, 441, 513
Willmore, N. 547
Willmott, H. 196, 581
Wilpert, B. 585
Wiltz, S. 584
Wisher, V. 277
women
 see also female workers
 equal opportunities 695–6
 Japan, recent trends 715–16
 progression 418–21
Wood, S. 25, 511, 578
work
 organisations 7
 orientations 193–7
 practices 147
 sampling 244
 systems 8
work tasks, deconstruction 183–4
work units, China 719, 720
workers
 adaptability 693
 consultation, Social Charter 686
 core 96, 104–6, 108, 110–11
 craft 108, 113, 155, 190